Blackstone's

Handbook for Policing Students

Blackstone's
Handbook for Policing Students

Ninth Edition

Edited by
Professor Robin Bryant
and
Sarah Bryant

Contributors:
Dr Sofia Graça, Kevin Lawton-Barrett,
Dr Martin O'Neill, Dr Steve Tong,
Robert Underwood, and
Dr Dominic Wood

OXFORD
UNIVERSITY PRESS

OXFORD
UNIVERSITY PRESS

Great Clarendon Street, Oxford, OX2 6DP,
United Kingdom

Oxford University Press is a department of the University of Oxford.
It furthers the University's objective of excellence in research, scholarship,
and education by publishing worldwide. Oxford is a registered trade mark of
Oxford University Press in the UK and in certain other countries

First Edition published in 2006
Ninth Edition published in 2014

Impression: 1

Published in the United States of America by Oxford University Press
198 Madison Avenue, New York, NY 10016, United States of America

British Library Cataloguing in Publication Data

Data available

ISBN 978–0–19–871335–7

Printed in Italy by
L.E.G.O. S.p.A.

Contents

Part III   Qualifications and Training

Part IV   General Procedures

Part V   Specific Incidents

Table of Cases

United Kingdom

European Court of Human Rights

Table of Legislation

International

Table of Secondary Legislation

Table of Codes of Practice

Table of Circulars

Introduction

This ninth edition of *Blackstone's Handbook for Policing Students* is designed and written to support trainee police officers and students on policing pre-join programmes at colleges, universities, or private sector training providers. The Handbook has six main parts (Overview, Policing in Context, Qualifications and Training, General Procedures, Specific Incidents, and Investigation and Prosecution). Each part is divided into a number of chapters and addresses a different aspect of policing and initial police training. The chapters focus in more detail on specific topics—such as Chapter 5 on the Criminal Justice System in England and Wales (in 'Policing in Context'), Chapter 15 on Unlawful Violence (in 'Specific Incidents'), and Chapter 24 on Interviewing (in 'Investigation and Prosecution').

The content has been revised and updated to reflect the needs of students undertaking pre-join programmes prior to joining the police. We have also included the content needed to meet most of the requirements of the Initial Police Learning and Development Programme (IPLDP) which underpins the training for all trainee police officers.

The authors of the Handbook have taken care to ensure the accuracy of the information contained within. However, neither the authors nor the publisher can accept any responsibility for any actions taken, or not taken, as a consequence of the information it contains. We would be grateful for feedback on the new Handbook, and for the identification of the occasional error. Reader feedback on the ninth edition is welcome. Please email police.uk@OUP.com with your comments or queries.

Please note that references throughout the Handbook to IPLDP materials have not been reviewed or endorsed by the IPLDP Central Authority Executive Services.

Introducing the Handbook

1.1 Introduction

In this chapter we provide you with guidance about how to use the Handbook and some background information and advice on studying policing. We are familiar with the wide range of experiences that learners (either on pre-join programmes at a college, university, or private training provider, or as trainee police officers) bring to their education and training, and the Handbook has been written and set out to be both accessible and of value to all our readers.

1.2 The Handbook as a Survival Guide

The Handbook is designed to assist you whilst you are preparing to join the police on an approved 'pre-join' programme such as the Certificate in Knowledge of Policing (CKP) or if you are already training to be a police officer. For example, to help you learn more effectively, we have omitted some of the more detailed aspects of the law and police procedure and instead provided a simplified version. Of course, this does not mean that the detail is not important; it is just that learning is usually easier when moving from the simple to the complex, so we start you off with the simple. In the case of the law, the full complexity will normally be introduced and explained to you by your tutors and trainers using a variety of teaching and learning methods. However, you may be expected to learn new material for yourself, and if this is so then you are likely to find Chapter 8 of the Handbook particularly useful.

The style of the Handbook represents a judgement concerning the best ways of introducing and describing a subject area. For many aspects of the law (eg as covered in Chapters 12 to 21 inclusive) we have adopted a bite-size approach for legislation and police practice. We have simplified and condensed the topics into relatively short sections of text and diagrams dealing with a particular topic. This would seem to suit the subject matter and the need for you, on many occasions, to assimilate and be able to reproduce the facts. In other parts of the book we have adopted a more holistic approach—for example to investigation and interviewing, covered in Chapters 23 and 24. This reflects the reality that learning the skills of investigation and interviewing involves more than adherence to codes and legislation. You will also need, for example, to appreciate the structure an interview can take, the forms of communication used (particularly for questioning), and the role of the interview within a wider criminal investigation.

1.3 Using the Handbook

You will sometimes look up a particular topic, but at other times you might read several sections to gain an overview. If you are an activist learner (see 8.6.5.2) you might find completing some of the tasks provides a welcome relief from simple reading! This Handbook, although large enough, does not contain the full level of detail you will need either to complete your pre-join programme or to qualify as a police officer, so we frequently refer you to further sources of information after hopefully providing you with a good general understanding of the topic in question.

1.3.1 Tasks, references, and further reading

In many chapters you are asked to undertake tasks. These are placed within the body of each chapter rather than, more traditionally, at the end of the chapter. If you are a student on a pre-join programme or a trainee police officer then these tasks will be useful to you for either checking your understanding or as stimulus material for your SOLAP or Learning Diary (see 8.5). Answers are provided at the end of each chapter. In many cases the tasks provide further ideas for you to explore, or point you in the direction of additional reading and study. For this reason it is helpful to read the answers to the tasks even though you may already be confident that you have a clear understanding of the answer to a question.

Referencing is a standard academic system for producing evidence for your arguments, or for directing the reader towards further information. We have deliberately kept the volume of referencing in this Handbook to a minimum, generally restricting it to where the source of the ideas and information might be useful. Referencing is a common courtesy to those authors whose work we have utilized, and respects the intellectual property rights of others, but we have minimized it to make the Handbook more accessible to a wider range of readers: the flow is not disturbed by frequent references to other material.

We also indicate where further reading might be useful as the Handbook is very much a survival guide (see 1.2) and you will find more detail and further explanation in many other textbooks in your college or university library (including electronic resources), in your College of Policing notes (if you are on a pre-join programme) or force notes (if you are also a special constable or undertaking initial training), and via websites such as NCALT and the PNLD. We frequently state that further information, or the source of the underpinning material we have utilized is available 'online'. The usual search techniques (using web-based search engines such as 'Google') will soon provide the relevant hypertext links.

1.3.2 Extracts from legislation, circulars, and Codes

Throughout the Handbook there are numerous extracts from primary legislation or Codes—often from Acts of Parliament. These are quoted in the original but sometimes with minor changes. Often an explanation in everyday language is also given, normally in a text box to the right of the original legislation. Quotations are signified by the use of a different font (or quotation marks), while explanations and comments are in ordinary text, like this:

if when not at [his/her] place of abode.

> The term 'place of abode' means the place or site where someone lives. It normally includes the garage and garden of a house and should be given its normal meaning, but it will be a question of fact for the court to decide. If a homeless person sleeps in his/her car, the car counts as an abode while he/she is asleep. However, when the same car is being driven by the same person, it is not considered as a place of abode for the purposes of the offence of going equipped (see *R v Bundy* 1977).

When changes have been made, this is usually because legislation tends to use the personal pronoun 'he' to cover 'he or she'. (However, in some legislation (eg for some sexual offences), 'he' really does mean just 'he'.) We have changed 'he' to 'he/she' and 'him' to 'him/her', and so on, where appropriate. We have also occasionally changed a particular word if it helps the sentence make more sense when quoted alone. Minor changes to the wording of legislation or Codes in the Handbook are shown in square brackets, as in the following example.

The original, from s 74 of the Sexual Offences Act 2003, states:

> For the purposes of this Part, a person consents if he agrees by choice, and has the freedom and capacity to make that choice.

Our revised version reads:

> For the purposes of this [offence], a person consents if [he/she] agrees by choice, and has the freedom and capacity to make that choice.

As you can see we have changed 'Part' to '[offence]' and 'he' to '[he/she]'. You will also find the detail of legislation covered in other publications. Most recent legislation is available from the government website <http://www.legislation.gov.uk>. Legislation can be confusing as it may have been subject to amendment and changed by subsequent legislation, for example the definition of a religiously aggravated offence to be found in the Crime and Disorder Act 1998 (see 14.10) was subsequently added to by the Anti-terrorism, Crime and Security Act of 2001. The 2001 legislation added a new subsection 28(5) to the four original subsections of the 1998 legislation. The government website at <http://www.legislation.gov.uk> provides 'updated' versions of original legislation.

It is also often the case that the words and phrases used in legislation have specific meanings that do not always correspond exactly to the same words or phrases used in everyday life. For example, you might think that a shotgun is an 'offensive weapon' and that 'assault' means physically hurting somebody but in both cases the legal meanings are somewhat at odds with our usual take on the meaning of these words.

Further explanation of legislation can be found (for example) in sources including:

- publications such as Butterworth's Police Law and the Blackstone's publications (notably the Police Operational Handbook and the annual Police Manuals);
- the PNLD website at <https://www.pnld.co.uk/docportal/content/commhome.mth>;
- legal guidance from the CPS at <http://www.cps.gov.uk/legal/index.html>;
- the 'official' home of UK legislation at <http://www.legislation.gov.uk>;
- the College of Policing digests at <http://www.college.police.uk/en/20002.htm>; and
- the online legal databases Westlaw (<http://www.westlaw.co.uk>) and Lawtel (<http://www.lawtel.com/UK/Home>) if you are studying at university or college.

Trainee police officers and special constables can also use force resources (eg the force intranet) and:

- the NCALT learning portal for the police service at <http://www.ncalt.com>;
- the Police OnLine Knowledge Area (POLKA) at <https://polka.pnn.police.uk>.

> **TASK 1** Use the internet to identify the definition of 'controlled area' in the law governing demonstrations in the vicinity of Parliament. It is defined within the Police Reform and Social Responsibility Act 2011.

1.3.3 Structure of the Handbook

As you might have already discovered through reading the Contents, the Handbook is divided into six parts and 26 chapters.

- **Overview**—this is mostly devoted to reference material that will be of value to students on pre-entry courses and trainee police officers. You are likely to use this part of the Handbook to check on the meaning of an acronym, remind yourself of a key date in policing, or practise the phonetic alphabet.
- **Policing in Context**—this provides the background and context to policing and law enforcement in England and Wales, including an overview of policing professional issues, the nature of crime and disorder, and the Criminal Justice System. If you are on a pre-join programme then this part of the Handbook provides you with a starting point for the required reading and research.
- **Qualifications and Training**—this is a description and discussion of what it means to work within the profession of policing, from standards of behaviour, to qualifications, to the detail of training itself.
- **General Procedures**—this examines general policing powers and procedures in detail, to the level required for initial training as a police officer.
- **Specific Incidents**—this covers the knowledge of criminal law required to undertake policing of a wide variety of incidents up to the stage of initial qualification, and hence is a particularly long and demanding part of the Handbook.
- **Investigation and Prosecution**—this looks at the processes involved within police investigation (including interviewing and forensic investigation), culminating in a chapter concerned with the prosecution of offenders.

1.4 Key Aspects of Police Education and Training

In Chapters 6 to 8 inclusive we provide more detail on education and training for pre-join programmes at a college or university and for trainee officers after joining the police. Here we offer a brief introduction to some key components: pre-join programmes, the IPLDP, the NOS, the Certificate in Knowledge of Policing, the Diploma in Policing, and the PAC. There are currently approximately 40 approved pre-join programmes (some available through distance learning) available in the UK. The IPLDP modules set out what you need to know and the skills you require to become a police officer. The National Occupational Standards (NOS) underpin both the Certificate in Knowledge of Policing and the Diploma in Policing (the latter forming the basis for qualification as a police constable). In many forces the Police Action Checklist (the PAC) is also a key requirement in the assessment of a trainee police officer for Independent Patrol.

The Handbook is linked throughout to the Certificate in Knowledge of Policing, the Diploma in Policing, and the associated NOS.

1.4.1　Pre-join programmes

Pre-join courses are provided by further education colleges, universities, and private training companies. The courses are either 'stand alone' (eg the Certificate in Knowledge of Policing) or embedded within longer programmes. If you are on a pre-join programme, your ambition is probably to join the police or other law enforcement agency as a full-time professional (eg as a PCSO or police constable). Or you might be a special constable; for some embedded pre-join programmes this is compulsory. Pre-join programmes are expected to articulate with the pre-join curriculum (see 1.4.2) and deliver the learning requirement of the Certificate in Knowledge of Policing (see 1.4.4).

1.4.2　IPLDP

The Initial Police Learning and Development Programme (IPLDP) forms the basis of initial policing training (that is, up to the point of confirmation as a police constable). The IPLDP consists of three sets of learning modules:

* the Induction modules (prefixed with 'IND');
* the Operational modules ('OP'); and
* the Legislation, Policy, and Guidelines modules ('LPG').

Taken together there are 7,720 separate learning outcomes (4,807 mandatory and 2,913 optional) described with the three sets of modules and it is not possible (or indeed appropriate) to cover them all in detail in a Handbook.

This Handbook covers most of the IND modules. However, some aspects of initial police training, such as First Aid, are more suited to specialist publications, and others (such as IND 8: 'Operation of information technology systems') are very dependent on individual force policy and equipment. In these instances we provide an overview of the training rather than describing the full detail. Similarly, a subject such as the multicultural nature of modern Britain and the diverse communities that you will police is better studied (we would wish to argue) using textbooks or other learning material specifically devoted to this task, rather than using this Handbook or College of Policing notes.

IPLDP Induction Modules

IND 1　Underpinning ethics/values of the police service

IND 2　Foster people's equality, diversity, and rights

IND 3　Develop one's own knowledge and practice

IND 4　Develop effective relationships with colleagues

IND 5　Ensure your own actions reduce the risks to health and safety

IND 6　Assess the needs of individuals and provide advice and support

IND 7　Develop effective partnerships with members of the community and other agencies

IND 8　Operation of information technology systems

IND 9　Administer First Aid

IND 10　Use police powers in a fair and justified way

IND 11　Social and community issues, and Neighbourhood Policing

---

The operational modules for the training of police officers are as follows. This Handbook covers the underpinning knowledge required for most of the OP modules.

IPLDP Operational Modules

OP 1   Deal with aggressive and abusive behaviour

OP 2   Obtain, evaluate, and submit information and intelligence to support local priorities

OP 3   Respond to incidents, conduct and evaluate investigations

OP 4   Participate in planned operations

OP 5(a)   Search premises

OP 5(b)   Search individuals

OP 5(c)   Search vehicles

OP 5(d)   Search open areas

OP 5(e)   Search missing person

OP 6(a)   Prepare, conduct, and evaluate interviews (witness/victim)

OP 6(b)   Prepare, conduct, and evaluate interviews (suspects)

OP 7   Arrest and report suspects

OP 8   Escort suspects and present to custody

OP 9   Prepare and present case information, present evidence, and finalize investigations

---

The Legislation, Policy, and Guidelines modules covered in this Handbook are as follows:

IPLDP Legislation, Policy, and Guidelines Modules

LPG 0   Underpinning legislation policy and guidelines (Phases 3 and 4)

LPG 1   Underpinning legislation policy and guidelines (Phase 3)

LPG 2   Underpinning legislation policy and guidelines (Phase 4)

This Handbook provides you with much of the basic knowledge required for LPG 1 and LPG 2, and the aspects we do not cover are inappropriate for a general textbook of this kind because they are related to local force policy, for example the use of the police radio system in LPG 1.4.07.

We cover the areas of LPG 0 we regard as essential for the trainee police officer or pre-join student (even though some of this is designated as optional under the IPLDP).

1.4.3   NOS Units for Policing

There are 21 National Occupational Standards (NOS) that relate to initial police training. It is unlikely you will be assessed directly against the NOS units particularly if you are on a pre-join programme. Instead, the NOS units are used as a basis for two qualifications, the Certificate in Knowledge of Policing and the Diploma in Policing (see 1.4.4 for a summary and 7.3 for further detail).

The 21 NOS Units for Initial Policing

AA1   Promote equality and value diversity

AB1   Communicate effectively with people

AE1   Maintain and develop your own knowledge, skills, and competence

AF1   Ensure your own actions reduce risks to health and safety

BE2   Provide initial support to victims, survivors, and witnesses and assess their needs for further support

CA1   Use law enforcement actions in a fair and justified way

CB1   Gather and submit information that has the potential to support law enforcement objectives

CD1   Provide an initial response to incidents

CD3   Prepare for, and participate in, planned law enforcement operations

CD5   Arrest, detain, or report individuals

CI101   Conduct priority and volume investigations

CJ101   Interview victims and witnesses in relation to priority and volume investigations

CJ201	Interview suspects in relation to priority and volume investigations
CK1	Search individuals
CK2	Search vehicles, premises, and open spaces
DA5	Present evidence in court and at other hearings
DA6	Prepare and submit case files
GC10	Manage conflict
2K1	Escort detained persons
2K2	Present detained persons to custody
4G4	Administer First Aid

Each of the NOS units is subdivided into learning outcomes, see 7.4 for details.

1.4.4 The Certificate in Knowledge of Policing and the Diploma in Policing

The Certificate in Knowledge of Policing (CKP) and the Diploma in Policing are QCF Level 3 qualifications. The Certificate is likely to be delivered as either an independent and stand-alone award or as part of a longer pre-join programme offered by a college, a university, a police force, or another education provider while the Diploma is more likely to be delivered by a police force as part of the initial training for trainee police officers.

The Diploma in Policing is the national minimum qualification for initial police training.

The units for the Certificate and the Diploma are drawn from the National Occupational Standards (NOS) for initial police training (see 1.4.3), for example BE2 which is concerned with 'providing initial support to victims and witnesses within a policing context'. In effect the Certificate represents the knowledge and understanding for each topic (hence it is often referred to as BE2K), while the Diploma covers the skills needed as well as the knowledge requirements. Each Certificate and Diploma unit is also indirectly linked with a number of other, more thematic NOS units such as NOS Unit AA1.

Certificate in Knowledge of Policing Units	No of credits	Main linked NOS Unit
Knowledge of providing initial support to victims and witnesses within a policing context	1	BE2
Knowledge of gathering and submitting information to support law enforcement objectives within a policing context	1	CB1
Knowledge of providing an initial response to incidents within a policing context	2	CD1
Knowledge of arresting, detaining, and reporting individuals within a policing context	3	CD5
Knowledge of conducting priority and volume investigations within a policing context	3	CI101
Knowledge of interviewing victims and witnesses in relation to priority and volume investigations within a policing context	4	CJ101
Knowledge of interviewing suspects in relation to priority and volume investigations within a policing context	3	CJ201
Knowledge of searching individuals within a policing context	2	CK1
Knowledge of searching vehicles, premises, and open spaces within a policing context	2	CK2
Knowledge of managing conflict within a policing context	2	GC10
TOTAL	23	

Diploma in Policing Units	No of credits	Main linked NOS Unit
Provide initial support to victims and witnesses	3	BE2
Gather and submit information to support law enforcement objectives	2	CB1
Provide an initial response to incidents	4	CD1
Arrest, detain, and report individuals	4	CD5

Conduct priority and volume investigations	5	CI101
Interview victims and witnesses in relation to priority and volume investigations	5	CJ101
Interview suspects in relation to priority and volume investigations	5	CJ201
Search individuals in a policing context	3	CK1
Search vehicles, premises, and open spaces	4	CK2
Manage conflict in a policing context	3	GC10
TOTAL	38	

This Handbook covers most of the content required for the CKP assessment apart from the associated curriculum content for two assessment criteria:

- 1.4 'Describe the National Intelligence Model or a model relevant to their organisation and explain how it fits within their organisation local policy'; and
- 2.2 'Explain how to select and apply an appropriate tactical option, based on a threat assessment, legislation, training and organisational policy, calling for any necessary assistance, back-up and support if required'.

The NIM is described in detail in 22.6 but you should also take note of your local force policies for further explanations. With respect to assessment criteria 2.2 on tactical options, the theoretical underpinning is largely covered in this Handbook but it also appears to require training which is normally restricted to special constable or PCSO initial training.

The Certificate in Knowledge of Policing and the Diploma in Policing are described in more detail in 7.3.

1.4.5 Local force policies

If you are a special constable or undertaking initial police training with a police force then this Handbook should always be read in conjunction with local force policies. This applies particularly for procedures such as writing a statement or making a pocket notebook entry. You are likely to find your local policies referred to as 'Force Orders', 'Standard Operating Procedures (SOP)', or 'Policies' on your organization's intranet.

Trainee police officers may also be required to learn verbatim definitions. Often concerned with the law, for example the definition of what constitutes theft. In this case we advise you to use the definitions given to you by your force rather than those reproduced in this Handbook or, indeed, in other textbooks. This is because there is sometimes a slight variation between forces in definitions of the same terms—for example, whether in the definition your force gives you to learn, 'he' in the original Act (a common occurrence) is replaced with 'he/she', 's/he', 'they', or is left in its original form.

1.5 Answer to Task

TASK 1 The Police Reform and Social Responsibility Act 2011 can be located at <http://www.legislation.gov.uk/ukpga/2011/13/contents/enacted>. Demonstrations in the vicinity of Parliament are dealt with in Part 3 of the Act, 'Parliament Square Garden and surrounding area' and in ss 142–147 inclusive. You should find a hypertext link to s 142 which explains that 'controlled area' of Parliament Square is its central garden and the immediately adjoining footways. However, s 142(2) explains that the definition of 'central garden of Parliament Square' is the site in Parliament Square on which the Minister of Works was authorized to lay out the 'new central garden' by the Parliament Square (Improvements) Act 1949. This Act will be difficult to locate unless you have access to a printed resource such as the All England Law Reports (eg through a university). However, the government produce explanatory notes for most new legislation, and in this case (by careful searching) you should be able to find Annex A to the document 'Police Reform and Social Responsibility Act 2011 Guidance on the Provisions Relating to Parliament Square and Surrounding Area' (<http://www.publications.parliament.uk/pa/cm201011/cmbills/116/en/2011116en.htm>) which provides a map of the controlled area.

2 Reference Material

2.1 Introduction

In this chapter of the Handbook we provide you with some background information as reference material. This is likely to be of value to you whilst undertaking a pre-join programme and subsequently during your initial training as a student police officer. For example, you might encounter more experienced police colleagues, or fellow students, using an acronym or a form of jargon that you have not encountered, and the glossary in 2.3 might well provide an answer. We also include in this chapter a list of dates and key events in the history of law enforcement and policing, and these might help you set present practices (and some reactions to proposed changes) in perspective.

We also provide you with an understanding of the basic configuration of the rank structure in policing and an overview of a typical police force organizational structure. Finally we describe and explain the conventions used by law enforcement agencies for conveying information, such as the phonetic alphabet and the codes for conveying or recording ethnicity.

2.2 Chronology of Law Enforcement and Policing

An understanding of the past is an important precursor to understanding the present. There are no CKP or IPLDP learning outcomes explicitly concerned with the history of policing, but IPLDP modules such as 'Understanding and being in the community' and 'Understanding social change' (both part of IND 11) are likely to be more meaningful if current practice is considered within a historical context. We do not provide a comprehensive history of law enforcement and the police in the UK, nor do we offer much in the way of analysis, but we do provide you with some of the background and a number of key dates in the history of policing. It is surprising to note that the police (in the UK and elsewhere) are a relatively modern phenomenon and there have been a number of notable occasions when their very existence has been challenged. If there is one key date in modern-day policing it is probably 1829 when Sir Robert Peel, then Home Secretary, introduced a Bill in Parliament for the establishment of a 'Metropolitan Police Force' for London. Perhaps this is the key observation here: the police service as we would recognize it today is barely 190 years old, and continues to be subject to fundamental changes regarding its purpose and structure.

Here we present a brief chronology (timeline) of the significant developments in the history of the police service of England and Wales, dominated (at least in the nineteenth century) by the Metropolitan Police in London.

1829   Sir Robert Peel established the first civilian police force in London, with two Justices of the Peace in charge of the force.

1831   Period of considerable unrest and mob violence, especially in the north of England and in London.

1835   The Municipal Corporations Act 1835 established 'watch committees' to oversee policing of areas outside London.

1839–40 Provincial constabularies were established across the country for the first time.

1842   Establishment of a detective force at the London Metropolitan Police HQ, Scotland Yard (still only ten staff in 1856).

1840s–50s There was considerable hostility towards the new police, with widespread resentment about the cost and the perceived lack of police officers when needed. Some believed that any police force was illiberal.

1856   It became mandatory for local government bodies to set up police forces. Financial support was awarded by central government to forces which proved to be efficient and reliable, paving the way for the modern inspection regime by the HMIC.

1860   Over 200 borough and county police forces in England and Wales in existence. Unrest in Ireland led to the formation of the Royal Irish Constabulary, which was paramilitary from the outset.

1872   Police officers went on strike for the first time.

1878   The Criminal Investigation Department (CID) was formed, with Scotland Yard detectives being called in by county forces to lead criminal investigations well into the 1930s.

1883   The Special Irish Branch was set up as part of the Metropolitan Police to deal with attacks by Irish republicans in London, and later became known simply as Special Branch.

1901   Scotland Yard's Fingerprint Bureau was formed.

1911   Police officers were armed for the first time, after assisting the military to end a siege of armed anarchists in a London house.

1912   Establishment of special constables on a permanent basis.

1914   NUPPO, the first Police Union (unofficial) was formed. The 'Women Police' were founded.

1914–18 The First World War put enormous pressure on the police due to enlistment in the armed forces, suspension of police recruitment, and new tasks such as the pursuit of deserters.

1916   The Commissioner of the Metropolitan Police ruled that any officer joining a union was liable to dismissal.

The regularizing of women police officers as equal members of the force is generally dated from 1916, though many would argue that women were not fully accepted in the police service until the Second World War, and even then, attitudes to female police officers were often negative. The Police Federation, for example, took until 1948 to admit female officers as members.

1918–19 The police, particularly in Liverpool and London, embarked on a series of strikes for better pay and conditions, and for recognition of police trades unions. New legislation then banned police trades unions and denied the police the right to strike, but allowed the formation of the Police Federation for negotiations over pay, etc.

1921   Police motorcycle patrols were established.

1922   After the creation of Eire in 1922, the RIC became the Royal Ulster Constabulary (RUC).

1931   A two-tier entry system to the police operated briefly, based on the officer/non-commissioned ranks recruitment in the armed forces. Police officers were trained at Hendon, but this experiment with 'officer entry' was short-lived.

1935   The first police forensic laboratory was opened by the Metropolitan Police.

1937   The emergency telephone number 999 was introduced.

1946   The number of forces was reduced to 125.

1948   The Police Federation started to admit female officers as members.

1950s   The so-called 'Golden Age' of policing, characterized by apparent widespread acceptance of the legitimacy of the police, and relatively low levels of crime and disorder. Popular belief in its existence probably derives at least in part from a television series of the time, *Dixon of Dock Green*.

1964   The number of separate and distinct forces was reduced to 49.

1965   Police officer personal radios were introduced.

1973   Women police officers were integrated directly into the police service.

1981   The Scarman Report into the Brixton riots in April 1981 (involving mostly young black men) gave rise to a concerted effort to improve relations between the police and minority ethnic groups.

1984   The Police and Criminal Evidence Act 1984 (PACE Act) created the Police Complaints Authority (PCA). This was in response to criticism of the police 'acting as judge and jury' in investigations into complaints from the public about the police.

1990   The Association of Chief Police Officers (ACPO) published its 'Statement of Common Purpose and Values', which emphasized that the police should be seen more as a service than as a force.

1994   Creation of a centralized computer database for criminal records.

1997   NAFIS, the National Automated Fingerprint Identification System was created.

1999   The Macpherson Inquiry into the death of Stephen Lawrence (a black teenager murdered in London in 1993) criticized the whole police service as institutionally racist.

        The RUC became the Police Service of Northern Ireland (PSNI), following the Patten Inquiry and Report.

2002   Introduction of Police Community Support Officers (PCSOs).

2003   TV airing by the BBC of *The Secret Policeman* video uncovering racism at a regional police training centre. The Independent Police Complaints Commission (IPCC) was established to replace the Police Complaints Authority.

2005   Formation of the Serious Organised Crime Agency (SOCA), combining several existing agencies to counter level 3 crime and criminality.

2006   Following a 2005 HMIC report, an amalgamation of police forces was proposed but then rescinded in 2006. The National Police Improvement Agency (NPIA) was formed, incorporating Centrex (police training) and other agencies such as Information Services.

2007   The Home Office was split into two parts: the 'justice' element was incorporated into a Ministry of Justice, whilst the 'security' element (including the police) became part of a new Interior Ministry. Such a division did not take into account that the police play a large role in justice as well as security (as stated in 1830 by Sir Richard Mayne at the founding of the 'new police' in London).

2008   Publication of the Flanagan Review of Policing, with recommendations on reducing unnecessary police bureaucracy and the implementation of Neighbourhood Policing.

2008–9 The 'Policing Pledge' was launched, setting out the public's right to a range of services from their local police force (eg that an emergency 999 call will be answered within ten seconds). It was subsequently withdrawn in 2010–11.

2010   A new government promises cuts in police bureaucracy, the return to the police of responsibility for charging suspects with 'low level' offences, and locally elected police and crime commissioners.

2011   The 2010 comprehensive spending review imposes budget reductions for police forces in England and Wales. By 2012 these cuts had led to a reduction in police staffing levels in many police forces in England and Wales.

2011   The first Winsor Review into police officer and staff remuneration and conditions is published with detailed recommendations on police pay.

2011   The Neyroud Review into police training and leadership recommends the establishment of a chartered professional body for policing.

2012   The first Police and Crime Commissioners (PCCs) were elected to replace the current Police Authorities. They are responsible for 'hiring and firing' the chief constable and setting out a five-year Police and Crime Plan. In London, the PCC role was adopted by the Mayor's Office.

2012   The publication of the second Winsor Review into entry routes into policing, promotion, health and fitness requirements, and contribution-related pay.

2012   The College of Policing was established as a professional body for policing.

2013   The Home Office consults on measures intended to maintain and enhance the integrity of the police, including: a new code of ethics (covering all ranks); a single set of professional standards; a national register of chief officers' pay packages, gifts, hospitality, and second jobs; and a national register of officers who have been 'struck off'.

2013   The Lord Stevens Independent Review of Policing makes 37 recommendations including reducing the number of police forces, scrapping PCCs, a new chartered status for police officers, and changes to the qualification structure of training.

2013   Allegations that the Government chief whip made particular derogatory remarks to police officers on duty in Downing Street lead to claims of collusion between some of the police officers involved (the repercussions were dubbed 'Plebgate' by some media).

2014   An MPS police officer is jailed for a year for misconduct in public office after falsely claiming that he witnessed an altercation between the chief whip and police officers in Downing Street in 2013.

TASK 1 What is the history of your local force? See if you can establish the dates of a few key events in the last 200 years or so.

2.3 Glossary of Terms Used in Policing

You will encounter many acronyms and forms of jargon during your training. The following glossary of terms covers a wide range of the often bewildering words and phrases used within policing. Note also that many police forces also publish their own glossary of terms.

5 × 5 × 5 A 'five by five by five' is an intelligence report. The numbers refer to a scale that is used to attempt to measure the reliability of, access to, and other factors about the source providing the intelligence.

16 + 1 Reference to the system used to record self-defined (as distinct from officer-defined (see IC1)) ethnicity: for example A1 is used for Indian.

ABC (1) Acceptable Behaviour Contract; (2) Activity-Based Costing, a finance/budgeting methodology that enables costs of an activity to be calculated (as opposed to a value which can only be assessed).

ABE ('A-B-E') *Achieving Best Evidence*, Guidance on Interviewing Victims and Witnesses, and Using Special Measures.

ABH Assault resulting in actual bodily harm.

ACC Assistant Chief Constable; a command rank (see 2.3 and 2.4).

ACPO ('Ack-poh') Association of Chief Police Officers. The term ACPO is also sometimes used as a vernacular proper noun for a chief officer (qv).

Active Defence A proactive approach to defence which involves a rigorous examination of police investigation procedures and the prosecution case; the title of an influential book by Roger Ede and Eric Shepherd.

ad hoc A Latin phrase meaning 'for this special purpose', which has come to mean 'off the cuff' or 'unrehearsed'.

ADVOKATE ('advokate') Mnemonic used in police training to assist the recollection of the so-called 'Turnbull' rules for witness recall (see 10.5).

AFO ('A-F-O') Authorized Firearms Officer.

Airwave The digital national police radio communication system.

AirwaveSpeak A standardized form of communication when using Airwave (qv).

Alpha/Bravo, etc The phonetic alphabet used in police communication (see 2.5).

AMHP Approved mental health professional.

Analyst A professional police staff member whose role (usually) is to analyse and assess crime data and intelligence, and present research findings.

ANPR Automatic Number Plate Recognition system: see 'Nexus'.

APA ('A-P-A') Association of Police Authorities (now replaced in part by APACE qv).

APACE Association of Policing & Crime Chief Executives.

APACS ('aippax') Association of Payments and Clearing Services.

APEL ('A-P-L' or sometimes 'aipull') Accreditation of Prior Experiential Learning.

APL ('A-P-L' or sometimes 'aipull') Accreditation of Prior Learning.

APP Authorised Professional Practice.

ARU ('A-R-U') Armed Response Unit.

ARV ('A-R-V') Armed Response Vehicle.

ASBO ('azboh') Anti-social Behaviour Order.

ASP ('asp') An informal term for an extendable metal baton (a reference to the US company Armament Systems and Procedures Inc).

ASU ('A-S-U') Air Support Unit.

Attestation The formal point at which the powers and responsibilities of the office of constable are assumed, accompanied by the swearing of an oath.

AVLS Automatic (or Automated) Vehicle Location System.

Awarding Bodies Organizations permitted to issue awards and qualifications such as NVQs (qv) and the Diploma in Policing (qv).

Baton A side-handled self-protection weapon carried by uniformed police officers.

Baton round The formal term for a rubber or plastic bullet.

BAWP ('B-A-W-P') British Association for Women in Policing.

BCE Bad-character evidence.

BCS British Crime Survey (now replaced by the Crime Survey for England and Wales).

BCU Basic Command Unit (Area, Division) or sometimes Borough Command Unit (particularly amongst MPS officers (qv)).

Biometrics The use of unique human physical characteristics (such as the iris of the eye) as identifiers.

BLS Basic Life Support (part of First Aid training: procedures in BLS for Adults differ from those in BLS for Infants and Children).

BME Black and Minority Ethnic (groups).

Bolt-on ASBO An informal term for an ASBO (qv) added after a conviction, usually by a magistrate.

BPA Black Police Association.

BTP British Transport Police.

Byford Report A review by Sir Lawrence Byford on the police investigation into the 'Yorkshire Ripper' (Peter Sutcliffe) murders between 1975 and 1981; the report was instrumental in the establishment of HOLMES (qv).

CAP ('C-A-P' or 'cap') Common Approach Path.

CAR (often 'car') Cumulative Assessment Record, used as part of assembling the SOLAP (qv).

Cat A/B/C murders ('cat A', etc) Categories of homicide (see 10.4.1 and 11.3.4).

CBRN Chemical, Biological, Radiological, or Nuclear (hazard, etc).

CCR Contact and Control Room.

CCTV Closed-Circuit Television.

CCU Computer Crime Unit.

CDRP(s) Crime and Disorder Reduction Partnership(s).

Centrex Central Police Training and Development Authority, previously responsible for national police training, subsequently subsumed within NPIA (qv).

CEOP ('see-op') Child Exploitation and Online Protection Centre, a command of the National Crime Agency (qv).

Certificate in Knowledge of Policing The knowledge requirement for the assessed units of the Police Diploma in Policing (qv), usually undertaken as part of a pre-join programme (qv).

cf Latin for 'compare'.

Chief Officer A police officer with the rank of assistant chief constable and above: command rank.

CHIS ('chiss') Covert Human Intelligence Source (informant).

CI ('C-I') (1) Cognitive Interview; (2) Cell Intervention.

CID ('C-I-D') Criminal Investigation(s) Department, now replaced in many police forces by Specialist Crime Investigations, SCI, or similar.

CIRA ('seera') Continuity Irish Republican Army.

CJPOA Criminal Justice and Public Order Act 1994.

CJ(S) A process or unit concerned with Criminal Justice (Systems).

CKP Certificate in Knowledge of Policing (qv).

CLDP Core Leadership Development Programme.

CLO ('C-L-O') Community Liaison Officer.

CLUE2 ('klue-too') A case-tracking data system.

CNC Civil Nuclear Constabulary.

CnC Command and Control system used by a number of police forces and other agencies.

Collar To make an arrest (vernacular).

College of Policing The professional body for policing.

Compromise When a criminal target (a suspect) detects covert surveillance.

Confirmation The final stage of successful initial training, normally after a period of two years, when a student police officer is confirmed as a police constable.

Continuity Continuity (of evidence): an audited and continuous trail from crime scene or suspect to court, such that evidential items can be accounted for at all times, to prevent interference or contamination.

CoP see College of Policing.

CPA (1) Crime Pattern Analysis; (2) Child Protection Agency.

CPIA Criminal Procedure and Investigations Act 1996.

CPOSA Chief Police Officers' Staff Association.

CPR Cardio-pulmonary resuscitation.

CPS Crown Prosecution Service, the governmental body of qualified lawyers who prosecute criminal cases before the courts.

CRaSH or CRASH Collision Recording and Sharing.

CRE Commission for Racial Equality; now the EHRC (qv).

CRFP Council for the Registration of Forensic Practitioners.

Crimelink Crime analysis software developed by the company Precision Computing Intelligence and used by some force analysts (qv).

CRO ('C-R-O') (1) Criminal Records Office; (2) Criminal (vernacular).

CROPS ('crops') Covert Rural Observation Posts (or Points).

CSI Crime Scene Investigator.

CSM Crime Scene Manager.

CSO Community Support Officer.

CSP (1) Communications Service Provider; (2) Community Safety Partnership.

CSU Community Safety Unit.

CTM Contact Trace Material.

Cuff (1) Police vernacular for not doing something which one is supposed to do as a matter of duty or obligation; (2) To handcuff (vernacular).

Custody or custody suite A designated area in a police station (usually where the cells are located), where arrested persons are logged and processed by trained custody staff.

CW Cannabis Warning.

Dabs Colloquial term for fingerprints.

DC Detective Constable.

DCC Deputy Chief Constable.

DCI Detective Chief Inspector.

DCS Detective Chief Superintendent; command rank.

DDA Normally a reference to the Disability Discrimination Act 1995.

DFU Digital Forensics Unit.

DI ('D-I') Detective Inspector.

DIC ('D-I-C') Drunk in charge (of a person or object).

Diploma in Policing The minimum national qualification for trainee police officers: a Level 3 QCF (qv) qualification consisting of ten assessment units totalling 38 credits: see 7.3.

Disclosure A reference to the requirement on the police and the prosecution to provide the defence with certain information and documents which might be pertinent evidence in a criminal case.

DNA Deoxyribonucleic Acid (genetic material used to obtain a 'genetic fingerprint').

Doctrine A body of knowledge and procedure concerned with police practice, notably criminal investigation—for example, as expressed in the MIM (qv) and Volume Crime Investigation Manuals of NCPE (qv).

DPP Director of Public Prosecutions.

DS Detective Sergeant.

DVCVA Domestic Violence, Crime and Victims Act 2004.

DVLA Driver and Vehicle Licensing Agency.

DVPN Domestic Violence Protection Notice.

DVPO Domestic Violence Protection Order.

EAW European Arrest Warrant.

ECHR European Convention on Human Rights.

EHRC Equality and Human Rights Commission: formerly the CRE (qv).

Element (of a unit of an NOS) The units of a NOS (qv) are usually divided into two or more elements which describe more precisely the skill or competence to be attained and measured.

ERO ('E-R-O') Evidence Review Officer.

ESDA ('ezzder') Electrostatic Detection Apparatus.

ETA ('E-T-A') Estimated time of arrival.

et al Latin for 'and others'.

Europol The European Union Law Enforcement Organisation.

Extended police family A reference to the wider group of law enforcement and pubic order staff, beyond the traditional full-time police—for example, special constables and PCSOs (qv).

FA ('F-A') Forensic Alliance (an independent forensic science laboratory and service).

Family of forces Term once used by the HMIC (qv) to describe those police forces which were considered to be very similar in structure, size, budget, and so on. Now largely replaced by the Home Office's designation of 'Most Similar Forces' (MSF (qv)).

FAO or FOAS ('F-A-O' or 'F-O-A-S') First Attending Officer/First Officer Attending the Scene/ first responder.

FASP ('farsp' or 'fasp') First Aid Skills for Policing. An NPIA (qv) programme of five modules. Module 2 (First Aid Skills) is often undertaken as part of IPLDP (qv).

FBO Football Banning Order.

FCA Forensic Computer Analyst.

FCC Force Communications (or Control) Centre.

FCP Forward Control Point.

'Federation' The Police Federation of England and Wales (qv).

Fence Vernacular for a person who buys or exchanges stolen goods.

FERRT ('fert') Fingerprint Evidence Recovery and Recording Techniques.

FIO ('F-I-O') Field Intelligence Officer or Financial Intelligence Officer.

Fishing Police vernacular for any speculative attempt, particularly where the intention is to try to recover evidence of potential value in a criminal case but the grounds for doing so (and the form of evidence to be seized) are uncertain.

FLA ('F-L-A') Family Law Act 1996.

FLINTS Forensic Linked Intelligence System: a database and comparative analysis system developed by West Midlands Police.

FLO ('F-L-O') (1) Family Liaison Officer (2) Forensic Laboratory Officer.

FOI ('F-O-I') Freedom of Information, as in a request under the Freedom of Information Act 2000.

Forensics21 An NPIA initiative to improve police forensic services (ended in 2012).

Foundation degree/FD A qualification at higher education level. There are a number of foundation degrees in Policing, many incorporating the NOS (qv) and the Diploma in Policing (qv) units for initial policing.

FPN Fixed Penalty Notice.

FSS (1) Forensic Science Service (closed in 2012); (2) Forensic Science Society.

FSU (1) Family Support Unit; (2) Firearms Support Unit.

FTS Forensic Telecommunications Services.

GBH Category of assault: Grievous Bodily Harm.

GMP Greater Manchester Police.

GPA Gay Police Association.

H2H House-to-house (as in conducting enquiries).

Handler Vernacular term for police officer responsible for liaising with and tasking a CHIS (qv).

Handling Taking illegal ownership of stolen or otherwise illegally obtained goods.

Hate crime ACPO (qv) defines a hate crime as any hate incident (qv), which constitutes a criminal offence and is perceived by the victim, or any other person, as being motivated by prejudice or hate.

Hate incident ACPO (qv) defines a hate incident as any incident, which may or may not constitute a criminal offence, that is perceived by the victim, or any other person, as being motivated by prejudice or hate.

Hearsay A reference to information that is not given directly (orally) to the court, but is somehow second-hand. It is generally not usable in a court as evidence, although there are many notable common law and other exceptions to this general rule.

Hermes A database of missing persons maintained by the MPB (qv).

Hit A DNA sample which can be matched with an identified person (not always criminal).

HMIC Her Majesty's Inspectorate of Constabulary. HMIC inspects at BCU (qv) and force levels and also carries out thematic inspections (eg into police training).

HMPS Her Majesty's Prison Service.

HMRC Her Majesty's Revenue and Customs (which has replaced 'Customs and Excise' and the 'Inland Revenue').

HOLMES, HOLMES2 Home Office Large Major Enquiry System: an information system designed to support large-scale police investigations (eg homicide).

Home Office A government department responsible for policy relating to policing and crime.

HORTies ('hortiz') Police vernacular reference to driving document production records HORT/1 and HORT/2.

HOSDB Home Office Scientific Development Branch, was part of NPIA (qv).

Hot spot A geographical location where there is a high incidence (or a perceived high incidence) of current crime and criminality.

HPDS High Potential Development Scheme.

HQ Headquarters.

HRA Human Rights Act 1998.

HSE Health and Safety Executive.

ibid Latin for 'in the same place'.

IC1, IC2 to IC9 (eg 'I-C-2') A reference to Identity Codes used by police officers to record ethnicity. IC1 is White European.

ICF Integrated Competency Framework. This combined descriptions of behavioural requirements with the National Occupational Standards (NOS (qv)) and profiles for a number of policing roles such as patrol constable. Replaced by the Policing Professional Framework (qv) during 2011.

ICIDP Initial Crime Investigators' Development Programme.

ICV Incident Command Vehicle used in situations where public order might be a problem.

IDENT1 ('ident-wun') The fingerprint database (replaced NAFIS (qv) in late 2004).

Idents Identifications (vernacular).

IDIOM Information Database for IOM; a database for tracking and monitoring PPOs (qv).

IED ('I-E-D') Improvised Explosive Device (a 'bomb').

IIMARCH ('eye-eye-march') Mnemonic for content of briefings: Information, Intention, Method, Administration, Risk assessment, Communications, Human rights compliance.

IL4SP Initial Learning for the Special Constabulary.

ILP/ILPM ('I-L-P') Intelligence-Led Policing and hence Intelligence-Led Policing Model; sometimes referred to as Intelligence-Based Policing, and also related to Information-Based Policing or Information-Led Policing.

IMPACT A College of Policing (qv) programme to improve police access to, and sharing of, information.

IMSC Initial Management of Serious Crime course.

IND Immigration and Nationality Directorate.

Independent Patrol The ability of a trainee police officer to conduct police patrol without the constant supervision of a qualified police officer. Usually achieved after successful completion of the PAC (qv).

Informant A person who passes intelligence to a source handler: a CHIS (qv). Often a criminal, an informant is known by other criminals as a snout, grass, or nark.

INI The IMPACT (qv) Nominal Index—a 'mega' database for searching of a number of smaller databases for information concerning named individuals.

Insp. or Ins. Abbreviation for 'Inspector', a policing rank.

Institutional racism A term used in 1999 by the Macpherson Inquiry (qv) which claims that institutions (eg the MPS), through their policies and procedures (both written and unwritten), can unintentionally behave in a manner prejudicial to ethnic minorities.

Inter-agency A term often employed in policing to describe approaches to crime investigation and reduction that involve partnership with non-police agencies: for example, collaboration with the Probation Service and Social Services. See also CDRP (qv).

inter alia Latin for 'among other things'.

Interpol International Criminal Police Organisation.

Intranet Often refers in police circles to a police internal electronic information system, with restricted access rights.

IO Investigating (police) Officer, usually a detective officer (for a crime), but can be a uniformed officer (eg for traffic collisions).

IP ('I-P') Injured Person or Party (often literally the person injured in a crime involving personal violence).

IPCC Independent Police Complaints Commission: deals with serious complaints against the police and investigates instances where police officers have used firearms.

IPLDP (I-P-L-D-P or 'ipple-dip') (1) Initial Police Learning and Development Programme: the programme of modernization of initial police training managed by the Home Office (qv). From April 2006 all new trainee police officers have been expected to undertake 'IPLDP-compliant' programmes of training in order to qualify as police officers; (2) Central Authority Responsible for the implementation and policy direction of IPLDP (qv), which includes representation from the Home Office, Police Federation, Superintendents' Association, and NPIA (qv).

ISO ('I-S-O') Individual Support Order. An ISO may be imposed upon a young person between the ages of 10 and 17 as a form of positive inducement to stop committing anti-social behaviour.

JAPAN: *J*ustification, *A*uthorization, *P*roportionality, *A*uditable, and *N*ecessary; a checklist for policing actions.

JBB Joint Branch Board of the Police Federation of England and Wales (qv).

JRFT Job-Related Fitness Test.

Justice Ministry Created in 2007 (from part of the Home Office) and responsible for the courts, prisons, probation, criminal law, and sentencing.

KUSAB ('queue-sab') *K*nowledge, *U*nderstanding, *S*kills, *A*ttitudes, and *B*ehaviours as developed in the training of student police officers.

Latent prints Prints (such as fingerprints) which are invisible until revealed by dusting or other techniques.

Lawrence, Stephen/the Lawrence Inquiry/the Macpherson Inquiry References to the death of the black teenager Stephen Lawrence in 1993, the subsequent investigation conducted by the MPS (qv), and the reports that followed (eg as conducted by Lord Macpherson, 1999).

LCN Low Copy Number; a tiny amount of DNA recovered through advanced scientific processes.

LDR Learning Development Review. These are regular reviews during training (typically three) as part of the IPLDP (qv) approach to monitoring achievement of a student police officer's skills and behaviour.

Learning Diary Under IPLDP (qv) trainee police officers keep a Learning Diary as part of the process of reflective learning. It may form part of the SOLAP (qv).

Learning Requirement A set of learning requirements that underpin the IPLDP (qv) curriculum designed by Professors John Elliott, Saville Kushner, and others (Elliott *et al*, 2003).

Level 1 Local crime signifier (used within NIM (qv)). Illegal possession of a controlled drug is a level 1 crime.

Level 2 Cross-BCU or cross-force crime signifier (used within NIM (qv)). Dealing in illegal drugs is a level 2 crime.

Level 3 National or international crime signifier (used within NIM (qv)). Organizing the importing or distribution of illegal drugs is a level 3 crime.

LGC Laboratory of Government Chemists (service provider for scientific analysis).

LIVESCAN Commercial computerized database for taking fingerprints digitally.

LOCARD Forensic database system.

loc cit Latin for 'at the place quoted'.

LPG Legislation, policy, and guidelines modules, part of the IPLDP curriculum (qv).

MAPPA ('mapper') Multi-Agency Public Protection Arrangements (part of the joint agency approach to managing violent and sex offenders).

MARAC Multi Agency Risk Assessment Conference.

Match An identified DNA (qv) sample.

MG 3 A form used to report to the CPS (qv) for an initial charging decision.

MG 11 Witness statement form.

MIM ('mim') Murder Investigation Manual (sometimes called the 'Murder Manual'), distributed by ACPO (qv). The MIM was the first example of a comprehensive doctrine (qv) to assist in the investigation of serious crime. It sets out the various investigative strategies that may be employed (eg the forensic strategy and the interview strategy). The MIM was written partly as a result of the enquiry into the death of Stephen Lawrence (qv).

minutiae Latin for 'of small parts'; the individuality of a fingerprint through examination of its ridge (qv) characteristics (up to 150 characteristics in a single finger print).

Misper Missing person or missing person forms.

MO ('M-O') *Modus operandi* is Latin for a characteristic way of doing something. Often used to refer to a particular way of committing a crime.

MoDP Ministry of Defence Police.

MOPAC Mayor's Office for Policing and Crime.

MoPI ('moppy') Management of Police Information.

Morris Inquiry An inquiry conducted by Sir William (Bill) Morris in 2004 into professional standards and employment issues in the MPS (qv).

MOU ('M-O-U') Memorandum of Understanding.

MPS Metropolitan Police Service: London's police force.

MSF Most Similar Force (for comparison).

Multi-agency A term employed in policing to describe approaches to crime investigation and reduction that involve partnership with non-police agencies.

NABIS ('nay-biss') National Ballistics Intelligence Service.

NACRO ('nak-roh') National Association for the Care and Resettlement of Offenders.

NAFIS ('naffiss') National Automated Fingerprint Identification System, now replaced by IDENT1 (qv).

National Crime Agency The National Crime Agency, the national law enforcement agency which has assumed responsibility for some of the work previously undertaken by the NPIA (qv), SOCA (qv), and the CEOP (qv).

National Injuries Database A searchable national database of (mainly) victim's wounds enabling comparisons.

National Missing Persons Bureau A missing persons information and expertise service located with SOCA (qv).

National Occupational Standards The National Occupational Standards (NOS) for policing were developed by Skills for Justice (qv). For initial police officer training there are currently 21 NOS which are required before confirmation (qv), but these are now embedded within a Level 3 Diploma in Policing (qv).

NB Latin for 'take especial note of'.

NBPA National Black Police Association.

NCA National Crime Agency (qv).

NCALT ('enn-kalt') National Centre for Applied Learning Technology. NCALT is a password-protected, internet-based learning portal for the police service.

NCIS National Criminal Intelligence Service, now subsumed within the now defunct SOCA (qv).

NCPE National Centre for Policing Excellence, part of the now defunct NPIA (qv).

NCS National Crime Squad, which was subsumed within the now defunct SOCA (qv).

NCSP National Community Safety Plan.

NDM National Decision Model.

NDNAD National DNA (qv) Database.

NDORS National Driver Offender Re-training Scheme.

NEFPN Non-endorsable Fixed Penalty Notice.

Nexus A combined computer database system.

NFA (1) No Further (police or CPS) Action; (2) No Fixed Abode; (3) National Fraud Authority (an executive agency of the Home Office (qv)).

NFFID National Firearms Forensic Intelligence Database.

NFIB National Fraud Intelligence Bureau, a central access point for individuals and organizations who suspect cybercrime, overseen by the City of London police.

NFIU National Football Intelligence Unit.

NFLMS National Firearms Licensing Management System: a database containing details of all firearm or shotgun certificate holders (and those in the process of applying for certificates).

NFRC National Footwear Reference Collection.

NHTCU National High Tech Crime Unit (part of the now defunct SOCA (qv)).

Nick Vernacular for: (1) a police station; (2) to arrest a person.

NID ('N-I-D' or 'nid') National Injuries Database (qv).

NIE ('N-I-E') National Investigators' Examination.

NIM ('nim' or 'N-I-M') National Intelligence Model. All police forces are required to follow the NIM, which is sometimes described as a business model for policing (see 22.1). The focus is largely, but by no means exclusively, on crime and criminality. It describes both strategic approaches (eg threat assessment) and tactical approaches (for example, the use of informants) for both police and inter-agency (qv) responses to crime and public disorder.

NMAT ('n-mat') National Mutual Aid Telephony, a national call-handling system for use in emergencies.

NMPR National Mobile Phone Register or the National Mobile Property Register.

Nominals Vernacular police term for those perceived to be active and often recidivist, high-volume criminals.

NOMS National Offenders Management Service.

Non-Home Office forces Somewhat misleading term that refers to police forces that are not one of the 43 county or city-based forces. Examples of non-Home Office forces include BTP (qv).

NOS ('N-O-S' or rarely 'noz') National Occupational Standards (qv).

NPAS National Police Air Service.

NPB National Policing Board.

NPIA National Police Improvement Agency: the umbrella term for organizations involved in police training, qualifications, assessment, scientific developments, and other means to improve the professional quality of policing. The NPIA was phased out during 2013. Much of its previous work is now managed by the College of Policing (qv), the National Crime Agency (qv), the Home Office (qv), and a police force (West Yorkshire Police and the National Police Air Service).

NPPF The National Police Promotion Framework (NPPF), a new system for promotion to Sergeant and Inspector ranks which is expected to replace the current arrangements.

NPT Neighbourhood Policing Team.

NSLEC National Specialist Law Enforcement Centre.

NSPIS National Strategy for Police Information Systems: a suite of databases and software to support case preparation, command and control, and custody processes.

NSY New Scotland Yard.

NTSU National Technical Services Unit.

NVQ National Vocational Qualification. There are NVQs at Levels 3 and 4 in Policing and other law enforcement roles, incorporating the relevant NOS (qv).

OCC Operations and Communications Centre.

OIC ('O-I-C') Officer in Charge.

OP ('O-P') Observation point for carrying out surveillance.

Op Operation, usually refers to a targeted police operation against a criminal problem, for example 'Op Damocles'. Note that the name of each operation is simply taken from a list and does not reflect the nature of the operation.

op cit Latin for 'see the work cited'.

ORC ('O-R-C' or 'ork') Operational Response Commander.

OSPRE® ('osspray') Objective Structured Performance-Related Examination, written tests for potential police sergeants or inspectors.

OST Officer Safety Training.

PAC ('P-A-C' or 'pack') Police Action Checklist. In many forces the satisfactory completion of a PAC is one of the criteria for the right to undertake Independent Patrol (qv).

PACE ('pace') Police and Criminal Evidence Act 1984.

PAS ('P-A-S') Police Advisers' (or Advisory) Service.

passim Latin for 'everywhere', but used in the sense of throughout.

PBE Pocket book entry.

PC or Pc Police constable.

PCC Police and Crime Commissioner.

PCeU Police Central e-Crime Unit, created in September 2008 and a national resource (partly funded by the Home Office (qv)), though based at the MPS (qv).

PCP Police and Crime Panel.

PCSO Police Community Support Officer.

PDP The Professional Development Portfolio is a tool for recording an individual police officer's professional development. The PDP for trainee police officers is effectively the Student Officer Learning and Assessment Portfolio (SOLAP (qv)).

PDU A dedicated Professional Development Unit for the development of trainee police officers, police officers, and other police employees.

PEACE ('peace') Mnemonic for an interviewing model, adopted by police forces in the UK. The letters represent the stages of an interview: *P*lanning and preparation; *E*ngage and explain; *A*ccount, clarification and challenge; *C*losure; and *E*valuation.

PentiP Penalty Notice Processing.

PI ('P-I') Performance Indicator; a type of quantitative measure which the Home Office often uses to assess the police service.

PIMS ('pimz') Performance Indicator Management System.

PIP ('pip') (levels 1, 2, 3, and 4) 'Professionalising Investigation Programme' originally developed by NCPE (qv). Level 1 is embedded in the initial training of student police officers (through mapping to the NOS (qv) 2G2, 2H1, and 2H2).

PIRA ('peer-ah') Provisional Irish Republican Army.

PKC Policing Knowledge Certificate, more properly known as the Certificate in Knowledge of Policing, a pre-join qualification.

PLO ('P-L-O') Prison Liaison Officer (a police officer).

PM Apart from its more common meaning (*post meridiem* or afternoon), it means a post mortem examination.

PNAC (sometimes 'p-nack') Police National Assessment Centre (sometimes 'Senior PNAC') for superintendents and chief superintendents who aspire to chief officer (qv) ranks.

PNB (1) Pocket notebook; (2) Police Negotiation Board.

PNC Police National Computer.

PND (1) Penalty Notice for Disorder; (2) Police National Database.

PNLD Police National Legal Database.

POCA ('poccah') Proceeds of Crime Act 2002.

Police Federation of England and Wales The national staff association for the federated ranks of constable, sergeant, inspector, and chief inspector, resembling a trade union.

Police Staff Official designation of support (civilian) staff, some of whom are operational but do not have the police officer warranted powers. Includes PCSOs (qv).

Police Superintendents' Association of England and Wales (PSAEW) The national staff association for the ranks of superintendent and chief superintendent.

POLKA ('polka') Police OnLine Knowledge Area, a restricted online collaborative site sharing policing knowledge and information.

PolSA/POLSA ('polsah') Police Search Adviser.

POP/BritPOP ('pop') Problem-Oriented Policing and its UK derivative.

PPF Policing Professional Framework—the replacement to the ICF (qv).

PPU Prisoner Process Unit.

PRDLDP Police Race and Diversity Learning and Development Programme.

Pre-entry programme or course See pre-join course or programme.

Pre-join programme or course A course of study and training, normally offered by a commercial provider, a further or higher education college or university, often in conjunction with a police force or forces and leading to entry to the police service as a student police officer. Many pre-join courses lead to a foreshortened period of subsequent training.

Probationer An informal term for a police officer in initial training and a reference to the probationary period. Now usually replaced by trainee police officer or trainee officer, but you may still hear the term used.

Profiling/Profilers An informal term often used in policing (as in 'offender profiling' and 'geographical profiling') but of uncertain meaning. Most often used to describe predicting the psychological traits of an unknown offender (eg when used to support the investigation into a linked serial rape case). However, the official ACPO (qv) term is behavioural analyst or behavioural adviser.

PS or Ps Police sergeant.

PSB or PSBM The basic personal safety course often included by forces as part of IPLDP (qv).

PSD Professional Standards Department.

PSNI Police Service of Northern Ireland (previously called the RUC, Royal Ulster Constabulary).

PWITS ('pee-wits') Possession (of drugs) with intent to supply.

QCF Qualifications and Credit Framework—the organization responsible for accrediting qualifications in England, Wales, and Northern Ireland.

QPM Queen's Police Medal.

qv Latin for 'for which, see'—reference to another item or word.

R&D Research and Development Unit (usually for intelligence analysis and tasking at BCU (qv) level).

Re-coursing/Back-coursing An informal term for the process of trainee police officers repeating elements of initial training, normally as a result of failure or for personal reasons.

Redcap Vernacular term for an officer of the RMP (qv).

Reflex Nationally funded project to deal with organized immigration crime.

Refs A vernacular reference to a refreshment break during a tour of duty.

Ridge and furrow Identifying features in fingerprints.

RIPA ('ripper') Regulation of Investigatory Powers Act 2000.

RIRA ('real I-R-A') Real Irish Republican Army.

RMP Royal Military Police.

ROTI ('roh-tee') A written record of a taped interview (audio-taped); a summarized account.

ROVI ('roh-vee') A written record of a video-taped interview; a summarized account.

RSHO Risk of Sexual Harm Order, a civil order to reduce grooming activities.

RTA (1) Road Traffic Act; (2) Road Traffic Accident—now largely replaced by RTI (qv) or RTC (qv).

RTC Road Traffic Collision. The term 'collision' is preferred to 'accident' as it is more suggestive of the fact that most collisions on roads are due to human error, negligence, or a criminal act, rather than a chance event. However, the term 'accident' is still present in legislation.

RTI Road Traffic Incident.

RV(P) Rendezvous (point) at a crime scene or major incident.

Sanitized Used to describe intelligence from which the identifying features and origins have been omitted.

SARA ('sarr-rer' or 'S-A-R-A') *S*can, *A*nalyse, *R*espond, and *A*ssess.

SARC ('sark') Sexual Assault Referral Centre.

SB Special Branch: a part of every police force that specializes in matters of national security and consists of non-uniformed police officers.

Scarman Inquiry (Scarman Report) An official inquiry into the circumstances surrounding rioting in the Brixton area of London in 1981, concluding with a number of recommendations on reforming the law, changing police training and practice, and improving community relations.

SCAS ('Scaz') Serious Crime Analysis Section. A database of homicides and stranger rapes housed at the Police College, Bramshill, housed by the NCA (qv).

SDE Self-defined Ethnicity.

SDN Short Descriptive Note (part of a case file, such as a reference to a transcription of an interview with a suspect).

Secret Policeman Reference to the video documentary made in 2003 by an undercover reporter and subsequently aired by BBC television. The documentary produced evidence of racist behaviour by police recruits at a police regional training centre.

SFO Serious Fraud Office (now part of SOCA (qv)).

SGM Second Generation Multiplex: a DNA-profiling system using seven areas for discrimination between people (1 in 50 million).

SGM+ A similar DNA-profiling system to SGM, using 11 areas for discrimination (1 in 1,000 million).

Sgt Abbreviation for 'sergeant', a policing rank.

Sheehy A reference to the Sheehy Report of 1993, which made a number of recommendations on police conditions, pay, and rank (most of which were not implemented at the time).

Shoe marks Informal term for footwear prints which can match a suspect to a crime scene, in the same way as DNA and fingerprints can.

Show out A vernacular reference to a security problem on a surveillance operation when the suspect realizes that he/she is being observed.

SIA ('S-I-A') Security Industry Association.

sic Latin for 'just as it is written'.

SIO ('S-I-O') Senior Investigating Officer (usually a detective officer) investigating a serious or major crime, such as a Category A or B murder (qv), or a rape or series of rapes.

SIODP Senior Investigating Officers' Development Programme.

SIU ('S-I-U') Special Investigation Unit (for child abuse and child protection investigations).

Skills for Justice/SfJ/S4J The Sector Skills Council (SSC) for Criminal Justice, including Policing. Skills for Justice is also responsible for the National Occupational Standards (qv) for Policing and other justice-related bodies and organizations (such as the Probation Service).

Skillsmark Quality assurance scheme introduced by Skills for Justice (qv).

SLA Service Level Agreement.

SLDP Senior Leadership Development Programmes (SLDP1 and SLDP2) for chief inspector roles or above.

SLP Senior Leadership Programme.

SMART(ER) Used in reference to objectives: *S*pecific, *M*easurable, *A*chievable, *R*ealistic, *T*imely (and *E*valuated and *R*eviewed).

SMT Senior Management Team (on a BCU (qv), it usually consists of the commander, a superintendent (or a chief superintendent on large BCUs), together with one or more chief inspectors (Crime and Operations) and a business manager).

SO 19 Firearms unit in the MPS (qv).

SOCA ('soccer') Serious Organised Crime Agency: established by the government in 2005 and phased out in 2013, its work (NCS, NCIS, SFO, and parts of HMCE (Investigation and Intelligence Divisions) and HM Immigration Service staff) is now carried out by the NCA (qv).

SOCO ('soccoh') Scenes of Crime Officer; outmoded term replaced in many police forces by CSI (qv).

SOCPA ('sockper') The Serious Organised Crime and Police Act 2005.

SOLAP ('soh-lap') Student Officer Learning Assessment Portfolio (see 8.4). In many forces this replaced the PDP (qv) for trainee police officers.

SOLO ('solo') Sex Offender Liaison Officer.

SOP ('S-O-P') Standard Operating Procedure.

SOPO ('sop-oh') Sexual Offences Protection Order.

SPoC/SPOC/spoc ('spock') Single Point of Contact.

SPP Strategic Policing Priorities.

Stinger Device for stopping cars by puncturing the tyres.

STO ('S-T-O') Specially trained officer.

STR Short Tandem Repeat: a DNA profiling methodology which replaces the SGM and SGM+ terms (qv).

Superintendents' Association The Police Superintendents' Association of England and Wales (qv).

Supervised Patrol Undertaken by trainee police officers under the supervision of a qualified police officer or officers.

T&CG Tasking and Coordinating Group.

Tac/TAC team (1) Tactical Support Team—for example, used to serve a warrant; (2) Terrorism and Crime Team (MPS (qv)).

TDA or TADA Taking and Driving Away: a reference to a form of vehicle crime. Also known as TWOC (qv).

Tenprint A fingerprinting process whereby all ten digits of a suspect or other individual are recorded.

Test Purchase The authorized purchase of drugs, alcohol, or other items (by an undercover police officer or another person) to provide evidence of illegal activity.

TFU Tactical Firearms Unit.

TIC ('T-I-C') Acronym for offences 'taken into consideration' by a court.

TIE (sometimes 'ty') Trace, Implicate, and/or Eliminate (in investigations).

TNA Training Needs Analysis.

TWOC ('twok') Taken Without (or Without Owner's) Consent—normally used in reference to a motor vehicle: TDA or TADA (qv).

UKAEAC United Kingdom Atomic Energy Authority Constabulary, replaced in 2005 by the CNC (qv).

UKBA UK Border Agency.

UKTA UK Threat Assessment (SOCA-derived).

Unit Part of a qualification. The NOS (qv) for initial policing consist of 21 units: for example, Unit CK1 to 'Search Individuals'.

UVP Ultra-Violet (Light) Photography.

VCSE Volume Crime Scene Examiner (forensic).

VDRS Vehicle Defect Rectification Scheme.

VEM ('V-E-M') Visible Ethnic Minority: refers to both individuals and communities.

VIAPOAR ('via-por') A mnemonic for the factors to take into account when making decisions; Values, Information, Powers and Policy, Options, Actions and Review.

VIPER ('viper') Video Identification Parade Electronic Recording.

ViCLAS ('vy-class') Violent Crime Linkage Analysis System—a database used by SCAS (qv) in the UK, originally devised by the Royal Canadian Mounted Police (RCMP).

ViSOR ('vy-zor') Violent and Sex Offender Register: a database of individuals considered a potential danger to the public because of their history of violence and/or sex offending.

Vol Volume.

VOO Violent Offender Order.

VPS Victim Personal Statement.

WBA Work-based Assessment.

'Whorl' With 'loop' and 'delta' etc, names given to fingerprint characteristics.

Winsor Review(s) Two reports (2011 and 2012) by Tom Winsor on pay, conditions, entry routes, and career pathways for police staff.

WPLDP Wider Police Learning and Development Programme.

YOT Youth Offending Team.

TASK 2 There could well be terms, acronyms, and jargon particular to your local police organizations and hence not on the preceding list. Your local force might have a list on its intranet, or on a publicly available website, or (more rarely) in a published form. Use the internet to try to track down a list.

2.4 Police Ranks

You may sometimes hear the police referred to as a 'disciplined organization'. This refers not only to the need for self-discipline and restraint but also to the fact that at least parts of the organization (those parts concerned with police officers) are organized into ranks in a hierarchical fashion, involving the issuing and receiving of orders. Apart from the MPS and one or two other forces, the rank structure (and the associated badges on the epaulettes of uniforms) are as follows:

Rank Structure

In order of decreasing superiority:
- Chief Constable;
- Deputy Chief Constable;
- Assistant Chief Constable;
- Chief Superintendent;
- Superintendent;
- Chief Inspector;
- Inspector;
- Sergeant; and
- Constable.

In the non-uniformed equivalents 'detective' often precedes the rank, for example Detective Chief Inspector.

The insignia of the ranks are as follows (as before, this may vary from force to force, as, for example, in the case of the PSNI):

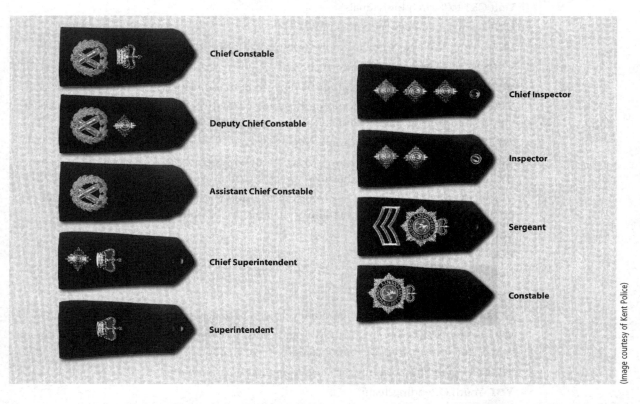

(Image courtesy of Kent Police)

In the MPS the rank structure is different above the chief superintendent rank; the three highest ranks are commissioners rather than chief constables; and there are two additional ranks marked with asterisks below:

MPS Rank Structure

- Commissioner;
- Deputy Commissioner;
- Assistant Commissioner;
- Deputy Assistant Commissioner;*
- Commander;*
- Chief Superintendent;
- Superintendent;
- Chief Inspector;
- Inspector;
- Sergeant; and
- Constable.

The City of London Police is a little different again.

You should also take the time to familiarize yourself with the insignia of uniformed members of the extended police family (see 3.4), such as special constables and PCSOs.

TASK 3 Construct a set of memory cards to help you learn the police ranks and their associated insignia. Memory cards are best made from thick paper or cardboard. (You may have used them as a child!) On one side of the card put the rank, on the other side the associated insignia, like so:

Superintendent

(Image courtesy of Kent Police)

Now take cards at random from your collection. If the name of the rank is given then describe the insignia. Reverse the card and check your answer. If the insignia is given, then you need to name the rank. As before, turn over to check your answer.

Keep playing (alone or in a group) until you have memorized all the ranks and insignia.

2.5 Typical Police Organizational Structure

The diagram shows a typical structure for a police force with 6,000-plus staff. There are likely to be small variations in different forces.

Overview

Overview

Typical police force structure

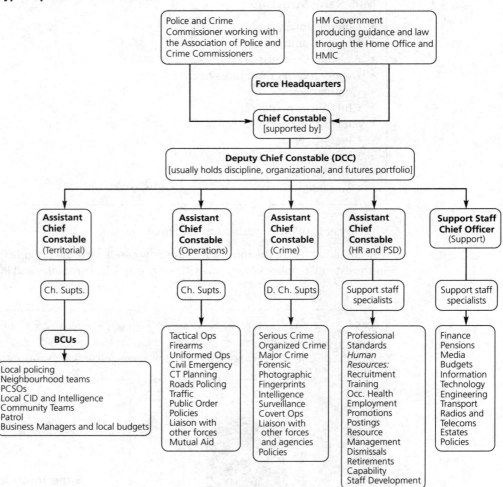

2.5.1   **Police and Crime Commissioners**

From November 2012, each police force now has an elected Police and Crime Commissioner (PCC), replacing the local police authorities as the body with the main responsibility for holding chief officers to account. Over three-quarters of the PCCs represent a political party, about one-third were previously involved with a police authority, about 20 per cent are former police officers, and only 15 per cent are women (APCCS, 2013). Each PCC is held to account by a Police and Crime Panel (PCP), the members of which are appointed. A minimum of ten of the panel members are local authority councillors (elected) and the other members individuals with specific skills or knowledge within their police locality. Although the PCP performs a similar role to existing local police authorities, the new system places much more emphasis on a single individual, the PCC. There are three important differences between a PCC and the previous local police authority:

- the PCC is a single person (as opposed to typically 17 individuals from different backgrounds, as was the case with the Police Authorities);
- the PCC is elected (rather than appointed, as is the case with local police authority members); and
- the PCC has a broader remit in holding other local crime-related agencies to account (compared with the much narrower scope of the local police authorities).

The introduction of PCCs will undoubtedly make the political dimensions of police work more explicit and transparent, but many also argue that the introduction of PCCs may undermine police independence and could hence lead to policing becoming more susceptible to political interference.

> **TASK 4** Find out the names and ranks of the individuals who lead your local police force. For example, who is the ACC responsible for training?

2.5.1.1 Police and crime plans

Every PCC in England and Wales is required (by the Police Reform and Social Responsibility Act 2011) to produce a police and crime plan setting out a strategy for policing and crime reduction. These plans will involve other community safety partners (eg health, local authorities, fire and rescue services) and other criminal justice agencies. Each plan covers a five-year period but they can be revised and updated each year. The plans are likely to contain specific objectives to be achieved. For example, one objective set by the PCC for Cumbria in 2013 was to 'Reduce the impact antisocial behaviour has on [Cumbrian] communities' with an associated priority to 'Promote restorative justice, encouraging a broader and more joined-up approach to the use of community resolutions to address offenders' behaviour, focussing on: antisocial behaviour, veterans, youth justice, rural crime' (Cumbria Police, 2014). Undoubtedly these police and crime plans have at least an indirect effect on the work of police service staff, and in many cases the effects will be relatively easy to see, in terms of changing priorities in operational policing.

2.6 Conventions for Conveying Information

If you have ever attempted to spell out a word on the phone to another person you have probably experienced the difficulty of clarifying the difference between 'm' and 'n', 's' and 'f', and so on. Mistakes made in the context of ordinary phone calls are seldom life-threatening, but if these same mistakes were made during a police communication it could prove costly, both in time and in terms of safety. This is the reason the 'phonetic alphabet' (sometimes referred to as the 'radio alphabet') and conventions for communicating numbers, time of day, and dates were developed and subsequently adopted by police forces throughout the UK.

2.6.1 The phonetic alphabet

With the phonetic alphabet each letter is given a phonetic equivalent. This is to avoid confusion over letters which sound the same, such as 'p', 'b', and 'd'; Instead of saying 'd' the police officer will say 'delta'. The following is a list of the phonetic alphabet as normally employed by police forces in the UK (and beyond). You may well be asked to memorize and use it after you join the police.

The Phonetic Alphabet

a Alpha	j Juliet	s Sierra
b Bravo	k Kilo	t Tango
c Charlie	l Lima	u Uniform
d Delta	m Mike	v Victor
e Echo	n November	w Whisky
f Foxtrot	o Oscar	x X-ray
g Golf	p Papa	y Yankee
h Hotel	q Quebec	z Zulu
i India	r Romeo	

(For a time 'Indigo' was used instead of 'India' but this practice is now very uncommon in police circles.)

> **TASK 5** Learn the phonetic alphabet. There are various ways of doing this, including using memory cards as in Task 3. One way of testing yourself is to spell out the names of family and friends.

2.6.2 Numbers

When communicating a number (eg the age of a person), then each digit of the number is said individually. There is a further convention that the number 0 is referred to as 'zero' and not 'naught' (nor as the letter 'O'). Hence the number 2,306 (two thousand, three hundred, and six) is communicated as 'two-three-zero-six'. A less common rule is to give large numbers in pairs such as 245,671 being conveyed as 'two-four, five-six, seven-one'. However, practice does vary with this (particularly with phone numbers).

2.6.3 Time and date

As you might guess, police forces tend to use the 24-hour clock for conveying the time of day. So 7.26 pm is written as 19.26 and hence said as 'one-nine, two-six hours' (see 2.6.2). Dates are given as the day-month-year, in the UK style.

2.7 IC and SDE Codes

There are a number of different situations in which a police officer might need to communicate or record a person's ethnicity, based upon an individual's appearance. The system used by some police forces to communicate the perceived ethnicity of a person is known variously as 'IC codes' 'IC 1 to 6 codes', 'PNC Codes', and 'ID codes'. An officer could use this to describe a suspect's ethnicity when searching for a record on the Police National Computer (or the Police National Database). The acronym IC probably now stands for 'Identity Code' (the system has been around for over 30 years). There are normally six or seven categories (IC 0/IC 7 not always being used):

Code	Definition	Nationality example*
IC 0 (sometimes IC 7)	Unknown	N/A
IC 1	White North European	Swedish
IC 2	White South European (sometimes 'Dark European' or 'Mediterranean')	Greek
IC 3	Black (sometimes 'Afro-Caribbean')	Nigerian
IC 4	Asian (sometimes 'South Asian')	Pakistani
IC 5	Chinese/Japanese/SE Asian (sometimes 'Oriental' or 'East Asian')	Chinese
IC 6	Middle Eastern (sometimes 'Arab')	Egyptian

*Ethnicity and nationality are not the same. Examples provided for illustration only.

Note that a different system might be used by a particular police force.

The Self-defined Ethnicity (SDE) codes (also known as '16 + 1') are codes used to record the ethnicity of a person as defined by that person him or herself. A student police officer will normally encounter these codes when completing forms. There are 16 ethnicity codes, plus one for 'not stated'. These are summarized in the following table.

General ethnic group	Self-declared ethnicity	Code
White	British	W1
	Irish	W2
	Any other White background	W9
Mixed	White and Black Caribbean	M1
	White and Black African	M2
	White and Asian	M3
	Any other mixed background	M9
Asian or Asian British	Indian	A1
	Pakistani	A2
	Bangladeshi	A3
	Any other Asian background	A9
Black or Black British	Caribbean	B1
	African	B2
	Any other Black background	B9
Chinese	Chinese	O1
Other ethnic group	Other ethnic group	O9
Not stated	Not stated	NS
Total		16 + 1 (not stated)

There is less variation between police forces in the use of these codes (when compared with the IC Codes—see previous table) as they are determined by the Home Office and adapted from the national UK census in 2001.

TASK 6 Use the internet to discover some of the previous IC codes employed by the police. (What 'unofficial' IC codes can you find?) What are the inherent problems when using police officer-defined codes for radio communication?

2.8 Answers to Tasks

TASK 1 Police websites sometimes include their force history (eg the extensive MPS site at <http://www.met.police.uk/history/>). Many forces also have museums (eg the Essex Police museum at Police HQ in Chelmsford) and some may also have a comprehensive and published written history (eg Ingleton, 2002).

TASK 2 Police forces often publish a glossary of terms used in their documentation, available under the Freedom of Information Act 2000. An example of a glossary may be found at <http://www.devon-cornwall.police.uk/AboutUs/LinksAbbreviations/Pages/Abbreviations.aspx>.

TASK 3 Using memory cards (sometimes also called 'flashcards') in the era of modern information technology may seem somewhat old-fashioned but they are a tried-and-tested method that works.

TASK 4 Many police websites have a 'Who's Who' section (although not always up to date), particularly for their Senior Management Team. Kent Police SMT for example is described on this page at their site: <http://www.kent.police.uk/about_us/our_organisation/our_org.html>.

TASK 5 You might like to test yourself by trying the NASA online phonetic alphabet tester available at <http://virtualskies.arc.nasa.gov/communication/2.html>.

TASK 6 In 1975 the police in London replaced their 'RC code' ('Race Code') with a new 'Identi-Coding'('IC') system. This assigned 'white-skinned European types—English, Scottish, Welsh, Scandinavian and Russian' to IC1; 'dark-skinned European types—Sardinian, Spanish, Italian' to IC2; 'Negroid types—Caribbean, West Indian, African, Nigerian' to IC3; 'Indians and Pakistanis' to IC4; 'Chinese, Japanese, Mongolians, Siamese' to IC5; and 'Arabians, Egyptians, Algerians, Moroccans and North Africans' to IC6. Even at the time this caused some controversy (Mackie, 1978).

An example of an unofficial IC code is 'IC 9' for people from the gypsy, Roma, or traveller community.

For operational reasons the police obviously require a quick, efficient, and timely means of communicating the ethnic appearance of a missing person, victim, or suspect. In terms of skin colour and other physical features a white South African does not resemble a black Nigerian and in some circumstances this is important. However, there are obvious definitional, empirical, and social problems in classifying individuals according to a perceived nominal categorization based on general physical appearance, skin colour, facial features, and so on. Put another way ethnicity is not defined by appearance, but the way someone looks might be part of their ethnicity. It is difficult because there is no reliable shared meaning of the descriptions 'black', white', 'Chinese', and so on when applied to people.

3 | Policing

3.1 Introduction

The title of this chapter is 'Policing' rather than 'The Police'. This reflects Reiner's distinction that the term '"Police" refers to a particular kind of social institution, while "policing" implies a set of processes with specific social functions' (Reiner, 2000, p 1). Policing is undertaken by a range of organizations and it is for this reason that Chapter 3 examines the 'extended policing family' and 'the multi-agency approach'. This chapter also engages with the aspects of learning and development (either as a student on a pre-join programme or as a trainee police officer) supporting the claim that policing is a profession. The demonstration of certain professional qualities will be required. These are sometimes less easy to pinpoint and identify than other aspects of learning and development (such as the acquisition of knowledge and demonstration of competencies and skills as outlined in Part III of this book), but they are just as important. If you can demonstrate these qualities you are very likely to have the potential to meet the requirements expected of a professional police officer in the twenty-first century.

Policing is always changing and evolving, but this is particularly true at the current time. The establishment of a professional body for policing is under way following the introduction of the College of Policing in December 2012. Alongside the introduction of the College of Policing, perhaps the most significant change for policing is the introduction of directly elected Police and Crime Commissioners (see 2.5.1) to replace local police authorities as the body with the main responsibility for holding chief officers to account. Without doubt, the current changes are profound, perhaps more dramatic and significant than any other changes in policing over the past 50 years or so.

3.2 Policing and Law Enforcement Agencies

The chronology of policing and law enforcement presented in 2.2 shows clearly that law enforcement in England and Wales has rarely been simply the province of the police alone. Many responsibilities for law enforcement and public order continue to be shared amongst a large number of agencies as shown in the table.

Type	Description	Examples	Comments
The 'territorial' or 'Home Office' police forces	The 43 county or metropolitan police forces in England and Wales, the single Police Services of Scotland and of Northern Ireland	Essex Police MPS Derbyshire Constabulary PSNI	What most people mean when they refer to the 'Police'
Sector-specific police forces	Police forces for specific sectors or industries (eg transport, nuclear power)	BTP CNC	Powers are at least equal to those of the territorial police forces

'Heritage' constabularies and police forces	Individual constabularies established previously under Acts of Parliament, restricted to small geographical areas	Port of Dover Police Royal Parks Constabulary Cambridge University Constabulary	Powers are the same as those for territorial police but the forces are small in size
Armed services police	Organizations responsible for policing the armed forces (eg the navy)	MoD Police Royal Military Police	Some armed services police are civilians and not members of the armed forces
Agencies	Home Office or non-statutory bodies with extensive powers of search, detention, arrest, and investigation	NCA (National Crime Agency) (for England and Wales)	The NCA is likely to subsume agencies such as SOCA in December 2013
National police 'units' or 'sections'	Normally ACPO or NPIA sponsored units offering specialist support to police forces	National Wildlife Crime Unit (NWCU) Serious Crime Analysis Section (SCAS)	Normally made up of seconded police officers, but not exclusively so
Other organizations with investigatory powers	Non-police organizations with limited powers of investigation (but which might include surveillance powers)	Local Authorities HM Revenue and Customs IPCC	Some powers are governed by RIPA 2000
Other organizations with enforcement and/or regulatory powers	Regulatory bodies with responsibility for enforcing regulations	Trading Standards HSE	Powers normally fall short of arrest although they can usually prosecute
Other 'emergency services'	Services, other than the police, usually involved in the case of fire, vehicle collisions, apparent accidents, and so on	Fire and Rescue Services	Some emergency services have powers for stopping people and vehicles, entry, investigation, and prosecution
'Private' security or investigatory services	Companies and individuals from the private security industry	Security guards 'Private detectives' Debt collectors	In some cases licensing is required or forms of self-regulation
Informal policing	Social control and enforcement as a secondary occupational responsibility	Teachers Park rangers Bus drivers	Normally no powers beyond that of the civilian

Informal policing activities are also undertaken at the so-called 'secondary' and 'tertiary' levels of social control, for example by teachers and bus conductors, and through institutions such as the church and trade union organizations. These informal policing mechanisms are not underpinned by powers beyond those of every citizen and are better understood as secondary occupational responsibilities or even less tangible societal responsibilities.

Despite the increased sharing of policing powers the 'public police' still retain unique and profound powers, including those surrounding discretion (see 3.6). We still often refer to our police organizations as 'forces' although you will also hear reference to the 'police service'. In 3.4 we examine some of the 'extended policing family' roles in more detail.

3.3 The Multi-agency Approach

We noted in 3.2 that policing responsibilities are shared among a number of agencies. The police in particular are encouraged (and sometimes required) to collaborate with a number of agencies in investigating crime, and on issues concerning public protection. A 'multi-agency' (sometimes 'inter-agency') approach to reducing crime and disorder and investigating crime is officially endorsed by the Home Office and others. The Diploma in Policing units to 'Provide initial support to victims and witnesses', 'Provide an initial response to incidents', 'Conduct priority and volume investigations', and to 'Interview victims and witnesses in relation to priority and volume investigations' make explicit reference to the police officer working and consulting with other agencies, organizations, and 'relevant others'. The Policing Professional Framework (PPF, see 8.5.2) states that one of the key personal qualities required for a police constable, is 'Work[ing] in partnership with other agencies to deliver the best possible overall service to the public'. Police forces have written force policy and protocols relating to multi- and inter-agency cooperation. Multi-agency collaboration is particularly evident in the following areas:

- **Child welfare and protection:** this is likely to involve cooperation between the police, health and social services, education and children's services. For example, if you are a trainee police officer on Independent Patrol you might attend an incident concerning alleged drink-driving but also notice at the scene a child who appears malnourished, bruised, and psychologically withdrawn. The trainee police officer will report this to their BCU's public protection desk. Children's services will then become involved and the circumstances further investigated.
- **Domestic abuse:** similarly, a police response to domestic abuse is likely to include working with specialist domestic abuse services (such as the local Women's Aid), social and health services, housing, education, and voluntary organizations (such as Relate). A multi-agency approach is recommended to provide protection and support to the victim and his or her dependants (see 15.7.3). A police force is also likely to have its own specialist domestic abuse investigation units. Note, however, that none of this detracts from the presumption that the police will arrest and take action against the alleged offender if possible (see 15.7).
- **Reducing crime and disorder:** the Crime and Disorder Act 1998 established on a statutory basis an obligation for the police and other agencies to work together to counter and reduce crime and disorder in their localities. This takes place formally within a Community Safety Partnership (see 3.3.2).
- **Partnerships with local councils or authorities over fixed-penalty notices:** fixed-penalty notices are often issued for parking infringements or driving offences (such as those recorded by speed cameras). The partnership is likely to include close cooperation with local authority CCTV monitoring teams, especially for city centres and popular club or pub venues.

3.3.1 Multi-Agency Public Protection Arrangements

Multi-Agency Public Protection Arrangements (MAPPA) are considered by many organizations as key to the successful management of violent and sexual offenders, especially their reintegration into society after a prison sentence. The Police, Probation, and the Prison Service in each area form a 'Responsible Authority' for MAPPA, and work together with other agencies such as social services, electronic monitoring providers, registered social landlords, youth offending teams, children's services, local health services, local housing authorities, and Jobcentre plus. MAPPA guidance identifies a framework with four core functions: identifying MAPPA offenders; ensuring relevant information is shared with appropriate agencies; assessing the risk of serious harm; and managing risk.

The guidance identifies three broad categories of offenders (with some overlap):

- Category 1—registered sexual offenders as defined in Part 2 of the Sexual Offences Act 2003;
- Category 2—violent offenders sentenced to 12 months or more imprisonment, sexual offenders not included in Category 1, and offenders disqualified from working with children; and
- Category 3—other dangerous offenders who are not included in the first two categories but are nonetheless still regarded by the Responsible Authority as presenting a serious risk to the public (eg they have a previous conviction or caution that indicates that they have the potential to cause serious harm to others).

There are three identified levels of risk management. Level 1 is for offenders who can be managed by one primary agency without necessarily involving other agencies. Level 2 management involves more than one agency but is not considered to be overly challenging or complex. Level 3 is used where managing the risk requires active conferencing and senior representation from the Responsible Authority and other agencies with a duty to cooperate.

In 2013 there were just over 60,000 'MAPPA offenders' in the UK (73 per cent Category 1; 27 per cent Category 2; and only 1 per cent Category 3) and over 95 per cent of cases were managed at Level 1 (MoJ, 2014).

In deciding on what course of action to take it is important that 'defensible decisions' are made. This is to ensure that the Responsible Authority has taken all reasonable steps, and that the assessment methods utilized are reliable. A thorough evaluation of the collected information needs to be demonstrated, and decisions need to have been recorded and acted upon. Throughout it is important to demonstrate that the appropriate policies and procedures have been followed, and that a proactive approach has been adopted by the practitioners and managers. An important function of MAPPA is to ensure that public protection work is communicated to the public in a consistent manner.

3.3.2   Community Safety Partnerships

The Crime and Disorder Act 1998 made partnership-working a statutory requirement for organizations such as police authorities, local authorities, fire and rescue authorities, primary care trusts, the Probation Service, and the Drug and Alcohol Action Team. These 'Community Safety Partnerships' (CSPs) work together to identify and respond to crime problems within a specific area (Rogers, 2006). There are about 320 CSPs in England and Wales. Trainee police officers are most likely to encounter CSPs in terms of the local force priorities.

CSPs meet regularly and discuss how to develop strategies to combat crime in the local area. Their key objectives are to:

- establish the level and extent of crime and disorder within the area;
- consult widely with the local population;
- develop a strategy aimed at tackling problems with a clear action plan with organizational responsibilities; and
- review the current strategy periodically.

The aim is to share information and working with other local public, voluntary, and private organizations to achieve agreed objectives, by means of an agreed strategy to reduce crime and improve community safety and quality of life.

3.3.3   Community Safety Units

Each police force contributes resources to a local Community Safety Unit (CSU) to coordinate the work of the police locally, in collaboration with the other local agencies such as district and county councils and primary health care trusts. (In some forces this coordinated multi-agency work might have a different name.) CSUs implement CSP strategic decisions and respond to local need through a full-time Community Safety Team. Given the local focus of CSUs there will be different priorities in different areas, but there are a number of common roles and functions. For example, they have an obligation under the Crime and Disorder Act 1998 to audit the crime and disorder problems in their respective areas and to devise suitable strategies (every three years) to prevent and reduce crime. This includes addressing quality of life issues and the fear of crime.

3.3.4   Youth Offending Teams

Youth Offending Teams (YOTs) are run by local authorities and bring together and help coordinate the work of a number of different agencies, including the police. They work with young people who are at risk of offending or reoffending, and offer support through education, employment, work placements, psychological support, and mentoring. YOTs also provide support for young people who have been arrested or have to attend court.

3.4   The Extended Policing Family

As can be seen from the previous paragraph, policing involves an array of providers to form an extended policing family. Here we draw attention to a number of significant players within the extended policing family. This is not an exhaustive list, but it does provide an indication of the various different kinds of policing arrangements, including voluntary, regulatory, and private policing providers.

In broad terms, in 2013 there were approximately 214,000 full-time equivalent (FTE) staff working for the police forces of England and Wales of which about 60 per cent were police officers, 30 per cent police support staff, and 7 per cent PCSOs (the remaining 3 per cent undertook roles such as traffic wardens) (House of Commons Library, 2014).

3.4.1 Special constables

Special constables ('Specials') are volunteers, and are sworn officers with full powers who undertake police duties on a part-time basis. They must be over the age of 18 and be a national of a country within the European Economic Area, or a national of a country outside the EEA, with the right to reside in this country without restrictions. Traditionally, most special constables have had day jobs; the system functions very much in the same way as the Territorial Army, or RAF, or Naval volunteer reserve forces. In most forces, they work alongside regular officers, go out on patrol, and deal with the range of activities which a patrol constable would encounter during an ordinary shift. Increasingly, individuals appear to be joining the specials as a route into the regular police force, particularly as part of a pre-join scheme. Recent developments in some police services have even required future applicants to the police service to serve as special constables before applying for full-time employment (Metropolitan Police Authority, 2010). Consequently, there are a growing number of specials who are in full- or part time education. Whilst such initiatives are currently welcomed, primarily on economic grounds, there might be issues further down the line for the status of specials as more focus is placed on what a police officer needs to know before being issued with a warrant card. For example, consider the implications if a special constable applies to his/her force to become a paid full-time police officer through the national SEARCH© assessment process (see 8.2), but is rejected (perhaps on the grounds of respect for diversity). This could raise concerns over whether he/she should retain the status of a warranted officer.

The training for specials is the IL4SC (Initial Learning for the Special Constabulary) programme, and utilizes both workplace assessments (against the NOS) and the assessment of knowledge and understanding (often deploying the Diploma in Policing learning descriptors as a basis).

3.4.2 Police support staff

In many forces, support staff can make up to a third of total numbers, and they undertake a wide range of tasks. There were approximately 63,000 police support staff in England and Wales in 2013. They were previously termed 'civilian' and this was often associated with administration or other 'non-police' work, but those days are long gone in most police forces. However, despite the extent to which police support staff have become increasingly integral to the wider policing family, such roles are undoubtedly most at risk when police budgets are cut.

> **TASK 1** Suggest some examples of the types of work police support staff might carry out.

You may be able to think of other police support staff roles (such as training) in a police force, but other important support staff include crime scene investigators, statement takers, detention officers, and lawyers. Other functions such as IT and finance are also carried out by support staff to complement the operational policing side of the work. For some areas in policing it may be more appropriate to employ specialist support staff (high-tech crime and fraud being two obvious examples) than to rely on 'omnicompetent' officers. This is part of a wider debate about the purpose of sworn officers, where police powers are needed, and where they are not.

3.4.3 Other police forces

As noted in 3.2, in addition to the Home Office 'territorial' forces of England and Wales there are other police forces such as:

- British Transport Police who are responsible primarily for policing the railway network in the UK (over- and underground). With its headquarters in London, BTP has uniformed and plain clothes officers travelling on the railways and performing police functions. BTP figured very prominently in cooperation with the MPS in the wake of the tube train bombings in London on 7 July 2005.
- The Ministry of Defence Police who guard MoD establishments (naval dockyards, airfields, and army regimental depots) across the UK (ie including Scotland). Other police forces within the armed forces are the Royal Military Police (RMP) and the RAF's Provost and Security Services (P&SS). These have jurisdiction only within their force establishments and then only for crimes which are not classified as major crimes. Murders and serious assaults are usually investigated by the local police force.

- The Civil Nuclear Constabulary (CNC) who protect civil nuclear installations and fuels in shipment and storage, and all its officers are firearms-trained.

3.4.4 Police Community Support Officers (PCSOs)

PCSOs work alongside police constables in policing local neighbourhoods. Their role is to help reduce crime and anti-social behaviour and provide reassurance to the public. They do this by engaging with the public and identifying their concerns and supporting those who are affected by anti-social behaviour, crime, or the fear of crime. They are encouraged to engage with the public, to walk or travel on a limited beat where they can be seen and spoken to, and there is an emphasis on their meeting and talking to young people. PCSO uniforms are similar to those of warranted police officers but they have blue ties and their epaulettes clearly identify them as Police Community Support Officers. Despite some initial hostility from quarters within the police themselves, the PCSO appears popular with the public, particularly in London.

PCSOs do not have a power of arrest but some have the power to detain. The 'standard' powers include entering premises to save life and limb, issuing fixed penalty notices for littering, requiring a person's name and address for anti-social behaviour. Additional powers can be granted at the discretion of chief officers, and include detaining a person for up to 30 minutes, using reasonable force to prevent a detained person from escaping, and issuing penalty notices for disorder. All PCSOs must carry documentation detailing the powers they have.

PCSO training involves being assessed against six of the ten Diploma in Policing units, but with one unit at level 2 rather than level 3. This is similar to the training and assessment of special constables. Some PCSOs are using the scheme as a route into regular policing. Many of the PPF personal qualities (see 8.5.2) for PCSOs are identical to those for police officers.

> **TASK 2** Think about what you know about PCSOs and the work they do. What form do you imagine PCSO training takes, and how long might it last?

3.4.5 Other policing and law enforcement agencies

Many aspects of our lives are predominantly policed by individuals other than sworn police officers, for example the policing within most football grounds is conducted by stewards. Likewise, the policing of the night-time economy in our town and city centres (to reduce the likelihood of serious disorder) involves many more privately employed individuals than sworn police officers. There are also non-police agencies which investigate and then turn their findings over to the police to take to court, while others have investigative powers and can also prosecute their own cases. HM Revenue and Customs, for example, has powers to investigate other crimes such as evasion of VAT or other taxes, improper importing, and other matters. Likewise, the United Kingdom Border Agency (UKBA) employees have specific powers in relation to immigration and customs matters. There have been moves to centralize and coordinate investigative capacities across different agencies initially through the introduction of the Serious and Organised Crime Agency (SOCA) in 2006 and more recently through the establishment of the National Crime Agency (NCA) in 2013. The NCA has subsumed the work of SOCA and has strong partnership links with other agencies such as the UKBA and has a number of different 'command' units, including its Border Policing Command, an Economic Crime Command, an Organised Crime Command, and a Child Exploitation and Online Protection Command.

3.4.6 Regulatory bodies

These are bodies which have a particular interest in specialized matters such as public health or environmental crime, and can prosecute offenders. This category includes:

- the Health and Safety Executive (HSE);
- Trading Standards Authorities;
- the National Society for the Prevention of Cruelty to Children (NSPCC);
- the Royal Society for the Prevention of Cruelty to Animals (RSPCA); and
- the Royal Society for the Protection of Birds (RSPB).

In a sense, most of these bodies focus on niche crime, such as maltreatment of animals and stealing birds' eggs. Only the work of the HSE and the NSPCC impact substantially on police work, although it seems likely that environmental crime will have a higher profile in the future.

3.4.7 The private sector

Despite the debacle of Group4's difficulties in providing the policing services it had agreed to for the 2012 London Olympics, the Coalition government remains firmly wedded to the idea that private companies, including Group4, have an important role to play within the extended policing family into the future. The private security industry is expanding rapidly and includes staff such as door stewards at clubs, and security guards who patrol areas frequented by the public. The last few years have seen an increase in the number of 'gated communities' (following a US model), where access to a group of private and exclusive dwellings is controlled by uniformed guards 24 hours a day. This reassures the householders that privacy is guaranteed, and increases physical security, making burglaries, robberies, and assaults more difficult to commit or attempt. Licensing for staff is being introduced for many security occupations such as door stewards and vehicle immobilizers personnel (clampers). More information is available on the SIA website.

Security extends across the community, for example through bailiffs and the use of CCTV. Bailiffs recover property that has not been fully paid for, or seize goods in lieu of debt, and may work with the police, particularly with evictions or where there is concern about public order. The extension of the policing family also includes the large surveillance system (eg monitored CCTV) across the UK, and automated number plate readers (ANPR) linked to cameras mounted on bridges and gantries (see 22.3.1) to monitor vehicle movements. The use of CCTV in police surveillance work is discussed in 22.3.1.

When considering the steady growth of private security, we should not ignore the large established security companies, such as Group4 and Securitas AB. They are involved in all aspects of private security, such as cash collection from businesses, the provision of physical security, and the transportation of prisoners. There can be a blurring of roles between public policing and private policing when private companies provide security for organizations, for example at some animal research facilities external security seems to be run by the police whilst internal security seems to be managed by a private company. The degree of cooperation that exists between the two, and the distinctions between 'accountable police activity' and 'unaccountable police activity' are not clear.

An important question raised in relation to private policing concerns the very purpose of the police. They carry out a variety of activities with a common purpose; to serve the public interest, and it is in this sense (perhaps more so than the question of how the police are funded), that the police are deemed to be public, as opposed to private. However, many police organizations receive private funding; for example, BTP are partially funded by the rail companies. Indeed, all public police services are increasingly generating income beyond that provided by government through the Home Office, and it seems likely that an increased reliance on private funding will make profitability rather than public interest a greater consideration. This concern has been raised in relation to announcements in 2012 by Surrey Police and West Midlands Police, indicating that they were considering contracting private companies to perform some aspects of police duties.

Finally (though we have by no means exhausted the examples of the private security industry), we may look at private investigators. These are small-scale enquiry companies (seldom exceeding half a dozen employees) which are usually staffed by ex-police officers. They are principally engaged in matters such as gathering evidence for presentation in divorce cases or tracking down missing persons. They present little in the way of conflict with the regular police, except when attempts are made to access official records or data such as vehicle number plates.

3.4.8 Policing cyberspace

Cybercrime is an example of a digital crime that has now taken on a more defined meaning. It refers to crimes occurring in a networked environment (such as the internet), but only to crimes that are more than simply facilitated by that environment. The term cybercrime therefore usually embraces the following criminal or anti-social activities: computer hacking and cracking; developing and/or spreading malicious code (eg viruses and Trojans); spamming; network intrusion; software piracy; network-based or network-enabled crimes (eg phishing and identity theft); IPR crimes (eg illegal file-sharing); and distribution of child sexual abuse imagery (Bryant and Bryant, 2014).

Police forces in the UK have their own locally based resources to investigate cybercrime. The centre of responsibility may vary, however, although typically it will involve variously either a 'High-Tech Crime Unit' (eg Lincolnshire Police); a 'Computer Crime Unit' (eg Strathclyde Police); 'Digital Forensics Unit' (eg Kent Police); or even be part of an 'Economic Crime Unit'. These units, often evolved from earlier force 'Fraud Squads', tend to be relatively small in size, and most of their work appears to be taken up with child abuse investigations.

The Police Central e-Crime Unit (PCeU) is based at the MPS, and is part of the NCA's new National Cyber Crime Unit (NCCU). The PCeU's Computer Crime Team has the remit to investigate and prosecute incidents such as 'Computer intrusion, Distribution of malicious code, Denial of service attack and internet-enabled fraud' (PCeU, 2014).

The PCeU works closely with the Child Exploitation and Online Protection (CEOP) Centre, which is also part of the NCA. A National Fraud Intelligence Bureau (NFIB) has been created as a central access point for individuals and organizations who suspect cybercrime. A UK-wide fraud and internet crime reporting centre (called 'Action Fraud' and run by the Home Office's National Fraud Authority) is responsible for collating all reports of fraud, including through cybercrime.

Thus responsibility for cybercrime investigation is not restricted to the police service, nor do they have the resources to investigate all reported cybercrimes. For example, it is widely acknowledged in the UK that the police are unable to investigate all reported credit and debit card offences. These may have been committed through phishing and pharming (eg through a 'botnet') or by more traditional methods (eg City of London Police, 2005). Cyber crimes are effectively 'screened' to decide whether further investigation is appropriate (see 23.4). Level 1 or 2 plastic card crimes, if investigated, are likely to be tackled by a force-based unit. Any Level 3 plastic card-related crime is likely to be passed to the NCA for investigation. The industry itself already supplements the police resources available to investigate plastic-card crime: for example, the industry body APACS sponsors the work of the Dedicated Cheque and Plastic Crime Unit (DCPCU).

Although the investigation of cybercrime will invariably involve the collection of 'traditional' forms of evidence (eg in written form) there might also be digitally based evidence such as a deleted file recovered from a PC hard drive, or the address book from a mobile phone SIM card. The actions police officers should take at crime scenes where such evidence may be required are covered in 25.7.3. The forensic techniques required from recovery to analysis (often known as digital forensics) are a specialist field within investigation. ACPO has published good practice guidelines for the handling of digital evidence and recommends that digital evidence strategies should form part of the wider investigative process (ACPO, 2007a and ACPO, 2012a). Police forces may choose to 'outsource' some digital forensic analysis to non-police contractors, who are also expected to meet the good practice guidelines.

3.5 Personal Authority and Legitimacy

Authority is a key concept for the police and of particular interest to the trainee police officer and students undertaking pre-join programmes. The exercise of authority is often viewed as a mark of a professional although 'authority' is often expressed or described instead as autonomy or credibility and related concepts. If you are a trainee police officer your authority will certainly be challenged on occasions, and you will no doubt find yourself thinking deeply about your authority, and maybe about how to increase it! There are a number of personal qualities that you need to exhibit before completing training (see the PPF in 8.5.2) and some of these are clearly related to personal authority.

In the 1960s and 1970s, the educational philosopher Richard Peters (often referred to as RS Peters, who usually wrote and worked in collaboration with Paul Hirst) argued that there are different forms of personal authority which nonetheless interrelate (Peters, 1973). Although Peters' focus was authority in education we have adapted his work here to apply to policing.

3.5.1   The main forms of personal authority

The main forms of personal authority are considered to be:

- **epistemic**: authority from knowledge (knowing more than the next person);
- **natural** (sometimes called 'charismatic authority'): derived from personality, demeanour (non-verbal communication);
- *de facto* (from fact): authority that exists through convention rather than as a matter of right;
- *de jure* (from right): authority as a matter of right; and
- **moral**: authority that arises from a moral high ground.

Note that these categories are not intended to be mutually exclusive. As we shall see later, *de facto* and moral authorities, for example, are often linked. It is also important to note that authority here can relate to two distinct concepts. There is the general authority of the police service, often thought about in terms of legitimacy and which is discussed in 3.5.3. The second is the authority of the individual police officer, which will vary from individual to individual, and it is that which concerns us here.

3.5.1.1   What do these mean for a police officer?

A police officer's *epistemic* authority stems from knowledge of the law and procedure. The public expect a police officer to know the rudiments of the law. Although members of the public may know that an offence has occurred (by applying their common sense), they will expect an officer to know which particular law or laws have been broken. In part, this expectation is fed by media portrayals of the police which often feature a police officer using the words 'I arrest you for [specifics of the offence]'. Therefore, if in a particular situation it is seen that a police officer's grasp of the law or proper procedure seems uncertain, then his or her epistemic authority will decrease. The law, policy, and guidelines studied during training (eg the IPLDP LPG modules: see 1.4.2) provide the basis for establishing epistemic authority.

Some people appear to have more *natural authority* than others through sheer presence (charisma), and are more able to take control when required. This form of authority can be developed, and trainee police officers will receive training on demeanour, use of language, non-verbal communication (body language), and other more subtle ways in which natural authority can be enhanced. Other factors are important too; being smartly dressed (polished shoes, clean and tidy uniform, etc) may seem a strangely old-fashioned topic for a Handbook of this kind but they are important aspects of a trainee officer's personal authority when, for example, giving evidence in court.

Police officers are seen to have *de facto* authority in certain circumstances, for example in the aftermath of a road traffic collision, or the expectation that road users will move out of the way of police patrol cars using their sirens and lights. This authority comes not just from the law, but through custom. In terms of the extent to which citizens trust the police and see the police as a legitimate authority, Tom Tyler in the USA and a number of academics in the UK have shown empirically that citizens appear to be more concerned with how police officers conduct themselves and carry out their duties, rather than what they achieve (see Tyler, 2003; Bradford *et al*, 2009; Myhill and Bradford, 2011; and Jackson *et al*, 2013). The focus of this research is on how perceptions of procedural justice inform the legitimacy of police authority. The *de facto* form of authority is easily lost if abused (or perceived as such), and members of the public will no doubt carry on making wry comments about the police using their sirens and lights to get back to the station more quickly for their cup of cocoa and a biscuit!

It is a simple fact that police officers have powers that are not granted to other members of society. These powers are the main source of an officer's *de jure* authority, and many are covered in this Handbook. The wearing of a uniform symbolizes this form of authority, to separate a police officer from the rest of society, as does the possession of a warrant card.

Police officers are expected to subscribe to a code of ethics and behaviour which is of a higher standard than the rest of society, and this gives them not only *moral authority but also moral responsibilities*. There are certainly greater moral obligations on the police when compared to many other occupational groups, for example in terms of honesty, integrity, fairness, impartiality, politeness, and general conduct. Gross examples of inappropriate police behaviour (such as the ill-treatment of prisoners) undermine the moral authority of the police service as a whole, but there are other less dramatic examples at the level of the individual. Put simply, members of the public do not expect to witness police officers swearing in public, smoking on duty, or acting other than seriously in the role. These restrictions on the personal behaviour of police officers and the effect on their moral authority also extend to life off-duty. Where is the moral authority of a police officer who arrests an acquaintance for possession of cocaine during a raid on Saturday, having smoked cannabis with him the previous evening? How is a police officer's moral authority affected if she uses her warrant card to gain free entry to a nightclub? Retaining moral authority also requires police officers to maintain a moral perspective when dealing with the public. It is not appropriate, for example, to judge a member of the public by the same high standards that a police officer must follow, and it is partly for this reason that the 'attitude test' (see 3.6.5) is an unacceptable means of deciding whether to arrest a person.

The College of Policing drafted a Code of Ethics for policing in late 2013, which was made available for consultation and a final version of the Code is due to come into effect in April 2014.

3.5.2 Development of personal authority

If you are a trainee police officer, then it is likely that there will be opportunities for you to develop your personal authority during your initial training. These may include:

- preparing and delivering presentations to others, including groups of students and training staff;
- increasing your knowledge and recall of the law and procedure;
- observing your own behaviour, including your demeanour and use of language, for example by analysing video of your performance whilst undertaking a particular task; or
- feedback from others, including your trainers, assessors, fellow trainees, and representatives of community groups (eg whilst undertaking your community attachment).

> **TASK 3** Imagine you are a police officer and you have arrested a woman on suspicion of assault and theft in a shopping centre. The victim has identified the suspect, who cannot explain her possession of the victim's mobile phone. Give examples of how the five forms of personal authority would feature in this particular scenario.

3.5.3 Legitimacy

The issue of legitimacy is central to debates about the police role in liberal democratic societies. The existence of police authority requires individuals to willingly sacrifice a degree of personal freedom and liberty in order to secure a greater degree of collective freedom and liberty. The logic behind this way of thinking is made explicit in the writings of the seventeenth-century English philosopher Thomas Hobbes: without authority in society there would exist 'a war of all against all'. For Hobbes, therefore, the existence of any authority is preferable to none at all. This is an important point to note because, as Nozick (1974) and Simmons (2001) argued, the necessity for authority must be considered before questioning the legitimacy of authority. The difficulty in justifying police authority is illustrated by the fact that it took six attempts (from 1785 onwards) to pass a Police Bill through the Houses of Parliament, to create the 'new' police in 1829. Clearly there was opposition at the time to the very existence of a professional standing body of police in England and Wales. Today, we largely take the existence of the police for granted, and very few people seriously question whether we would be better without any police.

Nonetheless, in terms of civil liberties, it is important to be able to justify a police presence, especially given the extent to which we could argue that such a presence may be expensive (eg at football matches) or disproportionate (such as in shopping malls). We may even go beyond justifying the mere existence of the police to consider the more pressing and ongoing debate concerning the legitimacy of the police. Here it is worth noting two distinct means through which it can be established: consensual and moral legitimacy.

3.5.3.1 Consensual legitimacy of the police

The police are quite rightly governed by the law, but the issue of legitimacy is central to debates about the police role in liberal democratic societies in other ways too. Consensual legitimacy is gained through the support of the people and communities who are being policed. It reflects the democratic aspect of policing within a liberal democracy, the notion of 'policing by consent'

(Reiner, 2000). In the early years of the police the discussion about legitimacy was almost exclusively concerned with consent, and today the Home Office's focus on neighbourhood policing (see 3.9.1) places great emphasis on the importance of this issue.

From the perspective of those advocating consensual legitimacy, the police are legitimate to the extent that the public consent to policing. Of course there are differing degrees to which we might say the public consents to the police. One view is to say that the public consents passively by not opposing what the police do. On the other hand we might insist on the public having an ongoing engagement with the police in order for consent to be given actively. In practice, the kind of consent gained will be dependent upon the type of police response and the particular problem addressed. For example, if the police are required to deal with a serious threat of terrorism, then the consent will have to be passive in order to allow the police to be effective. (The more the public knew about how the police intended to counter the terrorists, the more the terrorists would also know and the police intervention might fail as a consequence.) Conversely, when the police are required to resolve low-level but persistent offending, there is more need for the police to communicate with the local community, to establish and agree the best way to address the problem. In this latter case, the consent must be active and ongoing. The police need to negotiate their response to the problem and ensure that the community supports, as much as is possible, any police interventions. In this respect, to ensure consensual legitimacy of the police there must be appropriate public involvement in negotiating police responses, and the response must deal effectively with the particular problem. An appeal for witnesses to an event is a common form of this nexus between police and public.

There are limits to consensual legitimacy, for example the police could theoretically be too responsive to the views of the communities being policed. As Waddington (1999) has noted, the police are required to deal with conflicts in society and in the exercise of this function they may have to police 'against' some sections of the community. A real concern exists that the police might be overly responsive to one section of the community against another. This could lead to the exclusion and/or targeting of groups of individuals who are seen to be on the periphery of a community. Put another way, the popularity of the police, which is effectively what consent measures, is no guarantee that the police are acting in a legitimate way. Equally, people's fears or concerns may not necessarily match the prevailing crime patterns, and may not help the police to focus effort appropriately.

There are various ways of establishing the legitimacy of police authority, and approval from citizens is just one. As Simmons (2001) observes, this particular way of establishing legitimacy focuses on how an authority is perceived, rather than what it does. It measures the attitudes of the recipients of the authority, rather than measuring the authority itself. In a similar vein, Bottoms and Tankebe (2012) draw attention to the limits of the procedural justice approach to ascertaining police legitimacy (see 3.5.1.1) on the grounds that it captures the perspective of the 'audience', but not the power-brokers themselves.

We might say that consent is a necessary, but not sufficient, aspect of police legitimacy. In liberal democratic terms, consent reflects democratic, but not liberal concerns. The liberal concerns within liberal democratic contexts are expressed more through the moral legitimacy of the police, rather than consensual legitimacy.

3.5.3.2 The moral legitimacy of the police

It is also becoming increasingly important for the police to 'do the right thing' from a moral perspective. The course of action that would be supported by a local community is not always the moral one, and the community might not support all morally correct policing actions. For example, the police will not always be able to gain consensual support for protecting a known paedophile living within a residential area, or allowing a racist organization to march through the town centre. However, the reason why the police do what they do is often a matter of moral legitimacy rather than consensual legitimacy.

As far as possible, the police will try to achieve both moral and consensual legitimacy, but this is not always possible. The former Chief Constable of Devon and Cornwall, John Alderson, has been an advocate of what he refers to as 'principled policing' for a number of years (see Alderson, 1998). He has argued that policing should be more firmly founded upon moral principles, rather than pragmatic concerns. The Human Rights Act 1998 has given legislative support to this point of view. Increasingly, police officers must take into account a number of (often different or contradictory) moral considerations in order to make professional judgements. Policing by consent remains an important part of police legitimacy, but the police must operate primarily within both legal and moral boundaries if they are to be truly legitimate.

> **TASK 4** What would you need to take into account if (as a police officer) you had to control a march by the British National Party through your town, knowing that the Anti-Nazi League was planning to turn up in large numbers to oppose the march? (Note that our interest here is in judgements based on police legitimacy, rather than the detail of operational orders.)

3.6   Police Discretion

According to Jones (p 82 in Newburn and Neyroud, 2008) police discretion is the 'freedom of the individual officer to act according to his or her own judgement in particular situations'. It would perhaps be more precise to replace the word 'freedom' with the word 'duty' or 'obligation' and to add the word 'professional' before judgement, to emphasize the fact that police discretion is a concept founded within the notion of the 'office of constable'. This notion establishes the legal status of a police officer as a holder of original authority. A police officer cannot be ordered to arrest a person but must rather take responsibility for deciding whether arrest is appropriate or not, given the circumstances and context of a given situation (see 10.6). In this sense, discretion is better understood as a professional burden rather than a freedom, as freedom implies too much subjectivity. Importantly, police officers are not robots, programmed to respond to every crime they encounter by arrest and charge, and policing is about more than law enforcement; it is carried out in the public interest with a view to securing primarily a more peaceful society. In terms of good policing, law enforcement is just one means to an end, and would be inappropriate in some contexts. For example to arrest and charge for every offence:

- would not be practical, because police officers, their forces, and the criminal justice system as a whole do not have the time or resources to respond to all offences in society;
- could undermine the relationship between police and public—see 3.6.4;
- is not likely to have any significant impact on levels of crime (although see zero-tolerance policing models (3.9.4) and also the association between offences and criminality discussed in Chapter 4).

Thus the exercise of discretion is an important, even fundamental policing skill. Indeed, Lord Scarman stated:

> the exercise of discretion lies at the heart of the policing function. It is undeniable that there is only one law for all: and it is right that this should be so. But it is equally well recognised that successful policing depends on the exercise of discretion on how the law is enforced. . . . Discretion is the art of suiting action to particular circumstances. (Scarman, 1981, para 4.58)

Chan (2003) has noted that, in the early stages of initial police training, officers are hungry for basic technical knowledge; you might agree! This is understandable because police officers require the basic know-how skills in order to feel confident enough to perform duties (under the supervision of a tutor) in operational settings such as Supervised Patrol (see 3.5.1.1 on epistemic authority). Police discretion is a subject that does not fit easily under the umbrella of basic technical knowledge, unlike most of the other learning for trainee officers. Nonetheless, it is important to understand what police discretion is (and what it is not), because it is relevant to most of a police officer's everyday work. It is the vital ingredient which justifies police work as a profession, or in Neyroud and Beckley's words (2001, p 86), discretion is 'the essence of informed professionalism in policing'.

3.6.1   Defining and using discretion

Police discretion does not only apply to front-line officers. It also applies to the kinds of decisions that police managers and chief officers must make, described by Neyroud and Beckley (2001) as 'prioritizing decisions' and 'tactical decisions'. The former relates primarily to the allocation of limited resources and the latter relates to the balancing of liberty and order in a liberal democratic society. In a similar vein, Delattre (2002) discusses the need for senior investigative officers to make anticipatory and planning decisions about, for example, when to identify and release information about a serial killer. These are all good examples of police discretionary decisions and it is important for new police officers to be aware of why and how these kinds of decisions are made. However, here we will focus on discretion for front-line officers: in other words, the kind of decisions that patrol constables (and therefore trainee officers) are expected to make on a daily basis.

Discretion often involves choosing between different law enforcement options. For example, officers are regularly confronted with minor offences that present a choice of issuing fixed penalty tickets or making an arrest and taking the suspect to the police station. It has been argued that:

> Under-enforcement as opposed to choosing how to enforce the law, has led to concerns because it is seen by some to occur as a consequence of either an officer's 'misappropriation of judicial power' or an officer's 'discrimination'. (Neyroud and Beckley, 2001, pp 85–6)

Clearly anyone who is given a verbal warning or reprimand instead of being charged or arrested is unlikely to complain about it. At the same time, what defence can the perpetrator of an offence have when subjected to law enforcement? It could be argued that having committed an offence he/she has no defence, and merits the law's full weight of sanction. But, if one person deserves to be punished for committing an offence, why doesn't everyone (who has committed an identical offence) deserve to be punished in the same way too? The perceived unfairness of this situation is not so much that some are having the law enforced against them, but rather that others are not. Critics of under-enforcement therefore point to the inconsistency in applying the law which may result. As a consequence, the fundamental right of the police to employ discretionary powers is called into question.

One simple answer (proposed by the critics of police discretion) is to remove police discretion altogether, or at least reduce the extent to which officers can draw upon it. There would be practical problems with this. For instance, the criminal justice system already struggles to cope with the existing load presented to it; how would it cope if the police enforced the law without discretion? Another problem is that police work is extremely difficult to manage (Reiner, 2000, Ch 2). Most officers operate alone or with a partner and as Crawshaw *et al* (1998, p 24) note, police supervision tends to occur after the event. These problems illustrate the extent and relevance of police discretion, but they are not arguments for keeping it.

Governments have periodically introduced legislation and guidelines to restrict the amount of discretion a police officer can use. This may be reflected in force policies as well, for example in relation to the policing of domestic violence. 'Positive action' policies (including arrest at a domestic incident, see 15.7.2) have been applied across the UK, effectively reducing the use of discretion. If police discretion is to be maintained, however, it is important that we make a positive case for it. As part of the argument for discretion we need to identify a number of ways in which police discretion is often misrepresented. We begin by considering the view that police discretion is nothing more than applying common sense.

3.6.2 Discretion and common sense

The view that police discretion is a matter of applying common sense to policing situations would appear to have some merit. It helps police officers understand how real operational experiences complement the necessarily theoretical and abstract learning which takes place during the initial period of police training. Importantly, officers learn in this way to use the law as a means to an end rather than as an end in itself. However, the problem with viewing police discretion as the application of common sense is that it is too simplistic. It suggests that discretionary decisions are straightforward and could be applied by anyone. This view also fails to distinguish between decisions that are just simple, common-sense decisions and decisions that genuinely require the use of discretion. As Davis (1996) notes, not all choices are discretionary, and this is an important point. Police discretion cannot be simply reduced to being a matter of making choices or decisions.

3.6.3 Police discretion and subjectivity

Another way of understanding discretion is to consider the view that every police officer has a unique subjectivity that produces different approaches to how the law is interpreted and enforced. Within this perspective, police discretion is understood as the means by which individual subjectivity can be realized. However, although it is undoubtedly true to say that the individual subjectivities of officers play an important role in day-to-day policing, this should not be confused with police discretion. Indeed, police discretion is necessary precisely because it provides a way of curbing the influence of individual subjectivity.

To illustrate what this point means, consider the following question: should we expect all police officers to make the same decision in identical circumstances? We could say that there will be as many different decisions as there are officers making them, but others assert that every officer should make the same decision. So what is the correct answer? We should note that the question is not entirely fair because different contexts would probably produce different answers (in reality no two sets of circumstances are ever identical). Nonetheless, the existence of police discretion implies that we should not accept either of the extremes as an appropriate answer. If we expect every officer to make the same decision then why are we considering discretion at all? Alternatively, if every officer makes a different decision, in what sense are these decisions connected? That is, in what sense are these decisions related to policing principles and practice?

The answer is that we should expect officers' decisions to differ, but that there will be a finite number of decision categories, normally two or three. Ideally, each of these categories would represent good police decisions that could be justified and explained. (More realistically, we might expect a few officers to make decisions that fall into another separate category, one that represents bad police decisions.) There are only a limited number of valid options open for consideration because each option must adhere to professional standards, integrity, the law, and force policy. The legal philosopher Ronald Dworkin has explained this point by referring to discretion as the 'hole in the doughnut' (see Neyroud and Beckley, 2001, p 83). This analogy suggests that discretion is given meaning by the professionalism surrounding it, just as the hole in a ring doughnut is given meaning by the dough surrounding it. If we eat the ring, the hole disappears. Likewise, without professional standards, discretion becomes meaningless; police discretion cannot exist if there is no professional policing context.

Just as professional standards limit the number of options available to officers, the same standards also allow for different responses. We can say that subjectivity is not an adequate answer because it would mean that law enforcement is too arbitrary. It is not acceptable that a man is arrested only because he encountered officer A, rather than officer B or C. All police responses are only valid to the extent that they can be explained and justified in terms of professional standards, and not just as a product of a subjective perspective. To reiterate and emphasize the point, discretion reduces the influence of subjectivity by providing an objective, professional guide to decision-making.

3.6.4 Discretion and judicial misappropriation

It was noted earlier that some critics see police discretion as nothing more than an individual officer's misappropriation of judicial power. The reasoning behind this is that an officer is effectively acting as judge and jury if he/she decides not to enforce the law against an individual who has clearly committed an offence. This view is based upon a long-standing misconception of the police officer's role; that the police are merely law enforcers. Waddington (1999) observes (with reference to the surprise expressed by researchers into policing in the 1960s):

> the prevailing assumption had been that policing was little more than the application of the law...Criminals committed crimes and the police captured the criminals who were tried and convicted by the courts. (Waddington, 1999, p 31)

Indeed, Waddington refers to the discretionary powers of the police as being 'discovered' in the 1960s. Of course police officers had been exercising discretion since the creation of the modern police in 1829 but it was not an aspect of police work that had received much attention. As more research was conducted, it was found that the police would consistently enforce the law against certain sections of society and not against others, and to some extent this is still the case (see 3.6.5).

There can be no defence for the police discriminating against certain sections of society, but that does not mean in turn that the police should therefore have their discretion removed. Instead, what needs to be learnt from these experiences is that police officers are not so much law enforcers as 'peace officers' (Banton, 1964). Waddington (1999) has argued that the police use the law as and when appropriate in order to bring about a greater sense of peace and order in society. He refers also to Lord Scarman's warning following the Brixton riots in 1981 'that the maintenance of "public tranquillity" was a higher priority than "law enforcement"' (Waddington, 1999, p 42).

The police should make law-enforcement decisions based upon their interpretation of what is in the public interest. It is this balancing act between law enforcement and the needs of society that gives rise to police discretion. The police are expected to use the law to maintain order, and therefore they need discretionary powers in order to use the law as effectively as possible. This does not mean that the police can operate outside the law; they must work within legal boundaries. But they should not be required to enforce the law mechanically in every circumstance. In this respect the police are accountable not only to the law but also to the people they police.

3.6.5   Discretion and discrimination

The view that discretion is the means by which certain sections of society are discriminated against has arisen from research conducted since the 1960s. Why are some sections of society more likely than others to have the law enforced against them? In their defence, police officers have argued that they do not discriminate against any sections of society but respond to each individual they encounter depending on how that individual responds to them. This is referred to in police circles as the **attitude test**. (You will no doubt hear more experienced police officers using this phrase, or more colloquial versions.) Quite simply, an individual who is polite and repentant is less likely to have the law enforced against him/her. The supposed rationale is that he/she appears to have learnt a lesson and seems unlikely to reoffend. An intervention by a police officer is in itself an effective form of remonstration and can help to prevent repeat offending. It may not be in the public interest to pursue certain cases further, as this would contribute nothing towards achieving a more ordered society (and apart from the wasted expense, it could have a negative effect on the individual stopped). On the other hand, it is argued that if the individual stopped by the police officer is rude, abusive, and unrepentant, then it is assumed that further action needs to be taken against the individual in order to make sure he/she feels sufficiently reprimanded.

The problem with this kind of defence is that it perpetuates problems that exist in society. It is likely that those who regularly come into contact with the police will be immune to police warnings and will feel more confident in challenging the police officer's authority. They are more likely to be abusive and to have an existing antagonistic relationship with the police. Historically, individuals from certain ethnic minority groupings have had a disproportionately high interaction with the police and so the attitude test does nothing to break this cycle; indeed, it helps to perpetuate it. It is for this reason that police officers must take great care in such confrontations.

Earlier in this chapter we discussed epistemic authority (see 3.5.1.1), and noted the need for police officers to have a sound knowledge of the law. Increasingly, however, in relation to police discretion, police officers also need to know what actually works in policing; what is effective and what is not effective, and why different individuals are likely to respond in different ways to similar police interventions. Clearly, a police officer with a better knowledge and understanding of the contexts in which he/she is operating will be able to apply discretionary reasoning more effectively.

Efforts have been made to promote the absorption of this kind of information into police culture, and to rectify any resulting adverse or confrontational attitudes. There have undoubtedly been some low points; for example, see Macpherson (1999) and *The Secret Policeman* programme (2003). This programme, first screened on BBC television in October 2003, was about an undercover journalist, Mark Daly, who joined Greater Manchester Police as a trainee officer and then spent 15 weeks in training at the Bruche Centrex regional Police Training Centre, near Warrington. During his time at Bruche, Daly secretly filmed some of the behaviour of his fellow trainees and the trainers delivering the programme. He uncovered evidence of racist language and attitudes amongst some of his fellow trainees and inappropriate behaviour by some trainers. However, as Daly himself noted in 2003:

> The majority of the officers I met will undoubtedly turn out to be good, non-prejudiced ones intent on doing the job properly. But the next generation of officers from one of Britain's top police colleges contains a significant minority of people who are holding the progress of the police service back. (Daly, 2003)

Hopefully, today's police officers are in a better position to understand ethnic minority responses to the attitude test, and are able to respond to help break the cycle. The important difference between discriminatory decisions and discretionary decisions is that discrimination is based upon prejudice, whereas discretion is premised upon professional judgement (which incorporates many different factors, including the prevalence of discrimination in previous times). This requires officers to go beyond simply providing a common standard by which every individual encounter is measured. Officers are required to respond to each encounter individually, taking into account the specifics of each situation. As Rowe (2002) has noted, since the Macpherson Report (1999) policing no longer treats everyone equally but rather pursues specific policies aimed at reducing discrimination, for example by actively promoting an anti-racist agenda. It is now part of the police officer's role to break the cycle of discrimination.

TASK 5 In the following task you are given two scenarios to consider. The first is taken from the 1995 National Police Training notes and the second is our own invention.

1. You see a woman, who appears to be slightly drunk, pick up a street sign that has fallen from a wall, conceal it under her raincoat, and walk off. When stopped, she readily admits that she intends to keep it as a trophy. She is a medical student who is celebrating passing her final exam (NPT, 1995, p 4).
2. You are on duty outside a football ground when you observe a young man, clutching a can of super-strength lager, pick up an 'Away Supporters' sign that has fallen from a wall, conceal it under his hoodie and walk off. When stopped, he readily admits that he intends to keep it to start a collection. He is a football fan who is celebrating his club's victory in an important match.

In each case consider what discretion, if any, you would exercise.

3.7   Policing as a Profession

Trainee officers will often hear references during training to 'adopting a professional attitude' or that they need to 'behave in a professional manner'. But what does this actually mean? Here we consider what it means to professionalize policing and what this means for the trainee officer.

Before we examine what the 'professionalizing of policing' might mean, we need to consider what we might generally mean by the term 'profession'.

TASK 6 Make a list of professions. What features do you look for in an occupation that makes it a profession? Are there any common features that are found in all the professions you have listed?

3.7.1   What is a profession?

We encounter the word profession in many different contexts and applied to numerous occupational groups. You might have already suspected that there is not a universally accepted definition of the meaning of profession, though there is a general agreement that only some occupations qualify as professions. It is also potentially confusing that the word 'professional' is often appended to an activity simply to acknowledge that its practitioners receive some form of payment for it, or that it is undertaken more seriously. (For example, we know that a reference to a 'professional gambler' means that he/she probably earns a living from gambling.) However, there is likely to be more to a profession than this.

Traditionally, there were just four professions: law, medicine, the church, and the military. Later, accountancy became a profession, and now there are many more occupations commonly regarded as professions.

There is a broad consensus in the academic world that at least some of the following are required for an occupation to also be a profession:

- an accepted *corpus* of knowledge and theory underpinning the practice of the profession;
- controls on entry to the profession, normally through qualification, coupled with a need to maintain the currency of qualification;
- autonomy, discretion, and a degree of self-regulation;
- its practitioners have a form of vocational calling; and
- a code of ethics.

For most professions, many of the control and regulatory functions are carried out by a professional body.

To illustrate these ideas and to explore them further, we now consider medical practice as an example of a profession and measure it against our list of features for a profession.

Requirements of a profession	The medical profession
Corpus of knowledge and theory	The scientific basis to medical practice (eg physiology and biochemistry), knowledge of clinical practice (eg conducting physical examinations), aspects of the behavioural and social sciences
Controls on entry to the profession and continuing professional development	Completing a recognized medical degree, followed by a period of supervised practice (eg foundation training followed by postgraduate training). There is a need to demonstrate regular Continuous Professional Development under seven headings in order to maintain a place on the professional register
Autonomy, discretion, and self-regulation	Medical doctors have significant autonomy and discretion. Their conduct is regulated by the General Medical Council (GMC). Their representative body is the British Medical Association (BMA). Their authority is largely epistemic in nature (see 3.5.1)
Vocational calling	Difficult to prove, as no clear definitions of a vocation exist. However, interviews for entry to medical degrees often attempt to test applicants for this
Code of ethics	A code is published by the GMC. It includes the need for doctors to 'make the care of your patient their first concern', to 'respect patients' dignity and privacy', and 'to give patients information in a way they can understand'

We can see that medicine matches our working definition of a profession very closely.

3.7.2   Is policing a profession?

First attempt the following task.

TASK 7 Complete the following table for the occupation of policing:

Requirements of a profession	The policing profession
Corpus of knowledge and theory	?
Controls on entry to the profession and maintenance of position	?
Autonomy, discretion, and self-regulation	?
Vocational calling	?
Code of ethics	?

You probably found that policing in the UK meets some of our criteria for being a profession. Some of the 'missing' elements (such as the need to maintain skills and knowledge) were developed by the NPIA and others, and more recently the College of Policing has taken on this responsibility. In 2008 the NPIA introduced a 'Professional Register' for senior investigating officers (SIOs). It is envisaged that eventually it will contain the details of all investigators accredited through the Senior Investigating Officer Development Programme (SIODP), or through other means of demonstrating competence. In order to remain 'live' on the register an SIO will be required to provide details of the CPD activity they have undertaken in order to maintain their expertise (NPIA, 2008c). This is similar to the new requirements on medical practitioners who are now required to show evidence that they have kept up to date and are fit to practise, in order to retain their place on a professional register (GMC, 2008).

A key requirement for professionalization appears to be specialist knowledge and expertise. Sir Ian Blair during his BBC Jonathan Dimbleby lecture in 2005 commented on the role of the police service and the need for public engagement and the development of specific police knowledge (Blair, 2005). The 2011 Neyroud Review into police leadership and training (see 3.7.4) proposed further steps to align policing more fully with other professions, including the establishment of a new professional body. This is an ongoing remit of the College of Policing as indicated, for example, by the development of a Code of Ethics for policing.

3.7.3 Does it matter if policing is not yet a profession?

Some would argue that establishing and maintaining policing as a profession is important for the following reasons:

- to develop the body of knowledge (eg doctrine) and skills required for modern-day policing (as professions usually take the lead in determining what research and development best suit their clients' needs);
- to protect the right of the police, in certain key respects, to regulate themselves;
- to improve public confidence in the work of the police: for example, a professional register would almost certainly imply the need for its members to regularly demonstrate that they have met the requirement to maintain their skills and knowledge; and
- to distinguish the work and the professional standing of the police officer from other members of the extended police family (see 3.4) and other law enforcers (you might not agree that this is a good reason, but it is certainly behind some thinking).

There are alternative arguments. For example, many of the traditional professions such as law are not noted for their inclusivity, and striving for a professional status may reduce the representative nature of the policing family.

3.7.4 The 2011 Neyroud Review and the College of Policing

Many of the issues surrounding policing and professionalization discussed in 3.7.1 to 3.7.3 were addressed by Peter Neyroud (former Chief Constable of Thames Valley Police and the ex-Chief Executive of the NPIA) in his report into police leadership and training, commissioned by the Home Secretary and published in April 2011. The 'Neyroud Review' proposed moving policing towards 'a different model of professional approach' (Neyroud, 2011, p 44) and argued for the establishment of a chartered professional body for policing. The Review contrasted an artisan view of policing that is 'disengaged with science' with other established professions such as nursing. The established professions, he argued are developing 'transparency and public ethos' and the 'separation between professional standards, registration, qualification frameworks delivery of training and provision of services' (Neyroud, 2011, p 45). It also referred to developments in the professionalization of criminal investigators as an example of an alternative to the artisan approach (see 3.7.2). The Neyroud Review argued that a single professional body should be responsible for setting many of the key features of a profession (see 3.7.1), including maintaining professional standards in policing.

Following a period of consultation, the Home Office published a summary of the responses it had received regarding Peter Neyroud's proposals in December 2011, and stated its intention to establish a professional body for policing, albeit without chartered status. Details regarding the professional body have not been articulated at the time of writing, but it has given rise to much debate within the police service and academia. For an interesting perspective on the matter you can watch a podcast of the speech given by Professor Larry Sherman at the Royal Society for the encouragement of Arts, Manufactures and Commerce (RSA) in November 2011 at <http://www.thersa.org/events/video/vision-videos/professor-lawrence-sherman>.

Establishing a professional body for policing that is independent of government requires legislation, and this takes time. However, the Coalition government was keen to progress the recommendation made by Neyroud, and for this reason announced that the NPIA would close on 30 November 2012. In its place, the government introduced the College of Policing, an interim body tasked with steering the police towards establishing its own professional body. The College came into existence on 1 December 2012 but its Chief Executive Officer, Alex

Marshall, was still in post as the chief constable of Hampshire Police until 4 February 2013. It was also only after this date that the Chair of the College was appointed, Professor Shirley Pearce. The Board of Directors of the College had its first meeting chaired by Professor Pearce on 19 February 2013.

The College of Policing has been established with aspirations beyond that of its predecessor organizations (such as the NPIA). Whilst it is still relatively early in its development there are signs that it has intentions to significantly bolster the knowledge base of policing and it has begun to commission research from universities to this end. The College of Policing is also committed to developing evidence-based police practice and a 'what works' policy agenda, supported by other organizations such as the Society for Evidence Based Policing (the SEBP).

3.8   Diversity and the Police

Society is becoming increasingly more diverse, for example in terms of differences between people's ethnicity, religious beliefs, and sexual orientation. But more importantly we have become more conscious of such differences, and much more determined and willing to afford equal status to individuals from diverse backgrounds. Difference, expressed through the concept of diversity, has come to be represented as something to be celebrated, and it is now less common for difference to be seen as a barrier to the achievement of a harmonious society. Consider for example the changing ways in which anti-racist sentiments are expressed. A common slogan from previous times challenged racist views by stating that there is only one 'race' and that is the human race. Such a slogan seeks to diminish differences between people by saying that such differences are less important than the factors that unite humanity. Today though, anti-racism is expressed more commonly through the celebration of differences between individuals and groups in society, and is supported by the argument that the coming together of different values, beliefs, cultures, and perspectives makes life more interesting, more dynamic, and ultimately richer in a variety of ways.

It is important to note that diversity is about how we perceive differences between people as much as it is about the differences themselves. A simple illustration of this point is given with regards to the significance given to religious differences between communities in different contexts. For example, in most of the UK today the divisions within the Christian faith are of little significance for the majority of people. However, we know that historically this has not always been the case and more recently the divisions between Catholics and Protestants have been important factors in Northern Ireland. However, the existence of differences does not necessarily lead to tensions or problems as some may suggest, nor are differences necessarily the source of a dynamic society as others may claim. Either way, if you are (or plan to be) a professional police officer then you will be required to think carefully about issues of diversity within society, and about the various ways in which the concept of diversity informs policing. Moreover, it is the responsibility of police forces to end discrimination within their own organizations which means a heightened sensitivity towards the conduct of police officers when dealing with issues that involve diversity.

> **TASK 8** We have already referred to race and ethnicity as part of diversity. Suggest some other differences between people that contribute to diversity.

3.8.1   Diversity and vulnerability

One important way in which diversity informs policing is in relation to the responsibility that the police have towards vulnerable people (see Chapter 13). People who are clearly identifiable as minorities in society will often find themselves victimized by members of majority groups, for example when individuals from minority ethnic groups are targeted by racists. Sometimes the victimization can be more subtle, and trainee police officers or CKP students need to think carefully about how their own actions are perceived. Some actions could be deemed offensive by others, even though this was not the intention. As a professional, a police officer has the responsibility to do everything possible to resolve problems, and should certainly not be adding to them. This includes ensuring that police actions are not misunderstood or misinterpreted. But vulnerability does not only arise for individuals from minority groups. For example, women are not a minority group but are sometimes portrayed as being more vulnerable than men because of existing social inequalities which mean women are discriminated against.

It would be a mistake, however, to assume that an individual from a minority group or a group that has traditionally been discriminated against will feel vulnerable. Indeed in all respects of diversity police officers need to tread a fine line that recognizes diversity without imposing any preconceptions.

The issue of mental health is particularly useful in illustrating the complicated nature of diversity. Mental health issues exist to varying degrees in the general population and can have serious effects in terms of individual and collective well-being. But many people have preconceived ideas of what is healthy and is unhealthy, which makes recognizing diversity and difference in relation to mental health particularly difficult. Police actions in relation to mentally ill people are covered in 13.2.

3.8.2 Diversity and discrimination

Several of the strands of diversity are subject to law. It is unlawful to discriminate on the grounds of race, disability, age, sexual orientation, faith, or gender. Police forces have been under scrutiny for discrimination on the grounds of race for a number of years. The most notable incidents to date that reflect this are the Scarman Report, published in 1981 following a series of riots in the area of Brixton in London, and the Macpherson Report, published in 1999 following the death of Stephen Lawrence, which considered the Metropolitan Police to be 'institutionally racist'. Both reports relate a lack of ability to deal with racial discrimination by the police. In 2009 the Home Affairs Committee published an evaluation of the impact of the Macpherson Report on tackling racism in the police. It concluded that there were clear positive changes in the way that the police dealt with ethnic minorities and in the investigation of homicides where the victims were from ethnic minorities. There are, however, still concerns regarding the apparently disproportionate number of stop and searches being conducted on individuals from ethnic minorities, (black individuals are seven times more likely to be stopped and searched than individuals from other backgrounds, but see 9.1), as well as a disproportionate number of individuals from Afro-Caribbean backgrounds featuring on the National DNA Database.

The government introduced legislation to outlaw discrimination on the grounds of belief (ie, hatred against someone based on religion), but the subject is fraught with difficulty and it may be some time before a law is comprehensively framed which can allow criticism of belief but which prohibits actions that discriminate against belief systems.

Discrimination on the grounds of age is unlawful, but this is a complex area since age discrimination applies to the young as well as to the old (or indeed any age). In practical terms, trying to prevent discrimination on the grounds of age is closely related to the laws of employment and a progressively 'greying' population. It is more likely to concern employment of people who are past the conventional retirement age than about discriminating against people because they are young.

The Mental Health Act 2007 and the Disability and Equality Act 2010 reinforce the need to address ways in which people with mental health problems are discriminated against, especially since the majority of such individuals report having felt discriminated against. This is of particular relevance for police officers, given that people with mental health problems feature disproportionately within the criminal justice statistics (see Bradley, 2009). Many individuals with mental health problems come in contact with the police as a result of the Mental Health Act (see 13.2).

Gender discrimination is also subject to varied legislation to prevent discrimination. One area of recent particular interest for police forces is the legislation associated with forced marriages, which requires that special consideration is given when dealing with women who may be experiencing this form of victimization (see 15.7).

3.8.3 Promoting equality

It is important that police officers, given the powerful positions they hold in society, ensure that their own prejudices do not lead to discrimination. Prejudice can impact negatively on our relationship to others. Our culture, gender, life experiences, family, cultural, and social backgrounds can all influence our understanding and views of the world. They can be portrayed in a variety of verbal and non-verbal ways and need to be managed in order to reduce their potential impact during encounters with members of the public.

The Equality Act (2010) includes nine protected characteristics: age, disability, gender reassignment, marriage and civil partnership, pregnancy and maternity, race, sex, sexual orientation, and religion and belief. The Act provides an important requirement for any public authority to:

- eliminate discrimination, harassment, victimization, and any other conduct prohibited by the Act in relation to the protected characteristics;
- advance equality of opportunity between all people who share a protected characteristic and people who do not share it; and
- foster good relations between people who share a protected characteristic and those who do not share it.

A number of important principles that support equality have been integrated into the Standards of Professional Behaviour that apply for the police (see 6.3.1). These standards are reflected in specific requirements that apply for police responses to issues such as hate crime (see 14.10), harassment (14.5), confidentiality (6.8.1), human rights (5.4), and recording information in investigations (26.2.2). The intention is to avoid damage to minority groups that may otherwise feel angry, isolated, distrusting of the police, fearful, and distressed as a result of police failure to adequately address discrimination, harassment, and/or victimization. Equality and professionalism are crucial to maintaining police legitimacy across society and to building confidence in criminal investigations.

As a public service it is important that the police reflect a representative cross-section of society. This will benefit policing in terms of gaining confidence and cooperation across the full range of groups within the community. Recruiting from the full range of society allows the police service to attract a wider range of skills and knowledge as well as recruiting the best people to fill vacancies.

3.9 Models of Policing in England and Wales

Here we will consider some of the models of policing used in England and Wales.

> **TASK 9** What do you think characterizes our approach to policing? What can you point to that is essentially British about it?

It is perhaps misleading to suggest that the policing models that follow are somehow in competition or are mutually exclusive, although there are significant points of departure between them. Rather, they focus on different things. For example, the intelligence-led policing model tends to be seen as a response to the inevitable and unavoidable existence of criminals in society and the existence of high-volume repeat criminals. On the other hand, problem-oriented policing, as the label suggests, attempts to model crime or disorder in terms of problems that we analyse and attempt to solve. Community-based and neighbourhood policing favour the view that crime and disorder should be viewed in the wider context of the community or communities from which it originates. Zero-tolerance policing is based on the idea that an absence of effective police responses is likely to lead to an escalation from low-level anti-social behaviour and incivility towards more serious criminal activities. It therefore focuses on dealing robustly with all minor offending in order to make this outcome less likely. These different approaches to policing are premised upon conflicting views regarding what are the most pressing policing problems in society and what are the most appropriate and effective means of addressing them.

3.9.1 Community-based and neighbourhood policing

Government policies and media sound bites regularly focus on the policing of communities and neighbourhoods. Looking back at the history of policing, even before the creation of what we now know as the public police, there is clear evidence of participation of the community in policing (Rawlings, 2002). Consider for example the 'Hue and Cry', the pursuit of an offender in the King's name, as portrayed in historical accounts such as Dickens' *Oliver Twist* with the baying crowd pursuing Bill Sikes. Contrast this historical (and fictional) scenario with the present day; there is an increasingly distant relationship between the public and the police, particularly in relation to the contribution of communities to policing their own localities. Despite attempts over the last thirty years to improve police presence and community activism in protecting their own neighbourhoods, it is only in the past ten years that there have been fundamental changes in the structure and the development of legislation relating to these issues. Often perceived as the 'softer' side of policing and lower status than other policing roles (such as criminal investigation), community-orientated approaches to policing provide a crucial opportunity to engage with the public, proactively combat crime (through crime prevention strategies), and address community safety and quality of life issues. This engagement is important to community problem solving, developing public confidence in the police, and providing a visual presence.

The lack of partnership approaches has received substantial criticism since the 1980s with reforms in policing attempting to build partnerships and community engagement, for example the 1991 Morgan Report. The Crime and Disorder Act 1998 provided substantial powers in addition to a statutory requirement for partnership-working. The introduction of PCSOs (see 3.4.4) increased the visible uniformed presence, and the introduction of Neighbourhood Policing initiatives and the recent promotion of the 'big society' (Newburn, 2007; Herbert, 2011) was a further step forward. These changes represent attempts to develop local approaches to policing and improve police engagement with communities with the aim of increasing public contributions to policing objectives. The Home Office consultation document *Policing in the 21st Century: Reconnecting police and the people* (Home Office, 2010d) sets out the Coalition government's vision of 'cutting crime and protecting the public' and a more 'directly accountable' police service, offering 'value for money'. This vision also proposes to 'empower communities' and provide 'greater visibility and availability'. Although policing reforms are subject to consultation and implementation, the following subsections will provide a selective overview of key areas of recent initiatives to improve police community engagement.

3.9.1.1 Community policing approaches

In community policing the police seek to involve the various communities in their locality in terms of achieving local policing objectives. A key feature of this approach is the emphasis on communication and problem-solving activities between the police and community. It can also involve the community setting some priorities or engaging in policing activities. The community policing model has been widely recognized since the 1960s in the UK and strongly supported by John Alderson (former Chief Constable of Devon and Cornwall Constabulary) in the late 1970s (Mawby, 2008). The serious consequences of failing to work with communities or respond to their needs were apparently demonstrated through the Notting Hill disorders in 1958, the Brixton riots in 1981, and disturbances in Burnley, Bradford, and Oldham in 2001 (Fielding, 2005; Bowling, Parmar, and Philips, 2008). These outbreaks of community discontent resulted in civilian and police casualties and millions of pounds of damage, and sent local community relations with the police into decline. After such disturbances the inevitable examination of the causes usually results in recommendations to improve dialogue between the community and the police. Within the community policing umbrella there have been a number of approaches and activities that emphasize particular aspects of the community policing ethos, and we examine some of these in the following paragraphs.

3.9.1.2 Problem-orientated Policing (POP)

Herman Goldstein developed the concept of problem-orientated policing (POP) as a means of achieving the purposes of policing through tackling problems in communities (Tilley, 2008a). He defined POP as follows:

> In its broadest context, problem-orientated policing is a comprehensive plan for improving policing in which the high priority attached to addressing substantive problems shapes the police agency, influencing all changes in personnel, organisation, and procedures. Thus problem-orientated policing not only pushes policing beyond current improvement efforts, it calls for a major change in the direction of those efforts. (Goldstein, 1990, p 32)

This view was particularly important in the context of the police repeatedly dealing with particular crimes or calls for assistance (these could be non-crime anti-social behaviour) from the public in a reactive manner. This responsive approach or 'fire brigade policing' (Rowe, 2008, p 165) would not necessarily address underlying problems in the community; rather, it could stretch the police beyond their capacity without improving public safety. By reorganizing and reconfiguring police responses in the manner described by Goldstein the police would analyse the calls from the public and examine the underlying factors causing the need for police assistance. Particularly attention would be given to cases where repeat call-outs and minor cases could escalate to more serious problems (Rowe, 2008). The emphasis of POP in this context encourages a shift from reactive to proactive approaches to policing. This systematic way of dealing with community problems was not without challenges in terms of organizational and cultural resistance, including 'crude performance management regimes, staff turnover, lack of trained analysts and interagency hostilities' (Tilley, 2008b, p 226). In addressing underlying community problems Goldstein argues that the police frequently need to engage with other private, public, and voluntary organizations. Such partnership approaches (often referred to as 'inter-agency' or 'multi-agency' approaches) are not without tension, as there may be challenges due to different organizational culture, levels of authority, and objectives (Tong, 2008). So although POP might appear a sound proposal in principle we also need to consider the barriers to implementing such an approach. As with any concept or idea, the noble intentions to improve practice can face substantial barriers. Only through the support and willingness of practitioners to engage with new approaches will the intended objectives be met.

3.9.1.3 Neighbourhood policing

The Neighbourhood Policing initiative introduced by the then Labour government was rolled out to all police services during 2008. This initiative has been seen by some as a 're-morphed' version of community policing (Joyce, 2011, p 78). Since the late 1990s there had been a shift of emphasis in policing from a focus on crime-fighting to a broader recognition of behaviours that impact on the quality of life and the fear of crime. It is these underpinning influences and the public demand for a more accessible and visible police service that have provided the motivation for reform in policing.

Among the reforms that encouraged police engagement with communities was the Police Reform Act (2002) that paved the way for the introduction of Police Community Support Officers (see 3.4.4). Their role was specifically designed to provide presence and to be accessible so the community could contribute to Neighbourhood Policing Teams (NPT). These involve PCSOs and police constables being assigned to patrol and police particular geographical areas, and to use proactive, intelligence-led, and problem-solving approaches to tackle crime and anti-social incidents within their neighbourhood. There are approximately 3,700 NPTs in England and Wales (NPIA, 2011g). In addition to engaging with the public and hearing their concerns, NPTs are also tasked with providing solutions and engaging the community in creating safer neighbourhoods.

The NPIA (2011c) described Neighbourhood Policing as conforming to the AIIA model in that it provides:

- **Access**—to local policing services through a named point of contact;
- **Influence**—over policing priorities in their neighbourhood;
- **Interventions**—as joint actions with partners and the public;
- **Answers**—sustainable solutions and feedback on what is being done.

Neighbourhood policing aims to promote 'community interaction' and to control crime and reduce fear, 'with community members helping to identify suspects, detain vandals and bring problems to the attention of the police' (NPIA, 2011c). Although these aims would predominantly appear to target low-level crime, it should be noted that the fear of crime and nuisance behaviour, the role of intelligence collection, and effective communication with the police has wider implications. Sir Ian Blair (the former Commissioner of the Metropolitan Police) argued in his Jonathan Dimbleby lecture in 2005 that:

> national security depends on neighbourhood security. It will not be a Special Branch officer at Scotland Yard who first confronts a terrorist but a local cop or a local community support officer. (Blair, 2005)

3.9.1.4 Neighbourhood Watch

The Neighbourhood Watch (NhW) scheme involves bringing groups of residents together to 'create . . . communities where crime and anti-social behaviour are less likely to happen'

(Neighbourhood Watch, 2014). It was established in 1982 and there are now approximately 150,000 schemes in the UK covering 5 million households. NhW is usually organized by volunteers and led by a coordinator who is supported by a liaison officer linked to the local police station. These local networks are part of a larger national structure supported by the ACPO and the Home Office, and need to be registered with the police. NhW groups collect information about local concerns (eg criminal damage, anti-social behaviour, bogus callers, etc), and provide the police with any information regarding crimes or suspects. The police can also share information about crimes committed in their community and advise on how community members can protect themselves. Police officers can encourage members of the community to start up schemes or join established schemes by directing them to liaison officers or established coordinators. There are also other watch schemes such as Hospital Watch, Boat Watch, Business Watch, Pub Watch, Shed Watch, Church Watch, Forecourt Watch, Bicycle Watch, Country Eye, Horse Watch, Farm Watch, School Watch, and Shop Watch (Kent Police, 2010).

3.9.1.5 Volunteer roles in police work

There are two key volunteering roles in the police namely 'special constables' (see 3.4.1) and 'police support volunteers' (or simply 'police volunteers'). Police volunteers are individuals who work for the police in a variety of non-enforcement roles—these include helping with front desk responsibilities, neighbourhood watch support (see 3.9.1.4), and assisting neighbourhood policing teams with community initiatives. Typically a non-metropolitan police force will have between 100 and 200 volunteers. Police volunteers are security checked but do not hold any police powers.

3.9.2 Problem solving in the community

Attempting to solve problems within communities requires innovative responses, discretion, and imagination. It is difficult to provide an instruction manual or specific directions for practitioners to help solve community problems, as bespoke responses are often required to address specific problems in a unique context. With this in mind it is important to remember that problem solving is based upon personal judgement informed by individual values and the information available to the decision maker at the time. However, rather than provide no direction at all, there are models of problem solving that can be useful for individuals working in the community, for example the PAT (Problem Analysis Triangle) and the SARA (Scanning, Analysis, Response, and Assessment) process. These provide practitioners with a framework for tackling problems.

The PAT (see the following illustration) provides an officer with a basis to begin to analyse the problems he or she is confronted with.

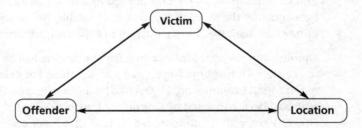

This approach has been associated with problem-orientated approaches and routine activities theory (Tilley, 2008a), and considers three main points of analysis (victim, location, and offender). Solutions are then found through identifying practical measures to address one or more of the three points of analysis. This could involve for example:

- protection of the victim through crime prevention or target-hardening measures;
- providing surveillance or additional patrols in the location concerned; and
- targeting or persuading offenders to cease their disruptive activities.

While some might consider this to be a simplistic model, it does provide a rationale to responding to problems and collecting the information needed to find solutions. It demands critical and objective thinking, and that in turn can provide inspiration for decision-making. Although this concept is predominantly aimed at uniformed work, there is clearly scope for it to be used more widely, including for non-crime problems.

The SARA process takes the process a step further through to assessment and review. This approach to the problem-orientated process continually re-evaluates decisions with the intention of improving practice. The key stages of the SARA process are as follows:

- **Scanning:** identifying a problem or a crime;
- **Analysis:** assessment of available information surrounding circumstances;
- **Response:** strategy chosen to deal with event;
- **Assessment:** review and evaluation of impact or effectiveness.

Although this model may be seen as rather mechanical, it does provide a practitioner with a framework in which to confront problems and make decisions (Bullock and Tilley, 2003, p 3).

There are other problem-solving models (with acronyms) which focus on different apsects of decision-making or problem-solving process. Practitioners need to identify a method of working that suits them.

3.9.3 Intelligence-led policing

Intelligence-led policing (ILP) was introduced in the UK in the 1990s as a new model of policing (and is also known as intelligence-based policing). Within this policing model, intelligence from a number of agencies is pooled with the explicit intention to 'disrupt, disable or undermine criminal behaviour' (Stelfox, 2008, in Newburn and Neyroud, 2008, p 146).

ILP was progressively adopted (with varying degrees of enthusiasm) by police forces in England and Wales during the late 1990s, and retains a significant influence on strategic and tactical policing methods in the UK. Thornton claims for example, that 'the concept of intelligence-led policing underpins all aspects of policing, from neighbourhood policing and partnership work to the investigation of serious and organised crime and terrorism' (Thornton, 2007, p 3).

ILP, at its outset at least, was a crime-focused model of policing which emphasizes the countering of crime through detection, disruption, or dissuasion. In practical terms, ILP derives its philosophy and principles from the recognition that crime and criminality can be understood at some level in terms of its perpetrators, its temporal and spatial patterns, and the linkages between crimes (eg common case analysis). In terms of the perpetrators of crime, the 1993 Audit Commission report (Audit Commission, 1993) and the unpublished research of Kent Police and others appeared to demonstrate clearly that a minority of criminals are responsible for the majority of most types of volume crime. The logic ran that this minority could be identified (eg through the use of paid informants) and then targeted and 'removed' through successful detection and prosecution. This, it was hoped, could be a more effective use of police resources, compared with more reactive models. Indeed, as Heaton (2008) and others have observed, this 'targeting' of high-volume and often recidivist offenders became a cornerstone of ILP. Thus the mantra of ILP became to 'target the criminal and not just the crime' (adapted from an observation made by the Audit Commission, 1993), and this led to a much greater emphasis on intelligence gathering (subsequently the '5 × 5 × 5'), the use of intelligence analysis (the employment of increasing numbers of analysts), and a reduction in apparently ineffective reactive policing.

Opinion and research continue to differ concerning just how small a minority of criminals are responsible for just how large a majority of crime. For example, the 1993 Audit Commission report (Audit Commission, 1993) cited Home Office research, which claimed that '7% of males who had been convicted of 6 or more offences accounted for 65% of all convictions' (Home Office, 1989, p 2). Heaton argued instead that 3 per cent of offenders being responsible for 24 per cent of offences is a more 'realistic' ratio (Heaton, 2000). Given that there was probably some exaggeration in early claims (particular as the oft-repeated '7% responsible for 65%' was derived in a particular context), there is nonetheless clear evidence for a skew in offending. For example, in a 2004 study in Brighton and Hove the 'top' 40 of the 400 identified high-volume offenders were responsible for 691 convictions out of the 3,453 total (Center for Problem Oriented Policing, 2009). Further, research on repeat victimization (eg Everson and Pease, 2001) suggests that prolific offenders may be responsible for the bulk of these repeated crimes against the same person or target.

The identification of 'patterns of crime' and linking crimes together is also an important (although not a unique) feature of ILP, giving rise to the ability to deploy policing resources more effectively. This is often combined with an increased multi-agency approach to the sharing of intelligence. The analysis of crime data and intelligence (see 22.6) by both the police and partner agencies (often through CSPs) is a key factor in identifying temporal and spatial aspects of crime. This can help ensure that resources are deployed appropriately, and proactively where possible.

3.9.4 Zero-tolerance policing

Zero-tolerance policing came to prominence in the 1990s under the mayoral leadership of Rudi Giuliani in New York City and the approach adopted by his Commissioner of Police, Bill Bratton. New York City had suffered high levels of crime throughout the 1970s and 1980s, and Bratton adopted a more aggressive and robust approach to policing. It came to be known as zero-tolerance policing because it responded vigorously to all acts of low-level criminality and incivility and behaviours that detracted from the quality of life for ordinary citizens. The approach was loosely premised upon the 'Broken Windows' thesis presented by Wilson and Kelling (1982). They argued that neglect and the consequent physical problems in a community foster social disorder and eventually crime, and outlined the need to 'nip bad behaviour in the bud'. The approach was accompanied by a systematic process of managerial accountability known as Compstat, which made the achievement of crime reduction outcomes more open and transparent.

Reductions in crime followed the introduction of zero-tolerance policing in New York, and Bill Bratton became an international star of policing. However, critics later pointed to the fact that similar reductions in crime had also occurred in parts of the USA that had not adopted zero-tolerance policing methods. The overzealous and aggressive approach adopted by officers enforcing a zero-tolerance policing strategy also began to attract criticisms from the citizens of New York City once crime rates had fallen.

In England and Wales, zero-tolerance policing was adopted in the late 1990s in Cleveland under the direction of Detective Superintendent Ray Mallon. However, controversy led to the suspension of Mallon and his eventual retirement from the force, and the image of zero-tolerance policing was somewhat tarnished by this experience.

Nonetheless, the notion of zero-tolerance policing regularly comes to the fore, for example following the outbreak of rioting across London and other English towns and cities in August 2011. Likewise, variations on the zero-tolerance policing approach have been developed and implemented by a number of police forces in England and Wales. The current Commissioner of the Metropolitan Police Service (MPS), Bernard Hogan-Howe, came to prominence during his time as Chief Constable of Merseyside Police through the successes of his strategy of 'Total Policing', which is seen by many as a form of zero-tolerance policing. In a speech delivered at the London School of Economics in January 2012 he announced his intention to lead the MPS, through promoting the strategy of Total Policing.

TASK 10 Consider the phenomenon of anti-social behaviour. How would intelligence-led policing, problem-orientated policing, and community-based or neighbourhood policing, adopted in their purest form (that is, to the exclusion of all other approaches), address this problem?

TASK 11 We have considered models of policing in England and Wales, but elsewhere in Europe other models are used. If you have travelled abroad, what differences have you noticed in policing?

3.10 Answers to Tasks

TASK 1 You might have included the following (which vary from force to force, of course, but which most forces have most support staff engaged in):

- **Crime Scene Investigators:** an operational role which in the past was undertaken exclusively by police officers, modern CSIs are often now police staff with training and qualifications in forensic investigation (see 25.3).
- **Statement takers:** many of the statements taken from witnesses and victims of crime, particularly volume crime, are taken, not by police officers but by support staff. The reason is that such statements do not have to be taken under caution (unlike statements by suspects) and therefore do not have to be taken by sworn officers. This can free up a great deal of time for police officers to pursue the investigation, and there can be a marked increase in the professionalism with which victims and witnesses are interviewed because the support staff involved are undertaking these tasks all the time.

- **Volume Crime Scene Examiners (VCSEs):** this role may not exist in all forces, but VCSEs are employed to undertake specialist forensic examination of extended areas of crime scenes on a large scale. They are particularly used in vehicle crimes.
- **Detention officers ('jailers'):** these are support staff trained in custody and holding prisoners.
- **Human resources (HR):** HR can include the whole range of specialists covering recruitment, promotions and postings, training, assessment and appraisal, retirement, secondment, dismissal, or capability issues. HR also deal with all matters relating to police support staff, including negotiations with staff associations.
- **Information technology:** these specialists are almost exclusively support staff, though some forces retain police officers where there is direct interface with police officers on patrol, for example in force communication centres or control rooms. IT often includes telephony and wireless communications (including personal radios) within its remit.
- **Lawyers:** force legal advice (civil and/or criminal) is now seen as an important resource, particularly for the chief officer team and the Police Authority, and in dealing with complaints from the public, or litigation by employees (eg employment tribunals).
- **Estates:** police forces occupy considerable numbers of buildings and possess vast stocks of property which need specialist handling, particularly in negotiations with planning authorities.
- **Finance:** with police budgets in the hundreds of millions of pounds annually, there is a need for specialist financial and budget management. In most forces, 80 per cent or more of the budget is spent on salaries or pensions, leaving a relatively small operational revenue budget to which is added the capital budget for aspects such as buildings and vehicles.
- **Administration:** from paper files to computerized records, from sickness certificates to awards ceremonies, from shotgun certificates to booking training courses, the administrative tasks in a police force are complex and numerous. The bureaucratic nature of policing inevitably creates a large administrative tail.

Force websites often provide descriptions of the roles undertaken by police staff. A good example is Essex Police and its website <http://www.essex.police.uk/recruitment/police_staff_vacancies.aspx>.

TASK 2 The volume and exact nature of the training is very much determined by the chief constable in each force, or the local BCU Commander in terms of any specific training. There is still debate about the outline of a training package which all PCSOs should receive. Training lasts for at least five weeks, but there have been calls for much longer and more specific PCSO training systems to be set up as a form of continuous development.

In most forces it would look something like this:

- **Week 1:** an induction course, which contains health and safety instruction, learning about diversity, and some introduction to the general nature of being a community support officer.
- **Weeks 2–4:** include attitude and behaviour development, combined with knowledge of outside agencies and other tools for successful community problem solving.
- **Week 5:** is the 'Powers' week, where PCSOs are provided with knowledge of their existing powers and their practical effectiveness. This would also include some rudimentary safety training and training to defuse potentially dangerous situations and how to calm and manage angry people.

Finally, there will be BCU or beat training and familiarization until independent patrol.

TASK 3 The following are examples of how the five forms of authority might feature in the scenario:

Form of authority	Examples
Epistemic	You have a clear understanding of the definition of the possible offences involved in this incident. You have knowledge of the appropriate procedures to be followed and this is conveyed in speech to those present, including the victim and the offender
Natural	You use your demeanour and language to take control of the situation, including indicating when you wish a person to answer a question and in which order
De facto	Your right to question those involved is probably accepted without challenge (but not necessarily with cooperation!)
De jure	You have the authority to arrest if the circumstances require this
Moral	You demonstrate, through your behaviour and attitudes, that you do not immediately jump to conclusions concerning the sequence of events, nor attribute guilt or innocence

TASK 4 You would have had to arbitrate between the right to freedom of expression (however extreme such views may be) and the need to sustain law and order. The legitimacy of your presence might not

be consensual, but it may be both legitimized in law and necessary for preservation of the peace. The police would endeavour to control the marchers by determining the safest route for the parade to follow whilst also ensuring that direct clashes with the protesters were avoided. However you managed the event, someone, somewhere would have individual freedoms circumscribed (even if only the rights of Saturday shoppers to go about their lawful business), and thus the police are using moral as well as legal legitimacy in the policing of the march.

TASK 5 You have probably spotted our intentions with this task; the two situations are very similar. The first scenario is the more serious in policing terms as you are told that the woman appears to be slightly drunk, whereas the young man is simply clutching a can of lager. In the first case the fact that she is a medical student who will soon (presumably) join the medical profession may well have influenced your thinking towards exercising discretion. However, you were not appointed to be a moral guardian of society: the place that a person holds in society should not feature in your decision whether or not to exercise discretion.

In terms of your answer you might well have considered other aspects such as the intentions of each person concerned, the precise nature of the apparent offence, and so on. The problem with presenting these scenarios in a written form (or as simulations in training) is the lack of this context; this is so important when making decisions.

When exercising discretion it is important that you are able to justify your actions to an outsider looking in—that is, to show how discretion is the result of rational decision-making rather than instinct or some other gut reaction. Doing so will also help you meet the assessment requirements of the Diploma in Policing units. During your training and assessment you must evidence your decision-making; your assessor cannot read your mind!

Taylor (1999) has produced a useful checklist for the exercise of discretion. You are asked to consider issues such as fairness, justice, accountability, consistency, and wider community interests and expectations.

TASK 6 It is highly likely that you included at least some of the following professions: medicine (eg a doctor); law (eg a barrister); Church (eg a vicar); and teaching (eg a school teacher). You may also have thought of the military (eg a General); nursing; accountancy. Did you include policing?

Professions are occupations that normally have the following qualities:

- They provide an income which is normally referred to as a salary. Interestingly, in many respects police officers are paid a wage rather than a salary—for example, below certain ranks they qualify for overtime payments calculated at an hourly rate.
- Entry to the profession is regulated and controlled. The title may be legally controlled, as in the case of the medical profession. Quite often a higher education degree in an approved area of study, or a licence is required. Members of the profession are then licensed to practise, but there are procedures for removal of the licence (which in some professions is referred to as being struck off).
- There is a code of ethics and behaviour that members of the profession subscribe to.

TASK 7 Some possible answers are:

Requirements of a profession	The policing profession
Corpus of knowledge and theory	There is underpinning knowledge and theory for some aspects of policing, for example the law. There was also doctrinal development, undertaken by the NPIA and now by the College of Policing (eg underpinning Authorised Professional Practice). However, there is yet no universally accepted *corpus* of knowledge which is unique to policing
Controls on entry to the profession and maintenance of position	Entry is controlled through the national selection process. However, there are no formal academic requirements to enter the profession, beyond relatively simple tests of English and numeracy, although this might well change in the future (see Chapter 8).
Autonomy, discretion, and self-regulation	Police officers enjoy relatively high levels of autonomy and discretion. The title of police constable is controlled so that only those that qualify are entitled to use it. Self-regulation of policing exists in a restricted form but is increasingly under challenge
Vocational calling	Policing is more than just a job and affects many aspects of an individual's life
Code of ethics	There is an established code of ethics

TASK 8 You would probably have picked up on race and gender, but did you get sexual orientation, age, or belief? And did you get disability?

TASK 9 You might have included:

- it is decentralized: public policing is still largely local, autonomous, and non-political (with shades of grey, viz the Miners' Strike in 1982–3);
- policing is consensual: it cannot operate without the active support of the public;
- approaches to policing are characterized by provisions in the Human Rights Act 1998 and the PACE Act 1984, which respect human dignity and ensure fairness of process;
- police officers, for the most part and on most occasions, are unarmed;
- police officers have independence in conducting investigations; they may still exercise initiative in whether to investigate or not;
- we have an adversarial criminal justice system, which requires the prosecution to disclose evidence;
- there is a presumption of innocence until proven guilty; the burden of proof lies with the prosecution.

TASK 10 In terms of anti-social behaviour you might have suggested the following:

- **Intelligence-led policing**—target the most active and serious contributors to the anti-social behaviour. This might require the use of informants and surveillance. When these individuals have been identified, then examine all appropriate means, within the law, of removing them from exercising leadership and direction over the rest. For example, consider what offences they might have committed, whether ASBOs might be suitable, what other agencies may be engaged to bring pressure to bear (eg do we have information that they are illegally claiming benefits?), what evidence we will need, and so on. If we cannot detect the crime, it could be disrupted instead.
- **Problem-orientated policing**—the fundamental problem needs to be identified. The anti-social behaviour may simply be the visible manifestation of a less obvious problem or change. For example, the removal of fences between the gardens of local-authority-owned houses could have created open areas which are vulnerable to anti-social behaviour. If so, other agencies might need to be involved in an agreed and concerted strategy to address the underlying problem.
- **Community-based or neighbourhood policing**—first we need to talk to those that can really help us: members and representatives of the local community and the patrol officers who work with them. If young people are involved then how can we mobilize their parents and others in the community to address both the anti-social behaviour and its underlying causes? What support can be offered? In summary, do not simply view this as a question of law enforcement but more as a wider question concerning the stability and cohesion of the local community.

TASK 11 You might have noticed that:

- uniformed police officers routinely and openly carry arms (so do detectives, but concealed);
- stop and search can be more widespread than in the UK; European citizens routinely carry an identification card or identifying papers;
- there are often several types of police officer (*gendarmes, carabinieri, guardia civil, police municipale,* city police as well as national police) in the same country;
- most European police forces are nationally organized, even when they have variations in police types (such as the paramilitary *gendarmes*, as against the *agents de police* in France); and
- particularly in Eastern Europe and Russia, as well as further afield, there may be a hostility to the police or even a fear of them, especially at border controls. This is a legacy and, in some cases, a continuation of the role of the police as an arm of the state, and is associated with repression and denial of freedom. Citizens in countries which have suffered under occupation or tight state control may show contempt and loathing of the police, to a degree seldom seen in the UK.

There are other differences which you will find only by close comparative study or by investigation into the individual country's criminal justice system. Did you know, for example, that the Dutch abolished the jury system in 1804 and never reinstated it? Or that Italy has provision for a jury trial system but has never used it?

4 | Crime and Criminality

4.1 Introduction

In this chapter we take a brief look at the nature of disorder, crime, and criminality in England and Wales. Every day, the contents of news bulletins on TV and radio and the pages of newspapers are dominated by disorder and crime; fraud investigations in the City, muggings on housing estates, the sadistic torture of young children through to the murder of a solicitor for her watch and mobile phone. Many articles and research papers are devoted to trying to understand criminal motivations, why people commit crimes, and why certain crimes are more prevalent than others. You will read some of these criminological texts and papers in the course of your study on a pre-join programme or as a trainee police officer.

We have deliberately simplified these issues because this is not a Handbook of crime or criminology, and the issues are very complex, drawing on psychological, philosophical, sociological, and political perspectives. In a very real sense, they are issues which you will be grappling with for the whole of your subsequent time in the police and certainly include matters on which you will have to reflect during your time as a student or police trainee.

TASK 1

- What makes a crime sensational?
- What makes a crime of little apparent interest?
- What makes a crime impact on a community?

Increasingly over the past 40 years, criminologists have become interested in studying the police. This has produced numerous publications concerning the organization, administration, and general understanding of police work. However, beyond this, criminology has also provided the police with a number of important theories about the nature of crime and criminal behaviour, which can help the police in a number of different ways. For example, the move towards proactive policing has been assisted by developments in criminological theories concerning crime prevention, the study of victims, and the spatial movements of criminals. The scope of criminological studies is too vast to cover here, but by providing a selection of important ways in which criminology informs contemporary policing, it is hoped that you will be encouraged to consult the growing body of criminological research concerning many different policing matters. But first we will consider some more basic questions, some possible definitions of crime, and some possible causes of crime.

4.2 Definitions of Crime

What is crime? We tend to think we know the answer until we begin to think through the details and test out our general ideas on some specific examples. We might say that crime is what is forbidden, that crime is activity which society would like to eradicate or prevent, or that crime is a measure of society's health: the more unbalanced the society, the more the crimes on the statute book. Technically, a particular activity is a crime because the law defines it as such. But remember that laws are made by people so, in the end, we are back to where we started: people (albeit only certain categories of people such as judges and MPs) decide which activities are crimes. Without reference to existing concepts of crime and laws there is nothing about an activity in itself that marks it out as a crime. Consider, for example, how some forms of sexual activity between consenting adult men were treated as crimes in the recent past but are no longer treated as such. There are a very few acts that have been consistently considered crimes throughout modern history (try Task 2). Other types and definitions of crime are mutable (they change as society changes). Think about our attitudes to the environment in which we live: note how activities like collecting birds' eggs or hunting foxes with dogs are now seen by many as unacceptable, and how laws have followed suit. Currently there is debate around so-called 'legal highs'; should they be 'criminalized'? And should drugs that are currently categorized as 'illegal' be legalized? These are debates that policy makers, practitioners, and academics will discuss at length, but until these activities are covered by legislation then they will not be a crime.

We will start with considering a narrow definition of crime—that is in terms of actions referred to in legislation. This provides us with a definitive statement but does not really explain why particular acts and behaviours are treated as criminal whilst others are not. However, if we look beyond the law as part of the definition of crime, we then find that the task becomes no easier. Finally, we consider the thoughts of JS Mill, a nineteenth-century philosopher who proposed that deviant behaviour might have a role in promoting beneficial changes in society (although he recognized that some deviant behaviours would be classed as crime if they caused harm to other people).

4.2.1 Crimes are defined by law

Originally, the word 'crime' actually meant judgement or accusation (from Latin *crimen*, a judgement), and it was only later that it came to be associated with the act of offence or wrongdoing. By the Middle Ages, crime was something 'against the law', and thus a crime was an action punishable by law. On one level, we now simply define crime as action which is against the law, and clearly the act needs to be against a specific criminal law. Critics of this definition of crime point to an obvious tautology—we are essentially saying the same thing twice but in a different form. Using such a circular argument, that crime is defined by law, takes us no further forward in our understanding.

4.2.2 Crimes are defined by society

Others have argued conversely that crime is a social construction. By this they mean that no act or behaviour is in itself wrong but rather that different societies will identify different activities as crimes, according to the specific needs of a given society at a particular point in history.

TASK 2

- List three crimes that would appear to be universal.
- List three offences that are considered criminal in the UK today but were not 100 years ago.
- List three offences that are considered criminal in other parts of the world but not in the UK.

Crime can also be defined more broadly as all social wrongdoings and anti-social behaviour. This sociological approach addresses the question from the perspective of why certain acts are criminalized, but can compromise the clarity of legal definitions of particular offences. A current example of this kind of approach occurs in debates over the best response to anti-social behaviour. Some have argued that the use of Anti-social Behaviour Orders (ASBOs, see 14.2.2) is an indirect means of criminalizing behaviour. (This is because imposing an ASBO is a civil procedure but breaking of the terms of an order may invoke criminal proceedings.) Others have argued that ASBOs are a civil procedure against criminal activities that are not readily and effectively dealt with by existing criminal proceedings.

4.2.3   Mill's principle of 'harm to others'

John Stuart Mill was an English philosopher writing in the nineteenth century. For Mill it was important for the development of a healthy society to allow individuals as much freedom as possible, primarily because he believed that individuals who deviate from the norm can help society to advance. However, the problem confronting any authority is establishing when a deviation from the norm might be beneficial and when it is not. In other words, it is not always possible to decide whether an individual acting differently is being innovative or criminal.

There are numerous examples throughout history of individuals (some of whom we now celebrate as heroes) who were considered a threat to society at an earlier time. Think, for example, about the suppression of scientific thinkers, such as Galileo, who were considered to be heretics, or (more recently) civil rights protesters such as Martin Luther King in the USA. In the UK today there are many examples of people and campaign groups willing to break the law, for example animal rights activists, Fathers 4 Justice, anti-abortionists, and environmentalists. These groups each believe they represent values that are not normal today but will become so in the future, in the same way that those fighting at previous times in history for equal rights for women or the abolition of the slave trade eventually came to be recognized as heroic figures.

For Mill, the way to permit individuals or groups to deviate from existing norms, and indeed to challenge them, is to allow people to make mistakes and act immorally, providing these acts do not harm others. This is Mill's famous 'harm to others' principle. It is largely from this perspective that we have established a separation between the law and morality; it is argued that the law pertains to public matters and morality to private individual concerns. This view was supported in the Wolfenden Report into homosexuality and prostitution, in which it was argued that private acts between consenting adults should not be the concern of law enforcement (Wolfenden Report, 1957). Campaigners for gay rights have criticized this finding for putting too much emphasis on the word private, as they feel this suggests that public expressions of homosexuality should be regulated and controlled.

However, other critics have challenged the view that law and morality can be so neatly separated. They argue that there is a significant grey area which we might characterize as social morality, that it is simply not possible to insulate our private activities completely, that there will always be leakage, and our actions will always have consequences in ways that we could not have predicted. This challenges Mill's 'harm to others' principle because it suggests that others are harmed by our actions even if this was not our intention. Perhaps a good example of this, to illustrate the point, is passive smoking. For many years it has been argued that smokers are harming themselves and campaigns have encouraged smokers to stop for their own sake. However, until recently, little was done to prohibit smoking. Increasingly though, smoking has come to be regulated on grounds of the health and safety of people in the vicinity (see 14.2.6).

This also illustrates that harm is more widely defined today than when Mill was writing. We have become more sophisticated in identifying different forms of harm. For example, consider the extent to which we have broadened our understanding of domestic violence to include psychological, emotional, and financial harm, in addition to physical damage.

4.3   The Causes of Crime

When examining the causes of crime an important starting point is to acknowledge some fundamental differences in how we might understand crime and how these differences in turn can inform police work. Blackburn (1995) makes a distinction between crimes and criminality. He discusses crimes as a rational response to the environment in which people find themselves, and criminality as a characteristic of an individual that emphasizes the propensity to commit crimes.

Policing in Context

4.3.1   Crime—a rational response?

Some crimes are apparently easily explained as a product of the social situation in which they occur. For example, an unemployed single mother shoplifting nappies for her baby is certainly committing a crime, but it could be said that a more serious problem is that she should be in such a difficult position in the first place. Others will point out that not all mothers in the same situation would resort to shoplifting but would find a legal solution to the problem. Irrespective of which moral position is adopted, from a policing perspective this particular crime can be understood more readily as a social response than as an individual failing. This view is associated with what is referred to as classical criminology, which emerged in the late eighteenth century and informed the thinking of law reformers at this time (eg Bentham, Howard, Beccaria). This view of crime suggests that anyone could become a criminal given the right circumstances, and that punishment is required to act as a deterrent to crime.

4.3.2   Criminals—a breed apart?

Conversely, it is difficult to understand the actions of a violent serial murderer as the consequence of injustices in society. No matter how bad society is, it is hard to view such brutality as a reasonable response in any sense. A contrasting explanation for the causes of crime is the concept of criminality. This view developed from what is referred to as the positivist school of criminology associated with Cesare Lombroso's *L'Uomo Delinquente* (The Criminal Man) published in 1876. Positivists differed from the classical approach to criminology by arguing that:

- criminality is determined by factors beyond the immediate control of an individual and is not a product of his or her free will;
- criminals are a certain type of individual distinct from non-criminal individuals; or
- criminals are pathological (see Jones and Newburn, 1998, pp 101–2).

4.3.3   Nature and nurture

These kinds of questions have been debated for centuries. It is often referred to as the nature/nurture debate. Nature refers to what we are born with or, in recent terms, our genetic make-up, and nurture relates to the environmental contexts in which we develop. This includes everything from our schooling, how our parents raised us, whom we chose to associate with, and every arbitrary experience that has good, bad, or indifferent outcomes. However, the nature/nurture dichotomy can often be misleading. The debates have frequently been polemical and exclusionary; that is, those favouring nature explanations would dismiss nurture as an influence and those supporting nurture explanations would exclude completely the view that nature has any part to play. Increasingly today we recognize that both nature and nurture form part of the explanation and, indeed, that it is not always easy to distinguish one from the other. Modern biology continues to uncover examples of genetic predispositions being either masked or revealed by environmental factors.

4.3.4   Hate crime

Although the term 'hate crime' is used widely among criminal justice agencies to identify criminality, there is no particular offence entitled 'hate crime'. Rather, legislation recognizes specific criminal offences allowing aggravating factors. The Criminal Justice Act 2003 dictates that if a crime is based on hostility influenced by actual or perceived religion, ethnicity, disability, or sexual orientation, then the court must state this as an aggravating factor in sentencing.

Interestingly, hate crime (including homophobic or racist crimes) can be defined as such by the victim(s) or any other person, irrespective of the views of the police officer dealing with it. This amendment arose from the enquiry into the death of the black London teenager Stephen Lawrence and a subsequent report into the police investigation chaired by Sir William Macpherson. (This report famously branded the MPS as 'institutionally racist'.) The following question then arises: 'If any person present can define a crime as a "hate crime", why cannot *any* individual define *any* incident in which they feel disadvantaged, wronged, or frightened, as a "crime"?' The law provides the answer. There must have been an identifiable criminal offence (such as assault) before the qualification of whether or not it is homophobic or racist can be considered. It is the hate which is defined by the individual and not the crime. Once again, the close interrelationship between the law, society, and individuals is a key factor in understanding crime. The law surrounding hate crime and harassment is covered in 14.5 and 14.10.

4.4 Measuring Crime

There are various means of measuring crime, for example police and criminal justice statistical records, large-scale (mostly government-sponsored) surveys, and small-scale academic studies. The government and criminal justice agencies use police recorded figures and the new Crime Survey in England & Wales (CSEW) and Northern Ireland Crime Survey (NICS) as their key sources of information. The new crime surveys employ the same methods and approaches as were used for the now defunct British Crime Survey (BCS); thousands of households are randomly selected and interviews are conducted with the aim of measuring both recorded and unrecorded crime (see 4.4.1). The crime survey in Scotland is entitled the 'Scottish Crime and Justice Survey' and is available from the Scottish Government Justice Analytical Services. The BCS ceased to cover Scotland in the late 1980s, and in April 2012 the responsibility for producing crime surveys was transferred from the Home Office and split between the National Statistics Office (ONS) for the CSEW and the Department of Justice for Northern Ireland for the NICS.

We know that the problems of under-reporting, under-recording, political interest, intellectual bias, and/or perspective all contribute to distortions in actually determining the levels of crime at any given time. This is particularly so if we wish to make comparisons with the past. The problems of under-reporting and under-recording are particularly problematic for the police and are factors that have been given much attention in recent years. We also know that any research design aimed at collecting data will have some weakness due to a range of factors such as sample size, access to research participants, ethical barriers, organizational limitations, funding restrictions, or the methods employed. Although historically the BCS was considered one of the most comprehensive crime surveys in the world, all research designs and methods are open to criticism. For example, it was only in January 2009 that the BCS began surveying 10- to 15-year-olds previously excluded from the survey, and clearly the experiences of crime from younger people are also important particularly for politicians, policy makers, and practitioners. Researchers constantly review their methods to ensure the crimes surveys are robust and as useful as possible.

Establishing a more accurate picture of the extent of crime and ensuring that it is recorded properly are important aspects of modern policing. However, what needs to be recorded?

4.4.1 Reported and recorded

An important distinction needs to be made between reported crime-related incidents (eg phoned reports made by a member of the public to the police) and recorded crime. It is obvious that not all crimes that occur will even be reported to the police. Setting this aside, let us consider a particular incident where the police are contacted. Imagine that I have witnessed a heated argument in the street, perhaps with some pushing, shoving, and screaming. I phone the police and report it; the police will register the contents of my call (it will be registered or 'logged' in police jargon). This registration is what most commentators mean when they refer to reported, but this is not the 'official' meaning of reported. The police then have to decide whether this reported incident should be then recorded as a crime (a so-called 'notifiable offence'). They are required to use the Home Office criterion which states that if (on the balance of probability) the circumstances as reported by the caller amount to an offence, and there is no credible evidence to the contrary, then it should be recorded as a crime (Home Office, 2013d). (The 'balance of probability' criterion is defined by the National Crime Reporting Standard.) The police response to incoming calls is discussed in more detail in 23.3.2.

Policing in Context

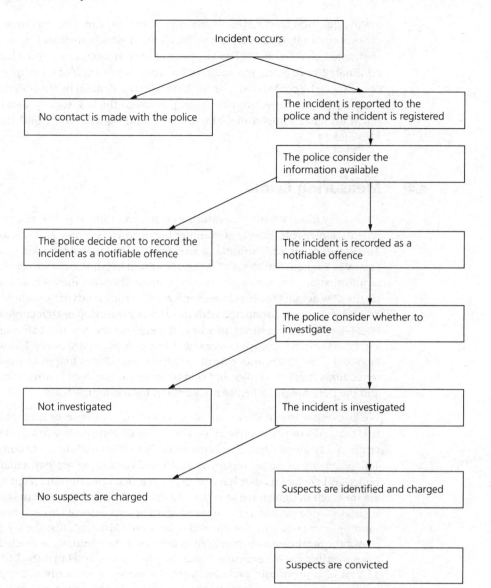

As our incident illustrates, the decision is far from simple. In response to my call the police are required to make all reasonable enquiries to identify specific victims and secure any supporting evidence. Although pushing and shoving could technically be an offence of assault or battery (see 15.2) or a public order offence (see 14.4), this would depend on the circumstances, and these would probably not be clear from my account over the phone. More importantly, a victim is unlikely to be identified and the basic recording rule of 'no victim, no crime' would be applied. (Note, however, that there are exceptions to this rule.) Hence in my example, it is highly unlikely that the pushing and shoving that I witnessed, although registered as an incident would actually result in the police recording a crime.

Crime recording and counting methods have in recent times become more consistent across police organizations, and are audited for accuracy and reliability. The three main group headings for classifying the status of a recorded crime are:

- detected (or 'cleared up'—that is a crime has been recorded and a suspect has been identified);
- undetected (a crime has been recorded but no suspect has been identified); and
- no crime (of which there are a number of possibilities, including that the crime as reported is already part of another recorded crime).

The processes of reporting and recording crime are complex and full details are provided by the Home Office (2011a).

In terms of statistics, the police service as a whole claimed to have cleared up 28 per cent of all recorded crime in 2011–12 (Taylor & Bond, 2012), which appeared to be an impressive record. However, in 1991 it was estimated that recorded crime represented only 7 per cent of all crime committed, and data from 2002 (see the pie chart) suggests that for all crimes occurring, 47 per cent are reported, 27 per cent are recorded, 5 per cent are cleared up, and 2 per cent result in conviction (Wright, 2002). It is interesting to note that in 1771, the clear-up rate for crime was estimated to be 24.6 per cent (Emsley, 1996) (although numerous other factors would need to be taken into account for any meaningful comparison to be made).

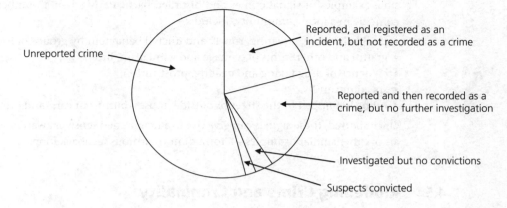

HMIC acknowledge that there is a 'degree of subjective interpretation in making decisions about how to record crimes' (HIMC, 2013, p 3). This is a subject of some concern. Indeed, the same HMIC report concluded that in at least one police force there was serious under-recording of crime which led to victims not receiving the service they required.

4.4.2 The perception of crime

There is a general acceptance that the fear of crime and disorder has increased in the last decade or so, despite the fact that most forms of recorded crime have shown a decrease in the same period (although see Farrall and Gadd (2004) for a critique). As Walker *et al* (2009, p 34) note, 'despite the total number of crimes estimated by the BCS falling over recent years, comparatively high proportions of people continue to believe crime has risen across the country as a whole and in their local area'. It would also appear that particular communities are more likely to believe that crime has risen significantly when compared to others, and also to worry more about crime. For example, the British Crime Survey for 2007/8 suggests the following demographic factors are significant (Kershaw *et al*, 2008, p 126 and table 5/06) in terms of perceptions and worry about crime:

- gender: women are more likely than men to feel that burglary and violent crime has risen;
- age: young people worry more about violence and car crime (although men and women in the 65 to 74 age group are most likely to perceive that there has been a significant increase in crime overall);
- ethnicity: people from non-white ethnic groups are more likely to be concerned about crime than those from white groups;
- location: those living in urban areas are more likely to worry about crime than those who live in rural areas; and
- newspapers: readers of the 'red top' (tabloid) newspapers are more likely to worry about crime than those who read the 'broadsheets' or 'quality press'.

However, it is important to note that according to official statistics, those who feel most worried about crime or who perceive crime to be increasing are not necessarily those who are actually the most likely to become victims. Although having said this, it could be argued that suffering from fear of crime is itself a form of harm to an individual. For some people who are very anxious and fearful about crime, the lifestyle implications can be profound: an elderly person's statistically 'irrational' fears about crime still need to be taken into account. Think of this as some kind of calculation: the risk may be low but the negative consequences are very high (eg in terms of recovery from an injury) and so overall the product is one of significant size for the individual concerned.

One possible reason for this apparently irrational overestimation of the volume of crime and disorder is that many of us may base our judgements about the level of insecurity of our communities not only on those 'invisible' but often very serious crimes (such as burglary or sexual crimes) but also on the more obvious and usually less serious local crimes such as repeated vandalism and graffiti, groups of young people shouting abuse at passers-by, and so on. These are examples of 'signal crimes' (Innes, 2004) or 'signal disorders' which are perceived as warning signals to people about the level of insecurity in their neighbourhoods. As Innes (2005, p 192) notes, 'major crimes such as homicides can and do function as signals, but (for most people, most of the time) the signals that they attend to and that assume particular salience for them are what have tended to be treated by the criminal justice agencies as less serious'. Possible examples of signal crimes and disorder, particularly when a number of these examples coincide in a local community, include:

- public drinking, swearing, rowdy and uncivil behaviour by groups of individuals;
- graffiti and other forms of damage and vandalism, litter;
- evidence of drug taking and dealing, prostitution;
- speeding; and
- rubbish dumped in the street or outside houses, burnt-out cars, and other vehicles.

Once spotted, these signals can give rise to a heightened sense of awareness amongst individuals of other similar examples—a form of non-virtuous feedback loop.

4.5   Modelling Crime and Criminality

In 4.3 we provided an overview of some of the theories that attempt to explain the existence of crime and criminality. We now move on from these general theories (often concerned with human nature and society) to more detailed explanatory models and also suggest some possible responses for the police and others.

4.5.1   Opportunities for crime

Pease (2002) notes three different ways in which crime has been understood, and he defines these in terms of structure, human psyche, and circumstance. 'Structure' covers major social issues that are seen to be linked to crime, for example poverty and inequality. Human psyche concerns the attributes of the criminal as a person, in other words the reasons why he/she has a propensity to commit offences. However, Pease proposes that the circumstance dimension of crime, or the opportunity for crime to occur, is the key factor for causing crime.

Rational-choice theory assumes that when criminals decide to commit offences they go through the same kind of thought process as non-criminals making everyday, non-criminal decisions:

> It is not the case (except for a tiny handful of pathological personalities) that criminals are so unlike the rest of us as to be indifferent to the costs and benefits of the opportunities open to them. (Wilson, 1996, p 312)

This suggests that crimes occur if and when they are easy to commit, and the results are sufficiently rewarding.

Routine-activity theory is also predicated upon an understanding of the relationship between an individual's everyday experiences and his/her criminal behaviour. Importantly, it defines criminal opportunities in terms of three interrelated and necessary components:

- a motivated offender;
- a suitable target; and
- the absence of a guardian.

Criminal opportunities arise when these three components coincide. We may observe that the number of offences might increase even if there is no increase in the number of motivated offenders. This occurs if a small number of motivated offenders are in situations where there are few guardians and plenty of suitable targets. Schools are a prime example of this kind of scenario: there are significant numbers of largely unsupervised vulnerable children with mobile phones, and there are other children who are keen to acquire these.

4.5.2   The 'hot' model

One way to consider the phenomenon of crime in society is to think about some of its constituent elements as being hot: that is, both frequently occurring and worthy of attention. (The following owes much to Clarke (1999), although terms such as 'hot offender' are ours.)

Hot spots are places that are particularly prone to crime, such as railway stations, shopping malls, town centres, particular shops and houses, post offices, or flats. This may be related to the easy pickings for the criminal intent on theft, shoplifting, mugging, or similar. In addition, it may also be related to opportunity, because these are places where people are more likely to be carrying large quantities of cash (railway stations close to race courses for example, or streets leading away from ATMs or cash machines). This leads to an unevenness of crime distribution: in a city there will be some particular and precise geographical areas that always or nearly always have a high crime rate (all types), but other areas will be virtually crime free. Until some preventative action is taken, these 'hot spots' will persist, and even if action is taken they may recur (see 4.6.3).

Hot offenders are defined as the relatively small number of people who are responsible for the majority of crime. However, opinion and research continue to differ over just how small a minority of criminals is responsible for just how large a majority of crime (see 3.9.3). Furthermore, research (eg Everson and Pease, 2001) on repeat victimization (see 'hot victims' discussed later) suggests that prolific offenders may be responsible for the bulk of these repeated crimes against the same person or target.

Hot products are the items we know are more attractive to burglars or street robbers, and there is a logic to what is stolen or snatched. In the 1970s, televisions were favoured by burglars due to their high value (despite being heavy, bulky, and difficult to steal without a car or van for transport) but became less so as the price of TVs dropped. Whilst flat-screen TVs are still objects of desire for burglars, the average, small-time, drug-abusing, volume criminal will go for small items of value which are easily transportable and not easily traced. This is why cash (pre-eminently) and jewellery are popular targets for thieves. Cash, of course, is easily disposed of and generally untraceable, and the bulk of rings and watches are easily converted into money. Satnavs are also a popular target.

As you might suppose, there is a mnemonic (Clarke, 1999) for rating hot products: CRAVED.

C	Concealable
R	Removable
A	Available
V	Valuable
E	Enjoyable
D	Disposable

The CRAVED model may be used as a means of judging just how attractive an object will be for a thief. A score can be assigned for each factor, and a high total CRAVED score would indicate that the object is more likely to be stolen. (Granted, it is not as simple as this, but the scoring system gives a relatively easy way of using the checklist.)

In the original work by Clarke (1999) disposability was considered to be one of the most important factors. Thieves prefer items which they can get rid of quickly and without fuss to a trusted 'fence', and will probably receive only a tenth or a fifth of the retail value of the item. Handling stolen goods is covered in 16.5.

TASK 3 Estimate how CRAVED the following articles might be:

- an iPod;
- an iphone 5 or equivalent smartphone;
- a laptop;
- £642.89 in coins;
- a computer with separate screen and keyboard;
- a CRT (non-flat-screen) television;
- a 2005 mobile phone;
- £350 in £50 notes;
- a manuscript copy of *The Lindisfarne Gospels*;
- 12 Japanese ivory *netsuke* dating from the late sixteenth century;
- a Rolex watch, engraved and dated; and
- an unframed oil painting by Rubens, measuring 23 × 19 cm.

Policing in Context

Hot victims are perhaps the least studied and least understood part of the equation. Intuitively, it could be expected that old age, frailty, and naïvety would make a person more vulnerable than the average person, but there is little empirical evidence to support this, other than for distraction burglary (see the start of 16.4). However, studies have shown that once someone has been a victim of certain types of crime on one occasion (particularly burglary), they are more likely than other people to be a victim again, even if all other variables are taken into account. Repeat victimization (if it occurs) generally takes place quite soon after the original incident. Often high crime rates and hot spots exist precisely because of repeat victimization (if not the same address, it could be the same street).

Why some people, or some premises, or some organizations should be repeat victims of crime is not always clear. There is some evidence (although not conclusive) that the original offender returns to the same places and reoffends. From a thief's perspective it may be that 'it worked once so it will work again'. Alternatively it could be that a thief intentionally gives a house-owner time to claim on insurance for a valuable item, and then returns to steal the replacement (see eg Bowers *et al*, 1998.) Whatever the explanation, we should emphasize that people who do not take elementary precautions after having been victims of crime on one occasion should not be surprised if they are targeted again.

Finally, we know that those who repeatedly victimize the same target tend to be more established lifestyle or career criminals. All this should suggest that intelligence about the nature of a crime and why it is repeated in the same spot with the same victim, should help police forces predict with a limited degree of accuracy where, when, and by whom the next attempt will be made (see eg Bowers *et al*, 2004 and more recently the claims made for 'PredPol', 2014).

TASK 4 Following what we have said about hot victims, what operational strategies do you think that the police should employ to help reduce repeat victimization?

Clearly, there are many possible interactions between hot spots, hot offenders, hot products, and hot victims. Hot offenders are more likely to want hot products. Hot victims are more likely to be in hot spots, and this is certainly the case for domestic burglary. Hot offenders are likely to target hot spots because, as we noted earlier, there are relatively easy opportunities for crime and relatively little chance of being caught. And, as previously mentioned, the same offenders may return to burgle the same house again. It is hard to disentangle cause and effect, but the unevenness of the distribution of crime cannot be ignored.

TASK 5 What practical policing implications can be derived from the following quotation, assuming that the argument being made is valid?

Becoming criminal can be explained in much the same way we explain becoming a midwife or buying a car. (Wilson, 1996, p 307)

4.6 Crime Reduction

We often hear the terms 'crime prevention', 'crime reduction', and 'community safety' used both within policing and more widely. Ekblom (2001) draws subtle distinctions between these concepts, whereas Pease (2002) suggests they are different expressions of the same thing and that the use of different terms is an indication of different political perspectives. We will follow Pease and use the terms interchangeably.

Crime prevention is a long-standing but often neglected policing priority. Today we recognize that all police officers have a crime prevention responsibility, and that this is not simply the role of a designated 'Crime Prevention Officer' (as was the case in the recent past). The police perspective on crime prevention has changed, and this is partly due to a better understanding of how preventative measures can be utilized to reduce crime. Two important lessons have been learnt. First, crime prevention can be seen as an integral aspect of a police officer's duties alongside, rather than in opposition to, a crime detection function. Secondly, we now understand better how crime prevention can be used in a targeted and directed manner to reduce crime and to thereby free more police resources for dedicated proactive police work.

Crime can be reduced to some extent through detecting crimes and imprisoning the offenders, with the result that fewer prospective offenders have the opportunity to commit crime. However, preventing crimes from happening in the first place represents a far more rational approach, and provides clear benefits to society. The targeted use of crime prevention is discussed in 3.9.2. It forms part of a problem-oriented approach to reducing crime informed by routine-activity theory and the insight into the three components of crime: the offender, the victim, and the location of a crime. Police officers can ask appropriate questions concerning why a crime has occurred, and in this way preventative measures become apparent: the police response becomes proactive as opposed to reactive.

The crime reduction agenda has also been bolstered by the move towards partnership approaches in policing (see 3.3), and in this respect the increasing emphasis on crime prevention has altered the role of the police. The local focus of crime prevention requires good intelligence and it is therefore important that police officers make the most of information from local intelligence officers. The quality of this information is likewise dependent on police officers sharing information with the local intelligence officers.

4.6.1   Reducing the opportunities for crime

A new emphasis on integrating crime prevention into everyday police work increases the need for police officers to anticipate, recognize, and assess the risk of criminal activity. Measures can then be taken to reduce the risk. These measures might be simple and straightforward, requiring little more than providing the public with crime prevention advice. At other times, a more concerted effort is required to reduce the crime risk. Police officers need to be adept at anticipating and appraising crime risks. For example, an unlit pathway provides criminals with an appropriate crime location. A police officer needs to be able to evaluate what short-term measures can be taken to reduce the criminal opportunity, for example increase the guardianship of the unlit pathway (through regular police patrol), but also to take the necessary action to ensure that a longer term solution is provided, for example by contacting the local council to ensure the lighting problem is addressed.

Routine-activity theory and rational-choice theory are also used to explain the causes of crime (see 4.3). Using these different factors we can suggest that preventative techniques could be organized under three headings:

- increasing the effort (eg target hardening);
- increasing the risks (eg CCTV); and
- reducing the rewards (eg marking property).

Pease (2002) adds a fourth heading: 'reducing the excuses'. The relative significance of each of these strategies depends upon the particular crime in question: which strategy is most likely to have the greatest deterrent impact on the potential criminal? These ideas are illustrated in Task 6.

TASK 6 Consider the following scenarios and identify whether increasing the effort, increasing the risk, or reducing the reward would be the most effective preventative measure. (We acknowledge that, to some extent, all three would be appropriate but try to identify the one that you think addresses the problem most directly.)

1. There have been a number of thefts from vehicles in a supermarket car park. The cars targeted have had valuable items stolen from them.
2. A shop is being repeatedly targeted at night by a group of known drug addicts.
3. Small amounts of money are being stolen by a member of staff from within a bank.

A consideration of routine-activity theory suggests some other approaches that may be used in crime reduction: for example, ensuring that motivated offenders are not left unobserved where there are easy criminal targets. From this perspective, we do not have to reduce the number of motivated offenders in order to reduce crime; we simply need to ensure that they are monitored more closely or that we design goods in a way that makes them less attractive to criminals.

4.6.2 The prevention of hot spots

A persistent police presence would undoubtedly have a deterrent effect, but that cannot be sustained over the long or even the medium term. Equally, the use of PCSOs or local authority wardens as a visible deterrent is costly, intermittent at best, and dubious as anything more than a temporary solution. CCTV cameras are a possible short-term solution, especially if coordinated with police action on the ground such as 'blitzes' on pickpockets, for example.

A longer-term (but potentially very effective) solution is to 'design out' crime through the use of features such as more carefully designed walkways and better street lighting. The use of intelligence (see Chapter 22) is likely to be an important part of any approach to dealing with hot spots. The kinds of crime, the times when the crimes take place, the sorts of people who commit those crimes, the seasonal impact (if any) upon the nature of the crime, and the likelihood of achieving a result will all be important considerations for the intelligence analyst. It is this intensity of knowledge, allied to detailed understanding about the hot spot and other contributory factors, which may lead to the cooling of a hot spot.

4.6.3 Crime prevention advice

Although it is stressed here that crime prevention is the responsibility of all police officers, a specialist Crime Prevention Officer (CPO) can provide further advice. Understanding crime through the prism of the victim, the offender, and the location, and asking the right questions as to why a crime has occurred, provide the basis for practical solutions aimed at preventing future crimes. The advice can be tailored to specific contexts. For example, in a home setting specific advice can be given regarding the most suitable locks, lighting, and other basic security measures.

Increasingly, we are also becoming more aware of the specific need to tailor crime prevention messages to children. Importantly, crime prevention should also feature as one aspect of a police criminal investigation to ensure that lessons from one crime are used to help prevent future criminal activities.

Police officers also need to make sure that communities as a whole are involved in implementing effective crime prevention strategies. There are many different 'watch' schemes in place that have built upon the success of Neighbourhood Watch schemes (see 3.9.1.4) including Street Watch. These are being provided in a targeted way to address the crime prevention needs of specific businesses. Neighbourhood Policing Teams (NPTs), Crime Prevention Panels (CPCs), and Local Policing and Confidence Units (LPCUs) provide a local focus for crime prevention measures alongside the national Crimestoppers Trust, which works in collaboration with the police. Crimestoppers is easily contacted by phone (a freephone number) or via their website.

4.6.4 Displacement

One problem that has been identified with crime prevention is that it leads to crime displacement: crimes are not prevented, but merely displaced to other places or other times. New types of crime may also occur through criminal innovation (see the following list). Displacement is often explained as a consequence of criminality: those with a disposition to commit crimes will adapt and find different ways in which to realize their criminal disposition. The following types of displacement have been identified.

- **Temporal displacement:** the crime takes place at a later time. As an example, consider the depot that introduces a security guard overnight to counter a string of night-time burglaries. However, there is a one-hour gap between the security guard finishing and the day staff arriving, so the criminals choose this time to commit the offence.
- **Spatial displacement:** the crime happens somewhere else. In this case imagine that a high police presence is introduced in Area 1 to curb incidents of anti-social behaviour from a group of teenagers. The teenagers simply move to Area 2 and behave in the same way.
- **Displacement by type of crime:** the criminals turn to different crimes. Suppose that the local council introduces better street lighting on an estate prone to street robberies. The number of robberies falls but the number of burglaries increases in the area.
- **Displacement by innovation:** the criminals become better at what they do. An example is the increasing use of credit cards; people no longer carry large amounts of cash. This reduces the cash reward for muggers but some turn to using stolen credit cards, thereby gaining access to even larger sums of money.

Pease (1997) has suggested that the extent of displacement is often exaggerated, and that the issue is raised on ideological rather than empirical grounds and used as an excuse for doing nothing. Furthermore, Pease argues that displacement is never likely to be 100 per cent, and he also illustrates ways in which it can be benevolent. For example, it might be beneficial to move a crime from one area to another to reduce its overall impact on society or to change the type of crimes that offenders are committing. For example, take a scenario in which prostitutes are operating in a residential area where many children live. We could assume that a high police presence there would move the prostitutes on to another area. The question would then be to establish whether this movement is beneficial or not. If the prostitutes move to a non-residential area it would clearly reduce the concern that children would be affected, although this might need to be balanced against a separate concern for the safety of the prostitutes. We might also consider that some of the prostitutes would potentially turn to other forms of crime, for example shoplifting, whilst others would innovate and use more discreet means of operating, for example by using cards in telephone boxes to advertise their services. We might also assume that some of the prostitutes will desist from any kind of criminal activity. The important point is that an assessment can be made as to what are the likely consequences following from anticipated displacement, which can then be tested empirically in order to establish what the effect actually was. As Pease puts it, displacement is positive as long as 'the deflected crime causes less harm and misery than the original crime' (Pease, 1997, p 978).

4.6.5 Crime reduction strategies in perspective

A final consideration follows from the recognition that the consequences of crime prevention strategies can be to varying degrees either benevolent or malevolent. This raises a fundamental question, and challenges our initial premise that prevention is necessarily better than cure.

By seeking to reduce crime, we are intending to make society better in some way. However, intervening in the lives of individuals will not always make things better and there are occasions when we have to accept that doing nothing is actually preferable to taking action. This may be hard to accept because we do not want to feel as though we are ignoring problems in society and just standing by, letting bad things happen. Police officers (especially) have a duty of care and they respond to problems, but it is important that any intervention is properly evaluated. To this end, policing in general (and crime reduction in particular) is increasingly subjected to research and evaluation, and the results of this research will help ensure that any claims used to justify preventative strategies are based on firm evidence (see eg Smith and Tilley, 2005).

The view that crimes are informed by rational considerations has been an important feature of situational crime prevention programmes. There are many examples of how this understanding has led to reductions in crime through architectural design and other measures aimed at making it more difficult for criminals to operate. This has made it more likely that they will be identified, caught, and prosecuted if they commit an offence. Other measures have been introduced to reduce the potential rewards of committing offences: for example the introduction of phone cards in place of the old coin-operated public telephone boxes.

However, critics of the rational view of crime argue that all crime prevention measures result in displacement. As we noted earlier, this criticism has been widely acknowledged but is countered by evidence that suggests displacement is never complete. In other words, we might expect some individuals to stop committing crime altogether as a consequence of crime prevention measures, because the extra effort and risk makes it less attractive. In this respect we begin to see a distinction between criminals who are driven by favourable opportunities and more prolific offenders who are driven by a desire to commit an offence. This can allow the police to concentrate resources against those offenders least affected by general crime prevention strategies.

4.7 Answers to Tasks

TASK 1 There are many different explanations for what registers as a sensational crime in public imagination and the media. A sensational crime is often one which has something out of the ordinary, something different, even a little outrageous, to make it stand out.

Some violent crimes involving children may feature highly in the media and thus public consciousness (possibly because many of us are expected to identify with the parents of the victim, or because the vulnerability of a child evokes sympathy and pity in us), as may crimes in which single young women are involved. (There is some suggestion of an ethnic bias in reporting crimes of this type, with victims of ethnic minorities less likely to receive extensive media coverage than their white counterparts. However, this discussion is beyond the scope of this Handbook.)

Crimes which tend not to make the headlines, unless really bizarre or huge, are the so-called victimless crimes such as defrauding a large company or embezzling insurance money. There are victims of course for any crime (because that helps to define the nature of a crime), but what frightens a community or spreads anxiety is the thought that some sort of terror or dread is stalking the streets. A series of rapes can do this, especially in a small community like a town or at a college, and the abduction of a child also causes widespread concern.

TASK 2 There are a large number of possible answers, and we provide some suggestions here. The answer for 'universal crimes' is somewhat speculative.

Crimes	Examples
Universal	Theft, murder, and rape
In the UK now, but not 100 years ago	Stalking, computer crimes (eg hacking), and some categories of outdoor music and dancing events at night
In other parts of the world, but not in the UK	Adultery (Nigeria), consuming alcohol (Saudi Arabia), keeping African pygmy hedgehogs (some states of the USA)

TASK 3 There is a difference between intrinsic value and 'CRAVED'. The thieves would probably leave the coins behind because they are bulky and very heavy, but they would pocket the £350 in notes immediately. The PC would probably be left; again it is bulky and heavy. The laptop would be easily picked up and sold on, as would the iPod, iphone, and the Rolex. Beware though—traffic in electronic goods is transient and short-lived. It is often the next-generation white goods that the fences demand. Stealing a mobile phone made in 2005 would yield no return. The Rolex might later cause problems because any engraving makes it potentially traceable, but in snatching or mugging for it the thieves would not stop to check. The engraving and date would knock pounds off the price, and the fence might subsequently file the engraving out.

The other items are small but would be very difficult to sell on. *The Gospels* and the Rubens' painting would be worth several million pounds, but they would be very difficult to fence on any art market. (However, organized drugs importers and traffickers have used valuable art such as paintings or sculptures as 'cash' for their transactions—the more so since the Proceeds of Crime Act 2002 made depositing large amounts of cash in a bank account subject to scrutiny and investigation.)

The *netsuke*, which are small carved figures, would be worth several thousand pounds each but only through an expert dealer, and it is doubtful that the average fence would know what they were. That said, some thieves steal to order and might target such items specifically, but these are not likely to be volume criminals working on hot spots.

TASK 4 In this task you were asked to consider police strategies to combat repeat victimization. Some useful suggestions are included in the Police research paper, 'Biting Back: Tackling Repeat Burglary and Car Crime' available online. The popular phrase, 'once bitten, twice shy' suggests that we become more vigilant after an unpleasant incident such as being the victim of a crime. Whilst it might be true that we become more wary, it is certainly not the case that we become less vulnerable. As we suggested in terms of burglary, by far the best predictor of future victimization is whether we have been a victim in the recent past. The police should ensure the householder receives advice on reducing the vulnerability of their property.

TASK 5 The quotation assumes that criminal behaviour will follow a rational pattern, thus hot products will be targeted by certain people in hot spots, and markets will exist for the products of crime. The predictability of this should allow the police to anticipate appropriate points at which to intervene.

TASK 6

1. Reducing the reward. The fact that the cars targeted have valuables on show suggests that the offenders are looking for easy rewards. Increasing the risk by introducing better lighting, CCTV cameras, or security guards would also be beneficial, but the most cost-effective measure is likely to be encouraging people not to leave valuables in the car.

2. Increasing the effort. We can assume that these particular offenders are desperate and therefore unlikely to be overly concerned at being caught (increasing the risk) and will be prepared to take risks for small rewards (reducing the reward). Therefore making it physically difficult to break in by installing metal bars and stronger locks is likely to be the most effective measure.

3. Increasing the risk. The rewards are already limited and making it more difficult to take the money is impractical because of the need for employees to handle money. Therefore increasing the risk, for example by installing CCTV, is likely to have a deterrent effect because the employees have a lot to lose if they are caught.

5 | The Criminal Justice System in England and Wales

5.1 Introduction

In the UK the concept of the criminal justice system refers to the law, law enforcement, and dealing with transgressions of the law. The criminal justice system (the CJS) in England and Wales includes the police, the courts of law, the National Offenders Management Service (NOMS), the Youth Justice Board, and the Crown Prosecution Service (CPS).

Both students on pre-join programmes and trainee police officers will need to understand a variety of different types of law and court procedures. A number of situations that involve specific types of legislation will be addressed in more detail in subsequent chapters (such as criminal and family law regarding domestic violence in 15.7), but here we will concentrate on the general aspects; how laws are made, some of the different branches of law, the principles behind criminal law, and the courts system. The system used by the courts in England and Wales is largely adversarial, whereas elsewhere in Europe (eg in France) the system is inquisitorial.

The adversarial model requires that a person, the defendant, is accused of an offence and is tried by a court (usually in open session), and that the defendant's guilt must be proved beyond reasonable doubt. The prosecution is conducted on behalf of the Crown, often referred to in written case law as 'R' ('Regina' or 'Rex', the Queen or King respectively, depending whether a King or a Queen is on the throne when the case is heard). The Crown Prosecutors and Senior Crown Prosecutors (SCP) are lawyers employed by the CPS to review, and when appropriate, prosecute cases investigated by the police. Associate Prosecutors (who are not lawyers) may also perform some of these functions at the level of the magistrates' courts. The defendant is normally represented by a solicitor and in some circumstances by a barrister. They are known as the 'defence counsel' or 'the defence'.

In an inquisitorial system (not used in England and Wales) the defendant is questioned by a judge during trial; correspondingly, the role taken by defence counsel is of much lower profile.

5.2 The Law in England and Wales

An understanding of the law in England and Wales is an important aspect of the police officer's epistemic authority (see 3.4), and is essential in relation to many of the NOS elements underpinning the Certificate in Knowledge of Policing and the Diploma in Policing. Law also features extensively during most Operational Modules and in LPG 1 and LPG 2.

You may have heard law referred to as: common law, statute law, case law, Acts of Parliament, Statutory Instruments, and by-laws. These all interrelate in a number of ways.

Common law (also known as judge-made law) can be traced back to the Norman invasion of Britain in the eleventh century. Local courts made decisions that were then passed by word of mouth to other courts, which with time became accepted by other courts throughout the country, creating a 'binding precedent'. Examples of common law offences which remain today are:

- murder;
- manslaughter;
- perverting the course of justice; and
- escape from lawful custody.

In the UK no new common law offences are created now apart from the setting of precedents by the courts when interpreting existing law.

Statute law is the foundation of the current legal system in England and Wales. These are primary sources of law, and can be accessed electronically via the UK Statute Law Database (<http://www.legislation.gov.uk>). The following are all commonly used:

- the Theft Act 1968 (principal offences of dishonesty);
- the Criminal Damage Act 1971 (some offences of damage);
- the Misuse of Drugs Act 1971 (the principal drug-related offences); and
- the Public Order Act 1986 (the main offences of public disorder).

Bills or 'draft law' are needed to create new legislation; ministry officials write a proposal and submit it to the Houses of Parliament for a decision. If accepted it is given Royal Assent before becoming an Act of Parliament.

Case law helps to establish the precise meaning of legislation. Decisions made by higher courts about legislation are then accepted by lower courts throughout the country. This 'doctrine of precedent' sets out how the legislation should be used by a court in similar circumstances. Although the specific circumstances of the case might change (referred to as *obiter dicta*), the court should use the same reasoning (or *ratio decidendi*) that was used by previous courts to reach a decision. An example of this would be the decisions made about identification evidence in the case *R v Turnbull* [1976] 3 All ER 549. (Note the system for referencing cases: 'R' stands for Regina (the Crown as prosecutor), 'v' for versus, and 'Turnbull' is the name of the defendant. This case can be found in Volume 3 of the 1976 All England Law Reports on p 549.)

Acts of Parliament are divided into sections containing, for example, definitions, offences, powers of arrest, exemptions, and interpretations of words and expressions used. An Act often includes technical details such as fines and penalties which may need frequent revision and updating. These will be provided in the form of Statutory Instruments such as Orders, Regulations, and Rules, and are often left to government ministers to reduce the pressure on parliamentary time.

Statutory Instruments (SIs) allow the details of an Act to be revised without using parliamentary procedures. They are as much part of the law of England and Wales as is the main body of the Act of Parliament. As with Acts of Parliament, SIs are given a number as well as a title, 'Criminal Justice (Electronic Monitoring) (Responsible Person) Order 2014' (SI 2014 No 163). The Home Secretary used this SI to enable private companies such as Capita and G4S to take responsibility for the electronic monitoring of people released on condition of bail or as part of a youth rehabilitation order, curfew, or community order.

By-laws are usually local laws which have been made by a local authority and approved by a Secretary of State of the government. They normally deal with local matters, for example dogs on leads in recreational areas. They can also refer to charters, which are documents created under a generic form of legislation to regulate certain activities within an organization. Examples of charters include Trades Union charters and the Department of Health Information Charter.

> **TASK 1** The Road Vehicle Lighting Regulations 1989 (SI 1989 No 1796) were introduced under s 41 of the Road Traffic Act 1988. Find out what regs 11–22 cover in relation to motor vehicles. (Use *Blackstone's Police Manual: Volume 3 Road Policing*, the internet, or other publications to look this up.)

5.3 Principles of Criminal Liability

Trainee police officers will of course be involved in non-crime incidents—for example, policing a picket line established during a strike—and will need to consider the relevant legislation. However, most of the law relevant to the first few years of service undoubtedly is of the criminal, rather than the civil form. Indeed, the list of subjects in the IPLDP LPG modules is dominated by criminal law.

We begin with the notion of 'criminal liability'—how do we *know* and then prove that a person has broken the law? There are two elements of criminal liability:

1. The *actus reus*—the action the defendant carried out, which must be proved beyond reasonable doubt (see 5.3.1).
2. The *mens rea*—guilty mindset that the defendant had at the time the action was taken, which also must be proved; that is, that the defendant intended to commit the crime. However, there are some exceptions to this (see 5.3.2).

Although the use of Latin can seem off-putting and exclusionary, these terms are commonly used in policing and so are worth remembering. We will now look at these two building blocks of criminal liability in more detail.

5.3.1   *Actus reus*

This is about a person's actions (including a lack of action). If a person is to be found guilty of a criminal offence, then it must be proved that he/she either:

- acted criminally in some way: for example committed murder;
- omitted to do an act which brought about a criminal outcome: for example knowing that someone was going to commit a crime but doing nothing to stop it or report it;
- caused a state of affairs to happen: for example, a man knowingly drinks a lot of alcohol which leads to him being found drunk and incapable at the wheel of a car; or
- failed to do an act which was required, and which brought about a criminal outcome: for example, by failing to ensure that a vehicle was roadworthy when offering it for hire, this leads to the criminal outcome of someone driving a car that is not in a safe condition to be driven.

5.3.2   *Mens rea*

This is about a person's thoughts or state of mind. Although the Latin term appears to be very narrow in its meaning, in reality there are a number of thought processes and levels of intent that satisfy the requirements of many offences, other than just having guilty knowledge. You will find these states of mind listed under different terms in a number of offences. The most common words are:

- 'dishonestly' such as for theft;
- 'wilfully' such as for neglect of children;
- 'recklessly' as in for causing criminal damage; and
- 'with intent' as in burglary with intent to steal.

The degree of *mens rea* in criminal offences varies between more serious situations where a person deliberately committed an offence, and less serious situations where a person failed to take appropriate care to avoid the criminal outcome of their action or inaction (usually called negligence). The level of intention is assessed by comparing the actions of the defendant with those of a hypothetical 'reasonable' or average person under the circumstances of the alleged offence. For more serious situations (eg murder and 'wounding or inflicting grievous bodily harm with intent') the law requires that the suspect has a certain intent or *mens rea*. This would also include offences for which there is an ulterior intent other than the main criminal act, for example when a defendant is charged with burglary with intent (see 16.4.1). Here, it would have to be proved that the defendant not only intended to enter a building as a trespasser, but also intended to inflict grievous bodily harm, cause damage, or steal.

'Strict liability' offences are those for which a *mens rea* is not required (or a diminished *mens rea* is sufficient) to convict someone for breaking the law. In such cases only the guilty act (*actus reus*) needs to have occurred. Examples of strict liability offences include:

- paying for sexual services of a prostitute who is being subjected to force (s 14 of the Policing and Crime Act 2009, see 17.5.3)—it is irrelevant whether the suspect knows about the force; and
- the sale of faulty goods (s 14 of the Sale of Goods Act 1979)—it is irrelevant whether the suspect knows the goods are faulty.

Cases of strict liability are considered less serious by the law and often correspond to statutory violations. However, it is not always clear whether a *mens rea* is required. Decisions concerning strict liability may be ultimately left to the courts.

5.3.3 Burden of proof

How do we prove that a person is guilty of a criminal offence? The law tells us that:

> throughout the web of the English criminal law one golden thread is always to be seen: that it is the duty of the prosecution to prove the prisoner's guilt. (*Woolmington v DPP* [1935] AC 462)

Therefore, in criminal proceedings the onus is on the prosecution to prove the guilt of the defendant, not on the defendant to prove his or her innocence. And furthermore, the degree of proof required for criminal cases is 'beyond reasonable doubt'. This was famously expressed by Geoffrey Lawrence (cited in Johnston and Hutton, 2005, p 133) in the following way:

> The possibility of guilt is not enough, suspicion is not enough, probability is not enough, likelihood is not enough. A criminal matter is not a question of balancing probabilities and deciding in favour of probability, a conviction must be formed beyond reasonable doubt that the accused is guilty, and this is done on the basis of the evidence provided in court.

5.4 Human Rights

The concept of human rights and the responsibilities of police officers in the preservation and maintenance of those rights runs throughout this Handbook. Human rights legislation stresses an individual's entitlement to expect certain fundamental rights as part of their social contract with the state and other forms of authority.

The protection of human rights in the UK has been significantly affected by the Human Rights Act 1998 (HRA) which came into force in the year 2000. The HRA took s 1 of the European Convention on the Protection of Human Rights and Fundamental Freedoms (which came into force in 1953, referred to as the ECHR) and to a large extent copied it into domestic law. There are several important features of human rights legislation under the HRA:

- all new statute law must be compatible with the rights, but there is no retrospective effect on existing law (*R v Lambert*, 2001);
- an individual may take a public authority to a UK court (rather than directly to the European Court of Human Rights) if the authority has not acted in a manner compatible with the rights;
- UK courts are required to interpret all legislation in a way which is compatible with the Convention's rights, so far as is possible (s 3); and
- public authorities (eg government and the police) cannot act in a way which is incompatible with the Convention.

Note, however, that although the HRA has no automatic retrospective effect, existing law may be examined to check its compatibility with human rights legislation. For example, Parliament's Joint Committee on Human Rights scrutinized the Terrorism Prevention and Investigation Measures Act 2011.

All ten of the Diploma in Policing assessed units include the requirement to address the need to 'Promote equality and value diversity' in the relevant context. For example, the assessed unit concerned with providing an initial response to incidents has an assessment criterion stating that the learner must be able to identify the legislation, policies, procedures, codes of practice, and/or guidelines that relate to race, diversity, and human rights when responding to an incident. The corresponding Certificate in Knowledge of Policing unit 'Knowledge of providing an initial response to incidents within a policing context' also requires knowledge of such matters.

5.4.1 What are the rights?

The rights are listed within the articles of the Human Rights Act 1998. Each right is considered as absolute (underlined), limited (L), or qualified (Q).

Article number	Article title
2	<u>Right to life</u>
3	<u>Prohibition of torture</u>
4	<u>Prohibition of slavery and forced labour</u>
5	Right to liberty and security (L)

6	Right to a fair trial (L)
7	<u>No punishment without law</u>
8	Right to respect for private and family life (Q)
9	Freedom of thought, conscience, and religion (Q)
10	Freedom of expression (Q)
11	Freedom of assembly and association (Q)
12	Right to marry (L)
14	Prohibition of discrimination (L)

The **Absolute rights** of an individual cannot be restricted by the interests of the community as a whole.

Limited rights do not apply in all circumstances and are limited in the articles which contain them—for example the right to liberty (part of Article 5) does not apply if the detention is lawful, such as after arrest. However, although the right to liberty may be limited, a lawfully arrested person would still have the right to security under Article 5. A further example occurs within Article 6, where there is a right for both the public and the press to have access to any court hearing, but this right is subject to certain restrictions in the interests of morality, public order, national security, or where the interests of those under 18, or the privacy of the parties require the exclusion of the press and public.

Qualified rights relate to matters where interference by the public authority is permissible if it is in the public interest and can be qualified, for example to prevent disorder or crime, for public safety, or for national security. However, a public authority (such as the police) may only interfere with a qualified right if the interference is:

* lawful and is part of existing common or statute law (see 5.2), such as the power to stop and search;
* made for one of the specifically listed permissible acts in the interests of the public, such as in order to prevent disorder for public safety; or
* necessary in a democratic society because the wider interests of the community as a whole often have to be balanced against the rights of an individual (but it must still be proportionate).

There are certain aspects of the HRA 1998 which may seem strange when compared to other Acts of Parliament (eg Article 1 does not contain any rights and Article 13 does not even exist). This is partly because the HRA is a transposition of s 1 of the ECHR into domestic law.

5.4.2 Applying the Human Rights Act to everyday policing

A police officer should consider the following questions in relation to an individual or group before 'interfering' with another person's qualified rights:

1. Are my actions lawful? Is there common or statute law to support my interference with their rights?
2. Are my actions permissible? Am I permitted to interfere with their rights because it is in support of a duty, such as preventing crime?
3. Are my actions necessary? Do the needs of the many outweigh the needs of the few; in other words, must I take into account the interests of the community and balance one individual's rights against another's?
4. Are my actions proportionate? Having considered everything, will my actions be excessive or could I do something less intrusive and more in proportion to the outcome I need to achieve?

During initial police training mnemonics may be used with regard to these questions, for example:

* **JAPAN** (Justifiable, Accountable, Proportionate, And Necessary) and
* **PLAN** (Proportionality, Legality, Accountability, and Necessity).

The ability to consider these matters is assessed in the Certificate in Knowledge of Policing, which includes the assessment criteria to be able to 'explain how to ensure that there is sufficient evidence and legal authority to justify actions' when arresting and detaining suspects (part of the unit 'Knowledge of arresting, detaining and reporting individuals within a policing context'). The ability is also required for the Diploma in Policing, for qualifying as a police officer. For example, one of the Diploma learning outcomes is to demonstrate the ability to 'Provide initial support to victims and witnesses', associated with the assessment criteria that actions when providing initial support should:

1. Follow the principles of equality, diversity, and anti-discrimination practice.
2. Manage risks to health and safety.

> **TASK 2** How would a trainee police officer seek to meet the first requirement, which is to 'follow the principles of equality, diversity, and anti-discrimination practice'? What evidence might an assessor be looking for?

5.5 The Criminal Justice System in Practice

Once an alleged crime has been reported, there will be an investigation at some level, mostly conducted by the police. The extent and nature of an investigation will inevitably vary with the circumstances (covered in more detail in Chapters 10 and 23). As subsequent prosecution is usually conducted by the CPS on behalf of the Crown (the state). Depending on the seriousness, the cases are dealt with at different courts (see 5.5.2). The defendant may choose to represent him/herself but it is more usual to use a solicitor or barrister. The courts may be assisted by Social Services and the Probation Service. Investigation, prosecution, and court procedures are covered in more detail in Chapters 22–26.

Certificate in Knowledge of Policing students will need to demonstrate underpinning knowledge and understanding about the UK criminal justice system in many of the units. Trainee police officers will obviously come into contact with the criminal justice system. Indeed, in many forces a criminal justice placement forms part of IPLDP Phase 2 of training, and this provides an opportunity for meeting other professionals working within the system. Many of them will also be on education and training programmes linked to NOS elements determined by Skills for Justice, as is the Diploma in Policing. A number of the Diploma assessed units such as 'Conduct priority and volume investigations' relate to carrying out investigations, preparing cases, and appearing in court. The PAC heading 'Finalize investigations' also requires a trainee officer to demonstrate the ability to 'adhere to court procedures' and 'give evidence at court' before being declared fit to undertake Independent Patrol.

5.5.1 The classification of criminal offences

Offences are classified according to their seriousness and the level of court at which they can be tried. The three main categories of offence are:

- **Summary offences**, which can only be tried in a magistrates' court. Examples are: common assault, assaulting a police officer in the execution of his/her duty, and most motoring offences.
- **Indictment-only offences**, which can only be dealt with in a Crown Court and are the most serious cases. Examples are: murder, manslaughter, causing death by dangerous driving, rape, robbery, aggravated burglary, and wounding with intent.
- **Either-way offences**, which can be tried in a magistrates' court or a Crown Court; the magistrate decides. Examples of either-way offences are: theft, obtaining by deception, assault occasioning actual bodily harm, and indecent assault.

There is a further term—**'indictable' offence**—a collective name for both 'indictment-only' and 'either-way' offences. (You may also hear the phrase 'arrestable offence', but this is out of date as offences are no longer classified in this way.)

The classification for each criminal offence and its mode of trial and penalty can be found either by reference to primary sources—that is, the legal texts themselves (eg through the Home Office website) or secondary sources, such as Blackstone's Police Manuals. As an example, the relevant legislation for the offence of theft is in s 7 of the Theft Act 1968. This, in conjunction with Sch 1 and s 32 of the Magistrates' Court Act 1980, states that theft is triable either way, with a maximum penalty of seven years' imprisonment on indictment, or if tried summarily six months' imprisonment and/or a fine.

TASK 3 Use an appropriate textbook or the internet to determine for the offence of robbery:

- the relevant Act, including section;
- the mode of trial; and
- the maximum penalty for a person found guilty.

5.5.2   The courts

The structure of the courts system in England and Wales relates to the nature of the matters in hand and the seriousness of the cases handled by each category of court.

The diagram shows some key elements in the relationships between the various types of court in England and Wales. The courts on the left side of the diagram deal with criminal cases while those on the right deal with civil cases. Police officers are only occasionally required to give evidence at a court dealing with civil cases, for example an officer who attended a road traffic collision in which a pedestrian was seriously injured might be called as a witness in a civil court case in which claims for damages were in dispute.

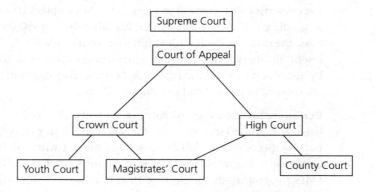

The role of the courts that deal with criminal cases is our primary concern here.

A magistrates' court conducts summary trials and deals with less serious criminal cases—about 95 per cent of all criminal cases. There are about 400 magistrates' courts across the UK. In a summary trial there is no committal (transfer to the Crown Court is not necessary) and no jury. The trial is before a bench of magistrates known as the Justices of the Peace, who are District Judges (qualified lawyers) or lay people (not professional judges or lawyers) drawn from the local community. Magistrates' courts also try non-criminal cases, such as family law disputes. The Specialist Domestic Violence Courts are set in magistrates' courts.

There are limits to the sentences that can be used at a magistrates' court. For custodial sentences the minimum is five days' imprisonment (s 132 of the Magistrates' Courts Act 1980) and the maximum is 12 months (s 154 of the Criminal Justice Act 2003), although many offences will incur a maximum of six months' imprisonment. Fines at magistrates' courts cannot exceed £5,000. For offences triable either way (see 5.5.1), the offender can be sent to the Crown Court for sentence if the magistrates believe that a more severe sentence is appropriate. If a defendant is dissatisfied with a verdict from the magistrates' courts, he/she may appeal to the Crown Court for matters of fact and law, and to the High Court for matters of law only.

A youth court is normally used for defendants aged between 10 and 17 years (unless being charged jointly with an adult or for murder or manslaughter). The procedures are very similar to those in a magistrates' court but are adapted to take account of the age of the defendant, and are not open to the public. A particular courtroom within a magistrates' court is often formally designated as a youth court. Appeals from a youth court generally go to the Crown Court.

The **Crown Court** is a first instance court (ie not an appeal court) for more serious criminal cases, including indictable offences such as murder, rape, or robbery. It also tries appeals from magistrates' courts, and 'either-way' cases (see 5.5.1) referred by magistrates' courts. The trial takes place before a judge and a jury, and members of the public may have to attend court as witnesses (see 26.5.1 on court cases). There are about 90 Crown Courts across the UK. On matters of fact and law, it is possible to appeal from the Crown Court to the Criminal Division of the Court of Appeal.

The **High Court** is, alongside the Crown Court and the Appeal Courts, part of the higher courts of justice in England and Wales. It hears cases at first instance and on appeal. The High Court consists of three divisions, the Queen's Bench Division, the Chancery Division, and the Family Division, and each hears different types of cases. Judges from the Queen's Bench Division hear the most important criminal cases at Crown Court.

The **Court of Appeal** is the highest court and normally sits in up to 12 courts in the Royal Courts of Justice in London. It considers appeals from the Crown Court (criminal cases) and the High Court (civil cases) but it also takes a few appeals from magistrates' and youth courts.

The **Supreme Court** is the final instance of appeal on points of law on important legal disputes for criminal and civil cases in England and Wales, and is presided over by 12 appointed senior judges. Prior to 2009 the House of Lords took this role.

Summary of the courts

Courts	Type of cases	Features	Appeals go to
Youth	Defendants aged 10 to 17 years	Not usually open to the public	Crown Court
Magistrates'	Offences triable summarily only Offences triable either way	Usually open to the public	Crown Court or High Court
Crown	Offences triable only on indictment Offences triable either way referred from magistrates' courts Appeals from magistrates' and youth courts	Judge and jury	Court of Appeal (Criminal Division)
Appeal	Appeals from Crown Court	Criminal and Civil Divisions	Supreme Court
Supreme	Appeals from Court of Appeal	Replaced the House of Lords in 2009	Final point of appeal

> **TASK 4** Find out the exact location of your nearest magistrates' court and Crown Court. Use as many resources as necessary including the web and local telephone directories. (Cross-check the results, identifying any inconsistencies in spelling, postcodes, and so on, if they are present.) Consider visiting one of the courts and sitting in the public gallery to observe proceedings.

5.6 The Police and Criminal Evidence Act 1984 (PACE)

The powers which police officers have to arrest individuals, to search people and property, to enter buildings, and to seize objects are considered in more detail later in this Handbook (Chapters 9 and 10). Many of these powers and the restrictions on their use are to be found in the Police and Criminal Evidence Act 1984 (known as the PACE Act 1984, or simply as PACE). A good understanding of a number of sections of the PACE Act 1984 (and particularly the associated Codes of Practice) is an essential prerequisite of meeting the Certificate in Knowledge of Policing unit 'Knowledge of arresting, detaining, and reporting individuals within a policing context' and the Diploma in Policing assessed unit to 'Arrest, detain or report individuals'. However, many other Certificate and Diploma assessed units also expect the candidate to meet assessment criteria concerned with 'legislation, policies, procedures, codes of practice and/or guidelines' in many practical policing contexts.

The demonstration of knowledge of the PACE Act 1984 in practical policing contexts is also an important milestone of the PAC—for example in relation to conducting searches. Trainee officers are likely to encounter this subject matter during Phase 3 of the IPLDP and within LPG 1 'Police Policies and Procedures', particularly parts of LPG 1.4(1) and LPG 1.4(8).

The PACE Act 1984 contains key legislation in relation to:

- criminal investigation procedures in England and Wales;
- applying the principles of justice, honesty, and workability in the investigative process;
- protection of the rights of all individuals; and
- police powers for search and arrest.

5.6.1   PACE Codes of Practice

The PACE Codes of Practice provide guidelines for the conduct of investigative processes. They are divided into eight main sections, and refer to contacts between the police and the public in the exercise of certain police powers.

Code	General areas covered
A	Stop and search
B	Search of premises
C	Detention, treatment, and questioning of suspects
D	Identification of suspects
E	Audio-only recording of interviews
F	Audio-visual recording of interviews
G	Power of arrest
H	Detention, treatment, and questioning of terrorist suspects

A brief summary of each code is provided here. Note that Codes A, B, C, E, F, and H were revised in October 2013. The Codes are available as an iPhone App and can be downloaded in full from the Home Office website.

Code A deals with the exercise by police officers of statutory powers of stop and search, and the requirements for police officers and police staff to record public encounters. It provides guidelines on searching people who are not under arrest, and the guiding principles for the justification needed for using a power of search, the circumstances in which the search can take place, and the responsibility of those making the search towards the individual. The considerations and recommendations for the protection of an individual's rights are also covered, leaving very little doubt about the proper extent of a search and where it can take place. In addition, the Code outlines what documentation must be completed at the end of such a search or encounter. Recent changes to Code A reflect the introduction of the Terrorism Prevention and Investigation Measures Act 2011 (TPIMS) and of the Protection of Freedoms Act 2012 and an associated statutory code of practice. As a result, references to stop and search under the Terrorism Act 2000 have been removed and other powers not related to terrorism added. Annex F on gender and searching has also been replaced by Annex L of Code C (Establishing Gender of Persons for the Purpose of Searching).

Code B deals with searches of premises by police officers, and the seizure of any property found (including property found on people present on the premises). It provides guidelines on how to protect a person's rights in relation to the conduct of the search and recording it afterwards. It includes pre-planned searches (with warrants issued by magistrates), as well as searches for the purposes of making an arrest, or a search for stolen or unlawfully possessed property in premises and on persons. Code B now includes the powers in Sch 5 to TPIMS to enter and search premises, and clarifies that a search warrant under PACE must be executed within three months of being issued

Codes A and B have been updated to require 'reasonable suspicion' for the search of individuals in school premises for weapons (as a result of the Violent Crime Reduction Act 2006, s 48). This represents a reduction of the previous requirement for 'reasonable belief'.

Code C deals with the detention, treatment, and questioning of suspects by police officers, and applies primarily to suspects under arrest. However, any person who is not under arrest but who is assisting with an investigation should be treated with 'no less' consideration (Note 1A). The Code outlines the procedure for protecting an arrested person's rights whilst in detention, and the care he/she must be given while in custody at a police station. It emphasizes that discrimination against a detained person with 'protected characteristics' (listed under the Equality Act 2012) is unlawful, and sets out how custody staff can give, and obtain, specified information from the detainee (including using interpreters and written translations of documents). Code C underlines the rights for detainees to communicate with other people, including legal representation, and describes how to protect those rights during questioning. Recent changes to Code C covers terrorism-related post-charge questioning and detention, and states that 10- to 17-year-olds detained in police custody must have an appropriate adult (see 24.4.2) and that a person responsible for his/her welfare (usually a parent or guardian) is informed.

Code D deals with the identification of persons by police officers. It protects the rights of a suspect regarding identification before and after arrest. Identification parade procedures and identification by body samples and fingerprints, and showing witnesses photographs of suspects are all covered.

Code E deals with audio recording of interviews with suspects (arrested or not), and safeguards the rights of an individual. It sets out that tapes must be handled securely and in confidence, and allows for breaks during interviews. Recordings can now also be made by secure digital network or removable media. The Code requires that the person is informed of the various aspects of the recording process at every stage (see 24.5.7).

Code F deals with audio-visually recorded interviews with suspects (arrested or not), and outlines the procedures to be followed. Such recordings can be made on tape or on a secure digital network or on removable media. At the time of writing there is no statutory requirement on the police to visually record interviews.

Code G deals with the statutory power of arrest by police officers. It outlines the correct procedures for arresting a person in order that his/her right to liberty is considered at all times (see 5.4). Code G defines a lawful arrest and explains that the justification for arrest is made up of two parts: involvement in the commission of the offence and that the arrest is necessary (s 24 of PACE, see 10.6.2). Police officers must consider all the information when deciding whether to make an arrest, particularly in situations where the suspect alleges self-defence (s 3(1) of the Criminal Law Act 1967), or when school staff allege using reasonable force to prevent pupils from committing an offence (s 93 of the Education and Inspections Act 2006). Information that may indicate a person's guilt as well as innocence should be taken into account (Code G, Notes for Guidance, 2A). Suspects should be warned that if they do not stop a certain behaviour, they may be arrested (2D), and should not be arrested simply for the purpose of interviewing (a result of *Richardson v The Chief Constable of West Midlands Police* [2011] 2 Cr App R 1; [2011] EWHC 773 (QB)) (2F). Arrests cannot be made with the sole intent of obtaining biometric data (2H).

Code H deals with suspects arrested on suspicion of being a terrorist under s 41 of the Terrorism Act 2000. It applies in no other circumstances, and ceases to apply once the suspect has been charged with an offence (Code C then applies), released without charge, or transferred to a prison. Code H was updated in 2012 and 2013 to incorporate the changes in Code C, such as the requirement to use interpreters and written translations where necessary.

If any of the Codes are breached there is a possibility of:

- disciplinary action, depending on the circumstances (see 6.6.5);
- a court deciding that evidence is inadmissible (s 78(1) PACE Act 1984);
- a court deciding that evidence poses a threat to fairness (s 78(1) PACE Act 1984); and/or
- liability for civil or criminal proceedings.

TASK 5 For each Code, write a brief description of a situation when it might be applied. If you are a trainee officer you might have witnessed such incidents while on Supervised Patrol, and descriptions of these may provide you with material for completion of your SOLAP.

5.7 Alternative Forms of Justice

Litigation in court is not always the best way to solve disputes between parties. Disadvantages include the costs involved with the judicial system, the length of the process, and the fact that the outcome may be perceived as unduly simplistic (there being a clear designated 'winner' and 'loser' within an adversarial system). To resolve a dispute without recourse to the judiciary, the parties may choose to reach an agreement between themselves or to involve a third party (deemed neutral) to conduct negotiations. This is done through a process known as alternative dispute resolution (ADR). A judicial decision can sometimes direct the parties to employ ADR.

The simplest forms of ADR are mediation and conciliation. Arbitration can also be used to resolve differences, and is regarded by some as a form of ADR. Restorative justice has a different emphasis in that it is less concerned with judgments or decisions—and instead aims more to help resolve a problem that arose from a criminal act.

5.7.1 Mediation and conciliation

Mediation is described by the Chartered Institute of Arbitrators (2009) as 'a voluntary and guided process whereby an independent mediator helps the parties to negotiate the settlement of a dispute'. Mediation is deemed particularly useful in civil and family cases and claims up to £5,000 (Justice, 2011), and is likely to be a quicker and cheaper process than using the courts.

The mediator should be properly trained as this is more likely to lead to a successful outcome, particularly as it should increase the parties' trust in the mediator and promote compliance with his/her suggestions. The parties may be advised or represented by legal representatives as the mediation negotiations take place. A legally qualified mediator should be used if a contract is to be drawn up at the end of the mediation.

Mediation sessions are conducted in private at any venue chosen by the parties. The mediator reads all the relevant documents beforehand and usually asks the parties the reasons for the dispute and their goals. The mediator then acts as a 'go-between' to help explore the solution(s) that would be acceptable for both sides. All discussion within the mediation process are 'without prejudice', which means that if a conclusion is not reached, the parties are free to move on to arbitration or litigation. (However, the mediator would not act as a witness in any subsequent arbitration or litigation.)

Conciliation is a particular type of mediation. A conciliator is usually more proactive and can make suggestions regarding the settlement or provide non-binding legal opinions. The distinction between conciliation and standard mediation is not always clear-cut.

5.7.2 Arbitration

This has been a popular way of solving disputes for a long time in areas such as construction, insurance, and shipping. It is often regarded as a type of ADR but in reality the process is more similar to a judicial procedure. Unlike in mediation and conciliation, the Arbitration Act 1996 requires that the relevant law is applied to the dispute, and therefore the arbitrator has a role similar to the role of a judge (s 46). The rules of arbitration are set in the Arbitration Acts of 1950 and 1996, but the parties can modify some of them by agreement. The arbitrators' decision (called an 'award') is binding and can be enforced by the courts of law if necessary.

5.7.3 Restorative justice

Restorative justice is a means of resolving conflicts without resorting to the criminal courts. It focuses on the victim's needs rather than on convicting the offender. Restorative justice aims to give victims more of a voice and to involve the offender in making amends directly to the victim. This often involves the offender acknowledging the impact of the criminal action, taking responsibility for it, and apologizing to the victim. There may be meetings between the offender and the victim(s), written and oral apologies, and making good the damage caused. It can help the victim overcome the trauma suffered and help reintegrate the offender back into the community.

Restorative justice can include mediation between victim and offender, victim and the community, the offender and the community, and between all three. It has been widely promoted as a means of dealing with youth crime but can be used for other forms of crime, and in schools and prisons.

5.8 Current Bills before Parliament

At the time of writing of the Handbook the following Bills were laid before Parliament and may become Acts at some point in the future. The list is not comprehensive and should only be used as a guide. More details about the passage of the Bills can be obtained on the Parliament website <http://services.parliament.uk/bills/>.

Age of Criminal Responsibility Bill [HL] 2013–14
Anti-social Behaviour, Crime and Policing Bill 2013–14
Assisted Dying Bill [HL] 2013–14
Asylum (Time Limit) Bill 2013–14
Asylum Seekers (Return to Nearest Safe Country) Bill 2013–14
Causing Death by Driving Whilst Disqualified Bill 2013–14
Child Maltreatment Bill 2013–14
Children and Families Bill 2012–13 to 2013–14
Clean Neighbourhoods and Environment (Amendment) Bill [HL] 2013–14
Defamation (Parliamentary Proceedings) (Amendment) Bill [HL] 2013–14
Drink Driving (Repeat Offenders) Bill 2013–14
Driving Whilst Disqualified (Repeat Offenders) Bill 2013–14
Drug Driving (Assessment of Drug Misuse) Bill 2013–14
Equality Act 2010 (Amendment) Bill [HL] 2013–14
Face Coverings (Prohibition) Bill 2013–14
Firearms (Amendment) Bill [HL] 2013–14
Foreign National Offenders (Exclusion from the United Kingdom) Bill 2013–14
Hate Crime (People with Learning Difficulties and Learning Disabilities) Bill 2013–14
Illegal Immigrants (Criminal Sanctions) Bill 2013–14
Intellectual Property Bill [HL] 2013–14
Offender Rehabilitation Bill [HL] 2013–14
Online Safety Bill [HL] 2013–14
Rights of the Sovereign and the Duchy of Cornwall Bill [HL] 2013–14
Surveillance of Telecommunications (Judicial Oversight) Bill 2013–14
Unsolicited Telephone Communications Bill [HL] 2013–14

5.9 Answers to Tasks

TASK 1 You should have found that these Regulations cover the fitting of lights, reflectors, and rear markings on vehicles.

TASK 2 You may have considered a number of possible scenarios that might take place on Supervised Patrol. Remember that these rights extend to suspects as well as victims and witnesses. For example, if you are a trainee officer then you may be involved in the arrest of an individual whose grasp of spoken English is poor or non-existent, and subsequently involved in the procedures used when suspects have difficulty communicating in English. The QCF indicate that, for this element, evidence **must** come from real-life situations. Your assessor may well be able to observe your actions directly in this case but you would also need to provide evidence of your knowledge and understanding—for example, through evidence in your SOLAP cross-referred to your Learning Diary or pocket notebook.

TASK 3 For the offence of robbery, you should have found:

- the Theft Act 1968, s 8(1);
- *mode of trial*: triable on indictment only;
- *maximum penalty for a person found guilty*: life imprisonment.

TASK 4 You will find the website <https://courttribunalfinder.service.gov.uk> a useful resource.

TASK 5 Your answers might include the following:

Code A: you may have seen searches of people being conducted under a number of powers. Bear in mind that s 1 of the PACE Act 1984 is only one power amongst 19 or so listed in Annex A of the PACE

Act 1984 Code A (see 9.4.3). You may therefore have seen searches taking place under s 23 of the Misuse of Drugs Act, s 47 of the Firearms Act, and s 1 of the PACE Act 1984.

Code B: you may have seen searches of premises take place using s 17 of the PACE Act 1984, in order to arrest a person. You may also have observed searches of premises at the time of an arrest under s 32 of the PACE Act 1984, and after arrest you may have witnessed searches of premises taking place under s 18 of the PACE Act 1984. You may also have seen a warrant executed and all these searches would have been carried out under the guidance of Code B.

Code C: you may have observed people suspected of committing road traffic offences interviewed at the roadside and the interview recorded in an officer's pocket notebook. You may also have seen suspects interviewed contemporaneously, perhaps as a result of their involvement in a road traffic collision.

Code D: you may have seen the identification by a witness or victim of a suspect take place in the local neighbourhood of an offence soon after it takes place. You may also have observed an identification parade in which a witness was requested to make a choice concerning the identity of a suspect in an offence.

Code E: you may have seen suspect interviews at the police station which were recorded on tape, and the steps taken to respect their rights—for example, offering a service to give the suspect the opportunity to have a copy made of the tape.

Code F: you may not have seen suspect interviews visually recorded with sound because there is no statutory requirement to record interviews this way, so not all forces do this.

Code G: you may have seen suspects arrested (see 10.6). You will also have seen them cautioned at the time of arrest.

6 Roles, Responsibilities, and Support

6.1 Introduction

This chapter of the Handbook covers applying to join the police service and your subsequent induction into a police organization. Induction is the process of 'bringing in' or initiation. In some senses it also refers to a kind of transformation—in this case from being a member of the public to becoming both a member of the public and a police constable. Normally, this transformation will take a significant length of time. Although it is suggested that the induction phase of IPLDP should take between three and five weeks (Home Office, 2004), the actual process of induction can be measured in months.

After you join the police you will discover that there are certain symbolic aspects to induction, such as the ceremony that surrounds attestation. We examine the Code of Conduct and Police Regulations, and we discuss conduct, misconduct, discipline, and complaints. Induction is also the assimilation into an organizational culture or cultures. In policing, the process of 'buying into' the existing organizational culture has not been without controversy. For some observers, the prevailing cultures within the police have often been characterized as male-dominated and exclusionary. Allied to this view is the suggestion that initial police training moves you from being an individual to being part of a group, and into a group where it is 'dangerous to be different'. (This is the so-called police 'canteen culture' that you may hear or read about.) The police service is aware of these criticisms and one of the driving forces behind recent changes to initial police training is to create a learning environment which is more inclusive.

We then introduce the staff association for police constables, the Police Federation, and mention some of the specialist support groups such as the British Association of Women Police Officers. This is followed by a description of police IT systems (an increasingly important part of information management) and how information is stored, processed, and communicated, including confidentiality and the implications of the Freedom of Information Act 2000. The importance of effective communication is also considered as this is an essential part of discharging the responsibilities of the police officer.

Understanding the role of health and safety is an important part of a police officer's ability to make risk assessments, and this is often covered in conjunction with First Aid, a vital skill for patrol constables. A police officer's own safety and that of others will be covered in Personal Safety Training (the title varies between forces). This will involve learning self-defence and about how to manage angry and tense situations, and the appropriate use of certain police equipment such as rigid-pattern handcuffs, the ASP baton, and incapacitant spray.

6.2 Attestation and the Role of the Police Constable

After attestation a trainee police officer holds the office of probationary constable, with the position being confirmed after about two calendar years. The origins of the office of constable within law enforcement in the UK can be traced back hundreds of years, although many commentators consider the most significant starting point for the modern-day police service as the year 1829 (see 2.2).

In recent years, constables have become just one of many members of the extended police family; they no longer have a monopoly on certain traditional policing powers. They nonetheless continue to hold a special position within a police organization, as you will discover when working through this chapter and those that follow. This privilege brings additional responsibilities to the role of constable, particularly in terms of attitudes, values, and professional knowledge. Many of the CKP and Diploma in Policing units are concerned with the need for a police trainee to demonstrate the appropriate attitudes and values, and, by extension, to have gained the appropriate underpinning skills and knowledge. Similarly, one of the Induction Modules of the IPLDP is concerned with the 'Underpinning Ethics/Values of the Police Service' (IND 1). The CKP unit 'Knowledge of managing conflict within a policing context' also contains the assessment criterion that learners should be able to 'explain how to communicate with people in a way that . . . is free from discrimination and oppressive behaviour'.

There has been much discussion about the possible effects of an individual's personal beliefs and values, and the manner in which these are expressed in their day-to-day actions and decisions. Trainees may feel (somewhat defensively) that they are 'entitled to their opinions' with the implication that their attitudes would have no bearing on their actions. This is obviously an important issue for those engaged in police training and education, and is addressed in other parts of this Handbook. Here, however, we are concerned with how the professional development of a trainee (and the progression to confirmation as constable) links up with the wider common purpose and values of the police service.

We noted in 3.7 that the existence of a code of professional conduct was a common feature of the professions. The Police Service Statement of Common Purpose and Values was first issued by ACPO in 1990 and is reflected today, almost word for word, in most police forces' own statements. It is a relatively consistent declaration of the guiding principles of the police service, and all police officers, including trainees, are required to work towards the achievement of this statement.

According to the statement, the purpose of the police service is to:

. . . *uphold the law firmly and fairly* . . .	be neither too weak nor too aggressive, and with no bias,
. . . *prevent crime* . . .	not let it happen if it can be stopped first,
. . . *pursue and bring to justice those who break the law* . . .	and hence we need to understand the requirements of the criminal justice system,
. . . *keep the Queen's peace* . . .	not allow public disorder and criminality to occur unchallenged,
. . . *protect, help and reassure the community* . . .	that is, all our communities and not just those that appear to support the police or those that we belong to.

In 2003 a BBC undercover reporter secretly filmed trainee officer training at the Centrex Bruche training centre (the BBC called the documentary *The Secret Policeman*). Examples of inappropriate behaviour by some trainee officers at Bruche uncovered by the documentary included:

- use of offensive racist terms to describe members of ethnic minorities, including unsubstantiated slurs on the character of the family of murdered black teenager Stephen Lawrence;
- donning an imitation Ku Klux Klan hood and threatening to knock on the door of a fellow trainee of British Asian heritage; and
- claims that they used police powers in a discriminating way against ethnic minorities.

One Centrex police trainer was also secretly filmed expressing his happiness to his group of trainees that the single police recruit of British Asian heritage had been re-coursed (required to retake certain aspects of his training), although there was no suggestion that this was as a result of racism.

> **TASK 1** If you are a trainee police officer, what does the Police Service Statement of Common Purpose and Values mean for you? Your reflections could be written up and used as evidence for your SOLAP—for example, as evidence cross-referring to the assessment criteria of one of your Diploma in Policing learning outcomes. Your reflections could also feature in your Learning Diary, under the heading 'Police Policies & Procedures'.

6.2.1 Attestation of police constables

Attestation is the stage at which a trainee police officer is formally given the powers of a police constable—for example, he/she is then able to arrest someone according to the law and Codes of Practice. The legal detail is set out in s 29 of and Sch 4 to the Police Act 1996, as amended by s 83 of the Police Reform Act 2002. (Parallel legislation covers the 'non-Home Office' forces, eg in s 24 of the Railways and Transport Safety Act 2003, for BTP.)

Attestation often coincides with the issuing of a warrant card, although practice may vary from force to force (some forces instead issue a form of 'trainee police officer identity card' at attestation). In many police organizations, attestation happens early on in a trainee officer's career—sometimes on initial appointment and certainly within the first few weeks.

The attestation often takes place during a formal ceremony to which family and friends may be invited. The declaration is usually taken by a Justice of the Peace (magistrate). The trainee will make a formal declaration (sometimes referred to as an 'Oath') as follows:

> I...of...do solemnly and sincerely declare and affirm that I will well and truly serve the Queen in the office of constable, with fairness, integrity, diligence, and impartiality, upholding fundamental human rights and according equal respect to all people; and that I will, to the best of my power, cause the peace to be kept and preserved and prevent all offences against people and property; and that while I continue to hold the said office I will, to the best of my skill and knowledge, discharge all the duties thereof faithfully according to law.

An alternative Welsh-language version can be used by in Dyfed-Powys, Gwent, North Wales, or South Wales. There are also alternatives for police officers in Scotland and Northern Ireland, and in the BTP.

The making of a declaration may seem somewhat old-fashioned. However, it is worth bearing in mind that the declaration police officers make has a statutory basis in law and its symbolic importance remains strong, both within police culture and in the wider political and social world.

> **TASK 2** Trainee police officers should learn the declaration for the attestation word for word! Note that you will probably be given an *aide mémoire* to read from at actual attestation, or be asked to follow another's lead. However, you are likely to be required to memorize information on a number of occasions during training (eg definitions) and this task is good practice.

6.3 The Standards of Professional Behaviour

Initial police training will frequently involve direct contact with both the public and fellow members of the extended policing family (eg PCSOs). Many of the Diploma in Policing learning outcomes are concerned with the nature and quality of these interactions.

Attested police officers are not employees in the conventional meaning of the term; they are instead holders of public office. One consequence of this is that all police officers' activities on and off duty are regulated by law through Statutory Instruments (see 5.2). For this reason, references to complaints, and misconduct, as well as a number of restrictions and expectations are contained in Police Acts and the Police Regulations.

All police officers must work towards the Standards of Professional Behaviour outlined in 6.3.1. We noted in 3.5 that the Standards of Professional Behaviour form an integral part of the developing moral authority of a trainee police officer, and also relate directly to a number of assessment criteria within the assessed Diploma in Policing units. The material covered here is likely to be relevant to Phase 3 of the IPLDP and the Induction Module IND 1: 'Underpinning Ethics/Values of the Police Service'.

The Standards of Professional Behaviour are the minimum standards that both trainee and confirmed police officers must maintain, and are listed in the Police (Conduct) Regulations 2008.

6.3.1   The ten standards of professional behaviour

1. Honesty and Integrity

Police officers are honest, act with integrity, and do not compromise or abuse their position.

2. Authority, Respect, and Courtesy

Police officers act with self-control and tolerance, treating members of the public and colleagues with respect and courtesy.

Police officers do not abuse their powers or authority and respect the rights of all individuals.

3. Equality and Diversity

Police officers act with fairness and impartiality. They do not discriminate unlawfully or unfairly.

4. Use of Force

Police officers only use force to the extent that it is necessary, proportionate, and reasonable in all the circumstances.

5. Orders and Instructions

Police officers only give and carry out lawful orders and instructions.

Police officers abide by police regulations, force policies, and lawful orders.

6. Duties and Responsibilities

Police officers are diligent in the exercise of their duties and responsibilities.

7. Confidentiality

Police officers treat information with respect and access or disclose it only in the proper course of police duties.

8. Fitness for Duty

Police officers when on duty or presenting themselves for duty are fit to carry out their responsibilities.

9. Discreditable Conduct

Police officers behave in a manner which does not discredit the police service or undermine public confidence in it, whether on or off duty.

Police officers report any action taken against them for a criminal offence, any conditions imposed on them by a court, or the receipt of any penalty notice.

10. Challenging and Reporting Improper Conduct

Police officers report, challenge, or take action against the conduct of colleagues which has fallen below the Standards of Professional Behaviour.

Note that the Police Service of Northern Ireland (PSNI) has its own Standards of Professional Behaviour.

> **TASK 3** In March 2010 a senior police officer from Thames Valley Police was arrested and suspended from duty after allegedly setting fire to a hire car he had used while on duty in order to destroy evidence that he was having an affair. Leaving aside the suspected criminal offences of arson, insurance fraud, and perverting the course of justice, which Standards of Professional Behaviour may have been breached during the alleged incident? What are the consequences of this for both the individual concerned and the police service as a whole?

If you are a trainee officer then your written reflections may be relevant to the knowledge requirements of the 'Underpinning Ethics/Values of the Police Service' sections of your SOLAP.

TASK 4 Consider standards 3, 4, and 7 of the Standards of Professional Behaviour, and list the assessed units of the Diploma in Policing that are most relevant. What sort of evidence could a trainee officer use to meet the learning criteria for these units? Bear in mind that evidence usually takes the form of tangible objects such as written documents and by direct observation and questioning by an assessor (see Chapter 8).

6.4 The Police Regulations and Conditions of Service

Conditions of service for police constables are also regulated by law under various Police Regulations contained in Statutory Instruments. Because of their length and complexity these will not be dealt with in their entirety here, but they are presented here in a summarized and simplified form, with extra explanations in places. Full details may be found in other textbooks such as *Blackstone's Police Manual: Volume 4 General Police Duties* and on the internet. At the moment of attestation a trainee police officer becomes subject to police regulations such as the 2003 Regulations as described in the following paragraphs. Note that the Police (Performance) Regulations 2012 do not apply for trainee officers during the probationary period.

6.4.1 Restrictions on private life and business interests

These are set out in Sch 1 to the Police Regulations 2003 which states that 'The restrictions on private life . . . shall apply to all members of a police force' (reg 6(1)) and that:

> A member of a police force shall at all times abstain from any activity which is likely to interfere with the impartial discharge of [his/her] duties or which is likely to give rise to the impression amongst members of the public that it may so interfere; and in particular a member of a police force shall not take any active part in politics. (Sch 1, para 1)

In other words, a police officer must not pursue a course of conduct which members of the public will perceive as favouritism and especially must not be active in politics. In addition, a police officer 'shall not wilfully refuse or neglect to discharge any lawful debt' (Sch 1, para 4). This does not mean a police officer cannot have a mortgage or a car loan (as these are lawful), but any debt which could place the officer in danger of being coerced is unacceptable.

The Police (Amendment No. 3) Regulations 2012 state in reg 8 that:

> [i]f a member of a police force has or proposes to have a business interest which has not previously been disclosed, or, is or becomes aware that a relative has or proposes to have a business interest which, in the opinion of the member, interferes or could be seen as interfering with the impartial discharge of the member's duties and has not previously been disclosed the member shall immediately give written notice of that business interest to the chief officer.

For the purposes of their integrity and credibility, police officers must disclose business interests in order that they may be checked for compatibility with the role of a constable.

TASK 5 Find out about the procedure used by a police force for declaring business interests.

6.4.2 Personal records, fingerprints, and samples

In relation to personal records, reg 15 of the Police Regulations 2003 states that the chief officer of a police force 'shall cause a personal record of each member of the police force to be kept' throughout a police officer's service. It will contain details of the officer and his/her relatives, a history of courses attended, expertise gained, promotions achieved, and the outcomes of any disciplinary investigations.

Regulation 18 of the Police Regulations 2003 concerns taking and recording a police officer's fingerprints, for the purposes of eliminating him/her from any forensic investigation. Quite often this takes place early on in training and sometimes as part of initial training on forensic awareness. Regulation 19 of the Police Regulations 2003 obliges an officer to supply a sample such as a mouth swab for DNA analysis, again for the purposes of elimination. From April 2012, the 2003 Police Regulations have been amended so that any officer can be selected for random drug testing according to protocols described within the Police (Amendment No. 2) Regulations 2012.

Qualifications and Training

6.4.3 Duty to carry out lawful orders

Regulation 20 of the Police Regulations 2003 states that every member of a police force:

> shall carry out all lawful orders and shall at all times punctually and promptly perform all appointed duties and attend to all matters within the scope of [his/her] office as a constable.

The police service has a rank structure in which supervisors and managers may require certain actions to be carried out. It is an expectation that a police officer will carry out these orders, but only if they are lawful.

6.4.4 Discharge of a trainee police officer

Under reg 13 of the Police Regulations 2003 a trainee officer can be dismissed. This is covered more fully in 8.4.4.3 along with extending the probationary period under reg 12. However, before being discharged, a trainee can give notice of retirement (in other words, resign).

> **TASK 6** If you are a trainee officer, take the opportunity to reflect upon these regulations. Which areas do you think are going to be easy for you to satisfy, and which areas do you need to consider at greater length? How for example would you know that an order was unlawful?
>
> The PSNI Code of Ethics, article 1.5 states that a police officer:
>
> > should carry out orders properly issued by [his/her] superior, but [he/she] shall refrain from carrying out any order [he/she] knows, or ought to know, is unlawful.

6.5 Ethical Decision-making in Policing

The legitimacy, authority, and even effectiveness of the police depend on the exercise of ethical decision-making. In essence this means that there is an expectation on the police, from the public and others, that they make decisions based on a set of ethical principles, and not in an arbitrary manner, or according to emotional response or prejudice. However, this presents a number of questions, including the fundamental question of 'Whose ethics?' We will examine the ethical basis to policing, how ethics are reflected in decision-making, and finally the ways in which police officers might fall short of the ethical requirements expected of the police service.

6.5.1 Ethics and policing

Ethics are important all police officers because if police methods and procedures do not meet high ethical standards then the authority of the police will be undermined, and the public may have less trust in the police and the law. The expected standards of behaviour are clearly defined in existing documents but ethics is also about personal ideas, and if a police officer's actions are to ring true, his/her own rules of moral behaviour (or personal ethics) need to correspond with the force's formal requirements. Diversity training (see 8.6.6) provides trainees with further opportunities for considering personal views and feelings about a range of possible attitudes and behaviours.

A number of official documents set out guidance (in varying degrees of detail and levels of official standing) concerning police ethics and behaviour. These documents include the PPF 'personal qualities' of the police constable (see 8.5.2); the Police (Conduct) Regulations 2008; the Police (Performance) Regulations 2008; the Police Regulations 2003; and the European Code of Police Ethics. The Police (Conduct) Regulations 2008 contain the 'Standards of Professional Behaviour' (see 6.3), guidance on police officer behaviour when off duty (see also 6.4), and misconduct procedures (see 6.6).

The police have always been affected by changes in customs, beliefs, and social morality. Policing norms are shaped by social norms, and so ethical questions concerning what police officers ought to do in particular circumstances are interpreted according to the moral values of the day. For example, there has been a shift in police practice from being responsive to being proactive, and more emphasis is placed on preventing crime.

TASK 7 What is policing by consent, and how might this differ from when police were introduced in 1829?

In recent years policing has been informed increasingly by the need to demonstrate value for money (sometimes through reductions in police staffing levels) and to meet targets set by government. This form of 'managerialism' has been criticized by some chief officers because it leads to police officers becoming over-concerned with meeting targets. This is problematic because it is not always easy to measure the things that police need to do.

The role of police in international peacekeeping (alongside a military presence and other supporting agencies from different parts of the world) demands an ethical consistency across different organizations with very different values and traditions. This might sometimes include British police officers working alongside officers from other countries where there is: widespread corruption; routine bribery of public officials; governments using their police as a political arm; very low rates of pay for police officers; very low status for police officers; and/or paramilitary-style force employed by the police.

TASK 8 Consider corruption, bribery, political use of the police, low pay, low status, and paramilitary policing. Draw a flow diagram showing how these factors might interact. Use arrows to show how one factor causes another. (An example of this particular use of arrows is shown in the diagram below: the arrow shows that poor pay leads to low status.)

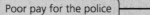

Poor pay for the police ⟶ Low status of police

Note that there are no certain answers to this exercise; you might argue that it is the low status that is causing the low pay.

One of the key skills trainee police officers have to develop during training is the ability to apply discretion (see 3.6), and this is linked with ethics. For example, imagine two trainees on Supervised Patrol are called to deal with a theft at a supermarket, with instructions to investigate the matter and decide upon a course of action. The offender is a confused 94-year-old man who has apparently picked up a bag of sweets and wandered out of the store, pursued by store detectives. The old man had technically committed a crime, but there were mitigating circumstances: his age and frailty must be taken into account, and proving 'intention permanently to deprive' (the basis of the Theft Act 1968 (see 16.2)) would be somewhat difficult. Enforcing the law might not be the most appropriate response, but a police officer has to be prepared to justify the reasons for his/her decision (see 6.5.2 on the NDM).

6.5.2 The National Decision Model (NDM)

Ethical decision-making in policing is informed by the NDM. The model was first introduced in 2012 and hence is yet to be fully implemented across the police service. It consists of six elements and five stages, which are interlinked and described in the table. The 'values' (ethical principles) should be applied throughout all stages of the model and could refer to, for example, the ACPO Statement of Mission and Values for the police service published in July 2011. In essence, the NDM is a risk-based model that is meant to provide the policy basis for taking ethical action, or deciding not to act. (Note, however, that police officers might need to work outside of policy if the circumstances require, but justification and documentation is still required.)

The NDM is intended for use by anyone making decisions in the police service (both operational and non-operational), which in effect means just about every employee. However, the language ACPO employ to describe the NDM is to a large extent drawn from operational police culture. Much of the NDM is self-evident and is summarized in the table (in the authors' own words). It can be recalled using ACPO's mnemonic 'VIAPOAR' which stands for Values, Information, Assessment, Powers and policy, Options, Action, and Review.

NDM elements

V	Decisions should reflect values of the police service: integrity, willingness to take risks, and to protect the human rights of all	Stage 1	I(nformation)	Collect information about the situation
A		Stage 2	A(ssessment)	Define and explore the problem, decide on the level of risk and immediate action that is required and begin developing a strategy to respond
L		Stage 3	P(owers) and P(olicy)	Identify feasible options in terms of either police powers or the implementation of policy
U		Stage 4	O(ptions)	Assess the options and be prepared to justify decisions (eg apply JAPAN principles)
E		Stage 5	A(ction) and R(eview)	Take action (respond, record, and monitor) and review outcomes of action
S				

(Table based on ACPO, 2012b)

6.5.3 Police corruption

In a culture where ethical decision-making in policing is not valued, corruption may flourish. Research has shown that corruption can occur in any part of the police service, and therefore we need to understand how widespread corruption is likely to be, and how we might prevent it. For example, in 2007 six men, five of whom were former police officers were sentenced to varying terms of imprisonment for conspiracy to intercept communications and for 'aiding and abetting misconduct in a public office'. The offences were committed over a period from 1999 to 2004 and were investigated by the Metropolitan Police's Anti-Corruption Command. The men had set up a company offering illegal private investigation services, and were paid by clients to hack into computers or bug telephone lines. More recently the MPS launched 'Operation Elveden' (supervised by the IPCC), an investigation into alleged illegal payments made by journalists to police officers during the earlier phone hacking scandal. The Home Secretary noted in Parliament on 18 July 2011 that the 'current allegations about phone hacking are not, unfortunately, the only recent example of alleged corruption in the police service'. Further arrests of former police officers were made as part of Operation Elveden and Operation Yewtree (the investigation into 'Savile and others') in 2013.

> **TASK 9** What sort of opportunities do you think there might be for corruption in relation to drugs policing?

Corruption can take a number of forms, for example, misfeasance—doing something you should not do; non-feasance—not doing something you should do; and malfeasance—the commission of indictable crimes.

What thought processes or experiences could lead officers to act this way? We suggest the following could all be potentially corrupting factors:

- corrupt police officers providing a role model;
- the pressure for results;
- abuse or assault from members of the public;
- the difficulties in securing convictions;
- belief that sentencing was not adequate for the crime committed;
- the first arrival at the scene of a crime, when cash or goods may be lying about;
- personal financial pressures;
- handling and storing drugs from police investigations;
- the 'long hours, low reward' culture, leading to envy of others more fortunately placed;
- lack of effective supervision;
- the excessive exercise of discretion without challenge;
- feelings of bitterness or resentment at not receiving expected promotion; and
- managing informants without adequate supervision or scrutiny.

> **TASK 10** Consider the list of factors that might contribute to an officer's decision to act corruptly. Most of them are about predisposition—motivations for an officer to act corruptly. But an opportunity is also required; list the five factors from the list which provide opportunities to act corruptly.

There are a number of theories about the causes of corruption. One such theory is that the metaphorical (in some cases, actual) free cup of coffee is enough to start a police officer on the slippery slope to corruption. The idea is that from a free cup of coffee it is but a short step to a free meal, then free entry to a club, then preferential treatment, then provision of goods and inducements, and finally the offer to engage in joint criminal exploits. By accepting the free cup of coffee the officer signals his or her willingness to be corrupted.

> **TASK 11** How convinced are you by the 'free cup of coffee' theory? Can you see any flaws in it? Can you think of examples that might challenge the theory?

The 'bad apple' theory argues that a corrupt police officer or staff member is an isolated instance, and that the solution is to simply remove the individual officer. The 'bent for the job' theory is a third explanation for corruption. It was argued that the law was so inadequately structured that substantial numbers of the guilty went unpunished and that officers were forced to be devious and underhand because that was the only way in which they could achieve results.

> **TASK 12** What sort of events or feelings would make a 'bad apple' officer more likely to act corruptly, and why might other officers not succumb to the same pressures or temptations?
>
> How convinced are you by the 'bent for the job' theory? Do you accept that the end is more important than the means, and, if so, does that mean that inexperienced officers have to be taught trickery or stealth?

6.6 Misconduct and Complaints Procedures

Police misconduct and complaint procedures are governed by three pieces of legislation namely; Police (Complaints and Misconduct) Regulations 2012, Police (Conduct) Regulations 2012, and Police (Performance) Regulations 2012. These regulations are outlined in the Home Office guidance document 'Police Office Misconduct, Unsatisfactory Performance and Attendance Management Procedures' published in November 2012, available on the Home Office website.

'Misconduct' includes any action by a police officer which does not meet the Standards of Professional Behaviour, and 'gross misconduct' is a more serious failure to meet the Standards (so serious that it could lead to dismissal). Allegations concerning the conduct of a police officer fall into one of two categories:

- 'conduct matters', which concern allegations made against a police officer by a colleague; and
- 'complaints' which are allegations made by a member of the public about the conduct of a police officer.

The process of making such allegations, the investigation and subsequent methods of disposal, are together known as the Police Complaints System.

Complaints and conduct matters can be handled by a line manager or supervisor, or if more serious by the 'appropriate authority' or the IPCC. The appropriate authority would be a chief officer (chief constable or commissioner), but he/she can delegate this function to a police officer of at least the rank of chief inspector, or another police staff member of at least a similar level of seniority. This will frequently be an officer within a Professional Standards Department.

6.6.1 Conduct matters

Police officers are required to abide by the Standards of Professional Behaviour (see 6.3). This includes the tenth Standard that requires a police officer to report, challenge, or take action against the conduct of any colleague whose behaviour has fallen below any of the other nine Standards. Failure to report such instances would render the officer liable for claims of misconduct. Normally, an officer should report any concerns to his/her supervisor or the Professional Standards Department. However, concerns can also be raised confidentially with the IPCC (see 6.6.3) as it is designated as an official body for the purposes of public interest disclosure.

The flowchart summarizes the procedures for handling an allegation relating to 'conduct matters'. These decisions would be taken by the appropriate authority—usually local senior officers (discussed earlier).

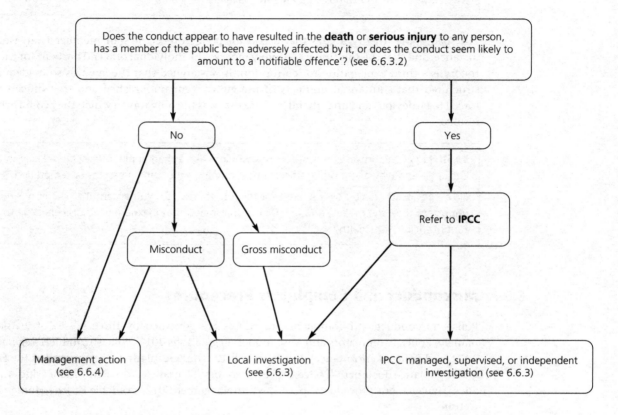

Management action includes setting expectations for future conduct and an improvement plan (see 6.6.4).

For a local investigation, the investigator will be appointed by the appropriate authority and the officer under investigation must be notified under reg 15 of the Police (Conduct) Regulations 2012 or reg 16 of the Police (Complaints and Misconduct) Regulations 2012 (see 6.6.3.2). A misconduct meeting or hearing (see 6.6.3.4) might be required, and the IPCC may be involved. The IPCC can decide to discontinue the proceedings if it becomes apparent that there is no case to answer. The possible sanctions are described in 6.6.4.

6.6.2   Complaints

Allegations made by members of the public concerning the conduct or behaviour of a police officer (trainee or confirmed) are called complaints. Examples might include complaints of rudeness, the use of excessive force, or unjustified arrest. Allegations can only be made by a member of the public who:

* claims to be the victim of the conduct;
* claims to have been adversely affected by the conduct (but is not the victim);
* claims to have witnessed the conduct; or
* is a person who is representing any of the above.

The appropriate course of action will be decided by the 'appropriate authority' (defined earlier). IPCC statutory guidance on the handling of complaints is available via its website (IPCC, 2013). The flowchart summarizes the process for managing complaints:

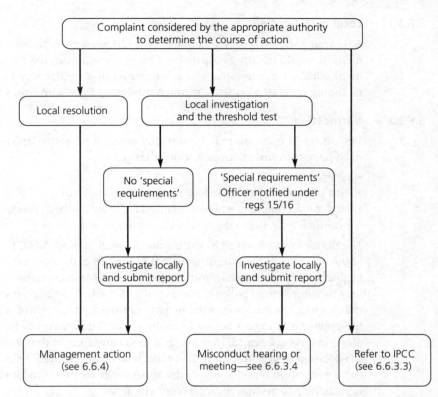

The threshold test establishes whether it appears likely that the officer who is the subject of the complaint has committed a criminal offence or behaved in such a way that disciplinary proceedings are likely to be required. If this applies, the investigation will be subject to 'special requirements', and the officer must be formally notified about the investigation (see 6.6.3.2).

6.6.3   Investigations and the Independent Police Complaints Commission

The diagram shows the different ways in which complaints and matters of misconduct are handled and the extent of the involvement of the IPCC. The diagram tapers towards the top as there are fewer high-level investigations. As you might expect, the more serious the matter, the higher the level of the investigation, and the greater the level of direct IPCC involvement.

IPCC stands for **Independent Police Complaints Commission**

Beginning with the lowest level, to dispense or withdraw means that a police organization is unable to bring about a successful conclusion to the matter, or it is no longer practicable to continue with an investigation. IPCC permission is sought to discontinue if:

1. the complainant is uncooperative;
2. the complaint or allegation of misconduct is harsh, is brought about with the intention of annoying, or an abuse of procedure;
3. the complaint or allegation of misconduct is repetitious; or
4. a local resolution is agreed (see 6.6.4).

6.6.3.1 Local investigations

A local investigation is carried out for less serious matters that do not warrant IPCC involvement. It would usually be carried out by personnel from the Professional Standards Department within a police force, and is structured in a similar way to any other police enquiry, including collecting evidence through interviews from witnesses and suspects.

6.6.3.2 Notification

The officer in question may be formally notified for some kinds of local investigations but must be notified for all investigations that are:

- referred to the IPCC;
- into a complaint where special requirements apply, or
- into conduct matters where it seems likely there has been misconduct or gross misconduct, a notifiable offence, a death or serious injury.

The notice must be served in writing and as soon as practicable. It will be served under reg 15 of the Police (Conduct) Regulations 2012 or reg 16 of the Police (Complaints and Misconduct) Regulations 2012. (The same form is used for both conduct matters and complaints.) The notice may be referred to in police circles as a 'reg 15' (with a hard 'g'). It will include a description of the conduct, the outcome of the severity or threshold test, and a reminder that the officer has the opportunity to seek advice from the Police Federation. The Police Federation advises any officer receiving a reg 15/16 notice not to say anything at that stage and to seek the advice of a Federation representative. If the officer is to be interviewed, once again the advice is to contact a Federation representative who will arrange to attend the interview or, in some circumstances, help to arrange for legal representation.

6.6.3.3 Investigations involving the IPCC

An IPCC-*supervised* investigation is used for complaints or allegations of misconduct which are of considerable significance and probable public concern. It will be supervised by an IPCC commissioner but conducted, directed, and controlled by the police. The complainant has the right of appeal to the IPCC.

An IPCC-*managed* investigation is used when the alleged incident is more serious and likely to cause higher levels of public concern, and therefore the subsequent investigation must have an independent element. The IPCC direct and control the process, whilst the police conduct the investigation.

An *independent* IPCC investigation is used for incidents that cause the greatest level of public concern, have the greatest potential to impact on communities, or have serious implications for the reputation of the police service (for deaths in custody). These require a wholly independent investigation conducted in its entirety by IPCC staff.

There is no right of appeal against an IPCC-managed or independent investigation except through judicial review, a form of court proceedings which checks that the correct procedures have been used.

6.6.3.4 Misconduct meetings and hearings

After the evidence has been collected in an investigation the appropriate authority decides if the officer's behaviour amounted to misconduct or gross misconduct, and there may be various outcomes, as shown in the flowchart.

A misconduct meeting may be held for an officer falling slightly short of the Standards of Professional Behaviour, and a misconduct hearing will be held for more serious failures or when the officer already has a final written warning. The evidence collected during the investigation will be considered and the outcomes and sanctions will be determined. The possible outcomes and sanctions are explained in 6.6.4.

6.6.4 Outcomes and sanctions

There are a number of methods of disposal available on the conclusion of an enquiry into conduct matters or complaints.

Qualifications and Training

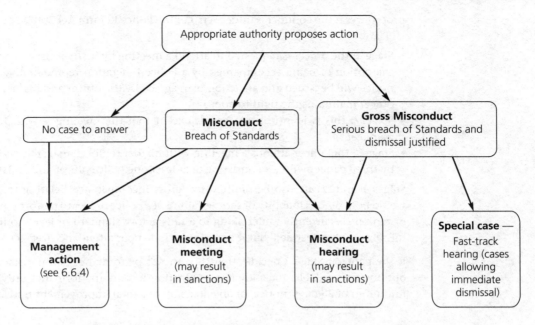

Local (or informal) resolution may be possible. Regulation 15/16 notices (see 6.6.3.2) are not required, no blame is attached, nor is there any need to involve disciplinary procedures. The process will not affect a trainee officer's personal development plan (usually the SOLAP, then the PDR), staff appraisal, or any subsequent misconduct hearing. Note that a police force cannot make an apology to the complainant unless the officer concerned (the officer against whom the complaint was made) authorizes such an apology.

Management action would involve pointing out how the behaviour fell short of the Standards of Professional Behaviour, and identifying expectations for future conduct. It could also include establishing an improvement plan and addressing any underlying causes of misconduct. It can therefore be seen as supportive.

After a **misconduct meeting** (for falling slightly short of the Standards of Professional Behaviour) the outcome could either be no further action, management action, a written warning, or a final written warning.

After a **misconduct hearing** the sanctions could be as for a misconduct meeting (see earlier) and also dismissal (with or without notice). The 'services' of a trainee officer can be dispensed with at any time under reg 13 of the Police Regulations 2003 (see 6.4.4).

In a complaints case, the complainant has the right of appeal against any decision to the Independent Police Complaints Commission.

6.6.5 Unsatisfactory performance or attendance

Unsatisfactory performance or attendance is an 'inability or failure of a police officer to perform the duties of the role or rank [he/she] is currently undertaking to a satisfactory standard or level' (Police (Performance) Regulations 2008). The Home Office document 'Guidance on Unsatisfactory Performance and Attendance Procedures' suggests that informal and early interventions by a manager ('management action') should be sufficient to improve and maintain a police officer's performance or attendance (see also 6.6.4). It also states that formal action should not be taken unless the police officer has earlier been offered supportive action but had declined or failed to cooperate, resulting in no improvement in performance or attendance (para 3.2).

The Unsatisfactory Performance Procedures (UPP) can also be invoked for officers on long-term sick-leave and supported by management action, but for whom returning to work during a reasonable time is unrealistic. Note that the UPP do not apply to trainee officers during their probationary period; reg 13 of the Police Regulations 2003 would be used instead (see 6.4.4).

There are three stages in the UPP with 3–12 months between each. During this time there must be improvement, and the satisfactory performance must be maintained for a year in order to avoid moving on to the next stage. However, recent changes to the regulations do allow the IPCC to recommend or direct police services to the Police (Performance) Regulation procedures if the conduct is under Sch 3 of the Police Reform Act 2002. The three stages of the UPP are:

- Stage 1: the officer is requested to attend a meeting by his/her first-line manager, and given the option of being accompanied by a Police Federation representative. An improvement notice will be issued and an action plan agreed by the officer and his/her line manager. The officer maintains the right to appeal.
- Stage 2: this is identical to Stage 1, except that the meeting is with his/her second-line manager.
- Stage 3: the officer attends a meeting with his/her senior manager. A decision will be made by three panel members consisting of at least one police officer and an HR professional.

Stages 1 and 2 can also be omitted for 'gross incompetence' relating to performance. This would be 'a serious inability or serious failure of a police officer to perform the duties of the role or rank he is currently undertaking to a satisfactory standard or level, to the extent that dismissal would be justified' but it does not include poor attendance (reg 4(1)).

If the panel at Stage 3 decides that the officer's performance is unsatisfactory the following options are available: redeployment, reduction in rank (performance only), dismissal with a minimum of 28 days' notice, or an extension of a final improvement notice.

6.7 The Police Federation and Other Police Representative Organizations

When a trainee joins the police service he/she automatically joins the Police Federation. Other staff organizations are described in 6.7.2.

6.7.1 The Police Federation

England and Wales have a single Police Federation (s 64(1) of the Police Act 1996, Membership of Trades Unions), as do each of Northern Ireland and Scotland. Here we describe the Police Federation of England and Wales, but many of the observations also apply to Scotland and Northern Ireland.

It is important to realize that the Federation is not a trades union in the usual sense of the term. Indeed, police officers are forbidden from joining a trades union:

> Subject to the following provisions of this section, a member of a police force shall not be a member of any trades union, or of any association having for its objects, or one of its objects, to control or influence the pay, pensions or conditions of service of any police force. (s 64(1) of the Police Act 1996, Membership of Trades Unions)

The Federation therefore does not have the right to call for any kind of industrial action such as a strike and cannot affiliate itself to the Labour Party or any other political organization. However, in many other respects the Federation has been established to represent the views of its members (police officers below the rank of superintendent) on local, regional, and national levels in much the same way as any other staff association.

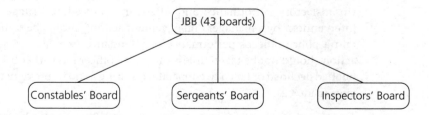

Each of the police forces in England and Wales has a Joint Branch Board (JBB). Within the JBB there are separate boards, representing the interests of constables, sergeants, and inspectors, as shown in the diagram. These boards each have separate agendas and meetings but also combine to form the force JBB. The JBB represents the views of police officers to the chief constable or commissioner, others in positions of responsibility, and members of the police authority.

The Federation of England and Wales has eight regions, with each region electing representatives to form the national Joint Central Committee. For example, Region No 2 of the Federation consists of the police forces of Cleveland, Durham, Humberside, Northumbria, North Yorkshire, South Yorkshire, and West Yorkshire. The Joint Central Committee is responsible for the national policy of the Federation.

6.7.1.1 The role of the Police Federation

On behalf of its members, the Police Federation negotiates aspects of pay, pensions, and allowances through a National Police Negotiating Board. The board consists of representatives from the Police Federations (England and Wales, Scotland, and Northern Ireland), the Superintendents' Association, and ACPO. These meet with representatives of the government ministers responsible for the police: the Home Secretary, the Scottish Secretary, the Northern Ireland Secretary, and representatives of the local authorities and magistrates. The Police Negotiating Board has an independent chairperson (appointed by the Prime Minister).

The Police Advisory Board (chaired by the Home Secretary) meets to discuss professional subjects such as training, promotion, and discipline. The Federation is also represented at these meetings. After taking these discussions into account, the Home Secretary may then make proposals to amend Police Regulations.

One of the primary functions of the Federation is to give advice and assistance to its members who are the subject of a formal complaint or internal investigation. In such circumstances the Federation's advice to an officer is to remain calm and contact his/her local Federation representative if unsure of what to do next. The IPCC have produced a leaflet concerning complaints which is downloadable from the IPCC's website (IPCC, 2014).

The Federation also offers advice and assistance to police officers (including trainee officers) who sustain injuries while on duty and who wish to claim compensation from the Criminal Injuries Compensation Authority (CICA). It also offers advice and assistance to police officers (including trainees) on matters arising from the conditions of service set out in the various Acts and regulations governing the police service.

6.7.2 Other police representative organizations

There are other organizations that represent particular groups and interests, and some have links with the Police Federation. For example, the British Association for Women in Policing (BAWP) is represented on the Equality Subcommittee of the Police Federation. The BAWP seeks to address women's issues in policing and not simply to represent women; membership is open to both men and women. Further information is available on their website.

The National Black Police Association UK (NBPA) is an independent charitable organization which seeks to further the position of all police officers of 'African, African-Caribbean, Middle-Eastern, Asian or Asian sub-continent origin'. A trainee officer may join the NBPA through membership of his or her local BPA, of which there are about 40 in the UK. Further information is available on their website.

The Gay Police Association (GPA) seeks to represent the interests of gay and lesbian police staff in the UK. Membership is on an individual basis and a trainee officer may join by contacting the national GPA via their website.

The National Disabled Police Association (NDPA) is a registered charity and staff association which seeks to support disabled people in both the police service and the wider community. It was launched in 2004 and aims to promote better access to policing for disabled people (see their website for further information).

The Police Superintendents' Association of England and Wales (PSAEW) represents the ranks of Superintendents and Chief Superintendents (there are similar organizations for Scotland and Northern Ireland). As with the Police Federation (see 6.7.1), the PSAEW represents its members at the national Police Negotiating Board (see 6.7.1.1).

The Association of Chief Police Officers (ACPO) represents the interests of chief officers in England, Wales, and Northern Ireland (there is a parallel body, ACPOS, for Scotland). Chief officers are defined as police officers of rank ACC or above (Commander in the MPS) and senior police staff equivalents. It is important to note that ACPO defines itself as a professional body and not as a staff association.

Qualifications and Training

> **TASK 13** If you are a trainee police officer, does your local force have a BPA? If it doesn't, try and find out why there is no BPA or equivalent.

6.8 Managing Police Information

Here we examine the need of police officers both to protect the confidentiality of information or data, and to share some information under the requirements of the Freedom of Information Act 2000 and the Data Protection Act 1998 (DPA). The recording of information and the confidentiality policies of the police service concerned should be explained to victims, survivors, and witnesses (IND 6.3).

Police data-gathering includes four principles, that the information gathered must be (1) Accurate, (2) Adequate, (3) Relevant, and (4) Timely. Once information is collected it is important the police adhere to legal requirements. Eight principles underpin the Data Protection Act 1998:

- Personal data must be processed fairly and lawfully and, in particular, must not be processed unless one or more of the 'conditions for processing' are met (covered in Schs 2 and 3 to the Act—for example, the individual concerned has consented or there is an urgent need because of the 'vital interests' of an individual, such as where medical history data is given to an A & E department in a hospital).
- Personal data can be obtained only for one or more specified and lawful purpose, and must not be further processed in any manner that is incompatible with that purpose or those purposes.
- Personal data must be adequate, relevant, and not excessive in relation to the purpose or purposes for which they are processed.
- Personal data must be accurate and, where necessary, kept up to date.
- Personal data processed for any purpose or purposes must not be kept for longer than is necessary for that purpose or those purposes.
- Personal data must be processed in accordance with the rights of data subjects under the DPA.
- Appropriate technical and organizational measures shall be taken against unauthorized or unlawful processing of personal data and against accidental loss or destruction of, or damage to, personal data.
- Personal data shall not be transferred to a country or territory outside the European Economic Area unless that country or territory ensures an adequate level of protection for the rights and freedoms of data subjects in relation to processing the personal data.

6.8.1 Confidentiality

Police officers (including trainee officers and special constables) will frequently encounter information of a sensitive and confidential nature. It is probably obvious, but confidentiality must be maintained, particularly in relation to witnesses, victims, and intelligence. Both the Data Protection Act 1998 and the Human Rights Act 1998 were enacted partly as a response to European legislation for protecting individual rights. Individual force policies may also make reference to the DPA and perhaps to the HRA (particularly those sections relevant to the right to privacy).

Police forces will collect and request information from a range of sources. The collection, storage, and disclosure of this information is subject to controls under the DPA and the Management of Police Information (MoPI). Each force has a 'data controller' who receives and considers applications for information, and decides whether the information requested can be disclosed. The DPA also provides certain rights to individuals (including witnesses and victims) for information. It is an offence under the DPA to disclose personal information without the consent of the data controller, except for the purposes of crime prevention or detection.

Confidentiality is one of the Standards of Professional Behaviour (see 6.3). Police officers are expected to 'treat information with respect and access or disclose it only in the proper course of police duties'. The new Policing Professional Framework (PPF) expects the police constable to 'uphold' these professional standards.

Respect for confidentiality is a theme running through many of the Diploma in Policing assessed units. The unit that requires a trainee to 'Gather and submit information to support law enforcement objectives' contains the assessment criterion that the trainee is able to 'explain the importance of maintaining the security...of information'. The evidence for meeting this assessment criterion is likely to be derived from activities on Supervised Patrol, and could take the form of artefacts such as records, or direct observation by an assessor (normally a tutor constable), or witness statements. It is very unlikely that simulations in a classroom environment would meet the requirements for this criterion. The Certificate in Knowledge of Policing contains a similar assessment criterion that covers only the knowledge aspects of this topic.

6.8.2   Management of Police Information (MoPI)

The means by which the police collect, record, share, and retain information has been the subject of some controversy in recent years, most notably as a result of the inquiry into the circumstances preceding the Soham murders (where a school caretaker killed two pupils) and the subsequent police investigations (see Bichard, 2004). A statutory Code of Practice on the Management of Police Information was published in 2005, followed by Guidance in 2006. These set out the basic principles that police organizations should adopt for the collection, recording, sharing, and retaining of information relevant to their usual work. At the level of the individual police officer, this information may take the form of intelligence and evidence gathering, details concerning domestic crime, search form completion, and pocket notebook entries. ACPO has published *Guidance on the Management of Police Information* which is available online (ACPO, 2011c).

Further, the HRA (see 5.4) requires all UK legislation to correspond with the European Convention on Human Rights. This means that any act by a public authority (such as the police) that contravenes the rights under the Convention will be unlawful. An individual's rights to privacy and family life (Article 8) can be 'interfered' with by the collection of personal information, and this interference is only permitted under certain circumstances.

Further constraints are placed upon holding personal data by the DPA. The Act defines personal data as any information which can identify a living person. However, when data is used for the prevention or detection of crime, or the apprehension or prosecution of offenders, exemptions are permitted. Finally, ACPO has also published its own *Manual of Guidance on Data Protection* (2010d) with a greater level of detail than provided by the Code.

The Code, the HRA, the DPA, and ACPO's manual all set out an obligation to manage police information in ways that are both effective and meet certain ethical and professional standards. Much of this is at the level of the organization (rather than the individual) and are made manifest through standing orders, policies, strategies (the force 'Information Management Strategy'), and similar instruments. However, the same principles also apply for all levels of police staff, regardless of rank or role, and are likely to feature in police training after joining the police, and even on some pre-entry courses. For example, there is the need to ensure that the information that a police officer records is necessary (for policing purposes); accurate (check the facts); adequate (do not omit important information); relevant (address the facts; record opinions only if necessary, and clearly mark as such); and timely (make the entry as soon as possible).

6.8.3   Freedom of information

The Freedom of Information Act 2000 (FoI) gives a general right of access to all types of recorded information held by public authorities. Police forces are included under the definition of public authorities, but ACPO, as a private company, is not. A police force will publish, normally on the internet, details concerning the public's right under the FoI to access information kept by the force, and the procedures for accessing it. The force will also have a publication scheme listing what information is available as a matter of routine, thereby reducing the number of requests for the same information. Not all requests for information will be successful—some of these are obvious, for example, requests relating to the identity of a Covert Human Intelligence Source (see 22.2 on the use of a CHIS). However, it is important to note that the right to information is the norm rather than the exception. Requests can be made, and are made, on all kinds of topics.

Qualifications and Training

There are two main ways that the FoI might directly affect a trainee police officer. First, he/she may personally receive a request for information under the FoI, perhaps in the form of a letter or by email. (Many people will know, for example, that a police work email is likely to be of the form x.y@force.pnn.police.uk where x is the first name, y is the surname, and 'force' is a shortened version of the name of a police force, for example BTP.) The officer should not normally respond in person but should promptly pass the request to the person responsible for handling FoI requests. Secondly, and put simply, all trainees and officers should always be aware when recording information as a police officer that someone, some day, may apply under the FoI to view that record. And unless there are very good reasons not to, this will be permitted, so it is very important to choose words accurately and carefully.

6.9 Operating IT and Communication Systems

Trainee police officers are expected to operate IT systems on both a general level (such as basic word-processing tasks and sending emails), and will also learn how to use specific police-related systems such as the Police National Computer (PNC) and the Airwave radio communication system. They might also be expected to use a particular police force information system. The ability to use 'force information management systems' is one of the requirements of the PAC under the 'Information Management' heading.

Many trainees and students on pre-join programmes are likely to already have many generic IT skills. Some police forces encourage their staff to take advantage of schemes such as the European Computer Driving Licence (ECDL). The basic skills include:

- searching the internet (vital for finding sites to help with all other IT skills!);
- creating folders;
- managing files (eg naming, saving, and retrieving files);
- word-processing documents;
- print documents;
- using presentational software (such as MS PowerPoint); and
- sending and receiving emails.

6.9.1 Police information systems and databases

There are two large databases of information for police use, the Police National Computer (PNC) and the more recently established Police National Database (PND). The PNC tends to be used by officers for 'street level' checks on a suspect, while the PND is usually employed in the context of an investigation, and is likely to contain much more than the PNC in the way of intelligence on individuals (both convicted and suspected).

6.9.1.1 The PNC

The PNC is a large database containing information on, amongst other things, people (eg those with criminal records), vehicles (including registered keepers), driving licences, and property. It is also used by agencies such as the Crown Court (for checking potential jurors) and the United Kingdom Border Agency. A police officer could use the PNC to establish, for example, whether a driver is disqualified, or to assess the potential for a particular suspect to respond with violence. However, the PNC can do more than perform these relatively simple checks. For example, the Vehicle Operator Services Agency (VOSA) database is linked to the PNC, so a police officer is able to check the expiry date of an MoT and other details (such as 'advisory notices'). The linked DVLA database will reveal information relating to tests, endorsements, and so on. The PNC can also be used to search for more 'fuzzy' information such as nicknames used by offenders, tattoos, scars, hair colour, and similar distinguishing features.

The PNC is normally accessed by radio and speaking to an operator based at the Force Control Room. There is a routine to be mastered; a particular sequence of requests is made to the operator, first specifying the nature of the request (eg a vehicle check). The officer then provides his/her name and force number before stating the reason for the check. The phonetic alphabet is used to spell out words to ensure there is no mistake in transmitting the information (see 2.6.1). Officers must make a PNB record (see 10.2) of the details of the checks carried out so that his/her work is auditable.

It will certainly be emphasized during police training that there is a requirement to access the PNC in a responsible and professional manner. Inappropriate use of the PNC is viewed by police forces as a serious matter and could lead to dismissal of a trainee police officer. (Not only is it a contravention of the PNC Code of Practice, but it is also against the law.) Unfortunately, examples of inappropriate use are only too easy to find. In the past these have included:

- checking on a daughter's new boyfriend (Wadham, 2004);
- accessing information about celebrities to sell to the red-top press; and
- selling information to private investigators (Wadham, 2004).

Alleged misuse of the PNC can lead to an IPCC inquiry (see 6.6.3).

TASK 14

1. What are VODS and QUEST? You may need to use the internet or (if you are a trainee officer) ask more experienced colleagues.
2. The HMIC has carried out PNC-compliance inspections of police forces. These may be viewed via the HMIC website. Check whether your local force has yet been inspected. If so, read the report. If not, read one from your Most Similar Force (MSF) comparator.

Trainee officers are likely to be instructed on using the PNC. Effective use of the PNC is part of LPG 1 of the IPLDP, and the ability to utilize the PNC is also listed under the 'Information Management' heading of the PAC (so this will need to be demonstrated before a trainee can undertake Independent Patrol).

6.9.1.2   The PND

The PND is a relatively new IT system (June 2011) for sharing information and intelligence between police forces. It was set up partly as a consequence of the inadequacies uncovered during the Bichard inquiry into the Soham murders in 2002, and replaces the IMPACT Nominal Index. The PND contains 'POLE' data which is information about:

- *People* (eg offenders and suspects);
- *Objects* (eg stolen vehicles);
- *Locations* (eg addresses of offenders); and
- *Events* (eg crime reports).

The data is located within five discrete but interconnected sets of records: custody, intelligence, crime, domestic abuse, and child abuse. A police force is able to check what information or intelligence is held on an individual (a 'nominal') by any other police force. Much of the information to be found on the PNC will also be present in the PND and vice versa.

6.9.2   TETRA and Airwave communication

The communication protocol used by police forces in England and Wales (as with most of the other countries in Europe) is known as 'TETRA'—Terrestrial Trunked Radio. 'Airwave' (the product of a commercial company, Airwave Solutions Ltd) employs the TETRA protocols, and is the radio communications network used by the police for voice communication (eg between a police patrol and the force control room) and for communication of data. The system has replaced what many people still think of as the police 'radio'. Airwave can also be used to communicate with other rescue and emergency services. Indeed, the Airwave equipment has an emergency button for use in the case of imminent personal danger. It is currently considered secure as it employs relatively sophisticated forms of encryption.

Trainee officers will be provided with full details about communication over Airwave, including codes and protocols which are restricted to the police service (and hence not reproduced here). The phonetic alphabet is used where appropriate (see 2.6.1). Trainee officers will also be required to learn 'AirwaveSpeak', which reduces the amount of time needed to communicate information, and reduces the incidence of error or ambiguity. The table describes some of the basic rules (but be aware that there are many more).

Airwave appears to function effectively in most circumstances, although there were claims made after the riots in England during the summer of 2011 that Airwave had become 'overloaded' and police officers were forced to use their own personal mobile phones to communicate (Police Federation, 2011, p 6) although this was subsequently denied by the company concerned.

	Description	Example
Starting the call ('calling up')	A police officer repeats the call-sign of the person (or control room) that he or she is calling and then adds his or her own call-sign	'Charlie romeo, charlie romeo...this is tango two three....'
Exchange	A police officer finishes his or her part of the exchange with the word 'Over'	'Charlie romeo, charlie romeo...this is tango two three...over'
Conveying information, asking questions, etc		'Charlie romeo, charlie romeo this is tango two three disturbance in Tontine Street over'
Confirming	A confirmation is often given that the message has been received and understood	'Tango two three, received, over'
Finishing the call	A police officer (or the control room) finishes the sequence of communication with 'Out'	'Charlie romeo, tango two three, suspects under arrest, out'

6.9.3 Mobile data devices

A number of police forces allocate mobile data devices such as smartphones, tablets, and laptops to their officers, with the intention of reducing the amount of 'paperwork'. A mobile data device provides an electronic means of:

1. entering and sharing data (eg a witness statement collected in electronic format at the scene of an incident);
2. recording and sharing location data (eg using GPS); and
3. printing some types of completed forms on a 'mini-printer' connected by Bluetooth or similar methods.

In recent years there has been considerable investment in other mobile data devices for the police service, typically in the form of BlackBerry smartphones and vehicle-mounted mobile data devices (eg in a patrol car). The intention is to free up police officer time and to improve efficiency. Deployment of these devices appears to be patchy; but the Home Office and the CoP have recently (2013) introduced a 'Digital Pathfinder' initiative, one aspect of which is to share good practice in the use of mobile data devices by police forces. Concerns have been expressed over both the cost of the devices and of ongoing data usage. However, the police use of mobile data devices is likely to grow and further expand into areas such as electronic completion of forms, particularly if the devices are linked with mini-printers. In addition, mobile data devices normally incorporate a digital camera which (in some forces) a police officer will use to record potential evidence.

In broad terms the devices allow a police officer to access the PNC, local force tasking and briefing bulletins, missing person reports, police intelligence systems, other information systems (eg the PNLD), and information relating to an individual's name and address (eg the electoral roll, the Quick Address System), and to send emails. The exact functions and applications used on the mobile data devices are specific to each force and normally kept confidential. It is also assumed that secure forms of data encryption are used, but the details of this are also confidential.

Trainee police officers issued with a mobile data device will be informed of the relevant protocols and rules. For example, when a force-issued mobile data device is switched on it is likely to become 'visible' to the control room and for this reason many police forces forbid their use whilst off duty.

6.10 Police Equipment and Technology

Police officers and Special Constables carry a range of equipment and technology when on patrol. The various items are used for personal protection (see 6.12.5), for controlling violent or potentially violent people, and for communication with other police staff. Training will be given in both the function and appropriate use of the issued equipment and technology. (Note that officers are usually prohibited from carrying unauthorized equipment or technology, but policy details vary between forces.) Here we provide a brief overview of police equipment and other items.

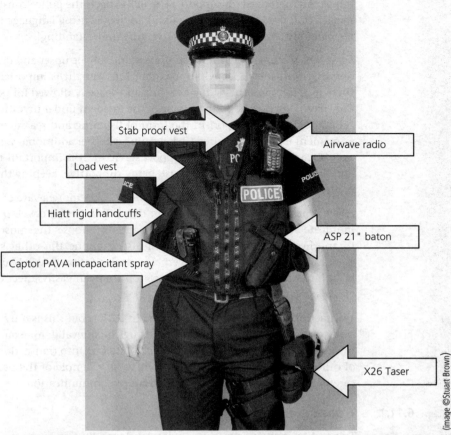

Stab proof vest

Load vest

Hiatt rigid handcuffs

Captor PAVA incapacitant spray

Airwave radio

ASP 21" baton

X26 Taser

(image ©Stuart Brown)

Typical clothing and equipment worn and carried by an operational police officer

Police uniforms vary from force to force, and according to the role a police officer may be performing at a particular time. A police officer on initial training will become familiar with the 'Standard' (or 'Default'), 'Ceremonial', 'Public Order', and 'Specialist' (eg Dog section) uniforms for his/her force. The 'Standard' uniform is worn on operational activities. It includes the custodian helmet (or the bowler for female officers) if on foot patrol, the cap if in a patrol car, and a black wicking shirt. 'Public Order' uniform includes a helmet, overalls, a face cover, and protective gloves. Every officer is also required to display a badge giving his/her name and/ or number.

Protective equipment such as body armour and/or a stab vest is also worn for operational duties. Police officers also carry equipment whilst on operational duties, such as a first aid kit, handcuffs, PAVA ('pepper') incapacitant spray (or CS spray), a baton (eg an ASP), an Airwaves terminal (see 6.9.2), and a torch. In some forces officers might also carry a mobile phone and a 'taser'.

Each force makes its own arrangements for purchasing equipment and technology, and some items (such as body armour) must meet Home Office quality assurance guidelines. There are opportunity costs in this approach for as the Home Office notes 'The police service currently procures equipment and services...in up to 43 different ways at a total cost of £3.3bn across 43 forces' (Home Office, 2012d, p 5). The government intends to legislate to encourage more bulk purchasing of equipment by consortia of police forces in the future.

6.11   Effective Interpersonal Communication

To 'communicate effectively' is an underpinning requirement of all the Diploma in Policing assessed units. For example, the unit 'Provide initial support to victims and witnesses' includes the assessment criterion requiring that an officer can 'communicate with individuals appropriately, taking account of pace, the victim or witnesses' level of understanding and their preferred forms of communication' (our interpretation). The Certificate in Knowledge of Policing requires that learners should 'understand the factors that affect victims and witnesses and

Qualifications and Training

impact on their need for support'. The PPF expects the police constable to 'Explain things well, focusing on the key points and talking to people using language they understand' and to 'listen carefully and to ask questions to clarify understanding'.

Survivors, victims, or witness can understandably be upset and disturbed by their experiences of crime, anti-social behaviour, or other incidents. It is important that officers are aware of these reactions and that sufficient time and space is allowed for people to communicate what they have experienced in the course of the incident under investigation. It may be that practical and emotional support in the form of listening and reassurance is sufficient, but careful assessment might be required to determine whether additional support is required (eg medical assistance, counselling, victim support services). It is important to communicate effectively, building a rapport and gaining trust, being supportive, keeping those affected up to date.

The ideas presented here should help you become more aware of the way you speak, and the effect it has on other people. In turn, this will help you develop strategies to help you communicate more clearly in the future, and to choose the most appropriate way to speak to another person. In 6.11.3 we will also examine the other side of the communication equation—listening skills. Non-verbal communication (NVC) is also covered (in 6.11.2) as this is an important means of communication that can easily affect exchanges between all individuals, including police officers.

Transactional analysis (TA) is explained in 6.11.1, but this is only one of many theories about human communication. Other theories are equally valid; for example, Shannon and Weaver's Information Theory. We are not asking you to buy into transactional analysis to the exclusion of other theories; instead we use it here as an example of the benefits that may flow from a careful and structured analysis of patterns of communication.

6.11.1 Transactional analysis

Transactional analysis was originally developed by Eric Berne (for an introduction see Berne, 1968), and is based upon the assumption that at any one time people tend to adopt the characteristics or 'ego states' of a parent (critical or nurturing), adult, or child (adapted or free). The ego state affects their attitudes and the way they speak to each other. The ego states and the type of language used and the associated typical behaviours and attitudes are shown in the table.

Ego state	Typical words/phrases	Typical behaviour	Typical attitudes
Critical parent	'That's disgraceful!' 'You ought to …!' 'Always do it!'	Furrowed brow, pointed finger.	Condescending, judgemental.
Nurturing parent	'Well done, that's clever!'	Benevolent smile, pat on back.	Caring, permissive.
Adult	'How …'? 'When …'? 'Where …'? 'What …'?	Relaxed, logical, attentive.	Open-minded, clear-thinking, interested.
Adapted child	'Please can I?' 'I'll try harder.'	Vigorous, nodding head, downcast eyes, whiny voice.	Compliant, defiant, complaining.
Free child	'I want …' 'I feel great.'	Laughing with someone, uninhibited.	Curious, fun-loving, spontaneous.

Note that no one operates in any of these states on a permanent basis, but switches between states, even within the course of a single conversation.

TASK 15 If this Handbook were a person, which of the ego states would fit best and most often?

According to the theory of TA, the way a person responds will vary, partly due to the way the other person behaves or speaks (influenced by their own ego state). A trainee officer needs to be able to analyse (to some extent) the way he/she speaks and responds and the ways that others speak and respond, and then to be able to identify the most appropriate way to manage the conversation. Having identified the ego states in play, the next task is to recognize the category of conversation or transaction, ie whether it is complementary, crossed, or ulterior.

Complementary transactions occur when the ego state of each side of the conversation correspond. Here is an example of a complementary transaction between a trainee police officer 'P' and a member of the public 'M'.

> P stops a car to give advice to the driver.
>
> M   I don't know why you've stopped me. Haven't you got anything better to do?
> P   Is this your car? I've stopped you because I've got the right, and what's your problem anyway?
> M   Get lost.
> P   You can't say that; any more lip and I'll have you.

The opening transaction is from M who appears to be in the child ego state. P's response is in the 'critical parent' ego state. The ego states correspond; it is a complementary transaction sequence:

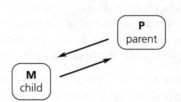

The exchange will continue in this way as long as the transactions are complementary. However, P can change the flow of the conversation by deliberately changing his/her tone and behaviour, and communicating a different ego state to create a 'crossed transaction'.

A **crossed transaction** breaks a complementary transaction. To change the style of the transaction, either P or M could employ a different ego state; let us begin the conversation again with P reacting differently.

> M   I don't know why you've stopped me. Haven't you got anything better to do?
> P   Hello, just a quick word, I'm PC Williams from Lewes police station. I've stopped you because one of your brake lights isn't working did you know? This could affect your safety as well as the safety of others.
> M   Oh right, I didn't realize—thanks for telling me—I'll get it fixed ... soon.
> P   Thanks for your cooperation. Good afternoon.

In this case P deliberately ignores M's child ego state and adopts an adult ego state. It is a reply that has reasoning in its content, and this has an effect on M, who may not have expected this type of response. M responds accordingly in the adult ego state, which brings about a satisfactory conclusion. This is referred to as a crossed transaction, as P's response has broken the parent–child–parent pattern, and the transaction has crossed over into a different style.

In an **ulterior transaction** there are actually two different messages, an open message and a hidden message. Frequently with ulterior transactions, the open message is adult–adult, but the hidden message is parent–child or child–parent.

> For example, M begins the transaction sarcastically, and emphasizes the word 'such'.
>
> M   It's nice to see the local police making such good use of their time.
> P   Yeah, it's all part of the service to you.

This transaction is not just about words: it is also about body language and the tone of voice. The opening transaction has a hidden meaning: M dislikes the police (or at least P) and feels that the police (or P in particular) waste his or her time, rather than catching real criminals; hence the sarcastic emphasis on the word 'such'. P's response also has a hidden meaning:

hence it is said with a smirk and an emphasis on the word 'you'. Each component is complementary. So, unless one of the participants crosses a transaction, the dialogue will continue in this manner. The skill, therefore, is to be aware of what is happening, and to be able to cross an unproductive transaction, and thereby change the ego state of the other person.

Try using these ideas to help you understand your own and other people's styles of communication, and then choose the most appropriate way of saying what it is that you want to say.

> **TASK 16** Over the next two days, listen carefully to conversations around you. What ego states are operating and what type of transactions are taking place? Write down three brief extracts and explain what is happening in terms of transactional analysis.

6.11.2   Non-verbal communication

People may communicate anxiety, confidence, despair, or any other emotion through body language, also known as non-verbal communication (NVC). You may be able to use NVC to help build up trust with other people. It has been observed that adopting similar body postures and mannerisms communicates a positive attitude. A trainee police officer or special constable could use such techniques (in a discreet manner) when communicating with witnesses, suspects, victims, or other members of the public.

However, be wary of popular accounts concerning NVC; particular actions never have definite meanings and hand gestures (for example) are not 'windows on the soul'. (Unfortunately these kinds of scientifically unjustified 'tips and tricks' have featured in police training in the past.) In particular, the use of 'body language' in an attempt to identify deception or lying is problematic (see Vrij, 2008, for a comprehensive consideration of this). In addition, you must be alert to 'ethnocentrism' in your interpretations of NVC, such as a refusal to make eye contact— for some ethnic groups this is related to cultural attitudes to authority, and does not necessarily indicate guilt or remorse.

6.11.3   Listening skills

Of all the skills that we develop during our lives, the ability to listen is probably the most difficult of all. We hear, but we do not always listen; this ability has to be learned and practised, and a trainee police officer will benefit from developing the ability more fully. Even the little things people say may be of critical importance when dealing with a public order situation or when investigating a crime.

Here we shall simply offer some basic advice on listening. Police training will include more detailed advice on listening skills. It is best to:

- pay full attention to the other person as he/she is speaking and to avoid looking away (think what it feels like for you when you are speaking to a person who keeps glancing away!). Use verbal and non-verbal feedback (eg nodding) to show you are listening'
- let the speaker finish before asking another question or make a comment, and don't interrupt. Most of us think we already do this but research shows that this is rarely the case! (However, there may be occasions when a police officer **must** interrupt for operational reasons.) A good way of training yourself to let someone finish is to mentally count a few seconds after he/she has stopped before you respond. You may also notice that he/she then fills this silence, and carries on speaking, almost as an afterthought. Sometimes, this extra information is of critical importance. Family doctors have long known this: often the most important part of the consultation is when the patient stands to leave and remarks, 'Oh yes doctor, there is one more thing …'
- try echoing back to the speaker if you need to clarify something, for example by using a phrase he/she has already used—'You said, "He asked me for a cigarette,"…'. The speaker is likely to pick up the thread and continue to explain further.

6.11.4   Communication with colleagues

There are many reasons why good working relationships are important including: maintaining trust, contributing to professional performance, effective cooperation, and encouraging commitment. There is a need to communicate effectively, but also to manage conflict, challenge some attitudes and behaviour, build relationships, and work in teams. It is important to be aware of the needs of work colleagues.

The ability to prioritize accordingly can be crucial in providing an effective response. Failure to do this can result in additional pressures placed on the supervisor and the team, put the public and police colleagues at greater risk, and undermine public confidence in the police. Often these situations can be highly pressured and having an appreciation of the available support and advice from colleagues and appropriate organizations (see 11.2) can improve the speed and quality of the service to the public.

Inappropriate behaviour in policing has been a source of criticism and one that the police service continually attempts to address. There are a variety of different ways in which inappropriate behaviour can occur such as unwittingly using potentially offensive language, ignorance, and intended insults and discrimination. All police officers are expected to understand cultural sensitivities, inappropriate sexist or racist behaviour, and language. If police officers disregard these important issues it undermines the police service, supports discrimination within the service, and can put police officers and the public at risk. It could also result in disciplinary action for the officers concerned. For this reason all police officers including trainees have a responsibility to address and where appropriate challenge inappropriate behaviour of colleagues. When taking such actions, however, it is important to recognize the limitations of your own abilities and when it may be better to seek advice or guidance from a supervisor.

6.11.4.1 Teamwork

The need to work effectively as a member of a team is reflected in a number of the Integrated Competency Framework (ICF) competencies. There are seven competencies: respect for equality and diversity, effective communication, personal responsibility, problem solving, team working, community and customer focus, and resilience.

The College of Policing lists several behaviours to build and maintain relations between team members, and also suggests a number of behaviours to avoid (see the table of dos and don'ts).

Effective team-working strategies	Poor team-working strategies
understand own role in a team,	fail to volunteer to help other team members,
actively take part in team tasks in the workplace,	only offer to take part in high-profile and interesting activities,
be open and approachable,	take credit for successes without recognizing the contribution of others,
make time to get to know people,	work to a single agenda rather than contributing to team performance,
cooperate with and support others,	allow small exclusive groups of people to develop,
offer to help other people,	play one person off against another,
ask for and accept help when needed,	restrict and control the sharing of information,
develop mutual trust and confidence in others,	prevent others from saying what they think,
willingly take on unpopular or routine tasks,	fail to offer advice or get advice from others,
contribute to team objectives no matter what the direct personal benefit may be,	show little interest in working jointly with other groups to meet the goals of everyone involved,
acknowledge that there is often a need to be a member of more than one team.	fail to discourage conflict within the organization.

Officers can demonstrate commitment by taking a full share of the workload and responding promptly to requests for help from other colleagues. It is also beneficial to clearly communicate about any difficulties encountered; this is far better than just trying to transfer the responsibility to someone else as the problems are unlikely to go away! A positive team spirit is beneficial to everyone, and all team members must take responsibility for maintaining productive working practices. The same principles apply for situations where an officer is working more as an individual rather than as part of a team; face up to responsibilities, take appropriate actions, and ensure all communications are clear.

6.11.4.2 Resolving conflicts

Occasionally, there can be disagreement between team members or with a supervisor. It is important to resolve disagreement diplomatically in order to avoid undermining police responses resulting in poor performance. Unless conflicts are resolved, a sense of distrust is very likely to develop between team members and supervisors, and they will no longer be able to work together effectively. Individual interpersonal skills are important in trying to avoid conflict by trying to understand the views and opinions of others and respond in an appropriate manner. Once a disagreement has occurred it is important to fully appreciate the issue concerned, understand the problem from the opposing perspective, identifying alternative solutions, and agree on the most appropriate way forward. One model of conflict resolution is 'CUDSA' (Confront, Understand, Define, Search, and Agree). This provides a step-by-step approach to resolving conflict, and begins with confronting and understanding the problem before moving on to search for and agree to solutions.

TASK 17 The QCF Diploma in Policing assessed unit 'Provide initial support to victims and witnesses' contains the following assessment criterion:

The trainee police officer can, when communicating with victims and witnesses, ensure that he or she 'applies principles of equality, diversity and anti-discrimination practice' (our interpretation).

List some examples of questions that a trainee police officer might ask people, to help demonstrate meeting this assessment criterion. (In practice, Skills for Justice expect this competency to be demonstrated in a practical context on at least two occasions.)

6.12 Health and Safety

By its very nature, policing has always been and will continue to be a potentially hazardous occupation. Whilst risks are present in all work activities, operational staff are more frequently exposed to risks, for example when dealing with environmental incidents or disorderly behaviour. All employers have a duty to ensure (as far as is reasonably practicable) the health, safety, and welfare of their employees. In turn, each employee has a duty to take reasonable care for his/her own health and safety and that of other persons who might be affected by his/her acts or omissions. It is important for front-line police officers to be fit and to be provided (and use) with suitable personal safety equipment.

Health and safety may seem at times to be just another bureaucratic burden, but it is an issue police officers must consider and have in mind at all times during their day-to-day work. Health and safety duties are covered by ss 2–7 of the Health and Safety at Work etc Act 1974, and became applicable to police officers, special constabulary officers, and cadets by virtue of the Police (Health and Safety) Act 1997. Home Office publications from 1996 onwards provide guidance for police managers. A police force will also have its own published health and safety policy.

Health and safety-related assessment criteria feature in many of the Diploma in Policing assessment units—indeed, health and safety assessment is embedded throughout the Diploma through articulation with the NOS Unit AF1 (see 7.4). For example, the Diploma assessed unit 'Search vehicles, premises and open spaces' has an assessment criterion to 'manage the health and safety of self and others prior to the search'. The Certificate in Knowledge of Policing unit 'Knowledge of searching vehicles, premises, and open spaces within a policing context' also requires learners to be able to 'explain how to maintain the health and safety of self and others during the search' when conducting vehicle searches.

Health and safety is also addressed during the IPLDP Induction Module IND 5, 'Ensure your own actions reduce the risks to health and safety'. The topics covered here are also linked with PAC heading 'Safety First' and in particular the subheadings 'Health and Safety—Legislation' and 'Health and Safety—Dynamic assessment'.

6.12.1   The employer's role in health and safety

Section 2(2) of the Health and Safety at Work etc Act (HSWA) 1974 sets out the employer's role for health and safety, stating that employers are responsible for:

- providing and maintaining plant and systems of work that are, so far as is reasonably practicable, safe, and without risks to health;
- making safe arrangements for the use, handling, storage, and transport of articles and substances;
- providing necessary information, instruction, training, and supervision for ensuring, so far as is reasonably practicable, the health and safety at work of employees;
- maintaining places of work under the employer's control in a condition which is safe and free from health risks, with safe means of entry and exit; and
- providing and maintaining a working environment for employees that is, so far as is reasonably practicable, safe, without risks to health, and has adequate facilities for their welfare at work.

(Adapted from the Home Office publication *A Guide for Police Managers*, 1997)

6.12.2   The employee's role in health and safety

Health and safety legislation places general duties on employees for example to:

- take reasonable care for their own health and safety and that of other persons who might be affected by his or her acts or omissions (s 7(a) HSWA);
- cooperate with the employer to enable the employer to comply with statutory duties for health and safety (s 7(b) HSWA);
- use correctly all work items provided by the employer, in accordance with training and instructions received (reg 14(1) of the Management of Health and Safety etc Work Regulations 1999); and
- inform their employer, or the person responsible for health and safety, of any work situation which might present a serious and imminent danger and any shortcoming in the health and safety arrangements (reg 14(2) of the Management of Health and Safety etc Work Regulations 1999).

(Adapted from the Home Office publication *A Guide for Police Managers*, 1997)

6.12.3   Hazards, risks, and threat level

Consider the potential threats to the health and safety of a trainee police officer on foot patrol. You have probably thought of several scenarios in which the trainee police officer could be harmed. But how much harm, and how likely is it to happen? This is a matter of judgement for each different situation, but it makes it easier to judge if you think of each type of harm in terms of the hazard, the risk, and the threat level.

A hazard is something with a potential to cause harm, for example, slipping over on a wet surface, being hit by moving traffic, seizing drugs and used needles, or being hit by a meteorite. The hazard criteria are about how serious the consequences would be if the event occurs. The formal levels of classification for the hazard level are:

- high—death, major injury, or serious illness may result;
- medium—serious injuries or ill health; off work for more than three days; and
- low—less serious illness or injury; off work for less than three days.

The risk is the likelihood of such an event actually happening. You might have already thought that some hazards are more likely to happen than others and that the likelihood of such events also needs to be taken into account. The risk criteria are about how likely an event is: a high risk means it is very likely or near certain to occur, and medium is when it is likely to occur, and low risk is when it is very unlikely to occur.

The threat level (sometimes referred to as overall risk) is a combination of the hazard and the risk. (Note the possibility of confusing risk and overall risk; the word 'risk' may be used in these two different ways, and you will need to seek clarification if the context does not make the meaning clear.) The grid shows different combinations of hazard and risk, and the resulting threat levels.

Qualifications and Training

THREAT LEVEL ↘		HAZARD		
		High	Medium	Low
RISK	High	INTOLERABLE **high** threat level	SUBSTANTIAL **high** threat level	MODERATE **medium** threat level
	Medium	SUBSTANTIAL **high** threat level	MODERATE **medium** threat level	ACCEPTABLE **low** threat level
	Low	MODERATE **medium** threat level	ACCEPTABLE **low** threat level	TRIVIAL **low** threat level

(Adapted from the Home Office, 1997)

Another way of looking at assessing the threat level is to multiply the hazard and risk in an equation: hazard × risk = threat level. For those of you who are more mathematically minded, this is not the conventional kind of formula—after all there are no numbers to put into the formula—it is just a way of summarizing the relationship to emphasize how the threat level is determined by the combination of the hazard and risk levels.

The following examples illustrate the interaction between hazard, risk, and threat level:

1. Death by meteorite—the hazard is very high as meteorites can be heavy and fall from the sky at high speeds. But the risk is low as this event is very unlikely to occur. So the threat level is low.
2. Bruising from arresting a drunken suspect—the hazard is minor. However, the risk is high as this is quite likely to occur. But the threat level is low as the consequences are unlikely to be serious.
3. Gunshot wounds when pursuing armed suspects—the hazard is serious, and there is quite a high risk of shots being fired. In this situation the threat level is high (and special precautions should be taken).

Consider another example. Imagine you are a trainee police officer on duty at the scene of a road traffic collision. Your colleague is dealing with an injured person in one of the vehicles and you are directing the traffic.

Hazards	You could be struck by a motor vehicle and your colleague could also be hit whilst attending to the injured person, therefore the hazard level is high, as death or major injury is likely to occur if another vehicle collides with you or your colleague.
Risk	Take into account day- or night-time, volume of traffic, weather conditions, and location: the risk level is medium as it is likely or possible that you might be struck by a vehicle.
Threat level	The threat level is therefore assessed as substantial.

There has been criticism of apparent 'risk aversion' amongst some police officers, and particularly when officers are confronted with situations that pose dangers to themselves and for members of the public. ACPO's position (as stated within its 'Statement of Risk Principles') is that 'maintaining or achieving the safety, security and well-being of individuals and communities is a primary consideration in risk decision making' (ACPO, 2011b).

6.12.4 Control measures

Control measures are steps that can be taken to lower the risk and therefore reduce the threat level. A five-step approach can be used, as illustrated in the following example; imagine you are a trainee police officer on foot patrol.

- **Step 1: Identify the hazards.** As a pedestrian you are exposed to danger from moving vehicles, and you could also face unpredictable confrontation with members of the public.

- **Step 2: Who may be harmed, and how?** You, a colleague, or a member of the public could be harmed by a moving vehicle, or a weapon used by a member of the public, resulting in death or major injury. Therefore the hazard level would be high.
- **Step 3: Evaluate the risks.** Your up-to-the minute location is not always known and you are sometimes alone, as a result of which harm is possible/likely to occur. You are always at risk of walking into an unexpected situation in which harm is possible/likely to occur. You may face difficulties with radio communication, reception, and transmission, or other faulty systems, which could lead to harm. Therefore the risk potential is medium.
- **Step 4: Record your findings.** The threat level grid shows the threat level would be substantial, so you should use control measures to lower it.
- **Step 5: Review your assessment from time to time, and revise it if necessary**.

The following control measures could be used to lower the threat level:

- in relation to the road network, adopting the correct procedures learnt during training, wearing the correct personal protective equipment (fluorescent), and using First Aid if required;
- applying techniques from training sessions for control and restraint, firearms and knife awareness, and using personal protection equipment;
- keeping the Control Room updated with your location;
- using your local knowledge and requesting all available information to assess situations; and
- being aware of the limitations of communications equipment.

> **TASK 18** We are not always good at judging overall risk. As an exercise, arrange the following risks in order of likelihood, putting the most likely first. They are given to you in a random order.
>
> The likelihood of death in the next year for the average person in the UK:
>
> - by falling down stairs;
> - through being struck by lightning;
> - in an aircraft crash;
> - in a train crash;
> - in a cycling accident;
> - as the victim of homicide;
> - by drowning in a bath; and
> - as a consequence of lung cancer.
>
> (Adapted from Haigh, 2006)

> **TASK 19** Imagine you are a trainee police officer carrying out a search of a person (under s 1 of the PACE Act 1984: see 9.4). What would be your considerations in relation to your own and your colleagues' safety whilst carrying out this search? What is your estimation of the threat level and what may be required to lower this level?

If you are a trainee or a student studying the CKP, completion of Task 19 might assist you in preparing to meet NOS standard AF1.1 'Identify the hazards and evaluate the risks in the workplace'. In turn, this links with PAC heading 'Safety First' and the checklist subheadings 'Health and Safety—Legislation' and 'Health and Safety—Dynamic assessment'.

6.12.5 Personal safety training

Police officers are permitted to use reasonable force if necessary to prevent crime or to arrest a person (see 15.5.1). This right exists under common law and s 3 of the Criminal Law Act 1967. In addition, s 117 of the PACE Act 1984 allows a police officer to use reasonable force to exercise powers granted by other parts of PACE. A police officer may also use reasonable force in self-defence (see *R v McInnes* [1971] 1 WLR 1600 (CA)). In all cases the force used must be proportionate and exercised with due regard to the human rights of the individuals concerned.

A trainee police officer will receive practical training in protecting both him/herself and others from attack, and also about how to use reasonable force against others. (Pre-join programmes are not likely to include practical training unless it is also for special constables, but the CKP does require learners to 'know the legislation and other relevant guidance related to managing conflict' and to 'understand how to apply conflict management skills and techniques'.) The precise title of the training may vary but in all cases, the relevant Diploma in Policing assessed unit is 'Manage conflict'. For example, this unit has an assessment criterion that the trainee is able to 'carry and use approved personal protective…equipment in line with organisational procedure'. The training normally takes place in specialist facilities over a period of five to ten days. (In most forces it is referred to as Personal Safety Training (PST) or the Personal Safety Programme, although you might also hear reference to Officer Safety Training (OST). The title PST is now preferred, partly because some or all of the training is also used for some members of the extended police family. Alternatively, a force may have contracted with the CoP to enable it to deliver the 'Personal Safety—Basic Course'.)

Further information is available in the ACPO Centrex 'Personal Safety Manual' and, if you are a trainee police officer, the ACPO 'Guidelines on the use of Handcuffs and Incapacitant Spray', are also useful, and available from your force.

These are the typical components of PST:

- **conflict management:** for example, recognizing typical signs of potential conflict;
- **searching people and places:** for example, health and safety when searching people who may have hidden weapons;
- **protective equipment:** for example, body armour, baton, and 'less lethal weaponry' such as the taser;
- **use of handcuffs and limb restraints:** for example, the use of the 'Speedcuff' rigid handcuffs and leg restraints;
- **'unarmed' self-protection skills:** for example, 'distraction strikes';
- **particular considerations when attending scenes:** for example, possible actions to be taken in the event of trying to help someone experiencing problems in water;
- **edged weapon skills:** for example, the appropriate responses to a person with a knife;
- **incapacitant sprays:** for example, the use of PAVA (Captor spray); and
- **use of batons and ASPs:** for example, the use of the 21-inch expandable baton (the ASP) and the Arnold baton.

Successful completion of PST is a target within the PAC (under the 'Safety First' heading), so trainee officers have to achieve it before Independent Patrol. However, many trainee officers will be expected to successfully complete PST before their first Supervised Patrol and, in many cases, before a community engagement. Police officers may also be expected to undertake and pass 'refresher' PST training courses later in their career.

> **TASK 20** Each force will have police officers trained in the use of equipment used for protection in Chemical, Biological, Radiological, or Nuclear incidents (CBRN incidents, see 11.5.3). What is the standard personal-protective equipment used by the UK police for such incidents?

6.12.6 First aid training

It is the duty of every police officer to 'protect life'. Inevitably police officers find themselves at incidents where there are seriously injured people, and they may also be called upon by members of the public to assist in helping with conditions ranging from a sprained ankle or scalding by hot water through to heart attacks or epileptic seizures. The public will expect a police officer to know what to do. Although specialized medical personnel will also be present (or on their way) on most occasions, a police officer will sometimes be the first person on the scene who has received any training for dealing with such emergencies.

It is for this reason that, pre-join programmes and the induction phase of training include instruction on how to administer basic First Aid. The training is likely to be based around the College of Policing programme 'First Aid Skills for Policing (FASP) Module 2—First Aid Skills'. There might also be assessment against the four elements of NOS Unit 4G4 'Administer First Aid'. Skills for Justice inform us that that the unit has been 'imported' from the Royal Marines Public Services NOS (Unit 4) and was developed by the British Red Cross in consultation with the St John Ambulance Service.

Qualifications and Training

> **Elements of Unit 4G4—Administer First Aid**
>
> 4G4.1   Respond to the needs of casualties with minor injuries
> 4G4.2   Respond to the needs of casualties with major injuries
> 4G4.3   Respond to the needs of unconscious casualties
> 4G4.4   Perform cardio-pulmonary resuscitation (CPR)

First Aid is also one of the headings in the Police Action Checklist and hence the successful completion of First Aid training is likely to be a necessary condition for Independent Patrol (see 8.4.2.1). First Aid training is likely to contain some or all of the following:

- **managing scenes and casualties:** for example, assessing the extent of casualties, communicating with others;
- **Basic Life Support (BLS) for Adults:** an algorithm of actions to administer immediate life support, including the need first to ensure the safety of yourself and others. It involves checking the injured person for a response, checking airways and breathing, and what to do next (recovery position, chest compression, rescue breaths, depending on the situation), and performing cardio-pulmonary resuscitation (CPR);
- **Basic Life Support (BLS) for Infants and Children:** variations on the system used for adults;
- **specific critical medical conditions:** eg shock, bleeding, spinal injuries, heart attacks, and epilepsy;
- **choking:** techniques employed to counter choking;
- **sprains, strains, and fractures:** dealing with broken bones and similar injuries;
- **scalds and burns:** what to do before more specialist medical treatment can be obtained; and
- **hypothermia, frostbite, heatstroke, and heat exhaustion:** how to treat potentially difficult medical conditions, especially when the individuals concerned are vulnerable.

Most police forces also expect police officers to maintain their level of First Aid training after the initial probationary period. Typically, this involves a 'refresher course' every three years or so. For more specialist roles, officers may be required to undertake specialist First Aid training, such as Kent Police's Tactical Emergency Aid Medical Support (TEAMS) First Aid Skills.

> **TASK 21** Read and reflect on the contents of Chapter 10 ('First Aid') of the 1999 Macpherson Inquiry into the death of Stephen Lawrence. It is freely available on the internet at: <https://www.gov.uk/government/publications/the-stephen-lawrence-inquiry>. Trainee officers may find this task provides stimulus material for completing a Learning Diary entry for Phase 1 under the 'Health & Safety' heading.

6.12.7   Coping with stressful situations

All professional work has the potential to create stress, but policing presents its own unique challenges in that it involves not only the usual sources of stress when working for a large organization (bureaucracy, differences with colleagues, etc) but also coping with crises, emergencies, and crime. These particular sources of stress also affect the other people involved, for example suspects, victims, and witnesses, and hence police officers often have to manage the reactions of others who are also experiencing stress. There has been a significant increase in the last few years in the number of sick days taken by police officers on the grounds of 'stress-related illness'.

It is difficult to scientifically define exactly what is meant when we say that somebody is suffering from 'stress' (as distinct from the perfectly normal short-term reactions most of us have to a challenging situation). However, most everyday definitions of stress emphasize that it is more continuous than a transient state and instead refers to a persistent collection of 'symptoms' such as psychological disturbances of anxiety, feelings of insecurity, and physiological changes such as palpitations or diarrhoea.

It is important to recognize the symptoms of long-term stress both within yourself, and others. These are many and varied and include feeling generally 'tensed up', irritable, having a short temper, sleep disturbance (particularly insomnia), problems in relationships, poor appetite, and physical symptoms such as headaches. However, professional medical advice is required to properly identify stress as a cause of these problems. Stressful situations do not necessarily give rise to long-term stress and, likewise, a person may be 'stressed' for no apparent reason.

The sources of stress in policing can be thought of as originating from three interrelated contexts: from within the person, from being a member of a police force, and from the external demands placed on police officers. It could well be that susceptibility to stress has a personality dimension. It could be that the very types of people who are attracted to policing are also more vulnerable to suffering from stress (although there is only limited research that supports this). Being a member of a large, complex, and demanding organization such as a police force can easily lead to exposure to sources of stress. The demands placed on police officers, in terms of dealing with the results of crime and disorder (including death and injury), interacting with members of the public, offenders, and the legal profession are also obvious sources of stress. The mistakes that police officers inevitably make are sometimes very visible ones. A particularly stressful event for police officers can be responding to a critical incident, when they may witness disturbing events. No doubt many readers would have heard of the phenomenon of 'Post-Traumatic Stress Disorder', or PTSD.

There are numerous articles, books, and websites with advice on coping with stressful situations. Police forces also have counselling facilities as well as occupational health support (eg through the 'Occupational Support Unit'). The usual advice typically centres on dealing with both the symptoms (which may require specialist medical help) and the causes of stress.

6.13 Answers to Tasks

TASK 1

Your response to the task may have centred on one or more of the following:

- **Ethical or moral reasons**: as a trainee police officer, you subscribe to the values of the Statement as they coincide (more or less) with your own values. Indeed, the reason you joined (or seek to join) the police was perhaps in order to 'protect, help and reassure the community'.
- **Professional reasons**: you have chosen to join a profession of your own free will and so should abide by the rules of that profession.
- **Instrumental reasons**: for example, in order to do my job as a police officer properly (or indeed, to keep my job) I need to subscribe to, and implement, the requirements of the Statement.

The circumstances surrounding the documentary and the political fallout are well documented on the internet and elsewhere. Many commentators have argued that the documentary gave added impetus to the reforms contained within the IPLDP, and particularly those aspects concerned with the values and attitudes of police officers.

TASK 2 There are many techniques for memorizing information (the author Tony Buzan, for example, has written extensively on the subject). We describe one straightforward technique here for memorizing the declaration:

1. Gather ample supplies of blank paper!
2. Now write out (or word-process) the declaration on a blank piece of paper by copying the original. Check and double-check that you have the words exactly as they should be.
3. Read the first sentence several times (not the whole paragraph) and try to commit this to memory.
4. Now turn the page and write down (or word-process), from memory, the first sentence on another piece of paper.
5. Check your recollected version against the original, correct, version word for word.
6. Repeat stages 3–5 until you have the sentence completely correct.
7. Now attempt to memorize the first two sentences together in order.
8. Repeat the process until you have the first two sentences completely correct.
9. Now add the third sentence and so on.
10. Continue until you have committed the complete declaration to memory.

This may take you some hours to achieve. The same technique can be used for memorizing other information—for example, your force might expect you to learn 'definitions'.

TASK 3 Although the police officer concerned was off duty when the alleged incidents took place you have probably noted that the standards for general conduct apply for officers both on and off duty. The standards apparently breached here include Honesty and Integrity, Duties and Responsibilities, and Discreditable Conduct.

TASK 4 The most appropriate Diploma in Policing assessed units would appear to be:

Standard	Relevant Diploma in Policing assessed unit
3. Equality and Diversity	All units
4. Use of Force	Manage conflict
7. Confidentiality	Gather and submit information to support law enforcement objectives

(However, some alternative answers are entirely possible.)

TASK 5 In many police forces, such as Kent Police, you would need permission from at least the BCU commander:

> A police officer or member of police staff who has, or proposes to have, a secondary employment or a business interest must give written notice to the Chief Constable on force e-form 3025NEW, which can be accessed via the list of General forms under MS Word. This is to be forwarded through the individual's line manager to their Divisional Commander/Head of Department for endorsement. (<http://www.kent.police.uk/about_us/policies/l/l087.html>)

In many forces, the responsibility for monitoring the 'secondary business interests' of police officers and police staff is delegated to the head of HR.

TASK 6 You will have your own response to the first part of the task. In relation to receiving an unlawful order, this is most unlikely to occur, but you should still be clear about your own position. The part of the PSNI Code of Ethics referred to in the task was inspired by the Council of Europe Declaration on the police, paras A(4) and A(7). This Declaration makes the case that obeying a superior's orders to undertake unlawful actions, such as the ill-treatment of an individual, or to carry out an unlawful killing, would be no defence for the individual concerned. Similarly, the Basic Principles on the Use of Force and Firearms by Law Enforcement Officials (as adopted by the Eighth Crime Congress of the United Nations Criminal Justice Information Network in 1990) states that:

> [o]bedience to superior orders shall be no defence if law enforcement officials knew that an order to use force and firearms resulting in the death or serious injury of a person was manifestly unlawful and had a reasonable opportunity to refuse to follow it.

TASK 7 The assumption is that consent should be achieved in a positive sense, through gaining the support of the public and involving them in policing decisions and strategies. There is also an emphasis on the need for police to be ever more responsive to community needs, see for example *Policing in the 21st Century: Reconnecting Police and the People* (Home Office, 2010c). In 1829, we would argue, the notion of consent was slightly different—it was measured negatively in the sense that people were consenting only to the extent that they were not proactively objecting to or protesting against policing initiatives.

TASK 8 As we suggested, there are no certain answers to this task. There are interesting examples of attempts by a number of countries to tackle, for example, corruption amongst their police officers through using the kind of analysis that you have just undertaken. For example, in Kenya, police wages in 2004 were almost doubled and corruption subsequently fell. (However, proving that this was cause and effect is somewhat more difficult.)

TASK 9 Drugs policing, in particular, gives rise to a number of opportunities for corruption both in type and frequency (Lee and South, 2003). These include theft from arrested drug dealers, planting drugs to imply guilt, illegally protecting drug dealers (eg by classifying them as a CHIS), and participation in dealing.

TASK 10 The five opportunities from the list are:

- first arrival at the scene of a crime where cash or goods are present;
- handling and storing drugs from police investigations;
- the excessive exercise of discretion without challenge;

- managing informants without adequate supervision or scrutiny; and
- lack of effective supervision.

TASK 11   The free cup of coffee theory may seem to you to be an unlikely explanation, but imagine if a police officer uses his warrant card to secure financial advantage—for example, to gain free entry to a club. Even if he justifies this to himself on the grounds that his (non-uniformed) presence would somehow be to the benefit of the club concerned, would this not lead to at least a small sense of obligation on his part and a potential compromise of his position? As they say in the USA, 'nobody ever gave a cop something for nothing'. The situation is even more complex when a police officer has a second job.

This is not to say that accepting gratuities is always wrong. The circumstances will be a guide, as will force policy. For example, you may be offered cups of tea (or coffee!) by well-meaning members of the public if you are engaged in long and tiring public order duties, and it seems there would be little to lose and much to be gained by accepting the offer on those occasions.

TASK 12   Remember that this theory assumes that the officer has a predisposition towards corruption or deviant behaviour. If this is the case, then he/she is likely to find many reasons that will justify undertaking corrupt acts.

For a comprehensive discussion of this and other aspects of police corruption you might want to read Caless (2008a and 2008b), as well as Newburn (1999) and Miller (2003).

TASK 13   You can establish whether your local force has a branch of the BPA by searching the database on their website.

TASK 14

1. They are both features of the PNC. VODS is a Vehicle Online Descriptive Search application for helping identify vehicles. It can search for combinations of details such as make and model, colour, and VIN (see 16.8.1.1). QUEST is a Query Using Extended Search Techniques facility within PNC, and is the fuzzy capability we referred to earlier. The operator can input partial descriptions of people and produce a list of names that match the characteristics. HMIC have reported the following example of a successful outcome when using QUEST:

In the West Midlands, counterfeit currency was used in a public house. A search was carried out on the description of a white male, 6' tall, thin build with a skinhead haircut, brown hair, aged 20–22 years. The offender had a tattoo of a swallow on his left hand. Enquiries at the scene suggested he lived in Solihull and may have been called 'Barry'. A QUEST search produced one suspect who was subsequently dealt with for the offence. (HMIC, 2005b, p 36)

You might like to conduct further research on the use of Boolean search techniques that use AND, OR, and NOT. These are also useful for conducting internet searches.

Further information is available at <http://www.inbrief.co.uk/police/police-national-computer.htm>. Interestingly there is some evidence that knowledge of these aspects of the PNC is not widespread amongst police officers in some forces (HMIC, 2006, p 9).

2. HMIC is interested in many aspects of a force's use of the PNC including accuracy, timeliness, completeness, relevance, and the overall security of the system.

TASK 15   Agreed, this task requires a gross oversimplification of the theory. However, on most occasions the Handbook would appear to be in adult mode—but there are certainly also aspects of the critical and nurturing parent.

TASK 16   We obviously provide a simplified version of transactional analysis (TA). You might want to read further. A good starting point is Berne's very readable and popular 1968 book *Games People Play* (reissued in the late 1990s), which you are likely to be able pick up second-hand on eBay or at boot sales for very little. The games that Berne refers to are transactions that lead inevitably to predictable outcomes.

Note that TA is not without its critics and some of its academic standing has been damaged by popularized and oversimplified accounts. Another frequent approach (in police training) to analysing the interactions between individuals (or groups) is the use of the so-called 'Johari' window. The unusual name Johari originates from its two inventors, Joseph Luft and Harry Ingham (Luft, 1970). It proposes that one way of analysing aspects of human interaction is to identify areas of personal awareness and ignorance:

	Known to self	Not known to self
Known to others	Open area	Blind area
Not known to others	Hidden area	Unknown area

For example, the blind area includes aspects which the person does not know about him/herself but which others know. This can range from straightforward information (such as a medical complaint like halitosis) to more developed personality features, such as feelings of inadequacy, which are barely discerned by the individuals concerned and yet can be easily seen by others.

TASK 17 The kind of questions you might ask are with reference to your actions, such as entering a person's home, touching a person when conducting a search, and religious requirements for the treatment of the dead.

TASK 18 The correct order starting with the most likely, based upon statistics for 2004, is:

1. as a consequence of lung cancer;
2. as the victim of homicide;
3. by falling down stairs;
4. in a cycling accident;
5. by drowning in a bath;
6. in a train crash;
7. in an aircraft crash; then
8. through being struck by lightning.

TASK 19 What hazards would you identify? The person you are searching could cause you injury as a result of using:

- physical force;
- a weapon or an object he/she is carrying or picks up or takes from you (eg your own personal safety equipment);
- infection such as hepatitis C, tuberculosis (TB), or influenza (flu), or infestation (eg scabies); and/or
- needle injury.

Therefore the hazard level is medium, as you could receive serious injuries or ill health and as a result could be absent from work for more than three days if the person does attack you.

In terms of the risks, you should take into account his/her level of agitation and aggression, how long the search will take, and what opportunity you give (or avoid giving) for the person to use force against you. You should also take into consideration:

- the locality of the search in terms of its proximity to other members of the public;
- how well lit the area is if it is carried out in the dark; and
- whether colleagues are present or nearby when you carry out the search.

The risk level is medium as it is likely or possible that you might be injured. What therefore is the threat level? The threat level is calculated to be moderate.

There are many control measures you could take, for example: request a cover officer if you are alone; carry out personal safety techniques such as standing at the person's side when conducting the search; be aware of the person's movements at all times during the search; engage the person in conversation (because it is difficult for them to think of answers to questions and do other things at the same time); wear gloves to reduce the risk of injury, and wash exposed body parts such as your hands afterwards; consider carrying out the search in the sight line of a town CCTV camera; and remain alert at all times.

TASK 20 The standard CBRN personal protection equipment issued to trained police officers in the event of an incident is the CR1 (CR stands for Civil Responder; the military are issued with their own version). The CR1 is identical to that used by the fire service in similar circumstances. Trainee police officers and special constables should be able to find the CBRN procedures *aide mémoire* on their force intranet.

TASK 21 Naturally, much media attention at the time of the Macpherson Inquiry report centred on the charge of institutional racism. Unfortunately, this inadvertently diverted national attention from the very serious issue of the training of police officers in First Aid and the need for them to maintain

Qualifications and Training

their skills, throughout their careers and at all ranks. Although the Report is clear that Stephen Lawrence's death from his injuries was probably unavoidable, Chapter 10 remains a shocking catalogue of incompetence and ineptitude. It concludes with the observation that:

> [t]his evidence reinforced the Inquiry's views as to the lack of satisfactory and proper training in First Aid for officers of all ranks. Not only should officers be properly trained and be given proper refresher training at regular intervals, but it must be made plain that more senior officers need instruction just as much as junior officers. An officer in the position of [name] must be able to ensure that what is being done by his juniors is proper and satisfactory and in accordance with well-coordinated and directed training. The notion that it may be good enough simply to wait for the ambulance and the paramedics must be exploded. (Macpherson, 1999, s 10.6)

7 Qualification and Professional Development

7.1 Introduction

In this chapter we examine the qualification process for training as a police officer (including pre-join programmes), and the formal assessment systems for the professional development of confirmed officers. By 'qualification' we mean the requirements on pre-join students and trainee police officers in terms of gaining access to a policing career, gaining advanced standing, and qualifying as a police officer.

7.2 Overview of Qualifications

Until relatively recently the usual qualification route for police officers was through joining a police force and undertaking a two-year full-time probationary period of training. There was little, if any, accreditation of prior learning involved and the same model applied to all entrants. There are now some alternative routes into policing and it might well be that the traditional model of entry and qualification will begin to fade away. A significant development in recent years has been the introduction of pre-join (or 'pre-entry') schemes and courses by some colleges, universities, and other providers, sometimes in conjunction with police forces. In late 2013 the Home Office confirmed its intention to introduce a fast-track inspector scheme, recruitment directly to the rank of superintendent, and to allow the appointment of chief constables from overseas (Home Office, 2013g).

The table summarizes the various routes to qualification currently available at the time of writing. APL is accredited prior learning (which will shorten the length of training and the probationary period for some trainee police officers).

Course	Qualification	APL arrangements	Comments
Traditional police training (two years)	Diploma in Policing	N/A	In the past this was the only form of training but it is offered less often now
Police, Law and Community Certificate (University of Portsmouth validated)	Higher Education Certificate or FE Level 3 credits	Towards the knowledge requirements only	Sometimes referred to as 'PLC'. Students complete Diploma in Policing after joining the police
Certificate in Knowledge of Policing	FE Level 3, but can be incorporated into HE programmes	Towards the knowledge requirements only	Sometimes called the 'CKP' or the Policing Knowledge Certificate, (PKC). Pre-employment qualification to be obtained before application. Students complete Diploma in Policing after joining the police
Foundation Degree in Policing, Police Studies, or related discipline	FdA or FdSc. Often linked with joining Special Constabulary	Towards knowledge requirements. Towards competence requirements if linked with Special Constabulary	For example, the University of Central Lancaster's Foundation Degree in Policing. Students complete Diploma in Policing before or after joining

Honours Degree in Policing, Police Studies or related discipline	BA (Hons) or BSc (Hons)	Towards knowledge requirements. Towards competence requirements if linked with Special Constabulary	Typically three years in duration (full-time), compared to two years for a FdA or FdSc. Students complete Diploma in Policing before or after joining

7.2.1 Pre-join programmes

Students on such programmes complete some of the learning and training required to become a full-time police constable before they join a police force. The College of Policing (CoP) expects the content of pre-join programmes to articulate with the Pre-join Knowledge Curriculum leading to a Certificate in Knowledge of Policing (CKP) within the Diploma in Policing (see 7.3) (NPIA, 2012, p 8). The CoP is also operating an 'Approved Provider Scheme' for pre-join programmes (particularly providers of the new Certificate) as part of its 'Pre-join Strategy'. At the time of writing (2014) 33 organizations have been approved including three distance-learning providers (CoP, 2014a). One important influence on the rapid growth in pre-join programmes is the ongoing economic necessity for police forces to reduce the cost of training. However, the development of pre-join courses is also linked with a wider move towards professionalization (see 3.7 and 3.10).

Pre-join programmes are either stand-alone (eg a course leading only to the CKP) or may be embedded within longer programmes of study, such as a Foundation degree in Policing or Police Studies.

Although pre-join programmes are relatively new, some concern has already been expressed regarding their possible adverse impact on the representation of particular social and ethnic groups in policing (particularly mature entrants—the CKP as offered by further and higher education tends to attract the 18–20-year-old cohort). This is especially the case where a pre-join programme is also a full-time undergraduate programme that also requires students to become special constables (CoP, 2014g).

Very few (if any) of the existing programmes (successfully completed) guarantee entry to the full-time police, or even an interview with a police force. (Even if a police force were willing in principle to guarantee entry, there would still be the hurdle of the nationally determined recruitment assessment process.) Nor are they always the only route into training as a police officer with a particular force. The APL value of a pre-join programme is likely to vary between 'receiving' police forces. (However, the CoP has established a set of 'principles' to guide force policy.) The CoP warn (CoP, 2014g, p 5) that the currency of a completed pre-join programme is normally three years, or four years for a PCSO or special constable continually engaged with operational duties. So entry to the police will need to be achieved within this time limit to gain the maximum APL for subsequent IPLDP training.

7.3 The Certificate in Knowledge of Policing and the Diploma in Policing

The Certificate in Knowledge of Policing and the Diploma in Policing are based around the 21 NOS units for initial policing (listed in 1.4.3, and explained in more detail in 7.4). The CKP essentially covers the knowledge aspects of the Diploma, and equates to roughly 50 per cent of the Diploma in Policing. The evidence collected as part of the assessment for the CKP can be used as a form of APL against the requirements of the Diploma when undertaking initial training with a police force. The CKP does not include any operational work-based policing assessments, and so successful completion of this qualification does not indicate operational competency.

Each of the Certificate and Diploma units are divided into learning outcomes with associated content and assessment criteria. For example, the content for the Certificate learning outcome to 'understand the relevant legal and organizational requirements relating to the arresting, detention and reporting of individuals' is likely to cover aspects of the PACE Codes of Practice and the HRA (see Chapter 5). The assessment criteria for each learning outcome give an indication of what the learner has to do to show that a learning outcome has been achieved. Further information concerning the assessment of the Certificate and the Diploma units and learning outcomes is provided in 8.5.1.

Both the Certificate and the Diploma are at QCF Level 3 which is roughly 'A' level standard, but it is invidious to draw simple comparisons between academic awards and hybrid occupational qualifications such as the Diploma in Policing. This is because the Diploma signifies occupational competence, which normally requires a combination of both theoretical understanding and practical application. It is reasonable that an HE Level 4 or 5 award (such as a Foundation degree) has a FE Level 3 Diploma representing competence embedded within it: after all, a person's practical ability to undertake a role within a profession often falls short of his/her theoretical understanding of the same set of tasks.

The Certificate and the Diploma are currently awarded by four awarding bodies (City and Guilds, SfJ Awards, Edexcel, and OCR), and can also be awarded by police forces, universities, and FE colleges, subject to registration with an awarding body and approval by the College of Policing. Some police forces are designated as an 'approved centre' for an awarding body and can therefore offer the Certificate and Diploma under licence, sometimes in partnership with a local college, university, or private sector provider.

The ten Certificate units cover the knowledge required for a range of policing activities. The Certificate carries a total of 23 credits (with the number of credits for each unit shown in brackets), and although it is a QCF Level 3 qualification overall, a few of the units are at Level 4.

Certificate in Knowledge of Policing Units	Learning outcome(s)
Knowledge of providing initial support to victims and witnesses within a policing context (1)	Understand the factors that affect victims and witnesses and impact on their need for support
Knowledge of gathering and submitting information to support law enforcement objectives within a policing context (1)	Understand relevant legal and organizational requirements related to gathering and submitting information
Knowledge of providing an initial response to incidents within a policing context (2)	Understand relevant legal and organizational requirements for responding to an incident Understand how to gather information and plan a response to an incident
Knowledge of arresting, detaining, and reporting individuals within a policing context (3)	Understand relevant legal and organizational requirements relating to the arresting, detention, and reporting of individuals
Knowledge of conducting priority and volume investigations within a policing context (4)	Understand the legal and organizational requirements in relation to conducting priority and volume investigations Understand the professional practice applicable to conducting priority and volume investigations
Knowledge of interviewing victims and witnesses in relation to priority and volume investigations within a policing context (3)	Understand relevant legal and organizational requirements in relation to interviewing victims and witnesses Understand the principles of interviewing victims and witnesses
Knowledge of interviewing suspects in relation to priority and volume investigations within a policing context (3)	Understand relevant legal and organizational requirements in relation to interviewing suspects Understand the principles of interviewing suspects
Knowledge of searching individuals in a policing context (2)	Understand legal and organizational requirements in relation to searching individuals
Knowledge of searching vehicles, premises, and open spaces within a policing context (2)	Understand legal and organizational requirements in relation to searching vehicles, premises, and open spaces
Knowledge of managing conflict in a policing context (2)	Know the legislation and other relevant guidance related to managing conflict Understand how to apply conflict management skills and techniques

(Table contents based on Ofqual, 2013a)

The ten Diploma units cover the knowledge required for a range of policing activities (as in the Certificate in Knowledge of Policing) but also cover the associated skills. Each Diploma unit carries between two and five credits, making a total of 38 credits (the credit value for each unit is shown in brackets in the table). For a QCF Diploma a minimum of 37 credits is generally required, with each credit involving a notional ten hours of learning. For the Diploma in Policing, and as part of the requirement for confirmation (see 8.4), all 38 credits are required.

Qualifications and Training

Diploma in Policing Unit	Learning outcomes
Provide initial support to victims and witnesses (3)	Know and understand the factors that affect victims and witnesses and impact on their need for support
	Be able to communicate effectively with victims and witnesses
	Be able to provide initial support to victims and witnesses
	Be able to assess the needs and wishes of victims and witnesses for further support
Gather and submit information to support law enforcement objectives (2)	Know and understand relevant legal and organizational requirements related to gathering and submitting information
	Be able to gather and submit information that has the potential to support law enforcement objectives
Provide an initial response to incidents (4)	Know and understand relevant legal and organizational requirements for responding to an incident
	Be able to gather information and plan a response to an incident
	Be able to respond to incidents
Arrest, detain, and report individuals (4)	Know and understand relevant legal and organizational requirements relating to the arresting, detention, and reporting of individuals
	Be able to arrest and detain individuals
	Be able to report individuals
Conduct priority and volume investigations (5)	Know and understand the legal and organizational requirements in relation to conducting priority and volume investigations
	Know and understand the professional practice applicable to conducting priority and volume investigations
	Be able to conduct priority and volume investigations
	Be able to complete and submit documentation relating to priority and volume investigations.
Interview victims and witnesses in relation to priority and volume investigations (5)	Know and understand relevant legal and organizational requirements in relation to interviewing victims and witnesses
	Know and understand the principles of interviewing victims and witnesses
	Be able to plan and prepare interviews with victims and witnesses
	Be able to conduct interview with victims and witnesses
	Know how to evaluate and carry out post-interview procedures with victims and witnesses
Interview suspects in relation to priority and volume investigations (5)	Know and understand relevant legal and organizational requirements in relation to interviewing suspects
	Know and understand the principles of interviewing suspects
	Be able to plan and prepare interviews with suspects
	Be able to conduct an interview with a suspect
	Be able to evaluate interviews with suspects and carry out post-interview procedures
Search individuals in a policing context (3)	Know and understand legal and organizational requirements in relation to searching individuals
	Be able to search individuals
Search vehicles, premises, and open spaces (4)	Understand legal and organizational requirements in relation to searching vehicles, premises, and open spaces
	Be able to prepare to search vehicles, premises, and open spaces
	Be able to conduct searches of vehicles, premises, and open spaces
Manage conflict in a policing context (3)	Understand legislation and other relevant guidance related to managing conflict
	Be able to apply conflict management skills and techniques
	Use personal safety skills and any issued equipment

(Adapted from Ofqual, 2013b)

Students who have taken an approved pre-entry programme (such as the Certificate in Knowledge of Policing), or who were previously a special constable or a PCSO should be able to claim 'advanced standing' against the assessment requirements of the Diploma through APL (see 7.2).

7.4 National Occupational Standards and NOS Units

The National Occupational Standards (NOS) are a set of statements that describe the competence required to undertake a certain occupation or to use a set of particular skills and form the basis of qualifications for certain occupations—for example, training to become a police officer. By inference (but sometimes explicitly) the standards relate competence to the knowledge and understanding required. The NOS are usually grouped together to form a number of units.

The initial training for trainee police officers is underpinned by 21 NOS units (see 1.4.3 for a list of the unit titles). Some of these units are the same as those used by other occupational groups—for example, in First Aid. This makes sense as some of the tasks performed by a police officer will be similar to those performed by parallel occupational groups. Indeed, the police often work alongside other professionals who have been trained to the same occupational standard. Trainee police officers will also find that some other professional requirements for initial training, for example PIP Level 1, are linked closely with some of the NOS.

If you have recently been assessed on academic courses at a college or university through taking exams or writing essays, then the approach adopted for assessment of the NOS units underpinning the Diploma in Policing may be unfamiliar. Assessment against NOS is much more like taking a driving test than sitting an examination in biology. First, the emphasis is on evidence of knowing how to do something. When you take a driving test, the examiner is not overly concerned with how you managed to gain the skills, but rather that you can actually drive— that you possess those skills. You could have been taught by your sister, or by the most expensive driving school in the country, or (most unlikely) have simply paid close attention to car-chase sequences in films. However, what matters is your ability to drive safely, competently, and to the agreed standards. Although the standards for initial policing do not work in quite the same way as for taking a driving test, the emphasis is still very much on the assessment of the end-product. You will also be assessed and judged in other ways whilst undertaking initial police training: for example, your attitudes and behaviour will come under close scrutiny against the Personal Qualities for a constable contained in the Policing Professional Framework (PPF—see 8.5.2) and you might well be expected to demonstrate that you have reached a certain level in your understanding of legislation and procedure. Nonetheless the main emphasis in a trainee's formal assessment is likely to be on the final 'threshold' standards that you will need to achieve before you can be confirmed as a constable.

Each of the NOS units is divided into elements (one or more, typically two or three in the case of initial policing) as shown in 7.4.1. The elements define more precisely the competence for each unit. Each element has a number of performance criteria, and these indicate the likely actions and behaviours expected from the trainee for demonstrating competence for the element. For example, as shown in the table the NOS unit to 'CJ201 Interview suspects in relation to priority and volume investigations' contains three elements, one of which is 'plan and prepare interviews with suspects'. One of that element's performance criteria is 'assess any factors affecting the suspect's fitness for interview and the necessity for appropriate people to be in attendance'. The performance criteria show what the student needs to do, and what the assessor needs to assess.

7.4.1 Links between the NOS units and the Diploma in Policing

The ten Diploma in Policing units are each based on one of the 21 NOS units. These ten NOS units are therefore fully assessed within the Diploma. A further five NOS units are embedded within the ten Diploma units, and the NOS unit on searching is partly assessed. Of the remaining five NOS units, four are not assessed within the Diploma and the final NOS unit (on First Aid) is assessed separately (see 7.4.1 for details). The ten NOS units and their elements that are wholly assessed in the Diploma are shown in the following table. You will notice that the titles of these ten NOS units are similar to the Unit titles for the Diploma; this is because their content is similar.

NOS initial policing units that are wholly assessed in the Diploma in Policing

NOS units		NOS elements	
BE2	Provide initial support to victims, survivors, and witnesses and assess their needs for further support	BE2.1	Provide initial support to victims, survivors, and witnesses
		BE2.2	Assess the needs and wishes of victims, survivors, and witnesses for further support

NOS units		NOS elements	
CB1	Gather and submit information that has the potential to support law enforcement objectives	CB1.1	Gather and submit information that has the potential to support law enforcement objectives
CD1	Provide an initial law enforcement response to incidents	CD1.1	Gather information and plan a response
		CD1.2	Respond to incidents
CD5	Arrest, detain, or report individuals	CD5.1	Arrest, detain, or report individuals
CI101	Conduct priority and volume investigations	CI101.1	Conduct priority and volume investigations
CJ101	Interview victims and witnesses in relation to priority and volume investigations	CJ101.1	Plan and prepare interviews with victims and witnesses
		CJ101.2	Conduct interviews with victims and witnesses
		CJ101.3	Evaluate interviews with victims and witnesses and carry out post-interview processes
CJ201	Interview suspects in relation to priority and volume investigations	CJ201.1	Plan and prepare interviews with suspects
		CJ201.2	Conduct interviews with suspects
		CJ201.3	Evaluate interviews with suspects and carry out post-interview processes
CK1	Search individuals in a policing context	CK1.1	Search individuals
CK2	Search vehicles, premises, and open spaces	CK2.1	Prepare to search vehicles, premises, and open spaces
		CK2.2	Conduct searches of vehicles, premises, and open spaces
GC10	Manage conflict in a policing context	GC10.1	Apply conflict management skills and techniques
		GC10.2	Use personal safety skills and equipment

A further five NOS units are relevant to many aspects of policing. These have therefore been 'embedded' within the ten NOS units that are formally assessed as part of the Diploma in Policing.

NOS initial policing units that are embedded in the Diploma

NOS units		NOS elements	
AA1	Promote equality and value diversity	AA1.1	Promote equality and value diversity
AB1	Communicate effectively	AB1.1	Develop and maintain communication with people
		AB1.2	Maintain the security of information
AE1	Maintain and develop your own knowledge, skills, and competence	AE1.1	Maintain and develop your own knowledge, skills, and competence
AF1	Ensure your own actions reduce risks to health and safety	AF1.1	Identify the hazards and evaluate the risks in the work place
		AF1.2	Reduce the risks to health and safety in the work place
CA1	Use law enforcement actions in a fair and justified way	CA1.1	Apply principles of reasonable suspicion or belief
		CA1.2	Use law enforcement actions proportionately
		CA1.3	Use law enforcement actions fairly

Qualifications and Training

Selected aspects of the NOS Unit CD3 are formally assessed and integrated into the two Diploma units that relate to searches (CK1 and CK2, see earlier table 'NOS initial policing units that are wholly assessed in the Diploma in Policing').

CD3	Prepare for, and participate in, planned law enforcement operations	CD3.1	Prepare for, and participate in, planned law enforcement operations

Four of the remaining five NOS units, although underpinning initial police training, are not likely to be formally assessed (although some of their elements may be mapped to specific assessment criteria of learning outcomes of the Diploma), and the remaining unit, concerned with administering First Aid, is assessed independently of the Diploma.

NOS initial policing units that are not formally assessed in the Diploma

NOS units		NOS elements	
2K1	Escort detained persons	2K1.1	Escort detained persons
2K2	Present detained persons to custody	2K2.1	Present detained persons for custody process
		2K2.2	Conduct initial custody reception actions
DA5	Present evidence in court and at other hearings	DA5.1	Prepare for court or other hearings
		DA5.2	Present evidence to court or other hearings
DA6	Prepare and submit case files	DA6.1	Prepare case files
		DA6.2	Submit case files and progress enquiries

NOS initial policing unit that is not assessed as part of the Diploma (but is separately assessed)

NOS unit		NOS elements	
4G4	Administer First Aid	4G4.1	Respond to the needs of casualties with minor injuries
		4G4.2	Respond to the needs of casualties with major injuries
		4G4.3	Respond to the needs of unconscious casualties
		4G4.4	Perform cardio-pulmonary resuscitation (CPR)

You should be aware that the requirements for assessments relating to the NOS can change quite quickly, both in terms of the number of units and their content.

7.5 PIP Level 1

In 2004, the Home Office and ACPO commissioned the NCPE to devise a Professionalizing Investigation Programme (PIP) in response to a widespread perceived need to improve the quality of police investigation of crime (Centrex, 2005). A total of four levels are available as shown in the table.

Level	Associated staff/police rank	Type of investigation or crime
1	Patrol Constable/Police Staff/Supervisors	Investigation of volume crime
2	Dedicated Investigator, eg CID officer	Substantive investigation into more serious and problem offences, including road traffic deaths
3	Senior Investigating Officer	Lead investigator in cases of murder, stranger rape, kidnap, or crimes of complexity—Category A–C
4	Principal Investigating Officer/Officer in Overall Command (OIOC)	Critical, complex, protracted, and/or linked serious crime—Category A+

(Derived from Centrex, 2005)

PIP Level 1 is included in initial pre-qualification police training and covers interviewing techniques, investigation methods and models, law, case files, major and serious crime procedures, ranging from petty theft to 'Cat C' murders. It is integrated into the IPLDP curriculum and has also been mapped against three of the NOS units used for the Diploma in Policing:

- CI101 Conduct priority and volume investigations;
- CJ101 Interview victims and witnesses in relation to priority and volume investigations; and
- CJ201 Interview suspects in relation to priority and volume investigations.

These units also feature within the operational modules of the IPLDP—for example, CJ101 and CJ201 have been mapped against OP6 'Prepare, conduct, and evaluate interviews'. It is therefore unlikely that a trainee officer will achieve PIP Level 1 until the end of his/her first year of training (at the earliest), and it is more likely to be during the second year.

After successfully completing PIP Level 1 a trainee officer will be 'signed off' as a Level 1 investigator and be registered with his/her force as having reached this standard. However, in order to remain registered all police officers have to demonstrate on a regular basis that their skills and knowledge have been maintained.

7.6 Professional Development

In this part of Chapter 7 we examine the professional development opportunities that might present themselves to you after (or even just before) you become a qualified police officer, including applying for promotion. Towards the end of your training (or in some forces, in the second year of training) you may be asked to consider the possibility of undertaking a specialist role within your force.

One of the first decisions will be whether to specialize or generalize. You should refer to the Policing Professional Framework (see 8.5.2) personal qualities for the constable role at this point, and remind yourself what is involved in reaching the required standard for the generic role.

You will already have the behavioural competencies; you are able to complete the administration procedures associated with the role, maintain the standards of professional practice, work as part of a team, provide First Aid when required, and comply with health and safety legislation. You will also make the best use of technology (both in IT and telephony) and you promote equality, diversity, and human rights in all your working practices, as well as being part of an organizational response which recognizes the needs of all communities. You employ an effective problem-solving approach to all community issues in which you become involved and you make good use of intelligence to support the policing objectives of your force.

Thus equipped, you should be ready to take on any general task as a constable, and to serve anywhere in the force that you are needed. For some people that is enough and they are perfectly happy refining these competencies and behaviours, building experience, and interacting with the public on a daily basis; some officers will never want to move away from this generic role for their entire careers.

7.6.1 Specialist roles

As a trainee police officer you will have been exposed to the work of three major divisions of policing during your initial training: investigation, patrol policing, and community policing. We now examine each of the three areas in turn.

7.6.1.1 Investigative policing

A decision to follow the investigative route does not mean that you are closing off the other avenues forever. It is quite common to move in and out of roles and across the streams of central police work, but as a rule you will stay within the detective branch or department if you specialize in investigation. In many forces, the route to becoming a skilled investigator is through service on an investigation team based locally in a BCU. In some forces, this is called a 'tactical criminal investigation department' or TAC CID.

Level 1 PIP is linked with the IPLDP and the NOS units/Diploma in Policing assessment units for initial policing, so Level 1 is automatically achieved on successful completion of initial training (see 7.5). The Initial Crime Investigators' Development Programme (ICIDP) is a police force programme for trainee Detective Constables (TDCs) and provides the basis for the investigation of more serious and complex criminal cases. (It is also sometimes referred to as the

National ICIDP (NICIDP).) The ICIDP is linked with PIP Level 2, which is in turn linked with three NOS units relevant to serious and complex investigations; CI102, CJ102, and CJ202 ('Conduct serious and complex investigations', 'Interview victims and witnesses in relation to serious and complex investigations', and 'Interview suspects in relation to serious and complex investigations', respectively). These are more demanding than the parallel NOS units for initial police training listed in 7.4.1.

The ICIDP consists of three phases, summarized as follows. Details are available from local police forces.

- **Phase 1** (for the trainee investigator) is a period of self-study using printed materials, and typically takes a minimum of 14 weeks to complete. The content is law-based and covers property offences, assaults, drugs, firearms, sexual offences, offences against children and other vulnerable persons, and evidence.

- **Phase 2** is typically a six-week taught course, and concludes with sitting the National Investigators Examination (NIE), a multiple-choice examination consisting of 80 questions which tests knowledge of the four sub-areas: property offences; assaults, drugs, firearms, and gun crime; sexual offences; and evidence (CoP, 2014h, p 68). There is some flexibility on how forces structure the course (eg some base it on a case study and might also incorporate a 'Hydra' simulation). However, all courses are likely to be linked to the NOS units and elements, to subscribe to the NPIA specified aims and objectives, and will at least cross-reference with the ACPO Core Investigative Doctrine. In many forces, before commencing Phase 2 there is also a requirement to complete a 'tier 2' investigating interview course after initial training. The methods used for assessment of the knowledge and understanding gained during Phase 2 vary between forces (eg whether a formal written examination is set or not).

- **Phase 3** will always involve demonstration and assessment of competence in the work place against the three NOS units (CI102, CJ102, and CJ202). A tutor (normally an Accredited Detective Constable (Level 2) or an Investigative Adviser) will provide supervision, and evidence must be collected in a Professional Development Portfolio (PDP). Experienced investigators (who will have been in position before the advent of the ICIDP) are able to access Phase 3 through APL procedures. On successful completion of Phase 3, investigators are 'registered' at the BCU level as qualified at PIP Level 2.

Officers may then move to internal force departments such as a central unit investigating Level 2 serious crime, or join a specialist homicide team, investigating 'Cat A' and 'Cat B' murders, manslaughter, or GBH. This will probably involve taking the **Initial Management of Serious Crime** (IMSC) course, which is designed primarily for detective sergeants and is, in effect, a bridging course between the ICIDP and the more advanced programmes for SIOs. After completing the IMSC course and attaining the rank of detective inspector, an investigator might choose to undertake the College of Policing three-week 'Detective Inspector Development Programme (DIDP)' as a further career step.

The Senior Investigating Officer Development Programme (SIODP) is designed for investigators who are already qualified to at least PIP Level 2 (eg through the ICIDP) or its equivalent, and who are likely to become responsible for investigating serious crime such as homicide and rape by a stranger. Students of the SIODP are typically of detective inspector rank or above. As with IPLDP and ICIDP, the SIODP is linked with the NOS, in this case the single unit CI103, 'Manage major investigations' (with a total of five elements). The course typically lasts 15 days. A one-week 'Hydra' simulation course (based on the investigation of a serious crime) is also often recommended as a follow-up, and is in some cases a compulsory element. The SIODP is usually delivered on a regional rather than local-force basis in order to provide good access to specialist inputs, and also for economy of scale (the numbers involved are significantly lower than for the ICIDP). The course usually covers the ACPO Core Investigative Doctrine (particularly in terms of initial response, gathering information, and the use of forensic investigation), multi-agency working, family liaison, resource management, the use of intelligence, record keeping (particularly in terms of policy logging and disclosure), self-evaluation and the evaluation of others, and handling the media. Evidence for claiming competence is presented in a PDP, and successful completion results in achievement of PIP Level 3.

Qualifications and Training

7.6.1.2 Patrol policing

If you decide that Patrol is your preferred interest, there are plenty of roles to take, such as Traffic, Tactical Operations, Firearms, and Public Order. In this type of work you will be at the forefront of visible uniformed policing. As for investigation, specializing within Patrol will involve a fair amount of training and will follow a systematic development route. One of the things you should consider, before opting to go into the Patrol stream, is what opportunities there are for you to obtain further qualifications, and to find out whether there is a partnership programme with academic institutions. If Patrol is a 'default option' in your force, and there is little evident development or systematic learning, you might want to think twice before committing yourself. If, on the other hand, your force is pursuing partnerships, links, and development opportunities, you will find that Patrol is far from a backwater and may be the most vibrant and innovative part of your force. It very much depends on your local circumstances.

There is no doubt that Patrol can be an immensely satisfying part of policing: you will often be the first officer attending a crime scene (with all the responsibilities we outline in Chapter 11, in terms of the 'golden hour' and your vital role in the preservation of life and of evidence), and you will have a major part to play in policing demonstrations, large gatherings, public events, and disorder. Your contact with the public will be an integral part of the reassurance agenda and you will be mainly involved with the policing of volume crime and public disorder. It is the most physically demanding of all police roles, and you will also be in the forefront of dealing with violence, collisions, tragedies, and human disaster. The dynamic risk assessments for many of the roles in Patrol will be crucial for police and public safety; you should not underestimate the strains and stresses of front-line police work.

7.6.1.3 Community (neighbourhood) policing

Community and neighbourhood policing is different again. Here, you will work with smaller teams, and the work will often help form an important bridge between Patrol and Investigation. You will learn new skills and your development will probably be geared to specializing in one of a number of roles. For example, you may opt to work as a Community Liaison Officer (CLO), in which case you will get to know the leaders and members of groups within your local community and help to develop sophisticated partnership-working arrangements to meet community needs. Diversity skills will be vital, as will the accumulation of intelligence on crime in the community. You will often be the first port of call from your detective colleagues when investigating crime within your area, and your advice will be needed, and usually respected and acted upon, especially when there are local sensitivities, such as minority ethnic communities or the investigation of a homophobic crime.

You may become part of a Neighbourhood Policing Team (NPT) alongside members of the wider policing family such as PCSOs and special constables. This will involve both responding to local issues and needs surrounding crime and disorder (often in collaboration with other agencies, such as local authorities), and taking proactive action in reassuring the public. You will be a named contact for members of the local community, and will help them access their local policing services. Community policing also involves providing feedback on actions taken and the consequences.

A Family Liaison Officer (FLO) has a specialist role within community policing. They are trained in negotiation, mediation, and some group-management techniques so that their work with families (usually the victims or witnesses of crime) is as productive, reassuring, and positive as possible. A FLO can provide a focus for the family in the wake of a crime, especially a crime of violence, and will help them through the difficulties of the search for the offender, arrest, charge, and the subsequent court proceedings. In a very real sense, a FLO is the 'face of policing' to that family, and will often help them provide vital evidence. For example a FLO played a leading part in obtaining evidence in the Russell murders case in Kent in 1996. This was a particularly disturbing crime, in which a mother and her two daughters on a rural footpath were attacked with a hammer or similar instrument. The mother and one of the daughters died but the older daughter survived. In the investigation which followed, the FLO's skills were vital in gaining her trust, and this was integral to the successful prosecution of Michael Stone for the murders.

Qualifications and Training

Working closely with neighbourhoods and their varied communities is, for many officers, what policing is really about, and offers its greatest rewards. This is not to say that the work is easy; to gain the community's trust and respect means working long hours, having highly developed personal skills, and understanding how community dynamics and partnerships work. The development of NPTs based on BCUs, in which there may be a mix of police officers, PCSOs, special constables, and members of other agencies, is a pointer to the importance of local and citizen-focused engagement. Should you opt for a community-policing role, you may well find yourself in time supervising the work of others, and/or managing a neighbourhood-policing team. Many officers find this a deeply satisfying activity and are reluctant to leave it. Other work, such as crime reduction, schools' liaison, and working with crime-reduction partnerships also provide considerable rewards in return for persistence, professionalism, and receptivity, but the results in terms of crime reduction are often long-term, rather than immediate. Communities appear to dislike frequent changes of police personnel and it takes time to build relationships. If you opt for community policing, you need to be aware that it is often for the long haul.

7.6.2   Personal development

Whether you seek promotion early or not, you have an obligation to sustain your continuous professional development (CPD). The nature of this CPD varies from force to force; in some it means gaining the necessary experience and qualification through training (such as in Firearms or the ICIDP programme—see 7.6.1.1). In other forces it can mean pursuing further study which links your professional development with an academic partner, resulting in a further academic award such as a two-year occupation-based Foundation degree, vocational qualifications such as an NVQ or SNVQ, or a higher education award such as a BSc (Hons) in Policing or a Master's degree. Some forces allow all these forms of CPD, which seek to develop the skills and capabilities you will need as you progress in policing (laterally or vertically). Your force is likely to have a number of academic partners through whom further professional study may be pursued, but, if not, plenty of institutions advertise their courses or programmes in publications and websites such as *Police Professional*.

Note that you will probably need permission to engage in further study, since the force has to balance your CPD with the demands of your current job. After all, studying could add up to 25 hours to the working week, although this could be justified in both organizational terms (increased professionalism) and individual aspiration. If the agreed further study is directly related to your policing function, your force might pay the fees and allow you some duty time to study, but always check first.

7.6.3   Achieving promotion

If you are a trainee police officer then your first priority will obviously be to achieve full confirmation at the end of two years' training. However, if not now, then probably at some time in the future, you may begin to think about promotion to a higher rank. Whenever possible you should talk to those already holding the substantive rank and find out what they do and why. You will also need to look at the competencies and role requirements of the generic sergeant role and any specialist functions which a supervisor performs. If you can, you should seek opportunities to 'act up' in the rank, perhaps by supervising a patrol of constables for a limited time, or by seeking temporary promotion whenever it is offered. It is helpful here to understand a difference in terminology: acting rank means that you do it for a short time, probably on a casual basis; temporary rank means that you perform the role of that rank for a period of at least three months, and you receive the pay of that rank. It is not a requirement in the police service, as it is in the armed forces, to spend some time in the acting rank before being eligible for consideration for promotion. However, the opportunity for an officer to act in the rank above is often a good opportunity for showing that he/she can do the next job; it accrues experience in the role and gives the opportunity for assessors to make judgements on a person's actual performance, rather than simply on potential.

OSPRE® (the Objective Structured Performance-Related Police Promotion Exam) forms part of the process for assessing candidates for promotion. The trademark is owned by the Home Sec-

Qualifications and Training

retary, and the only authorized licensee in 2013 was the College of Policing. Note that as a result of the recent introduction of the new College of Policing professional body, the approach to achieving promotion could change (see 7.6.3.3).

Whatever system is used, any officer who is likely to be seeking promotion should maintain the good practice from his/her initial training, such as:

- recording experiences and learning, and reflecting on the learning;
- evidencing competencies and showing how skills have developed;
- keeping detailed notes on the variety of policing experiences encountered; and
- ensuring that professional development portfolios are kept up to date.

7.6.3.1 Promotion from constable to sergeant

The statutory basis for promotion of constables to sergeant in England and Wales is to be found in the Police (Promotion) Regulations 1996, incorporating the Police (Promotion) (Amendment) Regulations 2005. In most police forces in England and Wales the current system for promotion from constable to sergeant requires the applicant to:

- be a 'substantive' constable (ie have successfully completed the probationary period of initial training and hence be confirmed);
- have passed the Sergeants' OSPRE® Parts I and II;
- have gained the support of their immediate line manager, for example an inspector;
- have no adverse disciplinary or attendance records;
- have evidence of potential or actual leadership ability (eg through the PDR); and then
- successfully pass an interview process (a 'Promotion Panel').

Part I of the Sergeants' OSPRE® is a three-hour multiple-choice examination paper with 150 questions. The syllabus may vary from year to year. In 2012 the syllabus was divided into four categories: crime, evidence and procedure, road policing, and general police duties (CoP, 2013f). Each of the four subject categories is then further divided into greater detail (eg 'handling stolen goods'), and related to legislation where applicable. The passmark for Part I is currently 55 per cent (CoP, 2013a).

Part II is an Assessment Centre based on assessing seven behavioural competencies (derived from the PPF competencies, see 8.5.2). The competencies are: Serving the Public, Leading Change, Leading People, Managing Performance, Professionalism, Decision-making, and Working with Others (CoP, 2013c). The Assessment Centre consists of pre-read material (including a detailed description of a fictitious police division), and then a series of five scenarios based around the day-to-day work of a police sergeant. Each scenario covers five of the seven competences, such that all seven are assessed on a number of occasions. For example, one scenario might consist of a letter from a member of the public complaining of acts of vandalism apparently directed at the property of a gay and lesbian support group, and a covering memo from an Inspector asking the candidate (in the role of Sergeant) to investigate the matter further. For each scenario the candidate's performance for each competency is marked by an assessor on a scale of 1 to 5 ('very effective task performance', 'purposeful', etc. through to 'very ineffective task performance', 'superficial' etc). All the scores are then used to calculate an overall grade (A to D) for each of the seven competencies. The College of Policing stated in 2012 that the pass-mark was 45 per cent (CoP, 2013g, p 12). Condonement appears to have been permitted for all the competency areas (that is, a low mark in one area can be compensated for by a high mark elsewhere), apart from for 'Working with Others'; here a D grade might lead to overall failure of Part II (CoP, 2013e).

Part II must be passed within 12 months of passing Part I (NPIA, 2011e, p 10). Passing the OSPRE® examinations alone is no guarantee of promotion from constable to sergeant because permanent promotion will depend upon the availability of vacant posts and meeting other criteria as outlined earlier.

7.6.3.2 Promotion from sergeant to inspector

In England and Wales the current system for promotion from sergeant to inspector is similar in structure to the system for promotion to sergeant (see 7.6.3.1), but of course at a higher level. Applicants are normally required to be of sergeant rank; to have passed the Inspectors' OSPRE® Parts I and II; to have no adverse disciplinary or attendance records; to have evidence of potential or actual leadership ability (eg through a number of recent PDRs); and then to successfully pass an interview process (a 'Promotion Panel'). As for promotion to sergeant, passing the relevant OSPRE® examinations does not guarantee permanent promotion. The structure, content, and requirements of Part I and II are very similar to the system for promotion to sergeant (see 7.6.3.1), except that the content is more demanding and the passmark for Part I is higher at 65 per cent.

7.6.3.3   The National Police Promotion Framework

The NPIA National Police Promotion Framework (NPPF) is a proposed new system for promotion to sergeant and inspector ranks, which might replace the current arrangements (NPIA, 2008b).

The NPPF involves four steps:

1. assessment of candidate's competence in his/her current rank through the PDR;
2. Part 1 OSPRE® examination process (described earlier);
3. assessment against role-specific competencies and matching these to the existing vacancies (eg by structured interviews or psychometric testing);
4. temporary promotion and work-based assessment (WBA) for a period of least 12 months, during which the individual will be required to demonstrate competence in the role (against the National Occupational Standards).

Seven police forces have been trialling this new 'Stepwise' approach. The NPIA's 2011 evaluation found mixed outcomes: police forces were better able to match candidate numbers to vacancy numbers, but the NPPF was also considered to be more bureaucratic than OSPRE®. In mid-2012 the Minister for Policing deferred the decision on national roll out of the NPPF to the College of Policing (CoP, 2013d), which at the time of writing (early 2014) had yet to make a decision (CoP, 2014f).

7.6.3.4   The High Potential Development Scheme

The High Potential Development Scheme (HPDS) is a programme to 'develop high calibre future leaders' (CoP, 2014c, p 3) for the police service. Successful 'graduates' of the HPDS are expected to reach at least the rank of superintendent during their careers, although in terms of promotion they must meet the same standards of other promoted officers (*ibid*, p 17). The HPDS is deliberately targeted only at constables (including trainees) and sergeants. Content of the HPDS includes 'Leadership and Public Value, Managing People and Change, Operations and Performance Management, Partnership Working, Stakeholder Management and Community Engagement, Policy Making and Strategy, and Managing and Using Resources' (CoP, 2014f). The HPDS is now a four- or five-year programme for those continuing to the Master's stage (this is unusual as most police learning programmes are much shorter and many officers exit the scheme before the end of the full five-year period). Academic accreditation is provided in the form of a Postgraduate Diploma in Police Leadership, which may then lead to a Master's degree from Warwick University Business School. However, applicants do not have to be university graduates to join the HPDS but are instead selected using a three-stage process to assess their suitability (the final stage is based on the Senior Police National Assessment Centre). The HPDS is currently under review and for the time being 2014 will be the final intake of students for the HPDS (CoP, 2014b).

8 | Education, Training, and Assessment

8.1 Introduction

In this chapter we examine the programmes of education and training that feature within police training, including entry through pre-join courses. The main emphasis, however, is on the training undertaken after you have joined the police and the forms of assessment that will be used to confirm your fitness to practise as a police officer.

Direct vocational training, which takes place for example in police forces, is often concerned with the 'mastery' of a skill or practical knowledge acquisition. The emphasis is on being able to do something, and to do it correctly. For this reason police forces often employ classroom-based techniques which involve problem-based learning punctuated with role-plays to provide more realism. Computer-based learning might also be used: for example, via the Managed Learning Environment (MLE) of the National Centre for Applied Learning Technologies (NCALT). The learning will assessed by sitting multiple-choice examination papers. Work-based learning will take place within the Basic Command Unit (BCU) and comprise of coaching by a tutor constable leading to competency-based assessment. This is discussed in more detail in 8.6.

In higher education, a student is likely to be given more responsibility for his or her own learning with teaching directed more towards further reading and independent research. However, in some cases practical application of the learning might also take place, although the realism of work-based learning may be limited unless the student is also a special constable. Emphasis in higher education will be placed on reflection, analysis, and criticality using libraries, e-libraries, and virtual learning environments such as Blackboard to locate resources. As a consequence, assessment will include writing academic assignments (eg essays) in addition to written formal examinations.

8.2 Applying to Join the Police

Some readers of the Handbook might already be full-time trainee officers, in which case this section might only have limited value to you. However, if you are a student on a pre-join programme at a college or university, or you are currently a special constable or a PCSO seeking to become a full-time police officer, then the following will provide a useful overview of gaining entry to the full-time police service. Note, however, that there are other options and positions within the wider police family (other than becoming a regular officer) and these are discussed in 3.4.

At the time of writing (early 2014) the police service in England and Wales is still adapting to the reduction in central government funding. Many police forces have had a temporary freeze on recruitment of new staff, although in some forces significant recruitment is now resuming. However, some have only been recruiting from the ranks of special constables studying for the CKP or via the PCSO route, so careful research is needed.

There are three main sources of information on becoming a 'regular' police officer:

- the recruitment departments of the police forces in England and Wales (accessible via the websites of the parent organizations)—consider not only the territorial police forces (such as the MPS) but also other police forces such as BTP;
- the 'official' Home Office Police Recruitment website (at <http://www.policecouldyou.co.uk>); and
- a website run by Chamberlain Place Ltd (at <http://www.allpolicejobs.co.uk>), which claims to be 'the only website that lists all current vacancies in all UK police forces'. However, at the time of writing this was a paid subscription-only service.

In 2011 Peter Neyroud (previously head of the NPIA) reported to the Home Secretary with recommendations on police training and leadership (see 3.7.4) and, if implemented, these recommendations might impact on the recruitment process. In addition, the second Winsor Review was published in 2012, containing recommendations on entry routes into policing, promotion, health and fitness requirements, and contribution-related pay. A number of the Winsor recommendations on recruitment were considered by the Police Advisory Board for England and Wales and the recommendations of the Board were accepted by the Home Office in early 2013. This means, for example, that at some stage the academic entry requirement will likely become a QCF Level 3 qualification (such as 'A' levels), or a police qualification which is recognized by Skills for Justice (such as the Certificate in Knowledge of Policing), or previous experience as a special constable or as a PCSO. Other changes in police recruitment requirements are also possible and you should check regularly for the latest information.

At the time of writing (2014), all of the following are requirements for joining the police service as a full-time police constable:

- You need to be **eligible** to join, for example in terms of age and nationality (see 8.2.1).
- Some police services require completion of a **pre-application questionnaire**.
- You need to submit and pass an **application process** at the level required by the force you have applied to (see 8.2.2).
- A **background** and security check and a medical check (including testing for use of illegal drugs) should indicate that there is no good reason to exclude you (discussed later).
- You need to undertake and pass a **fitness** and **eyesight test** (see 8.2.4.1).

In some forces you might also need to pass an in-force interview. Meeting all of these requirements does not guarantee you a job with the police force concerned. There have been occasions in the past where recruitment has been cancelled at short notice and otherwise successful applicants have been disappointed.

8.2.1   Eligibility

Eligibility in this context refers to both your general suitability for the police service and the technical requirements on you in terms of your age, fitness, and so on. There are many books and websites providing advice on the former. Many of the chapters of this Handbook will also provide insight into the skills, attitudes, and behaviour expected as part of the role of police constable. In terms of the technical requirements, in order to apply to become a full-time police constable you must be 18 years of age or over, and be in good health and reasonably fit. Officially there is no upper age limit, but the normal retirement age for police constables and sergeants is at 60 years of age and hence you are not likely to be selected if you are aged 57 or over.

The Home Office Police Recruitment website provides more detail on eligibility requirements, and detailed guidance from the College of Policing to police forces. Some key points are that:

- there is no height prerequisite;
- no formal educational qualifications are required (however, this might change in the near future as a result of a number of ongoing reviews, see the earlier discussion on the Winsor Review);
- convictions or cautions for serious offences will almost certainly disqualify an application;
- you must be a citizen in the UK, European Union, European Economic Area, or Commonwealth, or a foreign national with indefinite leave to remain in the UK;
- you need appropriate physical and mental fitness to perform police duties; and
- there may be additional local force requirements, such as the ability to drive or swim and in many cases, to prove that you have lived in the UK for a period of no less than three years (with no nationality exemptions).

It might be worth at this stage asking yourself 'Is there any reason that I know of now that will mean that I cannot join the police in the future?' For example, are your eyesight and level of health at the required levels? Do you have any convictions that might prohibit you from joining?

8.2.2 The application process

After careful consideration and research the next step after checking eligibility is to apply to a police force with vacancies. None of the stages of the application and recruitment process should be taken for granted! None are straightforward and there is always a possibility of failure, and this applies particularly for completing the application form. This will often need to be completed by hand (in writing) although some forces provide the opportunity to register and submit forms online. Many applicants fall at this first hurdle because they do not assign sufficient importance to the process. The guidance that accompanies the form should be read carefully. Common sense suggests that answers should be drafted before completing a handwritten form, thereby avoiding making spelling and grammatical mistakes.

The application form is likely to involve the following:

Section(s)	Notes
Biographical details—name, DoB, place of birth, nationality, address(es), family details, employment details, etc	Straightforward information is required, but double-check that you have these right
Convictions, tattoos, financial background, membership of BNP/National Front/Combat 18	Criminal convictions are likely to mean your application is rejected. Your family will also be subject to checks Be honest about tattoos, even if they are not on parts of the body normally exposed to the public. Offensive or racist tattoos are likely to be problematic Financial problems include County Court Judgments (CCJs) Membership of the BNP/National Front/Combat 18 will exclude you
Education and qualifications	List of your qualifications (exams passed) with dates, etc. Remember that you might be asked to show your certificates at some stage so check that you have the details correct
Personal referees	Choose your referees with care. Ensure that they can respond authoritatively on your employment or educational record
Competency questions	Usually four questions testing your understanding of the skills and qualities required of a police constable. In many respects the most important part of the form (see below)
Motivation questions	Usually five questions exploring the reasons why you wish to become a police officer

Your application form will join hundreds of others as part of an application 'sift'. The police staff responsible for assessing and grading your application (the 'assessors') deliberately do not see certain biographical details such as your ethnicity and so on, but instead judge how effectively you have answered the competency and motivation questions.

Assessors will look for evidence of specific behaviours from the National Competency Framework (NCF) in your answers and grade them accordingly. At the time of writing these are community and customer focus, effective communication, personal responsibility, problem solving, resilience, respect for race and diversity, and team working. (Note, however, that the NCF for police staff is currently being replaced.) Read and think carefully about these competency behaviours (the details are to be found via the CoP website under 'Examinations and Assessment' and then 'Police Constable Recruit Assessment Centre').

If you pass the paper sift then you will be invited to attend an 'Assessment Centre'. This is usually a reference to the assessment process itself rather than a physical location. The assessment will probably take place at a venue ('Centre') within the police force area applied to. It will be conducted according to national guidelines, as described in 8.2.3.

8.2.3   The Assessment Centre

Prior to attending the Assessment Centre all applicants are sent a 'Welcome Pack' containing a number of documents as preparation materials. The Assessment Centre process follows a nationally agreed format, often referred to as SEARCH© (a trademark registered with NPIA). The pack will include information about SEARCH although you can also download this information in advance from the CoP website.

The 'Welcome Pack' will also provide information about a fictitious shopping centre which will underpin the storyline for the interactive and written exercises which will take place at the Assessment Centre. The information about the shopping centre describes the applicant's role during these exercises: that of customer services officer. This might appear strange for applying for a position in policing (and not in commerce or business), but the intention behind this appears to be to ensure that all candidates have a fair chance regardless of background (eg a policing scenario might give a special constable an advantage). It assumes that the generic competences required by a constable can nonetheless be assessed. The Welcome Pack is also available via the CoP website (referred to as the 'Westshire Welcome Pack'). Note that the pack still makes references to the now defunct NPIA.

Preparation for the Assessment Centre could also include learning more about the force applied to (eg the name of the chief constable), practising for the interview (discussed later), and attempting numerical and reasoning tests.

The Assessment Centre takes about five hours. At the start all the candidates are divided into syndicates so that a number of exercises can be carried out in a 'carousel' arrangement. All the candidates will be under observation, even during breaks surreptitiously texting during a briefing will be noticed and will count against a candidate. More formal assessment will also take place during the five stages of the Assessment Centre. These will not necessarily be conducted in the same order as shown in the table. Grade A is highest and D is lowest.

Stage of Assessment Centre*	Number of assessments	Time allowed	Form of assessment
Interview	1	Up to 20 minutes (4 questions of 5 minutes each)	Using a subset of the NCF*, graded A–D
Numerical test	1	12 minutes for 25 questions	Simple right/wrong answers: the % correct converted to an A–D scale
Reasoning test	1	25 minutes for 31 questions	Simple right/wrong answers: the % correct converted to an A–D scale
Written exercises	2	20 minutes each	Using a subset of the NCF* graded A–D
Role-play exercises	4	10 minutes each (includes 5 minutes' preparation)	Using a subset of the NCF* graded A–D

* The competency 'respect for race and diversity'. Note also that details are subject to change by the CoP.

The **interview** consists of four questions and will focus on exploring how each candidate has handled situations in the past. Typically the questions begin with 'Can you give me an example of . . . ?' and then refer to a generic situation such as overcoming a particular challenge. Examples of 'mock' Assessment Centre interviews can be found on YouTube and these might be useful in terms of appreciating the format of the interview. But a candidate should avoid being too polished and calculating and must genuinely understand and mean what he/she says. His/her replies will be judged against a subset of the NCF competency criteria.

The **numerical test** consists of a 12-minute multiple-choice examination with 25 questions and five choices for each answer. Each of the number-based simple mental arithmetic problems requires a calculation (without a calculator) involving addition, subtraction, multiplication, division, and simple percentages.

The **reasoning test** involves 31 problems based on a short description of a situation (eg a suspicious fire) with some supporting facts. A number of possible inferences or deductions relating to those situations are provided, and the candidate has to decide whether each statement is 'true', 'false', or whether it is 'impossible to say'. Most people find this more demanding than the numerical test.

The two **written exercises** are more demanding still. The exercises are based on the contents of the Welcome Pack (discussed earlier). For each exercise written information is provided, relating to a problem that needs intervention (eg a memo from a colleague about problems at a shopping centre, a map of the centre, letters from those involved in the complaint, etc). Then the candidate as the customer services officer has to write a 'proposal document' using the template provided. As these are written exercises, it is likely that spelling, grammar, sentence construction, vocabulary, and clarity will also be assessed, as well as the NCF competencies. An example of the written exercises is available on the CoP website.

The four **role-play exercises** each consist of a ten-minute exercise; five minutes for preparation and five minutes for a role-play between the candidate and an actor playing a certain role, for example a customer with a complaint. During the preparation time the applicant is given written information relevant to the exercise, and again will be asked to assume the role of a customer services officer. This is an opportunity for using some of the information from the Welcome Pack such as the policies of the fictitious shopping centre. Making notes in advance is a good idea as these can be used during the role-play. The positive indicators described in the NCF should be used when acting out the role. For example, the candidate could say something like:

- 'I am going to take personal responsibility for this problem by doing the following...' (*personal responsibility*);
- 'I've looked at the centre's policy on... and I've decided to...' (*problem solving*);
- 'It may make me unpopular with... but I am still going to...' (*resilience*);
- 'I am going to challenge the attitude of... because it may have been discriminatory' (*respect for race and diversity*);
- 'I am going to offer support to... in order that they can...' (*team-working*); and
- 'I am going to keep you updated on my progress by...' (*community and customer focus*).

Each of the Assessment Centre stages is marked by the assessors and an overall mark is then calculated. Note, however, that the actual marking schemes are confidential. Candidates must score at least 50 per cent overall and have no Ds for Respect for Race and Diversity. They must also score at least 50 per cent for Respect for Race and Diversity, 50 per cent for Oral Communication, and at least 44 per cent for Written Communication (based in part on NPIA, 2008b, p 1). An example of how this works in principle is given in the following table:

Requirement	No of marks/ grades available	Example mark(s)	Example %	Minimum pass-mark/grade	Result
Overall Assessment Centre performance	123	70	57%	50%	'Pass'
Respect for race and diversity	21	14	67%	50%	'Pass'
Oral communication	15	8	53%	50%	'Pass'
Written communication	9	3	33%	44%	'Fail'
Respect for race and diversity	Grades available: A (high) to D (low)	C, C, A, A, B, C, A	N/A	D	'Pass'
				Overall result	Fail

Police forces are allowed to further prioritize applicants on the basis of their overall mark. For example, in 2013 Dorset Police required a pass-mark of 60 per cent or higher (Dorset Police, 2013) for entry. This is somewhat unsatisfactory given that in principle there should be no difference between the minimum standards police forces expect, but is largely the result of pragmatic 'gatekeeping' to match supply and demand in police training.

After a successful Assessment Centre (expect to hear after a couple of weeks or so) you may then be asked to attend an interview with your chosen police force (this does not apply in all forces). If you are going to be interviewed, then you should find out carefully what is involved, and why an interview is being conducted at this stage. As noted earlier, interviews are often used as further gatekeeping devices to reduce a pool of applicants to match force recruitment requirements.

8.2.4 Background, security, and medical checks

After a successful Assessment Centre (see 8.2.3) the police force concerned will conduct a background and security check on you and your family and associates. They are likely to take up the references you supplied in the application form (see 8.2.2) and check the PNC and other intelligence databases for your right to work in the UK, your address and other biographical details, any criminal convictions or cautions, your financial background, and whether you 'associate' with known criminals. Unfortunately, if you are refused entry to the police on grounds of security there is little you can do.

You will also be asked to complete and submit a detailed medical questionnaire (an example can be found on the Home Office Police Recruitment website) to be countersigned by your GP. The police force might request further information from you and/or your GP. You might then need to attend your chosen police force to undergo a 'medical' involving a hearing test, blood pressure measurements, a lung function test, and tests for alcohol, drug or substance abuse. Your BMI (Body Mass Index) might also be calculated which involves measuring your height and weight.

8.2.4.1 Fitness and eyesight test

If you are successful in the Assessment Centre (see 8.2.3) and you are selected for the next phase of recruitment, then you will be invited to attend a fitness assessment. At the same time you will be asked to have you eyesight examined by an optician (and the form completed and countersigned) or the force will carry out an eye-test. (This might also happen at an earlier stage—see 8.2.4.) Your unaided eyesight will need to meet certain minimum standards. Further details are available on the Home Office Police Recruitment website.

All applicants also undertake a 'multi-stage fitness test' (the MSFT). The MSFT consists of two tests:

- an endurance fitness test (the 'bleep test') which involves running backwards and forwards on a 15-metre track in time with a series of bleeps, with the time interval becoming increasing shorter. Some forces replace the bleep test with a 'circuit' of a 15-metre track.
- a dynamic strength test—the physical ability to push 34kg and to pull 35kg whilst seated.

Most reasonably fit applicants have no great problem in meeting these requirements. To test your level of fitness mark out a 15m distance (or use your local sports centre) and then download the mp3 file with the 'bleeps' from the CoP website (<http://www.college.police.uk/en/19834.htm>).

Note that after joining the police you will be required to undertake another fitness test, including a 15-metre 'shuttle' run (short bursts of speed, interspersed with slowing running), together with endurance testing (but no upper strength testing).

8.3 The Initial Police Learning and Development Programme (IPLDP)

The Initial Police Learning and Development Programme (IPLDP) is the form of police initial training used by all forces since April 2006. It also forms the basis, at least in part, of special constable training, PCSO training, and the growing number of pre-entry programmes available through colleges and universities. The full initial police training IPLDP (as distinct, for example, from a pre-entry IPLDP curriculum) contains three clusters of modules: Induction (IND), Operation (OP), and Legislation, Policy and Guidelines (LPG) as listed in 1.4.2.

The majority of the 'Induction' modules (eg IND 9 concerning First Aid), are covered in the first few weeks of police training, as you might expect. They could also be delivered as part of

Qualifications and Training

a pre-join scheme. Other modules however, such as IND 10: 'Use police actions in a fair and justified way' are introduced during the induction process after joining the police, but then developed and revisited during training. The IND modules link with the QCF Diploma in Policing assessment unit 'Provide initial support to victims and witnesses' (see 8.5.1.1).

The Operational modules are concerned with the routine but vital operational tasks of the police officer, often (but not exclusively) those most closely associated with patrol. For example, OP 5 is concerned with the ability of the police officer to 'search individuals and premises'. The OP modules link with all bar one of the QCF Diploma in Policing assessment units (see 7.3).

The three Legislation, Policy, and Guidelines modules of the IPLDP are the most closely linked with the acquisition of knowledge of the law, policy, and procedures associated with generic policing activities. For instance LPG 1 is concerned with crime; stop and search; protecting people; police policies and procedures; non-crime incidents; investigation and interview; and road policing.

The modules are spread over four phases of training and learning and are not normally delivered in a simple, linear serial manner. A typical pattern of delivery is shown in 8.4.1.

Colleges, universities, or forces may use different terminology from that used here. For example, instead of using the term 'modules' the term 'courses' may be used, and 'phases' might not mean the same as it does within the IPLDP. Police forces are expected to ensure that the entire mandatory IPLDP curriculum is taught (NPIA, 2010b, p 3), but can choose to structure their own training as long as they remain IPLDP-compliant (Home Office, 2005c). However, at the time of writing it was unclear how this requirement would be reconciled with the increasing availability of APL to applicants to the police. Note that the IPLDP curriculum is subject to regular review.

8.3.1 IPLDP and pre-join programmes

Educational and training providers have to demonstrate that the content and assessment of their pre-join programmes meets the IPLDP pre-join curriculum (NPIA, 2011a, p 12 and CoP, 2013e). This enables successful students to gain APL against parts of the full IPLDP on entry to the police. In practice it is often more straightforward for colleges and universities to deliver the underpinning knowledge requirement rather than the embedded professional skills requirement of IPLDP, for example through the new Certificate in Knowledge of Policing. (However, pre-join courses are sometimes coupled with special constabulary training, in which case practical skills training might well feature.)

Typically, a pre-join course will include subjects linking with the IPLDP LPG modules such as the context to law enforcement, the CJS, police powers, basic law and legislation relevant to policing (eg theft, traffic offences, etc), and more advanced criminal law (eg sexual offences). There is currently significant variation between pre-join course providers.

8.4 The Probationary Period and Confirmation

After joining the police all trainees undertake the Initial Police Learning and Development Programme through the Diploma in Policing (see 8.3). Trainees who have passed the CKP may only need to cover part of the Diploma as most of the knowledge aspects for each topic will have already been covered. This will involve acquiring the important knowledge and understanding required to work as a police officer, as well as the practical skills involved. In this part of Chapter 8 we examine the likely pattern of training over the two-year 'probationary period', how trainees are assessed as competent, the probationary period, and confirmation. We also consider what might happen to trainees who experience problems during training.

8.4.1 The pattern of training

The IPLDP approach to the initial training of police officers consists of four phases, and is likely to include certain content and activities as shown in the table. A community placement or engagement with a duration of at least 80 hours is likely to be included (Home Office, 2004 and NPIA, 2010c).

Phase	Typical activities
Phase 1: Induction	• Introduction to the force • Practical and organizational needs, eg dress code, uniform, Federation, etc • Learning about IPLDP, ethics, and diversity • Undertaking First Aid and Officer Safety Training (eg self-protection) • Introduction to the use of technology, eg Airwave, PNC, etc • Job-Related Fitness Test
Phase 2: Community safety and partnerships	• Receiving a crime and disorder 'package' • Community safety
Phase 3: Core police learning and Supervised Patrol	• Classroom learning of the bulk of LPG modules (including case studies, eg in public order) • Operating a 'Crime Investigation Model' • Undertaking Supervised Patrol
Phase 4: Additional learning and Independent Patrol	• Classroom learning (a minimum of 30 days/6 weeks) of the more complex LPG modules (including case studies), eg child abuse and sexual offences • Developing police practice (particularly local practice) • Undertaking Independent Patrol

The exact pattern of training will vary from force to force (particularly in the case of any link with a pre-entry course), but the following table describes a *typical* arrangement. Details concerning the Learning Diary, SOLAP, and PAC are given later in this chapter.

Time line in weeks	Stage	IPLDP phases	Typical duration	Activities	Milestones
1–2	Induction	1	2 weeks	Learning about the organization, Health & Safety, Personal Safety Training (PST), First Aid, etc	Undertaking the Job-Related Fitness Test completion of first Learning Diary entries, and attestation
3	Community engagement	2	1 week	Placement with a community group (this might occur instead at a later stage)	Completion of first SOLAP entry
4	Area familiarization	1	1 week	The work of a BCU	Completion of more Learning Diary and SOLAP entries
5–10	Taught courses	1 and 3	6 weeks	Legislation, procedures, and other subjects	Successful completion of assessments
11–12	Supervised Patrol	3	2 weeks	Coaching and assessment	Beginning Supervised Patrol and completion of some QCF Diploma unit learning outcomes
13–18	Taught courses	1 and 3	6 weeks	Legislation, procedures, and other subjects	Successful completion of knowledge element assessments
19–21	Supervised Patrol	3	3 weeks	Coaching and assessment	Completion of some QCF Diploma unit learning outcomes
22–27	Taught courses	4	6 weeks	Legislation, procedures, and other subjects	Successful completion of assessments
28	Supervised Investigation	3	1 week	Coaching and assessment	Completion of some QCF Diploma unit learning outcomes
29–32	Taught courses	4	4 weeks	Legislation, procedures, and other subjects	Successful completion of assessments, six of the QCF units and the PAC Satisfactory Learning Development Review and Independent Patrol status

Time line in weeks	Stage	IPLDP phases	Typical duration	Activities	Milestones
33–35	Supervised Patrol and Supervised Investigation	3	3 weeks	Coaching and assessment	Beginning Independent Patrol and completion of some remaining QCF Diploma assessment units
36–69	Independent Patrol	4	34 weeks	Patrol and/or investigation, assessment against QCF Diploma assessment units, taught courses	Completion of some remaining QCF Diploma assessment units
70	Independent Patrol	4	Part of 1 week	Meeting with supervisor	Second Learning Development Review
71–104	Independent Patrol	4	34 weeks	Patrol and/or investigation, assessment against QCF Diploma units	Completion of remaining QCF Diploma assessment units and the SOLAP Final Learning Development Review, and Confirmation

In practice the four phases might not be delivered in a discrete sequential pattern but instead might be 'interwoven' throughout the two-year probationary period.

For Supervised Patrol, Independent Patrol, and confirmation in particular, there are significant variations between forces. For example, in some forces Supervised Patrol occurs earlier than we suggest above, and may also occur more frequently and contain a greater coaching dimension. Similarly, attestation and Independent Patrol may take place earlier or later than in this typical model. More profound differences include the decision by some forces to concentrate most of the taught elements of training in the first 52 weeks.

Forces often elect to organize their training in terms of a series of courses or modules designed to deliver the requirements of the IPLDP. For example, West Yorkshire Police structures its training in the following way:

A typical structure for training (West Yorkshire Police)

Phase 1 (3 Weeks)

The first two weeks are an induction into the organisation at Bishopgarth, Wakefield. During this time recruits will be given more information about what the two years as a student officer will be like. They'll don the uniform for the first time and begin to see the responsibilities & obligations that come with it.

On week 3 the uniform is set aside for a while and they change location to the University of Huddersfield where they begin to develop the knowledge and understanding required by the modern Police Officer by looking at wider social issues affecting policing.

Phase 2 (4 Weeks)

Students continue at the University for a further three weeks covering such areas as: Equality, Diversity & Rights; Professional Development and delving further into Social & Community Issues. The final week of this phase consists of a five-day community placement, based in the Division (area) to which they'll be posted. They are there to observe and learn about a section of the community that they're likely to encounter and be expected to engage with, when on patrol. This allows them the opportunity to interact with the communities outside of the policing context. They don't wear uniform at all during Phase 2.

Phase 3 (24 Weeks)

This phase begins with 13 weeks of Legislation, Procedures and Guidelines training back at Bishopgarth. This is achieved through a combination of classroom-based training and practical exercises. It includes two weeks of detailed IT training in the key computer systems in general use within West Yorkshire Police. During this fortnight, one day is set aside

---

for Public Order training at our dedicated training site. By the end of this part students look forward to a week of annual leave. On their return from leave they begin gaining practical experience with a tutor constable in a Professional Development Unit (PDU) at an Operational Division for at least ten weeks. This may be extended if necessary, to accommodate individual development needs.

Phase 4 (Up to the end of Year 2)

Once a student is judged as fit for independent patrol, which is measured against set criteria, they commence Phase 4 and head out on their own for the first time. This doesn't mean they are alone; they are part of a team. Students will be monitored and assisted by colleagues and supervisors throughout the rest of the two years and beyond. During the second year they also receive a further five weeks of formal training which is split between Bishopgarth and the University; with a further community placement week. These will be grouped into three fortnights, spaced through the second year. Students actually spend 75 per cent of the first two years working at division, gaining practical experience.

Study

There will inevitably be some private study to do as you would expect with any training course or vocational qualification, but much of it is based upon students' experiences and how they have used those to develop. As the programme progresses they build a portfolio (Student Officer Learning & Assessment Portfolio—SOLAP) which catalogues learning and development, both in the training establishments and the work place. This substantially contributes towards two of the modules, which together with a handful of assignments for the University draw[s] on experiences of the programme.

As with many other vocational qualifications there will be a need to study outside work time, indeed some people will have family members who are currently doing that. Time invested now will result in successful completion of the programme and a rewarding career in the Police Service. Officers who fail to submit work when required will be failing to meet our standards.

Support

Don't worry—it is our aim to guide students through the programme and see them succeed but we do accept that some people will find it more taxing than others. Above all we want to see 100% effort and an officer who is prepared to respond positively to feedback. The first thing to realise is that this is a packed course, the majority of which is work place-based. It is important that recruits find time to complete the necessary study and work, as leaving things to the last minute will lead to huge problems. Any student who is unsure of anything must ASK. We can't help if no one speaks to us. Standards are set throughout the course, though 'pass' marks may vary from one aspect to another. Extra support is available at every stage and we aim to focus development based upon individual needs.

Beyond the first two years

When you have successfully completed the programme you are awarded a Foundation Degree in Police Studies. In terms of further study, you could, at your own expense, seek to turn this into a full degree in a suitably linked subject. There may also be the possibility in the future of being awarded further credits for work-related study which could also lead to a full degree.

Also, you will now be eligible to apply for one of the many diverse job opportunities that exist within the Organisation so you can begin to shape your own career.

(West Yorkshire Police, 2010, reproduced by kind permission of West Yorkshire Police.)

TASK 1 Find out about the pattern of training for the police force in your area, and how it relates to IPLDP Phases 1 to 4.

Qualifications and Training

8.4.2 The probationary period

The probationary period is the time that a trainee officer is technically under or in 'probation'. He/she is not a confirmed constable and is subject to the regulations that apply to trainee police officers (see 6.4.4). The probationary period is normally two years for full-time trainees. Part-time training (now increasingly available) will have an extended probationary period calculated according to Annex C of the Police Regulations 2003: training at half the full-time rate will take twice as long.

As with other aspects of initial training, the length of the probationary period may change in the future. In some forces APL (accredited prior learning) shortens the length of training and the probationary period. This may be particularly important for PCSOs and special constables who subsequently join up as police officers. Foreshortened training through APL might also be open to trainees joining from other professions, or through College of Policing-'approved' pre-join routes in higher and further education.

8.4.2.1 Independent Patrol

Attaining the right to undertake Independent Patrol is a key milestone in the professional development of a trainee police officer. It means that, although training is far from over, the trainee can undertake many police functions associated with fully qualified (confirmed) police officers without the need for constant supervision.

Independent Patrol normally occurs after about week 30 in training, although this does vary significantly from force to force. As with many aspects of initial police training, the timing of Independent Patrol remains under discussion. (The traditional approach was simply to say that, all other criteria being satisfied, it would happen on a certain week, but this makes less sense in an era of competence-based occupational standards.) A number of written reports have also highlighted problems that some forces faced in organizing and assessing the Independent Patrol phase of initial training.

A trainee's suitability for Independent Patrol is assessed against various criteria, including a subset of the QCF units, the Police Action Checklist (the PAC, see 8.5.3), and normally takes place after a Learning Development Review (see 8.5.4.3). As you would expect, the main aim is to ensure that the trainee is competent and safe to undertake Independent Patrol, including holding the appropriate values and behaviour (eg against the five PPF qualities of decision-making, leadership, professionalism, public service, and working with others: see 8.5.2). Although the PAC is a key component in this, it is important to realize that completing the PAC (according to the IPLDP) is only one trigger for Independent Patrol and does not automatically lead to it.

A trainee police officer normally receives confirmation of competence against the PAC from a Professional Development Unit (PDU) supervisor/assessor during phases 1, 2, or 3 of training (IPLDP terminology). In addition, some forces may also expect the acquisition of advanced driving skills before a trainee is granted Independent Patrol status.

8.4.3 Confirmation

All being well, after two years (104 weeks) a trainee police officer should expect to be deemed 'fit for confirmation of appointment'. However, in our view, the criteria for confirmation under the IPLDP remain less than clear and so you should seek a definitive statement of what is required. However, *some* or *all* of the following are likely to be involved:

- successful completion of the Level 3 Diploma in Policing (see 8.5.1);
- attainment of the five personal qualities of the PPF role profile for police constable (see 8.5.2);
- satisfactory completion of the SOLAP (see 8.5.4);
- satisfactory completion of the PAC (see 8.5.3);
- a 'successful' final Learning Development Review (see 8.5.4.3);
- a minimum academic attainment; and/or
- other requirements such as a level of fitness (the Job-Related Fitness Test), ability to administer First Aid, and being able to drive a car to a certain standard.

(Note that these requirements are not mutually exclusive because they interrelate and overlap. For example, the SOLAP is likely to cross-reference with the PAC, and the Learning Development Review will involve the five personal quality areas. The list could also be summarized in IPLDP language as the successful completion of Phases 1 to 4 inclusive.)

8.4.4   What can go wrong?

We have no wish to be negative, but things can sometimes go wrong.

8.4.4.1   Could I get sacked?

At the outset it is important to note that, as for qualified police officers, most trainee police officers are not employees in the usual sense of the term. Technically they are 'holders of public office' (and for BTP the situation is especially complicated). This means that the conditions of employment for trainee police officers are particularly complex. In terms of dismissal (officially called 'dispensing with your services') and resignation ('retirement'), the main source of definitive information are the Police Regulations 2003, Statutory Instrument No 527 (see 5.2 for an explanation of Statutory Instruments). The Regulations can be found on the www.legislation.gov.uk website. Note that there are a number of Annexes to the Determinants which set out the important detail.

For the student police officer, probably the most important paragraphs in the Police Regulations 2003 are regs 12 and 13 (often known colloquially as Reg (pronounced with a hard 'g') 12 and Reg 13). Other police regulations are covered in Chapter 6. As with many aspects of police training, the position regarding probation, the Regulations, and complaints may be reviewed. The Morris Inquiry in particular highlighted the complexity of current arrangements (Morris *et al*, 2004).

8.4.4.2   Extension of the probationary period

Regulation 12 provides for the usual probationary period (two years for full-time student police officers) to be extended. Details are given in Annex C to the Regulations. Normally the probationary period is extended for the following reasons:

- training has been interrupted for some reason, for example illness or personal problems; or
- a trainee officer has been 'back-coursed' (that is, required to retake a stage of training), perhaps because of failure.

Forces are unlikely to allow an indefinite extension to the probationary period and will usually provide a trainee officer with detailed information concerning the implementation of 'Reg 12' on the local level.

8.4.4.3   Dispensing with a trainee officer's 'services'

Regulation 13 allows for your dismissal. It is worth quoting in full:

Regulation 13

(1) Subject to the provisions of this regulation, during [his/her] period of probation in the force the services of a constable may be dispensed with at any time if the chief officer considers that [he/she] is not fitted, physically or mentally, to perform the duties of [his/her] office, or that [he/she] is not likely to become an efficient or well conducted constable.

(2) A constable whose services are dispensed with under this regulation shall be entitled to receive a month's notice or a month's pay in lieu thereof.

(3) A constable's services shall not be dispensed with in accordance with this regulation and any notice given for the purposes thereof shall cease to have effect if [he/she] gives written notice to the police authority of [his/her] intention to retire and retires in pursuance of the said notice on or before the date on which [his/her] services would otherwise be dispensed with; and such a notice taking effect on that date shall be accepted by the police authority notwithstanding that less than a month's notice is given.

(4) Where a constable has received a notice under this regulation that [his/her] services are to be dispensed with and [he/she] gives written notice of [his/her] intention to retire and retires under paragraph (3), [he/she] shall nevertheless be entitled to receive pay up to and until the date on which the month's notice [he/she] has received would have expired or where [he/she] has received or is due to receive a month's pay in lieu of notice [he/she] shall remain entitled to that pay notwithstanding the notice [he/she] has given under paragraph (3).

Regulation 13 dismissals are rare and would normally come at the end of a long process during which the trainee would have been offered support and guidance. If you are issued with a Reg 13 notice, then you are advised to contact your representative at the JBB (the Police Federation, see 6.7.1) or take other advice.

Note that the grounds for dismissal ('not fitted, physically or mentally, to perform the duties of [his/her] office, or that [he/she] is not likely to become an efficient or well conducted constable') are quite broad. For example, persistent failure in assessments or examinations could be considered grounds to consider that a trainee officer is not mentally fit to continue training.

However, more common reasons for being dismissed or resigning are examples of inappropriate behaviour, an inability to maintain a certain level of fitness, and so on.

There are obvious reasons for resigning before being dismissed, particularly in terms of future employment prospects. However, this would not mean that he/she would escape prosecution if the grounds for dismissal arose from a criminal act.

8.5 Assessment

If you are a student on a pre-join programme leading to the Certificate in Knowledge of Policing then you will be required to provide written explanations and descriptions which are assessed by your tutors against the assessment criteria. For example, one assessment requirement is that you 'understand relevant legal and police service requirements related to gathering and submitting information' in which case you might be asked to submit a description of a number of pieces of legislation and national policy or guidelines in relation to gathering, submitting, retaining, recording, and disseminating information. Other forms of assessment are also likely to be employed, consistent with the need for valid, reliable assessment of your knowledge and understanding (rather than the practical skills of policing). These forms of assessment are likely to include multiple-choice type examinations, timed essays, assignments, verbal questioning, formal written examinations, and assessed scenarios. However, the Certificate is still in its infancy and you should ask your provider about how they plan to assess you, what the pass-mark is and what to do if you do not agree with an assessment outcome. This is particularly the case with assessed scenarios where aspects of your behaviour such as your 'body language' might be assessed.

8.5.1 The assessed Diploma in Policing units

For trainee officers, summative assessments are used to determine whether he/she is fit to undertake Independent Patrol (see 8.4.2.1) and subsequent confirmation as a qualified police officer (see 8.4.3). They take place at the end of a phase or part of IPLDP. Formative assessment takes place throughout the learning period to help determine learning needs.

Successful completion of the QCF Diploma in Policing award is just one of the requirements for becoming a qualified police constable (see 8.4.3 for the others). Diploma units are also linked with the right to undertake Independent Patrol. As described in more detail in 7.4.1, each of the ten QCF units within the Diploma is linked with the National Occupational Standards (NOS) for initial policing. In effect, each Diploma unit consists of:

- one main NOS unit; and
- selected aspects of the five embedded NOS units (AA1, AB1, AE1, AF1, and CA1).

(The two 'Search' Diploma units also include part of NOS Unit CD3.)

The following table describes the relationship between attaining the units and gaining Independent Patrol status.

Name of Diploma in Policing assessed unit	Main NOS unit	Required *before* going on Independent Patrol	Final assessment *during* Independent Patrol
Provide initial support to victims and witnesses	BE2	✓	
Gather and submit information to support law enforcement objectives	CB1		
Provide an initial response to incidents	CD1	✓	
Arrest, detain, or report individuals	CD5	✓	
Conduct priority and volume investigations	CI101		✓
Interview victims and witnesses in relation to priority and volume investigations	CJ101		✓
Interview suspects in relation to priority and volume investigations	CJ201		✓
Search individuals	CK1	✓	
Search vehicles, premises, and open spaces	CK2	✓	
Manage conflict in a policing context	GC10	✓	

All of the units can be assessed incrementally during the two-year training period, and a number of the assessment units can be completely signed off in the work place during the taught phase of training. However, as shown in the table, before undertaking Independent Patrol a trainee officer must be assessed as competent on at least one occasion in six of the Diploma units (NPIA, 2010c, p 35), and three of the Diploma units can only be finally assessed during Independent Patrol and hence in the work place.

8.5.1.1   Components of a QCF Diploma unit

Each QCF Diploma unit is a self-contained and free-standing expression of a particular part of the role of police constable, with a description of how competence for this part of the role can be assessed. Each unit contains the following:

Learning outcomes	A list of two to five learning outcomes, for example the learner will 'be able to communicate effectively with victims and witnesses' (see 7.3 for a full list). The learning outcomes have been mapped with the IPLDP learning descriptors. There will be one or more assessment criteria for each learning outcome.
Assessment criteria	A list of 'can do' criteria that can be adapted for assessment, for example the learner can 'communicate with individuals appropriately taking account of pace, their level of understanding and their preferred form of communication'.
Additional information	Normally includes a description of the aims of the QCF unit, the linked NOS units, and specific assessment requirements, for example the number of times competence must be practically demonstrated.

The way these are used is explained here; we will work through an example of how a unit is likely to be assessed.

You achieve a QCF unit when you are competent to do so. You achieve the standard when it has been confirmed that you have provided reliable, valid, and sufficient evidence (in the correct format) to demonstrate your competence. Think of the analogy with the burden of proof in the courts—we are talking here of proof beyond reasonable doubt and not on the balance of probabilities, but remember (also) that it is the quality of evidence that is important, and not the volume.

Competence may be achieved at different times for different people. Indeed, you could be given credit if you can already meet a standard (perhaps having worked as a special constable before joining as a full-time trainee) through the accreditation of prior learning (APL), or prior experiential learning (APEL), but to date this has been difficult to implement. However, your force will almost certainly have systems in place to encourage (and even require) you to plan the phasing of your assessment against the QCF units, following a given schedule.

8.5.1.2   A detailed examination of one Diploma unit

We have chosen the unit **'Provide an initial response to incidents'** to look at its component parts in more detail. This unit is an average size for a QCF unit; it has a credit value of four, three learning outcomes (see 7.3), and a total of 13 assessment criteria. It is a good unit to consider here, as the underpinning training for this unit is likely to begin relatively early and this unit demonstrates the links between the Diploma, the NOS, and other aspects of training, for example the PAC. It also links with one of the embedded NOS units, AA1.

First, an overview of the unit itself. (We reproduce extracts from the QCF units, taken from the Register of Regulated Qualifications to be found at <http://register.ofqual.gov.uk/>, which are Crown copyright.)

The QCF provides the following summary:

> This unit covers providing an initial response to incidents, including: crime, non-crime and traffic incidents. The learner will need to be able to gather information on the incident, establish the nature of the incident, and plan their actions accordingly. In the case of a major or critical incident, when first on the scene, they will need to take control of the incident until relieved by the appropriate person.

It is clear that plenty of learning is required (including practising skills and acquiring knowledge and understanding) for this unit. The final assessment for it will probably be during Supervised or Independent Patrol.

First, adequate **knowledge** of legislation and police procedure concerning a whole range of incidents ('crime, non-crime and traffic incidents') is required. This will include at least a working knowledge of the legislation surrounding public order offences (eg s 4 of the Public Order Act 1986), violent incidents (eg s 47 of the Offences Against the Person Act 1861—Actual Bodily Harm), and so on. You will also need to be familiar with:

- police procedure, such as the correct use of the pocket notebook and making police statements (to be able to 'gather information on the incident');
- critical incident management ('take control of the incident'); and
- health and safety, human rights, and respect for diversity (as always).

This knowledge and understanding is likely to be achieved incrementally during the first year or so of training (and is covered in other parts of this Handbook).

In terms of **skills**, knowing how to communicate with the control room and fellow officers is essential, and personal safety training might also be required. You may also need to know how to support witnesses and victims, how to protect the scene (for forensic purposes), and possibly how to administer First Aid.

The unit has three **learning outcomes**, which effectively subdivide the unit into logical stages:

The learner will:
1. Know and understand relevant legal and organizational requirements for responding to an incident.
2. Be able to gather information and plan a response to an incident.
3. Be able to respond to incidents.

The first two learning outcomes are concerned with all those actions (mental as well as physical) that lead up to actual attendance at an incident. The third learning outcome relates to the events and police actions after arriving at the incident. It makes sense to group these learning outcomes together, since the quality of the police response is likely to depend (at least in part) on the quality of the planning.

Each learning outcome has a number of linked **assessment criteria**. For example, the third learning outcome, to 'be able to respond to incidents', requires the student police officer to be able to:

3.1 liaise and communicate effectively with the following people regarding the incident, requesting other resources as necessary:
- members of the public
- control room
- line management
- other specialists, including external agencies
3.2 respond and take control of incidents, within appropriate timescales, according to current policy, demonstrating the ability to:
- challenge and deal appropriately with unacceptable behaviour
- use appropriate personal safety techniques
- recognise individual needs with respect to race, diversity and human rights
3.3 demonstrate how to provide support to victims, witnesses and/or others
3.4 identify and prioritise casualties, and provide necessary assistance
3.5 take action to protect the scene of the incident and preserve evidence
3.6 record the following and submit for supervision within agreed timescales:
- information, intelligence and sources from the incident
- decisions
- actions
- rationale
3.7 respond to incidents ensuring that they:
- act in a way that values people as individuals
- use law enforcement actions proportionately, recording actions correctly, within agreed timescales

---

8.5.1.3 Demonstrating attainment of a QCF unit

The evidence for attainment of a QCF unit features at the level of the assessment criteria. One aspect is demonstrating that you have the required knowledge, and this applies for nine out of the ten QCF Diploma in Policing units. This means that a trainee officer usually needs to demonstrate formally that he/she has the appropriate knowledge (eg of legislation or police procedure) described within a unit. This must be demonstrated before he/she will be given the opportunity to demonstrate how to apply the knowledge in a real policing context.

The assessment of knowledge is most likely to occur when a trainee receives training in a classroom environment. It is assessed using a variety of means which include:

* responding to verbal questioning;
* multiple-choice or short-answer tests (sometimes called 'Knowledge Evaluation Exercises');
* written answers to questions;
* written assignments with deadlines;
* assessed practical exercises, role-plays, or discussions; and
* other means (eg online assessments).

The Diploma in Policing was first introduced in February 2010 and hence has yet to be fully evaluated. However, previous experience of IPLDP suggests that the assessment of knowledge can be one of the most confusing aspects of initial training. For this reason all trainee officers are strongly advised to carefully read the information provided by your force, about assessment of the knowledge element of the QCF assessment units, and to ask about the assessment strategies and criteria if you are unclear. A key question might be 'How do I pass the knowledge element for my QCF assessment units?'

You might also need to ask your trainers the following questions:

* Is there a pass-mark, and if so what is the pass-mark? (In some forces it is 60 per cent for each subject area.)
* If there is no pass-mark, then how are pass/fail decisions made for the knowledge element?
* What happens if I don't pass? (In some forces failure on one component of an assessment can be balanced by a particularly good mark for another ('condonement')).
* Who moderates the examinations or assessments and what is the process for external quality control?

For example, in other Level 3 Diploma units (such as those for the construction industry) the minimum pass-mark in written examinations is 70 per cent and moderation is carried out by the awarding bodies concerned.

Whatever the forms of assessment, it is important that you are clear on what is being formally assessed. For example, there are over 250 learning outcomes in the IPLDP Induction Modules alone, and the LPG 1 module has over 75!

8.5.1.4 Work place assessment

This is required for all QCF assessment units and is assessed using the Diploma unit assessment criteria. For example, the QCF Diploma in Policing unit 'Provide an initial response to incidents' (see 8.5.1.2) explains that competence must be demonstrated practically on three occasions, covering two different types of incident.

Work place competence is likely to be assessed by one or more of the following:

* **Direct observation** is a very common form of evidence for competence. Put simply, a suitably qualified person (normally a tutor, an assessor constable, or PDU assessor—the terms vary from force to force) observes a trainee carrying out a particular work-related task and confirms that the actions meet the standards. Before and after the event the assessor will explain the process. He/she will use the criteria to help decide whether the evidence is appropriate and sufficient.
* **Questioning** by the assessor might also be used, although during an observation the assessor should be as unobtrusive as possible.
* **Testimony from witnesses** can provide evidence to show that a trainee has met a particular assessment criterion. The witnesses are most likely to be the trainee's tutors and more experienced and qualified police colleagues. Other people can also provide testimony, but they need to be credible, and occupationally competent for the relevant unit.

- **Written evidence** or 'work products' come in a wide variety of forms. Common sources of written evidence include police statements written by the trainee, PNB entries, *pro forma* documents he or she has completed (eg FPNs), and reports. The assessor will obviously be interested in how far these products demonstrate that the trainee has achieved the assessment criteria for an assessment unit, but will also be checking on aspects such as authenticity (ie checking that it is the trainee's own work).
- **Artefacts** are tangible objects such as photographs (eg of a cordon the trainee helped establish) or tape recordings (eg of an interaction with a member of the public). This evidence is indexed and cross-referenced in the trainee's SOLAP (see 8.5.4). A written description of the background and context for the artefact will also be required.

In some circumstances a force may consider it more appropriate to test competence by using a **simulation** or role-play rather than by observing a real-life situation. All ten QCF Diploma in Policing assessment units permit simulation to some extent. This is an advantage in terms of safety and convenience; after all it might be difficult to arrange the necessary circumstances for a trainee whilst on Supervised Patrol, and some situations are so complex it makes sense to use simulation for each separate element. Certain first-aid skills are more appropriately evidenced through simulation (using realistic mannequins) than for real. For assessment through simulations you may need to think carefully: unless particularly carefully designed and organized, simulations always run the risk that applies to any hypothetical scenario (recollect those difficult interview questions that began with 'imagine the following'). They often lack the rich detail of real-life contexts, and this ambiguity can make it more difficult to devise an appropriate response.

> **TASK 2** Which learning outcomes of the QCF Diploma unit 'Arrest, detain and report individuals' must be practically demonstrated through competence in the work place, and on how many occasions?

8.5.1.5 Claiming achievement of a QCF unit

You should be proactive in claiming competence towards learning outcomes of a QCF unit: familiarize yourself with the assessment criteria—it is in your own interest. Do not slip into thinking that the learning outcomes are things that just happen to you; rather, think of the whole process as a series of opportunities to demonstrate your skills. Remember too that the assessment criteria for certain units may be demonstrated outside the context of traditional policing—for example, during a community placement in your second year of training. Although policy does differ from force to force, ask whether a suitably qualified person from outside your force is able to confirm competence.

A single incident you have attended, or one simple task that you have completed could potentially be used as the basis of evidence for a whole range of QCF units. These opportunities should be exploited as it will help you complete the assessment more quickly. You should certainly avoid leaving it to the last minute: if you leave it too long, you will discover that, as with stamp collecting, you will have many 'doubles' for 'Search individuals' but you are still looking for the elusive 'Manage conflict'!

If you feel that you do not have sufficient opportunity (particularly on Supervised Patrol) to demonstrate attainment of a learning outcome of a QCF unit, or if you feel that your assessor has it wrong, you should speak to one of your tutors. Forces are required to follow certain quality assurance procedures in assessing the QCF units and the linked NOS and these will almost certainly include the right to appeal against an assessment decision. All police forces will have a published policy concerning appeals against assessment decisions which sets out the grounds for an appeal and the processes involved. Normally the appeal is made to the person responsible for the PDU where the decision was made, rather than to the assessor who made the decision.

> **TASK 3** Use the internet to locate and download the specifications for the NOS Unit 4G4 'Administer First Aid' (see the Skills for Justice website (<http://www.sfjuk.com>)). This NOS unit is often assessed as part of your training but does not form part of the Diploma itself. What are the knowledge and understanding requirements?

8.5.2 The Policing Professional Framework (PPF)

The Policing Professional Framework (PPF) is relatively new, and replaced the Integrated Competency Framework (which had been widely criticized for being overly complicated and bureaucratic). The PPF describes and applies to all ranks (eg Superintendent) and roles (eg call controller) in the police service, and consists of a set of **role profiles** and the associated **personal qualities** needed to perform the role.

The role profile and personal qualities for trainee police officers are the same as for police constables. Skills for Justice (the sector skills council for the CJS and responsible for the PPF) describes a police constable as:

> The frontline of the criminal justice system and community engagement. Under general supervision, but often operating independently. Responsible for the protection of life and property, the prevention and detection of crime and the maintenance of public order through a range of sworn powers in line with organisational standards. (Skills for Justice, 2011)

The police constable role profile is essentially the NOS embedded within the ten QCF Diploma in Policing units (see 7.4.1). Hence if a trainee officer achieves the Diploma in Policing, he/she will also automatically attain the role profile of constable. However, trainee officers will also need to demonstrate the personal qualities required of a police constable. These are summarized in the following table.

Personal quality	Component	Description
Decision-making		Considers, makes, and reviews appropriate and timely decisions based on relevant information. Exercises professional discretion
Leadership	Openness to change	Embraces and encourages change, particularly in terms of new ways of operating
	Service delivery	Subscribes to a force's objectives with delivery and helps to achieve these
Professionalism		Behaves with integrity, is resilient, uses own initiative when appropriate, and upholds professional standards (such as a respect for diversity)
Public service		Responds to public needs and wants, builds links with the local communities
Working with others		Works well with others, good communication skills, shows politeness and tolerance

(Based on Skills for Justice, 2011, authors' interpretation)

Police forces are expected to contextualize the role profiles and personal qualities within their own training and HR processes. Also note that at the time of writing the PPF details were still awaited in terms of the implementation of the Framework within the IPLDP.

8.5.3 The PAC

The Police Action Checklist (the PAC) is part of the system for checking whether a trainee police officer is ready to begin Independent Patrol (see 8.4.2.1). It is cross-referenced to a subset of the NOS units and hence links with at least some of the QCF assessment units which form the Diploma in Policing. Therefore completing the PAC complements the achievement of the Diploma units and does not compete with or stand apart from this process.

The PAC has ten main headings and each heading is broken into a number of specific requirements.

Action Checklist

Safety first

- First Aid
- Health & Safety—Dynamic assessment
- Health & Safety—Reporting
- Personal Safety Training (PST/OST, etc)
- Fitness test—according to force policy

Qualifications and Training

Information management

- Utilize the PNC
- Utilize force information management systems (eg intelligence/crime reporting/command and despatch)

Patrol

- Demonstrate patrol priorities in accordance with NIM
- Demonstrate communication with control rooms

Search

- Conduct stops
- Demonstrate lawful search—persons
- Demonstrate lawful search—premises
- Demonstrate lawful search—vehicles

Investigation

- Use CCTV during an investigation
- Demonstrate initial crime scene management
- Conduct the initial investigation and report of missing persons
- Conduct the initial investigation and report of volume crime according to the National Policing Plan
- Conduct the initial investigation and report of volume crime according to the Local Policing Plan
- Conduct the initial investigation and report of a domestic incident
- Conduct the initial investigation and report of racist and/or hate crime
- Conduct the initial investigation and report in relation to a child protection and/or vulnerable person incident
- Conduct the initial investigation and report of a sudden death
- Demonstrate initial RTC scene management
- Interview—conduct a witness interview using the PEACE model
- Interview—conduct a suspect interview using the PEACE model
- Demonstrate correct handling of exhibits
- Provide support and advice to victims and witnesses
- Respond to developments during an investigation

Disposal

- Report for summons
- Make lawful arrests
- Convey a suspect into custody

Custody office procedures

- Present suspect to custody in accordance with force procedures
- Obtain fingerprints
- Obtain photographs
- Obtain DNA sample
- Complete pre-charge procedures

Finalize investigations

- Complete case files (eg summons and post-charge files)
- Prepare for court or other hearings
- Present evidence to court or other hearings

Road policing

- Check driving documents
- Demonstrate vehicle stops
- Complete traffic documents—including HO/RT1/FPN(E)/CLE2/VDRS
- Demonstrate correct administration of the appropriate tests for drink-/drugs-driving offences

Property

- Complete property register

The PAC is largely concerned with performance and, as the term 'checklist' suggests, it is not generally used as a tool for trainee officer development. It is also usually contextualized—that is, performance is also judged in the light of a trainee's developing personal qualities (part of the PPF role profile for police constables (see 8.5.2)).

Before a trainee officer can be considered for Independent Patrol an assessor will confirm his/her competence against all the PAC subheadings. Note that successful completion of the PAC does not necessarily guarantee eligibility for Independent Patrol. Some police forces will expect more—for example, a certain level of driving skills. In many forces there will still be formal training alongside Independent Patrol, and in all forces collecting evidence towards completion of the remaining QCF assessment units will certainly continue. Under the IPLDP, there should be at least 30 days of 'protected learning time' after being granted Independent Patrol, and before Confirmation.

Note that, as a result of the introduction of the Diploma in Policing, and the new PPF (see 8.5.2), the PAC is likely to change in the near future.

8.5.4 The SOLAP

The SOLAP is the Student Officer Learning and Assessment Portfolio. It is a record of achievement that trainee officers construct during initial training, and is a key document as it charts his/her progress towards becoming professional and competent, and eventually ready for confirmation as a constable. Some forces emphasize that the portfolio firmly belongs to the trainee officer, but in reality, this does not mean that the portfolio is confidential to him/her, nor does this ownership necessarily provide any kind of protection in the case of legal action.

The SOLAP is a physical or an electronic document (stored in a folder on the force intranet or housed on a Virtual Learning Environment such as Blackboard). It has to follow certain national requirements, but forces are permitted to customize it: from the relatively trivial act of adding a force logo to the more significant step of deciding to release the SOLAP requirements to trainees in stages, rather than as a whole at the outset.

Much of the advice we have provided concerning the assessment of the QCF Diploma units applies to the completion of the SOLAP. So, for example, the SOLAP should be started as soon as possible and any incidents attended and training should be fully exploited for evidence gathering. Records of crime and incident numbers should be kept so that the material for the SOLAP can be found when needed. Some forces provide SOLAPs from previous trainee officers (anonymized), to help show what is required.

8.5.4.1 Components of the SOLAP

A typical SOLAP will be made up of the following (the format may vary from force to force and is also subject to periodic revision):

The SOLAP

Chapter	Contents	Comments
1	Student Officer Personal Profile	You provide brief biographical details (name, DoB, etc), together with a list of your previous educational and other achievements. You are expected to keep this up to date
2	Student Officer Role Profile (to be reviewed and simplified)	Information concerning the Student Officer Role Profile, including the ICF (to become the PPF), QCF units, the NOS, the PAC, assessments, and appeals
3	Introduction to the Phases of Learning	A description of the four IPLDP phases
4	The Learning Modules	A description of the three sets of IPLDP Learning Modules (the IND, OP, and LPG modules described in 1.4.2) and how the curriculum is structured
5	Learner Development Framework	A description of Learning Diaries and Learning Development Reviews. You will be expected to keep a Learning Diary and take part in the Learning Development Reviews (or their equivalent in your own force)
6	Police Action Checklist	Information concerning the PAC. You need to achieve the PAC before Independent Patrol

Qualifications and Training

Chapter	Contents	Comments
7	Diploma in Policing/QCF units/ National Occupational Standards	Detailed information concerning the Diploma in Policing, the compulsory QCF units, and the links with the NOS
8	Assessment Process	Information concerning assessment of the knowledge element, competence, collecting evidence, the assessment process (induction, planning, etc), and a useful detailed example of an assessment activity
9	Overview of Assessment Methods	Note that this chapter is concerned with the assessment of your competence
10	Overview of Assessment	A description of the main forms of documentation involved in the assessment process. These include induction records, witness testimony forms, and an evidence index
11	Glossary of terms	A 'jargon-buster' of acronyms used in the IPLDP assessment process

In addition, there are a number of appendices which contain either additional information or templates to use in order to complete a SOLAP. We examine some of the key components of the SOLAP in more detail in 8.5.4.2 and 8.5.4.3.

8.5.4.2 The Learning Diary

This is included in Chapter 5 of the SOLAP. It is a structured account of learning during the probationary period. It is, however, unlikely to consist of entries beginning 'and then I did this'. Instead, most forces will expect more reflective and evidenced entries, using the subheadings provided. Some forces emphasize the need for structure and critical reflection by renaming the Learning Diary a Reflective Diary or Reflective Journal.

Under the IPLDP, the Learning Diary subheadings normally reflect the stage of training (Home Office, 2004). For example, in the first few weeks during the initial induction phase they might relate to a trainee officer's introduction to the organization, and during a community placement the subheadings are likely to encourage reflection on what has been learnt during the placement, and so on. Under IPLDP, the Learning Diary is related to the first three phases of training (up to Independent Patrol) in the following way (Home Office, 2004 updated with Home Office, 2005d):

Learning Diary and IPLDP phases

Phase	Learning diary activities
1. Induction	Critical reflections on, for example, the introduction to the police force and the IPLDP, the training received on Health & Safety, OST, the PNC, etc, how the student is going to balance work with other demands, the relationship with others in training, the ethics and values of policing
2. Community Safety and Partnerships	Critical reflections on, for example, working with the community, experiences and learning during the community placement, and how the student will develop in the future
3. Supervised Patrol	The entries may feature under seven headings that mirror the content of LPG 1: crime; stop and search; protecting people; police policies and procedures; non-crime incidents; investigation and interview; and road policing. A student may be asked to summarize the main learning points and reflect on how this learning will be put into practice

In most cases the Learning Diaries also have a 'golden thread' running through all components, about ethics, respect for diversity, relationships with colleagues, and health and safety. There is also normally a section for tutors and trainers to complete. As well as providing useful feedback, this is also a way in which a force can monitor completion of the Diary. It is not formally assessed (in the way that a written examination would be) but there is certainly some scope for using the entries as partial evidence towards completion of some of the QCF Diploma in Policing units' assessment criteria.

Trainee officers are normally asked to keep the Learning Diary throughout training, but the format of the Diary is likely to reflect the particular phase of training (eg the style used for community engagement will not be the same as that used for Supervised Patrol). This should be explained during the induction phase of training. The Learning Diary is for writing down personal reflections, so that judgements can be made on progress, evidence competency for assessment purposes, and to plan future development. During the first two phases of training officers are usually expected to make entries every week, and later on a monthly basis. Diary entries can be structured to address the following:

- What happened?
- How did you, and the others around you, respond?
- What was the outcome of the events?
- What could you do differently, or better, in the future?

The following (fictitious) Learning Diary entries provide an idea of what is generally expected.

Trainee Police Officer: PC Phillips

Crime

When we were on night duty mobile patrol, my tutor and I were sent along with other patrols to an alarm activation at a newsagents on a housing estate where suspects had been seen to make off on foot with cigarettes and alcohol.

Key learning points:

Choosing the right search parameters when called to incidents.

What surprised me?

My tutor did not drive us straight to the shop but began an area search for the suspects some way away. He said he had judged how long it took for the alarm to be notified to control, how long it took for us to be sent to the call, and how far the suspects could have travelled on foot in that time.

How will I put this learning into practice?

In the future, if that happens or similar I will also notify control that I will not go straight to the scene. I will judge how long it has been since the incident took place, judge the suspects direction of travel, and then begin my search away from the scene. I will also consider sitting in the car with engine switched off, waiting and listening, and also requesting a dog patrol (if there is one) to attend to track the suspect.

Intelligence

Today in our briefing we were given intelligence about a known criminal suspected of burglaries in our area during the daytime. The MO is to gain entry via insecure windows at the back of terraced houses, make an untidy search and take high-value electronic equipment in pillow cases from the house, and leave via the front door.

Key learning points:

The importance of intelligence to police operations.

What surprised me?

Whilst on foot patrol today, my tutor and I saw the suspect from the briefing on a housing estate, trying to hide from us in a back garden. We checked with the homeowner that the suspect did not have permission to be in the garden. His behaviour, the information we had, the time of day, and location were our grounds to look for stolen property and we carried out a s 1 PACE search. In a pillow case quite close to the suspect there was an iPod and another mp3 player. I arrested the suspect as this was necessary for one of the reasons we learnt about during training.

How will I put this learning into practice?

This incident really showed me the importance of intelligence. I will pay more attention to briefings from now on as the information in them helps my patrol skills and gives me the idea to pay attention to specific areas and to specific people. I can see that intelligence-led policing can really work and help me to add to my reasons for needing to do a s 1 PACE search. I will also go to the Intel unit when I've got time to get up to date information on disqual drivers and their cars.

Investigation and interview

When I saw what my tutor constable said when he interviewed a shoplifter I had arrested in the shopping centre, I saw how to prove the offence by interview.

Key learning points:

Questioning techniques for interviewing.

What surprised me?

I was expecting him to use the proper words like 'Did you dishonestly appropriate the property from the shop with the intention of keeping it?' But he just used open questions and everyday language and kind of managed the conversation and asked questions like 'Why did you go into the shop?', 'What were you thinking about when you picked up the bottle of scotch?', 'How much money did you take to go shopping today?', 'What did you want to do with the scotch?'

How will I put this learning into practice?

In my interviews I will try to get to the truth, but not by using the words from legislation but instead I will speak like in a general conversation, which should get a better response from the suspect for the points we may need to prove. I will try to use open questions to get as much information from the suspect and begin my questions with 'Tell me about . . .' This seems to be a better way of interviewing.

Non-crime incidents

Today my tutor and I were requested to attend a misper call about a 10-year-old boy who had gone missing from his home.

Key learning points:

An appropriate initial response to child mispers.

What surprised me?

Before we started to fill in the misper form my tutor asked the parents if they had looked for him. They said they had searched the whole house but he said that he still had to do another search. I watched him searching the house and garden looking for anywhere a child that age could be. We looked for any gaps or spaces which would be big enough. Then in an old shed at the bottom of the garden we found him. My tutor asked the parents some questions and the child about why he had hid himself like that. I didn't realise that there are two types of misper: absent or missing.

How will I put this learning into practice?

When I get the report of a misper (not just absent), esp a child, I will start by making a full search of the home, even if the family have said they have done it already. This might save a lot of time in the long run and might prevent a large-scale search involving lots of time and people. I will look for any spaces which would fit a child and try hard to find these spaces in the first place.

Police policies and procedures

Today we attended the scene of a road traffic collision with two cars. None of the drivers had passengers or were injured. The vehicles had very slight damage and the collision took place at a T-junction at very slow speed.

Key learning points:

The importance of following force policy.

What surprised me?

I did not have any suspicion that the drivers had been drinking, but my tutor reminded me it is force policy to give a breath test to every driver in a road traffic collision (Road Traffic Act powers). I was surprised that even though it was only 8.30 am, one of the drivers proved positive and I arrested him.

How will I put this learning into practice?

In the future I will take care to follow force policy and test every driver in a crash, whether I suspect them of drinking or not. I will do this whatever the situation for the crash and whether any other driving offences are suspected.

Protecting people

When we were on foot patrol in the shopping centre today, my tutor asked me to imagine I was a thief, to look around at the shoppers, and to consider who was the most likely to be a victim of a crime when out shopping.

Key learning points:

Crime prevention is just as important as crime detection.

What surprised me?

When I looked around I saw people paying no attention to their valuable property. I saw people (all ages) carrying mobiles in their hands, just giving a thief the chance to just snatch them. This was a similar thing for others with their ipods, they didn't see the dangers. There were also some people holding money in notes in their hands and a lot of older and more weaker looking women carrying their purses very high up in their handbags which could also easily be snatched. We began giving advice to some of these people about the risks of what could happen.

How will I put this learning into practice?

Whenever it is the situation to offer crime-prevention advice I will do it. For example, if I see an old person keeping their purse near the top of their bag I will go and tell them that it could be snatched and that they could think about fixing a chain onto the purse at one end and attaching the other end to their bag.

Stops and searches

While out with my tutor today I saw a number of searches being carried out by other officers. Some of the searches did not go that well and the suspects in some were clearly not that compliant.

Key learning points:

The importance of following a professional 'stop, account, and search' routine.

What surprised me?

Most of the searches where the suspects were more compliant were the ones where the searching officers said the PACE Codes of Practice requirements for searching. What I saw was the searching officers going through them using GO WISELY. This seemed to have the effect that the suspects thought they really knew they had the right so they did not try to obstruct or resist so much.

How will I put this learning into practice?

When I carry out my searches I will do exactly the same thing and use GO WISELY to remind me of what to say. Before today, I thought I was only taught it to help me remember it for my exam, but now I see how important it is and the good effect it has on people being searched.

> **Traffic**
>
> Today on mobile patrol, we must of stopped about 15 vehicles. Every time it was to give the driver some advice.
>
> **Key learning points:**
>
> The police can help with driver and passenger safety.
>
> **What surprised me?**
>
> The reasons why we stopped the vehicles did not seem to be major issues eg for no seat belts, children that were too small for the front seat, parking near crossings, and minor speeding. Then, after speaking to my tutor, I realized that we have a role for road safety and that it is part of our job to prevent injury to drivers, passengers, or pedestrians, not just 'catch criminals'. Because if we can prevent someone's head hitting the windscreen or another passenger if in a crash by reminding them to wear a seat belt or wearing it properly, then we might have saved a lot of pain and misery. Also parking near crossings needs to be stopped as it risks the lives of people crossing. Also we learnt recently in class that 30 mph areas are there for a purpose and going over the speed limit even a bit could be the difference between life and death for a pedestrian.
>
> **How will I put this learning into practice?**
>
> Even when I am v busy with calls to attend, I will try to take the time to give advice to road-users. I will say to them that the problem is in the unexpected situations that can happen very fast so cannot be avoided. It will be difficult for me sometimes to give advice to a road user like when I am tired and hungry, but I must remember that one day I might not take the chance to say something and just after he is involved in a crash and is injured or even dies. I would find that very hard to cope with.

8.5.4.3 Learning Development Reviews

A Learning Development Review (LDR) and other forms of self-assessment give rise to documents that are more formal than the Learning Diary. LDRs are based on structured meetings with tutors and assessors involving reviews and critical self-assessment. The trainee officer then writes this up as a formal document, based on the personal qualities and role profile of the police constable. The LDRs (usually around ten) are documented in Chapter 5 of the SOLAP. There are three key reviews during training:

- the review for Independent Patrol, involving completion of the PAC;
- an interim review, for example after the first year of training (week 52); and
- the final review for confirmation (at week 92, see 8.4.3), probably involving completion of the QCF Diploma assessed units plus other professional requirements.

These LDRs are essentially a progress report and an agreement of what actions might be needed within a specified timescale. The SMART model of objective setting may be used when agreeing targets for future development: that is, the trainee officer is expected to make the targets *S*pecific, *M*easurable, *R*elevant, *A*chievable, and *T*imed. Any disciplinary matters might be included in this part of the SOLAP.

Note that forces are permitted to replace the National IPLDP Learning Development Reviews with their own local approach if they can meet the criteria laid down by NPIA (2009d, p 4). This would include linking the LDR to the PFF role profile for police constables (see 8.5.2).

8.5.5 Fitness assessment for trainee police officers

Soon after joining, trainee officers may be required to take a new fitness test, the 'job related fitness test' (the JRFT). The present JRFT is usually taken after the third week of training and involves being tested for endurance and dynamic strength. It involves a bleep test and a dynamic strength test, and is very similar to the MSFT used during the selection for recruitment (see 8.2.4.1). The 2012 Winsor Review recommended that all police officers should undergo an annual fitness test based on the standard that is currently expected for recruits in England and Wales. From September 2013 all police officers and staff requiring personal safety training will be required to take a fitness test.

If a trainee officer fails the JRFT a retake is allowed, probably at about week nine. Obviously, he/she would be well advised to attempt to improve his/her fitness in the intervening weeks. Forces are normally supportive in this matter (they appreciate that there may have been a long period between taking the MSFT as part of the recruitment process and starting training). They may suggest a programme of activities such as swimming, road running, gymnasium circuits, rowing, or cycling, together with aerobic exercise. There may be a third and final chance to pass. Failure at this stage may lead to a 'Reg 13' and dismissal from the force (see 8.4.4), but policy can vary between forces, so in such circumstances the local force and perhaps also the local Police Federation representative should be consulted (see 6.7.1).

8.6 Learning as a Trainee Police Officer

In this part of the chapter we look at the various ways in which trainee officers learn as they make their way towards Confirmation. However, the ideas and information provided here might also be useful if you are on a pre-join programme at a local college or university. Police trainers tend to structure learning so that it starts off with relatively simple tasks, and will involve acquiring largely factual knowledge. But once this has been assimilated the learning moves on to how to apply the ideas in practice. This is all deliberate; trainers understand that most people find this the best way to learn, and they use such learning theories (see 8.6.5) to help everyone make progress. However, all learners can also apply these (and other) theories themselves, to help develop more effective ways of learning independently.

The IPLDP philosophy is to encourage police forces to adopt educational principles and practices that suit adults from all personal and educational backgrounds and with all learning styles. It is worth noting that police training has existed in the UK for over 150 years, and that hundreds of thousands of trainee officers have been successfully trained. This does not mean, of course, that police training was perfect in the past nor, indeed, that it is now (HMIC, 2002); we tend not to hear much from those who have been unsuccessful! However, it is clear that many people from all sorts of backgrounds have successfully trained to become police officers and moved on to rewarding careers in policing.

It will sometimes be appropriate to perform the simpler tasks in simulated situations, so that you can easily rectify mistakes and clarify any misunderstandings. Eventually, though, it will be appropriate for you to go onto the streets of your town or city and begin the process of policing the community, first on Supervised Patrol and then later on Independent Patrol. As this is initially a daunting prospect, trainees are allocated a tutor, coach, or mentor for support, and will probably be attached to a Professional Development Unit (PDU) as well.

8.6.1 Learning and PDUs

Professional Development Units (PDUs) are also known as Probationer Development Units in some forces. Some BCUs seem to struggle to support a large number of trainees (HMIC, 2005a, p 17), and there has also been some criticism concerning the lack of police management support for some force PDUs. A Skills for Justice report in 2007 noted that this 'has the potential to have a detrimental effect on the experience of Student Officers and their opportunities for development and assessment' (Skills for Justice, 2007a, p 4).

Usually PDUs are physically based within the BCU. They assist police officers who have transferred from other forces, support police officers back into policing duties (eg after a period of illness), and provide important aspects of initial police training. However, practice does vary significantly from force to force. In some forces there may be PDUs in every BCU, whilst in others a single PDU serves the whole force. Staffing also varies, as does the management structure and the types of resource available, so it is difficult to describe a typical PDU. A police officer of inspector rank or above is likely to be responsible for a PDU, and will line-manage sergeants and Pcs (sometimes referred to as training officers) based there.

The PDU is likely to work alongside the other departments in the police organization, and might be part of your training department (in fact you might receive all your training at the PDU, including classroom-based teaching). You can expect a PDU tutor (sometimes called a tutor constable or assessor constable) to be an experienced officer with skills in coaching and assessment. Whatever the particular arrangements, the PDU is likely to be of crucial importance for trainees, an observation supported by the Home Office (2005b, p 22): 'The importance of the role of the Professional Development Unit in providing and supporting … learning experiences throughout the whole of the probationary period cannot be overstated.'

8.6.1.1   The advantages of a PDU

PDUs provide trainee police officers with the opportunity to apply learning from the training room in a controlled environment. So, instead of being immediately plunged into a world of reactive policing, a trainee can reinforce selected aspects of his/her learning through simulations of genuine policing tasks. These may be based around particular policing needs of a force, especially towards the end of training.

The further advantages of this system include the opportunity for the tutor and student to carry out activities on a one-to-one basis (Home Office, 2005c). A trainee will be able to discuss what he/she intends to do and say at an incident (a pre-brief) and will then be able to deal with the incident itself in an effective, safe, and professional manner, albeit in a monitored or co-pilot fashion with the tutor/coach. The incident can then be discussed afterwards in a safe environment (debrief). This helps trainees use the different stages of the learning cycle (see 8.6.5.3). As further reinforcement, trainees could be asked to make Learning Diary entries (see 8.5.4.2), providing further opportunities for self-assessment and reflection.

Within the PDU, staff members assess trainees' competence against the QCF Diploma in Policing units and the PAC. In turn, the Home Office expects the assessors to be competent to perform this task, demonstrated through undertaking an assessor's award perhaps (Home Office, 2005b; NPIA, 2010c).

8.6.2   Teachers, trainers, and learning

In a class of up to 16 people, there is every chance that each learner will prefer learning in a different way (see 8.6.5.2 on 'preferred learning styles'). Therefore, it is obviously a challenge for the training staff to accommodate each learner with an appropriate activity. A popular approach in police training is 'facilitation', where trainers adopt styles and techniques to bring out (or 'tease out') ideas and views from the group whilst at the same time reducing their own role as conventional didactic 'stand at the front and talk' teachers.

We will describe a number of activities commonly employed by trainers. The intention is that all members of a group will be engaged at least once during a session. Some trainers will use evaluation sheets to find out more about the effectiveness of different methods.

The **'boardblast'** is a very popular teaching method used by police trainers. The tutor will invite responses which will be written down on a board or flipchart and then discussed. This will be assessed by the tutor and revisited at different stages of the lesson, and is often a very effective method (but is sometimes used to excess). Another occasional disadvantage to the boardblast approach is that most of the class will have very limited knowledge and hence the suggestions might not cover all the required aspects for the topic.

Written case studies involve working on a practical example of a police-related problem. Details will be given to an individual or a group, who will then read the material and form conclusions about its content to demonstrate understanding of the subject.

Demonstration can be used for practical topics involving the use of the body in the psycho-motor domain (see 8.6.5.1). The tutor will demonstrate the movements so the student can repeat the activity afterwards.

Small-group work is a very common method in police training. Students share ideas among the group and for this to work well, each member should be actively involved in the task. When the group reports back its findings, the trainer or trainers will probably act as a facilitator and will tease out the learning.

Large-group work usually involves allocating responsibility to small groups for researching part of a larger topic. They work away from the training room, and use books, reference material, and computer-based learning. After an agreed time the large group reassembles and the small groups each present their findings to everyone. Alternatively, a large group of students may be presented with information, perhaps from a specialist or a guest speaker, or by watching a video clip.

Individual work provides an opportunity for the student to work alone. This could take a variety of forms, ranging from conducting interviews for research to writing an assignment under exam conditions.

Electronic learning often uses computer-based learning (CBL) packages, which are now available both nationally and locally. CBL activity can be carried out individually or in small groups, both inside and outside the classroom environment. Trainee officers and/or special constables are likely to have access to the resources on the NCALT website (a username and password are needed). There are an increasing number of electronic resources available through NCALT, particularly case studies that link with the IPLDP learning outcomes and phases (see 1.4.2 and 8.3), Core Investigative Doctrine (the basis for investigative theory: see Chapter 23), and PIP Level 1 (see 7.5). For example, Phase 3 Case Studies include Public Order, Civil Dispute, Sudden Death, and Stop and Search, and Phase 4 includes Counter Terrorism, Missing Persons, Burglary, and Child Protection.

Facilitated discussions are particularly useful for exploring attitudes and behaviour. The discussion might be initiated by watching a DVD, or by reflecting on the presentation of a guest speaker. Trainers encourage students to share their thoughts with others. If this is the case, then trainee officers should be prepared to maintain confidentiality as private and sensitive matters may be disclosed (but remember that confidentiality does not protect a trainee from disciplinary action concerning inappropriate language, attitudes, or behaviour).

Presentations are used for some topics. If the subject matter is appropriate for this form of delivery (eg an introduction to the Theft Act 1968), or time is short, then trainers may well deliver a presentation, often using Microsoft PowerPoint software. Throughout the presentation, trainees are given the opportunity to ask questions and make notes. Different trainers will have different approaches to delivering presentations, which may or may not coincide with a student's learning style. For example, some may use the technique of progressively revealing bullet points which, although it will keep the attention of many in the class, can be irritating to some (most trainers welcome feedback on matters such as this). Finally, a Virtual Learning Environments (such as Blackboard) is likely to contain copies of the presentations.

Role-plays are where a trainee will 'play' a given role and act it out in an imaginary situation suggested by the trainer. For example, one of you may act the police officer and the other a member of the public in a simulated 'stop and account' scenario. In all cases, the brief for the role-play should be carefully explained to the trainee at the outset. Role-plays are normally used when a trainee has gained sufficient knowledge and skills (particularly in terms of police procedure) to make them meaningful. Some police forces use semi-professional actors or volunteers from the local community to play roles. The latter approach may also have certain added advantages in terms of diversity training. One underlying principle to the role-play approach is that adult learners are able to draw upon previous experiences to enhance their learning. Just as significant for a trainee's learning as the role-play itself is the debrief afterwards (a trainee could even be videoed to assist with this). Note that, as we discuss in 8.5.1.4, role-plays and simulations cannot normally be used as evidence against achievement of the assessment criteria of the Diploma in Policing units. However, a trainee officer can reflect on what has been learnt from a role-play in his/her Learning Diary Phase 3.

Undertaking a **community engagement** is seen as an important way in which trainee officers learn about the diverse communities they will police and their own attitudes towards the various community members (see 8.6.4). However, at this point note the importance that the IPLDP places on adopting a self-critical approach (Home Office, 2004) involving active self-questioning of his/her existing beliefs and attitudes. A police force will probably expect to see evidence of this self-critical approach in Learning Diary Phase 2 entries under headings such as 'What challenged you during the engagement, in what ways, and how did you respond?'

Syndicate exercises involve students working in small groups as a syndicate. A syndicate is a group of people where each assumes a certain role. For example, one student might be a member of the public complaining about anti-social behaviour in her street. Other members of the syndicate will play the role of the local PC, the police BCU commander, and so on. The various issues are explored from the different perspectives. Syndicate exercises can be useful learning devices but need to be carefully organized and managed by trainers, with detailed instructions and briefing on the roles played by students. For example, if the syndicate group is quite large (six or more) certain members of the group might not participate, or the issues might be only be examined in token and ineffective ways because of time restraints.

Finally, trainers will ensure that trainee officers have access to the NPIA 'blended' learning resources that support IPLDP. These include extensive student notes, audio notes (mp3 versions of the student notes), and the 'Quick Notes'—abridged versions of the full student notes that summarize key learning points.

8.6.3 Coaching

In police training, coaching is normally carried out one-to-one, and will be one of the responsibilities of a tutor or mentor, particularly when a trainee is based with a PDU (see 8.6.1).

As soon as you have been given details of your tutor(s) you should arrange to meet up. At the meeting you may find yourself talking about your background, how you came to join the police, and what you are aiming for. You should also mention the name you would like your tutor to use for you. However, bear in mind that your relationship with your tutor will develop over time—so do not say too much if it makes you feel uncomfortable. Take your SOLAP with you if it contains any feedback from your training staff at university or training centre, so that your tutor can start to get to know you. You could share entries from your Learning Diary (see 8.5.4.2) to help illustrate your strengths and weaknesses. Together you can use these to create a development plan for the future. Making a list of subjects that you have already learned in theory can help with planning on how to create opportunities for applying the learning in the work place.

Your tutor will use a variety of techniques to help you learn. Questioning can involve closed questions (with a yes or no answer), open questions which need fuller answers, and reflective questions to check your understanding; all of these are useful. If your tutor uses multiple questions you need to answer one question at a time to avoid confusion. And 'leading' questions might lead you to agree when you might in fact have a different opinion. (Remember, this could equally well apply to your own use of questions, so you should be aware of what style of questions you are using.)

Coaching often takes place before and after attending an incident as part of Supervised Patrol. The incidents may have been carefully selected by the PDU: that is, they wait for a particular type of incident to be reported (such as a suspected shoplifting incident) and then accompany you to that incident. In some cases, for practical or other reasons, you might attend any incident that day, regardless of its nature. Your response (but not necessarily on the first occasion) will be important in terms of your subsequent assessment against the Diploma in Policing units (see 8.5.1).

Pre-briefs are a good way of preparing. Your tutor will question you about the theory you have learned in the training room, and about how you intend to deal with the incident. At the debrief afterwards he/she will probably ask you to reflect and make notes about what went well, and what did not go quite so well (the notes can also be used for Learning Diary entries). Your tutor may help you reflect and learn by using the ELC (see 8.6.5.3). Important questions will include 'What happened at the incident?' and 'What are you going to do differently (or better) next time?'

The tutor feedback serves two main purposes: to reassure you that your contribution has been recognized and noted, and to help you develop the skills and abilities required. You may notice that feedback is often structured as a kind of sandwich; first an observation on something you did well, then discussing a developmental point, and then returning to something else you did well. This works well for most people.

8.6.4 Learning from the community

Under the IPLDP, all trainee police officers are expected to undertake at least 80 hours of community engagement, normally as part of Phase 2 or Phase 3 (if a police force uses this terminology). These hours could be a continuous week of block placement or perhaps one or two days per week for a number of months. For at least 24 of the 80 hours, a trainee will be based with a community group or a public, private, or voluntary organization such as a care home, a refugee support centre, or a youth-offending team. A particular emphasis is placed on the opportunities the placement provides in relation to ethnicity and diversity (by 'issues around diversity' the police service normally means gender, disability, gay and lesbian groups, and age). However, the community engagement can also be used to give the trainee an insight into the community's expectations of the police. Examples of this kind of placement include being based in local supermarkets, hospitals, schools, and housing authority units. Other examples of community placements (the other 56 hours) include attachments to 'low-profile' policing units and one-day visits to local community groups.

Trainee police officers on community engagement are not likely to be in uniform (or carrying personal safety equipment), and it may be decided that it is best not to reveal to the 'clients' at the placement that the fresh face is a trainee police officer. This is normally to allow trainees to interact as naturally as possible with the clients of the organization, particularly if some of them could be hostile to the police. If this is the case for you, bear the following in mind:

- Your force will have conducted a risk assessment concerning the placement but, if you feel uncomfortable in terms of your own personal safety, then you should make this known to your force. If the problem persists, then you may wish to contact your Police Federation representative (see 6.7.1).
- There will be standard operating procedures (SOPs) in place to govern the relationships between your force and the organizations involved and also what you should do under certain circumstances—for example, in the case of questions concerning health and safety. Familiarize yourself with these SOPs.

To make the most of a community engagement you should find out about the organization in advance. It may have a website setting out its aims and objectives. You should try and find out how it is funded and if it is inspected in some way (inspection reports may be available online). When on placement, you should engage with the people there—for example, staff and clients of the organization. They will be as interested in you as you are in them and so you will probably find this quite easy. You should keep in mind the objectives of the community placement; the aim is for you to learn about community issues. Think also about how you could evidence the skills and knowledge you gained from the placement. How could you demonstrate that your understanding of the ethics and values of the police service has been enhanced through engagement with the community?

You are sometimes required to present your findings to fellow trainee officers and perhaps even members of your Supervised Patrol BCU. Your experiences will also form the basis for some of your Learning Diary entries in the SOLAP (see 8.5.4), or could be used in a professional assignment. It is also likely to be relevant to some of the Diploma in Policing assessment unit learning outcomes and the relevant NOS units, in particular the embedded NOS Unit AA1 'Promote equality and value diversity'.

Your experience of learning from the community is unlikely to be restricted to the community engagement alone. As noted earlier, you will also receive inputs from guest speakers and community representatives during your training. You should make a real effort as a learner to engage with the guest speakers and achieve as much as possible from the session.

> **TASK 4** You are on community engagement at a centre that provides support for young people who have been excluded from full-time secondary education. The young people at the day centre have been told that you are a student and that you are there to learn about their experiences and the work of the support group. However, they have not been told that you are a student police officer. During a break you observe one young person offering to sell what appears to be Ecstasy, a class B drug (see 12.5) to his friend. What do you do?

8.6.5 Improving your learning

To understand how you will learn on pre-entry courses and during police training, you will need to understand something about how you learn as an adult, and this will vary and will depend in part on your educational background. You may be a student on a pre-join programme, or have entered the police family earlier in another police-related role (eg as a PCSO), or have recently left full-time further or higher education (up to 30 per cent in recent years), whilst a number of you might not have undertaken training or study for a long time.

8.6.5.1 Domains of learning

Many of our day-to-day actions centre on three main areas of activity and so it follows that these three areas are the ones in which learning or education often take place. Understanding these areas will help you to assess your own competencies and evaluate your own educational and training needs. This will make it easier for you to learn and revise for exams, and will provide you with a route map through any learning experience. The three areas are referred to as the 'learning domains' (eg Bloom *et al*, 1956 and subsequent publications in this series), and you will no doubt hear your trainers refer to them from time to time. In brief the three domains are:

- The cognitive domain which is associated with the ability to reason, and will include learning subject matter such as law, legislation, policy, and procedure, about which we have to think.
- The affective domain which is associated with feelings and emotions, for example, the way people react to situations (such as provocation), and their values and prejudices. A cliché in police training is that 'attitudes can be caught or taught', and therefore a great deal of your training will involve learning to adopt appropriate attitudes and behaviours towards the public and your colleagues, in areas such as respect, race and diversity, team working, community and customer focus, effective communication, problem solving, personal responsibility, and resilience.
- The psychomotor domain is associated with physical dexterity, for example, personal safety training, First Aid training, using a breath test machine, and traffic control.

Within these domains there are levels of complexity, beginning with the easiest (on the left) and progressively becoming more difficult towards the right, as shown in the table.

For the cognitive domain ('the head'):

Knowledge →	Comprehension →	Application
The ability to recall facts, words, or phrases, eg a definition of an Act or a section of law	To understand and be able to explain component parts of policy, procedure, or legislation, eg the meanings of words within definitions, the variations and exceptions	To use this knowledge and understanding to apply previous learning to a set task which is either simulated, paper-based, or in the work place

For the affective domain ('the heart'):

Receives →	Responds →	Values
Listens to or sees demonstrated an attitude which is to be learned eg 'We want you to be a non-discriminator, regardless of the prejudices you may actually have'	Outwardly shows the learned attitude or behaviour, but does not necessarily believe in it, eg 'I have prejudices, but I will not discriminate because I've been told I must not'	Adopts the learned attitude or behaviour and, without request or prompting, owns the feeling personally, eg 'Even though I have prejudices, I believe it is wrong to discriminate and therefore I will not do so'

For the psychomotor domain ('the hands'):

Imitation →	Manipulation →	Precision
Performs the skill as a result of copying or repeating what has been observed, eg resuscitation techniques in First Aid	Executes the skill with some instruction or coaching	Carries out the skill alone without copying, instruction, or the necessity for coaching

For a session involving mainly the cognitive domain, you will probably be asked to assimilate at least some of the knowledge about the subject in advance; for example, learning an offence in the form of a definition. This is sometimes referred to in police training as a 'pre-read' but you are of course required to *learn* material, and not just read it! The next stage will possibly involve a knowledge check to assess whether you have gained the appropriate level of understanding. A trainer or tutor will then probably move you on to the next level in the cognitive domain (from knowledge to comprehension) and check your understanding and clarify any misunderstandings. Finally, you will be given an opportunity to develop your learning further, using one or more of the methods listed in 8.6.5. This will involve the third level of the domain—applying your learning.

Similar activities will be used in the other two domains for attitudinal and skills-based subjects, but each time you will probably start at the simplest level and move incrementally to the more complex. Then, whether it is through assimilation or work-based learning in your PDU, you will be coached and mentored by your tutor to a level of competency in preparation for assessment against the Diploma in Policing units and the embedded National Occupational Standards (see 7.4).

8.6.5.2 Preferred learning styles

People seem to prefer to learn in different ways (Kolb, 1984) and researchers have discerned the existence of four main learning styles; activist, theorist, pragmatist, and reflective. Most people fit into one or two of these styles.

The **activist** learning style involves being actively involved with a task, for example taking part in simulations or role-plays; setting tasks or writing questions or case studies; taking part in computer-based learning, for example through the NCALT website; and/or using pre-formed questions before sessions so that learning can be continually checked.

The **theorist** learning style involves having a logical outlook and developing underlying theories; reading about a subject and drawing independent conclusions; challenging the underlying assumptions; and/or designing logical diagrams to summarize the subject matter as a sequence of points to be learned.

The **pragmatist** learning style involves thinking or dealing with the problem in a practical way, rather than using theory or abstract principles; finding the use of theory and discussion frustrating; and/or looking for the practical applications for learning.

The **reflective** learning style involves learning in a slow, deliberate way; taking a step back and looking at a subject from all angles before drawing a conclusion; discussing issues; and/or finding participation in simulations or role-plays less useful.

> **TASK 5** You can find out more about your own learning style(s) by taking part in an online questionnaire: go to the Learning Styles interactive website at Canterbury Christ Church University: <http://www.canterbury.ac.uk/graduate-skills/preview/audits/learning-styles/index.html>.

8.6.5.3 The Experiential Learning Cycle (ELC)

You have undoubtedly heard of the sayings 'if you don't succeed the first time, then try, try again' or 'we all learn by our mistakes'. Much of your learning will take place through your own experiences, and as adults we can actually teach ourselves, at least in part. This process can be represented as a diagram showing the experiential learning cycle (ELC), adapted from the work of David Kolb (Kolb, 1984).

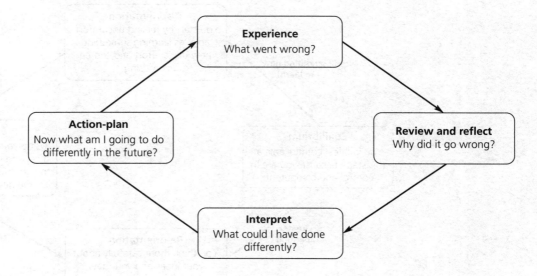

Qualifications and Training

> **TASK 6** Think of a situation you found yourself in recently where afterwards you decided to do something differently next time. Now relate those circumstances to the ELC diagram, starting with Experience and moving clockwise through the diagram.

The four stages to the cycle are as follows:

- *Experience* (called 'Concrete Experience' in the Kolb original): this is direct experience, often through practical application. As a trainee police officer you will often want to know what the practical applications of the session will be. You may want to get 'hands on' as soon as possible. The trainer may prompt you—for example, by prompting you to 'think of times in your own life when you have been subject to bullying or harassment'.
- *Review and reflect* ('Reflection'): what does the experience mean to me? This stage is the beginning of understanding. A task such as 'describe your feelings when you were bullied or harassed' may be given.
- *Interpret* ('Abstract Conceptualization'): this involves placing the experiences in some form of theoretical and more abstract framework such as 'How do victims feel about this?'
- *Action-plan* ('Active Experimentation'): the stage of action-planning is how we take this learning forward and test it against reality, such as 'How then do we act as a police service to support victims of harassment?'

> **TASK 7** A trainee police officer, as part of Personal Safety Training, starts learning how to handcuff a suspect by taking part in supervised practice using a manikin (dummy). The trainer, observing the student practise and testing the results, then asked: 'Were there any risks to you during the cuffing? How tight did that feel for the suspect? What might you have done differently?'
>
> That night the trainee reads up on how to handcuff suspects; the reasons for doing it in particular ways, force procedure, and the human rights of the suspect. The next day, presented with a fellow trainee to handcuff, she thinks: 'Now what did I do wrong yesterday and what did it say in those notes I read? I'll try it like this today.'
>
> Identify in the above, each of the four stages of Kolb's ELC.

8.6.5.4 Studying and study skills

We acknowledge that learning 'policing' is sometimes a confusing and disorientating experience. In some cases we even have to unlearn before we can learn. For example, if you do not know that there are major legal differences between the offences of robbery and burglary, you will have to unlearn what you thought you knew already, which can be a disconcerting experience! Taylor (1986) suggests that the discomfort we experience is actually a necessary part of adult learning. In particular, she discerned four distinct phases of the learning experience, as shown in the diagram.

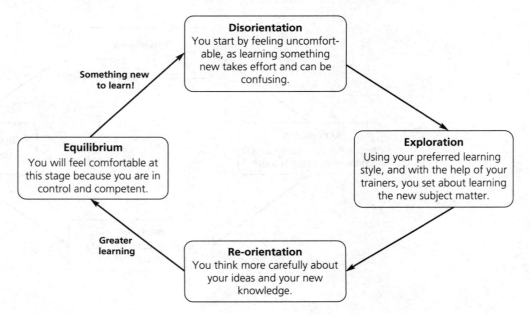

In summary, learning something new is often initially characterized by feelings of discomfort and anxiety. Bear this in mind when studying and it will help you cope; it is quite normal to have some ups and downs as you learn.

There are numerous guides, books, and websites which can be used to help develop your study skills. For example, if you are also undertaking a higher education award as part of your education and training, then you may find it useful to work through Dr Stella Cottrell's *Study Skills Handbook* (Cottrell, 2013). Students based at a college or university will almost certainly find that support for study skills is available. Broadly, trainee officers and students on pre-join programmes will need the following skills:

- reading skills;
- note taking and writing skills;
- memorizing and revising for assessments;
- using libraries, learning centres, and e-learning resources;
- researching and using internet search engines; and
- time management

Finally, note that you may have undiagnosed difficulties in learning which could affect your ability to study. If you are based in a college or university you may be offered screening for such problems at the outset of the programme.

> **TASK 8** Find out about the reading technique SQ3R, perhaps by using Google or another internet search engine. This will also prove useful to you if you decide to train as an investigator over the next few years.

8.6.6 Diversity training in the police

One of the reasons for undertaking a community engagement (see 8.6.4) is that it provides real and complex opportunities for a trainee police officer to witness and learn from the views and experiences of members of the diverse communities that make up the UK.

In general terms, diversity is about the range of features found in human life and culture including ethnicity, religion, gender, physical ability, age, sexual orientation, customs, and language. We ought perhaps to celebrate diversity as part of the richness of human cultures, but diversity is sometimes thought of as a form of 'otherness'—that is, qualities that make 'them' different from 'us'. We also examine diversity as a key theme in policing in 3.8.

Trainee officers need to think carefully about their own experiences and attitudes, and how these might affect the way they relate to the diverse range of people encountered in policing work. What skills are needed to work effectively in the community, and how can diversity training help with developing these skills? Diversity training is usually placed within IPLDP module IND 2, but it will be assessed in a variety of contexts. One of the assessment units embedded in the Diploma in Policing (NOS Unit AA1.1) includes the element to 'Promote equality and value diversity', and this is likely to be assessed through direct observation of a trainee's actions, the records he/she kept, and testimony from witnesses.

There is a tendency in some police environments to view diversity training as a form of inoculation. In fact, you sometimes hear police officers saying that they have 'had' their diversity training as if it were some form of one-off injection that would protect them for the rest of their careers. Perhaps it would be more appropriate to see diversity training as just the start of a process that will continue throughout your career.

8.6.6.1 Questions you might need to consider

You might need to consider the following questions during diversity training:

- What are my existing beliefs and attitudes about the diversity I encounter in people?
- How will my beliefs and attitudes affect the way that I behave during my everyday and professional life?
- How will my behaviour affect other people around me?

But at the outset, why is it important to consider these questions? It is important because our beliefs, attitudes, and values can spill over into our work, and for a police officer this includes whilst on duty. Hence if you hold prejudices and bias towards certain groups of people (as most of us do, to some extent at least), you are more likely to act upon your prejudices if you are not aware of them, and your conduct may fall short of the standards expected of trainee police officers.

Finally, respect for diversity makes good policing sense. You are more likely to gain the cooperation of others, to secure information and intelligence, and hence to progress an investigation, if you are aware of the pluralistic nature of the communities within the UK and have some understanding of how best to work in such contexts.

8.6.6.2   **Looking inwards**

As an individual, you will view the world in your own way, but you also need to remember that other individuals each have their own world-view that deserves respect. To consider these issues fully, you will need to genuinely engage with your lecturers, trainers, your colleagues, and most of all, yourself. In particular, you will need to examine what you know about yourself in relation to diversity and the following issues:

What I know about myself as an individual:

* how I currently behave;
* my current values, beliefs, and attitudes; and
* how my background has influenced me.

What I know about myself as a trainee police officer:

* my responsibilities and the duties I have to perform;
* my career history; and
* how the law affects me and the policies I have to follow.

TASK 9 Take the time to think, then jot down your thoughts about the points above—you might find it quite hard to see yourself in these ways. Reflect upon your ideas—which parts have you found easy, and which parts have been more puzzling? Do you know why? Through asking yourself these questions, you will be preparing yourself for genuine engagement with police service diversity training.

TASK 10 Consider:

* your experiences in life so far and those you are likely to have in the near future;
* your prejudices, assumptions, and stereotypical views, and their consequences;
* your view of the world you live in and the people within it; and
* your ability to mix well in a social environment with people from other backgrounds and cultures.

Again, take time to think about each point in turn. You may find it useful to think what your friends and family would say about any prejudices you might have. Make brief notes and reflect upon your answers.

8.7   Answers to Tasks

TASK 1 Well, how does it compare? Do not be surprised (or concerned) to find significant variation from the national template.

The internet will give you access to brief descriptions of a number of force approaches to structuring initial training, and it is surprising how varied these can be.

TASK 2 Outcomes 2 and 3 must each be demonstrated on two occasions.

TASK 3 You should have found that the knowledge and understanding requirements of Unit 4G4 are:

1. Limitations and risks of applying First Aid to others.
2. How to detect an obstructed airway and methods of clearing obstruction.
3. How to check for signs of life and for life-threatening conditions.

4. Methods of CPR and how to use this appropriately.
5. How to manage an unconscious casualty and the main causes of unconsciousness.
6. Precautions to be taken when performing CPR.
7. Different types of wound and their treatment.
8. Methods for controlling bleeding.
9. Signs and symptoms of shock.
10. Recognition and treatment of sprains, strains, and fractures.
11. Main safety considerations when dealing with burns or scalds.
12. How to recognize and assess the severity and extent of injuries.
13. Appropriate treatments for hypothermia, frostbite, heat-stroke, and heat exhaustion.
14. How to recognize and respond to local danger and risks when dealing with casualties.

TASK 4 This would be a difficult issue for any trainee police officer you. You have probably been attested, and hence have assumed the full responsibilities and powers of a constable and yet you are barely trained and even less experienced. You are with the organization to learn, not to disrupt their usual ways of working. However, dealing in drugs is a serious offence.

Your force will have standing operating procedures to help you decide what to do, and these often involve you taking advice from your supervisor and referring to the policies of the organization concerned. The important point is not to keep this to yourself.

TASK 5 You will find that the site will describe each of the categories as 'activist', 'theorist', 'pragmatist', and 'reflector' and undertaking the online questionnaire would have placed your preferred learning style into a grid:

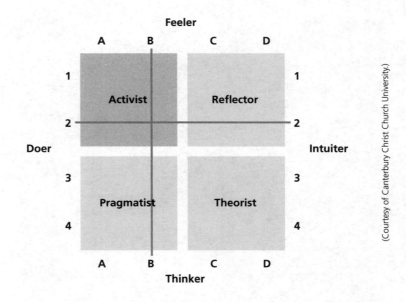

(Courtesy of Canterbury Christ Church University.)

Where the two lines intersect gives you some measure of your preferred learning style. It shows that I am a predominantly activist learner. According to the site this means that I seek hidden possibilities; I learn by talking with others; I get totally involved; I take risks; I am enthusiastic, working quickly and involving others, and my favourite question is 'What if'?

The site is not the only way of exploring your preferred learning styles. A popular method in police training is to use Honey and Mumford's Learning Styles Questionnaire. Further details may be found at <http://www.peterhoney.com/>.

TASK 6 Not everyone finds that the Kolb process works for them. Indeed, there are a number of more general critiques of the theory underlying ELC. Rogers, for example, has argued that 'learning includes goals, purposes, intentions, choice and decision-making, and it is not at all clear where these elements fit into the learning cycle' (Rogers, 1996, p 108).

TASK 7 The supervised practice with a dummy is the experience stage.

The trainer asked, 'Were there any risks to you during the cuffing? How tight might that feel for the suspect? What might you have done differently?'—this is the review and reflect stage.

The trainee reads up on how to handcuff suspects and reads about the reasons for doing it in particular ways, including force procedure and the human rights of the suspect—this is the interpret stage.

The next day she has the chance to practise handcuffing again and thinks, 'After what happened yesterday, and because of what I read last night I'll try it a bit looser'—this is the action-planning stage.

TASK 8 SQ3R stands for:

- Survey/Skim the material you need to read;
- formulate Questions that you expect the material to answer;
- do the Reading;
- Recall what you have read; and
- Review.

TASKS 9 and 10 Your answers will reflect your own particular experiences and thoughts.

As background reading you might wish to consider looking at the 2003 HMIC thematic inspection *Diversity Matters*, which examined training on matters of race and diversity in the police service. This report should be available from your police force. The Equality and Human Rights Commission document 'Police and racism: What has been achieved 10 years after the Stephen Lawrence Inquiry report?' is available online.

9 | Stop, Search, and Entry

9.1 Introduction

This chapter describes police procedures and duties in relation to stop and search for people and vehicles, searching premises, and powers of entry into premises. These procedures will be used by trainee police officers on Supervised and Independent Patrol.

'Stop and search' is an umbrella term given to the 19 or more powers to detain people for the purposes of search. The most widely used of these powers is s 1 of the PACE Act 1984. There is some controversy surrounding the use of stop, account, and search powers by the police in relation to people from visible ethnic minorities. Stop and search has been particularly associated with racial harassment; it is claimed that visible ethnic minority people have been subject to stop and search to a disproportionate extent compared with their proportion in the general population. There are, however, arguments concerning the statistical basis for this claim, which highlight the difference between the 'resident' and 'available' populations in particular policing areas (eg see Waddington *et al*, 2004). Put simply, the population 'available' for stop and search (eg on the streets) is not the same, in terms of ethnicity, as the population resident in an area. In fact, the numbers of young black men stopped and searched by the police is roughly equal to the proportion of such men in the 'available' population. However, as Newburn notes, 'irrespective of whether or not police stop and search powers are used...in a discriminatory fashion, it seems undeniable that this is how they are experienced by minority ethnic communities' (Newburn, 2007, p 787).

ACPO are clear that stop and search, when used with the support and confidence of communities, is a 'valuable tool in tackling criminality and terrorism' (ACPO, 2006b, p 3). Research also suggests that the use of stop and search, when employed properly, has the support of all communities in the UK (eg Stone and Pettigrew, 2000). On every occasion all police officers should ask themselves whether there is justification for conducting a particular stop and search within the context of the powers of search to be used. Their grounds and the reason must be able to withstand scrutiny. In addition, 'all stops and searches should be carried out with courtesy, consideration and respect for the person concerned. This has a significant impact on public confidence in the police' (PACE Code A, para 3.1 and the Terrorism Act 2000 Codes of Practice, para 5.1.1). Further commentary can be found in the 2013 HMIC report 'Stop and Search Powers: are the police using them effectively and fairly?' available online. The Home Secretary also launched a consultation into 'stop and search' in mid-2013, to look at whether police powers are used appropriately and fairly, and how they can be better targeted and more intelligence-led.

The record of all stops and searches is a conventional quantitative measurement of police performance, and each force has policy guidelines on when and how these powers may be used. The main thing to remember is that whatever search power is used, it must conform to the guidelines set out in the PACE Act 1984 Codes of Practice.

Powers of entry are also provided for searching, for example searching a property directly after an arrest for dangerous articles or property relating to a criminal offence (s 32 of the PACE Act 1984). Powers of entry are also available for other purposes, such as to make an arrest under s 17 of the PACE Act 1984. The precise circumstances are considered in 9.5 together with the procedures that must be followed.

General Procedures

9.2 Definitions of Places and Other Locations

Various categories of locations that apply to stop and account and searches are referred to in the legislation. The definitions of locations and places given here are also relevant to other aspects of law-enforcement work.

A **public place** is anywhere 'the public or any section of the public has access, on payment or otherwise, as of right or by virtue of express or implied permission' (s 1(1)(a) of the PACE Act 1984). The public have a right to use roads and footpaths, and other public areas during opening hours. They have express permission to enter cinemas, theatres, or football grounds having paid an entrance fee and they can remain there until that particular entertainment is over, when permission to be there ends. There is an implied permission for persons to enter privately owned buildings to carry out business transactions with the owners, and to use a footpath to the front door of a house to pay a lawful call on the householder. That implied permission remains until withdrawn by the householder or the owner of the business premises. Places to which the public has ready access include a private field (if that field is regularly used, even by trespassers), or a garden (if it is accessible by jumping over a low wall). Ultimately, it would be a question of fact for the court to consider whether all members of the general public can gain ready access to the place and whether a landowner has given permission for the public to use a privately owned place.

A **private place** is land or premises which are privately owned to which the general public does NOT have ready access, for example a private residence or a private office block. Privately owned land or premises that is used by the general public during opening hours (and is therefore a public place at that time) reverts to being a private place during closing times.

Premises is a very general term and under s 23 of the PACE Act 1984 includes:

(a) any vehicle, vessel, aircraft or hovercraft;
(b) any offshore installation;
(ba) any renewable energy installation; and
(c) a tent or moveable structure.

A **dwelling** is any place where a person or people live and is defined in two pieces of legislation. A dwelling is:

- '[a]ny structure or part of a structure occupied as a person's home or as other living accommodation (whether the occupation is separate or shared with others) but does not include any part not so occupied, and for this purpose "structure" includes a tent, caravan, vehicle, vessel or other temporary or moveable structure' (s 8 of the Public Order Act 1986);
- '[a]n inhabited building, or a vehicle or vessel which is, at the time of the offence, inhabited (irrespective of whether or not the person who occupies the vehicle/vessel is present at the time of the burglary)' (s 9(4) of the Theft Act 1968).

A **place of residence** is not defined in law so would be a question of fact for the court to decide, but is likely to be similar to a dwelling.

9.3 Stop and Account

Polices officers can speak to anyone in the ordinary course of their duties, and members of the public have a civic duty to help the police prevent crime and locate suspects (PACE Code of Practice A, Note 1). Paragraph 4.12 of PACE Code A explains that when a police officer asks a person in a public place to account for his/her behaviour, actions, presence in a public place, or possession of a particular item, there is no need to record the encounter or provide a receipt.

Police forces have discretion if there are concerns over local disproportionality; they can request officers to record the self-defined ethnicity of persons who are asked to account for themselves, or who are detained with a view to searching but are not searched (Code A, Note 22A). The person should be given information about how to report any dissatisfaction with respect to the way he/she has been treated, if he/she requests it (Code A, Note 22B).

9.4 Stop and Search Powers

There are over 19 different powers to stop and search, such as for drugs (see 9.4.3.1) and firearms (s 47 of the Firearms Act 1968). Section 1 of the PACE Act 1984 introduced a further power to stop and search for stolen items or 'prohibited articles' and is perhaps the most commonly used. The full list of stop and search powers is given in Annex A to the PACE Code of Practice A and we discuss some of these in more detail in 9.4.2. Finally, although not a power to stop and search *per se*, we will conclude with road checks for locating particular people, under s 4 of the PACE Act 1984.

The Certificate in Knowledge of Policing requires learners to 'understand legal and organizational requirements in relation to searching individuals' and to 'understand legal and organizational requirements in relation to searching vehicles, premises, and open spaces'. The ability to 'demonstrate lawful search of persons, premises, and vehicles' is a requirement within the PAC heading 'Search' and can also contribute evidence for the attainment of the Diploma in Policing assessed unit 'Search individuals'. Note that the unit requires that an officer can conduct searches on the appropriate 'grounds and legal authority', and identify and deal with any potential risks such as offensive weapons, assault, sharps (eg hypodermic needles), or hazardous substances. As with most Diploma assessment criteria, the evidence is likely to be through an assessor's direct observation of a real search. Competence will need to be demonstrated against the learning outcomes on at least two occasions in the work place.

9.4.1 Stop and search procedures

Whichever stop and search power is used, s 2 of the PACE Act 1984 and the PACE Codes of Practice always apply. This is to safeguard the rights of the individual concerned. The procedures to be followed are described in detail in 9.4.1.1 to 9.4.1.4.

9.4.1.1 Discrimination and 'protected characteristics'

Code A, para 1.1 of the Codes of Practice states that police officers must use their powers to stop and search fairly, responsibly, with respect for people being searched, and without unlawful discrimination. Indeed, the Equality Act 2010 makes it unlawful for police officers to discriminate against, harass, or victimize, any person on the grounds of the 'protected characteristics' of age, disability, race, religion or belief, sex, gender reassignment, sexual orientation, marriage and civil partnership, pregnancy or maternity.

9.4.1.2 Information a police officer must provide before the search

Reasonable steps must be taken to provide certain information to the person to be searched (or to the person in charge of a vehicle which is to be searched). These requirements are explained in s 2 of the PACE Act 1984 and Code A, para 3.8 of the Codes of Practice. The information to be provided is shown in the following table and can be summarized by the mnemonic GO WISELY.

G	Grounds of the suspicion for the search
O	Object/purpose of search
W	Warrant card (if the officer is in plain clothes or if requested by the person)
I	Identity of the officer performing the search
S	Station to which the officer is attached
E	Entitlement to a copy of the search record
L	Legal power used
Y	You are detained for the purposes of a search

It is important that police officers comply with all aspects of GO WISELY. In the case of *O (a juvenile) v DPP* (1999) 163 JP 725, it was decided that a breach of s 2 of the PACE Act 1984 would render a search (and probably any later arrest and detention) unlawful. This decision was confirmed in *R v Bristol* [2007] EWCA Crim 3214, a case that involved a search carried out under s 23 of the Misuse of Drugs Act 1971. The defendant was convicted of obstructing a police officer but the conviction was overturned on appeal because s 2 of the PACE Act 1984 had not been complied with during the search.

9.4.1.3 Conducting the search

The officer must comply with Code A throughout the search. The search must be kept **relevant**: the extent of the search must relate to the object the officer is looking for. For example, if a witness has seen someone putting an object into a certain jacket pocket or the glove compartment of a vehicle, then only that location can be searched (para 3.3). The person or vehicle can be detained for the purpose of such a search, but the length of time must be reasonable and kept to a minimum (para 3.3).

The following points also apply for searching a person under stop and search powers; the officer:

- must seek the **cooperation** of the person. Under s 117 of the PACE Act 1984 reasonable force may be used as a last resort (see 9.5.3 and 15.5.1), but only after attempts to search have been met with resistance (para 3.2);
- cannot search a member of the **opposite sex** if it involves removal of more than outer coat, jacket, gloves, headgear, or footwear, or be present at such a search unless the person being searched specifically requests it (para 3.6);
- cannot require any person to **remove any clothing in public** other than an outer coat, jacket, and gloves (however, the person can be asked to remove more clothing voluntarily (Note 7));
- can **place his/her hands** inside the pockets of outer clothing and feel round the inside of collars, socks, and shoes (para 3.5);
- can search a person's **hair**, but only if this does not require the removal of headgear (para 3.5);
- can carry out a **more thorough search**, for example requiring the removal of a T-shirt, but this must be undertaken out of public view, for example in a police van or at a nearby police station (see para 3.6).

Vehicle search procedures are covered in more detail in in 9.8.2.2.

9.4.1.4 Recording the search

If the person is not subsequently arrested, a record of a search must be made, either electronically or on paper (s 3, PACE 1984 and Code A, para 4.1). The record should be made as soon as possible after the search (s 3(2)(b) and Code A, para 4.1). Seven items of information must be recorded (Code A, para 4.3):

- the date, time, place, object, and grounds/authorization of the search;
- the person's ethnicity (as given, or if different, the officer's perception (see Code A, Annex B); and
- the officer's identity.

There is no requirement for an officer to record the name, address, and date of birth of the person searched (or the person in charge of a vehicle which has been searched) and the person is under no obligation to provide this information (Code A, para 4.3A).

The person must be asked if he/she wants a copy of the record, and if he/she does, it should be provided immediately if possible. Alternatively, a receipt can be provided, and this must explain how a copy of the full record can be obtained, including access to an electronic copy of the record (Code A, para 4.2). However, it may be completely out of the question to provide a record or a receipt at the time, for example during serious public disorder or if an officer is called to an incident of higher priority (Code A, para 4.2A). The person is entitled to a copy of the record at a later time, but must request it within three months (Code A, para 3.8(d)(ii)).

If the person is arrested and taken to a police station, the record of the search will be made on the custody record (s 3(2)(a) and Code A, para 4.2B). The custody officer must ask the person if he/she wants a copy of the search record and if so, it should be provided as soon as practicable (Code A, para 4.2B). This does not affect his/her entitlement to a copy of the custody record (Note 16).

After searching an unattended vehicle (or anything in or on it) a record of the search must be left, preferably inside the vehicle. If the vehicle has not been opened or it is not reasonable or practical to leave the record inside without causing damage, the record should be attached to the outside of the vehicle (see Code A, para 4.8 and s 2(7) of the PACE Act 1984).

9.4.2   Stop and search (s 1 of the PACE Act 1984)

This is often referred to simply as 'stop and search' although the Act refers to it as 'stop, search and detain'. We will refer to it here as 's 1 PACE stop and search' to distinguish it from the other 18 powers of stop and search. Any article for which there are reasonable grounds to suspect it to be stolen or prohibited, can be seized (s 1(6), PACE Act 1984). An officer does not have to be in uniform to carry out a s 1 PACE stop and search.

9.4.2.1   Grounds for an s 1 PACE stop and search

Under s 1(3) of the PACE Act 1984, an officer only has the power to search if he/she has reasonable grounds for suspecting that stolen or prohibited articles will be found. Reasonable grounds for suspicion obviously depend on the circumstances in each case (see Code A, para 2.2), but the following factors can all be considered:

- a suspect's behaviour, for example trying to hide something;
- accurate and current intelligence or information; and/or
- reliable information that members of a particular group habitually carry prohibited articles.

Unless the police have a description of a suspect, the reasonable grounds cannot be based upon physical appearance, including those listed as 'protected characteristics' (see 9.4.1.1) or previous convictions (either alone, or in combination with each other or with any other factor) (Code A, para 2.2).

Generalizing (ie stereotyping) groups of people as being more likely to take part in criminal activity must be avoided. However, when there is reliable and accurate intelligence about a particular group of people, it is not always necessary for the searching officer to reasonably suspect each individual member of the group of possessing the unlawful articles before carrying out the search(es) (*Howarth v Commissioner of Police of the Metropolis* [2011] EWHC 2818 (QB)).

The two scenarios provide further explanation on establishing the grounds for a s 1 PACE search.

9.4.2.2   Appropriate locations for an s 1 PACE stop and search

This type of search can be carried out in any public place (see 9.2). This can include a garden or yard, or other land attached to a dwelling, but not if the person is resident in the dwelling or has the resident's permission to be there (s 1(4)). A s 1 search cannot be carried out inside a dwelling (see 9.2) under any circumstances (s 1(1)(b)). The same principles apply to searching a vehicle on land attached to a dwelling: a vehicle cannot be searched under s 1 PACE if the resident of the dwelling is in charge of the vehicle or has permitted it to be on the land (s 1(5)(a) and (b)).

The search must be carried out at the place where the person or vehicle was first detained, or 'nearby'. Code A, para 3.4, note 6 defines being nearby as 'within a reasonable travelling distance', but gives no indication of actual distance, and as there is no guidance from case law the term should be interpreted relatively cautiously. If a vehicle is stopped for a search in a busy street, the officers might take it into the nearest side street. This would ease any possible traffic congestion, maintain the health and safety of all concerned, and is very likely to count as 'nearby'.

9.4.2.3   Who or what can be searched under s 1 PACE?

Having made sure that all of the requirements covered in 9.4.2.3 are satisfied concerning the location, under s 1(2)(a) of the PACE Act 1984 an officer can search:

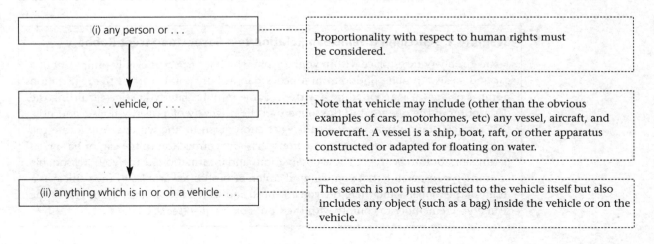

| (i) any person or . . . | Proportionality with respect to human rights must be considered. |

| . . . vehicle, or . . . | Note that vehicle may include (other than the obvious examples of cars, motorhomes, etc) any vessel, aircraft, and hovercraft. A vessel is a ship, boat, raft, or other apparatus constructed or adapted for floating on water. |

| (ii) anything which is in or on a vehicle . . . | The search is not just restricted to the vehicle itself but also includes any object (such as a bag) inside the vehicle or on the vehicle. |

General Procedures

9.4.2.4 **What items are included under s 1 PACE?**

The search can only be for stolen or 'prohibited' articles. Stolen articles include any article for which there are reasonable grounds for suspecting it to be stolen. The following table provides further details about prohibited articles.

Prohibited article	Description
Offensive weapons	Includes any article 'made, intended, or adapted' for causing injury to a person (see 18.2.1), for use either by the person having it with him/her or by someone else. See also s 1(9) of the PACE Act 1984 and Code A, Note 23
Bladed or sharply pointed articles	Includes any article which is bladed or sharply pointed, but excludes a small folding pocket-knife (see 18.2.2)
Any articles used in the course of or in connection with certain criminal offences	Includes any article made, intended, or adapted for use (by anyone) in the course of or in connection with burglary (see 16.4), taking a conveyance (see 16.8.2), fraud (see16.9), or criminal damage (see 20.2)
Fireworks	Only includes fireworks possessed in contravention of any of the firework regulations (see 14.9)

Note that some items (such as drugs and items for use in terrorist activities) do not fall within this definition of prohibited articles, and therefore other statutory powers of search must be used to search for such items (see Code A, Annex A).

Scenario 1: Searching a Suspected Burglar

One evening, at the start of a night duty, you are provided with an electronic briefing containing information that a number of burglaries have taken place on the local housing estate. The suspect's *modus operandi* (MO) is to enter the rear of dwellings through insecure doors or windows during the early hours of the morning, and take small electrical items.

Later on, at 02.00 hours, you are on mobile patrol when you are called to several reports from members of the public regarding a prowler in the rear gardens of a number of houses within the housing estate. You make a search of the area on foot and locate a suspect hiding in the back garden of a house carrying a small rucksack which obviously contains several items. You carry out a PNC check of the suspect on the details he provides, and there is a record of an individual with the same details who has previous convictions for burglary. A colleague speaks to the occupant of the house and asks if the suspect lives there and whether the suspect has permission to be in the garden. The occupant categorically replies 'no' to both questions.

Under these circumstances you can justify your 'reasonable grounds' to carry out a s 1 PACE search: you have the intelligence you gained from the earlier briefing regarding the burglaries in the area, the behaviour of the suspect and the fact that he is a trespasser, and your suspicion that the rucksack carried by the individual might contain stolen articles. Having established your reasonable grounds for suspecting that you will find stolen or prohibited articles on the person, and after you have complied with the Codes of Practice (see 5.5.5) you go ahead and detain the suspect for the purposes of a s 1 PACE search.

Scenario 2: Searching a Vehicle in Relation to a Suspected Street Robbery

A street robbery takes place within your area in which a suspect allegedly jumps out of a car and steals a mobile phone from a pedestrian at knifepoint. Part of the registration number of the car is reported by a witness. Some minutes later you see a car fitting the description of the one used in the robbery in the driveway of a nearby house, and note that the registration matches the part-registration given by the witness. You locate the resident, who says that nobody in the house has any connection to the car, or has given permission for it to be there. These observations and information justify your 'reasonable grounds' for suspecting that you will find stolen or prohibited articles in the vehicle as a result of the robbery, and therefore you go ahead and search the vehicle. At the end of the search you remember to comply with the Codes of Practice (see 9.4.1).

TASK 1 As you have seen, there are a number of requirements that must be met when making a search under any of the 19 statutory powers. Some of these relate to providing certain information to the person being searched. In order for this to become second nature, write down the list of things a police officer would have to say, in a way that will help you remember them (eg make a mind-map or your own mnemonic).

If you are a trainee police officer then completion of this task will help towards meeting the CK1 knowledge requirements in the SOLAP under the headings 'Legal and organizational requirements' and 'Searching individuals'.

9.4.3 Other stop and search powers

There are many other important and useful stop and search powers apart from under s 1 PACE. These include search powers under s 47 of the Firearms Act 1968 (for firearms) and s 7 of the Sporting Events (Control of Alcohol etc) Act 1985 (for alcohol and fireworks at sporting events).

Here we will cover in more detail:

- s 23 of the Misuse of Drugs Act 1971 stop and search for controlled drugs;
- s 60 of the Criminal Justice and Public Order Act 1994 stop and search powers for offensive weapons and bladed or sharply pointed articles;
- s 54(1) of the Animal Welfare Act 2006 stop and search powers to prevent cruelty to non-wild animals; and
- ss 43 and 47A of the Terrorism Act 2000 stop and search powers to prevent acts of terrorism.

Other stop and search powers are used less frequently (such as s 6 of the Public Stores Act 1875 and s 4 of the Crossbows Act 1987). The full list is to be found in Annex A to PACE Code of Practice A.

9.4.3.1 Stop and search for drugs

Drugs are not prohibited articles under s 1 of the PACE Act 1984. Section 23 of the Misuse of Drugs Act 1971 contains powers for searching persons and vehicles in relation to drugs offences, as shown in the flowchart. The offences relating to the unlawful possession, supply, and manufacture of controlled drugs are covered in Chapter 12.

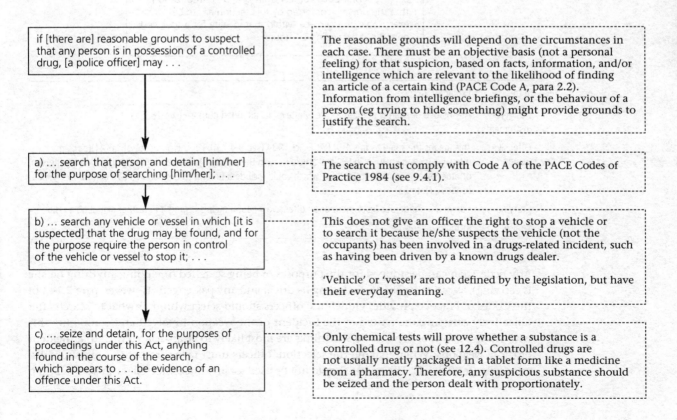

General Procedures

It is an offence to intentionally obstruct an officer during the course of a s 23 search, whether or not any drugs are found (s 23(4), Misuse of Drugs Act 1971). However, in *R v Pasaihou Garjo* [2011] EWCA Crim 1169 it was reiterated that for an offence of obstruction to be prosecuted, the detention of the suspect must first of all be lawful and have satisfied the requirements under s 2(2) of the PACE Act 1984 (see also *R v Bristol* [2007] EWCA Crim 3214 in 9.4.1.2).

This offence is triable either way and the penalty is a fine or imprisonment (summarily six months, and two years if on indictment).

9.4.3.2 Stop and search for incidents with serious violence

Section 60 of the Criminal Justice and Public Order Act 1994 applies in situations where it seems likely that a serious breakdown in public order has occurred or might occur. It empowers a senior police officer to authorize stop and search for offensive weapons or other dangerous instruments. This power applies even if there are no grounds for suspecting that the person or vehicle is carrying weapons or dangerous articles (s 60(5)). The table explains the meaning of key terms used in the wording of the legislation shown in the flowchart.

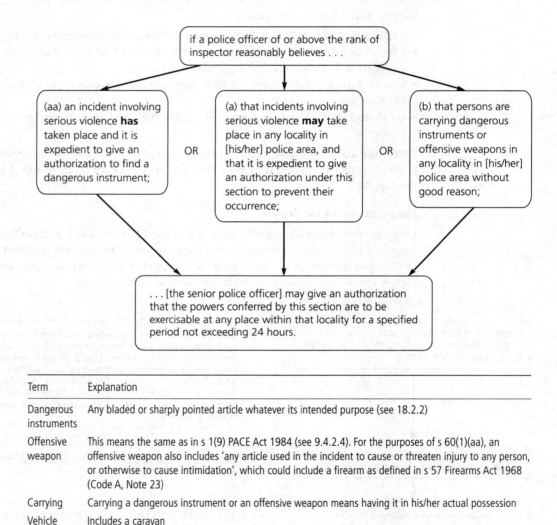

Term	Explanation
Dangerous instruments	Any bladed or sharply pointed article whatever its intended purpose (see 18.2.2)
Offensive weapon	This means the same as in s 1(9) PACE Act 1984 (see 9.4.2.4). For the purposes of s 60(1)(aa), an offensive weapon also includes 'any article used in the incident to cause or threaten injury to any person, or otherwise to cause intimidation', which could include a firearm as defined in s 57 Firearms Act 1968 (Code A, Note 23)
Carrying	Carrying a dangerous instrument or an offensive weapon means having it in his/her actual possession
Vehicle	Includes a caravan

Any pedestrian can be stopped for the purposes of being searched (including anything he/she is carrying), as can any vehicle, including its driver and any passengers. However, para 2.14A of the Codes of Practice provides guidelines; officers should select whom or what to search after objectively assessing the nature of the incident or the weapon involved and comparing this with those persons or vehicles he/she thinks are most likely to be associated with that incident or those weapons. When making the selection, officers must take care not to unlawfully discriminate (see 9.4.1.1). The power should not be used for any unconnected purpose other than the reasons for which the authorization was provided. The search must comply with s 2 of the PACE Act 1984 (see 9.4.1), and the person is entitled to a 'written statement' about the search within 12 months (para 2.14B). In *Roberts, R (on the application of) v The Commissioner of the Metropolitan Police* [2012] EWHC 1977 (Admin), it was agreed that although there was potential for racial discrimination in the exercise of a random search power such as s 60, it remains compatible with the Articles in the European Convention on Human Rights.

A driver or pedestrian who fails to stop when required commits a summary offence (s 60(8)) with a penalty of one month's imprisonment and/or a fine. A police officer may seize a dangerous instrument or an article which he/she reasonably suspects to be an offensive weapon (s 60(6)). The authorization also permits an officer in uniform to require any person to remove any item if the officer reasonably believes that the person is wearing it to try and conceal his/her identity, and it can also be seized (s 60AA(2)(b)). A person who fails to remove an item of clothing when required to do so by a constable (under this legislation) commits a summary offence (s 60AA(7)), with a penalty of six months' imprisonment and/or a fine.

TASK 2 A town has recently experienced several outbreaks of serious public disorder between two rival gangs. The disorder has mainly occurred in the local park. Subsequently, an order is in force under s 60 of the Criminal Justice and Public Order Act 1984.

An officer on patrol in the local park sees a young man wearing a full-face ski mask which is concealing the man's face. Under what circumstances can the officer ask the young man to remove the mask? Choose one of the following:

1. The officer reasonably believes that the person is carrying a dangerous instrument or an offensive weapon.
2. The officer reasonably believes that the person is attempting to conceal his/her identity.
3. No further circumstances are required as a s 60 order is in force.
4. The officer reasonably believes that the person is likely to be involved in violence.

9.4.3.3 Stop and search in relation to prevention of cruelty to animals

The Animal Welfare Act 2006 provides powers of stop and search to help prevent cruelty to non-wild animals. A vehicle may be stopped and detained under s 54(1) of the Animal Welfare Act 2006 to search it to prevent animal suffering (s 19(1)), or to seize an animal that is suspected of being involved in animal fighting (s 22(1)).

The officer must be in uniform to exercise this power. The vehicle may be detained for as long as is reasonably required (s 54(4)) for a search or inspection to be carried out (including the exercise of any related power under this Act). The search must take place where the vehicle was first detained or nearby.

Two other Acts provide powers of stop, search, and seize in relation to animal protection:

- the Wildlife and Countryside Act 1981 (s 19(1)) to help prevent taking and killing of wild birds and other animals; and
- the Wild Mammals (Protection) Act 1996 (s 4), which relates to vehicles as well as to persons.

9.4.3.4 Stop and search in relation to preventing acts of terrorism

The Terrorism Act 2000 (TACT) provides two types of stop and search powers to help prevent acts of terrorism; one for which reasonable suspicion is required to search persons and vehicles (ss 43 and 43A respectively), and the other for which suspicion is not required (s 47A) for searching persons and/or vehicles in specified locations (requires prior authorization by a senior police officer). The TACT Codes of Practice set out the basic principles for the use of powers by police officers under these sections and state that before any search under TACT the police officer conducting the search must provide the following information (para 5.2, TACT Codes of Practice):

One way to remember this list is to use the mnemonic 'GILPEYS'.

G	Grounds of the suspicion for the search (ss 43 and 43A only);
I	Identity of the officer performing the search;
L	Legal power used;
P	Purpose/object of search and that authorization has been given if it is under s 47A;
E	Entitlement to a copy of the search record;
Y	You are detained for the purposes of a search;
S	Station to which the officer is attached.

For a search under s 43 of TACT a police officer must reasonably suspect that a person is a terrorist. A police officer may stop and search a person (s 43(1)) if he/she reasonably suspects that the person is a terrorist to discover whether or not they have in their possession anything which may constitute evidence that they are involved in terrorism. This power may be used at any time or in any place if the criteria of reasonable suspicion has been met and no authorization is required (para 3.2.1). It extends to anything that the person is carrying with them, such as a bag, container, or other object (para 3.2.4). The police officer does not have to be of the same sex as the person to be searched (para 3.2.5) nor be in uniform (para 3.2.6). If a police officer stops a vehicle to search such a person (s 43(4A)), the officer can also search the vehicle and anything in or on it (s 43(4B)(a)) for anything which may constitute evidence that the person concerned is a terrorist (para 3.2.2). Any other person in the vehicle cannot be searched unless there are sufficient grounds for suspecting that he/she is also a terrorist. It is not sufficient that he/she is in the company of a person who is suspected of being a terrorist (para 3.2.3).

Under s 43A of TACT a vehicle can be stopped and searched if a police officer reasonably suspects that it is being used for the purposes of terrorism. An unattended vehicle can also be searched (para 3.3.1). The search must be for evidence that the vehicle is being used for terrorist purposes (para 3.3.1). The driver, any passengers, and anything on or in the vehicle can also be searched, as can anything carried by the driver or passengers. Items that are reasonably suspected to be related to terrorism can be seized and retained (s 43(4) and s 43A(3)).

Under s 47 of TACT an **authorization** from a senior police officer permits searches in a specified area or place (s 47A(1)) without the need for the searching officer to have reasonable suspicion in relation to the person or the vehicle (s 47A(5)). However, the authorizing officer must reasonably suspect a terrorist act will be forthcoming (s 47A(1)(a)) and that the authorization is necessary to prevent such an act (s 47A(1)(b)(i)). The area or place must be no larger than necessary, and the time period only as necessary to prevent such an act (s 47A(1)(b)(ii) and (iii)). When an authorization is in place, a police officer in uniform can stop any vehicle or pedestrian in the specified area or place in order to search:

- a pedestrian and anything he/she is carrying (s 47A(3));
- a vehicle and anything in or on the vehicle, its driver and any passengers, and anything carried by the driver or passenger(s) (s 47A(2)).

The search can only be for evidence that the vehicle is being used for terrorist purposes or that the person is a terrorist (s 47A(4)) (TACT Codes, para 4.9.2). Items that are reasonably suspected to be related to terrorism can be seized and retained (s 47A(6)).

9.4.4 Road checks (s 4 of the PACE Act 1984)

Section 4 of the PACE Act 1984 provides a senior officer with the power to authorize a road check for the specific purpose of determining whether a vehicle is carrying people connected with an indictable offence, or people who are unlawfully at large. Road checks cannot be used for road traffic or vehicle excise offences. They must be authorized by a senior officer because the rights of all the individuals stopped must be considered—every vehicle will be stopped in a certain area. Section 4 of the PACE Act 1984 sets out the circumstances under which a road check can take place—the time, place, and reason must all be specified.

The road check will be to find a person who:

- has committed or who is intending to commit an indictable offence; or
- is a witness to an indictable offence; or
- is unlawfully at large.

There must be reasonable grounds for suspecting that the person is, or is about to be, in the locality selected for the road check.

A police officer of the rank of superintendent or above must authorize the road check in writing, but if he/she is not available, then a road check may be authorized by an officer of a lower rank (see s 4(5) of the PACE Act 1984). Any use of the power to impose a road check must comply with PACE Code of Practice A. Section 163 of the Road Traffic Act 1988 must be followed when actually stopping the vehicles (see 19.4.1).

> **TASK 3** Consider the health and safety implications of holding a road check. What are the considerations applicable to police officers and to the general public?

9.5 Entry and Search to Arrest, or to Save Life or Property

Section 17 of the PACE Act 1984 provides a power to enter and search premises to arrest a person, or for saving life or limb, or to prevent serious damage to property. This power of search is limited to the extent that is reasonably required to achieve only the objective (s 17(4)). For example, if the entry and search was to find and arrest an adult, there is no justification for opening and looking inside a tobacco tin. Similarly, the s 17 power cannot be used to search a home in order to try and identify relatives of a person who is unconscious in hospital: the entry would be unlawful (there is no need to enter to save life or limb or to prevent serious damage to property). If an unlawful entry has been made, any evidence of criminality (such as the seizure of controlled drugs) may be excluded by the court under s 78 of the PACE Act 1984 (see *R v Veneroso* [2002] Crim LR 306 (Crown Ct)).

Inevitably there are risks when force is used to enter and search in unplanned situations: it is impossible to predict who or what might be encountered. Consideration should be given to whether it is really necessary to immediately enter the premises. It might be better to stay outside, watch the front and back, and secure the area until colleagues with appropriate equipment and resources arrive. Health and safety issues are examined in 6.12.

9.5.1 Power of entry to arrest

There are a number of situations where a power of entry applies in order to arrest a person, such as having a relevant warrant or in order to arrest for certain offences. Section 17 of the PACE Act 1984 explains the factors that must be taken into account, for example whether there are reasonable grounds for believing that the person is on the premises—can he/she be heard, or seen through a window?

In a block of flats or bedsit only communal areas such as hallways, stairs, and shared kitchens and bathrooms can be searched. A neighbouring flat cannot be searched 'just in case'. However, any of the individual dwellings can be searched if there is reason to believe that the person is in that particular dwelling.

9.5.1.1 Power of entry to arrest on warrant

A premises can be searched in order to arrest a person under the execution of the following warrants under s 17(1)(a):

- An arrest warrant issued in connection with or arising out of criminal proceedings (subsection (i)). Home Office Circular 88/1985, para 8 stated that this subsection 'is deliberately widely drawn and the words "in connection with" enable a constable to enter and search premises for the purpose among other things of executing a warrant for the arrest of a person for non-payment of a fine'. Other examples might include warrants to compel the attendance of witnesses, or require defendants to attend for disqualification.

• A warrant of commitment (subsection (ii)). This is for non-payment of fines and requires the offender to be taken straight to prison ('committed to prison') unless the fine is paid. The warrant itself would have been issued under s 76 of the Magistrates' Courts Act 1980.

9.5.1.2 Power of entry to arrest for specified offences

A premises can be searched in order to arrest a person for any indictable offence under s 17(1)(b). This includes indictable only offences and either-way offences (see 5.5.1). A premises can also be entered and searched under (s 17(1)(c)) to arrest for certain summary offences; a complete list is given in the table.

Summary offence with a power of entry in order to arrest	Legislation	Subsection of s 17(1) PACE 1984
Prohibition of uniforms in connection with political objectives	s 1 of the Public Order Act 1936	(c)(i)
Using violence to secure entry	s 6 of the Criminal Law Act 1977 (see 15.8)	
Trespassing with a weapon of offence	s 8 of the Criminal Law Act 1977 (see 16.4.3)	(c)(ii)
'Squatting' on premises	s 7 of the Criminal Law Act 1977	
Causing fear or provocation of violence s 4 public order offences	s 4 of the Public Order Act (see 14.4.3.3)	(c)(iii)
Failing to stop when driving a vehicle or cycle when requested	s 163 of the Road Traffic Act 1988 (see 19.4.1)	(c)(iiia)
Driving or being in charge of a vehicle when unfit through drink or drugs	s 4 of the Road Traffic Act 1988 (see 19.9.2)	
Being under the influence of drink or drugs when operating railways and trams, etc	s 27 of the Transport and Works Act 1992	(c)(iiib)
Trespassing on premises whilst an interim possession order is in place	s 76 of the Criminal Justice and Public Order Act 1994	(c)(iv)
Causing harm or distress to animals	ss 4,5, 6(1) and (2), 7, 8(1) and (2) of the Animal Welfare Act 2006 (see 13.7.1)	(c)(v)
Squatting in a residential building	s 144 of the Legal Aid, Sentencing and Punishment of Offenders Act 2012 (see 14.8.4)	(c)(vi)
Bringing animals into the UK (risk of rabies)	s 61 of the Animal Health Act 1981	(caa)

9.5.1.3 Power of entry to arrest in other specified circumstances

A police officer in pursuit of certain categories of person has a power of entry for arresting them (s 17(1)(d)), for example a person who had escaped after being arrested, or from involuntary custody at a psychiatric unit. Note, however, that the entry and (re)arrest must be under circumstances of hot pursuit, not after a period of days or weeks.

A separate power of entry exists for arresting a person who is liable to be detained in a prison, remand centre, young offenders' institution, or secure training centre (s 17(1)(cb)(i)). This could include an escapee from prison or from transport between establishments.

There is also a power of entry to arrest that applies to young people and children. A young person or child who has been detained having committed 'grave crimes' can be arrested if he/she was to escape, and the associated power of entry would also apply (s 17(1)(cb)(ii)). Section 32(1A) of the Children and Young Persons Act 1969 gives a power to arrest a child who is absent from care. This only applies to a child who has been remanded or committed to local authority accommodation (s 23(1) of the Children and Young Persons Act 1969). Section 17(1)(ca) of the PACE Act 1984 provides a power of entry to search premises for the purpose of arresting such a child.

9.5.2 Power of entry to save life and property

Subsection 17(1)(e) of the PACE Act 1984 provides a power to enter (and search) premises to save human life and limb and also to prevent serious damage to property. The officer does not need to have reasonable grounds for believing that anyone is on the premises. For blocks of flats, all the flats can be searched and not just one of them.

In the case of *Baker v Crown Prosecution Service* [2009] EWHC 299 (Admin), it was further decided that entry and search under subsection (e) can be carried out:

- without seeking the permission of the occupant (this might be self-defeating);
- without giving the occupant a reason if it is impossible, impracticable, or undesirable to do so;
- to save someone from him/herself as well as from a third party; but
- only to the extent that is reasonably required to satisfy the objective for using the power of entry (s 17(4) PACE Act 1984).

These powers should only be used if 'something serious' seemed to have occurred (or was likely to occur) within the property and should not be available 'simply on the basis of concern for the welfare' of someone in the premises, as shown in *Syed v DPP* [2010] EWHC 81 (Admin). In this incident the officers had attended a call from a neighbour reporting a disturbance at a nearby house. On arrival, there was no sign of a disturbance but the officers attempted to enter the premises, stating to the occupant that they were 'concerned about the welfare of person(s) within'. The occupant refused the officers entry, assaulting one and spitting at the other, and was subsequently charged with an offence under s 89 of the Police Act 1996 (see 15.4). On appeal the conviction was quashed; it was held that the officers had not been acting in the lawful execution of their duty as the criteria for using s 17(1)(e) had been too low.

9.5.3 The use of reasonable force to secure entry

Section 117 of the PACE Act 1984 states that 'where any part of the PACE Act 1984 grants a power … [an officer] may use reasonable force, if necessary, in the exercise of the power'. If met with force, an officer might have to equal that force to negate it, and then use even more force in order to take control. This is covered as part of personal safety training.

A court must determine whether an officer honestly believed that the force he/she used was reasonable (see 15.5.1) and proportionate in the circumstances. The principles are similar to the use of force during an arrest (s 3 of the Criminal Law Act 1967, see 10.8.2).

9.5.4 Power of entry and breach of the peace

Nothing in s 17(6) of the PACE Act 1984 affects any power of entry to deal with or prevent a breach of the peace. An officer is entitled to enter either private or public premises in order to make an arrest for a breach of the peace, or to prevent such a breach. However, the circumstances must really constitute a breach of the peace (see 14.3 on *R v Howell* [1982] QB 416).

Once the breach has finished an officer should not remain on private premises (unless there is another reason to do so) and should leave within a 'reasonable time'. If he/she is assaulted (eg by a resident of the property) during that reasonable time, this could be regarded as an assault on a police officer in the lawful execution of his/her duty. However, if the officer has not left within a reasonable time, his/her presence may be unlawful and therefore he/she might not be protected under criminal law (*Robson v Hallett* [1967] 2 QB 939).

9.6 Search of Premises after Arrest

Section 18 of the PACE Act 1984 provides for searches of premises associated with a suspect who has been arrested for an indictable offence. The search must be for evidence relating to that offence or to a similar one (s 18(1)). This power of search is useful because few suspects are likely to be still in possession of the items connected with the crime for which they have been arrested. In addition, it is reasonable to suppose that most suspects are not caught the first time they break the law, so the premises might contain evidence of previous and related criminal activity. The search must be authorized by a senior officer (see 9.6.1).

In addition, s 32 of the PACE Act 1984 provides the police with powers to search premises where a person was arrested for an indictable offence, or where he/she was immediately prior to the arrest (see 10.8.4).

The information here provides some of the underpinning knowledge required to achieve the PAC checklist heading 'Search' and in particular the ability to 'demonstrate a lawful s 18 PACE search'. The relevant Diploma in Policing assessed unit is 'Search vehicles, premises and open spaces'. The awarding bodies for the Diploma explain that competence must be demonstrated practically during three real searches (once for each type of search; vehicles, premises, land) ensuring that all assessment criteria are covered. The relevant Certificate in Knowledge of Policing unit is 'Knowledge of searching vehicles, premises, and open spaces within a policing context'.

9.6.1   Authorization

This is given in writing by an officer of the rank of inspector or above, and is normally obtained in advance of the search (s 18(4)). The authorizing officer must be satisfied that the necessary grounds exist and that the premises **are** actually occupied or controlled by the arrested person; mere suspicion of occupancy or control is not sufficient (Code B, para 4.3). If possible, the authority should be recorded on the Notice of Powers and Rights and signed. Details of the grounds and evidence which is sought should be recorded on the notice, the custody record, the search record, and in the officer's PNB.

However, if appropriate, the search can take place before the arrested person is taken to the police station (s 18(5)). For example, if a suspect arrested for theft of CDs at a store says she has some other stolen CDs at home, mixed up with her lawfully obtained collection, there would be justification to search her home before attending the police station so that she can identify the stolen CDs amongst the others. When a search is made without prior authorization, an inspector (or a higher ranking officer) must be informed as soon as practicable afterwards (Code B, para 4.3).

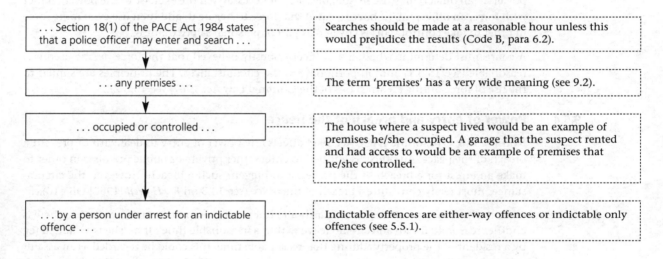

... Section 18(1) of the PACE Act 1984 states that a police officer may enter and search ...	Searches should be made at a reasonable hour unless this would prejudice the results (Code B, para 6.2).
... any premises ...	The term 'premises' has a very wide meaning (see 9.2).
... occupied or controlled ...	The house where a suspect lived would be an example of premises he/she occupied. A garage that the suspect rented and had access to would be an example of premises that he/she controlled.
... by a person under arrest for an indictable offence ...	Indictable offences are either-way offences or indictable only offences (see 5.5.1).

9.6.2   Evidence requirements

Section 18(1) of the PACE Act 1984 states that there must be reasonable grounds to suspect that there is evidence on the premises that relates to either the offence in question, a similar offence, or to some other related indictable offence. For example, a man who has been arrested for stealing a camera from a shop could have his car searched for other stolen property—he might have received other items for selling them on and the related offence would be handling stolen goods. Section 18(3) of the PACE Act 1984 limits the power to search to the extent that is reasonably required for the purpose of discovering relevant evidence. For example, in a search for motorcycles, there is no justification for looking in a handbag. (But there would be justification if the search was for documents associated with a motorcycle.)

Under s 18(2) anything found during a s 18(1) search can be seized and retained. These items may be referred to as exhibits in any subsequent statement the officer makes (see 10.12 on duty statements and 11.2.6 on exhibits). The use of photographic evidence should be considered to capture the property as found it in its original place and surroundings. If the evidence is stored electronically, for example on a computer, that computer can be seized (s 20 PACE Act 1984) in order that the evidence can be suitably reproduced (see 25.7.3 on seizing computers).

9.7   Search Warrants for Evidence of Indictable Offences

Section 8 of the PACE Act 1984 sets out the grounds and procedure to be followed when applying for a warrant to search premises as part of an investigation into an indictable offence, and also provides a power to seize certain evidence. A s 8 warrant would be used for a suspect who has not been arrested; after arrest s 18 or 32 of the PACE Act 1984 could be used (see 9.6 and 10.8.4). Other statutes provide particular powers for the police to enter and search premises in certain circumstances, such as the Theft Act 1968 (stolen property) or the Misuse of Drugs Act 1971 (controlled drugs). In such cases the police will be able to obtain a search warrant under that enactment. Any search warrant application (as well as the subsequent search) must comply with ss 15 and 16 of the PACE Act 1984.

The warrant is issued by a Justice of the Peace. There must be reasonable grounds for believing that an indictable offence has been committed, and that the object of the search is likely to be of substantial value to the investigation (but it must not be subject to legal privilege, excluded material, or special procedure material).

In addition, at least **one** of the following conditions must apply:

• It is not practicable to communicate with any person entitled to grant entry to the premises or to the evidence.
• Entry to the premises will not be granted without a warrant.
• The purpose of a search may be frustrated or seriously prejudiced unless a constable arriving at the premises can secure immediate entry.

There are two different types of search warrant; a 'specific premises warrant' (applies only to the premises specified in the application) and an 'all premises warrant' (applies to any premises occupied or controlled by the person specified in the application (and can include specified premises if required)). For the latter, the Justice of the Peace must be satisfied that an all premises warrant is necessary. This could be because of the particulars of the offence or because it is not reasonably practicable to specify every single premises which might need to be searched.

Premises may be entered and searched on more than one occasion under the same application, although the second and any other subsequent entries must be authorized by an officer of the rank of inspector or above.

TASK 4 Imagine you are a police officer, and you and a colleague are required to arrest a person on suspicion of theft. You follow the suspect to the vicinity of her house, but lose sight of her at the last moment. The house has a front and a rear entrance, so how are you going to carry out the arrest, and what are your considerations at this time?

9.8 Searching Premises, Vehicles, and Open Land

Here we cover the practicalities of conducting searches of vehicles, premises, and open spaces. In major and serious crimes the Senior Investigating Officer may require that a forensic examination is carried out first, followed by a search for intelligence materials. Then the building will be searched as described here.

It should be remembered that volume crime activities such as frauds (particularly card fraud) and drug sales can be used to fund terrorist activities. If premises and vehicles searches uncover evidence that leads to grounds for suspicion, the information should be passed to the appropriate authority.

9.8.1 Planning a search

Proper planning is essential for the success of a search, and for large or complex searches a Police Search Advisor (PolSA) should be consulted. ACPO (2006c) recommends using the IIMARCH mnemonic when planning a search, as a reminder to consider all of the following (see also 11.7.1):

• Information—why the search is needed, intelligence, local issues.
• Intention—the aim or reason for the search, the target material.
• Method—how the search and management of it will be conducted.
• Administration—maps, plans, transport, equipment.
• Risk assessment (see 6.12 to 6.12.4).
• Communications—such as which channel to use, mobile and landline numbers, code words.
• Human rights compliance.

A risk assessment of the venue will consider the physical risks, such as the safety of buildings and the contents, as well as the likelihood of resistance from occupants. Force intelligence systems and local knowledge could provide information on any contingency plans already in place for the premises, and any warnings regarding occupants. This will inform decisions regarding the number of officers and whether a PolSA and/or a specialist search team are required. For vehicle searches it is essential that roadside safety is considered: appropriate traffic control and safety systems must be in place. Searches should certainly not be carried out on blind bends or adjacent to fast-moving traffic.

The size of the search area and the relative size of the target objects are very important factors to consider when planning the size of the search team: searching for a small article in a large and cluttered house will be difficult. For outdoor searches, the terrain or surface vegetation is a further consideration—the search officers can obviously be more widely spaced when searching for a larger object on short grass. The officer in charge of a premises search may use a floor-plan or labels to identify the rooms to avoid confusion between, say, a large number of bedrooms. The search must be conducted systematically.

Personal safety equipment (helmets, gloves, knee protectors) and tools to access hides, dismantle equipment, or even dig in gardens may be required. Search dogs are an invaluable tool for specialist targets such drugs, cash, blood, and firearms (although dogs can damage fragile forensic evidence). A CSI may be useful for photographic recording and specialist packaging advice. In searches related to computer crime (or involving digital materials) a member of the Digital Forensics Unit may be required.

If it seems likely that more than a few items will be seized, it is good practice to appoint an exhibits officer. He/she will also be able to reduce problems associated with documentation and continuity, and will help ensure that force protocols regarding the handling, exhibiting, and storage of exhibits are closely followed. It is important that sufficient packaging material, transport, and storage facilities are available for the anticipated quantity of evidence. Officers should complete a PNB entry for finds in addition to completing any log entries.

9.8.2 Conducting the search

The correct authority, search records, and other paperwork must be in place prior to embarking on the search. The warrant or other authority should be served even if the occupier has agreed to the search. The officer in charge should manage the search closely and control the movements of personnel and effectively manage their deployment, depending on the complexity of each room or zone.

It is good practice for searchers to work in pairs inside buildings and vehicles and to maintain contact with each other. After the search is complete each could check the other's work as a form of 'peer review'—useful because no single person has 'seen it all before'. Everything moved and searched should be returned to the position in which it was found and damage should be meticulously recorded and (if necessary) authorized by the person in charge of the search.

9.8.2.1 Searching buildings

The search must be focused and detailed and start at a logical point, following the plan drawn up by the officer in charge of the search. Randomly poking about in a room is not a systematic procedure. It should be noted that work environments such as factories and commercial garages are exceptionally hazardous environments.

If there is anybody on the premises the officer in charge should identify him/herself and state the purpose and grounds of the search, and also identify and introduce any other officers involved (Code B, para 6.5). The officer does not have to communicate with people on the premises (Code B, para 6.4) if there are reasonable grounds for believing that alerting the occupier would frustrate the object of the search or put officers in danger. Consent is not required if the premises are unoccupied, or if no one who is entitled to grant access (an owner or tenant for example) is available. In a lodging house, a search should not be made solely on the basis of the landlord's consent; every reasonable effort should be made to obtain the consent of the tenant, lodger, or occupier (Code B, para 5.2). If practicable, the consent must be given in writing on the Notice of Powers and Rights before the search (Code B, para 5.1).

Section 117 of the PACE Act 1984 allows the use of reasonable force if, for example, the occupier is absent, or has refused entry or does not reply (see also Code B, para 6.6). A copy of the Notice of Powers and Rights should be given to the occupier, or left on the premises if they are empty (Code B, para 6.7). Specimen copies may be available during police training.

The precise choice of search pattern (spiral, zone, grid, or strip) is often a matter of personal choice but, above all, the search must encompass all possible parts of the building under scrutiny. In the case of a house the space is already divided into zones by the walls and floors, but larger structures can be more complex. It is essential that every effort is made to ensure all areas are searched effectively—there are likely to be voids behind drawers and under cupboards, and any access panels must be removed. Remember that many enterprising criminals attempt to hide evidence beneath floorboards and in water tanks.

9.8.2.2 Searching vehicles

Vehicles can be regarded as having five main areas: the engine bay, the passenger cabin, the boot, the exterior, and the underside. These should be searched systematically in turn. Vehicles contain a significant number of possible voids for the concealment of contraband, and indeed commercial vehicles intended for illegal drugs importations may have specially constructed voids built into their structure. For example, in Dover in the early 1990s a truck trailer was found to have drawers built into the chassis members of its box-frame; a customs officer spotted an unusual weld pattern at the rear of the trailer. The higher the stakes, the better and more professional the concealment is likely to be.

In terms of safety, apart from the danger of working alongside traffic, the specific dangers associated with all vehicles are moving parts and electricity, so always remove the ignition key and apply the handbrake. In addition, some vehicle owners have been known to place needles in seats and razor blades beneath access panels to prevent theft, so proceed cautiously.

9.8.2.3 Searching open spaces

External searches, whether for evidence or a missing person, can become very complicated, especially if the area to be covered is large, or there are outbuildings, vehicles, and/or drains. The weather, local dangers (such as capped wells and barbed wire), and the large distances that may be involved also make it more difficult. The assembled team must be motivated and effectively directed. Maps and plans of the area are essential, but so is local knowledge—all intelligence and information sources should be examined for useful information (this is likely to have also been done at the planning stage). A further complication is that the offender, any accomplices, the public, and the media may have access to the search area, especially when cordoning is impractical.

On open and featureless ground, police tape is normally used to divide the area into strips, grids, or zones. If a line search is used, on any return 'sweep' the boundary of the previous sweep is always covered again. The whole line stops when something (a ditch or hedge, for instance), bars the way, and the object is normally searched immediately.

A search of remote areas and woodland, in particular, can reveal caches of weapons or explosives, or hides containing stolen materials. Effective searches can be expected to turn up a wide variety of material that is unrelated to the offence under investigation, but any item such as a timer, electrical equipment, or a mobile phone found in a surprising, suspicious, or unexpected place should be treated with caution. These are rare events, but see 11.6 for more details on the actions that should be taken, in particular at the scenes of suspicious devices.

9.8.3 After a search

When finishing a search, officers should take away all their equipment and leave any paperwork required for the owner or occupant. The appropriate records must be made including details such as the people present, the area searched, and the evidence found. The records would be in the officer's PNB for a small search and in separate documents for a larger search. A large amount of evidence would be recorded in an exhibits register, and this would be referred to as an exhibit in individual officers' PNB entries.

At the end of the search the officer in charge will almost certainly debrief the team (if used) and conduct a final 'walk through' to assess the completeness of the search, particularly if the target material has not been found or if damage has been caused. If the occupier is present, then he/she should be shown the condition of the property. Photographs of damage (and the absence of damage) are very useful in this respect. The property must be left secure if force was used to secure entry.

TASK 5 Imagine you are a police officer. You are called to your custody area where your inspector is waiting to give you a signed 's 18' authority to search the premises of a person in custody for burglary of a shop which sells mobile phones. The burglary took place yesterday and the person in custody was not in possession of any stolen property at the time of arrest.

- What are your considerations before leaving the custody area?
- What are you going to do on arrival at the premises to be searched?
- How will you conduct the search?
- What will you do before leaving the premises?

9.9 Answers to Tasks

TASK 1 You are likely to find that making a mind-map and working on your own mnemonic or other way of remembering will really help fix the key points in your mind. Of course, you have GO WISELY to use, too.

TASK 2 The power is not absolute and cannot be exercised unless the officer reasonably believes that he is wearing the item to conceal his identity, so response 3 is incorrect. There is no reason to believe he was carrying a dangerous instrument or an offensive weapon, or that he was likely to be involved in violence, so responses 1 and 4 are incorrect.

Therefore, the answer is 2. The officer must reasonably believe that the young man was attempting to conceal his identity.

TASK 3 Considerations at road checks:

1. Wear personal safety equipment, including high-visibility clothing.
2. Carry out the road check in an area which is well lit by street lamps.
3. Use signs to reduce the speed of vehicles entering the checking area.
4. Remain alert to the presence of vehicles at all times.
5. Reduce the risk to the general public by asking them to stay in or near their vehicles.
6. Bear in mind the possibility that a vehicle might fail to stop at the road check.
7. Only use the correct techniques (from training) to bring to a halt a vehicle which has failed to stop.
8. Give clear indications to drivers of what the driver should do.
9. Communicate with colleagues and remain with the main group involved in the check.
10. Select a location with clear views of oncoming traffic.
11. Select a location which is suitable to stop vehicles (particularly large vehicles), such as a lay-by.
12. Provide the opportunity for vehicles to return to the traffic flow safely.
13. Consider the classification of the road and the speed of oncoming traffic if it is part of the 'fast road network' such as a dual carriageway.
14. Make allowances for the safe stopping distances of moving traffic during periods of adverse weather conditions.
15. Avoid certain locations if practicable, such as road junctions, bends, the brow of a hill, and crossings.

TASK 4 You probably considered the following:

1. How can you secure all entrances so she cannot escape (eg through the back door)?
2. Should and can you obtain further support from your colleagues to achieve this?
3. With the back door secured, knock on the door or ring the bell to locate the suspect.

4. If there is no response, consider what reasonable grounds you have for believing that she is on the premises—for example, can you see her through the window, or have you had the entrances and exits under continuous observation since she entered the premises?

5. Is this now developing into a pre-planned event for which you should consider calling for further assistance?

TASK 5 You probably considered the following:

1. Is there a door key in the prisoner's property that you can take in case there is no one at the premises to allow you entry?

2. Is the 's 18' authorization signed and in your possession?

3. At the premises you must follow the PACE Act 1984 Code of Practice in relation to the searching of premises; identify yourself, state the purpose and grounds of the search, identify and introduce anybody with you.

4. Limit your search to the extent that is reasonably required for the purpose of discovering evidence relating to burglary and mobile phones.

5. A copy of the 'Notice of Powers and Rights' should be given to the occupier or left on the premises if no one is present.

10 | Initial Investigation, Arrest, Detention, and Disposal

10.1 Introduction

In this chapter, we look in detail at the law surrounding detention and arrest, and collecting evidence—both from a crime scene and from people; victims, witnesses, or perpetrators of a crime. Police officers will have to conduct some form of initial investigation to help decide the appropriate course of action. Again, as we have commented throughout this Handbook, police officers will need to know the law and how to apply it, in relation to detaining a person, arresting someone, and taking him/her into custody. Further details on investigation, interviewing, and forensic procedures are covered in detail in Chapters 23 to 25.

The use of police powers to detain, arrest, and gather evidence must be shown to be justified and proportionate to what had taken place. The exercise of powers should be consistent with the Human Rights Act 1998 and the provisions of the Police and Criminal Evidence (PACE) Act 1984, and the associated Codes of Practice (see 5.6.1). A professional approach is nowhere more important than when processing a person's arrest and detention. A fundamental liberty is being taken away from the detained person, and officers must be entirely conversant with the powers to take such an action. Risk assessments must also be made when a person is detained, especially when there is a risk of self-harm. 'Death in custody' is a devastating occurrence to all concerned and treated very seriously by the IPCC investigators. In addition, any failure to follow proper procedure could lead to a criticism of police procedure, and can be a gift to defence counsel; a case could be lost as a result. A guilty person might walk free and possibly offend again, all because of a procedural or technical lapse.

An individual is more likely to respond positively if he/she is treated with respect. Over the years, police officers become very familiar with the layout of a police station, the location of the cells, the role of the custody officer, interview procedures, the use of the caution, the making of statements, and the use of legal jargon. They become so used to it in fact that much of it becomes automatic—part of the nature of professionalism. However, other people are not so likely to be familiar with the criminal justice. Witnesses, suspects, and victims might be anxious or confused, so they will need to have things explained, and their uneasiness or discomfort anticipated. A suspect may start to talk, a victim may feel able to describe what happened, a witness may explain what he/she saw, felt, smelt, touched, or tasted. Reassurance can be offered from day one in law enforcement.

10.2 The Pocket Notebook

The traditional police pocket notebook (the PNB) is a notebook used by a police officer to record in writing the details of incidents and other pertinent information, particularly whilst on patrol. This would include a statement made by a suspect or a description given by a witness. The making of an entry in the PNB is necessary to meet the requirements of PACE (see 5.6) and the rules of disclosure also apply (see 26.2). Typically a PNB is issued to trainees soon after joining a police force, and the local force policy will be explained concerning how to complete a PNB, where it should be stored, its surrender, the issuing of new PNBs, and so on (in accordance with the Management of Police Information procedures: see 6.8.2).

There are a number of fundamental aspects of the PNB common to virtually all police forces:

- at the very minimum it notes the start and finish time of each period of duty;
- it is used to keep a record of significant information collected during an incident in order to comply with the Criminal Procedures and Investigations Act 1996 (see 26.2);
- it is used to keep a contemporaneous account (this means at the same time as the events unfold) or if this is impossible, as soon as reasonably practicable afterwards;
- it should note clearly where another police officer (eg your assessor whilst on Supervised Patrol) has been consulted in the writing of an entry (see 10.2.3);
- where other official police documents exist such as 'stop and search' forms and FPNs it is not normally necessary to complete a PNB entry as well (but see local policy);
- it may be used to increase the extent and accuracy of recall in court (see 10.2.3 and 26.5.3), but the court must be satisfied that the notes were made contemporaneously to the event; and
- the language used in PNB entries must be clear, factually based, and avoid the use of exclusionary terms.

Police officers must keep it in a safe place whilst on and off duty and inform their supervisor straight away if it is lost.

Some forces (eg Surrey Police) now equip at least some officers with mobile data devices which can be used instead of the traditional, handwritten PNB for some tasks. The software used by current devices used (such as the BlackBerry) is designed to provide secure access to databases such as the PNC and electoral roll. These devices have a facility to complete standard *pro forma* documents that can then be uploaded to a force network, but they are not often used (at the time of writing) to record other information, for example statements made by suspects. Some forces are moving towards electronic alternatives to the written PNB, such the Motorola ES400 with dedicated software. However, in many forces the majority of police officers have yet to receive a mobile data device: for example, a report from the National Audit Office in 2012 found that in some forces only 1 per cent of officers had such devices (National Audit Office, 2012, p 25) and those that do tend to be in senior or specialist roles. Consequently, for the time being, most trainee officers will probably follow the time-honoured tradition of carrying a police pocket notebook.

10.2.1 How to use the pocket notebook

Although it may appear on the surface rather trivial, the importance of the PNB cannot be overemphasized. All police forces place obligations upon officers to record matters within it and, if it is used by an officer while giving evidence (see 26.5.3), the courts can examine it. Therefore, rules have been established in relation to its completion, and if these rules are not followed then the accuracy or even the authenticity of the entries could be questioned.

A number of Diploma in Policing assessed units refer to the need to keep accurate, legible, and complete records, and the PNB is in effect a set of records.

General Procedures

The following depicts some pages from a PNB outlining the general rules that police officers should apply for making PNB entries:

01

Write the day, date, and year at the beginning of entries for each day and underline them

	DO NOT LEAVE SPACES
	If spaces are left then ——— draw ——— a ——— line, to ——— indicate nothing further can be added. ———————
	Always make the pocket book entries in, black, ink. ———————
	Make all entries legible. ———————
WRITE	Entries should be made in the pocket book as the event happens. If the ———
THE	circumstances make it impossible to do so at the time, then the entry should be
TIME	made as soon as practicable after the event, and the reason for the delay should
IN THIS	also be noted eg: 'Whilst using officer safety techniques, I was unable to make any
COLUMN	entries'. ———————
USING	Each entry should include the time and name the location where the notes ———
THE	were made.———————
24 HR	Entries must only be written in single lines of writing on the lines of the pages of
CLOCK	the book (except when drawings are made, in which case, draw across the page). —
	Use every line and page of the pocket notebook and do not write anywhere else in
	the book such as inside the cover. ———————
	Do NOT overwrite errors. ———————
	Do NOT erase or obliterate errors. ———————
	Any mistake should be crossed out with a single line (~~so it can be read~~) and ———
	initialled beside the deletion. Any correction should then be written straight after
	the initials.———————
	If two pages are turned over by mistake a diagonal line should be ———
	drawn across the blank pages and 'omitted in error' written across the page. ———
	Do NOT tear out or remove any of the pages or parts of the pages. Write all ———
	SURNAMES in BLOCK CAPITALS. ———————
	Write down the names and addresses of victims, suspects, and witnesses. ———
	Write down all identifying features such as serial numbers of property, including
	vehicles or documents, e.g. the registration numbers of vehicles. ———————
	What a person says should be 'written down in direct speech!' and the conversation
	recorded verbatim or word for word. ———————

TASK 1 Why should we avoid the term 'Christian name' when referring to a witness?

10.2.2 Example of a PNB entry

The following shows how the rules are applied in a PNB entry.

		01
		Wednesday 16th January (0000)

	Duty 0600–1600 ———— Patrol ZZ 10 ————
	Refreshment time 0900 and 1400 ————
0545	Briefing at ZZ ————
0550	Collected keys for ZZ 10 patrol vehicle index number ZZ 00 ZZZ ————
0600	Checked vehicle seats and feet areas for property—no trace of any property ————
0605	Commenced patrol ————
0610	At the time stated on the date above, I was alone on mobile patrol in uniform ———— travelling in an easterly direction along Sheerbury Road, Ramstone, ———— approximately 50 metres east of the junction with Applebreaux Road, when I saw ———— a Fordover motor vehicle, index number YY 00 ZZZ being driven in the same ———— direction approximately 20 metres in front of me. There was a clear unobstructed ———— view of this vehicle. I caused the vehicle to stop in Sheerbury Road, 20 metres ———— West of the junction with Applebreaux Road and spoke to the driver who was the ———— sole occupant of the car. The driver identified him/herself to me as First Middle ———— LASTNAME, born 00/00/00 address 101 Hernegate Road, Ramstone, Kentshire. ————
Q	'May I see your driving licence and insurance for this vehicle please?' ————
R	'Haven't got my insurance with me because I have only just bought the car ———— yesterday, but here's my driving licence'. Driving licence details ———— LASTN000022FM9ZZ ————
Q	'As you are unable to produce your insurance to me right now and as I need to ———— ask you some more questions relating to your insurance, I would like to take the ———— opportunity to inform you of your rights at this point'. I cautioned Mr LASTNAME ———— and told him was not under arrest. ————
Q	Where is your insurance certificate right now?' ————
R	'I guess it's on its way in the post, I rang them yesterday' ————
Q	'What is the name of your insurance company?' ————
R	'I'm not sure—can't remember.' ————
Q	'How much did you pay for the insurance?' ————
R	'Again, sorry, I can't remember.' ————
Q	'How long have you owned this vehicle?' ————
R	'One day, I bought it yesterday.' ————
	PNC check no trace LASTNAME. PNC vehicle check LASTNAME RO at address ———— given. Voter's register check confirmed LASTNAME living at address I completed ———— an HO/RT/1 form. ————

Q	'As you haven't been able to produce your insurance to me now, please produce your certificate of insurance and this form at a police station within 7 days. Have you got any questions, and do you understand what you have to do?' LASTNAME gave no reply.
Q	'I have been making a record of our conversation, would you please read these notes I have made, and if you agree they are a true record of what we have said, and then sign my notes to that effect?'
	This is a true record. FM Lastname
Q	'As you have been unable to produce your certificate of insurance to me here, I am going to report you for the offence of failing to produce or not having a certificate of insurance for this vehicle.' I cautioned LASTNAME and there was no reply. These notes were made at the time between 0610 and 0630. CL Underwood PC 118118:
0630	Resumed patrol.
0900	Refs ZZ
0945	Resumed patrol.
V	No insurance—unacceptable because of possible consequences for passengers in the vehicle, pedestrians and property owners if vehicle was involved in a collision.
I	PNC check showed vehicle had no insurance.
A	Vehicle was stopped safely, driver spoken to on the footpath beside car.
P	S 136 RTA 1988 to stop vehicle, no insurance covered by s143 RTA 1988.
O	Could have used verbal warning, but due to the serious offence and possible outcome, prosecution is in public interest.
A	20 minutes for questioning and reporting the driver was proportionate here.
R	Driver remained calm. Safe environment throughout.

The reasons a police officer makes a particular decision need to be clear. National Decision Model (see 6.5.2) provides a suitable framework for making decisions, and the mnemonic VIAPOAR can be used to ensure that a PNB entry includes all the aspects that need to be taken into account. The College of Policing Authorised Professional Practice encourages its use and suggests that brief notes should be made against each letter of the mnemonic:

V	Values—which one(s) were considered during the decision-making process?
I	Information—where did it come from and what did it consist of?
A	Assessment—was there a risk, how was it assessed, and what was the outcome?
P	Powers and policy—which ones were used and were they legally justified?
O	Options—which ones were available and why were they selected?
A	Action—was it proportionate, legal, accountable, and necessary?
R	Review—what went well, did not go so well, or could be done differently in the future?

More information is provided on the College of Policing's Authorised Professional Practice website at <http://www.app.college.police.uk/>.

> **Top Ten Hints for Using a PNB**
>
> 1. It should be carried at all times on duty.
> 2. It should be used to record evidence (not opinion, except in cases of drunkenness).
> 3. It is a supervisor's responsibility to issue a new one when needed.
> 4. The general rules (see ELBOWS(S)) should always be applied.
> 5. Make use of the useful information it contains.
> 6. It may be referred to while giving evidence.
> 7. It remains police property.
> 8. Diagrams should be included (where appropriate) as part of the written notes.
> 9. On duty, additional pieces of paper should not be used to supplement the PNB, or as an alternative.
> 10. Don't lose it!

The rules concerning PNB entries can be summarized by the mnemonic 'no ELBOWS(S)', commonly used in police training.

E	no Erasures
L	no Leaves torn out/Lines missed
B	no Blank spaces
O	no Overwriting
W	no Writing between lines
S	no Spare pages
(S)	but Statements should be recorded in 'direct speech'

10.2.3 PNB entries and conferring with others

If other police officers have been involved in the same incident, then it may seem obvious and efficient for them to consult with each other to check facts. Police officers are (currently) legally entitled to confer with each in order to check on the factual accuracy of their respective PNB entries, and this is a relatively common occurrence in police practice (case law allows for this: notably *R v Bass* (1953) 17 Cr App R 51). However, in no circumstances should a police officer's PNB entries include material that the officer has not directly observed or recollected. Local force policy will apply in these matters.

In the inquest into the death of Jean-Charles de Menezes (shot by MPS firearms officers in 2005 in mistaken belief that he was a 'suicide bomber') the coroner criticized the practice of MPS firearms officers 'conferring' when writing their notes some 36 hours after the fatal shooting. In 2008 ACPO changed its guidance to recommend that in investigations concerning police discharge of firearms, normally officers should not confer with each other when making notes. In other cases (other than the discharge of firearms or incidents involving police contact leading to death or serious injury) it is probably good practice for police officers to record in writing (eg in their PNB) when they have conferred with another officer.

> **TASK 2** Formulate your own system for remembering the general rules concerning PNB entries— for example, a mind-map or mnemonic.

10.3 Cautions

From the moment a police officer suspects a person of committing an offence, the suspect has the right to certain information. This 'caution' or 'warning' is to protect the suspect's rights and keep him/her informed of the consequences of what he/she says during an investigation. Code C, para 10 of the PACE Codes of Practice outlines the necessity to give a suspect a warning

General Procedures

or caution at certain points during the investigative process. This has been confirmed by case law (*R v Nelson and Rose* [1998] 2 Cr App R 399) which states that a caution is required 'when, on an objective test, there are grounds for suspicion, falling short of evidence which would support a *prima facie* case of guilt, not simply that an offence has been committed, but committed by the person who is being questioned'.

There are three different cautions that are used at different stages of an investigation. The 'when questioned' caution is used at arrest and during interviews, at the stage of an investigation when questions are being asked. The 'now' caution is used right at the end of the investigation, just before a person is charged with an offence; at this stage the questioning is over. A 'restricted' caution is also used, but only for interviews after charge. In all cases the suspect is being warned about how his/her words can be used as evidence, and that whatever he/she says (or doesn't say) can be used in evidence.

There is no need to provide a caution:

- when asking for a person's identity or the identity of the owner of a vehicle;
- when asking for a driver's name and date of birth under the Road Traffic Act 1988 (see Code C, para 10.9, and 19.4.2);
- when asking a suspect to read and sign records of interviews and other comments (see Code C, para 11 and Note 11E, and 'unsolicited comments' in 10.5.1); or
- before a search (see Chapter 9).

A police officer using a caution must have a thorough understanding of the 'when questioned', 'now', and 'restricted' variations of the caution, so that the meaning can be passed on to the suspect. Minor deviations in the wording of cautions are acceptable, but if the Codes are clearly breached any evidence obtained will probably be rendered inadmissible. Police officers must always record when a caution has been given (a PNB entry or on a record of the interview) including the type of caution used (see Code C, para 10.13).

10.3.1 The importance of the proper use of a caution

The correct version of the caution must be used or the evidence obtained might be rejected by the court. For example, in *Charles v Crown Prosecution Service* [2009] EWHC 3521 (Admin) the defendant was arrested for being drunk in charge of a motor vehicle (s 5(1)(b) of the Road Traffic Act 1988: see 19.9.3). At the police station the suspect provided a positive specimen of breath for a breath test and was informed that he would be charged with a s 5(1)(b) offence. He was later interviewed about the incident (contrary to Code C, para 16.5, see 10.13.6), and incorrectly given the 'now' caution (see 10.3.4) rather than the 'restricted' version. During the interview, the suspect admitted to actually driving the vehicle and the charge was changed to driving a vehicle on a road above the prescribed limit (a more serious offence), but the conviction was quashed due to the incorrect procedures.

Some people, particularly those who do not speak English as their first language, may not understand the formal wording of a caution. There is an obligation under PACE (Code C, para 10.7 and Note 10D) to ensure that the detained person understands the caution. However, this may not be appropriate at the time of arrest: a full explanation of the caution might only be possible at the time of interview. When in doubt, an interpreter who is fluent in the suspect's own first language should attend (and may be needed during the interview process as well, see 24.4). The caution can be given in the Welsh language where appropriate. The wording of the Scottish caution is slightly different from the caution used in England and Wales, but officers in England and Wales are unlikely to use it. This is because a suspect who has committed an offence in Scotland but who is arrested in England or Wales would either be escorted back to Scotland for interview or a member of the Scottish police force would travel to interview the suspect.

10.3.2 The three parts to a caution

There are three parts to a caution (Code C, para 10.5), as shown in the diagram:

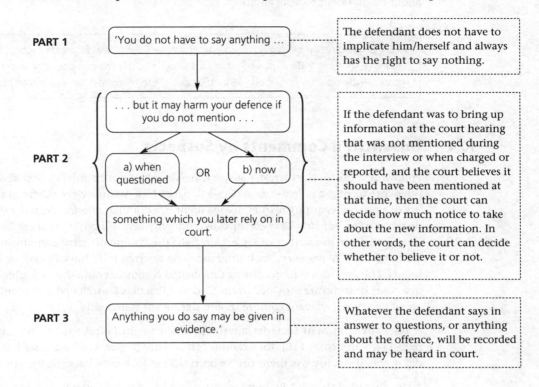

PART 1 'You do not have to say anything ...

The defendant does not have to implicate him/herself and always has the right to say nothing.

PART 2 . . . but it may harm your defence if you do not mention . . .

a) when questioned OR b) now

something which you later rely on in court.

If the defendant was to bring up information at the court hearing that was not mentioned during the interview or when charged or reported, and the court believes it should have been mentioned at that time, then the court can decide how much notice to take about the new information. In other words, the court can decide whether to believe it or not.

PART 3 Anything you do say may be given in evidence.'

Whatever the defendant says in answer to questions, or anything about the offence, will be recorded and may be heard in court.

10.3.3 Use of the 'when questioned' caution

The 'when questioned' caution is given to a suspect:

- at the time of arrest, unless this has been done earlier (eg in relation to being suspected of committing an offence) or it is impossible (eg he/she is unconscious or is fighting) (Code C, para 10.4 and Code G, para 3.4);
- at the start of an interview, and also when recommencing questioning after any break (see also Chapter 24 on interviewing).

At the same time as being cautioned, certain additional information must be provided to the suspect depending on the circumstances and location of the interview. For example, a suspect who has been arrested must also be reminded that he/she is entitled to free legal advice, and a suspect who has not been arrested (see 10.6) must be clearly told that he/she is not under arrest. Further details are provided in 24.5.5 which covers procedures to be followed at the start of an interview with a suspect.

10.3.4 The use of the 'now' caution

The 'now' caution is the last chance for the defendant to have anything recorded about the offence (see Code C, para 16.2). It could be used at the end of an investigation, for instance after a series of interviews when charging a detained person with an offence, or at the end of the process of reporting a person for an offence (see 10.13.1).

When informing a person who is not under arrest that he/she may be prosecuted, the Codes of Practice do not require a now caution to be administered. However, if the 'now' caution is not given at this time, the court cannot draw its own conclusions if the defendant then enters 'new information' at the hearing, and the court might be more likely to believe the new information (see Code C, Note 10 G and see 24.5.9.2). It is advisable therefore to use the 'now' caution after informing a person that they may be prosecuted.

10.3.5 The use of the 'restricted' caution

After being charged a detained person cannot be interviewed further unless it is necessary for the reasons listed in Code C, para 16.5 (see 10.13.6). If such an interview does take place, then the caution used is referred to as 'restricted', as it is shorter than the other cautions. The following words could be used: 'You do not have to say anything unless you wish to do so, but anything you do say may be given in evidence.' The interviewer should also remind the detainee about his/her right to legal advice.

TASK 3 Imagine an officer arrests a young woman. First, decide which caution he should use. Secondly, imagine that he uses the standard words but the woman does not understand what he means. Write down a simplified wording he could use to explain the caution to her.

10.4 Unsolicited Comments by Suspects

Following a decision to arrest a suspect, he/she must not be interviewed about the relevant offences except at a police station (Code C, para 11.1). An interview is defined as the 'questioning of a person regarding his/her involvement in a criminal offence'. So what should an officer do when a suspect who has been arrested suddenly says something that applies to the offence in question, or to another offence? After all, the comments may contain information that could be used in evidence. Such utterances are referred to as 'unsolicited' or voluntary comments. The procedures for recording unsolicited comments (and their possible subsequent use in a court hearing) are provided in the Codes of Practice. Unsolicited (or voluntary) comments are of two types: relevant comments and significant statements.

A **relevant comment** includes anything which might be relevant to the offence (Code C, para 11.13 and Note 11E), for example 'That other person you've arrested, it was them that did it, you'll see, just ask them you've been talking to, they'll back me up, you'll see!'

A **significant statement** includes anything which could be used in evidence against the suspect (Code C, para 11.4A). The term derives from Part III of the Criminal Justice and Public Order Act 1994:

> A significant statement or silence is one which appears capable of being used in evidence against the suspect, in particular a direct admission of guilt, or a failure or refusal to answer a question or to answer it satisfactorily which may give rise to an inference.

It may be part of a relevant comment but it must have been made in the presence and hearing of a police officer (or other police staff member), for example 'I wish I never done it now, but I lost it, the knife was on the table and I just kept stabbing, stabbing and stabbing!'

10.4.1 Recording unsolicited comments

All such comments made by the suspects should be recorded in a PNB entry, noting when the comment was made, signed by the police officer. When practicable, the suspect should be asked to read it and to check whether it is a true record of what was said. If the suspect agrees that it is a true record, he/she should endorse the record with the words 'I agree that this is a correct record of what was said' and then sign (Code C, Note 11E).

If the suspect does not agree with the record, the details of any disagreement should be recorded in a PNB entry. The suspect should then read the record and sign that it accurately reflects his/her disagreement. A refusal to sign should also be recorded (Code C, Note 11E).

10.5 Identification of Suspects by Witnesses

A significant number of the incidents encountered during Supervised or Independent Patrol will involve criminal offences which have been witnessed by members of the public. In many cases the witness will be able to remember something about what the perpetrator(s) looked like, and will feel able to recognize him/her. Obviously this could provide useful evidence.

Such an identification process can only be carried out when there is not enough information to justify the arrest of any particular person. In such circumstances the identity of the suspect, according to Code D, para 3.2 is 'not known'. (The identity of a suspect who has been arrested is regarded as 'known' (Code D, para 3.4) and other identification procedures will be used—eg video identification parades such as VIPER, and group identification, see <http://www.viper.police.uk/>.)

The Codes of Practice outline a process to safeguard the rights of a possible suspect. A record must be made of the witness's first description of the person, and the Codes also describe the procedures for taking a witness to a particular place to identify him/her. Finally, if the witness is successful in pointing out a person, the circumstances under which the identification was made must be recorded in line with the precedent set in the case of *R v Turnbull* (1976) 63 Cr App R 132.

10.5.1   The identification process

Before asking a witness to pick out a particular person a record should be made of the witness's 'first description' of the suspect if this is practicable (Code D, para 3.2a). Ideally, it should be recorded as a PNB entry.

Then the witness should be asked to identify the suspect. Care must be taken not to direct the witness's attention to any individual unless, taking all the circumstances into account, it cannot be avoided (Code D, para 3.2b). The identification may be compromised if the witness's attention is drawn to any individual (see Note 3F). However, a witness can be asked to look carefully at the people around, or to look towards a group, or in a particular direction. This might be necessary to ensure that the witness does not overlook a possible suspect, or to encourage him/her to make comparisons between several people in the area.

A trainee police officer or police support employee accompanying the witness must record as soon as possible in his/her PNB full details of the action taken (Code D, para 3.2e). If there is more than one witness, they must be taken separately to see whether they can identify the particular person independently (Code D, para 3.2c), and additional officers are likely to be required.

The witness has had two opportunities to see the suspect: first, around the time the offence was committed, and second, when taken to make an identification. The visual evidence from the first sighting may be disputed in court, but this is less likely if the 'Turnbull' guidelines have been followed. These were set by case law in *R v Turnbull* (1976) 63 Cr App R 132. The mnemonic ADVOKATE is a useful way to remember them:

A	Amount of time the suspect was under observation
D	Distance between the witness and the suspect
V	Visibility (eg what was the lighting like, what were the weather conditions?)
O	Obstructions to his/her view of the suspect
K	Known or seen before (does he/she know the suspect and, if so, how?)
A	Any reason for remembering the suspect
T	Time lapse between the first and any subsequent identification to the police
E	Errors between the first recorded description and the suspect's actual appearance

10.5.2   ADVOKATE in detail

In essence, the circumstances of an observation will alter from moment to moment and this needs to be recorded in detail.

In terms of the **Amount** of time the suspect was under observation, consider the following:

- During the time that the witness saw the suspect carrying out the criminal act, for how long was he/she looking at the suspect?
- Record the total time but also identify how long the witness observed the suspect at specific moments throughout the entire period; it is highly unlikely that a suspect stood in exactly the same position for the whole observation period.
- Was there a break (however brief) in his/her observation?
- What were the various distances involved (see below) and how long was the suspect observed at that particular distance?
- Was it a frontal view, rear view, profile view?

In terms of the **Distance** between the witness and the suspect consider the following:

- How far away was the witness from the suspect when the incident took place?
- If in the street, count kerbstones as a guide: they are usually one metre long.
- Record the distance between the suspect and the witness. The distance is likely to vary during the course of the observation and will rarely be one measurement.
- Record furthest distance, shortest distance, and timings involved at each level.
- Where was the witness in relation to the suspect?

In terms of the **Visibility**, consider the following:

- Was it day or night?
- Were the street lamps on?
- Was the witness wearing glasses or contact lenses?

Weather conditions must be included in detail (eg it is not sufficient to say 'It was raining'):

- Was it heavy rain, drizzle, etc?
- Was sunlight a factor?
- Where was the sun in relation to the suspect and the witness?
- Were there shadows cast?
- Include, if possible, the distance of available visibility.

In terms of **Obstructions** to his/her view of the suspect, consider the following:

- Any obstruction between the witness and the suspect should be described in detail. It is insufficient to say, for example, that the view was obstructed by a hedge. How tall, how wide, how dense was it?
- Obstructions include glass, and the glass would need to be described as well: its size, was it clean or dirty, frosted, open, closed, double-glazed, was there glare from the sun, etc?
- How did the obstruction actually obstruct the view of the witness and to what extent?
- Record the distance between the witness and any obstructions.

In terms of whether the suspect is **Known** to the witness or has been seen before, consider whether there is an association between the witness and the suspect, for example a relationship, friendship, or whether they work together. If there is an association then:

- How long has the witness known the suspect?
- How does he/she know the suspect?
- In what context and how well?
- When did he/she last see the suspect?
- Has his/her description changed in the interim period?

In terms of the existence of **Any** reason why the witness should remember the suspect, consider the following:

- This could be a distinguishing feature or peculiarity of the person, or the very nature of the incident itself that made the person memorable. This can relate to previous or present sightings.
- Was there anything unusual about the suspect's appearance (eg distinguishing features) or the prevailing circumstances?
- What, if anything, attracted the witness's attention?
- What has stuck in his/her mind?

In terms of the **Time** lapse between the first and any subsequent identification to the police consider the following (note that this is not the time between first seeing the suspect and the writing of the statement):

- How much time elapsed between recording or obtaining a description and the sighting of the suspect?
- How much time elapsed between recording or obtaining a description and the subsequent identification?

In terms of **Errors** between the first recorded description of the suspect and his/her actual appearance consider the following:

- Remember, a first description must been have recorded.
- Once the witness has made an identification, how similar is the first description to the actual appearance of the suspect?

- Record any errors, or differences between the first description, and the actual appearance of the suspect when he/she was identified (eg a suspect is identified while wearing a black sweatshirt without a hood when the original description recorded a hooded top).

Any differences must be recorded to show integrity of the evidence.

One of the most important issues to consider when using this process of identification is whether there was sufficient evidence to justify an arrest prior to taking the witness to make an identification. If there was, then the courts might consider that an identification method relating to 'known' identity of the suspect would have been more appropriate.

> **TASK 4** A police officer attends an incident involving criminal damage to a garden wall. The householder tells her that it all happened about 20 minutes ago and that he can definitely identify the person who did it, and knows where he is likely to be. What should the officer do, and what should she say?

10.6 Arrest Without Warrant

While on Supervised or Independent Patrol an officer may need to 'arrest without warrant' a person whom he/she suspects of committing a criminal offence. The term 'arrest without warrant' may need explaining. The phrase 'the judge ordered a warrant for his arrest' is often used by the media when reporting, for example, the failure of a person to attend court. This is when a warrant (in the form of a document) is issued by a court and it is the responsibility of the police, or in some cases a civilian enforcement officer, to serve the warrant on the person concerned (see 10.7). However, the police also have a general power to arrest without a warrant in relation to criminal offences (see Code G, Note 1) and separate powers of arrest for circumstances such as drink-driving offences, breach of the peace, and failing to answer or to satisfy conditions of bail (see Code G, Note 1A for the full list). The general power of arrest without warrant is derived from s 24 of the PACE Act 1984 and governed by Code G of the Codes of Practice. A police officer does not have to be in uniform to use this power.

It is no surprise that the right to liberty is an important principle under Article 5 of the European Convention on Human Rights set out in the Human Rights Act 1998 (see 5.4) and the power to arrest and take away a person's liberty clearly challenges that right (Code G, para 1.2). It is therefore obvious that the proper use of this power for the right reason and at the right time is paramount. The information provided here will contribute towards the Certificate in Knowledge of Policing unit 'Knowledge of arresting, detaining, and reporting individuals within a policing context' and the knowledge evidence to meet assessment criteria requirements of the Diploma in Policing assessed unit 'Arrest, detain or report individuals' and in particular the need to 'ensure that there is sufficient evidence and legal authority' to justify actions and to document 'decisions, actions and rationale' for making an arrest. It is also relevant to the PAC heading 'Disposal' and in particular 'make lawful arrests', and also contains material likely to be relevant to Phase 3 of the IPLDP LPG 1 under the 'Police Policies and Procedures' heading, particularly LPG 1.4(1).

The arrest of a suspect is not mandatory in every case where an offence has been committed. There are other ways of processing a suspect who has committed an offence, such as reporting the offence, granting street bail, or issuing a fixed penalty notice, and these are covered later in this chapter. A person can also attend a police station voluntarily to assist the police with the investigation of an offence, and may leave at any time unless he/she is subsequently arrested (Code C, para 3.21). The power to arrest without warrant is no different from any other power as a police officer, and if the rights of an individual are not observed, the investigation will be -discredited at best and at worst discontinued. There might also be an opportunity for the person to seek damages for an unlawful arrest and false imprisonment (Code G, para 1.3).

Code G, para 1.1 states that police officers must use their powers to arrest fairly, responsibly, with respect for people being arrested, and without unlawful discrimination. Indeed, the Equality Act 2010 makes it unlawful for police officers to discriminate against, harass, or victimize, any person on the grounds of the 'protected characteristics' of age, disability, gender reassignment, race, religion or belief, sex and sexual orientation, marriage and civil partnership, pregnancy and maternity.

10.6.1 The two elements for a s 24 PACE arrest to be lawful

PACE Code G, para 2.1 states two elements that must both be satisfied for a s 24 arrest to be lawful:

1. the person has been involved, has attempted to be involved or is suspected of involvement in the commission of a criminal offence; and
2. there are reasonable grounds for believing that the person's arrest is 'necessary' (see *Shields v Merseyside Police* [2010] EWCA Civ 1281).

10.6.2 Reasonable grounds for suspicion

It is important to bear in mind that although words such as 'suspicion', 'grounds', and 'belief' are in common usage, they have particular meanings within the context of policing and the law. In a law enforcement context the following meanings apply:

- Whether or not something is **reasonable** is a conclusion that one or more people reach in agreement as a result of personal experience or understanding. It is a practical, level-headed, and logical result.
- **Grounds** for something include a reason or argument for a thought to exist.
- To **suspect** something is to think that it is probably true, although you are not certain.
- To **believe** something is a stronger and more concrete conclusion.

Therefore, in order to decide whether there are reasonable grounds to suspect, the component parts of that offence must be considered, and whether or not a like-minded person would draw the same conclusions about the suspect and the offence. For example, did the person have the opportunity, the motive, the presence of mind, the means, and the incentive to commit the offence? Alternatively, certain facts might be known about the suspect, and a person could resemble him/her in terms of employment, description, name, or clothes, or have previous convictions for similar offences and live near the crime; any of these could contribute to grounds for suspecting (see *Chief Constable of West Yorkshire v Armstrong* [2008] EWCA Civ 1582).

The suspicion required to make an arrest must contain reasonable, objective grounds based on known facts and information. The suspicion must be related to both the likelihood that the offence has been committed and whether the person who is liable to arrest committed that offence (Code G, para 2.3A). Accordingly, a police officer must take account of not only the facts which might indicate a person's involvement but also information that might dispel suspicion, such as claims of innocence (Code G, Note 2). For example, defences to assault provided by common and statute law (see 10.8.2 and 15.5) and statutory powers given to school staff to use reasonable force against their pupils (under s 93 of the Education and Inspections Act 2006) should be taken into account (Code G, Note 2A). Indeed Code G, Note 2B reinforces the necessity for the arresting officer to pursue all lines of enquiry in order to fulfil his/her obligations as an investigator under para 3.5 of the Criminal Procedure and Investigations Act 1996 Code of Practice.

Note, however, that an arrest can never be justified simply on the basis of obeying the orders of a supervisor or manager (*O'Hara (AP) v CC of the RUC* [1997] 1 Cr App R 447). Equally, it is not sufficient to infer that a supervisor or manager had reasonable grounds for suspicion (see *Commissioner of Police of the Metropolis v Mohamed Raissi* [2008] EWCA Civ 1237); the arresting officer must have been given sufficient information by a supervisor or manager to generate his/her own reasonable grounds to suspect relating to that individual and that offence (see *(1) Sonia Raissi (2) Mohamed Raissi v Commissioner of Police of the Metropolis* [2007] EWHC 2842 (QB)). If the information was too sensitive to be passed to a more junior officer, then the supervisor or manager would have to make the arrest.

10.6.3 Involvement in the commission of a criminal offence

The first element of a lawful arrest under s 24 of the PACE Act is a person's involvement, suspected involvement, or attempted involvement in the commission of a criminal offence (Code G, para 2.1). The guidance in para 2.3 provides more detail on the circumstances in which this might apply. The table provides summaries and illustrative scenarios set in an electrical goods shop, with a police officer who is on duty but not in uniform. (Remember, however, before arresting the person the officer must be certain that element 2 is also satisfied: that it is **necessary** to arrest the suspect. The officer must have clear **reasons** in mind for the necessity (see 10.6.4).)

Level of involvement	Example
A person is about to commit an offence (s 24 (1)(a))	The officer sees a woman, who is obviously not a member of the shop staff, walk up to a display of batteries, select a multi-pack, and put it under her coat. She then walks towards the entry/exit of the shop, making no attempt to pay for it. The officer stops her as she is about to leave the shop.
A person is in the act of committing an offence (s 24(1)(b))	The officer sees a man walk up to a display of DAB radios, cut a security link, pick up a radio, and walk towards the door of the shop past the check-outs, without paying for the radio. The store alarm is activated and the man continues to walk out of the shop. The officer concludes that the man is stealing the radio and stops him just outside the shop.
There are reasonable grounds for suspecting a person to be about to commit an offence (s 24(1)(c))	The officer sees a man walk up to a display of mobile phones. He appears to be extremely nervous. The officer sees him take a metal cutter out of his pocket and reach out with the tool towards the security chain of the mobile and appears to be about to cut the chain. But then he is disturbed. He puts the tool back in his pocket and walks away. A few seconds later the same man returns to the display of mobiles, takes out the same tool, places the tool around the security chain, and sets off the alarm. At this moment the officer decides he has reasonable grounds for suspecting that the man is about to commit an offence
There are reasonable grounds for suspecting a person to be committing an offence (s 24(1)(d))	The officer is just outside the shop and notices a woman standing just inside, near the doorway. She is holding an unpacked, brand-new set of hair straighteners under her arm with the lead hanging down. She has a large handbag and appears nervous. The officer sees her use a tool to cut away the security tag from the straighteners before putting the straighteners into her bag. She then walks towards the door as if to leave the shop. The officer notes the obvious facts: • the straighteners should be boxed or at least in a bag supplied by the shop; • the woman should not be so anxious to leave the shop quickly, especially with the lead hanging free; • she should not have cut the security tag; and • she should not have put the straighteners in her bag. This all forms reasonable grounds for the officer to suspect that the woman is in the process of committing an offence of theft.
There are reasonable grounds for suspecting an offence has been committed and that a particular person is guilty of the offence (s 24(2))	The officer is just outside the shop and notices a woman run out of the shop clutching an apparently unpackaged white and chrome-coloured object. The store alarm is activated. He runs after her but loses sight of her in the crowd. A short while later the officer sees a woman fitting the description of the woman he ran after earlier. He decides he has reasonable grounds for suspecting she had stolen something from the shop, and has reasonable grounds for suspecting that she is the person he ran after earlier.

Section 24 of the PACE Act also caters for situations in which it will be clear that an offence has definitely been committed. For example, a camera shop owner who deals with *every* sale in his shop sees a woman walk up to a display of cameras, pick one up, and walk towards the door of the shop without paying for it. The store alarm is activated. The shop owner decides that she has stolen the camera and runs out and stops her, and then calls the police. In such circumstances, the officer (if it is also **necessary**) could arrest any person:

• **who is guilty of the offence** (s 24(3)(a)). For example, the shop owner describes the suspect's actions to the officer in the presence and hearing of the suspect and the suspect does not refute the allegations;
• **for whom there are reasonable grounds for suspecting to be guilty** (s 24(1)(b)). Imagine that the camera shop owner in the example had run after the suspect, but could not catch up with her. He calls the police and supplies a first description of the woman. The description is passed to an officer who the next day sees a woman fitting the description. He decides therefore that he has reasonable grounds for suspecting her of the theft.

10.6.4 Reasons that make an arrest necessary

In 10.6.1 we explained that there are two elements for a lawful arrest. The first concerns the involvement in the commission of an offence, as discussed earlier. The second element is that the arrest is necessary (Code G, para 2.4). An arrest is deemed to be necessary if one or more of the following reasons apply:

1 to ascertain a person's name;
2 to ascertain a person's address;
3 to prevent injury, damage, indecency, or obstruction;
4 to protect a vulnerable person;

5 to ensure prompt investigation; or

6 to prevent a suspect disappearing.

These six reasons are set out in full in s 24(5) of the PACE Act 1984 and Code G, para 2.9. Code G is available at <https://www.gov.uk/government/publications/pace-code-g-2012>. The table lists the six reasons and the mnemonic ID COP PLAN.

I	Investigation	To allow the prompt and effective investigation of the offence or of the conduct of the person in question.
D	Disappearance	To prevent any prosecution for the offence from being hindered by the disappearance of the person in question.
C	Child	To protect a child or other vulnerable person from the relevant person.
O	Obstruction	To prevent the relevant person causing an unlawful obstruction of the highway.
P	Physical injury	To prevent the relevant person causing physical injury to him/herself or any other person.
P	Public decency	To prevent the relevant person committing an offence against public decency.
L	Loss or damage	To prevent the relevant person causing loss of, or damage to, property.
A	Address	To enable the address of the relevant person to be ascertained.
N	Name	To enable the name of the relevant person to be ascertained.

(Note that unless it is unavoidable, a young person should not be arrested at his/her place of education. Should it become necessary and a young person is arrested, the principal or his/her nominee must be informed (Code G, Note 1B).)

10.6.4.1 To ascertain a person's name or address

If a person who is suspected in relation to an offence refuses to provide his/her name or address, the officer must always explain that it may lead to his/her arrest. Remember, this is not a power to arrest a person who simply refuses to give his/her name or address. Instead, this is just one of several reasons that make a person's arrest necessary in particular circumstances. An officer may arrest someone in a situation where:

1. The officer does not know and cannot readily ascertain the person's name or address (Code G, para 2.9(a)).

The officer should not just ask the person for his/her name and address once, or in a manner that lacks confidence. It should be made clear to him/her that his/her name and address is required in relation to an offence, in order that the process of investigation can be followed.

2. There are reasonable grounds for doubting whether a name or address given by the person is real (Code G, para 2.9(b)).

There must be a logical reason for not believing that the name or address he/she gave is correct, for example:

- he/she cannot provide anything which identifies him/her with the name or address (eg a driving licence with a photograph);
- the officer suspects that the person is using the name or address of a close relative with the same details;
- there is no record of the name or address he/she provided in the voters' register or telephone directory; or
- the officer suspects his/her name or address is fictitious because it is the name or address of a famous person or character.

Code D of the Codes of Practice provides more detailed information about the definition of a satisfactory address.

Examples of unsatisfactory addresses include:

- that of a person who is working in the UK and leaving very soon, never to return;
- that of a person of 'no fixed abode' who cannot supply any other permanent addresses;
- the address the person supplies does not exist; and
- the person's name does not appear on the voters' register at the address he/she has given.

However, an address will be satisfactory if some other person at that address (eg an employer or relative) will accept service of the written charge and requisition on his/her behalf. This could be used by a person whose home address is not in the UK.

10.6.4.2 To prevent injury, damage, indecency, or obstruction

A reason for arresting someone could be to prevent the person:

- **causing physical injury to any other person (Code G, para 2.9 (c)(i)):** for example, if investigating an offence of throwing fireworks in a street or public place under s 80 of the Explosives Act 1875, the officer might reach the conclusion that the suspect may harm somebody else;
- **suffering physical injury (Code G, para 2.9 (c)(ii)):** for example, if investigating a person for an offence of being a pedestrian on the carriageway of a motorway under s 17(4) of the Road Traffic Regulation Act 1984, the officer might reach the conclusion that the suspect may suffer physical injury from a passing vehicle veering off the main carriageway;
- **causing loss of or damage to property (Code G, para 2.9 (c)(iii)):** for example, if investigating a person for an offence of interference with a motor vehicle or trailer under s 9 of the Criminal Attempts Act 1981, the officer might reach the conclusion that the suspect could cause damage to a vehicle during the interference;
- **committing an offence against public decency (Code G, para 2.9 (c)(iv)):** for example, if investigating a person for an offence of using profane or obscene language under the Town Police Clauses Act 1847, an officer might reach the conclusion that the suspect was committing an offence against public decency; or
- **causing unlawful obstruction of the highway (Code G, para 2.9 (c)(v)):** for example, if a person was being investigated for an offence of wilful obstruction of the highway under s 137 of the Highways Act 1980 and the suspect was stopping or slowing vehicles on the highway, the officer might reach the conclusion that the person would need to be removed.

10.6.4.3 To protect a child or other vulnerable person

A reason for arresting someone could be if he/she was suspected of committing an offence which put the health and safety of a vulnerable person or child at risk (Code G, para 2.9 (d)). An example would be that the suspect was standing on the hard shoulder of a motorway holding a baby, and refused to move away from the traffic.

10.6.4.4 To allow the prompt and effective investigation of the offence or of the conduct

There may be many reasons why an investigation might be jeopardized if the suspect is not arrested (Code G, para 2.9 (e)), such as where it is necessary to obtain evidence by questioning or where there are grounds to believe that the person:

- has made false statements (eg dates of birth, denials of disqualification from driving);
- has made statements which cannot readily be verified (eg ownership of a car for which he/she has no records, such as vehicle registration documents);
- has presented false evidence (eg forged driving licences or MOT certificates);
- may steal or destroy evidence (eg disposing of stolen property from a burglary);
- may make contact with co-suspects or conspirators (eg a warning through the use of mobile telephones, which would make the co-suspects more difficult to locate); or
- may intimidate, threaten, or make contact with witnesses (eg in cases where the identities of the suspect and victim are known to each other).

This may include cases such as when an officer is considering an arrest in connection with an indictable offence. If the person has not been arrested, then it will not be possible to:

- enter and search any premises occupied or controlled by the person under s 18 of the PACE Act 1984;
- search the person under s 32 of the PACE Act 1984;
- prevent contact with others: it will not be possible to seek the authority to delay the right of the detained person to have someone informed of his/her detention;

- take fingerprints, footwear impressions, samples, or photographs of the suspect; or
- test him/her for drugs under s 63B of the PACE Act 1984.

10.6.4.5   To prevent the disappearance of the person in question

This may arise if there are reasonable grounds for believing that:

- if the person is not arrested, he/she will fail to attend court: for example, there is an existing warrant for his/her arrest for failing to appear at court for a previous offence;
- street bail after arrest would be sufficient to deter the suspect from trying to evade prosecution (Code G, para 2.9 (f)).

10.6.5   Arrest without warrant by other persons

Any person may arrest another person, although this only applies if the offence concerned is an indictable offence and a constable is not present to carry out the arrest (s 24A(3)(b) of the PACE Act 1984). The arrest must also be necessary in order to prevent the suspect escaping before a constable can arrest him/her, or to prevent injury (to the suspect or to another person) or to prevent damage to property.

Under s 24A(1) the person carrying out the arrest must:

- have seen the suspect committing an indictable offence; or
- have reasonable grounds for suspecting the suspect to be committing an indictable offence, such as a man that a member of the public sees climbing through a window into a house and suspects to be committing burglary (without actually knowing whether the man has the resident's permission).

The arrest can be carried out later (s 24A(2)); for example, if a store detective sees a woman commit a theft but is unable to apprehend her at the time. He sees her soon afterwards and arrests her then.

> **TASK 5** Think of a practical example for each of the offences of unlawful possession of drugs (see 12.5), criminal damage (see 20.2), robbery (see 16.3), and a s 5 Public Order Act offence (see 14.4.3.1). Consider the circumstances under which you (as a member of the public and not a police officer) could arrest for these offences and what possible reasons you could have for believing the arrest to be necessary.

10.7   Warrants of Arrest

A warrant is a formal written document of authority issued by a magistrate or judge. It is normally addressed to the police and directs them to carry out an action on behalf of the court. A warrant of arrest therefore authorizes the arrest of a named individual or a group. A police officer can execute a warrant even though the warrant might not be physically in his/her possession at the time (s 125 of the Magistrates' Courts Act 1980).

Commonly used warrants include those relating to failures to:

- pay fines (s 76(1) of the Magistrates' Courts Act 1980);
- appear at court (s 55(2) of the Magistrates' Courts Act 1980);
- answer bail (s 7(1) of the Bail Act 1976).

A warrant may also be issued for the arrest of a witness required in a court if the person in question has not attended despite having being summoned. For non-appearance at a magistrates' court the warrant will be issued under s 97 of the Magistrates' Courts Act 1980. To attend a Crown Court, the warrant will be issued under s 4 of the Criminal Procedure (Attendance of Witnesses) Act 1965.

> **TASK 6** Find out about and then describe in your own words how a police officer should execute a warrant.

TASK 7 What is the 'European Arrest Warrant'? How does it work?

10.8   Making an Arrest

Here, we deal with the process of making an arrest and a police officer's responsibility to protect the suspect's rights. Making an arrest is an important milestone to achieve within the Police Action Checklist. The 'Disposal' heading of the PAC is particularly relevant here, especially the confirmation that an officer can make lawful arrests. The relevant Diploma in Policing assessed unit is 'Arrest, detain or report individuals' and the learning outcome 'To be able to arrest and detain individuals'. This learning outcome has a total of five assessment criteria, including the requirement that, when making an arrest, an officer can ensure that his/her actions are lawful. The evidence for the achievement of these assessment criteria will come from successfully conducting arrests whilst under supervision on at least two different occasions. The information provided here is also relevant to the Certificate in Knowledge of Policing unit 'Knowledge of arresting, detaining, and reporting individuals within a policing context'.

10.8.1   Information to be given on arrest

Under s 28(1) of the PACE Act 1984 and Code G para 2.2, on arrest the officer must tell the person:

- that he/she is under arrest (even if it is obvious): and
- the reasons and the necessity for the arrest (see 10.6.1).

There is no need for the officer to use technical or precise language, and although it is recommended, it is not necessary to say 'I arrest you'. But it is definitely not sufficient for the officer to simply place a hand on the shoulder of the suspect; the suspect must be clearly informed in words (s 28(2)) and provided with sufficient information to understand what has happened and why (Code C Note 10B).

An arrest is not lawful unless the suspect is fully informed of the arrest and reasons at the time or as soon as practicable (Code C, para 10.3), unless this is not possible because, for example, the suspect runs off. The reason given must be correct for the arrest to be lawful.

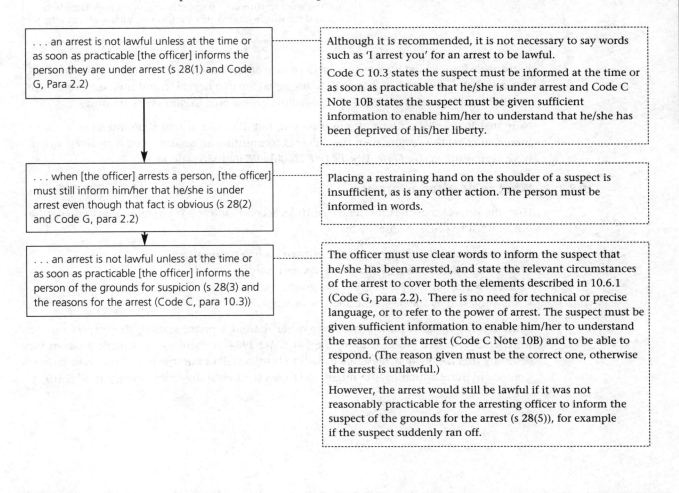

... an arrest is not lawful unless at the time or as soon as practicable [the officer] informs the person they are under arrest (s 28(1) and Code G, Para 2.2)

Although it is recommended, it is not necessary to say words such as 'I arrest you' for an arrest to be lawful.

Code C 10.3 states the suspect must be informed at the time or as soon as practicable that he/she is under arrest and Code C Note 10B states the suspect must be given sufficient information to enable him/her to understand that he/she has been deprived of his/her liberty.

... when [the officer] arrests a person, [the officer] must still inform him/her that he/she is under arrest even though that fact is obvious (s 28(2) and Code G, para 2.2)

Placing a restraining hand on the shoulder of a suspect is insufficient, as is any other action. The person must be informed in words.

... an arrest is not lawful unless at the time or as soon as practicable [the officer] informs the person of the grounds for suspicion (s 28(3) and the reasons for the arrest (Code C, para 10.3))

The officer must use clear words to inform the suspect that he/she has been arrested, and state the relevant circumstances of the arrest to cover both the elements described in 10.6.1 (Code G, para 2.2). There is no need for technical or precise language, or to refer to the power of arrest. The suspect must be given sufficient information to enable him/her to understand the reason for the arrest (Code C Note 10B) and to be able to respond. (The reason given must be the correct one, otherwise the arrest is unlawful.)

However, the arrest would still be lawful if it was not reasonably practicable for the arresting officer to inform the suspect of the grounds for the arrest (s 28(5)), for example if the suspect suddenly ran off.

General Procedures

To fulfil the requirements of both s 28 and Code G, para 2.2 an officer might say:

> I have just seen you run out of the shop with a brand-new digital radio under your arm. I heard the store alarm sound at the same time and I therefore suspect that you have stolen the radio. I am arresting you on suspicion of theft of that radio as the arrest is necessary to allow the prompt and effective investigation of the offence by interviewing you on tape at the police station and through the search of any premises occupied or controlled by you for evidence relating to similar offences of theft.

10.8.2 The use of force to arrest a person

During an arrest the use of force may be required, but the amount used must be reasonable. For example, s 117 of the PACE Act 1984 states that reasonable force may be used for arrests where the power of arrest is provided under PACE (see 9.5.3). The arresting officer must, however, have an honest belief that the force used was reasonable and appropriate in the circumstances (similar to the requirements under s 3 of the Criminal Law Act 1967).

Section 3 of the Criminal Law Act 1967 (see the flowchart) provides a defence for the use of force for law enforcement activities.

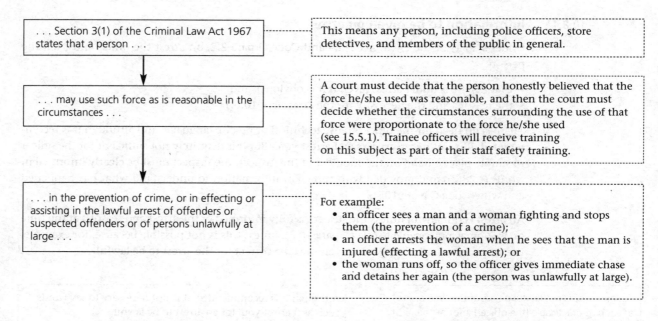

Reasonable force would have been used if a police officer acting in the course of a lawful arrest was met with force and had first of all to use equal force to negate it, and then use more force to take control (see also 15.5.1). Such procedures are covered in staff safety training.

Note that if a police officer restrains a person, but does not at that time intend or seem to intend to arrest the person, then the officer is committing an assault, even if an arrest would have been justified (see *Fraser Wood v DPP* [2008] EWHC 1056 (Admin)).

10.8.3 What to do after an arrest

First, the suspect must be cautioned (see 10.3). Second, unless it is impracticable to do so, the officer must record in his/her PNB:

- the nature and circumstances of the offence leading to the arrest;
- the reason or reasons why the arrest was necessary;
- that a 'when questioned' caution was given; and
- anything said by the person at the time of arrest.

If the arrest has taken place somewhere other than at a police station, the suspect can be searched by a police officer (s 32 of the PACE Act 1984) if there are reasonable grounds for believing that he/she may present a danger to him/herself or another (s 32(1)) or is in possession of anything which he/she might use to assist in escaping from custody (s 32(2)(i)) or which could be evidence relating to an offence (s 32(2)(ii)). The search must only be to the extent required to find the particular item—for example, if the search is for a plasma television, there is no reason to be looking in a trouser pocket (s 32(3)). In public, a person cannot be required to remove any clothing other than an outer coat, jacket, or gloves, but his/her mouth may be searched (s 32(4)).

A person who has been arrested can be photographed on the street (s 64A(1A) of the PACE Act 1984). This can be without consent (either withheld, or it is not practicable to obtain it). Before the photo is taken the person can be required to remove anything worn on or over any part of the head or face, and an officer can remove it if the person refuses (s 64A(2)). However, if it is a religious garment the person should be taken out of public view so that a photograph can be taken in private.

10.8.4   Searching premises after an arrest

After a person has been arrested for an indictable offence, the premises he/she was in immediately prior to the arrest can be searched (s 32(2)(b) of the PACE Act 1984) as shown in the flowchart. However, there must be reasonable grounds for believing that there is evidence relating to that offence on the premises and the search must be limited to this; it is not a 'fishing trip'. The search must only be to the extent required to find the particular item. For example, if searching for a petrol generator taken from a building site, there is no justification for looking in a toilet cistern (s 32(3)). In addition, when using these powers to search a block of flats or a bedsit the search must be limited to the dwelling where the arrest took place (or where the arrested person was immediately before) and communal areas, for example stairs, hallway, etc.

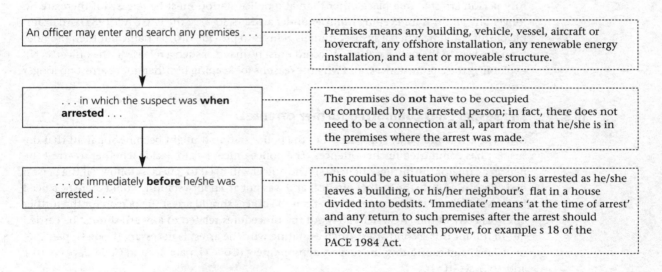

If the arrest is unlawful (eg if it was not necessary (see 10.6.4)) then a subsequent s 32 search would also be unlawful (see *Lord Hanningfield of Chelmsford v Chief Constable of Essex Police* [2013] EWHC 243 (QB)).

If permission is not given to search then reasonable force may be used to enter (s 117 of the PACE Act 1984). Further details on searching premises after an arrest are given in 9.8.2.1. Any item found on the person or premises can be seized, apart from items to do with legal privilege—for example, letters from the suspect's legal representative (ss 19, 32(8), and 32(9)) of the PACE Act 1984).

10.8.5   Taking the suspect to a police station

A person who has been arrested must be taken to a police station (s 30(1) of the PACE Act 1984 and Code C, para 11.1A) without delay. The only exception (s 30(10)) is if a delay could:

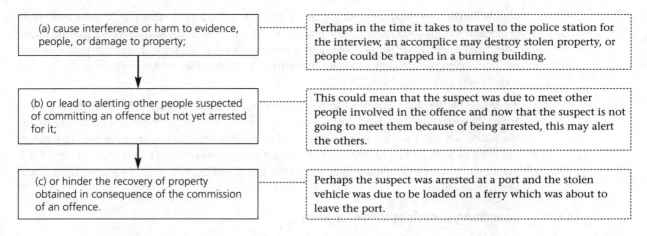

Any discussion of the alleged offence on the way to the police station should be avoided. This is because any questioning of a person regarding his/her involvement or suspected involvement in a criminal offence is considered to be an interview, and interviews must be carried out under caution in a suitable place (Code C, para 11.1A).

However, if the suspect freely provides information, then follow the guidelines in relation to significant statements and relevant comments (see 10.4, and see also how this is used during interviewing in 24.5.5).

10.8.6 'De-arresting' a suspect

Any person arrested in a place other than at a police station must be released if there are no longer any grounds for keeping him/her under arrest (s 30(7) of the PACE Act 1984). An example of this could be when a suspect initially refuses to provide his/her name but then provides it on the way to the police station. A record must be made of such a release in the officer's PNB explaining the circumstances, and why the reasons for keeping him/her under arrest no longer exist.

10.8.7 The suspect has committed further offences

After the arrest and taking the suspect to the police station it might become apparent that the suspect has committed further offences. The police officer has to decide whether to arrest the person again, for the further offences(s). The officer will need to reflect as follows: if the person had committed only the further offences and was not at a police station, would there be a need to arrest him/her? If the answer is 'yes' then the officer should arrest the person for the further offences (s 31 of the PACE Act 1984). All the procedures related to any arrest must be carried out in full for this second arrest (such as stating why the arrest is necessary (Code G, para 2.6, see 10.6.4) and cautioning the suspect appropriately (Code G, para 3.1 and Code C, paras 10.1 and 10.2, see 10.3).

TASK 8 Consider the following scenario:

An officer is on patrol just outside a tool shop. He sees a man run out of the shop carrying an unpacked, brand-new drill with the label still attached. The shop alarm is activated. During the earlier briefing at the police station the officer had been told that this shop had suffered a number of walk-in thefts over the last few days. He therefore decides to arrest him.
He says (on a bad day):

Hey... you're not going anywhere, you've got to come with me, I'll tell you why later... for now just do as I say... have you got a problem with that? Got anything to say, well it doesn't matter. Come on, give me that drill.

Take a moment to write down what is wrong as far as the PACE Act 1984 and the Codes of Practice are concerned.
Next write down what he should have said to the person.

This task will help develop the knowledge and understanding requirement of the Certificate in Knowledge of Policing unit 'Knowledge of arresting, detaining, and reporting individuals within a policing context' and the Diploma in Policing assessed unit competence 'Arrest, detain or report individuals'. It could also form the basis of an entry in the SOLAP and in particular the 'legal and organizational requirements' evidence sections.

10.9 Retaining Items in Relation to an Offence

Certain items found on a suspect or at a crime scene may be required as evidence during a subsequent investigation and prosecution for an offence. These items are often referred to as 'seized property'. (The use of the word 'property' in a policing context means any article, object, or item which comes into the possession of the police (whether ownership details are known or not) and includes 'found property' (eg items handed to the police which were found by a member of the public).)

Property can be seized directly from the suspect after his/her arrest. The item(s) may either be directly linked to the crime (eg objects suspected to have been stolen), or be other items which are to be sent for forensic examination, such as a weapon, a suspected illegal substance, or clothing. Other property that is relevant to an offence would include items that seem to have been abandoned after committing the crime, such as a safe which has been taken from a house and then left in a front drive because it was too heavy to carry. Such items are likely to require forensic examination in order to establish a link between the suspect and the offence.

10.9.1 Retention and storage of seized property

The main guidance regarding retention of seized property is found in s 22 of the PACE Act 1984, although detailed guidance will also be given during training with a police force. Note that s 22(4) states that 'nothing may be retained if a photograph or copy would be sufficient for that purpose'.

The legislation describes two main reasons for retaining items:

(a) anything seized for the purposes of a criminal investigation may be retained for use as evidence at a trial for an offence, or for forensic examination or for investigation in connection with an offence;

(b) anything may be retained in order to establish its lawful owner...where there are reasonable grounds for believing that it has been obtained in consequence of the commission of an offence.

Using the serial numbers of property such as mobile telephones, police officers can make an online search using the National Mobile Property Register (NMPR) to identify whether an item is stolen and to locate the registered owner. Further details are available online.

When seizing and retaining such items all officers should bear in mind the need to minimize contamination and to maintain a continuity record (see Chapter 11) and also the rules concerning 'Record, Retain, Reveal and Disclose' (see 26.2).

Seized items 'may be retained so long as is necessary in all the circumstances' (s 22) but this section does not elaborate further on the meanings of 'necessary' and 'circumstances'. However, common respect for the property rights of others (as described, for example, in the Human Rights Act 1998) would suggest that any item that is no longer relevant to an investigation should be returned to its owner as soon as possible. Each police force is likely to have a 'Property Management Policy' that sets out the protocols for return (see eg that of Merseyside Police, available online).

TASK 9 If you are a trainee police officer you should familiarize yourself with the forms and procedures relating to seized property. Once seized, where are such items initially stored and, if required, where are they stored for longer periods of time?

General Procedures

10.10 Presentation of Suspects to Custody Officers

The experience of being arrested can be a highly charged emotional event, and police officers must maintain a professional approach throughout. An arrest is the start of a long process for the suspect, and all staff involved have a responsibility to preserve his/her rights throughout the whole detention process. The suspect and the incident under investigation must receive the appropriate attention.

The information given here is relevant to the custody office procedures checklist in the PAC, in particular the requirement to 'provide grounds of arrest to custody officer' and 'search suspect and place in cell where appropriate', and the 'disposal' checklist, in relation to 'convey a suspect into custody'. The Diploma in Policing does not include a specific assessed unit addressing custody procedures, but the unit 'Conduct priority and volume investigations' has an assessment criterion that requires demonstration of the ability to 'deal with persons in custody diligently and expeditiously ensuring the custody officer is kept informed of progress to reach a decision on disposal'. Practical competence must be evidenced on at least two occasions in the work place.

10.10.1 Arrival at the police station with an arrested person

When an arrested person reaches the boundary of a police station, he/she should be taken before a custody officer as soon as practicable after arrival (Code C, para 2.1A). The time that the arrested person arrived at the police station is relevant because he/she can only be kept in custody for 24 hours after arrival. The arrival time is referred to as the 'relevant time' (s 41(2) of the PACE Act 1984). A police officer should make a note of this time in his/her PNB to provide continuity of evidence between time of arrest, arrival at the police station, and subsequent authorization and detention by the custody officer.

10.10.2 The custody officer

The custody officer's main duty is to ensure that any person in police detention is treated according to the PACE Act 1984 and the Codes of Practice, and that such treatment is recorded on a custody record. In the majority of cases the record will be created electronically (except in cases of technology malfunction), using the NSPIS Custody and Case Preparation Programme. Consequently, once the details of the detained person have been entered into a database, the information can be used electronically during the preparation of case files (see 26.3) and also mean that the Police National Computer (see 6.9.1.1) will be updated.

A custody officer will usually be a police officer of at least the rank of sergeant, but this role is sometimes provided by a police support employee designated as a staff custody officer.

When an arrested suspect is taken to the custody suite, the custody officer must be informed of the relevant circumstances of the arrest; the suspect's involvement in the commission of a criminal offence, and the reason(s) why the arrest was necessary. This is obligatory under s 24 of the PACE Act 1984 and Code G, para 2.2 (see 10.8.1). Here is an example of what an officer might say to the custody officer:

> At 11.00 hours today I was on duty outside an electrical shop in the High Street when I saw this person run out of the shop with a brand-new digital radio under his arm. I heard the store alarm sound at the same time and I therefore suspected that he had stolen the radio. I arrested him on suspicion of theft of the radio to allow the prompt and effective investigation of the offence by interviewing him on tape here at the police station, and also to obtain authority from an Inspector to search any premises occupied or controlled by him for evidence relating to similar offences of theft.

The officer should then stay with the suspect during the initial stages of the custody process.

10.10.3 Charging and detaining a suspect

The custody officer must decide if there is enough evidence to charge the arrested person at this point (s 37(2) of the PACE Act 1984). If the evidence is insufficient, the suspect can still be detained if the custody officer has reasonable grounds for believing that the detention is necessary to:

- secure or preserve evidence relating to an offence for which the suspect is under arrest (eg to carry out searches for evidence); or
- obtain such evidence by questioning the suspect.

The precise time that the custody officer authorizes the detention is called the 'authorized time'. The need for continued detention will be reviewed not more than six hours from the 'authorized time' and then at nine-hourly intervals after that. The reviews are carried out by an inspector, and the timings are sometimes referred to as the 'custody clock'.

10.10.4 The detainee's rights after arrest

If the custody officer decides to detain the arrested person he/she must record the grounds for detention in his/her presence and also inform the detainee of the grounds (Code C, para 3.4). If he/she is incapable of understanding, is violent, or is in need of medical attention, the grounds must be given as soon as practicable (para 1.8). The custody officer must also make sure the person is clearly informed about certain rights that apply throughout the whole period of detention (PACE Act 1984, Code C, para 3.1). The suspect's rights are:

1. to have someone informed of his/her arrest;
2. to consult privately with a solicitor and receive free legal advice; and
3. to consult the PACE Act 1984 Codes of Practice.

The detainee must be given two written notices explaining the rights and other arrangements (Code C, para 3.2). Detainees who need an interpreter must be given appropriately translated notices (Code C, para 13.1). The first notice sets out:

- the three rights noted above;
- the arrangements for obtaining legal advice;
- the right to a copy of the custody record; and
- an explanation of the caution, for example what it means to him/her (see 10.3).

The second notice sets out the detainee's entitlements while in custody, for example the provision of food and drink, access to toilets, and so on (see Code C, Notes 3A and 3B).

As well as providing the detainee with the two notices, the custody officer (or other custody staff as directed by the custody officer) must ask the detainee whether he/she would like legal advice (para 3.5 (a)(i)) and also whether he/she would like someone to be informed of his/her arrest (para 3.5 (a)(ii)). The detainee will be asked to sign the custody record to confirm these decisions (Code C, para 3.5). The custody officer will also determine and record (on the custody record) whether the detainee requires:

- medical attention, for example as a result of an injury or lack of medication;
- an appropriate adult, for example, the parent or guardian for a juvenile, or a relative or guardian for a mentally vulnerable person;
- help with checking documentation, for example providing clarification of any of the rights; or
- an interpreter, for example for detainees who cannot speak English, or detainees with speech or hearing impairments.

The custody officer will also initiate an assessment of the detainee to determine whether he/she will be a risk to him/herself or to others. Such assessment will include a check of the PNC, and consultation with the arresting officer and appropriate healthcare professionals, for example custody nurses (Code C, para 3.6).

10.10.4.1 The detainee's right to have someone informed of the arrest

The detainee may have one friend, relative, or interested person informed of his/her whereabouts as soon as practicable (s 56 of the PACE Act 1984 and Code C, para 5.1). If the attempt fails, the detainee can suggest two other people to be contacted, to try and ensure that at least one person knows the detainee's whereabouts. At the discretion of the custody officer or the officer in charge of the investigation, further attempts can be made to contact other people until the information has been conveyed to one person. In the case of a juvenile, the person responsible for his/her welfare must be informed of his/her detention.

The detainee should be given writing materials if requested, and be allowed to telephone one person (in addition to the person informed above) for a reasonable time.

General Procedures

10.10.4.2 Delaying the detainee's right to contact

The right to contact people and to legal advice can be delayed if the offence involved is an indictable offence or if it is believed that the communication is likely to lead to:

- interference with or harm to evidence or other people;
- alerting other people who are suspected of committing an indictable offence, but not yet arrested; or
- hindrance to the recovery of property.

Delaying a detainee's right to legal advice (s 58 of the PACE Act 1984 and Code C, Annex B) is very rare, and must be authorized by an officer of the rank of superintendent or above. Delaying contact with people must be authorized by an officer of at least the rank of inspector, and the delay must not be for more than 36 hours (s 56 of the PACE Act 1984 and Code C, Annex B).

10.10.4.3 Receiving visits

At the custody officer's discretion and if the detainee agrees, he/she may receive visits from friends, family or others likely to take an interest in his/her welfare, or in whose welfare the detainee has an interest (Code C, para 5.4). However, such visits are subject to the availability of supervising staff and the possible hindrance to the investigation (Code C, Note 5B).

10.10.5 Searching the detainee

The custody officer has the power to search detainees, but he/she may ask another officer to actually carry out the search. The custody officer will decide the extent of the search to be made (s 54(6)) of the PACE Act 1984), but it must not be intimate (s 54(7) and see also 25.6.1), and it must be carried out by a constable of the same sex as the detainee (s 54(9)). The forensic examination of suspects is covered in 25.6.

A strip search can be authorized, but only if it is necessary to remove an article which the detainee would not be allowed to keep (Code C, Annex A, para 10), and if it is reasonably considered that the detainee has concealed such an article. A strip search must be in accordance with Code C Annex A para 11. For example it must be carried out:

- by an officer of the same sex;
- in a safe place with at least two other people present, but in an area away from other people in general; and
- with regard to sensitivity but as quickly as reasonably possible.

To assist with the search, the detainee can be required to lift his/her arms and stand with his/her legs apart. In relation to establishing the gender of persons for the purposes of searching see Code A, Annex F.

10.10.5.1 Items found during a search

A record of all or any of the items found during a search can be made on the custody record, or elsewhere in which case the separate location must be recorded on the custody record (Code C, para 4.4). Clothes and effects can only be seized (s 54(3)) if there are reasonable grounds for believing they may provide evidence relating to an offence or if the custody officer believes the detainee would use the items to harm him/herself, to damage property, to interfere with evidence, or to try to escape (s 54(4)).

The custody officer is responsible for any of the arrested person's possessions that are unrelated to the offence and are not going to be used as evidence (Code C, para 4.1), and must arrange safekeeping of the property.

TASK 10 In Task 8 of this chapter a police officer saw a man run out of the shop carrying an unpacked, brand-new drill and heard the shop alarm go off. The officer knew from recent briefings that this shop had suffered a number of walk-in thefts over the last few days. He had therefore arrested the man and taken him to the police station. What should the police officer say to the custody officer?

Completion of this task would help towards achieving the knowledge requirements of the SOLAP.

10.11 Statements from Witnesses and Victims

A trainee officer will become increasingly involved, under supervision, in incidents involving the investigation of criminal offences, subsequent arrests, and the presentation of suspects to the custody officer. One important part of this is to support witnesses (including victims) through the process of making a witness statement. This is recorded on an MG 11 form and will be included in the case file for the incident (see 26.3 for more details on MG forms and case files). Victim personal statements (see 10.11.2) are also recorded on an MG 11 form, either following an evidential witness statement or as a separate statement.

The MG 11 form has a front sheet and continuation sheets if required. The back of the form (once completed) is for police and prosecution use only in order to protect witnesses. Two different versions of the MG forms are available; a paper version for completing by hand and an electronic version which is completed on a computer and then printed out. When completing MG 11 forms (or any other MG form):

• use black ink;
• do not use abbreviations or jargon;
• do not use correction fluid or overwrite a mistake; and
• do not staple the pages together (use a paperclip instead).

Any mistakes should be crossed out with a single line and initialled in the margin. Some of the following guidance is adapted from the unpublished document 'A Guide to Form MG 11, General Completion' by Kent Police.

10.11.1 Witness statements

Witness statements are generally written by the interviewing officer after he/she has interviewed the witness (see 24.6) and they have together agreed the facts that are to be recorded. The officer should outline to the witness the consequences of stating anything which is false or that he/she does not believe to be true, and draw the witness's attention to the need to sign a declaration to that effect at the end of the process. After the officer has written the statement the witness reads it through and signs it if he/she agrees with what has been written.

The witness's name should be written out in full at the top of the form, using capitals for the family name only. (If capitals are used throughout, then underline the family name.) Where a witness statement refers to a person, the name the witness gives that person should be used. For all descriptions of a person, object, or incident, ADVOKATE must be adhered to in full (see 10.5.3). Descriptions should be recorded in detail, and any uncertainties should also be fully recorded.

Witness statements must record only what he/she has experienced directly through his/her senses. Opinion should not be recorded apart from:

• a relevant expert providing an expert opinion; or
• a competent witness stating whether another person is drunk (see 12.2.1).

Exhibits (items that could be used as evidence in court) must be given a reference number that includes that person's initials. So, for example, the bag of shopping Alice Stoner gave to PC Hoddim will have the reference number AMS/1. PC Hoddim will refer to the exhibit as AMS/1 in his/her statement, having taken possession of it from Alice Stoner. The other bag (the orange bag held by the man on the pavement) will have the reference number CU/1 because it was the first item of evidence collected by PC Underwood in this incident. (In 11.2.6 further guidance is provided with respect to the numbering of exhibits.)

General Procedures

General Procedures

MG 11 (T)

RESTRICTED (when complete)

WITNESS STATEMENT

(CJ Act 1967, s.9; MC Act 1980, ss.5A(3) (a) and SB; MC Rules 1981, r.70)

URN ☐ ☐ ☐ ☐

The unique reference number will be generated by the unit or department that deals with case file.

Statement of: *Alice Marion STONER*

Age if under 18: *over 18* (if over 18 insert 'over 18') Occupation: *Customer service assistant*

Complete the number of pages **after** the statement is finished.

This statement (consisting of *one* page(s) each signed by me) is true to the best of my knowledge and belief and I make it knowing that, if it is tendered in evidence, I shall be liable to prosecution if I have wilfully stated anything in it, which I know to be false, or do not believe to be true.

Signature: *AMStoner*   Date: *01.03.14*

Tick if witness evidence is visually recorded ☐ *(supply witness details on rear)*

Always begin with the time, day, date, and location. Use the words used by the witnesses (for example 4 p.m. rather than the 24 hour clock).

At 4.00 p.m. on Wednesday 1st March 2014, I was in Kerrie's corner shop which is situated on the north pavement of the High Street at its junction with Hythewell Road, Maidbury. I was standing by the fruit which is located inside the shop approximately 10 metres from the front door but my view of the front door was obscured by upright shelving. The shop sells groceries and is approximately 15 metres by 15 metres with one door for customers in and out.

All descriptions must follow ADVOKATE

There is shelving fixed to the walls and three lines of upright shelving along the entire length of the shop which is approximately 2 metres high. I could not see any other customers inside the shop at the time, but I could see the shop

Any uncertainties must be included.

assistant but only when she leant over to the shelf. She was unpacking some bacon out of a box. I would describe the assistant as … [ADVOKATE]. I will refer to her as Assistant one.

For starting a new paragraph, do not leave any whole blank lines. There is no need to rule off the space at the end of a line.

I then heard some sort of a struggle approximately 10 metres away from me towards the back of the shop. I didn't see anything because there was shelving in between me and the scuffle. I heard a man's voice say in a cross way 'what's it to you if

Utterances must be recorded in direct speech. Hearsay evidence (she said that he said) should be recorded in direct speech.

some of us ain't got nothing to eat' or something like that and then I heard a long bang like a box falling over or a door slamming. Then I heard a thump and a shout outside. I picked up my bag and went over to the door and Assistant one was standing there rubbing her head like it was hurting. I could see a man in a dark blue or black jacket half lying on the ground outside, holding onto something orange, but I didn't have my glasses on so I couldn't see what it was quite. I would describe the man as… [ADVOKATE]. He was rubbing his leg like it was hurting him a lot.

The officer who wrote the statement on behalf of the witness must write this declaration at the end of the statement.

From the back of the shop, another assistant and a customer came walking towards me. I would describe the assistant as … [ADVOKATE] and will refer to her as Assistant two. Assistant two had a telephone in her hand. I would describe the customer as … [ADVOKATE].This customer and Assistant two went out of the front door and held on to the man, but he didn't look like he was struggling much. At 4.10 p.m. the same day two police officers arrived at the shop, one

The witness should sign at the foot of every page, and after the last word of the statement.

male and one femle. One of them (PC Hoddim) came into the shop and spoke with Assistant one. I found a bag with some shopping in it by the cold cabinet, which I gave to PC Hoddim (exhibit labelled and marked AMS/1). Then I went out and spoke to the lady officer. AMStoner

The officer must sign and date (including his/her rank and number) immediately after the last word of the declaration and at the end of each page.

This statement was taken by me at 13.26 hours on Saturday 28th March 2014 at Maidbury Police Station. At the end I read it over to Alice Stoner and she read and signed it in my presence. C.Underwood PC 118118, 01.03.14

Signature: *AMStoner*   Signature witnessed by: *C Underwood PC 118118*

PTO

MG 11 (T)

RESTRICTED—FOR POLICE AND PROSECUTION ONLY
(when complete)

Witness contact details

Home address: *31 JENNER ROAD, MAIDBURY, KENT*

.... Postcode: *MA99 1XX*

Home telephone No: *1234567* .... Work telephone No: *123456789*

Mobile/Pager No: *1234567* .... E-mail address: *N/A*

Preferred means of contact: *HOME PHONE*

~~Male~~/Female (delete as applicable) Date and place of birth: *12.00.65 BIG CITY*

Former Name: *N/A* .... Height: *163cm* Ethnicity Code: *W1*

Dates of witness non-availability: *see MG 10*

Witness care

(a) Is the witness willing and likely to attend court? ~~Yes~~/No. If 'No', include reason(s) on form MG6. What can be done to ensure attendance?

....

(b) Does the witness require 'special measures' as a vulnerable or intimidated witness? ~~Yes~~/No. If 'Yes' submit MG2 with file.

(c) Does the witness have any specific care needs? ~~Yes~~/No. If 'Yes' what are they? (Healthcare, childcare, transport, disability, language difficulties, visually impaired, restricted mobility or other concerns?)

....
....
....

Witness Consent (for witness completion)

a) The criminal justice process and Victim Personal Statement scheme (victims only) has been explained to me: Yes/~~No~~

b) I have been given the leaflet 'Giving a witness statement to the police—what happens next?' Yes/~~No~~

c) I consent to police having access to my medical record(s) in relation to this matter: Yes☐ No☐ N/A☑

d) I consent to my medical record in relation to this matter being disclosed to the defence: Yes☐ No☐ N/A☑

e) I consent to the statement being disclosed for the purposes of civil proceedings e.g. child care proceedings (if applicable): Yes☐ No☐ N/A☑

f) The information recorded above will be disclosed to the Witness Service so that they can offer help and support, unless you ask them not to. Tick this box to decline their services: ☑

Signature of witness: *AMStoner*

Statement taken by (print name): *PC 118118 UNDERWOOD* Station: *Maidbury Police Station*

Time and place statement taken: *17.50 01.03.14 MAIDBURY POLICE STATION*

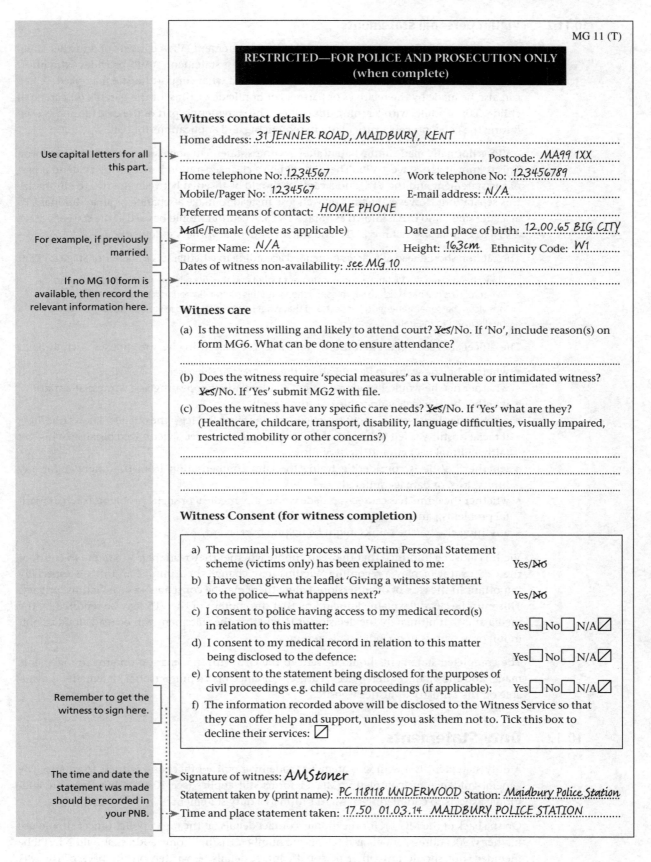

Sidebar notes (left margin):

- Use capital letters for all this part.
- For example, if previously married.
- If no MG 10 form is available, then record the relevant information here.
- Remember to get the witness to sign here.
- The time and date the statement was made should be recorded in your PNB.

Sidebar (right margin):

General Procedures

10.11.2 Victim personal statements

A witness may also be a victim. A victim personal statement (VPS) consists of a further statement by the victim in addition to the evidential witness statement. A VPS provides extra information on how the crime has affected the victim and what support he/she may need. A VPS can also be made by the relatives or partners of homicide victims, or the parents (or carers) of children or of adults with learning difficulties. The statement is part of the case file and is used during the court process, particularly in sentencing and applications for bail.

A VPS is normally made immediately after a witness statement and using the same MG 11 form. This is known as a Stage 1 VPS. There should be a clear separation between the evidential part of the statement and the VPS, and a caption should be inserted between the two to emphasize this separation. However, victims may choose instead to make a separate or an additional VPS at a later stage, and this is known as a Stage 2 VPS. A caption should be used at the start of a Stage 2 VPS to emphasize that it is a VPS and not an evidential witness statement.

The caption should read as follows (amended according to whether it is a Stage 1 or Stage 2 VPS):

> I have been given the Victim Personal Statement leaflet and the VPS scheme has been explained to me. What follows is what I wish to say in connection with this matter. [In addition to what I said in my previous victim personal statement] I understand that what I say may be used in various ways and that it may be disclosed to the defence.

The officer should explain that the victim can express anything he/she chooses, including:

- whether he/she wants to be told about the progress of the case;
- whether he/she would like extra support (particularly if appearing as a witness at a trial);
- whether he/she feels vulnerable or intimidated;
- whether he/she is worried about the offender being given bail (eg if the offender knows him/her);
- if racial hostility is felt to be part of the crime, or if he/she feels victimized because of his/her faith, cultural background, or disability;
- whether he/she is considering trying to claim compensation from the offender for any injury, loss, or damage suffered;
- whether the crime has caused, or made worse, any medical or social problems (such as marital problems); and
- anything else he/she thinks might be helpful or relevant.

Victims must be informed that they can choose whether they read their VPS aloud in court, or the CPS read it or play a recording. Victims may change their minds, and this is especially important in the case of open sessions where there may be consequences for victims' privacy. This must be clearly explained, including that the content of the VPS may be reported by the media and that ultimately the decision as to whether the statement will be read aloud or not, in full or in part, is up to judicial discretion.

The completed statement should be sent to the CPS with information on any arrangements made, and the victim's preferences. Further guidance on victim personal statements is available on the Ministry of Justice website.

10.12 Duty Statements

A duty statement is a witness statement made by a police officer as a witness to events. The general guidance for completing MG 11 forms still applies (see 10.11.1) but there are additional aspects to completing an MG 11 form as a duty statement.

On the back of the MG 11, for the 'home' contact details (at the top) a police officer should use his/her work address, email, and telephone number. His/her home address should NEVER be included, nor should any other personal contact details be written on the back of the MG 11—consider the potential consequences if a defendant obtained this information. Note that the lower sections on the back (Witness Care and Witness Consent) do not need to be filled in for a duty statement: simply put 'N/A' where appropriate.

10.12.1 How to write names in duty statements

When referring to other police officers, the first time the officer is mentioned in the statement his/her family name should be in capitals, with his/her rank and number. If the officer is men-

MG 11 (T)

RESTRICTED (when complete)

WITNESS STATEMENT

(CJ Act 1967, s.9; MC Act 1980, ss.5A(3) (a) and SB; MC Rules 1981, r.70)

Enter your rank and force number.

URN ☐ ☐ ☐ ☐

Statement of: *Charlotte UNDERWOOD*

Age if under 18: *over 18* (if over 18 insert 'over 18')   Occupation: *Police Constable 118118*

Sign with your rank and number.

This statement (consisting of *one* page(s) each signed by me) is true to the best of my knowledge and belief and I make it knowing that, if it is tendered in evidence, I shall be liable to prosecution if I have wilfully stated anything in it, which I know to be false, or do not believe to be true.

Signature: *C. Underwood PC 118118*   Date: *01.03.14*

Use the 24 hour clock and use 'at' not 'at approximately'.

Always begin with the time, day, date, location, and other persons present. Do not include your name, title, number, or station in the main body of the text.

Tick if witness evidence is visually recorded ☐ *(supply witness details on rear)*

At 1600 hours on Wednesday 1st March 2014 I was on uniformed patrol in a marked police vehicle with PC 69900 HODDIM. At this time we attended Kerrie's Corner shop, 98 High Street, Maidbury, Kentshire. As we arrived I saw a man who I now know to be Nathan JONAH born 09.09.1973 sitting on the pavement holding a plastic carrier bag approximately 1 metre from the front door of the shop on the pavement outside. I got out of the car and walked towards JONAH. I would describe JONAH as... The plastic carrier bag JONAH was holding looked as if it contained something lumpy. I heard JONAH shout 'That's it, you're all for it now!' and he tried to stand up, but stumbled and fell. As I approached him I could smell intoxicating liquor on his breath, his speech was slurred, and his eyes were glazed. He tried to stand up again but could not. He was drunk or otherwise intoxicated. He was groaning and looking downwards with his eyes shut sometimes.

This is hearsay evidence (she said that he said), and should be recorded in direct speech; see 10.9.

A woman came up to me and introduced herself as Mrs STONER. She said in the presence and hearing of the suspect 'I heard him say "what's it to you if some of us 'ain't got nothing to eat"' and then I heard a long bang—I think he pushed the shop assistant against the wall behind the door and ran out'. PC HODDIM came over with a shop assistant from the store, a person I now know to be Janis DEE. In the presence and hearing of the suspect I said to Mrs DEE 'Can you please tell me what happened?' Mrs DEE replied 'I was filling the refrigerator with packets of bacon when this bloke here took a pack from out of the box on the floor. He walked around the store for a little while, well staggered really. I tried to stop him and then he just walked out without paying for it.'

Arrests must be recorded in direct speech, but the caution does not have to be. Any response from the suspect must be accurately recorded.

At 1635 hours the same day I said to the suspect JONAH 'As a result of what this person has told me I am arresting you on suspicion of theft of a pack of meat from the shop. Your arrest is necessary for the prompt and effective investigation of the offence and because you are drunk you may suffer physical injury to yourself'. I then cautioned him to which he replied 'It wasn't me, you've got the wrong person ... why me?' ... As JONAH was drunk I believed that he may present a danger to himself or others if he had possession of a weapon. I also believed he may have other articles from the store which he had not paid for. Therefore I searched him before placing him into the police vehicle. I looked inside the bag he was carrying and it contained a large packet of meat which I seized (exhibit labelled and marked CW/1). JONAH was placed in a police vehicle and conveyed to Maidbury Police Station arriving at 1645 hours the same day where he was introduced to the custody officer PS BENN.

Sign and date after the last word of the statement, and include your rank and number.

C. Underwood PC 118118, 01.03.14

For a duty statement, the signature does not need to be witnessed.

Sign at the foot of every page, and include your rank and number.

Signature: *C. Underwood PC 118118*   Signature witnessed by: *n/a*

PTO

General Procedures

tioned again later in the statement, only the rank and name need be used. Witnesses should be referred to using either both names or Mr/Mrs (etc) and the family name in capitals. The first time a suspect is named in a duty statement, his/her full name should be used with the family name in capitals, but after that only his/her family name.

10.13 Methods of Disposal of Criminal Suspects

Here we describe the various methods of 'disposing' of a criminal suspect, including directing him/her to court or by imposing penalties without going to court, conditional cautions, and street bail.

10.13.1 Written charge and postal requisition by a public prosecutor

When a suspect is suspected of committing an offence, criminal proceedings can be instituted by way of a written charge and issue of a postal requisition (s 29(1) and (2) of the Criminal Justice Act 2003). An example of such criminal proceedings would be when a police officer reports a suspect at the roadside for a road traffic offence, or a suspect attends a police station voluntarily at an officer's request. To report a person for the purposes of issuing a written charge, the officer must:

1. state the offence(s) involved;
2. gather evidence in the usual way, ie using the senses, for example what was seen or heard;
3. point out the offence(s) to the suspect;
4. caution the suspect using the 'when questioned' caution (follow PACE Code C, para 10.2) and also inform him/her that he/she is not under arrest, but that any failure to cooperate or to answer particular questions may affect his/her immediate treatment;
5. make a written record of the questions and answers about the offence(s) in his/her PNB, including points to prove and negations to available defences;
6. offer the PNB to the suspect to read and sign that the notes are a true record of the interview (see Code C, para 11.11);
7. tell the suspect 'I am reporting you for the offence(s) of ...'; and
8. caution the suspect (using the 'now' caution: see 10.3).

Once the evidence has been gathered in relation to the suspect, it forms a case file and will be submitted. If a decision is reached to prosecute the suspect, a person authorized to institute criminal proceedings (a public prosecutor) will issue a written charge to the suspect. This will describe the offence for which the suspect is being prosecuted, including the title of the Act under which the offence was created. At the same time, the public prosecutor will issue a requisition which requires the suspect to appear before a magistrates' court. The written charge and requisition will be served on the person concerned by post, and copies sent to the court named in the requisition.

10.13.2 Penalty notices

A police officer who has reason to believe that a person aged 18 or over has committed a relevant offence can issue him/her with a penalty notice (s 2(1) of the Criminal Justice and Police Act 2001). These provide offenders with an opportunity to pay a fine for an offence without going to court. They were originally introduced for motoring and road traffic offences as Fixed Penalty Notices (FPNs: see 19.12.2) and following their success, the Penalty Notice for Disorder (PND) scheme was introduced (ss 1–11 of the Criminal Justice and Police Act 2001). PentiP (Penalty Notice Processing) is the national data-sharing system for recording PNDs, and it allows checks to be carried out on previously unpaid penalties. In some forces PNDs can be issued using hand-held computerized printers (instead of using the traditional paper-based booklets of PND tickets). Officers will need to be familiar with the type of PND forms used locally.

The key aims and objectives of penalty notice schemes are:

- to reduce the amount of time that police officers spend completing paperwork and attending court;
- to increase the amount of time officers spend on the street and dealing with more serious crime;
- to reduce the burden on the courts; and
- to deliver swift, simple, and effective justice that carries a deterrent effect.

A person who accepts a PND is not admitting to a crime; he/she is simply supporting a suspicion by a police officer that an offence has been committed and that there will be no further proceedings in relation to this. Consequently, accepting a PND is not admissible in a court as an admission of an offence that would affect a defendant's good character case (see *Regina v Hamer* [2010] WLR (D) 235).

Section 2A of the Criminal Justice and Police Act 2001 provides a power for chief police officers to develop education schemes within their area to enable police officers to issue a PND with an education option. On receipt of such a notice the person has to request to attend the relevant educational course, pay for it, and complete it, or pay the penalty within 21 days or ask to be tried at court. Failing to follow one of these options renders him/her liable to be fined 1.5 times the original penalty.

The following should also be noted in order to avoid confusion concerning terminology: first, the PND scheme involves fixed penalties (but a 'fixed penalty notice' issued by a police officer is usually for a motoring offence), and second, the Anti-Social Behaviour Act 2003 also provides for local authority personnel and PCSOs to issue penalty notices (also sometimes referred to as fixed penalty notices) for graffiti, littering, and other more minor disorder offences such as parking contraventions.

PND Offence with a fine of £90	Legislation
Wasting police time/giving false report	Criminal Law Act 1967, s 5(2)
Using public electronic communications network in order to cause annoyance, inconvenience, or needless anxiety	Communications Act 2003, s 127(2)
Knowingly giving a false alarm to a person acting on behalf of a fire and rescue authority	Fire and Rescue Services Act 2004, s 49 (England only) Fire Services Act 1947, s 31 (Wales only)
Causing harassment, alarm, or distress	Public Order Act 1986, s 5
Throwing fireworks	Explosives Act 1875, s 80
Drunk and disorderly	Criminal Justice Act 1967, s 91
Selling alcohol to person under 18 (anywhere)	Licensing Act 2003, s 146(1)
Supply of alcohol by or on behalf of a club to a person aged under 18	Licensing Act 2003, s 146(3)
Selling alcohol to a drunken person	Licensing Act 2003, s 141
Purchasing or attempting to purchase alcohol on behalf of a person under 18 (includes licensed premises and off-licences)	Licensing Act 2003, s 149(3)
Purchase of alcohol for consumption in licensed premises by person under 18	Licensing Act 2003, s 149(4)
Delivery of alcohol to person under 18 or allowing such delivery	Licensing Act 2003, s 151
Destroying or damaging property worth £300 or under	Criminal Damage Act 1971, s 1(1)
Unlawful possession of cannabis and its derivatives	Misuse of Drugs Act 1971, s 5(2)
Theft (retail) of property worth £100 or under (but see* at the end of this table)	Theft Act 1968, s 1
Breach of fireworks curfew (2300–0700hrs)	Firework Regulations 2004, reg 7 (Fireworks Act 2003, s 11)
Possession of a category 4 firework	Firework Regulations 2004, reg 5 (Fireworks Act 2003, s 11)
Possession by a person under 18 of an adult firework in public	Firework Regulations 2004, reg 4 (Fireworks Act 2003, s 11)

*For 'theft from a shop' other than by an employee only one PND should ever be issued to an individual, and only for incidents where the property has been recovered (consuming the stolen property may be an exception); the value of the goods does not exceed £100; and the recipient has never previously been issued a PND for theft.

PND Offence with a fine of £60	Legislation
Dropping or leaving litter or refuse except in a receptacle provided for the purpose	Royal Parks and Other Open Spaces Regulations 1997, reg 3(3) (Parks Regulation (Amendment) Act 1926, s 2(1)
Using a pedal cycle, a roller blade, etc except on a Park road or in a designated area	
Failing to remove immediately any faeces deposited by an animal of which that person is in charge	
Trespassing on a railway	British Transport Commission Act 1949, s 55
Throwing stones at a train	British Transport Commission Act 1949, s 56
Drunk in the highway	Licensing Act 1872, s 12
Consumption of alcohol in designated public place, contrary to a requirement by constable not to do so	Criminal Justice and Police Act 2001, s 12
Depositing and leaving litter	Environmental Protection Act 1990, ss 87(1) and 87(5)
Consumption of alcohol by a person under 18 in a bar	Licensing Act 2003, s 150(1)
Allowing consumption of alcohol by a young person (aged under 18) in a bar	Licensing Act 2003, s 150(2)
Buying or attempting to buy alcohol for a young person (aged under 18)	Licensing Act 2003, s 149(1)

10.13.2.1 The issuing and format of a PND

Under the Criminal Justice and Police Act 2001, if an officer has reason to believe that a person has committed a penalty offence, that person can be given a penalty notice. The notice may be issued either on the spot by an officer in uniform ('street issue'), or at a police station by an authorized officer, usually the custody officer in the custody area of a police station. The recipient then has 21 days to decide whether to pay the penalty or request a court hearing. Failure to take either option may result in either a fine (1.5 times the penalty amount) or court proceedings. If after receiving a PND it comes to light that the person may have committed a more serious and non-penalty offence during the same incident, the further offence can be investigated and prosecuted (see *R v Gore: R v Maker* [2009] EWCA Crim 1424; WLR (D) 240).

The flowchart shows the process model for issuing a PND (adapted from the current Home Office operational guidance (Home Office, 2013e)).

A person who has been given a penalty notice for disorder (by a police officer, a community support officer, or other accredited person) may be photographed on the street (s 64A(1A) of the PACE Act 1984). This can be without consent (either withheld, or it is not practicable to obtain it). Before the photo is taken the person can be required to remove anything worn on or over any part of the head or face, and if he/she refuses an officer can remove it (s 64A(2)). However, if it is a religious garment the person should be taken out of public view so that a photograph can be taken in private.

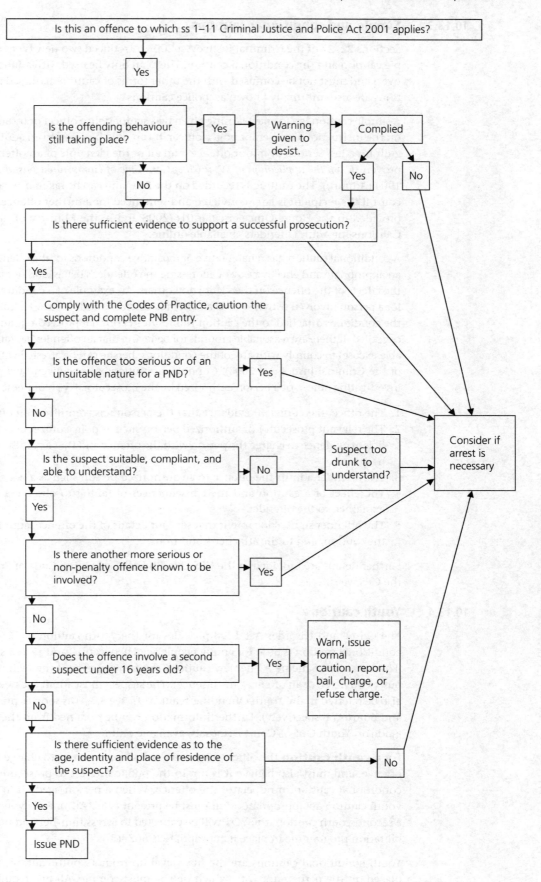

General Procedures

10.13.3 Simple and conditional cautions

Sections 22–27 of the Criminal Justice Act 2003 introduced two new types of caution, the simple caution and the conditional caution. They can only be used with adults (aged 18 years and over) and must not be confused with the other forms of caution discussed in 10.3. Simple cautions are also informally known as 'police cautions'

A simple caution is a formal warning given by a senior police officer or by another police officer on the instructions of a senior police officer. It can only be given to an adult who has admitted guilt for a less serious or minor offence, and all of the elements of an offence must have been proven (*R (on the application of W) v Chief Constable of Hampshire Constabulary* [2006] EWHC 1904 (Admin)). The caution is recorded on the PNC and can be taken into consideration by the court if the recipient is later convicted and sentenced for a further offence. Further details are provided in the Home Office circular 016/2008 and in the Ministry of Justice guide 'Simple Cautions for Adult Offenders' available online.

A conditional caution has rehabilitative or reparative conditions for the offender. It can be used as an appropriate and effective way of addressing the offender's behaviour, or making reparation for the effects of the offence on the victim and others. An example of a condition would be sobriety for a person involved with low-level alcohol-related crime and/or disorder. Failing to comply with the conditions attached to the caution will result in criminal proceedings and the caution being cancelled. If there are reasonable grounds for believing that an offender has failed (without reasonable excuse) to comply with any of the conditions, he/she can be arrested without warrant (s 24A of the Criminal Justice Act 2003). Conditional cautions can be given by a police constable, an investigating officer, or a person authorized by the prosecutor. Five requirements must be met:

1. The officer has sufficient evidence that the person has committed an offence.
2. The relevant prosecutor or authorized person such as police officer decides that there is sufficient evidence to charge the person with the offence and that a conditional caution should be given.
3. The offender admits the offence to an authorized person such as a police officer.
4. The effect of a caution and the consequences of failing to observe a condition must be explained to the offender.
5. The offender signs a document that sets out details of the offence, admits guilt, consents to the caution, and to the attached conditions.

Further details are provided in the CPS Conditional Cautioning Code of Practice, available on the CPS website.

10.13.4 Youth cautions

The Crime and Disorder Act 1998 provides for the youth caution (s 66Z(1)) and the youth conditional caution (s 66A) for young people aged between 10 and 17 years. (These replace the 'Final Warning Scheme'.) The new cautions can be used even if the recipient has been previously convicted of an offence (any offence). The suspect must admit the new offence, and must also be referred to the Youth Offending Team (YOT, see 3.3.4) as soon as practicable (ss 66ZB(1) and 66A(6A) respectively). Further information can be obtained from the Ministry of Justice guide on Youth Out-of-Court Disposals, available online.

For a **youth caution** the officer must have sufficient evidence to charge the person with an offence, and must also believe it is not in the public interest to prosecute or to give a youth conditional caution in respect of the offence. When a person aged 10 to 16 years is given a youth caution an appropriate adult must be present (s 66ZA(2)). For a young person receiving a second youth caution, the YOT will be expected to assess him/her and put a voluntary rehabilitation programme in place if appropriate (s 66ZB(2)).

Youth conditional cautions are the next level up from a youth caution, and conditions are placed on the perpetrator with which he/she must comply. All five requirements in 10.13.3 must be satisfied (ss 66A(1) and 66B(1)–(6)), and both the views of the victim and the behavioural needs of the young person should be taken into consideration.

10.13.5 'Street bail'

Under ss 30A–30D of the PACE Act 1984, street bail is a discretionary power which allows police officers to release an offender on bail (without taking him/her to a police station), on the condition that the offender must attend a specified police station at a later, specified date.

Benefits include:

- a reduction in the amount of time travelling to and from the police station;
- less time waiting at the police station; and
- more time available for investigation.

For legal representatives, parents, and appropriate adults, there are improved opportunities to plan and prepare for attendance.

10.13.5.1 Considerations for using street bail

Street bail enables 'front-line' officers to apply their discretion at the point of arrest. A decision to grant street bail should follow the normal arrest procedures in s 24 of the PACE Act 1984 (see 10.6). Statements concerning guilt are not relevant to the decision to grant bail—interview and examination of evidence will take place later.

Whilst on the street the following questions must be considered when deciding whether to grant street bail.

1. What type of offence has been committed and how serious is the offence? There is no definitive list of offences to which street bail can be granted; it is a matter for a police officer's discretion. However, it is unlikely that street bail would be granted in relation to a serious offence.
2. What has been the impact of the offence? The impact on the victim, the offender, and other persons should all be considered.
3. Would a delay in dealing with the offender result in loss of vital evidence? It might be necessary to take an arrested person to a police station to preserve and examine forensic evidence which could be lost if the suspect is released.
4. Is the arrested person fit to be released back onto the streets? A drunk driver or a person with mental health problems, for example, may not be in a fit state to be returned to the streets. In the case of a juvenile, consideration must be given to his/her welfare.
5. Does the arrested person understand what is happening? This particularly applies to vulnerable people who would normally require the assistance of an appropriate adult during an investigation (see 13.2 and 24.4).
6. If released on bail, is the arrested person likely to commit a further offence? Street bail should not be used if there are reasonable grounds to believe that the arrested person might continue to commit that or another offence if released; for example, where fighting is involved.
7. Has the arrested person provided a correct name and address? The identification and address details provided must be believed to be correct.

If street bail is appropriate the decision should be explained to the offender, and a street bail notice issued. He/she should then be released as soon as possible. It is important that the arrested person understands that he/she is not being legally discharged, may be subject to court proceedings or other disposal actions, and will be required to attend a police station on a specified date.

10.13.5.2 Using street bail

A verbal explanation covering the points in 10.13.5.1 should be given to the person granted street bail, even though these are also clearly stated on the notice provided. The length of time for street bail is partly determined by the time it takes to carry out investigations, but force policy might also apply (maximum periods may be specified).

Conditions may be imposed on the bail (s 30A(3A) of the PACE Act 1984) in order to ensure that the person surrenders to custody when required, does not commit an offence while on bail, and does not interfere with witnesses or otherwise obstruct the course of justice (whether in relation to him/herself or any other person). Some types of conditions are not permitted as a provision for his/her surrender to custody, such as a surety or bail hostel residency. A list of the conditions will be made on a bail sheet and given to the suspect. It will also name the police station at which the conditions can be varied.

There is a power to arrest without warrant if there are reasonable grounds for suspecting that the person has broken any of the conditions of bail (s 30D of the PACE Act 1984), or if he/she fails to answer bail at the specified time (s 30A of the PACE Act 1984).

General Procedures

10.13.6 Charge

A charge is a formal accusation that a person has carried out an illegal act and will be required to stand trial in a court of law. If there is sufficient evidence for a prosecution to succeed, either the custody officer (in the case of minor offences) or the CPS (for more serious offences) will decide whether the person should be charged with the offence or released, with or without bail. For a juvenile or a vulnerable adult, any action taken should be taken in the presence of an appropriate adult (Code C, para 16.1 and Note 16C). A decision to go ahead with the charge is referred to as 'accepting the charge'.

A person who is to be charged (or the appropriate adult) is given a written notice (an MG 4 form, see 26.3) which includes the following details:

- reference number of the case and custody record number;
- time and date the charge is made;
- the details of the person charged, including name, address, and date of birth;
- the name of the police officer who charged the suspect (not necessarily the 'officer in the case') and the name of the custody officer who accepted the charge; and
- any reply made by the suspect in response to charge.

The charge will always include the 'now' caution (see 10.3.4) and is likely to be worded as follows:

> You are charged with the offence(s) shown below. You do not have to say anything. But it may harm your defence if you do not mention now something which you later rely on in court. Anything you say may be given in evidence.
>   On (date) at (town) in the county of (name of county) you assaulted (name of victim) contrary to section 39 of the Criminal Justice Act 1988.

Having been charged with, or informed he/she may be prosecuted for an offence, a detained person may not be interviewed further unless the interview is necessary for the following reasons (listed in Code C, para 16.5):

- to prevent or minimize harm or loss to some other person, or the public;
- to clear up an ambiguity in a previous answer or statement; or
- in the interests of justice for the detainee, to have new information relevant to the offence put to him/her to comment on (new information having come to light since he/she was charged or informed that about the possibility of being prosecuted).

If an interview is needed a 'restricted' caution must be given at the start (see 10.3.5).

Once a person has been charged with an offence, he/she will be released by the custody officer (s 38(1) PACE) but bail may be denied in a variety of circumstances. This would include failing to identify the suspect, and for more serious offences; the full list is in s 38(1) PACE and s 25 of the Criminal Justice and Public Order Act. When bail is refused the suspect will be kept in custody and be brought before a magistrates' court.

10.13.7 Bail from a police station

Bail is a process of attempting to ensure that a person appears at a specified time at a specified place such as a police station or court. There are four main reasons for bail that police officers will encounter on a regular basis:

Circumstances for granting bail	PACE subsection	Return location	Conditions can apply?
Further investigation and evidence gathering is planned. Insufficient evidence to support a charge at present	s 34(5)	police station	no
Insufficient evidence to support a charge and no further investigation planned, but review is required	s 37(2)	police station	yes
Consultation with the CPS is required to agree charges	s 37(7)(a)	police station	yes
After a person has been charged with an offence	s 37(7)(d)	court	yes

If a person who has been released on bail fails to attend the police station or court at the appointed time, or is suspected of breaking attached conditions, then he/she can be arrested without warrant (s 46A(1) of the PACE Act 1984).

10.13.8 Refused charge

If there is insufficient evidence to charge a detainee and the investigating officer does not believe it is necessary to see the suspect again, the custody officer will release the person without charge. This process is called 'refused charge'. It will be the end of the matter unless fresh evidence is found.

> **TASK 11** What offence, if any, is committed by a person who fails to return on bail to a police station, or fails to surrender to custody at a court after having been bailed?

10.14 Handover Procedures

After initial enquiries into a suspected crime (eg taking statements, collecting potential evidence, the arrest of a suspect) the arresting officer may 'hand over' responsibility for the subsequent investigation to another colleague, for example a volume-crime investigator. Alternatively, the arresting officer may be required to hand the case files over to a Criminal Justice Unit or Department where 'case-builders' will obtain further statements and evidence. If appropriate they will then prepare files for submission to the CPS (using the 'MG' forms: see 26.3). Note, however, that practice does vary from force to force; in some cases the arresting officer may be expected to see the process through to a more advanced stage.

10.14.1 Handover packages

A fundamental principle underpinning the process of handover is that the information provided will enable the receiving colleague to become as familiar with the circumstances of the alleged offence as the arresting officer. This is done by means of a 'handover package', which will include documents (written and electronic) and references to artefacts (eg forensic evidence, special property). It will also contain a general checklist (sometimes called a 'Single Source Document'), which will be likely to include the following:

Checklist entry	Examples/notes
Names of the alleged offender(s)	Provide names, DoB, and custody numbers
The arresting officer's account of the circumstances leading up to arrest	Remember to avoid offering opinion in this section
Investigation checklist	• A series of tickbox lists addressing the arrest (including a copy of PNB entries); • searches; • exhibits; • scene and forensic evidence; • detainee and custody considerations; and • PNC/force intelligence database checks
Witness details and statements	• names, addresses, and contact numbers of witnesses; and • a summary of witness statements
Other officers involved	• details of those who also attended; and • copies of their PNB entries and statements

Note that the checklist itself is potentially 'relevant material' (see 26.2) and thus it has to be included on the MG 6C form.

10.15 Answers to Tasks

TASK 1 The 'first' or 'given' name is the term to use, rather than 'Christian' name. The latter is a reflection of a time when the assumption was made that all UK residents subscribed (at least notionally) to Christianity as a religion.

TASK 2 The use of mind-maps as tools for learning and analysis was pioneered by Tony Buzan and others. The website <http://www.mindtools.com/pages/article/newISS_01.htm> has some useful advice on the application of Buzan's ideas. Of course, we have provided you with the no ELBOWS(S) mnemonic already, but developing your own mnemonic is good practice and will help fix the ideas in your long-term memory.

TASK 3 There are many examples, but you might have considered the following:

The caution means that you have the right to silence and you do not have to say anything or reply to any question you are asked. Anything that you say now or during the rest of the investigation can be given to the court for consideration. However, if you choose not to say anything now or during the investigation and then you decide to say something during the court proceedings instead, the court can deal with this fresh evidence as they choose, including ignoring it.

TASK 4 She should:

1. obtain and record a first description from the householder;
2. ask the householder if he would consider accompanying her to the locations mentioned to attempt an identification;
3. explain to him that she will not direct his attention to any individual but that he should look carefully at all the people present.

TASK 5 Whatever examples you chose, each should have clearly addressed:

- a person's involvement, or suspected involvement, or attempted involvement in the commission of a criminal offence; and
- the reasonable grounds for believing that the person's arrest is necessary.

TASK 6 He should:

- locate the person who is subject of the warrant through the use of intelligence, a stop check, the PNC, or his local force database;
- identify himself, then confirm the identity of the person, and then arrest and caution the person;
- endorse the back of the warrant (also known as 'backing up');
- record the event in his PNB;
- send the 'backed-up' warrant to the appropriate court following local procedures.

If the officer is not in possession of that warrant at the time of the arrest and the person asks to see it, the officer must show the person the warrant as soon as is practicable.

TASK 7 The European Arrest Warrant (EAW) is an EU-wide arrest warrant which allows for the extradition of a person suspected of a serious crime from a participating EU country.

The important and relevant feature of the EAW is that application for a person to be 'surrendered to answer a warrant' is made from a judge in one country to a judge in another (where the suspect is). The process is therefore within and part of the criminal justice systems of both countries. Previously, 'extradition' was highly politicized and people or cases were subject to long delay, political processes, appeals, and so on. The aim of the EAW is to speed things up. Further details may be found at <http://www.asser.nl/Default.aspx?site_id=8&level1=10783>.

TASK 8 You probably considered the following:

1. An arrested person must be informed by the arresting officer that he/she is under arrest (s 28(2) and Code G, para 2.2).
2. The arrest is not lawful unless the arresting officer at the time or as soon as is practicable informs the person of the grounds for the suspicion (s 28(3)).
3. The arrested person must be informed about their involvement or suspected involvement or attempted involvement in the commission of a criminal offence and the reasonable grounds for believing that the person's arrest is 'necessary' (Code G, para 2.2).
4. The officer must caution the arrested person (Code G, para 3.4).

In the second half of the task your answer was probably along the following lines:

I have just seen you run out of the shop with a brand-new drill under your arm. I heard the store alarm go off at the same time and I suspect that you have stolen the drill. I am therefore arresting you on suspicion of theft of the drill. Your arrest is necessary to allow the prompt and effective investigation of the offence, and also, because you were running away, to prevent any prosecution for the offence being hindered by you leaving the area. You do not have to say anything, but it may harm your defence if you do not mention when questioned something which you later rely on in court. Anything you do say may be given in evidence.

TASK 9 The different categories of seized property might have separate forms for recording the details, but similar information is likely to be required such as:

- sequential number (to be attached to the item(s) for the purposes of recognition);
- name and address of the person from whom it was taken;
- place where taken;
- details of the police officer who took possession;
- exhibit reference (if known);
- description of article(s);
- reasons for taking into police possession;
- proposed method of disposal; and
- current location of the property.

Once the appropriate form has been completed and a copy attached to the property for the purposes of recognition, the property will have to be stored. Each force will have its own procedures but if there is no access to the main property store because it is closed (eg at night), the property will have to be placed in a 'transit store' (a secure cupboard) before it is transferred by the property officer to the main store.

TASK 10 You probably considered the following:

I have just seen this person run out of a shop with a brand-new drill under his arm. I heard the store alarm sound at the same time and I suspected he had stolen the drill. I therefore arrested him on suspicion of theft of the drill and the arrest was necessary to allow the prompt and effective investigation of the offence through a taped interview, and also, because he was running away, to prevent any prosecution for the offence from being hindered by him leaving the area.

TASK 11 Section 6(1) of the Bail Act 1976 states that it is an offence for person who has been released on bail in criminal proceedings to fail without reasonable cause to surrender to custody. This offence is triable summarily only and the penalty is three months' imprisonment and/or a fine.

Attending Incidents

11.1 Introduction

This chapter is primarily concerned with the general procedures to be followed when attending incidents, including crime scenes. Throughout we link the subject matter to police officer initial training, but the content will also be useful to those undertaking a pre-join programme at a college or university. We also examine attending and dealing with incidents involving loss of life, often sudden deaths, although not necessarily of a suspicious nature.

The police have a responsibility to respond and deal with many types of incident, but the majority of police everyday activities can be described as 'Steady State' policing. There are also 'Rising Tide' incidents, which are unexpected and cannot be planned for. Examples include large-scale rail, road, air, and sporting disasters or acts of terrorism. They may be classed as emergency, major, or critical incidents (see 11.5). 'Planned Operations' are where the police have had advanced warning of a situation (eg a large demonstration) and will have contingency plans in place (see 11.7).

The police will attend volume crime scenes and minor incidents more often than major crime scenes. In a number of key respects, the principles of attending a volume crime scene are no different to those employed when attending the scene of a major crime: the differences might simply be those of scale. However, as we note in 11.5 emergencies, major, and critical incidents may give rise to crime scenes of significant geographical size and complexity (such as the bombings in London in July 2005) and the events might require multi-agency emergency responses, adding to the demands of crime-scene management.

The material covered here is particularly relevant to two of the Diploma in Policing assessed units: 'Providing an initial response to incidents' and 'Conducting priority and volume investigations'. In particular, the following learning outcomes and assessment criteria are relevant:

Name of Diploma unit	Learning outcome	Assessment criteria
Conduct priority and volume investigations	Be able to conduct priority and volume investigations	• Identify and take the steps necessary to protect and preserve the scene • Identify and prioritize all lines of enquiry (eg forensic/scientific) • Gather all available material, retain and record in line with current legislation and policy
Provide an initial response to incidents	Be able to respond to incidents	• Take action to protect the scene of the incident and preserve evidence

It is also relevant to the Certificate in Knowledge of Policing units 'Knowledge of providing an initial response to incidents within a policing context' and 'Knowledge of conducting priority and volume investigations within a policing context'.

11.2 General Procedures at Crime Scenes

Deployment to any incident has the potential to generate numerous challenges, for example unlawful violence against persons and premises, and public disorder. Victims and witnesses may also need support, including first aid, and in the case of more serious injuries, an ambulance or paramedics may be required.

The crime scene is frequently the most important component of any investigation, because it is very likely to contain physical and electronic evidence which could identify suspects, corroborates or refutes statements made by witnesses, and demonstrate guilt or innocence. Early and effective protection of the crime scene ensures that the greatest amount of potential evidence is available for recovery and, therefore, maximizes its value to the investigation.

Crime scenes are not purely geographical locations to which we can apply an address, postcode, or map reference; a victim or suspect in a crime such as a sexual assault is also a crime scene. Treating a person (especially a victim) as a crime scene may be distressing and potentially offensive to the person and to his/her family or friends, but it is vital that we consider people as sources of evidence and intelligence. This is to ensure that we effectively 'protect and preserve' them, and recover the evidence or intelligence we need. Anything that could be a source of evidence or intelligence is also part of a crime scene, including articles related to the offence, such as weapons and vehicles, computer hard drives, digital storage media, as well as the intangible such as networked environments.

Some of the biggest 'offenders' in relation to poor scene preservation are victims of crime, so any opportunity to encourage good scene management is vital, and will pay dividends. Call centre staff should be trained to explain what the victims or informants could do to help preserve evidence, and the FAO (First Attending Officer) can instruct victims and the public on simple issues such as staying clear of the crime scene and not handling evidence. Victims are often vital sources of physical evidence (especially in offences against the person and sexual assault) and preventing their contamination by others (such as supportive family members) is important. Sexual assault victims should be forensically examined before they smoke, eat, drink, wash, or go to the toilet (unless absolutely necessary). This is sometimes very difficult to explain.

Nearly all officers carry a mobile phone with extensive features nowadays, including a camera. It might be tempting to use it to photograph a crime scene, and this may occasionally assist an investigation in the early stages (eg when a wet shoe mark is evaporating). However, generally, it is better not to use the camera on a personal mobile phone at a possible crime scene because the phone would then become a source of evidence and would normally be retained for analysis of the image in its original state.

11.2.1 Early priorities at crime scenes—the FAO

The overriding principle applied to the management of crime scenes is that all attending officers rigorously ensure the safety of the public, their colleagues, and themselves. Any physical location in which an offence has occurred may include emotional, aggressive, or confused people who might represent a danger. In addition, damage to premises, such as by fire, may weaken the structure of a building, resulting in further hazards.

While travelling to the scene of an incident, a risk assessment should be made based on the information gathered from the initial report (see the introduction to 23.3). The assessment should be based upon:

- what is known (objective fact/information) or believed (subjective fact/information) to have happened;
- the number of people likely to be present;
- any information on the PNC and local intelligence databases about the individuals involved (eg that a suspect has been violent in the past);
- any risks associated with the location;
- if any weapons are present at the scene;
- local community sensitivities.

11.2.1.1 Arriving at a crime scene

The first police officer who attends the scene (possibly as the result of an emergency call) is known variously as the FAO, the First Officer at the Scene (FOAS), or sometimes the Initial Responder; different forces use different acronyms. We use FAO in the remainder of this chapter. The FAO may be of any rank and position within the organization—indeed, it could be a trainee police officer—it depends on who happens to arrive first. For example, it was a special constable in Community Safety at Thetford (Norfolk) who was first on the scene of a serious assault, and he had to manage the scene and deal with first aid as well as keeping his control room informed.

The first few minutes after a **major crime** may be confusing and the FAO should control any person in the vicinity, including colleagues, and direct them to carry out urgent tasks where appropriate. The FAO may also have to arrest a suspect. It should be remembered that all physical evidence is expendable when balanced against human life. Hence the FAO should not preserve a crime scene to the extent that it causes delays which aggravate a victim's injuries or increase any risks to life and limb. This is not to say that physical evidence can be disregarded during the life-saving process; the FAO can advise the ambulance crew where not to tread and can carefully move furniture away from the victim to facilitate medical aid when *necessary*. However, if such actions are carried out, it is essential that moved items are left in their new position and not moved again in an attempt to recreate the original crime scene. This is because moving furniture, switching on lights, and even opening doors represents contamination (in its loosest sense) and may remove items from their original context. All these actions must be reported to the crime scene investigator (CSI) early on in the investigation and should also be recorded as PNB entries (see 10.2). Further details on investigative actions at crime scenes are covered in Chapter 23.

As soon as the initial response and emergency treatment of any casualties has been completed all police officers, including the FAO, and other personnel attending crime scenes should wear protective clothing for their own safety and to prevent the addition of misleading material to the scene.

11.2.1.2 The golden hour

The first period of any incident, particularly in major crime and critical incidents, is often described as the 'golden hour'. This is a shorthand reference to the need to identify witnesses and preserve a scene quickly so that evidence can be gathered while it is still fresh and undisturbed. For example, bloodstains should be sampled or protected before they are diluted by rain, shoe impressions (shoe marks) may need to be covered in poor weather, and the body of a deceased person could be initially examined before rigor mortis sets in.

It is also a real advantage to identify and interview witnesses whilst their recollections are still clear. A police officer should always listen carefully to witnesses and evaluate what they say in the light of what is already known. He/she will of course record what is said as a PNB entry, and may also make a note of further questions to ask or other lines of enquiry.

11.2.1.3 Cordons

Cordons are erected as a visible barrier to identify the parameters of crime scenes or other incidents, such as fires. A flimsy cordon tape is clearly not a physical barrier: it is more of a 'statement' to help limit and control access. In crime, cordons tend to be erected for the more serious offences such as major crimes and fatalities, rather than burglaries. Once any victims have been treated and removed (or confirmed dead), the scene must be cordoned off to prevent access by the public. The golden rule in cordoning is to make the cordon larger than seems immediately necessary. The inner cordon (sometimes known as the first cordon) must encompass specific areas:

- the venue of any suspected offence;
- all possible routes into or out of the venue;
- any location where physical evidence could possibly be found: for example, communal bins, under cars in the street, nearby gardens; and
- any location identified as significant by witnesses.

The cordon is set up using police tape and should be securely attached to carefully chosen fixed objects. It should not be attached to objects that might be sources of evidence, for instance a parked car, as the action of the wind or people moving the tape could erase evidence such as bloodstains and fingerprints. Nor should the location of convenient fixed objects determine the cordon size: if necessary, the tape can be affixed further out until poles are available. Whilst installing the tape the officer must also control witnesses and keep them out of the freshly cordoned area. This is sometimes difficult.

Once the initial cordon is in place a secondary cordon (the outer cordon) can be installed. The outer cordon is placed to manage the public's access and view, and is strictly a matter of control. If the public can see significant evidence then the cordon is almost certainly too small. It also makes sense to position the outer cordon so that vehicles can turn around, minimizing local congestion. At very large crime scenes the policy of some police forces is to position the cordons so that the area that might contain material of importance to the enquiry is between the inner and outer cordon. This could include a discarded weapon, clothing, telephone kiosks, or shoe marks.

Once the inner cordon is in place, nothing—not even a patrol car—may leave or enter it until sanctioned by a CSI, unless it is required to save life—for example, an ambulance or fire appliance. Vehicles moving through the cordoned area may damage vital evidence, for example at bomb scenes components of the device may be picked up by emergency vehicles and driven out of the scene. Additionally, the offender might have leant against a vehicle outside the venue of the offence when he made off, so CSIs may wish to examine every vehicle within the cordon or, on occasions, every vehicle in the street.

The powers available to the police to secure crime scenes were considered in the case of *DPP v Morrison* [2003] EWHC 683 (Admin). In a serious incident in a shopping centre involving groups of young people, the police had sought to cordon off four areas in the shopping centre to secure and preserve evidence. Morrison was arrested for obstruction of a police officer in the lawful execution of his duty (and a Public Order Act offence) after he had walked into one of the cordoned areas, despite being told not to do so by police. He was initially convicted but appealed, and the Crown Court allowed the appeal, stating that there was no lawful authority to erect the cordon, and therefore the police were not acting in the lawful execution of their duty. The prosecution in turn appealed to the High Court. The High Court considered case law and existing legislation and decided that where a public area is to be cordoned, it was unlikely that anyone would have a right to stop police from doing so, but that on private property the police were entitled to assume that the owner would consent to cordoning. The shopping area in the *Morrison* case was privately owned but had a public right of way, so the cordoned areas were a public place (see 9.2), and the police were therefore entitled to install a cordon there. The appeal was successful. On a practical level, this decision makes it clear that in certain circumstances police officers might need to obtain search warrants (under perhaps s 8 of the PACE Act 1984) in order to remain on private premises for the purposes of a crime scene search.

11.2.2 The rendezvous point and the Common Approach Path

The rendezvous point (RV point or RVP) is vital to the smooth running of the investigations at the scene, and should have been carefully chosen early on in the investigation. It may have to accommodate a number of vehicles, rest stations, food vans, major incident vehicles, and even a command tent. RVPs should never be placed in a narrow street with restricted access. They should always be in a roadway or on land with good access, which is unconnected to the investigation. When attending the scene of a suspicious explosion, care must be taken to search the RVP for secondary devices which have been deliberately placed to cause maximum casualties to the emergency services. In incidents involving firearms officers, forensic personnel and other emergency services will normally attend the RVP rather than the crime scene as a matter of safety.

The Common Approach Path (CAP) is the route from the edge of the cordon into the crime scene proper, and it should be guarded by a scene control officer. The CAP should not be the route likely to have been taken by victim or offender, nor should it necessarily be the same route taken by the FAO (who was initially acting without full knowledge of the facts). If the scene is 'empty' (there are no living victims on the crime scene) there will be more time to choose the most suitable route for the CAP.

The selected route should minimize damage to potential evidence, particularly material which is small or almost two-dimensional—such as shoe marks and blood. Wherever possible, the CAP should be laid on solid ground, as this will help prevent evidence being accidentally concealed; this could happen if personnel walked over a CAP consisting of softer materials such as grass and soil. Ideally the CAP should be marked with tape but, in the early stages, this may not be possible. Attending personnel should not be tempted to anchor the tape with rocks and other debris in the vicinity, since one of these may have been a weapon.

Some of the problems associated with CAPs are:

- The eagerness to establish a CAP through the rear of the premises: entering the premises via a back door and searching for a key may destroy vital evidence.
- How is the route for a CAP chosen in a flat, featureless field?
- There may be only one entrance to the building.
- There may be no available means to mark the CAP.

One of the early tasks of the CSI is to search the CAP for evidence, and if this is found the CSI may want to move the CAP, or record and remove potentially valuable material.

11.2.3 The crime scene log and attending personnel

Perhaps the most important document at the crime scene is the log. This is a booklet or sheet upon which the details of all attending personnel are recorded. In essence, it records any event that could have led to contamination of evidence. The log should contain details of:

- every person already at the scene when the FAO arrived;
- every person who subsequently attended the scene and the time of attendance;
- every person who entered the crime scene or inner cordon, with the time of attendance and the reason; and
- preferably, a description of the CAP so that every person attending the scene can familiarize themselves with it prior to entry.

Whilst the scene control officer should be visible (sometimes his or her car will be the only one with flashing blue lights at the scene) it is the responsibility of all attending personnel (including trainee police officers on Supervised or Independent Patrol) to seek him/her out. Logging or resourcing databases which manage deployments and information at incidents (such as STORM and the older systems like CAD and OIS) do not record deployments of officers at incidents in sufficient depth and should not be relied upon.

It is the responsibility of the scene control officer and every individual to ensure the log is completed correctly. The log must be copied and disclosed to the defence (see 26.2), who will study it and compare it to statements and other scene logs. Failure to properly maintain the log may mean that some or all of the evidence removed from the scene will be judged unusable by the CJS.

11.2.3.1 Non-police personnel at crime scenes

Ambulance crews should be allowed controlled access in order to save life. They are generally aware of how to behave in a crime scene but may have to be reminded not to touch anything needlessly and to show caution where they walk. Crews should be accompanied by the FAO, who should point out apparently significant evidence to be avoided and take their names for later elimination (particularly of shoes, clothing, and fingerprints). Clearly, ambulance personnel should wear gloves, as should the FAO. Efforts to resuscitate by ambulance staff can generate very considerable quantities of debris, such as wrappers and used medical equipment. This material should be left at the scene for the attending CSI.

A doctor is not always required to establish that a death has occurred since ambulance crews will make a 'recognition of life extinct' (ROLE), also referred to as 'Fact of Death'. In this case the attending officer should take any forms they produce and ensure these are returned to the police station. If a doctor attends, he/she should wear protective clothing, and disturb the body as little as possible. The use of oral, rectal, or deep-tissue thermometers is not generally permitted because this can interfere with biological evidence in particular, such as DNA. If there is any concern that the death may be suspicious (see 11.3) the doctor or ambulance crew will be requested not to turn the body nor search through clothing to view hypostasis or injuries until a CSI is in attendance. Certification of death is carried out by a doctor afterwards, but he/she could also be asked for an opinion as to the cause of death, particularly if the deceased has apparently suffered a sudden death and is known to the doctor.

Other police colleagues (including senior officers) are generally not allowed to enter the inner cordon unless:

- the offender is likely to be within and must be apprehended;
- they are saving life;

- they can assist in urgent and immediate acts to prevent loss of the scene (eg a fire); and/or
- a dog is required to pick up a track from within the cordon.

In the case of deaths, there is no requirement for a senior officer to enter the scene once death has been confirmed, or to confirm that a death is suspicious. Nor is it necessary for a senior officer to confirm any other observations made by other officers. Every additional person in the crime scene can potentially destroy or contaminate evidence.

The CSI will attend at the RVP (see 11.2.2) and will liaise with the FAO and other personnel, to decide how to proceed. In general terms, the CSI's initial role is to gather information, start with photography where appropriate, and advise detectives and uniformed police on the arrangements for any arrested persons. Once this has been achieved he/she will examine the CAP, record and recover vulnerable evidence from it, and occasionally move the CAP to another location. It is common for the CSI to enter the scene with the doctor to certify deaths.

The **Crime Scene Manager** (CSM) is appointed in a major crime enquiry to manage the scene and deal with scientific resources. In some cases a single CSM may be appointed, who will deal with all parts of the investigation. In a more serious or complex case there may be a number of CSMs and a **Crime Scene Coordinator** (CSC). Typically, the CSM will be hands-on, but will also be flexible enough to attend strategy meetings and deal with other issues.

A variety of emergency personnel may attend a scene and will be recorded in the log if they enter the crime scene, unless it is a serious incident and is impractical. The following groups will also keep their own records of attendance:

- the fire service;
- Explosives Ordnance Disposal (EOD) (in the case of explosions or suspected explosive devices);
- HM Coastguard and RNLI;
- mountain rescue and lowland search organizations (with dogs).

Other personnel who may attend as required include forensic scientists, borough or district surveyors and structural engineers (to assess the safety of damaged buildings), Transco (for gas leaks), and scaffolding contractors (to support damaged structures in order to prevent collapse). However, once cordons are in place, no one should enter the crime scene until sanctioned and briefed by a CSI unless the safety of the public or attending personnel is at risk.

11.2.3.2 Powers of entry for CSIs and experts

There is often confusion over powers of entry for CSIs, scientists, and computer experts at crime scenes as prior to the Police Reform Act 2002 very few people concerned themselves with this. However, the following now applies:

- section 18 of the PACE Act 1984 permits entry to a premises for police officers in relation to a person who is under arrest for an indictable offence, and s 38 of the Police Reform Act 2002 modified this to permit entry for a civilian designated as 'investigating officer';
- section 16 of the PACE Act 1984 (concerned with the execution of warrants by police officers) authorizes civilians and specialists to attend with the police. Code B, para 2.11 refers to any 'designated person' whose presence is needed to identify evidence sought by the investigator.

In many cases, however, formal permissions are not required because the occupier will invite the police to attend and enter the property.

11.2.4 Fast-track actions

In every major crime the senior investigating officer (SIO) will consider fast-track actions which might resolve the investigation rapidly. These decisions are taken after careful consideration, and are noted in the policy file (which records the decision-making process of the senior officer). However, in the very early minutes of an investigation, some actions may be necessary to prevent the loss of evidence or facilitate the apprehension of a suspect. These can include the following:

- the use of a dog to track the offender, particularly if the scent is not contaminated—the dog may have to enter the inner cordon;
- the immediate collection of evidence which is in danger of being lost, such as wadding and cartridge cases being blown down a street by the wind, photographing the image on a computer screen, powering off a smartphone (which might otherwise be remotely 'wiped');

- switching off a cooker if it might start a fire;
- covering shoe marks and tyre marks in poor weather, using boxes or bin lids taken from an area well away from the crime scene;
- an urgent search of the street (sometimes called a flash search) for evidence which has been discarded, especially when the area is busy; and
- controlling large groups of people in confined situations (eg a pub) which might cause the loss (or gain) of fibre evidence.

In these circumstances care must be taken to make the right decision. Protective clothing (at the least, clean medical-style gloves) might be needed to prevent contamination of the evidence. Police officers (including supervised trainees) should be prepared to justify their actions (or lack of them) to the senior investigating officer.

11.2.5 Forensic considerations at volume crime scenes

At volume crime scenes the actions of the CSI and others are likely to be far less extensive. Officers will also try to minimize disruption to normal life in the immediate vicinity of the crime. If the CSI is delayed, a police officer may be required to carry out these actions:

- close doors to control children and pets (instead of using cordon tape);
- close windows and consider boarding up in inclement weather;
- if boarding-up is to be arranged, ensure the original window is left, rather than being immediately removed by the contractor;
- cover shoe marks inside with a chair (not a piece of paper which is more likely to be moved or trodden on);
- bring broken glass and property inside, handling it by the edges and wearing gloves (as moisture makes fingerprinting difficult);
- cover shoe and tyre marks outside with bin lids, trays, or boxes, even in sunny weather;
- on a bed use the blanket or quilt to funnel any material to a corner of the room; and
- allow the victims to make drinks and food and facilitate this, unless doing so would damage good evidence or cause a health risk.

Whilst these actions may help a victim's state of mind, there are other considerations which must be borne in mind, such as the preservation of evidence. In the presence of DNA-rich material a mask should be worn (if available) to prevent contamination from the officer. Another important consideration is to protect any articles that have to be moved by wearing gloves and handling material carefully: **gloves do not prevent fingerprints from being destroyed**. Third, continuity must be considered, as the police officer who moves articles of interest should—technically—exhibit them. Local protocols should be followed on this issue. Details of investigative forensic procedures are covered in Chapter 25.

11.2.6 Exhibits and exhibiting

According to common law 'it is within the power of, and is the duty of, constables to retain for use in court things which may be evidence of crime' (*R v Lushington, ex p Otto* [1984] 1 QB 420). The ruling in *Lushington* later became s 19 of the PACE Act 1984 on the seizure of material, s 20 in relation to computers and digital evidence, and s 22 which describes police powers to retain seized material. The 'things' can include physical objects, such as knives, and are often referred to as exhibits (as they may be exhibited to a court). Under a Code of Practice within the Criminal Procedure and Investigations Act (CPIA) 1996, any police officer investigating alleged crimes 'has a duty to record and retain material which may be relevant to the investigation' (see 26.2 on recording and retaining).

Any police officer or member of the public who produces or finds an article which may be used as evidence should exhibit it—that is, formally record certain facts about the object. Police officers and CSIs are advised not to accept an unpackaged exhibit from anyone other than a member of the public, as this is a potential cause of contamination.

The procedures for packaging exhibits are covered in more detail in 25.7. Packaging materials often have labels printed on the outer surface which can be used for noting facts; otherwise a simple label can be affixed. The basic information required is:

- **name** of the person exhibiting;
- an **exhibit number**: normally the person's initials and a sequential number (see 10.11.1 for an example);

- a **description**, which should be brief and to the point—to prevent other people shortening the description for convenience (index numbers or serial numbers should be included for clarity); and
- the **date, time, and place** the exhibit was found;

It is the mark of a professional to make detailed notes about the exhibit to assist other investigators. If detailed and accurate records are not kept about the contents of a package, another person might be obliged to open it to check the contents, and this would be a possible source of contamination. Detailed notes should be made about any identifying marks, the size of clothing, any damage or stains, any logos or identifying features, serial numbers, and the precise location of the exhibit and its orientation. The procedures for storing items as they come into police possession are described in 10.9.

11.2.6.1 Signing exhibit labels

The exhibit label records the **continuity** (or chain of custody) of the exhibit. Ideally, the chain should be unbroken from its seizure until it arrives at court, so every person who takes control of the exhibit should sign the label (and later write a statement) unless local protocols dictate otherwise. The movement of bulk quantities of exhibits is often recorded on a *pro forma* by the driver, and major crime exhibits officers do not normally write a statement for every receipt of every exhibit. If, however, police officer X temporarily passes a packaged exhibit to officer Y for comment but it remains in X's custody, then Y need not sign the label. An example might be where X asks for a casual opinion, for example 'Is this a ball-peen hammer?' However, if another person Z gives a professional opinion or transports the exhibit to another place, then Z should sign the label and write a statement describing his/her actions.

11.2.6.2 Firearms as exhibits

Safety must always be considered when dealing with firearms as exhibits. That said, firearms are excellent sources of evidence. They provide ballistics evidence, and their smooth surfaces are good sources of fingerprints, and DNA can be collected from their rough control surfaces such as the grip, slide, and trigger (and from the muzzle if it has been in contact with skin or saliva). We will look at the different types of firearm and the associated law in Chapter 18.

All police forces will have strict protocols in place for entering firing ranges, accepting weapons from members of the public, and seizing them during searches, however, for health and safety, at a crime scene all personnel should:

- treat every weapon as if it is loaded;
- never handle or move a firearm unnecessarily;
- never stand in front of a firearm;
- never point a firearm at any person, even when 'made safe';
- never kick, move, or drop another article onto a firearm;
- ensure that every person who passes a firearm to him/her has clearly demonstrated that it is safe and vice versa;
- after appropriate training: never 'make a weapon safe' whilst pointing it at the floor or wall if it is possible that people may be below or on the other side of the wall;
- call for expert assistance—it is normal practice for a photographer or CSI to be present during the process of making safe by a firearms officer;
- never convey a loaded firearm to the police station or laboratory unless this is necessary and suitable safety measures are in place;
- never dry-fire a firearm or tamper with any controls apart from those necessary to make it safe; and
- never move a firearm by poking a pen, or any other object, into the barrel or trigger guard.

Above all: presume every firearm is loaded and ready to fire.
In truth, very few guns can fire by being dropped or knocked, since the majority of them have in-built safety features, but the consequence of a weapon firing by accident can obviously be extremely serious.

11.2.6.3 Contamination

Contamination is the transfer of trace evidence by any means other than direct or indirect involvement with the crime. It can be accidental or deliberate. The term is also broadly used to describe damage to an exhibit or altering its state in some way that is not required for its preservation. Consider the contamination issues regarding vehicles, prisoners, and colleagues. For example, if a police officer is tasked to deal with a suspect and has previously been to the crime scene, then he/she could potentially contaminate the suspect with material from the scene. This may reduce the value of evidence that links the suspect with the crime scene.

Certain forms of forensic evidence are, in all practical senses, incontrovertible (eg DNA evidence, see 25.5.3). Nonetheless, such evidence will be scrutinized by the defence in a criminal case, with the intention of casting doubt on the integrity of an exhibit and to have it disallowed by the judge. An effective defence team will look for errors in continuity, packaging, and handling, and for any possible source of contamination.

Proper packaging and storage can prevent contamination becoming an issue, and this is examined in detail in 25.7. However, the following general advice applies to reduce the risk of contamination:

• Attempt always to wear new surgical-type gloves and a face mask, as a minimum, when dealing with exhibits or whilst inside a crime scene. (In the absence of a face mask, at the very least, all persons present should avoid coughing or talking over exhibits.)
• Store exhibits properly to prevent decay and damage. Property stores should be cool and dry. Electronic exhibits should not be stored on plastic shelving or near motors and other sources of magnetic fields.
• Never deal with exhibits from two facets of the same offence, such as from the victim and the suspect. Care should also be taken when considering dealing with clothing from two people arrested together.
• Clothing from one person in an offence should not be dealt with (packaged; taken out of packaging) in a room that has previously been used for sampling another person.
• Do not place a prisoner in a cell until it has been cleaned.

In relation to vehicles, two people from the same offence (such as victim and suspect) should never be conveyed in the same vehicle, even at separate times, until all parties have been forensically examined. Police vehicles which could contain blood in any form should be cleaned or washed down once any forensic examination has been completed, and all patrol cars should be regularly and fastidiously valeted.

11.2.7 Attending major crime scenes

At the scene of a major crime many of the actions that should be taken by the first attending officer (the FAO: see 11.2.1) are common to the procedures to be followed at any crime scene. The FAO should attempt to:

• cordon off the scene and prevent unauthorized entry—make the cordon as wide as practicable (it can always be reduced later);
• refrain from entering the scene, except to preserve life;
• create a CAP for all who come to the crime scene, ensuring that this path does not trample on evidence or compromise the crime scene in any way;
• begin a 'scene attendance log' for recording all authorized persons who come to the site;
• refrain from covering bodies if deaths have occurred; if in public view, remove the public or screen off the view;
• record witness details and any comments they make: listen carefully to them;
• make a record of anything that is disturbed or moved;
• consider whether assistance is needed to preserve the scene;
• continue to be in communication with the force control centre and keep them informed and explain if it seems that specialist help, or a doctor, or other emergency service is needed; and
• remain calm, be positive, and manage the situation until help arrives.

> **TASK 1** In what ways might the subsequent investigation into a major crime differ from other investigations?

Most police forces have specialist (often centrally based) departments or units which deal with major crime investigations. The investigation is headed usually by a specially trained senior investigating officer, usually of detective inspector or detective chief inspector rank. Many of the elements involved in investigating major crime have been covered elsewhere in the Handbook and we do not repeat them here.

11.3 Incidents Involving Deaths

Police officers will almost certainly encounter death and injury as the result of major and critical incidents. However, for other incidents a person may have died through natural causes such as illness and old age; for example, the local police station might be called by the neighbour of an elderly person to report that they have not seen their neighbour for some time or that there are other circumstances which give cause for concern. Of course, these situations are not restricted to the elderly: it is a particularly distressing task to attend a scene of the death of a child or young person.

Any death which occurs outside the hospital environment and is in some way unexpected is referred to in police circles as a 'sudden death'. All sudden deaths will be subject to some form of investigation, but of course this does not mean that the death is associated with criminal activity. However, at any scene with fatalities it is essential that police officers are not afraid to ask questions. Senior officers may be grateful for this; a senior police colleague recounts the following story to every new group of trainees:

> After the death of a child in London, the body was returned to a hospital in the county concerned for a post-mortem examination. During the initial stages a new PC asked 'do bodies change colour after death?' The answer was 'yes, in fact they change colour quite a lot due to hypostasis, decay, and even mummification'. Later he asked if dead bodies could heal themselves. The curious pathologist answered that this was not possible and, incidentally, why was he asking? The answer was that the new PC had seen the deceased in London, where the child appeared Caucasian and had a hole in its forehead, yet here at the post mortem was an apparently Asian child and there was no hole. The hospital had handed the wrong body to the police.

The story may be apocryphal but the moral of the story is certainly not: asking questions will often help. In particular, a police officer in early attendance at a scene of a fatality could reflect on the following:

- Is the event which probably caused death at this scene likely or possible? (For example: could this banister support this body?)
- If it is a suicide, were the means available to the victim?
- Was the victim physically capable of the act? (Was he/she strong or tall enough? Could a woman of this stature pull the trigger on a rifle and shoot herself?)
- Is there any sign of a struggle? (It may appear that a struggle occurred because the location was particularly disordered, but it could have been like that anyway.)
- Is anything apparently missing? (eg an ornament, jewellery box, firearm, or car—and what is the evidence for this?)
- Is there evidence of a possible forced entry? (Damaged door locks, scratched or dented paintwork around windows, footwear marks on doors, and splintered frames are all suspicious, but there may be an entirely innocent explanation.)
- Does the position or state of the body fit logically with the information received?

If there is any uncertainty, the scene can be treated as 'suspicious' until proven otherwise.

11.3.1 Attending incidents with deaths

The general procedure to follow for sudden deaths will vary from force to force, although all subscribe to certain basic principles (and relate to the procedures for attendance at a crime scene: see 11.2). A police officer should:

1. ensure his/her own safety before approaching, as the scene of a death can be dangerous (particularly if there have been multiple deaths);
2. establish and use a CAP (see 11.2.2) to preserve the scene;
3. beware of bodies in contact with live electrical systems, as well as toxic fumes, poisons, firearms, needles, and body fluids;
4. touch nothing until a visual inspection has been made;
5. decide whether there is a chance the person is still alive: could First Aid be administered—is an ambulance required?
6. consider that any death might be the result of crime if it is in any way suspicious.

General Procedures

The officer should make a PNB entry (see 10.2) which records the location, position, and general description of the body, including any visible injuries. Any evidence should also be noted, such as physical evidence in the immediate area, or from witnesses. Obviously, if the identity of the deceased is known this should be included.

11.3.2 Certifying death

Where there might be the slightest chance a victim is alive, medical assistance should be obtained. A medical professional (a doctor, nurse, or ambulance crew) is required to attend the scene to certify that death has occurred or to make a ROLE (see 11.2.3.1). (This author, on one occasion, reluctantly called a police surgeon to a skeleton.)

> **TASK 2** Suggest a type of injury which would definitely cause death (and therefore not require a medical professional to certify death).

The procedure for certifying death depends on whether the death was expected or unexpected, as shown in the diagram. In April 2012 the system permitting doctors to certify death became more complex owing to the offences committed by Dr Harold Shipman. Doctors now prepare a Medical Certificate of Cause of Death (MCCD), which is scrutinized by newly appointed 'Medical Examiners' prior to the MCCD being fully issued.

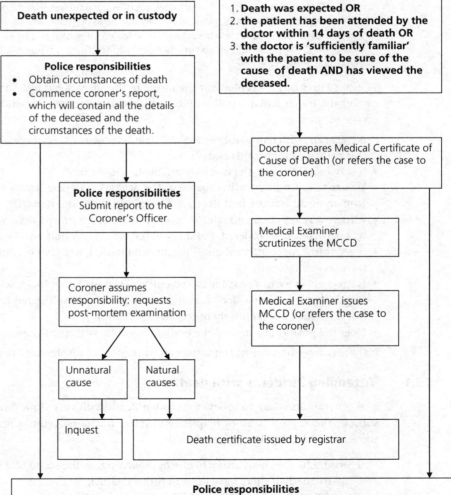

11.3.3   Changes to the body after death

There are several changes that take place in a body after death, and some of these are externally evident and may contribute to an investigation.

Hypostasis occurs when the blood settles to the lowest parts and enters the skin creating a port-wine-coloured stain. This is also known as post-mortem lividity or *livor mortis*. Where a body is upright, blood drains to the lower parts of the limbs, cheeks, and ears. After some time (around three to four hours), the blood clots (solidifies) and can no longer flow, so if the body is subsequently moved, the signs of hypostasis will no longer be on the lower or underside parts of the body.

Pressure can cause imprinting on the skin—blood and tissue fluid is squeezed out into adjacent areas of tissue. As a result, the deceased's skin may take on an impression of the surface beneath it (eg from a tiled floor). The pattern of the fabric or seams from the victim's clothing may also be very clearly imprinted on the skin.

Rigor mortis occurs when chemical changes in the muscles gradually cause them to stiffen. The process normally begins in the head and works down the body. In very general terms it might start after four hours and disappear after 24 hours (when the body begins to break down biologically). However, the process is dependent upon a number of factors, particularly the ambient temperature (the process is quicker at higher temperatures). Crucially, immediately after death the body becomes limp and will flop to rest on adjacent structures, and if left for a number of hours, rigor mortis will stiffen it in that position. If subsequently moved, the body will be rigid and fixed in that initial posture—it will not flop against the surrounding structures.

The core temperature of the deceased will equalize with the ambient temperature after death, so it will usually fall in the UK climate. The relationship between the lowering of the core temperature and the ambient temperature is well documented but not so reliable (as is commonly seen on television) that the pathologist can give an estimate of the time of death to within a few minutes. The ambient temperature, amount of clothing, and general health of the victim may all affect the temperature drop. Then, due to decay and insect activity, the body temperature may increase.

Other changes to the body will depend on the conditions. If the weather is not too cold it will begin to break down quite rapidly, which may attract a variety of animals which will feed upon it. Blowflies are the most mobile carrion feeders and will appear first, followed by successive waves of insects and other animals. The results include putrefaction and even dispersal of bones over time. In hot or dry environments the body may become mummified. The process of change in a body after death is covered by a specialist field: forensic taphonomy.

In relation to suicides there are some commonly held expectations, but many of these are untrue (or at least only partly true). These expectations (with the reality in brackets) include that:

- There should be a suicide note (but not every suicide victim writes a note);
- Women never shoot themselves in the face (some do);
- Farmers always use a shotgun (many do not);
- Vets always use animal tranquilizers or other drugs (many do);
- Those who cut their wrists or throats always make tentative cuts first (many do).

At any sudden death suspicion and an enquiring mind can be beneficial but investigators should rely on observation and experience rather than generalization.

11.3.4   Murder investigations

Murder investigations involve a huge investment of police time and resources. The majority of murders are committed by close family members, or others known to the victim, and although the circumstances leading to such events are often shocking on a domestic scale, it is the abduction and murder by strangers (particularly when children are victims) which attracts the majority of media attention and police resources.

> **TASK 3** What is the CATCHEM database and what does it tell us about a particular category of victims and their murderers?

General Procedures

The level of resources put into a murder investigation depends on the classification of the murder. Murders are classified as Category (Cat) A, B, or C within a more general system of categorizing major crime (see 23.2). Cat A and Cat B murder investigations will be led by an SIO who will probably be centrally based, while a Cat C murder could be investigated by detectives in a local BCU. However, there are variations on these basic categories, and a Cat C murder can often turn out to be more complicated than first thought, requiring more than just a local response.

The 'Murder Investigation Manual' ('MIM') (ACPO, 2006a) and the 'Practice Advice on Core Investigative Doctrine' (ACPO Centrex, 2005) offer an investigative model which most police forces will use as a template for enquiries into a major violent crime. The model consists of five stages (fast track, theoretical process, planned method of investigation, suspect enquiries, and disposal). In this Handbook, we have only briefly referred to the first stage concerning crime-scene and evidence preservation (see 11.2) and the initial police response to the reporting of the crime and the priority actions which follow.

> **TASK 4** Imagine you are a trainee police officer. You are called to a crime scene in a part of town with many multiple-occupancy dwellings. The body of a young woman is slumped on the floor of a blood-splattered bed-sitting room. Curious and worried onlookers are present, and the landlord of the property (who discovered the body) is nervously waiting for you just inside the bedsit door. He says that he heard a disturbance and a lot of screaming. He used his master key to open the door and has not touched anything. What do you do to ensure proper incident management, remembering Stage One of the MIM includes 'crime-scene and evidence preservation'? What are your tasks in priority order?

11.4 Railway Incidents and Fires

Railway property and any scene where there is a fire present particular risks. The policing of most railways and the London Underground is the responsibility of British Transport Police (BTP) but there are occasions where other forces will be engaged in activities relating to railway property. This could include the pursuit of suspects, searching railway property for missing persons or property related to crime, assisting at incidents and accidents, or providing cover when BTP are not immediately available. BTP officers' training is augmented by Personal Track Safety (PTS) courses: most other police forces do not offer this certification.

11.4.1 Incidents and offences on railway property

Railways and their associated infrastructure are exceptionally dangerous places. The risks include:

• being struck by a train whilst crossing a track (even at a level crossing or pedestrian gate);
• being struck by a train whilst walking onto a track to retrieve property, rescue a pet, or another person;
• electrocution by the 'third rail' or overhead power lines, or by signalling equipment;
• bumps, trips, and falls.

The electrical conductors which carry the power for trains are either a third rail or overhead, suspended between gantries. It should always be assumed that such conductors are 'live' because the power runs continuously and is not switched off when no train is present. Given that they carry so much power, death is almost certain if a person or anything they are touching comes into contact with railway power conductors. Overhead power lines can also arc, transmitting electricity through the air to nearby objects. If a person has fallen onto the third rail there is nothing which can realistically be done until the power is turned off, and police officers should be absolutely certain that this has been done before acting in such circumstances; there is no room for ambiguity. Further dangers are posed by 'rolling stock' (engines and carriages), particularly as in modern trains these are fast and relatively silent in operation. Railway apparatus (ie railway equipment other than rolling stock) is also dangerous: electrical components, moving parts, and trip hazards are universal. Therefore, police officers engaged on foot pursuits or assisting on railway property, for example at a station, should continuously consider their safety and those of colleagues and the public.

Essentially: there is no reward worth the risk of stepping onto a railway line. Most force policies will require the abandonment of foot pursuits if the suspect enters railway property.

For searches, special measures called 'Safe Systems of Work' (eg stopping trains and cutting the power) should be arranged before carrying out *any* search on operating railway lines or associated property, and it is wise to post a lookout for any carriages or engines that are still moving, however slowly. When searches of railway property are required, close negotiation with Railtrack and train operating companies is essential to reduce the risk of accidents and—where practicable—minimize disturbance to the network. BTP would be pleased to accommodate other forces in this respect. Under the Railway Safety Accreditation Scheme, BTP can accredit organizations and selected personnel with powers to deal with anti-social behaviour by issuing Fixed Penalty Notices and enforcing by-laws. Their presence is intended to act as a visible deterrent and reassurance as well as to free up BTP officers for more frontline duties.

Apart from the common offences which might be committed on railways, such as thefts (especially of cables), attacks on ticket machines, assaults, and criminal damage, specific legislation applies for crime and trespass on the railway network. Some of it is quite old, and 'translation' of the Victorian English can be difficult.

11.4.1.1 Trespass and authorized crossing point offences

Under s 16 of the Railway Regulation Act 1840 it is an offence to wilfully trespass on any railway or railway premises and to refuse to leave when asked to do so by any officer or agent of the railway company. The wilful behaviour is evidenced by a **refusal to leave**. The Regulation of Railways Act 1868 prohibits a person from crossing a railway line other than in an authorized place (eg level crossings or and pedestrian crossings). Under s 23 a person commits an offence if he/she crosses at an unauthorized place after being warned to desist by a servant or agent of the railway company.

Nearly a century later the British Transport Commission Act 1949 added legislation on trespass to cover trespass along 'railway lines, embankments, tunnels and sidings or any "works" (equipment) and electrical installations' (s 55). The section raises the issue of being in 'dangerous proximity' of lines and electrical installations. It is important to note that the investigating officer must produce evidence of a notice exhibited at the station nearest the place of the offence providing a clear public warning not to trespass on a railway. These signs are most obviously seen at the ends of platforms and at pedestrian and level crossings. The trespass is a summary offence and can be dealt with by a £60 PND (see 10.13.2).

11.4.1.2 Throwing objects and causing damage to railway property

Section 56 of the British Transport Commission Act 1949 makes it an offence to throw, or cause to fall, any object (stone, or thing likely to cause damage) into or upon any rolling stock or static equipment on any railway or siding or any 'works' or which is likely to cause injury. It is immaterial whether the train or equipment is in motion or is static. This is a summary offence and can be dealt with by a £60 PND (see 10.13.2).

The Offences Against the Person Act 1861 is a more complex but overarching piece of legislation which discusses 'unlawfully and maliciously' throwing or causing to fall objects such as stones, wood, or other matter or thing. If an intent to injure or endanger any person on or in a train or carriage etc can be proved, then the acts amount to an offence (ss 32 and 33). Section 34 contains misconduct offences such as drunkenness and not following by-laws. Section 17 of the Railway Regulation Act 1842 applies for misconduct by railway employees.

The Malicious Damage Act 1861 (s 35) covers placing items (eg a railway sleeper), on a railway, and also covers the removal of rails, turning (or switching) points, or showing or hiding signals. There must be intent to obstruct, upset, overthrow, injure, or destroy an engine, tender, carriage, or truck. This offence is triable on indictment only and the maximum penalty is life imprisonment. Section 36 deals with obstructing engines, or carriages, or railways. The offence is triable either way and it is not necessary to prove intent.

11.4.2 Attending scenes with fires

Fires are caused by the oxidation of fuel which creates heat. In order for a fire to occur three elements are required: a fuel source (such as furniture, hay, petrol), oxygen, and an external heat source to cause ignition. Once a fire has started the heat generated can accelerate the burning of the fuel load, which causes more heat energy to be liberated, causing a chain reaction effect. A fire can be extinguished by removing one of the three elements, such as by removing the fuel, starving the fire of oxygen, or reducing the temperature with water. Fires in buildings will often self-extinguish or reduce to a smoulder because they will consume all the available fuel or oxygen. If all the oxygen has been consumed, though, opening a door or window will introduce fresh air (containing oxygen) to the still-hot fuel and the fire can suddenly explode into an inferno within seconds. The heat from fires spreads by convection (hot air rises), conduction (heat travels through solid objects), and radiation (glowing heat that crosses empty space). This heat transfer can cause a fire to grow very fast, and the chain reaction effect means that small fires, which appear to be insignificant, can spread quite rapidly. During drought conditions the fuel load, such as grasslands, forests, and gardens, is so dry that the fire spreads far faster than would normally be expected.

Fires are emotional scenes: occupants of buildings and those whose homes have been damaged or destroyed will be suffering from a combination of fear, relief, anger, grief, and utter despair at, perhaps, losing everything they own. This combination of feelings may lead to irrational or angry outbursts levelled at anyone, and might include physical assault. A number of agencies are available to assist them, for example the local authority for temporary accommodation, and practical assistance may be sought from the Salvation Army or Citizens' Advice. If a family member or colleague has died or been injured as a result, then more specialist support can be arranged through Victim Support, the NHS, a Family Liaison Officer (FLO), and charities such as Cruse Bereavement Care.

11.4.2.1   The role of the police at fires

The overriding principle at fire scenes is to prevent the loss of life (including police officers' lives) and—when necessary and safe for the officer—to take action to save lives. The critical issue of your own safety as a police officer is covered in 6.12, and this principle extends to fighting fires: police officers should not attempt to take action against anything but the smallest of fires. Police officers have powers under s 17 of the PACE Act 1984 to enter a premises to save life or prevent damage, and PCSOs have powers under the Police Reform Act 2002, Sch 4, Part 1, but no unnecessary risks should be taken to save lives, protect property, or rescue animals.

Police officers at a fire scene where the Fire and Rescue Service (FRS) is not in attendance should employ the SAD-CHALETS mnemonic (see 11.5.2). During the survey and assessment phases officers may decide that a fire is small enough to tackle with available fire-fighting equipment (or imaginative use of a hose or towel). On the other hand it may seem that there is considerable potential for the fire to spread and grow. Whatever the verdict, the control room must be kept informed and they will contact the FRS who will decide whether or not to attend. Security companies, homeowners, and key holders of houses or businesses should be informed of the incident by the control room so that they can take appropriate action. Any conceivable risk to people (in nearby properties, the street, or in passing vehicles) means that decisive action must be taken: evacuate all nearby properties and keep everybody clear. Follow the old adage: GET OUT and STAY OUT. Police officers are often called to incidents where the FRS is already in attendance. The FAO should make contact with the senior fire officer present and act as a conduit for information at the scene. Police officers are likely to have relevant local knowledge about occupants, business activity on the premises, and/or information about any perceived risks or relevant force contingency plans in place in the area.

People in or near the fire may have burning clothes or hair, and these may also 'spontaneously combust' at a distance due to the radiant heat. Such victims may well panic and be unable to follow advice. They need to be pushed to the ground into a lying position, and the flames smothered with a coat or blanket. The horizontal position is particularly important to prevent convected heat rising from burning clothes, as this can cause damage to the eyes and mouth. Victims may need urgent first aid and hospitalization, but early decisive actions can save lives and reduce further injury.

Putting out the fire and saving lives is the role of the FRS, but police officers can assist by controlling the public (s 37 of the Road Traffic Act 1988), assisting with evacuations, and closing roads (ss 35 and 163) as appropriate. If the cause of the fire is unknown or suspicious then force policy will almost certainly require the attendance of a patrol supervisor or inspector, CID, and a CSI. An incident may be deemed to be 'serious' if injury or significant loss occurs, and an appropriate police response and investigation will take place.

Any large fire will inevitably attract onlookers, many of whom will merely wish to watch, but some may be intent on stealing rescued property or may even try to enter the property to steal. Scene security, management of the public, and a continuing eye on traffic problems need to be maintained. Some arsonists will return to observe the activity at the scene and a few may even obstruct attempts to extinguish the fire. At one fire in Kent, the offender repeatedly attempted to disable the fire hydrant in the street outside a fire until police arrived and arrested him. We cover offences that may be committed by persons obstructing firefighters in 11.4.2.2.

11.4.2.2 Fire and Rescue Service powers and obstruction offences

The Fire and Rescue Services Act 2004 confers a number of powers on the FRS and its members in relation to their responsibilities in emergencies, particularly for incidents which are likely to cause death or serious illness or injury, and where there may be serious harm to the environment and any plants or animals in it. This applies for fires or situations where there is a major risk of a fire, road traffic incidents, other types of emergency, and also covers actions required to prevent consequent damage to property (s 44(1)). Authorized FRS staff can enter premises by force, move or break into vehicles, close roads, control the traffic, and restrict access in order to achieve these aims (s 44(2)).

If a person interferes with or obstructs firefighters in the course of their work, they could be charged with an offence under the Emergency Workers (Obstruction) Act 2006 (EWOA) or the Fire and Rescue Services Act 2004, for example:

- obstructing or hindering personnel engaged in emergency operations when extinguishing a fire or protecting life and property in relation to a fire (or going anywhere to deal with it or prepare for it) (s 1 EWOA);
- obstruct a person who is assisting a firefighter (s 2 EWOA);
- obstructing or interfering with an employee of a fire authority who is entering a property or vehicle by force, or carrying out other emergency work under s 44 of the Fire and Rescue Services Act.

The full Acts are available on the www.legislation.gov.uk website.

11.5 Attending Emergency, Major, and Critical Incidents

Initial police training is likely to cover the police role in handling emergencies, major incidents, and critical incidents, and officers in training might even find themselves as an initial responder at the scene of an emergency. Useful background documents for this aspect of policing include the NPIA publications *Guidance on Emergency Procedures* (NPIA, 2009bc) and *Practice Advice on Critical Incident Management* (NPIA, 2007).

An **emergency** is defined by s 1 of the Civil Contingencies Act 2004 as 'an event or situation which threatens serious damage to human welfare in a place in the United Kingdom' including one or more of the following:

- human illness or injury or loss of life;
- homelessness or damage to property;
- disruption of a supply of money, food, water, energy, or fuel;
- disruption of transport, communication, or health systems and services;
- serious environmental damage (eg radioactive contamination);
- war or terrorism which threatens serious damage to the security of the UK.

A **major incident** is an emergency that requires the implementation of special arrangements by one or all of the emergency services for:

- the initial treatment, rescue, and transportation of a large number of casualties;
- the involvement either directly or indirectly of large numbers of people;
- the handling of a large number of enquiries likely to be generated both from the public and the news media, usually made to the police;
- the need for large-scale combined resources of the police, Fire and Rescue Service and Ambulance Service;
- the mobilization and organization of the emergency services and partner organizations, for example a local authority, to cater for the threat of death, serious injury, or homelessness to a large number of people.

(Wiltshire Police, no date)

A **critical incident** is any incident or event which has the potential to escalate and become a major incident. However, more recent thinking suggests that part of the definition of a critical incident may be that it creates a strong public perception of community vulnerability (ACPO, 2007b). The definitions of major and critical incidents vary from force to force, although they generally refer to either the size of the incident or its potential to escalate in some way, and often correspond closely with ACPO definitions given in the NPIA publications referred to earlier. It is for this reason that we have grouped together emergency, major incidents, and critical incidents in this part of Chapter 11.

Police officers in training will practise and rehearse effective ways to intervene to resolve a problem such as a domestic dispute, dealing with a shoplifter, or calming people down who have been involved in a minor road collision. They will learn to defuse, control, restrain, or manage any of a great variety of incidents. But what about an incident which has the potential to 'go major' and get really out of hand? There are fewer opportunities for practising for such events.

TASK 5 Try and imagine what your first response would be if you were the first police officer to arrive at:

- a serious road collision;
- the scene of a brawl in which someone had been knifed;
- an accident on a railway line;
- a burning house where people are trapped on upper floors; or
- a situation where a a child is being held hostage.

What would your responsibilities be, as opposed to your instincts? What would you be expected to do? Is there an order in which you should do things? What seem to be the priorities at the scene? What should be your priorities at the scene? What communication is needed and with whom?

Every force and every emergency service will have contingency plans to deal with a wide range of emergencies and incidents, and for some types of incident this will be a legal requirement under the Civil Contingencies Act 2004. There will be generic plans for certain types of emergency such as an aircraft crash, an influenza pandemic, or a siege incident with a hostage.

11.5.1 Early priorities at a major incident

The actions of first police officer on the scene are crucial to the proper and managed outcome of the incident, and relying on instinct is not sufficient in such situations. For example, at a large brawl in a club, bringing the scene under control is not best effected by an officer wading into the middle of the fracas and grabbing someone at random—this is likely to provoke more violence. House-fire incidents may also tempt a trainee officer to act heroically, but without the proper apparatus or an understanding of how fires develop (see 11.4.2) and the risk of structural collapse of the building, he/she may become a victim rather than a rescuer. A police officer needs to follow proper procedures, and to think and act calmly and rationally in order to:

- assess the situation and work out what is going on;
- communicate as quickly as possible; and
- prioritize actions.

> **TASK 6** Imagine you are a police officer attending an incident in which a man with a hostage appears to have barricaded himself into a semi-detached house in a cul-de-sac. About a dozen people are milling about, and the event has been described to you by two very excited and incoherent witnesses. You have one other police officer to assist you. Assuming that police back-up will arrive within ten minutes and other emergency services (fire and rescue service, ambulance) are also on their way (with an estimated time of arrival of 15 minutes), what would be your list of things to do in priority order at such an incident?

The FAO is in control of the incident (as 'Silver', the forward Commander: see 11.5.3) until he/she is relieved by someone of superior rank. The incident may include a crime scene, so preservation of evidence and keeping the scene clear and untouched is very important. In an emergency involving firearms or the risk of violence, the FAO would not let other emergency services go forward into the 'line of fire' either. Most ambulance trusts will not permit their personnel to enter firearms-related crime scenes as a matter of safety: consider that North West Ambulance Service forbade its staff from approaching the multiple scenes involved in the 'rampage' of Derrick Bird in 2010.

It is actually unlikely that a FAO would be alone for that long, unless the incident is in a really remote and inaccessible place, or there are corollary problems (such as a natural disaster of some kind) and access roads are blocked. A senior officer may arrive quite quickly but, if not, the golden hour is the responsibility of the officers present. All this sounds complicated and difficult to remember; however, training and experience enable police officers to maintain clear priorities and to follow procedures properly, acting calmly, positively, purposefully, and promptly.

11.5.2 CHALETS

The mnemonic **CHALETS** sets out the standard procedure for major incidents, in order of priority.

C	Casualties	How many, their location, and type of injuries
H	Hazards	• Immediate (fire, exposed electrical wires, flood water, chemicals, or hazardous substances) • Potential (gas cylinders near heat sources, spilled fuel, overhead power lines, firearms)
A	Access/egress	How to enter and leave the site, selecting RV points, setting up priority routes
L	Location	Where is the incident? (Are precise map references needed?)
E	Emergency services	• Are people hurt? • Is there a fire? • Are the services already on the scene or do they need to be called? • Is there a bomb or other explosive substance?
T	Type of incident	For example, vehicles in an accident, buildings in danger of collapse, affray in progress, underground tunnel collapse, public order, civil emergency, armed siege
S	Safety/start a log	Conduct a health and safety assessment, start an incident log in his/her PNB.

('SAD-CHALETS' is also sometimes used as a mnemonic, where 'SAD' stands for 'Survey, Assess, and Disseminate'.)

Out of all the services that may attend such an incident, only the police will be constantly alert to the possibility that a crime has been committed, and that the emergency, major, or critical incident could also be a crime scene (see 11.2). For example, after a road traffic collision, consideration must be given as to whether the driver was under the influence of drink or drugs. And after a fall from a height, did the woman fall or was she pushed; is this a natural or a suspicious death? Police officers should be suspicious and be alert to any signatures or characteristic signs that there is something wrong. For example, a witness may remark 'funny thing—that man hanging round all morning', or an officer may spot an article at the scene (or nearby) such as an empty wallet or purse. This might suggest that all is not what it seems, and problem-solving skills can help clarify ideas.

> **TASK 7** Describe a problem-solving and decision-making model you have encountered.

11.5.3   Control and responsibility

There is a standard command sequence in use in all police forces across the UK. The levels refer to the function of the command level and not necessarily to the rank of the officers concerned (see the College of Policing Authorised Professional Practice website for further information).

Levels of Command

Gold	Strategic command of the incident, usually at police headquarters or at a designated strategic police command centre
Silver	Tactical police command at a forward point closer to the scene of immediate crisis
Bronze	Operational local response at the crisis point itself (eg cordons or firearms), often carried out by a number of people (Operational Response Commanders or ORC), rather than one designated commander

When a more senior officer becomes available the command level will transfer to the officer with the higher rank. Therefore whilst on Independent or Supervised Patrol a trainee officer may be 'Silver' for a short period of time before a more senior or more experienced officer arrives on the scene. This tiered structure is considered by many in the police service to work effectively (and has been exhaustively tested) at local or force level and also at national level.

A risk assessment must be carried out to facilitate a proportionate response in the right sequence. The senior officer carrying out the assessment will ask the person who is 'Silver' at the time for information about the situation.

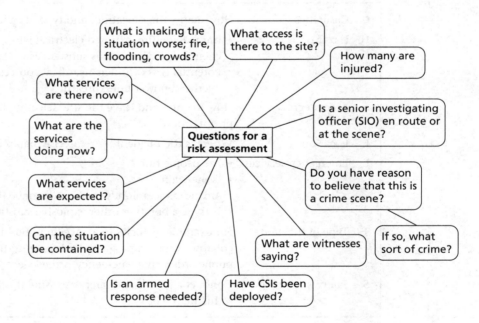

Resources should not be committed too early, unless there is a clear picture of what is happening on the ground, because over-resourcing is wasteful and inefficient. Police officers attending an incident are clearly not available for deployment elsewhere, and swamping a site with armed officers, dog teams, and underwater search teams is not necessary if the incident turns out to be trivial.

In the case of missing persons (especially when there may be other factors, possibly criminal) there are many components to the response: search teams are called out, assessments of transport needs are made, command and control, strategic, and tactical responses are all set up, and the control room will alert other emergency services. For larger incidents the invoking of 'military aid to the civil power' (MACP) might be required. Specialists such as explosives ordnance (bomb disposal), helicopters, search and rescue, engineers, nuclear, chemical, and radiological detection and containment units, and a host of others may be called upon. Note that deployment of armed officers is usually a top-level command decision ('Gold'), made by a chief superintendent or chief officer.

> **TASK 8** What problems might potentially arise within command structures? Make a list of what could go wrong and what would avoid problems.

At some incidents there may be bystanders, and they may be a help or a hindrance. Control of people's movements is essential, even at a relatively limited incident. Well-intentioned people may offer to help and any volunteers can be used effectively, to direct and contain people, to direct traffic, and conduct evacuation until more help arrives. However, bystanders may not always be so helpful; police and other emergency service support can be delayed because of 'rubber-neckers'—passers-by who want to see what is going on. This is often an impediment to effective scene management, and police officers should always be prepared to move such onlookers away from the incident.

There is another and very important reason why the area itself must be controlled. It could be a crime scene, and controlling access and the preservation of evidence is of absolutely vital importance (see 11.2).

11.5.4 Media interest

Newspapers, internet sites, Twitter, social network sites, radio, and television have apparently inexhaustible appetites for crime stories. This quest for the news story has produced an edgy, sometimes fraught, relationship between the media and the police. The media can definitely help with appeals for information to help solve complex crimes, raise awareness of danger, alert the public to emergencies or major disruption, or appeal for help with searches for missing people. The media offer the potential to engage with large numbers of people very quickly and locate suspects or witnesses who have left the local area. However, the media can also be rather superficial and sensationalist in an endless quest for headlines (see Leishman and Mason (2003) for more detail).

The management of information from the police must be carefully monitored. Too much information could put informants at risk, limit the range of questions that could be asked to a potential suspect, or result in the disposal of crucial evidence. Withholding information from the media can provide the police with a broader range of investigative tactics; unfair presentation of witness, victims, or suspects by the media can undermine their credibility before due process has taken place.

> **TASK 9** The media have a huge appetite for dramatic stories. How long do you think it might take for the media to respond to a major incident such as a train crash?

A police officer should never be tempted to give media interviews; each force will have a specialist unit for these functions (and some BCUs have their own media relations staff too). An officer's comments might inadvertently be misleading—he/she might not have the full picture and is unlikely to have much experience in communicating through the media. In major cases the police will hold a press conference to brief the press and provide up-to-date and appropriate information.

11.6 Attending Scenes with Suspect Devices

Suspect devices include bombs, incendiary devices (designed to start or sustain a fire), and CBRN (chemical, biological, radiological, and nuclear) devices, with or without explosive triggers. Any incident involving a suspect device is most certainly an extreme case of a major or critical incident. Incidents involving CBRN devices are still rare, but they have been known. In 1995, a small and secretive Japanese sect called AUM released small quantities of diluted Sarin (a nerve gas) inside a crowded Tokyo subway in the morning rush hour. Twelve people died and around 5,000 people required hospital treatment for their injuries. Had the gas been in concentrated form, the Japanese authorities believe that thousands could have died.

Terrorist incidents can be regarded as those incidents that involve the use or threat of violence (often extreme violence) to further or to publicize a political or extremist belief. The definitions of terrorism and extreme violence are considered further by Matassa *et al* (2003). The Terrorism Act 2000 provides particular powers for situations which might involve terrorism. Similar powers are available under other primary legislation or procedure, but the Terrorism Act 2000 provides wider powers than under other legislation to stop and search and to arrest (see 9.4.3.4).

If any suspect device is encountered, its precise nature cannot be determined by visual means alone. The cardinal rule is: do not touch it. The role of the FAO in managing such an ultra-critical incident is to create a very wide space around the suspect device (as wide as is practicable), and to get people out of the area. Whilst the requirement to preserve evidence is high, this is secondary to public safety at all times.

11.6.1 'Designated cordoned areas' under the Terrorism Act 2000

An area can be 'designated' as a cordoned area under s 34 of the Terrorism Act 2000 by a police officer holding the rank of superintendent or above (or under s 34(2), by any other constable if he/she considers it urgent). Police officers have certain additional powers in a designated cordoned area (s 34(1)). Under s 36(1) a police officer can:

* order a person to immediately leave a cordoned area or any premises adjacent to a cordoned area, and to move a vehicle from a cordoned area (if he/she is the driver or in charge of the vehicle);
* arrange for the removal of a vehicle from a cordoned area or for it to be moved within a cordoned area; or
* prohibit or restrict pedestrian or vehicular access to a cordoned area.

(Note that legislation regarding BTP and MOD police officers is slightly different.)

If a person fails to comply with any of these requests he/she commits an offence (s 36(2) of the Terrorism Act 2000). However, a defence is available to the accused if he/she can prove reasonable excuse for the non-compliance (s 36(3)). This offence is triable summarily only and the penalty is three months' imprisonment and/or a fine.

11.6.2 Suspected explosive devices

Alerts for suspected explosive devices present major demands on police and other emergency service resources, and hoaxes can be just as disruptive as the real thing (in the initial stages at least). Nonetheless, it must be assumed that every suspect device has the potential to kill and injure. **BOMB ALERT** is a useful mnemonic about the procedures to be followed.

B	Buildings: evacuate
O	Occupants: get them out and away
M	Move people right away from the scene
B	Back off: there could be secondary devices or other targets
A	Accurate information relayed back to control
L	Locate witnesses
E	Evacuate the neighbourhood of the device
R	Rendezvous (RV) points for arriving support
T	Tape off a cordon at the most practicable distance

As a general rule, cordons for small objects (up to briefcase size), should be placed at least 100 metres away from the device. For larger items (eg cars), the cordon should be a minimum of 200 metres, and for very large objects (eg large vans), the cordon should be a minimum of 400 metres.

Streets lined with buildings provide a blast corridor for an explosion so personnel are safer behind 'hard cover' (eg concrete buildings) with no line of sight of the suspected device. No person should be located behind or beneath windows or other glass panels, however far away from the device.

The CAP to the object should be marked out if practicable (see 11.2.2), consistent with the overriding priority of public safety. The force control room should be informed of the precise location of the device, especially if a wider evacuation is taking place outside the immediate cordon, but hand-held radios or mobile phones must not be used within 10 metres of the object, while vehicle-based radios must not be used to transmit within 50 metres.

11.6.3 CBRN incidents

A chemical, biological, radiological, or nuclear (CBRN) incident has the potential to cause extreme devastation and very widespread loss of life. Fortunately this type of incident is rare and all forces will have detailed contingency plans—the considerations and procedures are the same as for any other type of suspect device. A CBRN attack can be hard to recognize, but any reports of groups of people suddenly collapsing or feeling unwell, or of a strong or noxious smell could indicate the presence of chemicals. Other types of CBRN attack (eg involving nuclear radiation) will not be perceptible, in the early stages at least.

In a suspected CBRN incident the **Steps** procedure must be followed. The step number corresponds with the observed number of casualties.

For a Step 3 incident, a CHALETS assessment should be made if at all possible, but police safety must not be compromised.

Step	Number of casualties	Procedure
Step 1	One	Approach the site using the usual procedures.
Step 2	Two	Approach with caution and do not discount any possibility. Report arrival and do not touch any object. Report updates continually.
Step 3	Three or more	Do not enter the scene. Create an RV point outside the area and await instructions.

11.6.4 Attending the scene of a bomb explosion

After a bomb explosion there is likely to be devastation, wreckage, smoke, flames, badly injured people, dead bodies (and parts of bodies), noise, and confusion. The role of the FAO is the same in principle as for a train crash or major road traffic accident: take charge, clear those who can walk out of the area, close off the area with a cordon, attend to the injured if possible, and treat the area as a crime scene. In addition to the CHALETS principles (see 11.5.2), the mnemonic ICICLE provides guidance on the procedures to be followed:

I	Identify the source of threat or suspicion
C	Communicate all available details to force control
I	Investigate the circumstances
C	Contain the threat to people where possible
L	Lead and reassure people at the scene
E	Ensure that major incident procedures are put in hand

Nothing can prepare a trainee police officer (or anyone) for the emotional impact of witnessing such scenes; indeed, many police officers present at the immediate aftermath of a major disaster report experiencing an initial sense of helplessness. However, it has been said (and in our view rightly) that what distinguishes a police officer from the general public is not his/her exercise of powers, or uniform, or knowledge of the law, but knowing what to do in an emergency. That knowledge can only come from training and experience.

TASK 10 Note the priority actions now in response to (1) a suspect CBRN device; and (2) a subsequent detonation. What should be done first and thereafter?

General Procedures

11.7   Planned Operations

'Planned Operations' are where the police have had advanced warning of a situation or event and as a consequence will have been able to develop suitable contingency plans, tactics, and strategies. Examples include disruption at sea and airports due to strikes, pre-planned demonstrations, and large music festivals. As soon as the necessity for such an operation has been identified, it is given an operational name to distinguish it from other incidents. The 'operation' covers the period from instigation, through planning, execution, and debrief. We provide a summary here, but more details are available at the <http://www.app.college.police.uk> website.

11.7.1   Planning an operation

All police organizations have contingency plans for identified risks in their own areas, with a degree of flexibility to cover all eventualities. A range of tactical options are available for use for planned operations. Some of these are used as part of 'steady state' policing (see 11.1) such as police dogs, batons and building entry, while others are more specialized, for example the use of armed response personnel who can fire attenuating energy projectiles and CS smoke. Other tactical options include shield tactics, air support, vehicle tactics, barricade/obstacle removal, cordons and intercepts, water cannon, containment, and evidence-gathering teams.

The hierarchy of command, known as Gold, Silver, and Bronze (GSB) (see 11.5.3), is nationally recognized by the police, partner agencies, and other emergency services. At each level of GSB, tactical advisers from the police and external organizations provide knowledge, understanding, and skills for the planning phase and for responding to changing circumstances throughout the duration of the operation. For example, Gold Command could elect to convene a 'strategic coordinating group', or Silver Command could assemble a 'tactical planning group' to develop a strategy.

Commanders and coordinating groups require specific, accurate, and relevant information at each stage of the operation, so a dedicated intelligence function will be required (see Chapter 22). This will be located centrally within the GSB incident room, or elsewhere, for example at the Force Intelligence Bureau. A Community Impact Assessment (CIA) is made to judge the extent to which businesses, community groups, families, and individuals may be affected by the proposed police response, providing vital information for planning a successful operation. Personnel from within the police family (eg neighbourhood teams), and external representatives from the third sector (charitable and non-profit-making organizations, community bodies), can all provide input for the CIA.

Gold Command (or 'Gold') determines the strategy and plans the police response accordingly. All the relevant information is recorded in a single document, the 'operational order'. The personnel participating in the operation are briefed as required, following the categories set out in the IIMARCH model (see the table).

IIMARCH heading	Key features
Information	Such as evaluated intelligence, results of the community impact assessment, length, duration, and location of the operation
Intention	Objectives of GSB strategies, tactics, policies, powers, and procedures
Method	Process by which the tactics, policies, powers, and procedures will be used
Administration	Logistics pertaining to start times, location, and lengths of duty and periods of refreshment
Risk assessment	Based on gathered information from intelligence sources
Communications	Including media broadcasts and inter-operability between personnel
Human rights and other legalities	Preserving the rights of individuals and groups and adhering to codes of practice in the use of legislation

The police information (see 6.8.2) generated by an operation must be collected, recorded, shared, and retained in accordance with ACPO guidelines. These specify the use of the Government Security Classifications Policy (GSCP), under which information is classified as either: Official, Secret, or Top Secret.

11.7.2 Participating in a planned operation

In the course of a planned operation police officers will of course follow the tactics outlined in the operational order, but within these limits individual officers will probably need to decide what specific actions to take. They should use the National Decision Model (see 6.5.2) as a framework for taking a decision. Records of any decisions made and actions carried out should be made in accordance with the PACE Codes of Practice (see 5.6) and the rules of disclosure (see 26.2). Police officers will usually make a record as a PNB entry (see 10.2), although this might not be possible at the time, depending on the circumstances.

The operational order may specify the use of personal protective and operational equipment (see 6.10), particularly if the use of force is likely to be required. The use of force to challenge unacceptable behaviour will be covered under personal safety training (see 6.12.5) and limited by legislation such as the Human Rights Act 1998 (see 5.4) and common law. Each individual officer must remember that his/her own health and safety is just as important as maintaining the health and safety of others (see 6.12).

11.7.3 Effective communication for planned operations

Effective communication with partners, communities, and other stakeholders helps to build trust and confidence and ensure that the appropriate strategy is adopted. Openness and transparency can help identify the potential for further escalation of problems, and make it less likely that unplanned (and less suitable) police response tactics will be used. All officers participating in an operation have an individual responsibility to maintain effective interpersonal communication (see 6.11). Various communication channels are available to GSB during planning and during the operation itself, such as:

*   open data, for example POLICE.uk, Data.gov.uk and Ordnance Survey OpenData;
*   face-to-face, for example public meetings, under-represented groups, independent advisory groups, partnership working, and information sharing;
*   digital and social media, for example platforms such as Facebook, Twitter, YouTube, and Blog, social media monitoring, and digitally enabled meetings;
*   corporate communication (traditional media), for example press releases and statements, television, radio, and newspaper interviews.

After a planned operation there will be a debriefing process to identify examples of good practice and opportunities for improvement. This could help streamline procedures and reduce demands for frontline staff in the future. The information from the debrief should be recorded and retained for revelation and disclosure (see 26.2). Further information on debriefing can be found on the Authorised Professional Practice website at <http://www.app.college.police.uk>.

11.8 Answers to Tasks

TASK 1 You may have noted that major-crime investigations are often long term and complex, especially when dealing with 'stranger murders' or 'stranger rapes'.

You could note, too, that crimes of violence attract considerable media interest and widespread publicity which, whilst helpful in publicizing the crime, have the potential to adversely affect an investigation if not handled properly.

TASK 2 When a person is decapitated.

TASK 3 Although it is beyond the scope of this Handbook (and not something that you are likely to encounter unless you become an SIO) you might like to research the CATCHEM (Central Analytical Homicide and Expertise Management) database. Research conducted on child murder with a sexual motive revealed complex mathematical relationships between places of abduction, and aspects of the offender. This is described in Aitken *et al* (1995). One inferential model the authors describe suggests that, in the case of a boy victim aged 0–10 who has been abducted, there are high probabilities that the offender lives within five miles of the contact point (75 per cent chance) and is aged 21+ (77 per cent).

The pioneering work of Aitken *et al* continues to be developed and extended by, amongst others, the Serious Crime Analysis Section (now part of the NCA).

General Procedures

The research used has now been applied to the more general crime of homicide (Francis *et al*, 2004). For example, if the victim is aged 18–24, male, ethnically of Asian background, unemployed, and 'stabbed in a rage', then the model predicts that the offender is over 21 (68 per cent likelihood), also Asian (55 per cent), and an acquaintance of the victim (60 per cent).

TASK 4 The priority at the scene of a major violent crime is the preservation of life followed by the preservation of evidence.

You would probably note that the first priority would be not to let anyone else over the threshold of the crime scene, and that might well extend to the area outside the bedsit, to include stairs, stairwell, communal areas, and adjoining corridors or passages. You would clear people away (including the landlord), and close off the scene as swiftly as possible. You would enter the room, principally to ascertain whether the presumed victim is still alive. If she is you would follow the Airways, Breathing, Circulation (ABC) procedures, or possibly the 'Hands-only CPR' method as recommended by the British Heart Foundation and publicized by Vinnie Jones in early 2012 (see <http://www.bhf.org.uk>). Your duty is to support her until the paramedics arrive, and you would also ensure that nothing else was touched.

You would be in urgent communication with your force control centre, describing what you can see, the location, and any other relevant requirements, such as the attendance of paramedics, an ambulance, and a doctor. You would request the attendance of CSIs and probably the duty SIO or duty detective officer, since it is evident that a violent crime has been committed, possibly murder.

Then what? If you had a colleague with you, you could share the note taking, including the names and addresses of all those present, whether they have volunteered as witnesses or not. (Bear in mind the need to 'record, retain, reveal, and disclose' that we discuss in 26.2.) You would ask the landlord (whose details you have also recorded) for information about the victim and possible visitors she had had that day, including of course any information about the other person or persons present at the apparent altercation. You would log your actions, begin arranging the CAP, and note anything which you observed (such as a murder weapon, scattered possessions, blood splashes, and so on).

TASK 5 Your answers could well have been 'I do not know', which would have been entirely understandable even if you are a trainee police officer. (In fact your trainers might be more worried if you claimed already to know the answers to these questions.) We aim to go on to provide you with some general principles and some possible answers.

TASK 6 Your list could read something like this:
- Clear the immediate scene and note any injuries to anyone.
- Ensure that the area around the house (the 'stronghold') is evacuated and move people as far from the scene as possible.
- Continue to ask for information on what has happened, but calm any hysterical or over-excited people.
- Create a CAP in and out of the incident (see 11.2.2).
- Clear a wide area to receive the support which is coming (keep arriving vehicles away from the scene itself).
- Keep in constant communication with your control centre, making sure that they know what is happening and what you are doing.
- Use your colleague proactively to control the immediate area, to talk to witnesses, to communicate with the incoming support.
- Find out all you can about the alleged hostage-taker, including name and any relationship with anyone likely to be inside the house with him.
- Make notes: keep a careful log (see 11.2.3) of what has taken place to the best of your knowledge, recording names and addresses of witnesses (see 23.4).
- If it is safe to do so, try to open a dialogue with the hostage-taker, making sure that he understands that you are a police officer and emphasizing that your aim is to end this incident peacefully, without anyone getting hurt.

Trainee officers, could compare this list to the one provided during training. No doubt there will be many points in common.

TASK 7 There are many. The usual model taught during police training adopts a six-stage process, starting with defining the problem:

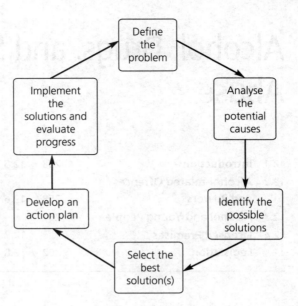

TASK 8 The 'Gold, Silver, Bronze' system has come under critical scrutiny in recent years. In his report into the investigation of the Soham murders, Sir Ronnie Flanagan made the following observation:

> Ironically, the overlaying of the Gold, Silver and Bronze command structure on this operation contributed to a lack of clarity of command of the incident, particularly in relation to the role of the SIO and was subject to comment in the internal review. (Flanagan, 2004, p 13)

The report also contained a recommendation that when applied to homicide the system should be clarified. A number of the Flanagan recommendations were subsequently adopted in NPIA guidance and subsequently feature in the CoP Authorised Professional Practice.

TASK 9 We were not exaggerating when we discussed the extent of media interest earlier. In the case of the Watford train crash in 1996, Hertfordshire police reported that media interest in the incident commenced within five minutes of the crash happening (Moses, 1997). And more recently, in January 2013, when a gunman began shooting at Lone Star College, near Houston, Texas, one student was tweeting during the incident. Justin Lear of CNN responded, and even asked if she had any photos. For an edited version of the tweets see <http://storify.com/mashable/student-tweets-during-school-shooting>.

TASK 10

1. The role of the police officer does not include identifying the type of device. His/her role would be to contain the scene, evacuate anyone within the cordon, and manage the site until help arrives. He/she should be communicating to the force control centre to tell them everything he/she can see and otherwise perceive, including the location of the device and its description.
2. Secondary devices would be a major concern. The ICICLE principles should be applied.

Further advice from the UK government concerning CBRN and 'aimed at those responsible for the safety of others in businesses and other public/private sector organisations' may be found in the NPIA document (2009b) *Guidance on Emergency Procedures*.

General Procedures

12 | Alcohol, Drugs, and Substance Abuse

12.1 Introduction

Many of the incidents encountered by a trainee police officer on Supervised and Independent Patrol will be alcohol or drug-related, particularly on late shifts. The health and safety of all persons present must be considered: the potential for injury can be very high. Intoxicated people are sometimes subject to rapid mood swings, happy one minute and then violent the next, and others who are normally quite reserved may lose some of their normal social inhibitions and behave unpredictably. Police training includes input to help trainee officers develop the skills to defuse such potentially dangerous situations. These skills will certainly be required; for example in *McMillan v Crown Prosecution Service* [2008] EWHC 1457 (Admin), police officers had warned a woman about her drunken behaviour in the street, but later the same day she was found still drunk, shouting and swearing at the front door of her daughter's house. One of the officers advised the woman to leave but she continued to shout and swear. As a result the officer took her by the arm and escorted her down the garden steps and onto the public footpath. It was held that the officer had not assaulted the woman and had been acting within generally accepted parameters.

Although this chapter is mainly concerned with the application of the law surrounding alcohol- and drugs-related incidents initial police training and pre-join programmes also provide an introduction to the wider issues surrounding alcohol and other forms of drug and substance abuse. For example, the police play a role in helping to reduce abuse of alcohol and drugs beyond law enforcement. In the case of Lincolnshire Police this takes the form of participation in the Lincolnshire Alcohol Arrest Referral (LARR) scheme (Lincolnshire Police, 2011), targeted at young people who may have encountered difficulties (with the police and others) in relation to alcohol abuse. It is also worth being aware of some of the complexities involved. For example, a common perception is of an increase in 'binge drinking' of alcohol amongst the young, but the reality appears somewhat more complex. The number of young people drinking to excess appears to have dropped in recent years, but those that do abuse alcohol do so more often and to a greater extent (Fuller, 2008). The use of potentially lethal intoxicating substances such as solvents is covered in 12.7.

Finally, note that drink- and drug-driving is covered separately in 19.9.

12.2 Alcohol-related Offences and Powers

The terms 'drunk' and 'drunkenness' are not defined in law. As a precedent, the case of *R v Tagg* [2002] 1 Cr App R 2 determined that the everyday meaning of 'drunk' should be used. The *Oxford English Dictionary* defines drunk as 'having drunk intoxicating liquor to an extent which affects steady self-control' (*Shorter Oxford English Dictionary*, 2002, although the 1933 edition was cited in that case). The Court of Appeal also accepted that the *Collins Dictionary* definition (used by the judge in the original case under appeal) and the *Shorter Oxford English Dictionary* definitions were essentially the same, and were helpful in determining the existence of a state of drunkenness.

The court itself must decide whether or not a suspect was drunk. The general rule that the opinion of a witness is inadmissible does not apply in this particular context: a competent witness may give evidence that, in his/her opinion, a person was drunk (*R v Davies* [1962] 1 WLR 1111). A competent witness is a person who understands questions put to them and gives answers that can be understood. Therefore a police officer can state his/her opinion (as a competent witness) on whether a particular person was drunk. He/she should also be able to give the facts on which that opinion is based, such as:

- he was unsteady on his feet;
- her eyes were glazed;
- his speech was slurred; or
- intoxicating liquor could be smelt on her breath.

The word 'alcohol' is used in some legislation. It is defined in s 191(1) of the Licensing Act 2003 as spirits, wine, beer, cider or any other fermented, distilled, or spirituous liquor.

12.2.1 Drunkenness as an offence

Section 12 of the Licensing Act 1872 states that it is an offence for a person to be:

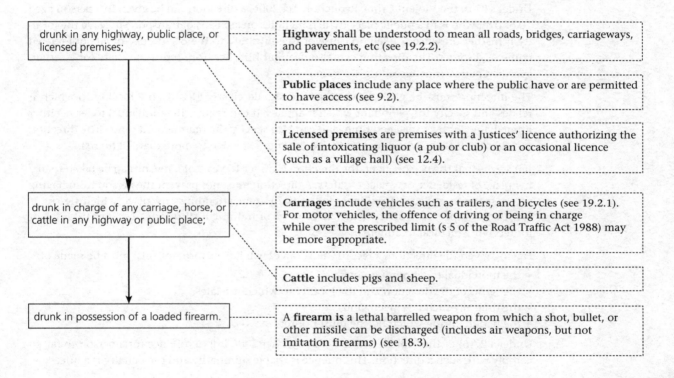

This offence is triable summarily and the penalty is one month's imprisonment or a fine. It is also a penalty offence for the purposes of s 1 of the Criminal Justice and Police Act 2001 (see 10.13.2).

12.2.2 Drunk and disorderly behaviour

The precise meaning of the term 'disorderly behaviour' is not defined by statute but its everyday meaning is 'unruly or offensive behaviour'. Under s 91(1) of the Criminal Justice Act 1967, it is an offence for any drunken person to display such behaviour in any highway, public place, or licensed premises.

This offence is triable summarily and the penalty is one month's imprisonment or a fine. It is also a penalty offence for the purposes of s 1 of the Criminal Justice and Police Act 2001 (see 10.13.2).

12.2.3 Drunk in charge of children

Under s 2 of the Licensing Act 1902, it is an offence for a person to be drunk while 'having charge' of a child under the age of 7 years in any highway, public place, or licensed premises. The precise meaning of 'having charge' is not defined by statute, but probably means some sort of care or control over the child(ren); the suspect must be the only person with the child, or alternatively everyone in a group with the child must be drunk. The offence is triable summarily and the penalty is one month's imprisonment or a fine.

12.2.4   Designated public place orders

A local authority can designate an area under a DPPO, also known as a 'controlled drinking zone'. In such an area a police officer has the power (s 12(2) of the Criminal Justice and Police Act 2001) to require a person to stop consuming alcohol and he/she may confiscate alcohol. However, Home Office advice is that 'it is not appropriate to challenge an individual consuming alcohol where that individual is not causing a problem' (Home Office, 2009b).

When a person is required to stop consuming alcohol he/she must be informed that it is an offence to fail to comply without reasonable excuse. The offence is triable summarily and the penalty is a fine. It is also a penalty offence for the purposes of s 1 of the Criminal Justice and Police Act 2001 (see 10.13.2).

12.2.5   Power to direct a person away from an area of alcohol-related crime and disorder

Under s 27 of the Violent Crime Reduction Act 2006, a direction can be given to a person aged 10 or over who is in a public place (which includes on a means of transport) to leave the locality if his/her presence is likely to cause or to contribute to the occurrence of alcohol-related crime or disorder. The direction can also prohibit him/her from returning there for a certain specified period (not exceeding 48 hours).

The direction must be given in writing, and should clearly identify the locality to which it relates and specify the period for which it applies. It can require the individual to leave either immediately or by a specified time, and can also specify the manner and route. The direction can subsequently be withdrawn or varied (but not extended to more than 48 hours).

If it seems that the person given the direction is under 16 years old, he/she can be taken to his/her place of residence or a place of safety. A direction must not prevent the person from having access to his/her place of residence or work or from attending any place which he/she is required or expected to attend (such as a college or training institution, a court or tribunal, or for receiving medical treatment).

Having given the direction, a record (most forces will have a form for this) must be made of:
* the individual to whom it is given;
* the terms of the direction and the locality to which it relates;
* the time at which it is given; and
* the period during which he/she must not return.

Under s 27(6) of the Violent Crime Reduction Act 2006 it is an offence for a person to fail to comply with such a direction. This offence is triable summarily and the penalty is a fine.

12.2.6   Drinking Banning Orders (DBOs)

Under s 1 of the Violent Crime Reduction Act 2006 a court may order a person aged 16 or over to be excluded from pubs and clubs in a defined geographic area for a specified length of time. An interim order may be used while a court considers an application for a full banning order.

It is an offence under s 11 of the Violent Crime Reduction Act 2006 for a person who is the subject of a drinking banning order (or interim order) to carry out any action prohibited by the order (without reasonable excuse). For further guidance, see Drinking Banning Orders (DBOs) on Conviction (Home Office, 2010b). This offence is triable summarily and the penalty is a fine.

TASK 1 Imagine you are a trainee police officer. In your area you often see a habitual drunk who often drinks large quantities of strong lager and then becomes very abusive to passing members of the public. You are requested to deal with this. How would you approach her and what long-term solution could you consider to try and resolve the situation? Look at s 34(1) of the Criminal Justice Act 1972 to help determine a suitable course of action.

12.3   **Alcohol and Young People**

Concern about young people drinking alcohol has increased considerably over the past few years. Certain legislation addresses this in relation to young people on licensed premises. Other legislation is available to help limit their alcohol consumption in other places to which the public has access.

On a more general note if an officer finds a child carrying unopened cans of alcohol, then he/she should at least consider where the child had bought the cans and his/her welfare, and take action accordingly. This applies even if there are no grounds to reasonably believe that the child has been consuming alcohol (or is about to consume it) at a relevant place.

12.3.1   **Confiscation of alcohol from young people**

A police officer (in or out of uniform) or a suitably designated PCSO may confiscate alcohol (or anything reasonably believed to be alcohol) from a young person in a 'relevant place' (s 1(1) of the Confiscation of Alcohol (Young Persons) Act 1997). A relevant place includes:

- any public place, for example streets, parks, and shopping centres (but not licensed premises such as pubs or clubs); and
- any other place to which the person has unlawfully gained access, such as gate-crashing a party at a private house where the trespasser did not have the consent of the homeowner to gain entry.

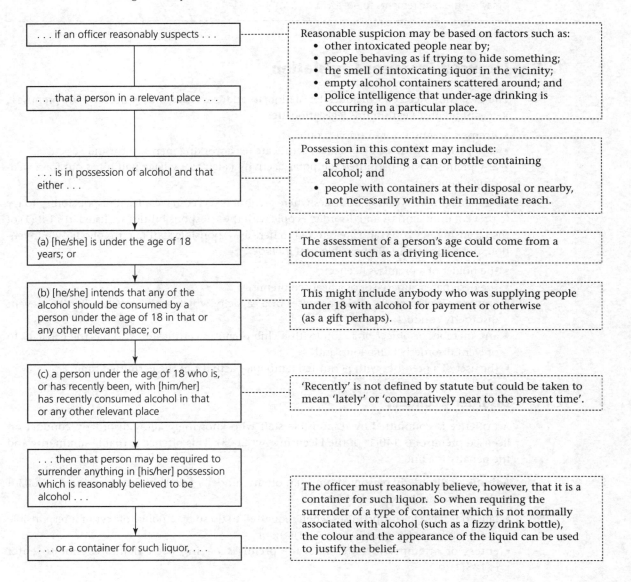

. . . if an officer reasonably suspects . . .

Reasonable suspicion may be based on factors such as:
- other intoxicated people near by;
- people behaving as if trying to hide something;
- the smell of intoxicating iquor in the vicinity;
- empty alcohol containers scattered around; and
- police intelligence that under-age drinking is occurring in a particular place.

. . . that a person in a relevant place . . .

. . . is in possession of alcohol and that either . . .

Possession in this context may include:
- a person holding a can or bottle containing alcohol; and
- people with containers at their disposal or nearby, not necessarily within their immediate reach.

(a) [he/she] is under the age of 18 years; or

The assessment of a person's age could come from a document such as a driving licence.

(b) [he/she] intends that any of the alcohol should be consumed by a person under the age of 18 in that or any other relevant place; or

This might include anybody who was supplying people under 18 with alcohol for payment or otherwise (as a gift perhaps).

(c) a person under the age of 18 who is, or has recently been, with [him/her] has recently consumed alcohol in that or any other relevant place

'Recently' is not defined by statute but could be taken to mean 'lately' or 'comparatively near to the present time'.

. . . then that person may be required to surrender anything in [his/her] possession which is reasonably believed to be alcohol . . .

The officer must reasonably believe, however, that it is a container for such liquor. So when requiring the surrender of a type of container which is not normally associated with alcohol (such as a fizzy drink bottle), the colour and the appearance of the liquid can be used to justify the belief.

. . . or a container for such liquor, . . .

Specific Incidents

As shown in the diagram an officer can require alcohol to be surrendered. When such a requirement is used the person:

- must be required to state his/her name and address (s 1AA); and
- may be removed to his/her place of residence or a place of safety if it is reasonably suspected that he/she is under 16 (s 1AB) (see 13.3.3 and 14.2.4.2).

Under s 1(4) of the Confiscation of Alcohol (Young Persons) Act 1997, the officer must inform the person of his/her suspicion under s 1(1) and state that it is an offence to fail to comply (without reasonable excuse) with a requirement under s 1(1) or (1AA). This offence is triable summarily and the penalty is a fine.

Anything surrendered under s 1(1) can be disposed of in such manner as the officer considers appropriate (s 1(2)); each force will have its own disposal policy.

12.3.2 Persistently possessing alcohol in a public place

Section 30 of the Police and Crime Act 2009 states that it is an offence for a person under 18 to be in possession of alcohol without reasonable excuse in any relevant place on three or more occasions within a year. The offence is triable summarily and the penalty is a fine.

> **TASK 2** Imagine you are a police officer and you see a young teenager at a bus station drinking alcohol. What requirements will you make of him? Write down a list of things you would have to say for the requirements to be lawful.

12.4 Licensed Premises Legislation

The Licensing Act 2003 includes legislation to address drunkenness in 'relevant premises'. Relevant premises within this legislation are:

- licensed premises, for example a pub;
- club premises with a club premises certificate (eg a working men's club); and
- any premises with permitted temporary activity (such as a village hall hired out for a wedding reception).

Staff managing or working in places where alcohol is served have a legal responsibility to try to prevent drunkenness and disorder. People with these responsibilities are listed in s 140(1) of the Licensing Act 2003, and are referred to here as responsible staff (a term of our own invention, not a legal term). Responsible staff include:

- the holder of a premises licence;
- the designated supervisor of a licensed premises;
- any person who works at the premises in a capacity which authorizes him/her to prevent disorderly conduct;
- any member or officer of a club (with a club premises certificate) who has the capacity to prevent disorderly behaviour; and
- the user of a premises with permitted temporary activity, at the permitted time.

12.4.1 Disorderly conduct

An offence is committed by responsible staff who knowingly allow disorderly conduct on licensed premises (s 140(1) of the Licensing Act 2003). This offence is triable summarily and the penalty is a fine.

A drunk or disorderly person commits an offence under s 143(1) of the Licensing Act 2003 if without reasonable excuse he/she:

- fails to leave relevant premises when requested to do so by a police officer or a responsible staff member at the premises (s 143(1)(a)); or
- enters or attempts to enter relevant premises having been requested not to enter (s 143(1)(b)).

This offence is triable summarily and the penalty is a fine.

A police officer must respond to requests for help from responsible staff to help expel or refuse entry to a drunken person (s 143(4) of the Licensing Act 2003). Reasonable force may be used to encourage the person to comply (see *Semple v Luton and South Bedfordshire Magistrates' Court* [2009] EWHC 3241 (Admin) and 15.5.1).

12.4.2 Providing a drunk person with intoxicating liquor

Responsible staff who knowingly sell (or attempt to sell) alcohol to a person who is drunk on relevant premises commit an offence under s 141(1) of the Licensing Act 2003. And in relation to customers, it is also an offence to obtain or attempt to obtain alcohol for a drunken person on relevant premises (s 142(1) of the Licensing Act 2003). These offences are triable summarily and the penalty is a fine. They are also penalty offences for the purposes of s 1 of the Criminal Justice and Police Act 2001.

12.4.3 Powers of entry into 'relevant premises'

Under s 180(1) of the Licensing Act 2003 reasonable force can be used (s 180(2)) to gain entry to any place if there is reason to believe that an offence under the Licensing Act 2003 is being committed (or is about to be committed). The term 'any place' is defined in s 193; it includes vehicles, vessels, or moveable structures, licensed or not.

There is also a power of entry under the Licensing Act 2003 to any place with a club premises certificate if there is reasonable cause to believe that:

- an offence relating to supplying a controlled drug has been committed (see 12.6.2), or is about to be, or is being committed at that moment (s 97(1)(a)); or
- a breach of the peace may occur (s 97(1)(b)).

Whilst exercising this power reasonable force may be used (s 97(2)).

For premises with permitted temporary activities, under s 108(1) of the Licensing Act 2003 a police officer may enter the premises at any reasonable time to assess the effect of the event in terms of the prevention of crime and disorder, public safety, the prevention of public nuisance, and the protection of children from harm. There is no specific offence of obstructing a police officer under this section, but the offence of obstruction in the lawful execution of police duties under the Police Act 1996 could be considered (see 15.4).

12.4.4 Selling alcohol to children and young people

Alcohol cannot legally be sold to a child (any person under the age of 18 years).

An offence is committed by a person who:

- sells alcohol to a person under 18 in any place (s 146(1) of the Licensing Act 2003)—this is also a penalty offence under s 1 of the Criminal Justice and Police Act 2001 (see 10.13.2); or
- knowingly allows the sale of alcohol on relevant premises to an individual aged under 18 (s 147(1) of the Licensing Act 2003).

A further more serious offence is committed if on two or more different occasions (within a period of three consecutive months) alcohol is unlawfully sold on the same licensed premises to an individual aged under 18 (s 147A of the Licensing Act 2003).

These offences are triable summarily and the penalty is a fine.

> **TASK 3** In the course of an investigation into offences concerning public indecency and criminal damage it is found that many of these offences are committed by people who have consumed large amounts of intoxicating liquor on relevant premises. This intake of alcohol may have contributed towards these offences being committed.
>
> How could the licensing authority of the premises be informed about such activities?

12.5 Unlawful Possession of a Controlled Drug

The legislation for the offence of 'unlawful possession of a controlled drug' is covered in s 5(2) of the Misuse of Drugs Act 1971. Drugs that are subject to legal control are referred to as controlled drugs. Some controlled drugs are addictive and/or dangerous, and the results of their

Specific Incidents

misuse are obvious to us all. The Misuse of Drugs Act 1971 was enacted to curb the use of controlled drugs and to outlaw various actions by those people who are unlawfully in possession of them. Drugs are not prohibited articles under s 1 of the PACE Act 1984, but s 23(2) of the Misuse of Drugs Act 1971 has its own power of search (see 9.4.3.1).

Recognizing controlled drugs is very difficult as there are so many different forms, shapes, colours, and sizes including pills, tablets, liquids, powders, and resins. Therefore, when finding such substances without pharmaceutical company packaging a police officer should not try and work out exactly what drug it is. He/she should instead suspect that the person might be in possession of controlled drugs and act accordingly.

Risk and hazard levels should be carefully assessed when dealing with people who have been taking drugs. Personal safety equipment may be required; the consequences of contamination from bodily fluids or equipment used by a drug addict can be very serious. The merest micro-cut from a sharp article contaminated by a transferable virus could cause an infection that might even be life-threatening. Demonstration of appropriate health and safety measures will count towards the PAC Safety First requirements and the assessment criteria across most of the Diploma in Policing assessed units.

12.5.1 What is a controlled drug?

A controlled drug is a drug that is controlled because of its effect on the human body. They are divided into classes A, B, and C (Misuse of Drugs Act 1971) according to the potential for harm they are thought to present to individuals and to society at large.

Class A	eg Ecstasy, heroin, cocaine, crack cocaine, 'magic mushrooms' (containing psilocin), and LSD
Class B	eg cannabis leaves, cannabis resin, amphetamines, and barbiturates
Class C	eg tranquillizers (such as Temazepam), and some painkillers

A full list of controlled drugs can be found on the Home Office website. A controlled drug also includes any substance or product made the subject of a temporary class drug order by the Secretary of State (s 2(1)(a)(ii)).

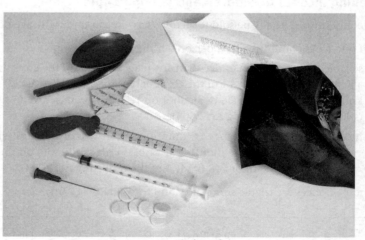

Heroin 'gear'

Crack Smoking equipment
(Photographs from Drugscope 2013, copyright free)

12.5.2 The offence of 'unlawful possession'

As a police officer in training, the offence of unlawful possession is the most frequently encountered drugs offence. In order to commit this offence (s 5(2) of the Misuse of Drugs Act) a person must:

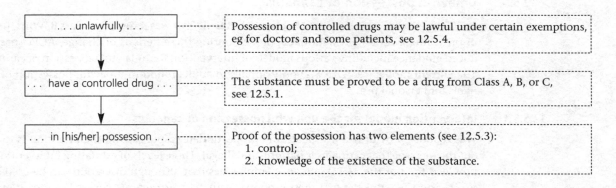

As an example, imagine that during a search of a man under the powers under s 23 of the Misuse of Drugs Act 1971 (see 9.4.3.1), a cigarette lighter and aluminium foil with traces of brown powder on it are found in the man's pocket. After examination of the substance it is found to be heroin. To prove the offence of possession it must therefore be shown that:

- the foil was in his pocket and he knew it was there;
- he knew there was powder on the foil (it does not matter whether or not he knew the substance was a controlled drug);
- the powder was heroin; and
- he was not lawfully entitled to possess the drug.

12.5.3 Proving that a person is in possession of a substance

Through case law it has been established that two elements are required in order to establish possession of a substance; control of the substance and knowledge of its existence.

Elements required to prove possession	Explanation
1. Control of the substance itself or a container in which it is held	Control of a substance is indicated by the rights the person has over the substance, and generally amounts to ownership. It would certainly include items found on a person or in his/her property, but would also include items that a person has ordered and paid for by post but has not yet received. Having control would also include having custody when a person knows he/she has temporary or partial responsibility for an item, with the owner's consent or knowledge.
2. Knowledge of the existence of a substance	What is important is that the suspect knows of, or suspects the existence of a substance. If it was inside a container, it must be proved that the suspect knew about the container and that it contained a substance.

Both of these elements must be present in order to prove that the person was in possession of the substance. It is not sufficient for a person to have something in his/her pocket (ie control) if he/she is not aware it is there. Nor can a person be said to be in possession if he/she knows that a substance is in a particular bag, but the bag is not in that same person's custody or control. The situation is less straightforward if the substance was found on shared premises.

Possession can be actual (on his/her person), or constructive (eg under his/her control in a vehicle or house some distance away).

12.5.4 Exemptions permitting lawful possession of a controlled drug

Most people who are in possession of a controlled drug will be in unlawful possession. Exemptions are provided under the Misuse of Drugs Regulations 2001 and are made by the Home Secretary under s 7 of the Misuse of Drugs Act 1971. Possession is lawful for some workers during their employment, for example for suppliers to the pharmaceutical trade, and for medical practitioners as long as they keep proper prescribing records. Patients who have been prescribed controlled drugs are also provided for under the exemptions. Regulation 6 allows the police officers, police support employees, customs officers, and postal workers to possess drugs whilst acting in the course of their duties.

12.5.5 Unlawful possession of cannabis

In 2004 cannabis was reclassified to class C, but in 2009 it was returned to class B. With the aim of providing a consistent national approach during these periods of change, ACPO has produced guidance including various models of intervention for unlawful possession of cannabis. The current model (see 12.5.5.1) only applies to adults found in unlawful possession of cannabis for personal use.

12.5.5.1 Intervention model for the unlawful possession of cannabis

This is about providing a justifiable and proportionate response, and the intention is to send out the message that cannabis is harmful and illegal. Three levels of escalating intervention are provided for, but the ACPO guidance emphasizes that although discretion can be used at all times, arrest remains the first presumption. Cannabis warnings are covered in more detail in 12.5.5.2.

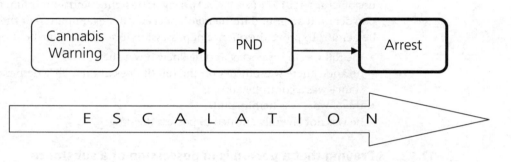

The model only applies to a person who:

- is aged 18 years or over and has verifiable personal details, for example name, date of birth, and address;
- is not vulnerable (see 13.2);
- is competent enough to grasp the meaning of the officer's questions and his/her own replies;
- is not under the influence of alcohol or drugs at the time a warning or a PND (Penalty Notice for Disorder, see 10.13.2) is issued;
- possesses an amount of cannabis only suitable for personal use (in the officer's judgement); and
- is not in possession of any other drug.

Suspects aged 17 years and under cannot be issued with a Cannabis Warning or a PND for unlawful possession of cannabis. They will have to be given a youth caution (see 10.13.4) or be prosecuted.

Aggravating factors must be taken into consideration when deciding which option to take in the intervention model. If there are no aggravating factors then a Cannabis Warning is the likely outcome. If there are one or more aggravating factors, then discretion should be used to decide whether to issue a PND or make an arrest.

Aggravating factors include a suspect who:

- was smoking cannabis in a public place or in the view of the public, for example at a sports ground, on a bus, near a pub, or on educational premises;
- is a repeat offender (other criminal offences) or someone who continually engages in anti-social behaviour; or
- appears not to recognize the seriousness of possessing cannabis.

The location where the person is found to be in possession of cannabis may also be an aggravating factor. This could be a previously identified 'hot spot' for anti-social behaviour due to cannabis use (eg a corner of a park) or any place young people are more likely to come into contact with cannabis users such as a playground or youth club.

The PNC can be used to find out whether the suspect has received a Cannabis Warning or a PND in relation to cannabis. Even if the suspect has never received a Cannabis Warning he/she can be offered a PND or be arrested, depending on the officer's discretion. If a warning or a PND has been previously received, then a Cannabis Warning cannot be used—a PND or arrest must be used instead. If he/she has already received a PND for cannabis the only option is to arrest (see the diagram of the escalation model). If the suspect does not admit the unlawful possession of cannabis, a PND can only be used if there is sufficient evidence (see 12.5.3) to prove the offence.

The large flowchart with the shaded boxes shows the main factors to take into account when dealing with suspects in possession of cannabis. Individual circumstances and the use of discretion mean that the diagram can only provide an indication of the more usual outcomes, and does not cover every eventuality. The shaded boxes relate only to the intervention model.

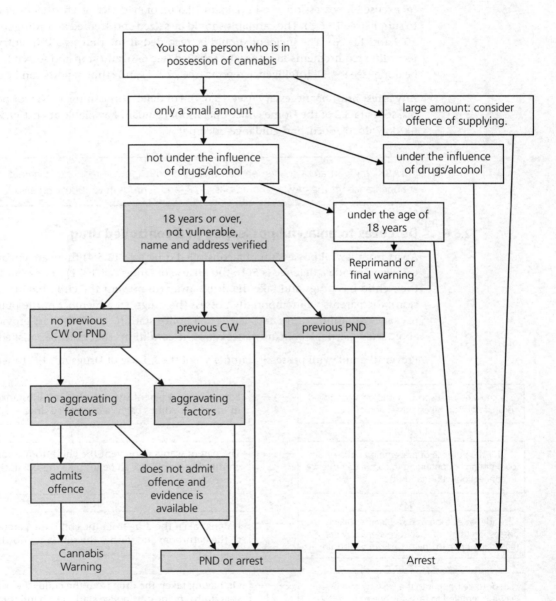

12.5.5.2 Cannabis Warnings

These can only be issued when there are no aggravating factors (see 12.5.5.1), and only to a person who is compliant with the procedure, admits to the offence, and has no previous records of Cannabis Warnings, PNDs, or convictions. The general principle stated in the current guidance is that no more than one Cannabis Warning should be issued to an individual; however, the previous guidance was slightly different and considered two warnings to be a cut-off point. Therefore, Cannabis Warnings issued after 26 January 2009 must be taken into account when deciding a level of intervention, whereas those issued before this date should be considered only as part of any previous offending history.

There is no formal group of words that make up a Cannabis Warning, but ACPO still recommend that the term 'cannabis warning' is used (rather than 'street warning'). The officer should tell the suspect that the cannabis warning will:

- be recorded and added to local police databases for future reference;
- produce a record of a detected crime for the purposes of statistics as a recordable crime;
- not amount to a criminal record or conviction; and
- lead to the issuing of a PND or arrest if he/she is found in unlawful possession of cannabis in the future.

12.5.5.3 Unlawful possession of small amounts of cannabis: practical aspects

For suspects in possession of small amounts of cannabis a police officer should investigate the suspected unlawful possession, remembering the obligations under the PACE Codes of Practice to protect the rights of the individual (see 10.3 on cautions), and determine if there is any lawful excuse for possession (see 12.5.4 and 12.5.6), or evidence of a further offence such as intent to supply (see 12.6.3). The cannabis should be seized and secured according to local policy (see 10.9 and 11.2.6). The incident should be recorded at the time as a PNB entry (see 10.2). The recording requirements must also be satisfied (see 6.8), and stop and search forms will need to be done (see 9.4.1). Intelligence reports (see 22.5.1) and crime reports can be completed later.

Any arrest must be 'necessary' (see 10.6.4). For details on issuing a PND for possessing cannabis, see para 3.2 of the Home Office operational guidance available at <http://www.justice.gov.uk/downloads/oocd/pnd-guidance-oocd.pdf>.

> **TASK 4** If you are a trainee police officer, find out the common street names, prices, and the appearance for the most common class A, B, and C drugs in your policing area.

12.5.6 Defences to unlawful possession of a controlled drug

Apart from lawful possession of a controlled drug (see 12.5.4) there are circumstances which can also provide a defence (s 5(4), the Misuse of Drugs Act 1971), for example if parents find their child has drugs and take the drugs away (to prevent the child having unlawful possession), the parents will temporarily possess the drugs. Or a member of the public might find a package containing drugs and take it to a police station. The flowchart provides more details about these particular circumstances and the conditions that must be satisfied.

Preventing unlawful possession under s 5 of the Misuse of Drugs Act 1971 means:

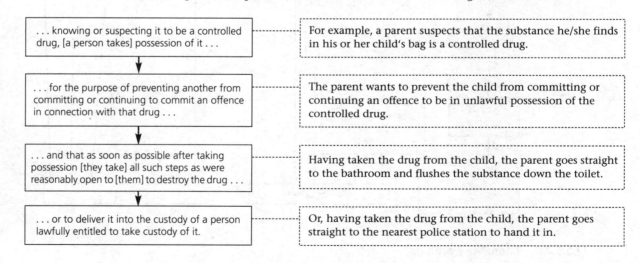

Other defences are available under s 28 of the Misuse of Drugs Act 1971. These relate to two main issues; the suspect's knowledge and beliefs about whether the substance was a controlled drug (s 28(3)(b)(i)) and whether the suspect was entitled to possess a particular controlled drug (s 28(3)(b)(ii)). The onus is on the suspect to prove that he/she did not know or suspect some relevant point of fact alleged by the prosecution. Trainee police officers are unlikely to be involved in this process.

12.5.7 **Mode of trial and penalty for unlawful possession of drugs**

Offences involving class A, B, or C drugs are triable either way and the penalty is imprisonment and or a fine. The lengths of prison sentences are shown in the table.

Under the Criminal Justice and Police Act 2001, unlawful possession of cannabis can also be dealt with by way of a PND for £80 (see 10.13.2 and 12.5.5).

Class	As a summary offence	As an indictable offence
A	Six months	Seven years
B	Three months	Five years
C	Three months	Two years

> **TASK 5** Establishing whether someone is in unlawful possession of controlled drugs is not always straightforward. It is relatively easy to identify the substance in question as a controlled drug but proving possession is more complicated. Consider the following three scenarios and try and decide whether possession has been established in each case.
>
> 1. Before going out to a party one night person E puts some cannabis into a wallet. He goes out and gets very drunk and can't remember the night's events. He returns home the next day and puts his coat containing the wallet back into his wardrobe. Some days later he puts the coat on again forgetting it contains the wallet with the cannabis. He is subsequently stopped and searched by the police and the cannabis is found. Is he guilty of unlawful possession?
>
> 2. During a s 23 search, controlled drugs in the form of tablets are found in the jeans pocket of person F. He claimed that the tablets had been prescribed to him by a doctor some months ago but that he had lost them and thought they had been destroyed when he had washed his jeans. As a consequence he obtained another prescription from his doctor for some more tablets. Later on, he finds the missing tablets at the back of a drawer and puts them in his jeans pocket where they are found by the police. Was he in unlawful possession of the tablets at the time?
>
> 3. Person G was entertaining visitors when a search warrant under s 23(3) of the Misuse of Drugs Act 1971 was executed. A small quantity of heroin was found on the sofa in between two guests, and G admitted to the police officers present that she was the owner. But when she was formally interviewed she withdrew the admission but provided information about what she claimed was the identity of the true owner of the heroin, and stated that one of her visitors probably had drugs in his possession in her flat and that another had been preparing to take heroin before the search took place. Are the circumstances sufficient for G to be in control of the drugs?

12.6 **Production and Supply of Controlled Drugs**

Drugs legislation has been carefully worded so that it is not only the illegal end user of controlled drugs who is subject to prosecution, but also (and perhaps more importantly) the people involved in supplying the drugs.

Possible defences to production and supply offences relate to proving possession and whether the substance in question actually is a controlled drug. The relevant legislation is in ss 4–6 of Misuse of Drugs Act 1971, but see also 12.5.6 on s 28 and other defences for possession.

12.6.1 **Production of a controlled drug**

Home Office Circular 82/1980 recommends that cultivation of cannabis is charged under s 4(2) as the charge of 'cultivation of cannabis' under s 6(2) does not allow for confiscation proceedings. The defences outlined in s 28 of the Misuse of Drugs Act 1971 (see 12.5.6) apply to both these offences.

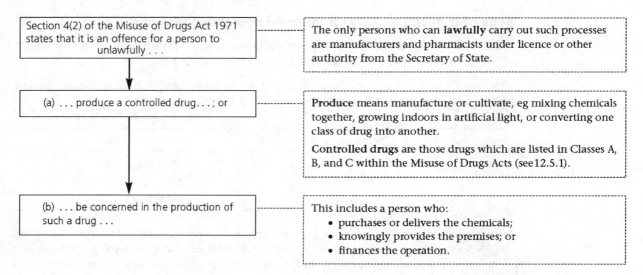

Section 4(2) of the Misuse of Drugs Act 1971 states that it is an offence for a person to unlawfully . . .

The only persons who can **lawfully** carry out such processes are manufacturers and pharmacists under licence or other authority from the Secretary of State.

(a) . . . produce a controlled drug. . . ; or

Produce means manufacture or cultivate, eg mixing chemicals together, growing indoors in artificial light, or converting one class of drug into another.

Controlled drugs are those drugs which are listed in Classes A, B, and C within the Misuse of Drugs Acts (see12.5.1).

(b) . . . be concerned in the production of such a drug . . .

This includes a person who:
- purchases or delivers the chemicals;
- knowingly provides the premises; or
- finances the operation.

Offences involving production of drugs are triable either way and the penalty is imprisonment and/or a fine. The lengths of prison sentences are shown in the following table.

Class	As a summary offence	As an indictable offence
A	Six months	Life
B	Six months	14 years
C	Three months	Five years

The s 4(2) offences in relation to a class A drug are 'trigger' offences under s 63B of the PACE Act 1984: a sample can be demanded from a person in police custody (see 25.6 on taking samples from people).

12.6.2 Supplying a controlled drug

This is covered under s 4(3) of the Misuse of Drugs Act 1971 as shown in the diagram.

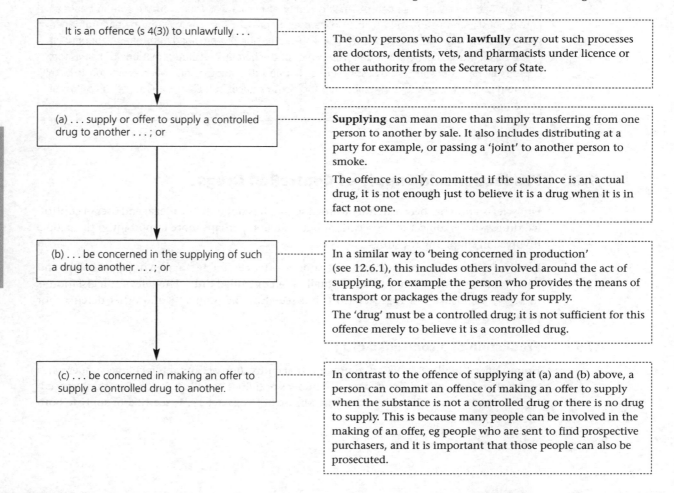

It is an offence (s 4(3)) to unlawfully . . .

The only persons who can **lawfully** carry out such processes are doctors, dentists, vets, and pharmacists under licence or other authority from the Secretary of State.

(a) . . . supply or offer to supply a controlled drug to another . . . ; or

Supplying can mean more than simply transferring from one person to another by sale. It also includes distributing at a party for example, or passing a 'joint' to another person to smoke.

The offence is only committed if the substance is an actual drug, it is not enough just to believe it is a drug when it is in fact not one.

(b) . . . be concerned in the supplying of such a drug to another . . . ; or

In a similar way to 'being concerned in production' (see 12.6.1), this includes others involved around the act of supplying, for example the person who provides the means of transport or packages the drugs ready for supply.

The 'drug' must be a controlled drug; it is not sufficient for this offence merely to believe it is a controlled drug.

(c) . . . be concerned in making an offer to supply a controlled drug to another.

In contrast to the offence of supplying at (a) and (b) above, a person can commit an offence of making an offer to supply when the substance is not a controlled drug or there is no drug to supply. This is because many people can be involved in the making of an offer, eg people who are sent to find prospective purchasers, and it is important that those people can also be prosecuted.

Specific Incidents

Under s 4A of the Misuse of Drugs Act 1971, a court must treat this offence more seriously if it was committed in or in the vicinity of a school, or the suspect used a courier who was under the age of 18 years. The defences outlined in s 28 of the Misuse of Drugs Act 1971 (see 12.5.6) apply to s 4(3).

The penalties are the same as for the production or supply of a controlled drug (see 12.6.1), and the offence is a trigger offence: a police officer can demand a sample from a suspect in custody.

12.6.3 Possession with intent to supply a controlled drug

Section 5(3) of the Misuse of Drugs Act 1971 states it is an offence for a person to:

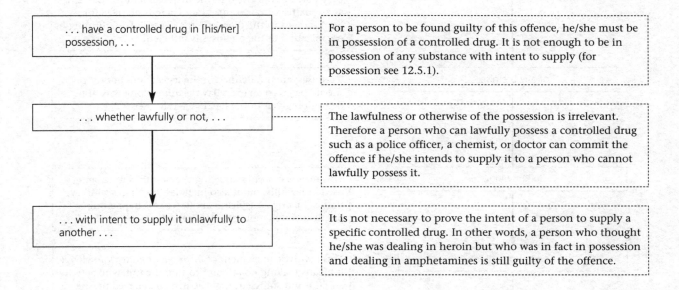

. . . have a controlled drug in [his/her] possession, . . .	For a person to be found guilty of this offence, he/she must be in possession of a controlled drug. It is not enough to be in possession of any substance with intent to supply (for possession see 12.5.1).
. . . whether lawfully or not, . . .	The lawfulness or otherwise of the possession is irrelevant. Therefore a person who can lawfully possess a controlled drug such as a police officer, a chemist, or doctor can commit the offence if he/she intends to supply it to a person who cannot lawfully possess it.
. . . with intent to supply it unlawfully to another . . .	It is not necessary to prove the intent of a person to supply a specific controlled drug. In other words, a person who thought he/she was dealing in heroin but who was in fact in possession and dealing in amphetamines is still guilty of the offence.

The defences outlined in s 28 of the Misuse of Drugs Act 1971 (see 12.5.6) apply to s 5(3). The penalties are the same as for the production of, supply, or intent to supply a controlled drug, and the s 4(3) offence is a trigger offence: a police officer can demand a sample from a suspect held in custody (see 12.6.1).

12.6.4 Occupier or manager of premises used for controlled drug offences

This offence (s 8 of the Misuse of Drugs Act 1971) concerns persons who occupy or are concerned in the management of a premises, and who knowingly permit or suffer any of the following activities to take place there:

(a) producing or attempting to produce a controlled drug;
(b) supplying, attempting to supply, or offering to supply a controlled drug to another;
(c) preparing opium for smoking;
(d) smoking cannabis, cannabis resin, or prepared opium.

There must be evidence that one of these activities has actually occurred (see *R v Auguste* [2003] EWCA Crim 3329). For example, in relation to (b) above, there must be evidence of a controlled drug actually being supplied on the premises: the simple existence of sufficient quantities and equipment for supplying controlled drugs is insufficient to prove the offence (see *Regina v McGee* [2012] EWCA Crim 613).

To be an 'occupier' the person does not have to be a tenant or owner, but needs to have sufficient control over the premises such that he/she could prevent drug-related activities. A student who pays for a room on campus would be regarded as an occupier. A person 'concerned in the management' does not have to have a legal interest in the premises, and would include a trespassing squatter (see *R v Tao* [1976] 3 All ER 65). A cleaner would be neither an occupier nor concerned in the management.

To 'knowingly permit or suffer' the activity would include having suspicions but choosing to take no action, and also trying to stop the activity but without success. The suspect does not need to know what type of controlled drug is involved.

Offences under s 8 are triable either way and the penalty is:

- summarily: a prescribed fine and/or imprisonment (six months for classes A and B, and three months for class C);
- on indictment: 14 years' imprisonment and/or fine.

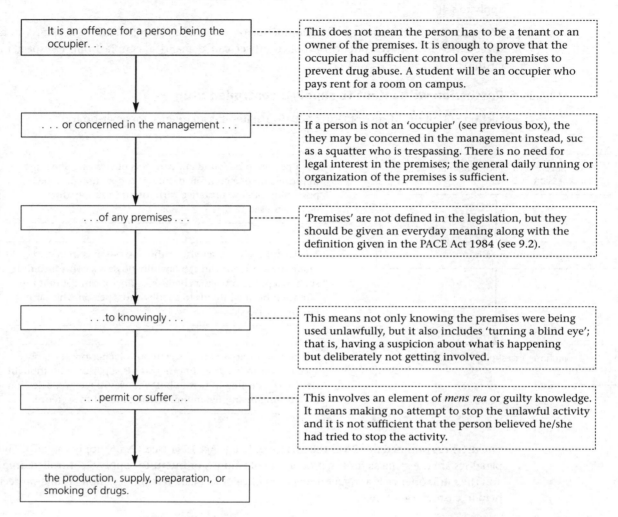

It is an offence for a person being the occupier. . .	This does not mean the person has to be a tenant or an owner of the premises. It is enough to prove that the occupier had sufficient control over the premises to prevent drug abuse. A student will be an occupier who pays rent for a room on campus.
. . . or concerned in the management . . .	If a person is not an 'occupier' (see previous box), the they may be concerned in the management instead, suc as a squatter who is trespassing. There is no need for legal interest in the premises; the general daily running or organization of the premises is sufficient.
. . .of any premises . . .	'Premises' are not defined in the legislation, but they should be given an everyday meaning along with the definition given in the PACE Act 1984 (see 9.2).
. . .to knowingly . . .	This means not only knowing the premises were being used unlawfully, but it also includes 'turning a blind eye'; that is, having a suspicion about what is happening but deliberately not getting involved.
. . .permit or suffer. . .	This involves an element of *mens rea* or guilty knowledge. It means making no attempt to stop the unlawful activity and it is not sufficient that the person believed he/she had tried to stop the activity.
the production, supply, preparation, or smoking of drugs.	

TASK 6

- Make a list of factors and circumstances that would provide reasonable grounds for suspecting a person is in unlawful possession of drugs with intent to supply.

- What would a police officer have to say to a person before carrying out a search under s 23 of the Misuse of Drugs Act 1971?

- Having found an unidentifiable substance, what are some of the reasons that would make it necessary to arrest the person?

12.7   Volatile Substance Abuse

Volatile Substance Abuse (VSA), also known as solvent abuse, provides some people with a quick and inexpensive form of intoxication. The substances are easily accessible and include household products such as aerosols, spray cans, and cigarette lighter refills. Other volatile substances abused by people include petrol, industrial adhesives (not household glues), and products containing Tetrachloroethlene (used in some dry-cleaning products) or alkyl nitrite room odourizers (known as 'poppers'). These substances are volatile—they evaporate quickly at room temperature to form vapours, allowing them to be inhaled.

According to the charity 'Re-Solv', VSA has killed more children under 15 than all other illegal drugs combined (Re-Solv, 2013). VSA is also present in adult populations. The abuse is often difficult to detect as its effects pass quickly, but signs include 'chemical smell, runny nose, watery eyes and rashes or spots around the nose and mouth' as well as 'throat irritation, nausea and "drunken", withdrawn, irritable or inattentive behaviour' (Re-Solv, 2013). People abuse volatile substances for a number a reasons such as curiosity and peer pressure, but it can also indicate the existence of underlying psychological problems for some individuals.

It is difficult to prevent VSA through control measures because many of the chemicals abused can be found in common household products. Controls exist mainly on the supply side, for example it is illegal:

- to sell a substance to anyone believed to be under the age of 18 if there is reasonable cause to think that the substance may be used for intoxication (Intoxicating Substances (Supply) Act 1985);
- to supply cigarette lighter refills containing butane to anyone under the age of 18 (Cigarette Lighter Refill (Safety) Regulations 1999);
- to sell spray paint to anyone under the age of 16 (s 54 of the Anti-Social Behaviour Act 2003);
- to sell nitrous oxide for inhalation (the Medicines Act 1968);
- to sell petrol to anyone under the age of 16 (this breach of licence conditions would be prosecuted under the Petroleum (Consolidation) Act 1928).

Although the consumption of volatile products is not in itself illegal, intoxicated behaviour may lead to anti-social behaviour or other forms of behaviour prohibited by law.

12.8 Answers to Tasks

TASK 1 Look at s 34(1) of the Criminal Justice Act 1972 to help with the answer.
- The health and safety of the individual is paramount—is she injured in any way?
- How drunk is she?
- What offence has she committed? Is she just drunk or drunk and disorderly?
- Is arrest necessary to prevent her from causing physical injury (to herself or others)?
- Can the matter be dealt with in another way?
- What other agencies could you involve?

Some forces have a local agreement whereby a person can be taken to an approved treatment centre for alcoholism. If this was the case the police officer could treat her as being in lawful custody for the purposes of the journey (s 34(1) of the Criminal Justice Act 1972).

TASK 2
- Introduce yourself, giving your name and the station you are from.
- Explain to him that you suspect he is under 18 years of age.
- Tell him that he is in a public place.
- Make clear to him that you wish him to surrender any intoxicating liquor in his possession and state his name and address, and that failure without reasonable excuse to comply with your requirement is an offence.

TASK 3 Some forces have a member of staff who is responsible for representing the police at applications for premises licences or renewals. He/she should be notified of incidents where suspects have been drinking excessively, and the information can then be taken into account when deciding on granting or renewing licences.

TASK 4 Some common unlawfully used controlled drugs are:
- **amphetamines** (speed, whizz, w, billy, uppers, phet, amph, wizz, white, sulphate, snow, sprint, bomb, base, paste, dexies). The average UK street price is £13 per gram;
- **cocaine** (coke, crack, charlie, sniff, white, ching, powder, snow white, snuff, rock, nose candy, okey cokey, fairy dust, bolivian marching powder, toot, wrap). The average UK street price is £46 per gram, and £16 for a 'rock' of crack cocaine weighing 0.25 grams;
- **heroin** (smack, crack, brown, gear, shit, jack, skag, henry, horse, needles); and

- **cannabis** (weed, skunk, pot, dope, bud, green, blow, hash, ganja, grass, draw, puff, gange, shit, spliff, wacky backy, pukka, rocky, joint, hashish, resin, doobie, gear, bush, smoke, leaf, stash, buddha, rasta pasta, chill, mary jane, to blaze, marijuana, squidgy black, rock, purple haze, sensimilia, hemp, herb, blow, soap, blunt). The average UK street price for cannabis resin is £27 per quarter ounce.

More information is available at <http://www.drugscope.org.uk/>.

TASK 5

1. Yes. In *R v Martindale* (1986) 84 Cr App R 31 (CA), Lord Laine stated that:

   Possession does not depend upon the alleged possessor's powers of memory. Nor does possession come and go as memory revives or fails. If it were to do so, a man with a poor memory would be acquitted, he with a good memory would be convicted.

2. Yes, his possession was lawful. The original possession of the tablets was lawful and the lawfulness continues with time (see *R v Buswell* [1972] 1 WLR 64).
3. No, she cannot be said to be in control of the drug. There is insufficient actual or physical control of the heroin in this situation (see *Adams v DPP* [2002] All ER (D) 125 (Mar)).

TASK 6 Factors and circumstances that would provide reasonable grounds for suspecting a person is in unlawful possession of drugs with intent to supply might include:

- intelligence that drugs are being supplied or used in that particular area;
- information on the descriptions of people supplying or using drugs in that area;
- behaviour of the person (eg is he/she trying to hide something? Or preparing to throw away something small, seemingly with the intention that you will not notice?); and
- behaviour of people who approach the person (eg do a number of individuals walk up to the person from different directions, exchange small items, and walk away again? Note that these may be very open acts to try and avoid attracting attention).

Before the search, the police officer must explain the purpose of the search, explain the grounds, tell the person about his/her entitlement to a copy of the record of search, show a warrant card if he/she is not in uniform, explain to the person that he/she is being detained for a search, state the legal search power title to be used (s 23 of the Misuse of Drugs Act), and provide the name of his/her police station and his/her (the officer's) name. This can be summarized by the mnemonic GO WISELY (see 9.4.1 for full details).

See 10.6.4 for the reasons that can apply for making an arrest.

Providing Protection and Support

13.1 Introduction

People often need protection, support, and guidance from a number of organizations, and the police service will often be tasked with the initial protection of young people, vulnerable people, missing persons, and other people who may lack the mental capacity to make decisions. In this chapter we explore the response of the police to these situations, and describe the procedures and available powers. The police inevitably come into contact with people with mental health issues, but they are not obliged to assume direct or indirect responsibility. Other partner agencies are often better equipped to deal with such issues and may have statutory responsibility for providing support and services, although the police will often assist (see the College of Policing, Authorised Professional Practice, particular the practice surrounding 'Engagement and communication', 'Major investigation and public protection', 'Public order', and 'Detention and custody'). We conclude with an examination of how the law seeks to prevent harm to animals.

13.2 Mentally Vulnerable People

When working in law enforcement, it is common to encounter people who behave in ways that may seem strange, or who seem to be unable to think clearly. They may be suffering from a mental illness with distorted thoughts and feelings, or may just find it hard to take in basic facts and make decisions, or they might be under the influence of drugs (illegal or otherwise). There is often an association between mental disorder and an impaired decision-making capacity. This incapacity may be transient during severe periods of illness, or more persistent during periods of enduring mental illness. In 2010, ACPO produced comprehensive guidance on responding to people with mental health problems or learning disabilities (NPIA, 2010a). In addition, the mental health charity MIND has published a good practice guide for the police (2013), and a guide ('a toolkit') for prosecutors and advocates (2010).

The Mental Health Act 1983 (MHA) is used in relation to people with mental illness, although for a person in a private place such as his/her home only some sections can be used by police officers. The Mental Capacity Act 2005 (MCA) is used if a person is incapable of making a decision and requires care for any other reason, such as a medical condition. The scenario in 13.2.4 illustrates this further.

A common misconception is that many people who suffer from mental disorder (mental illness) are also violent, but this is not the case: most pose no physical threat to others, but they may be confused or unable to cope. Police training will include guidance on how to recognize the symptoms of mental illness. Here we will examine the relevant legislation and parts of the MHA Code of Practice (Department of Health, 2008). Note that dependence on alcohol or drugs is not considered a disability or a disorder (s 1(3) MHA).

Learning disabilities cover a wide range of conditions with 'significant impairment of intelligence and social functioning' (s 1(4) MHA). With such a wide definition, officers need to assess each situation on an individual basis—there can be no general rules. Individuals with learning disabilities can be especially vulnerable. They are likely to have a limited understanding of police work and the justice system. Some may have difficulty recalling events, understanding questions, and communicating effectively. Others may acquiesce to suggestions of events and actions in order to appease the interviewer. It is therefore very important that individuals with learning disabilities are identified as such when giving witness statements, and that this information is passed to the CPS. You may also want to engage the help of a doctor or a mental health practitioner to help identify whether an individual has a learning disability. Support agencies such as Victim Support can provide assistance to individuals with mental disabilities, for example if they are asked to testify in court.

13.2.1 Interacting with mentally vulnerable people

Mental ill health includes a variety of disorders, including psychotic disorders (such as schizophrenia), mood disorders (such as depression or bipolar disorder), and a variety of personality and anxiety disorders (such as panic attacks and phobias). To some extent the requirements for interacting with a person with mental ill health are similar to what is required for a person with a learning disability. It is important to remember, however, that individuals with learning disabilities, like any other member of the public, may or may not experience mental ill health and the two concepts should not be confused.

It is important that trainee police officers learn to deal with these situations effectively and maintain their own and others' safety. Factors such as fear, paranoia, confusion, anger, hearing voices, and frustration may lead to aggressive behaviour and you need to be aware of ways to minimize their impact. For example, when dealing with individuals displaying signs of mental ill health, pay careful attention to potential signs of aggression such as sweating, clenched fists, eyes moving rapidly, frowning, increased reaction to sound, raised voices, and threats.

When interacting with individuals experiencing mental ill health you should avoid any physical contact with them unless you are sure that it will not be perceived as threatening. You should maintain an adequate distance and you may want to remove your headwear, as this may be seen as threatening. However, you should be cautious in your approach and maintain yourself in a safe position. You should explain what you are doing and repeat yourself to ensure that you are being understood. Do not act in a rushed way, stay calm and assess the situation with time. Do not reinforce behaviour that results from mental illness (eg by acknowledging that the delusions from someone with schizophrenia are real) but show understanding towards someone's feelings of distress. Be respectful and do not stare.

Establishing good communication may be difficult, but is essential when dealing with a person with mental ill health. Keep the person informed of your actions instead of leaving them to guess what you are doing or likely to do. Individuals with mental ill health may be unpredictable and it is important that they are prevented from engaging in harmful behaviour. Call for further assistance but ask for lights and sirens to be turned off. A Medic Alert bracelet could provide useful information and the individual should be asked about it. Ask the person why they are upset and what they want you to do. Avoid challenging or reasoning against delusions. Use a calm low-pitched tone and reassure the individual of what you are trying to achieve. Keep noise to a minimum and ensure that only one officer talks at a time, and do not whisper to your colleagues. Also, avoid using your radio where possible. Consider taking a step backwards to show you are giving the person space, move slowly, and as little as possible, but keep your hands visible. If necessary, reduce your height to appear less threatening. Make a visual check for weapons and remove anything dangerous, particularly sharp objects, from the individual's reach. Remove any onlookers from the scene.

There may be situations when you may need to use force, for example to ensure that the individual experiencing mental ill health does not harm him/herself. But make sure that it is only used as a last resort and that it is absolutely necessary and proportional to the situation you are dealing with. You may also need to use force to protect the public and to protect yourself. In both situations, the force must be necessary and reasonable, and consideration should be given to the strategies to minimize aggression, discussed previously, before deploying the use of force.

It is common for local policies to be established between law enforcement agencies and practitioners to ensure a fair and adequate treatment of individuals experiencing mental ill health. You may want to familiarize yourself with the local policy in your area to ensure that you can provide best service in such situations.

13.2.2 Disturbed behaviour in public places

It is not an offence to be mentally disordered in a place to which the public have access (see 9.2 for further information on the definition of a public place). There are a great many people who live in the community who suffer from such conditions who cope well with their everyday lives. However, if such a person is in a public place and in need of immediate care and control, a police officer has the power to remove such a person and take him/her to a place of safety (s 136 MHA).

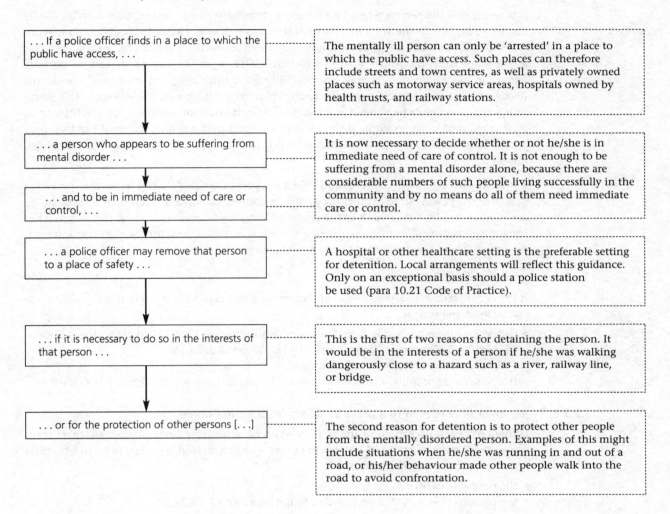

. . . If a police officer finds in a place to which the public have access, . . .	The mentally ill person can only be 'arrested' in a place to which the public have access. Such places can therefore include streets and town centres, as well as privately owned places such as motorway service areas, hospitals owned by health trusts, and railway stations.
. . . a person who appears to be suffering from mental disorder . . .	It is now necessary to decide whether or not he/she is in immediate need of care of control. It is not enough to be suffering from a mental disorder alone, because there are considerable numbers of such people living successfully in the community and by no means do all of them need immediate care or control.
. . . and to be in immediate need of care or control, . . .	
. . . a police officer may remove that person to a place of safety . . .	A hospital or other healthcare setting is the preferable setting for detenition. Local arrangements will reflect this guidance. Only on an exceptional basis should a police station be used (para 10.21 Code of Practice).
. . . if it is necessary to do so in the interests of that person . . .	This is the first of two reasons for detaining the person. It would be in the interests of a person if he/she was walking dangerously close to a hazard such as a river, railway line, or bridge.
. . . or for the protection of other persons [. . .]	The second reason for detention is to protect other people from the mentally disordered person. Examples of this might include situations when he/she was running in and out of a road, or his/her behaviour made other people walk into the road to avoid confrontation.

The person cannot be arrested under s 24 of PACE if no offence has been committed. However the Code of Practice (para 10.45) states that a person who is removed under s 136 of the MHA is deemed to be 'arrested' for the purposes of the PACE Act 1984, and therefore a police officer has a power to search him/her under s 32 PACE (see 10.8.3).

Hospital or ambulance transport will be used if a person needs to be transported to a place of safety (as set out in agreed local policies). Only exceptionally, such as in cases of extreme urgency or where there is a risk of violence, should police transport be used (Code of Practice, para 10.17).

An appropriate adult will need to be present when interviewing 'mentally vulnerable' or 'mentally disordered' individuals (see 24.4.2). There are exceptions to this requirement, namely if there is a likelihood of interference with evidence related to an offence, an individual, or property, or may lead to alerting someone else suspected of committing an offence or the inability to recover property obtain from an illegal act. An officer of the rank of superintendent or above must approve the interview without an appropriate adult and that it will not represent harm to the individual (PACE Code C).

13.2.2.1 Detention in a place of safety

A person removed from a public place to a place of safety may be detained there but only for examination and assessment by a registered medical practitioner, being interviewed by an approved social worker, or for making any necessary arrangements for his/her treatment or care. The detention period must not exceed 72 hours.

13.2.3 Disturbed behaviour in private places

A police officer might need to help or restrain a mentally disordered person in a private place, such as the person's home. The powers of removal and detention are not the same as in a public place.

If it seems that the person might be a danger to him/herself or to others, then a police officer can try to explain the need for treatment. If the person does not agree to this, then police control should be contacted to request the attendance of an AMHP. A police officer should remain at the scene until the AMHP arrives. Once an AMHP begins to assess a person for possible detention he/she assumes overall responsibility for coordinating the process of assessment (Code of Practice, para 4.40), and for arranging transport to hospital if required. The police officer may leave once he/she has provided the relevant information unless the AMHP requests further assistance, for example if the patient is violent or dangerous (Code of Practice, para 11.18). The AMHP might ask for assistance during the transportation of the patient to hospital, but see 13.2.3.2.

If it seems that an AMHP is not required, then the person can be detained in order to prevent a breach of the peace, but remember the particular conditions which must be met relating to the use of force (see 14.3 on 'breach of the peace'). There may be reasons to arrest the person if he/she is suspected of committing an offence, but arrest will not necessarily be the most appropriate way of dealing with a mentally disordered person.

13.2.3.1 Using force to enter

If the person refuses to let anyone in and there is no one else present to grant entry, then force can be used, but only if:

- the police officer has a magistrate's warrant (granted under s 135 MHA) authorizing a search to remove persons believed to be suffering from mental disorder;
- there is a breach of the peace (see 14.3); or
- it is to save life or limb or to prevent serious damage to property (s 17(1)(e) PACE, see 9.5).

13.2.3.2 Removing the person to a place of safety from his/her home

If there has been no breach of the peace and no offences have been committed, there is no power available under the MHA to detain or convey a person from a private place to a hospital (or other place of safety) unless:

- the person consents;
- the person is 'sectioned' for admission to hospital (see 13.2.3.3); or
- a magistrate's warrant (see 13.2.3.1) already exists for that private place.

If an AMHP arranges for the detention of a person and his/her removal to hospital, the police may be involved in transportation but only for more challenging patients. The extent of such police involvement will be set out in locally agreed policies (Code of Practice, para 1.19).

13.2.3.3 'Sectioning'

This is an unofficial term normally associated with the process carried out by an AMHP and medical practitioner(s) in a person's home or another private place. If a person clearly requires urgent psychiatric hospital treatment, but will not seek it voluntarily and is a danger to him/herself or to others, then he/she can be 'sectioned' (the term is used with reference to a section of the MHA). The application is made by an AMHP or the nearest relative, and is considered by two medical health practitioners (or just one in an emergency). If the application is agreed, a police officer may be asked to help remove the person to hospital (but see 13.2.3.2), by force if necessary (s 6 MHA). It is essential that a 'section application form' is completed and signed prior to any such police involvement.

13.2.4 The Mental Capacity Act 2005

The Mental Capacity Act 2005 (MCA) provides a broad legal framework which aims to protect vulnerable people aged 16 years or over (s 2(5)) who do not have the capacity (ability) to make their own decisions. (This could be through illness, unconsciousness, alcohol, drugs, or a severe learning disability that has been present since birth.) The Act also empowers and offers protection to carers and others (such as police officers) who find themselves involved in the protection of vulnerable people. Of particular interest is s 5, which provides the power to carry out acts related to the care or treatment (including restraint) of a person who lacks capacity. The MCA Code of Practice (Department for Constitutional Affairs, 2007) is available online. It provides guidance on how the Act should be interpreted, and is not just for police officers and health care professionals.

As you read on about the meaning of the term 'capacity' and making decisions, you might find it useful to consider how the Act might apply in practice; one such scenario is presented here from the perspective of a police officer.

> Two police officers have been asked by a paramedic team to attend a bedsit in town. An extremely thin and naked man is lying in bed with several open wounds on his body which look as if they could have been caused by hypodermic needles. He appears heavily intoxicated, and is suspected of using controlled drugs. Blood-filled syringes are strewn all around the bed and the floor of the room and the man appears to be bleeding from body orifices. The police officers consider the health and safety of the people around them as a priority so they and the paramedics don protective clothing and remove dangerous and contagious items to a toxic chemical receptacle and a 'sharps box'. The paramedics have tried to persuade the man to go to hospital but every time they have got close to him he has mumbled and moved away violently. The police officers also try to communicate with him, but without success. They must now decide how to help him, and under which legislation.
>
> In these circumstances the use of the Mental Health Act 1983 is inappropriate partly because the person is not in a public place (and so s 136 would not apply), but also because the man is in need of immediate medical and not psychiatric care. Although he might be suffering from a temporary mental disorder, it is his inability to make a decision and gain medical attention that is the immediate concern. The use of the Mental Capacity Act in these circumstances would seem logical, so that he can be transported to hospital for medical treatment.

13.2.4.1 General principles underlying the Mental Capacity Act 2005

Section 1(1) of the MCA provides some key principles, for example that a person:

- must be treated as if he/she has capacity (see 13.2.4.2) unless it can be established otherwise (s 1(2));
- must not be treated as incapable of making a decision unless all practicable steps have been taken to help him/her to do so, without success (s 1(3)); and
- must not be treated as if he/she is unable to make a decision just because he/she is known to have made an unwise decision previously (s 1(4)).

The Act also specifies that any decision or action that is taken must be in the person's best interests (s 1(5)) and must avoid (as far as possible) interfering with his/her rights and freedom (s 1(6)).

13.2.4.2 Judging a person's mental capacity

Capacity is the ability to take in information and use that information to make decisions. A lack of capacity could be caused by an impairment or disturbance in the functioning of the mind or brain (s 2(1)), for example through a learning disability, dementia, brain damage, or toxic confusion caused by drugs or another noxious substance. The lack of capacity could be permanent or temporary (s 2(2)). Of course, any evaluation can only be made on the balance of probabilities.

The process of judging of a person's capacity will focus on the person's ability to make decisions. Section 3 of the Act provides specific guidance on how to judge a person's ability to make a decision. No reference can be made to the person's age or appearance, nor should any unjustified assumptions be made based solely on the person's condition or behaviour (s 2(3)). A functional test may be used to check, for example, if he/she is able to do any of the following:

- understand and retain any information relevant to a decision;
- use information to help make a decision; or
- inform another person of a decision.

Specific Incidents

The means of communication used by either party is not important; it could be talking, writing or typed text, a sign language, or other gestures.

13.2.4.3 Acting on behalf of a person who lacks capacity

Under s 4 of the MCA the decision made and any subsequent action must be in the person's best interests. He/she must be encouraged to participate as fully as possible in any act or decision, and all reasonably practicable steps should be taken to achieve this. The likelihood of the person having the capacity at some point in the future must be considered, and if there is no immediate need to make a particular decision and the person is likely to regain the capacity to make the decision, then making it should be delayed until he/she has recovered sufficiently.

If the person cannot make decisions and therefore lacks capacity, a decision might need to be made on his/her behalf.

As far as possible, the person's wishes and feelings should be considered, especially his/her beliefs and values from the past (when he/she might have had a greater capacity than at the present time). The views of the following people should also be taken into account:

- his/her carer;
- anyone else he/she would like to be consulted; and/or
- anyone with power of attorney or a deputy appointed by a court.

Actions carried out in connection with the care or treatment of a person do not incur any liability (s 5) if prior to those acts, reasonable steps have been taken to establish that the person lacks capacity, and it is reasonably believed that the actions are in the person's best interests. If a decision relates to life-sustaining treatment, any consideration that a person should be allowed to die should be avoided.

If the actions are resisted (despite efforts to communicate and to encourage participation) restraint may be needed. However, it may only be used if it is reasonably believed to be necessary in order to prevent harm to him/her and the restraint is proportional to the likelihood and seriousness of that harm (s 6).

Actions defined as restraint under s 6 include using force (or threatening to use it) in order to apply care or treatment, and restricting a person's liberty of movement, whether or not he/she resists. However, such restraint does not include depriving a person of his/her liberty within the meaning of Article 5 of the ECHR, or contravening a decision made by a court or a person with a relevant power of attorney.

13.2.4.4 Applying the Mental Capacity Act 2005

In the scenario at the start of 13.2.4, all practicable steps to help the man have been unsuccessful. The attending police officers and paramedics believe he needs urgent treatment in hospital. On the balance of probabilities he is suffering from toxic confusion which has caused an impairment or disturbance of his mind or brain. He is therefore unlikely to have the capacity to make the decision to go to hospital and appears to be incapable of understanding the information relevant to the decision—that he is seriously ill and needs treatment. The police officers and paramedics have tried to communicate with him and to encourage him to participate in making the decision to go to hospital but their efforts have failed. It is unlikely that there is any information pertaining to any of his family friends, or carers (or indeed if he has any), and there is no indication of how he might have wished to be treated when he had capacity.

The police officers and paramedics have taken all reasonable steps required to establish that he does in fact lack capacity, and that he cannot make the relevant decision. Therefore they need to make a decision on his behalf. The least restrictive action or decision to avoid interfering with his rights and freedom is to ensure he receives hospital treatment. They judge that the least restraint required under the circumstances is to help him onto a stretcher for transportation to hospital.

13.2.4.5 Ill-treatment or neglect of a person who lacks capacity

Some people have particular caring or legal responsibilities for an individual who lacks capacity, and may also have a power of attorney. It is an offence under s 44 of the MCA for any such carer or responsible person to ill-treat or wilfully neglect the relevant individual.

The offence is triable either way and the penalty is a fine or imprisonment (summarily 12 months, and five years on indictment).

> **TASK 1**
> 1. What is your local force's policy in terms of the use of s 136 MHA powers?
> 2. A police officer is called to the home of the parents of a young man (over 18) who seems to be suffering from a mental disorder. On arrival, the parents inform her that he is in his bedroom holding onto the door handle to stop anyone opening the door. Using the minimum force necessary (and limiting your answers to the Mental Health Act 1983):
>   (a) how could she gain entrance for the parents, and
>   (b) what options are available should she decide that the young man is in need of medical attention in relation to his apparent mental disorder?

13.3 Safeguarding Children

The Children Act 1989 was seen as an important development in safeguarding the welfare of children in the UK. Its accent upon encouraging multi-agency working and supporting children and families heralded an approach to child welfare that made children the primary concern. This also led to the 'Working together to safeguard children' national guidance. However, cases such as the tragic death of Victoria Climbié demonstrated that more needed to be done to protect children from harm. The Victoria Climbié inquiry, headed by Lord Laming (2003) provided a number of key recommendations designed to ensure thorough investigation of potential crimes, proper training for investigators, and appropriate and effective inter-agency working. In response to the Laming recommendations, the government produced 'Every Child Matters', and eventually the Children Act 2004. These promoted child welfare, and inter-agency working, placing statutory obligations upon local authorities to cooperate with other agencies. The role of child commissioner was created, and Local Safeguarding Children Boards (LSCBs) were set up in regions throughout the country. The role of LSCBs was to ensure that clear guidance and procedures were in place, and to provide multi-agency training.

Note that the age definition of a child in the Children Act 1989 is any person under the age of 18 (s 105). Legislation often refers to children or young people of a particular age, for example 'a child under the age of 12'.

13.3.1 Investigating child abuse

Each police force will have a specialist Child Abuse Investigation Unit. Whilst there may be regional differences in the exact nature and scope of their work, these teams will usually be staffed by nationally trained investigators (trained in ICIDP or equivalent), who will have also undertaken the National Specialist Child Abuse Investigation Development Programme (SCAIDP). Naturally, some officers will be working towards achieving accreditation in these areas. There is an expectation that all officers interviewing children in relation to abuse will be trained to a very high standard in witness interviewing.

Once a referral is made to such a team, either from an internal notification or from an external agency (ie from one of the social services), the investigators will decide what type of investigation to undertake. These may often begin as joint agency investigations, and where criminal offences are suspected the police will take a lead role.

According to s 47 of the Children Act 1989, the local authority has a duty to investigate where it believes that a child might be suffering from significant harm. The police have certain powers under s 46 of the same Act in relation to police protection (see 13.3.3). The first consideration will be to secure the welfare of a child or children, following which a thorough criminal investigation can take place. At the same time other agencies will work to assure the current and future welfare of the child.

It is important to stress that specialist units are available to assist trainee officers with decision-making where a child's welfare is a concern. There are many examples of cases where the police become involved with children where child abuse might be an underlying factor. Trainee officers need to be aware of a range of incidents that may be associated with child abuse, such as:

- domestic abuse;
- missing children, including those truanting from school;

- children engaged in criminality, including bullying and abusing others;
- children abusing animals;
- children involved in sexual exploitation or prostitution;
- parental drug or alcohol abuse.

13.3.2 Protecting children from harm

Children are sometimes exposed to significant harm by their parents, relatives, and other people involved in their care and supervision. Harm can be defined in a number of ways. The Children Act 1989 (s 31(9)) states that harm means 'ill-treatment or the impairment of health or development, including for example, impairment suffered from seeing or hearing the ill-treatment of another' (eg ill-treatment of a sibling or parent). It further suggests that ill-treatment includes 'sexual abuse and forms of ill-treatment which are not physical'. ACPO *Guidance on Investigating Child Abuse and Safeguarding Children* (2nd edn) (2009) on the other hand categorizes child abuse into four distinct types: physical, emotional, sexual, and neglect.

Some of the legislation in the Children and Young Persons Act 1933 (CYPA) is considered here and in 13.1.1.2. The Offences Against the Person Act 1861 and the Sexual Offences Act 2003 are also relevant (see Chapters 15 and 17 respectively).

13.3.2.1 The offence of child cruelty

An offence is committed by a person aged 16 or over who is responsible for caring for a child under 16 if he/she wilfully 'assaults, ill-treats, neglects, abandons or exposes' the child or causes (or procures) him/her to be treated in such a way, if this is likely to cause the child or young person unnecessary suffering or 'injury to health' (s 1(1) of the CYPA). The 'injury to health' includes:

- physical injury or loss of 'sight, hearing, limb or organ of the body'; or
- psychological problems such as 'mental derangement'.

The offence is triable either way and the penalty is a fine or imprisonment (summarily six months, and ten years on indictment).

13.3.2.2 Cigarettes and young people

A constable in uniform has a duty to seize any cigarettes, tobacco, or cigarette papers in the possession of a young person who is smoking in any street or public place (s 7(3) of the CYPA). This applies for any young person who is or appears to be younger than 16. Any seized items should be disposed of according to local force policies and procedures.

Selling cigarettes, cigarette papers, or tobacco to young people under the age of 18 years is an offence under s 7(1) of the CYPA. However, shopkeepers may be relieved to know that under s 7(1A) it is a defence if it can be proved that he/she 'took all reasonable precautions and exercised all due diligence to avoid the commission of the offence'. The offence is triable summarily and the penalty is a fine.

Should a person be convicted of a s 7(1) or 7(2) offence on two or more occasions within two years a magistrates' court can apply a restriction order under s 12. This bans the offender from selling or managing premises for selling tobacco-related products. It is a summary offence for a person to knowingly contravene such an order; the penalty is a fine.

13.3.2.3 Injuries to children from heating appliances

Carers have a responsibility to ensure that children are kept safe when heating appliances are in use. Under s 11 of the CYPA a person over 16 commits an offence if a child under 12 is killed or suffers serious injury because the carer allowed 'the child to be in a room containing an open fire grate or any heating appliance'. The appliance must have been such that it was 'liable to cause injury to a person by contact with it' and 'not sufficiently protected to guard against the risk of being burnt or scalded without taking reasonable precautions against that risk'. The penalty for this summary offence is a fine.

13.3.3 Police protection

The Children Act 1989 provides police officers with the powers to take children under 18 who are at risk of significant harm into police protection. Any child's welfare is paramount and officers should take action if they fear that significant harm is likely to occur if no action is taken. It will be matter for a police officer to decide whether or not a child would be likely to suffer significant harm if no action was taken. However, Home Office Circular 17/2008 states that police protection:

> is an emergency power and should only be used when necessary, the principle being that wherever possible the decision to remove a child/children from a parent or carer should be made by a court. (para 15)

Apart from in exceptional circumstances (eg an imminent threat to a child's welfare), no child should be taken into police protection until the initiating officer (see 13.3.3.2) has seen the child and assessed the circumstances. A child can be in police protection for up to 72 hours (s 46(6) of the Children Act 1989).

Where possible, officers should speak with the child establishing what, when, where, and who was involved, restricting themselves to these questions to avoid 'contaminating' any future interviews. The responses should be recorded word for word. Once officers have secured the safety and well-being of the child, the case should be referred to the Specialist Child Abuse Investigation Unit or its equivalent (see 13.3.1).

13.3.3.1   Procedure for police protection

Section 46(1) of the Children Act 1989 states that:

> where [a police officer has] reasonable cause to believe that a child would otherwise be likely to suffer significant harm, [he/she] may . . .
>
> (a) remove [the child] to suitable accommodation and keep [him/her] there; or
> (b) take all reasonable steps to ensure that [his/her] removal from a hospital, or other place, in which [he/she] is accommodated, is prevented.

There are two separate and distinct roles for the police in relation to police protection: the initiating officer and the designated officer (Home Office Circular 17/2008). The **initiating officer** takes the child into police protection, undertakes the initial enquiries, and completes a Police Protection Form as soon as possible. The **designated officer** will have at least the rank of inspector and cannot be the initiating officer for the same case. He/she must independently overview the circumstances in which the child was taken into protection.

13.3.3.2   The role of the initiating officer

Under s 46(3) of the Children Act 1989, having taken a child into police protection the initiating officer must as soon as is reasonably practicable:

(a) inform the local authority where the child was found, of the police protection steps that have been taken (and are proposed to be taken) concerning the child, and the reasons for taking these actions;
(b) tell the authority in which the child usually lives ('the appropriate authority') where he/she is now being accommodated;
(c) inform the child (if he/she appears capable of understanding) about the steps taken with respect to him/her and the reasons, and about any further police protection steps that may be taken;
(d) try and establish the wishes and feelings of the child;
(e) ensure that a designated officer has been assigned for the case; and
(f) arrange for the child to be moved to local authority-provided accommodation ('suitable accommodation' (see 13.3.3.4), if the child is not already in such a place.

In addition, as soon as is reasonably practicable, the initiating officer must contact the adults who have been caring for the child (s 46(4)). As well as the child's parents, this would include every person who has parental responsibility for the child (see 13.3.3.3) and any other person with whom the child was living immediately before being taken into police protection. The adults who have most recently been caring for the child must be told about the police protection steps taken (or planned) concerning the child, and the reasons.

13.3.3.3   The meaning of 'parental responsibility'

In s 3(1) of the Children Act 1989 parental responsibility means 'all the rights, duties, powers, responsibilities and authority which by law a parent of a child has in relation to that child and [his/her] property'. It can be held by the parents, the step-parents, and in certain circumstances, by other people or administrative bodies such as a local authority. The question of who has parental responsibility is dealt with in ss 2 and 3 of the Children Act 1989. The key points are:

- If the father and mother were married to each other when the child was born, they will each have parental responsibility (s 2(1)). (The rule of law that a father is the natural guardian of his legitimate child has been abolished (s 2(4)).)
- If the father and mother were not married to each other when the child was born, the mother will have parental responsibility, as will the father if the child was jointly registered after 1 December 2003 (s 2(2)).
- More than one person can have parental responsibility for the same child at the same time (s 2(5)) and each may act alone to meet that responsibility (s 2(7)).
- A person who has parental responsibility for a child at any time does not cease to have that responsibility simply because another person acquires such responsibility for that child (s 2(6)).

The spirit of the legislation is that all the parties including the parents, the child, and the local authority must be kept informed and given reasons for any actions. The child's wishes must be listened to but do not necessarily have to be acted upon.

13.3.3.4 Suitable accommodation

A definition of suitable accommodation is given in Home Office Circular 44/2003 as local authority accommodation, a registered children's home, or foster care. Alternatively, if the designated officer and social services consider it appropriate, the child may also be placed with relatives or other appropriate carers. The child may also be taken to hospital if he/she requires medical attention.

The circular also emphasizes that a child under police protection should not be taken to a police station unless there is absolutely no alternative, and under no circumstances should he/she be taken into the custody suite or cell area.

TASK 2 Jo is a single parent struggling to care for 4-year-old Sam. The child has been ill, and Jo does not want to take any more time off work. Her parents often care for Sam while Jo is at work.

However, on one occasion the grandparents are unavailable to supervise Sam. Jo realizes that there is no food in the house and, when Sam falls asleep, Jo decides to go to buy some food at the supermarket. During the journey, Jo's car breaks down.

Sam awakes and is distraught. Having heard the child screaming hysterically, the neighbours call the police. Although the officer can clearly hear Sam inside, all the doors and windows are shut and Sam refuses to open the door.

1. What power of entry, if any, is available?
2. What offence might Jo have committed?

13.4 Missing Persons

The vast majority of absent or missing persons are found very quickly and have suffered no harm (or the report turns out to be unfounded). A few are found dead after many weeks, and some are never found. ACPO (2013, p 5) now use the following definitions:

- 'Absent'—a person not at a place where he/she is expected or required to be.
- 'Missing'—anyone whose whereabouts cannot be established and where the circumstances are out of character or the context suggests he/she might be subject of crime or at risk of harm to him or herself or another.

(Note, however, that these definitions have been adopted by 14 police forces in the UK with the remainder still using the older ACPO definition of 'missing'.) A person will be categorized as 'absent' if their disappearance does not feature with any apparent risk or they are simply not where they should be. In these circumstances the police are not likely to launch an investigation. However, 'absent' cases must be carefully monitored and if the level of risk increases, an escalation to the category of 'missing' should be considered. The onus is to view 'going absent' as a possible indicator of potentially something else, and not just as an event in its own right. For example, a child might go absent because he/she is being abused at home, and in such circumstances the safe recovery of the child might be just the start of further investigations.

There are a number of reasons for a person to 'go absent or missing'. These include:

- children or young people (predominantly teenage girls) who run away from home, normally for one or two days, often because of some recent or chronic issues at home. This is the single biggest demographic group of absent or missing persons (NPIA, 2010d, p 11);
- children who are missing through abduction (either by a non-custodial parent, direct physical abduction by a stranger, or through other means such as internet grooming (see 17.7.2.4));
- adults (predominantly men) who go absent probably in an attempt to escape from problems in their home lives. These cases are much less likely to be resolved quickly;
- vulnerable adults such as the aged and the mentally ill who become lost;
- adults who have been abducted, for example for purposes of sexual assault or people trafficking.

Missing person incidents sometimes become critical incidents (see 11.5), requiring the support of services other than the local force. A search for a missing person can entail a considerable expenditure of resources and time, including rural and urban searches, dragging of waterways, and exhaustive enquiries, particularly if the missing person is in some way vulnerable, such as a child or a mentally ill adult. Some investigations reveal a criminal aspect to the disappearance, and this can involve a major crime unit (or equivalent), especially if the circumstances involve a suspicious death.

The national policy on the police response to 'misper' incidents was extensively redrafted in the light of the Soham murders in 2002. That case highlighted the reliance of smaller police forces on 'mutual aid' for large-scale searches. This is part of the argument for merging forces into larger organizations which are capable of mounting such searches independently.

13.4.1 Missing person enquiries

The requirements of each case are specific to the case, but there are standard considerations, not least of which is to identify whether the person is 'missing' or 'absent' (see 13.4).

One of the first things to be done in a 'misper' (missing person) enquiry, is to conduct a risk assessment. Information is required about the person and his/her circumstances prior to the disappearance, particularly any factors which indicate vulnerability. Some of what follows is drawn from ACPO (2005a, updated 2010a).

The majority of cases involving missing persons relate to missing children, so a thorough knowledge of the procedures related to the disappearance of a child is vital. The main guidance is to be found in:

- 'Missing Children and Adults—A Cross Government Strategy' (Home Office, 2011b);
- 'Guidance on the Management, Recording and Investigation of Missing Persons' (ACPO, 2010c); and
- 'Interim Guidance on the Management, Recording and Investigation of Missing Persons 2013' (ACPO, 2013).

All these documents are available online.

13.4.1.1 Questions to ask about the missing person

The personal details of the missing person need to be considered. Is he/she, for example, vulnerable in any way? The disappearance of a child (ie under 18) is always be medium- or high-risk, and concern would be even higher for a child who was on the Child Protection Register.

Police officers will complete a checklist such as:

Factor	Yes/No/Unknown
1. Is the person likely to self-harm or attempt suicide?	
2. Is the person likely to be the subject of a crime in progress, eg abduction?	
3. Is the person vulnerable due to age, infirmity, or any other factor?	
4. Are the weather conditions inclement to the extent that this would seriously increase the risk to health, especially where the missing person is a child or an elderly person?	
5. Does the missing person need essential medication or treatment not readily available to them?	

Factor	Yes/No/Unknown
6. Does the missing person have any physical illness, disability, or mental health problems?	
7. Does the person have the ability to interact safely with others in an unknown environment?	
8. Has the person been involved in a violent, homophobic, and/or racist incident or confrontation immediately prior to his/her disappearance?	
9. Has the person been subject to recent bullying?	
10. Has the person previously disappeared and suffered or been exposed to harm?	

If a person had left intentionally then items he/she may have taken would be missing (are credit cards or money missing?). He/she might be involved with crime or have employment or financial problems.

If there is evidence of a violent struggle the person may have been abducted, and the scene of the disappearance must be preserved for evidential and investigative purposes.

13.4.1.2 Furthering the investigation

The level of risk to the missing person must be evaluated. ACPO (2010a) suggest that police forces use a 'low, medium or high' scale as shown in the table (our summary):

Level of risk	Criteria
High	The risk posed to the missing person is immediate and there are substantial grounds for believing that he or she is in danger through her vulnerability; or he or she may have been the victim of a serious crime; or the risk posed is immediate and there are substantial grounds for believing that the public is in danger
Medium	The risk posed is likely to place the person in danger or the person is a threat to him- or herself or others
Low	There is no apparent threat of danger to either the person or the public

The particular actions needed for each level of risk form part of police training. However, searching for the missing person is an obvious early step to take. This would probably initially involve a thorough search of the person's house, garden, and any adjoining premises (children can hide away in very small spaces) and could be extended to include the surrounding area concentrating first on the person's 'habitual haunts', and then hazardous places such as pools, streams, caves, empty buildings, and so on.

Preparation should be made to widen the search systematically, including making house-to-house enquiries.

The person's recent movements and activities need to be established, and this could involve checking work place or school absence records. Personal papers belonging to the individual who has gone missing should be viewed (diaries, work schedules, planners, and financial information) and these would all need to be retained as evidence. Local and national police databases should also be interrogated. A list should be made of all relatives, friends, contacts, and work colleagues/fellow trainees in case these are needed, and recent photographs that are a good likeness should be obtained.

The reliability of any person giving information should be considered; he/she may be involved in the disappearance. For example, Ian Huntley, a caretaker at a school in Soham murdered two young girls, and provided information (false information) to the police early in the investigation about where he had last seen them.

13.4.1.3 Special considerations for missing children

Missing children are particularly at risk of abuse. The Human Rights Act 1998 places a duty on states to protect any person who may be at risk; police forces therefore have a duty of positive action on the investigation of missing persons. All reports of missing children must be properly investigated, and should never be considered as low risk.

Children in care make up a large proportion of cases of missing children. They often have other needs that compound their vulnerability and the fact that they are often considered to be 'street wise' can expose them to further long-term risks. Carers may use the term 'unauthorized absence' in relation to some missing children. The police, however, should not use the same expression when recording a missing child (ACPO, 2010a, p 17). If a child in care is missing but his/her whereabouts are known or thought to be known (eg staying with a friend), it is the responsibility of the care staff to search the area and make enquiries as to where the child might be. If the child is then reported missing, the police might want to consider searching the area again.

TASK 3 Consider the following scenario:

A 16-year-old boy has been reported missing by his mother. Checks with his school showed that he did not arrive at school that morning, despite having left his house (an isolated farm) at the normal time and in school uniform. His whereabouts are unknown and he may have been missing for as long as ten hours. There are indications that the boy has recently become moody and depressed, and that he may have been subject to some bullying at school. He is asthmatic and needs regular medication. He is a keen shot and has his own shotgun, properly licensed, for using on the farm. He had a quarrel with his father the night before; his father had refused to allow him to attend a party. The father says the boy acts rebelliously.

1. You might note that there are a number of vulnerabilities, or potential areas for concern, in this case. What further information is required?
2. If the missing person enquiry becomes prolonged, what national guidance is available to help plan the ongoing police investigation?

13.5 Human Trafficking

Human trafficking is a complex phenomenon of significant national and international importance. It impacts different areas of policing and incorporates a variety of offences, offenders, and forms of victimization. Police officers may come across human trafficking whilst on patrol or when responding to incidents. Human trafficking may involve adults and children, UK and foreign citizens, and a combination of all these. It is therefore important to have a general awareness of what human trafficking involves and how to respond to it.

Human trafficking should not be confused with human smuggling. Smuggling involves an immigrant or asylum seeker paying someone to bring them into a country illegally, after which the relationship between the parties ceases (Article 3 of the Protocol against the Smuggling of Migrants by Land, Sea and Air supplementing the UN Convention against Transnational Organized Crime). Trafficking may involve smuggling in an initial stage but afterwards the victims are coerced or deceived into a situation of exploitation by either the trafficker or someone else to whom they are delivered. Trafficking therefore involves the movement of people by force or deception for the purpose of exploitation.

13.5.1 Types of human trafficking

There are different ways in which this exploitation can take place. According to Article 3 of the Protocol to Prevent, Suppress and Punish Trafficking in Persons, Especially Women and Children (also known as the Palermo Protocol), these include: sexual exploitation, forced labour or services, slavery or similar practices and servitude, or the removal or organs. Some of these will now be explored in more detail:

Sexual exploitation is more likely to affect women and girls. Some victims are forcibly taken from their homes and used in the sex trade, while others voluntarily travel to another destination, unaware of the exploitation that will ensue. This is further complicated by the fact that some victims agree to travel for the purposes of working in the sex industry but not to the conditions that they are forced to work under (eg number of clients, type of sexual activity, and pay). Many of the offences that entail sexual exploitation are covered in the Sexual Offences Act 2003, see especially s 1 (rape, see 17.6.3), s 52 (causing or inciting prostitution for gain), s 53 (controlling prostitution for gain, see 17.5.3), and ss 57–59 (trafficking into the UK for sexual exploitation, trafficking within the UK for sexual exploitation, and trafficking out of the UK for sexual exploitation). Section 33A of the Sexual Offences Act 1956, related to the offence of keeping a brothel, is also important.

Labour exploitation is when the victim is forced to work under unacceptable conditions. It is often achieved through the use of threats or physical harm, restrictions of movement, debt-bondage, withholding wages or significantly reducing them, retention of identity documents such as passports, threats of denunciation to the authorities of the illegal status of the worker. Labour exploitation can be found in a variety of industries, such as factory work, construction, and catering and hotels. The principal offences related to labour exploitation can be found in s 4 of the Asylum and Immigration Act 2004. For situations in which trafficking does not exist or cannot be proved, s 71 of the Coroners and Justice Act 2009 may be applied (regarding slavery, servitude, and forced or compulsory labour).

Domestic servitude is when victims are forced to work in a domestic setting and are also often the target of sexual abuse. Offenders may have attracted victims through the promise of employment or patronage (eg promising the parents of a child that they will provide her with an education). The principal offences related to labour exploitation can be found in s 4 of the Asylum and Immigration Act 2004. As above, for situations in which trafficking does not exist or cannot be proved, s 71 of the Coroners and Justice Act 2009 may be applied (regarding slavery, servitude, and forced or compulsory labour).

Organ harvesting involves the removal of an organ from an individual for transplantation into another. It has not been identified as problematic in the UK but in some countries, 'transplant tourism' is a major concern.

There may be a perception that human trafficking only involves the exploitation of foreign victims who are brought to the UK for the purpose of exploitation. This is only partly true. All types of exploitation mentioned previously may occur in a domestic or international setting. Internal trafficking consists in the movement of victims within the UK for the purpose of exploitation. Victims may be UK or foreign nationals. It is also important to notice that not all human trafficking entails a sophisticated complex operation. The exploitation of an individual by another, for example with the promise of work in another part of the country, may fall into this category also.

13.5.2 The context of human trafficking

Victims are often poor, relative to the average person in the country of destination and to people in their country of origin. Poverty places individuals at a greater risk of victimization, especially in situations where there is pressing need for money (such as a relative becoming ill). This also makes countries with a relatively lower socio-economic status better targets for human traffickers, as individuals in these countries are more likely to be attracted by the promise of a relatively better income in a more developed country. Corruption and the involvement of government officials in human trafficking in the countries of origin can impede the prevention and investigation of human trafficking. Although both men and women are victims of human trafficking, women are more likely to be victimized due to a number of socio-economic circumstances in the country of origin (eg lower wages and greater difficulty in accessing education) and demand in the country of destination (eg greater demand for female sex workers).

They will have been recruited in a variety of ways, from advertisements for work to abduction and kidnapping. One way of controlling victims is by retaining their travel documents, which may or may not be legitimate and may or may not have been arranged by the traffickers themselves. For example, a trafficker may arrange a new identity for a child and appoint themselves the child's guardian, thus controlling almost every aspect of the child's life. A variety of points of entry into the UK and forms of transportation may then be used to bring victims into the country.

13.5.3 Interacting with victims of trafficking

Trafficking is a serious organized crime. Its victims are not exploited by their own volition but were led into exploitation. Possible indicators that a victim may have been trafficked include: human rights breaches, threats or actual harm to family members, food, water, and sleep deprivation, the withholding of medical care, being forced to perform sexual acts, having wages partly or totally withheld, debt-bondage, working excessive hours, not having access to identity documents such as a passport, being threatened with denunciation of the illegal immigrant status, or having restricted freedom of movement. It is important not to judge or stereotype victims of human trafficking, as their circumstances are often unique and difficult to understand for the outsider. Cooperation from victims is often essential for the successful investigation and prosecution of human trafficking, and therefore an effort must be made to understand their background and how they may benefit from support.

When the victims are children, other indicators of trafficking might be present, such as possession of goods and money not accounted for, exhibiting self-confidence and maturity beyond their years, being unable to give details of a contact person or an address, not appearing to have money but having a mobile phone, going missing from local authority care, being cared for by adults who are not their parents, having a difficult relationship with their 'parents', being one of several unrelated children living at an address, not being registered with a GP or not attending a medical practice, not being enrolled in school, having to pay debts, or being especially afraid of deportation. Additional factors that may be particularly relevant for children trafficked within the UK include signs of physical abuse, being sexually active and having sexually transmitted diseases or unwanted pregnancies, existence of reports of sexual exploitation, evidence of substance abuse, contact or relationships with significantly older adults or adults outside their normal circle, accounts of social activities with no plausible explanation for funding, street homelessness, self-harming behaviour, and forming online relationships with adults.

Some children may not be aware that they are being trafficked and others may actively hide the trafficking. Children are not deemed capable of consent and are therefore seen as victims of trafficking even if they were not forced or deceived but are being transported for the purpose of exploitation. If an officer suspects that a child may be a victim of human trafficking, he/she has the power to remove the child to a safe place or to prevent the child's removal from it for a maximum of 72 hours (s 46 of the Children Act 1989 (see 13.3.3)). If there is a risk of life or likelihood of serious harm, the police can apply to court for an Emergency Protection Order, under s 44 of the same Act.

It is sometimes very difficult to respond effectively to victims of human trafficking. For example, the victim may not understand English, might have learning and communication disabilities, or have suffered trauma leading to mental ill health. Other difficulties include the victim needing medical assistance or having dependants relying on the victim's financial assistance. They might also fear reprisals, or fear any authority, having an insecure or illegal immigration status. Their cultural or religious beliefs, shame and fear of dishonour, and the need to conduct forensic medical examination, especially in victims of sexual abuse, can present additional difficulties. Each of these aspects should be taken into account when interviewing victims of human trafficking and an effort should be made to communicate with them effectively and reassure them of the role of the police and any required procedures. Victims of human trafficking are especially vulnerable and any contact must be undertaken with great care and respect. Trainee officers should be mindful of their conduct, gender, and appearance and the effects that these may have on victims. Some victims may have experienced long periods of isolation and therefore may not want to cooperate in bringing the offender (on whom they feel dependent) to justice. Adequate physical and psychological support should be provided from the early stages of the investigation and some may require immediate medical attention due to the conditions that they have been exposed to.

The UK has two authorities with trained 'case-owners' who make decisions on whether someone is a victim of trafficking. These are the UK Human Trafficking Centre (UKHTC) and the UK Border Agency (UKBA). As a trainee police officer dealing with a potential victim of human trafficking, you should ensure that victims are safe and receive required medical assistance, and inform a supervisor and a senior detective officer of the situation. The UKHTC should also be notified as soon as possible using the National Referral Forms. When dealing with children, you should also notify the local authority children's social care service and police Child Abuse Investigation Unit. An intelligence report should also be submitted.

13.6 Support for Victims, Witnesses, and the General Public

Whilst it could be argued that law enforcement is the main priority of the police, it could also be said that their position within the CJS and society as a whole places further demands upon them. Discourse surrounding police legitimacy (see 3.5.3 and 3.5.4) suggests a need to engage with the community, and to act as much as a 'police service' as a 'police force'. It is also important that victims and witnesses are supported so they can provide good evidence during prosecutions.

13.6.1 Providing support for members of the general public

In the following sections, we cover some of the services provided by the police that are unrelated to law enforcement. A few might argue that the role of the police in the twenty-first century should not include these time-honoured and traditional activities. Others might suggest that they serve to enhance and secure police legitimacy in an evermore demanding society.

13.6.1.1 Lost property

Traditionally, although not a statutory obligation, the police service has been the repository for property found in public spaces. The police also maintain records of property reported as lost so that any article that has been found can be reunited with its owner at the earliest opportunity. Other organizations provide a similar service, such as road and rail transport companies, but only for property lost or found in their own vehicles or premises.

A person finding property is not obliged to hand over the article to the police, but should take all reasonable steps to find the owner in order to negate being suspected of committing theft (see 16.2). This might include reporting the find to the police, and indeed, items such as passports and driving licences are more likely to be quickly and safely returned to the owner if the police take responsibility for making the contact. The local policy of most police organizations is that members of the extended police family finding property must not personally retain it. They should instead record and deposit the find at the police station.

Police staff on patrol or at the front counter of police stations will inevitably have people handing in items they have found and reporting items as lost. It is vital that accurate records are made, and a full entry should be written if a PNB is employed (see 10.2). The description of the item(s) should refer to simple facts such as measurements, and unique identifying features such as serial numbers. Assumptions should be avoided; just because the face of a watch incorporates the word of a leading manufacturer and appears to be made of gold, it may not be the genuine article. A description of such an article should state that it is a wrist-worn timepiece made of yellow metal, and a record should also be made of the wording on the face.

13.6.1.2 Illness in the street

Police officers on patrol will often encounter individuals who are ill, or appear to be ill. This will range from minor illnesses to more serious conditions, such as heart attacks, and will also include people suffering from severe mental health problems. People who appear to be drunk or under the influence of drugs might actually be suffering from an allergic reaction or some other ailment. They might even be the victim of an assault.

A first task for a police officer in this situation is to decide whether the person is ill, and if so to determine the nature of the illness. It is worth checking to see if the person is carrying documentation or wearing MedicAlert jewellery relating to an illness or its treatment. This might show that he/she is taking prescribed drugs, has an allergy or other illness, and help ascertain the nature of the illness or indeed explain why the person is acting in an unusual manner.

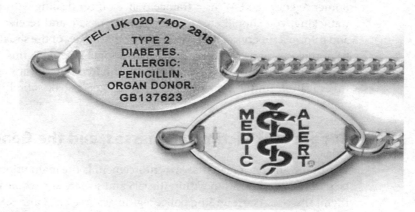

Image reproduced with permission of the MedicAlert foundation.

Police officers are trained to call for an ambulance if it seems necessary without assuming that a bystander or witness has done so (even if he/she claims to have called). A person cannot be obliged to go to hospital but a police officer should be prepared to go against the wishes of a person if it is felt that the illness is serious enough to require professional and immediate treatment at a hospital (see 13.2.4 on mental capacity and the ability of a person to make proper decisions). Where possible and appropriate the police officer should be prepared to provide first aid medical assistance. The preservation of life is always paramount.

It is also necessary to try to establish the identity of the person, and this will not always be straightforward. After asking the person questions and checking his/her personal documentation (including checking any MedicAlert jewellery) it may be necessary for an officer to ask if anyone else at the scene knows the ill person. It might also be necessary to check descriptions on the PNC to see if there are any matches on the wanted and/or missing persons indexes. If a person remains unidentified CCTV can also be checked to elucidate the person's movements prior to the collapse or crisis. It might be necessary to speak to a supervisor to ensure a description of the person can be circulated as soon as possible if all else fails.

Some individuals encountered by police officers will be suffering from memory loss. In these situations, in addition to the previous points, it is important to find out whether the person's loss of memory is a result of an injury or some pre-existing condition, such as Alzheimer's disease or simply old age. Witnesses might be of assistance in establishing the facts here. An officer should administer medical treatment if and when appropriate to do so.

An officer also has a responsibility to safeguard any property that an ill person might have with them. If possible, this should be kept with the person if, for example, they need to go to hospital. However, if this is not practical, the property should be taken to the police station for safekeeping or preferably taken to a known relative. Beyond the immediate care given to the ill person a police officer should where possible ensure that the appropriate relatives are notified. A person may not wish a relative to be informed and the police officer might need to make a judgement call. In these cases the priority for a police officer is to ensure that decisions are clearly documented and, if required to do so, the officer should be able to justify the decision taken. A supervisor should be consulted if necessary.

A police officer should accompany a person to hospital if the illness seems to be especially serious and/or life-threatening. This helps to ensure continuity in piecing together a sequence of events.

13.6.2 Providing support for victims and witnesses

Officers at the scene need to consider the needs for support of victims, witnesses, or suspects and those affected by the incident in an ethical (see professional standards of behaviour) and appropriate manner. Victims and witnesses may suffer from physical injury and visible signs of stress. They may appear emotional, confused, aggressive, angry, and/or scared. The type of support required will vary depending on the incident and those involved, and could involve providing reassurance, first aid, and information on issues on procedures relating to the incident (legislation, courts, and available services). Specialist medical help might also be required. It is important that the appropriate procedures and legislation are followed and that anxiety or vulnerability is not increased. With this in mind officers should keep victims and witness informed, and where vulnerability has been identified the wishes of those concerned have been discussed with them and met where appropriate. This may result in further support being put in place such as 'Special Measures' (see 26.5.2.4). For all witnesses, survivors, and victims, the needs for support can change over time, and the needs can be related to their experience of the incident concerned or be totally unrelated.

One reason that it is important to offer suitable support is that it will facilitate the collection of evidence. Victims and witnesses can often provide key information for the prosecution of a suspect. For further guidance in relation to intimidated survivors, victims, and witnesses see 14.6 and 24.4.

13.6.2.1 Information and support for victims

Working with victims of crime is an important part of police work, but victims and their families have often stated that they do not understand the complexities of criminal investigations and legal proceedings. Establishing a good relationship with victims increases the chances that they will cooperate effectively with the investigation and prosecution. Victims must be treated with dignity and respect, regardless of the specific circumstances of the crime. It is important to understand that victims may have experienced events particularly traumatic and require adequate support. Some victims are considered vulnerable (eg due to their age or the type of crime suffered) and require additional forms of support. Police officers should consider the well-being of individuals from a broad perspective and be aware of the full range of support services. Specialist support for victims of domestic abuse is covered in 15.7.2.4, and in 17.6.1 for victims of sexually motivated offences.

Victims have certain rights as enshrined in *The Code of Practice for Victims of Crime* (available online). A victim is defined in the Code as someone who:

- has 'suffered harm, including physical, mental or emotional harm or economic loss which was directly caused by criminal conduct'; or
- is a close relative of someone 'whose death was directly caused by criminal conduct'.

The Code **requires** enhanced levels of support for victims, particularly those who may have to attend court, and require the police and other members of the CJS to supply them with information on from whom and how to get support. It extends to businesses, and to the families of the deceased as appropriate. There are separate entitlements for adult victims (Chapter 2, Part A) and child victims (Chapter 3, Part B). The entitlement for services remains regardless of anyone being charged or convicted of the crime and regardless of the person entitled wanting to collaborate with the investigation.

The Code also sets up duties for service providers, including the police. We will provide a brief summary of these in relation to adult victims. All victims making an allegation of criminal conduct should be provided within five days with the 'Information for Victims of Crime' leaflet (or be referred to a relevant website where they can find the same information). Some victims will be identified by the police as priority victims who are entitled to an enhanced service, and must be given this information within one day. This would include victims of the most serious crimes, persistently targeted victims, and vulnerable or intimidated victims. Victims must also be informed of the existence of the Victims' Code and how they can find out more about its provisions. Victims entitled to special measures should have these clearly explained. Any specific measures that have been identified as necessary to help victims give evidence should be recorded and shared with Witness Care Units and the CPS.

Victims must be given information about relevant victims' services, including contact details. They should be informed that their details will be passed to victims' services unless they ask the police not to do so. Special consideration must be given to victims of sexual offences or domestic violence, or bereaved close relatives, as their explicit consent must be obtained before sending their details to victims' services. Victims can refer themselves to victims' services at a later date. The referral to the appropriate services should be done within two working days of an allegation being reported by a victim. Victims of the 'most serious crime' should also be informed of the availability of pre-trial therapy if needed.

A Victim Personal Statement (VPS) can also be made (see 10.11.2). Victims of the most serious crimes, persistently targeted, and vulnerable or intimidated victims, and parents or guardians of vulnerable or child victims, must also be informed of the possibility of making a VPS. (Other categories of victim must be informed of this opportunity only when completing a witness statement.) The police retain the discretion, however, to offer the opportunity to make a VPS to any victims whenever deemed appropriate.

The police must keep victims informed about the suspect. Victims must be informed within five days (one day for enhanced service) of a suspect being arrested, interviewed under caution, released without charge, released on police bail, or if there are changes in the conditions to their bail or it is cancelled. Any decisions to prosecute or to give the suspect an out-of-court disposal must be communicated to the victim within the relevant time limits (one or five days), including all police cautions and decisions and reasons not to prosecute. The police must also inform victims of the date, time, and location of the first court hearing and bail conditions (including any decisions regarding breaches of these conditions). When considering out-of-court disposals, victims should also be asked for their views when practicable, and these should be taken into account.

Once a trial has started the CPS, Witness Care Units, and other agencies take over responsibility for providing information to victims. The exception is when the police are nominated as the single point of contact with victims, in which case it may be necessary to keep victims updated of any developments.

13.6.2.2 Support services for victims

Police officers will sometimes need to seek advice from colleagues of other services and should look to Family Liaison Officers (FLO), call centre staff, other public service agencies (private, public, or third sector), scenes of crimes officer, other colleagues, supervisor, or the crime reduction officer. Various support groups are available outside the police service including Victim Support, Citizens Advice Bureau, social services, mental health, bereavement, or marriage councillors, and medical practitioners. Particular care needs to be taken with vulnerable people (eg age, disability, individuals suffering from trauma or mental health issues, children, and the intimidated). Note that police officers are in a good position to inform victims of violent crime about the Criminal Injuries Compensation Scheme.

Victim Support (VS) is a non-governmental agency that offers support to victims of crime. It offers help not only to victims of crime but to all those who may have been affected by it, such as the family members of a victim. Victim Support also provides assistance to witnesses and runs the Witness Services in courts across the country. The full range of VS services are listed and described on their website. Victim Support is staffed by specially trained volunteers who offer free and confidential service to victims of crime. (All VS volunteers carry photographic identity cards.) The support offered by this institution includes short-term assistance (such as how to improve personal safety or how the criminal justice system works), crisis management, and long-term help. A crisis is often due to a serious form of crime but can also result from any major disruption of daily life that does not necessarily result from crime (eg a road traffic collision or a sudden death). Specially trained support staff can provide assistance to bereaved family members of victims of violent deaths. Finally, Victim Support also offers information on compensation and insurance schemes.

13.6.2.3 Advice for victims on crime prevention

The security of a building should be considered after a fire (see 11.4.2) or a crime has occurred (see 4.5.2) as other criminals can exploit perceived weaknesses and commit further crimes. Simple crime prevention and reduction advice, access to good information perhaps from a Crime Reduction Officer, ideas on alarm installation, and other 'target hardening' techniques can be useful to the victim. Some victims are repeatedly targeted by offenders (see 4.5.2 on 'hot victims') and, in many cases, the scale of the offences can become quite alarming, particularly in relation to property-repair scams carried out by bogus callers who target the vulnerable, or in households where domestic violence is an issue.

A basic level of support can be offered by patrols occasionally visiting vulnerable victims to check on their welfare and give advice to prevent further problems. Neighbourhood Watch schemes should be encouraged; victims and their neighbours can be told how to contact Neighbourhood Policing Teams to help them engage more with the local police and build a rapport.

13.7 The Prevention of Harm to Animals

The first legislation to protect animals in the UK was 'An Act to Prevent the Cruel and Improper Treatment of Cattle' in 1822. Indeed, this was the first animal welfare legislation passed by a parliament anywhere in the world. Research indicates that there may be links between animal abuse and human abuse (see <http://petaf.org.uk/CrueltyToA-InterpersonalV.asp>).

The legislation covered here is from:

- the Animal Welfare Act 2006 (for non-wild animals; 'gardens, farms and zoos');
- the Wildlife and Countryside Act 1981 (for all types of wild animals, including invertebrates); and
- the Wild Mammals (Protection) Act 1996 (for wild mammals only).

Note that the definition of 'animal' and 'wild animal' varies slightly between the Acts.

Specific Incidents

13.7.1 The Animal Welfare Act 2006

This Act applies only to animals that are vertebrates; that is, mammals, birds, reptiles (eg snakes), and amphibians (eg frogs). It does not cover invertebrates (animals without a backbone) such as insects, snails, or worms. It also refers to 'protected animals', which are defined as a type of animal that is either:

- normally domesticated in the UK (such as a cat);
- under the control of a person (such as a cow kept in a farmer's field); or
- not living wild (such as a lion; note that a lion that has escaped from a zoo is not truly living wild).

The Animal Welfare Act 2006 places a 'duty of care' on animal owners (eg farmers and pet owners) in an attempt to ensure the basic needs of animals are met, as well as outlawing certain forms of suffering. Offences which can be committed under the Animal Welfare Act 2006 include:

- causing or permitting unnecessary suffering (s 4);
- mutilation (s 5);
- docking of dogs' tails (s 6);
- administration of poisons (s 7);
- arranging animal fighting (s 8);
- failure of person responsible for animal to ensure welfare (s 9); and
- transfer of animals by way of sale or prize to persons under 16 (s 11).

Other parties involved in investigating possible animal welfare offences include local authorities and the state veterinary service. The RSPCA in association with ACPO and Centrex published guidance notes for the Animal Welfare Act 2006, and these are available online. Guidance for dealing with dangerous dogs is available from Defra (Defra, 2009).

All the offences listed in the following paragraphs under the Animal Welfare Act 2006 are triable summarily and the penalty is imprisonment not exceeding 51 weeks and/or a fine.

13.7.1.1 Causing unnecessary suffering to an animal

Section 4(1) of the Animal Welfare Act 2006 concerns causing unnecessary suffering to a protected animal (defined at the start of 13.7.1).

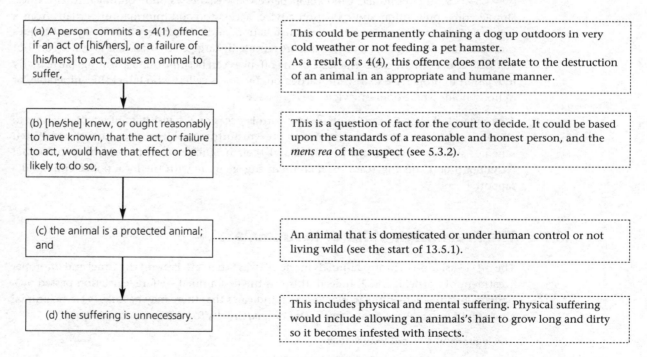

(a) A person commits a s 4(1) offence if an act of [his/hers], or a failure of [his/hers] to act, causes an animal to suffer,	This could be permanently chaining a dog up outdoors in very cold weather or not feeding a pet hamster. As a result of s 4(4), this offence does not relate to the destruction of an animal in an appropriate and humane manner.
(b) [he/she] knew, or ought reasonably to have known, that the act, or failure to act, would have that effect or be likely to do so,	This is a question of fact for the court to decide. It could be based upon the standards of a reasonable and honest person, and the *mens rea* of the suspect (see 5.3.2).
(c) the animal is a protected animal; and	An animal that is domesticated or under human control or not living wild (see the start of 13.5.1).
(d) the suffering is unnecessary.	This includes physical and mental suffering. Physical suffering would include allowing an animals's hair to grow long and dirty so it becomes infested with insects.

The meaning of 'unnecessary' includes a consideration (s 4(3)) of whether the suffering could reasonably have been avoided or reduced. It could also be that the conduct causing the suffering could be justified because it was:

- for a legitimate purpose, such as for the animal's benefit, or to protect a person, property, or another animal;

- in compliance with an enactment such as the Animals (Scientific Procedures) Act 1986 (or with the provisions of a licence granted for specified permissible purposes under such an Act).

However, any justified conduct should be proportionate to its purpose.

There is a separate offence (s 4(2)) where the offender does not directly cause the unnecessary suffering but instead permits it to be caused by another person (or fails to prevent this). Here, a person (A) can commit an offence through the actions of another person (B) if:

- A is responsible for, owns, or is in charge of the animal (permanently or on a temporary basis); or
- B is under the age of 16 and has responsibility for the animal, and A has the care of or control over B.

A court will decide what person A could reasonably have done in the circumstances to prevent the unnecessary suffering.

13.7.1.2 The duty to ensure welfare

A person who is responsible for an animal has a duty to ensure its welfare. Section 9(1) of the Animal Welfare Act 2006 states that a person commits an offence if he/she does not meet an animal's needs, which under s 9(2) include its need:

- for a suitable environment and diet;
- to be able to exhibit normal behaviour patterns, including any need it has to be housed with, or apart from, other animals; and
- to be protected from pain, suffering, injury, and disease.

13.7.1.3 Mutilation of a protected animal and docking dogs' tails

Under s 5(1) of the Animal Welfare Act 2006 a person commits an offence if he/she mutilates a protected animal. The definition of mutilate is interference with the sensitive tissues or bone structure of an animal (excluding permitted procedures carried out by a veterinary surgeon). It is also an offence for a person who is responsible for an animal to permit another person to mutilate, or to fail to prevent another person from mutilating a protected animal (s 5(2)). This legislation does not apply to the removal of a dog's tail, or in certain circumstances specified by the regulations of an appropriate national authority (eg the armed services).

The docking of a dog's tail is covered in s 6 of the Animal Welfare Act 2006. It is an offence to remove (or cause to be removed) a dog's tail (or part of it), other than for medical treatment. The legislation is mainly intended to prevent the removal of dogs' tails for purely cosmetic reasons, and does not apply if the dog is a 'certified working dog' that is less than six days old. A dog is a certified working dog if:

- evidence has been given to a vet;
- a national authority has proved the dog will be used for work (eg pest control or emergency rescue); or
- the dog is of a specified working type.

13.7.1.4 Administration of poisons

Section 7(1) of the Animal Welfare Act 2006 states that a person commits an offence if without lawful authority or reasonable excuse he/she administers (or causes to be administered) any poisonous or injurious drug or substance to a protected animal, knowing it to be poisonous or injurious. This includes any drug or substance which, due to the quantity or manner in which it is administered or taken, has a harmful effect (such as large amounts of salt).

A person responsible for any animal also commits an offence by permitting or failing to stop someone else allowing the animal to take poisonous substances (s 7(2) of the Animal Welfare Act 2006). This only applies if the person responsible for the animal knew that the substance was poisonous and did not intervene.

13.7.1.5 Transfer of animals by way of sale or prize to persons under 16

Section 11(1) of the Animal Welfare Act 2006 states that it is an offence to sell an animal to a person whom the seller has reasonable cause to believe is under the age of 16 years. Here, selling an animal includes 'transferring, or agreeing to transfer, ownership of the animal' (s 11(2)).

Specific Incidents

Section 11(3) explains what this means for a person offering an animal as a prize to a person aged under 16 years. The person offering the prize does not commit the offence if the arrangement takes place:

- face to face and the young person is accompanied by a person aged 16 years or over;
- not face to face (eg by telephone) but with the consent of the relevant carer; or
- in a family context.

13.7.1.6 Animal fighting

An animal fight involves placing a 'protected animal' with any animal (including a human) for 'fighting, wrestling, or baiting'. Section 8(1) of the Animal Welfare Act 2006 states that a person commits an offence if he/she either:

- causes an animal fight to take place, or attempts to do so;
- knowingly receives money for admission to an animal fight;
- provides information about an animal fight to another with the intention of enabling or encouraging attendance at the fight, or knowingly publicizes a proposed animal fight;
- makes or accepts a bet on the outcome of an animal fight or the occurrence of a particular event during an animal fight;
- takes part in an animal fight;
- possesses any item for use in an animal fight, with the intention of it being used;
- keeps or trains an animal for fights; or
- keeps any premises for animal fighting.

It is also an offence to be present at an animal fight, without lawful authority or reasonable excuse (s 8 (2)), or to knowingly supply, publish, show, or possess with intent to supply a video-recording of an animal fight (s 8(3)).

Section 22(1) of the Animal Welfare Act 2006 states that a police officer may seize an animal if it appears that it has been involved in a s 8(1) or (2) offence. There is also a power to enter and search (s 22(2)) for the purpose of exercising a power under s 8(1) if the premises is not a private dwelling and the officer reasonably believes that there is a relevant animal on the premises.

13.7.1.7 Protected animals in distress

Animals in distress may need to be taken into police possession, and some might need to be destroyed. The powers are provided under ss 18 and 19 of the Animal Welfare Act 2006 but local force policy should be considered in relation to their use. Animal inspectors also have the same powers. It is an offence to intentionally obstruct a person acting under s 18 of the Animal Welfare Act 2006 (s 18(12)).

Section 18(1) of the Animal Welfare Act 2006 states that, if there is a reasonable belief that a protected animal is suffering, an officer may 'take, or arrange for the taking of, such steps as appear to be immediately necessary to alleviate the animal's suffering'. This in itself would not authorize destruction of an animal (s 18(2)).

An animal inspector or police officer may destroy a protected animal (or arrange for another person to do so), either at the site or at another location. However, this only applies if the animal's condition is so poor that this would be in its own interest and this is:

- certified by an attending vet as such (s 18(3)): or
- there is no reasonable alternative and the need is so urgent that it is not reasonably practicable to wait for a vet to attend (s 18(4)).

A protected animal may be taken into possession by an animal inspector or police officer if a veterinary surgeon certifies that it is suffering, or is likely to suffer if its circumstances do not change (s 18(5)). If the officer believes that action is needed urgently (and it is not reasonably practicable to wait for a vet) then he/she may act alone (s 18(6)). Any dependent offspring may also be taken into possession (s 18(7)). When an animal is taken into possession under s 18(5), it can be removed to a place of safety, cared for (either on the premises where it was being kept or at another suitable place), and marked for identification purposes (s 18(8)).

There is a power of entry (s 19(1)) to non-residential premises to search for a protected animal and to exercise any power under s 18. A warrant under s 19(4) would be required for a similar entry and search of a private dwelling. A police officer or animal inspector must reasonably believe that there is a protected animal on the premises, and that it is suffering (or if the circumstances of the animal do not change, it is likely to suffer). Reasonable force may be used if necessary, but only if it appears that entry is required before a s 19(4) warrant can be obtained and executed.

13.7.1.8 Other powers under the Animal Welfare Act 2006

Police officers may enter and search any premises to arrest any person they reasonably suspect of committing an offence under ss 4, 5, 6(1), 6(2), 7, 8(1), and 8(2) of the Animal Welfare Act. This power is provided under s 17 of the PACE Act 1984: see 9.5.1.

A vehicle may be stopped and detained under s 54(1) of the Animal Welfare Act 2006 in order to search it to prevent animal suffering (s 19(1)) or to seize an animal that is suspected to have been involved in animal fighting (s 22(2)). A police officer must be in uniform to exercise this power. The vehicle may be detained for as long as is reasonably required (s 54(4)) for a search or inspection to be carried out (including the exercise of any related power under this Act). It may be searched either at the place where it was first detained or nearby (see 9.4.1 on procedures for searches).

13.7.2 Cruelty to wild animals

The law concerning cruelty to wild animals is to be found largely in:

* the Wildlife and Countryside Act 1981 (for most types of wild animal—mammals, birds, frogs, toads, fish, insects, and snakes, but there are notable exclusions, see 13.7.2.1); and
* the Wild Mammals (Protection) Act 1996 (a mammal is an animal whose female produces milk for the nourishment of its young, such as rabbits, foxes, squirrels, hedgehogs, bats, and dolphins).

A recently published report (Environmental Audit Committee, 2012) calls for a consolidation of the more recently enacted wildlife crime laws as these are seen collectively to be over-complex. It also suggests better training for magistrates and prosecutors regarding wildlife crime and improving guidelines to enable a more consistent sentencing strategy.

The offences of cruelty to wild animals described here are all summary offences, and the penalty is six months' imprisonment and/or a fine.

13.7.2.1 The Wildlife and Countryside Act 1981

Section 1 of the Wildlife and Countryside Act 1981 covers wild birds. A 'wild bird' is any bird of a species that lives wild as a resident or visitor to the European territory of any member state. Game birds (such as pheasants) are not considered as wild birds for the purposes of this Act, and there are also other current exceptions (as determined by the Secretary of State for the Environment), such as wood pigeons and herring gulls.

Under s 1 of the Wildlife and Countryside Act 1981 it is an offence to intentionally:

(a) kill, injure, or take any wild bird;
(b) take, damage, or destroy the nest of any wild bird while that nest is in use or being built; or
(c) take or destroy an egg of any wild bird.

Other types of wild animal are protected under s 9 of the Wildlife and Countryside Act 1981, under which it is an offence to intentionally kill, injure, or take 'any' wild animal. However, there are some exclusions including rats and rabbits, and it will be for a court to decide whether a particular animal is covered under s 9.

Section 19 of the Wildlife and Countryside Act states that if a police officer suspects with reasonable cause that any person has committed an offence under this Act he/she may search that person and anything in his/her possession and seize and detain evidence (see 9.4.1 on searching). He/she may also enter premises other than a dwelling to arrest a person in relation to these offences (see 9.5.1).

13.7.2.2 The Wild Mammals (Protection) Act 1996

Under this Act a mammal is wild if it is not of a kind which is commonly domesticated in the British Islands, and is not the kind of animal that would normally be under the control of a person. It is an offence to mutilate, kick, beat, nail, or otherwise impale, stab, burn, stone, crush, drown, drag, or asphyxiate any wild mammal with intent to inflict unnecessary suffering (s 1 of the Wild Mammals (Protection) Act 1996).

The following are not offences under the Wild Mammals (Protection) Act 1996:

- mercy-killing (and attempts) such as putting an injured badger 'out of its misery';
- actions under authorization, for example by a vet; and
- lawful killing by traps, dogs, birds, or poisons.

If a police officer has reasonable grounds for suspecting that a person has committed an offence under the Wild Mammals (Protection) Act 1996 he/she may stop and search the person (including a vehicle) and seize any relevant items. Code A of the PACE Act 1984 Codes of Practice would apply (see 9.4.1).

TASK 4

1. In the Animal Welfare Act 2006 an animal can only 'suffer' physically. True or false?
2. What are the three different ways a 'protected animal' may be defined under the Animal Welfare Act 2006?
3. There have been anonymous reports about a flat where a dog has been left alone while the residents have gone on holiday. Could a police officer enter the premises under s 19 of the Animal Welfare Act?
4. A police officer attends an incident where a cat has been found with a discharged firework taped to its body which had been recently ignited. The cat is still alive but badly injured. The suspects were seen running into a nearby house. Restricting your answer to the Animal Welfare Act 2006, what power of entry, if any, could she use if required to enter and arrest the suspects?

13.8 Answers to Tasks

TASK 1

1. There are likely to be policy agreements with local Social Services and the Healthcare Trusts.
2. (a) A dynamic risk assessment of the situation should be made first. Can she safely enter the room or should she seek the assistance of other officers with appropriate personal safety equipment? Entrance can be gained by seeking the permission of the parents/owners of the property to unscrew the door handle and withdrawing the bar a little, so the handle on the other side no longer works. Then she could turn the handle herself to open the door.
   (b) She should find out if the young man will voluntarily go to hospital. If not, an AMHP should be called to see if he can be taken into hospital under one of the sections within the MHA.

TASK 2

1. Under s 17(1)(e) PACE an officer 'may enter and search any premises for the purposes of saving life or limb or preventing serious damage to property'. The witness evidence of hysterical screaming and the suspicion that the child is alone and does not open the door together justify the use of s 17 to save the life and limb of the child.
2. It would appear that Jo has committed an offence under s 1 of the Children and Young Persons Act 1933. This is committed by any person who is 16 years old or over who has responsibility for a child under the age of 16 years and who 'wilfully assaults, ill-treats, neglects, abandons or exposes the child in a manner likely to cause unnecessary suffering or injury to health'. In these circumstances Jo has 'abandoned' Sam in a manner likely to cause unnecessary suffering or injury to health. It appears that, although an offence has been committed, the child is no longer in immediate danger and arrangements could be made perhaps with the neighbours or the grandparents for the child's safety while Jo is absent. If there was any reason to believe the child was in immediate danger the officer could consider taking Sam into police protection and arresting the mother. However, prosecution guidelines must be followed and the guidance of a CPS representative would be required. Whatever action is taken, it must be proportionate.

TASK 3

1. The boy needs regular medication: has he taken that medication with him? Are there factors which will make his medical condition worse (such as stress-induced asthma)? Can the condition be life-threatening in any way? Is his shotgun (and any other weapons on the farm) accounted for? Has any ammunition gone missing? Has the boy mentioned any particular individuals in

connection with the apparent bullying at school, or about revenge? Was the quarrel with his father more serious than usual? What could have caused his depression and anxiety? Has he ever talked (or hinted) about suicide? Does he have a religious belief or strong ethical principles? Has he taken drugs? Has he ever been in trouble with the police?

2. ACPO has produced an updated guide; 'Interim Guidance on the Management, Recording and Investigation of Missing Persons 2013' to accompany their 2010 guidance. Both are available online.

TASK 4

1. False. In the Act, 'suffering' means physical or mental suffering and related expressions shall be construed accordingly.

2. Section 2 states an animal is protected if it is:

   • of a kind which is commonly domesticated in the British Islands;

   • under human control (permanently or temporarily); or

   • otherwise not living in a wild state.

3. Section 19 does not authorize entry to any part of premises which is used as a private dwelling. Under these circumstances a warrant will need to be obtained under s 19(4).

4. She may enter and search any premises to arrest any person she reasonably suspects of committing an offence under s 4 of the Animal Welfare Act 2006 using s 17 of the PACE Act 1984 (see 9.5). Local force policy must be followed in relation to using force to gain entry in such circumstances.

14 Policing Public Order, Anti-social Behaviour, and Harassment

14.1 Introduction

In their 'Stop the rot' report HMIC (2010) observed that tackling crime appeared to be given a higher priority than keeping the peace and controlling anti-social behaviour (ASB). The report outlined that in the period 2009–10 approximately 3.5 million calls were made to the police about anti-social behaviour problems, but that this was probably only just over a quarter of the total number of anti-social incidents that had actually occurred. In comparison, around 4.3 million crimes were recorded in the same period. Critically, the report highlighted the 'growing importance' of anti-social behaviour 'as an indicator of failure to control the streets' (HMIC, 2010, p 5).

The Crime Survey for England and Wales (Home Office, 2013a) estimates the effects of crime and disorder on the quality of people's lives. In the 2013 Survey 13 per cent of people perceived the levels of ASB as 'high'. Anti-social behaviour is not a 'crime' as such, but a label placed on a number of disruptive activities which may or may not in themselves be criminal offences. Consequently, this chapter looks not only at offences but also considers some of the powers designed for the policing of social disorder generally, both in private and public places. Note that in 2012 the government signalled its intention to replace the existing anti-social behaviour measures and instead introduce alternative 'community-based' approaches.

Dealing with civil disputes (eg trespass or debt) and court orders (concerning, eg, access to children or repossession of property) is not normally the responsibility of the police service in England and Wales, but the police are often first at the scene when a situation escalates. Of course, an incident which began as a civil dispute may also erupt into an incident in which criminal offences are committed. For some cases of civil dispute, an alternative remedy in the civil courts can be suggested by the police. If, for example, a person is harassed by a neighbour, an injunction can be brought about under s 3(1) of the Protection from Harassment Act 1997 (see 14.5.1.4). In other circumstances, the police can apply for a civil order such as a Domestic Violence Protection Order (see 15.7.1).

The policing of demonstrations has been considered in recent years, particularly in terms of police strategy to contain and control crowds (eg the controversial use of 'kettling'). The police have a duty not only to maintain public order but also to facilitate the democratic right of citizens to lawfully protest and demonstrate; 'the right to peaceful assembly' in the European Convention on Human Rights (ECHR), subsequently enshrined in the Human Rights Act 1998 (in particular the freedom of expression (Article 10) and the freedom of assembly (Article 11)—see 5.4). There have been a number of HMIC reports on the policing of protest, including a major review in 2009 after the protests at the G20 summit (HMIC, 2009, revised 2011). An HMIC report in 2011 recommended that the police retain an adaptable response to the changing nature of protest (HMIC, 2011). Hence it could well be that any training you may receive after joining the police has been designed to reflect these ongoing changes. In this chapter we examine the common law employed by the police to contain protesters to reduce the threat of large-scale disorder.

14.2 Police Action against Anti-social Behaviour

Here we examine some relatively new approaches to countering anti-social behaviour. Areas with particular problems can be targeted by the police, who can then provide support for communities by reducing intimidation and other forms of anti-social behaviour. The target area can be as small as a parking area or as large as a whole housing estate.

14.2.1 Power to require name and address

If a police officer has reason to believe that a person has been acting (or is acting) in an 'anti-social manner' a police officer may require that person to give his/her name and address (s 50(1) of the Police Reform Act 2002). An anti-social manner is one that 'caused or was likely to cause harassment, alarm or distress to one or more persons not of the same household as [him/herself]' (s 1 of the Crime and Disorder Act 1998). It is an offence for such a person to fail to give his/her name and address when required (including giving a false or inaccurate name or address (s 50(2) of the Police Reform Act 2002)). This offence is triable summarily and the penalty is a fine.

14.2.2 Anti-social Behaviour Orders

At the time of writing Anti-social Behaviour Orders (or ASBOs as they are commonly known) can be used for individuals over 10 years of age who continually behave in such a way as to cause harassment, alarm, or distress to members of the local community. Section 1 of the Crime and Disorder Act 1998 allows a magistrates' court to make an ASBO against such an individual. The order is intended to prevent problem behaviour in the future rather than punishing behaviour that has already occurred, but if the individual breaches an ASBO, he/she commits a criminal offence (s 1(1) of the Crime and Disorder Act 1998). This is intended to act as a deterrent.

An ASBO is made following a complaint about behaviour occurring in the preceding six months and:

- lists the types of behaviour that are prohibited for that particular individual;
- lasts at least two years;
- can be discharged (discontinued) if both parties agree; and
- may be varied (changed) if new and different complaints are made.

In some situations, a banned behaviour might not be in breach of the ASBO if it can be proved that the behaviour was reasonable under those particular circumstances.

A breach of an ASBO is a strict liability offence (see 5.3.2). However a court is still entitled to consider a defendant's state of mind in relation to a 'reasonable excuse' (*JB v Director of Public Prosecutions* [2012] EWHC 72 (Admin)). The offence is triable either way and the penalty is a fine and/or imprisonment (six months summarily and five years on indictment).

At the time of writing, the Home Office had presented its draft Anti-Social Behaviour Crime and Policing Bill 2013–14 to Parliament. This may amend the Crime and Disorder Act 1998 and thereby implement the policies set out in the white paper 'Putting Victims First' available online.

14.2.3 Local child curfews

Local child curfews ban children under 16 from being in a specified area of a public place between 9 pm and 6 am unless they are under the effective control of a parent or a responsible person aged 18 or over (s 14 of the Crime and Disorder Act 1998). A local authority or a chief officer of police can introduce a local child curfew scheme for a specified period, which cannot be more than 90 days.

Before implementing a local child curfew scheme, the applicant must consult with the chief officer of police and appropriate bodies such as the local authority, and the scheme cannot come into effect until it is confirmed by the Secretary of State. The notice will be given by displaying it in the area or by any other suitable method. Section 15 of the Crime and Disorder Act 1998 describes the action a police officer should take if he/she finds a child contravening a local child curfew. If there is reasonable cause to believe that a child is in contravention of a ban imposed by a curfew notice the local authority must be informed (s 15(1)). The child can be taken back to his/her home unless there is reasonable cause to believe that the child would be likely to suffer significant harm (s 15(3)).

14.2.4 Dispersal and removal powers for anti-social behaviour

Section 30 of the Anti-Social Behaviour Act 2003 describes police powers that may be used if a senior police officer of superintendent rank or above has reasonable grounds for believing that in the relevant locality:

1. members of the public have been intimidated, harassed, alarmed, or distressed as a result of the presence or behaviour of groups of two or more persons; and
2. anti-social behaviour is a significant and persistent problem.

The senior police officer can make an authorization under s 30(2) that provides a police officer in uniform with dispersal and removal powers to address such issues should the need arise. The authorization can last for up to six months.

14.2.4.1 Dispersal of groups

The term 'group' is not defined in the legislation but has been held to include protesters (see *R (on the application of Singh and another) v CC of West Midlands Police* [2006] EWCA Civ 1118) and must be two or more persons. Once the authorization has been made (see 14.2.4), and if the circumstances recur, a police officer has the power (s 30(4)) to give a direction requiring the people in a group to disperse (either immediately or within a certain time limit). Any person in the group whose place of residence is not within the relevant locality can be directed to leave (either immediately or within a certain time limit) and not to return within a specified period (24 hours or less).

Section 32 of the Anti-Social Behaviour Act 2003 provides more guidance on how to give a direction for the purposes of s 30(4). Under s 32(1) a direction may be:

1. given orally;
2. given to any person individually or to two or more persons together; and
3. withdrawn or varied by the person who gave it.

Section 32(2) states that it is an offence to knowingly contravene a direction. The offence is triable summarily and the penalty is three months' imprisonment and/or a fine.

14.2.4.2 Removal of young people under 16

A young person found in any public place within the relevant locality at night (between 9 pm and 6 am) can be 'removed' if a s 30 authorization is in place. The officer must have reasonable grounds for believing that he/she is under 16 and is not under the effective control of a parent or a responsible person aged 18 or over. Under s 30(6), such a young person can be removed to his/her place of residence (unless there are reasonable grounds for believing that he/she would be likely to suffer significant harm once at the residence). If he/she is unwilling to go voluntarily, the word 'remove' has been held to mean 'take away using reasonable force if necessary' (*R (W) v Commissioner of Police for the Metropolis and another, Secretary of State for the Home Department, interested party* [2004] EWCA Civ 458).

> **TASK 1** What power can a police officer use to help identify a person who is acting in an anti-social manner?

14.2.5 Nuisance or disturbance on hospital premises

It is an offence (s 119(1) of the Criminal Justice and Immigration Act 2008) for a person on NHS premises to cause a nuisance or disturbance (without reasonable excuse) to an NHS staff member who is working there or is otherwise there in connection with work, and to refuse (without reasonable excuse) to leave when asked to do so by a police officer or an NHS staff member.

Here, NHS premises includes:

- English NHS hospitals and any building or other structure on hospital grounds (land in the vicinity of the hospital and associated with it); and
- vehicles associated with the hospital and situated on hospital grounds (includes an air ambulance).

This offence cannot be committed by a person who is on the NHS premises for the purpose of obtaining medical advice, treatment, or care for him/herself, but can be committed by someone who has already received it or has been refused it during the previous eight hours. An NHS staff member is anyone employed (or otherwise working for) a relevant English NHS body, and includes agency and contract workers, students, and volunteers.

A police officer who reasonably suspects that a person is committing or has committed a s 119(1) offence can remove him/her from the premises using reasonable force if necessary (s 120(1)). The offence of causing a nuisance (s 119(1)) is triable summarily and the penalty is a fine.

14.2.6 Smoking in a smoke-free place

Under s 7 of the Health Act 2006, a person commits an offence if he/she smokes in a 'smoke-free' place. Smoking includes the smoking of cigarettes (hand-rolled and manufactured), pipes, cigars, herbal cigarettes, and the use of water-pipes (eg 'hubble-bubble' pipes).

Smoke-free places include 'enclosed or substantially enclosed premises which are open to the public, and shared workplaces', and are defined more fully in the Smoke-free (Premises and Enforcement) Regulations 2006. Briefly, enclosed premises have a ceiling or roof and are wholly enclosed except for doors, windows, or passageways, and substantially enclosed premises have a ceiling or roof but the permanent openings in the walls are less than half of the total areas of walls, known as the '50% rule'. (Here, 'walls' include structures which 'serve the purpose of walls and constitute the perimeter of premises', and a 'roof' includes any fixed or moveable structure or device which is capable of covering all or part of the premises as a roof, including, for example, a canvas awning.) Therefore premises with a ceiling or roof that have large permanent openings in the wall (more than half of the total wall area) are not subject to this legislation.

This offence is triable summarily and the penalty is a fine.

14.2.7 Dangerous dogs and anti-social behaviour

Some owners of dangerous dogs (defined in s 1 of the Dangerous Dogs Act 1991) handle the dogs in public in an anti-social manner. Guidance for dealing with such incidents, and allegations of people owning or breeding prohibited dogs can be found in 'Dangerous Dogs Law Guidance for Enforcers' (Defra, 2009). Legislation in relation to protecting the dogs from cruelty can also be considered (see 13.7.1).

14.2.8 Injunctions for gang-related violence

Section 34(3) of the Policing and Crime Act 2009 enables the police or a local authority to apply to a county court (or the High Court) for an injunction against an individual, in order to prevent him/her from engaging in, or encouraging or assisting, gang-related violence. An injunction may also be issued to protect a person from gang-related violence. Section 34(5) of the 2009 Act defines a gang as a group that:

- consists of at least three people;
- uses a name, emblem, or colour or any other identifiable characteristic; and
- is associated with a particular area.

A power of arrest (s 43(2)) may be attached to an injunction in case of it being breached. The Home Office has issued Statutory Guidance on s 34(3) injunctions (Home Office, 2010d).

> **TASK 2** Imagine you are a trainee police officer on Supervised Patrol in a part of a city which has a significant and persistent problem with anti-social behaviour, and is therefore subject to an order under s 30 of the Anti-Social Behaviour Act 2003. The order allows you to disperse people from the locality if you believe this is required. During your patrol, you see a group of about a dozen young people who appear to be local residents. A member of the group appears to intimidate a passer-by. What precise powers would you have to deal with the young people involved?

14.3 Breach of the Peace

You have no doubt heard of the phrase 'breach of the peace'. There is some considerable debate concerning both its meaning and whether the police should still have powers in this respect.

This is partly because the law surrounding a breach of the peace is somewhat unusual: it is not a criminal offence, nor is it part of statute law, but is instead part of common law (see 5.2). Case law has set a precedent in defining its meaning (see 14.3.1). Some police forces discourage their officers from the use of police powers in relation to a breach of the peace, whereas others continue to view it as an important means of reducing the likelihood of harm taking place. In all cases the police use of breach of the peace should be consistent with Article 5 (the right to liberty and security), Article 10 (the right to freedom of expression), and Article 11 (the right to freedom of assembly and association) of the Human Rights Act 1998 (see 5.4). During recent protests the police have used likelihood of an imminent breach of the peace as the reason for the containing ('kettling') of large numbers of protesters at the same location for extended periods of time. The use of 'containment' as a public order measure remains controversial, as does the use of breach of the peace legislation.

Any person committing a breach of the peace can in law be arrested by any other person (although in most cases this will be a police officer, rather than a member of the public). Having been arrested, individuals can be detained until there is no likelihood of a breach of the peace recurring. They may then be released without further action or be 'bound over' (see 14.3.3).

14.3.1 Definition of breach of the peace

The case of *R v Howell* [1981] 3 All ER 383 provides a definition of the meaning of breach of the peace:

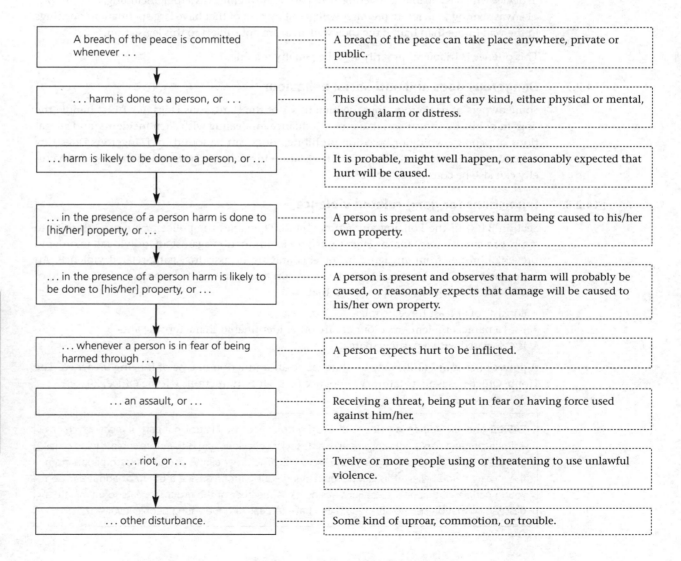

14.3.2 Powers of arrest for breach of the peace

Breach of the peace is unique. It can take place in many different ways, but whatever the situation, it must satisfy the elements set out in the case *R v Howell*.

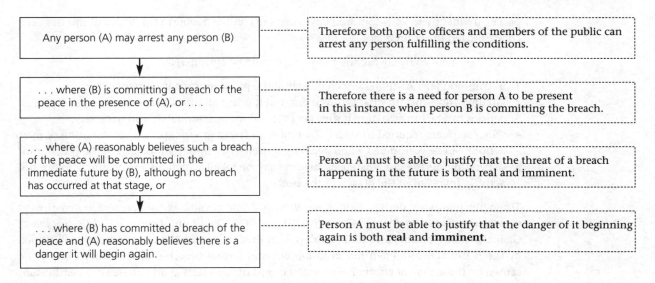

Any person (A) may arrest any person (B)	Therefore both police officers and members of the public can arrest any person fulfilling the conditions.
... where (B) is committing a breach of the peace in the presence of (A), or ...	Therefore there is a need for person A to be present in this instance when person B is committing the breach.
... where (A) reasonably believes such a breach of the peace will be committed in the immediate future by (B), although no breach has occurred at that stage, or	Person A must be able to justify that the threat of a breach happening in the future is both real and imminent.
... where (B) has committed a breach of the peace and (A) reasonably believes there is a danger it will begin again.	Person A must be able to justify that the danger of it beginning again is both **real** and **imminent**.

For the arrest to be lawful, the person making the arrest must identify the all-important ingredients of harm and compare the actual circumstances with the definition. The breach must have taken place in his/her presence, or the threat or its renewal must be both real and imminent.

14.3.3 Binding-over after an arrest for breach of the peace

After arrest for breach of the peace a person may be released by the police without further action when it is deemed that a risk of a breach no longer exists. However, in other circumstances the CPS may decide (s 3(2)(c) of the Prosecution of Offences Act 1986) that further action is needed to reduce the risk of a further breach. The person arrested for breach of the peace will appear before a magistrates' court, which can issue a binding-over order. This can refer to general terms of protection, or it can be more specific by naming people. The order can also require the recipient to:

- enter into a recognizance for a specified sum (an agreement to pay some monies if brought back to court after any subsequent breaches); and
- keep the peace for a specified time.

TASK 3 In August 2012 at King's Cross underground station in London a group of around 30 to 40 individuals were stopped from making their way to the Notting Hill Carnival in order to 'prevent a breach of the peace'. Some of the men were reported by the press to be wearing 'body armour'. The men were believed to have travelled from north London in order to 'cause trouble' at the carnival. They were held until the police judged there was no risk of disorder and then released without charge. An MPS Commander was reported as saying 'On the arrests at King's Cross we received intelligence that members of a north London gang were heading towards the carnival. They were spotted on the Underground and they were detained until the carnival was over. There was no doubt they were planning on causing trouble' (London Evening Standard, 2012).

In November 2003, a woman climbed the gates of Buckingham Palace to protest at the visit of US President George W. Bush. She then unfurled the Stars and Stripes flag on top of the gates with the words 'ELIZABETH WINDSOR AND CO...HE'S NOT WELCOME' written on the flag. After about two hours she voluntarily climbed down from the gates and was reportedly arrested by the police on suspicion of criminal damage and breach of the peace.

Compare the use of breach of peace powers in the two examples.

14.3.4 Containment

Containment (also known as 'kettling') is used by the police to maintain public order and safety. It involves putting a cordon around a large number of people and confining them to a relatively small, easily managed public area, and police officers control who remains inside the cordon and for how long. The police argue that the likelihood of an imminent breach of the peace provides them with common law powers to confine people in this way, but this has been challenged in the courts.

For containment to be lawful, the following should be considered:

1. at common law, an apprehended breach of the peace must be imminent;
2. circumstances dictate what is imminent, but it is not an inflexible concept;
3. actions can be justified only if they are proportionate, reasonable, and necessary;
4. when steps are required to keep two or more different groups apart, a combination of their actions can be considered when deciding if there is an imminent breach of the peace; and
5. depending on the circumstances, action may be taken which affects people who are not actively involved in the breach of the peace.

These five points are derived from *R (on the application of Hannah McClure and Joshua Moos) v Commissioner of Police for the Metropolis* [2012] EWCA Civ 12 and *Laporte v Chief Constable of Gloucestershire Constabulary* [2007] 2 AC 105. In the former case the containment was justified by the reasonable apprehension of imminent and serious breaches of the peace likely to be caused by the arrival of another substantial crowd of protesters at an airbase. The justification was not the violent and unruly behaviour of the main crowd. (See also *Moss v McLachlan* [1985] 1 RLR 76 in relation to policing the 1984 miners' strike.)

The police must take all other possible steps to prevent the breach or imminent breach of the peace and to protect the rights of third parties before using containment (*Austin v Commissioner of Police of the Metropolis* [2009] 1 AC 564). The containment of children is lawful if s 11 of the Children Act 2004 is followed, regarding the welfare of the children (*R (on the application of Castle and others) v Commissioner of Police for the Metropolis* [2011] EWHC 2317). It should be noted that people released from containment have no obligation to provide personal information, nor is it acceptable for them to be photographed (*Susannah Mengesha v Commissioner of Police of the Metropolis* [2013] EWHC 1695 (Admin)). Further information on the use of containment can be found in the *Manual of Guidance on Keeping the Peace* (ACPO, 2010e)

14.4 The Public Order Act 1986

The Public Order Act 1986 deals with a wide range of behaviours and offences as follows:

- riot (s 1);
- violent disorder (s 2);
- affray (s 3);
- fear or provocation of violence (s 4);
- intentional harassment, alarm, or distress (s 4A);
- non-intentional harassment, alarm, or distress (s 5).

The most commonly committed public order offences (under s 4A and s 5) are the least serious.

14.4.1 Intoxication is not a defence

Some people accused of Public Order Act 1986 offences may claim in their defence that they were intoxicated at the time of the offence. However, s 6(5) of the Public Order Act 1986 specifically states that in these circumstances a person will be taken by the court to have the same level of awareness as if he/she had not been intoxicated, unless it can be proved that either the intoxication:

- was not self-induced (eg 'spiked' drinks); or
- was caused solely by the taking or administration of a substance in the course of medical treatment (eg prescribed medicine).

Note that s 6(5) does not apply to s 4A of the Act, as s 4A was introduced at a later date.

14.4.2 Locations for public order offences

Offences under ss 4, 4A, and 5 of the Public Order Act 1986 are for the most part only committed in a public place, but in certain circumstances they can also be committed within the confines of a private place, for example a communal area such as a shared laundry in a block of flats (see *Le Vine v DPP* (2010) DC (Elias LJ, Keith J) 6/5/2010). An offence can also be committed when the conduct occurs in the confines of a private place which causes a person who is outside in a public place to be harassed, alarmed, or distressed. For example, if a neighbour attaches an offensive poster to the inside of a window, which offends a person in the public street outside, the offence has been committed. (However, if the poster was seen by the same person but from inside his own house next door (perhaps through a side window), then the offence has not been committed. Other legislation is available for circumstances which are completely private, for example the Protection from Harassment Act 1997 (see 14.5.1).)

The more serious public order offences (riot, violent disorder, and affray) can take place in private, as well as in public places (see 9.2 for definitions of public places).

14.4.3　Offences under ss 5, 4A, and 4

Members of the public generally like to be able to walk along the street without being intimidated, frightened, or stressed by other people's actions. Sections 5 and 4A of the Public Order Act 1986 are used for relatively minor forms of public disorder such as persistent swearing and shouting. Section 4, on the other hand, deals with a more serious type of public disorder, involving fear or provocation of violence.

Before looking at the sections in detail, you might find it useful to consider the definitions of key terms used in the legislation, as shown here in the table. The distinctions between offences under ss 5, 4A, and 4 require careful consideration and still cause some debate in legal and police circles. The offences will be described individually, and then compared in order to highlight important differences between them. Please note that the Crime and Courts Act 2013 removed the word 'insulting' from s 5.

Definitions	
Abusive	Using or containing insulting or degrading language
Alarm	A state of surprise, fright, fear, terror, and panic
Behaviour	Display of conduct involving the treatment of others
Disorderly behaviour	Rowdy, unruly, boisterous, loud, raucous, or unrestrained conduct
Distress	A feeling of suffering, anguish, and misery
Distribute	To hand out, share out, give out, or issue to a particular person or people, not just simply leave 'lying about'
Harassment	A feeling of annoyance, persecution, irritation, and aggravation
Insulting	Disrespectful, especially if done in a way that is offensive or suggesting that a person is beneath consideration (but in a way that is more than causing annoyance or bitterness)
Threatening	Describes a physical or verbal act which indicates that harm will be inflicted. It can also include violent conduct
To display	To show or exhibit for all to see, such as placing a sign or poster in a window
Words	Spoken or shouted
Writing, sign, or other visual representation	A notice containing lettering or other visible form of copied picture, text, or image, leaflet, pamphlet, or fly poster

14.4.3.1　Section 5 of the Public Order Act 1986

The offence is also referred to as causing non-intentional harassment, alarm, or distress. Section 5 of the Public Order Act 1986 states that a person is guilty of this offence if he/she uses threatening or abusive words or behaviour, or disorderly behaviour, or if he/she displays any writing, sign, or other visible representation which is threatening or abusive, and this is done within the hearing or sight of a person likely to be caused harassment, alarm, or distress thereby.

The key features of s 5 offences are that:

- the conduct does not have to be aimed towards a specific person;
- the conduct must take place within the presence of a person who can see or hear the conduct, but that person does not need to be identifiable;
- the type of conduct must be likely to cause harassment, alarm, or distress;
- any material used (such as a poster) is not distributed;
- the suspect must intend or be aware that their conduct is threatening or abusive in general terms; however,

- there is no need to prove he/she actually intended to cause any person to be harassed, alarmed, or distressed.

You may feel that the last two bullet points appear contradictory, but consider the example shown here. A police officer (PO) is interviewing a suspect (S), and the precise nature of a s 5 offence becomes more clear; the suspect might intend his/her conduct to be threatening or abusive but still have no intention to make any person harassed, alarmed, or distressed.

> **PO** Why did you behave like that, back there in the street?
> **S** I was trying to be...hard in front of my mates.
> **PO** Didn't you think about the effect it might have on other people?
> **S** Not really, it didn't even cross my mind they'd take any notice—I was only messing about.
> **PO** What was the point of it all then?
> **S** Not a lot—I was only showing off, I'd had a couple of drinks, but I wasn't drunk. I knew what I was doing and I wanted to be as loud and proud as I could, just to show my mates I could do it. They just laughed and made out I was acting stupid.
> **PO** Yes, and you might have upset a few elderly people passing by; how do you think they felt hearing that lot?
> **S** I just didn't think—yeah, I knew they were there...But if I did, I didn't mean to upset them...

There are three defences to this offence (listed in s 5(3)):

- that he/she had no reason to believe, whilst in public, that anybody could hear or see his/her conduct and had become harassed, alarmed, or distressed as a result—in other words, the suspect believed that his/her poster or behaviour could not be seen or heard by anybody else;
- that he/she had no reason to believe, whilst inside a dwelling (place of residence), that his/her words, behaviour, or conduct could be seen or heard by a person outside that same or another dwelling: for example, a poster was positioned on a wall inside the front room, and could not be clearly seen from the road outside; or
- that his/her conduct was reasonable and did not cause anybody to be harassed, alarmed, or distressed. For example he/she shouted at a group of people who were carrying out an unlawful act outside his/her home.

This offence is triable summarily and the penalty is a fine. It can also be racially or religiously aggravated (see 14.10.4).

> **TASK 4** Take a moment now to consider what evidence a police officer would need before making a decision whether to consider a person for a s 5 Public Order Act 1986 offence.
>
> 1. Who would provide evidence?
> 2. What evidence would they be able to provide?
> 3. What evidence would a police officer present at the scene be able to provide?

14.4.3.2 Section 4A of the Public Order Act 1986

A s 4A offence is often referred to as causing intentional harassment, alarm, or distress. A person is guilty of this offence if he/she uses threatening, abusive, or insulting words or behaviour, or disorderly behaviour, or displays any writing, sign, or other visible representation which is threatening, abusive, or insulting, with intent to cause a person harassment, alarm, or distress thereby causing that or another person harassment, alarm, or distress.

The key features of s 4A offences are that:

- the suspect intends the conduct to be threatening, abusive, or insulting and to cause a person harassment, alarm, or distress;
- the conduct does not have to be aimed towards a specific person;
- at least one identifiable person must be harassed, alarmed, or distressed; and
- material (if used) cannot be distributed.

This piece of legislation is aimed at supporting the most vulnerable members of the community, who may be specifically targeted because of their inability to respond appropriately to intentionally directed acts which cause them harassment, alarm, or distress. These victims may feel particularly uncomfortable as witnesses, so every opportunity should be taken to support them throughout any police or legal process.

As a possible defence, a suspect could demonstrate that:

- he/she had no reason to believe his/her words, behaviour, or conduct inside a dwelling (a place of residence) could be seen or heard by a person anywhere outside, for example a poster hanging on an inside wall within a house was difficult to see from the road outside (s 4A(3)(a)); or
- his/her conduct was reasonable, for example if a person shouted at a group of people who were carrying out an unlawful act outside his/her home (s 4A(3)(b)).

This offence is triable summarily and the penalty is six months' imprisonment and/or a fine. This offence can be racially or religiously aggravated (see 14.10.4).

14.4.3.3 Section 4 of the Public Order Act 1986

A s 4 offence is also referred to as fear or provocation of violence. A person is guilty of this offence if he/she uses towards another person threatening, abusive, or insulting words or behaviour, or if he/she distributes or displays to another person any writing, sign, or other visible representation which is threatening, abusive, or insulting. The intent must be to:

- cause that person to believe that immediate unlawful violence will be used (against him/her or another) by any person; or
- provoke the immediate use of unlawful violence (by that person or another);
- cause that person to believe it is likely either that such violence will be used or be provoked.

For this offence, the intentions of the suspect are the key issue; the actual effect of the behaviour on other people is not relevant. The intention must be to make the recipient (the person (or persons) to whom the conduct is addressed) feel fear, or to provoke anyone to be violent. Despite the fact that the actual effect of the conduct is not relevant for this offence, for the intentions of the suspect to be held to be genuine, his/her conduct must be directed towards a recipient who must be present at the time when the words or behaviour are used. The recipient must be able to see or hear the conduct (or the suspect must at least believe that the recipient is able to see or hear the conduct (see *Atkin v DPP* [1989] Crim LR 581)).

The suspect's intentions may be to cause fear of violence. If so, the suspect must intend the recipient to fear that violence will be used (or is likely to be used). The key point is that if the suspect is intent on causing the recipient to fear violence, the threatened violent acts do not need to involve the suspect or the recipient directly. The violent acts could be threatened by the suspect against the recipient, or against another person. Also, the suspect can intend to cause fear in the recipient that such violent acts will be carried out by another person, and not by the suspect.

Alternatively, the suspect could have the intention (a determined state of mind) to provoke any person to use violence. For example, an extremist shouts at an animal research worker at a demonstration, 'A dog is for life, not just for you to torture and experiment on, you sadist! You'll get the same, I promise you that!' If the intention is to provoke immediate violence on the part of a group of animal rights activists who are nearby, the offence is committed.

The key features of s 4 offences are that:

- the conduct must be directed towards a person or persons present at the scene;
- any material used is distributed and not just displayed;
- the suspect must intend or be aware that his/her conduct is potentially threatening, abusive, or insulting (but it does not matter whether the recipient actually feels threatened, abused, or insulted);
- the suspect may intend to cause fear or provoke a reaction of violence (but it does not matter whether the conduct actually has either of these effects);
- if the suspect intends to cause fear (that violence will be or is likely to be used), the intention need only be to cause the recipient to feel fear; and
- if the suspect intends to provoke violence, the intention can be to provoke any person present.

Specific Incidents

A police officer may enter any premises to arrest any person reasonably suspected of committing an offence under s 4 of the Public Order Act 1986 (s 17 of the PACE Act 1984: see 9.5.1.2). The offence is triable summarily and the penalty is six months' imprisonment and/or a fine. This offence can be racially aggravated (see 14.10.4).

	s 4	s 4A	s 5
Awareness and intentions of the suspect	Intends to cause fear of violence or to provoke violence	Intends to be threatening, abusive, or insulting	No intention, but is aware that the conduct is threatening or abusive
Recipient of the conduct	Conduct aimed towards a specific person	Conduct does not have to be aimed towards a specific person	Conduct does not have to be aimed towards a specific person (but has to be carried out in the hearing or sight of a person likely to be caused harassment, alarm, or distress)
Includes disorderly behaviour?	Does not include disorderly behaviour	Includes disorderly behaviour	
Distribution of material?	Includes distribution of material	Does not include distribution of material	
Outcome of the behaviour	No specific outcome is required to prove this offence	An identifiable person must be harassed, alarmed, or distressed	No specific outcome is required to prove this offence

TASK 5 Imagine you are a trainee police officer on Independent Patrol. You encounter a man who is shouting in an incoherent and aggressive manner, and it seems to you that the behaviour is likely to be capable of causing harassment, alarm, or distress. Consider how you will deal with this situation if there is no one else in the area at the time to whom this conduct is aimed and hence it appears to be directed solely at you.

While drawing your conclusions, refer to *DPP v Orum* [1988] Crim LR 848 and *Harvey v DPP* [2011] EWCA Crim B1.

TASK 6 Imagine you are a trainee police officer on Independent Patrol. You see a man walk up to the door of a club and adopt an aggressive posture towards the door supervisor. You are about two metres away. The aggressor has clenched fists, bulging eyes, and has taken up a 'boxing' position. The suspect then pushes his shoulder into the door supervisor's chest causing the door supervisor to move back. You hear the suspect say 'You're a dead man'. You believe that the door supervisor is about to be attacked and so you arrest the suspect under s 4 of the Public Order Act 1986.

When you return to the club to obtain a statement from the door supervisor, you are informed that he is not willing to make a statement. In your opinion could a successful prosecution be brought against the suspect under these circumstances?

When drawing a conclusion, consider *Swanston v DPP* (1997) 161 JP 203.

14.4.4 Serious public order offences

These offences under the Public Order Act 1986 are, in increasing order of seriousness:

- affray (s 3);
- violent disorder (s 2); and
- riot (s 1).

Remember, these more serious public order offences can be committed in private as well as in public. Offences under ss 1–3 all involve unlawful violence. Briefly, violence is aggressive or hostile conduct towards property or persons, and includes acts capable of causing injury even if no injury or damage is caused. Section 8 of the Public Order Act offers guidance on the meaning of unlawful violence in this context:

(a) except in the context of affray, it includes violent conduct towards property as well as violent conduct towards persons; and

(b) it is not restricted to conduct causing or intended to cause injury or damage but includes any other violent conduct (eg throwing a full can of beer towards a person, even if it falls short).

The legislation describing offences under ss 1–3 also uses the term a 'person of reasonable firmness' (sometimes referred to as the 'hypothetical bystander'). This is not defined under law but can be taken to mean an average person in terms of their reaction to violent incidents around them (ie not someone who is unduly frightened by the most minor of incidents, nor someone who is completely hardened to acts of violent behaviour).

14.4.4.1 Affray

For an affray (s 3 of the Public Order Act 1986) the threat of violence needs to be capable of upsetting others. The primary objective of the law is to protect the general public around the affray and therefore the court will consider how a hypothetical person of reasonable firmness (see 14.4.4) who witnessed the incident would feel (*R v Sanchez*, The Times, 6 March 1996).

Therefore, there are in effect three parties involved in an affray:

1. the individual making the threats;
2. the person subject to the threats who must be present; and
3. at least one bystander.

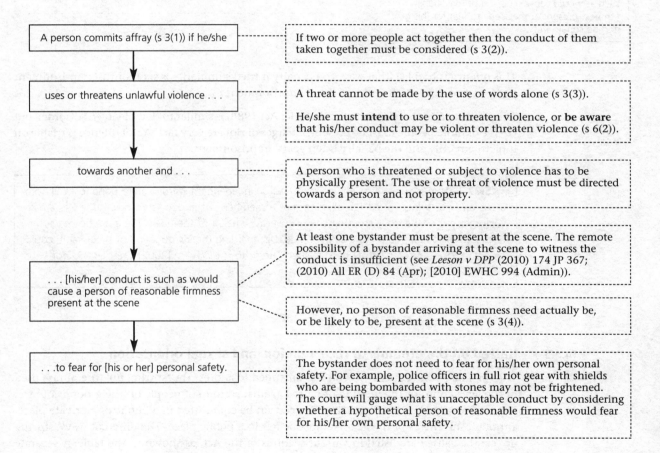

In drawing a conclusion about the conduct of the suspects and the person of reasonable firmness, the court can consider evidence from witnesses at the incident (including police officers), the extent of any injuries, and recordings such as from CCTV or the media.

This offence is triable either way. The penalty if tried summarily is six months' imprisonment, and/or a fine, and on indictment three years' imprisonment.

14.4.4.2 Violent disorder and riot

For the offence of violent disorder (s 2 of the Public Order Act 1986), three or more persons must be present together and use (or threaten to use) unlawful violence. If it is only possible to arrest and investigate one person out of such a group, then he/she can still be charged with this offence, but it must still be proved that at least two other people using or threatening violence were present, and they must be mentioned in the charge. However, there is no requirement for a common purpose to be held by those using or threatening behaviour. For example, a man becomes violent towards a police officer for personal reasons and a short while later a crowd forms around the officer threatening violence but for a different reason to that of the man (see *R v NW* [2010] EWCA Crim 404).

Section 6(2) states that as for affray a person is guilty of violent disorder only if he/she:

- intends to use or threaten violence; or
- is aware that his/her conduct may be violent or may threaten violence.

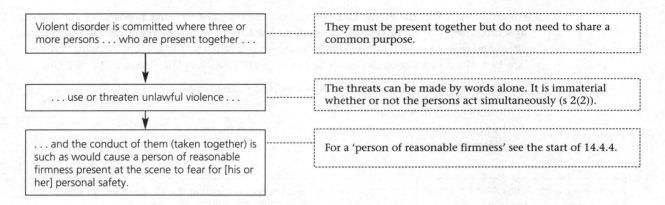

This offence is triable either way. The penalty if tried summarily is six months' imprisonment and/or a fine, on indictment five years' imprisonment.

The offence of riot (s 1(1) of the Public Order Act 1986) is similar to that of violent disorder, but twelve or more people must be present. Charges of riot are very rare. A riot offence is triable on indictment only and the penalty is ten years' imprisonment.

> **TASK 7** Imagine you are a trainee police officer on Independent Patrol. You respond to a call from a customer of a local nightclub alleging that a member of the door staff has pushed a female customer out of the door and that she fell over as a result of the push. There are no other witnesses to the incident and no CCTV footage. Disregarding the investigation of the assault, could an investigation into an affray be sustained? Refer to *R v Plavecz* [2002] Crim LR 837 for your answer.

14.4.5 Hatred on the grounds of race, religion, and sexual orientation

The original Public Order Act 1986 was amended to address the 'stirring up' (the phrase used in the legislation) or the inciting of hatred against a group of people on the grounds of race, religion, or sexual orientation. The offences can be committed in a public or a private place, although the effects of the actions must be felt in a public place. The different ways 'stirring up' can be caused are listed in various sections of the Act, as shown in the table. A separate offence such as criminal damage can also be aggravated on these grounds, and this is covered in 14.10.

Racial hatred means 'hatred against a group of persons defined by reference to colour, race, nationality (including citizenship) or ethnic or national origins' (s 17 of the Public Order Act 1986).

Religious hatred (s 29A of the Public Order Act 1986) means hatred against a group of persons defined by reference to:

- religious belief, for example Christianity, Islam, Hinduism, Judaism, Buddhism, Sikhism, Rastafarianism, Baha'ism, Zoroastrianism, and Jainism; or
- a lack of religious belief, for example atheists and humanists.

Hatred on the grounds of sexual orientation means 'hatred against a group of persons defined by reference to sexual orientation whether towards persons of the same sex, the opposite sex or both' (s 29AB of the Public Order Act 1986). Further guidance on this is provided in a Ministry of Justice Circular (2010).

Grounds/Activity	Racial	Religious or sexual orientation
Using threatening words or behaviour, or displaying written material	s 18	s 29B
Publishing or distributing written material	s 19	s 29C
Public performance of a play	s 20	s 29D
Distributing, showing, or playing a recording	s 21	s 29E
Broadcasting threatening images or sounds	s 22	s 29F
Possessing racially inflammatory material	s 23	s 29G

In practice, the offences a police officer is most likely to encounter are those involving the use of threatening words or behaviour or the display of written material. Some possible defences are that:

- the acts were part of a programme service (eg on a television programme);
- the acts took place in a private place and were not noticeable to a person in a public place; or
- the suspect was not fully aware of the possible effects of his/her actions.

These offences are triable either way and the penalty is a fine or imprisonment (six months summarily and seven years on indictment).

14.5 Protection from Harassment

Harassment exists in a variety of forms, for example during episodes of stalking, pestering, persecution, and causing annoyance. A number of offences are available to help to deal with the often traumatic experience of being harassed. If complaints are not investigated and addressed in the first instance, relatively minor incidents may develop into much more serious offences such as kidnap, assault, and even murder.

14.5.1 The Protection from Harassment Act 1997

Sections 1 to 5 of the Protection from Harassment Act 1997 can be applied in a wide range of situations, including disputes between partners in a relationship, disputes between neighbours, stalking, and campaigning. Companies or corporate bodies cannot be harassed, but their employees can, so references to 'a person' in the context of harassment refer to a person or persons as individuals (s 7(5) of the Protection from Harassment Act 1997).

The behaviour must be oppressive, unreasonable, and unacceptable, such as that displayed during an act of stalking (for which the offence was originally designed), and be of the sort that a reasonable person would see as harassing (s 1(2) of the Protection from Harassment Act 1997). Harassing a person includes alarming the person or causing the person distress (s 7(2)). For the various offences to be committed it is necessary that the perpetrator knows or ought to know that his/her actions are likely to cause the relevant effect on the victim. The judgement on whether a suspect 'ought to know' is made by considering whether a reasonable person in possession of the same information would know that the actions would have these effects. The final decision whether or not particular behaviour led to a person being alarmed, distressed, or fearful is taken by the court.

The offences described in the Protection from Harassment Act 1997 are:

- harassment (without violence) (s 2);
- stalking (s 2A);
- breaching an injunction (s 3(6));
- putting people in fear of violence (s 4);
- stalking involving fear of violence or serious alarm or distress (s4A); and
- breaching a restraining order (s 5(5)).

Clearly, the Protection from Harassment Act 1997 is a potentially valuable piece of legislation which offers a number of options for providing support to victims of harassment. However, a considerable amount of evidence is required to secure a successful prosecution under this Act, and proving a course of conduct in particular can be difficult. Advice from the CPS should be sought at an early stage.

14.5.1.1 A 'course of conduct'

Under s 1(1) of the Protection from Harassment Act 1997 a person must not pursue a course of conduct which amounts to harassment of another (s 1(1)(a)) or of two or more persons (s 1(1A) (a)), and which he/she knows or ought to know amounts to harassment (ss 1(1)(b) and 1(1A) (b)). The conduct cannot be just a one-off event; it must be a course of conduct which means it must occur on more than one occasion. A course of conduct exists when conduct is directed towards:

- an individual on at least two occasions (s 7(3)(a)); or
- two or more people, and on at least one occasion in relation to each of those persons (s 7(3) (b)).

By precedent it has been decided that it is not just the number of incidents that is important, but whether those incidents are connected (*Lau v DPP* [2000] All ER (D) 224). However, it is less likely that the court will accept that behaviour constitutes a course of conduct if there is a long period of time between the events under consideration. The course of conduct does not have to comprise similar types of conduct: indeed, often it is not obvious that separate incidents are connected, so be aware of this during any investigation. However, a number of irregular and unconnected incidents in a turbulent and unpredictable relationship in which all parties concerned play a part, does not amount to a course of conduct (see *R v Curtis* [2010] EWCA Crim 123 and *R v David Roger Widdows* [2011] EWCA Crim 1500). A court may decide that there was a sequence of separate incidents instead (see *(1) Buckley (2) Smith v DPP* [2008] EWHC 136 (Admin)).

Conduct includes speech, letters, and emails so evidence will need to be gathered from a wide range of sources such as diary entries, emails, letters, photographs, and interviews with witnesses. What might begin as a bona fide enquiry to a company, for example, could become harassing if it is followed up in a manner that is persistent (see *DPP v Hardy* [2008] All ER (D) 315 (Oct)).

The conduct can also involve more than one person. An example of where a group of people could be guilty of harassment would involve three people, X, Y, and Z, who stand along the route which H takes to work in order to give her a threatening letter. They give her the letter, and later Z makes a threatening phone call to her. Provided that H feels alarmed or distressed, and X, Y, and Z knew (or ought to have known) that their actions were likely to be alarming or distressing, then X, Y, and Z would all be committing an offence (s 7(3A) of the Protection from Harassment Act 1997).

That a suspect did not make contact himself was held to be irrelevant: in *James v CPS* [2009] EWHC 2925 (Admin), a client who was receiving local authority care made repeated calls to the office but received no reply. The eventual victim returned the calls on a number of occasions and was verbally abused. Also the offence of harassment does not have to include actually carrying out the conduct; mere planning or otherwise assisting with the course of conduct can amount to the offence.

14.5.1.2 Harassment without violence

It is an offence under s 2(1) of the Protection from Harassment Act 1997 for a person to pursue a course of conduct which involves harassment of one (s 1(1)(a)) or more persons (s 1(1A)(a)). Once initiated a person continues to pursue a course of conduct even when he/she does not personally harass the victim but aids, abets, counsels, or procures another who carries it out instead (s 7(3A)). The suspect(s) must know (or ought to know) that the behaviour amounts to harassment (s 1(1A)(b)).

The course of conduct can be to persuade a person to carry out a particular act or to omit to carry out a particular act. The offender might try to persuade a person to do something that he/she is **not** under any obligation to do (s 1(1A)(c)(ii)). For example, an animal rights extremist might pressurize a person working with animals in research to supply information on work practices. This offence can also be committed when there is an intention to persuade a person to omit to do something that he/she is entitled or required to do (s 1(1A)(c)(i)). For example, an animal rights extremist might pressurize a person to stop working for a company that uses animals for research.

The offence can also be committed when the course of conduct is intended to persuade *any person* to change his/her current routine (s 1(1A)(c)(i) and (ii)). This may form part of a wider campaign about political or social issues. It must be directed towards two or more person(s) in the first instance and occur on at least one occasion in relation to each of those persons.

As a possible defence to a s 2 offence, the suspect could try to show on the balance of probabilities that he/she acted either 'in reasonable circumstances' (this will be for the court to decide, probably using the 'reasonable person' test as in s 1(2)), or in the course of his/her work, for example as a police officer or court official. Full details of the defences are given in s 1(3) of the Protection from Harassment Act 1997.

This offence is triable summarily and the penalty is six months' imprisonment and/or a fine. It can also be racially or religiously aggravated (see 14.10.4).

14.5.1.3   Stalking

The offence of stalking is covered under s 2A of the Protection from Harassment Act 1997. The suspect's acts (or omissions, although no examples are provided) must be associated with stalking (s 2A(1)(b)) and include:

- following a person (s 2A(3)(a));
- contacting, or attempting to contact, a person by any means (s 2A(3)(b));
- publishing any statement or other material relating or purporting to relate to a person, or purporting to originate from a person (s 2A(3)(c)(i) and (ii));
- monitoring the use by a person of the internet, email, or any other form of electronic communication (s 2A(3)(d));
- loitering in any place (whether public or private) (s 2A(3)(e));
- interfering with any property in the possession of a person (s 2A(3)(f));
- watching or spying on a person (s 2A(3)(g)).

As for s 2(1) offences, the suspect must pursue a course of conduct that involves harassment (s 2A (2)(a)), and it can be targeted at one (s 1(1)(a)) or more persons (s 1(1A)(a)). Once initiated, a person continues to pursue a course of conduct even when he/she does not personally harass the victim but aids, abets, counsels, or procures another who carries it out instead (s 7(3A)). The suspect(s) must know (or ought to know) that the behaviour amounts to harassment (s 2A (2)(c)).

This offence is triable summarily and the penalty is six months' imprisonment and/or a fine. It can be racially or religiously aggravated (see 14.10.4).

14.5.1.4   Isolated events causing distress

If distress is caused only on one occasion this does not constitute a course of conduct, and may instead be the subject of a claim in civil proceedings under s 3(1) of the Protection from Harassment Act 1997. The legislation has recently been amended so that a company (as well as a person) can apply for an injunction against individuals. The result of a civil claim can be damages (a court order to pay money) and/or an injunction (a court order to impose sanctions on the offender). If an injunction is breached, an offence is committed. It is triable either way and the penalties are a fine or imprisonment (six months summarily and five years on indictment).

There are no racially or religiously aggravated versions of the civil proceedings under s 3 of the Protection from Harassment Act 1997.

14.5.1.5   Putting people in fear of violence

This offence is described in s 4 of the Protection of Harassment Act 1997 and involves more than sending insulting or abusive letters or emails. The conduct must be targeted at an individual and be calculated to alarm or cause distress. It must also be oppressive and unreasonable (as identified in *Thomas v News Group Newspapers Ltd* [2001] EWCA Civ 1233, [2002] EMLR 78).

There are several key differences from the harassment (s 2) offence we described earlier. For s 4 offences:

- the victim must believe the violence will happen (as opposed to believing it might happen);
- the victim must fear the violence personally (and not on behalf of somebody else, such as a family member) (*Caurti v DPP* [2002] Crim LR 131); and
- the fear of violence cannot be conveyed through a third party.

In most other ways, the conditions for this offence are similar to those for the offence of harassment (s 2) described in detail (see 14.5.1.2); the court decides what is reasonable or unreasonable, it is an offence to pursue or assist the conduct, and there must be a course of conduct amounting to harassment within the meaning of s 1 (see 14.5.1, and *Haque v R* [2011] EWCA Crim 1871). Other relevant case law includes *R v Curtis (James Daniel)* [2010] EWCA Crim 123, [2010] 1 WLR 2770 and *R v Widdows (David Roger)* [2011] EWCA Crim 1500, (2011) 175 JP 345.

The defences to this offence are similar to the defences for s 2 but with one major addition: that the suspect's course of conduct was pursued reasonably for his/her own protection, for protection of another, or for the protection of property (belonging to him/her or another).

This offence can be racially or religiously aggravated (see 14.10.4) and is triable either way. The penalty is a fine or imprisonment (six months summarily, and five years on indictment).

14.5.1.6 Stalking involving fear of violence or serious alarm or distress

These offences are covered under s 4A(1) of the Protection from Harassment Act 1997. Under s 4A(1)(a) the suspect's course of conduct must amount to stalking (see 14.5.1.3) and also cause the victim:

- on at least two occasions to fear that violence will be used against him/her (s 4A(1)(b)(i)); or
- serious alarm or distress which has a substantial adverse effect on his/her usual day-to-day activities (s 4A(1)(b)(ii)).

For these offences the suspect must know (or ought to know) that his/her acts will have these effects on the victim (ss 4A(2) and 4A(3)).

The defences to this offence are given in s 4A(4), and are similar to the defences for s 4. A suspect found not guilty of this offence could instead be found guilty of an offence under ss 2 or 2A (s 4A(7)). This offence is triable either way and the penalty is a fine or imprisonment (twelve months summarily, and five years on indictment).

The offence can be racially or religiously aggravated (see 14.10.4).

14.5.1.7 Restraining orders

A court can make a restraining order under s 5 of the Protection from Harassment Act 1997 against a person who has been convicted (s 5(1)) or acquitted (s 5A) of **any** offence, to protect a person from harassment. A restraining order will place restrictions on a person's future behaviour. It may last indefinitely or for a period stated by the court, and it can be varied or discharged on application. The PNC, the police local intelligence database, and the PND hold records showing whether a person is subject to a restraining order. If such an order is breached an offence is committed (s 5(5)). It is triable either way and the penalty is a fine or imprisonment (six months summarily, and five years on indictment).

TASK 8 Imagine you are a police officer. You are requested to attend an address in your area where a complaint of harassment has been made. Write brief answers to the following questions:

1. What evidence would you need to collect to prove an offence under either s 2 or s 4 of the Protection from Harassment Act 1997?
2. What other methods could be used to stop the conduct?
3. How could future evidence be recorded?
4. What reason(s) would make an arrest necessary in these circumstances?

14.5.2   **Preventing harassment and the Criminal Justice and Police Act 2001**

Harassing or intimidating behaviour by individuals towards a person in his/her home is an offence under the Criminal Justice and Police Act 2001. A person can also be given 'a direction' to leave a particular area, and this can be used with protesters if appropriate. There is a power to arrest a person who knowingly contravenes such a direction.

This legislation should not be seen as a way of stopping people from carrying out their lawful rights to protest peacefully or express strong opinions. Nor is it intended to prevent a fan from standing outside the home of his/her favourite television celebrity or to stop media commentators from trying to record first-hand comments from people in the news. Rather, this legislation aims to provide a balance between the right to carry out such activities and the right of other individuals in their own homes to be protected from harassment, alarm, or distress.

The legislation referred to here provides more than one tool to deal with this type of situation (see 3.6 on discretion). The direction to leave is useful, but of course it does not prevent the same protesters from returning and continuing with the same type of behaviour. Charging a person with an offence (causing harassment, distress, or alarm), however, is a more serious matter. Therefore you will need to consider carefully which of the powers to use and this will depend on factors such as the number of people in the vicinity of the person's home, their behaviour and purpose, and the impact of their presence on the resident(s) and people in the surrounding area.

14.5.2.1   **Causing harassment of a resident**

Behaviour that may cause harassment, alarm, or distress (ss 42 and 42A of the Criminal Justice and Police Act 2001) includes:

- persistent, sustained, and aggressive hammering on a door;
- ringing a doorbell or shouting through the letter box;
- climbing onto the roof of a dwelling;
- shouting abusive slogans or continuous loud chanting; and
- aggressive use of banners or placards to block or impede access.

As well as causing distress to a resident inside his/her dwelling, other categories of people can also be affected such as other people present with the resident or people living nearby. Courts will use the 'reasonable person' test to decide whether a person would find the relevant activities significantly disturbing. A police officer does not have to be present when the behaviour occurs; for example, recordings from a resident's CCTV could be used as evidence of the protestors' activities and the distress caused. This offence is triable summarily and the penalty is six months' imprisonment and/or a fine.

14.5.2.2   **Giving directions in order to prevent harassment, alarm, or distress**

Under s 42(1) of the Criminal Justice and Police 2001 Act a police officer has the power to give 'directions' to a person (or a group) in order to prevent him/her/them from causing harassment, alarm, or distress to residents (or other people in the vicinity). The wording of a direction (s 42(2)) might be 'You have caused harassment and distress to people living in this area. I therefore require you to leave immediately'.

The direction can be given orally or in writing, and will instruct the person(s) to leave the vicinity and for a specified period (not exceeding three months) and conditions may be attached. An officer of any rank can give the direction (s 42(6)) but it will usually be given by the most senior officer present. An offence is committed under the Criminal Justice and Police Act 2001 by any person who having received a direction to leave:

- knowingly fails to comply with a direction (s 42(7)); or
- returns (within the specified period to the vicinity of the premises in question) to try to persuade a resident to follow a particular course of action (s 7A).

This offence is triable summarily and the penalty is six months' imprisonment and/or a fine.

14.5.3   **Sending nuisance communications**

If the nuisance behaviour involves a form of communication such as telephone calls or letters, then alternative offences can be considered. This is particularly useful if a course of conduct is not evident.

14.5.3.1   Sending items to cause distress or anxiety

Under s 1 of the Malicious Communications Act 1988 it is an offence for a person to send, for the purpose of causing distress or anxiety, any item (including electronic communications) which contains:

- indecent or grossly offensive content (s 1(1)(a)(i));
- a threat (s 1(1)(a)(ii)) (unless it was made reasonably to reinforce a demand (s 2));
- information which is false and known or believed to be false (s 1(1)(a)(iii)); or
- any article which is entirely or partly, indecent or grossly offensive (s 1(1)(b)).

This offence includes letters, parcels, and other articles sent by post. It also includes electronic communication such as emails, text messages, and oral or other communication transmitted by means of a telecommunication system, for example landline or mobile telephone (s 2A(a) and (b)). Sending includes delivering by hand, transmitting, and causing to be sent (s 3) by the sender, but does not include the actions of the service provider. The offence is triable summarily and the penalty is six months' imprisonment and/or a fine.

14.5.3.2   Improper use of public electronic communications network

Section 127 of the Communications Act 2003 states that it is an offence for a person to send (or cause to be sent) by means of a public electronic communications network (eg mobile and landline telephones), a message which is:

- grossly offensive, indecent, obscene, or menacing (s 127(1)); or
- false, or persistently uses the network for the purpose of causing annoyance, inconvenience, or needless anxiety to another (s 127(2)).

These offences are triable summarily and the penalty is six months' imprisonment and/or a fine. Section 127(2) is also a penalty offence for the purposes of s 1 of the Criminal Justice and Police Act 2001 (see 10.13.2).

> **TASK 9** Imagine you are a trainee police officer on Supervised Patrol and you have been asked to attend the address of a person who reports being harassed by people in the street outside his house. Suggest some factors you would need to consider in order to decide whether to direct anybody away from the house and whether to investigate for an offence.

14.6   Intimidation of Witnesses, Jurors, and Others

Witnesses often feel vulnerable and concerned about the consequences of their actions, and some become victims of intimidation by the suspect(s) in the case. For example, suspects or their associates might attempt to intimidate witnesses and victims to dissuade them from giving evidence in court. The 'No witness, No justice' project is a joint initiative between the CPS, ACPO, the Home Office, and the Cabinet Office's Office of Public Service Reform. It highlights the importance of providing support to people who are crucial in the successful prosecution of offenders, and that the police have a duty of care towards them. The Home Office report (1998) 'Speaking Up for Justice' argues that in this context intimidation is not simply a matter of explicit threats of physical harm to a witness or victim but also includes other less tangible forms: for example, threats made to third parties such as a wife, son, or daughter; financial threats (such as withdrawing support for a dependant). It is important therefore that police officers involved assess the needs of intimidated witnesses and be aware of the various supporting agencies including: Victim Support, the Witness Service, Anti-Social Behaviour Units, Housing Associations, Witness Care Units, Crown Prosecution Service, Prison Service, and other voluntary organizations (eg specific support such as sexual violence or domestic violence).

In *Osman v United Kingdom* (1998) 29 EHRR 245, it was decided that national authorities (such as the police) have an obligation to take preventative measures to protect an individual whose life is at risk through the criminal acts of others. In cases involving death threats, there must be a real and immediate risk to the life of the identified individual(s). Reasonable steps must be taken to assess those threats (known as the Osman threshold) and protect the individuals concerned. However, if the assessment does not suggest that there is a real and immediate risk, the police and other authorities cannot be held negligent if subsequent harm falls upon the victim (*Chief Constable of Hertfordshire v Van Colle (Administrator of the estate of GC, deceased) & Anor: Smith v Chief Constable of Sussex* [2008] UKHL 50).

There are four offences in relation to this type of intimidation; these are to be found in the Criminal Justice and Police Act 2001 (for civil proceedings), and the Criminal Justice and Public Order Act 1994 (for criminal proceedings).

Under the latter Act, the following definitions apply:

* an 'investigation' is a process carried out by the police or another person charged with the duty of investigating offences or charging offenders;
* an 'offence' can be either alleged or suspected; and
* a 'potential juror' is a person who has been summoned for jury service at the court at which the offence will be tried (s 51(9)).

The person making the threat in the first place commits an offence even if a third party is used to convey that threat (s 51(3)). The threatened harm or intimidatory act can be financial or physical, and can be directed against either the person or his/her property (s 51(4)). During the relevant periods there is a presumption of an intention to intimidate unless the suspect can prove otherwise (s 51(7) and (8)).

14.6.1 Intimidation relating to current proceedings

The suspect must have carried out an act which causes intimidation and is intended to either obstruct, pervert, or otherwise interfere with the course of justice. The act must occur between the start of the investigation and the end of the proceedings, for example at the conclusion of a court hearing.

Intimidation relating to current civil proceedings is covered under s 39(1) of the Criminal Justice and Police Act 2001, and the victim of the intimidation can be a witness in any civil proceedings in the Court of Appeal, the High Court, the Crown Court, a county court, or a magistrates' court.

Intimidation relating to current criminal proceedings is covered under s 51(1) of the Criminal Justice and Public Order Act 1994. The victim of the intimidation must be either assisting in the investigation of an offence, a witness or potential witness, or a juror or potential juror in proceedings for an offence.

14.6.2 Intimidation relating to proceedings in the past

The person suspected of intimidation must have carried out an act (or acts) which either:

* caused harm to, and was intended to harm, another person; or
* threatened to harm another person, and was intended to cause the other person to fear harm.

Intimidation in relation to civil proceedings in the past is covered under s 40(1) of the Criminal Justice and Police Act 2001. The person suspected of intimidation must know (or believe) that his/her victim had been a witness in the relevant proceedings, and the intimidation must take place within the period from the start of the proceedings until 12 months after the end of the proceedings.

Intimidation in relation to criminal proceedings in the past is covered under s 51(2) of the Criminal Justice and Public Order Act 1994. The person suspected of intimidation must know (or believe) whilst carrying out the relevant acts that his/her victim has either:

* assisted in an investigation into an offence including as a witness;
* acted as a juror; or
* concurred in a particular verdict in proceedings for an offence.

In addition, the intimidatory acts must take place within a certain time frame. Note that a person can of course both assist with an investigation and be a witness in court, in which case the longer time frame applies.

Role of the intimidated victim in criminal proceedings	Time period in which the intimidation occurs	
	Starts	Ends
A person who assisted with an investigation	The start of any assistance in the investigation (or the start date as believed by the suspect)	Twelve months after any assistance was given
A witness or juror during the court hearing	The start of the court proceedings	Twelve months after the end of the trial or appeal

The offences of intimidation are triable either way and the penalty is a fine or imprisonment (six months summarily, and five years on indictment).

14.7 Sports-related Offences

Sports-related offences do not feature within the compulsory LPG modules of the IPLDP, but we cover them here since the policing of football matches often features as part of the training of trainee police officers whilst on Supervised or Independent Patrol. Hence, although the policing of football matches is not a common occurrence for every police officer in England and Wales, trainee officers might be involved in it, particularly in forces covering large towns and cities.

Many football clubs will take steps to inform their supporters of the main points of the law and the regulations governing behaviour, for example see Stoke City's 'Customer Charter' online.

The offences described in this section are covered under two Acts:

* the Sporting Events (Control of Alcohol etc) Act 1985; and
* the Football (Offences) Act 1991.

The Sporting Events (Control of Alcohol etc) Act 1985 applies only to sports grounds, certain sporting events, and designated periods relating to those sporting events. Currently, football is the only sport which it is considered necessary to control. Statistics on football-related arrests and banning orders can be found on the www.gov.uk website. The CPS website provides the prosecution policy guidelines for football offences.

14.7.1 The Sporting Events (Control of Alcohol etc) Act 1985

The Sporting Events (Control of Alcohol etc) Act 1985 applies to football matches only if both the particular sports ground and match have been 'designated' by the Secretary of State (see Sch 1, Art 2(1) of Statutory Instrument 2005 No 3204, available online). Note that the list may vary from year to year to reflect changes in the organization of football leagues.

The following events are examples of matches which would be likely to be designated for the purposes of the Sporting Events (Control of Alcohol etc) Act 1985, as they meet both the ground and the match (teams) criteria:

* A football match played between Bristol City and Scunthorpe United at Bristol City's ground, Ashton Gate. This is because Ashton Gate is a designated sports ground and both teams are currently members of the Football League.
* A match played between Dover Athletic and Manchester United at Dover, because the Crabble is a designated sports ground and Manchester United is currently a member of the Football Association Premier League (although Dover Athletic is not).

The legislation does not apply to any sporting event in which players are not paid, nor if spectators are admitted free of charge, such as amateur weekend matches on school sports fields or recreation grounds.

Offences under the Sporting Events (Control of Alcohol etc) Act 1985 can only be considered if they occur during the period commencing two hours before the start of a football match and ending one hour after the end of the match. For example, if a football match is scheduled to start at 7.45 pm and the match ends at approximately 9.30 pm, the period of this match would be from 5.45 pm to 10.30 pm. (We ignore here the added complexity of added time being played to compensate for stoppages, or extra time to decide a match, or the match starting late.)

Specific Incidents

14.7.1.1   Transport of passengers to sports events

Drivers, owners, and passengers of some types of vehicle which are used for the principal purpose of carrying passengers for the whole or part of a journey to or from a designated sporting event are subject to legislation under s 1 of the Sporting Events (Control of Alcohol etc) Act 1985.

Public service vehicles covered by this legislation include buses and coaches, passenger trains, and minibuses. It is an offence under s 1(2) to knowingly cause or permit intoxicating liquor to be carried on such a vehicle. This applies to the operator of the public service vehicle and to the person who has hired it. (It also applies to a 'servant or agent' of the operator or hirer.) It is also an offence for such a person to have intoxicating liquor in his/her possession (s 1(3)) or to be drunk (s 1(4)) while on a vehicle to which this section applies. This offence is triable summarily only and the penalty is a fine for s 1(2) or (4) offences, and three months' imprisonment and/or a fine for an offence under s 1(3).

Minibuses and larger motor vehicles (that are not public service) vehicles are covered by s 1A of the Sporting Events (Control of Alcohol etc) Act 1985. They must be adapted to carry more than eight passengers and be in use for the principal purpose of carrying two or more passengers. It is an offence for the following persons to knowingly cause or permit intoxicating liquor to be carried (s 1A(2)) on such a vehicle:

- the driver;
- the vehicle's keeper or his/her servant or agent; and
- any person to whom it is made available (by hire, loan, or otherwise) by its keeper (or his/her servant or agent), or the servant or agent of the person to whom the vehicle is so made available.

It is an offence for such a person to have intoxicating liquor in his or her possession (s 1A(3)) or to be drunk (s 1A(4)) on a vehicle to which this section applies. This offence is triable summarily only and the penalty is a fine for s 1A(2) or (4) offences, and three months' imprisonment and/or a fine for an offence under s 1A(3).

14.7.1.2   Alcohol and drinks containers at a designated sporting event

Section 2(1) of the Sporting Events (Control of Alcohol etc) Act 1985 is generally imposed for football matches where there is a potential for disorder. Under this legislation it is an offence to possess alcohol or drinks containers likely to contain alcohol. The containers covered by this legislation are defined in s 2(3) as any article or other portable container for holding any drink, which when empty is normally discarded or returned to (or left to be recovered by) the supplier and which is capable of causing injury to a person struck by it. This obviously includes bottles and cans. It also includes such containers when crushed or broken, and parts of such containers. (Containers for holding any medicinal product (within the meaning of the Medicines Act 1968) are not included.)

Section 2(1) applies at any time during the period of a designated sporting event when the person is either in any area of the sports ground from which the event may be directly viewed, or entering (or trying to enter) the sports ground. The offence is triable summarily and the penalty is three months' imprisonment and/or a fine.

It is also an offence for a person to be drunk inside the ground, or to be drunk while entering or trying to enter a ground at any time during the period of a designated sporting event at that ground (s 2(2)). This offence is triable summarily and the penalty is a fine.

14.7.1.3   Fireworks, flares, and similar articles during a designated sporting event

Section 2A of the Sporting Events (Control of Alcohol etc) Act 1985 covers the possession of fireworks and similar objects at designated sporting events. The prohibited objects (s 2A(3) and (4)) include fireworks, rockets, distress flares, fog signals, pellets and fumigator capsules (for testing pipes), and any other item which is for 'the emission of a flare for purposes of illuminating or signalling, or the emission of smoke or a visible gas'. It does not include matches, cigarette lighters, or heaters.

The times and places to which this legislation applies are the same as for the possession of alcohol at a sports ground. Therefore a person is guilty of a s 2A offence if he/she has a firework or similar object (see earlier) at any time during the period of a designated sporting event when the person is in any area of the sports ground from which the event may be directly viewed, or entering (or trying to enter) the sports ground. The offence is triable summarily and the penalty is three months' imprisonment and/or a fine.

14.7.1.4 Powers of entry for sports grounds

Section 7 of the Sporting Events (Control of Alcohol etc) Act 1985 allows a police officer to enter and search any part of the ground if he/she has reasonable grounds to suspect that an offence under the same Act is being committed (or is about to be committed), or to enforce the provisions of the Act. This relates to the possession of alcohol, fireworks, and similar articles and applies during the period of a designated sporting event at any designated sports ground (see 14.7.1).

There is a power of search a person (s 7(2)) or a vehicle (s 7(3)) if there are reasonable grounds to suspect that an offence under this Act has been committed (or is about to be committed). See 9.4.1 for details on search procedures.

14.7.2 The Football (Offences) Act 1991

The Football (Offences) Act 1991 also deals with problem behaviour at football matches. It covers the throwing of objects, racist chanting, and pitch invasions. The definition of a designated match is very similar to the definition for the Sporting Events (Control of Alcohol etc) Act 1985, as is the time period. The time period is from two hours before the start of the match (or its advertised starting time if earlier) and one hour after the end of the match. This also applies if the match does not take place, using the advertised starting time as a point of reference.

Throwing objects at a designated football match is an offence under s 2 of the Football (Offences) Act 1991. The objects must be thrown without lawful authority or excuse (for the suspect to prove) at or towards the playing area, or any adjacent area to which spectators are not generally admitted, or any area in which spectators or other persons are or may be present. This offence is triable summarily and the penalty is a fine.

Indecent or racist chanting at a designated football match is an offence under s 3(1) of the Football (Offences) Act 1991 if the chanting is of an 'indecent or racialist nature'. Chanting means the repeated uttering of any words or sounds, by one or more people (s 3(2)) and 'racialist nature' means it is 'threatening, abusive or insulting to a person by reason of [his/her] colour, race, nationality (including citizenship) or ethnic or national origins'. The offence is triable summarily and the penalty is a fine.

Spectators going onto the playing area (a 'pitch invasion') at a designated football match commit an offence under s 4 of the Football (Offences) Act 1991. This includes 'any area adjacent to the playing area to which spectators are not generally admitted, without lawful authority or lawful excuse (which shall be for [the suspect] to prove)'. This offence is triable summarily and the penalty is a fine.

TASK 10 As a trainee officer on Supervised Patrol, you are deployed to a football match. The club concerned plays within the Football Conference National Division (currently the Blue Square Premier), so you can therefore assume that both the ground and the matches played in the ground are designated under both the Sporting Events (Control of Alcohol etc) Act 1985 and the Football (Offences) Act 1991. Consider each of the following offences and match them against the situations given in the table by putting the appropriate letter(s) in the right-hand column. The first answer has been given to you. You may need to consult the original legislation for the detail.

(a) s 2(1) of the Sporting Events (Control of Alcohol etc) Act 1985;
(b) s 2(2) of the Sporting Events (Control of Alcohol etc) Act 1985;
(c) s 2 of the Football (Offences) Act 1991;
(d) s 3 of the Football (Offences) Act 1991;
(e) s 4 of the Football (Offences) Act 1991;
(f) s 1(2) of the Sporting Events (Control of Alcohol etc) Act 1985;
(g) s 1(3) of the Sporting Events (Control of Alcohol etc) Act 1985;
(h) s 1(4) of the Sporting Events (Control of Alcohol etc) Act 1985; and
(i) s 2A of the Sporting Events (Control of Alcohol etc) Act 1985.

| 1. | You see a fan fumbling for money to pay for a cup of tea from the refreshment stand. When you approach, he is hardly able to stand and his breath smells of intoxicating liquor, his eyes are glazed, and his speech is slurred. | b |

2.	You are on duty at the edge of the pitch near the entrance to the players' tunnel as the teams enter after half-time. Whilst observing the crowd, you see a dark metal object hit the ground near your feet and notice one of the players stop in his stride and grab his head in pain. You look up and see a youth in the crowd with his right hand raised as if he has just thrown an object.
3.	One of the mid-field players is black. Every time he receives the ball you hear opposition supporters make 'monkey' sounds and shout racist abuse.
4.	Whilst on duty outside the ground you see a fan waiting to get a ticket and enter. Under his arm you clearly see a four-pack of lager cans.
5.	Before the start of a match you see a supporter waiting to purchase a ticket to enter the ground. He finishes drinking from a can, drops it to the ground, and stands on it to crush it. He is now at the front of the queue to get in, looks around, picks up the crushed tin, and puts it in a coat pocket out of view.
6.	One of your responsibilities is to monitor the away supporters arriving by coaches and minibuses hired for the occasion. On one of the minibuses you observe a person drinking from a bottle of cider. As the vehicle stops, the door of the minibus is opened by the driver; at that moment you see one of the other passengers offer the driver a can of lager. Just then a third passenger gets up from a seat and falls down the steps of the minibus, apparently drunk.
7.	At the end of one of the matches, when the final whistle is blown the two teams leave the pitch and a group of fans go onto the pitch to follow the players and congratulate them.
8.	At the end of a match in early November, you see a youth reach into his pocket as the crowd is leaving the ground. As he withdraws his hand from his pocket, a firework falls to the ground.

14.8 Criminal Trespass and Outdoor Gatherings

Travelling people with no fixed abode sometimes find a temporary place to live on land that is privately owned by others. This may cause anxiety and distress for the owners of the land or for local residents. However, if the intention of the trespassers is not to reside, gather, or disrupt lawful activity or if only one trespasser is involved, then the situation might be a civil matter (see 14.8.5). On other occasions a trespasser might have the clear intent of disrupting lawful activity and this is much more likely to be a criminal matter. Separate legislation is available to deal with difficulties arising from large outdoor music and dancing events.

14.8.1 Criminal trespass or nuisance on land

This offence is described under s 61(1) of the Criminal Justice and Public Order Act 1994. At least two suspects must be planning to live on the land for a period of time, and they must have been asked to leave by the owner or legal occupier. In addition, the suspects must have either:

* caused damage to the land or to property on the land, or used threatening, abusive, or insulting words or behaviour towards the occupier, a member of his/her family, or an employee or agent of his/hers; or
* have six or more vehicles with them on the land (a vehicle includes caravans and unroadworthy vehicles).

A senior police officer present at the scene must reasonably believe that these conditions have been fulfilled. He/she may then direct those persons to leave the land, and to remove any of their vehicles and other property from the land. It is an offence (s 61(4)) for a person to fail to leave as soon as is reasonably practicable, or to leave and then re-enter within three months. These offences are triable summarily and the penalty is three months' imprisonment and/or a fine.

If the trespassers will not leave (having been given an order to do so), s 62 of the Criminal Justice and Public Order Act 1994 provides a power to seize and remove their vehicles. This also applies if a person fails to remove any vehicle on the land, or leaves and returns within three months (s 62(1)).

14.8.2 Aggravated trespass on land

Sections 68 and 69 of the Criminal Justice and Public Order Act 1994 cover trespassers who disrupt or obstruct any lawful activity taking place on land or adjoining land (hence the 'aggravated' nature of the trespass). This would include protesters at a military base. Land would include agricultural buildings, footpaths, bridleways, and cycle tracks that cross the land. The summary offence of aggravated trespass is provided under s 68(1). The penalty is three months' imprisonment and/or a fine.

14.8.2.1 Powers to direct trespassers to leave

Section 69 of the Criminal Justice and Public Order Act 1994 provides the senior police officer at the scene of an aggravated trespass with the power to direct a person to leave the land. The senior police officer must reasonably believe that the person is committing (or has committed or intends to commit) the offence of aggravated trespass (s 69(1)), as shown in the diagram.

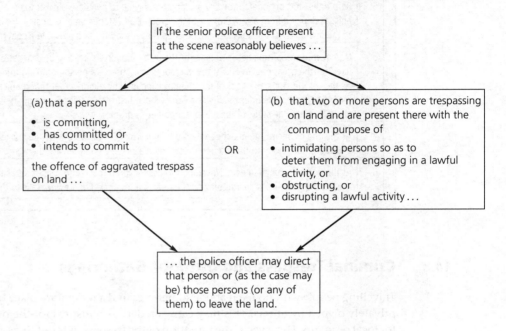

Under s 69(3), it is an offence for a person who has been directed to leave if he/she fails to leave the land as soon as practicable, or having left, re-enters as a trespasser within three months (beginning with the day on which the direction was given). It is a defence if the accused can show that he/she was not trespassing, or that he/she had a reasonable excuse for failing to leave as soon as practicable or for re-entering as a trespasser. The offence is triable summarily and the penalty is three months' imprisonment (maximum) and/or a fine.

14.8.3 Open-air gatherings with music at night

Although complaints about excessive noise from gatherings in residential properties are often dealt with by staff from local authorities, complaints about larger gatherings in the open air may sometimes require police action. Sections 63, 64, and 65 of the Criminal Justice and Public Order Act 1994 can be used to deal with such situations. The type of gathering (also referred to as an 'open-air rave') is defined in s 63; more than 20 people must be present and the gathering must be out of doors at night with music. The music must be amplified with repetitive beats, and be loud or go on for a long time. It should also be 'likely to cause serious distress to local residents'.

The Act includes the power for you to give directions to people present at such gatherings (and to people travelling to the locality). There are some predictable exemptions; the following categories of people cannot be given directions under ss 63–65:

- the occupier of the land ('the person entitled to possession of the land by virtue of an estate or interest held by him [or her]' (s 61(9));
- any member of the occupier's family;
- any employee or agent of the occupier; and
- any person whose home is situated on the land.

14.8.3.1 Dispersal powers for open-air gatherings with music at night

A power is available to disperse people who are at a gathering with music at night. This power (under s 63(2)) also applies to people preparing for such a gathering or waiting for it to start.

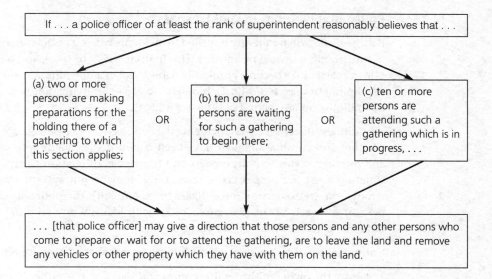

Such a direction, if not communicated by the police officer giving the direction, may be communicated by any constable at the scene (s 63(3)). A person will be treated as having had the direction communicated to him/her if reasonable steps have been taken to bring it to his/her attention (s 63(4)). It is an offence (s 63(6)) if a person (knowing that a direction has been given which applies to him/her) then fails to leave the land as soon as reasonably practicable, or leaves and re-enters within seven days. If the suspect can show that he/she had a reasonable excuse for his/her actions, this may be a defence (s 63(7)). A person who has been directed to leave a gathering who then moves on to (or prepares for) another similar gathering within 24 hours commits an offence under s 63(7A). He/she must know about the direction. The offences are triable summarily and the penalty is three months' imprisonment and/or a fine.

Section 65 of the Criminal Justice and Public Order Act 1994 provides powers to direct persons not to proceed towards a gathering to which s 63 applies. The police officer must be in uniform and within five miles of the gathering. It is a summary offence (s 65(1)) for a person not to comply with such a direction and the penalty is a fine.

14.8.3.2 Powers of entry and seizure for open-air gatherings with music at night

Section 64 of the Criminal Justice and Public Order Act 1994 gives powers of entry to the police when dealing with night-time open-air musical gatherings; police officers may need to be deployed to find out what is happening at such gatherings. A warrant is not required (s 64(3)). Under s 64(1) if a police officer of at least the rank of superintendent reasonably believes that the relevant circumstances exist (see the start of 14.8.3), then he/she may authorize any constable to enter the land. This will be to ascertain whether such circumstances exist, and if they do s 63 directions can be given.

Vehicles and sound equipment may be seized if a direction has been given under s 63 and a constable reasonably suspects that any person to whom the direction applies has, without reasonable excuse, failed to remove any vehicle or sound equipment which appears to belong to him/her (or to be in his/her possession or under his/her control). In addition, if within seven days of the direction being given, a person with a vehicle or sound equipment enters the land as a trespasser, then their vehicle and equipment can also be seized.

14.8.4 Squatting in a residential building

Under s 144(1) of the Legal Aid, Sentencing and Punishment of Offenders Act 2012 it is an offence for a trespasser in a residential building to live or intend to live there for any period of time (s 144(1)(c)). The person must have entered as a trespasser (s 144(1)(a)) and must know (or should know) this (s 144(1)(b)).

The offence does not apply if the person remains in occupation after the end of a lease or licence (s 144(2)). A building includes any temporary or moveable structure or part of a structure (s 144(3)(a)) and it is residential if it had been designed or adapted before the time of entry for use as a place to live (s 144(3)(b)). Section 17 of the PACE Act 1984 provides a police officer in uniform with the power to enter and search premises for the purpose of arresting a person for this offence (see 9.5.1.2). The offence is triable summarily and the penalty is six months' imprisonment and/or a fine.

Specific Incidents

14.8.5 Police involvement in civil trespass

Police officers will frequently be called to incidents where a person unlawfully enters onto land or into premises owned by another. This in itself is civil trespass, and is not a criminal offence. The trespasser may become criminally liable if, for example, the acts and/or the intent amount to criminal trespass (see 14.8.1), burglary (see 16.4), or living or intending to live in a residential building for any period of time (see 14.8.4).

Accordingly, in civil trespass incidents the actions of police officers are limited to identifying whether any criminal offences have been committed, remaining to prevent any take place, and offering advice to both owners and trespassers in relation to civil remedies. The owner should request the trespassers to leave, but if they do not and the owner decides to try and remove the trespassers by force (likely to be difficult), the police should remain in order to prevent a breach of the peace (see 14.3) or to identify any criminal offences, for example unlawful personal violence (see 15.1).

Consequently, at an incident where civil trespass is alleged, a police officer should:

1. Locate the owner of the land/premises and speak with him/her to try and establish the circumstances surrounding the complaint, the identity of the trespassers and their location, and what criminal acts, if any, have taken place. The limitation of police involvement (if no criminal offences have taken place) should be emphasized.
2. Locate the alleged trespassers and seek to establish their identity (should they wish) and any claim to lawful entry they might have (in order to help the owner and the trespassers come to a common understanding). The officer should also explain that if they commit a criminal offence or a breach of the peace, they may be liable to arrest and prosecution, and that the owner can obtain an order from a civil court to eject them.
3. Attempt to bring about an amicable agreement between the two parties through dialogue, if no criminal offences have been committed.
4. Remain at the incident if it seems that any criminal offences may be committed.
5. Make a full PNB entry (see 10.2) of the events and what was said.

14.9 Firework Offences

Under the law, a firework is any device which burns and/or explodes to produce a visual and/or audible effect; and is intended for use as a form of entertainment. Some offences relating to fireworks are about misuse that could cause danger or annoyance, some relate to the time of year, and some relate to the age of the person buying fireworks. Of particular concern in recent years has been the use of powerful fireworks such as 'aerial shells, aerial maroons, shells-in-mortar and maroons-in-mortar', which can register sound levels above 120 dB—about the noise level of a jet aircraft 100 metres away. The sale of these products to the public is now banned, but people can still purchase them abroad and bring them back to the UK. Concern has also been expressed about the use of fireworks to damage or even destroy objects such as phone boxes or cars. It is for these reasons that we include fireworks as a subject for the Handbook. Relevant legislation includes the Explosives Act 1875, the Fireworks Act 2003, the Fireworks Regulations 2004, and the Fireworks (Safety) Regulations 1997.

It is an offence for any person:

- to throw, cast, or fire any firework in or into any highway, street, thoroughfare, or public place (s 80 of the Explosives Act 1875);
- to wantonly (deliberately) throw or set fire to a firework in the street to the obstruction, annoyance, or danger of residents or passengers (s 28 of the Town Police Clauses Act 1847).

It is also an offence for anyone under the age of 18 years to possess fireworks in a public place, except for indoor fireworks (reg 4 of the Fireworks Regulations 2004). Indoor fireworks include caps, sparklers, and 'throwdowns'. (A throwdown is a paper or foil wrapped firework containing impact-sensitive explosive which produces a sound when thrown onto the ground.)

These offences are triable summarily. Alternatively a PND can be used (see 10.13.2), apart from an offence under s 28 of the Town Police Clauses Act 1847.

14.9.1 Selling fireworks

A special licence is required for a trader to sell fireworks to the public throughout the year. Traders without a special licence can only sell fireworks to members of the public during the following periods:

- first day of Chinese New Year and three days prior to this;
- Diwali and three days prior to this;
- between 15 October and 10 November; and
- between 26 and 31 December.

Under s 12(1) of the Consumer Protection Act 1987 it is an offence to supply fireworks (including sparklers but excluding all other indoor fireworks) to persons under the age of 18 years. This offence is triable summarily, and the penalty is a fine.

14.9.2 Firework curfews

A 'firework curfew' is a period of time where the general use of fireworks is not permitted. Under reg 7(1) of the Fireworks Regulations 2004 it is an offence for a person to use an 'adult firework' (essentially all fireworks other than indoor fireworks) between 2300 and 0700 hrs the next day except for during the periods shown in the table. Other exemptions apply for local authority employees using a firework during a local authority display or national commemorative event.

Curfew exemption event or date	Exemption period ends
First day of the Chinese New Year	0100 hrs the following day
5 November	Midnight
Diwali	0100 hrs the following day
31 December	0100 hrs the following day

This offence is triable summarily and the penalty is six months' imprisonment and/or a fine, or a PND can be used (see 10.13.2 on PNDs).

14.9.3 Restrictions on large fireworks for public displays

Public displays frequently use large fireworks, known as category 4 fireworks. They may only be used by an appropriately qualified person (reg 5 of the Fireworks Regulations 2004). Members of the general public are prohibited from possessing such fireworks, except for any person who is employed by a local authority, or who is involved in public or commercial firework displays. A breach of reg 4 or 5 is a criminal offence under s 11 of the Fireworks Act 2003. The offence is triable summarily, and the penalty is a fine.

14.10 Hate Crime

'Hate crime' is defined by ACPO and the CPS as

> [a]ny criminal offence which is perceived by the victim or any other person, to be motivated by hostility or prejudice based on a person's race or perceived race; religion or perceived religion; sexual orientation or perceived sexual orientation; disability or perceived disability and any crime motivated by hostility or prejudice against a person who is transgender or perceived to be transgender (CPS, 2014).

A key consideration for the police when identifying a potential hate crime is the victim's perception. Most police force written policy is to record a crime as a 'hate crime' if the victim perceives it as such. Hate crimes can sometimes develop into critical incidents (see 11.5)

In all cases of hate crime the police are expected to identify and record crimes as such, to thoroughly investigate hate crimes and to offer a level of support to victims and others that reflects the issues surrounding hate crime. Trainee officers are unlikely to be involved beyond the early stages of an investigation (see 23.3). In addition to the usual considerations (eg forensic awareness) extra sensitivity around the needs of victims from minority communities is often needed. Further details are to be found in the 2005 ACPO 'Hate Crime Manual' (ACPO, 2005b). Training on this is likely to be included in the IPLDP, and this often involves a contribution from local minority communities or groups.

Specific Incidents

There are several specific Acts that cover hate crime offences, including:

• Public Order Act 1986 (see 14.4.5 on inciting hatred);
• Football Offences Act 1991 (see 14.7.2); and
• Crime and Disorder Act 1998 (see 14.10.1 on aggravated offences).

The perpetrators of some hate crimes can be charged with the 'aggravated' version of the basic offence and this is regarded as more serious and as a separate offence (all under the Crime and Disorder Act 1998), and will carry a heavier sentence on conviction. Currently this applies to racially or religiously motivated hate crime. At the time of writing (2014) there are no 'aggravated' versions of charging for hate crimes motivated by a person's disability, sexual orientation, or transgender identity. However, if such a motivation is shown to be present, then this would be taken into account in the sentencing of an offender. The term 'racially or religiously aggravated' is defined by s 28 of the Crime and Disorder Act (see 14.10.1).

The following categories of offence can be racially or religiously aggravated:

• assaults (s 29 of the Crime and Disorder Act 1998);
• criminal damage (s 30 of the Crime and Disorder Act 1998);
• public order offences (s 31 of the Crime and Disorder Act 1998); and
• harassment (s 32 of the Crime and Disorder Act 1998).

For a basic offence that is triable on indictment, a person who is found 'not guilty' of the aggravated version of that offence can still be found guilty of the basic offence. This is known as the 'alternative verdict' (s 6(3) of the Criminal Law Act 1967). In summary cases, there is no power for the court to return an alternative verdict; therefore the defendant is more likely to be charged with both the basic and the racially or religiously aggravated offence. An overview of hate crime in England and Wales is available on the www.gov.uk website.

14.10.1 The definition of racially or religiously aggravated

The definition is provided in s 28(1) of the Crime and Disorder Act 1998. An offence becomes racially or religiously aggravated for the purposes of ss 29–32 if the offender 'demonstrates...hostility' or 'is motivated...by hostility' (on racial or religious grounds).

Clearly, it is easier to prove that the suspect 'demonstrated hostility' (s 28(1)(a)) than to prove that the suspect's behaviour was motivated by hostility (s 28(1)(b)).

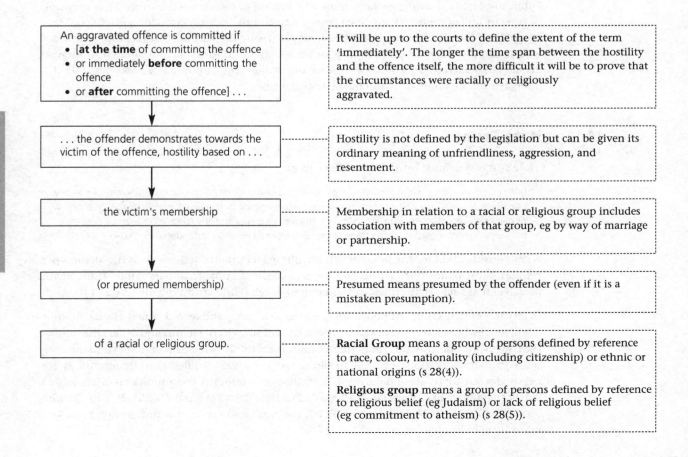

An aggravated offence is committed if
• [**at the time** of committing the offence
• or immediately **before** committing the offence
• or **after** committing the offence] ...

It will be up to the courts to define the extent of the term 'immediately'. The longer the time span between the hostility and the offence itself, the more difficult it will be to prove that the circumstances were racially or religiously aggravated.

... the offender demonstrates towards the victim of the offence, hostility based on ...

Hostility is not defined by the legislation but can be given its ordinary meaning of unfriendliness, aggression, and resentment.

the victim's membership

Membership in relation to a racial or religious group includes association with members of that group, eg by way of marriage or partnership.

(or presumed membership)

Presumed means presumed by the offender (even if it is a mistaken presumption).

of a racial or religious group.

Racial Group means a group of persons defined by reference to race, colour, nationality (including citizenship) or ethnic or national origins (s 28(4)).

Religious group means a group of persons defined by reference to religious belief (eg Judaism) or lack of religious belief (eg commitment to atheism) (s 28(5)).

Specific Incidents

For s 28(1)(a), the offender is held to have demonstrated hostility even if his/her behaviour might be partly motivated by other factors with no racial or religious basis (s 28(3)), but this is a question of fact for the court to decide. For example, in the case of *Johnson v DPP* [2008] EWHC 509 (Admin), two car park attendants were the victims of hostility, partly based upon their job status and partly upon their membership of a racial group. It was subsequently held that a racially aggravated s 5 Public Order Act 1986 offence had been committed against them. The accused had made reference to the skin colour of the attendants ('white'), and told them to leave the black community in which they were working and to go instead to a predominantly white area.

Note that people working in law enforcement are of course fully entitled to protection from any racial or religious aggravation.

14.10.2   Racially or religiously aggravated assaults

Under s 29(1) of the Crime and Disorder Act 1998, the following types of assault as a basic offence can be racially or religiously aggravated.

Basic offence	Notes
Any offence under s 20 of the Offences Against the Person Act 1861	Includes malicious wounding or grievous bodily harm, but excludes s 18 'with intent' (see 15.3)
Any offence under s 47 of the Offences Against the Person Act 1861	See 15.2 on occasioning actual bodily harm
Common assault	See 15.2 on unlawful personal violence

The motivation for the basic offence must be taken into account—it must be racially motivated or based on racial hostility. For example, in the case of *DPP v Roshan Kumar Pal* (unreported, 3 February 2000) the charge of racially aggravated common assault was not proved. Even though the assault on an Asian-heritage caretaker was accompanied by abuse, the assault was held to be motivated by the perceived low status of the victim's job, and not by racism. If the racial or religious aggravation aspect of the offence charged is not proved, the basic offence may be substituted by the court in most cases.

Aggravated s 20 and s 47 offences from the Offences Against the Person Act 1861 are triable either way and the penalty is a fine or imprisonment (summarily, six months and seven years on indictment). Aggravated common assault offences are triable either way and the penalty is a fine or imprisonment (summarily, six months and two years on indictment).

14.10.3   Racially or religiously aggravated criminal damage

These offences are covered in s 30 of the Crime and Disorder Act 1998. A person is guilty of this offence if he/she destroys or damages property belonging to another (see 20.2) and the acts are racially or religiously motivated. Case law extends the meaning of the term 'belonging' to include having control or custody for property (as used in the Criminal Damage Act 1971 and the Theft Act 1968). There is no need to identify a specific victim and therefore spray-painting racist graffiti on a wall would be likely to constitute an example of this offence.

The offence is triable either way, regardless of the value of the property damaged. The penalty is a fine or imprisonment (summarily, six months and up to 14 years on indictment).

14.10.4   Racially or religiously aggravated public order offences

Section 31 of the Crime and Disorder Act 1998 covers offences that are aggravated forms of basic public order offences. The table shows the basic public order offences (see 14.4) that may be racially or religiously aggravated, and also identifies the corresponding subsections of the Crime and Disorder Act 1998 for the aggravated forms of the offences.

Basic offence (Public Order Act 1986)	Aggravated offence (Crime and Disorder Act 1998)
Fear or provocation of violence (s 4)	s 31(1)(a)
Intentional harassment, alarm, or distress (s 4A)	s 31(1)(b)
Causing harassment, alarm, or distress (s 5)	s 31(1)(c)

Specific Incidents

In *Norwood v DPP* [2003] EWHC 1564 the regional organizer of the British National Party for Shropshire was found guilty of a racially aggravated s 5 Public Order Act 1986 offence. A few weeks after the 9/11 terrorist attack in New York he displayed a poster which included the words 'Islam out of Britain' and 'Protect the British People' and an image showing one of the 'twin towers' in flames, along with a crescent and star surrounded by a prohibition sign. It was displayed in his flat window and could clearly be seen in the street outside. However, where the offence is motivated towards the individual victim (and not towards members of his/her racial group) it is not held to be racially aggravated. For example, in the case *DPP v Howard* [2008] EWHC 608 (Admin), an off-duty police officer heard his neighbour shouting 'I'd rather be a paki than a cop.' It was held that the only motivation for the neighbour's shouting was his intense dislike and hostility towards the police officer (and as a consequence an offence under s 5 of the Public Order Act 1986), and therefore that the comments had not been racially aggravated.

The penalty for a s 31(1)(a) or (b) offence (triable either way) is a fine or imprisonment (summarily, six months and two years on indictment). An offence under s 31(1)(c) is triable only summarily as it relates to a summary-only basic offence (s 5 of the Public Order Act), and therefore has no alternative verdict. The penalty is a fine.

14.10.5 Racially or religiously aggravated harassment

This is covered in s 32 of the Crime and Disorder Act 1998. The offences are racially and religiously aggravated forms of basic offences from the Protection from Harassment Act 1997, s 2 (harassment) and s 4 (putting people in fear of violence).

The offences of aggravated harassment (s 32(1)(a)) and aggravated putting people in fear of violence (s 32(1)(b)) are triable either way and the penalty is a fine or imprisonment (six months for a summary offence, and on indictment two years (s 32(1)(a)) and seven years (s 32(1)(b)). For trials on indictment, a person who is found not guilty can still be found guilty of the relevant basic harassment offence (s 32(5) and (6) of the Crime and Disorder Act 1998).

> **TASK 11** Consider the following groups of people. In relation to racially or religiously aggravated offences, decide whether they constitute a racial or a religious group, or neither or both:
>
> 1. Jews (see *Seide v Gillette Industries* [1980] IRLR 427);
> 2. Rastafarians (see *Dawkins v Crown Suppliers (Property Services Agency)*, The Times, 4 February 1993, [1993] ICR 517);
> 3. Muslims (see *J H Walker v Hussain* [1996] ICR 291); and
> 4. Gypsies (see *Commissioner for Racial Equality v Dutton* [1989] QB 783).

14.11 Answers to Tasks

TASK 1 A constable in uniform may require a person to give his or her name and address if the constable has reason to believe that a person has been acting (or is acting) in an anti-social manner (within the meaning of s 1 of the Crime and Disorder Act 1998). This power is given under s 50(1) of the Police Reform Act 2002.

Further, s 50(2) states that an offence is committed by any person who:

(a) fails to give [his or her] name and address when required to do so under subsection (1), or
(b) gives a false or inaccurate name or address in response to a requirement under that subsection.

TASK 2 Since the young people in the group appear to be local residents, you would only be able to require them to disperse (either immediately or by a time you specify). As they are all local residents, you would not be able to prohibit them from returning within 24 hours. Even though apparently only one of the group was actually intimidating a member of the public, you would have the power to disperse the whole group, since two or more persons were present.

TASK 3 In the first example the intelligence available and the body armour being worn would appear to provide reasonable grounds for believing that harm was likely to be down to a person or persons at the carnival.

In terms of the second example there was no evidence in the description given:
- of harm being done or being likely to be done to a person;
- that, in the presence of a person, harm was done to his/her property;
- of a person fearing being harmed through assault, riot, or other disturbance.

It would therefore be very difficult from the information in the description alone to prove a breach of the peace in this case.

TASK 4 You probably considered the following:

1. The officer would collect evidence from the suspect and other people in the area.
2. They could provide evidence that the suspect was aware that:
   - while he/she was in public anyone could hear or see his/her conduct or (if the behaviour took place inside a dwelling) it could be heard outside that same or another dwelling; and
   - his/her conduct was unreasonable and was likely to cause harassment, alarm, or distress. Evidence could be gathered from people in the public area at the time confirming that they felt alarmed or distressed.
3. The officer could provide evidence of what he/she saw and heard in relation to the suspect's conduct, and that there were other people in the public area at the time.

TASK 5 A police officer can also be harassed, alarmed, or distressed, but remember that this is a question of fact to be decided in each case by the magistrates. In determining this, the magistrates may take into account the familiarity that police officers have with the words and conduct typically seen in incidents of disorderly conduct. The evidence of other people in the area is an important factor.

TASK 6 In the case of *Swanston v DPP* (1997) 161 JP 203, the incident had occurred in a very small area and the officer was within 5 feet (about 1.5 m) of the suspect. Unless the door supervisor had impaired hearing or sight, he could not have failed to understand what was said and the actions committed by the suspect. In the *Swanston* case, the prosecution proved that the suspect had the intention of causing the door supervisor to fear that violence was going to be used against him. Those facts were proved by the admissible evidence, including evidence of the police officer who was a witness to the incident.

TASK 7 In *R v Plavecz* [2002] Crim LR 837, having been found guilty of affray, the defendant appealed and the court decided that affray is a public order offence and is inappropriate where the incident is essentially 'one on one'. The conviction was therefore quashed. It is doubtful therefore, given these circumstances, that an investigation for affray could be sustained, but always seek guidance from the CPS in such matters.

TASK 8

1. For either of these two offences to be proven, you would have to investigate what evidence existed to prove a course of conduct: for example letters, photographs, or eyewitness accounts.
   - If the harassment involved phone calls, you would seek police force assistance to liaise with the service provider in order to obtain evidence of the calls.
   - You would clarify with the victim whether there had been any previous instances of harassment or being put in fear of violence, and whether the police were informed or any civil remedy taken under s 3 of the Act.
   - You would collect statements from colleagues who had seen the victim on previous occasions, and collect evidence from any other witnesses and paperwork, letters, and photographs from the victim, and exhibit them in a statement (see 10.12).
     The case could be discussed with a CPS Evidence Review representative or anyone involved in the investigation in an advisory capacity.
2. If the suspect was known and a course of conduct could not be proved but the victim had been harassed or put in fear of violence, you could warn the suspect. The warning would be recorded as a PNB entry, and you would also make sure it is recorded on the force database for future reference. This could be evidence towards proving a course of conduct in the future. The victim should be advised to:
   - seek legal advice, if pursuing a civil remedy under s 3 of the Act was appropriate;
   - contact Victim Support representatives;
   - contact his/her phone service provider if the phone was being used to harass or put him/her in fear of violence, to arrange for a block to be placed on 'number withheld' incoming calls.
3. The victim should keep a diary of events, retain physical evidence (such as letters), and take photographs of any visible evidence.

Specific Incidents

4. If a course of conduct could be proved or suspected, then consideration would need to be given as to the most appropriate course of action. If arrest was considered, a reason for the arrest being necessary would be required. This could be to protect a child, or to allow the prompt and effective investigation of the conduct of the person in question, or to prevent any prosecution for the offence being hindered by the disappearance of the person in question.

TASK 9 The following are factors for consideration:

- How many times has the victim been harassed by people congregating outside his own home?
- Has he asked the people to leave the area?
- How many people are in the vicinity?
- What is their behaviour?
- What is the purpose of their gathering?
- What is the impact on the person in his home?
- Is there sufficient evidence to investigate the offence, or can the situation be better resolved in its early stages by directing the people to leave the area?

TASK 10 The answers are as follows:

1b, 2c, 3d, 4a, 5a, 6fgh, 7e, 8i.

TASK 11 The answers are:

1. Racial group and religious group.
2. Not a racial group but a religious one.
3. Not a racial group but a religious one.
4. Racial group but not a religious one.

15 Unlawful Violence Against Persons and Premises

15.1 Introduction

Unlawful personal violence is a very common occurrence, and police officers are called to investigate such incidents with alarming frequency. The Crime Survey for England and Wales (CSEW) estimates that there were 1.9 million violent incidents in England and Wales in 2012–13, amounting to some 22 per cent of all incidents considered in the survey. However, not all incidents will come to the attention of the police. A total of 598,273 offences of violence against a person were recorded by the police in 2012–13 (Office for National Statistics, 2013). This was in fact a decrease of 3 per cent compared with 2011–12.

A number of different offences are covered in this chapter, both against individuals and premises. These offences include:

- common assault under s 39 of the Criminal Justice Act 1988;
- common assault by beating under s 39 of the Criminal Justice Act 1988;
- assault occasioning actual bodily harm under s 47 of the Offences Against the Person Act 1861;
- unlawful and malicious wounding, or inflicting grievous bodily harm (GBH) under s 20 of the Offences Against the Person Act 1861;
- wounding or causing grievous bodily harm with intent to do grievous bodily harm, or to resist or prevent arrest (referred to as 'GBH with Intent') under s 18 of the Offences Against the Person Act 1861;
- assaults on the police and obstructing a police officer under s 89(1) of the Police Act 1996; and
- assault with intent to resist arrest under s 38 of the Offences Against the Person Act 1861.

The general provisions of criminal law of course apply to violence and abuse in domestic settings; there are no offences that relate specifically to domestic violence.

The health and safety of the officer(s) and the general public is paramount: therefore where the use of unlawful violence is likely police officers should always consider whether personal protective equipment is required.

The information given here is likely to be relevant to trainee police officers during Phase 3 of the IPLDP and for LPG 1 under the 'Crime' heading.

Before going into the details of the offences, the various meanings of the word 'assault' must be considered. There is no legal definition of assault. In *R v Brown* [1993] 2 All ER 75, Lord Templeman referred to the definition of assault as that which was adopted by the Law Commission in their Consultation Paper No 122, *Legislating the Criminal Code: Offences against the Person and General Principles* (1992), para 9.1. This stated:

> in common law an assault is an act by which a person intentionally or recklessly causes another to apprehend immediate and unlawful personal violence and a battery is an act by which a person intentionally

or recklessly inflicts personal violence upon another. However, the term assault is now, in both ordinary legal usage and in statutes, regularly used to cover both assault and battery.

So whenever the word assault is used, the intended meaning must be considered.

15.2 Common Assault and Occasioning Actual Bodily Harm

Historically, the Offences Against the Persons Act 1861 provided magistrates with the opportunity to imprison or fine anyone committing the common law offences of assault or battery (see 15.2.1). The same statute provided the offences of assault occasioning actual harm, GBH, and GBH with intent. Assault and battery remained as common law offences until they became summary offences by virtue of s 39 of the Criminal Justice Act 1988.

The CPS advises prosecutors and police to consider both the level of injuries and the likely sentence that a court would apply when deciding how to charge a case of assault. They should take into account the 'Sentencing Council's Definitive Guideline on Assault' (published in March 2011). In general, if there are no serious injuries, then the offence should be charged as common assault. The charge should be ABH if the injury is serious and the sentence is likely to exceed six months' imprisonment. For an injury which is considered to be 'really serious', the charge should be GBH. There may be instances where it is necessary to deviate from this general principle (Sentencing Council, 2012).

15.2.1 Common assault offences

Under s 39 of the Criminal Justice Act 1988 there are two possible offences:

- common assault—this is not a physical attack, but is instead any act (eg a threat) which makes a victim understand he/she is going to be immediately subjected to some personal violence. An example of this would be: 'I'm going to smash your head in!';
- common assault by beating—this involves the actual use of force by an assailant on a victim but only results in very minor or no perceivable injury.

These are alternatives and should never be charged together (see *DPP v Little* [1992] 1 All ER 299). The naming of these offences is widely acknowledged to be confusing; attempts (as yet unsuccessful) have been made to revise the legislation concerned.

In the context of common assault, an assault is:

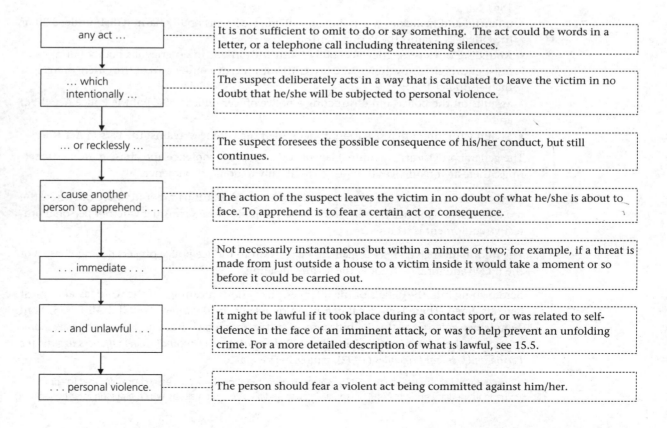

| any act ... | It is not sufficient to omit to do or say something. The act could be words in a letter, or a telephone call including threatening silences. |

| ... which intentionally ... | The suspect deliberately acts in a way that is calculated to leave the victim in no doubt that he/she will be subjected to personal violence. |

| ... or recklessly ... | The suspect foresees the possible consequence of his/her conduct, but still continues. |

| ... cause another person to apprehend ... | The action of the suspect leaves the victim in no doubt of what he/she is about to face. To apprehend is to fear a certain act or consequence. |

| ... immediate ... | Not necessarily instantaneous but within a minute or two; for example, if a threat is made from just outside a house to a victim inside it would take a moment or so before it could be carried out. |

| ... and unlawful ... | It might be lawful if it took place during a contact sport, or was related to self-defence in the face of an imminent attack, or was to help prevent an unfolding crime. For a more detailed description of what is lawful, see 15.5. |

| ... personal violence. | The person should fear a violent act being committed against him/her. |

A battery (as in common assault by beating) is any act by which a person:

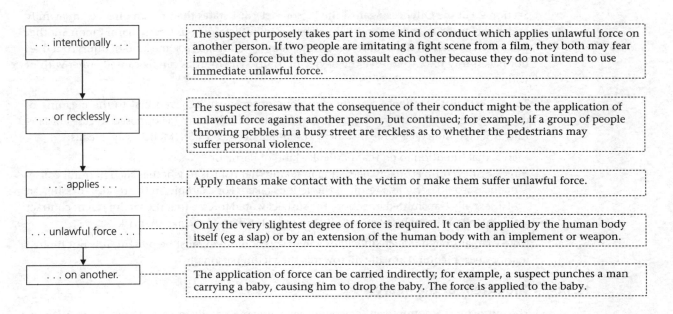

These common assault offences are triable summarily only, and the penalty is six months' imprisonment. Note that these offences can be racially or religiously aggravated (see 14.10.2).

> **TASK 1** Consider the following incidents in relation to s 39 of the Criminal Justice Act 1988, and state for each which offence has been committed:
>
> 1. Two men have been arguing in the street and one man has pushed and shoved the other, but very little force has been used upon the victim, who is therefore uninjured. What offence has been committed, common assault or common assault by beating?
> 2. During a dispute between two women in a car park no force was used, but one of them was left in no doubt that she was about to face unlawful personal violence. What offence has been committed?

15.2.2 Actual Bodily Harm (ABH)

This offence is usually referred to as Assault Occasioning Actual Bodily Harm (AOABH) and is covered under s 47 of the Offences Against the Person Act 1861. Note that here the word assault is being used to mean some sort of physical attack. The main factor which distinguishes common assault by beating from AOABH is the degree of injury. *R v Donovan* [1934] 2 KB 498 at 509, [1934] All ER Rep 207 suggested that 'bodily harm'

> has its ordinary meaning and includes any hurt or injury calculated to interfere with the health or comfort of the prosecutor. Such hurt or injury need not be permanent, but must, no doubt, be more than merely transient and trifling.

The injury must therefore be real and it should be capable of being seen or felt by the victim (or by witnesses such as a police officer). It includes psychiatric injury/illness or psychological damage (*R v Ireland* [1998] AC 147 (HL)).

The aspects of intention or recklessness are the same for actual bodily harm as they are for common assault by beating; it only needs to be proved that the assault was intended or that it was carried out recklessly. There is no need to prove that the accused intended to cause injuries amounting to actual bodily harm (or was reckless as to whether injuries amounting to actual bodily harm would be caused).

This offence is triable either way. The penalty if tried summarily is six months' imprisonment and/or fine, and five years' imprisonment on indictment. This offence can be racially or religiously aggravated (see 14.10.2).

Specific Incidents

15.3 Unlawful and Malicious Wounding or Inflicting GBH

Section 20 of the Offences Against the Person Act 1861 states that it is an offence 'unlawfully and maliciously' to 'wound another person' or to 'inflict grievous bodily harm [upon another person]'. The suspect must know that the actions would result in some kind of injury, but does not necessarily have to foresee the degree of injury. The injuries can be caused either with or without a weapon.

To understand this offence, careful consideration needs to be given first to the meaning of certain words. 'Unlawfully' means 'without lawful justification' (as opposed to cases of lawfully inflicted injury, eg some instances of self-defence, see 15.5). 'Maliciously' means:

- an actual intention to do that particular kind of harm; or
- recklessness (unreasonably persisting in taking that risk) as to whether such harmful consequences would occur as a result of the actions taken. For example, in the reckless passing-on of a sexually transmitted infection, the suspect would foresee that the victim might contract the infection through sexual activity but would still go on to take that risk.

Note that, although malice (ill-will or a malevolent motive) must be present, it is not limited to (nor does it require) any ill-will towards the victim personally.

15.3.1 The extent of the injury

The injury must amount to either wounding or grievous ('really serious') bodily harm. Wounding is defined as breaking of all the layers of the skin. It is not necessary to cause the wound with a weapon (though of course this is often the case, eg using a deliberately smashed glass for the attack). Grievous bodily harm is not defined in the Act but case law has established that it should be given its ordinary meaning, which is 'really serious bodily harm' (*DPP v Smith* [1960] 3 All ER 161). The bodily harm must be serious, but not necessarily dangerous or permanent.

Examples of GBH include:

- injury resulting in some permanent disability, that is loss of function;
- visible disfigurement;
- broken or displaced limbs or bones;
- injuries with substantial blood loss, usually requiring blood transfusion;
- injuries resulting in lengthy treatment or incapacity;
- psychiatric injury (expert evidence is required).

(This list is adapted from CPS, 2009b.)

GBH does not have to include an assault or a battery (see 15.2.1). For example, a person infecting his/her partner knowingly with the HIV AIDS virus while concealing the infection from the partner is committing the offence of grievous bodily harm. There have been at least ten convictions for GBH based on the reckless transmission of HIV in England and Wales. Telephone calls that would result in serious psychiatric injury to the victim can also amount to grievous bodily harm.

This offence is triable either way. The penalty if tried summarily is six months' imprisonment and/or fine, and five years' imprisonment on indictment. This offence can be racially or religiously aggravated (see 14.10.2).

15.3.2 GBH with intent

The full name for this offence is 'wounding or causing grievous bodily harm with intent to do grievous bodily harm or to resist or prevent arrest'.

Section 18 of the Offences Against the Person Act 1861 states it is an offence to:

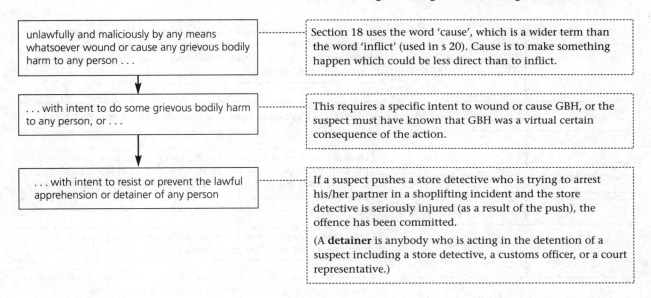

| unlawfully and maliciously by any means whatsoever wound or cause any grievous bodily harm to any person . . . | Section 18 uses the word 'cause', which is a wider term than the word 'inflict' (used in s 20). Cause is to make something happen which could be less direct than to inflict. |

| . . . with intent to do some grievous bodily harm to any person, or . . . | This requires a specific intent to wound or cause GBH, or the suspect must have known that GBH was a virtual certain consequence of the action. |

| . . . with intent to resist or prevent the lawful apprehension or detainer of any person | If a suspect pushes a store detective who is trying to arrest his/her partner in a shoplifting incident and the store detective is seriously injured (as a result of the push), the offence has been committed.

(A **detainer** is anybody who is acting in the detention of a suspect including a store detective, a customs officer, or a court representative.) |

The main difference between plain GBH and this offence is the element of intent. Of course intent is sometimes difficult to prove, although there will be some obvious examples, for instance if a weapon is used.

This offence is triable on indictment only and the penalty is life imprisonment. There was no perceived need to create a racially or religiously aggravated offence for this offence as the maximum sentence is already life imprisonment.

15.3.3 Violent Offender Orders

The Criminal Justice and Immigration Act 2008 introduced Violent Offender Orders (VOO) in 2009. The purpose of a VOO is to limit the possibility of violent reoffending (Home Office, 2009a). VOOs are civil orders with a duration of between two and five years, and set restrictions or conditions that limit an individual's behaviour, for example preventing him/her from going to certain locations, attending certain events, or having contact with specified individuals (s 102 of the Criminal Justice and Immigration Act 2008).

Such an order is requested by a chief officer of the police and issued by a magistrates' court. The court must be satisfied that the measure is necessary to protect the public or any particular member of the public from serious physical or psychological harm. VOOs are applicable to 'qualifying offenders', who must be over 18 and have been previously convicted to at least 12 months' imprisonment for a serious violent offence, or having been found not guilty due to insanity, are subject to an order equivalent to a hospital order or supervision order (s 99). VOOs are also applicable to offenders whose crimes were committed outside the UK (s 99(4)).

15.4 Assaulting, Resisting, or Obstructing Police Officers

This applies to police officers acting in the lawful execution of their duties, and to anyone assisting a police officer in the lawful execution of his/her duties. Assault to resist arrest is a separate offence. Note that here the word 'assault' is being used to mean some sort of physical attack.

Section 89 of the Police Act 1996 states it is an offence for any person:

Specific Incidents

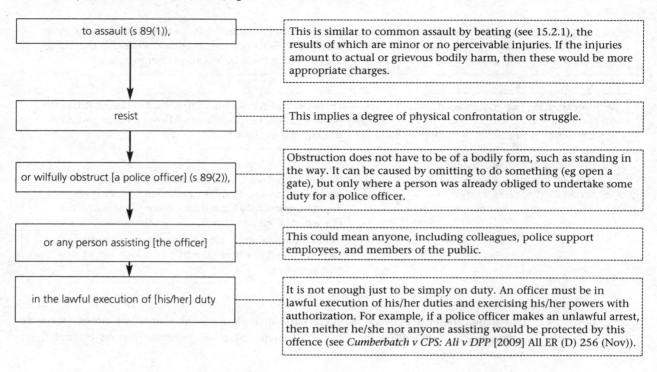

to assault (s 89(1)),
— This is similar to common assault by beating (see 15.2.1), the results of which are minor or no perceivable injuries. If the injuries amount to actual or grievous bodily harm, then these would be more appropriate charges.

resist
— This implies a degree of physical confrontation or struggle.

or wilfully obstruct [a police officer] (s 89(2)),
— Obstruction does not have to be of a bodily form, such as standing in the way. It can be caused by omitting to do something (eg open a gate), but only where a person was already obliged to undertake some duty for a police officer.

or any person assisting [the officer]
— This could mean anyone, including colleagues, police support employees, and members of the public.

in the lawful execution of [his/her] duty
— It is not enough just to be simply on duty. An officer must be in lawful execution of his/her duties and exercising his/her powers with authorization. For example, if a police officer makes an unlawful arrest, then neither he/she nor anyone assisting would be protected by this offence (see *Cumberbatch v CPS: Ali v DPP* [2009] All ER (D) 256 (Nov)).

These offences are triable summarily and the penalties are a fine or imprisonment (six months for a s 89(1) offence and one month for a s 89(2) offence).

Section 38 of the Offences Against the Person Act 1861 states it is an offence to:

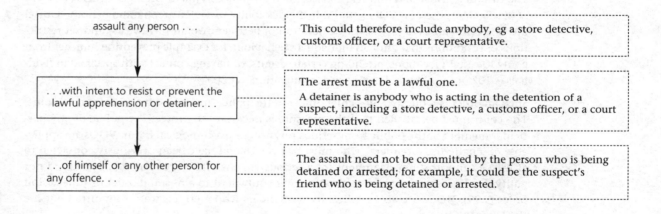

assault any person . . .
— This could therefore include anybody, eg a store detective, customs officer, or a court representative.

. . .with intent to resist or prevent the lawful apprehension or detainer. . .
— The arrest must be a lawful one. A detainer is anybody who is acting in the detention of a suspect, including a store detective, a customs officer, or a court representative.

. . .of himself or any other person for any offence. . .
— The assault need not be committed by the person who is being detained or arrested; for example, it could be the suspect's friend who is being detained or arrested.

If the suspect believes that the arrest is unlawful, it is still an offence. This would include a belief that the arrested person was innocent. This offence is triable summarily and the penalty is two years' imprisonment.

15.5 General Defences to the Use of Violence

There are several defences, such as consent or the lawful application of force. Actions taken in order to prevent a crime or in relation to effecting a lawful arrest can also be used as a defence (see 10.8.2) as long as the force used was reasonable in the circumstances (see 15.5.1). Note that s 58(1) of the Children Act 2004 removes the opportunity for a suspect to claim the defence of 'lawful chastisement' of a child in relation to ss 18, 20, and 47 of the Offences Against the Persons Act 1861 (GBH with or without intent and ABH) and s 1 of the Children and Young Persons Act 1933 (see 13.2). It does, however, remain available as a defence to offences under s 39 of the Criminal Justice Act 1988 (see 15.2.2).

One possible defence is that consent was given for the act. This could be for being tattooed, having a piercing, or being operated on for a medical condition. Consent does not include:

- being reckless as to whether consent was or was not actually given, for example knowing an injury might occur and still taking a risk of causing it; or
- submitting to an assault, actual or grievous bodily harm, for example by giving in.

Lawful sports such as boxing and rugby are contact sports and as such the participants consent to the injuries they may receive while engaged in the sport and abiding with its rules. However, if the rules are broken and the injuries are caused as a consequence, then this defence no longer applies.

Self-defence (often referred to as common law self-defence) may also be used as a legal defence. It is not defined by statute and therefore it is a question of fact for the courts to decide. In *Dewar v DPP* [2010] EWHC 1050 (Admin) it was reaffirmed that there is a two-part test to self-defence: that the individual believes that he/she was acting in self-defence and that the force used was reasonable in the circumstances (15.5.1).

15.5.1 The meaning of 'reasonable force'

The use of reasonable force for self-defence, defence of property, and law enforcement is defined in law, for example its use for certain powers of arrest and entry provided under s 117 PACE (see 9.5.3). The general meaning of 'reasonable force' is expanded upon in s 76 of the Criminal Justice and Immigration Act 2008 (subsections 1–10). This can be applied in criminal offence proceedings in relation to the use of force and the following defences:

- the common law defence of self-defence (s 76(2)(a));
- the common law defence of defence of property (s 76(2)(aa)); and
- the defence provided by s 3(1) of the Criminal Law Act (s 76(2)(b)), use of force in prevention of crime or making arrest (see 10.8.2).

The defence is available to a person who holds an honest belief that it was necessary to use force and that in the circumstances as he/she saw them, the degree of force used was not disproportionate (see *Palmer v R* [1971] AC 814). A person who uses force will be judged on how he/she perceived the circumstances in which the force had to be used. For example, in the heat of the moment the defendant may not be expected to have judged exactly what degree of force was required. A person, who uses the force honestly and instinctively, thinking that it was necessary, will be provided with some leeway. Even if the belief of the defendant was mistaken, and the degree of force used was disproportionate, he/she is still entitled to have his/her actions judged on the basis of his/her view of the facts as he/she honestly believed at the time. Although the level of force used must be reasonable according to the circumstances, a person who uses a disproportionate amount of force will not be automatically perceived as having acted unlawfully. If a person honestly and instinctively believes that the action taken was reasonable in those circumstances, then he/she will not have committed an offence if eventually the action is considered disproportionate. The possibility of retreating (rather than reacting with force) will be taken into account, but only as far as it would have been relevant in the particular circumstances. Whether the use of force was reasonable in the circumstances will have to be assessed on an individual basis.

However, note that a police officer commits an assault (as in common assault by beating, ABH, or GBH) if he/she restrains a person without intending or purporting to arrest him/her. This applies even if an arrest could have been justified (see *Fraser Wood v DPP* [2008] EWHC 1056 (Admin)).

Further information regarding the defence of property is available in the Parliament briefing paper 'Householders and the criminal law of self-defence' available online.

15.5.2 Positional asphyxia

In some, thankfully, very rare circumstances the use of restraint in the course of law enforcement can result in serious injury or death. Leaving aside the possibility of a cardiac arrest, one of the more serious risks is positional asphyxia (PA), also referred to as postural asphyxia. This is when a person's body position or posture affects the ability to breathe, and can be exacerbated by pressure applied to the person's back. It may occur through poorly executed or ill-thought-out restraint techniques, or be consequent to some form of accident, such as fainting onto a chair or other raised surface. Asphyxiation can also be caused by obliging a person (particularly if overweight) to remain seated with his/her chest close to his/her knees.

To reduce the risk of PA, police forces, prisons, and medical organizations generally recommend that restrained persons are held face down for only the shortest possible period of time. In addition, pressure on the back or chest (such as controlling the person with a knee or the restrainer's body weight) must be limited as much as possible. The risk of PA is increased for people who are under the influence of alcohol or drugs, or unconscious, who are overweight, who have engaged in a violent struggle or heavy exercise, or who are under extreme stress. Prevention is relatively simple: pressure should not be applied to the chest area or the back; a seated person should not be forced or left to lean forward; and detained persons should be made to stand or sit upright as soon as possible, for example after handcuffs have been applied.

The warning signs of impending PA are relatively clear and include:

- suddenly becoming quiet, limp, or agitated—any change in consciousness should be considered;
- complaining of not being able to breathe—even if the detainee seems generally obstructive and complaining, any such complaint should be taken seriously;
- noisy breathing, gurgling or choking, foaming saliva, convulsions;
- signs of cyanosis (such as blue lips, eyelids, gums—often difficult to spot);
- signs of force or stress in the face and neck, such as raised blood vessels or haemorrhaging.

In the event of asphyxiation, any hold or position potentially affecting the subject should be removed and his/her clothing should be loosened. If this does not improve the person's condition then CPR should be performed. However, it should be noted that resuscitation often fails. More details can be found in Belviso *et al* (2003).

15.6 Threats to Kill

Section 16 of the Offences Against the Person Act 1861 (as amended by Sch 12 to the Criminal Law Act 1977) is about making threats to kill. One way this offence can be committed is straightforward: A threatens to kill B and intends that B will believe the threat.

- Annie says to Bob 'You've 'ad it, you're dead, I'll see to it..., you're dead': Annie wants Bob to believe that her threat to kill him is real.

The other way this offence can be committed is slightly more complicated: person A communicates a threat to kill, and intends that B should believe the threat. But the threat is not about killing B, it is about killing another person C. (It is irrelevant whether C knows about the threats.)

- Adam says to Babs 'That Colin—he's finished now, I'll sort it—final like, stone cold, dead': Adam intends that Babs should believe that his threat to kill Colin is real.

To prove this offence, it is not necessary for A to actually intend to kill anyone, but it must be proved that A intends that B should believe and fear that this would be carried out. The threats made by A can be premeditated, or spoken during the heat of an argument. They can be communicated by various means (eg through email or on a social networking site), and do not need to be such that the threat can be carried out immediately. The offence could be useful where there has been no assault (eg if an assault has been prevented), yet the victim B was in fear that it would be carried out.

Threats to kill are relatively common and it is often difficult to prove an offence has occurred because it is often one person's word against another. There are also defences such as A only made the threat against B in self-defence. If the threat to kill does not involve an obvious seriousness, then perhaps a charge under s 4 of the Public Order Act 1986 or a charge of affray would be more appropriate (see 14.4).

This offence is triable either way. The penalty if tried summarily is six months' imprisonment and/or a fine, and on indictment ten years' imprisonment.

> **TASK 2** A police officer attends each of the following incidents. Using the information given here decide what offence or offences may have been committed in relation to the injuries sustained by the victims. In some cases you may wish to give more than a single answer.
>
> 1. Two people are arguing in the street. The dispute reaches a point where one of the couple head-butts the other, who then has a severe nosebleed.
> 2. An apparently drunken man throws a glass bottle from a moving car in the direction of a woman waiting at a bus stop. The bottle hits the shelter and breaks. A large fragment of flying glass hits the woman on her head, causing a deep wound which bleeds profusely. The woman's skull can easily be seen through the wound. Subsequently, the victim attended accident and emergency at a local hospital and had several stitches inserted.
> 3. CCTV images show a woman taking goods from a clothes shop and hiding them under her jacket. A store detective follows her out and into the street and stops her. He explains who he is and why he is detaining her. She makes a sudden move, pushing the store detective backwards. He falls over and grazes his hand.
> 4. After months of alleged harassment by local youths in the street outside her house, the occupant comes out and slaps one of the youths, leaving a large red mark on his cheek.

15.7 Domestic Violence

There is currently no legal definition of domestic violence. The Home Office (2013), however, proposes the following definition:

> any incident or pattern of incidents of controlling, coercive, threatening behaviour, violence or abuse between those aged 16 or over who are, or have been, intimate partners or family members regardless of gender or sexuality. The abuse can encompass, but is not limited to psychological, physical, sexual, financial and emotional [abuse].

Domestic violence should be prosecuted as any other violent crime. The Sentencing Guidelines Council states that incidents occurring in a domestic environment should not be treated more leniently than incidents occurring in other contexts. In terms of police action, Home Office Circulars 60/1990 and 19/2000 already encouraged a more proactive and professional approach from the police, even before the introduction of the Domestic Violence, Crime and Victims Act 2004. Part of this approach is a pro-arrest policy and gathering as much evidence as possible. Detailed guidance on the investigation of domestic violence was published on behalf of ACPO (NPIA, 2008a), and underpins much of what is written here. It emphasizes a multi-agency approach and the need for officers to take 'positive action' whenever reasonable and within their powers.

A 'Domestic Violence Disclosure Scheme' (also known as Claire's Law) will be rolled out to police forces across the UK in 2014 (UK Parliament, 2013) after a two-year pilot in a number of forces. The scheme allows individuals to find out whether their partner has a history of violence. Members of the public have a 'right to ask' (similar to the Child Sex Offender Disclosure Scheme) and a 'right to know'. If the police receive relevant information, they can disclose it to the person at risk after making the appropriate checks (Home Office, 2012b).

15.7.1 Civil law and domestic violence

The Family Law Act 1996 (FLA) provides opportunities under civil law to counter domestic violence and abuse. The FLA was modified by the Domestic Violence, Crime and Victims Act 2004 and provides the basis for most of the provisions covered here.

A **non-molestation order** requires a person to refrain from molesting another named person. The applicant (an 'associated person' (s 62(3) of the FLA)) could be a spouse, ex-spouse, civil partner, or a current or former cohabitant. Under s 42A of the FLA it is a criminal offence to breach a non-molestation order without reasonable excuse (the person must know of the existence of the order). If the CPS fails to act, the victim may be able to use contempt of court proceedings. The offence of breaching a non-molestation order is triable either way and the penalty is a fine or a maximum of five years' imprisonment.

An **occupation order** allows an owner, tenant, spouse, or a civil partner to seek the removal of one occupant (the abuser) from his/her home (s 33, FLA). The abuser will be forbidden from entering the property (s 33(3)). A power of arrest may be included under s 47(1)) for a breach of the order (although this is only a civil offence). These orders can be difficult to obtain, often because of the abuser's property rights (Herring, 2007, p 270). The lengthy procedures involved are an obvious disadvantage for victims.

Domestic Violence Protection Orders (DVPOs) and **Domestic Violence Protection Notices** (DVPNs) are to be rolled out across police forces in the UK from 2014, after a two-year pilot in a number of forces. A DVPN is imposed by the police in the immediate aftermath of a domestic violence incident, and prevents the abuser from having contact with the victim or returning to the victim's home for a maximum of 48 hours. (The authorizing officer for this notice needs to be at least at superintendent rank.) Within 48 hours of a DVPN being issued, an application needs to be made to a magistrates' court for a DVPO, a civil order under which there will be a further no-contact period (14–28 days' duration) for the victim and the offender. The aim of DVPNs and DVPOs is to give victims more time to decide whether to leave the abuser or to apply for a non-molestation or occupation order.

15.7.2 Responding to domestic violence incidents

The Crime Survey for England and Wales reports 2 million victims of domestic violence in the year 2010/11. Of these victims, 1.2 million were women and 800,000 men (Home Office, 2013c). For most incidents of domestic violence reported to the police there are likely to be numerous previously unreported incidents—47 per cent of the victims interviewed for the BCS 2009/10 had been victimized more than once and 30 per cent three or more times (Flatley *et al*, 2010), and two people (on average) are killed by their current or former partner every week in England and Wales (Women's Aid, 2006). It is also common for victims of domestic violence to also experience other forms of inter-personal violence such as sexual assault and stalking (Walby and Allen, 2004). Hence it is essential that positive action is taken from the start.

The first part of the response is the call taker. He/she must ensure the safety of the caller as well as gathering and recording information. The following information will be required: the location and identity of the people involved, whether anyone at the scene is disabled or intoxicated, the presence of any injuries or weapons, whether an interpreter will be required, and finally whether a court order has been breached. The victim's demeanour (and that of others present) and the possible significance of any background noise should also be noted.

The caller should be told when the police are likely to arrive, and that he/she should avoid disturbing any possible evidence. The call taker should inform the attending officer in advance whether any children are present, and about other relevant factors such as court orders and child protection matters. He/she should also be told whether his/her supervisors have been briefed of the incident. Officer safety must be considered; back-up may be necessary.

15.7.2.1 Attending a domestic violence crime scene

The first priority is the safety of everyone at the scene. An officer has a power of entry under s 17 of the PACE Act 1984 (see 9.5.1) to arrest for an indictable offence or to save life and limb. Arrest for a breach of the peace (see 9.5.4) may also be considered.

If a suspect has left the scene, then a description of the suspect should be circulated. Officers should then speak in more detail with the persons present and consider whether photographic and video evidence will be required. If any children are at the scene, a general perception of their welfare, communication ability, and demeanour should be recorded along with his/her name, date of birth, sex, address, doctor, primary carer, and school. If no children are immediately apparent, officers should be alert for signs that indicate the presence of children.

First accounts should be obtained from each individual as soon as possible after the events. They should be seen separately and in a safe environment (see 15.7.2.2). The witness account should be recorded, especially any description of an absent suspect. In serious cases video-recording should be considered. When the versions of the events differ considerably there is a need to establish whether justifiable force was used (eg by the 'victim' as self-defence), or if the suspect is making a false counter-allegation, but the arrest of both parties should be avoided if possible. Support for the victim(s) should also be offered at this stage (see 15.7.2.4).

Forensic evidence should be gathered to avoid over-reliance on the victim's statement in a future prosecution. Officers should be proactive in gathering and using photographic evidence in domestic violence investigations. A victim's non-intimate injuries should be photographed as soon as possible after the event, and again when injuries may become more apparent. Photographs should be used to assist interviewing, given to custody officers to help decide bail, and attached to the evidence file to be sent to the CPS and judiciary. Chapter 11 provides more details on general procedures to be followed when attending crime scenes.

The decision to arrest a suspect (see 10.6) should not be influenced by the victim's opinion or whether previous complaints have been withdrawn. If the decision is not to arrest, the reasons need to be recorded. Alternatives to arrest include:

- reporting the suspect for an offence and proceeding by way of a written charge; or
- informing the suspect (verbally and/or in writing) that a renewal or repeat of his/her actions may constitute an offence under the Protection from Harassment Act 1997 (see 14.5.1). Such a verbal or written communication is known as a police information notice.

The decision on the method of disposal should be explained to the victim and reassurance provided, including that support services are available. It should also be explained that the incident will be recorded on police IT systems, and that the information and evidence from the current incident could be used to support future prosecutions.

A risk assessment must be carried out for all incidents involving domestic violence. Many forces use an *aide mémoire* to assist with this. In some forces a risk assessment is the responsibility of specially trained staff such as the domestic abuse officer or coordinator, but the first officer at the scene might conduct the risk assessment under supervision. Relevant information includes the frequency of repeat victimization, the seriousness of the injuries, any escalation of violence, and details of the victim and the suspect. All staff involved with the ongoing investigation, including the custody officer, should be encouraged to contribute information. If several risk factors are identified it may be necessary to inform the victim and notify the relevant support services.

15.7.2.2 Investigating and follow-up for domestic violence incidents

The management of the investigation is dependent on local practices and on general guidance. The investigating officer must find out whether there is a history of domestic abuse, and relevant police intelligence (eg of sexual abuse or incidents witnessed by children) should be sought at local and national levels. Sources of intelligence include:

- the Police National Database (see 6.9.1.2);
- the Violent Offenders and Sex Offenders Register (with further guidance in ACPO's ViSOR Standards of 2008);
- house-to-house enquiries;
- information gathered from witnesses who came forward with information on other criminal activities of the suspect; and
- CCTV images and covert surveillance (see 22.3).

Relevant medical information should also be sought (with consent), as well as information held by housing, social care, and probation services, and the existence of civil orders, and child contact agreements (including disputes). Any professionals who witnessed the abuse and staff from the emergency services may also be able to provide important information for the prosecution. Some hearsay evidence may be acceptable as evidence, for example a witness's report of something said by a suspect (see 26.4.4).

Interviews should explore details of the incident and possible existing evidence. This will include information such as details of witnesses; the extent of the victim's physical and emotional injuries; details of family members; the history of the relationship and any previous incidents or threats (including with other partners); whether children were present; whether the parties are separated; whether any civil action has been taken; whether any sexual offences have been disclosed; the points to prove; and the victim's perception of the future relationship in terms of the likelihood of further abuse. When interviewing the suspect, it is important to consider the victim's safety if disclosing information provided by the victim. The first officer at the scene should also be interviewed when relevant. The interview should be recorded and the welfare of the officer considered, as he/she may have witnessed distressing events.

If a witness decides to withdraw from the investigation the domestic abuse officer should take a comprehensive withdrawal statement including the witness's reasons for withdrawal, confirmation of the truthfulness of his/her original statement, whether he/she was put under pressure to withdraw, with whom he/she has discussed the matters, whether he/she is considering civil proceedings, and also the perceived impact on him/her and any children were the prosecution to continue. This statement and a report from the officer for the case should then be sent to the CPS. The statement may be used as evidence in the prosecution of the current or other incidents. The risk assessment and safety plan for the victim should also be reviewed.

All reports of domestic violence must be recorded following the National Crime Recording Standards, particularly as domestic violence may be associated with other crimes, such as child abuse and harassment. All relevant information should be passed to police domestic abuse coordinators, who will liaise with the Tasking and Co-ordination Group (see 22.6). The accuracy of the existing data can then be monitored and further statistical information can be produced for sharing with partner agencies and other police personnel.

TASK 3 One of the partners in a long-term domestic relationship complains that she has been punched by the other. What offence has been committed?

15.7.2.3 Methods of disposal of suspects

General codes of practice and CPS guidance on domestic violence (CPS, 2009a) should be used when deciding whether to charge a suspect. The victim should be informed if the decision is against prosecution. The use of cautions and ASBOs in cases of domestic violence is discouraged (in NPIA guidance) although cautions may be used in some situations, for example a first incident with no intelligence of related incidents. ASBOs can only be used if individuals outside the household have been affected.

When considering releasing the suspect on bail (see 10.13.7), risk factors should be taken into account and the victim should be consulted. Any conditions attached to bail should ensure that the victim, children, and witnesses are protected. The conditions must be such that they can be policed effectively, and not conflict with existing court orders. It is important to make clear to the suspect that *he/she* (and not the victim) needs to comply with the conditions of bail, and that breaches of bail will be treated seriously, even if the suspect and the victim become reconciled. Before a suspect is released from a police station (on bail or otherwise), the victim should be informed where possible (Code of Practice (Home Office, 2005a)), and this notification should be recorded. The police should facilitate the removal of belongings by the suspect and the victim from each other's property, especially if this could otherwise lead to a breach of conditions for bail. All control rooms and databases should be updated regarding the suspect's bail conditions.

15.7.2.4 Support for the victim and victim safety

Victims should be told about the support available, including referral details for an IDVA (Independent Domestic Violence Advisor). Officers should only refer victims to victim support services when they have the victim's explicit consent (NPIA, 2008a, p 39). Temporary emergency accommodation may be used, but the location should never be revealed to the suspect.

The police should assist the victim and the IDVA in developing and implementing a safety plan. Any existing safety measures should be taken into account and it should not include any element of victim accountability. Advice on home security (from Crime Prevention Officers), personal alarms, mobile phones, and CCTV can all form part of a plan. Other safety schemes include:

- cocoon watch schemes (neighbours, family, and relevant agencies contact the police in case of further incidents);
- police watch schemes (regular patrolling of a certain area); and
- sanctuary schemes (provision of extra support so the victim does not have to go out and the creation of a safe room from where he/she can call the police).

Neighbourhood policing teams should be kept informed about domestic violence and associated levels of risk in their geographic area.

For victims of domestic violence with an unstable immigration status, there may be additional difficulties as the government has a general policy of no recourse to public funds for immigrants (eg housing benefit). However, the Home Office recognizes that victims of domestic violence with uncertain immigration status may be in a particularly vulnerable situation, and allows for an appeal for indefinite stay in the UK if the violence had occurred within the first two years of the relationship.

When a person is killed by a partner or former partner, the Secretary of State can direct a person or body listed in s 9 of the Domestic Violence, Crime and Victims Act 2004 to conduct a 'domestic homicide review' with the aim of learning from that incident in order to prevent further deaths. The reviews can include chief officers of police, local authorities, probation officers, and health and social services.

15.7.3 Multi-agency work and wider initiatives to counter domestic violence

The NPIA guidance emphasizes the importance of multi-agency work in preventing and addressing domestic violence incidents (and College of Policing Authorised Professional Practice guidance is expected in the first quarter of 2014). Provision varies across the country, but good practice often involves a Local Strategic Partnership (LSP), which brings together representatives from local authorities, public and private sectors, community and voluntary organizations. Multi-agency work is also facilitated through:

- MAPPA (Multi-Agency Public Protection Arrangements), where the police, the Prison Service, and the Probation Service help to manage risk from violent and sexual offenders in the area (see 3.3.1).
- MARACs (Multi-Agency Risk Assessment Conferences), often coordinated by local police forces. They provide a forum for the sharing of information developing a multi-agency risk management plan for each case. The police have a significant role in the work of a MARAC, particularly in detaining perpetrators and referring cases.
- IDVAs, who work with police officers to provide independent support, risk assessment, and safety planning for victims. They are important in helping the police fast-track the investigation of domestic abuse incidents and can testify as an expert witness.
- SDVCs (Specialist Domestic Violence Courts), set up to improve victim protection, increase offender accountability, and to promote multi-agency cooperation.

Other strategies to reduce domestic violence include the DASH risk assessment checklist (Home Office, 2009d, p 32) and a College of Policing course on domestic violence for police officers and CPS professionals.

Three further aspects which have been at the forefront of governmental policy regarding domestic and gender violence are 'honour'-based violence, female genital mutilation, and forced marriages (Home Office, 2009c). These present particular difficulties, for example, investigations into 'honour'-based violence may be hampered by the non-cooperation of the extended family or the community. In addition, officers should be aware that when a victim has an insecure immigration status, records of the investigation may become part of the victim's application to stay in the UK. ACPO issued an 'honour'-based violence strategy in 2008, in relation to engaging with local communities encouraging victims to come forward. The international dimension of domestic violence needs to be taken into account, and international cooperation encouraged.

The current government's long-term strategy to address violence against women especially within domestic and sexual contexts can be found in the policy 'Call to end violence against women and girls: strategic vision' (Home Office, 2010a) and subsequent action plans. Practical guidance for helping women and children of black and ethnic minority background to escape domestic violence is also available (Home Office, 2011c).

15.8 The Use of Violence to Enter Premises

It is an offence under s 6 of the Criminal Law Act 1977 to use violence to gain entry into premises which are being occupied by any person opposing the entry. Defences are available for residents and intended residents concerning trespassers but generally, it makes no difference that the person using the violence has a right or interest in the property.

Originally, forced entry was identified as an offence in order to prevent the owners, tenants, or occupiers of premises from using violence to gain entry when 'squatters' were in occupation. More recently, however, convictions for this offence are likely to be in relation to serious and violent domestic disputes. For example, a person trying to force his way into his own flat is committing an offence if his live-in partner is inside the flat and she does not want him to come in. A police officer suspecting that such an offence may have been committed should run through a mental checklist before acting, to ensure that the circumstances match all the requirements of the relevant legislation.

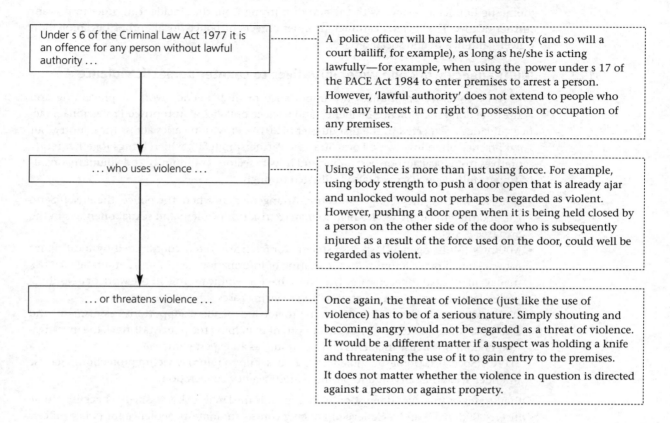

Under s 6 of the Criminal Law Act 1977 it is an offence for any person without lawful authority . . .	A police officer will have lawful authority (and so will a court bailiff, for example), as long as he/she is acting lawfully—for example, when using the power under s 17 of the PACE Act 1984 to enter premises to arrest a person. However, 'lawful authority' does not extend to people who have any interest in or right to possession or occupation of any premises.
. . . who uses violence . . .	Using violence is more than just using force. For example, using body strength to push a door open that is already ajar and unlocked would not perhaps be regarded as violent. However, pushing a door open when it is being held closed by a person on the other side of the door who is subsequently injured as a result of the force used on the door, could well be regarded as violent.
. . . or threatens violence . . .	Once again, the threat of violence (just like the use of violence) has to be of a serious nature. Simply shouting and becoming angry would not be regarded as a threat of violence. It would be a different matter if a suspect was holding a knife and threatening the use of it to gain entry to the premises.\n\nIt does not matter whether the violence in question is directed against a person or against property.

So for this offence, the suspect must not have lawful authority, and must either use violence or threaten to use violence.

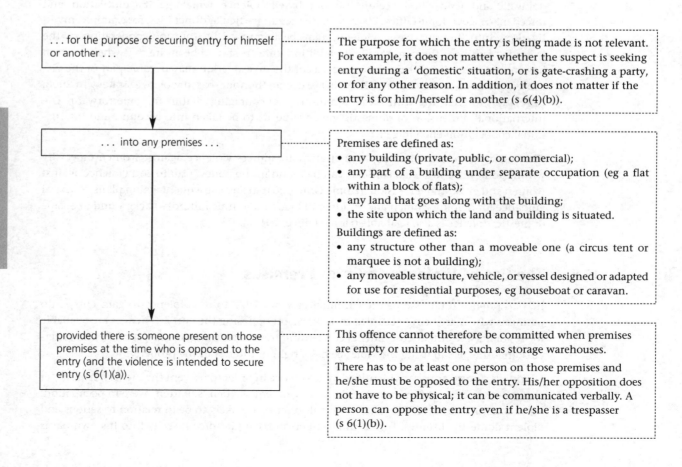

. . . for the purpose of securing entry for himself or another . . .	The purpose for which the entry is being made is not relevant. For example, it does not matter whether the suspect is seeking entry during a 'domestic' situation, or is gate-crashing a party, or for any other reason. In addition, it does not matter if the entry is for him/herself or another (s 6(4)(b)).
. . . into any premises . . .	Premises are defined as: • any building (private, public, or commercial); • any part of a building under separate occupation (eg a flat within a block of flats); • any land that goes along with the building; • the site upon which the land and building is situated. Buildings are defined as: • any structure other than a moveable one (a circus tent or marquee is not a building); • any moveable structure, vehicle, or vessel designed or adapted for use for residential purposes, eg houseboat or caravan.
provided there is someone present on those premises at the time who is opposed to the entry (and the violence is intended to secure entry (s 6(1)(a)).	This offence cannot therefore be committed when premises are empty or uninhabited, such as storage warehouses. There has to be at least one person on those premises and he/she must be opposed to the entry. His/her opposition does not have to be physical; it can be communicated verbally. A person can oppose the entry even if he/she is a trespasser (s 6(1)(b)).

A home owner does not commit an offence under s 6 of the Criminal Law Act 1977 if there are trespassers inside and he/she enters by force, but only if the home owners are:

- Displaced residential occupiers (defined in s 12 of the Criminal Law Act 1977): this would include people who leave the home they live in for a short while, and during the time they are away a person enters the premises as a trespasser to take up residence.
- Protected intended occupiers (defined in s 12A of the Criminal Law Act 1977): this would include people who are intending to take up occupancy (having completed the legal process to buy or rent the premises).

This offence is triable summarily and the penalty is six months' imprisonment and/or a fine. There is a power of entry to arrest under s 17 of the PACE Act 1984 for this offence (see 9.5.1).

TASK 4 Charlie and partner Sam have been facing up to the fact that their three-year relationship is drawing to an end. Recently there have been several episodes where they shouted angrily at each other, and both of them have taken to going out separately and getting very drunk. They share a house which is owned jointly.

One evening Charlie stays at home while Sam goes out to a club. Sam arrives home in the early hours of the following morning, very drunk, to find the front door will not open with the key. Sam begins to bang on the door with his fists, and the awakened neighbours hear Charlie shouting from inside the house to stop the banging and to go away. One of the neighbours calls the police who attend the scene to find Sam still banging the door. In relation to s 6(1) of the Criminal Law Act 1977, has Sam committed an offence?

15.9 Gang-related Violence

The issue of 'gang'-related violence is one that has featured highly in recent years. For example, ACPO claimed in 2009 that 'the issue of violent street gangs is one that unfortunately blights a number of our areas' and that 'there are a number of our cities and towns that have considerable problems with violent groups of young people' (Akers, 2009). There have certainly been tragic cases of the killing of innocent individuals by groups of young men in our larger cities, some members of the group being armed with knives and guns. It is also the case, as almost all research has demonstrated, that where gangs exist they tend to be made up of young people, with members being no older than about 25 years of age (Marshall *et al*, 2005). However, there are questions around how a 'gang' is defined and these discussions go beyond simply academic interest. For example, in the UK we often appear to subscribe to the assumption that our 'gang problem' is similar in nature, if not in extent, to that of the United States. However, research indicates that the two key characteristics of US gangs are that they are 'business' orientated and provide a mechanism for group identity (Campbell and Muncer, 1989), which is in contrast to our understanding of British gangs, which tend to exhibit a much broader range of characteristics (Stelfox, 1998).

The law provides a definition of a 'gang' in s 34(5) of the Policing and Crime Act 2009 as a group that consists of at least three people; uses a name, emblem, or colour or any other identifiable characteristic; and is associated with a particular area. This definition may sometimes prove a little vague. More recently ACPO has been using a working definition of gang that includes the notion of a

> relatively durable, predominantly street-based group of young people who:
> (1) see themselves (and are seen by others) as a discernible group; and
> (2) engage in a range of criminal activity and violence.
>
> They may also [...]
> (3) identify with or lay claim over territory;
> (4) have some form of identifying structural feature; and/or
> (5) be in conflict with other similar gangs
>
> (Home Office, 2012c).

Some research (eg Harris *et al*, 2011) suggests that we need to be cautious about labelling offenders as gang members. This is because such labelling may have the unwanted effect of a 'self-fulfilling' prophecy, with supposed gang members finding it more difficult to break associations with other criminally active individuals.

15.9.1 Tackling gang violence

For investigations into gang-related crime the police can apply for an 'Investigation Anonymity Order' for an individual. This can be used to protect individual gang members who give information to the police (see 24.7). An injunction can be used against an individual in order to prevent him/her from engaging in, or encouraging or assisting, gang-related violence under s 34(3) of the Policing and Crime Act 2009 (see 14.2.8).

In November 2012, the Home Office published a report on gang-related violence called 'Ending Gang and Youth Violence: one year on' (Home Office, 2012a). This was a follow-up to a previous initiative published in November 2011, in the wake of the 2011 summer riots. The new report summarizes a number of government ministries' recent work on tackling gang-related violence, including providing support for vulnerable youngsters, the development of gang injunctions for 14- to 18-year-olds, and a new offence of threatening with a knife in a public place or school. Other plans include introducing a further new offence: possessing illegal firearms with intent to supply, with a potential maximum penalty of life imprisonment, and also increasing the maximum penalty for importation of firearms to life imprisonment. The implementation of these provisions is currently being addressed in Parliament under the Anti-social Behaviour, Crime and Policing Bill 2013–14. The report also proposes continuing the work developed during the past year in terms of promoting inter-agency communication and sharing of good practice to address gang-related violence (including ACPO, NOMS, and local initiatives), supporting local intervention to address youth crime as a matter of public health, and developing initiatives to understand, prevent, and support girls involved in gangs (who are often then victimized).

15.10 Answers to Tasks

TASK 1

1. Common assault by beating (battery): only the very slightest degree of force is required to constitute a battery and little or no visible injury is necessary to prove the offence.
2. Common assault: if a person is threatened with immediate unlawful personal violence of a minor nature, he/she is the victim of common assault (remember that assault is the threat of violence or harm, not the harm itself).

The suspect can only be charged or reported for the offence of common assault, or common assault by beating (battery), not both.

TASK 2 The problem with these kinds of scenario is that you lack all the other information that would be available in a real incident. However, based entirely on the limited information available to you in the questions, the following are the possible offences that could be considered:

1. Here, in order to have sustained a nosebleed the health and/or comfort of the victim is most likely to have been 'interfered with', so AOABH under s 47 of the Offences Against the Person Act 1861 is most likely to be the appropriate offence.
2. All layers of the victim's skin have been broken and therefore the injury is a wound. More evidence is required to ascertain the suspect's intentions (this will come from witnesses and by interviewing the suspect). The offence could be GBH or GBH with intent.
3. Two options here perhaps; as far as the injury is concerned, a graze may have interfered with the health and comfort of the store detective, therefore AOABH under s 47 of the Offences Against the Person Act 1861 could be considered. When the aspect of detention/arrest is also taken into consideration, then assault with intent to resist lawful arrest under s 38 of the Offences Against the Person Act 1861 may also be appropriate.
4. Once again, a large red mark may have interfered with the health and comfort of the young man, therefore AOABH under s 47 of the Offences Against the Person Act 1861 could be considered. Alternatively, the red mark could be considered as a minor or hardly perceivable injury, so this might be a common assault by beating (s 39 of the Criminal Justice Act 1988).

Prosecution guidelines or charging standards are available on the CPS website.

TASK 3 You probably considered the following:

1. Through questioning, a police officer would be able to determine whether the injury affects the health or comfort of the victim in more than a trivial way.
2. Through questioning and observation, a police officer would be able to collect and collate evidence concerning the injury and whether it can be seen or felt by the victim or witnesses. Remember that the police officer him/herself is a witness too.
3. If there is no evidence of the offence of actual bodily harm, then common assault could be considered as an alternative.

TASK 4 Section 6(1) of the Criminal Law Act 1977 states that any person who, without lawful authority, uses or threatens violence for the purpose of securing entry into any premises for [him/her]self or for any other person is guilty of an offence provided that:

- 'a person is present on those premises, and he/she is opposed to the entry which the violence is intended to secure'; and
- 'the person using violence or threatening the violence knows that that is the case'.

In the circumstances it appears that Sam is only hammering on the door with his fists and therefore the actions of Sam fall short of the 'violence' that is required for this offence. If Sam's actions escalate to the likelihood of damage being caused, or threats or use of violence, then the offence would be committed provided that Sam knew Charlie was on the premises and opposed the entry.

16 | Theft, Fraud, and Related Offences

16.1 Introduction

This chapter examines the law and procedure concerned with a number of criminal offences associated with theft and fraud. We present the basic knowledge of the criminal law required for many pre-join programmes and for initial police training. This Handbook will provide you with the essence of the individual law and some interpretations (both academic and from case law or precedent), but there is no substitute for reading and understanding the law itself.

Of all the dishonest criminal offences police officers will deal with early in their careers, theft will probably be the most common. Theft includes shoplifting and stealing from an employer, as well as a number of other similar crimes. The primary source of legislation relating to theft is to be found in ss 1–6 of the Theft Act 1968. There are many legal complexities surrounding theft and we will simply examine the basic principles involved. Trainee officers are likely to be involved in most stages of the investigation of theft and 'simple' types of fraud, from reporting to investigation and possibly prosecution. They are less likely to become involved in complex fraud investigations, beyond the initial stages. This is particularly the case for large-scale credit card fraud, where difficult decisions need to be made concerning the 'screening' of reported offences to decide which should be the subject of a secondary investigation (see 23.4) and in reference to the NIM (see 22.6). The investigation is likely to be handled by a specialist unit (which might also deal with cybercrime).

The information is this chapter is relevant to the PAC requirement that trainee police officers conduct initial investigations and report volume crime according to National/Local Policing Plans. It will also provide the opportunity to develop the underpinning knowledge required for a number of Certificate in Knowledge of Policing and Diploma in Policing assessed units, and for trainees' Phase 3 Learning Diary entries (particularly the 'Crime' heading) and SOLAP. Note, however, that the IPLDP curriculum is subject to periodic 'maintenance' and hence a check should be made with each force to find out precisely what aspects of the criminal law and police procedure around theft, fraud, and related offences are required.

16.2 The Definition of Theft

A person is guilty of theft (s 1 of the Theft Act 1968) if he/she 'dishonestly appropriates property belonging to another with the intention of permanently depriving the other of it'. A thief is a person who commits a theft or in everyday language, steals something. We examine each of the five key concepts for theft in turn.

Dishonesty is not defined by the Act, but s 2(1) of the Theft Act 1968 defines where a person will not be treated as dishonest. The person is not acting dishonestly if he/she believes that:

- he/she had the lawful right to take the item (eg a man sees a woman leaving with his bag and decides to take it back from her);

- he/she would have had the owner's consent if the owner had known the circumstances (eg your neighbour is on holiday and you are looking after his garden, but your lawnmower breaks down so you take his from his shed to cut your grass); and
- the owner cannot be discovered by taking reasonable steps (eg a person finds cash in the street).

But s 2(2) of the Theft Act 1968 states that a person may be treated as dishonest if property is taken, even if the person would have been willing to pay for it. A court must decide if a person acted dishonestly. To prove dishonesty, it would need to be shown that a reasonable person would consider the action(s) dishonest **and** that the defendant knew that his/her actions would be viewed as dishonest by those standards (see *R v Ghosh* [1982] QB 1053).

Appropriation is given the following meaning in s 3(1) of the Theft Act 1968. It is:

- assuming the rights of an owner of property by keeping it or controlling its movements (eg a girl takes a pen from a shop display and puts it in her pocket); or
- obtaining property innocently and later keeping it and using it as his or her own (eg hiring a ladder and not returning it).

However, when an innocent purchaser pays the right price for property which later turns out to be stolen, he/she will not have committed theft. For example, if a man buys a second-hand bicycle in good faith and then discovers it is stolen, he will not have committed theft (s 3(2) of the Theft Act 1968). It will then be a matter for a civil court to decide who is now the rightful owner—the prior owner or the innocent purchaser.

Property within the Theft Act 1968 (s 4) covers a wide range of items and other things such as ideas. As you might expect, it includes money and personal property (eg personal effects and pets), and real property ('real estate'); for example, land and things forming part of the land such as buildings and some plants. But it also includes:

- plants or fungi growing wild, but only if they are picked for sale, reward, or a commercial purpose (but always consider other legislation that might prohibit such activities, such as the Wildlife and Countryside Act 1981);
- wild creatures, but only if they are tamed and have not been lost or abandoned since they were kept in captivity;
- things in action; for example, patents, copyrights, and trade marks; and
- tangible property; for example, gas (but not electricity, see 16.7).

Note, however, real property (property which relates to land and buildings) can only be stolen:

1. by a trustee (someone who has the legal control over the land), for example, during its transfer in some kind of a legal process;
2. by persons who do not own the land, for example by removing turf, top soil, or digging up cultivated trees and shrubs; or
3. by tenants, for example by removing fixtures and fittings.

Belonging to a person (s 5) means that the person has:

- a proprietary right or interest, for example the owner of a pair of boots that needs repair;
- possession, for example the owner of the shoe repairers where the boots are taken for repair; or
- control, for example a woman repairing the boots.

The intention to permanently deprive (s 6(1)) is shown by a person treating another person's property as if it were his or her own. This could include:

- lending and borrowing over an extended time scale (eg borrowing a sewing machine from somebody and then lending it to someone else); or
- pawning an item (eg going to a pawnbroker's shop with another person's laptop and receiving a loan of money in exchange).

The offence of theft is triable either way. The penalty if tried summarily is six months' imprisonment and/or a fine, and seven years' imprisonment on indictment.

> **TASK 1** Now that you know what constitutes a theft, think of three incidents of theft that you are aware of, either through the media or other means, and try and identify the five elements of theft within each of those incidents.

16.3 Robbery and Blackmail

Robbery and blackmail are two separate offences under the Theft Act 1968, but there are some similarities. Robbery is theft involving the use of physical force (or the threat of force) to appropriate property belonging to another person. For blackmail, pressure is also put on the victim with the aim of causing him/her a loss. However, for blackmail no property needs to have been taken and no physical force needs to be involved for the offence to be proved.

16.3.1 Robbery

Robbery is the act of stealing from a person whilst using (or threatening the use of) force or violence. It is an aggravated form of the primary offence of theft and therefore, for robbery to be proved, theft has to be proved first. Robbery is covered in s 8 of the Theft Act 1968.

A robbery must involve at least one of the following elements:

- force or a threat of force is used on any person, immediately before, at the time of the theft, and in order to carry out the theft; or
- any person is 'put in fear' that force will be used to carry out the theft.

There are two main ways of establishing the 'put in fear' element of the offence:

- Actually to put in fear: this can be proved from the victim's statement. The fear of being subjected to force must be genuine and it could be evidenced by what the victim saw the suspect do and the way that made him/her feel as a result.
- To seek to put in fear: the state of mind of the suspect is what is important, and this could be evidenced from the suspect's statement. He/she must seek to put some person in fear of force. However, it is not necessary to prove that any person was actually put in fear; if the victim is not intimidated by the suspect, it is enough that the suspect tried to frighten the victim. This might be proved by evidence from other witnesses or circumstantial evidence, such as the suspect wielding an offensive weapon.

Note that all five elements of theft must be proven (see 16.2) to have applied at the time of the robbery. For example, in *R v Vinall and another* [2011] EWCA Crim 6252, it was held that although violence had been used at the time a pedal bike was initially taken, there was no intention to permanently deprive. An intention to permanently deprive would only be demonstrated if the pedal cycle was abandoned, at which point the theft would be complete. But at this moment (when the theft was complete) there was no use or threat of force, and hence no robbery.

The offence of robbery is triable on indictment only and the maximum penalty is life imprisonment.

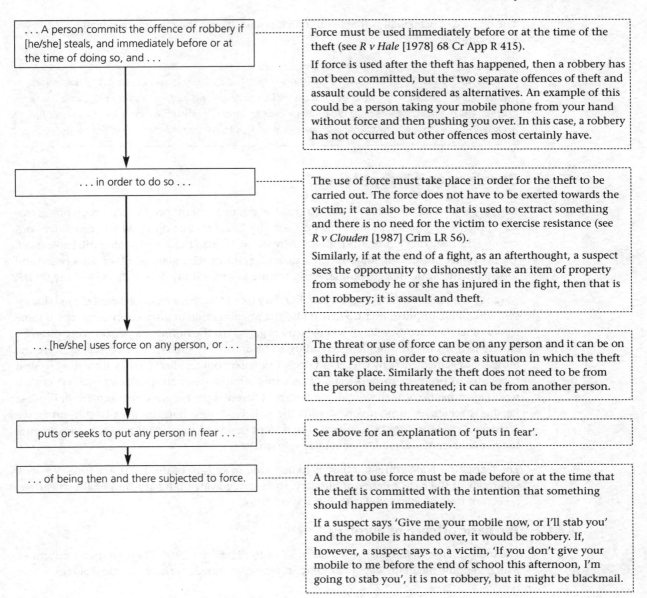

... A person commits the offence of robbery if [he/she] steals, and immediately before or at the time of doing so, and ...	Force must be used immediately before or at the time of the theft (see *R v Hale* [1978] 68 Cr App R 415).
	If force is used after the theft has happened, then a robbery has not been committed, but the two separate offences of theft and assault could be considered as alternatives. An example of this could be a person taking your mobile phone from your hand without force and then pushing you over. In this case, a robbery has not occurred but other offences most certainly have.
... in order to do so ...	The use of force must take place in order for the theft to be carried out. The force does not have to be exerted towards the victim; it can also be force that is used to extract something and there is no need for the victim to exercise resistance (see *R v Clouden* [1987] Crim LR 56).
	Similarly, if at the end of a fight, as an afterthought, a suspect sees the opportunity to dishonestly take an item of property from somebody he or she has injured in the fight, then that is not robbery; it is assault and theft.
... [he/she] uses force on any person, or ...	The threat or use of force can be on any person and it can be on a third person in order to create a situation in which the theft can take place. Similarly the theft does not need to be from the person being threatened; it can be from another person.
puts or seeks to put any person in fear ...	See above for an explanation of 'puts in fear'.
... of being then and there subjected to force.	A threat to use force must be made before or at the time that the theft is committed with the intention that something should happen immediately.
	If a suspect says 'Give me your mobile now, or I'll stab you' and the mobile is handed over, it would be robbery. If, however, a suspect says to a victim, 'If you don't give your mobile to me before the end of school this afternoon, I'm going to stab you', it is not robbery, but it might be blackmail.

16.3.2   Blackmail

Section 21(1) of the Theft Act 1968 states that a person commits an offence if he/she makes any unwarranted demand with menaces, with a view to making a gain for him/herself or any other person, or with intent to cause a loss to any other person. The demand must be unwarranted and unreasonable. Some demands may be considered reasonable, for example in relation to the repayment of a debt.

The evidential requirements are shown in the following table.

Evidential requirement	Explanation
Demand	The demand can be made orally or in writing
With a view to gain or loss	The loss or gain must be financial in nature
Menaces	This should be given its ordinary dictionary meaning, for example has a threatening quality or action
The demand must be unwarranted	The court must decide whether the demand was unreasonable, and whether the suspect believes it was reasonable and proper

Specific Incidents

The offence of blackmail is triable on indictment only and the maximum penalty is 14 years' imprisonment.

> **TASK 2** Chris is carrying a bag full of shopping in her local shopping centre when the handle breaks and the bag falls to the ground. Jo grabs the grabs the bag and makes off, but it breaks open, spilling the contents onto the ground. Jo picks up one of the items and then runs into Chris, causing her to fall over heavily and break her arm. Has Jo committed the offence of robbery?

16.4 Burglary and Trespassing

Burglary is a so-called 'volume' and 'acquisitive' crime. Students on pre-join programmes (see 7.2.1) might well be set an 'investigation' activity based on a burglary when knowledge concerning the needs of victims, the legislation involved, human rights and similar will be assessed. Trainee police officers will undoubtedly encounter crimes of burglary whilst on Supervised and Independent Patrol. Indeed, burglary may feature as a case study during Phase 3 of the IPLDP.

Burglary is a serious offence; aggravated burglary (see 16.4.2), for example, carries a maximum sentence of life imprisonment. There is also the phenomenon of distraction burglary (in some forces called 'artifice' burglary), where entry is gained to the home of a person (very often an elderly person) by an offender pretending to be an official such as a meter reader. Here the burglar has gained entry by trickery or deceptive behaviour (artifice) so they have not received true consent from the owner/occupier and are therefore trespassing. Not all such crimes are reported, either because the victim is unaware at first that the burglary has occurred or because he/she is reluctant to be involved with the police. Artifice burglars usually commit 'spree offences' (a series of similar crimes within a short period of time). This is likely to be because the net haul from each residence is relatively small.

The legislation concerning burglary is to be found in ss 9–10 of the Theft Act 1968. We look separately at the basic offence of burglary, then at aggravated burglary, and finally at various aspects of trespass associated with this type of crime.

16.4.1 The basic offence of burglary

The basic offence of burglary is set out in s 9 of the Theft Act 1968. There are two subsections which describe the main ways the offence can be committed, as shown in the diagram.

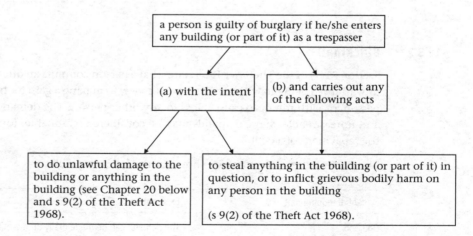

Certain terms, such as 'entry', 'trespasser', and 'building' need to be carefully defined in order to fully appreciate the range of activities that might count as burglary under s 9(1) of the Theft Act 1968.

Entry can be gained in a number of clearly defined ways:

- In person, by walking or climbing into a building, either completely or by inserting a body part (eg an arm or a leg) through a window or letter box. However, there must be more than minimal insertion; sliding a hand between a window and frame from the outside of a building in order to release the catch would be insufficient.
- Using a tool or article as an extension of the human body to carry out one of the relevant offences. In these circumstances no part of the body needs to be inserted, only the article that is being used to gain entry. The article must be used for more than just gaining entry; using a crowbar just to prise open a door would not qualify as the full offence, but a length of garden cane pushed through the letter box of a shop to hook a scarf from a display would qualify as the full offence.
- Using a blameless accomplice in a similar way to using an article as an extension of the suspect's body. Here, for example, a child below the age of criminal responsibility (10 years of age) could be lifted through a small window to obtain property from inside. On the other hand, if the child is used for the purposes of preparing an entry point for the burglar only and nothing is stolen, then the full offence is not committed; it has only been attempted.

Trespass involves a person entering a building or part of a building (for the purpose of committing one of the relevant offences) in one of the following ways:

- entering a building for a purpose other than the intended purpose of that building, for example going into a shop with the intention to steal (rather than an intent to browse or buy);
- entering by some kind of deception, for example pretending to represent a utility company for the purpose of reading a meter and being invited into the building ('distraction burglary', referred to earlier);
- crossing over a demarcation line of some kind, unlawfully and without invitation or permission, whether or not the owner knows he/she is trespassing.

The person must have guilty knowledge (*mens rea*: see 5.3.2) that what he/she is doing amounts to trespass, or alternatively, not care about whether he/she is trespassing.

(Image © Zoe Lawton-Barrett)

Burglary involves entering a building as a trespasser

The word '**building**' is used within the Theft Act, but is not defined there. However, the meaning of 'a building' is reasonably well established through case law:

- 'building is an ordinary word, which is a matter of fact' (*Brutus v Cozens* [1973] AC 854, 861);
- a building is 'a structure of considerable size and intended to be permanent or at least to endure for a considerable time' (*Stevens v Gourley* (1859) 7 CBNS 99); and

Specific Incidents

- 'a building need not necessarily be a completed structure; it is sufficient that it should be a connected and entire structure' (Judge Lush in *R v Manning & Rogers* (1871) CA). Therefore an unfinished building becomes a building when it reaches a point at which it has all its walls and a roof.

Examples of buildings other than houses include garages and garden sheds, but force policy and procedures may vary with regard to burglary from different types of building.

A dwelling is defined within the Theft Act as an inhabited building or a vehicle or vessel which at the time of the offence is inhabited (irrespective of whether or not the person who occupies the vehicle/vessel is present at the time of the burglary). For example, a houseboat which is moored alongside a river bank, and is inhabited by its owners, is regarded as a building for the purposes of the Theft Act 1968. Similarly, a motor home or caravan inhabited during a holiday is a building (but not when it is parked and empty during the winter). However, an inhabited tent would not be included since it is not a semi-permanent structure. We provide further information on the definitions of premises and locations in 9.2.

This legislation also covers the circumstances where a person is lawfully within a building but enters a part of it that he/she is not meant to enter. For example:

- a customer who leaves the front of a shop where purchases are made and walks through to the back, past a sign clearly stating 'Staff Only—No Unauthorized Entry' and into a storeroom;
- a customer in a pub who hides behind the bar at closing time; and
- a student at evening classes in an adult education centre who, during a break in lessons, goes into the administrative offices of the centre which are only staffed during the day.

16.4.1.1   Sections 9(1)(a) and 9(1)(b)

Subsection 9(1)(a) relates to intent only, while s 9(1)(b) relates to actually carrying out the acts (as shown in the diagram at the start of 16.4.1).

For an offence under s 9(1)(a) of the Theft Act 1968 the suspect must enter a building (or part of a building) as a trespasser and intend to:

- steal anything in the building;
- inflict grievous bodily harm on anyone in the building; or
- unlawfully damage the building or anything inside it.

However, the acts do not have to be committed, only intended. The intent can be proved in a number of ways (or in combination), such as the suspect admitting to having guilty knowledge or criminal intent to commit the offence. Alternatively, other suspects (who admit to involvement in committing the offence) might name the suspect as an accomplice.

Circumstantial evidence can also help prove intent, and this might include:

- witness statements;
- observations of the arresting officer(s) in relation to the suspect's proximity to the crime scene when he/she was arrested;
- property known to originate from the premises being found in the suspect's possession before he/she has left the building; and
- the results of forensic examination of the suspect's clothes or fingerprint evidence indicating that he/she was present at the crime scene (see 25.6).

If the offence relates to an intent to inflict GBH then the entry must have been made with that intent. Consequently, in relation to proving the offence, the same degree of evidence of intent will be required as would be needed to prove intent under s 18 of the Offences Against the Person Act 1861 (see 15.3.2).

Under s 9(1)(b) of the Theft Act 1968, burglary involves trespassing and then **committing** acts (or attempted acts) of theft or injury.

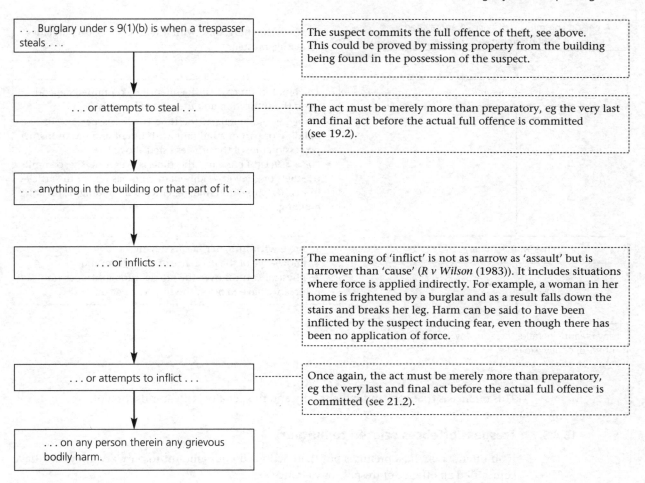

| ... Burglary under s 9(1)(b) is when a trespasser steals ... | ┄┄ | The suspect commits the full offence of theft, see above. This could be proved by missing property from the building being found in the possession of the suspect. |

| ... or attempts to steal ... | ┄┄ | The act must be merely more than preparatory, eg the very last and final act before the actual full offence is committed (see 19.2). |

| ... anything in the building or that part of it ... |

| ... or inflicts ... | ┄┄ | The meaning of 'inflict' is not as narrow as 'assault' but is narrower than 'cause' (*R v Wilson* (1983)). It includes situations where force is applied indirectly. For example, a woman in her home is frightened by a burglar and as a result falls down the stairs and breaks her leg. Harm can be said to have been inflicted by the suspect inducing fear, even though there has been no application of force. |

| ... or attempts to inflict ... | ┄┄ | Once again, the act must be merely more than preparatory, eg the very last and final act before the actual full offence is committed (see 21.2). |

| ... on any person therein any grievous bodily harm. |

An offence under either subsection is triable either way. The penalty if tried summarily is six months' imprisonment and/or a fine. If tried on indictment the maximum penalty is ten years' imprisonment (14 years if the building or part of the building was a dwelling), and three years minimum on conviction for a third domestic burglary.

16.4.2   Aggravated burglary

Aggravated burglary (s 10 of the Theft Act 1968) is a more serious offence than burglary and may involve the use of weapons or explosives. The types of weapon or explosive (articles) covered by this legislation are shown in the table.

Article	Details	Theft Act 1968
Firearm	Includes an airgun or air pistol (see 18.6)	s 10(1)(a)
Imitation firearm	Anything which has the appearance of being a firearm, whether capable of being discharged or not (see 18.8)	
Weapon of offence	Any article made or adapted for use for causing injury to or incapacitating a person, or intended by the person having it with him for such use (see 18.2.1)	s 10(1)(b)
Explosive	Any article manufactured for the purpose of producing a practical effect by explosion, or intended by the person having it with [him/her] for that purpose	s 10(1)(c)

Specific Incidents

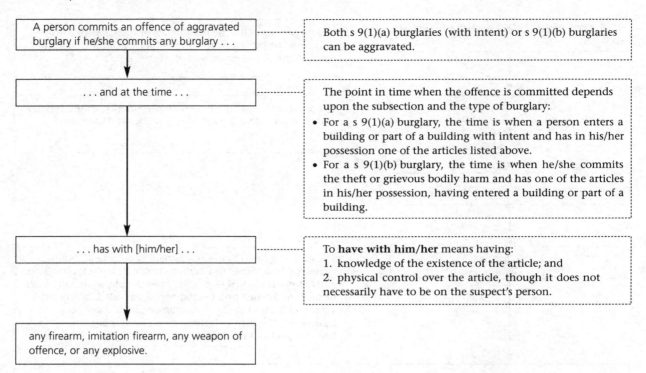

This offence is triable by indictment only and the penalty is life imprisonment.

16.4.3   Trespass offences related to burglary

If an offender enters a premises but their actions do not amount to burglary, they may have committed an offence of trespass or vagrancy.

Trespassing with a weapon of offence is when a person is on any premises as a trespasser (after having entered as such) and has in his/her possession any weapon of offence without lawful authority or reasonable excuse (s 8 of the Criminal law Act 1977). This offence is not committed if the person has innocently entered and is then subsequently asked to leave (even if he/she possesses the weapon of offence). The offence is triable summarily and the penalty is three months' imprisonment and/or a fine.

Trespassing with an intent to commit a sexual offence is covered under s 63 of the Sexual Offences Act 2003. The offender must be on premises or land without the owner's or the occupier's consent and know that he/she is trespassing (or be reckless as to whether he/she is trespassing). There must also be an intent to commit a sexual offence on the premises or land, and this could be proved from statements from the offender or intended victim, or items seized from the offender at the scene (such as a knife). The intention to commit the sexual offence can be formed at any time the suspect is trespassing, for example before entering the premises, or while on the premises (having entered without any intention to commit a sexual offence). It is immaterial whether any sexual offence is actually committed.

The offence is triable either way. The penalty if tried summarily is six months' imprisonment and/or a fine not exceeding the statutory maximum, and on indictment ten years' imprisonment.

The Vagrancy Act 1824 particularly s 4, could be used when a suspect is found on enclosed premises in the open air or land for any unlawful purpose, such as preparing to commit a burglary or theft. Enclosed premises in the open air would include a house, a shed, or a warehouse, and can mean inside a room or a building. But it does not include the situation where a person is found in a room having made his/her way from another part of the same premises where he/she was entitled to be. For example, a man could not be found guilty of this offence if he wandered from a communal public area such as a hallway into a private room which was part of the same premises, because the room itself would not be an enclosed area in the open air (*Talbot v Oxford City Justices*, The Times, 15 February 2000). Enclosed premises can also include an outdoor area such as an enclosed garden or yard that has a defined boundary, and it does not matter if there are gaps in the fence or boundary enclosure. It would not include a university campus truncated by roads and footpaths (see *Akhurst v DPP* [2009] WLR (D) 96).

The person must be on the enclosed premises for an unlawful purpose, so it would not include a person who is hiding from the police following a burglary because the unlawful purpose must be current (*JL v CPS* [2007] WLR (D) 202). It would definitely not include a homeless person who sleeps in a shed for the night if he/she has no criminal intention, and does not carry out a criminal activity. However, under s 144(1) of the Legal Aid, Sentencing and Punishment of Offenders Act 2012 it is an offence for a trespasser in a residential building to live or intend to live there for any period of time (see 14.8.4). The offence under s 4 of the Vagrancy Act 1824 is triable summarily and the penalty is three months' imprisonment and/or a fine.

TASK 3

Georgia enters a house as a trespasser with intent to steal jewellery for which there is a demand at local car boot sales. While she is on the premises, and as a precaution against capture, she takes a screwdriver from a cupboard under the stairs. She continues the search, still with the screwdriver. Twenty minutes later, the occupier returns and Georgia stabs her, causing serious injury. Has burglary been committed? Give reasons for your answers. (Consider only the offences relating to burglary here.)

16.5 Stolen Goods and the Proceeds of Crime

The definition of stolen goods include 'money and every other description of property, except land, and includes things severed from the land by stealing' (s 34(2)(b) of the Theft Act 1968). For this offence goods are considered to be 'stolen goods' if they have been obtained through theft, blackmail, or fraud (ss 1 and 21 of the Theft Act 1968, and s 1 of the Fraud Act 2006, respectively).

Stolen goods also include the proceeds of the disposal of the original stolen items such as money or other items which have been received in exchange (s 24(2) of the Theft Act 1968). After the original theft there is often a whole chain of events, and each of the handlers in this process commits the offence of handling stolen goods, so long as each has guilty knowledge (*mens rea*) that the goods represent the original stolen goods. The chain will only be broken when a person receiving the goods is unaware of their origins.

It is not always possible for a criminal to benefit from a crime if the proceeds of the felony remain in their original state. In the majority of cases, the profits have to be realized, exchanged, or hidden to be of any worth. The Proceeds of Crime Act 2002 (POCA) makes it an offence to benefit from any kind of proceeds.

16.5.1 Handling stolen goods

This offence is committed when a person handles goods that they know or believe to have been stolen. It is described in s 22 of the Theft Act 1968. The person can:

(i) receive the stolen goods, or
(ii) agree to their retention, removal, disposal or realisation by or for the benefit of another person, or
(iii) assists in their retention, removal, disposal or realisation by or for the benefit of another person, or
(iv) arrange to do any of (i), (ii) or (iii) above.

The various aspects of the offence and the meanings in law of some of the key terms are explained presently. Further aspects of this offence are shown in the diagram.

The meaning of receiving has been established through case law as 'gaining possession or control'. Therefore it can mean actual physical possession such as carrying or holding the goods. Having control over goods is when a person has remote possession; the goods could be kept in storage in a garage or lock-up, for example.

The receiver does not need to gain in any way from handling the goods, but he/she must know that the goods are stolen at the time of their receipt, and there must be proof that the goods were actually received. If the receiver is still negotiating the receipt of the goods, then another aspect of the handling might apply.

The retention, removal, disposal, or realization of stolen goods can also be a way of committing the offence of handling stolen goods:

- retention means continuing to possess something (especially when someone else wants it);
- removal means taking something away from the place where it was;
- disposal means passing on, getting rid of, giving away;
- realization means obtaining money or profit by selling something.

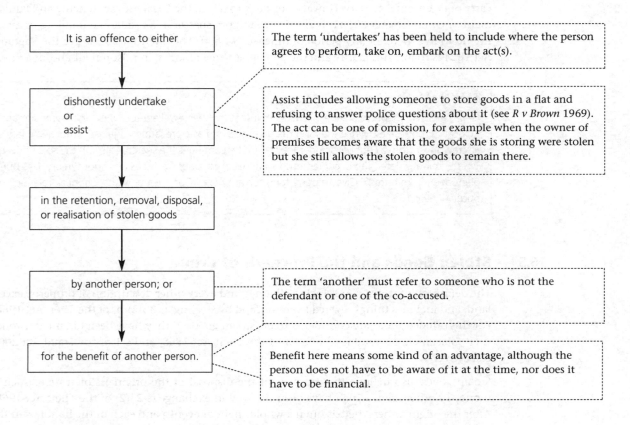

It is an offence to either

The term 'undertakes' has been held to include where the person agrees to perform, take on, embark on the act(s).

dishonestly undertake
or
assist

Assist includes allowing someone to store goods in a flat and refusing to answer police questions about it (see *R v Brown* 1969). The act can be one of omission, for example when the owner of premises becomes aware that the goods she is storing were stolen but she still allows the stolen goods to remain there.

in the retention, removal, disposal, or realisation of stolen goods

by another person; or

The term 'another' must refer to someone who is not the defendant or one of the co-accused.

for the benefit of another person.

Benefit here means some kind of an advantage, although the person does not have to be aware of it at the time, nor does it have to be financial.

16.5.1.1 Knowing or believing that goods are 'stolen goods'

Another key issue for this offence is that the handler must know or believe that the goods are stolen for the handling to be dishonest. The court has to decide what is dishonest by everyday standards, and whether the suspect was aware he/she was dishonest by those standards. Dishonesty in relation to handling goods would not include believing he/she has a right to the property in law, or that he/she would have the owner's consent. Nor would it include a belief that the owner cannot be traced.

The difference between knowing and believing is not clear-cut; the following points could be considered:

- knowing them to be stolen goods means having actually been told that the goods are stolen by the thief or burglar or someone with first-hand knowledge; and
- believing them to be stolen goods means being uncertain as to whether or not the goods are stolen, but then thinking there is no other likely explanation in those particular circumstances (see *R v Hall* [1985] 1 QB 496).

Knowledge or belief could be proved by direct evidence from the thief, admission by the handler, or circumstantial evidence, such as non-standard packaging, or where the goods were offered for sale.

16.5.1.2 The distinction between 'handling' and 'theft'

It is important to distinguish clearly between 'handling' and 'theft', and this is largely to do with whether the actions of the suspect followed on from the theft continuously (ie without a break). The following factors will be taken into account: whether the theft was complete, whether there was a break in the proceedings, and whether the suspected handler became involved only after the theft had occurred.

For example, Ellis goes to a large out-of-town electrical store. She steals two digital radios from the store, goes outside, and hides them in a rubbish bin to evade detection. Sal then takes the radios. The table presents a number of different scenarios and shows whether the activity amounts to handling or theft.

Offences committed by Sal the accomplice

Sal's actions …	Offence committed by Sal	Other factors to be taken into account
Sal is waiting by pre-arrangement and takes the radios away	Theft	
Sal arrives half an hour later by pre-arrangement, and takes the radios away	Theft	Particularly if the proceeds are to be shared out between Ellis and Sal
	Handling	May be considered if Sal subsequently pays Ellis for the goods
Sal is told where the radios are, but only *after* they have been stolen. Sal then collects the radios	Handling	

A thief can become a handler of the property that he/she originally stole, but only if he/she loses control of the property and later decides (whilst the goods can still be referred to as stolen goods) to have dealings with the property once again.

The offence of handling stolen goods is triable either way. The penalty if tried summarily is six months' imprisonment and/or a fine, and 14 years' imprisonment on indictment.

16.5.1.3 Wrongful credits

If a person knows that his/her bank account has been 'wrongly' credited but does not take any action this may be a handling offence. In this context a credit is 'wrongful' if the funds concerned were derived from theft, blackmail, fraud, or stolen goods. A person is guilty of an offence under s 24A of the Theft Act 1968 (inserted by 2(1) Theft (Amendment) Act 1996) if:

(a) a wrongful credit has been made to an account which is either kept by him/her or in which he/she has any right or interest;

(b) he/she knows or believes that the credit is wrongful; and

(c) he/she dishonestly fails to take reasonable steps (in the circumstances) to secure that the credit is cancelled.

The maximum sentence upon conviction is ten years' imprisonment.

16.5.2 Proceeds of crime offences

The proceeds of crime can be converted into assets in order to make their origin appear legitimate, and this would include money laundering. It is an offence to benefit from any kind of proceeds, not just money. There are three main offences which cover most eventualities in benefiting from the proceeds of crime and these are described presently. The Proceeds of Crime Act 2002 (POCA) makes reference to 'criminal property' with reference to the proceeds of crime. Criminal property (for the purposes of the POCA 2002) is any property which the suspect knows or suspects to be or represent, the benefit from any criminal conduct (s 340(3)). Criminal conduct is conduct which constitutes (or would constitute) an offence in the UK (s 340(2)). Criminal property (s 340(9)) includes:

- money;
- property (real, personal, inherited, and moveable);
- things in action such as patents, copyrights, and trade marks; and
- other intangible or incorporeal property such as property rights, leases, or mortgages.

(Real property is land and things forming part of the land, such as plants and buildings, and moveable property is not attached to the land (eg furniture, art, books, or household goods).)

Concealing, converting, or transferring criminal property is an offence under s 327(1) of the POCA 2002. A person commits an offence if he/she conceals, disguises, converts, transfers, or removes from the UK any criminal property. For example, a man knows that his wife brings back large quantities of alcohol from cross-Channel ferry trips to sell on to local young people.

Their 'business' is thriving, but she does not want to raise suspicions by depositing the money in their bank account so he hides the money from the sales in a secure cash box, which he places behind the panel of the bath in their house. He is guilty of concealment of criminal property.

Involvement in arrangements for criminal property is an offence under s 328(1) of the POCA 2002. A person commits an offence if he/she enters into (or becomes concerned in) an arrangement which he/she knows (or suspects) will help with the acquisition, retention, use, or control of criminal property, by (or on behalf of) another person. The suspect defendant must know or believe at the time when the arrangement was made that the property was criminal property (see *R v Geary* [2010] WLR (D) 228). For example, a man derives a considerable income from targeting vulnerable people living alone. He carries out a roof inspection and deceives the victim about its condition, and carries out unnecessary 'repairs' for cash. His live-in partner knows how the money is obtained, and has opened several bank accounts for depositing the profits. Therefore she has been concerned in an arrangement that will help in the retention or control of criminal property.

Acquisition, use, and possession of criminal property is an offence under s 329(1) of the POCA 2002. For example a small-time drug supplier gives some of her profits from selling drugs to a friend. He knows where the money comes from as she discusses it freely with him (and they first met when she was supplying drugs to him). He uses the money to buy food; he has 'used' criminal property.

16.5.2.1   Defences and penalties

There are three shared defences available for ss 327(1), 328(1), and 329(1) of the POCA 2002:

- the suspect makes or intends to make (with reasonable excuse) an 'authorized disclosure' to a police, customs, or nominated officer, concerning his/her actions;
- law enforcement authorities (such as the police) have a defence if they convert or transfer seized criminal property, placing it, for example, in an interest-earning account; and
- the suspect knows (or reasonably believes) that the criminal conduct took place outside the UK and that it was not unlawful in that other country (s 327(2) and (2)A).

There is an additional defence available for s 329(1) where a person acquires, uses, or has possession of the criminal property for 'adequate consideration'. For example, a shopkeeper could claim this defence if she sells goods to a customer and the customer pays with money that comes from crime. Similarly, solicitors or accountants who receive money for costs also have this defence.

These offences under ss 327, 328, and 329 are all triable either way and the penalty is a fine or imprisonment (six months summarily or 14 years on indictment).

TASK 4

1. In the context of 'handling stolen goods', which, if either, of the following statements is true?
   (a) For the purposes of committing an offence of handling, 'stolen goods' includes money but not land.
   (b) Property obtained as a result of a fraud under s 1 of the Fraud Act 2006 is considered to be 'stolen goods' for the purposes of the offence of handling.

2. A police officer carries out a lawful s 1 PACE Act 1984 stop and search on Terri and complies with the PACE Codes of Practice throughout the process. Terri is an 18-year-old persistent offender and prolific shoplifter. His current favoured MO is to steal items such as chocolate and clothes from shops, to sell on quickly and cheaply. Local intelligence has indicated that Terri has also become a courier for local drug suppliers. Intelligence also indicates that he has an extremely modest lifestyle; he does not own any vehicles, lives alone in a one-room bedsit, doesn't drink, but occasionally smokes cannabis. He is registered unemployed, receives state benefits, and has no close family. During the search, £100,000 in used £50 notes is found concealed in various locations in his clothing. Terri cannot account for this money and there is no evidence of its origin. What would be the likelihood of a successful prosecution for acquiring, retaining, using, or controlling the criminal property under s 328(1) of the POCA 2002? Refer to the cases of *R v NW, SW, RC & CC* [2008] EWCA Crim 2 and the conjoined cases of *R v Allpress; R v Symeou; R v Casal; R v Morris; R v Martin* [2009] EWCA Crim 8 for your answer.

16.6   **Going Equipped**

This offence is described in s 25 of the Theft Act 1968. A wide range of articles are used to carry out burglary or theft, such as:

- equipment for removing security tags from clothing;
- instruments used for gaining entry to vehicles, including keys; and
- tools used to gain entry to buildings or vehicles.

The offence is not committed simply by the suspect being in possession of the articles. In order to commit the offence of going equipped, the suspect must have possession of the articles and be on his/her way to carry out a theft or burglary (see *R v Ellames* [1974] 3 All ER 130). A direct connection to a specific burglary or theft does not need to be established, but it must be possible to prove that the article is intended to be used to commit crime by the suspect (or another person). The offence cannot be committed when coming away from the crime.

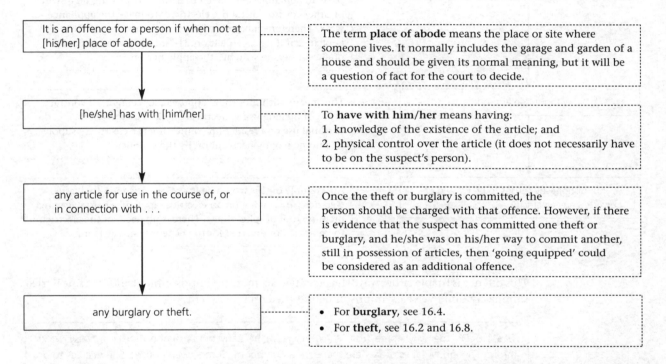

It is an offence for a person if when not at [his/her] place of abode,

> The term **place of abode** means the place or site where someone lives. It normally includes the garage and garden of a house and should be given its normal meaning, but it will be a question of fact for the court to decide.

[he/she] has with [him/her]

> To **have with him/her** means having:
> 1. knowledge of the existence of the article; and
> 2. physical control over the article (it does not necessarily have to be on the suspect's person).

any article for use in the course of, or in connection with . . .

> Once the theft or burglary is committed, the person should be charged with that offence. However, if there is evidence that the suspect has committed one theft or burglary, and he/she was on his/her way to commit another, still in possession of articles, then 'going equipped' could be considered as an additional offence.

any burglary or theft.

> - For **burglary**, see 16.4.
> - For **theft**, see 16.2 and 16.8.

This offence is triable either way. The penalty is six months' imprisonment and/or a fine if tried summarily, or three years' imprisonment on indictment.

TASK 5

1. At each of her BCU briefings throughout the past week, a police constable has been informed about a series of car thefts in her area. One night, she is on patrol in a narrow street of terraced houses with no front gardens or driveways. She knows that a prolific car thief lives there. She notices a car being parked in the street outside his house and goes over. She speaks to the driver and notices gloves, a large bunch of approximately 40 car keys, and a short length of scaffolding pole in the footwell of the passenger's seat. What could she say to him? Could the offence of 'going equipped' have been committed? What questions does she need to ask in order to establish if this offence has actually been committed?

2. Which of the following offence(s) are neither a 'theft' nor a 'burglary':
   (a) robbery;
   (b) taking a conveyance; and
   (c) abstracting electricity?

16.7 Abstracting Electricity

Electricity does not fall within the definition of property in the Theft Act 1968, and therefore it cannot be stolen, in legal terms. Instead, 'abstracting' is the legal term used for the offence of illegally taking and using. The electricity could be from the mains or from a battery, in a caravan for example. As electricity is not property within the Theft Act 1968, an entry into premises with the sole intention of abstracting electricity will not amount to burglary.

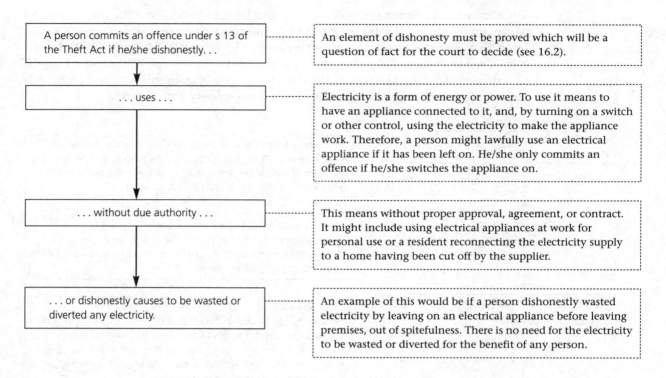

This offence is triable either way. The penalty is six months' imprisonment and/or a fine if tried summarily, and five years' imprisonment if tried on indictment.

> **TASK 6** On the way home from a nightclub in the early hours of the morning, Daisy walks through an industrial estate where there are a number of storage warehouses. She decides to go into one of the warehouses without permission, through an open door, with the intention of finding somewhere to sleep for the night. Having entered the warehouse, she forces open a door to another room and in so doing damages the lock. Once inside the room, she switches on an electric fire to keep warm and falls asleep until awoken by a security guard patrolling the industrial estate. Has burglary been committed? Give reasons for your answers.

16.8 Theft of Vehicles and Related Offences

Every year thousands of cars are stolen in England and Wales. Where do they go and why are they stolen? How do we identify stolen vehicles? Here we examine some of the legal aspects and police procedures surrounding a number of vehicle crimes.

Some vehicles are stolen for resale, and will be provided with new and false identifying features. Other vehicles may be broken down for parts as the overall value of an older vehicle is often much higher if it is broken down into parts. The cost of vehicle repairs motivates some people to arrange (or merely claim) that the vehicle has been stolen, so that the owner can claim on the insurance.

Other vehicles are taken for 'joyriding'; the vehicle is driven for excitement or as a means of transport, usually for only a brief period of time. This is not theft because although the suspects take the vehicle, they do not have the intention to permanently deprive the owner of it; consequently the offence cannot be proven. The offence of TWOC (taking a conveyance without consent) was created as a separate offence in the Theft Act 1968 to cover these circumstances. TWOC may also result in damage and injury, so we also describe 'aggravated vehicle taking' in this part of the Handbook. Prior to a TWOC offence the offender will often manipulate parts of the vehicle (eg locks or ignition systems). As TWOC is a summary offence it cannot be attempted, so a separate offence has been created, that of 'interference and tampering with motor vehicles'. This is also covered along with the theft of pedal cycles.

16.8.1 Detection of stolen vehicles

There are a number of ways of establishing that a particular vehicle is a stolen vehicle and some everyday clues can trigger an alert police officer to investigate a little further. For example:

- Does it belong to a group of vehicles more likely to be stolen (see Task 7)?
- Is the vehicle displaying the correct registration plates? Do the plates look as though they have been replaced or have new plates been stuck over the old plates? Do the plates seem different from the rest of the car—for example, is the car clean and the plates old and dirty, or the other way round; or are the plates plain, with no reference to the dealership that sold the car?

To investigate further, a police officer will need to establish the specific identifying features of a vehicle such as the VIN number (see 16.8.1.1).

16.8.1.1 The identifying features of a vehicle

Vehicles normally have a number of identifying features unique to each vehicle, and these can be easily recalled by using the police mnemonic VICE. The identifying features are recorded on DVLA databases along with the colour, make, and model of the vehicle. Police control-room staff have access to databases listing the positions of the stamped-in VIN, the VIN plate, and the engine number, for each make and model of vehicle.

V	Vehicle Identification Number (VIN)	The 17-character VIN unique to that vehicle is on a metal plate attached to a part of the vehicle not normally subject to replacement, and in a conspicuous and readily accessible position. All vehicles used on or after 1 April 1980 have such a plate. Many modern vehicles have a visible VIN, which is located on the dashboard and can be seen through the windscreen.
I	Index number or registration plate	All mechanically propelled vehicles used on public roads require a registration mark (number).
C	Chassis number (same as VIN)	All vehicles used on or after 1 April 1980 will have their 17-character VIN stamped into the chassis or frame of the car. The location is often described in the vehicle Handbook.
E	Engine number	Engine numbers are often tucked away in locations most easily seen when (or if) the engine is taken out of the vehicle. Engines are also sometimes replaced, so the fact that an engine number cannot be found should not in itself be a cause for suspicion.

(Image © Kevin Lawton-Barrett)

Example of a VIN on the chassis of a VW camper van

16.8.1.2   **Disguising stolen vehicles**

When a vehicle is reported as stolen it is recorded on police and other databases using the VICE identifying features. So if it is to be sold on or used long term it needs to have a new 'identity'. The new VIN and other VICE features have to be taken from a similar vehicle so that the colour and make, etc will match that of the stolen vehicle. Often, the new identifying features will be taken from a vehicle that has been severely damaged, and has been reported as such to the DVLA on a V23 form. (A V23 is sent to the DVLA either by an insurance company whenever a total loss payment is made on a vehicle, or by a police officer to make a report on a vehicle written off in an accident. It is legal to repair these vehicles and use them on the roads.)

The thief will usually:

- obtain the identifying features of a vehicle (see 16.8.1.1) that has been declared uneconomical to repair using a V23 form;
- steal a similar vehicle;
- remove the identifying features from the stolen vehicle and replace them with those from the badly damaged vehicle (which is usually then scrapped).

The stolen vehicle (with its new identity) is then sold to an innocent purchaser. Some vehicles are exported as their resale value may be higher in other countries.

Thus police officers must be alert to vehicles with identifying features that do not match with the database records. In addition, a legitimate vehicle with a V23 will have been extensively repaired to get it back on the road. Therefore, if there are no indications of major repairs, the vehicle's VICE details do not belong to the vehicle and it is likely to have been stolen.

16.8.1.3   **Procedure for checking for stolen vehicles**

The recommended procedure is outlined in the diagram. If the vehicle needs further examination, a force vehicle examiner can carry this out.

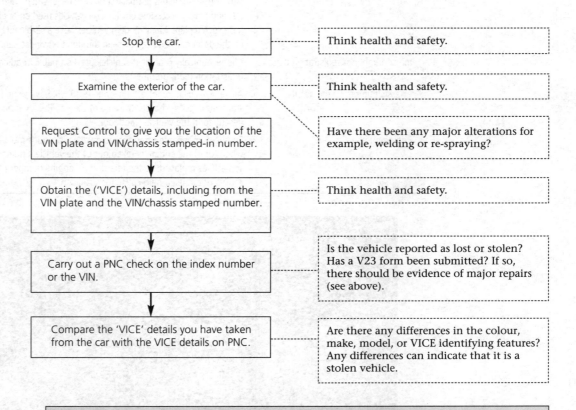

TASK 7 In 16.8.1.3, references are made to stopping the car, examining the car, and locating the VIN and VIN/chassis number. What powers or regulations (1) allows a police officer to stop and examine a car; and (2) require the car to be equipped with a VIN or chassis number?

16.8.2 Taking a Conveyance without the Owner's Consent or Authority (TWOC)

This offence (TWOC) is described in s 12 of the Theft Act 1968. 'Taking a conveyance' is a very common offence in England and Wales and unfortunately, modern technology has so far failed to deter criminals from this activity. Note that a conveyance is any equipment constructed or adapted for the carriage of a person or persons whether by land, water, or air. (It does not include a conveyance constructed or adapted for carrying items other than people, such as the pedestrian-controlled vehicle used by postal workers to transport mail. Pedal cycles are not included under this legislation either; taking a cycle is covered by another subsection described in 16.8.3.)

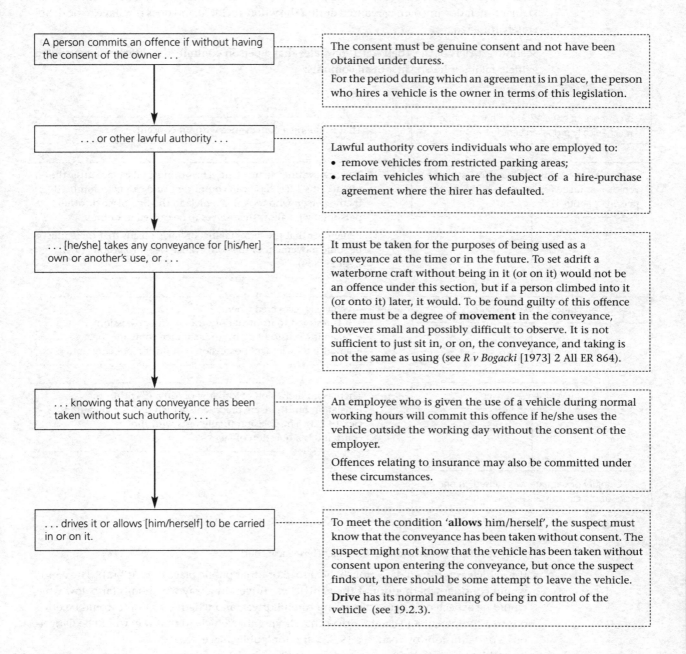

A person commits an offence if without having the consent of the owner . . .

The consent must be genuine consent and not have been obtained under duress.

For the period during which an agreement is in place, the person who hires a vehicle is the owner in terms of this legislation.

. . . or other lawful authority . . .

Lawful authority covers individuals who are employed to:
- remove vehicles from restricted parking areas;
- reclaim vehicles which are the subject of a hire-purchase agreement where the hirer has defaulted.

. . . [he/she] takes any conveyance for [his/her] own or another's use, or . . .

It must be taken for the purposes of being used as a conveyance at the time or in the future. To set adrift a waterborne craft without being in it (or on it) would not be an offence under this section, but if a person climbed into it (or onto it) later, it would. To be found guilty of this offence there must be a degree of **movement** in the conveyance, however small and possibly difficult to observe. It is not sufficient to just sit in, or on, the conveyance, and taking is not the same as using (see *R v Bogacki* [1973] 2 All ER 864).

. . . knowing that any conveyance has been taken without such authority, . . .

An employee who is given the use of a vehicle during normal working hours will commit this offence if he/she uses the vehicle outside the working day without the consent of the employer.

Offences relating to insurance may also be committed under these circumstances.

. . . drives it or allows [him/herself] to be carried in or on it.

To meet the condition '**allows** him/herself', the suspect must know that the conveyance has been taken without consent. The suspect might not know that the vehicle has been taken without consent upon entering the conveyance, but once the suspect finds out, there should be some attempt to leave the vehicle.

Drive has its normal meaning of being in control of the vehicle (see 19.2.3).

A possible defence (s 12(6) of the Theft Act 1968) is that the person believes that he/she has the consent of the owner or had other lawful authority. This offence is triable summarily and the penalty is six months' imprisonment and/or a fine.

The basic offence of taking a conveyance cannot be attempted (see 21.2 on criminal attempts), as the offence is not indictable; more appropriate offences might include vehicle interference or tampering with a motor vehicle (see 16.8.2.2). Note that as theft is an indictable offence, the offence of theft could also be considered if some form of attempt has taken place.

Specific Incidents

> **TASK 8** Approximately 1,000 vehicles are taken without the owner's consent in the UK every day. What type of vehicle seems most likely to be taken in your area? If you are a trainee police officer, your area should be able to provide you with factual information on this, including where the vehicles are stolen from, and what happens to them.

16.8.2.1 Aggravated vehicle-taking

A further offence may have been committed under s 12A(1) of the Theft Act 1968 if damage or injury is caused when a vehicle is taken without consent. Injuries may also include shock. Damage includes any damage caused during the whole incident and does not have to be deliberately inflicted.

Section 12(A)(1) of the Theft Act 1968 states that a person commits the offence of aggravated vehicle-taking if he/she first of all commits:

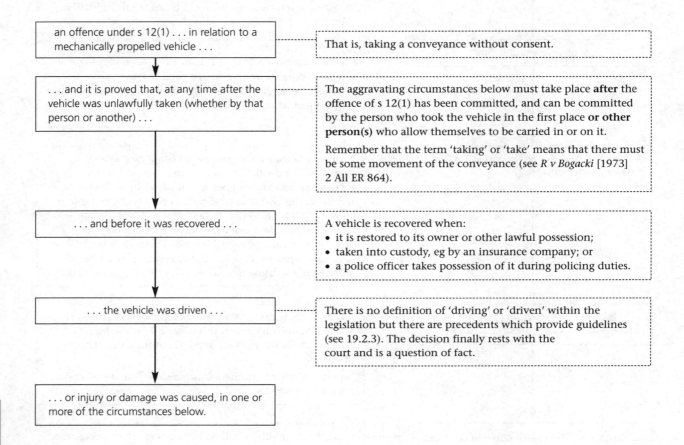

The aggravating circumstances for this offence are that:

- the vehicle was driven dangerously on a road or other public place (s 12A(2)(a)). The courts would consider whether or not the vehicle was driven in a way which falls far below what would be expected of a competent and careful driver, and whether or not it would be obvious to a competent and careful driver that driving the vehicle in that way would be dangerous. For definitions of 'road' see 19.2.2, and for 'public place' see 9.2;
- an accident occurred (due to the driving of the vehicle) which caused an injury to a person in or outside the vehicle (s 12A(2)(b)) or damage to property other than the vehicle (s 12A(2)(c)). Here an 'accident' is an unintended occurrence which has an adverse physical result, and the court can also take into account what an 'ordinary' person would consider to be an accident (see *R v Morris* [1972] RTR 201);
- the vehicle was damaged (s 12A(2)(d)), eg by the vehicle colliding with something, or by a person when avoiding arrest. It can be caused by a person other than the person who first took the vehicle.

Specific Incidents

Possible defences include that the suspect:

- committed the basic offence of taking the vehicle before the aggravating circumstances occurred (s 12A(3)(b)); or
- was not in or on the vehicle, or in its 'immediate vicinity' when the driving, accident, or damage occurred (s 12A(3)(b)). Immediate vicinity is a question of fact for the court to decide.

Even if the suspect can disprove aggravating factors, he/she can still be found guilty of the basic offence (s 12A(5)). This offence is triable either way and the penalty is a fine or imprisonment (six months summarily or two years on indictment). If the accident (under s 12A(2)(b)) caused death, the penalty is 14 years' imprisonment.

16.8.2.2 Interference and tampering with motor vehicles

When a suspect takes a conveyance without the consent of the owner, in many cases he/she will go through a process of selecting a vehicle, gaining entry either forcibly or by trying door handles, overcoming anti-theft devices such as alarms and steering locks, and then applying a technique such as hot wiring to start the engine. This process inevitably takes time, and sometimes the suspect can be apprehended before the vehicle is taken. However, TWOC is a summary offence (and therefore cannot be attempted under s 1(1) of the Criminal Attempts Act 1981: see 21.2). Therefore, the Criminal Attempts Act 1981 includes a specific offence of 'interference and tampering with motor vehicles'.

Interference, in everyday language, is when a person is interfering with a motor vehicle and it is apparent that he/she is attempting to commit a crime such as stealing the car. However, actually proving intent is tricky. In 5.3, we discussed the two main building blocks to a criminal act: *actus reus* (the act itself), and *mens rea* (an intention to commit an act). In this case, the act cannot simply be preparation but needs to go further than this. Unfortunately, case law provides us with little guidance on what interference actually means in practice.

Nonetheless, s 9(1) of the Criminal Attempts Act 1981 states that it is an offence for a person to interfere with a motor vehicle or trailer, or with anything carried in or on a motor vehicle or trailer with the intention of committing:

- 'theft of the motor vehicle or part of it';
- 'theft of anything carried in or on the motor vehicle or trailer'; or
- the offence of taking a conveyance.

It must be proved that the suspect had at least one of the three intentions, but it is not necessary to prove which particular one. This is a summary offence and the penalty is three months' imprisonment and/or a fine.

Tampering as an activity is more readily understood than interference, and the legislation (s 25(1) of the Road Traffic Act 1988) refers specifically to vehicle brakes. It is an offence for a person without lawful authority or reasonable cause to tamper with the brake or any other part of its mechanism, or to get on or into the vehicle. This applies to motor vehicles on a road or in a parking place provided by a local authority. It is a summary offence and the penalty is a fine.

16.8.3 Taking a pedal cycle

A pedal cycle is not a conveyance for the purposes of s 12(1) of the Theft Act 1968, so the taking of a cycle is not a TWOC offence, but is covered as a separate offence under s 12(5). It includes riding a pedal cycle knowing it to have been taken by another person without consent or lawful authority. The penalty for this offence is six months' imprisonment and/or a fine.

> **TASK 9** Which of the following would constitute an offence of interfering with a motor vehicle?
>
> 1. Trying to removing a horse box from the tow bar of a vehicle in order to steal the horse box.
> 2. Attempting to remove a go-kart from the garden of a house in order to steal it.
> 3. Opening the unlocked front driver's door of a car to steal a satnav fixed to the dashboard.
> 4. Putting super glue in a car door lock to prevent the owner from opening the door.

16.9 Fraud and Bribery Offences

The various Theft Acts (1968, 1978, and 1996) also contained sections addressing aspects of what we tend to call fraud and deception. This proved confusing and much of the law surrounding the crime of fraud is now encapsulated instead in the Fraud Act 2006.

Section 1 of the Fraud Act 2006 states that the offence of fraud can be committed in one or more of three distinctive ways:

1. by false representation, for example returning stolen goods to a shop to try to obtain a refund (s 2);
2. by failing to disclose information, for example omitting important information when applying for a job or health insurance (s 3); and
3. through abuse of position, for example whilst driving a local authority minibus, demanding fares from local residents when the service is actually free (s 4).

For all of these offences there is the same intent; to make a gain for him/herself or another or to cause a loss to another or to expose another to a risk of loss. The gain or loss can be temporary or permanent and could involve 'personal' property, 'real' property, things in action, and other intangible property, such as the name of a company or the copyright to a product. This is similar to the definitions of property under the Theft Act 1968.

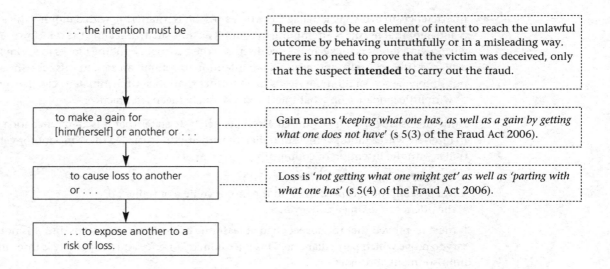

The offences are all triable either way and the penalty is a fine or imprisonment (12 months summarily or ten years on indictment).

16.9.1 False representation

Section 2 of the Fraud Act 2006 states that a person commits an offence if he/she 'dishonestly makes a false representation and intends...to make a gain for [him/herself] or another, or to cause loss to another or to expose another to a risk of loss'.

The term 'dishonesty' is not defined in the Act, but in case law it has been held to relate to the test of whether the dishonesty would challenge the standards of a reasonable and honest person, and whether the conduct was considered dishonest by the suspect him- or herself (see *R v Ghosh* [1982] QB 1053).

A representation can be made to a device or machine which is designed to receive, convey, or respond to communication; for example, bank ATMs or coin-operated cigarette dispensers (s 2(5)). A representation is **false** (s 2(2)) if it is 'untrue'; for example, using foreign coins or objects to obtain cigarettes from a machine; or 'misleading'; for example, assuming the identity of a charity worker and shaking a stolen charity collection tin in a busy shopping centre. Recent case law makes it clear that the suspect must intend that the false representation will cause the gain or loss (*R v Gilbert* [2012] EWCA Crim 2392).

16.9.2   Failure to disclose information

Section 3 of the Fraud Act 2006 states that a person commits an offence if he/she 'dishonestly fails to disclose to another person information which [he/she] is under a legal duty to disclose, and intends, by failing to disclose the information to make a gain for [him/herself] or another, or to cause loss to another or to expose another to a risk of loss'.

The failure to disclose can be made by an oral or written omission. The legal duty to disclose derives from:

* statute, for example where a company must publish yearly accounts under company law, but fails to do so;
* good faith, such as not disclosing a serious illness in order to reduce health insurance premiums;
* the express or implied terms of a contract, such as an estate agent not revealing all bids for a property to a client, so his friend can buy it at a lower price;
* the custom of a particular trade or market;
* the existence of a fiduciary relationship (where a person is entrusted with another person's financial arrangements), for example where the entrusted person does not notify the other person that there is another beneficiary to a contract.

16.9.3   Abuse of position

This offence (s 4) can be committed by a person who occupies a position in which he/she is expected to safeguard (or not to act against) the financial interests of another. The offence is committed if he/she dishonestly abuses that position intending to make a gain for him/herself or another, or to cause loss to another or to expose another to a risk of loss.

The offence could apply for anyone who has relied upon or has knowledge of another person's financial affairs, such as between an employer and an employee, between a trustee and a beneficiary or between cohabitees. The meaning of the term 'abuse' in this context is not defined in law but is held to have its normal everyday meaning. It can be an act or a failure to act (s 4(2)). Examples might include a person who has access to the bank account of a vulnerable relative and takes money for their own use, or where housemates pool money to pay bills and one of them is entrusted to pay the bills, but instead misuses the money dishonestly.

16.9.4   Possession, making, or supplying of articles for committing fraud

A person can commit an offence by 'going equipped' (see 16.6) to carry out a fraud, rather than actually having committed the fraud itself. In this context, going equipped means being in possession or control of articles for use in frauds (s 6 of the Fraud Act 2006) or making or supplying such articles (s 7).

The articles can include clothing to imitate company representatives, mechanisms to slow down electricity meters, and bogus satellite TV cards, as well as false identity cards, credit cards, cheque books, shopping bags, till receipts, passports, and driving licences. It also includes a computer program or data held in electronic form.

Section 6 of the Fraud Act 2006 covers possession or having the article under his/her control. For possession, the person must have immediate physical control over the article and know that it is there. Having control would include having physical control at a distance (eg possessing the key to a cupboard where the item is kept) and also knowing that the article was there.

Unlike most other statutory preventative measures, this offence can be committed anywhere, including when the articles are located in the suspect's home. (Statutory preventative measures are pieces of legislation designed to prevent criminal offences from taking place, for example 'going equipped' to steal and 'carrying offensive weapons'.)

Section 7 of the Fraud Act 2006 states that a person commits an offence if he/she makes, adapts, supplies (or offers to supply) any article, knowing that it is designed or adapted for use in the course of or in connection with fraud (or intending it to be used to commit or assist with the commission of fraud). An example of this could be a man offering to make a false ID card for a woman, when he knows she is going to use it to pose as a charity collector and collect donations from the public. Under s 1 of the PACE Act 1984, a police officer has the power to search (see 9.4.2) for articles made or adapted for use in fraud.

The offences are triable either way and the penalty is a fine or imprisonment (12 months summarily, five years on indictment for a s 6 offence, and ten years on indictment for a s 7 offence).

16.9.5 Dishonest obtaining of services

In the fraud offences described in 16.9.1–16.9.3 the gain or loss related to tangible and intangible property. However, in circumstances where a service has been provided, for example a taxi ride, there is no gain or loss of property, only the provision of a facility or service. For this reason, an additional offence is provided for by s 11 of the Fraud Act 2006, for when a service is obtained by dishonest means.

The services must be of a type for which payment is generally required and would include bus or train rides, haircuts, a stay in a hotel room, dry-cleaning, table attention at a restaurant, and tuition. The service must be obtained through a dishonest act (not an omission), and this would include using a false credit card, giving false personal details, and making false promises or agreements. The proof of the dishonesty should follow the guidelines in *R v Ghosh* [1982] QB 1053 (see 16.2 on dishonesty).

The offence is triable either way and the penalty is a fine or imprisonment (12 months summarily or five years on indictment).

16.9.6 Making off without payment ('bilking')

If no dishonest representation takes place and a person had every intention to pay for goods before the property was obtained, but then makes off without paying, an offence is committed under s 3 of the Theft Act 1978 (rather than fraud under s 1 of the Fraud Act 2006). This particular offence is often referred to as 'bilking'. For example, a person might fill up with petrol on the forecourt of a filling station with every intention of paying for the petrol, but on seeing the staff otherwise engaged and no other customers around, decide to drive off without paying.

Note that this offence only applies if 'payment on the spot' is the norm in that particular situation, such as collecting goods on which work has been done (eg shoe repairs) or paying for a service which has been provided (eg a haircut). This offence does not cover circumstances in which a customer has a credit arrangement or a 'tab' with the service provider.

The offence is triable either way and the penalty is a fine or imprisonment (six months summarily or two years on indictment).

Specific Incidents

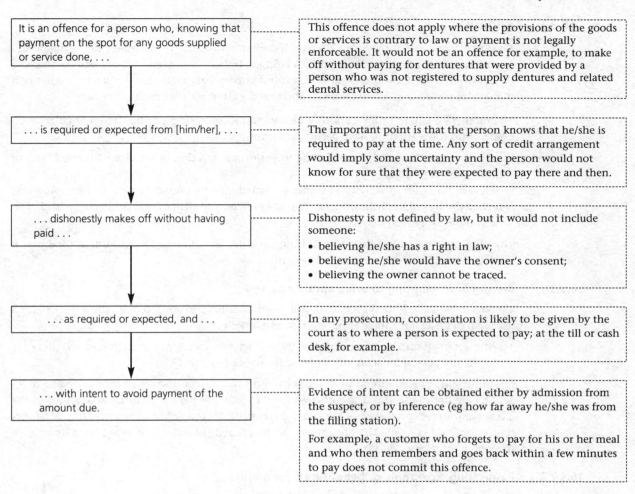

It is an offence for a person who, knowing that payment on the spot for any goods supplied or service done, . . .	This offence does not apply where the provisions of the goods or services is contrary to law or payment is not legally enforceable. It would not be an offence for example, to make off without paying for dentures that were provided by a person who was not registered to supply dentures and related dental services.
. . . is required or expected from [him/her], . . .	The important point is that the person knows that he/she is required to pay at the time. Any sort of credit arrangement would imply some uncertainty and the person would not know for sure that they were expected to pay there and then.
. . . dishonestly makes off without having paid . . .	Dishonesty is not defined by law, but it would not include someone: • believing he/she has a right in law; • believing he/she would have the owner's consent; • believing the owner cannot be traced.
. . . as required or expected, and . . .	In any prosecution, consideration is likely to be given by the court as to where a person is expected to pay; at the till or cash desk, for example.
. . . with intent to avoid payment of the amount due.	Evidence of intent can be obtained either by admission from the suspect, or by inference (eg how far away he/she was from the filling station). For example, a customer who forgets to pay for his or her meal and who then remembers and goes back within a few minutes to pay does not commit this offence.

TASK 10 At what stage of a visit to a restaurant are the following offences potentially committed by people who fail to pay for a meal:

• s 1 of the Fraud Act 2006;
• s 3 of the Theft Act 1978; and
• s 11 of the Fraud Act 2006?

To answer the question, complete the table by describing in the right-hand column the likely actions and thought processes of the customers at each stage of the visit to the restaurant, linking these to ss 1 and 11 of the Fraud Act 2006 and s 3 of the Theft Act 1978. The case of *DPP v Ray* [1974] AC 370 may assist.

People enter the restaurant and order a meal	
Having ordered the meal, they wait at the table for it to be served	
The meal is served to the table	
Having consumed the meal, they are expected to pay	
They leave the restaurant	

Specific Incidents

16.9.7 Bribery

The Bribery Act 2010 provides an effective legal framework to combat bribery in the public and private sectors. It also includes offences relating to bribery of foreign officials, and commercial organizations that allow their agents to commit bribery. An organization will have a defence if it provides evidence of having policies and practices in place that prohibit bribery.

The offences relate to bribing another person and to accepting a bribe. Two particular terms used within the legislation have particular meanings:

- 'improper performance' means failing to perform a function or activity with good faith or impartially (s 4); and
- 'relevant function or activity' includes all functions of a public nature, for example those carried out by public authorities (such as the police), and all activities connected with a business, trade, or profession (s 3).

The offences are triable either way and the penalties are a fine or imprisonment (one year if tried summarily, and 12 years on indictment).

16.9.7.1 Bribing or attempting to bribe another person

Under s 1(1) of the Bribery Act 2010, it is an offence for person P to offer, promise, or give a financial or other advantage another person in order to:

- bring about an improper performance by any person of a relevant function or activity; or
- reward any person for such improper performance (s 1(2)).

It is sufficient for P to intend to induce or reward the misconduct; the actual outcome of P's actions are irrelevant. It is also sufficient for P to know or believe that the acceptance of the advantage offered, promised, or given in itself constitutes the improper performance of a function or activity (s 1(3)). The advantage can be offered, promised, or given by P directly or through a third party (s 1(5)).

16.9.7.2 Requesting, accepting, or benefiting from a bribe

Under s 2(1) of the Bribery Act 2010, it is an offence for person R to request, agree to receive, or accept an advantage if:

- R intends improper performance (by anyone) to follow as a consequence (s 2(2));
- R's request (in itself), agreement, or acceptance amounts to improper performance (s 2(3));
- R accepts the reward for anyone's subsequent improper performance (s 2(4)).

It is irrelevant whether he/she actually receives any advantage. The meaning of 'advantage' is a question of fact for the court to decide.

16.10 Answers to Tasks

TASK 1 You probably considered the following:

1. Was the person dishonest?
2. Did he/she take the property?
3. To whom did the property belong?
4. Did the person show an intention never to give the property back to its owner?

TASK 2 The circumstances do not amount to an offence of robbery because violence was not used in order to steal. This is because Jo picked up the bag and attempted to run off with it; she did not use force to steal it. Jo then picked up an item from the floor of the shopping centre and ran into Chris, causing her to fall over and break her arm, and it is only now that force is used. However, this force is used after the theft has taken place. Force was not used immediately before, at the time, nor in order to steal the bag and the goods, and therefore robbery has not been committed.

TASK 3

The following offences are likely to have been committed:

- burglary with intent to steal (s 9(1)(a) of the Theft Act 1968), since Georgia entered as a trespasser with the necessary intent;

- burglary (s 9(1)(b) of the Theft Act 1968) has been committed since Georgia, having entered as a trespasser, inflicts grievous bodily harm on the occupier; and
- aggravated burglary (s 10 of the Theft Act 1968) has taken place because, whilst committing the s 9(1)(b) burglary, Georgia was armed with a weapon of offence at the time of the search for something to steal.

TASK 4

1. Both statements are true.
2. Without identifying the specific criminal conduct (or at least recognizing the type of criminal conduct which produced the money in the first place), there is unlikely to be a successful prosecution. The case of *R v NW, SW, RC & CC* [2008] EWCA Crim 2 was important with respect to the interpretation of the POCA 2002. The Court of Appeal ruled that the CPS could not just focus on inexplicable affluence, make the assumption that there was no lawful reason for its presence, and then presuppose that the affluence must result from the proceeds of crime. Unless there is evidence that Terri had the necessary knowledge or suspicion that the property represented a benefit from criminal conduct, there could not be a successful prosecution under s 328(1) of the POCA 2002. Even if it could have been proved that the money was from the unlawful supply of controlled drugs, it was decided in *R v Allpress; R v Symeou; R v Casal; R v Morris; R v Martin* [2009] EWCA Crim 8 that, if a suspect's only role in relation to the drug money was to act as a courier on behalf of another, such property did not amount to property for which the court could have ordered confiscation from him under the POCA 2002. Therefore, only if it could have been proved that Terri had benefited (eg by receiving payments for passing on the money), could he have been successfully prosecuted under s 328(1) of the POCA 2002.

TASK 5

1. In response to this task you may have considered:

- **Has he 'control' over a pair of gloves, a large bunch of approximately 40 car keys, and a short length of scaffold pole?** Yes, they are in his car and in his sight.
- **Can the gloves, a large bunch of approximately 40 car keys, and a short length of scaffold pole be considered as 'any article'?** Yes.
- **Could the articles be used in the course of or in connection with any 'burglary' or 'theft'?** Yes, these are articles which are often used for breaking into cars. (Eg the short length of scaffold pole can be used to break a steering lock.) However, it is not clear at this point whether or not the person has used the articles for any burglary or theft, or whether he was going to use them for such in the future. In order to be found guilty of going equipped the suspect must have some future intention to carry out a burglary or theft and therefore this would need further investigation.

A further consideration is whether the suspect is 'at his place of abode'. There are two issues here. Is the man is parked outside his own house? The police officer will need to verify whether it is his house; confirmation could be acquired by making a personal visit to ask inhabitants of the house, checking the voters register, or perhaps asking to see utility bills. And if it is his house, is sitting in a parked car outside a house (with no driveway) equivalent to being 'at his place of abode'? This would be a question of fact for a court to decide.

2. (c) only; abstracting electricity. Interestingly, even though it was mentioned in 16.8 that TWOC is not theft, the Theft Act 1968 (s 25(5)) specifically states that for purpose of going equipped, TWOC will be treated as theft.

TASK 6

No burglary has been committed. Although Daisy entered the storage warehouse as a trespasser, her intention was to sleep, and not to commit any of the offences specified in s 9(1)(a) of the Theft Act 1968. Once inside the warehouse, she damaged the door (which is property), and also abstracted electricity by using the fire, but neither damage to property nor abstraction of electricity are included in the acts listed under s 9(1)(b) of the Theft Act 1968 (which is confined to theft and grievous bodily harm).

TASK 7

1. Section 163 of the Road Traffic Act 1988 states that 'a person driving a mechanically propelled vehicle on a road must stop on being required to do so by a constable in uniform' (see 19.4.1). A police officer will be authorized as an examiner by his/her chief officer (see 19.5) and will therefore have the authority to test a vehicle on a road, for the purposes of ascertaining compliance with:

- the construction and use requirements including lighting; and
- the requirement that the condition of the vehicle is not such that its use on the road would involve a danger of injury to any person.

2. All wheeled vehicles first used on or after 1 April 1980 should be equipped with a plate which clearly shows the vehicle identification number, the name of manufacturer, and the type approval number (possibly on a separate plate). The plate should be in a conspicuous and readily accessible location on a part not normally subject to replacement. This is described under reg 67 of the Road Vehicles (Construction and Use) Regulations 1986. The VIN should also be stamped on the chassis or frame and together these identifying features can be matched against details on PNC to enable identification of stolen vehicles.

TASK 8 Note that reliable statistics for the cars most likely to be stolen are not available, as the Home Office no longer collect these figures. But the Honest John website provided the following information on the most frequently stolen cars based on analysis of 500,000 car crime reports, between October 2011 and September 2012.

1. Mitsubishi Pajero	6. Rover Metro
2. Nissan Sunny	7. Vauxhall Nova
3. Nissan Bluebird	8. Vauxhall Cavalier
4. BMW X6	9. Toyota Previa
5. Ford Orion	10. Ford Granada

TASK 9

1. This would be interference (a horse box is a trailer).
2. No, because a go-kart is not a motor vehicle adapted or intended for use on the road.
3. Yes, there is an intention to commit theft of an item which is 'carried in or on the motor vehicle' so this counts as interference.
4. No, there is no intention to steal the vehicle, anything in or on it, or take it without the owner's consent so this would not count as interference.

TASK 10 People enter the restaurant and order a meal. There is an expectation that people who enter a restaurant will pay for food which is prepared for them and served accordingly. By entering a restaurant, therefore, people imply that they have the means by which to pay for goods which are ordered and the intention to do so unless there is a special credit agreement whereby payment can be delayed until a later date. If people enter the restaurant with the appearance of being paying customers (the false representation), but with an express intention not to pay for the meal they are about to order and consume (the property), or knowing they do not have the means to pay for it, they will commit a s 1 Fraud Act 2006 offence of 'fraud by false representation'. This is because the 'dishonest representation' took place before the property was obtained.

Having ordered the meal, they wait at the table for it to be served. When people enter a restaurant and order the meal, initially intending to pay but then change their mind about paying before it is obtained, then the offence is again one of s 1 'dishonest representation', as once more they assume the role of paying customers (the false representation) before the meal is obtained (the property).

The meal is served to the table. When obtaining a meal at a restaurant, some of the charge is for the service that the customer receives. If the customer implies that he/she is an ordinary customer but intends not to pay for the service of the meal, then a s 11 Fraud Act offence of 'obtaining services dishonestly' may be committed.

Having consumed the meal, they are expected to pay. If people who enter a restaurant intend at the start to pay for their meal, but then change their minds after their meal is served, then the dishonesty has occurred after obtaining the property, so this cannot be a s 1 Fraud Act offence. However, because the meal was served to the table, a s 11 Fraud Act offence of 'obtaining services dishonestly' may be committed.

They leave the restaurant. If the people continue to make out that they are ordinary customers, intending to pay (eg waiting for the bill), and then slip out of the restaurant at a convenient moment without paying, there is dishonesty, but it takes place after obtaining the property and the offence is more likely to be s 3 Theft Act 1978; that is, 'bilking'. Seek the advice of a CPS representative in such cases for the most appropriate charge.

Sexual Offences

17.1 Introduction

In this chapter we examine the law surrounding sexual offences such as rape and indecent exposure. The incidence of sexual offences in England and Wales is notoriously difficult to determine, beset as it is by issues of under-reporting and lack of definitional clarity. The most recent crime survey, the Crime Survey for England and Wales (the CSEW, replacing the British Crime Survey) explains that the police recorded 55,812 sexual offences in 2012–13. This represents an increase of 9 per cent compared with the previous year. According to the CSEW, this can be partly explained by a higher number of victims coming forward as a result of investigating historical cases of sexual abuse under Operation Yewtree (Office for National Statistics, 2013, p 11). In 2012–13 the CSEW (Table 2) states that the police recorded 17,061 rapes and 38,751 'other sexual offences'. For female victims of the most serious sexual offences, around 90 per cent knew their attackers, and only 15 per cent had reported the case to the police (Ministry of Justice *et al*, 2013, p 6).

A number of assumptions surrounding sexual offences have been disproved by researchers over the years. These include 'rape myths', such as assuming that rape only occurs to certain types of women or that women in some way provoke the offence (Croall, 2011, p 267). An example of this is the prosecution of the rape when the victim is a prostitute; their complaints were sometimes not taken seriously due to nature of their work.

Establishing that the victim did not consent to a sexual act is also a problematic aspect of this type of offence. The Sexual Offences Act 2003 defines consent and presumptions about consent (ss 74 to 76), and it is also presumed that there is no consent if the victim is under 16. In 1991, a landmark case made it clear that it was never the case that by marriage a woman had irrevocably consented to sexual intercourse with her husband, irrespective of her state of health or any objections to the act (*R v R* [1992] 1 AC 599, HL). A more recent case convicted a husband of raping his wife on a number of occasions from 1970 onwards, citing the *R v R* decision as exploding the myth that it was ever acceptable (*R v C* [2004] EWCA Crim 292). The situation is not always clear in relation to consent, and it is often debated whether consent was granted when a victim had consumed large amounts of alcohol, or changed his/her mind about engaging in sexual activity. The issue of consent will be discussed in more detail in 17.6.2.

More recently, there has been increasing concern about the sexual abuse of children, and particularly the use of technology to facilitate grooming of victims and to share images of child abuse. The possession and sharing of illicit images of children will be covered in more detail in 17.4.2. Individuals concerned with the safety of children can raise concerns with the police, who in certain circumstances will be able to disclose information in order to protect children, under the Child Sex Offender (CSO) Disclosure Scheme.

The investigation of sexual offences has been a problematic area for the police, although the situation has improved markedly since the documentary made by Roger Graef in 1982. This showed the unsympathetic manner in which three male police officers interviewed a female who alleged she had been raped. Given the particular controversies surrounding the police investigation of rape in the past it is perhaps not surprising that there is detailed guidance in this area, particularly from NPIA/College of Policing, ACPO, and the CPS (eg ACPO, 2010a for an abridged version; a fuller version is made available to police forces).

The rate of attrition (between a report being made to the police and successful prosecution) is particularly high in sexual offences cases and has been the subject of much official, professional, academic, and media interest. There is undoubtedly an increased emphasis within the police service on improving both the rate of reporting of sexual crimes and the proportion that are brought to a successful prosecution or outcome.

The police tend to define policy in terms of 'serious' sexual offences and 'other' sexual offences. There is no collective official definition of 'serious' and in a sense every sexual offence is a serious one (eg 'flashing' (see 17.2) is not normally included within the category of serious sexual offences, but its impact on victims might well be serious). However, the police consider that a distinction is needed for a number of reasons, including the pragmatic necessity to make decisions on the deployment of resources and the development of policy. Many police forces will make reference to the use of the word 'serious' in the context of the Sexual Offences Acts of 1956 and 2003 and derive definitions in this way. In broad terms the following are normally considered as serious sexual offences (including attempts to commit these offences):

- rape (vaginal, anal, and oral);
- sexual assault by penetration;
- sexual assault where the assault is particularly serious (or is aggravated such as by including a child under 13 or a person with a mental disorder or involving child abuse pornography);
- causing a person to engage in sexual activity without consent; and
- any other offence of a sexual nature deemed especially serious by the investigating officer.

Reports to the police of sexual offences will arise from a variety of circumstances and in a number of forms. For example, the police may attend the scene of rape that has occurred within a household or on waste ground in a city centre or a victim might phone the police or attend in person at a local police station. There may also be referrals from a Sexual Assault Referral Centre (SARC). The report might be of a very recent sexual assault or of a rape that took place some 20 or more years ago.

Records of sexual offenders are kept by the police. Part 2 of the Sexual Offences Act 2003 determines that offenders convicted for certain sexual offences, for example rape and certain child sex offences committed by adults, are required to notify the police of personal information such as their name and address (s 80). These details are entered on what is commonly called the 'sex offenders register'. This requirement was extended in 2012 to include other offender information such as his/her bank and credit card details and if he/she is living in a household with a child (s 83(5A)(h)). In circumstances where notification requirements are not automatic (eg for a crime committed before the Sexual Offences Act 1997), a chief constable can apply to a magistrates' court for a notification order to the same effect (s 97). Notification requirements are imposed for a fixed or indefinite period, depending on the sentence received, and offenders have three days to notify the police of any relevant changes. The offender can appeal against the notification requirements and these can be revised (s 82). Failure to comply with a notification order is an offence under s 91, triable either way, with punishment ranging from a fine to five years' imprisonment.

A court may issue a Sexual Offences Protection Order (SOPO) if it deems the order necessary to protect the public or a specific member of the public from serious sexual harm caused by the offender committing any of the acts in Sch 3 or 5 to the Sexual Offences Act 2003 (s 104). A SOPO may also be applied for by a chief police officer in relation to an offender residing in his/her police area. A SOPO may prohibit certain conduct by the defendant. *R v Smith and others* [2011] EWCA Crim 1772 determined that the terms of the SOPO must be necessary, proportional, and not oppressive for the defendant (eg by prohibiting the defendant from accessing the internet altogether). The breach of an SOPO is an offence, triable either way. The punishment is up to six months' imprisonment or fine if tried summarily, and a maximum of five years' imprisonment if tried on indictment.

17.2 Acts of a Sexual Nature in Public Places

Exposure is covered by s 66(1) of the Sexual Offences Act 2003. It is commonly referred to as 'flashing'. A person commits an offence if he/she exposes his/her genitals and intends that someone will see this and be caused alarm or distress. It is not necessary for a person to actually have seen the exposed genitals or to have been distressed as a result; the offence is still committed.

However, a 'streaker' intending 'merely' to cause amusement does not commit this offence, and neither does a nudist who, on a site specifically set aside for naturism, does not conceal his or her genitals, but whose purpose is not for onlookers to become alarmed or distressed.

This offence is triable either way and the penalty is imprisonment (summarily, six months and two years on indictment).

Outraging public decency is covered by common law which states that it is an offence:

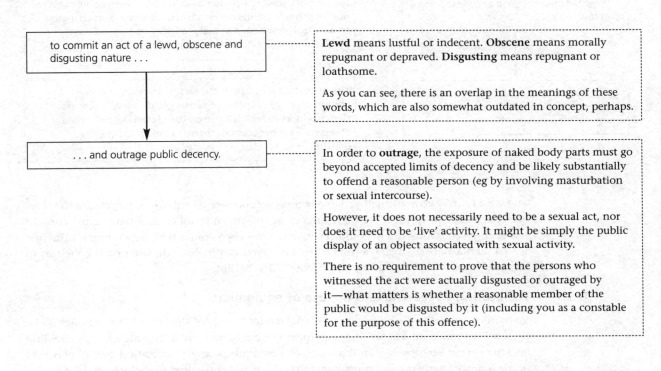

to commit an act of a lewd, obscene and disgusting nature . . .

Lewd means lustful or indecent. **Obscene** means morally repugnant or depraved. **Disgusting** means repugnant or loathsome.

As you can see, there is an overlap in the meanings of these words, which are also somewhat outdated in concept, perhaps.

. . . and outrage public decency.

In order to **outrage**, the exposure of naked body parts must go beyond accepted limits of decency and be likely substantially to offend a reasonable person (eg by involving masturbation or sexual intercourse).

However, it does not necessarily need to be a sexual act, nor does it need to be 'live' activity. It might be simply the public display of an object associated with sexual activity.

There is no requirement to prove that the persons who witnessed the act were actually disgusted or outraged by it—what matters is whether a reasonable member of the public would be disgusted by it (including you as a constable for the purpose of this offence).

The public must have access to (whether they have a right to such access or not), or be able to see the relevant location, such as a private balcony in public view (*R v Walker* [1996] 1 Cr App R 111; *Smith v Hughes* [1960] 1 WLR 830). It must also have been possible for more than one person to witness the act.

This offence is triable either way and the penalty is imprisonment (summarily, six months and unlimited on indictment).

Sexual activity in a public lavatory is an offence under s 71 of the Sexual Offences Act 2003. There is no need for any person to witness the activity, and if there are witnesses, they do not have to be in any way outraged or distressed. The activity must be such that a reasonable person would regard it as sexual in nature. This offence is triable summarily only and the penalty is six months' imprisonment and/or a fine.

17.3 Voyeurism

Voyeurism is an offence under s 67(1) of the Sexual Offences Act 2003. Usually a suspect (commonly known as a Peeping Tom) secretly observes another person undressing or having sexual intercourse (a 'private act') for the purposes of the suspect's own sexual gratification.

Section 68(1) of the Sexual Offences Act 2003 explains that, for the purposes of s 67, a person does a private act if he/she is in a place which would reasonably be expected to provide privacy, such as in a home or hotel (but not on a beach or in an open-plan changing room) **and** at least one of the following conditions is met:

- his/her genitals or buttocks, or her breasts are exposed or covered only with underwear (see *R v Bassett* [2008] EWCA Crim 1174);
- he/she is using a lavatory; or
- he/she is participating in 'a sexual act that is not of a kind ordinarily done in public' such as sexual intercourse or oral sex.

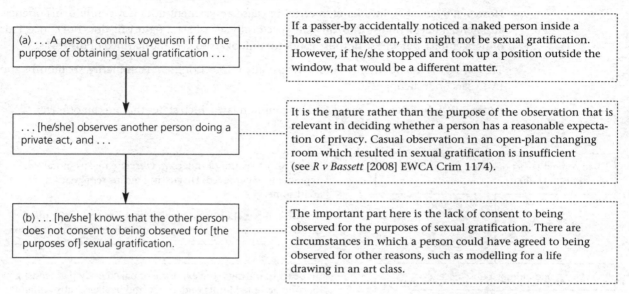

(a) . . . A person commits voyeurism if for the purpose of obtaining sexual gratification . . .	If a passer-by accidentally noticed a naked person inside a house and walked on, this might not be sexual gratification. However, if he/she stopped and took up a position outside the window, that would be a different matter.
. . . [he/she] observes another person doing a private act, and . . .	It is the nature rather than the purpose of the observation that is relevant in deciding whether a person has a reasonable expectation of privacy. Casual observation in an open-plan changing room which resulted in sexual gratification is insufficient (see *R v Bassett* [2008] EWCA Crim 1174).
(b) . . . [he/she] knows that the other person does not consent to being observed for [the purposes of] sexual gratification.	The important part here is the lack of consent to being observed for the purposes of sexual gratification. There are circumstances in which a person could have agreed to being observed for other reasons, such as modelling for a life drawing in an art class.

There is a form of voyeurism linked to dogging (outdoor sexual activities); however, if the 'doggers' encourage people to watch, the offence of voyeurism is not committed because consent has been given. Other offences, however, may have been committed, depending on the particular circumstances. Aggravating factors for voyeurism include threatening the victims to dissuade him/her from reporting the offence (CPS, 2012b).

17.3.1 Facilitating voyeurism and the use of equipment

Voyeurism using live link equipment is covered by s 67(2) of the Sexual Offences Act 2003; person E commits an offence if he/she operates equipment with the intention of enabling another person F to observe, for the purpose of obtaining sexual gratification, a third person G doing a private act. Person E must know that G has not consented to the operation of equipment to that end. For example, a landlord commits an offence if he operates a webcam so that people on the internet can gain sexual gratification from viewing his tenant having sexual intercourse. The landlord must know that the tenant did not agree to this. There is no need to prove that the landlord personally gained sexual gratification.

The recording of images in relation to voyeurism is covered by s 67(3) of the Sexual Offences Act 2003. It is similar to the legislation under s 67(2), except that the acts are recorded and not just transmitted. For example, an offence is committed by a person who secretly photographs a man masturbating in a bedroom and intends to show the photos to others for their sexual gratification. The photographer must know that the man does not consent to the photos being taken with that intention. Proof that the intention was sexual gratification could be that the image was posted on a pornographic website or that it was offered for sale to a pornographic magazine. Circulating images or recordings are deemed aggravating factors by the Sentencing Guidelines Council, particularly when offenders record sexual activity and place it on a website or circulate it for commercial gain (Sentencing Guidelines Council, 2007).

Installing equipment and adapting structures for voyeurism is covered by s 67(4) of the Sexual Offences Act 2003. It is an offence to install equipment or construct or adapt a structure (or part of a structure) with the intention of enabling him/herself or another person to commit an offence of voyeurism (under s 67(1)). The offence is still committed even if the installation or adaptation is never used. Note that a 'structure' (a site where the equipment is installed) can include a tent, vehicle, vessel, or some other temporary or moveable structure.

These offences are triable either way and the penalty is imprisonment (summarily, six months and two years on indictment).

> **TASK 1** On the drive back to their home ground, four members of a rugby club team have taken to celebrating their wins by exposing their naked buttocks ('mooning') out of the rear window of the team bus. A police officer is asked to deal with the most recent incident in the busy main high street. What offence might have been committed?

17.4 Pornography

Many aspects of adult pornography are completely legitimate, but if it involves 'extreme images' or indecent images of children, it will be illegal.

17.4.1 Possession of extreme pornographic images

This offence is covered by s 63(1) of the Criminal Justice and Immigration Act 2008. It is an offence to be in possession of an 'extreme pornographic image' (s 63(2)). An image is said to be *pornographic* if it appears to have been produced solely or principally for the purpose of sexual arousal (s 63(3)). An image includes moving images and electronic data that can be converted into an image, and/or stored on mobile phones or a computer drive, for example (s 63(8)). An *extreme image* is any image of an act which depicts (or appears to depict) activities which:

- threaten a person's life;
- result in (or are likely to result in) serious injury to a person's anus, breasts, or genitals (including surgical reconstructions);
- involve sexual interference with a human corpse (necrophilia); or
- involve a person performing an act of intercourse or oral sex with an animal (bestiality), where any such act, person, or animal depicted in the image is or appears to be real (s 63(7)).

The Prime Minister announced in 2013 that he would endorse the creation of legislation regarding images that depict rape in the catalogue of extreme pornographic images (Woodhouse, 2013). The offence of possession of an extreme pornographic image does not apply for 'excluded images' (s 64(2)). (These are defined in 17.4.1.1.)

The defences for possessing extreme images (s 65 of the Criminal Justice and Immigration Act 2008) include that the person:

- had a legitimate reason for possessing the image (s 65(1));
- had not seen the image and did not know (nor had any cause to suspect) it was an extreme pornographic image (s 65(1)); or
- had received the image without any previous request having been made, and did not keep it for an unreasonable time (s 65(2)).

The offence cannot be prosecuted without the consent of the Director of Public Prosecutions. It is triable either way and the penalty is 12 months' imprisonment and/or a fine if tried summarily. For trials on indictment the penalty is imprisonment (three years for images which depict life-threatening acts or involve serious injury, and two years for images which involve necrophilia or bestiality).

The Ministry of Justice has issued guidance for dealing with the offence of possession of extreme pornographic images, available on the CPS website. The Internet Watch Foundation (IWF) now operates an internet hotline for the public and IT professionals to report potentially illegal websites.

17.4.1.1 Excluded images

These images are excluded in the sense that they would not be of concern for the offences contained in s 63(1) of the Criminal Justice and Immigration Act 2008 (see 17.4.1) and s 62(1) of the Coroners and Justice Act 2009 (child pornography, see 17.4.2.3). An excluded image must be part of a full-length mainstream or documentary film classified by the British Board of Film Classification (BBFC), and if the image appears as part of a series in the complete film, it will not be considered as pornographic.

However, if parts of the classified work have been extracted solely or principally for the purpose of sexual arousal, they will no longer count as 'excluded' (s 63(3)). Such cases will be a question of fact for the court to decide. For example, a recording of a particular short section of a film could have been unintentional, due to incorrectly set recording times. Alternatively, part of a film could have been reproduced for a purpose other than for use as pornography.

17.4.2 Images of children and pornography

Sexualized images of children are used by paedophiles as both 'stimulus' masturbatory fantasy material and also as a possible disinhibitor for actual abuse of children. To help protect children from harm and exploitation, in addition to the general legislation relating to extreme pornography (see 17.4.1), further legislation is available in relation to images of children. Early legislation only applied to photographs and pseudo-photographs, but more recently it has been recognized that drawings and other fantasy-style images of explicit child sexual abuse can be created using computers, so new legislation that is specific to image production has been introduced. For the purpose of legislation relating to child sexual abuse imagery (or 'child pornography'), any person under the age of 18 is a child, except in cases where defences of marriage apply.

Some photographs of children may appear indecent but are not indecent in terms of the legislation. These exceptions are listed in s 1 of the Protection of Children Act 1978—the suspect is required to prove that:

- the photograph was of a person aged 16 or over, and that at the time of the alleged offence, the person and the suspect were married or lived together as partners in an enduring family relationship (exception 1A);
- it was necessary to make the photograph for the purposes of the prevention, detection, or investigation of crime, or for the purposes of criminal proceedings in any part of the world (exception 1B).

17.4.2.1 Possession of indecent photograph of child

Section160(1) of the Criminal Justice Act 1988 states that it is an offence for a person to have in his/her possession any indecent photograph or pseudo-photograph of a child. The law does not define 'indecent'. According to *R v Stamford* [1972] 2 QB 391, it is up to the jury to decide whether an image is indecent or not based on 'recognized standards of propriety' (and not necessarily their own subjective views—see *R v Neil* [2011] EWCA Crim 461).

Defences (s 160(2)) include:

- having a legitimate reason for possessing the image;
- having not seen the image, nor having cause to suspect what it was; and
- receiving the image without requesting it and not keeping it for an unreasonable time.

The offence is triable either way, and the penalty is a fine or imprisonment (six months if tried summarily, and five years on indictment).

17.4.2.2 Producing and distributing indecent photographs of children

This offence is covered in s 1 of the Protection of Children Act 1978, and is explained in more detail in the flowchart.

Two defences to this offence are listed in s 1(4) of the Protection of Children Act 1978:

- the defendant had a legitimate reason for distributing, showing, or having possession of the photographs or pseudo-photographs; and
- the defendant did not see the photographs or pseudo-photographs or saw them and did not know they were, nor had any cause to suspect them to be, indecent.

The offence is triable either way. If tried summarily the penalty is six months' imprisonment and/or a fine, and on indictment the penalty is ten years' imprisonment.

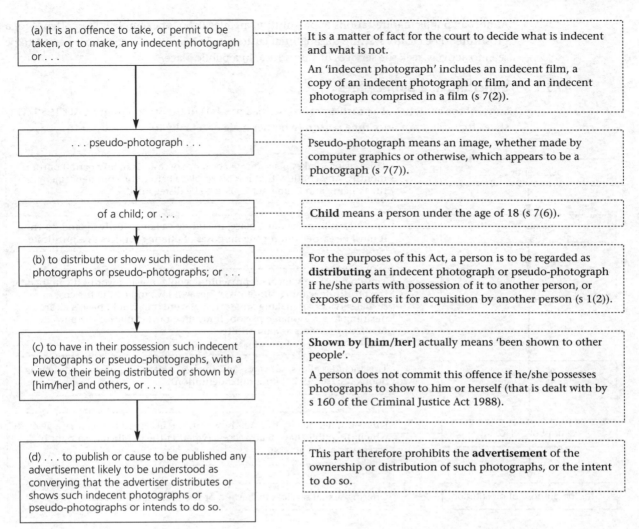

(a) It is an offence to take, or permit to be taken, or to make, any indecent photograph or . . .	It is a matter of fact for the court to decide what is indecent and what is not. An 'indecent photograph' includes an indecent film, a copy of an indecent photograph or film, and an indecent photograph comprised in a film (s 7(2)).
. . . pseudo-photograph . . .	Pseudo-photograph means an image, whether made by computer graphics or otherwise, which appears to be a photograph (s 7(7)).
of a child; or . . .	**Child** means a person under the age of 18 (s 7(6)).
(b) to distribute or show such indecent photographs or pseudo-photographs; or . . .	For the purposes of this Act, a person is to be regarded as **distributing** an indecent photograph or pseudo-photograph if he/she parts with possession of it to another person, or exposes or offers it for acquisition by another person (s 1(2)).
(c) to have in their possession such indecent photographs or pseudo-photographs, with a view to their being distributed or shown by [him/her] and others, or . . .	**Shown by [him/her]** actually means 'been shown to other people'. A person does not commit this offence if he/she possesses photographs to show to him or herself (that is dealt with by s 160 of the Criminal Justice Act 1988).
(d) . . . to publish or cause to be published any advertisement likely to be understood as conveying that the advertiser distributes or shows such indecent photographs or pseudo-photographs or intends to do so.	This part therefore prohibits the **advertisement** of the ownership or distribution of such photographs, or the intent to do so.

17.4.2.3 Possession of a prohibited image of a child

Under s 62(1) of the Coroners and Justice Act 2009 it is an offence to be in possession of a prohibited image of a child (under 18). An image (moving, still, or in data form) is said to be prohibited if it is either pornographic (produced for the purpose of sexual arousal) or 'grossly offensive, disgusting or otherwise of an obscene character'. In addition, the image must either focus solely or principally on a child's genitals or anal region, or portray a child as a witness or participant for at least one of the following activities:

- sexual intercourse or oral sex with a person or an animal (the animal can be dead, alive, or imaginary);
- masturbation;
- penetration of the anus or vagina (with a part of the body or anything else).

For the purposes of this legislation an image does not include an indecent photograph or pseudo-photograph (s 65(3)), as these are dealt with by other legislation (see 17.4.1), nor does it apply to excluded images (see 17.4.1.1).

Defences for the offence of possession of a prohibited image of a child (s 64) are similar to those for possession of an indecent photograph of a child (see 17.4.2.1). The offence is triable either way and the penalty is a fine or imprisonment (12 months if tried summarily, and three years on indictment).

17.5 Prostitution

A prostitute is defined as 'a person . . . who, on at least one occasion and whether or not compelled to do so, offers or provides sexual services to another person in return for payment or a promise of payment to [him/her] or a third person' (s 51(2) of the Sexual Offences Act 2003).

Specific Incidents

Almost all public manifestations of prostitution are illegal. So for example it is an offence for a prostitute to be clearly waiting for potential customers in a public place, or for a person to be seen to actively seek the services of a prostitute in a public place.

17.5.1 Soliciting in a public place

Some of the activities of a prostitute are described in s 1(1) of the Street Offences Act 1959. This states that it is an offence for a person (whether male or female) to:

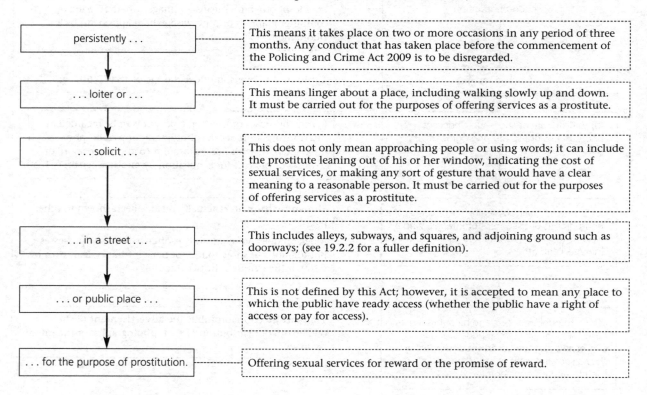

persistently . . .	This means it takes place on two or more occasions in any period of three months. Any conduct that has taken place before the commencement of the Policing and Crime Act 2009 is to be disregarded.
. . . loiter or . . .	This means linger about a place, including walking slowly up and down. It must be carried out for the purposes of offering services as a prostitute.
. . . solicit . . .	This does not only mean approaching people or using words; it can include the prostitute leaning out of his or her window, indicating the cost of sexual services, or making any sort of gesture that would have a clear meaning to a reasonable person. It must be carried out for the purposes of offering services as a prostitute.
. . . in a street . . .	This includes alleys, subways, and squares, and adjoining ground such as doorways; (see 19.2.2 for a fuller definition).
. . . or public place . . .	This is not defined by this Act; however, it is accepted to mean any place to which the public have ready access (whether the public have a right of access or pay for access).
. . . for the purpose of prostitution.	Offering sexual services for reward or the promise of reward.

This offence is triable summarily and the penalty is a fine or a court order requiring the offender to attend three meetings with a 'suitable person' (specified in the order).

17.5.2 Procuring the services of a prostitute

It is an offence under s 51(A) of the Sexual Offences Act 2003 for potential clients (either on foot or in a vehicle) to 'solicit' the services of a prostitute in a public place. This offence is known as 'kerb crawling' when carried out from a vehicle. It is an offence for a person in a street or any other public place to solicit another person for the purpose of obtaining sexual service as a prostitute from them. The meanings of solicit and prostitute are covered in 17.5.1. A street is defined in 19.2.2 (but see also 17.5.1). **Public place** is not defined in this Act, but in the Public Order Act 1986 and the Crime and Disorder Act 1998 it means 'any highway and any place to which at the material time the public has access, on payment or otherwise, as of right or by virtue of express or implied permission'. This offence is triable summarily and the penalty is a fine.

17.5.3 Paying for the sexual services of an exploited prostitute

Section 53A of the Sexual Offences Act 2003 states that in some circumstances it is an offence to pay (or promise to pay) for the sexual services of a prostitute. This only applies if a third person has induced or encouraged the provision of payment for the sexual services, and that third person is motivated by gain (for him/herself or another) and has used exploitative conduct. The conduct can include the use of force or threats (not necessarily violent), the use of coercion, or by deceiving the prostitute. It is irrelevant whether the services are actually provided or whether the suspect is aware that the third person has participated in the exploitative conduct. The offence need not take place in the UK. This offence is triable summarily and the penalty is a fine.

TASK 2

1. Two police officers are on uniformed patrol near a railway station when they notice a woman standing in the car park. As they approach she walks away towards the town centre, but is back in the same place a few minutes later. Later on in the evening the same police officers see two cars stop next to the woman. Each time the occupants of the cars talk to the woman and then drive off. What do you consider the police officers could do in these circumstances in relation to the woman?

2. A person offering a professional body-piercing service passes round a mobile phone amongst a group of strangers. On the screen of the phone can be clearly seen the images of female breasts and genitals into which sharp metal objects of various shapes and sizes have been inserted. In relation to the possession of extreme pornographic images, have any offences been committed?

17.6 Sexual Assault, Rape, and Other Sexual Offences

This part of Chapter 17 covers the following offences under the Sexual Offences Act 2003:

- rape (s 1);
- assault by penetration (s 2);
- sexual assault (touching) (s 3); and
- causing another person to engage in sexual activity without consent (s 4).

In law, for these offences the offender and victim can be of any age. Remember that the question of consent is of paramount importance when considering whether a sexual act amounts to an offence.

The term 'sexual' now appears in ss 2, 3, and 4, as well as many of the child sex offences. An activity will be sexual if a reasonable person would consider it is obviously sexual (s 78 of the Sexual Offences Act 2003). This would cover, for example, masturbation, which most people would consider to be sexual.

Paragraph (b) of s 78 covers more ambiguous activities which may or may not be sexual, depending on the circumstances or the intentions of the perpetrator (or both). A two-stage test may be applied:

1. Would a reasonable person consider the general nature of the act to be potentially sexual in nature? For example, the digital penetration of the vagina of a woman is likely to be considered by most reasonable people to be a potentially sexual act.
2. What are the specific circumstances (which might include the intentions of the person carrying out the potential sexual act). For example, if the digital penetration of the vagina of a woman were carried out by a GP as part of a necessary medical examination, it would not be likely to be considered sexual.

If a person has a hidden sexual motive to an apparently innocent activity, this will not be considered sexual for the purpose of the Act; in effect the activity would fail the first part of the test. The general opinion is that the definition under s 78 excludes obscure sexual fetishes.

Whatever the situation, the term 'sexual' is defined so as to make it clear that not every potentially sexual activity will automatically be considered as sexual under s 78. However, a number of observers have pointed to the possible tautological problems with s 78 definitions of sexual (it defines sexual in terms of itself) and you might consider researching this further.

17.6.1 Initial response to sexual crime

All reports of serious sexual assault made by victims or 'third parties' (eg a witness or a confidant of the victim) should be assumed to be true, and an investigation should be initiated. The initial investigation into an alleged serious sexual offence is conducted by a specially trained officer (an 'STO', although the title will vary from force to force) who will become the single point of contact (SPOC) for the victim, and also provide early support. If the victim is a child (under 16) then other specialist police staff will also be involved. A detective sergeant will be appointed to lead the investigation, the progress of which is expected to be reviewed on a regular basis.

ACPO guidance for the investigation and prosecution of rape (ACPO, 2010a) is also applicable to other types of 'serious' sexual offences. The guidance promotes the use of a multi-agency approach to the investigation of rape.

A number of the Diploma in Policing units are relevant to the early stages of a sexual offence enquiry, notably the units 'Provide initial support to victims and witnesses' and 'Provide an initial response to incidents'. The material covered here is also likely to be relevant to the CKP units 'Knowledge of providing initial support to victims and witnesses within a policing context' and 'Knowledge of providing an initial response to incidents within a policing context'.

17.6.1.1 Information from the victim

A rape is often first reported to the police by the victim, but victims often do not report rape or serious sexual assaults immediately after the event. Also, the victim might not define it as such or at least not immediately (eg it may initially be reported as domestic violence). This can be due to mistrust in the justice system, fear of not being believed, or fear for his/her own or children's personal safety. Officers dealing with victims of rape or other serious sexual offences should be mindful that the victim may be reluctant to disclose events of a traumatic and intimate nature.

A trainee officer is unlikely to be involved much beyond the initial stages of investigation into an alleged serious sexual offence. As for other incidents, the priority of the 'first officer on the scene' will be the protection of the victim and any other individuals at risk (see 11.2.1). They will not be expected to take a detailed account from the victim (this is the responsibility of an STO) but still need to be mindful that this could be the first stage of a prolonged investigation. An initial report should be taken (eg location, identity, times, description of suspect, etc) and accurate and relevant entries made in the PNB (see 10.2), followed by rapid referral to line managers and the STOs. The FAO should remain the single point of contact with the victim until an STO is appointed to the case, and should communicate the complaint to the relevant departments (usually criminal investigation and specialist investigation teams).

Report-takers should display active listening (see 6.11.3) and concern for the victim when taking the statement. It is important to establish a relationship of trust with the victim early on as this will encourage the victim to provide as much detailed information as possible at a later stage, but a detailed interview of the victim is not appropriate during the first response stage, because the events are likely to have been highly traumatic. The focus should be on assessing the immediate safety of the victim, and be sufficient for briefing of the officers investigating the events.

The ACPO guidance provides a list of questions for the initial stages. These depend on the urgency of the report and include, amongst other things, asking the identity of the person making the report (and for phone calls, his/her location), the location and time of the incident, whether the person making the report is the victim or a third party (and if the latter, in what capacity), the nature of the incident, the location and identity of the suspect, and details of any known injuries (ACPO, 2010a, pp 24–5). Victims should be provided with information on rape crisis centres and local victims support organizations. Any decision to arrest the offender (or involve him/her in any other way in the investigation) should consider the risk that this may present to the victim.

Forensic requirements must be considered (see 11.2), including the use of evidence-recovery methods if appropriate (see 25.6). Sexual assault victims should not smoke, eat, drink, wash, or go to the toilet (unless absolutely necessary) until they have been forensically examined. The preservation of physical evidence is essential.

17.6.1.2 Information from others

Reports may be made by third parties, in which case the report-taker should try to establish in which capacity the third party is acting (eg as a witness or a member of a victim support organization). The third party should be provided with the contact details of an IO so that any further information can later be provided. Direct police contact with the victim should usually be avoided without the knowledge of the third party. This does not mean, however, that contact with the victim should be avoided altogether; a risk assessment should be made under the supervision of an IO, who should consider using a STO to take matters forward. If the third party identifies an offender, the IO should consider further investigation and an arrest if there is reasonable suspicion of the offence having taken place. If the third party making the report is from another agency, the recording and investigation should follow the pre-agreed information-sharing protocols. The information should be auditable (eg recorded in an IT system) and can be used, for example, to analyse trends and patterns of offending.

Specialist sexual violence services should be made aware of any anonymous reports. The IO should consider ways to corroborate whether there is enough evidence to amount to reasonable suspicion and a subsequent arrest.

17.6.2 Consent

In many sexual offence cases the court will focus on the issue of consent. A defence is available if the suspect believes that consent was given, but he/she would also have to prove that this belief was reasonable. In any prosecution the court will decide whether the belief was reasonable after considering the circumstances and the steps that the suspect took to obtain consent (s 1(2) of the Sexual Offences Act 2003).

In general terms, the court will seek to establish whether the suspect made a conscious effort to

* establish consent; and
* monitor the consent—the other person might change his/her mind and withdraw consent, indicated by a change of physical expression or voice tone, for example.

Section 74 of the Sexual Offences Act 2003 states that a person consents if he/she agrees by choice, and has the freedom and capacity to make that choice. A choice has not been made freely if the person has taken part under duress or through being put in fear of violence. Capacity to agree means the ability to decide either way, and to be able to communicate the decision. If a person is 'unable to refuse', through intoxication (see *R v Bree* [2007] EWCA Crim 256) or mental disorder, for example, then he/she does not have the capacity to make the choice. The general definition of consent under s 74 of the Act is wide enough to encompass circumstances where the victim feels compelled to have sex (eg in *R v Jheeta* [2007] EWCA Crim 1699 the victim mistakenly feared she would be fined by the police), and therefore could not be said to have consented. It covers a multitude of circumstances.

In order to increase the conviction rate for those guilty of sexual assault, the Sexual Offences Act 2003 introduced two sets of presumptions which courts can make in relation to the guilty knowledge of the defendant: evidential and conclusive presumptions about consent.

Evidential presumptions about consent are covered in s 75 of the Sexual Offences Act 2003. The defence can provide evidence that the victim did in fact consent (to contradict the presumption that consent was not given). The defence will need to convince the judge (through the use of evidence) that there is a definite issue about consent, and then produce relevant evidence from the defendant, a witness, or the victim under cross-examination. If the judge is not convinced, the jury will be directed to find that the victim did not consent, and that the defendant could not have reasonably believed that consent was given. The jury will only be asked to assess whether the defendant's belief that consent had been granted was reasonable if his/her reasoning is not merely 'fanciful or speculative' (*R v Ciccarelli* [2011] EWCA Crim 2665).

Under s 75 the court will presume that the victim did not consent if evidence presented in court proves that the circumstances involved:

* use of and fear of immediate violence against that or another person;
* unlawful detention;
* unconsciousness;
* inability to communicate due to physical disability; and/or
* substances (such as drugs) non-consensually administered, that are capable of stupefying or overpowering.

It also has to be proved that the defendant knew of these circumstances and that the defendant carried out the act in question.

Conclusive presumptions about consent are covered in s 76 of the Sexual Offences Act 2003. This covers circumstances in which the victim has been deceived. The presumption about consent (ie the lack of consent) is conclusive and final: if the victim has been deceived, no amount of evidence can prove that consent had been given. The court will presume that the victim did not legally consent if it is proved in court that the defendant intentionally:

- deceived the complainant about the nature or purpose of the relevant act (eg telling the victim it was a necessary medical procedure); or
- impersonated an individual personally known to the victim, with whom the victim would have consented to such activity (eg the defendant pretends to be the victim's current sexual partner and engages in sexual activity during complete darkness).

(Of course, it also has to be proved that the defendant carried out the relevant act.)

Interestingly, recent case law has made it clear that certain deceptions that fall outside s 76 can be dealt with as lack of consent under s 74. These include deceptions concerning the gender of the perpetrator, whether a condom will be used, and blackmail. It has also been suggested that where a person lies about his/her HIV status this too could negate consent under s 74 of the Sexual Offences Act 2003. This will surprise many as a previous case (*R v B* [2006] EWCA Crim 2945) seemed to suggest that this would amount to GBH rather than rape. However, in *R v Justine McNally* [2013] EWCA Crim 1051 the Court of Appeal clarified that in *R v B* the assailant was silent about his HIV status, and that this is different from an actual deception.

17.6.3   Rape

This is covered under s 1 of the Sexual Offences Act 2003 and can only be committed by a man, but the victim can be male or female. Further details are shown in the flowchart, and some other key points about the definition of penetration are shown in the list.

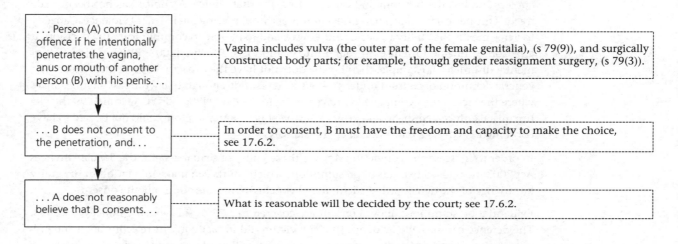

There are some important points to consider about penetration:

- the penetration does not need to be more than just the slightest degree (*R v Hughes*, 1841);
- penetration is a continuing act from entry to withdrawal (s 79(2)); a person (A) may have penetrated person (B) consensually, but then B changes his/her mind (quite legitimately) and no longer consents. If A does not withdraw, this amounts to a continuing penetration and therefore satisfies that particular point to prove; and
- references to a part of the body also include parts that may have been surgically constructed (in particular through gender reassignment surgery) (s 79(3)).

The offence of rape is triable on indictment only and the maximum penalty is life imprisonment.

17.6.4   Assault by penetration

This is an offence under s 2 of the Sexual Offences Act 2003 and is very similar to rape in terms of the guilty knowledge of the suspect; evidential and conclusive presumptions about consent must be considered (see 17.6.2). Note that as for rape, penetration is a continuing act from entry to withdrawal (s 79(2)) and that references to a part of the body also include parts that to may have been surgically constructed (in particular through gender reassignment surgery) (s 79(3)). The issue of consent can be considered by looking at the general definition under s 74, or any of the evidential or conclusive presumptions in ss 75 or 76 (see 17.6.2).

Under s 2 a person A commits an offence if:

- he/she intentionally penetrates the vagina or anus of another person B (with a part of his/her (A's) body or anything else);
- the penetration is sexual;
- B does not consent to the penetration; and
- A does not reasonably believe that B consents.

This offence is triable by indictment only and the maximum penalty is life imprisonment.

17.6.5 Sexual assault

This is covered under s 3 of the Sexual Offences Act 2003, and the details are shown in the flowchart.

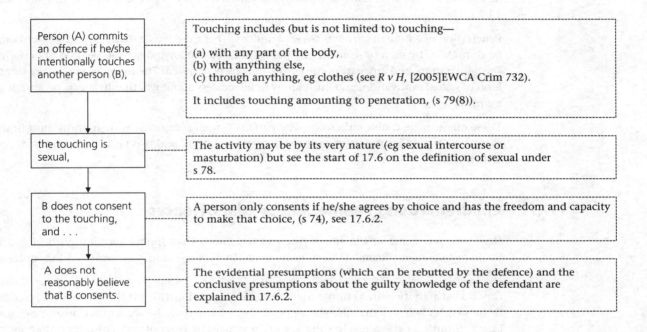

Unlike the old offence of indecent assault, the s 3 offence requires an actual touching of the person (along with the other relevant points to prove) before an offence is complete. In circumstances where the suspect has only tried to touch in a sexual manner, then consideration should be given as to whether it is instead an attempted offence.

This offence is triable either way. The penalty is six months' imprisonment and/or a fine if tried summarily, and ten years' imprisonment on indictment.

17.6.6 Causing another person to engage in sexual activity without consent

Section 4(1) of the Sexual Offences Act 2003 states that person (A) commits an offence if he/she intentionally causes another person (B) to engage in sexual activity, and B does not consent, and A does not reasonably believe that B consents. An extreme age difference between offender and victim, and general vulnerability of the victim are aggravating factors. The penalty is six months' imprisonment and/or a fine if tried summarily, and ten years' imprisonment on indictment.

Causing another person to engage in penetration without consent is an offence under s 4(4), and is similar to the s 4(1) offence described earlier, but also involves:

(a) penetration of B's anus or vagina;
(b) penetration of B's mouth with a person's penis;
(c) penetration of a person's anus or vagina with a part of B's body, or carried out by B with any item; or
(d) penetration of a person's mouth with B's penis.

It is triable on indictment only and the penalty is life imprisonment.

TASK 3 Many victims of rape will be concerned about their identity becoming known during the investigation and any subsequent court case. What legislation is available to provide anonymity in relation to complaints of rape and restrictions on evidence at trials for rape?

17.6.7 Sexual activity with an animal or a human corpse

Sexual intercourse with an animal is covered under s 69 of the Sexual Offences Act 2003. It involves penile penetration of animals by humans, and of humans by animals. The animals and the human participants must be alive and the penetration can be of the vagina or the anus. This activity is also known as bestiality. The offence can also be committed by allowing or causing such an act. (Note that penetration of an animal with an object does not come under this legislation but could be pursued through legislation for prevention of cruelty to animals—see 13.7.)

Penetration of a human corpse is covered under s 70 of the Sexual Offences Act 2003 and can be committed by men or women. Any part of the body or any object can be used to perform the penetration, and any part of the corpse may be penetrated. The offender must have some kind of sexual motivation, and must know or be reckless about whether he/she is penetrating a corpse.

These offences are triable either way. The penalty if tried summarily is six months' imprisonment and/or a fine not exceeding the statutory maximum, and two years' imprisonment on indictment.

17.7 Children, Young People, and Sexual Offences

Here we cover some of the sexual offences legislation that applies specifically to offences involving younger victims. (The offences listed in 17.6 can also be considered for younger victims.)

Any sexual activity with a child under the age of 16 is unlawful, but there may be a defence if the suspect believes that the young person was more than 16 years old. Consent cannot be given until a person reaches the age of 16 years. The issue of consent does not apply if the child is under 13 years of age: such a young person cannot legally give consent. However, the law considers that there is a possibility that children aged 13 to 15 might have 'voluntarily agreed' to sexual activities with other children or young people, provided there was no use of coercion or corruption. In these circumstances a prosecution is not always considered in the public interest. Further information concerning this complex and sensitive area of the law may be found in the 'Rape and Sexual Offences' section of the CPS website.

The offences fall into two main groups, relating to the age of the victim and the suspect:

- where the victim is under 13 (see 17.7.1); and
- where the victim is under 16 (see 17.7.2) and the offender is over the age of 18 years (however, s 13 of the Sexual Offences Act 2003 does make exceptions to this rule).

17.7.1 Sexual offences where the victim is under the age of 13

This is important legislation as it applies to younger suspects (10 years of age and over) as well as to adult suspects over the age of 18. Proof that the victim was under the age of 13 must be provided. Whether the victim appears to consent or otherwise agree to the activity is of absolutely no relevance.

17.7.1.1 Rape and sexual assault of a child under 13

Rape of a child under the age of 13 is an offence under s 5 of the Sexual Offences Act 2003. It can only be committed by a man, but the victim can be male or female. The victim's anus, vagina, or mouth must be penetrated by the offender's penis. The sexual organs can include those constructed through surgery (as with s 1 rape: see 17.6.3).

Sexual assault by penetration of a child under the age of 13 is an offence under s 6 of the Sexual Offences Act 2003, and can be committed by a man or a woman. The penetration can be carried out using any part of the body (such as a finger) or a separate object. The child does not need to be aware of the nature of the penetrating object.

These two offences are both triable on indictment only and the maximum penalty is life imprisonment.

Sexual assault on a child under the age of 13 without penetration is covered by s 7(1) of the Sexual Offences Act 2003. It is an offence for a person (male or female) to intentionally touch a child under the age of 13 in a sexual manner. Further explanation of the terms 'touching' and 'sexual' is given in 17.6.5. This offence (s 7(1)) is triable either way. The penalty is six months' imprisonment and/or a fine if tried summarily, and 14 years' imprisonment on indictment.

17.7.1.2   Causing or Inciting a child under the age of 13 to engage in sexual activity

This is covered by s 8 of the Sexual Offences Act 2003 and can be committed by a man or a woman. The sexual activity caused or incited will involve touching and/or penetration (s 8(1) for no penetration and s 8(2) if penetration is involved) and might involve the child acting alone or with another person. The offender might not be physically involved and no sexual activity actually has to occur; it is the incitement that is the offence. Section 8 therefore creates four separate offences: 1. causing non-penetrative sexual activity; 2. causing penetrative sexual activity; 3. inciting non-penetrative sexual activity; and 4. inciting penetrative sexual activity.

Section 8(1) offences (no penetration) are triable either way. The penalty is six months' imprisonment and/or a fine if tried summarily, and 14 years' imprisonment on indictment. Section 8(2) offences (these involve penetration) are triable on indictment only and the maximum penalty is life imprisonment.

17.7.2   Other Sexual offences in relation to children

For all the offences listed here the relevant sections state they apply to offenders aged 18 years of age or over. However, s 13 of the Act also makes it an offence for anyone under 18 to commit these offences but limits the maximum sentence applicable to five years' imprisonment. The CPS decide on whether offenders under 18 will be charged with these offences by considering the ages of the young people or children involved, the existence or otherwise of coercion, and other factors.

If the victim is aged 13 to 15, there is a defence available if the suspect reasonably believed that the victim was 16 or over and appeared to consent, but there is no defence available if the victim is under 13. Proof that the victim is under 16 must be entered as evidence (eg birth certificate).

17.7.2.1   Sexual activity with a child

It is an offence under s 9 of the Sexual Offences Act 2003 for a person (male or female) to intentionally touch a child, when the touching is sexual in nature. For further explanation of the terms 'touching' and 'sexual', see 17.6.5. This offence is very similar to the s 7 offence (see 17.7.1.1) except that the child does not have to be under 13. It is triable either way. The penalty is six months' imprisonment and/or a fine if tried summarily, and 14 years' imprisonment on indictment.

If the sexual activity involves penetration, then a more serious offence is committed. Under s 9(2) of the Sexual Offences Act 2003 this could be:

(a) penetration of B's anus or vagina with a part of A's body or anything else;
(b) penetration of B's mouth with A's penis;
(c) penetration of A's anus or vagina with a part of B's body; or
(d) penetration of A's mouth with B's penis.

As for other sexual offences, penetration is a continuous act from entry to withdrawal (s 79(2)) and that references to a part of the body also include parts that may have been surgically constructed (s 79(3)). This offence is triable by indictment only, and the penalty is up to 14 years' imprisonment.

Specific Incidents

17.7.2.2 Causing or inciting a child to engage in sexual activity

This is covered by s 10 of the Sexual Offences Act 2003 and is very similar to the s 8 offence (see 17.7.1.2) except that the child does not have to be under the age of 13. Non-penetrative sexual activity is covered under s 10(1) and penetrative sexual activity under s 10(2).

The s 10(1) offence is triable either way. The penalty is six months' imprisonment and/or a fine if tried summarily, and 14 years' imprisonment on indictment. An offence under s 10(2) is triable on indictment only and the penalty is imprisonment for up to 14 years.

17.7.2.3 Children witnessing sexual acts

There are two offences under the Sexual Offences Act 2003: one where the offender him/herself commits the sexual acts and the other where the offender arranges for the child to witness other people committing sexual acts.

For the offence of engaging in sexual activity in the presence of a child (s 11) the offender commits a sexual act with the intention that a child will be aware of the activity in some way (eg seeing the activity live, or on a webcam, or hearing it). The offender has to gain some sexual gratification from his/her knowledge or belief that the child is aware of the activity. However, the victim does not actually have to be aware of the activity (eg if the child does not notice or falls asleep without the offender noticing).

For the s 12 offence of causing a child to watch a sexual act the offender must gain sexual gratification from causing a child to watch a third party involved in sexual activity. The activity could take place live in front of the child, or a recording could be shown, for instance pornographic films on a TV screen. The child need not be coerced to watch, and may even agree to watch; this is irrelevant to whether the offence has been committed.

These offences are both triable either way. The penalty is six months' imprisonment and/or a fine if tried summarily, and ten years' imprisonment on indictment.

17.7.2.4 Meeting a child following sexual grooming

Section 15 of the Sexual Offences Act 2003 provides an offence of meeting or travelling to meet a child following sexual grooming. The person committing the offence (A) must be aged at least 18 years and the victim (B) must be under 16 years of age. The suspect (A) must not reasonably believe that B is 16 or over.

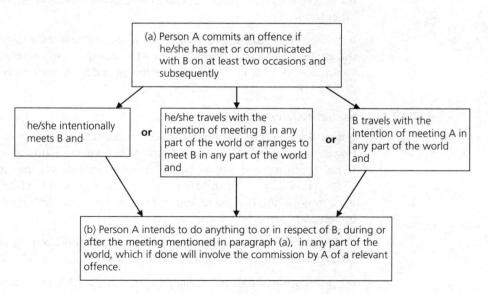

The overall aim of this legislation is to criminalize behaviour where an adult contacts a child on at least two occasions and meets or intends to meet that child in order to commit a relevant sexual offence against the child. Whilst it is popularly considered that the previous communications between the two need be sexualized, this is not in fact the case. A relationship between, for instance, an adult swimming coach and a child swimmer could fall within this section if they have previously communicated (on at least two occasions) and the meeting is arranged in some way or occurs with the relevant intention. The communication can be by way of meeting, letter, email, text, or any other means of communication.

17.7.2.5   Anti-grooming measures

A Risk of Sexual Harm Order (RSHO) can be used to try and prevent online sexual approaches to children under 16, if it is feared that the subject of the order intends to meet and sexually abuse the child. A chief officer of police must apply for the order (a civil order) and there must be a reasonable belief that it is necessary. The subject of the order must be aged 18 years old or over (s 123 of the Sexual Offences Act 2003), and must have committed on at least two occasions acts described in s 123(3) of the Sexual Offences Act 2003, which are:

(a) engaging in sexual activity involving a child or in the presence of a child;

(b) causing or inciting a child to watch a person engaging in sexual activity or to look at a moving or still image that is sexual;

(c) giving a child anything that relates to sexual activity or contains a reference to such activity;

(d) communicating with a child, where any part of the communication is sexual.

RSHOs have a fixed term and cannot be for less than two years (s 123(5)b)). Any breach of such an order amounts to a criminal offence (*Commissioner of Police of the Metropolis v Ebanks* [2012] EWHC 2368 (Admin) (CLW 12/43/9)).

> **TASK 4** Imagine you are a trainee officer and you are asked to attend the home of a 15-year-old girl. She alleges that a family friend has been visiting the house on a regular basis, and he has sometimes massaged her genitals. If the allegations are substantiated could he have a defence to any possible charge? Would it make a difference if the victim was 12 years old?

17.8   Answers to Tasks

TASK 1 Section 66 of the Sexual Offences Act only applies to exposure of a person's genitals, not the buttocks (although it is possible that 'mooning' may also result in exposure of the genitals, even though this was not intended). However, in any case the suspects might excuse themselves by stating that their intention was to entertain or amuse, not to alarm or distress.

In the common law offence of Outraging Public Decency, there must be a deliberate act that is lewd, obscene, or disgusting. In *R v Rowley* [1991] 4 All ER 649, Lord Simon decided that outraging public decency goes considerably beyond offending the sensibilities of 'reasonable' people.

Therefore the local evidence-review representative or CPS representative should be asked whether the common law offence might be committed by members of the rugby team. The public order offences could also be considered, for example s 5 of the Public Order Act—non-intentional harassment, alarm, or distress.

TASK 2

1. The woman could be investigated under s 1(1) of the Street Offences Act 1959 as 'persistently loitering or soliciting in a street or public place for the purposes of prostitution'. However, in order to prove 'persistently' there must be evidence of the behaviour on two or more occasions in any period of three months. The police officers should speak to the woman and, having found out her name, address and date of birth, check whether she has any record of soliciting in the last three months. If she is a persistent offender they may need to consider further action. Otherwise they could warn her about the possible consequences of continuing her behaviour, ensuring of course that the warning is recorded in the appropriate place according to local procedures. This will provide evidence that she has already been acting in this way to any police officer who may need to check in the future. Each police officer should record the incident in his/her PNB.

2. It depends: this offence can certainly be committed by the possession of extreme images stored on a mobile telephone. However, body piercing carried out hygienically and with consent is unlikely to result in serious injury to a person's breasts or genitals. Also, if the owner of the mobile was a professional piercer trying to get business he/she could claim the images were for advertising and not for sexual arousal, and is likely to have a defence.

TASK 3 Section 7 of the Sexual Offences (Amendment) Act 1976 provides anonymity for victims of rape. This includes attempted rape, aiding, abetting, counselling, and procuring rape or attempted rape, incitement to rape, and conspiracy to rape.

TASK 4 For the offence of sexual activity with a child (s 9(1) of the Sexual Offences Act 2003), there is a defence available if the family friend reasonably believed that the girl was over 16. There would be no defence if the girl was younger than 13 years.

18 | Weapons Offences

18.1 Introduction

According to the Crime Survey for England and Wales (the CSEW), in the year ending September 2013 the police recorded 25,953 offences involving a knife or sharp instrument (Office for National Statistics, 2014). Knives or sharp instruments were used in 20 per cent of robberies. Firearms (excluding air weapons) were used in 5,075 recorded offences in England and Wales during the year ending September 2013.

In this chapter we outline the legislation that covers the use and ownership of firearms, and prohibits possession of weapons in certain circumstances. In recent years governments and ACPO have encouraged a more 'robust' approach to charging individuals found carrying offensive weapons, with the intention of deterring those who might otherwise choose to do so. The expectation now is that all people aged 16 or over found involved in knife crime (including possession) will be charged. Those aged 15 or under will be issued with a warning (ACPO, 2010b) and referred to a Youth Offending Team (see 3.3.4). Policies aimed at reducing the number of offensive weapons being carried in public are also often examples of the multi-agency approach described in 3.3. For example, the Violent Crime Reduction Act 2006 makes provision for members of school staff to search pupils, including walk-through scanners for detecting weapons. Part 7 of the Education and Inspections Act 2006 describes the use of reasonable force by school staff, and the circumstances when confiscation from pupils would be lawful. In most cases school policies on searching and seizing of offensive weapons will have been agreed with the local police.

18.2 Offensive Weapons, Bladed and Sharply Pointed Articles

Serious wounding and possibly death can result from the use of these items, but many people possessing such items seem relatively unconcerned about this and offer some sort of excuse. In some cases, individuals found in possession of such articles may be genuinely vulnerable to attack by others, but whatever the circumstances, it is a police officer's responsibility to attempt to prevent crimes involving the use of these weapons and, if at all possible, to detect the presence and removal of such items before they are used.

The legislation covered here concerns offensive weapons, bladed and sharply pointed articles in public places and on school premises, and is to be found in:

- s 1 of the Prevention of Crime Act 1953; and
- s 139 of the Criminal Justice Act 1988.

A police officer has the power to search for offensive weapons, or bladed, or sharply pointed articles under s 1 of the PACE Act 1984 (see 9.4.2).

18.2.1 Possessing an offensive weapon in a public place

An offensive weapon for the purposes of the Prevention of Crime Act 1953 is any article made, adapted, or intended for causing injury (s 1(4)):

- A made article has been made or manufactured for the purposes of causing injury to people, for example a flick knife or telescopic baton. These are offensive weapons per se; the courts

Specific Incidents

need no proof of their intended use, but do require proof that the defendant had no reasonable excuse for possessing such an item.

- An adapted article is any article which has been modified in some way for the purposes of causing injury, for example a broken bottle with sharp edges, or a potato embedded with protruding razor blades. A jury can decide whether or not articles have been specifically adapted to be offensive weapons, but proof that the defendant had no reasonable excuse for possessing such an item is still required. For example, in the case of *Prosecution right of appeal (No 23 of 2007), sub nom R v R* [2007] EWCA Crim 3312 it was decided that gloves filled with sand were offensive weapons as the prosecution had produced evidence that similar gloves had been advertised for sale on a website as 'self-defence gloves'.
- An intended article is any article in the suspect's possession, with which he/she intends to cause injury. The precise nature of the article is not important: it is what the suspect intends to do with it. A pillow could become an offensive weapon if it can be proved that the suspect intended to use it to cause injury to an elderly relative. Once again, gathering evidence through interview is important in relation to this kind of offensive weapon because possession alone is insufficient to prove the offence; it must be proved that the suspect intended to cause injury with the article. Only then will any reasonable excuse be considered (see *R v Sundas* [2011] EWCA Crim 985).

Of course, some items that might be classed as offensive weapons may have innocent uses, and the person would therefore have a reasonable excuse for carrying such an item (see 18.2.1.1).

Section 1(1) of the Prevention of Crime Act 1953 states that it is an offence for:

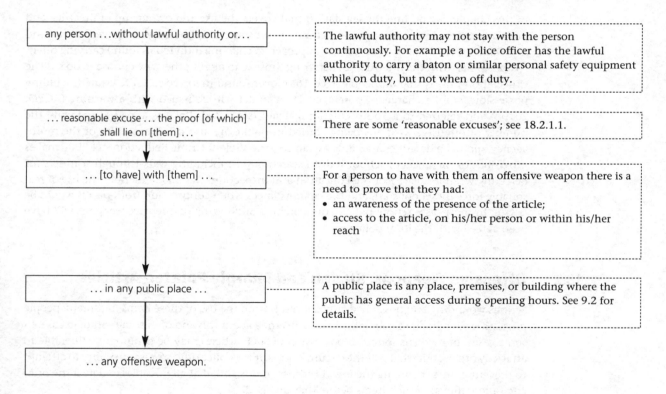

Health and safety should be of primary concern when searching for offensive weapons—the PAC Safety First checklist is relevant as are many of the Diploma in Policing assessed units ('Ensure your own actions reduce risks to health and safety' is one of the NOS units that is 'embedded' within the Diploma (see 7.4.1)).

This offence is triable either way and the penalty is a fine or imprisonment (six months if tried summarily and four years if tried on indictment).

18.2.1.1   Reasonable excuses

A person may have a reasonable excuse for possession of an offensive weapon in a public place if he/she fears for his/her safety: for example, a security guard who fears attack while picking up or dropping off money at a bank, or a person who feels he/she is about to be assaulted (and cannot escape) and picks up a chair to defend him- or herself. Other reasonable excuses include having an innocent reason, such as a chef carrying knives.

Unreasonable excuses include:

- Forgetfulness—for example forgetting that there is a machete under the seat in his/her car; see *R v McCalla* (1988) 87 Cr App R 372. However, when the forgetfulness is combined with other circumstances (eg 'relating to the original acquisition of the article') it will be for the court to decide whether there was a reasonable excuse (see *R v Vasil Tsap* [2008] EWCA Crim 2679). An example might be when a weapon is left by a passenger in a taxi and the driver moves it to the front of the vehicle for the purposes of disposing of it. If the taxi is subsequently stopped by the police the driver may claim to have forgotten that the weapon was there (see *R v Glidewell* LTL 19/5/99, The Times, 14 May 1999).
- Ignorance—not knowing the true identity of the item, for example, believing that a truncheon is a telescope.
- General self-defence—'just in case' he/she is attacked.

In any prosecution the burden of proving a reasonable excuse for possession of an offensive weapon lies with the defendant. Therefore, officers should gather as much evidence as possible—before, during, and after interview under caution, in relation to any likely reasonable excuse.

18.2.2   Possessing a bladed or sharply pointed article in a public place

Historically, under the Prevention of Crimes Act 1953, if the defendant was able to persuade the court on the balance of probabilities that he/she had reasonable excuse (see 18.2.1.1) for having an offensive weapon, such as a kitchen knife, pair of scissors, or large pocket knife, he/she would not be found guilty. The offence of having a bladed or sharply pointed article (s 139(1) of the Criminal Justice Act 1988) was created in an attempt to prevent serious crimes involving the use of everyday items. An offence is committed by any person who possesses a bladed and sharply pointed article in a public place. These terms are defined as follows:

- 'Bladed' includes any kind of bladed article, for example a kitchen knife, scissors, a craft knife, a pocket knife, a dagger, or any other article which has been given a cutting edge or blade. Pocket knives with a blade less than 7.62 cm (3 inches) long which cannot be locked in the open position are exempt from this legislation.
- 'Sharply pointed' includes any kind of sharply pointed article, for example a needle, geometry compasses, or any other article which has been given a sharp point.

This is in contrast to the Prevention of Crimes Act 1953, which is more concerned with objects that are more obviously weapons than everyday articles. A court must decide whether or not an article has a blade or is sharply pointed, and therefore the onus is on the prosecution to prove that the article fits the relevant description. For example, in *R v Davis* [1998] Crim LR 564 the suspect was carrying a screwdriver which the court was asked to consider as a 'bladed article capable of causing injury'. The court decided that it was more important to decide whether the screwdriver had a cutting edge or point than to consider whether it was capable of causing injury. Therefore, unless a screwdriver has a pointed end or has been sharpened to make a blade, it is not an article for the purposes of this Act.

18.2.2.1   Defences

General self-defence, ignorance, or forgetfulness are not defences: see the description of reasonable excuses for carrying an offensive weapon in 18.2.1.1. Some defences that are likely to be considered are shown in the table.

Other grounds for defence (s 139 of the Criminal Justice Act 1988)

Defence	Example
Lawful authority	The lawful authority may not stay with the person continuously. For example, a police officer would have lawful authority to have a bladed or sharply pointed article after seizure and before placing it into a property store. Members of the armed services will also have lawful authority to carry articles such as bayonets whilst on duty, but may be liable for prosecution if such an article was carried off duty

Defence	Example
For use at work	A joiner uses wood chisels with very sharp cutting edges and may need to carry them in a bag in the street while moving between jobs. The work can be casual and the bladed article does not have to be used on a regular basis (see *Chahal v DPP* [2010] EWHC 439 (Admin)). He/she, however, would not be able to use this claim if he/she had a chisel in a nightclub whilst socializing
Religious reasons	Followers of the Sikh religion may carry *kirpans* (a small rigid knife) for religious reasons
Part of any national costume	Whilst wearing national costume, some Scots carry a skean dhu (a small dagger, tucked in the top of the socks). However, this defence could not be used if the person was carrying the knife but not wearing national costume

As mentioned earlier, when investigating a person for this offence, it is very important to gather evidence to counter any defences that may be offered later. The offence is triable either way and the penalty is a fine or imprisonment (six months if tried summarily and four years on indictment).

18.2.3 Threatening with a weapon in a public place

These are new offences that relate to the aggravated use of offensive weapons or bladed or sharply pointed articles in a public place where these are used to intentionally threaten a person, thereby creating an immediate risk of serious physical harm to that other person. The legislation for 'offensive weapons' is under s 1A of the Prevention of Crime Act 1953 (POCA), and under s 139AA of the Criminal Justice Act 1988 (CJA) for an article with a blade or sharp point.

The use of the weapon must be unlawful (see 18.2.2.1) and 'serious physical harm' is that which amounts to grievous bodily harm (see 15.3.1) for the purposes of the Offences against the Person Act 1861. Public place and school premises have the same meaning as s 1 of the Prevention of Crime Act (see 18.2.1) and s 139A of the Criminal Justice Act (see 18.2.4) respectively. If the suspect is found not guilty of either of the aggravated offences at court, he/she can be found guilty of one of the relevant basic possession offences, as long as it is proved (s 10 of the Prevention of Crime Act and s 12 of the Criminal Justice Act).

The offences are triable either way with a penalty of a fine or imprisonment (12 months if tried summarily and four years on indictment).

> **TASK 1** A police officer on patrol notices scissors and several craft knives inside a vehicle on the floor by the passenger seat. What needs to be considered and what action might be needed?

18.2.4 Weapons in schools

The Criminal Justice Act 1988 states that it is an offence for any person to have with him/her on school premises an offensive weapon (s 139 A(2)) or a bladed or sharply pointed article (s 139A(1)). School premises include land used for the purposes of a 'school', including open land such as playing fields or playgrounds (s 139A(6)), and a 'school' is also defined by s 14(5) of the Further and Higher Education Act 1992 as an educational institution providing primary and secondary education. Further and higher educational establishments (eg FE colleges or universities) are not covered by this Act.

The classification of these offences and powers of search are the same as for possessing an offensive weapon in a public place (see 18.2.1). A police officer does not have to be in uniform to enter school premises if he/she suspects an offence under this section is being committed (or has been committed).

Reasonable force may be used to secure an entry. If offensive weapons, or bladed, or sharply pointed articles are found, they can be seized (s 139B of the Criminal Justice Act 1988). At the time of writing the Legal Aid, Sentencing and Punishment of Offenders Bill 2010–2012 intended that a new section (s 139AA) should be added to the Criminal Justice Act 1988.

This would make it an offence for a person to unlawfully and intentionally threaten another person with an offensive weapon in a public place or on school premises, in such a way that there was an immediate risk of grievous bodily harm. The offence would be triable either way with a penalty of a fine or imprisonment (12 months if tried summarily and four years on indictment).

18.2.5   Arranging the minding of a dangerous weapon

Under s 28 of the Violent Crime Reduction Act 2006, a person commits an offence if he/she uses another person to look after, hide, or transport a 'dangerous weapon' for him/her. The way this is done must help make the weapon available for an unlawful purpose; that is that the weapon is available for him/her to use at a particular time and place, and that its possession would either constitute an offence or be likely to lead to the commission of an offence. The offence is triable either way.

The table lists those items which are classified as dangerous weapons for the purposes of s 28 of the Violent Crime Reduction Act 2006. Some descriptions (in quotes) are taken from the relevant Acts and Statutory Instruments.

Item	Comments
Bladed or sharply pointed article	'Any article which has a blade or which is sharply pointed and which is made or adapted for use for causing injury to [a] person'
Firearm	'Other than an air weapon or a component part of, or accessory to, an air weapon' (see 18.3.1)
Axe	The usual meaning of the term
Knife	With the exception of a 'folding pocket-knife if the cutting edge of its blade does not exceed 7.62 cm (3 inches)'
Disguised knife	'Any knife which has a concealed blade or concealed sharp point and is designed to appear to be an everyday object of a kind commonly carried on the person or in a handbag, briefcase, or other hand luggage (such as a comb, brush, writing instrument, cigarette lighter, key, lipstick or telephone)'
Stealth knife	'A knife or spike, which has a blade, or sharp point, made from a material that is not readily detectable by apparatus used for detecting metal and which is not designed for domestic use or for use in the processing, preparation or consumption of food or as a toy'
Razor blades	With the exception of 'razor blades permanently enclosed in a cartridge or housing where less than 2 millimetres of any blade is exposed beyond the plane which intersects the highest point of the surfaces preceding and following such blades'
Knuckleduster	'Band of metal or other hard material worn on one or more fingers, and designed to cause injury'
Telescopic truncheon	'A truncheon which extends automatically by hand pressure applied to a button, spring or other device in or attached to its handle'
Baton	'A straight, side-handled or friction-lock truncheon'
Shuriken, *Shaken* or Death Star	'A hard non-flexible plate having three or more sharp radiating points and designed to be thrown'
Push dagger	'A knife the handle of which fits within a clenched fist and the blade of which protrudes from between two fingers'
Belt-buckle knife	'A buckle which incorporates or conceals a knife'
Swordstick	'A hollow walking-stick or cane containing a blade which may be used as a sword'
Handclaw	'A band of metal or other hard material from which a number of sharp spikes protrude, and worn around the hand'
Hollow *kubotan*	'A cylindrical container containing a number of sharp spikes'
Footclaw	'A bar of metal or other hard material from which a number of sharp spikes protrude, and worn strapped to the foot'
Balisong or Butterfly knife	'A blade enclosed by its handle, which is designed to split down the middle, without the operation of a spring or other mechanical means, to reveal the blade'
Blowpipe or blow gun	'A hollow tube out of which hard pellets or darts are shot by the use of breath'
Kusari gama	'A length of rope, cord, wire or chain fastened at one end to a sickle'
Kyoketsu shoge	'A length of rope, cord, wire or chain fastened at one end to a hooked knife'
Manrikigusari or *kusari*	'A length of rope, cord, wire or chain fastened at each end to a hard weight or hand grip'
Samurai sword	'A sword with a curved blade of 50 cms or over in length which is measured in a straight line from the top of the handle to the tip of the blade'

Specific Incidents

The seizure of weapons may prevent further and perhaps more serious offences taking place. The law regarding weapons is different in some other countries, and therefore certain weapons are easily obtainable elsewhere and then brought into the UK.

18.2.6 Possession of an item for causing injury

The offences we have discussed so far relate to the possession of weapons in public places or on educational property. Faced with a situation in which the possession of an 'instrument' or other article is on private property (eg inside a dwelling) an offence under the Offences Against the Person Act 1861 could be considered. Under s 64 it is an offence for a person to have in his/her possession, make, or manufacture anything with intent to commit, or enable any other person to commit, any of the offences within the Act. The items or things covered here include explosive substances (eg gunpowder), 'engines', machines, instruments, and 'any other dangerous or noxious thing'. The penalty for this offence is imprisonment for up to two years.

> **TASK 2** Ahmed, a 17-year-old at a local FE College carries a knife 'for his own personal protection'. He is under threat from others at the college and has good grounds to fear for his safety. Putting aside any discussion of whether Ahmed has a reasonable excuse: what factors should be taken into account when deciding what action (if any) to take?
>
> Note that these considerations may be relevant to the Certificate in Knowledge of Policing assessed unit 'Knowledge of providing initial support to victims and witnesses within a policing context' and the knowledge element of the Diploma in Policing assessed unit 'Provide initial support to victims, survivors and witnesses'.

18.3 General Firearms Legislation

Each force will have specially trained and equipped personnel to deal with all firearms incidents and the deployment of firearms officers will be considered for all such incidents. However, there always remains the possibility that a trainee police officer could find him/herself unexpectedly at the scene of a firearms incident. He/she may also come across firearms during a search of a premises, or may be deployed to investigate people using air weapons, or required to investigate whether a firearm is legally owned or not. The procedures to be followed when attending an incident where a firearm has been found are covered in 11.2.6.2, and forensic aspects of firearms are covered in 25.5.6. Further information can be found on the www.gov.uk website.

18.3.1 Definition of a firearm

Section 57(1) of the Firearms Act 1968 provides a definition of a firearm as shown in the flowchart.

Firearms are loosely grouped into four categories under the Act:

1. Section 1 firearms (covered under s 1 of the Firearms Act 1968).
2. Shotguns.
3. Air weapons.
4. Prohibited weapons.

All the working parts of a firearm (the trigger mechanism, the firing pin, and so on) also fall within the definition of a firearm, but not additions such as a trigger guard. With regard to a silencer or a flash eliminator it will be for a court to decide whether it could be used with the firearm in question, and whether the suspect had the accessory for that purpose. An item referred to as an imitation firearm may or may not be a firearm in a legal sense, but might instead be a replica (see 18.8).

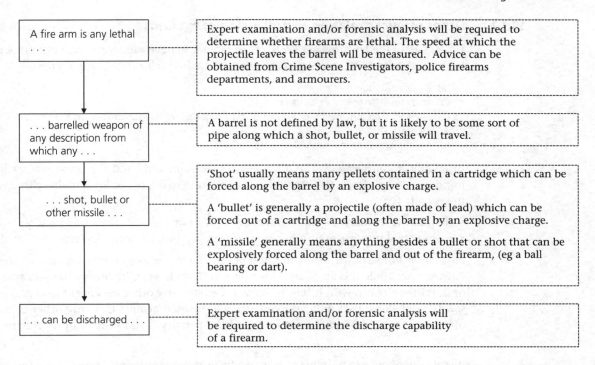

| A fire arm is any lethal . . . | Expert examination and/or forensic analysis will be required to determine whether firearms are lethal. The speed at which the projectile leaves the barrel will be measured. Advice can be obtained from Crime Scene Investigators, police firearms departments, and armourers. |

| . . . barrelled weapon of any description from which any . . . | A barrel is not defined by law, but it is likely to be some sort of pipe along which a shot, bullet, or missile will travel. |

| . . . shot, bullet or other missile . . . | 'Shot' usually means many pellets contained in a cartridge which can be forced along the barrel by an explosive charge.

A 'bullet' is generally a projectile (often made of lead) which can be forced out of a cartridge and along the barrel by an explosive charge.

A 'missile' generally means anything besides a bullet or shot that can be explosively forced along the barrel and out of the firearm, (eg a ball bearing or dart). |

| . . . can be discharged . . . | Expert examination and/or forensic analysis will be required to determine the discharge capability of a firearm. |

The design of a firearm will vary depending largely on its intended use. **Smooth-bore** weapons have a barrel which is smooth inside to enable the easy passage of shot. Although normally associated with lead shot, as used in sport shooting, these weapons can also fire a single or several larger lead 'slugs'. Generally, smooth-bore weapons have a limited range, but find popular use in crime because accuracy is not required due to the spread of shot. For **rifled-bore weapons** the inside of the barrel is grooved (rifled) in a spiral pattern, with 2–16 clockwise or anti-clockwise grooves. These impart a spin to the bullet, giving it stability and increasing the firing accuracy and range.

Calibre is the measurement of the diameter of the barrel. In rifled weapons this figure is normally expressed in metric or imperial figures (eg 7.62 mm, 9 mm, .38inch, .357inch). The units are readily convertible between the two measuring systems. In Britain and the USA, calibre is measured differently for smooth-bore weapons because it was difficult for engineers in the past to be accurate to hundredths of one inch. The calibre is determined by the mass of a lead sphere that would exactly fit the barrel and the sphere's mass as a fraction of a pound. A 12-bore (UK) or 12 gauge (US) is a barrel diameter into which a lead ball with a mass of one-twelfth of a pound would just fit (approximately 1.33 ounces or about 37g).

A bulleted **cartridge** has a lead bullet at the front, with a brass cartridge containing explosive powder behind it. At the other end of the cartridge ('the head' which faces backwards) is the primer, a sensitive powder which is ignited by the action of the trigger and the firing pin. This causes the main powder charge to burn and explode, forcing the bullet out through the barrel. Shotgun cartridges are described in more detail in 18.5.

18.3.2 Firearms certificates

A certificate is needed for s 1 firearms, shotguns, and some types of ammunition. Other categories of firearm such as air weapons and some imitation firearms do not require certificates.

Under s 48(1) of the Firearms Act 1968 a police officer may demand the production of a firearm certificate from any person whom he/she believes to be in possession of any firearm(s) or ammunition requiring a firearms certificate. The interpretation of the term 'demand' varies between forces; for some it means the certificate should be produced on the spot, while in others it could be produced at some specified time in the future. If the person does not produce the certificate and permit a police officer to read it (or otherwise show that he/she is entitled to have the items in his/her possession), then the firearm or ammunition may be seized and retained (s 48(2)). A police officer can also require such a person to give his/her name and address. It is an offence for a person to have a s 1 firearm or a shotgun without the requisite certificate (see 18.4 and 18.5, respectively).

Specific Incidents

18.3.3 Other offences relating to possession of firearms

Under s 19 of the Firearms Act 1968 it is an offence to have a firearm in a public place without lawful authority or reasonable excuse (see 18.2.1.1 on excuses). This applies to:

(a) a loaded shotgun;
(b) an air weapon (whether loaded or not);
(c) any other firearm (whether loaded or not) together with ammunition suitable for use in that firearm;
(d) an imitation firearm.

In relation to air weapons the offence is triable summarily and the penalty is six months' imprisonment and/or a fine. The offence in relation to (a), (c), or (d) is triable either way and the penalty is:

• summarily: six months' imprisonment and/or a fine;
• on indictment: a fine or imprisonment (seven years for (a) or (c), and one year for (d)).

Possessing a firearm with the intention of causing fear is also an offence under s 16A of the Firearms Act 1968. It is an offence for a person (A) to have in his/her possession any firearm or imitation firearm with intent to cause (or enable any other person (B) to cause) any person (C) to believe that unlawful violence will be used against C or any other person. The offence is triable on indictment only and the penalty is ten years' imprisonment and/or a fine.

It is also an offence to be in possession of a firearm or an imitation firearm at the time of arrest (s 17(2)). In *R v Bentham* [2005] UKHL 18, it was decided that putting a hand inside a jacket and extending the fingers to provide the appearance of a firearm did not constitute an imitation for the purpose of committing an offence under s 17(2).

18.3.4 Requesting a person to hand over a firearm or ammunition

Health and safety always come first. Health and safety in relation to firearms found at crime scenes is covered in 11.2.6.2.

Under s 47(1) a police officer can require any person to hand over a firearm (and/or ammunition) for examination if the officer has reasonable cause to suspect that he/she has a firearm (with or without ammunition) in a public place, or if he/she is committing or is about to commit a 'relevant offence'. Relevant offences for the purposes of this legislation include other offences from the Firearms Act 1968, such as carrying a firearm with criminal intent (s 18), trespassing in a building with a firearm (s 20(1)), or trespassing on land with a firearm (s 20(2)).

It is a summary offence to fail to hand over a firearm or ammunition when required to do so (s 47(2)). The penalty is three months' imprisonment and/or a fine.

18.3.5 The power to stop and search for firearms

This is provided by s 47 of the Firearms Act 1968 (s 47(3) for a person and s 47(4) for a vehicle). It applies if a firearms offence has been committed or is about to be committed, but, as ever, health and safety comes first. In order to carry out such a search, s 2 of the PACE Act 1984 and the associated Codes of Practice must be followed (see 9.4.1). A power of entry (s 47(5)) is available to search for firearms.

18.3.6 Young people and access to firearms

For all types of firearms (including imitations) and ammunition it is a summary offence under the Firearms Act 1968 for any person to sell or hire such an item to a person under 18 (s 24(1)) and for a young person under 18 to purchase such an item (s 22(1)). It is also an offence to give or lend (s 24(2)(a)) or otherwise part with (s 24(2)(b)) any s 1 firearm or ammunition to a person under 14. A defence is available for the s 24 offences if it can be shown that there were reasonable grounds to believe the young person was older than the relevant age limit (as applicable, s 24(5)).

Other legislation applies to only particular types of firearms and this is covered where the various categories of firearm are described separately.

18.3.7   Trading in firearms

Section 3(1) of the Firearms Act 1968 prevents any person from trading or carrying out any business with firearms without being registered as a firearms dealer. Activities will include manufacturing, selling, exposing for sale, repairing, and testing firearms, including air weapons. These offences are triable either way. The penalty is six months' imprisonment and/or a fine if tried summarily, and five years' imprisonment on indictment.

18.3.8   Ball bearing ('BB') guns

A typical BB gun will not be classified as a firearm as they are not lethal, neither do they fit the definition of an imitation firearm (see 18.8) for the purposes of offences under the Firearms Act 1968. However, many 'firearms incidents' involve BB guns; a national overview can be found at <http://www.infertrust.org/issues_bb_guns.asp>.

The term 'BB gun' is derived from the small round plastic or aluminium balls they fire, which resemble ball bearings. They are powered by a spring, batteries, or gas (eg carbon dioxide) from an external aerosol canister. However, if the gun appears to be more powerful than a typical BB gun or has large projectiles, the power level may need to be assessed by a forensic laboratory, because it might be sufficiently powerful to be classified as an air weapon or a 's 1 firearm'. If the projectiles are forced out by gas from a self-contained cartridge (resembles a bullet and casing), then the weapon will be classed as a prohibited weapon (see 18.7).

18.4   Section 1 Firearms

Section 1 firearms include a broad range of firearms. They are defined in s 1 of the Firearms Act 1968 as any firearm except for shotguns, legal air weapons, prohibited weapons, and imitation firearms. A sawn-off shotgun (see 18.5) is classed as a s 1 firearm. However, a blank firing revolver which had been modified to render the barrel unobstructed was judged not to require certification under s 1 because it had no cylinder or other structure for containing the bullets or rounds (*Simon Rogers v R* [2011] EWCA Crim 1549). It is an offence to have a s 1 firearm without a certificate (s 1) as shown in the diagram.

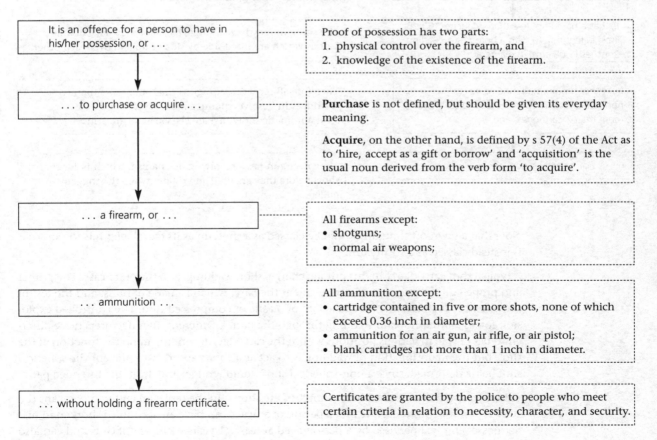

It is an offence for a person to have in his/her possession, or ...	Proof of possession has two parts: 1. physical control over the firearm, and 2. knowledge of the existence of the firearm.
... to purchase or acquire ...	**Purchase** is not defined, but should be given its everyday meaning. **Acquire**, on the other hand, is defined by s 57(4) of the Act as to 'hire, accept as a gift or borrow' and 'acquisition' is the usual noun derived from the verb form 'to acquire'.
... a firearm, or ...	All firearms except: • shotguns; • normal air weapons;
... ammunition ...	All ammunition except: • cartridge contained in five or more shots, none of which exceed 0.36 inch in diameter; • ammunition for an air gun, air rifle, or air pistol; • blank cartridges not more than 1 inch in diameter.
... without holding a firearm certificate.	Certificates are granted by the police to people who meet certain criteria in relation to necessity, character, and security.

Specific Incidents

This offence is triable either way and the penalty is a fine or imprisonment (six months if tried summarily, but if on indictment five years, and seven for a sawn-off shotgun).

In some circumstances a s 1 firearm might not require a certificate. This is a complex area, but special arrangements are in place for certain types of firearm, including antique firearms and handguns used for killing animals. Members of rifle and pistol clubs, visiting overseas forces, and theatrical performers in a show are also excluded from the requirement to hold a firearms certificate.

The age restrictions for s 1 firearms are shown in the table. An empty box means the activity is not permitted. Note that a person of any age can carry a s 1 firearm for a person over 18 during a sporting activity.

The person may	Under 14	Age 14+	Age 15+	Age 17+	Age 18+
Hold a firearm certificate	*	✓	✓	✓	✓
Carry a firearm for a person over 18 during a sporting activity	✓	✓	✓	✓	✓
Receive a s 1 firearm as a gift		✓	✓	✓	✓
Purchase or hire a s 1 firearm					✓

* It may be possible for a parent to be granted a certificate or to have an existing certificate varied to include a child under 14. This could apply if the child intends to participate in competitive target shooting.

18.5 Shotguns

Subsection 1(3)(a) of the Firearms Act 1968 provides the definition of a shotgun as shown in the flowchart.

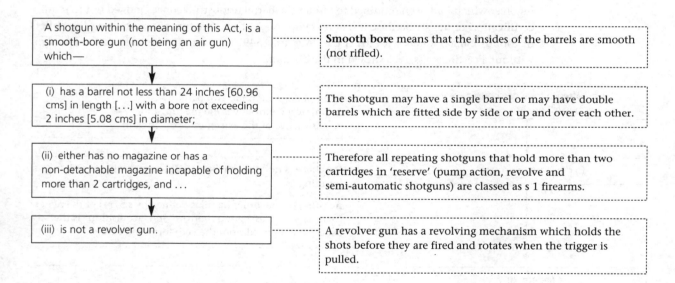

Note that a sawn-off shotgun cannot be classed as a shotgun as its barrel length is too short; it is instead classed as a s 1 firearm.

A typical shot cartridge contains primer, charge, shot, wadding, and the outer case. The primer and propellant are stored in a battery cup at the base, which is made of brass, and the rest of the assembly is stored in a tube made up of plastic or compressed card. The controlled explosion forces all the shot and wadding through the barrel. Different manufacturers place different types of wad in various positions within the cartridge, depending upon the function of the shot, but the main function of wadding is to act as a shock absorber to prevent the spherical shot being deformed, since a non-spherical shot would tend to stray from the intended path.

The age restrictions specifically for shotguns are shown in the table; an empty box means the activity is not permitted. Note that a person of any age can have an assembled shotgun in his/her possession if supervised by a person aged at least 21 years with a certificate, and can also have a shotgun certificate. The age restrictions that apply for firearms in general are covered in 18.3.6.

The person may	Under 14	Age 14+	Age 15+	Age 17+	Age 18+
Hold a shotgun certificate	*	✓	✓	✓	✓
Possess an assembled shotgun if supervised by a person aged 21 or over with a certificate	✓	✓	✓	✓	✓
Receive a shotgun as a gift			✓	✓	✓
Have an uncovered/unsecured shotgun			✓	✓	✓
Purchase or hire a shotgun					✓

It is an offence to gift a shotgun or ammunition to a young person under 15 (s 24(3)). A defence is available if it can be shown that there were reasonable grounds to believe the young person was not that young (s 24(5)).

18.5.1 Shotgun certificates

A shotgun certificate (also referred to as a 'licence') is granted by the chief police officer of the force in which the applicant lives. Shotguns are frequently used for sporting purposes (eg clay pigeon shooting) and for shooting game. Therefore, unless there is a specific reason to refuse the application it will normally be granted, in marked contrast to the issue of certificates for s 1 firearms. Possessing, purchasing, or acquiring a shotgun without holding a relevant certificate is an offence under s 2(1) of the Firearms Act 1968. The offence is triable either way and the penalty is a fine or imprisonment (six months if tried summarily and five years on indictment).

A number of conditions are placed upon the holder of a shotgun certificate. An important requirement is that shotguns will be kept secure when not in use, for example in a specially designed steel gun cabinet. It is an offence for a person to fail to comply with a condition relating to a shotgun certificate (s 2(2)). This offence is triable summarily and the penalty is six months' imprisonment and/or a fine.

In certain circumstances, however, a person may 'have' a shotgun without a shotgun certificate, such as when borrowing a shotgun from a person (who holds a certificate) and then using it on that person's land in his/her presence. Nor is a certificate required in order to possess the type of shotgun cartridge that has many small pellets (ie five or more shot pellets in a cartridge with pellets not more than 0.36 inches in diameter).

TASK 3

1. Describe the general characteristics of a firearm.
2. What are the powers to demand production of certificates?
3. Under what circumstances can a person be required to hand over a firearm or ammunition for examination?
4. What firearms are covered by s 1 and so require a s 1 certificate?
5. What ammunition is covered by s 1 and therefore requires a s 1 certificate?
6. Describe the specifications of a shotgun that would be legal in the UK.

18.6 Air Weapons

Air weapons include air pistols, air guns, and air rifles. They are usually less dangerous than other firearms because the pellets are discharged from the barrel relatively slowly and have less mass than, for example, a handgun bullet. (Remember that kinetic energy is related to both the square of the speed and the mass.) The velocity is relatively low because the pellets are propelled by air pressure alone, rather than by an explosive charge. However, air weapons are capable of causing serious injury including blindness. Fatalities are also not unknown, particularly with children—in 2013, a 24-year-old man died in Sheffield after being shot in the head with an air rifle. Air weapon offences make up more than half of all recorded firearms offences and it is clear they should be taken very seriously.

(Photo by Kevin Lawton-Barrett)

Air rifle

A lawful air weapon does not require a certificate under s 1 of the Firearms Act 1968 unless it exceeds the authorized kinetic energy. To be classified as an air weapon the kinetic energy (the energy used to fire the pellet) must not exceed 6 ft lb (for air pistols), or 12 ft lb (for air weapons other than air pistols). For further information see the Firearms (Dangerous Air Weapons) Rules 1969. A forensic laboratory will be able to measure the energy of the pellets produced by an air weapon. Any weapon with a self-contained gas cartridge system (containing both a charge of compressed air or other gas and the pellet) is classed as a prohibited weapon under s 5 of the Firearms Act (see 18.7).

18.6.1 Age limits for possessing and firing air weapons

Age restrictions applying to all firearms (including air weapons) are covered in 18.3.6; for example, persons under 18 cannot purchase firearms (s 22(1)). Other legislation applies specifically to air weapons and this is covered here.

For a person under the age of 18 it is an offence to 'have' with him/her an air weapon or ammunition for an air weapon anywhere and at any time (s 22(4)) unless he/she is a member at a rifle club and firing at targets (s 23(2)(a)), or the weapon is being fired at a gallery and does not exceed .23 calibre (s 23(2)(b)).

A young person under 14 can use (ie fire) an air weapon on private land but must have permission from the landowner and be supervised by a person of 21 years or over. If the pellets go beyond the premises, both the firer and the supervisor commit an offence (s 23(1)), but a defence is available if it can be proved that the owner of the adjoining property gave permission (s 23(1A)). 'Premises' is not defined in this Act, but examples will include houses and gardens and other private places which are enclosed.

A young person between 14 and 17 years can use an air weapon:

- unsupervised on private land with permission of the owner (s 23(3)). An offence is committed if any pellets go beyond the premises (s 21A(1)), but a defence is available if the owner of the adjoining property also gave permission (s 21A(2));
- anywhere if supervised by a person aged over 21 (s 23(1)). However, it must be remembered that unless a person has lawful authority or reasonable excuse it is an offence to carry any firearm (includes air weapons) in a public place (see 18.3.3).

These offences are triable summarily and the penalty is a fine.

18.6.2 Preventing access to air weapons for young people

The legislation described in 18.3.3 helps prevent young people having access to firearms in general, including air weapons. But further legislation applies specifically to air weapons. Subject to the exemptions to supervisors of young people outlined in 18.6.1, it is an offence:

- to make a gift (s 24(4)(a)), or to otherwise part with (s 24(4)(b)) any air weapon or ammunition to a young person (under 18);
- for a person in possession of an air weapon to fail to take reasonable precautions to prevent a young person (under 18) from having an air weapon (s 24(ZA)(1)).

A defence is available if it can be shown that there were reasonable grounds to believe the young person was aged 18 or over (s 24(5)).

These offences are triable summarily and the penalty is a fine.

TASK 4

1. A 16-year-old boy has been firing an air rifle from his parents' bedroom window at baked-bean cans on top of their garden wall and some of the pellets have clearly gone into the neighbour's garden. What offence has the boy committed?
2. A young person is seen carrying an air rifle in a street. Police questioning establishes that she is 17 years old. What offence, if any, has she committed?

18.7 Prohibited Weapons

Parliament decided that the general public have no reasonable need to possess certain types of potentially highly dangerous weapon such as machine guns, PAVA (an incapacitating pepper spray), or CS spray. Under s 5 of the Firearms Act 1968, no one may possess or make such items without special authority. The table shows some of the more significant prohibited features along with some examples. There are some exceptions to these prohibitions (ie such firearms would not be prohibited) as shown in the final column of the table (information derived from the CPS website.)

Prohibited feature	Example of a prohibited firearm	Permitted exceptions
Short barrel (less than 30cm) or short overall (less than 60cm)	handguns, revolvers	If also an air weapon, a muzzle-loading gun or a firearm designed as signalling apparatus
Can discharge a noxious liquid, gas, or other thing.	stun guns, aerosol incapacitant sprays, eg CS	
Two or more missiles can be successively discharged without repeated pressure on the trigger	machine guns	
Self-loading or pump-action with a rifled barrel	short-barrelled rifles	If chambered for .22 rim-fire cartridges
Self-loading or pump-action with a short smooth-bore barrel (barrel less than 24", or overall length less than 40")	self-loading shotguns	If chambered for .22 rim-fire cartridges, or an air weapon

Prohibited feature	Example of a prohibited firearm	Permitted exceptions
Smooth-bore revolver gun	'Dragon'	If also designed for 9mm rim-fire cartridges or a muzzle-loading gun
Can project a stabilized missile	rocket launcher	If also for line-throwing or pyrotechnics, or designed as signalling apparatus
Has a self-contained gas cartridge system	Brococks	
Ammunition designed to explode on or just before impact, or containing a noxious substance		
A firearm disguised as another object	pen guns, key fob guns, and phone guns	

It is an offence to possess, purchase, acquire, manufacture, sell, or transfer a prohibited weapon or ammunition (s 5(1) of the Firearms Act 1968) without written authority from the Defence Council (the Secretary of State for Defence, other MoD Ministers, the Chiefs of Staff, and senior civil servants). This offence is triable either way and the penalty is a fine or imprisonment (six months if tried summarily and ten years on indictment).

(Images courtesy of Kent Police)

The two canisters on the left are examples of CS Spray and those on the right, pepper spray. All are examples of s 5 prohibited weapons.

TASK 5 A firearms incident at Hungerford in Berkshire in 1987 shocked the public and led to calls for changes in legislation (there are numerous websites that will provide the details). Consider the subsequent White Paper, *Firearms Act 1968: Proposals for Reform* (Cm 261, 1987) and the amendment to the 1968 Act effected by s 1 of the Firearms (Amendment) Act 1988. Why was a change in the list of prohibited weapons thought to be necessary at this time?

18.8 Imitation Firearms

The original definition of an imitation firearm provided in s 57(4) of the Firearms Act 1968 was 'anything which has the appearance of being a firearm whether or not it is capable of discharging any shot, bullet or other missile.' But the Firearms Act 1982 added two further conditions for an imitation firearm:

- it *can* be readily converted (see 18.8.1) into a firearm of a type requiring a firearm certificate under s 1 of the Firearms Act 1968 (see 18.4); and
- it has the appearance of a firearm of a type requiring a firearm certificate under s 1 of the Firearms Act 1968 (see 18.4).

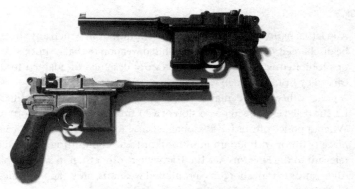

(Images courtesy of Kent Police)

On the left a real Mauser, on the right the imitation

This provided clarification on the difference between imitation firearms and replica firearms. A replica firearm merely resembles a firearm, and is not an imitation firearm for the purposes of the Firearms Act 1968 unless it can be readily converted to a s 1 firearm. However, a replica may require a certificate (see 18.4) if one or more of its working parts constitute components of a firearm (see 18.3.1).

18.8.1 Readily converted imitation firearms

An imitation firearm is 'readily convertible' if it can be converted without special skills or special tools (s 1(6) of the Firearms Act 1982). Here, a 'special tool' is a tool which would not generally be used in the home for construction and maintenance. Therefore if the conversion only required the simple use of a normal screwdriver, the imitation firearm could be described as readily convertible.

Ultimately only a court can decide whether an item requires a certificate, and testing at a forensic laboratory would usually be required before commencing any prosecution. If a certificate is required but none is held, an offence will have been committed. The accused might have a defence if it can be shown that he/she did not know (and had no reason to suspect) that the imitation firearm was readily convertible (s 1(5) of the Firearms Act 1982). It is an offence to buy or sell imitation firearms (see 18.8) if the buyer is under 18 (s 24A of the Firearms Act 1968). This offence is triable summarily and the penalty is 12 months' imprisonment and/or a fine.

18.8.2 Other offences relating to imitation firearms

It is an offence to buy or sell imitation firearms if the buyer is under 18 (s 24A of the Firearms Act 1968). This offence is triable summarily and the penalty is 12 months' imprisonment and/or a fine. It is an offence under s 19 of the Firearms Act 1968 to have an imitation firearm (or any other firearm, see 18.3.3) in a public place without lawful authority or reasonable excuse. It is not an offence to have a replica of a firearm in a public place.

18.9 Answers to Tasks

TASK 1 You probably considered the following:

1. Do the occupants have a reasonable excuse for the presence of the items?
2. Who do the items belong to?
3. Does it seem likely that a crime could be prevented if the matter is investigated further?
4. How would a police officer progress this matter further? Are the circumstances such that an arrest is necessary?
5. Could a police officer deal with the matter by reporting the suspect?

TASK 2 You probably considered the following:

1. Is Ahmed above the age of criminal responsibility?
2. What type of knife is it?
3. Has it been made, adapted, or intended to cause injury?
4. How long has Ahmed carried the knife?
5. Will he hand over the knife?

Specific Incidents

TASK 3

1. Any lethal barrelled weapon of any description from which any shot, bullet, or other missile can be discharged. This includes a prohibited weapon (lethal or not), any component part of a lethal or prohibited weapon, and any accessory designed or adapted to diminish the noise or flash caused by firing any such weapon.

2. A police officer may demand the production of the relevant certificate from any person whom he/she believes to be in possession of a s 1 firearm (or ammunition) or a shotgun.

3. When a police officer has reasonable cause to suspect a person of having a firearm in a public place (with or without ammunition), or to be committing (or be about to commit) an offence relevant to the Firearms Act 1968, anywhere other than in a public place.

4. All firearms except shotguns, prohibited weapons, air weapons (unless 'specially dangerous'), or imitation firearms (unless converted).

5. Any ammunition for a firearm except:
   • cartridges containing five or more shot, none of which exceeds .36 inch in diameter;
   • ammunition for an air gun, air rifle, or air pistol; and
   • blank cartridges with 1 inch maximum diameter.

6. The shotgun must have a smooth bore and the barrel must be at least 60.96cm long and no more than 5.08cm in diameter. It must not be a revolver gun, and must have either no magazine, or a non-detachable magazine that can hold only one or two cartridges.

TASK 4

1. It is generally an offence for a person under the age of 18 to have an air weapon (or ammunition for an air weapon), but there are exceptions. For example, it is not an offence for a person aged 14 years or over to possess the air weapon on private premises with the consent of the occupier, and he/she does not have to be supervised. However, it is an offence to use an air weapon to fire a missile beyond those premises (s 21A of the Firearms Act 1968).

2. A person commits an offence if, without lawful authority or reasonable excuse, he/she has with him/her in a public place any loaded or unloaded air weapon (s 19 of the Firearms Act 1968).

TASK 5 As a result of the shootings at Hungerford on 12 August 1987, it was considered that certain firearms were so dangerous that they should be classified as prohibited weapons. These include self-loading and pump-action rifles (other than those chambered for .22 rim-fire), and certain self-loading and pump-action shotguns (see the White Paper *Firearms Act 1968: Proposals for Reform* (Cm 261, 1987) and the amendment to the 1968 Act (effected by s 1 of the Firearms (Amendment) Act 1988)). The 1968 Act was also amended so that a firearm certificate was required for certain shotguns.

19 Road and Traffic Policing

19.1 Introduction

This chapter describes legislation and police procedures and practice relevant to road and traffic policing. Trainee police officers will probably be expected to demonstrate competence in many of the areas described in this chapter whilst on Supervised and Independent Patrol. In the pages which follow you will learn about the law about highways, driving, road traffic collisions (the preferred term for accidents), insurance, offences, driving standards, drink- and drug-driving, and arcane subjects such as 'fireworks and highways'.

Road accidents and injuries are often personal tragedies to those involved but are also incur significant economic costs. In 2012 for example, it was estimated that road fatalities cost approximately £3.1 billion to the public purse (Department for Transport, 2013b). In terms of road users, motorcyclists are particularly at risk of being involved in incidents leading to death or serious injury.

We should also perhaps note the link between road and traffic offences and other forms of criminality. Research by Rose (2000) demonstrated that 79 per cent of disqualified drivers had a criminal record (four times the average), and that approximately 50 per cent of dangerous drivers had a previous conviction and approximately 25 per cent were reconvicted within a year (three times the average). Interestingly, drink-drivers had less extensive criminal records than other groups of serious traffic offenders (40 per cent had a criminal record), the average time since their last court appearance was eight years, and 12 per cent were subsequently reconvicted within a year. However, these figures are still twice the average. Junger *et al* (2001) also identified links between 'risky' traffic behaviour and more general violent crime, and similarly in a famous study, Chenery *et al* (1999) demonstrated the links between the relatively minor offence of illegal parking in disabled bays, active criminals, and illegal vehicles. All of this leads us to the notion of 'self-selecting' road and traffic behaviour that police officers could usefully consider as indicators of perhaps more serious criminal predisposition.

A significant number of people routinely drive too fast for the legal speed limit. The table gives the proportion of vehicles observed to be moving either at or over the speed limit in surveys conducted in Great Britain in 2012.

Vehicles exceeding (or at) the speed limit (%) 2012

	Motorways 70 mph	Dual carriageways 70 mph	Single carriageways 60 mph	Urban 40 mph	Urban 30 mph
Cars	48	40	8	22	47
HGVs*	1	82	73	16	43
Motorcycles	48	51	21	33	50
Coaches/ buses	18	50	28	12	25

* Speed limit for HGVs on motorways is 60 mph (many are fitted with speed limiters), 50 mph on dual carriageways and 40 mph on single carriageways.

(Adapted by the authors from Department for Transport data (2013a, 2013b).)

The same survey showed that in 2012, 11 per cent of HGVs travelled at speeds of more than 35 mph in 30-mph urban speed limit areas, where of course there are more pedestrians, particularly children. On a more positive note, however, this percentage represents a decrease of one-third on the previous year's figures

The majority of urban accidents are caused by excessive speed, sometimes in combination with drink or drugs. Very few drivers keep to the legal limit all the time, and those who do are often abused by those who do not. The consequences for pedestrians of even small increases in speed can be very significant. The injury caused by a vehicle is directly related to its kinetic (moving) energy which is given by $\frac{1}{2}mv^2$, where m is the mass ('weight') of the vehicle and v the velocity ('speed'). The kinetic energy, and hence the severity of injury increases linearly with weight of the vehicle as to be expected but also increases with a square of the speed. So a small increase in speed of, say from 30 to 33 mph (10 per cent), actually gives rise proportionally to a much larger increase in energy (21 per cent) and hence the likely severity of injuries caused. This is one of the reasons why the law insists on a strict adherence to speed limits in residential areas.

Trainee police officers will be instructed, shown, and assessed on the detail of police procedure in terms of stopping a vehicle, actions to be taken when attending the scene of a recent collision, and so on. Where appropriate, some of this detail is provided here; in 19.4.1 for example on stopping vehicles. However, police officers should also be guided by local force policy and the ACPO guidelines in *Policing the Roads—5 Year Strategy 2011—2015,* and *Investigating Road Deaths* from the College of Policing, both available online.

19.2   Definitions Relating to Vehicles and Roads

Numerous terms for vehicles and roads are used in the various Acts relating to road traffic policing. Some of these were written over a hundred years ago, and the terminology in every-day use has inevitably changed over the years. The term 'public place' is also widely used within legislation relating to roads and driving; it is defined (along with other definitions relating to locations) in 9.2.

19.2.1   Definitions of vehicles

Within the legislation, there are named references to different types of vehicle and to other wheeled objects such as carriages, conveyances, and cycles. The following table explains some of these terms, but is by no means comprehensive.

Vehicle type	Definition	Examples
'Vehicle'	According to the Vehicle Excise and Registration Act 1994, a vehicle is: 'a mechanically propelled vehicle, or anything (whether or not it is a vehicle) that has been, but has ceased to be, a mechanically propelled vehicle' The ordinary dictionary meaning can also be used	Milk float, ride-on grass cutter
'Mechanically propelled vehicle'	'Mechanically propelled' means that the vehicle is powered by a motor (driven by electricity, petrol, diesel, or other fuels). The meaning is not defined by any Act of Parliament, so whether a particular vehicle is a mechanically propelled vehicle is therefore a question of fact for a court to decide	Car, van, lorry, go-ped, quad bike, speedway motorcycles, Formula One racing cars, invalid carriages such as powered wheelchairs and scooters (for footway use only)
'Motor vehicle'	This is a mechanically propelled vehicle that is intended or adapted for use on roads (s 185, Road Traffic Act 1988)	Car, van, lorry
'Motor bicycle'	This means a motor vehicle which has two wheels and a maximum design speed exceeding 45 kph. If powered by an internal combustion engine, the cylinder capacity must exceed 50cc. It includes a combination, such as a motor vehicle and a side-car (s 108, Road Traffic Act 1988)	Motorcycle with two wheels
'Bicycle'	This includes a 'motor bicycle' (ie a motorcycle) for the purposes of vehicle excise duty	

'Moped'*	Moped means a motor vehicle which has fewer than four wheels and: (a) if first used before 1 August 1977, has a cylinder capacity not exceeding 50cc and is equipped with pedals by means of which the vehicle is capable of being propelled; and (b) in any other case, has a maximum design speed not exceeding 50 kph and, if propelled by an internal combustion engine, has a cylinder capacity not exceeding 50cc (s 108, Road Traffic Act 1988)	
'Pedal cycle'	This is either propelled only by pedals or is an electrically assisted pedal cycle (reg 3, Pedal Cycles (Construction and Use) Regulations 1983).	Mountain bike, racing bike, BMX bike
'Carriage'	This means a motor vehicle or trailer (s 191, Road Traffic Act 1988). The ordinary dictionary meaning also applies	Any motor vehicle described above, and caravans
'Conveyance'	This is a vehicle constructed or adapted for transporting person(s) by land, water, or air, but not one constructed or adapted for use 'only under the control of a person not carried in or on it' (s 12(7), Theft Act 1968)	Motorcycle, bus, boat, and plane

* De-restriction kits are available which enable the moped to go faster than 50 kph and/or the cylinder capacity is increased. If such alterations are made it becomes a motorcycle and the rider must conform to the licence requirements accordingly (see 19.3.1.1).

(Images courtesy of Kent Police)

This adapted bicycle would be classified as a moped under s 108 of the Road Traffic Act 1988, as it has a small engine but can also be propelled by its pedals.

The Department for Transport have clarified that mini-motos and go-peds are in fact 'lightweight powered motor vehicles' (not the same as a 'motor vehicle') and must comply with the usual road traffic and vehicle excise licence laws (a 'tax disc' is required). On the other hand, they are not categorized for the purposes of driving licences.

19.2.2 Definitions of roads, highways, and related terms

Legislation relating to road and traffic policing often includes the words 'road' and 'highway'. Each term is used in different pieces of legislation, though the term 'road' is used far more frequently, particularly since the introduction of the Road Traffic Act 1988.

- A road is defined as any (length of) highway to which the public has access, and includes bridges over which a road passes (s 192 of the Road Traffic Act 1988). The limits of a road are the hedgerows on either side, so a public footpath alongside a road is part of the road.
- A highway (s 5 of the Highways Act 1835) is defined as a road, bridge, carriageway, cartway, horseway, bridleway, footway, causeway, church way, or pavement.

Specific Incidents

- A public road is a road maintained at the public's expense (for the purposes of vehicle excise duty legislation), as defined in s 62 of the Vehicle Excise and Registration Act 1994.

Note the potentially confusing overlap between a road and a highway: in practice this does not matter as each relates to individual pieces of legislation.

A number of other terms are also used:

- A carriageway is a way marked or arranged in a highway over which the public have a right of way for the passage of vehicles, but does not include cycle tracks (s 329 of the Highways Act 1980).
- A bridleway is a highway over which the public have a right of way on foot, on horseback, or leading a horse (s 329 of the Highways Act 1980).
- A footpath is a highway not adjacent to a road, over which the public have a right of way on foot only (s 329 of the Highways Act 1980).
- A footway (such as a pavement) is a highway adjacent to a road over which the public have a right of way on foot only (s 329(1) of the Highways Act 1980).
- A street includes roads, lanes, alleys, subways, squares, and any other similar places open to the public. It also includes doorways, entrances to premises, and any ground adjoining a street (*Smith v Hughes* [1960] 2 All ER 859).

The maintenance of a private road is usually the responsibility of the landowner; this one is in a good state of repair. Private roads may or may not be subject to public rights of way.

(Photo by Kevin Lawton-Barrett)

19.2.3 Definitions relating to driving

Legislation relating to road and traffic policing often refers to 'driving' and 'attempting to drive', and these are defined and explained here.

Driving is not defined within any Act, but there are precedents which provide guidelines. The decision finally rests with the court and is therefore a question of fact. The court will consider:

- the degree to which the person had control over the direction and movement of the vehicle;
- the length of time the person had control;
- the point at which the person stopped the driving; and
- the use of the vehicle's controls by the person in order to direct its movement.

Attempting to drive is not defined by statute, but the general principles of attempting should be applied and these are that an attempt is:

- the last action before the full offence is committed; and
- more than merely preparatory to the act (see 21.2.1).

For example, trying to drive a vehicle which has a fault and therefore will not start could be considered as attempting to drive.

19.2.4 Using, causing, and permitting use of, and keeping a vehicle

Many road traffic offences relating to vehicles can be committed not only by the people who use the vehicle (eg the driver), but also by people associated with the vehicle who may cause or permit its use (eg owners and people who hold supervisory responsibilities). You need to have a clear understanding about the meanings of these terms. We will illustrate the principles using an employer and employee as an example, but 'using', 'causing', and 'permitting' also occur in other circumstances, for example within families or between friends. It is also important to note that it will be for the courts to decide as a question of fact whether any of these offences has been committed in particular circumstances; the descriptions we provide here are only general guidelines.

Using a vehicle is not the same as driving a vehicle under road traffic law; for example, a vehicle can be 'in use' while parked, or while being towed. The user of a vehicle can be:

- the driver of a vehicle, including an employee driving a company vehicle for business purposes (the employee is likely to be held responsible if the vehicle was being used for purposes other than company business);
- the employer of the driver if the vehicle is a company vehicle used on company business (the employer can be held responsible for committing an offence relating to a vehicle defect even if he/she is unaware of the defect: in some circumstances, both the employer and the driver (an employee) can be held responsible);
- the owner of a vehicle driven by another person, but with the owner present and for the benefit of the owner; or
- a person steering the vehicle, for example when it is being towed.

Causing use of a vehicle must involve both of the following:

- The 'causer' must have the authority to make a subordinate carry out a particular action (eg the line manager of a transport company orders one of the company's drivers to make an urgent delivery using a particular company vehicle).
- The causer must also have knowledge about the unroadworthy state of that vehicle.

If either one of these elements cannot be proved, then 'causing' cannot be considered as an offence (although the 'use' of the vehicle might be considered as an alternative offence). In some cases, a company can be held responsible for causing the use of an unroadworthy vehicle if the company director knows the vehicle is defective. Also, note that if a person tows a vehicle, then this person is causing that vehicle to be used on a road.

Permitting use of a vehicle has two elements that must be satisfied. The 'permitter' must:

- be in a position to either allow or forbid its use—such permission can be given verbally, in writing or merely implied; and
- have knowledge of (or 'turn a blind eye' to) the unroadworthy state of the vehicle or its lack of documentation.

Therefore an offence is committed by an employer who knows about a defect on a company vehicle and allows an employee to use it for business purposes. However, many companies give a general permission to their employees to use company vehicles for private purposes and in such circumstances it is unlikely that the employer could be held responsible for permitting the vehicle to be used. If one of these elements cannot be proved, then the 'use' of the vehicle is an alternative to 'permitting the use' because there will be no requirement to prove the existence of a permission or knowledge of the defect.

Keeping a vehicle is when a person ('the keeper') has day-to-day responsibility for a vehicle. It is a question of fact for a court to decide who is a keeper as no legislative definition exists. The 'registered keeper', on the other hand, is the person to whom a vehicle is registered for the purposes of state records. Consequently a registered keeper may either be the keeper or he/she may not; (see *Mohindra v DPP* [2004] EWHC 490 (Admin)).

TASK 1 Imagine you are a police officer. You see a car being towed by a van. There is no one in the car and one wheel is not turning. You stop both vehicles and examine the car briefly. It appears to have many defects (apart from the wheel that won't turn), including steering defects, and the engine will not start.

What offence is the van driver committing in relation to the presence of an unroadworthy vehicle on a road and what evidence will you need to prove the offence?

19.3 Vehicle and Driver Documents

Certain documents and licences are required for the use of vehicles. Some of these relate to the driver while others relate to the vehicle. Here we consider driving licences, insurance arrangements and insurance certificates, MOT certificates, vehicle registration documents, and vehicle excise duty ('road tax'). We also describe some of the offences that are committed if the documents are not held in accordance with legislative requirements.

19.3.1 Driving licences

Over the years, the government has introduced new policies and procedures (eg updated driving tests and compulsory basic training for motorcyclists) with the aim of improving driving standards. A driver who has passed the relevant test for a category of vehicle will have a full licence for that category. A driver who is learning to drive a certain category of vehicle must have the relevant provisional licence before going on the road (see 19.3.1.4). Full details of driving licences, including the meaning of the various symbols and codes are available on the www.gov.uk website.

Offences relating to driving licences under the Road Traffic Act 1988 include:

- driving a motor vehicle on a road otherwise than in accordance with a licence authorizing him/her to drive a motor vehicle of that class (s 87(1));
- causing or permitting another person to drive on a road if that other person does not have a licence authorizing him/her to drive a motor vehicle of that class (s 87(2)); and
- failure to update a change of address on a driving licence (s 99(5)).

19.3.1.1 Vehicle categories and codes used on driving licences

The table shows the vehicle categories and age requirements for driving particular categories of vehicle. Some of the motorcycle categories were changed or discontinued after 19 January 2013 (marked with an asterisk). The new categories for motorcycles are shown in the second table. The older categories will of course still appear on older licences.

Licence category	Type of vehicle	Minimum age
A1*	Light motorcycles with an engine size of up to 125cc and a power output of up to 11 kW (14.6 bhp)	17
A*	Medium-sized motorcycles up to 25 kW (33 bhp) and a power-to-weight ratio up to 0.16 kW/kg (with or without a side-car)	17
	Large motorcycles (over 25 kW (33 bhp) and a power-to-weight ratio over 0.16 kW/kg)	19
B	Cars and light vans	17
B1*	Motor tricycles, quadricycles, and other three- or four-wheeled vehicles with an unladen weight no more than 550 kg	17
C1	Vehicles weighing between 3500 kg and 7500 kg, (with or without a trailer; 750 kg maximum trailer weight)	18
C	Vehicles over 3500 kg, with a trailer up to 750 kg	21
D	Passenger-carrying vehicles with 9 to 16 passenger seats	21
F	Agricultural tractors	17
G	Road rollers	21
H	Tracked vehicles	21
K	Mowing machines or pedestrian-controlled vehicles	16
P*	Mopeds with an engine size of up to 50cc and a maximum speed of up to 50 kph	16

The second table shows the age requirements for the new bike categories, ages, and licence requirements that have applied since 19 January 2013. The requirements for obtaining a motorcycle licence are complex, but all require a practical test on the relevant category of machine, and the majority require CBT (Compulsory Basic Training). We provide a summary of the requirements here, but see also 'The Routes to your motorcycle licence' flowchart available on the www.gov.uk website. Note that the requirements for category A may be subject to change between now and 2018.

Licence category	Type of motorbike	Requirements for licence in addition to a practical test	Minimum age
AM	Mopeds with speed range of 25–45 km/h Small 3-wheelers (up to 50 cc and below 4 kW) Light quadricycles (under 350 kg, top speed 45 km/h)	CBT, theory test	16
Q	As for AM plus 2- or 3-wheeled mopeds with top speed of 25 km/h		
A1	Small motorbikes up to 11 kW and 125cc (power-to-weight ratio not more than 0.1 kW per kg)	CBT, theory test	17
	Motor tricycles with a power output 15 kW or less		
A2	Medium motorbikes up to 35 kW (power-to-weight ratio not more than 0.2 kW per kg). Must not be derived from vehicle more than twice its power	Direct access—CBT, theory test	19
		Staged access—A1 licence held, but if for less than 2 years, theory test needed too	
A	Motorbikes, unlimited size/power, with or without a side-car Motor tricycles with power output over 15 kW	Direct access—CBT, theory test	24
		Staged access route—A2 licence held for a minimum of 2 years	21

Drivers of mini-motos (miniature motorbikes) and go-peds (petrol-driven scooters) do not require a driving licence because these vehicles do not fit any of the vehicle categories for driving licences. An electrically assisted pedal cycle is classified as a pedal cycle (see 19.2.1) so a driving licence is not required. Similar exemptions are made for powered wheelchairs and powered scooters designed for people with disabilities.

19.3.1.2   **The driver number**

The driver number contains information about the driver. The information can be seen as three clusters which provide information on the holder's:

- family name (five characters);
- gender and date of birth (six numbers); and
- initials.

How to interpret the driver number	
The Driver Number is:	MORGA 657054 SM9IJ
The first cluster is the first five letters of the family name:	If the name has less than five characters the remaining spaces will be made up using the figure 9
The first and last digits of the DoB cluster are derived from the year of birth:	657054 shows the year of birth is 1964
The second and third digits represent the month of birth and the gender of the licence holder:	657054 shows this person was born in July and is female. For women, 5 is added to the second digit so for a male born in July the number would be 607054, and for a female born in December, it would be 662054
The fourth and fifth digits show the day of birth:	657054 shows that the date of birth was the 5th of the month
The first two characters of the final cluster represent the person's initials:	MORGA 657054 SM9IJ (if there is only one initial, 9 is used in place of a second initial)
The following number and the final two letters are computer-generated and are used to avoid duplicate records:	MORGA 657054 SM9IJ

Specific Incidents

19.3.1.3 **The driving licence photocard and counterpart**

Driving licences are made up of two parts: the photocard and the counterpart. Both parts store the essential information relating to the driver and the vehicles he/she is licensed to drive. The photocard has to be renewed every ten years when the photo expires.

Photocard licences are about the size of a credit card, and are pink for a full licence and green for a provisional licence. A new type of card has been issued since 19 January 2013 to meet the European Union Third Directive. The layout is similar to the old cards, but the new cards have new security features such as tactile (raised) surfaces, tactile engraved text, changing colours, as well as complex background designs.

The annotated diagram shows one of the older type photocards. The new-style photocard is shown below. The front of the old-style photocard shows:

- the holder's family name and first names (items 1 and 2);
- the holder's date and place of birth (item 3);
- the licence issue date and the issuing authority (items 4a and 4c);
- the photo expiry date (item 4b);
- the driver number (item 5);
- the holder's photo (in black and white for more recent cards, and in colour for older cards);
- the holder's signature and address (items 7 and 8); and
- the entitlement categories (item 9).
- feature 10 is similar to a hologram but clearer as it has definite lines and brilliant colours. It contains a steering wheel that appears to turn as the card is tilted in different directions;
- feature 11a is an image that changes when the licence is tilted. On a full licence it is a blue road sign or a black triangle, and on provisional licences it is a red road sign or a black triangle;
- feature 11b also changes on tilting and shows the last five characters of the driver number or the photo expiry date (month and year).

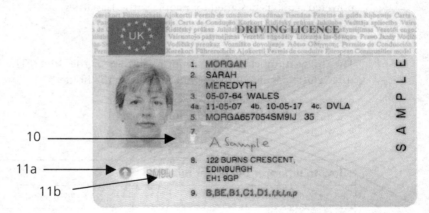

The new-style cards differ slightly in that the dates are shown as DD.MM.YYYY, the vehicle categories in item 9 are separated by slashes rather than by commas, and the date in 4b shows the licence expiry date (rather than the photo expiry date).

The reverse of the old-style photocard shows the licence categories with pictograms (column 9), and the start and finish dates periods for each category (columns 10 and 11). Column 12 of the older style cards shows any restrictions that apply to the adjoining categories; code 101 means the licence holder cannot drive that category of vehicle for hire or reward. On the new-style card (the second image) a full table is shown, including categories that do not apply for that driver. A legend explains the contents of each field, and a space in the bottom left corner shows the restriction codes and any extra information Both types of card show a unique identifier code indicated with an arrow. The old-style card has an image of a steering wheel as a security feature (this changes from green to gold when the licence is tilted).

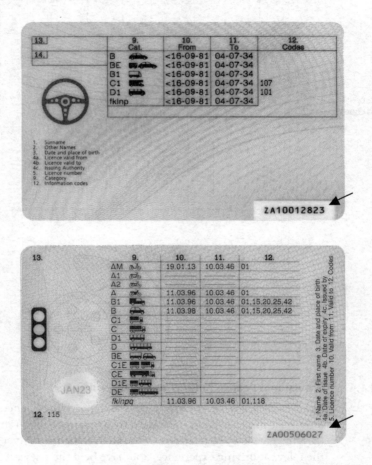

The counterpart is a paper document showing additional information, such as the vehicle categories the holder is entitled to drive provisionally, the entitlement history (superseded categories), and any endorsements. It is pink for a full licence and green for a provisional licence (as for the photocard).

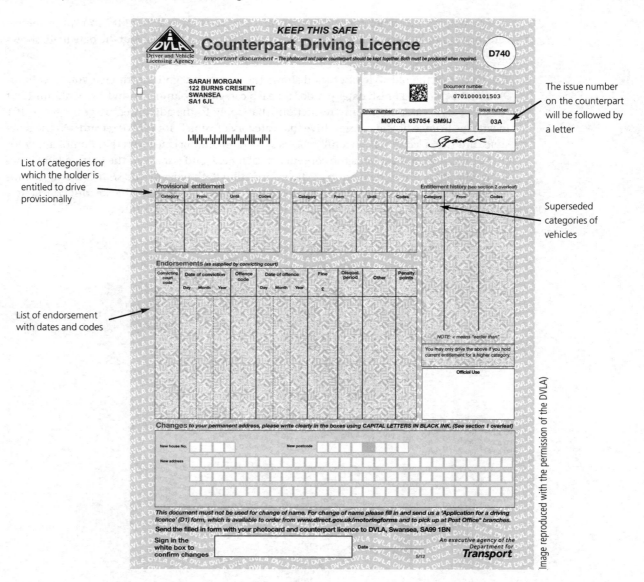

List of categories for which the holder is entitled to drive provisionally

List of endorsement with dates and codes

The issue number on the counterpart will be followed by a letter

Superseded categories of vehicles

Image reproduced with the permission of the DVLA)

19.3.1.4 Provisional licence holders and learner drivers

Apart from a few exceptions, a provisional driving-licence holder must not drive a vehicle unless accompanied and supervised by a 'qualified driver' (reg 16(2)(a) of the Motor Vehicles (Driving Licences) Regulations 1999). Such a qualified driver must be at least 21 years old, have the relevant driving experience, and have held the relevant licence for at least three years (reg 17(1) and (2) of the Motor Vehicles (Driving Licences) Regulations 1999). The licence must be a full British (including Northern Ireland) or a Community (EC) licence.

There are exceptions in relation to the requirement for supervision. It is not required when:

- driving a motor vehicle of certain categories: for example, three-wheeled vehicles;
- riding a moped, or a motorcycle (with or without a side-car);
- driving a motor vehicle on an exempted island (except large goods vehicles and passenger-carrying vehicles); or
- driving a motor vehicle having just passed a test (but he/she must have a certificate authorizing him/her to drive the respective class of vehicle).

'L' plates must be displayed on front and back of the vehicle while it is being driven by a provisional driving-licence holder in England. The plates must be clearly visible to other road users within a reasonable distance. Details are provided in reg 16(2)(b) of the Motor Vehicles (Driving Licences) Regulations 1999. The appropriate sizes and measurements of an 'L' plate are shown in the diagram. The corners can be rounded, but the dimensions of the 'L' plate must be as shown. 'D' plates can be displayed in Wales, but if driven in England these must be replaced with 'L' plates.

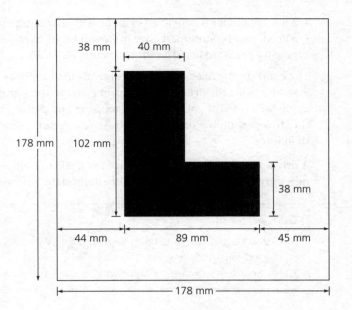

A provisional driving-licence holder must not drive a vehicle with a trailer (reg 16(2)(c) of the Motor Vehicles (Driving Licences) Regulations 1999). There are obvious exceptions, for example learner drivers for articulated lorries. A breach of any of the requirements relating to a provisional licence (outlined earlier) will be driving otherwise than in accordance with a driving licence (s 87(1) of the Road Traffic Act 1988).

19.3.1.5   Disqualification or revocation of a driving licence

Disqualification can occur in a number of different ways, as shown in the table.

Main ways in which a driver may be disqualified

Endorsement and penalty points	Penalty points are awarded according to the type and seriousness of the offence and are endorsed on the driving licence. When 12 points have been accumulated ('totted up') in a three-year period, the driver is disqualified
Discretionary disqualification	This is the penalty for certain offences including 'failing to stop after an accident' (see 19.7.2). The court may disqualify for a period of its choosing (but not for an indefinite period)
Obligatory disqualification	The Road Traffic Act 1988 sets out minimum periods of compulsory disqualification for certain offences such as drink-driving. In some cases, the court can disqualify a person until he/she has retaken and passed the appropriate driving test again. In such a case, the driver will hold a provisional licence during the period leading up to the test. A failure to satisfy any of the requirements of a provisional licence (see 19.3.1.4) means the person will commit the offence of disqualified driving

A person is guilty of an offence under s 103(1) of the Road Traffic Act 1988 if, while disqualified from holding or obtaining a licence, he/she obtains a licence (s 103(1)(a)) or drives a motor vehicle on a road (s 103(1)(b)). Admissible evidence of the original disqualification must be provided to the court (see *Mills v DPP* [2008] EWHC 3304 (Admin)). This could be:

• a certificate of conviction under s 73 of the PACE Act 1984;
• the defendant's admission (at interview or in court); or
• evidence of a person who was in court when the original disqualification was imposed.

These offences are triable summarily. The penalty for obtaining a licence while disqualified is a fine, and for driving a motor vehicle on a road while disqualified imprisonment for up to six months and/or a fine, discretionary extension of the disqualification, and obligatory endorsement (six penalty points).

Revocation is when a new driver's licence is cancelled within two years of passing his/her test on the first occasion. It was introduced (in the Road Traffic (New Drivers) Act 1995) with the intention of reducing the number of road accidents involving inexperienced and newly qualified drivers. A licence may be revoked when:

Specific Incidents

- a licence holder is convicted of an offence involving obligatory endorsement (s 2(1)(b)); or
- a licence and counterpart have been sent to the fixed-penalty clerk, and there are six or more penalty points to be taken into account (s 2(1)(d)).

The court (or the fixed-penalty clerk) sends the licence and the counterpart to the Secretary of State to revoke the licence. The driver reverts to the status of a learner driver, and will have to apply for a provisional licence. On retaking and passing the driving test again there is no further two-year probationary period (s 7), so a person cannot have his/her licence revoked more than once.

A driver who has had his/her licence revoked commits an offence if he/she drives without a new provisional licence, 'L' plates, or appropriate supervision (see 19.3.1.4).

TASK 2

1. How could a disqualified driver or 'new driver' with a revoked licence conceal the fact that he/she is disqualified?
2. How could a police officer on patrol check whether a person is disqualified?

19.3.2 Insurance

All users of cars, motorcycles, and other vehicles are required by law to have third-party insurance as a minimum level of cover. Additions such as cover for fire and theft of the vehicle are made at the discretion of the insured person, as is fully comprehensive insurance. Comprehensive insurance covers damage to the insured and his/her vehicle, as well as proving cover for third parties, fire, and theft.

There are over 50 companies in the UK offering insurance to drivers. An insured driver will receive a certificate of insurance from the company, and this will include at least the following features:

Insurance Company Name and Address:
AAA Insurance Ltd.
The High Street
Maidbury MB1 1AB

Registration Number: AA 00 AAA

Certificate number: 000/999/123
Policyholder's name: Orlando SMITH Expiry date: Noon 16th April 2014

Permitted Drivers: Verity SMITH, Noah KAY
Limitations as to use: Use for social, domestic, and pleasure purposes, including travel between the driver's home and place of work.

(The policyholder and any 'permitted drivers' must have a licence to drive the vehicle and must not be disqualified from driving it.)

19.3.2.1 Vehicles without adequate insurance cover

Third-party motor insurance is the minimum level of insurance allowed and guarantees that injuries or damage to third parties can be compensated. Third parties include passengers in the user's car and other people's property (damaged due to an accident caused by the insured person).

Section 143(1) and (2) of the Road Traffic Act 1988 states that:

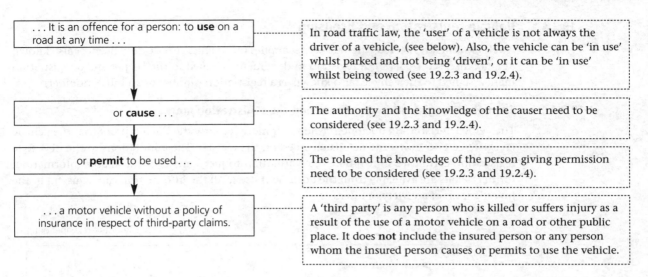

There are a number of exceptions to this offence which, if produced, must be substantiated. These exceptions include vehicles:

- kept by the registered keeper, but not on a road or other public place;
- not kept by the registered keeper at the relevant time, for example whilst lent to another person;
- that have been stolen and not recovered before the relevant time;
- driven by an owner who has deposited £500,000 with the Accountant General; or
- owned by authorities (such as councils, police authorities, the NHS, Army, or Air Force).

It is a defence (s 143(3) of the Road Traffic Act 1988) if it can be proved that the user did not own the vehicle, nor had he/she hired it, or if he/she was acting in the course of her/his employment and had no reason to believe that the vehicle was not properly insured (an employee is unlikely to know about his/her employer's insurance arrangements).

If a vehicle is not properly insured, the person named as its registered keeper on the vehicle's registration document (see 19.3.4) is also guilty of an offence (s 144A of the Road Traffic Act 1988). A vehicle without adequate insurance can be seized under s 165A of the Road Traffic Act 1988. Details of the procedure are described in 19.4.3.

19.3.3 MOT test certificates

Certain categories of vehicle must have passed an MOT test if they are to be used on the road (s 47 of the Road Traffic Act). The following vehicles must be submitted for annual tests from the third anniversary of their registration (s 47(2)):

- passenger vehicles with up to eight passenger seats, for example family cars;
- rigid goods motor cars (unladen weight not exceeding 1,525 kg), for example small vans;
- dual-purpose vehicles, for example pick-up trucks;
- motorcycles (including three-wheelers and mopeds); and
- motor caravans (motorhomes).

However, other categories of vehicle must be submitted for annual testing from the first anniversary of their registration (s 47(3)). This includes taxis licensed to ply for hire, ambulances, and vehicles with more than eight passenger seats.

When the vehicle is used on a road in the UK or elsewhere before it is registered in the UK, then a test certificate must be obtained three years from the date of manufacture. The date of manufacture of a vehicle is taken to be the last day of the year during which its final assembly was completed. This is relevant for people moving to the UK from abroad and bringing a vehicle.

It is an offence under s 47 for a person at any time to use (or cause or permit to be used) a motor vehicle on a road without a test certificate apart from:

- being driven to a pre-arranged MOT test;
- being driven from a failed MOT test to a garage for repairs by previous arrangement (reg 6(2)(a)(i) of the Motor Vehicle (Test) Regulations 1981); or
- towing it to a place where the vehicle is to be broken up for scrap (reg 6(2)(a)(iii)(B)).

19.3.4 Vehicle registration and licensing

A vehicle is first registered when its keeper applies for a vehicle excise duty licence (also known as a tax disc, see 19.3.4.2). A registration document is issued to the keeper and a registration mark assigned to the vehicle (also known as a registration number or an index number).

19.3.4.1 The vehicle registration document and the registration mark

The vehicle registration document (the V5 or more recently the V5C) is proof that the vehicle is registered and shows the details recorded on the register. The annotations to the new style registration certificate shown here draw attention to just some of the available information; further details are available from the document itself. All the information can be useful in the investigation of a variety of offences.

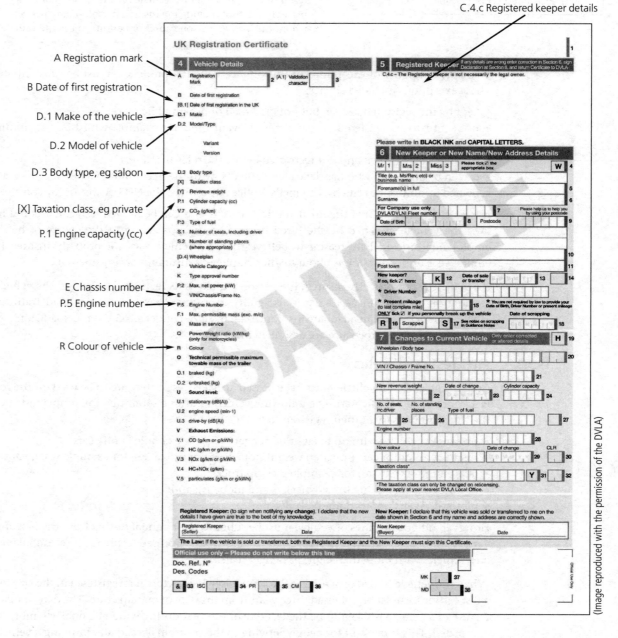

(Image reproduced with the permission of the DVLA)

A vehicle is not properly registered if any of the particulars recorded in the register are incorrect or incomplete. Defences for using a vehicle that is not properly registered include that no reasonable opportunity was given to supply the name and address of the registered keeper (eg if the road purchaser had only just bought the vehicle), or if there were reasonable grounds for believing that the recorded particulars were correct.

It is an offence to use a vehicle that is not properly registered on a road or in a public place (s 43C(1) of the Vehicle Excise and Registration Act 1994). Other offences related to registration documents include failure to notify the DVLA about the disposal of a vehicle, or a change of vehicle details. (Most of these offences will be committed under the Road Vehicles (Display of Registration Marks) Regulations 2001 and the Vehicle Excise and Registration Act 1994.)

The registration mark or index number is shown on the 'number plate' of a vehicle. This should use a standard font, and the font should not be customized in any way. These and further details on number plates may be found on the DVLA website.

Local memory tag denoting where a vehicle is first registered. AB refers to Peterborough.

Age identifier which changes twice yearly in March and September. The number 51 refers to September 2001.

Random letters which will never include I or Q and which uniquely define the vehicle.

(Image reproduced with the permission of the DVLA)

Offences relating to number plates (mostly under the Road Vehicles (Display of Registration Marks) Regulations 2001) include:

- no number plate or an obscured number plate;
- forgery of a number plate;
- incorrect fitting, number, or position of plates; and
- incorrect style, size, and spacing of characters.

These offences are all triable summarily.

19.3.4.2 Vehicle excise duty

Most vehicles used on a road are also subject to vehicle excise duty, otherwise known as road tax. This is also referred to as 'vehicle licensing' and is covered under s 1 of the Vehicle Excise and Registration Act 1994. There are a number of taxation classes such as 'bicycle' (ie two-wheeled motorcycle), private/light goods vehicles (PLG) such as family cars, buses, and heavy goods vehicles.

Exempted vehicles include goods and passenger vehicles being used for current commercial purposes, fire engines, ambulances, and vehicles for disabled people (s 5(2) of the Vehicle Excise and Registration Act 1994). The full list is available on the www.legislation.gov.uk website. Exempted vehicles are issued with a 'nil licence' and will still appear on the vehicle licensing register.

The vehicle excise duty licence is commonly known as a tax disc. At the time of writing, it had been announced that tax discs would be replaced with an electronic system beginning in October 2014.

The person keeping the vehicle (see 19.2.4) is responsible for arranging the purchase and display of the tax disc. It must be displayed in the vehicle so it is clearly visible in daylight from the nearside of the road (reg 16 of the Road Vehicle (Registration and Licensing) Regulations 1971), and protected from the weather.

Required position of tax disc

Type of vehicle	Position for licence disc
Cars and most common vehicles	On or adjacent to the nearside
Other vehicles	On the nearside in front of the driver's seat, between 0.76 m and 1.8 m above the road surface.
Solo motorcycles, motor tricycles, and invalid vehicles	On the nearside in front of the driving seat
Motorcycle and side-car	On the nearside of the handlebars of the motorcycle or on the nearside of the side-car in front of the driving seat

Date of expiry

Registration/index mark

Make of vehicle

Weight/engine size/
number of seats
(no data shown on this example)

Period of duty (6 or
12 months)

Rate of duty

Class of vehicle

Issuing authority stamp

Image reproduced with the permission of the DVLA.

It is an offence under the Vehicle Excise and Registration Act 1994:

*   to use or keep an unlicensed vehicle on a public road (s 29(1));
*   to forge or fraudulently use, alter, lend a vehicle licence, or allow it to be used by another person (s 44(1)); or
*   to use or keep a vehicle on a public road without a vehicle licence on display in the manner prescribed earlier (s 33(1)).

A person 'keeps' a vehicle on a public road if he/she is not using it but causes it to be there for any period, however short (s 62 of the Vehicle Excise and Registration Act 1994), and see also 19.2.4 regarding the definition of the 'keeper'.

> **TASK 3** Imagine you are a trainee police officer and that while you are on Supervised Patrol in your BCU area, you see a vehicle not displaying a licence.
>
> *   How could you report the user (or keeper) of the vehicle?
> *   What would you do if the driver or keeper of the vehicle is not present?
>
> What forms could be used for these processes?

19.4 Powers to Stop a Vehicle, Examine Documents, and Seize a Vehicle

Whilst on foot or mobile patrol a police officer may need to investigate offences connected with the use of a variety of vehicles on roads. These offences may relate to the way in which a vehicle has been driven (it might seem that a driver's ability has been impaired through drink or drugs), or the condition of a vehicle. Or the officer might suspect that the occupants of a vehicle have been involved in committing other offences using the vehicle, or he/she may wish to speak to them about other matters. For whatever reason, if a vehicle is in motion on a road, the officer will need to stop it safely in order to speak to the people inside.

19.4.1 Police powers to stop a vehicle

The power to stop a mechanically propelled vehicle on a road is provided in s 163 of the Road Traffic Act 1988 and does not require any form of suspicion or authorization to be used. The police officer must be on duty in full uniform, and give a clear direction to the driver (whether from a police vehicle or while on foot patrol). The drive commits a summary offence if he/she fails to comply, and the penalty is a fine. A power of entry into premises in order to arrest a person for this offence is provided in s 17 of the PACE Act 1984 (see 9.5.1.2).

19.4.2 Requesting documents and information from drivers

A police officer can request a 'driver' to produce certain documents or provide information in relation to his/her status as a driver and the vehicle.

Here, a 'driver' is:

- any person driving a motor vehicle on a road;
- any person the officer has reasonable cause to believe was driving a motor vehicle on a road at the time it was involved in an accident; or
- any person who the officer has reasonable cause to believe has committed an offence in relation to the use of a motor vehicle on a road, for example 'quitting' (see 19.5.2.3).

19.4.2.1 Requiring to see documents

A police officer can request a driver to produce the following documents:

- his/her driving licence (photocard and counterpart) (s 164(1));
- an appropriate insurance certificate (s 165(1));
- the vehicle's MOT test certificate (s 165(1)); and/or
- CBT certificate (motorcyclists only) (s 164(4A)).

The requirement to produce a licence also applies to a person supervising a provisional-licence holder who is a 'driver' in any of the three circumstances listed at the start of 19.4.2 (s 164(1)(d)).

TASK 4

1. What form would a police officer need to use to request a person to produce his/her driving licence within seven days?
2. What problems might there be in establishing the person's true identity?
3. What extra checks could a police officer carry out to make sure he/has been given the person's real name and address?

A police officer can also request any person using a registered vehicle (see 19.2.4) to produce the vehicle's registration document (s 28A(1) of the Vehicle Excise and Registration Act 1994).

19.4.2.2 Requesting information from a driver

A police officer may require a 'driver' (see 19.4.2) to state his/her date of birth (s 164(2)) if he/she:

- has failed to produce his/her licence;
- has produced a licence that is unsatisfactory (eg it seems to have been altered or if it contains information that seems incorrect); and/or
- is the supervisor of a learner driver at the time of an accident or an offence, and there is reason to suspect that he/she (the supervisor) is under 21 years of age.

If the insurance or MOT certificate are not produced when required (see 19.4.2.1), a police officer can require the person to state his/her name and address and the name and address of the owner of the vehicle (s 165(1) of the Road Traffic Act 1988).

For drivers of mechanically propelled vehicles and pedal cyclists suspected of dangerous, careless, or inconsiderate driving or cycling (ss 2, 3, 28, and 29; see 19.8 onwards) there is a separate offence (under s 168) of failing to provide his/her name and address to any person having reasonable grounds (including a police officer) for requiring them.

19.4.2.3 Offences relating to failing to produce documents or provide information

Under the Road Traffic Act 1988 it is a summary offence for a person to fail when required to:

Specific Incidents

- produce his/her licence and its counterpart or state his/her date of birth (s 164(6));
- produce his/her CBT certificate (motorcyclists only) (s 164(6));
- state his/her name and address and the name and address of the owner of the vehicle (s 165(3));
- produce a certificate of insurance or an MOT certificate (s 165(3)).

The failure to produce the registration document when required is an offence under s 28A(3) of the Vehicle Excise and Registration Act 1994 (except when the vehicle is subject to a lease or hire agreement).

However, a person will not be prosecuted for failing to produce a document if the relevant document or information can be produced within certain time limits. The time limits are as follows:

- within seven days in person at a police station (specified by the driver at the time of the request);
- as soon as reasonably practicable (a question of fact for a court to decide); or
- at a later time if the driver can prove it was not reasonably practicable to do so before the day on which written charge proceedings were commenced).

Insurers can provide insurance certificates electronically, for example by email or via a website (s 147 of the Road Traffic Act 1988). An insured driver who is required to produce his/her insurance certificate can use such an electronic version to provide electronic access or to produce legible printed copies (s 165(2A)).

19.4.3 Seizing a vehicle

Under s 165A of the Road Traffic Act 1988, a police officer has the power to seize a vehicle if he/she has reasonable grounds for believing that the driver does not have a suitable licence or that the vehicle is not adequately insured. Around 1,500 uninsured vehicles are seized by police every week (Directgov, 2011).

To seize a vehicle a police officer must be in uniform and have requested to see the relevant documents. He/she must also warn the driver that the vehicle will be seized unless the documents are produced immediately. (However, if it is impractical to warn the driver then a warning is not required (s 165A(6)).)

If the driver has failed to stop or has driven off, the vehicle may be seized at any time in the 24-hour period following the incident. In order to seize a vehicle a police officer may enter premises (other than a private dwelling-house) if he/she has reasonable grounds for believing the vehicle to be present. Reasonable force may be used if necessary. Note that a private dwelling-house does not include any outbuildings or adjacent land, so vehicles can be seized from areas such as driveways and garages.

TASK 5 Imagine you are a police officer. You stop a vehicle using your powers under the Road Traffic Act 1988. The driver is very young and the vehicle is large and looks powerful. You establish from the Police National Computer that the vehicle he is driving has a large engine capacity.

- What questions would you put to him about his insurance policy?
- How would you check that the insurance company has been notified of the large engine capacity, and that the insurance cover is adequate?

TASK 6

Imagine you are a police officer. Whilst on Independent Patrol you have stopped a vehicle using your powers under the Road Traffic Act 1988 and have asked the driver to produce a valid test certificate.

- How will you establish the date of first registration of a UK-registered vehicle?
- If the driver does not have a valid test certificate, what questions will you put to the driver to negate any defences?

19.5   **Construction and Use of Vehicles**

The responsibility to prevent crime not only applies to preventing crimes associated with theft or violence; criminal acts can also be committed by people driving motor vehicles on the road, and the potential to cause danger to other road users is very high. There is also the responsibility to 'pursue and bring to justice those who break the law', and 'protect, help and reassure the community'. Police officers are therefore involved with investigating offences relating to the use of vehicles, and also contribute to road-safety campaigns.

Under s 67 of the Road Traffic Act 1988 a police officer will be designated as an authorized vehicle examiner by his/her chief officer of police. An examiner is authorized to test a vehicle (and drawn trailer) on a road for the purposes of ascertaining compliance with requirements relating to the vehicle's construction and use (including lighting) and its condition (if used on the road), so that it is not a danger to any person.

19.5.1   **Tyres**

The component parts of a tyre profile are shown in the diagram.

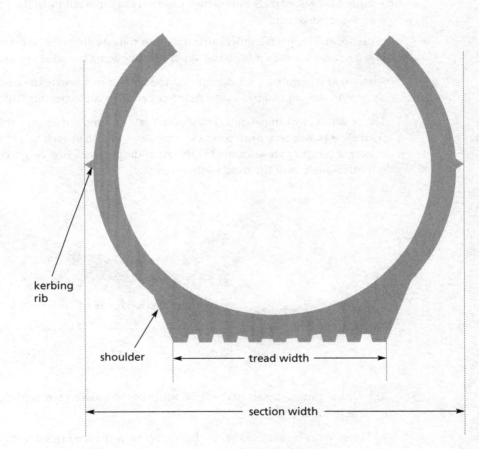

For use as evidence all the identifying codes and features on the wall of a tyre should be noted, including serial numbers and characters relating to the type of tyre. Full details of the meaning of the letters and number refers can be found at <http://www.blackcircles.com/general/sidewall>.

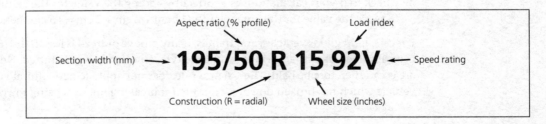

Specific Incidents

19.5.1.1   **Offences relating to the condition and maintenance of tyres**

Regulation 27 of the Road Vehicle Construction and Use Regulations 1986 describes a range of tyre problems relating to tyre condition and the circumstances in which they are being used. These regulations only apply to vehicles and trailers used on roads with pneumatic (inflatable) tyres.

Tyres must be correctly **maintained** and inflated to the correct pressure for the purpose so they are fit for the use to which the vehicle or trailer is being put. They must not have defects which might cause damage to the road surface or persons in the vehicle or road.

The tyre must be the correct type for the vehicle (taking into account the type of tyres fitted to the other wheels) and for the road conditions or purpose. (This does not apply for agricultural motor vehicles with a maximum speed of 20 mph.)

Tyres must not have damage such as:

• cuts in excess of 25 mm or 10 per cent of the section width of the tyre (whichever is the greater), measured in any direction on the outside of the tyre, and deep enough to reach the ply or cord;
• lumps, bulges, or tears caused by separation or partial failure of the structure;
• exposed ply or cord.

(This does not apply for agricultural trailers or trailed appliances; for vehicles that have broken down or are en route for breaking up; or vehicles being towed at not more than 20 mph.)

Some wear is permitted, for example on the tyres of cars, where the base of the grooves which showed in the original tread pattern are not clearly visible creating 'bald' patches.

The position of worn patches is significant. For cars and passenger vehicles carrying no more than eight passengers, worn patches on the outer eighth of each side of the tread width do not matter unless they are associated with cuts or deeper wear. However, worn patches on the central three-quarters of the tread width do matter.

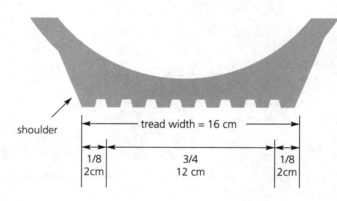

The central three-quarters of the tread width of the unworn tyre in the diagram, can be calculated as follows:

1. Measure the breadth of the tyre in contact with the road (total width = 16 cm).
2. Obtain the width of the central three-quarters of the tyre by dividing the total width by 4, then multiplying by 3 (16 cm/4 = 4 cm, and then 4 cm × 3 = 12 cm).
3. Obtain the width of each of the two outer eighths of the tyre by dividing the total width by 8 (16 cm/8 = 2 cm).
4. Check that your calculations are correct by adding the value for the central three-quarters to twice the value for the outer eighth (12 cm + 2 cm + 2 cm = 16 cm, hence correct).

For cars, light goods vehicles, and trailers, if any groove or tread is less than 1.6 mm deep in the central three-quarters anywhere round the tyre, an offence is committed. Note that the outer areas can therefore be bald. The 1.6 mm rule does not apply to agricultural vehicles, or to any vehicle which has broken down, is en route for breaking up, or is being towed at a maximum speed of 20 mph. For other types of vehicle (such as motorcycles, larger passenger vehicles, and larger goods vehicles) the groove depth over the central three-quarters of the tread must be at least 1.0 mm. Note that the tyres for some vehicles, such as motorcycles, are manufactured with no grooves or tread on the outer eighths of the tread width.

19.5.2 Lights on vehicles

The importance of lights could be underestimated, particularly when compared with incidents involving violent criminal activity. However, the position, style, maintenance, and colour of vehicle lights are all very important for road safety. Police responsibilities include identifying vehicles with faulty lights, testing and inspecting lights, and bringing the faults to the attention of the owner and/or driver.

Drivers are also expected to employ their lights with consideration towards other road users. Police officers can offer advice to drivers about how they use their vehicles' lights; for example, lights should not cause undue dazzle or discomfort to other persons using the road.

The following information relates in part to the Road Vehicles Lighting Regulations 1989. To help explain the extensive lighting regulations, a family car has been chosen as an example to illustrate the two main categories of lights on vehicles: obligatory lights (must be fitted and maintained), and optional lights.

> **TASK 7** List all the types of light that you think are obligatory for a car. Then compare your list with the list in 19.5.2.1 (no peeping!).

19.5.2.1 Obligatory lights

On the front of a car front-position lights ('side lights'), dipped, and main-beam headlights, and direction indicators are all obligatory. On the back of the car position lights, direction indicators, stop lights (brake lights), fog lights, a registration-plate lamp, and a rear reflector (not strictly a light) are obligatory. A 'hazard warning-signal device' to operate the direction indicator lights on the front and back of the car is also obligatory.

These obligatory lights are often clustered under a plastic or glass cover: some typical arrangements are shown in the photographs, but there is significant variation between makes and models of cars.

Position lights must be present on all four corners of a vehicle, to indicate the vehicle's presence and width to other road users. The front position lights (also known as side lights) are white and not particularly bright, and are often switched on by the first click of the switch near the steering wheel. The back position lights (also known as tail lights) are red, and are operated by the same switch as the front position lights. They are less bright than brake lights.

Position lights must be lit when the vehicle is moving at night (between sunset and sunrise) and during the day if visibility is reduced. When a vehicle is parked on a road at night, the position lights must be illuminated, unless it is parked with its nearside against the nearside kerb on a 30-mph road with street lighting (and see 19.5.2.4).

Dipped-beam headlamps are powerful white lights at the front of the car. They illuminate the road ahead, but should shine downward and to the left to avoid dazzling drivers of oncoming vehicles. The headlights are often switched on with two clicks of the light switch. They must be lit when the car is being driven during hours of darkness, except on a 30-mph road with street lighting or if the vehicle's fog lights are illuminated. They should also be used during the day in seriously reduced visibility. The headlights do not need to be illuminated if the car is being towed.

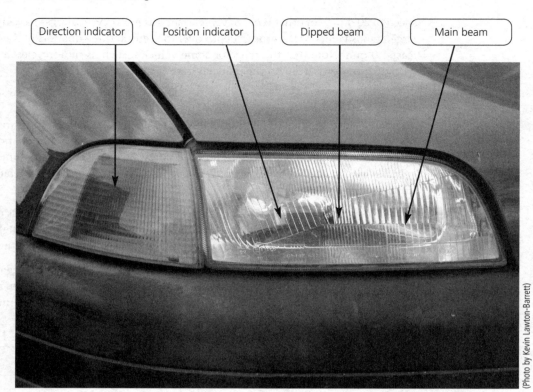

Direction indicator | Position indicator | Dipped beam | Main beam

(Photo by Kevin Lawton-Barrett)

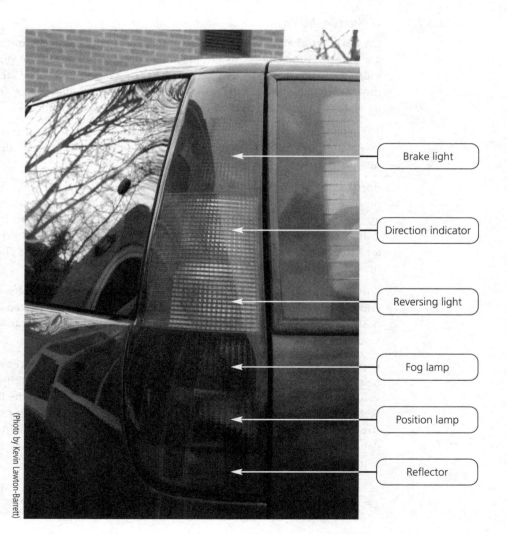

Brake light

Direction indicator

Reversing light

Fog lamp

Position lamp

Reflector

(Photo by Kevin Lawton-Barrett)

Specific Incidents

Main-beam headlights are very bright white lights at the front of the car which shine straight ahead to illuminate the road over a long distance. They are usually operated with a pull or push of a switch near the steering wheel when headlamps are already on. If front fog lamps are in use (in seriously reduced visibility), there is usually no need to use the main-beam headlights.

The main-beam headlight switch must be wired so that they can be 'deflected' by the driver in order to avoid dazzling oncoming traffic. This does not involve any movement in the headlamp unit; it switches on the dipped-beam headlights and switches off the main-beam headlights.

Direction indicators are found at each corner of the car (and sometimes at the sides) and are used to indicate to other road users that the driver is intending to move the car to the right or left. They must be amber and flash on and off between 60 and 120 times a minute. They are usually operated by pushing a switch near the steering column upwards or downwards, and there must be some sort of indicator near the driver to show that the direction indicators are 'on'.

The **rear registration-plate lamp** is a small white light at the rear shining on to the registration plate which automatically illuminates when the position indicator lights are switched on. It should not shine directly into the eyes of the driver of the vehicle behind.

Rear fog lamps are very bright red and are operated by an independent switch that will only work when the headlights are illuminated. They should be used only if visibility is reduced and do not need to be used when the car is towing a trailer.

Rear stop lamps are also known as brake lights and are very bright red. They are positioned at the rear corners of the car and must operate when the braking system (eg foot brake) of the car is applied. They warn other road users that the vehicle is slowing down or stopping.

Hazard warning signalling uses the same lamps as the direction indicators. It is controlled by a switching device that makes all the direction indicators flash at the same time. It operates automatically in some vehicles when the driver brakes hard. It should only be used:

- when the vehicle is stationary to alert other road users of the obstruction; or
- on a motorway or dual carriageway to warn drivers behind of an obstruction ahead; or
- by the driver of a bus to summon help; or
- by the driver of a bus when children under 16 are getting on or off.

The switch of this device must be in reach of the driver. The switch button surface often has a small triangle which will be illuminated when the hazard warning lights are switched on.

19.5.2.2   Optional lamps

Some optional lamps perform the same function as obligatory lights: for example, extra front-position lights (side lights), extra stop lamps, extra direction indicators, and extra dim/dipping and hazard warning devices. As they have the same functions as obligatory lights, they must be maintained and in full working order, just like the obligatory lights (which must still be fitted as described earlier).

Other optional lamps include lamps such as reversing lights and front fog lights. They are not obligatory in type so do not have to be maintained. They must not, however, be used in such a way that they cause undue dazzle or discomfort to other road users.

19.5.2.3   Sunrise, sunset, lighting-up times, and hours of darkness

To establish when position lamps or side lights must be illuminated, published sunrise and sunset times may be consulted. Police officers can use police databases (via the control room), but these times can also be found in diaries, the internet, or local publications such as newspapers.

Remember: Hours of Darkness for Dipped headlights

The 'hours of darkness' start half an hour after sunset and end half an hour before sunrise.

Remember: Sunset and Sunrise for Sidelights

Specific Incidents

19.5.2.4 Parking without lights between sunset and sunrise

Parking without lights of passenger vehicles other than buses, light goods vehicles, motorcycles, and invalid carriages is permitted between sunset and sunrise on a road with a speed limit of 30 mph or less. A vehicle must also be:

* in a designated parking area or lay-by;
* parked facing the right way and ten or more metres from a junction; or
* parked on a one-way street, facing the right way (on either side of the road).

19.5.2.5 Legitimate use of a vehicle with defective lights

A vehicle with defective lights may be driven in some circumstances without an offence being committed. This is only permitted during the day (between sunrise and sunset), and the lights must have become defective during that journey, or arrangements must have already been made to repair the fault (reg 23(3) of the Road Vehicles Lighting Regulations 1989).

Note that the examples given earlier relate only to a family car; other regulations apply to other forms of transport.

> **TASK 8** Consider each of the following statements in turn, and decide if each statement is true or false:
>
> 1. The term 'hours of darkness' refers to a period from half an hour after sunset to half an hour before sunrise.
> 2. The legislation that covers the use of lights on vehicles is the Road Vehicles (Construction and Use) Regulations 1986.
> 3. The permitted flash rate of an indicator lamp fitted to a vehicle is between 80 and 100 pulses per minute.
> 4. Hazard-warning signals on a vehicle may be used lawfully when the vehicle is being towed by another vehicle.
> 5. A defect occurring during a journey during daylight hours is a defence to a defective light fitted to a vehicle.
> 6. A reversing light is an optional lamp.
> 7. The term 'obligatory light' means a light that is required by the legislation to be fitted to a vehicle.

19.5.3 Danger of injury from the use of vehicles or trailers

A person is guilty of an offence under s 40A of the Road Traffic Act 1988 if he/she uses, causes, or permits another person to use a motor vehicle or trailer on a road when its use involves a danger of injury to any person because of:

* the condition of the motor vehicle or trailer (or of its accessories or equipment);
* the purpose for which it is used;
* the number of passengers carried by it or the manner in which they are carried; or
* the weight, position, or distribution of its load or the manner in which it is secured.

See 19.2.4 for an explanation of 'use, cause, or permit'. Details of the types of situation that could lead to injury or the danger of injury are listed in 19.5.3.1 and 19.5.3.2.

19.5.3.1 Poor maintenance and some associated offences

When considering the condition of a vehicle, a general rule is to consider how it was first constructed: this will be a guide to how it should be maintained. If a component part is missing or not working, an offence is likely to have been committed. Here we list just some of the offences that relate to poor maintenance of a vehicle:

* The wipers and washers (those that are required to be fitted) must be maintained in efficient working order and be properly adjusted (reg 34).
* An audible warning instrument (horn) must be fitted to any motor vehicle with a maximum speed of more than 20 mph (reg 37).
* The braking systems (including the handbrake) must be maintained in good working order and be properly adjusted (reg 18(1)).

- Exhaust systems and silencers must be maintained in good working order, and must not be altered to increase the noise made by escaping exhaust gases (reg 54).
- Motorcycle exhausts must be the correct type (only for a moped or motorbike first used after 1 January 1985, reg 579A(1) or (4)). The silencer should be either the original fitted by the manufacturer or an approved British Standard replacement. (A motorcycle should not be used on a road if its exhaust is marked 'not for road use' or similar.)
- Vehicle emissions must not contain any smoke, visible vapour, grit, sparks, ashes, cinders, or oily substance that causes (or is likely to cause) damage to property, or injury or danger to other road users (reg 61). Police forces sometimes have instruments to test vehicle emissions.

Using a vehicle in a dangerous condition (eg with jagged edges to bodywork) may lead to disqualification, and this will be obligatory if the offence is committed within three years of a previous conviction under s 40A of the Road Traffic Offenders Act 1988 (reg 100(1)).

19.5.3.2 Incorrect use of a vehicle and some associated offences

There are many ways in which a vehicle can be used incorrectly, and only a few of the more commonly encountered means are covered here, such as:

- Loads carried by a vehicle must not be a danger or nuisance to any person or property. The weight, packing, distribution, and adjustment of a load must be taken into account (reg 100(1)). The load carried by a motor vehicle or trailer must be secured if necessary, by physical restraint other than its own weight: for example, the luggage on the roof bars of a car must be tied down (reg 100(2)).
- Passenger numbers must not exceed the number that seats allow (reg 100(1) and (3)). For example, passengers must not be carried in the rear of a small van with no fixed seating.
- The horn (reg 99) must not be used when the vehicle is stationary (other than an emergency involving another vehicle, or when using a reversing or boarding-aid alarm). In addition, the horn must not be used by vehicles in motion on restricted roads between 2330 hours and 0700 hours.
- Excessive noise from motor vehicles on roads must be avoided by the exercise of reasonable care on the part of the driver (reg 97).

19.5.3.3 Stationary vehicles offences

The following practices must be observed, though exemptions apply to emergency services vehicles and to vehicles that need to keep the engine running, for example to power machinery (such as a crane) or to charge the battery. The engine must be turned off when the vehicle:

- is stationary for any length of time to prevent noise or exhaust emissions (reg 98). It is an offence to leave the engine running whilst stationary in a confined space with other vehicles.
- is unattended ('quitting') unless there is another person in the vehicle who is licensed to drive it (reg 107, and s 42 of the Road Traffic Act 1988). This would apply to a driver who parks outside a shop and runs inside to buy something. The parking brake must also be applied.

19.5.3.4 Head and eye protection for motorcyclists

Helmets or other suitable protective headgear must be worn by anyone driving or riding on a motor bicycle (defined in 19.2.1). It is an offence under s 16 of the Road Traffic Act 1988 to drive or ride on a road without such protection. Helmets must be securely fastened by straps or other fastening provided for that purpose, and an additional strap under the jaw must be used to secure a chin cup. The helmet must also bear a mark indicating compliance with the British Standard (BS 6658:1985) or the equivalent EU standard, or it must be of a type which seems likely to afford similar protection.

Helmets are not required for some people in some circumstances, such as:

- a person using a ride-on motor mower;
- turban-wearing followers of the Sikh religion, whilst on a two-wheeled motorcycle;
- riders or drivers of three-wheeled vehicles (unladen weight no more than 550 kg and at least 460 mm between the centre of contact of the rear wheels);
- passengers in a side-car; and
- any person pushing the two-wheeled motorcycle on foot.

Specific Incidents

Eye protection is not required to be used by law. However, if eye protection is used an offence is committed if it does not meet the British Standards EN 1938:1999 (s 18(3) of the Road Traffic Act 1988).

19.5.3.5 Seatbelts

The requirements for the use of seatbelts depend on the age of the person and where he/she is sitting (s 14(3) of the Road Traffic Act 1988). Details are shown in the following table (based on extracts from the Highway Code, 2004 and *Child Car Seats—The New Law 2006* available online). Note that there are a few very limited exceptions for children in taxis or the rear seats of family cars. In addition, some older cars such as classic cars may not have seatbelts fitted.

Seatbelt requirements

	Front seat	Rear seat	Who is responsible?
Driver	Must be worn if fitted	Not applicable	Driver
Babies and children up to 135 cm tall or 12 years	Correct child restraint must be used; this might employ an adult seatbelt as part of the restraining mechanism		Driver
Child 12–13 years, or under 12 years and over 135 cm tall	Adult seatbelt must be worn if fitted		Driver
Passenger over 14 years	Adult seatbelt must be worn if fitted		Passenger

Child restraints consist of four types as described in the following table:

	Child weight and age	Notes
Baby seats	Less than 13 kg (approx birth to 9–12 months)	Rear-facing
Child seats	Between 9–18 kg (approx 9 months to 4 years)	Forward-facing
Booster seats	Over 15 kg (approx 4 years and up)	May or may not have a back
Booster cushions	Over 22 kg (approx 6 years and up)	Do not normally have backs

In some situations a seatbelt does not have to be worn, such as:

- a driver engaged in deliveries (eg delivering post or newspapers) or collections;
- a driver reversing a vehicle, or supervising provisional-licence holders who are reversing a vehicle (or conducting a manoeuvre which includes reversing);
- an examiner conducting a driving test, if wearing the belt would be dangerous;
- people in vehicles being used for police purposes (force policy may vary in relation to people under arrest) and vehicles being used for fire brigade purposes;
- taxi drivers while 'plying for hire', answering calls for hire, or carrying passengers, and private-hire drivers while carrying passengers;
- people taking part in processions organized by, or on behalf of, the Crown;
- people holding a medical certificate exempting them from wearing a seatbelt (provided the certificate is produced at the time or within seven days) and disabled people wearing a disabled person's belt;
- the vehicle is driven under a trade licence for the purposes of investigating or remedying mechanical fault; or
- where the seatbelt is an inertia type which is locked as a result of being, or having been, on a steep incline.

19.5.4 Vehicle identification regulations

Under reg 67 all wheeled vehicles registered after 1 April 1980 should be equipped with a VIN plate in a conspicuous and readily accessible location (on a part not normally subject to replacement) which clearly shows the Vehicle Identification Number, the manufacturer, and type approval number (providing confirmation that the specifications (eg brakes and lights) meet UK standards). The VIN will also be stamped on the chassis or frame. The type approval number is sometimes on a separate plate. These identifying features can be matched against details on the PNC to help identify a suspected stolen vehicle (see 16.8.1).

> **TASK 9** Imagine you are a police officer. You suspect a particular vehicle has a number of serious defects so you signal to the driver to stop (using powers under the Road Traffic Act 1988).
>
> 1. In terms of health and safety, what factors must you consider?
> 2. What will you to say to the driver, and if you find a defect what will you do next?

19.6 Pedestrian Crossings and Road Signs

Over the years, the number of road signs and regulations in England and Wales has increased in an attempt to keep the road environment as safe as possible for all road users. These signs and regulations, however, are only of value if road users comply with them. Police officers, however, can do more than detect offences; they are also in a position to help the public develop their road-safety awareness.

19.6.1 Pedestrian crossings

The following table shows the key characteristics of the three main types of pedestrian crossing described in the Zebra, Pelican, and Puffin Pedestrian Crossings Regulations 1997.

Pelican	Pedestrians can push a button to operate traffic lights to bring vehicles to a stop. The traffic light sequence is the usual one except that, after the red light, the amber light flashes to indicate that vehicles may proceed, but only if the crossing is clear
Puffin	Sensors detect anyone waiting to cross and change the traffic lights accordingly for vehicles to stop. The traffic light signal is the same as regular traffic lights
Zebra	These are not supported by traffic lights. Pedestrians walk across a section of road indicated by alternate white and black stripes. Drivers and riders of vehicles are warned of the presence of a crossing by two black and white striped poles with yellow flashing beacons on top, on each pavement

19.6.1.1 Layout of crossings

The limits of crossings are by marked out by two parallel lines of studs across the carriageway.

The stop line for a Pelican or Puffin crossing is a solid white line across the road, just before the first line of studs. The give-way line at the start of a Zebra crossing is the same, apart from being a broken white line. Drivers and riders must not cross the stop or give-way line if pedestrians are on the crossing (or of course if the traffic lights are red for a Pelican or Puffin crossing).

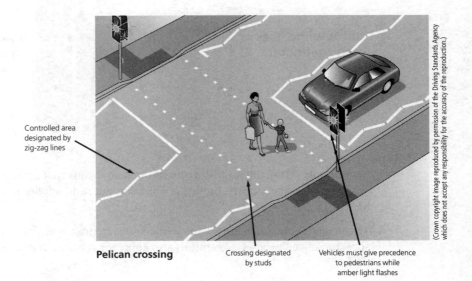

Controlled area designated by zig-zag lines

Pelican crossing

Crossing designated by studs

Vehicles must give precedence to pedestrians while amber light flashes

(Crown copyright image reproduced by permission of the Driving Standards Agency which does not accept any responsibility for the accuracy of the reproduction.)

Specific Incidents

The controlled area of a crossing is a certain length of road before and after a crossing. It is indicated by white zigzag lines painted along the edge and the middle of the road (between two and 18 zigzags, depending on the road layout in the immediate vicinity). It is an offence to park anywhere in the controlled area of a crossing. Overtaking in a controlled area when approaching a crossing is also an offence (but overtaking in the controlled area after a crossing is not).

Where there is a refuge for pedestrians or a central reservation on a zebra crossing, each part of the crossing is treated as a separate crossing.

19.6.1.2   The correct use of crossings

The regulations for the use of crossings are given in the Zebra, Pelican, and Puffin Pedestrian Crossings Regulations 1997. The regulations give rise to several offences which can be committed by the drivers or pedestrians. The offences listed are committed under the Zebra, Pelican, and Puffin Pedestrian Crossings Regulations 1997, s 25(5) of the Road Traffic Regulation Act 1984, and Sch 2 to the Road Traffic Offenders Act 1988. Many of the offences apply to all types of crossing, so the regulations relating to these are listed first.

1. Vehicles must not stop within the limits of any crossing, unless the way is blocked or it is necessary to avoid injury to persons or damage to property (reg 18).
2. Pedestrians must not delay on any crossing longer than is necessary to use the crossing in a reasonable time (reg 19).
3. Vehicles must not stop in the controlled area of any crossings (reg 20) unless it is to allow pedestrians to cross, to prevent injury or damage, to make a right or left turn, to carry out building work or maintenance of the road or crossing, or to remove obstructions from the road (regs 21 and 22). This does not apply to pedal cycles or public service vehicles, nor if the vehicle is beyond the driver's control.
4. Vehicles approaching any crossing must not overtake within the limits of the controlled area (reg 24).
5. Vehicles must stop at red/steady amber lights at Pelican or Puffin crossings (reg 23).
6. Pedestrians have precedence over vehicles at (or approaching) Pelican crossings when the amber light is flashing (reg 26).
7. Pedestrians have precedence over vehicles at (or approaching) Zebra crossings (reg 25).

19.6.2   White lines along the centre of the road

These are covered in reg 26 of the Traffic Signs Regulations and General Directions 2002. The lines may be continuous on both sides, or continuous on one side and broken on the other. The lines are used to indicate parts of the road where vehicles may not be permitted to stop, or to cross the lines:

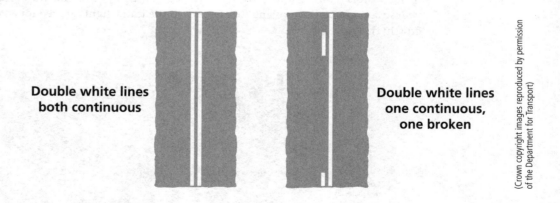

Double white lines both continuous

Double white lines one continuous, one broken

A continuous white line in the centre of the road means that no vehicle is permitted to stop. This applies to roads with a broken line on one side, and applies to vehicles on either side of the road (reg 26(2)(a)).

This regulation does not apply to dual carriageways, nor to vehicles used for fire brigade, ambulance, or police purposes. Exceptions also apply for vehicles that have stopped in order to:

- allow passengers to board/alight from a vehicle;
- allow goods to be loaded or unloaded from the vehicle;
- facilitate building or demolition work;
- enable the removal of any obstruction to traffic, road works, or public utility work; or
- avoid an accident.

Exceptions also apply for vehicles that are prevented from proceeding by circumstances outside the driver's control, or are required to stop by law or with the permission or direction of a constable in uniform or a traffic warden.

It is also an offence for a vehicle to cross or straddle a continuous line when the line is to the left of the broken line or another continuous line (reg 26(2)(b)). This does not apply when a vehicle is turning right, or passing a stationary vehicle, overtaking a pedal cycle, horse, or road-maintenance vehicle moving at a speed of 10 mph or less, when the action is unavoidable, or to avoid an accident or when complying with directions from a police officer or a traffic warden in uniform.

The offences relating to crossing white lines are committed under s 36(1) of the Road Traffic Act 1988, reg 10 of the Traffic Signs Regulations 2002, and Sch 2 to the Road Traffic Offenders Act 1988.

19.6.3 Disobeying a traffic sign

This is an offence only in relation to signs of the prescribed type (listed under reg 10 of the Traffic Signs Regulations and General Directions 2002) that have been lawfully placed on or near a road (s 36 of the Road Traffic Act 1988). Drivers are therefore under no obligation to heed informal signs erected by members of the public.

Regulation 10 of the Traffic Signs Regulations and General Directions 2002 creates two lists of relevance to s 36 of the Road Traffic Act 1988:

List 1: contravention of a List 1 sign is an offence under s 36 of the Road Traffic Act 1988.
List 2: contravention of a List 2 sign may lead to disqualification or endorsement of the driver's licence.

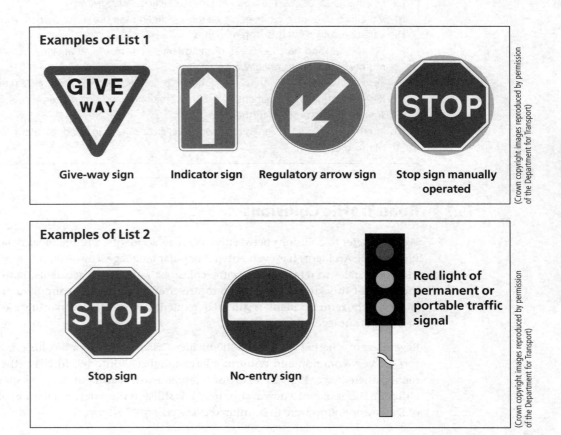

19.6.4 **School crossing patrols**

Local councils can designate places where children cross roads on their way to and from schools (or from one part of a school to another) as a 'patrolling place'. This is where a school crossing patrol (in uniform) can hold up a prescribed sign to stop traffic for a person to cross. This power is given under s 28 of the Road Traffic Regulations Act 1984 and states that if required to do so by a school crossing patrol, a vehicle must stop:

• before reaching the crossing place (so it does not impede people crossing the road (s 28(2) (a)); and
• for as long as the sign continues to be exhibited (s 28(2)(b)).

It is an offence to fail to comply to the requirements of a school crossing patrol or cause a vehicle to be put in motion whilst the sign is exhibited (s 28(3)). The offence is triable summarily and the penalty is a fine. The driver may also be disqualified.

TASK 10 For each of the following road traffic signs, find an image to show either the symbol for the sign or the sign as marked on the road surface itself.

1. Vehicular traffic entering the junction must give priority to vehicles from the right: for example, a mini-roundabout.
2. Priority is to be given to vehicles from the opposite direction.
3. Warning of a weak bridge.
4. Prohibition of vehicles exceeding a stated height.
5. Drivers of large or slow vehicles to stop and phone for permission to cross a level crossing.
6. Route for use by buses and pedal cycles only.
7. Route for tramcars only.
8. Stop sign, manually operated.
9. Convoy vehicle, no overtaking.
10. Stop for road works.
11. Vehicles to stay to the right of a vehicle involved with mobile road works.
12. Zigzag lines for an equestrian (horse) crossing (also called 'Pegasus') or Toucan crossing (crossing for pedestrian and cyclists to use together).
13. Line markings across a junction at which a vehicle must give way.
14. Variations of double white-line markings, including the use of hatched areas.
15. Variations of yellow bus-stop markings.
16. White lines and hatched areas dividing lanes or a main carriageway from a slip road (on motorways or dual carriageways).
17. Yellow grid markings within a box junction preventing entry without a clear exit.
18. Red-light signal of permanent/portable traffic signals and green filter arrows.
19. Tramcar not to proceed further.
20. Intermittent red-light signals at railway level crossings, swing bridges, etc.
21. Matrix prohibition.

19.7 Road Traffic Collisions

We often refer to collisions between vehicles as 'accidents' and the older police term RTA (for Road Traffic Accident) has even entered popular language. However, it is more common now in police circles to refer to road traffic collisions rather than accidents, partly to reflect that incidents of this kind are often due to driver error, rather than simply a random accident. However, the term 'accident' is still used frequently during police training and is used in much of the relevant legislation.

Regardless of whether we refer to the incident as an accident or a collision, incidents of this sort are very common and result in a large number of injuries. In 2012 (the latest available report) there were 195,723 road user casualties (Department for Transport, 2013b), and although this is part of a downward trend it is still as if the whole population of a town the size of Dudley or Bolton were to be injured every year, year after year.

Officers attending collisions where it seems that no criminal offence has been committed should still make a full record of the events (see 10.2). This is because the attending officers might be called upon as witnesses in a civil court case in which claims for damages are in dispute, for example if a pedestrian had been seriously injured in a collision. In such situations, the importance of detailed notes taken, even if no criminal offences are identified, cannot be underestimated.

19.7.1   Management of collision scenes

The police have a number of key responsibilities when responding to road traffic incidents, such as vehicle collisions ('crashes'). These include the need to preserve life, to coordinate the emergencies services involved (eg the Fire and Rescue Service), to secure, protect, and preserve the scene (see 11.2), to lead and manage the subsequent investigation into the incident, and to carry out liaison with relatives of the injured or killed. In the first response to a collision on the strategic road network such as motorways, the police will be working very closely with the Highways Agency. Highway Agency Traffic Officers (HATO) have restricted powers related to the control and direction of traffic and are under direction of the police when the circumstances dictate.

Here, we provide a summary of the key police responsibilities, but for further information see also *CLEAR Keeping Traffic Moving* available online. CLEAR is a mnemonic for Clear, Lead, Evaluate, Act, and Re-open.

19.7.1.1   Dynamic risk assessments

When attending incidents on roads, police officers should conduct a dynamic risk assessment in terms of the location, and the vehicles and the people involved.

The location may increase the risks if it is on a dangerous bend or there is reduced visibility due to weather conditions. The volume of passing traffic should also be considered as should any addition problems such as fallen trees or electricity lines. Some locations may also hinder effective communication between officers at the scene and with their control rooms.

All the vehicles involved should be identified, and as you might expect, a larger number of vehicles is generally associated with a higher risk. The contents and the post-impact condition of some vehicles may present additional hazards, and some might have been involved in criminal activity (PNC checks can be made) creating additional complications. Sufficient lighting is also important, particularly if there are special recovery requirements, for example for abnormally heavy loads.

All the people at the scene (driver(s), passenger(s), pedestrian(s), and witness(es)) should be accounted for. Their demeanour and any need for medical attention should be taken into account, and support provided as appropriate. The PNC could be used to help establish whether any of them have been involved in criminal activity that could present additional risks at the scene.

19.7.1.2   ACE-CARD actions for road traffic incidents

The 'ACE-CARD' mnemonic can be used to help remember the sequence of considerations and actions required when responding to a road or traffic incident. This approach is summarized in the table.

Letter:	Abbreviation for:	Meaning:
A	**A**pproach	Before approaching gather as much information as possible. Where possible approach incidents from the rear. Obey police 'hard shoulder' driving rules
C	**C**aution (signs)	Place warning signs and cones correctly (see 19.7.1.3). Make contact with FCC if matrix signs (on a motorway) of speed restrictions need activating. Establish an appropriate 'exclusion zone' around the incident
E	**E**xamine (the scene)	Decide whether further assistance is needed. Employ the critical incident procedures if required (see 11.5)

Specific Incidents

Letter:	Abbreviation for:	Meaning:
C	**C**asualties	After protecting the scene check that all casualties have been found and administer first aid if required. Take details of casualties before they are taken from the scene
A	**A**mbulance (and Fire and Rescue Service and other support agencies)	Control and manage the scene. Provide a safe working area for the support agencies
R	**R**emove (the obstructions)	Recovery services should be contacted (via FCC) asap but no vehicle should be removed until potential evidence is secured. Breakdown vehicles should be controlled by police or HATOs
D	**D**etailed (investigation)	Reporting and subsequent investigation according to local and national policy

19.7.1.3 The correct locations for signs

It may be necessary to cone off part of the carriageway, and a cone taper will be used to guide motorists into the lanes that are still open. Signs are placed to warn motorists of a cone taper, with more than one sign required for roads with higher speed traffic. On single carriageways signs should be placed on both directions of approach to the incident.

The following minimum suggestions apply for placing cone taper warning signs:

Speed limit	Number of signs	Clear view to the first sign	Distance for the signs (before the start of the cone taper)
70 mph	3	100 metres	300, 600, and 900 metres
50–60 mph	3	100 metres	300, 600, and 900 metres
40–50 mph	2	100 metres	200 and 400 metres
30 mph or less	1	100 metres	300 metres

(Adapted from College of Policing, 2013b)

19.7.2 Driver actions required after a collision

The Road Traffic Act 1988 takes a common sense approach to collisions (referred to as accidents in this Act) and dictates that the drivers involved must stop and be prepared to provide details to anyone who reasonably requires information (s 170). The information might be needed for compensation claims for repairs, injuries, or deaths. Police officers in training will no doubt be carefully assessed on what information must be exchanged after a collision, and the offences committed by a person who fails to meet his/her obligations in this regard.

19.7.2.1 The definition of a section 170 road traffic accident

The meaning of 'accident' has not been defined by statute and remains a question of fact for the courts to decide. However, in *R v Morris* [1972] RTR 201 'accident' was held to be 'an unintended occurrence which has an adverse physical result'. If the accident meets certain criteria, then the driver has to provide particular information to other people, or failing that, report the incident to the police (s 170(1) of the Road Traffic Act 1988). The criteria for a 'section 170 accident' are the location of the accident, the vehicle, and the result.

The location of the vehicle at the time of the accident is important. It must have been on a road or other public place such as hospital grounds, household garage blocks, private roads, or motorway service areas (see 9.2 for further discussion on the definition of a public place). If the vehicle leaves the road or other public place and ends up in a private dwelling, or grounds adjacent to the road or public place, an accident to which s 170 of the Road Traffic Act 1988 applies has still occurred. If a collision takes place at any location other than a road maintained at public expense, evidence will be required to prove that it is a public place. (This evidence could relate to the frequency of use, by whom, and under what circumstances.)

The vehicle must be mechanically propelled (see 19.2.1) and the collision must be due to its presence on a road or other public place. The type of vehicle would include those intended or adapted for use off-road (eg dumper trucks and off-road motorcycles).

The damage must be to another vehicle such as a bicycle, or to property such as a road sign, garden wall, or certain animals. The damage can be to private property, but the vehicle must have been travelling along a road or other public place immediately before the incident. Damage does not have to be permanent or beyond repair, but the physical appearance must have been altered in some way. Certain types of animals (horses, cattle, asses, mules, pigs, sheep, goats, and dogs) are classed as property. The injury must be to a person other than the driver of the vehicle, for example passengers, pedestrians, or people in other vehicles, and includes shock as well as actual bodily harm. If the only injury or damage caused is to the driver or his/her vehicle itself (or an animal in or on it), it is not an accident for the purposes of s 170 of the Road Traffic Act 1988.

19.7.2.2 Providing information and documents after a section 170 accident

After a s 170 accident the drivers must stop and remain at the scene for as long as necessary to provide information to others (s 170(2) of the Road Traffic Act 1988). Failing to stop at an accident is a serious offence and is committed even if the person reports the accident to the police at a later time.

At the scene, a driver must provide particulars to anyone who has reasonable grounds for needing the information, such as the driver or rider of any other vehicle involved, the passengers in any of the vehicles, property owners, pedestrians, or their representatives. The driver must provide:

- his/her name and address;
- the name and address of the vehicle's owner; and
- the identification marks of the vehicle (eg the vehicle registration number).

Failing to stop or report an accident is an offence under s 170(4) of the Road Traffic Act 1988. This offence is triable summarily, the penalty is six months' imprisonment and/or a fine, and the offender may also be disqualified.

If the driver cannot or does not provide the relevant information to anyone who has reasonable grounds for it at the time of the accident, then he/she must 'report' the accident and provide the relevant information to the police. This must be done as soon as reasonably practicable and certainly within 24 hours (s 170(3) and (6) of the Road Traffic Act 1988). He/she must report in person to a constable or police station; it is not sufficient to telephone, or send a fax or email, nor should the driver just wait for the police to make contact. It is a matter for a court to decide what is 'reasonably practicable' for the particular circumstances.

A certificate of insurance must be produced by the driver where personal injury is caused to a person other than him/herself (an 'injury accident'). The certificate should be shown to a police officer and any person having reasonable grounds for requiring it to be produced, for example the injured person (s 170(5)). If this is not possible at the time the driver must report the accident to the police and produce the insurance as soon as is reasonably practicable and, in any case, within 24 hours (s 170(6)). Failing to produce proof of insurance after an injury accident is a summary offence under s 170(7) of the Road Traffic Act 1988 and the penalty is a fine.

Specific Incidents

TASK 11 In many police forces the policy is to use a preliminary breath test on every driver involved in a road traffic collision. What legislation provides the power to carry out such a test? What computer checks could be carried out on the drivers involved?

(Photo by Kevin Lawton-Barrett)

19.8   Offences Relating to Standards of Driving

Standards of driving are assessed as sufficient when a driver passes his/her driving test, but this minimum standard should be maintained. Careless and inconsiderate driving can result in damage to property or injury to a person, but poor driving can also be alarming, distressing, or annoying to members of the public. Police officers have powers to stop, seize, and remove the vehicle in such situations.

Here we cover the following offences:

- dangerous driving (s 2 of the Road Traffic Act 1988);
- careless and inconsiderate driving (s 3 of the Road Traffic Act 1988);
- wanton and furious driving (s 35 of the Offences Against the Person Act 1861);
- careless and inconsiderate cycling (s 29 of the Road Traffic Act 1988);
- causing death by dangerous driving (s 1 of the Road Traffic Act 1988);
- causing death by careless or inconsiderate driving (s 2B of the Road Traffic Act 1988);
- causing death by driving whilst unlicensed, disqualified, or uninsured (s 3ZB of the Road Traffic Act 1988);
- causing the death of another person whilst under the influence of drink or drugs (s 3A of the Road Traffic Act 1988); and
- unauthorized off-road driving (s 34 of the Road Traffic Act 1988).

19.8.1   Dangerous driving

There are two main causes of dangerous driving defined in s 2 of the Road Traffic Act 1988. These are 'bad driving' due to the driver's style of driving, and driving a vehicle that is in a dangerous condition.

Bad driving is defined in s 2A(1) of the Road Traffic Act 1988, which explains that a person is to be regarded as driving dangerously if (a) the way he/she drives falls far below what would be expected of a competent and careful driver; and (b) it would be obvious to a competent and careful driver that the driving would be dangerous (a question of fact for the court to decide). The minimum standard of driving is set by the Driver and Vehicle Licensing Authority during the driving test although even learner drivers will be expected to maintain a degree of competency. The Highway Code also sets the standard at which a competent and careful person should drive and the knowledge and application of its contents are a useful guide as to how to gather evidence in the interview of a person suspected of driving badly.

The following are examples of driving activities which may support an allegation of bad driving under s 2A(1):

- racing or competitive driving style;
- driving at a speed which is highly inappropriate for the prevailing road or traffic conditions;
- aggressive driving, such as sudden lane changes, cutting into a line of vehicles, or driving much too close to the vehicle in front;
- disregard for traffic lights and other road signs which, on careful analysis, would appear to be deliberate, or disregard for warnings from fellow passengers;
- overtaking in circumstances where it could not have been carried out safely;
- impaired driver ability, such as having an arm or leg in plaster, or impaired eyesight, or too tired to stay awake;
- using a mobile phone for talking or text messages (*R v Browning* [2001] EWCA Crim 1831; [2002] 1 Cr App R (S) 88).

The dangerous state of a vehicle is judged from the perspective of a 'competent and careful driver' (s 2A(2) of the Road Traffic Act 1988) 'if it would be obvious...that driving the vehicle in its current state would be dangerous'. In determining the state of a vehicle for the purposes of s 2A(2), the weight or height of the vehicle, as well as any load carried, should be considered in relation to restrictions on the road. Examples of s 2A(2) offences might include driving a vehicle with a load which presents a danger to other road users and driving with actual knowledge of a dangerous vehicle defect.

The Highway Code and Construction and Use Regulations 1986 should be used as benchmarks when gathering evidence through interviews with witnesses and suspects. When interviewing a driver, it is advisable to consider the wide range of defences for this offence (see 19.8.3), and if appropriate, evidence must be collected to contradict these. It is for the jury or magistrates to decide whether it would be 'obvious' (to a competent and careful driver) that driving the vehicle in such a state would be dangerous. The offence of dangerous driving is triable either way and the penalty is a fine or imprisonment (six months if tried summarily and two years on indictment).

19.8.1.1 Causing serious injury by dangerous driving

Section 1A of the Road Traffic Act 1988 states that it is an offence for a person to cause serious physical injury to another by driving a mechanically propelled vehicle dangerously on a road or other public place. Serious injury means physical harm, which amounts to grievous bodily harm as in the Offences Against the Person Act 1861 (see 15.3.1).

If the court finds the suspect not guilty of this offence, the defendant may alternatively be convicted of dangerous driving (see 19.8.1) or careless, or inconsiderate, driving (see 19.8.2).

The offence is triable either way and the penalty is a fine or imprisonment (12 months if tried summarily and five years on indictment).

19.8.2 Careless or inconsiderate driving

Legislation concerning careless or inconsiderate driving is provided by s 3 of the Road Traffic Act 1988. An offence is committed by a person who drives a mechanically propelled vehicle on a road or other public place without due care or attention or without reasonable consideration for other persons using the road or public place. Whether the driving was careless or inconsiderate is a question of fact for the court to decide.

Driving without due care and attention is defined in law as when the standard of driving falls below what would be expected of a competent and careful driver (s 3ZA(2)). The driver's knowledge of the circumstances can be taken into account, and any factors that he/she should have been aware of. Examples of careless driving would include a driver who fails to look behind whilst reversing, or crosses the white line when overtaking without checking for oncoming vehicles, or using the right-turn direction indicator and then turning left.

For inconsiderate driving, another person must be inconvenienced by the suspect's driving. This would include:

- 'cutting across' the path of another vehicle, eg when turning or changing lanes without prior warning;
- causing traffic problems by failing to conform to directional arrows;

- forcing other drivers to take evasive action by failing to drive correctly;
- deliberately performing skids at high speed or making 'handbrake turns';
- driving on footpaths; or
- driving off-road across grassland, with disregard for other users of these public spaces.

A driver can only be charged with careless or inconsiderate driving, not both. These offences are triable summarily and the penalty is a fine. The driver may also be disqualified.

19.8.3 Defences to dangerous, careless, or inconsiderate driving

There are various defences that may be offered by a suspect in respect of committing the offences of dangerous or careless or inconsiderate driving. These are summarized in the following table.

List of defences

Automatism	Automatism is 'the involuntary movement of a person's body or limbs' (*Watmore v Jenkins* [1961] 2 All ER 868), and it must occur very suddenly with little or no warning. This could be an epileptic fit or a wasp sting. Case law has established that falling asleep at the wheel or a hypoglycaemic diabetic coma are not included
Unconsciousness or sudden illness	This would include situations where a person suddenly becomes unconscious as a result of circumstances beyond his/her control, such as being hit on the head by a stone that has smashed through the windscreen
Assisting in the arrest of offenders	Here, the driver might have a defence (even though he/she was driving dangerously) if for example he/she intentionally shunted a suspect's car off the road in order to help the police arrest the suspect (*R v Renouf* [1986] 2 All ER 449)
Duress by threats	The suspect must be able to show that he/she drove dangerously as a result of a threat. However, he/she must not have voluntarily placed him/herself under the threat, nor avoid the opportunity to escape from it
Duress of necessity (of circumstances)	The suspect must be able to show that he/she drove dangerously out of necessity in order to avoid death or serious injury to him/herself or anybody else, and that he/she could not reasonably have been expected to act otherwise in the circumstances
Sudden mechanical defect	This does not apply if the driver is already aware of the defect or it could have been easily discovered by superficial examination, for example of tyres (*R v Spurge* [1961] 2 All ER 688)
Authorized motoring event	A person will not be guilty under s 1, 2, or 3 of the Road Traffic Act if he/she drove in accordance with an authorization for a motoring event given by the Secretary of State (s 13(A) of the Road Traffic Act 1988)

19.8.4 Other offences involving dangerous driving

Section 35 of the Offences Against the Person Act 1861 states that it is an offence for anyone 'having the charge of any carriage or vehicle...[to cause] or cause to be done bodily harm to any person' by wanton or furious driving, racing, other wilful misconduct, or wilful neglect. This could be used on occasions when dangerous driving has taken place, but the Road Traffic Act 1988 cannot be used as the basis of a prosecution. This could be when:

- the driving was not on a road or other public place;
- the vehicle used was not a mechanically propelled vehicle (eg it was a bicycle or horse-drawn vehicle); or
- the statutory Notice of Intended Prosecution was not given (see 19.12.4).

The offence can only be committed if the driver has a degree of subjective recklessness: he/she must appreciate that harm was possible or probable as a result of his/her bad driving (*R v Okosi* [1996] CLR 666). It is triable by indictment only and the penalty is two years' imprisonment. Disqualification is discretionary, although endorsement (three to nine points) is obligatory if the offence is committed in a mechanically propelled vehicle.

Riding a cycle carelessly, inconsiderately, or dangerously on a road is an offence under the Road Traffic Act 1988. This can be riding 'without due care and attention, reasonable consideration for other persons using the road' (s 29), or riding dangerously (s 28(1)). These offences are triable summarily and the penalty is a fine.

19.8.5   Causing death by driving

The offences of causing death by dangerous driving, careless, or inconsiderate driving, or whilst being unlicensed, disqualified, or uninsured are shown in the table, along with the corresponding section number of the Road Traffic Act 1988 for each offence. It is not relevant whether the deceased person was inside or outside the suspect's vehicle at the time of the incident.

The offence	dangerous driving	careless or inconsiderate driving	driving whilst unlicensed, disqualified, or uninsured
Section	(s 1)	(s 2B)	(s 3ZB)
Type of vehicle	mechanically propelled vehicle		motor vehicle
Description of the driving	Dangerously	without due care and attention, or without reasonable consideration for other persons using the road	The manner contributes in some way to causing the death, and the driver did not have the appropriate licence (s 87(1)) or insurance (s 143), or was disqualified (s 103(1)(b))
The location	on a road or other public place		on a road
Mode of trial	indictment only	either way	
Non-custodial penalty	obligatory disqualification or obligatory endorsement—licence endorsed between 3 and 11 points		
Prison term for a custodial penalty	14 years	one year if tried summarily	
		five years on indictment	two years on indictment

Note that for a s 3ZB offence (causing death by driving whilst unlicensed, disqualified, or uninsured) it must be a motor vehicle (defined in 19.2.1) being driven on a road (defined in 19.2.3). This sets it apart from the other offences shown here. The manner of the driving must have contributed to causing the death. It is not necessary to prove careless or inconsiderate driving, but the mere presence of a vehicle on a road is insufficient (see *R v Hughes* [2013] UKSC 56).

19.8.5.1   Causing a death whilst under the influence of drink or drugs

Under s 3A of the Road Traffic Act 1988 it is an offence for a person to cause the death of another person by driving a mechanically propelled vehicle on a road or in a public place. The style of the driving must be 'without due care or attention' or 'without reasonable consideration for other people using the road or the place'. For the offence to be committed the driver must also either:

(a) have been unfit to drive through drink or drugs, at the time;

(b) have consumed so much alcohol that the proportion of it in his/her breath, blood, or urine exceeded the prescribed limit;

(c) failed without reasonable excuse to provide a specimen when required under s 7 (see 19.9.5 onwards) within 18 hours of the incident; or

(d) failed without reasonable excuse to give permission for his/her blood to be tested (see 19.9.5), when required by a police officer.

This offence is triable on indictment only and the penalty is 14 years' imprisonment.

TASK 12

1. The following is a list of some of the main contributory factors to reported road accidents in 20012 (taken from 'Contributory factors of reported accidents, Great Britain, 2008–2012', available on the www.gov.uk website). Put them in order, with the most frequently occurring first.

(a) Pedestrian failed to look properly

(b) Slippery road (due to weather)

(c) Sudden braking

(d) Driver failed to look properly

(e) Loss of control

(f) Careless, reckless or in a hurry

(g) Failed to judge other person's path or speed

(h) Following too close

(i) Vehicle travelling too fast for conditions
(j) Poor turn or manoeuvre.

2. List three national road policing priorities.

TASK 13

1. Who would be held to be 'driving' in each of the following scenarios? Use the case suggested as guidance.

(a) Jerry sits in the driver's seat and lets the car freewheel downhill with the steering lock on. See *Burgoyne v Phillips* [1982] RTR 49.

(b) Maz, a passenger in a car 'driven' by Mel, sees a friend walking along the roadside towards the moving car. To frighten the friend, Maz snatches the steering wheel from Mel's grasp towards himself in order to make the car veer in that direction. Would Maz be held to be 'driving'? See *DPP v Hastings* [1993] 158 JP 118.

(c) Hari is in the driving seat of the car and 'driving' along the road. Pat leans over from the front passenger seat and steers the car, while Hari manipulates the other controls. Hari's view forward is partially obscured by Pat. After some distance, the car runs into a ditch, while Pat is steering. Pat had been able to reach both the handbrake and the ignition key and knew the consequences of using the various controls, but did not have access to the foot pedals. See *Tyler v Whatmore* [1975] RTR 83. Who was driving?

2. Answer questions (a) and (b) by selecting the correct option(s) from the following list.

(a) Where can dangerous driving and causing death by dangerous driving be committed?
(b) In what location(s) does s 35 of the Offences Against the Person Act 1861 apply?
  (i) Anywhere?
  (ii) On a road?
  (iii) In a public place other than a road?
  (iv) In a public place only?

19.8.6 Other offences involving standards of driving

Other offences relating to poor standards of driving are described in the Road Vehicles (Construction and Use) Regulations 1986. The term 'driving' has a wide meaning under s 192 of the Road Traffic Act: pulling up by the side of a road with the engine running, for example, could be considered as driving. The offences apply not only to the driver, but also to any person causing or permitting (see 19.2.4) another person to drive inappropriately. The following regulations are relevant to offences involving standards of driving:

- No person shall drive (or cause or permit any other person to drive) a motor vehicle on a road if the driver is in such a position in the vehicle that he/she cannot have proper control of the vehicle or have a full view of the road and traffic ahead (reg 104). The penalty is an obligatory endorsement (three points) and a discretionary disqualification.
- No person shall open, or cause or permit to be opened, any door of a vehicle on a road so as to injure or endanger any person (reg 105).
- No person shall drive a motor vehicle on a road if the driver is in such a position as to be able to see directly, or by reflection, a TV or similar apparatus (reg 109). (This does not apply to satnav apparatus or other apparatus used to display information about the state of the vehicle, nor to devices that assist the driver to see the road adjacent to the vehicle.)
- Driving a motor vehicle on a road while using a hand-held phone (eg a 'mobile') is an offence, and also applies to similar devices with an 'interactive communication function' (reg 110). (Communication by two-way radio, such as 'CB', is excluded from this offence, although obviously the general need for safe driving still applies.) Apart from applying to drivers, this offence can also be committed by anyone supervising a driver with a provisional licence. Employers providing the employee with a company hand-held phone can be held liable if they fail to prohibit their employee from using it while driving on company business. The penalty is an obligatory endorsement (three points),

a discretionary disqualification and a fine. Alternatively a fixed penalty notice can be issued (see 19.12.2).

It is important to note that members of the police service and members of other emergency services are granted some exemptions from road traffic regulations. However, police officers are expected to drive at least as well as other motorists; and should aim to provide a positive role model for other drivers—consider this in relation to personal authority (see 3.5). It is very important that a police officer's driving meets the relevant standards and that he/she is fully aware of force policies before taking on any emergency response.

TASK 14

1. What other offences might be considered for a person using a hand-held mobile telephone while driving, apart from the offence derived from reg 110 in the Road Vehicles (Construction and Use) Regulations 1986?

2. Driving while using a phone is clearly dangerous; what other circumstances or activities might adversely affect standards of driving?

19.8.7   Off-road driving

The law surrounding off-road driving is covered in s 34 of the Road Traffic Act 1988. This states that an offence is committed by a person who:

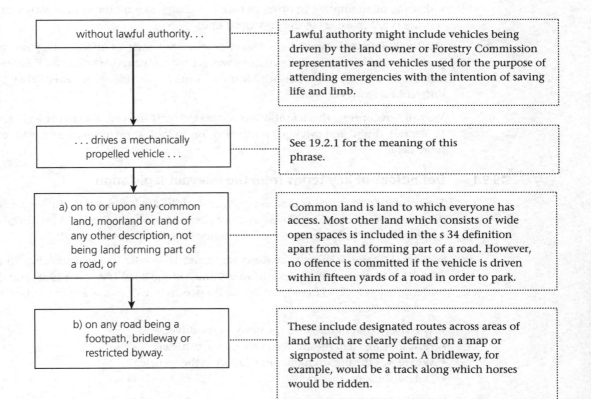

without lawful authority. . .
— Lawful authority might include vehicles being driven by the land owner or Forestry Commission representatives and vehicles used for the purpose of attending emergencies with the intention of saving life and limb.

. . . drives a mechanically propelled vehicle . . .
— See 19.2.1 for the meaning of this phrase.

a) on to or upon any common land, moorland or land of any other description, not being land forming part of a road, or
— Common land is land to which everyone has access. Most other land which consists of wide open spaces is included in the s 34 definition apart from land forming part of a road. However, no offence is committed if the vehicle is driven within fifteen yards of a road in order to park.

b) on any road being a footpath, bridleway or restricted byway.
— These include designated routes across areas of land which are clearly defined on a map or signposted at some point. A bridleway, for example, would be a track along which horses would be ridden.

This offence is triable summarily only and the penalty is a fine.

19.9   Drink- and Drug-driving

Police officers can only test a person for alcohol or drugs if he/she has reason to suspect the driver might be under the influence of alcohol, or if a moving traffic offence has been committed, or if the vehicle has been involved in an accident. Random testing is not permitted.

Scenarios for testing for drink/drug-driving offences

General scenario	Example
An accident	A vehicle runs into the back of another vehicle at a junction
A moving traffic offence	A driver crosses a red traffic light
Inappropriate style of driving	A driver cannot restart his stalled vehicle which causes a traffic jam. The attending police officer notices the driver's speech is slurred
Vehicle stopped for another reason	A vehicle is stopped under s 163 of the Road Traffic Act 1988 (see 19.4.1) to inspect for roadworthiness. The driver's breath smells of intoxicating liquor
Other information about drink/ drug consumption	A witness reports the registration number of a car being driven by a woman who had consumed a large amount of alcohol in a pub

The level of alcohol or drugs in a driver's blood is not always easy to judge. If a police officer suspects that alcohol or other drugs may be present, a 'preliminary test' is administered at the roadside. The best known of these tests is the so-called 'breath test'. The result of a preliminary test does not form part of the evidence for a prosecution; it only provides grounds for suspicion that the proportion of alcohol in the person's breath or blood exceeds the prescribed limit (an offence under s 5 of the Road Traffic Act 1988: see 19.9.3.1).

There are two main driving offences relating to driving while under the influence of alcohol or other drugs, and these are both covered under the Road Traffic Act 1988:

- driving, or attempting to drive, or being in charge of a mechanically propelled vehicle while unfit to drive through drink or drugs (s 4); and
- driving, or attempting to drive, or being in charge of a motor vehicle with alcohol (s 5) or drugs (s 5A) in excess of the prescribed limit

The key difference between these two offences is that, for a s 4 offence, the prosecution has to prove that the suspect's ability to drive was actually impaired, whereas for s 5 offences a high alcohol level in the blood, breath, or urine is the only evidence required. They also involve different categories of vehicle.

We will first consider the definitions of some key terms and concepts in the legislation relating to alcohol, drugs, and driving, and then go on to look at preliminary and evidential tests in more detail.

19.9.1 Definitions of key terms from the relevant legislation

The legislation relating to offences committed whilst driving under the influence of alcohol or drugs uses many terms employed in other pieces of road policing legislation. The definitions of mechanically propelled vehicles and motor vehicles are covered in 19.2.1.

Sections 4(2) and 5(1)(b) of the Road Traffic Act 1988 refer to a person being 'in charge of a vehicle'. (This term only occurs within ss 4 and 5 of the Road Traffic Act 1988, and is not therefore covered in 19.2.3.) In order to decide if a person is in charge of a vehicle, the court is likely to consider the following:

- Was the person in question the most recent driver?
- How long ago had he/she been driving the vehicle?
- Where was the person found, in relation to the vehicle?
- Did he/she have the keys?

It may be necessary to negate defences in relation to being 'in charge'. For example, the defendant might attempt to prove that there was no likelihood of his/her driving the vehicle in the near future (while still under the influence of alcohol or drugs), but a stated intention to not drive is insufficient (see *CPS v Thompson* [2007] EWHC 1841 (Admin)). A suitable defence might include that he/she had booked a hotel room for the night, or that the vehicle had been wheel-clamped (see *Sheldrake v DPP* [2003] 2 All ER 497). The defence might also claim that the driver was so badly injured that he/she was unable to drive the vehicle, or that the vehicle was severely damaged, but the court may choose to disregard any injury or damage when assessing the likelihood of the suspect driving.

19.9.2 Unfit to drive through drink or drugs

These offences are covered under s 4 of the Road Traffic Act 1988. The diagram shows this in detail (s 4(1)).

There is no need to administer a preliminary test for breath alcohol levels or for drug consumption before arresting a driver for this offence. The suspect's level of impairment and ability to drive properly is assessed by a police medical practitioner at a police station using an evidential test. Specimens of breath, blood, or urine may also be taken for other evidential tests, particularly to prove the presence of drugs in the body (which would imply impairment). In addition, even though a suspect has been arrested for a s 4 offence, he/she might eventually be charged with an offence under s 5, depending on the results of evidential tests measuring the level of alcohol in the body. Section 4 can also be used if the driver is over the limit for alcohol but the vehicle involved is not a motor vehicle.

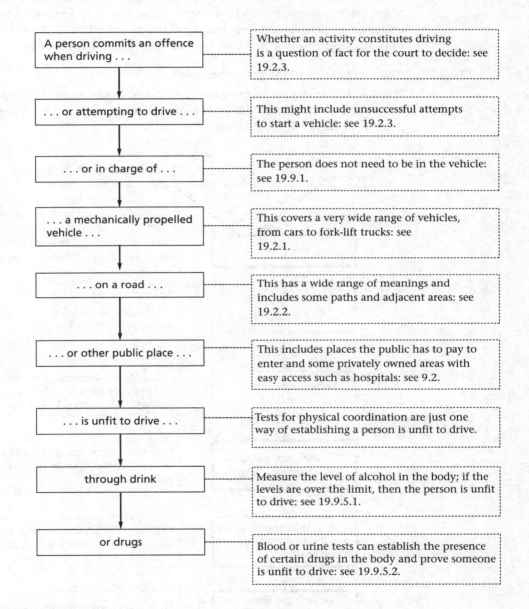

The evidence presented to a court for a s 4 offence is likely to include:

- the style of driving before the accused was stopped;
- his/her demeanour at time of stop (speech, unsteadiness);
- the report by a medical examiner whilst in custody (particularly if evidential specimens are not obtained to prove the presence of drugs in the body); and
- the results of evidential drug tests (using blood or urine samples).

Remember that it might be necessary to present evidence to counter a defence that the driver was not likely to drive whilst under the influence of drugs or alcohol, when investigating an 'in charge' offence (see 19.9.1).

There is no power of arrest for a s 4 offence under the Road Traffic Act 1988. An arrest for this offence would be under s 24 of the PACE Act 1984. A power of entry to arrest for a s 4 offence is available under s 17(1)(c)(iiia) of the PACE Act 1984, but note that this only applies if there are reasonable grounds for believing that the suspect is on the premises (see 9.5.1).

Offences under s 4 of the Road Traffic Act 1988 are triable summarily and the penalties are:

- for driving and attempting to drive whilst unfit due to drink or drugs (s 4(1)): six months' imprisonment and/or a fine, and obligatory disqualification; and
- for being in charge of a vehicle whilst unfit due to drink or drugs (s 4(2)): three months' imprisonment and/or a fine, and discretionary disqualification.

19.9.3 Driving or being in charge of a motor vehicle when over the prescribed limit

For these offences (under ss 5 and 5A of the Road Traffic Act 1988) the evidence required is a blood, breath, or urine evidential test result showing that the level of alcohol or specified controlled drug in the driver's body was above the prescribed limit. There is no need to provide evidence that the suspect was unfit to drive in terms of his/her demeanour or behaviour.

19.9.3.1 Alcohol in excess of the prescribed limit

The flowchart shows the wording for a s 5 offence; bold-edged boxes emphasize the features that distinguish a s 5 offence from a s 4 offence. Section 5 of the Road Traffic Act 1988 states that it is an offence for a person to:

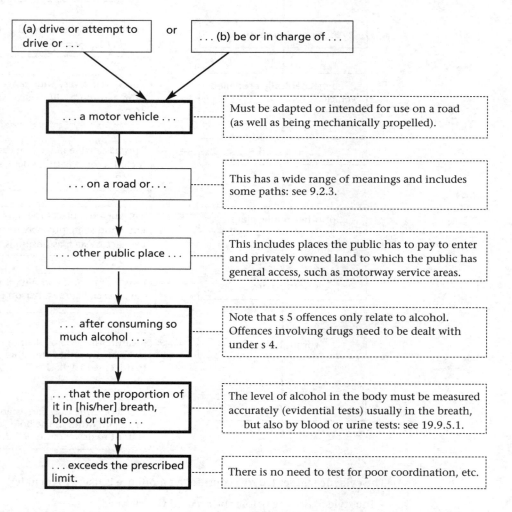

The prescribed limits are shown in the table. Note the units: microgrammes (µg), milligrammes (mg), and millilitres (ml). A good way to help memorize these figures is to remember that the digits in each measurement add up to 8.

Type of sample	Amount of alcohol per 100 millilitres
Breath	35 μg (microgrammes)
Blood	80 mg (milligrammes)
Urine	107 mg (milligrammes)

These offences are triable summarily and the penalties are:

- for driving or attempting to drive above the prescribed limit (s 5(1)(a)): six months' imprisonment and/or a fine, and obligatory disqualification; and
- for being in charge of a vehicle above the prescribed limit (s 5(1)(b)): three months' imprisonment and/or a fine, and discretionary disqualification.

19.9.3.2 Specified controlled drug in excess of the prescribed limit

Although not effective at the time of writing, the Crime and Courts Act 2013 will introduce a s 5A offence of driving or being in charge of a motor vehicle with the concentration of a specified controlled drug above a specified limit for that drug (s 5A(2)). It will include driving or attempting to drive (s 5A(1)(a)), or being in charge of (s 5A(1)(b)), a motor vehicle on a road or other public place, and the limit will be specified for blood or urine. Statutory regulations will be produced by the Secretary of State to indicate which controlled drugs and what limit will be 'specified' (s 5A(8)).

A preliminary impairment or drug test (see 19.9.4.2) can be administered to find out if it is likely that a drug-related driving offence has been committed. If the test is positive then the suspect will be asked to provide a specimen of blood or urine for an evidential test (see 19.9.5). In order to decide if a person is in charge of a vehicle, the court is likely to consider the points mentioned in 19.9.1.

Defences are available if the suspect can show that the specified controlled drug had been prescribed or supplied for medical or dental purposes (s 5A(3)(a)), and he/she had taken the drug in accordance with any instruction (s 5A(3)(b)), and that immediately before taking the drug, its possession was not unlawful under s 5(1) of the Misuse of Drugs Act 1971 (s 5A(3)(c)) (see 12.5.2). However, the defences are not available if the suspect's actions were contrary to any advice or instructions given by the person prescribing, supplying, manufacturing, or distributing the drug, in relation to the amount of time that should elapse between taking the drug and driving a motor vehicle (s 5A(4)(a)and (b)).

The penalty and punishment for this offence are the same as for a s 5 offence; see 19.9.3.1.

19.9.4 Preliminary tests

Preliminary tests are frequently referred to as roadside tests and are covered in ss 6A, 6B, and 6C of the Road Traffic Act 1988, but they can also be used in police stations and hospitals. They are only used for drivers of motor vehicles (and not other mechanically propelled vehicles). Preliminary tests are used to find out if it is likely that a drug- or alcohol-related driving offence has been committed: they only provide grounds for suspicion. More detailed tests (evidential tests, see 19.9.5) are required to provide evidence for a subsequent prosecution. The three main types of preliminary test are:

- a preliminary breath test to indicate whether the proportion of alcohol in the breath or blood is likely to exceed the prescribed limit (s 6A of the Road Traffic Act 1988);
- a preliminary impairment test of whether a person is unfit to drive (whether due to drink or drugs), which is done by observing the person's performance during a set of tasks or observing his/her physical state—a police officer can only carry out such a test if he/she is approved for that purpose by the chief officer of his/her force (s 6B of the Road Traffic Act 1988); and
- a preliminary drug test to indicate the presence of drugs in a person's body: a specimen of sweat or saliva is obtained and tested with an approved device (s 6C of the Road Traffic Act 1988).

A police officer does not need to be in uniform to require a person to take part in a preliminary test. However, the police officer actually administering a preliminary test must be in uniform (except after an accident). A Home Office statistical return form must be completed after administering a preliminary test. More recent equipment will do this automatically.

In some situations it might not be clear who was driving, so it should first be clarified who was in the vehicle at the time of the accident; witnesses may be able to help on this matter. However, remember that a police officer only has to 'reasonably believe' that a person was driving a vehicle at the time of the accident, and therefore if no one admits to being the driver, then more than one person from the vehicle can be tested.

There is a power of entry (s 6E of the Road Traffic Act 1988) in order to administer preliminary tests, but only after an accident in which the police officer reasonably suspects a person has been injured. The power can be used for any place, using reasonable force if necessary.

The flowchart summarizes the circumstances for administering preliminary tests.

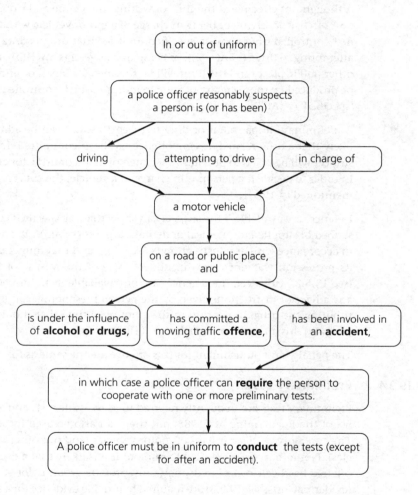

The meaning of the term 'accident' has not been defined by statute and remains a question of fact for the courts to decide. However, in *R v Morris* [1972] RTR 201 'accident' was held to be 'an unintended occurrence which has an adverse physical result' and when such a situation arises out of the presence of a motor vehicle on a road it 'is a fair basis on which a police officer may request the provision of a specimen of breath'.

19.9.4.1   Preliminary breath tests

There are currently two styles of preliminary breath-test device approved by the Secretary of State. Electronic devices include models such as the Lion Alcolmeter, the Alcosensor IV, the Draeger Alert, and the Draeger Alcotest 7410. Others (such as Alcotest 80 and R80A and the

Alcolyser) are not electronic and involve the inflation of a bag. All of the devices test air that has come from deep within the lungs. It is most important that the manufacturer's instructions and force policies are followed when using these devices.

The police officer must say to the suspect (when requesting a specimen of breath):

> I suspect that you are driving a motor vehicle on a road under the influence of alcohol. I require you to provide a specimen of breath for a breath test here. Failure to do so may make you liable to arrest and prosecution.

He/she must also ask the person when he/she had last drunk alcohol or smoked: if the person has been drinking or smoking recently the police officer must comply with the manufacturer's instructions to wait a period of minutes before administering the test (as recent smoking of a cigarette or cigar can 'mask' the measurement of alcohol content). Failure to ask these questions will not invalidate the test (*DPP v Kay* 1998) and innocent failure to follow the instructions will not make the arrest and subsequent evidential test unlawful, although the results may be considered as less reliable.

To carry out the test the driver should be asked to take a deep breath and to blow into the machine in one continuous breath until requested to stop. The person should then be told the result of the test. A positive result from a preliminary breath test directly justifies arrest; the suspect must be told that he/she is under arrest (s 6D(1) of the Road Traffic Act 1988) on suspicion that the proportion of alcohol in his/her breath or blood exceeds the prescribed limit and must be cautioned. The reason for the arrest is not that the breath test has produced a positive result. An evidential breath test should then be carried out (see 19.9.5.1).

A patient in a hospital must never be arrested (s 6D(3)). However, should such a wrongful arrest take place, a subsequent and lawfully obtained evidential specimen will not become unlawful (*DPP v Wilson* [2009] EWHC 1988 (Admin)).

19.9.4.2 Preliminary drug tests

The Drager DrugTest 5000 equipment has been approved by the Home Office for analysing mouth swabs for traces of cannabis. It can be used in police stations, and is also portable as it has an integrated battery. The swab is placed in the analyser, and the result is shown on a digital display.

19.9.4.3 What to do after a preliminary test

If the results of a preliminary breath test are negative but (due to his/her demeanour) the police officer still suspects the driver of being under the influence of drugs then he/she should consider:

1. administering a preliminary impairment or drugs test if he/she is qualified and has the apparatus available; or
2. arresting the driver on suspicion of the s 4 offence of driving whilst unfit, using s 24 of the PACE Act 1984 powers of arrest.

If no other offences have been committed, then the driver is free to leave.

The diagram summarizes the actions that should be taken in relation to other outcomes from preliminary tests.

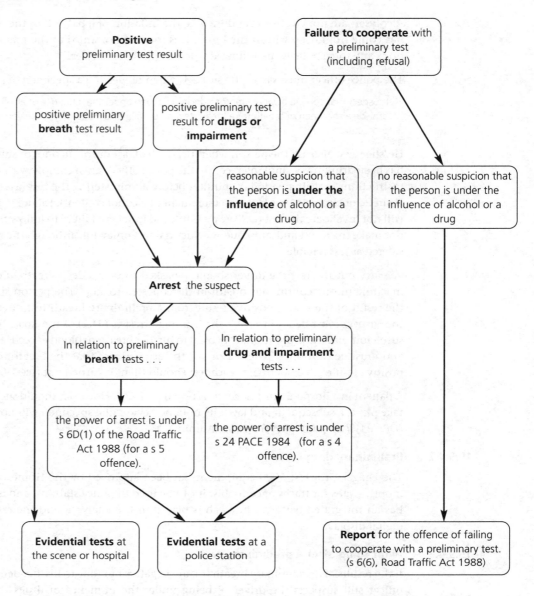

There is a power of entry in order to arrest a person who has provided a positive preliminary test and has been involved in an injury accident. This power is given under s 6 of the Road Traffic Act 1988.

19.9.4.4 Failure to cooperate with a preliminary test

The number of opportunities that should be provided for completing a preliminary test will be stated by each force. If, despite further opportunities, a person still fails to complete a preliminary test, the action that should be taken next depends on whether there is any suspicion about the influence of alcohol or drugs, as shown in the previous chart.

If the driver cannot complete a preliminary test (eg due to a medical condition) and there is reasonable suspicion that he/she is under the influence of alcohol or a drug then he/she should be arrested and blood or urine tests arranged. However, a patient in a hospital must never be arrested (s 6D(3)).

If alcohol or drugs are not suspected, he/she cannot be arrested under s 6D(1) of the Road Traffic Act 1988 (see 19.9.4.1) and should instead be reported for the offence of failing to cooperate with the provision of a specimen for a preliminary test under s 6(6) of the Road Traffic Act 1988. The person's true identity will need to be ascertained (through computer checks with control), and identification documentation obtained from the person. The address he/she gives must be checked as genuine. He/she should be interviewed under caution (all recorded in the pocket notebook), and then reported for the offence of failing to cooperate with a preliminary test and cautioned again. This offence is triable summarily and the penalty is obligatory endorsement (four points) and discretionary disqualification.

19.9.5 Evidential tests

When investigating whether a person has committed an offence under ss 3A, 4, or 5 of the Road Traffic Act 1988 (see 19.8.5.1, 19.9.2, or 19.9.3 respectively) a constable may require a person to provide:

- two specimens of breath for analysis by means of a device of a type approved by the Secretary of State (s 7(1)(a)); or
- a specimen of blood or urine for a laboratory test (s 7(1)(b)).

The results of these tests (for drugs, alcohol, and impairment) can be used as evidence in a court. The tests are usually carried out at a police station (or hospital if the suspect is a hospital patient) but some may also be conducted at the roadside. The requirement for an evidential test (all types) is made at a police station or hospital, but the requirement for an evidential breath test can also be made at the roadside. It is usual to arrest a suspect before making the requirement for an evidential test, although this is not compulsory by law. A suspect who is also a hospital patient cannot be arrested (s 6D(3) of the Road Traffic Act 1988).

At a police station, a suspect cannot delay providing a specimen for an evidential test in order to obtain legal advice. There can only be a delay in exceptional circumstances and where a legal representative is available for immediate consultation (*Chalupa v CPS* [2009] EWHC 3082 (Admin)).

For alcohol, an evidential breath test will always be used in preference to blood or urine tests, even at a police station, unless (s 7(3) of the Road Traffic Act 1988):

- there is reasonable cause to believe that a medical reason prevents the use of a breath test;
- the approved device for conducting a breath test is not available;
- there is cause to believe the approved device for a breath test gave an unreliable result; and/or
- a preliminary drug-test result or the medical examiner's opinion suggests there is reasonable cause to believe that the suspect has a drug in his/her body.

19.9.5.1 Evidential breath tests

The test can be required and conducted at (or near) a place where a relevant preliminary breath test has been administered, at a police station, or in a hospital (s 7(2), Road Traffic Act 1988). There is no need to have already carried out a preliminary breath test if the suspect is being investigated for the offences of causing death by careless driving when under the influence of drink or drugs, or for being unfit to drive (ss 3A and 4 of the Road Traffic Act 1988 respectively).

Two samples of breath are required for the test, and the process and period of time in which the two samples are collected is called a 'cycle'. The two samples must be obtained from the same cycle in order for the test to be valid. Only the sample containing the lower proportion of alcohol will be used as evidence—the other will be disregarded (s 8(1) of the Road Traffic Act 1988). The samples will be analysed by a device approved by the Secretary of State (currently the Camic Datamaster, the Lion Intoxilyzer 6000, or the Intoximeter EC/IR). The person operating the machine (often the custody officer) will have been trained to use it and will check that it is working properly. MG DD forms must be used to record the breath-test procedure, as these completed forms will constitute the 'notes made at the time'.

The suspect must be warned that failing to provide a suitable specimen (two samples) may render him/her liable to prosecution (s 7(7) of the Road Traffic Act 1988). Each organization will have its own policy on how many attempts can be allowed for the suspect to provide a sufficient volume of air in a proper manner (s 11(3) of the Road Traffic Act 1988). Note that regurgitation of stomach contents does not affect the accuracy of the measurements (see *McNeil v DPP* [2008] EWHC 1254).

The prescribed limit for alcohol in the breath is 35 µg of alcohol per 100 ml of breath (see 19.9.3), but some forces do not proceed unless the level is above 40 µg. If the result is between 35 and 50 µg of alcohol in 100 ml of breath, the driver can choose to replace it with a blood or urine sample (s 8 of the Road Traffic Act 1988). This is known as the 'statutory option', and the driver must be informed that it is available. After the test, the MG DD forms are completed and if the result is above the prescribed limit the driver can be charged and bailed to court.

If the driver fails to provide two samples of breath, the offence of 'failing to provide a specimen of breath for an evidential breath test' (s 7(6)) has been committed. Refusing to provide suitable samples is equivalent to failure (s 11(2) of the Road Traffic Act 1988), including when not enough breath is provided (see *Rweikiza v DPP* [2008] EWHC 386 (Admin)). The suspect must be allowed sufficient time to provide the samples in each subsequent cycle; otherwise a subsequent prosecution may fail (see *Plackett v DPP* [2008] EWHC 1335 (Admin)). The suspect is not obliged to mention any medical condition which could account for failing to provide enough breath, but the court does not have to accept the excuse if he/she later claims that this is the case (see *Piggott v DPP* [2008] WLR (D) 44). If the testing machine registers an error on the second sample in each of two cycles, then further breath samples can be required (at another police station or using another machine for example) and failing to comply is an offence (s 7(6)), even though previous samples were supplied (see *Hussain v DPP* [2008] EWHC 901). In *Bielecki v DPP* [2011] EWHC 2245 (Admin) it was decided that a court could draw an inference (ie draw their own conclusions) whether a request for a specimen of breath that was translated by an accredited interpreter will have been understood by a non-English speaking suspect.

19.9.5.2 Blood and urine tests

These may either be requested by the suspect (the 'statutory option', see 19.9.5.1), or be required under s 7(3) of the Road Traffic Act 1988 (see the start of 19.9.5). The requirement to provide a specimen of blood or urine can only be made at a police station or hospital.

Before such a blood or urine sample is taken the driver must be told:

- the reason(s) why breath specimens cannot be taken (from the list under s 7(3) in 19.9.5); and
- that he/she is therefore required to give a sample of blood or urine; and
- that failing to provide the specimen could result in his/her prosecution.

Apart from medical considerations, the driver cannot choose whether the sample will be blood or urine. Before proceeding with a blood test the driver should be asked if there are any medical reasons for not taking a blood sample. A blood sample must of course be taken by a medical examiner. After the sample has been obtained the driver can be bailed to return to the police station when the results arrive back from the laboratory. Blood and urine samples are usually sent to the laboratory by post. If the driver refuses (or is unable) to provide blood or urine samples, then he/she will have committed the offence of failing to provide samples for an evidential test (s 7(6), Road Traffic Act 1988).

19.9.5.3 Allowing for the delay between the offence and taking samples

As the human body continually breaks down alcohol it is assumed that the level of alcohol in a suspect's breath, blood, or urine at the time of an alleged offence will gradually decrease over time (if no more alcohol is consumed). It is a fact of law that a court will assume the level of intoxicants in the body at the time of the alleged offence were not less than the levels measured in the evidential test (s 15(2) of the Road Traffic Offenders Act 1988).

However, the accused may claim the 'hip-flask defence', insisting that he/she consumed alcohol or drugs after the offence but before the evidential sample was taken (eg that he/she ran off after a collision and went for a drink before the police arrived), or that he/she consumed intoxicants from a container (the proverbial (and sometimes actual) hip flask) in the vehicle after the preliminary test. This is formally referred to as 'post-incident drinking'. If he/she can prove this, the assumption under s 15(2) (see previous paragraph) cannot be made.

If a driver provides an evidential specimen and alleges he/she has consumed further intoxicants since the time of the alleged offence, 'back calculations' can be used to establish that the driver was in excess of the legal limit when the offence occurred. These calculations are based on the time elapsed since the offence, the subsequent consumption of alcohol, and the estimated rate of elimination of alcohol from the human body. Evidence for back calculations should be recorded on Form MG DD/D at the police station. However, if this defence is not raised until later, the relevant laboratory should be provided with as much information as can be obtained from the case papers and the officer in charge of the case.

The following information is relevant, where available:

* the type and quantity of alcohol consumed before the offence and, if possible, the times at which individual units of alcohol were consumed;
* the type and quantity of alcohol allegedly consumed after the offence but before the test;
* the driver's characteristics: weight, height, build, age, sex, and any medical conditions;
* details of any food consumed from six hours before the offence until the provision of a breath or laboratory specimen; and
* details of any medication taken regularly or within four hours prior to drinking.

19.9.6 Key differences between ss 4 and 5 Road Traffic Act 1988 offences

	s 4 'Unfit to drive'	s 5 'Over the prescribed limit'
Vehicle	Mechanically propelled vehicle; includes motor vehicles (see 19.2.1)	Motor vehicle only (see 19.2.1)
Offence	Unfit through drink or drugs	The proportion of alcohol in breath (or blood or urine) exceeds the prescribed limit. Failing/refusing to provide a specimen
Preliminary tests	Not mandatory. However, if a motor vehicle is being used a drugs or impairment test can be carried out (assuming the equipment is available and the officer has been trained in its use)	Preliminary breath test required (unless arrested or being investigated for s 3A or s 4 offences)
Evidence	Impairment test, and blood or urine test results for drugs or alcohol (if available)	Breath, or blood, or urine test results for alcohol
Arrest	The power is provided by s 24 of the PACE Act 1984, which requires the officer to have a reason why it is necessary, such as 'to allow the prompt and effective investigation of the offence' (see 10.6.4)	After a positive preliminary breath test the power to arrest (on suspicion that the proportion of alcohol in the person's breath or blood exceeds the prescribed limit) is provided by s 6D(1) of the Road Traffic Act 1988

	s 4 'Unfit to drive'	s 5 'Over the prescribed limit'
Power of entry	Power of entry to arrest (s 17(1)(c)(iiia) of the PACE Act 1984, see 9.5.1)	Power of entry (s 6E(1) of the Road Traffic Act 1988) for the purposes of: • making the requirement for a preliminary test; • arresting on suspicion that the proportion of alcohol in the person's breath or blood exceeds the prescribed limit; but only after an accident involving injury to any person

TASK 15

1. If you are a trainee police officer, find out what preliminary test equipment is available for you to use and how to use it. This information should be available at your police station or from your force policy documents.

   • Would you only be authorized to use equipment to test for breath alcohol, or could you test for drugs as well?
   • Would you be able to carry out a preliminary impairment test?

2. The suspected commission of a moving traffic offence is one reason for requiring a driver to be tested for the presence of alcohol in his/her body. Give some examples of moving traffic offences under the Public Passenger Vehicles Act 1981, the Road Traffic Regulation Act 1984, and the Road Traffic Offenders Act 1988.

19.9.7   Drink- and drug-driving, and admission to hospital

Here we consider situations where a driver has been admitted to hospital after an accident. This is covered under s 9 of the Road Traffic Act 1988. A hospital is defined by the Act to mean an institution which provides medical or surgical treatment for in-patients or out-patients. The term 'patient' is not defined and will be a question of fact for the court to decide, but generally speaking a patient is a person who is currently on hospital grounds receiving medical treatment (or waiting to receive medical treatment).

Before a requirement is made or any test carried out on the person, the medical practitioner (usually a doctor) in immediate charge of his/her case must be notified of the proposals for tests. The procedures must be explained and the doctor must be given the opportunity to object (s 9(1) of the Road Traffic Act 1988), as the welfare of a patient is of primary importance. A further complicating factor is that the suspect might receive drugs as part of his/her medical treatment, and these could interfere with the accuracy of the police investigation alcohol and drugs tests.

19.9.7.1   Obtaining samples from a hospital patient

The regulations governing such procedures are given in s 9(1) of the Road Traffic Act 1988. Before making any requirements the relevant medical practitioner must be notified. A general description of preliminary and evidential tests is given in 19.9.4 and 19.9.5.

Preliminary tests in a hospital can only be requested and carried out if the doctor agrees, and he/she will object if the process is prejudicial to the care or treatment of the patient. If the doctor does not object, the patient can be asked to cooperate with a preliminary test. If the result of the test is negative, the patient must be told that no further action will be taken with regard to tests for alcohol. If he/she does not cooperate and refuses to have the test, he/she should be reported for an offence under s 6(6) of the Road Traffic Act 1988. Note that a person who is a patient in hospital cannot be arrested for failing to cooperate with a preliminary test (s 6D(3)).

Evidential tests will be carried out if the result of the preliminary test is positive (or the patient fails to complete the test). The outline procedure is shown in the diagram.

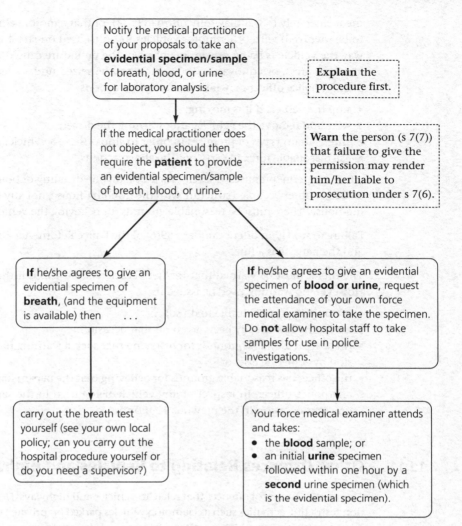

For a blood test, a police medical practitioner must take the specimen of blood. If this is not possible, then another medical practitioner may be asked (this is very rare), but he/she should not have a responsibility for the clinical care of the patient.

An unconscious patient is not able to take part in a breath test and so a blood sample will be required, and once again the relevant medical practitioner must be notified (see s 9(1A) of the Road Traffic Act 1988). Consent cannot be given by an unconscious patient, so in such circumstances it is lawful for a medical practitioner to obtain a specimen of blood (s 7A(3)). However, this must not be subjected to a laboratory analysis until the patient comes round and gives permission (s 7A(4)). It is an offence to refuse such permission (s 7A(6)).

TASK 16 A trainee police officer is required to attend the accident and emergency department at the local hospital. There she makes a lawful requirement for a sample of breath, blood, or urine from a patient who was driving a vehicle at the time of a collision. Unfortunately, whilst waiting for the police medical practitioner to arrive, the patient is discharged from hospital and leaves the building.

Does the obligation for the patient to provide that sample still stand? Refer to *Webber v DPP* [1998] RTR 111 for your answer.

19.10 Vehicles and Harassment

What powers are available to the police when people are racing in cars and therefore causing concern for other people in the area? There may be reasonable grounds under the Road Traffic Act 1988 for believing that a mechanically propelled vehicle has been driven carelessly or inconsiderately (s 3), unlawfully off-road (s 34), or that a motor vehicle is involved (or is likely to be involved) with other motor vehicles in unlicensed on-street racing. If, as a result of the way the vehicle is being driven, members of the public are caused (or are likely to be caused) alarm, distress, or annoyance, the vehicle can be seized under s 59 of the Police Reform Act 2002. A police officer may take the following actions:

- stop the vehicle if it is moving;
- seize and remove the vehicle, after warning the driver;
- enter certain types of premises in order to stop or seize a vehicle; and
- use reasonable force to carry out the above actions.

(Here, the term 'premises' does not include a private dwelling or home, nor does it include any garage or other occupied structure with the dwelling-house, nor any land attached to the dwelling-house. There must be reasonable grounds for believing the vehicle is on the premises.)

Failure to stop is an offence under s 59(6) of the Police Reform Act 2002. It is triable summarily, and the penalty is a fine.

The driver must be warned that his/her vehicle will be seized if the improper use continues. However, no warning need be issued if:

- it would be impracticable to do so;
- a warning has already been given on that occasion;
- there are reasonable grounds for believing that such a warning has been given on that occasion by someone else; or
- the officer has reasonable grounds for believing that the person has been given a warning (by any police officer, in respect of any vehicle being used in the same or a similar way) on a previous occasion in the previous 12 months.

19.11 Other Offences Relating to Vehicles and Highways

There are a number of offences that relate to vehicles and highways. Here we cover the new legislation restricting activities such as clamping vehicles parked on private land, and some offences that relate to activities on a highway that might cause distress or inconvenience to other road users.

19.11.1 Immobilizing vehicles parked on private land

Private individuals and organizations who immobilize or move vehicles parked on private land, obliging the owner/driver to pay a release fee, may commit an offence under the Protection of Freedoms Act 2012.

It is an offence under s 54(1) for a person without lawful authority to:

- immobilize a motor vehicle by attaching to it (or to part of it) an immobilizing device, for example a wheel clamp (s 54(1)(a); or
- move or restrict the movement of a vehicle, for example by towing it away or blocking its movement with another vehicle (s 54(1)(b).

The offence requires an intention to prevent or inhibit the removal of the vehicle by a person otherwise entitled to remove it. Consequently, a householder who moves a vehicle a few metres away from the entrance to his/her driveway does not commit the offence as he/she does not intend to prevent the driver from eventually retrieving the vehicle.

The 'law of contract' does not provide lawful authority to the landowner or operator of a commercially run car park to immobilize or move a vehicle, even when the terms and conditions of the parking are clearly displayed and the vehicle is parked for a longer period than permitted (s 54(2)). So a car park operator who clamps a vehicle in such circumstances is likely to have committed an offence. However, for a car park where the movement of vehicles in and out is restricted by the use of a rising-arm barrier the situation is different. If a car driver does not pay the parking fee and therefore cannot leave because the barrier remains down, no offence is committed by the car park owner or operator (s 54(3)). Anyone entitled to remove a vehicle cannot commit this offence. An example might be the representative of a hire company who retrieves one of her vehicles after the hire agreement has expired (s 54(4)).

This offence is triable either way and the penalty is a fine.

19.11.2   **Non-driving offences on highways**

Some of the more common offences are described here.

Wilful obstruction is an offence under s 137 of the Highways Act 1980. It is an offence for a person:

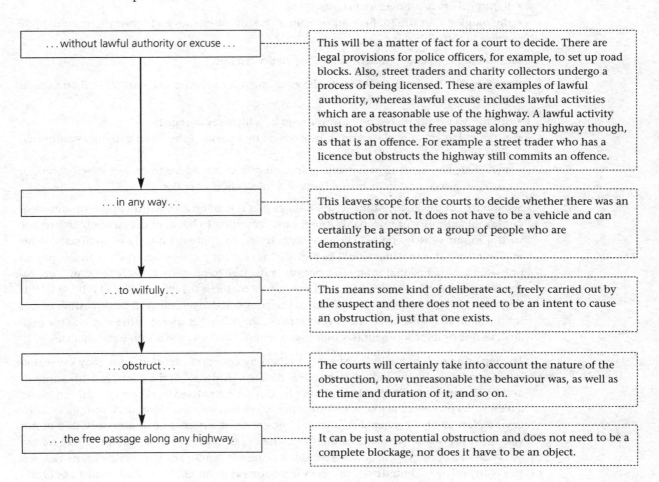

. . . without lawful authority or excuse . . .	This will be a matter of fact for a court to decide. There are legal provisions for police officers, for example, to set up road blocks. Also, street traders and charity collectors undergo a process of being licensed. These are examples of lawful authority, whereas lawful excuse includes lawful activities which are a reasonable use of the highway. A lawful activity must not obstruct the free passage along any highway though, as that is an offence. For example a street trader who has a licence but obstructs the highway still commits an offence.
. . . in any way . . .	This leaves scope for the courts to decide whether there was an obstruction or not. It does not have to be a vehicle and can certainly be a person or a group of people who are demonstrating.
. . . to wilfully . . .	This means some kind of deliberate act, freely carried out by the suspect and there does not need to be an intent to cause an obstruction, just that one exists.
. . . obstruct . . .	The courts will certainly take into account the nature of the obstruction, how unreasonable the behaviour was, as well as the time and duration of it, and so on.
. . . the free passage along any highway.	It can be just a potential obstruction and does not need to be a complete blockage, nor does it have to be an object.

This offence is triable summarily and the penalty is a fine.

'Unauthorized campers' can be directed away from a roadside under s 77 of the Criminal Justice and Public Order Act 1994. This provides local authorities with the procedure for removing persons residing in vehicles 'on any land forming part of a highway; on any other unoccupied property, or on any occupied land without the consent of the owner'.

Vehicles or trailers must not be left in a dangerous position on a road (s 22 of the Road Traffic Act 1988). It is an offence for a person in charge of a vehicle to cause or permit:

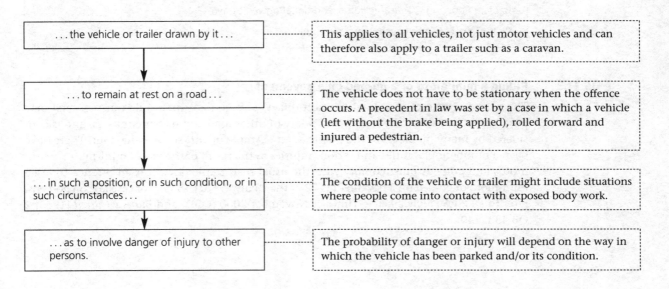

. . . the vehicle or trailer drawn by it . . .	This applies to all vehicles, not just motor vehicles and can therefore also apply to a trailer such as a caravan.
. . . to remain at rest on a road . . .	The vehicle does not have to be stationary when the offence occurs. A precedent in law was set by a case in which a vehicle (left without the brake being applied), rolled forward and injured a pedestrian.
. . . in such a position, or in such condition, or in such circumstances . . .	The condition of the vehicle or trailer might include situations where people come into contact with exposed body work.
. . . as to involve danger of injury to other persons.	The probability of danger or injury will depend on the way in which the vehicle has been parked and/or its condition.

Specific Incidents

This offence is triable summarily and the penalty is a fine.

Lighting fires or letting off firearms near a highway is an offence under s 161 of the Highways Act 1980. This prohibits any person (without lawful authority or excuse) from:

- depositing anything on a highway which leads to someone getting injured;
- lighting a fire on or over a carriageway; or
- discharging a firearm (or firework) within 50 feet of the centre of a highway if it could injure a user of the highway.

This offence is triable summarily and the penalty is a fine.

Interfering with road signs, other traffic equipment, or vehicles may put other road users at risk. Traffic equipment is defined as:

- anything lawfully placed on or near a road by a highway authority;
- a traffic sign lawfully placed on or near a road by a person other than a highway authority; and
- any fence, barrier, or light lawfully placed on or near a road (eg to protect street works), or any item placed under the instructions of a chief officer of police.

Section 22A of the Road Traffic Act 1988 states that it is an offence to (intentionally and without lawful authority or reasonable cause) cause anything to be on or over a road, or interfere with a motor vehicle, trailer, cycle, or with traffic equipment (directly or indirectly). This applies only if the activities would be regarded as obviously dangerous to a reasonable person or bystander; that is, that injury to a person or damage to property is likely to occur. The reasonable person or bystander does not have to be a motorist (*DPP v D* [2006] EWHC 314). It is irrelevant that the suspect was unaware of the potential danger; this will be a question of fact for the court to decide given the circumstances. The offence is triable either way and the penalty is a fine or imprisonment (six months summarily and seven years on indictment).

The repairing of vehicles in the street is a relatively common occurrence but may cause nuisance to other residents and environmental damage. Under s 4 of the Clean Neighbourhoods and Environment Act 2005, it is an offence to 'carry out restricted works on a motor vehicle on a road'. This includes the repair, maintenance, servicing, improvement, dismantling, installation, replacement, or renewal of a motor vehicle or of any part of or accessory to a motor vehicle. However, no offence is committed if the works were not carried out for gain or reward or as part of a business, and gave no reasonable cause for annoyance to persons in the vicinity. Nor is any offence committed if the work is required as a consequence of an accident or breakdown and repairs were necessary on the spot or carried out within 72 hours.

Holding or getting onto a motor vehicle (or an attached trailer) that is moving and on a road, in order to be towed or carried is an offence (s 26(1) of the Road Traffic Act 1988). This is a summary offence and the penalty is a fine.

TASK 17 Several complaints have been made by residents in the neighbourhood of a club. They say that at closing time they have seen people throwing rubbish bins and other items about the streets, tampering with traffic lights, and deflating vehicle tyres.

What offences might have been committed?

19.11.3 Riding a mini-moto or a go-ped on a pavement

The use of mini-motos (miniature motorbikes) and go-peds (petrol-driven scooters) may pose potential risks to the health and safety of other road and pavement users, and is considered by many members of the public as an example of anti-social behaviour. There have been a number of fatalities and serious injuries as the result of the use of mini-motos. Mini-motos and go-peds must comply with the usual road traffic laws. It is an offence to use a mini-moto or go-ped on a pavement (s 72 of the Highways Act 1835). For case law on go-peds, refer to *DPP v Saddington*, The Times, 1 November 2000 (QBD) and *Burns v Currell* [1963] 2 QB 433, 440.

19.12 Methods of Disposal for Motoring Offences

When investigating the kind of road traffic offences we have described so far, there are several ways of dealing with a suspect. The decision will be based upon a number of issues, including local force policy and the police officer's discretion (see 3.6). The methods of disposal for such offences include:

- a verbal warning;
- the VDRS (Vehicle Defect Rectification Scheme);
- an FPN (fixed penalty notice); and
- reporting a suspect for the purposes of issuing a written charge.

The flowchart summarizes the investigative process for dealing with motoring offences.

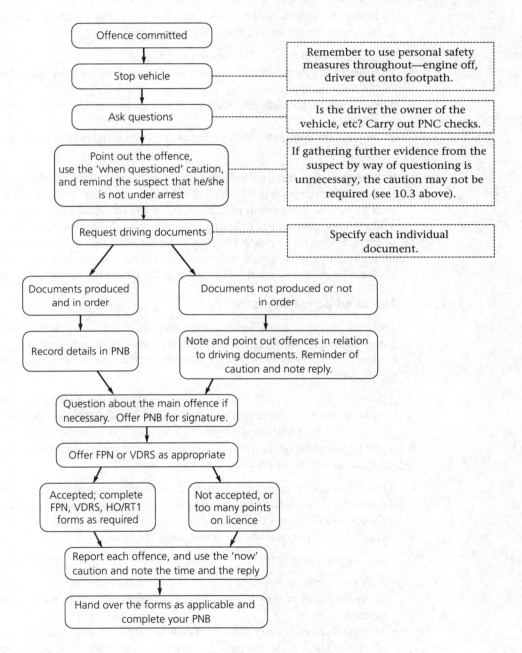

19.12.1 Vehicle Defect Rectification Scheme

Drivers in possession of a vehicle found to be in an unsuitable condition can be given the opportunity to join the Vehicle Defect Rectification Scheme (VDRS). This will depend upon both the circumstances of the offence and the officer's discretion. The VDRS is a way of dealing with certain minor vehicle defects without the need to prosecute or issue a fixed penalty notice.

The advantages of this scheme include:

- the defects are rectified, which contributes to road safety;
- the offender does not have to go to court; and
- better police and public relations: the only time many people will come into contact with the police is during the investigation of road traffic matters and VDRS is partly supportive, rather than wholly punitive.

When considering using the VDRS the police officer must point out the offence to the person responsible for the vehicle and inform him/her that no further action will be taken if he/she agrees to participate in the scheme. However, he/she should also be informed that participation in the VDRS is voluntary. If the driver declines to participate in the VDRS, he/she will be issued with a fixed penalty notice, or reported for the offence.

To avoid the possibility of prosecution when using the VDRS, the driver must complete the following within 14 days of the ticket being issued:

1. Repair the defect or renew the faulty body part.
2. Submit the vehicle for examination at a Department for Transport approved testing station (an MOT testing station).
3. Have the VDRS form endorsed at the MOT testing station to confirm that the fault is rectified.
4. Forward the completed VDRS form to the Central Ticket Office within the time specified on the ticket.

If the driver fails to return the form within the specified time, he/she can be prosecuted by way of written charge (as if the VDRS had not been used). The copy of the form will be returned after 21 days to the relevant police officer, for the reporting process. He/she will need to write a duty statement (see 10.12) which will include evidence relating to the offence, in the same way as for reporting a suspect for the purposes of issuing a written charge (see 19.12.3). The officer will submit a case file (see 26.3), including a report requesting the issue of a written charge. The charge will outline the offences for which the driver was reported.

19.12.2 The fixed penalty system

The fixed penalty system for motoring offences (Pt III, Road Traffic Offenders Act 1988) provides offenders with the opportunity to pay a fixed fine instead of going to court. The system is similar to the Penalty Notice for Disorder (PND) system for anti-social behaviour offences (see 10.13.2).

A fixed penalty notice (FPN) can only be issued to the person actually committing the offence or driving the vehicle involved; a FPN cannot be used for people who cause or permit an offence (see 19.2.4 for 'cause' or 'permit'). In some circumstances a FPN can be issued by leaving the documents on the vehicle without the need for the driver to be present, such as a parking ticket affixed to a car's windscreen.

If the FPN is not accepted by the driver, there is no further action to be taken on the street, and the driver will have to be reported and prosecuted. A fine for a FPN must be paid within 28 days (to the Central Ticket Office in the area). If the fine is not paid within this time, it will be increased by 50 per cent and be recovered by the courts.

There are two kinds of FPN:

- Non-endorsable fixed penalty notices (NEFPN), for offences which do not add penalty points to an offender's driving licence, such as offences relating to parking, seatbelts, and vehicle lighting.
- Endorsable fixed penalty notices (EFPN), for offences which add penalty points to an offender's driving licence. Such offences include contravening a red traffic light, failing to conform to a stop sign, and driving a vehicle with defective tyres.

19.12.2.1 Issuing a non-endorsable fixed penalty notice

When a police officer in uniform has reasonable grounds to believe that a person is committing or has committed a fixed penalty offence, a FPN can be issued in respect to that offence (s 54 of the Road Traffic Offenders Act 1988). If the driver is present the police officer should:

1. point out the offence;
2. caution the driver using 'when questioned' and inform him/her that he/she is not under arrest (PACE Code C, para 10.2) but that a failure to cooperate or to answer a particular question may make him/her liable to detention or arrest (see 10.3.1);
3. question the driver and allow him/her to ask questions (in relation to the offence(s));
4. check that the driver wishes to proceed with a FPN;
5. complete and issue the NEFPN;
6. report the driver or owner for the offence;
7. use the 'now' caution (see 10.3.4).

If the driver is not present and the offence relates only to the vehicle, an NEFPN can be attached to a stationary vehicle (s 62(1)). Note that it is an offence for any other person to remove or interfere with any FPN fixed to a vehicle.

The flowchart below summarizes the process.

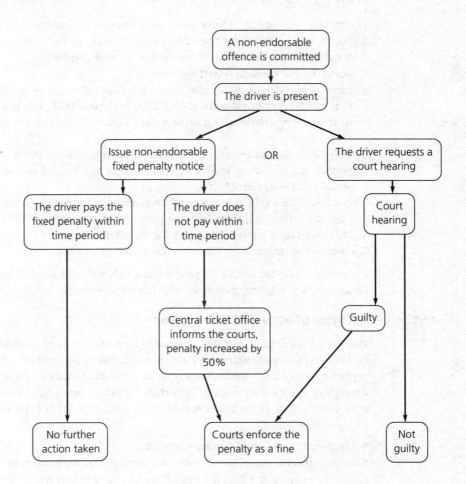

19.12.2.2 Endorsable fixed penalty notices

Where the penalty for the offence is obligatory endorsement, s 54 of the Road Traffic Offenders Act 1988 states that an EFPN may only be used if:

- the driver produces a licence and its counterpart for inspection and surrender;
- the driver would not be liable to disqualification (due to the number of points already on the licence); and
- the driver accepts an EFPN.

The procedure for issuing an EFPN is the same as that for a NEFPN, except for checking and retaining the driving licence and providing the driver with a receipt for the licence.

If the licence contains more than 12 points then an EFPN cannot be used and the driver will have to be reported for prosecution. If the driver does not have a driving licence available, a provisional EFPN should be issued and the driver must produce his/her licence for inspection at a police station (of his/her choice) within seven days.

Specific Incidents

19.12.2.3 Conditional offer of fixed penalty

If the FPN cannot be handed to a driver or attached to a static and unattended vehicle, then a conditional offer can be sent to the alleged offender (s 75 of the Road Traffic Offenders Act 1988). This could apply for speeding offences detected by automatic camera devices, or when a police officer sees a driver disobeying a road sign but it is impossible or too dangerous to follow. The conditional offer will state the circumstances of the alleged offence, the relevant fixed penalty, and explain that no further proceedings will take place in relation to the offence for 28 days from the date of issue. If payment is made within that period (and the licence is surrendered for obligatory endorsement offences), there will be no court proceedings. Police officers and staff at Central Ticket Offices can arrange for conditional offers to be sent.

19.12.3 Reporting for the purposes of issuing a written charge

To report a person for the purposes of issuing a written charge, the following procedure is used. The police officer must:

1. examine the vehicle or have seen the offence being committed;
2. decide what offence has been committed (having gathered evidence in the usual way, that is using his/her senses, what was seen, felt, smelt, and so on);
3. point out the offence(s) to the driver;
4. caution the driver using the 'when questioned' form of caution and inform him/her that he/she is not under arrest (PACE Code C, para 10.2), but that any failure to cooperate or to answer a particular question may make him/her liable to detention or arrest (see 10.3.1);
5. make PNB entries recording the questions and answers about the offences (eg when the person last inspected the vehicle, how long ago he/she began the journey, was he/she already aware of the defect?);
6. offer the PNB to the driver to read and sign as a true record of the interview;
7. offer the driver (if appropriate) the opportunity to use the VDRS or a FPN;
8. tell the driver 'I am reporting you for the offence(s) of...';
9. caution the driver using the 'now' caution—(see 10.3.4).

A driver electing for the VDRS scheme or a FPN will still need to be reported for the offence because he/she might not comply with the requirements.

19.12.4 A Notice of Intended Prosecution

The Road Traffic Offenders Act 1988 safeguards the rights of an individual suspected of committing certain road offences by informing them at the earliest opportunity of his/her suspected involvement. This is usually done through a Notice of Intended Prosecution (NIP), which will specify the nature of the offence and the time and place where it is alleged to have been committed. This applies for offences listed in s 1(1) of the Road Traffic Offenders Act 1988, such as:

- dangerous driving and dangerous cycling;
- careless and inconsiderate driving and careless and inconsiderate cycling;
- failing to conform with the indication of a police officer when directing traffic;
- failing to comply with a traffic sign; and
- speeding offences.

The full list is contained in Sch 1 to the Road Traffic Offenders Act 1988, available on the www. legislation.gov.uk website.

Section 1(1) states that a person cannot be prosecuted for any of these offences, unless he/she has been either:

- warned (a verbal NIP) at the time of the offence of the possibility of prosecution (s 1(1)(a)); or
- served with a NIP (s 1(1)(c)) within 14 days of commission of the offence, setting out the possibility of prosecution; or
- served with a written charge within 14 days of commission of the offence (s 1(1)(b)).

It is advisable to provide the NIP as a document, because if the suspect later claims not to have fully understood a verbal NIP it would be the responsibility of the prosecution to prove the contrary (see *Gibson v Dalton* [1980] RTR 410). The NIP can also be served by post when necessary. This could be, for example, in relation to a speeding offence detected by an automatic camera device, or when a police officer observes a vehicle go through a red traffic light and it is too dangerous to follow. A PNC check (see 6.9.1) on the registration number of the vehicle will provide the name and address of the registered keeper (see 19.2.4). The registered keeper must then state who was driving the vehicle at the time of the incident (s 172(2) of the Road Traffic Act 1988); a failure to comply is an offence (s 172(3)). In *Whiteside v DPP* [2011] EWCA 3471(Admin) it was decided that:

- a NIP has been lawfully served as long as it has been posted (even if the recipient does not receive it);
- the recipient does not have a defence simply because he/she has no knowledge of the NIP being sent, unless it can be proved that under the circumstances it was not reasonably practicable to have been made aware of the Notice;
- the offence is committed even if a recipient of the NIP does not know that he/she is obliged to state who was driving.

A NIP is not required when the vehicle concerned has been involved in an accident (s 2(1)), unless the driver failed to stop (see 19.7.2). Neither is it required if a FPN (see 19.12.2) has been issued at the time the offence was committed (s 2(2)). Final methods of disposal after the NIP has been served will include a written charge or a conditional offer of a fixed penalty (see 19.12.2.3).

TASK 18

1. Imagine you are a police officer. Write down the sequence of what you would need to say and do when dealing with a driver in each of the following three situations:

   (a) driver unable to produce driving documents;
   (b) an offence for which you can use a fixed penalty notice; and
   (c) an offence for which you can use the Vehicle Defect Rectification Scheme.

2. Find out about and list the road traffic offences for which a non-endorsable fixed penalty notice can be used.

19.13 Answers to Tasks

TASK 1 As you approach and examine the vehicle, you would consider health and safety implications (see the answer to Task 6 for more details). You would need to consider gathering the following evidence:

1. whether the wheels of the car can rotate freely (at least one wheel appears to have seized);
2. whether the normal vehicular controls are operative (the steering appears locked); and
3. if the engine can be started.

In such cases (where proof is required to determine whether or not a motor vehicle is still a motor vehicle for the purposes of the Road Traffic Act 1988), evidence would be more appropriately obtained by a thorough examination by a qualified and authorized vehicle examiner. If the results of the examination reveal that the car can still be classified as a motor vehicle, then the van driver will be 'using' the car in a legal sense.

TASK 2

1. Knowing that he/she was likely to be disqualified from driving, a person might contact the DVLA to obtain a duplicate licence before the court hearing and then submit one and keep the other. Alternatively, the person could obtain a stolen licence and produce it to assume the identity of another person (if it was an old-style licence without a photograph).
2. He/she should carry out PNC checks, local database checks such as the voters' register, and question the person about his/her identity to match the details given with the details held on police computer databases. Local knowledge would be very important here as he/she would be able to ask about the description of localities and names of places to help verify the identity of the driver.

TASK 3

- You could use your investigative skills to locate the user or keeper by accessing the PNC or undertaking house-to-house ('H2H') enquiries in the vicinity of the vehicle.
- If you could not find the driver or keeper, you could use a DVLA form CLE 2/8. The DVLA can be notified through their website.

TASK 4

1. The form is a HORT/1 (Home Office Road Traffic Form 1), known colloquially as a 'Horti' or 'producer'.
2. One major problem associated with the use of this form is that, if the driver has not given details of his/her true identity, the police will probably not be able to find the driver again, and he/she will continue to drive, and will avoid prosecution.
3. The details should be checked; a police officer should:
   - always check the driver and vehicle details with the PNC to establish if they match;
   - use the PNC to check whether the driver has a criminal record;
   - request further proof of identity, for example passports and credit cards;
   - request a voters' register check through the control room; and
   - request telephone numbers and ask control room to call the numbers to verify the existence of the person.

There may be no need to use an HORT/1 if the person's verified address is nearby.

TASK 5 You might ask the driver about his insurance; whether he is insured to drive the vehicle, the name of his insurance company, the starting and expiry date of his policy, the cost of the policy, and the type of vehicle (including the engine size) that he is entitled to drive.

Further questions could be asked about the vehicle such as its engine size and whether it has been modified in any way. If it seems that the engine size of the vehicle differs from the size given on the PNC, a request could be made for the vehicle to be examined by an authorized vehicle examiner.

The police officer should then contact the insurance company and speak to a police liaison representative to find out exactly what type of vehicle the person is insured to drive.

TASK 6 The date of first registration could be obtained from the Certificate of Registration and/or the PNC.

Possible defences to not having a valid test certificate could be countered by asking the driver what was the starting point and destination of his/her journey. If the answer to either of those questions involves the testing of the vehicle, then further questioning may be necessary to counter the possible defences of vehicles travelling to a pre-arranged test and where the vehicle has failed the test.

TASK 7 How did your list compare?

No vehicle is permitted to use blue flashing lights unless it belongs to a defined list (such as police vehicles); however, the number of types of vehicles on the list continues to grow. A decision was made a few years ago to allow vehicles owned by HM Revenue and Customs and used in pursuit of serious crime to be fitted with blue warning beacons (Explanatory Memorandum to the Road Vehicles Lighting (Amendment) Regulations 2005 No 2559).

TASK 8

1. True. The term 'hours of darkness' refers to a period from half an hour after sunset to half an hour before sunrise.
2. False. It is the Road Vehicles Lighting Regulations 1989 as amended by the Road Vehicles Lighting (Amendment) Regulations 1994.
3. False. The correct rate is 60 to 120 pulses per minute.
4. False. The lawful circumstances are:
   (a) while stationary, to warn other road users of a temporary obstruction;
   (b) to summon assistance to the driver, conductor, or inspector of a bus (PSV);
   (c) on a motorway or unrestricted dual carriageway to warn following drivers of the need to slow down due to a temporary obstruction ahead; and
   (d) in the case of a school bus, while loading or unloading (or about to do so) passengers (under 16 years of age), provided the bus displays the statutory yellow reflective signs indicating the presence of schoolchildren.

5. True.
6. True.
7. True.

TASK 9 As you approach the vehicle, you would need to consider health and safety implications and consider the potential problems associated with the:

- the driver attempting to move off in the vehicle;
- traffic passing by the location;
- engine running;
- driver making off;
- location of the ignition keys; and
- handbrake not being applied.

You could follow the following sequence:

1. Speak to the driver and introduce yourself.
2. Outline your reason for stopping the vehicle.
3. Ask the driver for his/her name, address, and date of birth.
4. Ask the driver for his/her connection with the vehicle (is he/she the owner too?).
5. Ask the driver for details of his/her intended destination and the place where he/she began the journey.
6. Examine the vehicle whilst considering the potential health and safety implications associated with:

   - moving parts inside the engine compartment such as thermostatically controlled cooling fans;
   - high temperatures associated with parts such as brakes, exhaust systems, radiators, and engines;
   - harmful liquids such as hydraulic fluids, battery acid, anti-freeze, and hot engine coolant;
   - sharp objects such as exposed tyre cords or faulty bodywork;
   - movement of the vehicle and anything in, on, or under the vehicle;
   - movement of other vehicles and persons around you; and
   - the surface upon which you and the vehicle are positioned and the existence of harmful objects or substances.

7. Note any possible offence(s) detected in the usual way, through gathering evidence using your senses (ie what you saw, felt, smelt, and so on).
8. Point out the possible offence(s) to the driver.
9. Caution the driver using the 'when questioned' form and ensure that you satisfy PACE Code C, para 10.2 by informing the person that he/she is not under arrest, but that failing to cooperate or answer a particular question may affect his/her immediate treatment (see 10.3.1).
10. A police officer would write down the questions and answers about the offences in his/her PNB, for example when the person last inspected the vehicle, was he/she already aware of the defect, and how long ago did he/she begin the journey?
11. The PNB entry would then be offered to the driver to read and sign that the notes are a true record of the interview.
12. The driver could then be reported for the offences and cautioned.

* Note that the total is over 100 per cent as some collisions/accidents have more than one contributory factor.

TASK 10 See the Highway Code (available online) for answers. You can also practise your understanding using the 'Practise your driving theory test' page on the www.gov.uk website.

TASK 11 The legislation that provides the power to implement such a policy is s 6A of the Road Traffic Act 1988; whilst in uniform or not, if a police officer reasonably believes that a person is driving, has been driving, is attempting to drive, or is in charge of a motor vehicle on a road or public place at the time of an accident, he/she may require the person to cooperate with one or more preliminary tests including a breath test. The officer must be in uniform to administer the test.

The computer checks that could be carried out on the drivers involved include:

1. a PNC check to:

   - discover if the drivers are wanted, or disqualified from driving;
   - ascertain if there are any reports regarding the vehicles being stolen; or
   - establish details of the keepers of the vehicles;

2. local checks to determine whether the drivers' names and addresses are valid and/or if they are locally wanted on warrant.

TASK 12

1. The order is as follows, with percentages for 2012:

Order	Factor	Percentage of main contributory factors*
(d)	Driver failed to look properly	45%
(g)	Driver failed to judge other person's path or speed	23%
(f)	Driver careless, reckless, or in a hurry	16%
(j)	Poor turn or manoeuvre	15%
(e)	Loss of control	14%
(b)	Slippery road (due to weather)	10%
(a)	Pedestrian failed to look properly	10%
(c)	Sudden braking	8%
(i)	Travelling too fast for conditions	8%
(h)	Following too close	7%

2. The ACPO document *Policing the Roads—5 Year Strategy 2011–2015* (available online) lists five priorities: reducing road casualties, disrupting criminality, countering terrorism, patrolling the roads, and combating anti-social road use. The document *Road Policing* on the College of Policing Authorised Professional Practice website contains further relevant information.

TASK 13

1. (a) Jerry is driving.
   (b) Maz is not driving.
   (c) Both Hari and Pat are driving.
2. (a) (ii) and (iii): it applies on a road or in a public place.
   (b) (i): it applies anywhere.

TASK 14

1. Using a hand-held mobile telephone (mobile) while driving could easily amount to failing to have proper control of the vehicle, or even dangerous driving (see 19.8.1).
2. Other 'careless driving' activities may include lighting a cigarette, turning round and shouting at children, searching for a station on the radio, changing CDs, looking for sunglasses, looking in the mirror and applying make-up, or any other similar action that diverts the attention from driving.

TASK 15

1. Trainee police officers are likely to receive instruction quite early on in the use of an Electronic Breath Screening Device (ESD), and be provided with opportunities to use one during Supervised Patrol. It is usually a hand-held device, with a mouthpiece that will need to be changed for each test.
   In relation to preliminary drug test devices, each force has different policies relating to which staff can carry out this procedure, so trainee officers might not be trained in the use of such a device straight away.
   A preliminary impairment test can only be conducted by an officer who has been approved for it by his/her chief officer.
2. Moving traffic offences include:
   • contravention of traffic regulations, for example speed limits; and
   • failing to comply with traffic signs and directions, for example traffic lights.

TASK 16 Yes, in such circumstances the required sample may then be taken at a police station, regardless of whether an appropriate breath-analysis machine is available. See *Webber v DPP* [1998] RTR 111.

TASK 17

Section 22A of the Road Traffic Act 1988 states that a person is guilty of an offence if he/she intentionally and without lawful authority or reasonable cause:

(a) causes anything to be on or over a road;
(b) interferes with a motor vehicle, trailer, or cycle; or
(c) interferes (directly or indirectly) with traffic equipment.

TASK 18

For all of these situations the officer should first point out offence(s), then caution and inform the driver that he/she is not under arrest, but that a failure to cooperate or to answer particular questions may make him/her liable for detention or arrest (see 10.3.1). Then the officer should question the suspect and note the answers given. The next stage will vary:

1(a) Driver is unable to produce driving documents when required: the next stage is to complete HO/RT/1 to produce the documents at a police station, report the suspect, and caution the suspect ('now' version).

1(b) Fixed penalty notice offence: for a non-endorsable offence with driver present the officer should then: complete and issue NEFPN, and report and caution the suspect (the 'now' caution). The driver can refuse the offer of a FPN and elect to go to court instead. If the driver is not present the completed NEFPN should be fixed to the vehicle.

For an endorsable offence when the driver is present the next stage is to offer FPN in lieu of court, report the suspect, and give the caution (the 'now' version). The driver must be in possession of his/her licence and be willing to submit it, and it must have less than 12 points. If the licence is not available, a provisional FPN can be issued. If the licence has more than 12 points or the driver refuses the offer of a FPN, then no further action can be taken on the street.

1(c) VDRS offence: offer VDRS and issue form if accepted, then report the suspect and caution him/her ('now' version). If the VDRS offer is refused then no further action can be taken on the street.

2. The following offences can all be dealt with by a non-endorsable fixed penalty notice:

Road Traffic Act 1988

s 14	No seatbelt—adult, front or rear
s 15(2)	No seatbelt—child in front of vehicle
s 15(4)	No seatbelt—child in rear of vehicle
s 16	No helmet—motorcycles
s 19	Parking heavy goods vehicle on verge or footway
s 22	Leaving vehicle in dangerous position
s 23	Unlawful carrying of passengers on motorcycles
s 24	More than one person on a pedal cycle
s 34	Driving a motor vehicle off-road
s 35	Failure to comply with traffic directions
s 36	Failure to comply with traffic signs
s 40A	Using vehicle in dangerous condition, etc
s 41A	Construction and Use Regulations relating to brakes, steering, and tyres
s 41B	Construction and Use Regulations relating to weight (goods and passenger vehicles)
s 42	Other Construction and Use Regulations relating to lighting offences

Road Traffic Act 1988

s 87(1)	Driving other than in accordance with a driving licence
s 163	Failing to stop vehicle for constable in uniform
s 172	Failing to notify the police of driver's identity

Specific Incidents

Highways Act 1835

| s 72 | Cycling on the footway (not Scotland) |

Highways Act 1980

| s 137 | Obstruction of highway by a vehicle |

Road Traffic Regulation Act 1984

s 5(1)	Contravention of Traffic Regulation Order outside London
s 8(1)	Contravention of Traffic Regulation Order inside London
s 11	Breach of experimental traffic order
s 13	Breach of experimental traffic scheme inside London
s 16(1)	Use of vehicle contrary to temporary prohibition/restriction orders at roadworks
s 17(4)	Contravention of motorway regulations
s 18(3)	Contravention of one-way traffic on trunk road
s 20(5)	Contravention of restriction/prohibition of use of vehicle on a particular road
s 25(5)	Breach of pedestrian crossing regulations
s 29(3)	Use of vehicle in street playground
s 35A(1)	On-road parking restrictions, etc
s 47(1)	Failure to pay excess charge at parking place
s 53(5)	Breach of parking place Designation Order, etc
s 53(6)	Breach of parking place Designation Order, etc
s 88(7)	Contravention of minimum speed limit
s 89(1)	Speeding offences

Vehicle Excise and Registration Act 1994

s 33	Using or keeping vehicle without excise licence
s 42	Driving or keeping vehicle without registration mark
s 43	Driving or keeping a vehicle with obscured registration mark
s 43C	Using incorrectly registered vehicle

Road Vehicles (Display of Registration Marks) Regulations 2001

| | Registration mark not in prescribed format |

Greater London Council (General Powers) Act 1974

| s 59 | Parking on footways, verges, etc |

Zebra, Pelican and Puffin Pedestrian Crossing Regulations and General Directions 1997

| reg 24 | Overtaking a moving or stationary vehicle in controlled area of a crossing |

20 Damage to Buildings and Other Property

20.1 Introduction

In this chapter we examine the law surrounding damage to property, much of which stems from the Criminal Damage Act 1971. We also look at legislation to help protect ancient monuments and heritage sites in the UK. An understanding of these aspects of the law will help a trainee officer with achieving the requirement to 'Conduct the Initial Investigation and Report of Volume Crime According to (the) National Policing Plan' under the PAC heading 'Investigation'.

Criminal damage is both one of the most common crimes in England Wales and often one of the most visible (it is an example of one of the so-called 'signal crimes' described in 4.4.2). It often comes to the notice of the police through reports from the public, property owners, and others. However, intelligence might also feature, particularly in terms of identifying and taking action for 'taggers' (individuals who spray graffiti on buildings or trains or other objects as a form of stylized self-identification). Likewise, the tags themselves might also provide useful information for building intelligence about the activities of a local criminal 'gang' (see 15.9 and 22.6.4).

The investigation of criminal damage, arson, and 'heritage crime' (eg the illegal removal of objects from archaeological sites) provides good examples of the multi- and inter-agency approach to crime reduction described in 3.3. For example, detection of criminal damage might well involve (or be led by) PCSOs and Local Authorities, suspected arson investigation is often carried out by specialist fire and emergency service investigation teams (subject to local agreements), and cultural crime detection might well involve partnership with English Heritage and others.

20.2 Criminal Damage

In terms of criminal damage, a trainee officer is most likely to encounter graffiti and minor damage to fences, cars, and bus shelters. Occasionally, the damage can be much more serious, when, for example, the damage has been caused by fire or involves culturally important buildings. Graffiti is among the most common forms of criminal damage, and to help reduce its prevalence it is a summary offence under the Anti-Social Behaviour Act 2003 to sell aerosol paint containers to a young person under the age of 16 (s 54(1)).

Section 1(1) of the Criminal Damage Act 1971 describes the offence of criminal damage. It states that an offence is committed by a person who 'without lawful excuse destroys or damages property belonging to another, intending to destroy or damage any such property or being reckless as to whether any such property would be destroyed or damaged'.

The damage must be to something 'real'; that is, something that you could touch. It can be land ('real estate') or personal items including money (eg a wad of notes). It includes wild animals in captivity (but not wild flowers). Criminal damage also includes destroying an item (ie the property is no longer any use and cannot be repaired). The cost of such 'damage' would be the cost of replacing the item.

The property must belong to another person who has custody, control, a right, an interest, or is in charge of the property. (This is in contrast with the offence of criminal damage, life endangered (see 20.2.1)). It is possible for a person to criminally damage their own property but only if it also belongs to somebody else (eg if the property is jointly owned).

The person carrying out the offence must either intend to cause the damage, or be reckless as to whether the property would be damaged. Recklessness is explained in the flowchart.

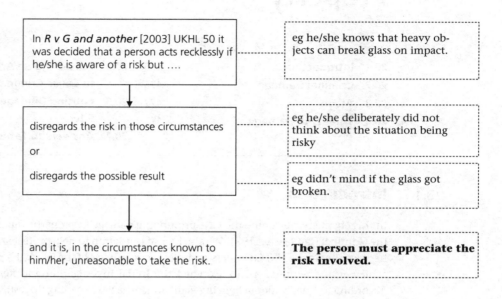

In *R v G and another* [2003] UKHL 50 it was decided that a person acts recklessly if he/she is aware of a risk but ....

eg he/she knows that heavy objects can break glass on impact.

disregards the risk in those circumstances

or

disregards the possible result

eg he/she deliberately did not think about the situation being risky

eg didn't mind if the glass got broken.

and it is, in the circumstances known to him/her, unreasonable to take the risk.

The person must appreciate the risk involved.

The person must also not have a lawful excuse for causing the damage. A person would have lawful excuse if they had an honestly held belief that:

- he/she had **permission** from the owner of the property (or an appropriate person) to cause the damage; for example, a recovery operator is authorized by a car owner to load the car onto a recovery vehicle, and damages it in the process. This would also apply if the operator believed that the owner would have given permission but is unable to do so (eg having been taken to hospital unconscious);
- that his/her own or another's property was in immediate need of **protection** by reasonable means, if for example a car had slipped down a steep embankment and was likely to slip still further, and a recovery operator damages it when pulling it back up onto the road.

This offence is triable either way. If the value of the property damaged or destroyed is less than £5,000, the offence is tried summarily (s 22 of the Magistrates' Courts Act 1980). The penalty is six months' imprisonment and/or a fine if tried summarily, and ten years' imprisonment on indictment.

TASK 1 Robyn, after her arrest for being drunk and disorderly, smears her own excrement on the walls of the police station cell. Discuss whether this constitutes criminal damage.

20.2.1 Criminal damage, life endangered

The offence of 'criminal damage, life endangered' (s 1(2) of the Criminal Damage Act 1971) is committed by a person who destroys or damages property intending (or being reckless as) to endanger life. To prove the offence, there is no requirement for the offender to try to kill someone or for any actual injury or harm to occur. There is only a necessity to prove that the damage was caused intentionally or recklessly and that there was potential for another to be harmed as a result of that damage being caused.

For this offence the property can belong to the offender or to another person. For example, an angry man deliberately damages the brakes of his own car knowing that his partner will be driving it later that day, and intending her life to be endangered. The damage caused must also be the cause of the danger: for example, shooting at someone in a room through a window both endangers life and damages the window, but it is the bullet that endangers the life, not the damage from the window, so this would not be criminal damage life endangered.

This offence is triable by indictment only and the penalty is life imprisonment.

20.3 **Arson**

Arson is destroying or damaging property by fire. It is covered under s 1(3) of the Criminal Damage Act 1971. For a person to be found guilty of this offence at least some of the damage must have been caused by fire (excluding smoke damage). For the offence to be proved there must be an intent or an element of recklessness in relation to the use of fire.

The penalty is six months' imprisonment and/or a fine if tried summarily, and up to life imprisonment on indictment.

> **TASK 2** For what reasons might the crime of arson be committed? Can the behavioural profiling of arsonists be of potential value to the police and others?

20.4 **Threats to Damage**

This offence is covered in s 2 of the Criminal Damage Act 1971 and there are two points to prove in relation to such a threat:

- the conduct that is threatened must refer to damage; and
- the extent of the threatened damage must constitute an offence under s 1 of the Criminal Damage Act 1971. This can include acts of simple damage under s 1(1), as well as criminal damage where life is endangered (s 1(2)).

However, the offence of making threats to damage **cannot** be committed if the threat involves an element of recklessness as to whether the property would actually be destroyed or damaged (see 20.2 in relation to the meaning of 'reckless'). For example, imagine an angry woman shouts to a neighbour 'If your kid keeps throwing stones over my wall, I'll start chucking them back, and no, I don't care where they land'. She is reckless as to whether damage is caused so she would not have committed the offence of 'threats to damage'.

A stated intention to destroy or damage the property can be communicated in any way—for example, email, text message, fax, letter, or phone call—and it could be an idle threat: there need be no intention to actually carry it out. The recipient does not have to believe the threat will be carried out immediately (if at all), nor does the recipient need to be put in fear. In any prosecution it will be for the court to decide whether what was communicated had enough substance and immediacy to constitute a threat. In some circumstances it might be more appropriate to consider an offence under s 4 of the Public Order Act 1986 (see 14.4.3.3).

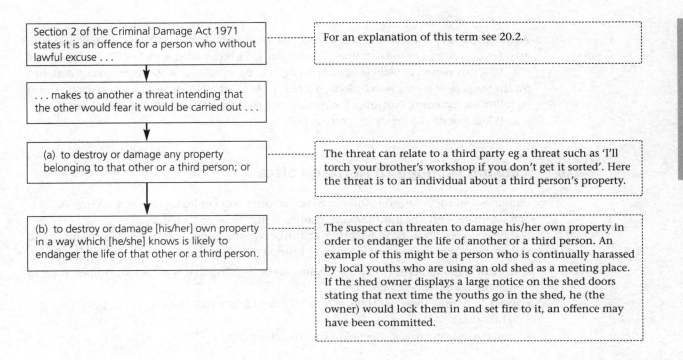

Section 2 of the Criminal Damage Act 1971 states it is an offence for a person who without lawful excuse . . .

For an explanation of this term see 20.2.

. . . makes to another a threat intending that the other would fear it would be carried out . . .

(a) to destroy or damage any property belonging to that other or a third person; or

The threat can relate to a third party eg a threat such as 'I'll torch your brother's workshop if you don't get it sorted'. Here the threat is to an individual about a third person's property.

(b) to destroy or damage [his/her] own property in a way which [he/she] knows is likely to endanger the life of that other or a third person.

The suspect can threaten to damage his/her own property in order to endanger the life of another or a third person. An example of this might be a person who is continually harassed by local youths who are using an old shed as a meeting place. If the shed owner displays a large notice on the shed doors stating that next time the youths go in the shed, he (the owner) would lock them in and set fire to it, an offence may have been committed.

Specific Incidents

This offence is triable either way and the penalty is six months' imprisonment and/or a fine if tried summarily, and ten years' imprisonment on indictment.

20.5 Possessing an Article with Intent to Cause Criminal Damage

This offence is covered in s 3 of the Criminal Damage Act 1971. The type of article involved here can be literally anything. The Law Commission, who advised on the Act, explained that:

> [t]he essential feature of the proposed offence is to be found, not so much in the nature of the thing, as in the intention with which it is held. (Law Commission No 29, para 59)

This offence is triable either way. The penalty is six months' imprisonment and/or a fine not exceeding the statutory maximum if tried summarily, and ten years' imprisonment on indictment.

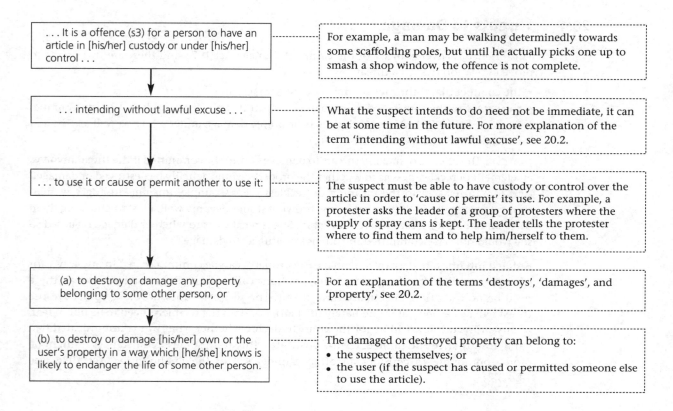

A power to search for articles made or adapted for use in the course of or in connection with an offence under s 1 of the Criminal Damage Act 1971 is provided under s 1(2)(a) of the PACE Act 1984. Any person or vehicle (and anything in or on a vehicle) can be searched and detained for the purpose of such a search. Section 2 of the PACE Act 1984 and its Codes of Practice must be followed, including providing the person with the information listed in para 3.8 of Code A (GO WISELY, see 9.4.1 on search procedures).

20.6 Causing Damage to Heritage Sites

Buildings and sites of historic interest have had some form of legal protection in the UK since 1882. Initially only the most important ancient sites were protected, such as Stonehenge and the great castles. Over the years, however, further specific legislation has been introduced and this provides protection to many types of historic site such as:

- scheduled monuments (an archaeological site or building that is of national importance, eg Stonehenge or Dover Castle);
- listed buildings (over 500,000 in the UK including small houses, street furniture, and lighthouses);
- protected marine wreck sites (46 in UK coastal waters);

- protected military remains of aircraft and vessels of historic interest (includes losses during peacetime);
- conservation areas (local authority designated areas of special architectural or historic interest; around 9,000 in the UK);
- Registered Parks and Gardens (gardens of stately homes, public parks, and cemeteries on a national register; over 1,600 in the UK);
- Registered Battlefields (43 in the UK, eg at Hastings); and
- World Heritage Sites (17 in the UK, eg Canterbury Cathedral, Stonehenge, and Hadrian's Wall).

20.6.1 Legislation to protect heritage sites

A number of authorities (local authorities, the police, and English Heritage) share the responsibility to enforce legislation designed to protect heritage sites. Partnership-working (see 3.3) plays a fundamental role in tackling heritage crime, both at a local operational level and nationally at a strategic level. However, this is a challenging task due to the shared responsibility, the relative rarity of incidents, and the lack of expertise and understanding of the nature of the possible 'harm'.

20.6.1.1 The Ancient Monuments and Archaeological Areas Act 1979

It is an offence under s 28 of the Act to damage or destroy (without lawful excuse) a 'protected monument' (defined in s 28, and includes a scheduled monument). The person must know that it is a protected monument and intend to destroy or damage it, or be reckless as to whether it would be destroyed or damaged. The offence is triable either way and the penalty is a fine and/or imprisonment (six months if tried summarily and two years on indictment).

Other sections of this Act may also be relevant to the trainee police officer:

- s 42 under which it is a summary offence to use a metal detector in a 'protected place' without the written consent of English Heritage, and an either-way offence to remove an object in such circumstances;
- s 9 under which it is an either-way offence to damage, demolish, or alter a listed building.

20.6.1.2 The protection of wrecks and military remains

The Protection of Wrecks Act 1973 can be used to designate an area containing a 'protected wreck'. All wreck material (eg fixtures and fittings, coins, cannon, and wreck timbers) must be reported to the 'Receiver' at the Maritime and Coastguard Agency.

The Protection of Military Remains Act 1986 makes it an offence to interfere (without a licence) with the wreckage of any crashed, sunken, or stranded military aircraft or designated vessel. The Act provides two levels of protection, depending on whether the site is designated as a 'protected place' or a 'controlled site'. Greater restrictions are placed upon activities at the latter. Investigations under this Act usually relate to diving and are undertaken by the Ministry of Defence supported by the police and English Heritage. Most of the offences in relation to this Act are triable either way.

20.6.2 Offences relating to cultural objects and treasure

We have already referred to the legislation around the use of metal detectors (see 20.6.1.1). Further legislation is available to help regulate the trade in 'cultural objects' and 'treasure' found at archaeological or other heritage sites. It is an offence to:

- dishonestly deal in a tainted cultural object knowing or believing that the object is tainted (s 1 of the Dealing in Cultural Objects (Offences) Act 2003). A 'cultural object' is defined as an object of historical, architectural, or archaeological interest. It is 'tainted' if a person illegally excavates an object from its original position in the ground, or removes it from a building, structure, or monument of historical, architectural, or archaeological interest in the UK or elsewhere (after 30 December 2003). The offence is triable either way.
- fail to notify the district coroner within 14 days of finding 'treasure' (s 8(3) of the Treasure Act 1996). 'Treasure' includes old gold, silver, or bronze coins, collections of prehistoric metalwork, and objects found with such coins or metalwork (s 1 of the Treasure Act 1996). The reporting of treasure is dealt with through the Portable Antiquities Scheme. This is a summary offence.

20.7 Answers to Tasks

TASK 1 The excrement will not have destroyed the walls of the police cell, but the walls will need to be cleaned and have therefore been damaged. The cost of the damage will be equal to the cost of the cleaning operation. The suspect will need to be interviewed to prove or disprove whether she intended to damage the walls or was reckless as to whether or not the damage was caused. If the drunken state was self-induced, it will not be a defence.

TASK 2 Arson is regularly found to be the single biggest cause of fire. In 2007 a Home Office analysis of incidents identified particular motives for setting arson in the UK, as shown in the table.

Form of arson	Motive	Proportion of all arson (year 2000 data)	
		Property	Vehicles
Youth disorder and nuisance	Vandalism and boredom	36%	39%
Malicious	Revenge, racism, clashes of beliefs/ rivalries, or personal animosities	25%	3%
Psychological	Mental illness or suicide	26%	13%
Criminal	Financial gain and fraud, or the concealment of other crimes (theft, murder, etc)	13%	45%

(Based on Home Office, 2007)

However, there are alternative but complementary ways of understanding the causes of arson. For example Canter and Fritzon (1998) identified two main categories; person-orientated (towards self or others) arson and object-orientated arson. A further distinction is possible, namely in terms of the motive being either expressive (eg to express some form of emotion or psychological need) or instrumental (eg to serve as a means of achieving another goal). This gives rise to fourfold typology, as summarized in the table:

	Person-orientated	Object-orientated
Expressive	Directed inwards (towards the offender) possibly as the result of anxiety, depression, or suicidal tendencies	Direct at an object (eg building) but for symbolic or emotional needs of the offender
Instrumental	Directed outwards (to others), possibly as revenge for perceived wrongdoing	Directed at an object (eg building), but where arson is a consequence of another motive, for example to hide evidence of a burglary

(Based on Canter and Fritzon, 1998 and Fineman, 1995)

Canter and Fritzon (1998) found that there were statistically significant associations between each of the four motive categories and the offender's social and psychological background. For example, repeat arsonists tended to fall into the expressive/object-orientated category, whereas an expressive/person-orientated arson was more likely to be committed by a person with a history of psychiatric problems. This approach thus provides a potential basis to 'profile' unknown offenders on the basis of the types of arson incidents observed. The Home Office and others see some virtue in this approach in terms of aiding arson investigation (Home Office, 2007, p 15).

21 | Attempted Offences and Encouraging or Assisting Crime

21.1 Introduction

In this chapter we discuss legislation designed to deal with suspects who stop just short of committing an indictable offence but can nevertheless be prosecuted for attempting to commit the full offence. In addition, those accomplices who are not the actual perpetrators of an offence who encourage or assist in the commission of a crime from a distance are also considered.

21.2 Criminal Attempts

A person planning a criminal offence might not actually commit the full offence. This could be because the suspect lost his/her nerve, or was disturbed, or simply found that his/her plans were impracticable. The offence of a criminal attempt can be used to penalize a criminal for carrying out an act just short of committing a full offence. This offence (a criminal attempt) is described under s 1(1) of the Criminal Attempts Act 1981:

> If with intent to commit the offence to which this section applies, a person does an act which is more than merely preparatory to the commission of the offence, [he/she] is guilty of attempting to commit the offence.

The attempted offence must be an indictable offence (ie it can be tried on indictment in a Crown Court or either way at a magistrates' court or a Crown Court—see 5.5.1), however, see 21.2.3 for certain indictable offences which cannot be attempted. Summary offences cannot be attempted in terms of this legislation, but see 21.2.4.

The mode of trial is the same as for the main offence. For either-way offences the penalty is the same maximum penalty as the substantive offence when tried summarily. For an indictment-only offence the maximum penalty is the same as for the substantive offence.

21.2.1 Criminal intent

The suspect must have formed criminal intent (*mens rea*) in all three of the areas shown in the table:

The suspect must have the intent to	Example
Commit the full offence	The suspect intended to steal a car or to rob a person
Take part in a series of acts which will lead to a final outcome of committing the full offence	The suspect made a point of collecting the tools together, going to a house, and forcing a window in order to break in
Carry out **all** the elements of the offence	In order to attempt a theft, for example, the suspect must have acted dishonestly with the intention of appropriating the property belonging to another **and** of permanently depriving the other of it

For a person to be found guilty of an attempt to commit an offence, the suspect must have more than an intention to do it (*R v Campbell* [1991] Crim LR 268). The suspect must demonstrate his or her guilty intent by carrying out acts, and these must be more than just preparing to commit the full offence. Therefore, it would not be enough if the suspect had some cloth and a container of petrol in a bag, and transported them to the rival's house; his/her actions might still be considered as preparatory. If, on the other hand, the suspect went to the front door of his/her rival's house with cloth soaked in petrol, put it in the letter box, and then used a lighter to try to set light to the cloth, this would show a clear intent to carry out the offence of arson. These acts would probably be considered as more than merely preparatory and could therefore constitute an attempt under the Criminal Attempts Act 1981.

The final act carried out by the accused must be in combination with all the other preparatory acts, and have no aim other than to complete the full offence. For example, a group of people might be seen getting out of a van close to a fenced enclosure containing scrap copper. They cut a hole in the fence that would be big enough for someone to climb through. On seeing a security guard, they quickly leave but are stopped some miles away. One of the group still has some wire clippers in his pocket and another throws a pair of bolt croppers out of the van. They have done more than merely prepare to steal the metal; they have committed an attempt under s 1(1) of the Criminal Attempts Act 1981 (see *Davey v Lee* (1967) 51 Cr App R 303).

It is sometimes difficult to identify the fine line between preparatory acts and attempts to commit crime. However this is primarily a jury's decision, based upon 'common sense'. In *R v Geddes* (1996) the court provided a useful suggestion on how to interpret the statute: does the available evidence demonstrate that the defendant has performed an action which shows that he/she has actually tried to commit the offence in question, or has he/she merely become ready to put him/herself in a position or equipped him/herself to do so? (*R v Geddes* (1996) 160 JP 697).

In addition, s 1(3)(b) states that, if the person **believes** that he/she is committing an offence, he/she will still be regarded as having attempted it, even if it is proved later that it would not have been possible to commit the full offence. For example, a woman is paid money to travel from another country to the UK with a suitcase that she believes contains heroin. On arrival at the UK port her suitcase is searched and she admits to importing heroin into the UK. However, tests on the substance in the suitcase reveal it to be harmless vegetable matter, and not drugs. The offence of importing controlled drugs has not been committed, therefore, but the person has still attempted to commit the crime (*R v Shivpuri*, [1987], AC 1).

The recent case of *L v CPS* (2013) QBD (Admin) demonstrates that the prosecution need to prove more than mere presence at the scene of a robbery to convict a person of involvement in attempted robbery. A group of youths were accused of acting together to attempt to rob young children of their phones. All were convicted. However, the appeal was allowed in the case of L as there was insufficient evidence to demonstrate that he encouraged the attempted robbery at any stage. His mere presence amongst the group of offenders was found to be insufficient to convict him of attempted robbery.

21.2.2 Thorough planning and practical preparation

Section 1(2) of the Criminal Attempts Act 1981 states that there must be evidence that the person actually planned to personally carry out the act, rather than just planning it (in which case someone else could have carried it out): 'the person does an act which is more than merely preparatory to the commission of the offence'. If there is something else to be done before the completion of the offence, it does not amount to an attempt.

It does not matter (for the offence of criminal attempt) whether the attempted offence would actually have been impossible to carry out (s 1(2)). An example would be a woman who shoots a man lying on a bed intending to kill him, but the man unbeknown to her was already dead. Even though the full offence of murder is impossible, she has still in fact attempted to kill someone.

21.2.3 Offences which cannot be criminally attempted

Section 1(4) of the Criminal Attempts Act 1981 lists several categories of offence that cannot be 'attempted', such as summary offences. There are also a number of ways in which indictable offences cannot be attempted. These include:

- conspiracy to commit an indictable offence: that is, an agreement between people to commit an offence;

- aiding, abetting, counselling, procuring, or suborning the commission of an indictable offence: for example, a person knew all the circumstances concerning a particular murder and did everything apart from deliver the fatal kick to the head; and
- assisting offenders: for example, knowingly helping offenders avoid arrest or concealing information, perhaps by paying money to a witness to stop him/her giving testimony in any trial.

21.2.4 Summary offences and attempted criminal acts

As we have already noted, summary-only offences cannot be attempted in terms of the Criminal Attempts Act 1981. However, certain summary offences amount to attempts to commit certain acts, for example:

- 'attempting to drive whilst unfit through drink or drugs' (see 19.9.2); and
- 'interfering with vehicles' (see 16.8.2.2).

The latter was created to cover situations where a person's actions effectively amount to an attempted 'Taking a conveyance without the owner's consent' offence (see 16.8.2), but could not be charged as such because TWOC is a summary offence.

> **TASK 1** The following case relating to an attempt subsequently went to appeal. Predict the result of the appeal and explain your reasoning.
>
> A man was seen by a teacher in the lavatory block at a school. A cider can carrying the man's fingerprints was found in one of the cubicles and his rucksack, containing a large kitchen knife, some rope, and a roll of masking tape, was found in some nearby bushes. He was charged and convicted of attempted child abduction, the prosecution putting forward the argument that he had been hiding in the lavatories to abduct a child. He appealed on the grounds that he had not attempted to commit the offence (*R v Geddes* [1996] Crim LR 894).

21.3 Encouraging or Assisting Crime

Quite commonly, criminal offences involve two or more accomplices. However, more often than not, they do not all actually perpetrate (carry out) the offence; some accomplices at the scene 'merely' offer encouragement. Other accomplices might assist in the commission of a crime from a distance, providing information, transport, or financial support.

A person who encourages or assists in a crime (but does not perpetrate the main offence) may believe or claim that he/she was not a true accomplice. However, under the Serious Crime Act 2007 there are three criminal offences in which a person becomes criminally liable for encouraging or assisting another person to commit an offence. Together they replace the common law offence of incitement (now abolished), and also provide additional scope for prosecution in cases where the crime has not yet taken place; previously there was no criminal liability for assisting the commission of an offence unless the offence had been committed or attempted. The legislation providing for these offences came into force on 1 October 2008 and does not apply retrospectively, so would only apply for conduct since that time.

Note that a person cannot be convicted of encouraging or assisting a crime for which he/she is the intended victim. For instance, a 16-year-old schoolgirl could not be convicted of encouraging or assisting her teacher to engage in sexual activity with her. The teacher would commit the sexual offence of breach of a position of trust, but the girl could not be convicted of encouraging or assisting it as she is the person protected by that particular piece of legislation (s 51 of the Serious Crime Act 2007).

21.3.1 Intentionally encouraging or assisting an offence

This is covered by s 44 of the Serious Crime Act 2007, which states that an offence is committed by a person who:

Specific Incidents

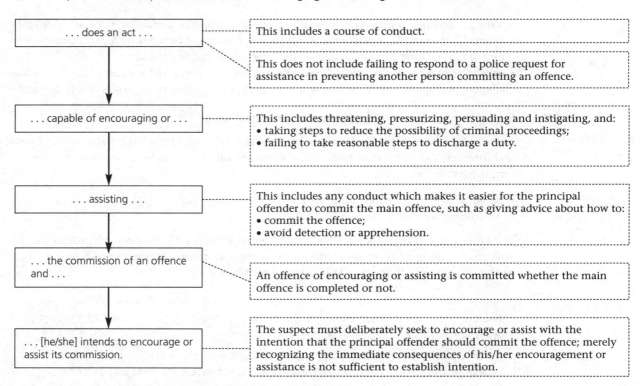

. . . does an act . . .	This includes a course of conduct.
	This does not include failing to respond to a police request for assistance in preventing another person committing an offence.
. . . capable of encouraging or . . .	This includes threatening, pressurizing, persuading and instigating, and: • taking steps to reduce the possibility of criminal proceedings; • failing to take reasonable steps to discharge a duty.
. . . assisting . . .	This includes any conduct which makes it easier for the principal offender to commit the main offence, such as giving advice about how to: • commit the offence; • avoid detection or apprehension.
. . . the commission of an offence and . . .	An offence of encouraging or assisting is committed whether the main offence is completed or not.
. . . [he/she] intends to encourage or assist its commission.	The suspect must deliberately seek to encourage or assist with the intention that the principal offender should commit the offence; merely recognizing the immediate consequences of his/her encouragement or assistance is not sufficient to establish intention.

We provide a few examples to illustrate some key points:

1. At a noisy and angry street demo, a police officer speaks to Dodie (a protestor) to try and help him calm down, but Dodie becomes increasingly irate and aggressive. Due to the loud noise, the officer is unable to summon assistance from a colleague. Instead the officer requests Neil, another protestor, to help restrain Dodie, but Neil refuses. Neil's refusal would probably not be regarded as encouraging or assisting a person to commit a criminal act.
2. Frankie lends a baseball bat to a neighbour who is scared that someone might possibly break into his house to steal some antiques. Frankie knows that a baseball bat is sometimes used as a weapon to injure people, but gives it to her neighbour with the sole purpose of helping him feel more confident. Subsequently an intruder is seriously injured by the neighbour using the baseball bat. For Frankie, this would probably not amount to assistance or encouragement to cause grievous bodily harm.
3. Kristoff is having an affair with Bella, one of his wife's (Shazia) workmates. Kristoff intends to murder Shazia and dispose of the body and make it seem that she has moved away. Bella knows all about Kristoff's plan and agrees to provide him with up-to-date information on Shazia's whereabouts during the day to give Kristoff a better opportunity to act without being caught. In the meantime, another work colleague overhears Bella talking about the plan, and she alerts Shazia, who flees the country. Bella has intentionally assisted in the commission of murder.
4. Brown works for a double-glazing firm and in return for payment gives his friend Mal a spare key from a recently installed door, knowing that Mal will use the key to burgle a particular house. One night Mal enters the house, takes the keys of an expensive car, and drives off in it with the intention of selling it. Brown has intentionally assisted in the commission of burglary (for burglary, see 16.4).

21.3.2 Believing one or more offences will be committed

This relates to belief rather than intent. An offence is committed under s 45 of the Serious Crime Act 2007, when a person 'does an act capable of encouraging or assisting the commission of an offence' (the main offence) believing that the main offence will be committed and that his/her act will encourage or assist its commission.

This differs from the s 44 offence in that for a s 45 offence the person (A) offering the encouragement and assistance to B must believe that B will commit the offence, and that his act will encourage or assist its commission. It is immaterial whether the main offence is completed or not.

The following is likely to constitute a s 45 offence.

> Black is a car salesman who makes a copy of a key to the most expensive car on his fore-court. During an evening out, he gives the spare key to his friend Steve, knowing that Steve will probably steal the car in the near future. Steve does not steal the car but is arrested during a burglary and is found in possession of the spare key. During his interview, Steve outlines his reasons for possessing the spare key, including Black's involvement. In this example, Black has committed the s 45 offence because, although he did not intend that Steve should commit theft, Black still believed that Steve would commit the offence. It is irrelevant that the offence was not actually committed by Steve.

The s 46 offence is very similar to the s 45 offence, but applies in circumstances where there are a number of possible main offences planned by person B (rather than just one), and person A (providing the encouragement or assistance) does not know which offence(s) B is going to commit.

It is immaterial whether A has any belief as to **which** main offence will be encouraged or assisted, nor does any main offence need to be completed.

> As an example of a possible s 46 offence the following:
> Tilly has been disqualified from driving and is now concerned that the local police will recognize her if she drives. Late one night she pays Jas to drive her to the next town. From what Tilly has said recently, Jas has a good idea that Tilly plans to carry out three offences: a serious assault in one house and two burglaries. Scared of getting caught, Jas drops Tilly off around the corner from the first house and drives off. However, Tilly suddenly decides to delay her plans until another time. Here, Jas believed that at least one of the three offences was going to be committed, and therefore she can be prosecuted and convicted for encouraging or assisting the commission of offences that she believed were going to be committed.

Other examples include a gun shop owner providing guns to a criminal gang knowing they will use them in criminal enterprises such as robbery, but being unclear as to specifics, and providing cutting agents to drug dealers to mix with illegal drugs in order to supply them to others, being unaware of what class of drugs they may be supplying and to whom (*R v Omar Saddique* [2013] EWCA Crim 1150). A further example in relation to organized crime would be where a person supplies a crime gang with various number plates for vehicles upon request. He knows they commit robbery, burglary, and murder, and often do so using stolen cars on false number plates. He is unaware which crime will be committed, but he knows the false number plates will be used.

21.3.3 Possible defences to encouraging or assisting offences

If the defendant can prove that it was reasonable for him/her to act the way he/she did (in the circumstances he/she was aware of or believed existed) this may be a defence (s 50) to an offence under s 44, 45, or 46. When determining what was reasonable, the following will be considered:

- The seriousness of the anticipated main offence: it might be reasonable to encourage or assist in the commission of a minor offence in order to prevent a more serious offence being committed. For example, Peta infiltrates a gang who are conspiring to commit an armed robbery. He tells one of the other members of the gang to steal a car for the gang to use when making off from the robbery. Peta's intention is to look credible in front of the other gang members so he can achieve his main objective of preventing the robbery from taking place. Therefore he may have a 'reasonable' defence.
- The purpose of the act of encouragement or assistance: it might be reasonable to encourage or assist in the commission of a minor offence in order to prevent more serious harm from

being inflicted. For example, Manny and Sam are members of a teenage gang on a housing estate. Sam meets with other members of the gang and together they plan to attack a rival gang and stab the leader, Taz. However, Manny does not want to attack Taz and succeeds in persuading Sam and the others to smash the windows of Taz's car instead. Manny is charged with encouraging Sam to commit criminal damage, but may have a 'reasonable' defence that his actions were to prevent a more serious offence.

- The authority under which he/she was acting: it might be reasonable to encourage or assist in the commission of an offence if it was done for the benefit of collecting evidence during an investigation by law enforcement agencies. For example, Boris, a 15-year-old, is tasked by a local authority trading standards department with going into a local shop and purchasing a lottery ticket.

The defendant may be able to plead impossibility as a defence if appropriate. If the crime that he/she encourages or assists would be impossible to commit, then he/she cannot be convicted. This is because a person can only be convicted if his/her acts are genuinely capable of encouraging or assisting a crime, which cannot apply if it is impossible for the main offence to be committed. However, a person could still be convicted of a criminal attempt as an alternative (see 21.2.2). Remember also a person cannot be convicted of encouraging or assisting a crime for which he/she is the intended victim (see the introduction to 21.3).

The maximum penalties for an offence under s 44, 45, or 46 of the Serious Crime Act 2007 will be the same as the maximum available on conviction for the relevant main offence.

21.4 Answer to Task

TASK 1 The suspect had never had any communication nor made any other contact with any of the pupils. As a result, the Court of Appeal concluded that the acts of the suspect were merely preparatory and that the suspect had not attempted to abduct a child or children.

22 | Intelligence

22.1 Introduction

This chapter examines in detail the place of criminal intelligence and how it is used to support policing objectives. We will also consider some of the components of intelligence gathering: sources, source handling, surveillance, research and development, the intelligence 'target package', and some of the laws and rules about what can and cannot be done with intelligence. Some of the material may not appear immediately relevant to the work of a trainee police officer, but after you join you will discover its importance as you move through your training. Many of the serious and organized-crime investigations which result in a successful prosecution have their origins in good intelligence. Very few investigations into Level 2 crime (and few of those at Level 1) would be effective without intelligence, and certainly much police time would be ill directed and fruitless. However, intelligence is not the only tool available; this Handbook also describes other complementary approaches, such as forensic investigation.

Significant cases such as the Rhys Jones murder on Merseyside and some arrests for suspected terrorist offences have highlighted both the importance and the difficulty of converting intelligence into evidence. In each case the police had information and intelligence from numerous sources but it proved highly problematic to convert the intelligence into admissible evidence. In the case of Rhys Jones, the police were able to use new legislation under which a key witness gave evidence of fact as a 'protected' witness (under the 'Assisting the Prosecution' programme, see 24.6.1.1), and the police also obtained recordings of conversations (using hidden audio devices) and key forensic DNA evidence. Through these means the identity of the offenders was confirmed. However, in the case of the terrorist suspects, these evidential links could not be established in the same way and the suspects were released without charge.

The Certificate in Knowledge of Policing includes the assessment criterion that learners should be able to 'describe the National Intelligence Model or a model relevant to their organisation and explain how it fits within their organisation'. The Diploma in Policing assessment unit concerned with gathering and submitting information requires the trainee to be able to 'describe the National Intelligence Model...and explain how it fits within their organisation'. An understanding of the NIM is an important requirement for trainee police officers, and it features either explicitly or implicitly within many parts of the IPLDP, including PIP Level 1, the IND modules, and particularly the OP 2 module. The NIM is covered in 22.6.

22.1.1 The definition of intelligence

Intelligence, in the investigative context, may be considered a form of information, but of a special kind—that is, it is information which has taken on meaning.

Simply put, the police deal with three distinguishable forms of incoming data:

- **Information**: normally from a source that needs no confidentiality constraints or protection. It is overt information, such as a call from the public advising the police of an occurrence.
- **Intelligence**: is more difficult to define but is generally considered to be information derived from many sources (some confidential) that has been recorded, graded, and evaluated.
- **Evidence**: can be either information or intelligence, and is generally material that can be admitted in a court of law and abides by the 'rules of evidence'—that is to say, it is admissible.

It is essential that a police officer is able to recognize these three as distinct because each requires different types of action. The Diploma in Policing requires that a trainee police officer is able to 'distinguish between information and evidence' (part of the assessed unit 'Gather and submit information to support law enforcement objectives'), and the Certificate in Knowledge of Policing requires learners to be able to 'define how to distinguish between information and evidence, and the procedures to follow for each'.

For example, we might have information concerning an increase in the number of thefts of radios from cars in a particular area. If we link this information to a change in payment policy by a local drug dealer (who is now accepting goods in lieu of money in payment for drugs) we begin to derive intelligence from the information.

Criminals will usually go to some lengths to prevent knowledge about what they do leaking out. They often seek to protect key questions about a crime or a criminal; the when, where, how, and why. Finding out about criminal intentions before a crime is committed, or using covert (hidden) methods after a crime has been committed, is one aspect of intelligence-led policing (ILP). Some of the methods for obtaining intelligence, information, and evidence (and how they are managed) are explained in the remainder of this chapter.

22.2   Covert Human Intelligence Sources

The police term for an informant or source is 'CHIS', which stands for Covert Human Intelligence Source. Criminals use many more descriptions (mostly unflattering) such as 'grass', 'snout', and 'nark'. Many intelligence sources are themselves criminals as they are normally the only people with real access to criminals, their plans, and their activities.

It is interesting to note that many government agencies are permitted to use sources to gain intelligence (provided for in the Home Office Codes of Practice under the Regulation of Investigatory Powers Act 2000 (RIPA)). Such agencies and departments include HM Revenue and Customs, the Ministry of Defence, the Department of Health, the Department for Work and Pensions, the Environment Agency, the Armed Forces, and the Food Standards Agency. Any agency using a CHIS must have a responsible authorizing officer and observe the other RIPA requirements. Local authorities must obtain judicial approval for surveillance activities and the use of CHIS (ss 37 and 38 of the Protection of Freedoms Act 2012).

22.2.1   The definition of a CHIS

We need to look closely at the definition of a CHIS. Members of the public who volunteer information about criminals or crimes are not generally defined as sources. A source is a person who has access to hidden criminal intentions or plans, and enters into arrangements to reveal this information.

The law is clear about what constitutes a source. Under s 26(8) of RIPA a person is a source if he/she establishes or maintains a personal or other relationship with a person for the covert purpose of:

• obtaining information or providing access to information to another person; or
• disclosing information obtained by the use of such a relationship, or as the consequence of the existence of such a relationship.

In essence it means that a CHIS is someone who cultivates another person to obtain information, or who provides access to information, or who discloses information. Notice that the words criminal or unlawful are not used here. This is because the information need not necessarily be crime-related, at least to start with. It is the 'covert' part which is important. (Thus, people like solicitors or bank officials who pass details of suspicious activity to the police are not sources because they are working in an open relationship with the police and not acting covertly.)

In general terms the term 'covert' usually means hidden, but RIPA provides a precise legal definition (s 26(9)(b)–(c)):

> a purpose is covert in . . . a relationship if it is conducted in a manner which is calculated to ensure that only one of the parties to the relationship is unaware of the purpose [and]

[a] relationship is used covertly, and information obtained is used or disclosed in a manner that is calculated to ensure that one of the parties to the relationship is unaware of the use or disclosure in question.

What this means in straightforward terms is that the person being cultivated by the CHIS (or from whom information is obtained because of that relationship) does not know that the CHIS is informing the police. As an alternative, consider this as a working (but strictly speaking, 'non-legal') definition: a CHIS is tasked by the police with cultivating or sustaining a relationship with a third person, and that third person doesn't know about the police involvement.

Under RIPA, any use or conduct of a CHIS by the police will always require authorization granted by the force authorizing officer (a senior police officer, usually a detective superintendent or higher) who is answerable to a surveillance commissioner with a national remit. The authorization (or 'authority') will normally last 12 months.

22.2.2 Source handling

Most forces use a qualified and experienced detective constable as a source handler, probably paired with another (perhaps less experienced) handler. It is good practice to have two handlers so that a CHIS (who could be manipulative and might have his/her own agenda) has less chance of exerting control over the handlers. A further advantage is that two can share the responsibility of handling, welfare issues, and recording of meetings with a CHIS. Sometimes, especially when meetings or intelligence taskings are urgent, there have to be 'singleton' meets between one handler and a source, but most forces recommend that this should never be routine.

The dedicated source-management unit is staffed by a CHIS controller, CHIS handlers, and support staff. The CHIS controller is responsible for the supervision, management, and control of all the staff in the unit. The CHIS handlers are responsible for the day-to-day management and recruitment of CHISs.

> **TASK 1** What qualities do you think would make a good source handler? Discuss this with your colleagues and produce a list of attributes, skills, and competencies necessary to handle a covert source with access to criminal information.

Handlers are usually detectives who have undergone an intensive training programme during which they learn (through scenarios and role-play) how to keep control when tasking informants, arranging secure meetings, and handling devious, dishonest, manipulative, and fantasizing sources.

A handler submits a report with details of the intelligence he/she has obtained from the CHIS, and writes a separate note to his/her controller detailing the meeting itself. The intelligence is passed in its raw state to the Research and Development unit or Force Intelligence Bureau, where it is assessed against what is already known, considered in the wider context, and then sanitized (see 22.5.1).

22.2.3 Restrictions on the use of sources

We have already noted that RIPA provides the definitions of a source and what is meant by covert, but the Act also determines the legal and practical parameters for handling a CHIS. We do not need to go into all the detail of the Act here, but there are special safeguards for vulnerable or young people, and a regular audit of authorizations by a surveillance commissioner, appointed nationally under a chief surveillance commissioner.

Attention is also drawn throughout RIPA to proportionality and to Articles in the Human Rights Act 1998 legislation, particularly with respect to the right to a private life. RIPA provides the necessary framework for the ethical and legal use of CHISs by properly trained source handlers who are aware of the full extent of their powers (but will not abuse them), as well as ensuring that the risks are proportionate to the expected gain. To make this a little more concrete, a source with excellent access to the upper echelons of criminality would not be used to establish the identity of a local graffitist.

Investigation and Prosecution

> **TASK 2** We noted earlier that a police CHIS is often a criminal, because it is usually through criminals that access can be gained to other criminals. What do you think the problems might be for a police force when recruiting and using an active criminal as a CHIS? Aside from the ethical and moral considerations, what practical difficulties might there be? How might they be met and overcome?

22.2.4 The consequences for the CHIS

When allowing a crime to go ahead, the CHIS can be designated as a participating informant (PI). This does not mean that the source will not be charged if he/she is involved in a crime (particularly if any pre-arranged limit to involvement in the crime has been exceeded). However, the sentencing judge will be made aware of the assistance provided by the accused.

Even when not active as a PI, an informant may be able to take advantage of the new 'assisting prosecutions' legislation contained within the Serious Organised Crime and Police Act 2005. A formal agreement can be made with an offender in order to secure evidence for the prosecution of other offenders.

The police and the Crown Prosecution Service usually adopt what they see as a pragmatic approach: if there is a risk to the source, the prosecution is very likely to be withdrawn and charges dropped and the source can be used again. No one can pretend that these are easy judgements; you may like to read further on this matter: see Harfield and Harfield (2005 and 2008).

22.2.4.1 Motivation of informants

The handler should identify a potential source's primary motive or motives (even before recruitment takes place), because this will affect how the CHIS should be handled. The primary motivation at the outset needs to be sufficient to sustain the source throughout the long period of gathering intelligence. This is a very under-researched area and hence what follows should be treated with some caution.

> **TASK 3** Consider for a moment why someone might decide to become a source for the police. Why would you betray your criminal colleagues? How would you keep it up, week after week, month after month? How do you keep the secret of your relationship over a period of time that may extend to many years?

Many sources will suggest that money is a key motivator. However, a CHIS might well make more money from the criminal enterprise he/she is reporting on, so we must look a little deeper; motivation is psychologically complex. For example, an experienced and 'lifestyle' criminal might inform on other criminals threatening his/her dominance. Other sources may be motivated by distaste for the crimes committed by the target criminal. In one contemporary case a young woman (with two young children) was motivated to inform on her brother, a prominent local criminal, because she had seen him downloading child pornography on his computer and suspected that he was an active paedophile.

It is easy to overlook the human needs of sources: like most people, they want affection, praise, contact, reward, encouragement, and a sense of being valued. Handlers can provide all these things for a source, but he/she might become too emotionally dependent upon a handler and be unable to function adequately (in other aspects of his/her life) without the handler's help. This can lead to problems. Other ethical dilemmas may also arise: for example, imagine a CHIS drug-user overdoses on drugs purchased with the money he received from the police. To what extent would the police be ethically or morally responsible?

22.2.5 Undercover officers and 'test purchase' operations

A highly trained police officer can work to penetrate a group of criminals, for example posing as a drugs importer or as a document supplier (eg for passports). However, the risk must be proportionate to the outcome. An undercover officer would only be used in relation to very serious crimes, such as high-profile robberies or conspiracy to murder. All operations using an undercover officer require authorization, and the risk assessment for this must be very detailed. Officers cannot sustain undercover roles for long and need to be reintegrated into the police force before they are compromised or exhausted by the continuous strain ('turned or burned'). This requires fastidious timing by the handler and supervisors, in order to maximize the benefits. Recent problems with undercover police activities have led to calls for more stringent supervision of such police practices. In 2012 a HMIC report criticized an undercover police officer for defying management instructions (HMIC, 2012); the trial against environmental activists subsequently collapsed.

Test purchase operations are used relatively frequently, and involve a police officer posing as a potential buyer for an illegally acquired item such as drugs. The whole transaction is monitored carefully (surveillance teams deployed and uniformed officers on hand), and when the moment is right, the dealer or seller is arrested and charged. The advantage for the police of such 'sting' operations is that an officer only needs to appear once in one location, thereby reducing the risk. The advantage in terms of criminal justice is that the criminal is caught in the act, and is therefore more likely to plead guilty. This saves time and expense, both for the police and the criminal justice system.

Officers planning and undertaking such operations must be sure that the proposed operation is proportionate and does not entrap individuals into committing offences they would not normally commit. If there is a lack of proportionality, or obvious entrapment, this could lead to either an application under s 78 of the PACE Act 1984 to have the evidence obtained rendered inadmissible, or the defence will put forward an abuse of process argument for illegality (that is a court will not allow a prosecution to continue as it is 'unfair').

> **TASK 4** What qualities and competences are required for a good undercover officer? What logistical and operational problems might arise? What needs to be considered when planning a test purchase operation?

22.3 Surveillance

The term 'surveillance' is used in an everyday sense and in a legal sense, and the meanings are slightly different. For the general public, surveillance generally means watching over something, but in a police and legal sense it generally means covert surveillance, where the subject of the surveillance is unaware that he/she is being monitored, and the monitoring is planned in advance. The use of covert surveillance is tightly controlled by the Regulation of investigatory Powers Act 2000 (RIPA, see 22.3.1). However, other types of monitoring, such as the use of CCTV by local authorities, generally do not involve the planned observation of a particular person and so are not regulated so closely (but see 22.3.1).

Principles about liberty and freedom must be respected; the surveillance might risk infringing the 'right to privacy and family life' (see 5.4). For obvious reasons we only provide a general description of what is involved here. Details are provided during initial training, as and when appropriate.

22.3.1 CCTV

The simplest and most obvious form of open surveillance is the ubiquitous CCTV camera, overlooking public and private premises, walkways, town centres, banks, railway stations, airports, and even police stations. The benefit of CCTV is that it gives 24-hour coverage of a location and its images are retrievable within a certain period; the disadvantage is that the location of the cameras is fixed—cameras cannot follow a target round a corner. In addition, CCTV cameras are usually easy to spot, so an aware criminal will note the locations of cameras and avoid them, or wear something which disguises his/her features.

CCTV cameras are principally operated by local authorities or shop security officers. If an operator spots a person behaving suspiciously and decides to observe him/her using the CCTV for a while, this is not covert surveillance as it is not part of a planned operation; the observation is spontaneous as it is in response to immediate circumstances. The police can arrange to have access to recordings from a particular CCTV camera (as in the Jamie Bulger case, when two children enticed a toddler away and later killed him). Furthermore, some forces have live access to CCTV coverage and can therefore respond immediately to any incidents unfolding on the screens. The procedures for arranging to view CCTV footage are covered in 23.4.2.

Some local authorities and other organizations (see Sch 1 to RIPA for a full list) carry out directed surveillance using CCTV for their own enforcement activities, for example to monitor criminal behaviour such as fly-tipping. Sections 29 to 35 of The Protection of Freedoms Act 2012 introduce powers for the Secretary of State to issue codes of practice for surveillance camera systems, as well as a system for regulating such activities, spearheaded by a Surveillance Camera Commissioner. These provisions came into force on the 1 July 2012, and the codes of practice were issued in June 2013 (Home Office, 2013f).

Recently the use of automatic number plate recognition systems (ANPR) has come under scrutiny by the surveillance commissioners, who concluded that ANPR cameras are sometimes utilized for covert purposes (see 22.3.2). In such circumstances authorization under RIPA will be required (see 22.3.2.2).

22.3.2 Covert surveillance

Covert surveillance does not include discreet spontaneous observations of a crime that is unexpectedly taking place. Surveillance is planned in advance and is defined as covert:

> if, and only if, it is carried out in a manner that is calculated to ensure that the persons who are subject to surveillance are unaware that it is or may be taking place. (s 26(9), RIPA)

The Act divides covert surveillance into two types; directed and intrusive, depending on the location of the target and hence the level of intrusion. Directed surveillance is when the person is anywhere other than residential premises or in a vehicle, and intrusive surveillance is when the person is in residential premises or in a vehicle.

Directed surveillance is defined in s 26(2) of the RIPA, as shown in the flow-diagram.

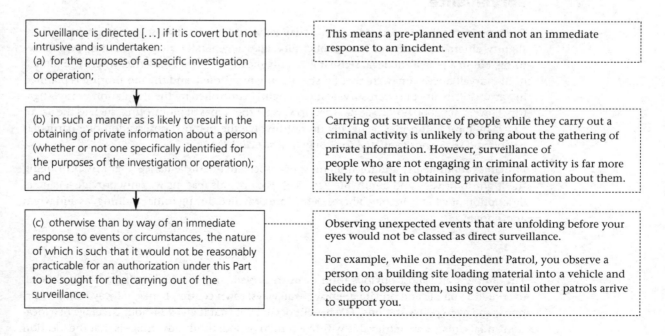

The provisions in RIPA are intended to ensure that police actions are proportionate and justified; the JAPAN principles apply here: Justification, Authorization, Proportionality, Auditable, and Necessary. An example of directed surveillance might be the installation of a concealed camera in a tree opposite a suspect's residence so a surveillance team could see when the subject was about to leave. The camera would have to be positioned so that only the suspect's premises was under surveillance. If the camera captured the neighbours' house and their activities, this would be 'collateral intrusion' and authority could be withheld until it is minimized or avoided. If CCTV is to be used for a covert pre-planned investigation, then authority should be sought.

Intrusive surveillance (s 26(3) of RIPA) is described in the second flow-diagram. An example of intrusive surveillance would be using a hidden listening device in a hotel room. It would also be intrusive if the listening device was installed outside the room but consistently provided information of the same quality and detail, as might be expected from a device installed inside the room (s 28(5)).

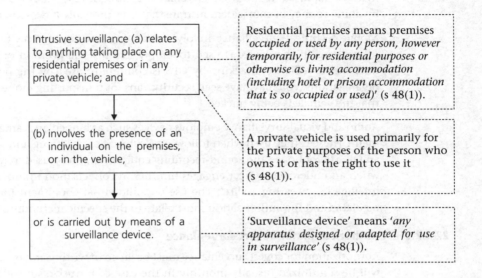

Surveillance is not intrusive if it is carried out by a tracking device designed or adapted principally for the purpose of providing information about the location of a vehicle (s 28(4)(a)), or if it is a one-sided consensual interception (eg of a postal service or telecommunication system) with no intercept warrant (s 28(4)(b)). In a recent landmark case relating to the lawfulness of monitoring communications between suspects and a solicitor, the House of Lords concluded that RIPA Pt II allowed the covert surveillance of communications between lawyers and their clients, even though those communications might be covered by legal professional privilege, and despite the fact that a person in custody has enshrined rights to consult privately with his/her legal representative (*In re McE (Appellant) (Northern Ireland) & In re M (Appellant) (Northern Ireland) & In re C (AP) and another (AP) (Appellants) (Northern Ireland)* [2009] UKHL 15).

More recently, the Court of Appeal was asked to deliberate on the case of two men who had been arrested for violent robbery and burglary. The police had bugged the prison van they had been transported in on three occasions, and overheard incriminating remarks. Amongst other arguments, the defendants argued that the prison van should be regarded as akin to a prison cell, which in their view made it a private residential premises within the context of intrusive surveillance. If this was the case, then the authority for the surveillance should have been by a chief officer of police not the superintendent. They also argued that the surveillance in itself was not necessary or proportionate, and that their convictions should be quashed because the surveillance evidence should have been rendered inadmissible under s 78 PACE (see 24.5.1.1). In a clear judgment, the Court of Appeal did not agree that the prison van was private or residential, and accepted that as one offender was yet to be found, the police action had been necessary and proportionate. The appeal was dismissed (*R v Plunkett and Plunkett* [2013] EWCA Crim 261). The case is a good illustration of the importance of clear decision-making by the investigators, to demonstrate both reasonableness and good faith.

22.3.2.1 Covert surveillance methods

Surveillance work involves a variety of approaches, depending on the information required.

Static observations can be carried out from a fixed vantage point (an Observation Point or OP); for example, from a park bench or an unmarked parked police vehicle. If the OP is on private property, then special provisions apply: the identity and safety of the property's owner or user must not be compromised. The surveillance could be either directed or intrusive, depending on the location of the subject under observation.

Mobile conventional surveillance involves officers following the subject on foot or in a vehicle. If only the position and movements of the subject are recorded, then this is directed surveillance. The teams who undertake this type of work are highly trained and such operations are carefully planned. Two key factors to consider are the awareness of the subject and the location. A tightly knit rural community would be a difficult location as strangers and unknown cars will 'stand out' in a small village or a quiet residential street. Different but equally complex problems occur in busy high streets, where it is difficult to keep the target in sight. Some criminals use sophisticated counter-surveillance techniques to shake off such surveillance, though by doing so they of course demonstrate that they probably have something to hide.

Mobile technical surveillance involves attaching tracking devices to vehicles, packages, or other items. If the device is used to simply identify the position of an object, then this is directed surveillance. Tracking by GPS is commonly used by the police and private-sector organizations; you may have seen security vans for transporting money with a sign indicating that the vehicle is being tracked.

Audio and visual surveillance employs devices such as binoculars, cameras, or recording equipment. These can be used when following a subject, or observing and recording him/her from an OP. Microphones and sound-recording equipment can be used to record a subject's speech when an undercover officer engages him/her in conversation in order to obtain evidence or intelligence; 'wearing a wire'. The use of audio-visual equipment for surveillance is tightly regulated and the authorization must relate to the specific methods to be used.

22.3.2.2 Authorization for covert surveillance

Authorization for covert surveillance must be given in writing and is valid for three months. It will be scrutinized (usually monthly in the case of intrusive surveillance) by a surveillance commissioner. The authorization can be withdrawn and the operation cancelled if he/she is not satisfied that the grounds were reasonable and the justification proportionate. Any intelligence obtained is also likely to be destroyed.

For directed surveillance, the authorization should be given in writing by a police officer not below the rank of superintendent. In urgent cases, oral authorizations may be given by a superintendent, but only for 72 hours (and written authority should be provided within the 72-hour period). Intrusive surveillance is a highly specialized area of police work and will only be authorized if it involves serious crime. All such operations must be authorized by a person holding the rank of chief officer (ie assistant chief constable rank and above) and the authorization must be approved by a surveillance commissioner.

Some operations involve the use of a CHIS, OPs, and mobile surveillance, and therefore multiple applications for authority need to be considered. These complex procedures ensure that the police (and other agencies) operate in a system which is open to both scrutiny and monitoring, and in compliance with the Human Rights Act 1988.

22.3.3 Communication Service Provider data

Other sources of covert intelligence available to the police include data gathered from Communication Service Providers (CSPs). The term CSP is not defined under the relevant legislation (largely RIPA, which uses phrases such as 'public telecommunications service' instead). But it normally refers to a wide range of public and commercial companies whose business it is to provide telecommunication services (eg mobile phone and landline), internet services, cable and satellite services, and so on. Examples of CSPs in the UK include BT Group plc, and Virgin Media Inc CSPs will often offer combinations of services to their customers (eg a 'bundle' of landline, broadband, and TV). The regulation of the gathering of CSP data is complex, and involves statute law, case law, and EU Directives. Trainee police officers are unlikely to be involved in the collection of intelligence gained from communications data transmitted or held by a CSP but need to be broadly aware of the controls surrounding its request and collection.

'Communications data' is defined under RIPA and refers to the 'who', 'when', and 'where' of a communication (CPS, 2007, p 13), but not the content (ie what was said or written). There are three forms of 'communications data':

Communications data	Explanation (derived from s 21 of RIPA)	Examples
Traffic data	This covers data which identifies the location of the communication equipment being used and/or the network through which the data is being transmitted	The 'header' of an email which identifies the IP address of a sender (but not the contents of the email) The postal address on a letter that is being sent through the post (but not the contents of the letter) The location of a mobile phone (eg using cell site analysis)
Service user data	This is concerned with data about how the service has been used	List of numbers called by a particular mobile phone Records listing delivery of registered letters
Subscriber data	Essentially CSP data about a person other than traffic or service data	'Reverse look ups' (eg whose mobile phone is this?) What password did the subscriber use to sign up?

Communications data can provide valuable intelligence to the police and other agencies involved, particularly in terms of investigating organized crime and terrorism. However, the gathering of communications data is only lawful if it meets the usual JAPAN requirements under the HRA. The necessity criteria are defined under RIPA, and this includes for the purposes of preventing or detecting crime. A police officer who determines that it is necessary and proportionate to oblige a CSP to provide communications data must first channel the request through the force's Single Point of Contact (SPoC). The SPoC is a specially trained officer standing outside the investigation, who has the responsibility of deciding whether the request meets the criteria for authorization. If it does, the request is passed to a designated senior officer (inspector and above for subscriber data, and superintendent or above for all other communications data) for authorization. Authorized requests are passed back to the SPoC, who will then arrange to collect the data from the CSP.

22.4 Other Sources of Intelligence

Information may be obtained from police interviews, either with the criminal or with people who know him/her. A police officer can let colleagues know that he/she is interested in a particular individual, and would welcome any useful information gleaned in the course of interviews. The same applies of course to police patrols, who should spend some part of their duty deployment on open observation and interaction with the public. Information can also be obtained from prisons. The formal intelligence gathering in prisons is subject to strict protocols and risk assessments, but plenty of miscellaneous and open information about criminal targets is available from prison visits, interviews, preparations for release, and so on.

Police forces also share information with other forces. The Bichard Report concluded that police forces should routinely communicate information which, though itself trivial or incomplete, might have a bearing on the activities of someone in another police force area (Bichard, 2004). However, as we have noted elsewhere, the infrastructure for such information exchange is only just (at the time of writing) being implemented through the Police National Database (see 6.9.1.2). An important document in terms of the police use of intelligence is the NPIA's Management of Police Information 2010 ('MoPI'), available online.

Information can also be obtained under the provisions of the Proceeds of Crime Act 2002. This places obligations on certain occupational groups such as bank managers and solicitors; they must report the handling of sums of money for which there is little or no apparent justification as this may indicate criminal activity.

We should not think that the only sources of information or intelligence about crimes or criminality are covert or clandestine (or 'closed'). For example, there are also 'open' (or 'overt') sources.

> **TASK 5** Can you suggest some open sources of intelligence? These would be available to any member of the public.

The first and most obvious source of 'open' intelligence about crime and criminality is likely to come from the general public. People notice all kinds of things and should be encouraged to report to the police anything that is odd, suspicious, or out of character. There is much to be gleaned about the lifestyles of criminals from simple observation or from general conversations with members of the public. Criminals live within communities, they have to go shopping, wear clothes, and socialize, and of course they are very likely to have families, hobbies, or interests which have nothing to do with crime. A profile can be built up of a criminal's daily habits: where he/she shops or goes for a drink, what cars he/she drives, and so on. Neighbours, garage mechanics, newsagents, dog walkers, joggers, parking attendants, crossing attendants, fitness instructors, and the like may all have information that could be useful in an investigation.

Local newspapers can also provide useful information for police officers. Most provincial newspapers are served by a small army of volunteers who send in reports every week, and it is sometimes possible to pick up open references to criminal targets. Similarly, the internet is increasingly becoming a valuable source of open intelligence—for example, through social networking sites and online forums.

22.5 Managing, Processing, and Using Intelligence

Intelligence should be managed, processed, and analysed so that it can be used effectively and legally by the police and other agencies. We might note, in passing, that for crime at Level 3 the national intelligence agencies link closely with the police. For example, HM Revenue and Customs includes an investigation branch (part of the National Crime Agency) and uses intelligence-led principles to track illegal imports (of any kind: drugs, people, contraband). The Security Service (MI5) also uses intelligence from police sources to counter threats to national (internal) security.

22.5.1 Intelligence reports

Intelligence is usually reported by police officers on a $5 \times 5 \times 5$ form (a 'five-by-five-by-five' when said out loud). The numbers refer to 'qualities' of the intelligence, measured in three categories, using ordinal scales of A to E and 1 to 5. For example, in relation to a CHIS the scales refer to the reliability of the CHIS, the reliability of the intelligence, and the level of security to be implemented. There are a number of assessment criteria within the Diploma in Policing assessed units that are concerned with the ability to complete parts of such forms.

A summary of the $5 \times 5 \times 5$ approach is given in the table (note that headings might vary from force to force).

Reliability of source (Do we trust him, her, or it?)	Reliability of intelligence (Do we believe the specific intelligence?)	Distribution (Who can see it?)
A *Always reliable* (not normally used for human sources)	1 *Known to be true without any doubts* (eg direct observation by CCTV)	1 *May be distributed to other LEAs outside the force but within Europe*, eg to the UKBA, Europol
B *Mostly reliable* (ie intelligence has mostly turned out to be correct in the past)	2 *Known to source but not to police officer* (eg through the source being told something by a fellow criminal)	2 *May be distributed to non-prosecuting authorities in the UK*, eg to a credit card issuer
C *Sometimes reliable* (ie intelligence has mostly turned out to be incorrect in the past)	3 *Not personally confirmed by source but corroborated* (eg as the result of the source 'eavesdropping' and which has also been confirmed by another source)	3 *May be distributed to non-European LEAs if in public interest and risk-assessed*, eg to the Turkish Police
D *Unreliable* (ie intelligence has normally turned out to be incorrect in the past)	4 *Impossible to say*	4 *Only to be distributed within force* (to specified individuals)
E *Unknown/untested* (ie not necessarily unreliable but perhaps a new source, eg through Crimestoppers)	5 *Probably false*	5 *Conditional dissemination*, eg to Social Services but with conditions imposed

All combinations of scales are possible, for example a piece of intelligence may be graded as 'C by 2 by 4'. A police officer will complete the main body of the form with the intelligence (the who, when, where, why, and how). The grade concerned with distribution (sometimes referred to as the 'Handling Code') is normally completed by the force Intelligence Unit. These 5 × 5 × 5 forms are a major part of the intelligence in-flow into a police force's 'Research & Development' unit (or 'Force Intelligence Bureau'—the name varies from force to force). They ensure that reports are circulated to those who need to know; this will usually be the Tasking & Coordination Group (see 22.6). Reports dealing with a common theme may be collated from a number of sources and be circulated as a single composite intelligence item (further protecting each source).

The information may be 'sanitized'—this is the removal of any features of the intelligence that could identify the source or the circumstances in which the intelligence was obtained. For example, no R&D staff would allow a report to go into circulation which began:

At 5.30 pm, on Tuesday 15 August, 'Fat Jimmy' saw Sam 'Toucan' Belmont in the Three Feathers pub in Harpenden, and gave Jimmy . . .

Such obvious indicators could quickly identify the source, which would be likely to compromise his/her access as well as putting him/her at personal risk. The 'need to know' principle applies to protecting sources, because the police want the source to continue his/her covert relationship with the target. R&D staff may return to the handler(s) with requests for directions to pursue and more targets; a productive source will be heavily tasked.

22.5.2   Analysing intelligence

At some point in the distribution chain (this varies from force to force), analysts will analyse the intelligence, for example establish and identify the MO (the *modus operandi*). This is how the criminal has carried out the offence—how did the burglar gain access to the property, what type of items were taken, where did he/she look? If the offender is known, the findings may be incorporated into a subject profile, or a problem profile if the identity of the offender has not yet been established.

The next stage will be to try and match a particular event with what is already known about other similar crimes. In some forces, this happens with the raw intelligence, in others with the sanitized version. Either way, the assessed intelligence helps analysts to fill out the picture.

The NIM (see 22.6) suggests that intelligence analysis should be undertaken within four main areas:

* Problem profiling—for example, the identification of crime hot spots (see 4.6.2).
* Subject profiling—analysing the actions of suspected criminals and their associates, and of victims. This will involve building up an understanding of the criminal networks involved, through link and association analysis.
* Tactical assessment—essentially a management-support function undertaken by the analyst and involves recommendation of the deployment of resources based on the intelligence available.
* Strategic assessment—involves likely future developments in criminal activity (eg the impact of an international event or the introduction of new technologies). Strategic assessment is normally undertaken by a senior or principal analyst.

Crime pattern analysis, network analysis, and case analysis are just three of the techniques which might be employed by the analysts. There are up to ten different analytical techniques (ACPO, 2008), although research shows that in practice often significantly fewer than ten are used (eg Cope *et al*, 2005). The theoretical and empirical methods that underpin the ten techniques include the creation and testing of hypotheses and the drawing of inferences. Analysts also use various software packages, for example the i2 company's 'Analyst's Notebook'.

The R&D unit in turn will try to gather enough intelligence to construct a 'targeting package' for the Tasking and Coordination Groups to consider (see 22.6.2).

22.5.3   Intelligence 'packages'

An intelligence package is a number of items of intelligence with related content (the term comes from the idea of bundling different items together). An ideal package would a be highly accurate picture of how particular crimes are carried out in a given locality, by whom, with what success, how the acquisitions from the crime are fenced, how money is laundered and by whom, what the likelihood is of repeat victimization, and how the crime series is likely to develop. However, many lack such detail and are much more likely to combine hard intelligence and reasoned speculation.

The intelligence package is fundamental to police operational planning at the T&CG level (and above). Intelligence packages are not just put together as a response to crime, but may also be used to support other objectives, such as planning appropriate levels of policing for a demonstration.

22.6   The National Intelligence Model

The NIM was launched by NCIS in 2000, and is concerned with using intelligence to determine priorities for policing. The Home Office describes the NIM as 'a validated model of policing...representing best practice in the use of intelligence to fight crime' (Home Office, 2001, p 45). All police forces in England and Wales are required to implement the NIM. The NIM is also utilized by the National Crime Agency and local Community Safety Partnerships (see 3.3.2).

The NIM should perhaps be clearly distinguished from ILP, although the two are often juxtaposed. (For example, the 2007 ACPO practice advice 'Introduction to Intelligence-led Policing' is almost entirely devoted to the NIM, and the Bichard Inquiry explains that the purpose of the NIM is to 'enhance intelligence-led policing' (Bichard, 2004, p 119).) The key difference between the two is that whereas ILP is essentially concerned with using intelligence to counter crime, the NIM is more concerned with using intelligence to determine priorities for policing.

22.6.1   Key features of the NIM

The key part of the NIM process is shown in the centre of the diagram: the Tasking and Coordinating Process, overseen by Tasking and Coordination Groups (T&CG). This determines the operational responses to crime and disorder, and prioritizes intelligence requirements (eg identifying car-crime hot spots, or obtaining information about a series of burglaries). The arrows on the diagram show how intelligence and other factors influence decision-making.

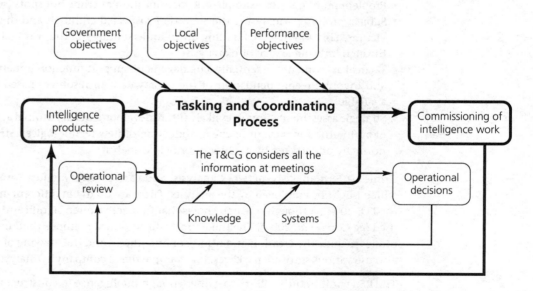

The bold lines indicate the key aspects of the process and emphasize the use of intelligence products to determine what further intelligence work needs to be commissioned. It is a continual cycle of policy development, implementation, and review, and bears some resemblance to Kolb's learning cycle, referred to in 8.6.5.3.

The Tasking and Coordinating Process is conducted at three levels to correspond with the specified levels of incident:

- Level 1 (local BCU level) in relation to local crime capable of being managed by local resources (which may include the most serious crime) and anti-social behaviour;
- Level 2 (force and regional) in relation to force, inter-force, and regional criminal activity, usually requiring additional resources; and
- Level 3 (national) in relation to the most serious and organized crime.

The classification of the crime is significant for resourcing. A single BCU does not have the resources to cope with, say, a group of criminal associates carrying out thefts from ATMs (cash machines) across the force area. A force-level response (Level 2) would be needed, and this would usually be centrally coordinated and directed. Level 3 crime is dealt with by linking with national agencies such as the NCA, in cooperation with its international counterparts.

Whether on a national, regional, or local scale, the use of assessed intelligence to inform operational decision-making follows the same principles as set out in the NIM. Care must be taken to avoid isolating the work at one level from the work at other levels. Related issues at different levels must be taken into account to ensure that opportunities are not missed, and that appropriate resources are allocated.

22.6.2 The Tasking and Coordinating Process

At the heart of the business process are the **Strategic** Tasking and Coordination Group (Strategic T&CG) meetings. Most forces will have a Strategic-level T&CG dealing with serious Level 2 crime. The purpose of the meetings is to initiate a Control Strategy which will establish the intelligence requirements and set the agenda for prevention, intelligence, and enforcement priorities. The Strategic T&CG do not routinely determine the operational tactics to be deployed, but instead maintain an overview of priorities. So, for example, if the Strategic T&CG required that ATM raids were to be made a priority, then specialist operations such as surveillance and CHIS recruitment would be 'tasked' to challenge that criminal network. Strategic issues are considered every six months at force-level Strategic T&CG meetings. Members of a Strategic T&CG include the force-wide senior management team, intelligence specialists, crime analysts, and other senior staff as required.

A second category of T&CG meetings also takes place: the **Tactical** Tasking and Coordination Group meetings. At a BCU level (Level 1) the Tactical T&CG meets at least every two weeks. The group comprises the senior supervisory officers and support staff from the local area, and they apply the planned response to the Control Strategy, review progress, and make changes to plans if judged appropriate. They can call on other agencies to assist in tactical decisions, but compared with Strategic T&CG meetings there is generally not such a wide range of senior staff present at Tactical T&CG meetings.

22.6.2.1 Inputs to the tasking and coordinating process

The T&CGs are informed by intelligence products which have been researched and written by analysts working with police officers (see 22.5.3). Both the strategic planning at force level and the local-tasking operational planning at BCU level are guided by these intelligence products and other forms of analysis.

Strategic Assessments are long-term strategy documents, usually produced every six months. Tactical Assessments review the progress of current operations and approaches. The T&CGs also commission, and are subsequently informed by intelligence products. These include target/subject profiles about named offenders, victims, or networks and problem profiles about issues of concern such as a hot spot or the increased availability of a particular street drug.

The decisions taken by the T&CG will be influenced by a number of other factors such as:

- Government objectives: for example, to raise the profile of thefts from cars, or deal with public order issues.
- Local objectives: including force objectives, such as dealing with problem families, problem estates, local disorder, and so on. These views will have been canvassed both by the police, through community liaison officers, and through local government councillors, local authority officials, and other parts of local government. All will be conveyed to the area or BCU commander (usually a superintendent) through routine meetings and consultations, and will be arranged into local objectives.

Investigation and Prosecution

- Performance objectives: the long-term (yearly) objectives for the BCU will also be taken into account. These may be to develop strategies to reduce all crime locally (and might include reducing burglaries by a specific percentage, for example), or dealing with anti-social behaviour, or arrest rates, or 'brought to justice' data. These determine the BCU Commander's strategic approach.
- Knowledge: the professional knowledge required by staff in order to contribute fully to the NIM and other aspects of police work. It includes knowledge of legislation, codes of practice, and force policies.
- Systems: the IT systems and associated procedures for the storage, retrieval, analysis, and dissemination of intelligence information.

22.6.2.2 Outputs from the tasking and coordinating process

Implementation of the Control Strategy will include the commissioning of new intelligence work and making operational decisions to improve the management of crime and the local community. Teams may be assembled to tackle particular issues, and budgets are set; the overtime budget is frequently of particular significance.

As well as the weekly or fortnightly Tactical T&CG meetings at BCU level there are likely to be daily meetings to monitor and direct daily aspects of police work. The daily meetings (sometimes known as 'Intelligence Daily Briefing' meetings, or more colloquially in some forces as 'Morning Prayers') are part of the process of ensuring that the T&CG strategy is implemented and kept on track.

22.6.3 Links with the wider policing role

The NIM is intended to be the engine room that drives the policing machine. Police officers undertake much of their non-reactive work at the direction of the T&CG, to help policing in their area to be coordinated, specific, and focused. The full picture is considered at T&CG meetings, of which the intelligence on criminal matters is only a part. For example, it would not be appropriate for the T&CG to recommend an operation targeting thefts from cars when local priorities were largely focused on reducing alcohol-related violence. (However, the BCU Commander may still judge that disrupting car thefts is a temporary but urgent priority.)

22.6.4 The NIM in practice

To illustrate the way in the NIM is used in policing we will track through a crime from start to finish.

Suppose we receive several reports of an 'artifice burglary' (see the start of 16.4). The reports will enter the process as information, and a key early requirement will be for analysts to assess the criminal's MO such as the type and location of targeted property (see 22.5.2). The findings may be incorporated into a subject profile (if the offender is known) or a problem profile (if his/her identity has not yet been established).

The T&CG may then task the police staff who are responsible for gathering intelligence to find out whether there is access to this type of criminal (perhaps through a regular 'fence'), and whether there is knowledge locally of such individuals. The T&CG will assign a priority to the investigation and will commission further work, such as checking the force's criminal databases, and trying to match other spree offences in the force area or in neighbouring forces. (Artifice burglars tend not to 'work their own patch', perhaps because they run the risk of being recognized.) Analysts might note, for example, that the offences have all taken place within half a mile of a railway station, in which case the force may approach British Transport Police for help, and look at relevant CCTV footage.

Suppose the frequency of artifice burglaries increases, and one of the victims becomes seriously ill as an indirect consequence of the theft (quite a common occurrence). At the next T&CG meeting, the priority level of the case is raised and the operational plans developed accordingly. The BCU Commander will take into account government objectives, local feelings about the nature of the crime, media pressures, and the chances of catching the culprit.

Now imagine that a CHIS (see 22.2) provides useful information to her handler and a report is submitted. It is assessed by the R&D unit and compared with other intelligence. We now have a name, a preferred location, and a clear idea of the MO. An operation is mounted, two people are arrested, and a case is prepared. The final outcome for the offender could be a prison sentence, a caution (see

10.13.3), a fine, seizure of assets, or community service. Other outcomes might include displacing the activity of artifice burglars (see 4.6.4), the development and implementation of a crime reduction (prevention or disruption) strategy (see 4.6.1), and probably some useful media coverage.

The NIM process has led to an assessment of the nature of the crime, to tasking the intelligence-gathering parts of the force, and giving the crime a higher priority level in the midst of competing claims for attention. The newly acquired intelligence was assessed and used to develop a package of operational measures through the T&CG, the resulting police action disrupted that type of crime, and probably reassured the community to some extent. This is a simple example of the business-process model of policing, and the same principles will operate whether the issue is the vandalizing of cars or a more serious crime enquiry, such as systematic violent assaults on young people near a sports centre.

> **TASK 6** Now it is your turn: using the NIM, describe what would happen if the BCU Commander wanted to deal with:
>
> 1. a crime hot spot involving alcohol-fuelled violence;
> 2. a spate of break-ins into vehicles;
> 3. a series of attacks on students to steal credit cards.
>
> What factors do you think would influence the prioritizing of the crimes? What would you expect the crime analysts to provide? How would you task the collection of intelligence? What operational considerations would there be?

22.7   Answers to Tasks

TASK 1 You may have come up with a list like the following (which is not exhaustive!):

- integrity and honesty;
- patience and attention to detail;
- strong-minded and not easily diverted;
- knowledgeable about crime and criminals;
- ordinary/normal in appearance, so can blend into a crowd;
- reticent or discreet;
- firm sense of duty but objective;
- understands the 'bigger picture' of force needs and intelligence requirements;
- adaptable (can think on his/her feet) and flexible;
- professional in the relationship (courteous but not close);
- willing to work long or unsocial hours;
- resilient and stable as a personality;
- good listener, empathetic ('emotional intelligence').

These qualities, skills, or attributes are not common in such combinations. A good source handler can be trained to a high level, but there must be strong character traits already there upon which the training can build. You can see that it takes someone with considerable investigative experience and 'life skills' to succeed in this role.

TASK 2 The first consideration for the police is whether, if the identity of the informant is made known, there will be a serious risk to his/her life (or of serious harm or injury). In such circumstances the identity of the 'informant' will never be revealed. The prosecution of a case in open court would probably be abandoned if the informant was the main source of evidence.

You might also have referred to the difficulty of using an active criminal as a source. If a CHIS takes part in an organized crime, or is involved in criminal planning, these are offences for which the CHIS could be charged and brought before a court. A further difficulty is whether, in order to obtain the intelligence they need, the police have to allow a crime to go ahead and let their source take part.

The use of informants is discussed further in Dunnighan and Norris (1996 and 1999).

TASK 3 Motivation is notoriously difficult to understand and identify, and particularly so with informants. As Canter and Alison (2000) noted, the motivation that a person may put forward for their actions is not necessarily the most useful for understanding that person's actions, and will be only one of a number of possible explanations.

TASK 4 For a good undercover officer the following would all be relevant; resilience, self-sufficiency, strong professionalism, the ability to work alone, the ability to pass yourself off as something you are not, the focus and concentration to know what intelligence is needed, a very good relationship and trust with your handler, and a personal inclination towards the clandestine.

Logistical and support problems include a good cover story (both for the criminal target and to explain the officer's absence back in the force), payment, nothing to identify the officer as from the police (in clothing, residence, possessions), career planning, reassuring family members, diverting curious colleagues, and so on. There are a host of problems associated with going undercover long term and a team of people are used to support the lone officer.

In planning a Test Purchase (TP) operation, you would have to think about the original intelligence and its reliability, the patterns of movement (and MO) of the target criminal, when to insert the TP officer, how to monitor what is happening, how to intervene and disrupt or arrest, and whether you have the authorization to proceed.

TASK 5 Open sources of intelligence have grown rapidly in recent years, largely as a result of the availability of electronic resources such as the internet. Whereas in the past we might have needed to search manually through paper copies of newspapers and magazines selling used cars for evidence of possible 'ringing', now we can use the search facilities available on most websites. Indeed, the widespread availability of information is causing some concern with the advent of crimes such as identity theft (putting aside the obvious general desire to maintain personal privacy). As an experiment, try to find out as much about yourself as you can by using freely available internet resources. For example, start with <http://www.192.com> and enter your own name. You may be surprised at what you (and others) can find out.

TASK 6

1. You should consider where the hot spot is. Is it in a town centre? Close to a series of pubs or clubs? When does crime happen? Would a police presence act as a deterrent? Who is likely to have brought the incidents to police attention? What would be the feelings and fears of the local community?

2. Are the vehicle owners reporting the crime? What is taken? Is there a pattern? What is the location? Are particular kinds of car targeted? What preventative action would help? (Eg leafleting car owners, warnings in the media not to leave valuables on view, or CCTV coverage.)

3. Are the credit card thefts seasonal (ie do they occur in the summer, at the start of a new term, or in the run-up to Christmas)? What is the MO? What do students do about it? Is violence involved? How is the crime reported? Are women students more at risk than men? Are there criminals on the database who specialize in this sort of crime? What preventative action might you recommend? (Hint: think about crime prevention, raising awareness, liaison with college and university authorities to put cash points on campuses, credit card theft-prevention schemes, talking to the banks, posters near ATMs, security awareness, CCTV, and so on.)

23 | Criminal Investigation

23.1 Introduction

Harfield (in Newburn and Neyroud, 2008, pp 67–8) suggest that criminal-investigation management has many facets, the main ones being: intelligence-led policing; the statutory framework of investigative powers; managing evidence; the management of key resources; the community; and third-party oversight. We examine many of these elsewhere in the Handbook (eg in terms of the forensic investigation strategy, the use of intelligence) but here we provide an overview of the processes involved and describe some of the particular responsibilities of the trainee police officer. The police are required to make strategic decisions concerning the investigation of crime, and for this reason we begin Chapter 23 with a discussion of volume, priority, and major crime.

An important change in recent years is an attempt to 'recast' the process of investigation as a 'seeking after the truth', rather than the 'building of a case' against a suspect from the outset. (This is not to say that case-building does not feature in investigation; it is just that it should not be the focus.) A police officer is therefore expected to pursue just as vigorously those reasonable lines of enquiry which point towards the innocence of the suspect, and to be seen to have done so.

A criminal investigation is defined in s 22 of the Criminal Procedure and Investigations Act 1996 (CPIA) as an investigation conducted by police officers with a view to it being ascertained:

- whether a person should be charged with an offence; or
- whether a person charged with an offence is guilty of it.

It is vital that investigators know when any particular investigation has begun, so they can ensure compliance with the CPIA 1996 and the associated Codes of Practice. The CPIA Codes of Practice state that this includes investigations set up in the belief that a crime is about to be committed.

The CPIA 1996 is clearly central to the correct procedures being followed for an investigation. It defines the roles of investigator (wide enough to encompass both detectives and others), disclosure officer, and officer in the case. (No distinction is made between detectives and others within a police investigation.) Each role is accorded particular duties in a criminal investigation. Amongst the most important duties are the need to record, retain, and ultimately reveal (to the prosecutor) relevant material, and the necessity to pursue all reasonable lines of enquiry whether they point towards or away from the suspect. Much of the recent legislation in relation to investigation was enacted to combat fears that the police had historically withheld important information, ignored exonerating facts, and simply constructed cases against individuals who were sometimes innocent. High profile miscarriages of justice often demonstrated these failings in abundance (such as the 'Guildford Four' and the 'Maguire Seven', the 'Birmingham Six', the case of the Taylor sisters, and Stefan Kiszko). For more information on these and other miscarriage of justice cases, see Eddlestone (2012).

The following legislation is also relevant to undertaking investigations and therefore underpins what we describe here:

- the Criminal Justice and Public Order Act 1994 (CJPOA);
- the Police and Criminal Evidence Act 1984 (PACE Act) and Codes of Practice 2004;

Investigation and Prosecution

504 Chapter 23: Criminal Investigation

- the Human Rights Act 1998 (HRA);
- the Regulation of Investigatory Powers Act 2000 (RIPA); and
- the Serious Organised Crime and Police Act 2005 (SOCPA).

Students undertaking the Certificate in Knowledge of Policing (see 7.2.1 and 7.3) will study the underpinning knowledge required to 'conduct priority and volume investigations within a policing context' and may also be assessed when undertaking an investigation scenario (eg, a simulated burglary). Trainee officers may encounter the IPLDP 'Crime Investigation Model' during Phases 3 and 4 of training. It consists of seven stages: instigation, initial response, investigative assessment, suspect management, evidence assessment, charge and post-charge activity, and finally court (Home Office, 2004). In other chapters we have already examined many aspects of the IPLDP's seven stages and we discuss most of the remaining ones here. However, during initial training you may also be taught a model of investigation drawn from the NCPE Practice Advice on Core Investigative Doctrine (Home Office, 2005d), which posits five groups of tasks: initial investigation, scene management, further investigation, investigative and evidential evaluation, and finally, suspect and case management. There are a number of activities within these groups of tasks, which we have interpreted in the table. The Core Investigative Doctrine informed the development of PIP Level 1 (see 7.5), which trainee police officers are also expected to attain before the end of their initial training.

The links between Core Investigation Doctrine and NOS Units/QCF Diploma Units

Core investigative doctrine activity	Example of activity	Linked NOS units	Linked QCF Diploma unit
Initial Report	Control room instruction, incident log, etc	BE2	Provide initial support to victims and witnesses
Police Response	Risk assessment, recording the incident, etc	BE2, CJ101, CK1, CK2, CD1	Provide initial support to victims and witnesses. Interview victims and witnesses in relation to priority and volume investigations
Scene Attendance	Provide immediate support to victims, etc	CI101, 4G4	Provide initial support to victims and witnesses
Crime Scene Assessment	CPIA 1996, protecting the scene, minimizing contamination, etc	CD1	Provide an initial response to incidents
Witnesses	Identify and question witnesses, CCTV, etc	CI101	Conduct priority and volume investigations
Information/ Intelligence	Force intelligence reports, CHIS, etc	CI101	Conduct priority and volume investigations
Suspect	Initial lines of enquiry, description, names, etc	CI101	Conduct priority and volume investigations
Enquiries to trace offender	PNC, NDNAD	CI101	Conduct priority and volume investigations
Arrest	Arrest strategy, PACE Act 1984/SOCPA 2005 powers of arrest, etc	CD5	Arrest, detain, or report individuals
Searches	Legal authority, seizure of items, proportionality, etc	DA5, DA6	Search individuals. Search vehicles, premises, and open spaces
Custody Procedures	Escort to custody, give grounds for detention, etc	CJ101, CJ201	Not explicitly covered
Interview(s)	PEACE, interview strategy, etc	CJ101, CJ201	Interview victims and witnesses in relation to priority and volume investigation. Interview suspects in relation to priority and volume investigations
Charge, Caution, Bail, NFA (No Further Action), etc	CPS charging standards, prepare case files, evaluate investigation, etc	DA5, DA6, 2G4	Gather and submit information to support law enforcement objectives

(Based on Home Office, 2005e and NPIA, 2010c)

Trainee police officers may be directly involved in undertaking criminal investigation, and this will provide many opportunities for collecting evidence for the Diploma in Policing assessed units. The evidence could include PNB entries and witness statements.

23.2   Defining Volume, Priority, and Major Crime

The distinction between volume, priority, and major crime is determined largely at the BCU level by the Tactical Tasking and Coordinating Group. They will also decide how to tackle volume crime in their particular area (see 22.6.2).

Volume crime as defined by the NPIA (on behalf of ACPO) is 'any type of crime which, through its sheer volume, has a significant impact on the community and the workload of the local police...' (NPIA/ACPO, 2009, p 8). It usually includes:

- street robbery;
- burglary, of dwelling-house and other ('non-dwelling');
- theft (including shoplifting);
- theft of vehicles and from vehicles;
- criminal damage;
- common assault; and
- illegal possession of controlled drugs (often linked with acquisitive crime).

Priority crimes for many BCUs in recent years have included street robbery, burglary, and car crime. Hence a priority crime might also be a volume crime, and vice versa, but the terms are not synonymous.

Major crime generally includes any crime that includes serious violence (eg murder, manslaughter, and stranger rape) or the potential for serious violence, and that requires resources beyond those of a single BCU. Any crime of grave public concern (eg the abduction of a child), terrorism, or the threat of terrorism is also likely to come under the umbrella of major crime. The official classification for major crimes as shown in the table.

Category	Definition
A+	Public concern and the associated response to media intervention are such that 'normal' staffing levels are not adequate to keep pace with the investigation
A	An incident of grave concern or where vulnerable members of the public are at risk; where the identity of the offender/s is not apparent, or the investigation and the securing of evidence requires significant resource allocation
B	The identity of the offender/s is not apparent, the continued risk to the public is low, and the investigation or securing of evidence can be achieved within normal resourcing arrangements
C	The identity of the offender/s is apparent from the outset and the investigation and/or securing of evidence can easily be achieved

For each force a senior officer (eg a detective superintendent) will head up a Major Crime Unit. He/she can designate any crime as a major crime, in order that the appropriate resources may be made available for its subsequent investigation.

23.3   Initial Investigation

The response to priority and volume crimes involves many different police staff, from call handlers to trained investigators. The majority of incidents attended by members of the police family are usually dealt with by the first attending officer (FAO). In many circumstances he/she may in the end be the only investigator.

The quality of an investigation and the chances of a successful prosecution are enhanced by actions taken early on in the investigation. These actions include locating, gathering, and retaining material, and making an initial report. Call handlers, public-facing support staff, and police officers are all obliged to record, retain, and reveal information to the investigating officer, and must follow the specified procedures described for Management of Police Information (see 6.8.2) and in the Criminal Procedure and Investigations Act 1996 and its associated Code of Practice (see 26.2). If other investigators are subsequently involved they should not underestimate the potential benefits of questioning and gathering evidence from the person reporting the crime and the person who received and wrote the initial report.

A criminal investigation can be instigated proactively as a consequence, for example, of research and development of intelligence gathering, or reactively when new information becomes available from sources such as:

- the general public;
- partnership agency reports;
- intelligence derived from other crimes or new information received about an old crime leading to a subsequent re-investigation;
- self-generated police actions, for example discovering a cannabis factory through the use of a thermal imaging camera.

Some of what follows is an interpretation of the NPIA/ACPO 2009 document *Practice Advice on the Management of Priority and Volume Crime (The Volume Crime Management Model)*, 2nd edn (NPIA/ACPO, 2009), see this document for further detail. We have attempted to describe the procedures adopted in a 'typical' police force, and present the investigation of priority and volume crime as a series of separate activities (for simplicity) but in practice they are more likely to overlap and merge into a single process. The various activities described here will not all necessarily feature in any particular investigation, or in the precise order implied.

The trainee police officer is more likely to be involved in the early stages. The actions outlined here could provide evidence of competence at PIP Level 1.

23.3.1 Call handling and initial investigation

In many cases the start of an investigation is a phone call made by a member of the public to the police or emergency services. Call handlers play a key role in the initial investigation and screening. For example, their guidance to a caller may help preserve forensic material at a scene.

Call handlers collect a large amount of information, and may use scripts or computer drop-down menus to help ensure all relevant information is gathered. Their questions effectively amount to an initial investigation and the appropriate response can then be determined. Depending on the BCU deployment policy, officers may be dispatched to a location (there may be a dedicated team of officers for attending volume crime scenes). If immediate attendance is not required the caller may be transferred to a 'crime bureau' where details of the incident will be considered and recorded.

23.3.2 Obtaining first accounts

Police officers may be deployed to a location based upon the decisions of the call handlers (or for other reasons, such as encountering an incident whilst on patrol). An officer's initial appraisal of the situation and a few preliminary questions will often be all that is needed to determine whether any persons present could be reasonably suspected to have been involved in a criminal offence. The answers to these questions comprise the 'first account', sometimes referred to as an initial account, and would aim to establish:

- the type of alleged offence;
- the approximate time of the alleged offence;
- the scene of the alleged offence—only sufficient general knowledge to understand what might be said in an interview; and
- how the alleged offence came to the notice of the police.

A police officer who is trying to discover whether, or by whom, an offence has been committed can question any person from whom useful information might be obtained (PACE Code A, Note 1). If there are reasonable grounds for suspecting that the person has been involved in a criminal offence then a caution should be given before asking any further questions (see 10.3 on cautions). Any conversation that takes place with a suspect before a caution is given should be summarized in a PNB entry, as the court may wish to take it into consideration. It might be necessary to arrest a suspect (see 10.6). Once a suspect has been arrested he/she cannot be interviewed about the offence except at a police station (Code C, para 11.1) unless the delay would irretrievably hinder the investigation (see 10.8.5).

In the majority of cases, the most beneficial way of using witness evidence is to ask the witness in the presence and hearing of the suspect(s) to explain to what he/she saw or heard. Care must be taken in cases of domestic abuse or sexual offences where the victim might be reluctant to speak in front of the suspected abuser. This will be a judgement call by the officer, based upon the circumstances of the case. The answers given by a witness should be recorded word for word in a PNB entry or equivalent. The record could later be used as evidence in court as part of an officer's duty statement (see 10.12 on duty statements, and 26.5.3.2 on using a PNB in court).

First accounts from witnesses can also provide the information required for planning an interview with the suspect, or for constructing a 'handover pack' for other officers to conduct the interviews (see Chapter 24 on interviews and 10.14 on handover procedures). A first account can also be compared with an account given under oath verbally at court, and any inconsistencies between the two accounts would require an explanation from the witness.

Information about all the witnesses, and any actions, statements, comments, or other relevant material (see 26.2) must be recorded, ensuring compliance with the CPIA. A case could be undermined in court if the defence asked a police officer about something a witness had said and the officer had no record of it (see 26.5.3). If for some reason a PNB record cannot be made, the record can be made separately, on a clip board for example. The use of the PNB and making PNB entries is covered in 10.2.

If a witness or a victim cannot appear in court in person (eg if he/she is dead or seriously ill, or cannot be found, or is too scared to give evidence even with special measures) written police records of victim and witness early accounts may be admissible as evidence (s 116 of the Criminal Justice Act 2003). The police records of such accounts must be recorded verbatim. In addition a victim might tell a third party about the events in relation to the offence, and this 'hearsay' is potentially admissible as evidence in court (see 26.4.4). A record must be made of the names and addresses of any other people the victim has told about the incident so these can be followed up. Concerning the account from the third party, it is vital that a verbatim PNB record is made if the police record is to be admissible in court.

23.3.3 Early investigative actions

Investigating begins at the very moment a police officer arrives at an incident or a call handler answers a call from a member of the public. This could lead to a more formal type of investigation, but in order to decide whether this is appropriate some initial information has to be gathered and assessed. A trainee police officer is most likely to be involved in the early stages of a response to volume crime.

In addition to obtaining first accounts, other actions are required, as shown in the table. These actions would generally be taken during the 'golden hour' or as 'fast track actions' (see 11.2.4). A trainee police officer is most likely to be involved in the early stages of a response to volume crime, and could undertake any of the actions listed here. The National Decision Model (see 6.5) would be used to help decide what actions to take.

Much of the information gathered (as shown in the table) could contribute to a primary investigation. The trainee officer will need to prioritize those early actions that can be realistically pursued at the time. If the case continues, the remainder of the actions can be followed up within the primary investigation phase.

Taking a report of a crime	All actions taken to trace witnesses and suspects should be recorded. A list should be made of any other enquiries that have been made, or could be made
The crime scene	The scene should be preserved for the CSI, to avoid contamination. This might require a cordon (see 11.2) for a large or serious crime scene
CCTV evidence	The location of cameras that could have recorded the incident should be recorded (for CPIA purposes and evidence recovery). The CCTV hard copy should be preserved, recovered, and exhibited where possible (see 23.4.2)
Managing witnesses	First accounts must be recorded, including full names and addresses. These accounts might suggest further potential witnesses, and these should be recorded in full

House-to-house enquiries	These are likely to concern witnesses or potential witnesses. A record should be made of all persons spoken to, and of any absent potential witnesses (for a future visit). The content of the discussions should be carefully noted, including any refusal to reply
Other evidence	Photographs, plans, and maps might suggest opportunities for obtaining forensic evidence. All documents, captured texts, images, or sequences from electronic devices should be retained
Taking statements	Statements should be obtained as a matter of urgency where violence has occurred (or been threatened), where a suspect has been detained, or if witness contamination must be avoided (eg where a description of a person is relevant)
Recording actions taken	Before going off duty, full details of all actions taken must be recorded, as handwritten PNB entries or electronic entries (depending on the circumstances)

(Adapted from Practice Advice on The Management of Priority and Volume Crime (The Volume Crime Management Model, 2nd edn (NPIA/ACPO, 2009))

With regard to possible witnesses, any people in the vicinity who were not involved or who did not see what happened should be eliminated from the enquiry. Careful judgement is needed to establish who was a material witness to the event (who actually saw it) and who was not. This is not as easy as it sounds because people can become over excited when they think they have witnessed a crime and will be keen to provide their (possibly derivative) account. Note, however, that an effective response to supporting survivors, victims, and witnesses will improve the quality of investigation by maximizing the availability of evidence while also increasing the confidence in the police to those receiving the support.

23.4 Further Investigation

If further investigation into the alleged crime is required then a primary investigation is initiated. The aim would be to complete all the actions listed in the table. In this way the information can be pieced together. It is important to realize that a primary investigation is an integral part of the whole investigation (eg as a precursor to a secondary investigation) which may lead to prosecution; the primary investigation is not simply a collection of information concerning an alleged crime.

Trainee police officers will be involved in both the primary and secondary investigations into priority and volume crimes during their second year of initial training (or earlier in some forces). Senior Investigating Officers (SIOs) will record decisions on the investigation in a policy file.

23.4.1 Primary investigation

A primary investigation includes:

- taking (or checking) the basic details of victims (eg name, DOB, age, contact details) and the alleged offence (eg location, description of alleged offender(s));
- taking (or checking) the basic details of witnesses together with an assessment of the potential evidence they could provide;
- assessing the likelihood of other forms of intelligence or evidence (eg CCTV video footage, house-to-house enquiries);
- initial enquiries to trace suspects (eg PNC checks);
- preserving the crime scene if appropriate (see 11.2);
- an immediate arrest (if necessary, see 10.6.4), for example at the scene of an alleged crime; and
- ensuring all necessary statements have been taken.

The primary investigator produces a crime report which is sent to the principal screener. It is important that the FAO is thorough in considering all of these initial actions, so that a professional product is either handed to an investigator who may take the investigation further, or it is filed with no further investigation necessary.

23.4.2   Obtaining CCTV evidence

CCTV evidence can be used to establish the sequence of events and to provide evidence, including supporting the defence case. Relevant material would include footage that showed the suspects were near to the relevant vicinity around the time the crime was committed. ACPO has produced Practice Advice on the use of CCTV in Criminal Investigations, available online; we summarize the key points here.

Ideally CCTV footage should be obtained early on during the 'golden hour' to avoid it being lost, but it is sometimes difficult to obtain straight away. In theory, any officer could seize and exhibit CCTV evidence but when and who depends on the circumstances. A trainee officer could ensure that the recording system is safe and secure before referring the matter to his/her supervisor; specialist services might be required.

The storage format and technical requirements for recovering recordings should be established before accessing the equipment. If the footage contains relevant material, it should be seized in accordance with the rules about the preservation of evidence (see 11.2.6 on exhibits and 26.2.1 on relevant material). Working copies must be made for any further viewings.

Often the images are stored on a disc, and taking away the machine (or its hard drive) is not always possible. For copying digital storage media footage, ACPO's four principles must be followed (see 25.7.3). The ACPO Good Practice Guide for Digital Evidence, Version 5 (available online) makes it clear that seized hard drives should be placed in anti-static bags, tough paper bags, tamper evident cardboard packaging, or wrapped in paper and placed in aerated plastic bags.

23.4.3   Screening

The principal screener will normally be an experienced police officer with investigative skills at PIP Level 2 or above. (The exact role title can vary from force to force.) He/she will:

- decide if the crime should be classed as mandatory, priority, or non-priority;
- assess the quality of the initial and primary investigation, and ensure that all evidence-gathering opportunities are exploited (for the current incident and for other related incidents).

Non-volume serious crimes such as homicide and rape will be classed as mandatory and will certainly be assigned for secondary investigation. The probable 'solvability' of priority and or non-priority crimes will also be assessed, and a secondary investigation will be allocated for any crimes which are part of a series, involve a named suspect, or for which there is good evidence or credible intelligence linked to a named offender. An investigation plan, sometimes part of a 'handover package' (see 10.14), will be prepared for the secondary investigation team.

If the decision is not to investigate any further then the crime report is filed ('finalized') and the reasons for the decision are recorded.

23.4.4   Secondary investigation

The investigation plan will help direct the secondary investigation and will identify relevant lines of enquiry. This could involve further forensic work, e-fit circulation, statements from witnesses with full descriptions, and capturing text or other electronically generated data. In most police forces there will be identified supervisors who regularly review progress and help ensure that the investigation plan is carried to a conclusion. After the secondary investigation there may be:

- continuing investigation into and gathering intelligence about the alleged crimes—this might include further interviews (eg with witnesses—see 24.6), seizure of property, and conducting searches;
- reviews of the available evidence and a decision on charging or disposal (see 10.13);
- discussion about any other offences to be 'taken into consideration'; and
- documents to complete, for example an MG 3 for the Crown Prosecutor (see 26.3).

A successful priority or volume crime secondary investigation is likely to give rise to the arrest of a suspect or suspects. Trainee police officers early in training would be unlikely to have any further involvement at this stage.

23.4.5 The 'investigative mindset' and 'gap analysis'

There is plenty of guidance from ACPO, the College of Policing, and others about the law surrounding investigation, procedural matters, and the application of forensic investigation. However, there is comparatively little available guidance on the actual process of investigation: that is, the forms of cognition and decision-making required to see an investigation to a successful conclusion. The phrase often found in the professional literature is the 'investigative mindset' (eg see ACPO Centrex, 2005, p 60) but it is far from clear what this means in practice. Most often it is a reference to what are considered the best ways for investigators to both make sense of the information (eg an eyewitness statement) and potential evidence (eg a DNA sample) gathered during an investigation (usually referred to in the professional literature as 'material', a term taken from CPIA), and to make decisions based on that information. ACPO describe five principles underpinning the investigative mindset and we summarize these in the table.

Principle	Explanation
Understanding the source of material	Understanding how a deleted SMS has been recovered from a mobile phone
Planning and preparation	This in terms of the gathering of material, eg planning a witness interview
Examination	This comprises: • account (eg given by a victim); • clarification (eg investigate any apparent contradictions); and • challenge (both the meaning and reliability of material)
Recording and collation	Making adequate records, storing material correctly, establishing access arrangements
Evaluation	Identify further action that may be needed (eg fast-track actions to find other materials). 'Gap analysis' (see 23.4.5.1)

(Based on ACPO Centrex, 2005, pp 60–3 but authors' own interpretation)

ACPO argue that the application of the mindset by investigators helps ensure that the maximum amount of information is gathered, that the reliability of this information is effectively tested, appropriate actions are initiated, proper record keeping is undertaken, and material is stored appropriately (ACPO Centrex , 2005, p 63).

23.4.5.1 Gap analysis

Allied to the concept of the investigative mindset, and particularly to the principle of investigative and evidential 'Evaluation', is the notion of a 'gap analysis'. This is the periodic analysis of material gathered during an investigation in order to identify and then fill any gaps in investigative and evidential knowledge. It is often referred to as the '5WH' approach; that is, identifying the gaps in knowledge concerning the 'Who? What? When? Where? Why? and How?' of the alleged offence.

Gap in Knowledge	Explanation
Who?	The identities of witnesses, suspects, victims, etc
What?	The sequence of events leading up to, during, and after an alleged offence
When?	The time(s) of events linked with the alleged offence
Where?	The locations linked with the alleged offences
Why?	Motivation—why this place, this time, this alleged victim?
How?	The means of conducting the alleged offence

24 Interviewing

24.1 Introduction

Interviewing witnesses, victims, and suspects is a key part of the police investigation process, and is something that a 'frontline' police officer will do nearly every day. Interviews are an important means of obtaining accurate and reliable information about events or matters under police investigation.

The modern approach to police interviewing in the UK is to see the interview as a means of seeking to establish the truth. This sounds obvious but it does in fact represent a marked change in emphasis from the past: it is no longer simply a case of working through a list of 'points to prove'. Instead, interviewing is now much more of an 'inquisitorial approach' (see 5.1). In the past (particularly in the 1970s and 1980s) the police were sometimes accused of using oppressive techniques for obtaining a 'cough' (confession) and there were a number of notorious miscarriages of justice where innocent people were wrongly convicted. Both the PACE Act 1984 and the PEACE interview technique (see 24.3 onwards) were a reaction to the perceived shortcomings in police interviewing. However, a remarkably high proportion of suspects still confess to crime during the interview process. For example, Gudjonnson *et al* observed in 2004 that about 60 per cent of suspects in England confessed to the police during interviewing, and that this proportion had remained relatively constant for the previous 25 years (Gudjonnson *et al*, 2004). The precise reasons for this are unclear.

Here we will examine interviewing procedures in detail, and the recommended methods for conducting interviews. The IPLDP covers this in detail, and trainee officers will also practise interviewing procedures and techniques, including how to follow the relevant codes and legislation. The information provided here is also relevant to the 'Investigation and interview' heading in the Learning Diary (Phase 3). If you are on a pre-join course at a university, college, or with a private training provider (see 7.2.1) you might have the opportunity to explore some of the underpinning theory and research involved in police interviewing in more detail—for example, in relation to memory enhancement, lying and deception, and false confessions. The Certificate in Knowledge of Policing has two assessed units that are relevant: 'Knowledge of interviewing suspects in relation to priority and volume investigations within a policing context' and 'Knowledge of interviewing victims and witnesses within a policing context'.

24.2 Key Principles for Interviewing

Some general principles apply to all interviews and will help with effective planning and implementation. Home Office circular 2/1992 on investigative interviewing provides the following seven principles:

1. The role of investigative interviewing is to obtain accurate and reliable information from suspects, witnesses, and victims in order to discover the truth about matters under police investigation.
2. Investigative interviewing should be approached with an open mind.

3. Information obtained from the person who is being interviewed should always be tested against what the interviewing officer already knows or what can reasonably be established. When questioning anyone, a police officer must act fairly in the circumstances of each individual case.

4. The police officer is not bound to accept the first answer given. Questioning is not unfair merely because it is persistent. Even when a suspect exercises the right of silence, the police still have a right to put questions.

5. When conducting an interview, police officers are free to ask questions in order to establish the truth: except for interviews with child victims of sexual or violent abuse which are to be used in criminal proceedings, they are not constrained by the rules applied to lawyers in court.

6. Vulnerable people, whether victims, witnesses, or suspects, must be treated with particular consideration at all times. The interviewing of victims, witnesses, and suspects is an every-day part of the police role.

7. The interview is the formal means by which vital information and evidence is obtained in relation to incidents. This requires specific skills to obtain this information and evidence in a way that conforms to the laws of the land.

The legislation around police interviewing is complex, and here we cover the basics, sufficient for the trainee officer. The following legislation is also important for interviewing:

- ss 76 and 78 of the PACE Act 1984, including provisions under Code C, Code E, and Code F;
- Part III and ss 34, 36, and 37 of the Criminal Justice and Public Order Act 1994 (CJPOA), including 'special warnings' (see 24.5.9);
- the criminal law relating to the offence(s) for which suspects are charged;
- the Human Rights Act 1998 (see 5.4);
- the CPIA 1996; and
- the Youth Justice and Criminal Evidence Act 1999 (especially on 'vulnerable', 'intimidated', and child witnesses).

Other legislation covers specific provisions which we will refer to later, but those noted here are the principal sources governing the legality of what a police officer can do and say during an interview. Legislation such as the PACE Act 1984 has certainly helped to reassure the public, lawyers, academic commentators, and the police themselves that interviewing is now more tightly controlled, more ethical, and often more effective. Of course, simply knowing the law is not enough: applying the law is the key role for a police officer. If mistakes are made through incompetence, poor practice, or acting in 'bad faith' during the interview process, parts of the evidence may be rendered void or inadmissible. This could mean that a guilty person might avoid prosecution and be free to offend again, or an innocent person might be wrongly charged and convicted.

Copies of the PACE Act 1984 and the CJPOA 1994 (available on the www.legislation.gov.uk website) should be to hand while reading this chapter.

24.3 The 'PEACE' Approach to Interviewing

Police forces in England and Wales use the 'PEACE' approach to interviewing:

- Planning and Preparation
- Engage and Explain
- Account, Clarification, and Challenge
- Closure
- Evaluation

Each of these elements will be considered in turn, but the detail will depend on whether the interview is with a suspect or a witness.

The key points to consider are as follows:

- the objectives (what is to be achieved and how: remember, the emphasis is on establishing the truth (see Chapter 23 on investigation));
- the relevant law (eg recent stated cases, and intention, effect of drink/drugs on intention, recklessness, etc);

- possible defences (eg, statutory defences, reasonableness, mistake, coercion, duress, self-defence);
- possible mitigating and aggravating factors; and
- pre-interview disclosure (to solicitors or legal representatives: see 24.5.4).

We devote considerable time to looking at the preliminaries, because establishing an appropriate tone, mood, and format for an interview from the very start is beneficial to the overall process. Most interviewees will not know what is happening and will need reassurance; he/she may have never even been in a police station before.

For an evaluation of the use of PEACE by police forces in England and Wales, see Clarke and Milne (2001) and more recently Walsh and Milne (2008). In the latter case the two researchers found particular concerns within the PEACE stages of rapport building, and the lack of summarizing during the interview. Clarke, Milne, and Bull looked at PEACE interviewing again in 2011 and found that further improvement in training was required, particularly in terms of the communication skills of interviewers (Clarke *et al*, 2011). It might be worth thinking about this as you read through the rest of Chapter 24.

For further information on the history of PEACE together with a detailed explanation, see 'Investigative Interviewing: the conversation management approach' (Shepherd and Griffiths, 2013).

24.3.1   PEACE—planning and preparation

Many aspects of an interview appear to be merely practical issues, but on closer inspection several of these factors could also influence the whole outcome of the interview, so careful planning is essential. For example, will other officers be present? This is likely to affect the approach taken for the interview. There is no substitute for careful and detailed planning; every interview is different and every witness, victim, or suspect will behave differently, so interviewers must be prepared for these differences and plan accordingly. The plan should be in writing.

Practical aspects to be covered in the plan include:

- the order of interview if more than one person is to be interviewed;
- who will be present, and the seating plan;
- the time and location;
- the timing of breaks; and
- the number of tapes required.

For interviews with suspects (see 24.5), there are other practical considerations, such as recording the interview and the PACE requirements for rest and review times. Reference should be made to the PACE Codes of Practice.

As well as covering the practical aspects listed previously, the following points should be included:

- the range of topics to be covered;
- the points needed to prove the possible offence(s) under investigation; and
- evidence that the suspect committed the offence(s) and the specific parts of the criminal law under which the suspect may be charged.

One of the first things to decide is what potential offence or offences are being investigated. The relevant legislation should be consulted and the key points established. Using information such as witness accounts or statements, the contribution the interview will make to the investigation becomes clear. Remember that, if an offence has actually occurred, the following must be proved:

1. **Criminal intent** (*mens rea*): What was in the suspect's mind at the time? Why did he/she commit the offence?
2. **Criminal action** (*actus reus*): What did he/she actually do? How did he/she do it?

An interview should explore these aspects carefully (see 5.3 for further details). The suspect may be guilty or, if the course of the interview suggests otherwise, a 'refused charge' may be the outcome (see 10.13.8 on methods of disposal).

The key questions in the interview should be planned in advance. The first main question is very important as it tends to set the agenda for the rest of the interview and also, to a certain extent, dictates interviewing tactics. Open questions (which normally cannot be answered with a simple yes or no) are preferable, as this invites a fuller response and the more detail given in the interviewee's own words, the more powerful the evidence. The use of leading questions which might lead a person to overstate or understate the truth should be avoided. In a suspect interview, in order to prove the *mens rea* the interviewer might ask an open question, for instance starting with the words 'What were you feeling when you...?' or 'What were you thinking when you were...?' There are various approaches to interviewing; SE3R is widely used ('survey, extract, read, review, and respond').

A plan helps an interviewer keep track of what has been covered and what remains to be explored. It will also help if the accounts from different interviewees contradict each other or vary significantly from what seem to be the facts. The plan may contain a series of prompts or be used as an *aide mémoire* during the interview itself, but prompts need to be used with care if the interviewer is to appear professional and in control of the interview. Remember that whatever sort of plan is used, the interview plan is relevant material (as set out in the CPIA 1996) and must therefore be retained as a document to be revealed (see 26.2.4).

Certain information is required about the interviewee, and establishing this is part of the preparation process. The following questions will need to be answered before the interview begins:

- Has his/her identity been confirmed? A Livescan and IDENT1 check could be done (see 25.5.4).
- How old is he/she? (Establishing the age of a person is not necessarily a simple process. Some adults will claim to be younger than they are in an attempt to avoid prosecution.)
- Does he/she have any relevant previous convictions or reprehensible behaviour; if so could they be used in interview as evidence of 'bad character'—to rebut an innocent explanation, to suggest a propensity to commit the type of offence suspected, untruthfulness or even the unlikelihood of coincidence. (For example, a person's offending history might make it seem more likely that he/she is the offender for the current offence (*R v McAllister* [2009] 1 Cr App R 129). This type of bad character evidence (see 26.4.5) was used recently in the conviction of Levi Bellfield for the murder of Millie Dowler (*R v Bellfield*, 2011).)
- Is he/she on the force's intelligence database? Is he/she suspected of other crimes elsewhere or flagged as active or of interest to other police forces or agencies?
- Is he/she already on bail? Is he/she in breach of bail, an ASBO, or a court order, or wanted for a crime elsewhere?

Normally the same interview team would conduct all interviews relating to one incident. However, after arrest and detention procedures are complete the responsibility for an interview is sometimes handed over to another officer (perhaps from a dedicated unit for prisoner handling). In such circumstances, the interviewing officer will need to be very fully briefed so he/she can prepare properly for the interview (see 10.14 on handover procedures).

24.3.2 PEACE—engage and explain

The interviewer should explain what is going to happen and how things will proceed in order to reassure and relax the interviewee. If this is all done in a friendly and non-threatening manner, he/she is far more likely to cooperate, and encouraging the person to talk is a primary aim of the interview process. The interviewer should not simply read from his/her plan, as this is likely to convey a general lack of flexibility and alertness, and rapport may suffer as a consequence (see 6.11 on communication).

In this stage of a PEACE interview, the interviewer should:

- **establish a rapport** by including introductions, concerns, considerations, and by using appropriate humour. This will help create a compatible atmosphere and establish common ground;
- **explain the reasons for the interview** (for a suspect, this should include an explanation of the alleged offence, the grounds for arrest, and that the interview provides an opportunity for the suspect to put his/her account of what happened, and for the police to seek the truth);
- **describe the routines**—depending on the nature of the interview this might include explaining why certain persons are present, the recording procedures, the need for interviewers to refer to their notes and make further notes, the production of exhibits, etc;
- **set out the route map**—what happens during and after the interview process, and the general (not the specific) line of questioning;

- **state the expectations**—ground rules such as no over-talking or interruptions, politeness, time to think, and the need to seek clarification of questions and answers; and
- **explain legal rights** and the role of the solicitor and legal advisers.

Setting the right tone is very important. For each interviewee any cultural or behavioural factors (eg how to address him/her) should be noted and taken into account. Asking directly how he/she wishes to be addressed might provide an easy ice-breaker at the beginning of the interview. An interviewer could also offer the interviewee a cup of tea or other refreshment (if available—there is a certain loss of face otherwise!).

24.3.3 PEACE—account, clarifications, and challenge

This is the main part of the interview. In the following order, the interviewer should:

- seek a 'free' account, without any interruption if possible;
- develop the account by first phasing the incident, and then moving systematically from one phase to another, clarifying or seeking greater detail—*Turnbull* and the ADVOKATE checklist could be used here (see 10.5.3);
- summarize the account and then select topics that are relevant, in dispute, and checkable for examination in greater detail. Does the account make chronological sense?
- seek new/additional information and summarize each topic with commitment and agreement if possible;
- clarify and challenge but restrict challenges to inconsistencies and checkable, provable, and admissible facts. When challenging, the interviewer should take care not to criticize or accuse—instead he/she should ask for explanation, especially where discrepancies emerge;
- consider whether a special warning is needed (see 24.5.9); and
- consider whether bad-character evidence is appropriate (see 26.4.5), and if so has it been introduced in a way that is relevant to the nature of any likely charges?

TASK 1 What special interview techniques may be used to help the interviewee's recall, particularly for witness interviews?

Breaks are useful for making arrangements and gathering thoughts, particularly if the interview has taken an unexpected turn; the plan for the rest of the interview may even need to be revised. After a break it is good practice to summarize what has been said and to invite the interviewee to comment on the accuracy of the summary. This demonstrates that the interviewer has been listening carefully and has realized the significance of what has been said, and that the interviewee is being taken seriously.

24.3.4 PEACE—closure

The interviewer should aim to maintain the good rapport built up during an interview as it might be necessary to interview the same person again, especially if any new evidence emerges or if CPS guidance is received. Before finishing the interview the interviewer should:

- review the interviewee's account in full;
- allow the interviewee the chance to correct, confirm, deny, alter, or add to his/her account;
- ensure that all the planned questions have been covered;
- check whether the interviewee (or the solicitor, if present) wants to ask any questions; and
- explain what will happen in the future.

Once this has been done the interview can be formally closed. This is likely to include recording the time when the interview finishes. For interviews with suspects, there are additional requirements relating to recording the interview (see 24.5.7).

24.3.5 PEACE—evaluation

The evaluation stage includes not only an evaluation of what has been achieved but also how well the aims and objectives set by the interviewer were met. The interviewer should refer to his/her plan and reflect on what went well, what might have gone better, and (for next time) which areas he/she would try to develop or improve. The following questions might be relevant:

- Have other reasonable lines of enquiry (such as an alibi) been discovered?
- Have other forensic opportunities been discovered?
- Have all the points to prove from the offence under investigation been covered?
- Have the statutory defences, mitigation, or explanation, perhaps pointing to innocence been considered?
- Have the objectives been achieved?
- Does the interview add to the investigation as a whole?
- Have the requirements of the CPIA 1996 been satisfied?

Trainee police officers could assess their personal level of skills and knowledge about interviewing and use this as a basis for Learning Diary entries.

24.4 The Needs of the Interviewee

Many suspects will be anxious and want to know what is going to happen next and in the longer term. The common questions are 'Will I be released?', 'Will I get bail?', and 'How long will I be here?' If the suspect asks, then the interviewer should answer fairly and honestly but should also explain that he/she cannot determine the decisions of the custody officer or the CPS reviewing lawyer.

24.4.1 Meeting the needs of all interviewees

The interviewer and the custody officer should be alert to the special circumstances involved in interviewing a person with a physical or mental impairment. They should always try to ascertain the nature and extent of the impairment, although the individual may or may not be willing to divulge it and the PACE Act 1984 'allows police officers to proceed on an assumption'. This obviously needs careful and sensitive handling; bluntly asking a witness, suspect, or victim 'Are you deaf?' is inappropriate. It is far better to use more neutral language such as 'Do you have a physical impairment we should be aware of?'

For a profoundly deaf individual a signer may be required for the interview. A partially deaf person will find it easier if he/she can see the interviewer's face in order to lip-read, and people should speak one at a time. A deaf person's attention could be attracted by lightly touching his/her sleeve. The force diversity team may provide Braille texts which explain, for example, a suspect's rights, the caution, and the management of tapes after interview, but it should be remembered that not all blind people can read Braille.

Other impairments such as speech impediments may be more difficult to deal with, but interviewers should always be sensitive to the individual's needs and requirements, and should try to meet them. The simple question is: 'Have I done all I can to ensure that this person is not disadvantaged in any way because of a disability or impairment?' If this is the case, then all reasonable steps have been taken. No one should be placed at a disadvantage in a police interview because of physical or mental impairment; the criminal justice system is not well served unless this principle is upheld.

24.4.2 The presence of an 'appropriate adult'

It is usually the custody officer who considers whether an appropriate adult is required. The PACE Act 1984, Code C, para 1.4 states that an 'appropriate adult' must be provided for any person (victim, witness, or suspect) suspected or known to be:

- 'mentally disordered or otherwise mentally vulnerable' (see 13.2);
- under the age of 18 (since October 2013, PACE Code C, para 1.5A); or
- likely to find an interview problematic due to an impairment such as a serious visual handicap, deafness, illiteracy, or who has difficulty in articulation because of a speech impediment.

The appropriate adult acts on behalf of the interviewee. The legal adviser does not play this role: they seldom have the relevant experience or expertise, and in any case his/her role is confined to the legal interests (and to a lesser extent the longer term welfare) of the client.

PACE Code C, para 1.7 sets out the categories of person who can be an appropriate adult, and his/her duties are also described. The appropriate adult for a juvenile is, first, a parent or guardian, or, if the juvenile is in care, a suitable representative from the care authority or voluntary organization. If neither of these is available a social worker may stand *in loco parentis* (in the place of a parent). As a last resort, any responsible person aged 18 or over who is not a police officer or employed by the police may act as the appropriate adult. The PACE Act 1984 does not define what is meant by responsible. PACE Code of Practice C Note 1B states that 'A person, including a parent or guardian, should not be an appropriate adult if they are: suspected of involvement in the offence; the victim; a witness; involved in the investigation, or have received admissions prior to attending to act as the appropriate adult.' For a person who is 'mentally disordered' or has a reduced mental capacity (see 13.2), an appropriate adult is a relative, guardian, or other person responsible for his/her care and custody. Alternatively, it could be someone who has experience of dealing with mentally vulnerable people, such as an approved mental health professional (AMHP) or a specialist social worker. Failing this, any responsible person aged 18 or over can act as the appropriate adult, but as stated earlier, anyone connected with the police is not eligible.

The appropriate adult does not have a passive role as a mere observer. He/she will be informed by the custody officer that:

> Where you are present at an interview, you are not expected to act simply as an observer. The purpose of your presence is to advise the person being questioned, to observe whether or not the interview is being conducted properly and fairly and to facilitate communication with the person being interviewed.

The appropriate adult will be invited to sign the custody record to show that he/she understands the responsibilities involved. The interviewer should check that this has been done before the interview begins.

A couple of other practical points: such an interview may take longer, especially if it involves interpretation, for example by a signer. Translation from one language to another takes at least twice as long as normal, so allowances should be made for this. There are advantages: the interviewee has more time to consider his/her replies, and the interviewer will have more time to observe and consider the suspect's NVC and demeanour (although of course any interpretations must always allow for cultural and linguistic diversity, see 6.11.2).

24.5 Interviews with Suspects

A suspect interview is defined as 'the questioning of a person regarding his/her involvement or suspected involvement in a criminal offence or offences which must be carried out under caution' (PACE Code C, para 11.1A). This applies to any conversation (no matter how short and wherever it takes place) once a caution has been given and it is irrelevant whether or not the suspect has been arrested. Not all suspects are arrested, for example a suspect on the street being reported for a road traffic offence (see 10.13.1), or a suspect who volunteers to be interviewed to assist with the investigation of an offence.

Interviews with suspects will often take place at a police station. Suspects who have been arrested must be interviewed at a police station (PACE Code C, para 11.1). Suspects who have not been arrested and who volunteer to be interviewed to assist with an investigation would normally be interviewed at a police station, but could be interviewed at another location such as his/her home. Suspects being reported for a road traffic offence would usually be 'interviewed' in the street.

24.5.1 General rights of the suspect

The suspect has the normal rights of being treated with dignity, fairness, and objectivity, and the right to a legal adviser during interview, and for a vulnerable person, an 'appropriate adult' should also be present (see 24.4.1). A number of laws and associated Codes regulate the process of police interviews, in order to protect the interviewee. The suspect should be assessed as 'fit for interview'. Normally a doctor or custody nurse will make this decision considering whether the suspect is ill, hurt, or suffering from a psychological condition, but it can be decided on the person's own say, supported by the custody officer's independent observations.

Unquestionably, there have been many instances in the past of the police abusing their powers to question suspects (some of which may have been motivated in part by the so-called 'noble cause corruption' discussed in 6.5.3). This could range from oppressive behaviour used to obtain confessions under duress, to a lack of safety provisions when interviewing a vulnerable person (eg due to a disability or learning difficulty). A recent example of where the suspect's rights were denied prior to arrival at the police station was the Halliwell case (see 24.5.1.1).

The custody officer and the suspect's legal adviser both have a responsibility to monitor the suspect's rights and the process of interviewing, and this has greatly reduced the opportunities for foul play. The suspect should have his/her rights explained, and this should be reinforced with a written explanation.

24.5.1.1 Confessions, oppression, and unfairness

Many of the unfair practices that were adopted by the police to secure a 'confession' from a suspect in custody have been identified and made more difficult, if not impossible, by legislation and practice guidelines. Any statement that is in any way adverse to a person (eg admitting to a crime or even to being present at the scene of a crime) can amount to a confession under s 82 PACE. The statement can be made to any person, not just a police officer, and can include written or spoken words, actions, or even silence. Even though a person may have confessed in one of these recognized ways, the evidence might not be admissible in court (for example in the Halliwell case, see later). The defence can argue that a confession should be rendered inadmissible because:

- it was or may have been obtained by oppression (s 76 PACE);
- if something was said or done likely to render the confession unreliable (s 76 PACE) (eg inducements were offered, threats were made, or the caution was not properly given);
- the manner in which the evidence was obtained would mean that it would be unfair to admit it (s 78 PACE); or
- it is too prejudicial to admit it (eg that the offender has previously confessed to a similar but more serious offence, and the bench or the jury might concentrate on the seriousness of that offence rather than fully consider the evidence in the current case) (s 82 PACE).

Oppression usually means behaviour akin to breaching a person's human rights under Article 3 (this refers to torture, inhumane or degrading treatment, or the use or threat of violence). Case law has widened the definition of oppression to include 'exercise of authority in a burdensome, harsh or wrongful manner' (*R v Fulling* [1987] 2 All ER 65), as well as 'questioning which by its very nature, duration or other circumstances (including the fact of custody) excites hope (such as the hope of release) or fears, or so affects the mind of the subject that his will crumbles and he speaks when otherwise he would have stayed silent' (*R v Prager* [1972] 1 WLR 260, 266, adopted by the House of Lords in *R v Mushtaq* [2005] UKHL 25). This definition can encompass many situations, and it is unsurprising that defence solicitors often argue that a confession has been obtained by oppression. If the court or the defence raise the issue of oppression, the burden of proof is on the prosecution to prove that it was not obtained in that manner.

Inducements to confess could include offers to grant bail, or for the police to refrain from arresting family members. Threats could be suggesting that bail would not be granted or that family members might be arrested.

Section 78 of PACE provides an important basis for many defence arguments, as it allows for any potential prosecution evidence to be rendered inadmissible (not just confessions, see *R v Mason* [1987] 3 All ER 481). The defence has to show that the manner in which the evidence was obtained would mean that it would be unfair to the proceedings to admit it. The defence might argue, for instance, that DNA should not be admissible because the prosecution have not proven continuity of the evidence from the moment it was found to the moment it was examined at the laboratory. Note, therefore, that the defence could argue that a confession should be rendered inadmissible under s 78 if the s 76 argument does not succeed.

A recent example of where the suspect's rights were denied was the Halliwell case. A superintendent was judged to have breached PACE by interviewing the suspect in circumstances that were oppressive and that deliberately denied him his rights (both ss 76 and 78 PACE arguments were employed by the defence). Halliwell was arrested for abduction of Sian O'Callaghan who had been missing for several days, but some of the interviews were conducted prior to arrival at a police station, under the guise of an urgent interview, without caution, and without a solicitor. This was also without Halliwell's express agreement. He confessed to the murder of O'Callaghan and another woman, and was subsequently charged with both murders. After lengthy legal arguments at the start of the trial, all of Halliwell's confessions were ruled inadmissible and the second murder case failed. The O'Callaghan case continued based upon other evidence and Halliwell was convicted. There was extensive media coverage and an IPCC investigation ensued. The superintendent was found guilty of gross misconduct for the breaches and was given a final written warning.

24.5.2 Planning suspect interviews

As well as the general PEACE considerations for planning interviews covered in 24.3.1, there are other factors that apply only to suspect interviews to consider, such as:

- the legal framework for interviews with suspects;
- the suspect's right to a free independent legal adviser and for the adviser to be present throughout the interview; and
- the arrangements for recording the interview.

These requirements need to be covered in the interview plan. The interviewer also needs to consider what defences the suspect might employ and how these might be countered.

24.5.3 Defence solicitors

The defence solicitor is the defendant's legal adviser. A 'duty solicitor' is drawn from a retained panel of solicitors available to advise an arrested person who does not have a solicitor of his/her own available for the interview. They provide 'free and independent legal advice' (FILA) and are there to advise their clients at any time. They are of course independent of the police and the CPS. The custody officer will make the initial contact with the solicitor, following a request from the detained suspect (see 10.10), and the interviewer will then become the point of contact for the defence solicitor. (Note that confidential handover documents or witness statements should not be attached to the custody record.)

The defence solicitor is obliged to prevent his/her client from further assisting the police by way of self-incrimination, if that is not in the client's interest (Note 6D of PACE Code C).

24.5.3.1 Active defence

A solicitor might adopt an 'active defence' role (Ede and Shepherd, 2000). If the evidence looks weak or merely circumstantial, the solicitor will probably advise the suspect to remain silent or to submit a jointly prepared statement. It is sometimes difficult for a trainee officer to accept as proper that a solicitor can advise a suspect from providing details about a crime or admitting guilt, and more experienced police officers may also argue that there is no 'level playing field'. (However, later in court a jury may adversely interpret a suspect's silence at interview, if he/she relies on evidence which he/she could have provided earlier (see 24.5.9.2 on adverse inference).)

The solicitor is very likely to try and find out about the line of questioning planned for the interview in order to try and head off any lines of enquiry which will be difficult for the suspect. If the evidence is very strong the solicitor may try to depict the suspect as a victim who has been manipulated by unscrupulous others. Sometimes an admission of guilt is better for the client, especially if there is strong or irrefutable evidence, or strong mitigation (an excuse or reason for what has been done).

The solicitor might try to dominate an interview (an accepted tactic), particularly if the interviewing officer seems to lack experience or is unprofessional during the interview. If a solicitor is disruptive there is a risk of 'losing the interview', so the interviewer may need to speak out and take control. However, it is very rare for a solicitor to behave so inappropriately that the police interviewer has to exclude him/her from the interview, and in any case the whole interview is on tape; the court will take a negative view of a disruptive solicitor, and this might even prejudice the suspect's chances.

24.5.4 Briefing a solicitor before an interview

Before the interview begins the solicitor must be briefed (provided with the relevant information) so that his/her client may be properly advised. The interviewer must plan what he/she will disclose, considering:

- What is the evidence?
- What evidence should be disclosed immediately?
- What evidence should be withheld (at least for the time being)?
- When will this evidence be disclosed in the interview process?
- Can withholding this evidence be justified?

Any evidence derived from intelligence, vital forensic evidence, or details which relate to a particular MO should not be disclosed until there is no choice, and disclosure becomes inevitable (see 26.2.5). However, there are some cases where fuller disclosure might facilitate a frank and productive interaction between the suspect and the police. The skill is to be able to recognize the types of cases where fuller disclosure would be beneficial. Where a decision is made to provide limited disclosure, the solicitor is more likely to ask difficult questions and to advise the suspect to remain silent at interview. If further material is disclosed during an interview, the solicitor is likely to immediately ask for a private consultation with his/her client. These consequences should be considered and planned for, but the interviewer is free to determine the nature and extent of disclosure on a case-by-case basis. There are two major warnings which must be heeded when briefing the solicitor: never overstate or understate the evidence, and never express a view on the likely outcome for the client.

In a well-planned meeting, the encounter between the police officer and the defence solicitor will take place in a quiet room without interruptions. (Sometimes, though, the encounter will take place in a busy corridor or by phone, and the interviewer must guard against saying too much.) At the start of the meeting the interviewer should explain that he/she will answer the solicitor's questions when the disclosure of evidence is complete. Sufficient time should be allowed for the solicitor to take notes, although in serious cases an audio-recording will be made. The case against the suspect should be outlined, including the evidence upon which the interview will be based, and up-to-date information about the welfare of the client should also be provided. Then the solicitor can be invited to ask questions; this needs careful handling, as being over-defensive and disclosing only in response to the solicitor's questions may increase the likelihood of a 'no comment' interview. The interviewing officer needs to remain calm and self-possessed. A solicitor may try different tactics, such as switching abruptly from questions about evidence to questions about other aspects of the case. The interviewer will of course be able to deal more confidently with such situations if he/she knows all the details of the case, and has a thorough understanding of the relevant law.

24.5.5 The start of a suspect interview

The time spent on relaxing the suspect, engaging with him/her, explaining what is going to happen and following procedure properly, may prove productive later. In addition, no irregularities will have been provided for the solicitor to use in the defence of his/her client.

At the start of the interview (or after a break) and before any questions about the offence are put, the interviewer must caution the suspect (see PACE Code C, paras 10.8 and 11.4) and check his/her understanding. A detailed account of the various cautions and their use is given in 10.3. The interviewer might say to the suspect, for example:

> You have an absolute right to remain silent if you wish, you cannot be compelled to answer my questions. However, if you choose not to tell me something in answer to a question I ask you now, but later in court you do then answer to the same question, then the magistrate or jury are entitled to ask themselves why—why you did not answer the question earlier, when I asked you. They might think that the answer you give in court is untrue and is a lie. I must warn you that a recording of this interview can be played back in court.

The solicitor should not be asked to explain the caution, or to acknowledge that his/her client understands it—this is the responsibility of the interviewing officer.

Certain additional information must be provided to the suspect depending on the circumstances and location of the interview. A suspect who has been arrested and who is being interviewed at a police station must also be reminded that he/she is entitled to free legal advice and that the interview can be delayed until it is obtained. Such reminders and the suspect's response should be recorded in the interview record (Code C, para 11.2). Other information that must be provided to the suspect is given in the table.

Circumstances and location of interview with a suspect who has not been arrested	Additional information to be provided
Suspect is on the street being reported for an offence	The failure to cooperate (eg by not providing a name and address when he/she is being reported for an offence) could amount to committing a further offence or make him/her liable for arrest (Code C, para 10.9)
Suspect has volunteered to assist with the investigation of an offence. The location for the interview could be a police station or another location such as the suspect's home (Code C, para 3.22)	The suspect must also be told that he/she can leave whenever he/she wants, and can obtain free and independent legal advice if he/she agrees to remain (Code C, para 3.21)

Any significant statement (see 10.4) should also be discussed. The suspect must be given the opportunity to confirm, deny, or add to an earlier statement. Sometimes it may be difficult to distinguish between a significant statement and a 'relevant comment' (again see 10.4), but if there is any doubt, the statement or comment should be put to the suspect at the beginning of the interview.

24.5.6 Tactics during interviews

The interviewing officer should be polite, rational, and relaxed (or at least appear relaxed), and proceed with the questioning as planned. However, interviewees are often hostile and refuse to cooperate. The common tendency for an interviewing officer in such circumstances is to confront the solicitor or to start rushing the questions, but this must be avoided. The interviewing officer must not be drawn into:

- asking closed questions (requiring a yes or no reply);
- speeding up, allowing little time for answers (as if no answer is expected);
- asking the suspect to justify why he/she is not answering the questions; or
- showing any hostility to the suspect or the solicitor.

The simple advice in this situation is to adhere to the PEACE model of interviewing, and not to be thrown. Skilful and persistent questioning may slip under a hostile suspect's defences, and following a new line of questioning he/she may forget to brazen it out with a repeated 'no comment' and suddenly provide vital evidence or information.

Most defence solicitors, particularly duty solicitors, will have a good understanding and plenty of experience of the PEACE interview model and the approaches which an interviewing officer is likely to adopt. For example, the solicitor will know that the interviewer will try to build a rapport with the interviewee but it is very unlikely that he/she will assist with the process. If the interviewing officer starts with a few informal words about a non-contentious topic (such as whether the suspect would like a drink) to encourage the suspect to open up, the solicitor is likely to challenge its relevance unless it relates directly to the suspect's welfare.

The PACE Codes of Practice provide some guidance on what is acceptable behaviour by the solicitor in an interview. A legal adviser is permitted to seek clarification offer the client their advice (including not to answer a question), and can also challenge an improper question or the manner in which it is put. A legal adviser may not, however, answer questions on the client's behalf or provide him/her with written responses to quote.

The solicitor will also closely monitor the interview process itself. This is because, however overwhelming the evidence, any flaw in police procedure can lead to charges against the suspect being dismissed, or an application at trial to have the evidence ruled inadmissible. A solicitor has no obligation to immediately point out any police failing or non-adherence to the appropriate Codes, and may only mention it later when it is of particular advantage to the client, for instance in court. This is one of the reasons why the interviewing officer needs to know the law and the associated police procedures very well indeed. Asking leading questions, adopting a threatening or bullying manner, or seeking to offer the suspect a lighter sentence in exchange for giving more evidence will all prompt the solicitor to intervene (and rightly so). If, however, the interviewing officer is acting fairly, proportionately, and properly, then the solicitor's grounds for intervention are much reduced.

Investigation and Prosecution

24.5.7 Recording suspect interviews

The tenet of Code E (para 3.1) is that an audio-recording should be made of all interviews under caution with suspects (including those attending voluntarily).

24.5.7.1 Recording interviews with suspects who have not been arrested

If a suspect is not under arrest but is interviewed voluntarily at a police station, then the interview should be recorded whenever possible, for example on tape. Codes E and F (in force since October 2013) state that an officer of the rank of sergeant or above can authorize an interview to continue without an audio-recording in prescribed circumstances, for instance where:

- the custody officer believes there will be no prosecution from the outset:
- equipment has failed or no room is available and the custody officer believes it would cause unnecessary delay (Code E, para 3.3A);
- the suspect objects to an audio-recorded interview (Code E para 4.8).

If the suspect refuses to be audio-recorded, a written record must be made of the interview. The decision to continue recording the interview against the wishes of the suspect may be commented upon in court, as this could be seen as being oppressive (PACE Code F, Note 4G). The evidence could then be rendered inadmissible under s 76 or 78 (see 24.5.1.1).

If the interview takes place other than at a police station, for example at the roadside in relation to a motoring offence, or at a juvenile's home (with an appropriate adult), the PNB is the most appropriate place to record such an interview in writing, complying with PACE Code C, para 11.7.

24.5.7.2 Procedures for recording interviews

The sealed tapes must be shown to the suspect at the start so that he/she can see that they are new and have not been tampered with. The following information must be recorded as a PNB entry or on the paper seals to be wrapped around the tapes at the end of the interview (see PACE Code C, para 11.7, PACE Act 1984):

- the time, day, date, location of the interview;
- the name, rank, role of the interviewer;
- the name, address, date of birth of the interviewee;
- the persons present; and
- a description of the layout of the room and the equipment.

When the tape recorder is first switched on there will be a continuous sound from the machine during which time nothing can be recorded (while the tape is winding on to the recording part of the tape). This must be explained to the suspect.

Two tapes are recorded simultaneously. At the end of the interview one of them will be sealed (the master tape) and the other (the working copy) will remain with the case file. A further copy will also be provided for the solicitor on request. The master tape is filed by the designated responsible person, and will not be opened unless it is needed in exceptional circumstances, or is to be examined on direction of a judge or a senior member of the CPS.

> **TASK 2** Find out what happens to the working copy of the tape.

At the end of the interview:

- the interviewing officer must record the time when the interview finishes (before switching off the machine);
- the labels for the tapes (if used) must be signed by the suspect, the interviewing officer, and the solicitor (note that no signing is required for a recording made on a secure digital network); and
- the master tape must be sealed in the presence of the suspect.

If a suspect or the solicitor refuses to sign the labels, this has to be recorded. The suspect should be told what will happen to the tapes, and this is reinforced by providing a written explanation on a pre-printed card.

Interviews are sometimes video recorded. PACE Code F states that there is no statutory requirement to visually record interviews, and the suspect has the right to refuse visual recording. (Code F describes in some detail the process to be followed in such circumstances.) Further details concerning recorded interviews may be found in the ACPO *Investigation of Volume Crime Manual*, Appendix H (ACPO, 2001). Note that the suspects's non-verbal communication (NVC) is not recorded in an interview under the PACE Act 1984, apart from the interviewing officer making references to actions.

24.5.8 Taking offences into consideration

Admissions of other offences can sometimes be treated as TICs (Taken Into Consideration). These assist police to solve crimes, they allow victims closure, they allow victims to claim compensation, and they allow the police to gather essential intelligence relating to criminal activity. A suspect may wish to tell the police about other offending behaviour in order to 'get it all over and done with', fearing for instance that further evidence of his/her offending behaviour could emerge over time, leading to repeated arrests.

TICs should be discussed with suspects, of that there is no doubt. However, no admissions to crimes should be obtained by inducements or favour (see 24.5.1.1). Safeguards have been put in place to prevent abuse of the TIC system; in the past, some criminals undoubtedly 'assisted' the police by admitting to offences they had not committed, hoping for more lenient treatment. But in fact the opposite applies—the Sentencing Council (2012) make it clear that where a defendant has admitted TICs, the sentence should reflect the totality of the offending.

It is legitimate for an officer to ask if a suspect if he/she wishes any further offences to be taken into consideration, as long as the officer adheres to the warnings above. Where a suspect discusses another crime he/she has committed, the officer should obtain sufficient detail of the crime to be able to satisfy the points to prove, as if the case was going to court as a charge. This includes seeking out any evidential material that may already exist, for example forensic evidence. Each subsequent admission should be dealt with in the same manner, providing a thorough and professional response to the investigation of the other crimes. Officers will also need to check whether the admitted crimes have already been reported or whether they are new crimes that should be recorded as such. The MG 18 form must be completed so that the prosecutor and the court are made aware of any relevant factors, and also the MG 19 form which relates to possible compensation for victims. If the suspect refuses to accept the TICs in court at a later stage, then they will already have been warned that the offences concerned could be investigated separately.

Sentencing guidelines (2012) make it clear that TICs for sexual or violent offences, or for offences more serious than the main charge, are unlikely to be accepted. If an officer is in doubt about the appropriateness of any charges or TICs, advice can be sought from the CPS, custody officers, or PIP Level 2 investigators. For further information see the CPS website.

24.5.9 Special warnings and adverse inference

Special warnings are used when the suspect fails to, or refuses to answer questions satisfactorily after due warning. If he/she presents a 'no comment' interview when asked questions, or fails to respond to questions based on special warnings, then at trial a judge may advise the jury that they are entitled to draw an 'adverse inference'.

24.5.9.1 Special warnings

The use of a special warning (ss 36 and 37 of the CJPOA 1994) is, in a sense, a further caution to the suspect and his/her legal adviser. A special warning may be needed for a suspect who has been caught directly in the commission of a crime (*in flagrante* or 'red-handed').

Section 36 warnings relate to a suspect's refusal to account for objects, marks, or substances, or marks on such objects. Further details are shown in the flowchart.

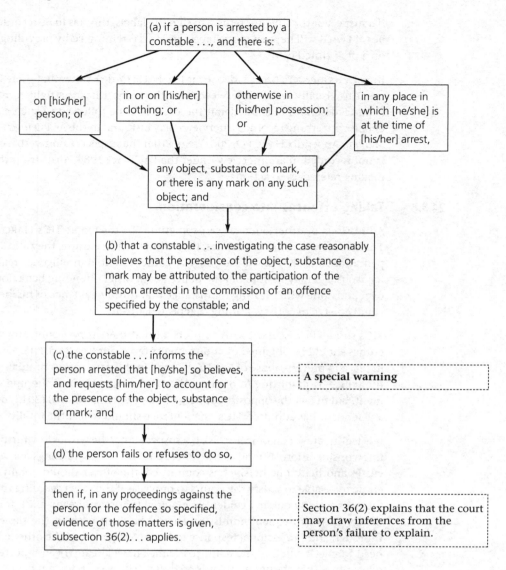

Section 37 warnings relate to the failure of a person to account for his/her presence at a place at or about the time that the offence is alleged to have been committed. If he/she cannot explain and a police officer believes that the suspect's presence is attributable to his/her participation in the offence, then the suspect must be warned that 'adverse inference' could be drawn. If a suspect has given a reasonable account of the fact in question, a special warning should not be used. This is because it is inappropriate and could be interpreted as oppressive behaviour and it would almost certainly entail an intervention by the suspect's legal adviser.

The special warning should include the following five points, put in language which the suspect will understand:

1. the offence being investigated;
2. the particular fact the suspect needs to account for;
3. that the interviewing officer believes that the fact arose because the suspect was involved in the offence;
4. that inference may be properly drawn if the suspect fails to account for that specific fact; and
5. that a record of the interview is being made.

Suggested wording and more guidance on special warnings may be found in Appendix H of the ACPO *Investigation of Volume Crime Manual* (ACPO, 2001).

24.5.9.2 Adverse inference

'Adverse inference' can be drawn if the suspect presents new significant information in court, and its significance is such that the court would expect the suspect to have already divulged it earlier at interview. The jury would be entitled to ask themselves 'Why didn't he/she mention this earlier?' and may conclude that the suspect is concealing something that might count against him/her, or that he/she might be lying in court. Therefore during a police interview the suspect **must** be asked all the relevant questions; the questions that would make it possible to draw adverse inference in court. After all, if the crucial question was not asked during the interview, then the defence might be able to convince the court that the suspect would have provided the crucial information at interview 'if only he/she had been given the opportunity'.

> **TASK 3** When should the special warning be used—before caution, during the 'engagement' phase, or at the end of the interview, as things are being brought to a close?

24.6 Witnesses in Investigations

The evidence of a witness (including victim(s)) may be vital in obtaining a conviction. Many, if not all, witnesses will cooperate if officers provide reassurance and information about what to expect: see, for example, <http://www.cps.gov.uk/victims_witnesses/resources/index.html>.

24.6.1 Categories of witness

There are various categories of witness, and these are important for determining the form of the dialogue between the witness and the police officer, the means by which evidence is obtained, and how it is subsequently used in court. The term 'victim' is normally associated with a person who has been disadvantaged, suffered injury, or been damaged as a result of an event, but a victim is usually also a witness.

A **defence witness** is a person who the accused is going to call to give evidence at his/her trial in relation to an alibi or to other matters. The name, address, and date of birth of any such witness must be disclosed in advance to the prosecution (s 6 of the Criminal Procedure and Investigations Act 1996) as the police may wish to interview him/her. Some defence witnesses may be intimidated or reluctant to assist, fearing, for example, police coercion to change his/her account. In these circumstances consultation with the CPS is advised. Any interview with a defence witness has to comply with the relevant Code of Practice (under s 21A of the Criminal Procedure and Investigations Act 1996).

A **significant witness** (also referred to as a key witness) is designated as such by an SIO, usually during a serious or major crime enquiry involving an indictable offence. Such a person may have witnessed the offence (or part of it) or may stand in a particular relationship to the victim, or have evidence or intelligence to offer in relation to the offence, possibly because of a close relationship with the suspect. An interview with a significant witness may be visually recorded if it seems that this will contribute significantly to the investigation (see 24.6.2.1).

Vulnerable and intimated witnesses may require 'special measures' during investigations and any subsequent court appearances (see 26.5.2.4). Definitions of these two categories of witness are given in Part II of the Youth Justice and Criminal Evidence Act 1999.

A vulnerable witness (s 16) is any person:

- under the age of 17;
- with a 'mental disorder' (this is the phrase used in the Act);
- with significant impairment of intelligence and social functioning (eg a learning disability); or
- with a physical disability or a physical disorder.

An intimidated witness (s 17) is:

- any elderly and frail person;
- a witness suffering from fear or distress in relation to testifying in the case;
- any witness who self-neglects or self-harms;
- any complainant in a sexual assault case;
- a victim of domestic violence, racially motivated crime, or repeat victimization; or
- a relative of the victim in a homicide case.

Witnesses who are under 17 years of age or complainants in sexual cases always require special measures. Vulnerable or intimidated witnesses in the other categories may require special measures, but further assessment will be required through the use of an MG 2 form. Trainee officers will probably only engage with such witnesses in obtaining a first account. However, this is an essential part of an investigation, and the record of what was said will later be scrutinized very carefully. Interviewing officers must take account of and use the 'special measures' available so they can offer reassurance in the face of questions such as 'Will I have to face him in court?' or 'Will the general public be able to hear all this?' Interviews that are likely to be more difficult or protracted will be conducted by specialist officers qualified to at least PIP Level 2 (see 7.6.1.1) and will follow ABE (*Achieving Best Evidence*) guidelines. A trainee officer might attend such an interview to brief and assist the interviewing officers. More information on special measures can be found on the CPS website.

Reluctant witnesses include those who decline to cooperate from the start, or who make a statement but then refuse to attend court. He/she could claim issues of confidentiality (eg involving a bank), or might fear repercussions or reprisal, or simply might not want to assist the police. If the police can establish that he/she has important material evidence to offer, a witness summons can be issued to compel attendance in court (see Home Office Circular 35/2005).

Anonymous witnesses are allowed in the interests of justice. For example, a witness against the accused may also be a co-accused, as in the Rhys Jones murder. In that case the CPS was originally going to charge a co-accused with firearms offences but instead offered him immunity from prosecution provided he met certain conditions, including attending court and giving a truthful account. He accepted these terms and the new evidence enabled the CPS to charge a suspect with murder.

However, a key principle of criminal justice is that the defendant must receive a fair trial. Therefore the police must obtain as much corroborative evidence as possible in any case where witness anonymity might be involved. Certain conditions must be met for a 'witness anonymity order' (under the Coroners and Justice Act 2009) to be issued by a court:

- the order is necessary to protect the safety of the witness or another person, or to prevent any serious damage to property, or to prevent real harm to the public interest—the court must take the witness's feelings into account on these matters;
- the order is necessary to help the defendant receive a fair trial; and
- the witness's testimony is important in the interests of justice (and without the order either the witness would not testify or the public interest would be harmed if the witness were to testify without anonymity).

Some of the methods for maintaining witness anonymity in court are covered in 26.5.2.4. Investigation Anonymity Orders are covered in 24.7.

24.6.1.1 Offenders as witnesses for the prosecution

The Serious Organised Crime and Police Act 2005 (SOCPA) established a number of important new powers to help the police tackle serious organized crime. For example, agreements can be made with offenders who offer to assist with the investigation or prosecution of offences committed by others. The agreement must be in writing and could state (eg) that the person will not be prosecuted (an immunity notice under s 71), or that certain pieces of evidence will not be used (a 'restricted use undertaking' under s 72).

In order to benefit from the agreement the person must fully admit his/her own criminality, agree to cooperate in full, provide all the information he/she has regarding the matters under investigation, and give evidence in court if required.

24.6.2 Interviews with witnesses

The PEACE process applies to all interviews (see 24.3) but interviews with witnesses are not governed by the PACE Codes of Practice, which allows for greater flexibility. Different approaches and techniques for gathering witness testimony can be adopted (eg video- or audio-recording), depending on the category of the witness and the nature of the interview in prospect.

Ideally, interviewers should only know a little about the alleged offence(s) before the interview. This is because too much knowledge might result in the interviewer contaminating the interview by inadvertently introducing information not already mentioned by the witness. Another pitfall can be the interviewer failing to asking all the questions which would be needed to fill any 'gaps' in a witness's account. This can happen when the interviewer subconsciously supplements the account with his/her own knowledge of the offence.

24.6.2.1 Recording witness interviews

The account from a witness is usually written up on an MG 11 as a witness statement (see 10.11). Some categories of witnesses and victims (eg vulnerable or intimidated witnesses) are interviewed away from a police station at designated facilities with suitable recording facilities.

In a serious crime the interview with a significant witness is often video-recorded to capture his/her initial oral account of events. This has numerous advantages for the investigator; for example, it is less obtrusive and more fluent than the stop/start approach required for a written statement, so the witness may be more forthcoming. In addition, the witness's own words and intonation are recorded, thus reducing the risk of the statement-taker unintentionally influencing the content. A video-recording can also help assess the witness's ability to provide convincing oral evidence from the witness box ('come up to proof')—some witnesses may not be able to perform reliably in court due to nervousness, forgetfulness, or confusion. After the interview a ROVI (record of a video-interview) document may be prepared by the police to help inform decisions on criminal charges, or a full witness statement (MG 11) can be prepared. The existence of the video-recording must be revealed (see 26.4) to the CPS. The subsequent use in court of evidence derived from video-recordings is covered in 26.5.2.4.

24.7 Interviews and Criminal Intelligence

An often overlooked by-product of a formal police interview is the 'intelligence interview'. An intelligence interview is the process through which the police attempt to gather criminal intelligence on the activities and lifestyle of the interviewee and others. It is a separate process from an investigative interview, and must be undertaken by specialist intelligence officers. A trainee officer is unlikely to be involved in the detail of any of this, but it helps to know that it happens.

All police officers should be alert to the potential for an intelligence interview and carefully note those people (known as 'subjects' in this context) who would have access to information about targets whose criminality comes within the force's strategic intelligence requirement. The access which the subject has should be reported to the BCU Intelligence Unit, who will arrange for an interview. This is often carried out by a fully trained intelligence analyst or researcher who does not work 'in the field' (so that other criminals who may be in the vicinity will not recognize him/her). Any interview conducted whilst the subject is in custody (and this is often the only opportunity for a secure approach) must be recorded on the custody record, but there must be no specific reference to the interview's purpose. The record will simply show the transfer of custody from one police officer to another. In order to enhance confidentiality intelligence interviews should not be recorded on tape and no other people should be present. Any information obtained will be recorded on a 5 × 5 × 5 (see 22.5.1).

An Investigation Anonymity Order (IAO) can be used when a person (other than a witness) can assist the police with relevant information or intelligence, but he/she wants to remain anonymous. This is only possible in certain circumstances and for certain offences, as set out in the Coroners and Justice Act 2009. The legislation is primarily intended to tackle 'gang culture' crime, but may in time be extended to cover a wider range of criminal acts. An IAO prohibits the disclosure of information that identifies the person or might lead to his/her identification. The case must involve murder or manslaughter where the death was caused by a firearm or knife, and the suspect must be between 11 and 30 years of age and belong to a group of people of a similar age. This group ('gang') should also be identifiable by the types of criminal activity undertaken by its members, and also be likely to use intimidation against any member providing relevant information to the police regarding the offence in question.

24.8   **Answers to Tasks**

TASK 1 For interviews with cooperative witnesses the 'cognitive interview' (CI) technique could be used. This uses memory-enhancing techniques such as context reinstatement, which involves recreating the other events that were also encoded at the same time (or before or after) the event of interest. You are probably familiar already with this idea—for example, what techniques do you use to locate misplaced keys? If you want to know more about the cognitive interview and other interview techniques then *Investigative Interviewing—Psychology and Practice* by Rebecca Milne and Ray Bull is a good start (Milne and Bull, 1999). Although CI may be part of PEACE training, it is not often used by police officers investigating volume crimes.

TASK 2 A shortened version of the interview will be prepared as a transcript for the reviewing lawyer (a Short Descriptive Note (SDN)). It is not usual practice for a full transcript (Record of Taped Interview or ROTI) to be made, as this is very time-consuming and therefore costly.

TASK 3 Many police practitioners argue that the best place to use a special warning is after the suspect has had a full opportunity to account for what happened, but has not done so. This would probably be in the 'challenge' phase of the PEACE interview (see 24.3.3).

Forensic Investigation

25.1 Introduction

This chapter is concerned with the use of forensic investigation and the role it plays in policing. We will concentrate on the aspects of forensic investigation that are most relevant to initial training, exploring not only the subject of forensic investigation itself (and its relationship with forensic science) but also the role of police officers in assisting the CSI, such as 'bagging and tagging' evidence, and collecting evidence from suspects. An understanding of forensic investigation and how a police officer supports that process is vitally important in terms of both convicting the guilty and exonerating the innocent. This importance is reflected in the IPLDP: there are a large number of learning outcomes that relate to forensic investigation in the modules OP 3, LP 1, and LPG 2.

This chapter will help a police officer in training to develop the underpinning knowledge required for a number of Certificate in Knowledge of Policing and the Diploma in Policing assessed units, several of the PAC headings, and entries for the Learning Diary Phase 3 and SOLAP. It will also be of interest and value to students on pre-join programmes (see 7.2.1) at a university, college, or with a private training company leading to the Certificate in Knowledge of Policing (see 7.3): many such courses will include modules that cover basic forensic science and investigation.

The apparent obsession with detail in packaging and exhibiting can seem odd to the uninitiated but there are serious consequences in making errors or from failing to follow accepted procedure. As an example, this is an extract from the judgment in *R v Hoey*, by Weir J (2007):

> It is not my function to criticise the seemingly thoughtless and slapdash approach of police and SOCO officers to the collection, storage and transmission of what must obviously have been potential exhibits in a possible future criminal trial but it is difficult to avoid some expression of surprise that in an era in which the potential for fibre, if not DNA, contamination was well known to the police such items were so widely and routinely handled with cavalier disregard for their integrity.

(R v Hoey [2007] NICC 49 (20 December 2007))

25.2 Principles of Forensic Investigation

Some key principles underpin the application of forensic science to criminal investigation. For example that:

- all things are unique;
- when two objects come into contact they exchange material; and
- forensic science is context-sensitive, which means that forensic evidence is given meaning when its place or role within the investigation is understood.

Forensic investigation is a tripartite arrangement which involves forensic science, the investigator, and the CJS. It supports criminal (and civil) investigations.

25.2.1 Locard's Principle

We take a knife from a drawer and replace it. In so doing, material (eg sweaty deposits from our fingertips) is transferred from the hand to the knife and may remain there, for a little time at least. Material is also transferred from the knife to our hand—for example, particles of dust or even tiny fragments of the wooden handle. Edmond Locard (1877–1966) is credited with the development of this Principle of Exchange. His assertion was that material from the crime scene would be found on the suspect and vice versa and is commonly expressed as 'every contact leaves a trace'. As a simple example, an offender could leave fingerprints, blood, and shoe marks at the crime scene and might take away glass fragments on his/her clothing; the contacts have left a trace.

Locard's Principle has been a mainstay of forensic investigation, despite the fact that some contacts cannot actually be proven because the quantities of the physical material transferred are too small to be located by current technology. Where a transfer of physical material cannot be found the principle can be extended to include the impressions left at crime scenes by tools, weapons, and other materials. The principle is really inductive reasoning by another name and hence cannot be considered a scientific law in the usual sense, but until relatively recently this did not much concern the courts. (Inductive reasoning involves generalizing from a number of previous examples to establish a rule or theory. The fingerprint, for example, is still assumed to be unique and this is based on the assertion by fingerprint experts that no two fingerprints have yet been found to be the same. Perhaps the most famous example of inductive reasoning is that 'all swans are white', which is based upon repeated observations of white swans. It would be entirely natural, therefore, to have every confidence in the statement until the day that a black swan is observed.) In practice, Locard's Principle manifests itself in reverse in forensic investigation—evidence of transfer is used as a demonstration of contact.

Trust in the principle requires a leap of faith but, even after assuming we can find the transferred material or impressions, we then need to show that it came from the particular source in question. This brings us to the concept of individualization or uniqueness.

25.2.2 Individualization

No two things can actually be identical, apart from at an atomic or molecular level. Thus, everything we are concerned with in forensic investigation should be considered as unique, or a one-off. This represents another leap of faith on the part of the investigator and forensic scientist because, again, this concept is not strictly a scientific law. (It cannot be considered to be a scientific law because there is no way it could ever be falsified.) However, as with Locard's Principle, the criminal justice system does not consider this a particular problem and it is doubtful whether it has ever featured in deliberations in the courts.

Many objects which appear to be identical are markedly different, and those that are very similar (perhaps too similar to measure any differences) become visibly or measurably unique during use. This unique quality is brought about by the development of individual characteristics. The majority of industrial processes impart very similar characteristics to the same products, so they appear identical to the naked eye. Consider a standard 'slot' screwdriver:

- the shaft is typically cylindrical and appears identical in each screwdriver made on the production line; and
- the tip is hammered flat and a subsequent sharpening process grinds the blade tip to pre-set dimensions, creating an edge which is generally very similar in every screwdriver of that type.

The end-products of the manufacturing process are thousands of screwdrivers which—to unaided eyes—are identical in every way. During subsequent use (and misuse) each screwdriver develops measurable unique characteristics, which provide the means for the forensic scientist to tell them apart, or individualize them.

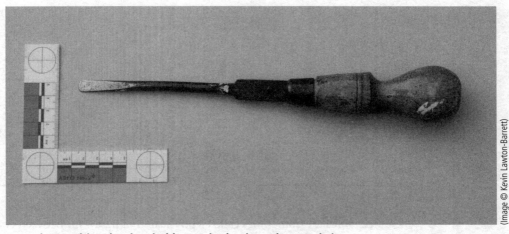

(Image © Kevin Lawton-Barrett)

A used screwdriver has inevitably acquired unique characteristics

Anything which can be associated with its source is said to have individual characteristics: for instance, a fingerprint to a finger, a tool-mark to a tool, and so on. There are different types of characteristic. Consider, for example, a number of unused, apparently identical screwdrivers of the same brand. These will have:

- class characteristics which are qualities produced by a controlled process, typically a manufacturing process: for instance, the manufacture of the screwdrivers, where each one is similar to the naked eye;
- sub-class characteristics which are the features on a batch of screwdrivers, particularly those which distinguish them from other batches—these features may be imparted by poor quality control or minute changes in settings, grinders, and so on.

Individualization follows from the premise that two items are derived from a common source, but that each will be modified during use and this individualizes them: any marks a screwdriver makes can potentially be matched with the screwdriver in question. This process is easier if the screwdriver has been damaged or modified by use.

25.2.3 Applications to criminal investigation

An investigator will use evidence of transfer in an attempt to prove that contact has occurred. Transfer can be demonstrated by the so-called traces that comprise debris (eg glass, paint flakes, hairs, and fibres). Traces can also include saliva, blood, and other DNA-rich material which is often classified separately as biological or DNA evidence. Trace evidence is covered in more detail in 25.5.1. Second, there are 'impressions' (see 25.5.2) which include 'prints' made by fingers, shoes, tools, typewriters, and printers. Note also that Locard's Principle is not restricted to these traditional and tangible examples: it can also be extended to intangible digital data held by electronic media, such as computers, discs, and mobile phones.

Locard's Principle is primarily used to create physical links between the differing parts of an investigation. This is set out in its simplest form in the following diagram.

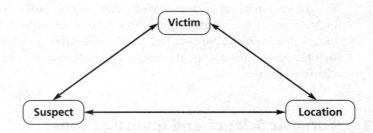

The links are normally created by forensic scientists comparing a 'questioned sample' with a 'control'. It is the examination of articles for individualizing features and subsequent comparison to another object which creates evidence that can be used by the CJS.

Clearly, the link may be between two or more people, a suspect and the scene only, or any permutation of these. A chief aim of forensic investigation is to locate and recover the physical material which will allow the links to be made. Although any police officer may be involved in searching a crime scene—whether a place, person, or thing—the majority of scenes are examined by specially trained CSIs. The best links are two-way, and are sometimes referred to as 'best evidence'.

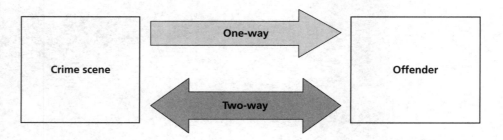

A mechanical fit (sometimes called a physical fit or jigsaw fit) between two or more fragments is an extended application of the theory that all things are unique and can be individualized. In its simplest form, imagine that an object breaks into several parts, and that those parts are later found separately. If the parts can be reconstructed as 'a fit', then they must all originate from the same source. This would provide exceptionally powerful evidence in a police investigation. For example, small fragments of a blade were found in the chin of a deceased male and a suspect was found in possession of a damaged craft knife. The blade of the craft knife and the metal fragments were reconstructed successfully to rebuild the blade in its original form. (However, whilst this is acceptable to the court as proof of the craft knife's involvement in the murder, it does not prove who committed the offence.)

In a more common scenario, imagine that a window has been forced using a screwdriver. The CSI will recover control samples from the crime scene (see 25.6.2.1), perhaps a sample of paint and a cast of a tool-mark, and will aim to have these compared with the 'questioned samples'—a screwdriver and a sweater taken from a suspect. This may provide evidence of association. However, if a corner of the screwdriver blade had broken off and become lodged in the window frame it would fit almost exactly with the damaged screwdriver blade, and this would provide stronger evidence of association. (The 'exactness' of fit would depend on a number of factors, including whether the screwdriver had been used after the break occurred.) However, there are further issues to be investigated before Locard's Principle can be properly employed in the investigative context: Who was holding the screwdriver when it forced the window? The investigator needs to be able to 'put the suspect at the scene', so evidence of transfer between the suspect and the window (or other parts of the crime scene) would be important here. Any paint flakes on the suspect's clothing could be compared to the control of paint removed from the crime scene. Thus: two forms of evidence would have been employed—the mechanical fit *proves* the involvement of the screwdriver and the paint flakes are *strongly supportive* of the notion that the suspect was present during the commission of the offence. One role of the CSI is to provide a variety of types of physical evidence for analysis by experts in order to support the contention that the suspect committed the offence in question.

Locard's Principle does not cease to apply after the commission of the offence, because each subsequent contact will leave a trace which can mask (or partly mask) previous traces. In this way all trace material or articles which leave an impression continue to change: fibres on the guilty party are lost, shoes continue to wear out, screwdrivers become blunter and their individual characteristics are modified, and DNA decays. The objective of the police is, therefore, to intervene as quickly after the crime as possible to recover the potential evidence and stop it changing further.

25.3 Forensic Science and Investigations

Forensic science is commonly described as the application of scientific disciplines to the legal system. The fields of science so employed are many and varied: from archaeology through every conceivable speciality to zoology, and any of these may have a role in the investigation of an offence. Experts in these fields produce evidence for the investigator by interpreting the material provided. It is the responsibility of the forensic scientist to analyse and test materials supplied from an investigation in order to determine facts about the case. The scientist can later make statements of fact (what he did during the examination) and opinion (what he believes his analysis means).

The evidence may point to the guilt or innocence of a suspect, neither of which should be a consideration for the scientist. There are a number of important principles which the scientist is bound by, and chief amongst these is to discover the truth and to be unbiased. This is also the essence of a police investigation and the primary focus of the criminal court.

Forensic investigation is often concerned with two main forms of (largely physical) evidence:

1. Corroborative evidence: material that will confirm or refute a hypothesis about the crime, for instance that a powder is, or is not, heroin.
2. Inceptive evidence, which identifies an unknown, for example a person.

The investigator may employ forensic investigation and forensic science in a variety of ways when considering these two main forms of evidence. These include:

- Describing the *modus operandi* (MO): the attending CSI or scientist can help form a hypothesis about the method used by the offender to commit the crime. This would be at an early stage in a forensic investigation. The data can be analysed for patterns to link offences. For example, scientists may analyse a fire scene to establish the MO for a series of arson attacks, or a CSI may link a number of burglaries based upon MO.
- Answering investigative questions in order to progress an enquiry: for instance, whose DNA is on this knife? Is there a connection between the weapon used in this crime and this suspect?
- Establishing that an offence has occurred: by examining exhibits it may be shown that an offence has been committed, for instance: following the analysis of a white powder; the classification of a firearm; the calculation of alcohol in urine or blood.
- To corroborate or refute witness statements: this is particularly useful when applied to very specific issues raised during interview.
- To establish physical links in two ways, by demonstrating that the same tool was used in a series of burglaries, and second that there are links between the suspect, crime scene, and victim (although the route for this may be circuitous, for instance by linking the suspect to a weapon and the weapon to the incident).
- To identify an individual: fingerprints and DNA (and some other techniques) can be employed to identify people, including suspects, arrested persons, or the body of a deceased person.
- To further inform an enquiry: often by clarifying issues or providing some form of descriptive information or intelligence. An example would be a specialist helping to identify the make and model of a vehicle involved in a hit-and-run RTC.

25.3.1 Working with forensic scientists

Efficient communication with forensic scientists is vital to the investigative process. In volume crime this is normally carried out by the CSI, but in major crime it will be a senior CSI, and sometimes one or more investigators assist at a case conference held by a Forensic Management Team (FMT). In order to provide an efficient and effective service to the police, the forensic scientist expects:

- unbroken continuity (or 'chain of custody') of evidence (see 11.2.6);
- correct packaging with intact integrity seals;
- utmost care in preventing contamination (see 11.2.6.3);
- a clear communication which explains the investigative need and describes the perceived relevance and place of the evidence (context);
- guidance regarding 'points to prove';
- up-to-date information whenever the investigation changes tack; and
- clear guidance on any deadlines, such as bail dates or court appearances.

It should also be remembered that forensic evidence is context-sensitive. Issues of context can be difficult to understand, which is often based upon the notion that a particular type of evidence is 'good' or 'poor'. Ask any forensic science student or trainee police officer whether fingerprints are 'good' or 'poor' evidence and they will almost certainly say that they are good. This is because fingerprints can be differentiated by using the individual characteristics of the marks that fingers make on surfaces. This happens all the time during innocent activities as well as during the commission of crimes so, when context is added, these commonplace fingerprint patterns and DNA are elevated from the mundane to become evidence:

- A fingerprint found near the point of entry in the female toilets of a burgled pub was found to belong to the barman. The context of this apparently innocent mark changed when, during interview, he categorically denied ever having been in the toilet.
- Blood on a suspect's clothing was explicable because he had provided First Aid to a victim when flagged down in his car, but the person who stopped him for assistance had disappeared. Upon closer analysis it was apparent that the blood must have spattered onto his clothing during the commission of the offence, which indicated his involvement.

In order to provide the correct information and to explain its importance to the case, a form is used to guide the investigator through the submissions process. The Forensic Science Service provided a form called the MG FSP, and something similar will almost certainly continue to be used now that the FSS has closed. Different police forces have different systems and policies regarding the submission of exhibits to laboratories. Police officers must follow their own force procedures to avoid problems in any subsequent prosecution.

25.3.2   The role of the Crime Scene Investigator

The CSI is typically the first port of call for all enquiries regarding forensic science, such as taking samples from suspects and victims and the examination of crime scenes. (Some forces use the term Scenes of Crime Officer (SOCO), or Crime-Scene Examiner (CSE).)

Chief amongst the CSI's crime-based activities are:

- the photography of crime scenes, articles, or people associated with crime, such as weapons, injuries, victims, and suspects (but not photographs taken for storage in data systems, so-called 'mug shots');
- the location, assessment, and recovery of physical or biological evidence (including fingerprints) from crime scenes such as burglary, murder, arson, and theft;
- the packaging, storage, and documentation of recovered material;
- attending post-mortem examinations for sudden and suspicious deaths;
- providing advice to police officers and investigators on matters related to physical evidence, photography, and laboratory submissions; and
- gathering intelligence in support of the NIM, whether the spoken word, personal observations, or physical material for use in databases (see 22.6).

CSIs are also involved at non-crime-related events such as the investigation, photography, and scene analysis of some sudden deaths, most suicides, and fatal industrial accidents (on behalf of HM Coroners and in support of Health and Safety Executive investigations). CSIs are likely to become even more involved in 'accidents' and work-related deaths following the Corporate Manslaughter and Corporate Homicide Act 2007. CSIs may also be involved in the recording of loss through fire (especially at high-value scenes, prior to arson being ruled out).

The majority of CSIs in the UK police are police support staff attached to a force's Scientific Support Department (sometimes shared with the facilities in another county). This includes other complementary services such as a photography unit, a fingerprint bureau, and a laboratory for the enhancement of fingerprint evidence. There may also be Computer Forensic Investigators and Technical Services (responsible for covert intelligence and evidence-gathering technology) within the same department.

25.4   Establishing the Time and Date of an Event

This is about establishing the precise time that an event occurred (eg an image on a computer hard drive was accessed) and is sometimes known as 'time-and-date-stamping'. Some evidence may occur in a form which shows it was created during the commission of the offence, and this is potentially of great value. For example:

- in the investigation of an assault, the distribution of blood on the suspect could indicate that she had been present during an assault, and even establish her distance and position in relation to the victim. DNA analysis of the blood on the suspect's clothing could establish it was from the victim, so proving the suspect's clothing (and probably the suspect) was present when *the* offence was committed;

- when investigating a case of criminal damage to a church window the presence of unusual stained glass from the window on the suspect's upper clothing may indicate that he was present when *the* window was smashed;
- for an offence where a firearm was used, finding firearm discharge residue (FDR) on a suspect may show that he was present when *a* firearm was discharged. However, it does not prove that he fired *the* gun in question during the offence.

Note the stress placed on the words 'the' and 'a'.

Challenging suspects in interviews, however, can be used to reinforce many forms of evidence. CSIs and forensic managers prefer absolute statements from suspects because this can make the context of the evidence stronger. There are two important points here:

1. When a laboratory result is received (either in statement form or by other means) officers must consider their interview strategy; that is, how best to employ the information received. This is an example of forensic science driving the investigation forward.
2. If a suspect or other person makes an early statement, this information should be carefully considered: it may be of value to the scientist and must, at least, describe any admissions made by the suspect.

For example where a man is suspected of a shooting, the forensic manager and scientist will consider the value of any potential FDR evidence after interview thus:

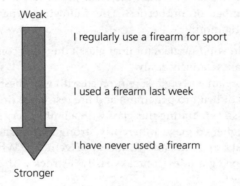

Clearly, if the man denies the use of firearms on any occasion then any FDR located on his body or his clothes would provide the basis for challenging the veracity of any statement he makes in his defence. If this were the case, consideration must be given to his activity in recent days:

- Has he been in the vicinity of a firearm which has been used?
- Was he arrested by an officer who recently used a firearm, say, for sport?
- Was he conveyed in a vehicle which had contained people who were contaminated with firearms residues?
- Was he arrested by an officer who was environmentally contaminated through using firearms at work?

The forensic scientist would need to know this sort of information so that an informed assessment of contamination can be made. This in turn may impact on the guilt or innocence of a suspect.

TASK 1

1. What does FSS stand for?
2. Who is credited with the development of the Principle of Exchange?
3. List three things for which an investigator might employ forensic science.

25.5   Types of Forensic Evidence

Forensic evidence can be classified in a number of different ways, but in this section we have chosen a relatively simple method:

- trace evidence; very small quantities of material (DNA is considered separately);
- impressions or marks (fingerprints are considered separately);

- DNA evidence (a type of trace evidence, but with special features);
- fingerprints (impressions, which also leave a trace of sweat, and can be printed in blood or other materials); and
- documents, firearms, digital evidence, and CCTV.

25.5.1 Trace materials as forensic evidence

Trace material can be any material transferred from the suspect to the crime scene (or a victim) and vice versa. It ranges from common materials such as glass fragments and paint flakes transferred during property crimes to the more exotic, such as pollens, soils, and even insects or their fragments. Imagination is important here and consideration should not be limited to any specific groups: creativity is a vital element in forensic investigation. DNA evidence is covered separately in 25.5.3.

25.5.1.1 Glass

The manufacturing processes vary depending on the type of glass required and this provides varying degrees of discriminatory power (ie the ability to distinguish one object made of glass from another). The addition of colourants and physical processes can make this outwardly common material very useful in the right criminal circumstances. Glass is a mix of silica, sodium carbonate, and calcium compounds which are smelted to form the base material to which physical processes or chemical additives are applied, imparting a number of properties. The following types of glass are often encountered in an investigation:

- Plain window glass (or float glass): the most common window glass manufactured today. It breaks relatively easily.
- Georgian wired glass: reinforced with wire mesh of varying sizes, used for security (because it is difficult to penetrate) and fire resistance (it remains in situ in fires for longer than float glass). Penetrating this glass with a limb is very serious, since escape is difficult.
- Toughened glass: inherently strong and normally difficult to break—used in telephone kiosks and the side windows of vehicles. When it breaks it forms thousands of cube-shaped granules. It breaks easily if struck with force near the edge, particularly by a sharp object.
- Laminated glass: two sheets of glass which sandwich a plastic filling which prevents the pane shattering and it retains its position in the frame. Windscreens and many low-level windows are constructed in this way.
- Container glass: eg bottles, drinking vessels, older TV and computer screens.
- Optical glass: found in lenses.
- Mirrors.

Health and Safety considerations apply for glass. Shards may be exceptionally sharp and small, and can be very dangerous. Always wear goggles and gloves when dealing with broken glass. Large, unsupported broken windows are a particular hazard if they are not laminated, as they can collapse without warning. Fortunately there are very few non-laminated large panes still in existence because of their inherent dangers and subsequent legislation governing glazing practices.

Glass found on the suspect or other articles can be compared to samples recovered from the broken window frame by a variety of chemical and physical techniques. Where the glass is unusual (perhaps very old or specially coloured) the scientist may provide a forensically important statement. Glass can be broken in a variety of ways and different authors have different views on classification. In a criminal context, glass is typically broken by moving objects (varying speeds), by some form of stress, by heat, or by an explosion. Frequently, the cause is deduced at the scene, but windows and glass objects can be reconstructed in order to demonstrate the cause, point, and direction of the breakage. One of the most valuable attributes of breaking glass is a process called backward fragmentation, where a breaking window throws out fine particles of glass. These may land on the offender in a characteristic way, which can demonstrate that he/she was in the vicinity of the window when it broke. In addition, fractures develop through glass when it breaks, either radiating from or running concentrically around the point of impact. The edges of some of these fractures (viewed 'end on') can assist in determining from which side a window was broken.

25.5.1.2 Fibres and paint

Fibres can be natural, man-made, or mixed. They are frequently transferred from clothing, seats, and carpets on to receptive surfaces, especially when the contact has been violent or has occurred over a long period. There is some police reluctance about using fibres as a form of evidence because they are (wrongly) thought by many to be very similar and common. However, manufacturers use different fibre mixes and dyes and so a garment or other fabric may have an unusual or characteristic mix. Man-made fibres, in particular, can survive conditions which cause decay in natural materials such as wool or cotton. A process called fibre mapping can be carried out in significant crime scenes, where every fibre is lifted onto hundreds of adhesive tapes. This can demonstrate the position of, for instance, the suspect at a crime scene. Note, however, that the success of such procedures is exceptionally vulnerable to poor crime scene management.

Paint is applied to window and door frames, manufactured objects, and cars as a protective or cosmetic coating. Its chemical components are designed to give the paint specific properties, such as rust-proofing, weather-proofing, fungal resistance, and even as an identification measure. These elements and the enormous variety of colour and finish types ensure that any surface which has been chipped or scraped may be usefully examined and compared with paint fragments found on a suspect's clothing, tools, or other objects in his/her possession.

Since the paint on houses is applied a number of times over the years according to individual tastes and changing fashions, the profile of the layers of coatings on, say, a forced window frame, can be unique. The more layers of paint, the more likely the profile will be unique. Unusual colourings or paint types can also be very useful. They include military (infrared absorbing) coatings, colour-coded scaffold poles and Indsol Tracer (manufactured by Smart-Water Technology Ltd), a polymer emulsion paint which is visible under ultraviolet light. The chemical contains unique identifiers so that the owner of stolen property can be identified. Other dye and marker traps are normally categorized separately to paints.

25.5.1.3 Soil, plants, and insects

Soils are found nearly everywhere, but they can vary significantly over short distances because of a number of important geological and geomorphological ('rock shape') factors, such as the source rock contributing to the soil. In a simplified description, the scientist examines the source minerals, amounts of organic material, and grain size of the sample. Of particular note are areas where the soil has been modified by the inclusion of chemicals and waste material from industrial and other processes. Soil is almost always sampled during exhumations to demonstrate that any toxins found in the body of the deceased have not leached in from the surrounding soil. The main general limitation for soil evidence is demonstrating that it came from a very specific location related to the offence (perhaps a few square metres of a field) but it should be noted that—while difficult—it is not necessarily impossible.

Vegetative material can often be used by *forensic botanists* to identify the species of a plant from small fragments of leaf, stem, seed, flower, or wood. *Palynologists* can identify the species of plant from the pollen transferred onto clothing, vehicles, and illegal substances such as cannabis resin. If the knowledge of both scientific specialists is pooled or synthesized, the source species of vegetable material is likely to be accurately identified. In many circumstances, an association between scene and suspect can be made by the mix of botanical debris, and if this is linked with other forms of evidence such as paint, the results can be powerful. Many plants occur naturally in specific locations owing to climate, soil type, and plants' relationships with animal and insect species, so plant material can also identify a broad location, such as heathland, deciduous forest, proximity to the sea, and so on. Of further note is the fact that plant material, especially wood, is used in thousands of domestic and industrial applications, and some of these require unusual imported species. The treatments carried out on woods for cosmetic or protective purposes may also be valuable to the investigator.

Insects are generally sensitive to their food source and climate (apart from the common pest species). As a result, many species are found in limited ranges and, when insects are identified during forensic investigation, they may be helpful in determining the geographic origin of materials such as cannabis resin, or the previous locations of vehicles and people. Forensic entomologists can also use known data on insect life cycles—especially that of blowflies—to identify when a body became available for them to feed upon. It is possible that this information may be of value when attempting to determine the time of death.

25.5.1.4 Toxicology

This is a specialist field engaged in the analysis of poisons and drugs and may be crucial to an investigation, for example:

- to calculate whether a person is over the drink-drive limit;
- to establish that alcohol or drugs may explain behaviour such as violence or drowsiness (particularly relevant to 'date-rape' offences); or
- to establish cause of illness and death.

Roadside breath tests are the most common forms of toxicological measurement carried out by the police, but these are normally used as screening tests (see 19.9.4) prior to more stringent evidential tests (see 19.9.5). A variety of field-test kits and covert-sampling devices can be employed to screen for drugs, but the opinion of an expert toxicologist should be sought to provide evidence suitable for a prosecution unless force policy allows the suspect to make a guilty plea prior to caution or if there is an intervention model in place at the time (see 12.5.5). Elaborate analysis would therefore not normally be required (or at best, not even embarked upon), since the case will not go to court.

In driving cases, laboratory submission forms MG/DD A to E should be used in cases where a back calculation is required (to establish a previous level of alcohol in a suspect: see 19.9.5.3). Police officers should always seek the advice of a CSI based at the BCU (or a Scientific Support Unit adviser), since the forms required for such a calculation can be quite complex. Regardless of this, original bottles and glasses should be seized where possible, and marked up to show what the suspect claims to have drunk—remembering that a 'gulp' or 'swig' is not a scientifically accepted measurement of alcohol consumption!

Commonly, blood or urine is sent for analysis for toxins, but other samples from the body tissue of deceased victims (including the eyes) may also be used, depending upon the circumstances. Toxicology samples must always be treated as a potential health hazard.

25.5.2 Impressions as forensic evidence

These are the marks left by fingers, shoes, tools, tyres, stamping machines, printers, and typewriters, etc. Whilst these can be a direct 'stamped' effect, many are made up of irregular scrapes and smudges and even cutting or drilling marks. Fingerprints are covered separately in 25.5.4.

25.5.2.1 Footwear marks

Shoe or other footwear marks are a useful but potentially short-lived form of evidence. Footwear is readily modified by use when people walk over surfaces which scratch and tear the soles or add particles such as glass and stones. The resultant damage occurs at random and is therefore unique to every sole. When a shoe leaves an impression at a crime scene the mark can easily be compared with the shoe in question. However, the shoe must be located and recovered before the relevant damage to the sole is further eroded, as this would reduce the value of making a comparison.

The marks can be on a flat, apparently two-dimensional surface, or they can be impressed into a soft substrate to form a three-dimensional pattern. Importantly, the surface must be fine enough to receive the mark: soft clay is clearly better than coarse sand.

Trainers in particular are readily identifiable (either from databases or by an expert in the field) and this data can be used for intelligence purposes in order tentatively to link crime scenes.

In theory, marks should be present at almost every crime scene, since almost all offenders will walk within the venue. All personnel in attendance should be aware of this and take care to use the Common Approach Path (CAP) to a crime scene (see 11.2.2). A variety of techniques can be used to recover the marks: photography, casting, lifting, or removal of the surface upon which the mark rests.

The National Footwear Reference Collection provides a valuable intelligence tool (see also 25.6.1.5). The addition of MO, times of offence, and target properties can make such databases invaluable. Under the PACE Act, 1984, (as amended) police forces can make good use of shoe marks and their intelligence databases by taking shoes from prisoners in custody and scanning the sole patterns for future use (see 25.6.1). It should be noted that this would of course only provide intelligence data on the shoes worn at the time of arrest. The database can also provide information on offences where a *similar* sole pattern has occurred.

25.5.2.2   Tyre marks

Vehicle tyres leave impressions which are commonly found in soft soils, on roads, smooth concrete floors, glass, and paper—particularly at 'ram raids'. As for footwear, tyres are modified during use by the surfaces over which they pass, and may pick up 'inclusions' such as glass and gravel. On a suitable surface these individual details will be impressed as a two or three-dimensional pattern. The impression may be of a rotating tyre or a skidding tyre. The full circumference of a car tyre is approximately 3.14 times the diameter, so a car tyre that is 50 cm in diameter needs over 150 cm to leave a print of one full rotation. (Finally, that school geometry has proved useful!) Never assume that only part of a print needs to be preserved: as much as possible should be retained for the CSI. The laboratory can assist in identifying the make of tyre from a recovered print, which may include or exclude vehicles from the enquiry.

25.5.2.3   Other types of marks

Tool or instrument marks are marks imparted to receptive surfaces by the application of force, normally by some form of tool. These marks can also be left by objects such as rocks, baseball bats, and any suitably hard object which meets a receptive surface, but typical examples are those made by forcing a window or cashbox. The marks can be made by:

- levering, to force open a window, door, or cashbox—one edge of the target surface acts as a fulcrum or pivot and both this and the opening part will be marked;
- striking an object, or person, with a weapon or similar;
- cutting—the action caused by scissors, wire cutters, and bolt croppers; and
- drilling—the waste material and hole from drilling can bear the impression of the cutting edge of the drill bit.

The actions used will cut into or impress into the surface with the shape of the tip or edge of the device. This will have been individualized through its previous use, as can be clearly seen on the milled edges of scissors and pliers for example.

Stamps, dyes, and manufacturing marks are impressions into a surface, similar to tool or instrument marks, and can be made by any item. This includes plastic-label printers, metal-numbering dyes, franking machines, rubber stamps, and other such devices. All are modified by accidental damage and ageing. Any material which is set in a mould or extruded also takes on an impression of the mould or extrusion head, particularly where debris has built up. Examples include copper pipes, plastic bags, and plastic components. Many of these latter marks are visible as lines and dimples, and may need to be viewed using microscopy or polarized light. The sequence of manufacture of rolls of bags, in particular, can be demonstrated by the scientist and may help to show that an offender used a bin bag from a particular place, for instance to carry away goods from a burglary.

Printers, copiers, and typewriters can also provide useful evidence. Modern copiers (and all printers) are digital, which means that the pages which have been printed are digitally stored within the device's limited memory for some time after printing. Paper feeders and rollers may also impart marks. When the metal letters, golf ball, or daisy wheel are damaged or aged they take on individual characteristics which are easily compared with characters contained in seized documents. Photocopiers superimpose an image of the glass screen (the platen) on the copies they produce. The more damage (or dried correction fluid) on the platen, the better the scientist's chances of demonstrating an association between a particular copier and paper evidence. Most colour printers are also capable of 'printer steganography' where the serial number of the machine and date are printed onto the document; this can be used for tracking forged documents and money.

The fonts chosen by typewriter manufacturers can be identified when found on letters or other material, even with the demise of traditional typewriters in favour of computers. In electric typewriters the text is impressed from an ink-coated ribbon, and mistakes are lifted from the page by an adhesive tape on a similar spool—both of these can be used to transcribe what has previously been written. Following advice from a scientist a targeted search of premises can be made to locate a particular design of typewriter.

Bite marks are valuable sources of evidence. The position, number, layout, orientation, and cutting surfaces of teeth make our dentition highly individual. It is the role of the *forensic odontologist* to compare marks found on victims and in foodstuffs with the teeth of the suspect. This is carried out by taking a three-dimensional dental impression of the suspect's teeth and comparing it with photographs or with impressions of the injury or damage. Older bite marks on skin may be visible under ultraviolet (UV) lighting and can be photographed some time after the incident. The apparent lack of a bite mark is not, therefore, a 'lost cause'. (Whenever bite marks are found, then DNA may be present and consideration must be given to preserving this evidence.)

25.5.3 DNA evidence

Every cell in the human body—with a few exceptions—contains a nucleus with chromosomes. Chromosomes are made up of genes which instruct the body to manufacture proteins and therefore govern the biological and physical processes within the cell and, consequently, the body. The genes are made of DNA and every nucleus contains a copy of the DNA for the entire organism, so a cell from a person's cheek contains exactly the same material as a white cell from his/her blood. A large proportion of DNA is the same for all humans, but small differences occur between individuals and these account for variations such as hair and eye colour, other physical characteristics, and genetically related illness. However, the chromosomes also contain sections of DNA which have no apparent function ('junk DNA'). The coding in junk DNA varies significantly between individuals so it is therefore very useful for forensic analysis. Many texts refer to DNA as the 'blueprint' for humans and other living things, but the term 'DNA fingerprinting' is not to be taken literally—fingerprint patterns cannot be established through DNA analysis.

DNA is typically found on articles or at scenes yielding blood, semen, saliva, hair with roots, some bodily secretions, and pieces of body tissue. (It is important to treat all body fluids as potential health hazards as they might contain pathogens or disease-carrying bacteria.) However, this biological material also needs protecting from us if it is to be used as evidence because our own DNA can easily contaminate it.

At the laboratory the DNA is removed from the swab or material upon which it is found, then copied many times using a process called Polymerase Chain Reaction (PCR) to ensure enough is available for analysis. The term DNA LCN means that only a very small amount of DNA is available ('low copy number'). In such circumstances extra cycles of the PCR copying process are carried out to ensure enough is present for subsequent analysis. This has yielded sufficient DNA for analysis from a number of unexpected sources such as tools, clothing grabbed by the suspect, and weapons.

25.5.3.1 DNA variability and forensics

Clearly, there would be no mileage in employing common genetic material in order to identify suspects. The analysis of DNA samples must highlight the differences between the DNA of different individuals. One serious problem with DNA is that, because it is inherited from both parents, identical twins and identical triplets are almost certain to share the same DNA profiles. This is because the twins (or triplets) came from the same fertilized egg which later split into individual foetuses. (There is a very small possibility that their DNA has mutated, but this is not likely to be discovered in routine forensic tests.) Twins or triplets from different eggs are called fraternal (or non-identical) twins or triplets and their DNA differs considerably.

Short Tandem Repeats (STRs) are short sections of DNA that are different in different people and are not part of the genes that code for a person's characteristics. These STRs ('junk DNA') are highly variable between individuals and, as a result, can be used to distinguish between people. A DNA 'hit' is a calculation concerning a selection of a person's STRs and is supplied by the scientist as a 'match probability'. If the match probability is one in a billion, it means that there is one chance in a billion that another person selected at random has the same profile. It does not mean that there is a one in a billion chance that the suspect is innocent, nor does it mean that one in every billion people shares the same profile. If the DNA recovered for analysis is degraded through age or lack of proper handling, the match probability applied to the comparison may be reduced, which can cause some concern, but remember that other evidence should be used to support the prosecution case.

Mitochondrial DNA (Mt DNA) is a different form of DNA which can be extracted from bone, hair, faeces, and teeth. Mt DNA is doughnut-shaped and is found within all cells inside tiny structures called 'mitochondria', rather than in the nucleus of the cell. The doughnut shape makes the DNA more resilient to external influences so it may last for many years. It does, however, have limitations in that it cannot uniquely identify a person: it can only identify the maternal line. This means, for example, that a person shares his/her Mt DNA with:

- his/her brothers and sisters (because they had the same mother);
- his/her mother and her siblings (his/her mother and her siblings had the same mother); and
- his/her grandmother and her siblings (his/her grandmother and her siblings had the same mother).

So mothers share their Mt DNA with their children, but fathers share none with their children.

Mt DNA can be beneficial when applied to the study of old and degraded samples where normal (nuclear) DNA is unavailable. It was famously used by the FSS to identify Tsar Nicholas II and Tsarina Alexandra, whose bodies (along with those of three children) were found near Yekaterinburg in Russia, in 1991 (the royal family having been killed by the Bolsheviks in 1919).

Y STRs are a variable genetic feature found on the Y chromosome, so can only be used for the identification of men (as women do not have a Y chromosome). It can be used to determine paternal ancestry by studying a specific set of STRs. Since females have no Y chromosome to pass on to a son, Y chromosomes only pass from father to son. In Western culture (though not in Iceland, where surnames are constructed differently), this is traditionally paralleled by the transfer of the surname; hence Y chromosome analysis has gained commercial popularity as a genealogical tool and may assist in some investigations. The value of Y STRs is, of course, diminished in males whose paternity is not ascertained.

25.5.3.2 The National DNA Database

The National DNA Database (NDNAD) is a database containing records of the DNA of persons who are arrested, cautioned, convicted, and charged for recordable offences, and also some volunteers and vulnerable people. It is the property of the police and is managed by the Home Office. The database stores records on DNA recovered from crime scenes (where applicable) and from all people who have been sampled under legal and operational criteria. The Home Office reports that on 31 March 2013 the UK database held 6,737,973 samples from individuals (though some 11.6 per cent are duplicates) and 428,634 profiles from crime scenes. The samples from individuals include the DNA of 6,847 pairs of identical twins and ten sets from triplets (however: remember that their fingerprints are different). Some 161,766 crime samples (and their associated DNA profiles) are currently loaded and are available for matching with currently unknown offenders. In 2013 nearly 593,000 'innocent' profiles were deleted for a variety of reasons including DNA taken from volunteers ('innocent') samples (*ibid*), which significantly reduced the size of the database (Home Office, 2014). The NDNAD's true strength lies in making 'cold hits' which is when a sample from a crime scene or victim identifies a suspect. In many of these offences there was no other way that this might have occurred.

The elegance of the system is that although many offenders who commit minor crimes will move away from criminal activities, others will continue as volume-crime offenders or will step up their activity to more serious offences. Very few armed robbers, for example, do not already have a criminal record. By taking the DNA sample of new volume-crime offenders, the police effectively 'bank' this information for future investigations, as for fingerprints. There may also be a deterrent effect.

Each time a new crime-scene or suspect sample is received it is entered in the database and cross-checking occurs. The NDNAD can also identify links between crimes. This may not seem hugely significant, but consider the case of John Wood who sexually assaulted two young girls in 1988 in Canterbury in Kent, and was not apprehended at the time. Many years later in 2001 he was arrested in Derbyshire for shoplifting £10 worth of groceries, and the arresting PC took the suspect's sample in accordance with local instructions. The DNA in the sample was matched to DNA found at the crime scene in Canterbury. The officer was directly credited for Wood's arrest and for the detection of the Canterbury offences. Wood admitted the offences and was sentenced to 15 years in prison.

25.5.4 Fingerprints

About 5 per cent of the human body is covered in a horny layer of skin bearing ridge detail. This is found on the fingers, palms, soles, and toes. Every finger and toe pattern on every person is considered by the criminal justice system to be unique, including those of so-called identical siblings. The prints left by any part of the hand or foot are, therefore, capable of identifying an individual with certainty. The ridges form classifiable patterns on the horny layer which are clearly visible to the naked eye. Upon close examination it is apparent that the ridges are not uniform lines: they split (bifurcate), they start and stop, and the lines sometimes cross over. These features are normally referred to as '*minutiae*'. The ridges develop in the womb and remain identical (apart from size) until death—or well past death if the body is sufficiently preserved.

Fingerprints are marks or impressions which are left on a surface by sweat and contaminants and can potentially be found on all the finely textured surfaces we touch. There is analogy here with the pattern of a shoe impressed into soft clay compared to one impressed into shingle: the surface must be capable of receiving the mark. The easiest test to determine whether a non-porous surface might yield fingerprints or not is to scratch it gently with a fingernail: if the surface makes a noise (due to it being rough) then the surface might be unsuitable. A completely smooth surface will be virtually silent. (Clearly, this practice should be carried out with caution, and never at serious or major crime scenes.) This rule holds fast for most surfaces though, curiously, not normally melamine.

25.5.4.1 Locating fingerprints

Latent marks are present but invisible. They can be made visible by dusting with powders using a fine brush and searching with a torch. This is the most common procedure; the fabric of the building can be examined, and bulky items left in place, rather than being recovered as evidence. After 'visualizing' the mark, it should be photographed and, where appropriate, lifted with an adhesive material and placed onto an acetate sheet. **Positive** (or patent) marks are visible, often printed in dirt or blood, and can be photographed. Plastic marks are three-dimensional patterns impressed into putty, clay, or chocolate for example. They can also be photographed and even cast using a silica gel if the surface is firm enough.

On some items, such as paper, there may be no visible marks, but it is presumed that marks are very likely to be present. Such an item can be seized and packaged for later chemical or physical enhancement. Laboratory analysis normally involves using different wavelengths of light which cause the mark to fluoresce, or by the application of chemicals which react with the non-aqueous components of the print to produce colours. (Sweat is approximately 98.5 per cent water and the remainder is made up of other components such as salts, fats, and amino acids which readily respond to a number of chemical dyes.) Occasionally, laboratory services go out to complex scenes and search the fabric of the building using chemicals and light sources. Whilst CSIs routinely 'dust' smooth non-porous surfaces, it should be borne in mind that marks may be found on many other surfaces such as textured plastics, polythene bags, paper, smooth wood, and even wall coatings. The majority of marks at scenes or on exhibits are invisible, which means they are easily damaged by clumsy actions.

It should also be noted that as an initially nervous and sweaty-palmed offender moves through a building, the hands dry out sufficiently to leave marks of good quality further inside the scene. Because of this, it is always better to preserve a whole crime scene rather than just the point of entry.

25.5.4.2 IDENT1

The IDENT1 database contains the fingerprints (so-called 'tenprints') and palm prints of arrested persons, and crime-scene marks recovered by CSIs and other personnel. It is a truly national database which incorporates Scottish fingerprint and palm-print collections. The system covers England, Scotland, and Wales, and includes Home Office forces as well as British

Transport Police, MOD Police, and the National Crime Agency and other organizations absorbed by it. The database contains in excess of eight million sets of fingerprints and palm prints.

The basic functionality of IDENT1 is not especially new; it essentially compares:

- crime-scene marks to crime-scene marks to search for links between offences;
- tenprints and palm prints against crime-scene marks (and vice versa); and
- new tenprints to those already on file to confirm identity or to establish that an arrested person is using a pseudonym.

Once the system identifies a suspect print, a chain of at least three experts then verify the result before providing a statement of evidence.

A chief benefit is that IDENT1 is linked to 441 Livescan tenprint scanners (in police stations) which electronically capture suspects' fingerprints. The use of this digital technology means that the identity of a suspect can be verified in about ten minutes, a so-called Live Identification. Portable 'Lantern units' are also linked to the system for identifications while on patrol. People can be required to provide fingerprints when those taken previously have proved unsatisfactory for analytical purposes—this was a serious issue when tenprints were taken using ink and a copper plate. Tenprints taken by Livescan are unlikely to be of poor quality, but for the police this power is still is an important right that directly affects the performance of the IDENT1 database.

25.5.5 Evidence from documents, digital sources, and CCTV

Here we examine the evidence available from handwritten and printed documents, digital devices such as computers, and PDAs, and public safety or security CCTV systems.

25.5.5.1 Evidence from documents

Under the term 'documents', forensic investigators normally include all letters, paperwork, invoices, cheques, transfers, application forms, handwriting, and any other written material, whether handwritten or printed by typewriter, computer printer, photocopier, or other device.

The writing on a document (eg a hate-mail letter) can be analysed through a comparison of material obtained during the investigation with samples provided by a suspect. Handwriting samples are used most effectively when a variety of material is submitted for comparison. This can include:

- samples produced in front of a police officer;
- material sourced from the suspect's home address, work, or other places—such as diaries, letters, general paperwork—which is identifiably written by the suspect (this is referred to as 'course of business' handwriting). Some samples may be *known* to have definitely been written by the suspect, but for others this might not be certain.

A document can also be analysed for 'impressed' handwriting. Typically this is found when a pad of paper is used and an impression of writing on one page is transferred to the pages below. It is enhanced using Electrostatic Detection Apparatus (referred to as ESDA).

Printers and typewriters can also be analysed and compared with a specimen document. The presence of printer-head faults, 'banding', or damage to typefaces may be reproduced under laboratory conditions and compared with the suspect document (see also 25.5.2.3). Research is under way to link printers without apparent faults to specific pages of text.

The physical features of paper can also be compared, such as tear marks, staple holes, and altered text. Other document features such as watermarks, obliterations, paper type, security inks, concealed marks, and 'reactive fibres' can be analysed in a number of ways, for example by microscopy and by using a Video Spectral Comparator (VSC). A VSC uses different wavelengths of light and is particularly useful in identifying handwritten text added to cheques and payment forms, and for revealing obliterated text. When a suspect is identified, the investigator should also exploit any fingerprints on paper or probable DNA on envelope flaps and stamps.

25.5.5.2 Intelligence and evidence from digital sources

Digitally stored data is retrievable from USB pen drives, hard drives, discs, CDs, DVDs, mobile phones, smartphones, tablet computers (eg iPads), media players (eg iPods), satnavs, games consoles (eg Xbox 360, particularly the removable hard drive), telecoms equipment, credit cards and credit card reading devices, video systems, and any other electronic recording or processing device. It is also sometimes retrievable from 'volatile' data sources such as networks and Cloud storage facilities. Social networks, online forums, and websites are also potential sources of data. These data can provide evidence of the commission of a crime, and support investigations by producing evidence and intelligence. Special protocols exist for the seizure of digital evidence in every force in the UK. We provide an overview of the particular issues surrounding the seizure of electronic equipment in 25.7.3.

Analysis of networks, objects such as smartphones, computers, and associated storage media can provide evidence about:

- network communication;
- SMS text messages;
- emails;
- images and text, whether downloaded or created locally;
- address books and contact details;
- hidden files and data;
- times and dates of activity; and
- deleted files and images.

However, even reasonably unsophisticated criminals may have sufficient ability to booby-trap their computers so that the machines can execute certain procedures when interfered with—officers should be particularly aware of wireless networks. Whilst data can normally be recovered even after deletion (and often after erasure), any police action that causes deletion to happen is a form of contamination and must be avoided if at all possible.

The forensic techniques required from recovery to analysis of digitally based evidence (such as a deleted file recovered from a PC hard drive, or the address book from a mobile phone SIM card) are a specialist field within investigation. ACPO has published good practice guidelines for the handling of digital evidence and recommends that digital evidence strategies should form part of the wider investigative process (ACPO, 2012a). Typically, the responsibility for the recovery and the analysis of digitally based intelligence and evidence is undertaken by a specialist unit within a force, such as a Digital Forensics Unit. However, police forces may choose to 'outsource' some digital forensic analysis to non-police contractors, who are expected to meet the good practice guidelines.

25.5.5.3 CCTV footage

At some crime scenes, CCTV footage might provide vital information. Most CCTV cameras are automatic and many are actually unmonitored, with tapes being renewed on average about every seven days. Copies of CCTV recordings can be obtained with appropriate authorization so that a forensic analyst can enhance the images and conduct a more thorough analysis (see 23.3.1). CCTV footage should not be ignored or simply deleted if the activity which concerns the investigator is not seen on the tape or disc. Such actions may be challenged at appeal: in *R (Ebrahim) v Feltham Magistrates Court* (2001) the investigating officer did not seize a CCTV tape because he saw nothing of significance on it, but this was challenged on the ground that a fair trial would not be received as a result. CCTV tapes and discs are disclosable material under the CPIA (see 26.2).

25.5.6 Firearms and forensics

Firearms such as rifles and revolvers have bulleted cartridges and the CSI and scientists can use these to provide evidence. Cartridge and bullet design varies depending on the manufacturer, the type of weapon, the loading system, and the firing mechanism. The intended function of the bullet (anti-personnel, tracer, armour-piercing) will also affect the design. The categories of firearms and the associated legislation are covered more fully in Chapter 18.

Bulleted cartridge component	Available evidence
Cartridge case	The actions of loading, firing, and ejecting the cartridge will scratch the polished brass casing and leave comparable marks upon it. These marks are caused by the magazine (if used), the ejector, extractor, breech face, and firing pin. Since bullets, cartridge design, and extractors vary, it may be possible to identify the type of weapon from which the cartridge was ejected. Manufacturer's details, calibre, and type of round are normally engraved on the head stamp (the base) of cartridges. Despite the high temperature generated during firing fingerprints can potentially be recovered from the case
Bullet	This will normally identify the calibre of the weapon used, and since there is huge variation in bullet design, specialist rounds and sometimes the type of weapon can be identified. Most important, though, is the scratched impression on the bullet of the rifling grooves within the gun barrel. Variations in the twist (left or right) and the number of grooves may assist in the identification of the make and model of the gun used, and can be compared to a suspect weapon. Even badly deformed bullets are useful to the scientist
Powder	During burning, the powder gives off quantities of smoke and particulates which are emitted from the muzzle and frequently around the mechanism of the firearm itself. Minute particles of the bullet, unburnt powder, and other debris are ejected in several directions. Some also contain small particles of lead, barium, and antimony which form small granules. These firearm discharge residues (FDRs) can be found on the clothing, face, and hands of the offender and other people and items in the vicinity. Swabbing kits are available to retrieve this material. Suspects should be swabbed as soon as possible because the residues fall off easily. It should be noted that the presence of FDRs does not necessarily prove involvement in the offence

Shotgun cartridges vary both in their overall design and the number and size of lead shot they contain (see 18.5). CSIs and forensic scientists can use these features to derive evidence.

Shot cartridge component	Available evidence
Cartridge case	This is normally retained in the weapon until reloading; however, it may be ejected by automatic or self-loading weapons. It can be used to establish the bore of the weapon and the manufacturer and type of cartridge. Scratches on the brass base and the impression of the firing pin and breech face can be compared to suspect weapons. In automatic weapons marks from the extractor, ejector, and magazine may be found
The shot	The size of the shot may eliminate some types of cartridge from an enquiry. The spread of the shot is useful in establishing the range of the weapon (when the possible use of a 'choke' is taken into consideration)
Powder	FDRs are available, but in most sporting shotguns the FDRs are ejected through the muzzle, since the breech is sealed
Wadding	The presence of wadding indicates that a shotgun has been discharged. It can frequently give an indication as to the bore of weapon used, and a hint as to the cartridge manufacturer. Wadding is normally badly deformed during discharge, so irregular lumps of plastic, felt, or cork at the scene should be collected and preserved. Plastic wadding fired from a sawn-off weapon can sometimes be compared to the finish at the sawn-off muzzle end: if the finish is poor, the wadding may bear scratches which can be reproduced during controlled tests

The most frequently asked questions at the laboratory are:

- Is this a firearm as defined by the Act(s) (see 18.3.1)?
- Is this an imitation firearm (see 18.8)?
- What type of weapon fired this bullet (or cartridge case)?
- Did this weapon fire this bullet (or cartridge case)?
- How far was the weapon from the victim?
- Can this weapon fire accidentally?
- Do these swabs/items of clothing bear FDR?
- Which is the entry wound/exit wound on this victim?

(Adapted from a number of unpublished Forensic Science Service publications.)

> **TASK 2**
>
> 1. List three types of trace evidence or material which might be found at a burglary.
> 2. List three types of impression.
> 3. List three sources of DNA.
> 4. Which does mitochondrial DNA establish: male or female lines?

25.6 Taking Samples in Investigations

The objective of taking samples from suspects, victims, and crime scenes is to demonstrate a link between them, preferably during the offence in question (see 25.4). Forensic evidence has the potential to produce powerful forms of evidence which might 'include' or 'exclude' people and other things from an enquiry, and can also produce investigative leads. In some crimes the victim is an important component of a crime scene: for example, in a kidnapping one key objective is to demonstrate that the victim had been in a certain place.

Procedures must be strictly followed in order that samples have a clear provenance and do not become contaminated with other material. Typically, if a sample is taken from one person or place then a corresponding sample should be recovered from elsewhere for comparison. This is known as a 'control' and is covered in 25.6.2.1.

Whilst the crime scene is normally examined by CSIs, any people who are suspected of having been involved in the offence will also need to have samples taken. This can be carried out by custody staff, a medical practitioner or police officer in the custody area, a hospital, or at a person's home or place of work (depending on the person and the circumstances).

25.6.1 Taking samples from people

We have already discussed the requirement to link suspects, victims, and venues as part of an investigation. Samples are also occasionally used to establish identity.

The samples taken from people can include a variety of trace evidence and DNA-rich material in or on any part of the body, including:

- foreign blood, saliva, and semen (all are sources of DNA);
- firearm and explosive residues;
- trace material such as glass, paint flakes, fibres, grease, plant debris, or soil;
- bite marks, weapon marks, and bruises;
- chemicals, such as alcohol, toxins, and drugs within the blood and urine, or chemical traces upon the skin;
- fingerprints; and
- handwriting characteristics.

There is an important distinction between people in custody and others who are voluntarily providing evidence or material which can eliminate them from the scene. When taking forensic samples from suspects (whether arrested or not) the procedures set out in PACE Code D must be followed (see 25.6.1.1). However, there is no PACE Act requirement for people such as victims and witnesses who provide samples to assist police investigations. This means it might not *always* be necessary for a police surgeon or other medical practitioner to take certain types of sample. Police officers must, however, treat victims, witnesses, and volunteers in accordance with the Human Rights Act 1998 (see 5.4). This is an important consideration when arriving at a scene or dealing with a victim who attends the police station where no CSI or medical assistance is immediately available.

As noted earlier, people are crime scenes and are sources both of evidence (potentially to be used in court) and intelligence (eg to provide leads in an investigation). Hence samples from a person can be used to:

- prove or disprove his/her involvement in the offence;
- corroborate or refute statements;
- show a link between him/her and another person, the scene, or an exhibit;
- establish drug, toxin, or alcohol levels in the body;

- further inform the enquiry; and
- provide a reference sample (DNA, fingerprints, or footwear impressions) for direct comparison, for elimination, or for a database.

Normally DNA and fingerprint samples provided by suspects are retained in databases for 'speculative' (untargeted) searches, but most other samples are destroyed after the case is complete.

25.6.1.1 PACE Code D

When taking forensic samples from suspects, parts 4–6 of PACE Code D must be followed. This includes suspects attending a police station 'voluntarily' (para 5.19). Note that when PACE refers to a suspect attending a police station 'voluntarily' (para 5.19) this is not referring to a member of the public who 'volunteers' to submit to some form of sampling.

Some of the key points from this part of Code D are that:

- samples should be relevant and should be proportional to the offence (unless they are for speculative searching and are covered by blanket policies, such as taking fingerprints, DNA identification, and photographs);
- appropriate adults are required in many circumstances, including taking samples from juveniles, the mentally disordered, or the visually impaired; and
- records must be kept about consent, authority, and warnings to the detained person.

Part in Code D	Procedure covered
4	Identification by fingerprints and footwear impressions
5	Examinations to establish identity and the taking of photographs
6	Identification by body samples and impressions

The PACE Act 1984 defines two types of sample: non-intimate and intimate. The easiest way of remembering what sample falls under each category is this: if the area to be sampled is an orifice or it is within the underwear (including a bra) then it is intimate. If it is not an orifice or is outside the underwear then it is non-intimate.

A non-intimate sample may be taken by a police officer, detention officer, or CSI and includes:

- a sample of hair, other than pubic hair, which includes hair plucked with the root;
- a sample taken from a nail or from under a nail;
- a swab taken from any part of a person's body other than a part from which a swab taken would be an intimate sample (a sample from the hands and face is permissible but not from inside a nostril or ear);
- saliva;
- skin impressions from non-intimate areas.

Police personnel must not take an intimate sample from a detained person. A registered medical practitioner (a doctor, dentist, nurse, or paramedic) must be called to take intimate samples. An intimate sample is:

- a dental impression;
- a sample of blood, semen, or any other tissue fluid;
- urine;
- pubic hair; or
- a swab taken from any part of a person's genitals or from a person's body orifices other than the mouth.

Intimate samples are essential when attempting to prove a sexual assault or rape and other serious offences against the person in order to establish the existence, or otherwise, of a 'two-way transfer' between the parties (see 25.2.3). Note that in cases of sexual assault and murder the intimate *and* non-intimate sampling of prisoners and victims must be conducted by a specially trained police surgeon (Forensic Medical Examiner (FME)) or other registered medical practitioner. Police officers and CSIs may assist.

25.6.1.2   What samples should be taken?

The types of sample taken from victims and suspects will depend on the nature of the criminal offence. The following table describes the minimum samples for *consideration* (represented by a tick in the table). Note that PACE Code D and the Human Rights Act 1998 must be complied with, and the reasons for taking a particular sample must be noted in each case.

Minimum samples

	Cheque or other fraud. Hate mail	Burglary or other property crime	Sexual assault or rape	Theft from motor vehicle with damage caused	ABH and other assaults	Homicide victims and suspects
Blood and/or urine for toxicology			✓		✓	✓
Clothing (inner)			✓		✓	✓
Clothing (outer)		✓	✓	✓	✓	✓
DNA	✓	✓	✓	✓	✓	✓
Fingerprints	✓	✓	✓	✓	✓	✓
Hair (combing)		✓	✓	✓	✓	✓
Hair (pulled/cut)		✓	✓	✓	✓	✓
Handwriting sample	✓					
Photographs of injuries		When relevant	When relevant	When relevant	When relevant	Effectively mandatory
Sexual offence kit			Mandatory			Normally used
Shoes		✓	✓	✓	✓	✓

25.6.1.3   The sampling procedure for taking evidence from people

Upon delivery to a custody area all arrested persons are subject to mandatory sampling where their fingerprints, DNA, and a photograph are taken. In the case of DNA this will not be required if a successful profile has been created previously. Sampling of suspects for evidence to link them to crime scenes should be carried out as soon after arrest as possible to recover the maximum available material and to prevent evidence being lost during Livescan fingerprinting or DNA swabbing. If there is a long delay between offence and arrest (even years), the CSI should be consulted because non-intimate samples, and material recovered from the crime scene, may still be potentially useful.

Brand-new, unused packaging equipment must be used, since old equipment is a source of contamination. Specific kits are available, for example for the sampling of hair or urine, and these should be used where accessible. Personnel should wear gloves as a minimum form of protection. For serious offences, or where health warnings exist, officers should wear protective clothing to protect themselves and the evidence from contamination. The CSI should be informed when samples have been taken, so that correct transport, storage, and subsequent preservation can be arranged. Blood, semen, and saliva contain DNA and should normally be frozen immediately. Where DNA is not required, for instance for the comparison of paints and oils, it is best practice to air-dry the samples securely or to freeze them if this is not possible.

Samples from the exposed skin, hands, head, and mouth should be taken first (before clothing samples) in order to prevent material from those areas contaminating the clothing or vice versa. For example, pulling a sweater covered in glass fragments over head hair which does not contain glass would cause contamination: the head hair should be dealt with first. Swabs from the body include skin swabs from hands and face, as well as elsewhere. Skin impressions include ear-prints, lip-prints, and prints of the skin: elbows, cheeks, feet, etc. Non-intimate samples may be taken from a detainee by a police officer at a police station and reasonable force may be used (but see 25.6.1.7 for buccal swabs and the relevant documentation).

25.6.1.4 Head hair samples

Head hair (including beard hair) may contain glass, plant material, foreign hairs, and so on and should be dealt with before clothing is removed. This will limit contamination by or from other samples (especially important in offences where windows have been smashed). Head hair samples can be used for the following purposes:

- recovery of fibres, hair, and particulate material and traces, wet or dry blood;
- comparison (as a control) with the subject's hair (structure, length, colour, and treatments) when found at scenes or on other people;
- chemical analysis to demonstrate long-term drug use or metals poisoning; and
- DNA analysis from the cells forming part of a hair root.

Any hat should be removed and exhibited first. Where religious head coverings are worn, such as turbans, it is good practice to ask permission from the person first and, time permitting, make arrangements for alternative head coverings prior to removal.

The samples must be taken over a sheet of pre-folded paper (at least A4 size) which catches debris. The hair should be combed from front to back all over the head so that debris falls onto the paper, continuing until no more debris is found. Clearly, this is not easy when the person is not compliant. The paper and comb should both be exhibited. For a person with matted hair or dreadlocks, a glove can be worn and the hair gently 'brushed' with the hands, or a new small hairbrush can be used with care. The paper containing the debris, the glove, and the brush should be exhibited. Any blood or other matted material in the hair should be cut out over a sheet of pre-folded paper, and the scissors should be exhibited along with the cut section and the paper.

A 'control' of head hair is also required and ideally this is pulled out (so it contains the root material and can be identified as belonging to that person through DNA). Alternatively the hair can be cut, but it should never be simply combed out as it could have come from someone else. At least 25 hairs should be taken, including all colours and length variations.

25.6.1.5 Clothing and footwear samples

Clothing and footwear can be used as a source for samples for impressions, or for other materials they have picked up from a crime scene (fibres, hair, and particulate material and traces, wet or dry blood, and chemicals). They can be used for comparison as a control of a fibre mix, and to recreate impressions left by clothing or shoes on vehicles following RTCs and at crime scenes. They can also provide information about weapons used on a victim (damage to clothing) and indicate proximity to fire or explosion (through the damage to fibres).

When taking clothing from suspects and victims, the subject must stand on a clean paper sheet to catch any debris which may fall. Material recovered from the floor of custody areas or medical facilities is not suitable for laboratory examination since it has no provenance (and most force quality-control systems will as a matter of course prevent the submission of such articles). The clothing should be removed in a logical manner. Each piece should be separately exhibited and packaged in front of the subject. Notes should be made about the condition of clothing: its size, the presence of blood, colour, logos, and any damage. (This avoids the need for another person to open the packaging in order to screen or describe the contents.) A final search of pockets may be carried out within the bag to prevent the unnecessary loss of material.

When all the clothing has been taken the officer should ask the subject to brush off his/her bare feet onto the paper sheet before stepping off, because otherwise material on the sheet will adhere to sweaty feet. The paper sheet on the floor is now an exhibit, and must be treated with care before being dispatched for analysis.

Footwear impressions can provide important intelligence information since they can be compared using the National Footwear Reference Collection (NFRC) for England and Wales. This can be searched for footwear matches, which is particularly relevant for premises-related crimes such as burglary. Taking footwear impressions was previously an ill-defined area, but s 118(3) of SOCPA 2005 now includes 'impressions of footwear' as well as fingerprints. These procedures in the context of a criminal investigation are covered in Code D, paras 4.16–4.21. Shoes which may be needed for the analysis of trace materials and DNA should not be scanned or copied as this can contaminate the shoes or cause the loss of material.

25.6.1.6 Skin swabs

Swabs from the skin may show the presence of blood, saliva, or chemical residues such as explosives traces. Generally, this is best left to a CSI (particularly explosive and firearm traces and the photography of blood) or a medical examiner, but do not permit unnecessary delays to occur.

CSI training officers or a CSI 'on area' will be able to provide information on the latest protocols for recovering blood and other fluids from non-intimate areas on suspects' skin. Note that bite marks on people may contain DNA from another person that will need to be preserved; a CSI should be contacted immediately.

25.6.1.7 Buccal swabs and other samples for DNA analysis

Buccal (mouth) swabs and pulled hair can be analysed for DNA for inclusion in the NDNAD. DNA required for the database or comparison to crime scene material is normally taken from suspects (and victims) using a buccal swab since it is a cheap and effective method.

In general terms, the subject should not eat, drink, or smoke for at least 20 minutes before the test. This allows the mouth to regenerate dead or damaged cells. The sampling pack contains a buccal swab kit and a hair sampling kit. The gloves must be worn and every effort must be made to avoid contamination. Biological material can be very easily contaminated by people talking, coughing, or sneezing over it, or otherwise mishandling the material. The sampling process should be carried out before completing the associated paperwork, because if the swab is accidentally dropped, a new form would have to be completed for the replacement swab kit. After taking the sample it should all be sealed in the 'tamper-evident' bag, arranged so the forms can be read through the bag. Force protocols must be followed regarding subsequent handling and storage.

Under the PACE Act 1984, a suspect may refuse to provide a buccal swab, in which case he/she may elect to provide a hair sample (pulled, to include the root). The hair sampling site can be chosen by the suspect on condition that it is not in an intimate area. Note that although Code D, para 6.7 refers to the use of 'reasonable' force to take non-intimate samples, buccal swabs should not be taken by force because the swab tip can be dislodged inside the mouth and presents a risk of choking.

25.6.1.8 Prints and impressions from people

Fingerprints are a useful and non-invasive form of evidence and the regulations governing their use by the police are in Code D, paras 4.1–4.15. Police officers receive training on how to fingerprint suspects and victims at police stations using either:

- Livescan—a digital finger and palm-scanning device which is found in all main police stations.
- Ink—the traditional copper plate and printers' ink system or simpler, portable systems such as an ink pad or peel-apart, pre-inked strips, now mainly used to take elimination fingerprints from, for example, victims of crime.
- Lantern—a portable digital device which can be used on patrol to identify people who have previously had their fingerprints taken.

Fingerprints can be used to identify a person as part of immigration enquiries, such as for a person detained under the Immigration Act 1971, Sch 2, para 18(2). They are also used for identification in relation to s 141(7) of the Immigration and Asylum Act 1999 when a person:

(a) fails to produce identity and nationality upon arrival to the UK;

(b) is refused entry but temporarily admitted;

(c) is to be removed as an illegal entrant or deported;

(d) is arrested under the Immigration Act 1971;

(e) has made a claim for asylum;

(f) is a dependant of any person listed in (b) to (e).

All police officers should be qualified to take fingerprints, but other impressions are problematic. For instance, Code D, para 6 covers the more unusual body impressions (eg ears and feet) and other forms of evidence comprehensively, but does not permit the taking of impressions from an intimate area. CSIs can provide guidance in this respect. A registered dentist is required under PACE to take impressions of a suspect's teeth (an intimate sample under Code D).

25.6.1.9   Handwriting samples

Not all subjects who are providing handwriting samples are under arrest and subject to the PACE Act 1984 but, in any case, relatively strict rules apply. The person should sit at a table without being able to view any of the existing handwriting evidence. He/she is then given a well-used ballpoint pen—pencils and felt tips are not used because they do not necessarily show the construction of each letter, which is important. The officer then dictates what is to be written. Under no circumstances should the subject be asked to write 'the quick brown fox jumps over the lazy dog'. This sentence would be of little use since a person's writing style is partly determined by the letters before and after every other letter, so it might not provide the combinations required for the investigation.

The sample material must be written in the same format as the document for comparison: if the original is in capitals, then the sample piece must be in capitals, and so on. If the writing was on a specific form, the supplier should be asked to supply blank samples; dummy cheques are available from CSI or Fraud Units if necessary. The person should be asked to write out the contents of the document a *minimum* of five times (unless this would be unreasonable), and for cheques, at least 15 samples are needed. He/she should sign and date every page, and each completed sample should be removed so the writing style used previously cannot be seen and copied. The subject may, obviously, attempt to conceal his/her true handwriting style but may start to revert to type after several samples. Indeed there is nothing wrong with stopping the process several times (to make it harder for the subject to remember a writing style) or to ask for 20 samples, as long as this is not unreasonable. Even though the final results may be 'obvious', the samples should still be submitted to a suitable facility for expert opinion.

25.6.1.10   Photographs

Taking photographs is covered in Code D (paras 5.1–5.18 for a detained person and paras 5.19–5.24 for a person who is at a police station but not detained). The Code is not explicit regarding injuries, but it is common, especially in major crimes, for suspects to be examined by a doctor (or nurse) and to be photographed by a suitable person to provide injury evidence. Photographs of a recent injury may indicate a suspect's involvement in an offence, for example burns from arson attacks, and bruises or lacerations caused by one or more parties defending themselves in an assault case. Valuable identification evidence can also be provided by taking photographs of certain features, such as tattoos and scars.

TASK 3 Imagine you are a police officer. Consider what you might do if:

- A woman attends the police station and claims to have been 'date-raped'. GHB and Rohypnol (examples of so-called 'date-rape' drugs) are rapidly excreted from the human body. Would you find a 'urine module' and request an immediate urine sample? How might this affect potential DNA evidence?
- You attend a robbery and a man says he bit the offender. He can still taste blood in his mouth. Would you ask him to spit into a sterile bottle?
- A victim claims a man sexually assaulted her and ejaculated over her hand. Would you glove or bag her hand, or even take a swab from it (if trained)?

25.6.2 Sampling from crime scenes

This is a complex area. CSI trainers will provide training for new officers and for more experienced officers on detective training. This Handbook can be used as a guide, but CSIs are able to provide the most up-to-date information on local force protocols.

A force is likely to employ specialist CSI staff whose chief role is the recovery of physical material from crime scenes. However, there will be many occasions where a police officer may seize exhibits in the course of duty, for example when:

- a police officer is part of a search team;
- there is no apparent evidence apart from one or two items which can be safely recovered without a CSI (eg documents, cheques, or a single moveable shoe mark)—note that local policies must be followed;
- the CSI is unable to attend; and
- evidence may be lost if not recovered immediately (eg a shotgun cartridge on a windy day).

Material taken from crime scenes can include a wide range of potentially valuable material. Crime scene investigators are specially trained to 'recognize' potential evidence from amongst the often chaotic venues of offences, but this skill can be learned by anyone, particularly police officers who have an eye for investigative aims. The best way to identify sources of potential evidence at volume crime scenes is to speak to the victim. The CSI will question the victim at a common domestic burglary regarding probable entry and exit routes, what has been disturbed, and what was stolen. This informs the search for evidence which, typically, follows a pattern:

- an assessment of the scene in its context;
- a brief health and safety assessment, which continues throughout the search;
- an examination of external areas for evidence (which may otherwise be lost due to wind, rain, curious passers-by, children, and pets);
- early action to recover evidence which could otherwise be lost;
- a search of the internal areas, guided by (but not controlled by) the victim.

Typically (though not normally at volume crimes), photographs are taken first, because it is a non-destructive recording method. Then DNA and other trace evidence are taken, with fingerprinting carried out last, because the powders are contaminants. Each piece of evidence is packaged, marked, and labelled according to force protocols, and its position and description recorded on a worksheet.

In a standard volume crime scene, common forms of evidence to be searched for and probably found include:

- tool-marks and shoe marks outside the premises, particularly near to the point of entry (these are photographed and cast using a silicon gel and plaster of Paris, respectively);
- broken glass (which could have been broken as a means to gain entry or when a window was forced). A control of the glass is required to match to any suspect's hair and clothing;
- shoe marks on windowsills, (can be photographed and lifted onto gel or tape). Shoes can also leave prints some distance into a crime scene, especially on recently waxed floors and gloss doors;
- fingerprints left by a suspect climbing into the premises. These can be developed with a powder and brush, lifted onto tape, and encapsulated on an acetate sheet. Fingerprints may also be left on moved articles, papers, glossy or polished surfaces, and bags. The treatment of these depends upon the nature of the surface; fingerprint powder can be used on non-porous surfaces but paper, plastic, and cellophane yield better prints if sent to the force chemical treatment laboratory;
- DNA, if the suspect has sustained injuries, left strands of pulled hair, consumed food or drinks, or discarded a cigarette;
- glove and fabric patterns, prints left by the ears, nose, elbows, and even lips, which have all been found at crime scenes, and can be used by the scientist with varying degrees of success.

25.6.2.1 Recovering 'controls'

A control is for comparing with other samples, for instance comparing a fibre from a blanket found at a crime scene with fibres found on a suspect. A control (in crime scene investigation terms) comes from a known source. Where only a simple control of material is needed without a full scene examination, then a suitably trained police officer may gather the samples, but for anything more complex the CSI should be tasked. Police officers can, however, take glass and paint controls in order to save time and inconvenience.

Glass controls should always be taken from the supporting frame because glass on the ground has 'no provenance' (its origins are unknown). Where no glass remains in the frame a police officer must satisfy him/herself, and also be able to satisfy the forensic scientist, and a potential jury that the glass originally came from the frame. Thick gloves and goggles should be worn to prevent injury. At least six pieces should be taken and marked on both sides with an indelible felt pen or 'chinagraph' pencil. Samples from all around the break should be included. For a hole in toughened glass, the cube-shaped debris should be removed from around the hole (see 25.5.1.1 on different types of glass). If a large laminate window has been broken, the slabs can be extremely dangerous, but the complete thickness must be sampled and not just the dusty ground glass on the surface. Shoe marks may also be present on window glass.

All glass fragments should be placed into a suitable sturdy box with every edge sealed with tape. No fragments should puncture or escape through the box, and an outer polythene bag is essential. The window void and its exact position above the ground should be measured, and the information recorded on a plan drawing (not required for vehicle windows).

Paint controls from window and door frames should be sliced with a new sharp knife from several areas around the damage. (However, if a tool mark is present, it may be advisable to call a CSI before taking paint samples.) The sections of the paint should be at least 20 mm, and some base material should be included if possible. On vehicles, a 10p-sized section of paint should be cut out, all the way to base metal, including filler where present. This should be done from several places near to, and remote from, the damage in question, and from any part where foreign paint is found. On vehicles with damaged panels the paint sometimes falls away in rectangular slabs and these should be taken from the car, and not from the ground beneath it.

The fragments of paint should be placed into a paper fold (see 25.7.1) and then put into a polythene bag. Because paint is brittle it may lend itself to a mechanical fit, and if this seems likely the entire object and all the chipped paint are needed, so a CSI is almost certainly required. Note that adhesive tapes should never be used to recover paint samples.

25.7   Packaging Techniques

Using the correct packaging prevents damage and contamination and is, effectively, a demonstration of the care and skill that accompanied the seizure of the exhibits. Local force protocols will be based on those laid down by forensic science laboratories and these must be followed. Specifically, guidance can be found in the FSS publication *The Scenes of Crime Handbook* (not publicly available, although probably available to police officers through their local force).

25.7.1   Types of packaging and how to use them

Paper bags should have the top folded over twice (approximately 25 mm (one inch) per fold). The joint should be sealed over with a signature seal (an adhesive label with the officer's signature, name, and number). The entire join between folds and bag should then be completely sealed. An exhibit label can also be attached if required. Note that some forces require the factory-sealed base of the bag to be folded and sealed in the same way as the folded top.

For **polythene bags** a tamper-evident bag should be used if available. For a plain bag a signature seal and a complete seal of tape is tented over the open top. The ends of the tape should be pinched off and cut off about 10 mm from the bag. An exhibit label can also be attached if required.

Nylon bags should be sealed by twisting into a 'swan neck' (as shown in the photograph), and then secured with tape or a cable tie without 'teeth' (as these could puncture the bag).

The sealed nylon bag is then placed in a polythene bag, swan necked, and sealed. The entire package should then be placed in a rigid container, signature sealed, and labelled. The type of items stored in nylon bags should not be stored in proximity to other samples (see 25.7.2).

Boxes are used for some items, but they must be secured with string or cable ties; special perforated inserts can be used, but if unavailable the box can be punctured to accept the string or ties, and the holes then signed and sealed over. All open edges of the box must be sealed with tape and signature-sealed as shown in the photograph.

(Image © Kevin Lawton-Barrett)

A Nylon bag 'swan necked' prior to securing with a cable tie

(Image © Kevin Lawton-Barrett)

Police evidence box

Paper folds are required for the safe collection and storage of dry materials such as powders, paint fragments, and hair combings, but they are not adequate for storing glass. The diagram shows a common technique used to construct a 'paper-fold' container. The paper should be pre-folded before use, and the debris worked down into the greyed section before refolding and sealing into a suitable polythene bag.

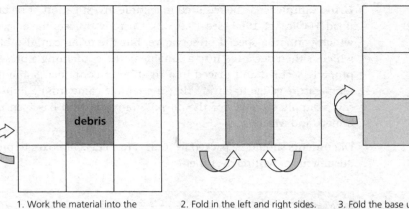

1. Work the material into the grey area and fold the base up.

2. Fold in the left and right sides.

3. Fold the base upwards and tuck the last fold in.

25.7.2   Packaging procedures for some common items

Bedding and recently worn clothes or shoes must be sealed into paper bags which allow them to breathe. Sealing articles which are even slightly damp into plastic encourages the growth of mould and bacteria. A health hazard warning label should be used if any biological material might be present or where it is known or believed that articles have come from a potentially contaminated source (eg a known drug addict). If paper bags are not pre-printed, an exhibit label should also be attached but it is advisable to write the exhibit details onto the bag as a fail-safe measure, simply because labels routinely fall off the bags.

Articles that are **slightly wet or soaked** with non-flammable liquids (including blood) need to be dried. A CSI should be contacted urgently for advice and assistance with drying. Fabric items bearing wet blood must not be folded as this causes the blood to transfer to other parts of the article. In an emergency the wet items could be placed in a polythene sack for transport but urgent CSI advice is required, and it should all be sealed into a robust paper sack for protection.

Articles which may bear **flammable substances** should not be stored in paper bags because flammable chemicals (accelerants) will evaporate through paper sacks and be lost, as well as contaminating other material in storage and transit. A nylon bag should be used for hydro-carbons (eg petrol, diesel, or paraffin). For non-hydrocarbons such as methylated spirits, alcohol, and acetone (or any uncertainty over whether a substance is a hydrocarbon) a nylon bag *within* a polythene bag should be used. Where biological material such as blood or semen is also believed present, the CSI should be consulted, since DNA may be destroyed by flammable substances. It is likely that the CSI will recommend immediate transport to a laboratory.

Sharps, bladed weapons, screwdrivers, and other pointed objects represent a very serious health hazard. When working with hypodermic needles at crime scenes a sharps storage pack for needles should be used, but hypodermic needles are in fact rarely dispatched to laborator-ies. Needles from syringes can be disposed of in a sharps bin prior to packaging the syringe (if specialist syringe and needle storage boxes are not available) but this does not apply in major-crime cases: advice will be required. For knives and blades a knife tube should be used, but if unavailable, a clean, unused, sturdy box can be used. Care should be taken with screw-thread knife tubes as the screwing action can easily force the point of a knife blade through the lid into the hand. The two halves of knife tubes and sharps packs should be sealed together with tape and signature-sealed prior to packaging in a polythene bag.

Firearms represent a serious and immediate high-risk hazard. It is best practice to call for the assistance of a Firearms Officer and CSI to properly record the making-safe process. Once made safe firearms of forensic interest are sealed in boxes. If they are of no forensic interest, they may be removed to the police station for safety, for example, when the owner of a firearm is consid-ered to be unfit to continue to possess it.

Bottles and glasses must be immobilized in a sturdy box. This will protect fingerprints or DNA, and prevent damage from any sharp edges. Bottles and glasses for back-calculation alco-hol analysis (see 19.9.5.3) must be marked to show the levels the suspect claims to have drunk.

Urine samples may be required in a crime investigation or be taken from drivers under the Road Traffic Act 1988 (see 19.9.5.2). Custody officers have access to 'RTA-type' urine kits which contain a special preservative, but the urine can also be collected in a plastic pot, which is then decanted into a suitable bottle containing a preservative. The bottle must be properly secured and placed in a rigid outer container. Some urine collection pots bear a temperature gauge to ensure that the sample came from a living person, rather than from, say, a supply secreted for the purpose (anyone who has seen the film *Withnail and I* will understand why).

Documents should be packed in stout card folders or boxes to prevent people leaning on the documents or writing over them.

TASK 4 If you are a trainee police officer discuss the following questions with a BCU, CSI, or your trainers. If you are a student you could raise them in a seminar:

1. At a major crime scene, what are the usual problems with the CAP and cordons?
2. What is the better form of evidence: a fingerprint or DNA? (People are very likely to have different views, based almost entirely upon the perceived context of the evidence.)
3. What is worse, genuine contamination of an exhibit, or the suspicion of contamination?

25.7.3 Seizure and packaging of computers and other digital devices

Where a computer seizure is planned, the Digital Forensics Unit (or Computer Crime Unit) should be contacted in advance for advice and, where necessary, attendance at the scene. DFU personnel are specially trained to recover data and present it in a form acceptable to the criminal justice system. In doing so they will be mindful of ss 19 and 20 of the PACE Act 1984 (which provide the legal basis for the seizure of data) and the ACPO good practice guidelines for Computer-Based Electronic Evidence (ACPO, 2012a). The latter outlines four principles of digital evidence which must be adhered to:

* Principle 1: *No action taken by law enforcement agencies, persons employed within those agencies or their agents should change data which may subsequently be relied upon in court* (ACPO, 2012a, p 6). For the trainee police officer this means, for example, that they shouldn't turn on a PC that is off (see 25.7.3.1).

The remaining three principles are more relevant to specialists but are included here for completeness:

* Principle 2: *In circumstances where a person finds it necessary to access original data, that person must be competent to do so and be able to give evidence explaining the relevance and the implications of their actions* (ACPO, 2012a, p 6).
* Principle 3: *An audit trail or other record of all processes applied to digital evidence should be created and preserved. An independent third party should be able to examine those processes and achieve the same result* (ACPO, 2012a, p 6)
* Principle 4: *The person in charge of the investigation has overall responsibility for ensuring that the law and these principles are adhered to* (ACPO, 2012a, p 6).

Apart from data and programs that may be stored on a digital device, its plastic, metal, and glass surface may provide useful evidence. The outer skin of most computers is mildly textured and commonly will not yield fingerprints (in volume crime) but the screen and areas which are not normally seen, such as the inside, under the support foot and at the rear, are often very smooth and may yield fingerprints. Local policy must be followed for all seizures and storage of computers and associated equipment, particularly relating to packaging. In serious or major crimes great care must be taken: the whole device may be required for DNA and fingerprint analysis. This may present a conflict between the physical and digital evidence retrieval—and must be resolved prior to any activity.

A key point is that a computer that is to be seized as part of an investigation should never be turned off by going through the usual domestic or workplace routine (by first closing down Windows, etc). Instead, the power supply must be interrupted, see 25.7.3.2. Just as important—a digital device that is turned off must not be turned on. More information may be found in Bryant (2008).

25.7.3.1 Unplanned seizures of digital equipment

Where a seizure is unplanned, contact should be made with the Digital Forensics Unit (or Computer Crime Unit) for advice. The scene should be secured and people moved away from the equipment and any power supplies. If the printer is still printing then it should be allowed to complete its run and the screen should be photographed (if it is displaying).

In the meantime:

- do not turn on or off any device;
- do not touch any key or the mouse;
- do not interfere with any other device on a network;
- do not use the telephone system in any scene; and
- treat with caution the advice of the owner or user.

The layout of the devices and associated cabling should be photographed or sketched where practicable.

For small, portable devices local policy should be followed but in any case call lists, pictures, or any other files should not be viewed. If the devices are unconnected to other devices, then the DFU may suggest a simple seizure, but remember that some of these devices can still communicate with other systems, through Bluetooth and infrared. In this case, the employment of a Faraday bag, which prevents communication with the network, may be advisable.

The ACPO Good Practice Guide for Digital Evidence, Version 5 (available online) also makes it clear that seized hard drives should be placed in anti-static bags, tough paper bags, tamper evident cardboard packaging, or wrapped in paper and place in aerated plastic bags.

25.7.3.2 Procedures for mobile devices and computers that are switched on

The power supply to a computer (PC, laptop, netbook, iPad, etc) should not be interrupted unless the person has received the relevant training. However, the exception to this rule is when the computer is executing instructions to format the logical drives or other 'destructive' activity; this will be explained during initial training.

Following DFU advice, an appropriately trained person should interrupt the power supply, and this is normally done by removing the power lead from the back of the PC base unit. (Unplugging it from the mains would not cut the power supply if the computer had an Uninterruptible Power Supply (UPS).) Removing the power supply to a computer prevents automated routines from being activated—these might destroy vital evidence on the hard drive. Laptops can be a particular problem in unplanned seizures because removing the power lead will not close them down. DFU procedure may be to remove both the battery and the power cable, but as in all matters concerning the seizure of digital equipment, local force policy must be followed. A removed battery must also be seized.

For mobile phones and smartphones that are switched on similar general advice applies (but check local policy)—photograph the device (particularly the screen) and make a note in your PNB of any on-screen text and imagery that might be visible and in what state (loading a web page?) the device is in, then power down. (However, there are some circumstances where local policy might determine that you leave the device on.)

25.7.3.3 Packaging digital equipment

Force policy must be followed for 'bagging and tagging' digital equipment. This will usually be to use see-through plastic bags, and to use one bag per PC base unit if these are seized. The bag must be properly sealed and a cardboard exhibit label attached if the bag has no pre-printed label.

However, polythene bags will obliterate fingerprints if they touch any smooth surfaces, so care must be taken. In serious or major crimes great care must be taken: remember that the whole device may be required for DNA and fingerprint analysis.

For small, portable digital devices the following procedures are likely to apply:

- package different media separately (eg USB pens separately from CDs);
- note the exact number of items in each bag (eg 'a large quantity of CDs' is not likely to be an adequate description);
- where applicable, keep media in their cases (remember to check inside cases);

- do not fold or bend or put any labels on discs;
- seize cradles/power packs for tablets, smartphones, PDAs and similar equipment; and
- keep packaged devices away from sources of magnetism, including during transport (eg not close to car radios).

Force-specific policies will exist in relation to seizure and packaging of smartphones and mobile phones. This may include storage in Faraday bags and boxes to prevent them communicating with the network.

TASK 5

1. A police officer is taking a DNA sample from an arrested person. He accidentally drops the swab on the floor. What should he do now?
2. Which PACE Act 1984 Code applies to fingerprinting suspects?
3. Imagine you have a quantity of fine debris you wish to store. Taking a sheet of A4 paper, make a paper fold to retain it.
4. Clothing thought to be contaminated with hydrocarbons (like petrol) is packed into what sort of bag?
5. In an emergency, can a police officer lawfully ask a victim to provide a urine sample if he/she says he/she was the victim of a drug-induced rape?
6. A police officer attends a crime scene and takes a control sample of glass. How many pieces should she take? From where? How should she mark them (if at all)?

25.8 Answers to Tasks

TASK 1

1. Forensic Science Service or the Forensic Science Society (sometimes FSSoc): see the Glossary in Chapter 2. The Forensic Science Service has now closed and its services have been transferred to the private sector. The archive still exists.
2. Edmond Locard.
3. A possible list:
   - describing the *modus operandi* (MO);
   - answering investigative questions;
   - to establish that an offence has occurred;
   - to identify an offender or suspect;
   - to corroborate or refute witness statements;
   - to establish a physical link between suspect, crime scene, and victim;
   - to identify an individual; and
   - to further inform an enquiry.

TASK 2

1. Fibres, glass, paint, soil, pollen, fibres, etc.
2. Tool-marks, shoe marks, impressions from stamps and dyes, extrusion marks, finger marks, clothing, gloves, etc.
3. Blood, semen, ear wax, mucus, saliva, etc.
4. Mitochondrial DNA comes from the female line, that is, from the mother.

TASK 3 In all these instances you could lawfully have taken the evidence. If you elected not to do so the evidence could quite possibly be lost.

It is acceptable, in an emergency and when a CSI or medical assistance is not available, for anyone to take a sample from a victim in a case such as this. Clearly, the dignity and psychological well-being of the victim must be uppermost in your mind, but there are occasions when decisive action will benefit the investigation. Crucially, you would have to have access to the appropriate sterile equipment for the task and you would preferably have received previous training.

Many police forces have evidence kits at the front counter for just these unlikely situations. Out on Supervised or Independent Patrol these kits might not be available, so personnel may have to 'make do', but immediate actions like these can be required at any time.

TASK 4

1. Common Approach Paths sound simple but raise many problems, not least of which being where to put them. Essentially, they should be on a hard surface and should not be the likely route that the offender or victim took to, or from, the crime scene. The next issue is: how can they be marked on a windy day without anything to secure the tape? This cannot really be done until assistance arrives. CSIs will probably be able to explain that, with hindsight, the FAO could have employed better tactics.

2. Fingerprints are assumed to be unique, but there is disagreement over this issue since it is difficult to actually prove this point in a scientific sense. Our DNA is unique, too, but many people feel more comfortable with DNA because it has been the subject of much recent research. The best evidence, ultimately, only occurs where the context for it is right: thus on one occasion DNA can be of no use, whilst the next day it is very powerful.

   If speed is the best measurement, then fingerprints win since the turnaround for a fingerprint in an emergency can be a few hours, at most, from any point in the UK by using Livescan or Lantern, digital photography and secure email, or by driving the fingerprints direct to a fingerprint bureau. The best that DNA can manage is around 12 hours.

3. If the CSI knows contamination has occurred he/she can warn the scientist and, occasionally, there may be a way to overcome the problem. If there is a suspicion or accusation that it has occurred then there may be no resolution, particularly if the Crown is 'ambushed' in court. By ensuring rigorous standards at the scene (or elsewhere) and by admitting mistakes the prosecution might be able to rebut these accusations. The most important point is: never allow contamination to occur. But if it does then honesty is the best policy.

TASK 5

1. Destroy the entire kit and start again with a new kit.
2. Code D.
3. Compare the result to the diagram in 25.7.1.
4. Nylon. Nylon bags are crinkly and rustle like a crisp packet: remember 'Nylon is Noisy'.
5. Yes. There is nothing to prevent an officer asking for a sample in an emergency (and assisting, to an extent, in its collection). However; the human rights of the individual must be respected and officers should act with common decency.
6. Six pieces from the frame (around the hole), and mark the inside or outside of each piece.

26 Prosecution and Court Procedures

26.1   Introduction

It is tempting to see prosecution as simply the final stage of a process which often starts with a report of a crime, its recording, the charging of suspects, and investigation. However, as all experienced police officers know, prosecution is often a lengthy and complex affair, and many aspects are not solely in the control of the police.

Statements, MG forms, and other information will often be an important element in the decision to prosecute a person for a crime, and could also be influential in the decision by the accused to plead guilty to a charge (as so-called 'advanced information', which is provided in advance of a 'guilty' or 'not guilty' plea).

There are two forms of prosecution: written and criminal charge. Relatively minor offences such as traffic violations are normally dealt with by the former. This is a relatively straightforward process, although care has to be taken to ensure that time limits are met and policy guidelines followed. Since April 2010, either the police or the CPS can take the responsibility to charge (a resumption of earlier practice—until recently the CPS had sole responsibility). In broad terms the police decide on charging in the case of most 'volume crimes' that are either summary only or (in the case of an envisaged guilty plea) either-way offences normally dealt with at magistrates' courts. The offences that can be prosecuted by the police are known as 'specified proceedings' and are listed in the Prosecution of Offences Act 1985 (Specified Proceedings) Order 1999. Additional offences were added to the list in November 2012 through the Prosecution of Offences Act 1985 (Specified Proceedings) (Amendment No. 3) Order 2012. These include: careless or inconsiderate driving; failing to comply with a traffic direction; failing to stop, report an accident or give information or documents; being drunk in a highway, other public place or licensed premises; and throwing fireworks in a thoroughfare.

The CPS take responsibility for decisions on charging those individuals suspected of committing an indictable offence and/or more complex cases; hence in general the more 'serious' crimes. The test used by both the police and the CPS (called the 'Full Code Test') to decide on prosecution is based on two questions: Is there enough evidence to prosecute? Is prosecution in the public interest? If the answer is yes to both questions, then a prosecution is expected to take place. (Further details are to be found in the Code for Crown Prosecutors, which can be accessed online through the CPS website.) A CPS 'charging standard' might be used to determine the precise charge or charges made against an individual. For example, a suspected shoplifter might be charged with 'Theft contrary to section 1(1) and 7 of the Theft Act 1968' and in this case the charging standard would involve a consideration of the five elements of the offence (dishonesty, appropriation, property, belonging to another, permanent intention to deprive). It is around this stage that the 'suspect' becomes a 'defendant'.

The 'police officer in the case' prepares the case files or is in charge of a team of people for this purpose. He/she is also likely to have made the arrest, arranged for the charge, carried out the interview, and prepared the case papers for the CPS. The officer will liaise with the CPS lawyer(s) and is expected to ensure that any exhibits in police possession are made available to the court, and will then give evidence in court. The CPS will review the prosecution on a regular basis and offer advice to the police about the evidential requirements and even what lines of enquiry might need further exploration. The prosecution may be discontinued if the CPS decide that the Full Code Test is not satisfied.

In this chapter we examine those aspects of prosecution and court procedures which are most relevant to trainee officers and students on pre-join programmes.

26.2 Record, Retain, Reveal, and Disclose

Here we look at the need to 'record, retain, and reveal' information gathered during an investigation. *Record*, *Retain*, and *Reveal* is often referred to as the '3 Rs' in police training. The CPS then decides which information should be disclosed to the defence. You should note that 'revealing to the CPS' and 'disclosing to the defence' are two separate processes, but both are often (perhaps confusingly) referred to as 'disclosure'.

These matters are covered during initial police training as part of the IPLDP module LPG 1.7. Your ability to properly record and retain material is also addressed explicitly in a number of Diploma in Policing assessed units, notably the unit 'Gather and submit information to support law enforcement objectives' and the Certificate in Knowledge of Policing unit 'Knowledge of gathering and submitting information to support law enforcement objectives within a policing context'. The legislation around disclosure is complex, as recent research continues to demonstrate. The information presented here is drawn largely (but not exclusively) from the Criminal Procedure and Investigations Act 1996 (CPIA) and its associated Code of Practice, but we also refer to the Disclosure Manual (CPS, 2006).

Some officers regard revelation and disclosure as a process that both confuses the courts and facilitates the work of the defence. However, investigations need to be conducted as a search for the truth and so the police investigator has to actively search out evidence which will not only point to guilt, but also (with equal enthusiasm) any evidence which points to innocence. The prosecution has access to significant professional services and capabilities for producing evidence for the prosecution, while the defence case may be constructed by only one person, the defence solicitor. Put another way, it could be said that disclosure helps create a 'level playing field' or 'equality of arms'.

Before we examine the 3 Rs in detail we will first illustrate the importance of this topic with an example. Imagine a case in a local magistrates' court where the prosecution counsel opens the case by outlining the circumstances in which a major public disturbance had taken place in the town centre. The incident had been witnessed by a number of people. Officers from the nearby police station and surrounding areas had attended and a woman was arrested. The arresting officer consequently provided a statement regarding the arrest and other statements were taken from a number of independent witnesses. These provided good evidence of an assault by the defendant. The CPS decided to prosecute, a case file was built, and the suspect is now in court.

A witness of the disturbance first gives evidence for the prosecution, and is then cross-examined by the defence counsel. Next, the arresting officer takes the witness stand and the prosecution asks him to outline the evidence of the arrest. After this has been done, the defence counsel rises, and says:

> **Defence:** Officer, I have only two questions for you…we will hear shortly from my client that there were several other police officers at the scene of the alleged assault. Who were these other officers and why are they not giving evidence today?
> **AO:** There were approximately ten officers at the scene; I do not know their names as they came from a neighbouring police area.
> **Defence:** Officer, the last witness has told this court that, when you arrived at the location, you had a conversation with him about what actually happened. Where are your notes of that conversation?
> **AO:** I have no record of the conversation; I remembered the name and address and then a statement was taken later.

The defendant now takes the stand and tells the court the reason for the assault was self-defence and that the arresting officer was completely wrong about how drunk she was. The defence counsel asks his client if there is anyone who can corroborate what she is saying and she replies that, if the other police officers and witnesses had been at court, they would be able to confirm her account, but not the police officer's account.

Investigation and Prosecution

The focus of the lawyer has now switched from what his client actually did at the scene (which is what you are probably thinking is the most important issue), to examining the efficiency of the police officer in relation to recording the verbal transactions with the accused, and ensuring that the lines of enquiry to identify the other police officers had been adequately undertaken. The defence applies to stay the proceedings on the basis that their client is being deprived of the right to a fair trial under Sch1, Art 6 to the Human Rights Act 1998 (see 5.4), stating that the prosecution have effectively prevented their access to a number of witnesses who are crucial to the defence of their client. Alternatively they might apply for a stay of proceedings on the grounds of an abuse of process. The magistrates retire to deliberate.

Whether the application would have been successful or not in this imaginary case is irrelevant here. The point we wish to make is that a lot of time and effort can be wasted if important information is not recorded, and that cases can be lost as a consequence.

> **TASK 1** What sort of information could the arresting officer have recorded in relation to this case?

26.2.1   Relevant material

These two words have a precise meaning in law and it is important to note that relevant material has a much wider meaning than, for example, 'evidential material'. The Disclosure Manual (CPS, 2006) suggests the following meanings (rephrased in our words):

* material refers to information and objects obtained in the course of a criminal investigation, and includes written materials, videotapes, and information given orally; and
* these materials are relevant when they have a bearing on any offence under investigation or any person being investigated, or on the surrounding circumstances of the case.

In general terms, all relevant material obtained or generated during the course of an investigation must be recorded and retained, even if it is not subsequently used by the prosecution. If it is not recorded, (or is recorded wrongly), or is not retained then it is 'lost' to the defence, and hence has not been properly shared with them through the CPS. This could be a serious loophole that the defence may exploit as in the example in 26.2.

It may be difficult to recognize whether materials are relevant (whether they do or do not have a bearing on an investigation and any possible subsequent criminal case). It is impossible to accurately predict a defence strategy, but the decision on retention often needs to be made very quickly. It is important to remember that the responsibility to record and retain relevant material does not relate just to prosecution material, but also to material which might assist the defence.

As an example, imagine that CCTV recordings of an incident involving assault outside a nightclub in the centre of a town have been collected. The recording would need to be reviewed and considered in terms of whether it contains relevant material with a bearing on:

* the offence under investigation;
* any person being investigated; or
* the circumstances surrounding the alleged offence.

That much is obvious. However, the test of relevance applies to both the potential defence and the prosecution in a case. The recording is relevant material if it is of potential use to either party involved in any subsequent prosecution. It may portray events that do not provide evidence on who hit whom, and when, with what force, and at what time, and so on. However, if the tape shows the suspect talking to a bouncer outside the club, this could be an alibi for the suspect and the material would be relevant. If, on the other hand, the content of the recording is considered irrelevant, then there is no legal requirement to retain it, but a summary should be made of what it showed.

26.2.2   Record

The officer in charge of the investigation is responsible for ensuring that relevant material is recorded in a durable or retrievable form. This could be in writing, on video- or audiotape, or on a computer drive. The record should be made when received or as soon as possible afterwards.

The following is a list of material which is routinely recorded and retained, as described in para 5.4 of the CPIA Code of Practice:

1. **Crime reports** (including crime report forms, relevant parts of incident report books, and your PNB).
2. **Custody records**.
3. Records which are derived from **tapes of telephone messages** (eg 999 and 112 calls) containing descriptions of an alleged offence or offender.
4. Final versions of **witness statements** (and draft versions, where their content differs from the final version), including any exhibits mentioned (unless these have been returned to their owner on the understanding that they will be produced in court if required).
5. **Interview records** (written records, or audio- or videotapes, of interviews with actual or potential witnesses or suspects).
6. **Communications between the police and experts** such as forensic scientists, reports of work carried out by experts, and schedules of scientific material prepared by the expert for the investigator, for the purposes of criminal proceedings.
7. Records of the **first description of a suspect** by each potential witness who purports to identify or describe the suspect, whether or not the description differs from subsequent descriptions by that or other witnesses.
8. Any material casting **doubt** on the reliability of a witness.

There is a particularly important point concerning potential witnesses, known to exist by the police, but not interviewed. In the case of *R v Heggart and Heggart* (November 2000 (CA)), it was determined that the courts should assume that any evidence from un-interviewed witnesses would either undermine the prosecution case or assist the defence case. Therefore, in the example of the court case given earlier a record should have been made of any witness details and what they observed in relation to the incident at the scene. There is, however, a notion of proportionality here: there would be no expectation to record the details of all 25,000 spectators at a large football match.

26.2.3 Retain

Material relevant to an investigation must be retained for a certain period of time. The amount of time is dependent upon a number of factors, such as whether the case continues to court and the outcome if it does, such as whether the suspect is acquitted, or the length of sentence following conviction. This is explained in more detail in para 5.8 of the CPIA Code.

26.2.4 Reveal

Material that forms part of the prosecution case is referred to as evidential and will be exhibited and form part of the prosecution case. But it is very likely that there will be other relevant material that is not used by the prosecution for the case. This 'unused material' will be revealed to the CPS by the 'disclosure officer' on form MG 6C (see 26.3.1 on MG forms).

The type of offence under investigation and local force procedures will determine who will be designated as the 'disclosure officer' for a case. In routine and minor cases, the arresting officer or the case officer will also be the disclosure officer. In more serious cases it is a specific and dedicated specialist role, and it will not necessarily be a police officer.

26.2.5 Disclosure

Disclosure is a term used in policing and legal circles, and according to the Prosecution Team Manual of Guidance (drawing on the Criminal Justice Act 2003 amendments) it refers to:

> providing the defence with copies of, or access to, any material which might reasonably be considered capable of undermining the case for the prosecution against the accused, or of assisting the case for the accused, and which has not previously been disclosed.

This is referred to as 'the disclosure test'.

There are four disclosure forms: MG 6 B to E. The items which are going to be disclosed are recorded on a form MG 6E, and the disclosure officer ensures that copies of these items are provided to the defence. The CPS then reviews all the disclosure forms and decides what else should be disclosed and when. Some of the more sensitive information revealed to the CPS will not be disclosed, such as personal details of a CHIS (see 22.2 on the use of a CHIS) or of a person giving information through the Crimestoppers scheme. It would be marked confidential and recorded on an MG 6D form.

Failure to disclose the activity of an undercover police officer and evidence which may have helped the defence's case led to the convictions of 20 appellants being quashed in the high-profile case of *R v Barkshire and others* ([2011] EWCA Crim 1885). The appellants had been convicted of conspiracy to commit aggravated trespass in preparation for protests against climate change at a power station at Ratcliffe-on-Soar. The prosecution failed, amongst other things, to disclose the action of an undercover police officer who had infiltrated the group and could have been seen to be inciting the events himself.

TASK 2

1. Reference is made earlier to material that is relevant but non-evidential and therefore will not be used as evidence. In relation to the disclosure process, what title will this material be given?
2. Who is responsible for examining the records created during the investigation with a view to revealing the material to the prosecutor?
3. What forms are used when non-evidential relevant material is revealed to the prosecutor?

26.3 Preparing and Submitting Case Files

The interview record (see 24.5.7) and the MG 6 forms (see 26.2) would be included in the case file for any subsequent prosecution. But numerous other forms will be involved, including charge sheets, lists of exhibits (often forensic evidence), and so on. Successful investigations require the preparation and submitting of good quality and accurate case files. Paperwork is rarely popular, but all officers acknowledge the particular importance of case files. Case-file preparation must not be regarded as a mere technical exercise—the successful prosecution of a person who is guilty of a serious offence will depend on the case file. The topic is usually covered during the second year of initial police training. The 'Finalize Investigation' PAC heading lists the following as targets to be achieved before Independent Patrol; 'Complete pre-charge files', 'Complete post-charge files', and 'Complete summons files'.

In addition to any notes and training you may receive, you could also download and read section 1 of the 2011 edition of the *Prosecution Team Manual of Guidance* (ACPO, 2011d).

26.3.1 MG forms

The forms for case files are often referred to as 'MG forms' (the MG stands for Manual of Guidance). Information such as the suspect's details and the case file reference number will be common on each form. It is likely that such information will be accessed through an interface with the NSPIS Custody and Case Preparation Programme which will have been uploaded when the suspect was first presented to the custody officer upon arrest (see 10.10.2).

Here we cover only the MG forms that a trainee police officer is likely to require. These are for:

- straightforward cases (ie, without complications such as certain sensitive disclosure issues) where a guilty plea is entered; and
- contested ('not guilty' pleas) or Crown Court cases.

Charging decisions are usually based on the information received by the CPS. This will include forms MG 3 and MG 3A and any key evidence (ACPO, 2011d). Before a charging decision has been made, the required case file is known as a Pre-charge Expedited file. Once the charge has been made, a Post-charge Expedited File is required for the court. If a 'not guilty' plea is entered, or if the case is to be heard in Crown Court, upgrading to a Full File is required. If the case is disposed of at the first court appearance, then upgrading is not required.

The likely case-file forms in each eventuality are summarized in the table (CPS, 2004). A tick indicates that it is very likely a particular form will be needed, and a question mark indicates that the form might be needed. The *Prosecution Team Manual of Guidance* (section 3) provides detailed guidance on the completion of MG forms (ACPO, 2011d).

Form	Description	Straightforward		Contested		Full file
		pre-	post-	pre-	post-	
MG 1	File front sheet		✓		✓	✓
MG 2	Initial witness assessment		?		?	?
MG 3	Report to Crown Prosecutor		?			
MG 3A	Further report to Crown Prosecutor		?		?	
MG 4	Charge sheet		✓		✓	
MG 4A	Conditional bail form		?		?	
MG 4B	Request to vary police conditional bail		?		?	
MG 4C	Surety/security		?		?	
MG 5	Case file summary; might include SDN (see later in table)		✓			
MG 6	Case file information		✓		?	
MG 6B	Police officer's disciplinary record					?
MG 6C	Schedule of non-sensitive unused material					✓
MG 6D	Schedule of sensitive material					✓
MG 6E	Disclosure officer's report					✓
MG 7	Remand application		?		?	?
MG 8	Breach of bail conditions		?			
MG 9	Witness list					✓
MG 10	Witness non-availability	✓	✓		✓	
MG 11	Witness statement(s)		✓			
MG 12	Exhibits list			✓	✓	✓
MG 13	Application for order on conviction		?		?	
MG 15	Interview record (SDN, ROTI, or ROVI*)	✓		✓	✓	✓
MG 18	Offences taken into consideration		?		?	?
MG 19	Compensation form (plus supporting documents)		?		?	?
SDN	Short Descriptive Note; may be written on MG 15, MG 5, or officer's MG 11		✓			✓
Phoenix print	Computer print-out of the suspect's previous convictions, cautions, etc	✓	✓	✓	✓	✓
Copy of documentary exhibits/photos			✓	✓		✓
Police racist incident form/crime report			?		?	?
Crime report and incident log			✓			
Any unused material which might undermine the case					✓	
Custody record						✓

* ROTI: Record Of a Taped Interview; ROVI: Record Of a Video-recorded Interview; both are written documents summarizing the content of the recordings

26.4 Forms of Evidence

Evidence is information which is presented to a court so that it may decide upon a fact ('Did the accused do this act by this means?'). In the sense that we use the word throughout this Handbook, evidence is almost always linked with crime in some way. Evidence is usually regarded as consisting of four kinds:

- oral (also called verbal or spoken);
- real (an article, object, or thing with material existence; that is, it can be produced in court);
- documentary (a document, paper, or record, which can be electronic);
- hearsay.

We also consider bad character evidence. The nature and types of evidence are covered during initial police training, for example in LPG 1.7 'Investigation and Interviews'.

26.4.1 Oral evidence

This is the most common form of evidence presented to a court. A witness will say 'I saw him push the block over the parapet of the bridge', or 'I heard her scream and then felt a hand on my bottom', or 'The drink tasted really bitter after I came back from the toilet'. It is what has been directly experienced by someone on the spot at the time that the alleged offence was committed. A witness to an act must have perceived (seen, heard, felt, tasted, or smelled) that act directly, through his/her senses.

Under s 9 of the Criminal Justice Act 1967, a witness statement can be read out in court in the place of oral evidence from the witness (and hence is often referred to as a 'section 9 statement').

26.4.2 Real evidence

This is any article or thing which can be produced for the court, however large or small. Real evidence can range from microscopic bloodstains or particles of explosive, through to objects which the court will have to see *in situ* (eg a large lorry, a crash site, or piece of machinery). It must have a material existence independent of anything else, but its link to the accused generally has to have supporting testimony, such as 'This is the iron bar which I saw him holding', or 'These bloodstains were recovered from the clothing worn by the accused at the time of his arrest, and which match the blood type of the man found lying in the stairwell'. The significance of a piece of real evidence usually has to be explained in court, especially if the relevant item is not within everyone's common experience, such as an explosive detonator for triggering a bomb, or the motherboard from a computer.

> **TASK 3** Can you think of potential problems associated with the use of, and production in court, of 'real evidence'?

It is the responsibility of the reporting or arresting police officer to ensure the secure retention of exhibits and their production to the court. There must be an auditable trail for the article produced as real evidence, from the moment it was discovered or recovered until it is produced in court. This is referred to as 'continuity of evidence' or the 'chain of evidence', and it simply means that the prosecution must be able to prove that the article has been held securely and that it has not been tampered with, modified, or changed in any way. In complex cases, an exhibits officer will be appointed to the case, and in some police forces a designated specialist is responsible for safeguarding certain materials, such as forensic items or CCTV footage. Further details on the procedures for ensuring the continuity of evidence are provided in 11.2.6 and Chapter 25.

26.4.3 Documentary evidence

This is written material (including electronic records of documents) which is produced in court. The medium through which it is written can vary from a 'Last Will and Testament' on parchment with spidery copperplate writing, to an electronic file recording the use of a credit card over the internet. A document is of course also 'real evidence', but is separately classed because of its referential nature and because often authorship can be proven (which would be more difficult with a common-pattern kitchen knife, for instance).

The rules about the legal status of documents are complex but the general point is that the document should be produced in court by the person who created it and who can testify to its contents. This is not always possible (eg for a will) but a court can ask for a handwriting expert to testify that, within limitations, the author of one particular document is likely to be the author of another particular document. This becomes even more complex when it comes to electronic text, and specialists differ over degrees of certainty about the authorship of, for example, web documents, particularly if they are not signed or copyrighted. Some documents are seized as evidence by the police and are submitted to the court—the classic example is a suicide note. The points made about 'continuity of evidence' in 26.4.2 also apply to documents.

26.4.4 Hearsay evidence

This is evidence provided by one person about what another person said. Hearsay can also include documents whose existence cannot be proven by the author, or whose contents cannot be similarly proven. It is generally inadmissible in court because of the potential for ambiguity or malice ('She told me that he threw the knife…' is not evidence). The acceptability of hearsay evidence in the UK was debated in the European Court of Human Rights (ECHR). It was feared it might breach Article 6 of the ECHR (which establishes the right to a fair and public hearing) by not allowing the defence the opportunity, for example, to cross-examine an absent witness. The ECHR recently found that hearsay evidence does not necessarily represent a breach of Article 6 and that the circumstances of each trial need to be taken into account (*Al-Khawaja & Tahery v UK* [2012] 2 Costs LO 139).

> **TASK 4** There are a number of exceptions which allow for hearsay evidence to be used. Can you think of any possible exceptions that might apply?

26.4.4.1 Hearsay evidence and the Criminal Justice Act 2003

In legal terms, s 114 of the Criminal Justice Act 2003 defines hearsay evidence as 'any statement not made in oral evidence in the proceedings'. For example, the victim might say something significant to a friend, who then makes a statement about it to the police (see 23.3.2). The friend's statement would be 'hearsay' because the friend only knows what he/she has been told by the victim. The CJA changed the law relating to the admissibility of hearsay evidence in criminal proceedings. The old law was criticized for being too complicated and difficult to obtain (because it was in different Acts of Parliament or case law), and too inflexible. In an infamous trial for indecent assault (*R v Sparks* (1964)) the court would not allow a defendant to use certain evidence and he was convicted. (He subsequently appealed and was successful, but only on other grounds.)

The new law can be seen as a major shift in attitude towards hearsay evidence. The four 'gateways' to admissibility of hearsay evidence are:

1. The CJA or any other Act indicates it may be used. (This will include, for instance, when a witness has given evidence to police but cannot attend court due to illness, and statements from a person (eg a victim's friend) about what the victim had told them about the incident (s 120 CJA).)
2. Any of the common law exceptions which have been preserved by the CJA (including confession evidence).
3. All parties to the proceedings agree to the evidence being given.
4. The court concludes that in the interests of justice the hearsay evidence should be admitted.

Gateway 4 is particularly welcomed by the prosecution for hearsay evidence that does not fit any of the recognized exceptions (sometimes referred to as the 'safety valve'). A recent example can be found in the decision by the Court of Appeal (Criminal Division), which accepted hearsay evidence consisting of a police officer's record of a conversation with a 14-year-old witness. This contained details of the witness's relationship with the offender, and was accepted on the grounds that it was useful to confirm the evidence that had been given by the offender and later denied (*Burton v R* [2011] EWCA Crim 1990).

A trainee officer does not have to learn all the details of all these provisions, but he/she must remember to record (in his/her PNB) exactly what is said.

26.4.5 Bad Character Evidence (BCE)

When dealing with criminal cases, officers should always consider whether relevant bad character exists. The law makes it clear that reprehensible behaviour falling short of a conviction counts as bad character, as well as obvious instances, such as previous convictions. For instance, a person may have a propensity to be violent if he/she gets drunk, and this may become relevant in a case of assault against a family member, irrespective of whether the accused has been previously convicted in relation to similar behaviour.

Bad character evidence (BCE) is likely to be covered during initial police training as it features in IPLDP Operational Module 9 'Prepare and present case information, present evidence, and finalise investigations' and under LPG 1.4 'Bad character evidence'. Here we provide an overview of bad character evidence introduced by the Criminal Justice Act 2003 and which is relevant to the trainee officer. The CPS website provides information on bad character evidence and the NPIA produced Practice Advice on Evidence of Bad Character on behalf of ACPO, which trainee officers may wish to consult via their force. The College of Policing Authorised Professional Practice website also contains further information (under the heading 'Prosecution and case management').

26.4.5.1 The definition of bad character

Bad character is defined by s 98 of the Criminal Justice Act 2003 as evidence of:

- misconduct, including pre-convictions (offences for which a person has been charged, but the charge has not been heard or the person was acquitted (s 112));
- a disposition towards misconduct, for example 'other reprehensible behaviour' (s 112), which is likely to include anti-social behaviour, persistent lying, and racist behaviour.

The evidence for BCE cannot come from the offence currently under investigation, nor can it be related to the process of the current proceeding (eg the defendant not attending court when required). Therefore police officers should record matters that might relate to bad character evidence contemporaneously, and provide such intelligence to the relevant department. This information could be crucial to a subsequent criminal investigation.

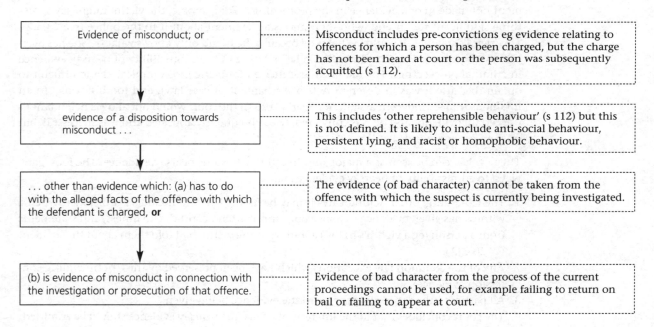

| Evidence of misconduct; or | Misconduct includes pre-convictions eg evidence relating to offences for which a person has been charged, but the charge has not been heard at court or the person was subsequently acquitted (s 112). |

| evidence of a disposition towards misconduct ... | This includes 'other reprehensible behaviour' (s 112) but this is not defined. It is likely to include anti-social behaviour, persistent lying, and racist or homophobic behaviour. |

| ... other than evidence which: (a) has to do with the alleged facts of the offence with which the defendant is charged, **or** | The evidence (of bad character) cannot be taken from the offence with which the suspect is currently being investigated. |

| (b) is evidence of misconduct in connection with the investigation or prosecution of that offence. | Evidence of bad character from the process of the current proceedings cannot be used, for example failing to return on bail or failing to appear at court. |

26.4.5.2 Introducing BCE in court

The defence or the prosecution can apply to the judge under s 100 of the Criminal Justice Act 2003 for BCE to be used in court. The main principle is to protect witnesses and victims from having their previous history brought up unless it is relevant to the case. Where the defendant wishes to raise the previous sexual history of a complainant, this is likely to be excluded by virtue of s 41 of the Youth Justice and Criminal Evidence Act 1999 (YJCEA 1999), unless it is relevant and admissible. Case law shows that judges are unlikely to allow BCE evidence to be introduced unless it is really significant and relevant (see *R v Bovell* [2005] 2 Cr App R 401).

For a defendant, s 101(1) of the Criminal Justice Act 2003 lists the seven circumstances where BCE is admissible. This does not require leave of the judge, but does require the prosecution to give notice to the defence regarding the BCE they propose to call. In some cases, the defence can apply to disallow its use.

> **TASK 5** Find out which MG form is used to record BCE in a defendant's case file.

26.5 Giving Evidence in Court

Now we have come to the stage where the final phases of the investigative process will be played out: the courts. The role of magistrates' courts and the Crown Court is explained in 5.5. Here, we will concentrate on what happens during a case, with particular emphasis on the likely role of a trainee officer.

The course of events in a magistrates' court, and more so in the Crown Court, could be said to bear a striking resemblance to scenes in a theatre. The participants perform very particular roles and many of the 'rituals' are quite theatrical, and may appear strange to people who are not familiar with the system.

The 'actors' in the court

Participants and others	Description of the role
The Magistrate(s)	Concerned local citizens who act 'for the people' in hearing petty offences or the evidence of crimes
District Judge	The paid professional dealing with local offences
Justices' Clerk	The paid professional who knows the law and advises the lay magistrates
The Accused	In the dock and trying to create the best possible impression, whether guilty or not
Prosecution	The retributive voice of the people; a professional lawyer (Crown Prosecution Service)
Defence	The upholder of justice acting for the client(s); a professional barrister or solicitor
The Public	The 'theatre audience' (but can include relatives of the victim and the accused, with a definite interest in the outcome)
The Judge	In Crown Court, a professional lawyer whose legal experience qualifies him/her to assume the role of objective and dispassionate 'arbiter'
The Jury	The jury is nominally '12 good persons and true' and is present in Crown Court trials at which the defendant has pleaded 'not guilty'. The members of the jury are theoretically drawn from any walk of life (including police officers)
Witnesses	Some witnesses may be overwhelmed by the big occasion but specialists with expert knowledge (eg pathologists or forensic scientists) are more accustomed to appearing in court
The Media	Usually present at big trials and apt to dramatize events as much as possible. Court reporters are almost always present at the petty level

This is the cast of players, with the first likely to appear at the magistrates' court (where the drama is often brief and low-key) and the remainder at the Crown Court (where tensions can run high). Add to this heady mix the panelled courtroom, the eighteenth-century costumes and wigs, the rituals, and the ceremony, and you have a stage set. The bowing to the coats of arms as representing the presence of the Queen is one such formality. It may be considered somewhat trivializing or even inappropriate to refer to the enactment of justice as a play, and the venue as a stage set. However, the analogy may help you appreciate some aspects of the culture of a courtroom. There is, of course, no substitute for familiarizing yourself directly with court procedure at all levels by visiting courts and observing the procedures live.

For a trainee police officer, giving evidence features as one of the PAC headings, a key aspect of qualifying to undertake Independent Patrol. However, after qualifying a police officer might not attend court again for years; indeed, to some extent the opportunities to experience court during training are specially arranged. Police officers are unlikely to need to give evidence in court unless they are a detective working on volume crime or involved in a major police operation. Part of the reason for this is that the proportion of 'guilty' pleas has increased over the years, probably because of advances in DNA evidence and the increased availability of discounted sentences in return for a guilty plea at an early stage. Also statutory fines or penalties are used to a much greater extent (see 10.13.2). However, as court appearances by police officers now tend to relate to more serious offences and involve a substantial criminal trial, it is all the more important to get it right.

26.5.1 The adversarial justice system in court

In the dramatic setting of the court, the contest is played out between the two adversaries or opponents, the defence and prosecution lawyers. The defendant can choose to conduct his/her own defence, although this is rare in a criminal trial.

The defence and the prosecution must comply with the rules of evidence. The prosecution has a duty to ensure that all relevant evidence is disclosed (see 26.2.5), but the defence has no such obligation unless it is expert witness testimony. The defence occasionally challenges the prosecution's case and asks for the prosecution to cease. For example, the judge can be asked to dismiss the case at a Plea and Direction hearing (PDH) before the trial begins. The admissibility of critical evidence might be challenged, and if successful the case for the prosecution inevitably fails. Alternatively, the challenge might come later on in the trial, and is very likely to occur if a key witness fails to confirm (orally) the evidence in his/her written statements. The judge can also halt a trial for similar reasons and direct a jury to acquit, but this is rare.

The defence will challenge (in the following order) whether:

- the alleged offence actually took place (eg in a rape case, when a point to prove has not been established in the evidence);
- the defendant did it (perhaps he/she has an alibi);
- the defendant had the requisite intention (the act was unintentional or there were justifiable reasons for the act, such as self-defence); and/or
- something was wrong in the process which brought the defendant to court.

This last point can be used even if it seems very likely the defendant clearly did commit the crime (eg if there is very strong DNA prosecution evidence) and there is little to be said in mitigation. The defence could claim for example that the relevant PACE 1984 and CPIA 1996 Codes of Practice had not been followed, and suggest that the trial is flawed and unfair, and the judge will be asked to dismiss the evidence and any related charges.

Indeed, it is the role of the defence counsel to expose flaws in the prosecution case if that helps the defendant. Some people feel uncomfortable with these aspects of the defence counsel's role, believing such approaches to be morally ambiguous. This misses the point: the role of the defence is to do anything it can (within legal and ethical bounds) to act in the defendant's best interest, including exploiting loopholes in the law.

So, in this sense, the police have to get it absolutely right every time, whilst the defence does not. That is why we place so much emphasis here on getting the procedure right every time.

26.5.1.1 A court as a public arena

Both the Crown Court and magistrates' courts have a public gallery, and anyone can watch any trial or hearing in progress (although in exceptional circumstances a case is held in camera and the public are excluded).

When friends or relatives of the defendant and the accuser attend, public order problems may occasionally occur. If this seems likely the ushers and security staff should be alerted to this possibility. The judge or chairman of the bench may warn the public gallery about the possible consequences of disruptive behaviour, such as removal or arrest for contempt of court. Whilst efforts have been made to alter courtroom layouts to avoid such a possibility, a member of a jury may still be intimidated by glares and gestures ('eyeballed') from the defendant's circle of associates. In such circumstances the public gallery may be cleared, leaving the press bench to represent the public's interest. It is not just in the courtroom that these problems arise, however: in communal corridors, cafes, and smoking areas, the defendant's associates and the witnesses for the prosecution have opportunities to meet. If necessary, separate rooms are available in most courts for witnesses to sit away from other people. Intimidation of juries and witnesses is covered in 14.6.

Police officers are not immune from threats or intimidation, and should identify and bring to the court's attention any person who challenges, or seeks to threaten or intimidate an officer. Common times for this are when a police officer is leaving court at the close of the day, or is away from the court during a lunch break.

26.5.2 Court procedures

Evidence is usually presented in court in the form of the testimony of a witness. As we noted earlier, witnesses give evidence of what they heard, saw, smelled, tasted, or felt. Sometimes, an expert witness may be asked to give an opinion, such as a pathologist giving an opinion on the cause of death in a murder case, but ordinary witnesses (including police officers) will seldom be asked for an opinion. Witnesses who attend courts frequently (eg police officers) are known as professional witnesses, as distinct from expert witnesses.

On the basis of the given evidence, the bench or district judge (in a magistrates' court) or the jury (in the Crown court) will decide whether the accused is guilty or not. In the case of the Crown Court, if the accused pleads guilty, there will be no need for a jury, and the hearing or trial will be much shorter.

26.5.2.1 The notification to attend court

At the outset witnesses are 'warned for court'. For a magistrates' court the notification to attend will be a simple letter or notice stating the date and time. For the Crown Court, there are two forms of witness warning—a 'conditional' and a 'full' warning. A conditional warning is used when the witness's evidence is not likely to be contested and so the witness may not be required to attend court. If nothing more is announced or communicated then he/she can 'stand by' and is unlikely to give evidence (unless either side move to have the witness called—perhaps if the trial takes an unexpected turn). Note, however, that he/she still should not discuss the evidence with any third party. A witness receiving a full warning will certainly be called to attend, but still might not be called to give evidence.

Waiting for a notification to attend court can be a frustratingly long, drawn-out process. It could be said that the delay serves the purposes of the defence team as, the longer a case is delayed, the fainter are the witnesses' recollections, and the less detail people can remember. Most magistrates and judges are wise to this defence tactic and will deal with it after a reasonable period, but some will not. If the defence appears to be postponing or prolonging matters unnecessarily the CPS lawyer can make a representation to the defence, or if necessary to the judge. Once in court, a case may still not be heard quickly: it may be put back, postponed, rescheduled, or otherwise not heard on that day for any number of technical or procedural reasons.

26.5.2.2 The oath

Evidence must be given on oath by any witness or defendant at a statutory legal process, including a magistrates' court or the Crown Court. The Perjury Act 1911 and the Oaths Act 1978 require that a person must be sworn in the particular form or manner which is binding on his/her conscience.

Taking the oath

Belief system or religion	Wording of the oath
Most Christians	'I swear by almighty God...'
Hindus	'I swear by the Gita...'
Muslims	'I swear by Allah...'
Sikhs	'I swear by Guru Nanak...'
All non-believers, most Buddhists, some Quakers, Jehovah's Witnesses, and others	'I do solemnly, sincerely, and truly declare and affirm...'

Those adhering to a religious belief touch or hold (covered or uncovered) their respective holy books when giving the oath, but there may be other observances involved such as a ritual washing.

Perjury is when a person lies under oath. It is a serious criminal offence under the Perjury Act 1911. A person commits perjury when he/she wilfully makes a 'statement material in that proceeding, which he knows to be false or does not believe to be true' (s 1(1) and (2)), having been lawfully sworn as a witness or as an interpreter in a court or tribunal, or before any person legally empowered to hear and assess evidence. A court determines whether the statement was 'material' or not for the proceedings (s 1(6)). The false statement must have been made deliberately and not merely by mistake, and the testimony of only one witness (alleging that the statement was false) is not sufficient for a conviction (s 13).

Perjury is an offence in criminal and civil proceedings, punishable on indictment with a maximum of seven years' imprisonment or a fine (CPS, 2012a), and the punishment must reflect the seriousness of the original offence (*R v Dunlop* [2001] 2 Cr App R (S) 27). Although perjury will in most cases amount to perverting the course of justice, the two offences (perjury and perverting the course of justice) should not be confused. Perverting the course of justice could be arranging a false alibi, but lying about it in court would be perjury. A prosecution for perjury is appropriate when making a false statement in court is the principal act, but not if the false statement is part of a series of acts aimed at perverting the course of justice (SFO, 2010). Aiding, abetting, counselling, procuring, or suborning another person to commit perjury carries the same penalty as perjury itself (s 7(1)).

26.5.2.3 Giving evidence and cross-examination

Witness evidence is given from the witness box (often surprisingly small and modest in reality, unlike those you may have seen on TV or film). The witness should face towards the judge or the bench when giving evidence. Evidence can take a number of forms such as oral, real, documentary, or hearsay, and these are covered in detail in 26.4. Evidence-in-chief is evidence given by the witness in response to the party that called him/her as a witness.

In most straightforward cases oral evidence is given 'directly', which means providing a detailed and accurate chronology of events without any prompting. Under s 9 of the Criminal Justice Act 1967, a witness statement can be read out in court in the place of oral evidence from the witness (and hence is often referred to as a 'section 9 statement'). In more complex cases, and always at the Crown Court, evidence is given in response to questions seeking to draw out detail from the witness, and this usually follows the chronology of the events.

A visual recording of an interview with a significant witness (see 24.6.1) may be shown to the court, particularly if there are inconsistencies between the oral evidence and the recorded evidence, but a recording cannot be shown as evidence-in-chief. The court can exclude a recording if there is insufficient information about where it was made, or if the recording contains serious violations of the rules of evidence.

Once the evidence has been given (either directly or in response to the counsel's questions), the opposing counsel is likely to ask questions. This is known as cross-examination and may be quite stressful for the witness. Indeed, for some witnesses a live link may be used (see 26.5.2.4). After the cross-examination, the counsel that called the witness has the right to ask yet further questions (re-examination), but this questioning is restricted solely to matters that arose in the cross-examination, and is usually seeking clarification and removing ambiguity. And finally the judge may need to ask questions of a witness, though he/she will be very careful not to take over the role of either counsel.

After a witness has finished giving evidence the magistrate or judge gives permission for him/her to leave the witness box. There are two forms of 'permission to leave' and these are:

- to be stood down, which usually requires a witness to be available for recall; and
- to be discharged, which means the court does not expect him/her to be recalled so he/she may leave the court.

The witness can sit in the public gallery once he/she has been discharged.

26.5.2.4 Special measures in court

Some witnesses need extra help to provide their evidence effectively. This extra help is known as 'special measures' and is available for all vulnerable and intimidated witnesses (defined in 24.6.1). The special measures in court include:

- screens to shield the witness from the defendant;
- a live televised link for a witness to give evidence from outside the courtroom; and
- judges and barristers removing their wigs and gowns.

Evidence may also be given in private for cases involving sexual offences or intimidation. Members of the public and the media (except for one named person to represent the press) will be excluded from the court.

The witness's name and other identifying details may be withheld or removed from materials disclosed to any party to the proceedings. In addition, the types of questions that may be asked can be restricted if the questions and answers could lead to the witness's identification. Pseudonyms, concealing screens, and voice modulation equipment are also used.

Vulnerable witnesses may be provided with extra support in court, such as the use of an intermediary to assist the witness in giving evidence. Interpreters and other communication aids or techniques are also allowed (provided that the communication can be independently verified and understood by the court).

Video-recordings of interviews with vulnerable witnesses and ABE interviews can be shown in court as evidence-in-chief, with cross-examination being conducted by live-link CCTV from elsewhere within the court building. This applies only for vulnerable witnesses in the Crown Court, and for complainants for serious sexual offences (an intimidated witness).

Special provisions apply for child witnesses under the age of 17. The provisions (which apply equally for child witnesses for the prosecution and the defence) vary depending on the type of case but include the use of video-recordings for evidence. Any child witness can be deemed to be in need of special measures, but the need is automatically assumed for sexual cases involving violence, abduction, or neglect but the court must be satisfied that the special measures will improve the quality of the evidence.

26.5.2.5 Hostile witnesses

A barrister can ask for a witness to be deemed 'hostile' by the judge. This is when a witness has made a statement previously but declines to confirm certain details in court, and is assumed to be deliberately not telling the truth. (He/she may have been asked to change his/her story or fall silent rather than incriminate the accused.) The judge will announce his/her decision to the court, often giving reasons. The witness can then be cross-examined and challenged about his/her change of evidence, and inconsistencies between previous statements and accounts will be explored.

26.5.3 Giving evidence as a police officer

Early on in his/her career a police officer is most likely to give evidence in court as the 'officer in the case'. If this applies to you, your BCU Administrative Unit will help arrange a suitable date for the hearing.

This is the final phase of the investigation in a sense, because it is the calling to account of the case against the accused and a consideration (a weighing) of the evidence. His/her role would be to explain what he/she has done, heard, seen, or recorded, as clearly and as concisely as possible. Any witness, including you as a police officer, should avoid discussing the case in detail with colleagues or associates before, and certainly during, the trial, because recollections can be contaminated by verbally revisiting the circumstances.

26.5.3.1 Preparing for giving evidence as a police officer

After the case file has been prepared, further planning and preparation is needed for the actual process of giving evidence. As the officer in the case you would have to:

- review the case, reread the case papers, and reread your PNB;
- ensure you have a copy of your duty statement to use as a reminder, if required, while giving evidence (permitted under s 139 of the Criminal Justice Act 2003);
- familiarize yourself with the rules of evidence (particularly on hearsay evidence and opinion);
- speak to the CPS lawyer who will be prosecuting;
- prepare for dealing with predictable but difficult questions from the defence, for example on certain points of evidence;

- check that everything in the case is administratively in order, including labelling the exhibits; and
- check the arrangements for witnesses, payment of witnesses, and holding areas, particularly if they feel vulnerable to intimidation—often a room is set aside for witnesses.

You could also visit the court premises and sit through part of a case, before checking the exact location of the courtroom to be used for the case.

26.5.3.2 In the witness box as a police officer

You would introduce yourself by rank, police number, name, and the police station where you are based. When you are speaking to a person (or being spoken to) you should turn towards the other person—you will probably find yourself doing this automatically.

If you want to refer to your PNB in court, you should ask for permission. The defence may ask you to explain the manner and time of making your notes, and whether your notes represent a 'contemporaneous account' (written at the time) or whether you wrote up your PNB afterwards. Any notes made reasonably soon after the event should be acceptable, but if there is a significant time lag (two days or longer) the defence is likely to question you very closely and probably in a hostile manner. The court, prosecution, or defence may want to examine the entry itself, so make sure that your grammar and spelling are always up to scratch and that your handwriting is at least legible! They might also examine it to look for any evidence of collusion with other officers (see 10.2.3).

When giving evidence you could be tempted to try to learn your evidence by heart and then recite from memory, but this is most inadvisable. For a start it will sound rehearsed and artificial. Secondly, the defence may try to put you off with questions so that you lose your thread and flounder, and finally it suggests that maybe you do not have the confidence to rely on your recall of events. There is nothing wrong with referring to your PNB entries—after all, the lawyers and the judge constantly refer to their notes. However, you should not rely on your PNB exclusively as you will not create a good impression. It is much better to speak clearly and confidently to the court, referring only now and then to your PNB to refresh your memory, or to quote a particular detail. We discuss how to create a good impression in more detail in 26.5.3.4.

26.5.3.3 Cross-examination

As a witness you can ask the defence or anyone else to repeat a question which you did not hear, did not understand, or which you want clarified. (It also gives you an extra moment to think.) You should be prepared for the unexpected, such as 'PC Winn, what formal training have you had in interview techniques and did that training, if indeed you had it, cover the use of oppressive interrogation?' Here the defence is using a common tactic of double questioning, as well as launching straight into querying the officer's qualifications. She might choose to reply as follows:

> [to the judge] I was accredited Tier 2 Investigative Interviewing, which means I am qualified by the police in investigative interviewing, which incorporates questioning styles. I did the training at the Police training centre in August last year. I routinely undertake interviews at this level and believe I have an understanding of the term 'oppressive' as it applies in the Police and Criminal Evidence Act 1984, section 76.
> [turning back to the defence] Would you repeat the second part of your question, sir?

Note her politeness and refusal to be flustered or stampeded by the defence's approach. In fact, the completeness of her first reply establishes her as a professional and credible witness, and the defence may seem merely querulous (questioning for its own sake). If the defence persisted in making an innuendo in such a deliberately challenging tone the judge might intervene to ask where it is leading and how is it relevant, and whether the defence is raising an issue for consideration for exclusion of the evidence. You might also have noticed how PC Winn 'collects' the question from the lawyer and delivers her answer directly to the judge, before politely asking the defence lawyer for the second part of his question. This emphasizes that she has been attentive and is not to be hurried into giving confused (or confusing) answers to compound or complex questions.

The use of body language can certainly help control pace and speed. It would be best to turn back to a person asking a question only when you think you have given a complete answer and you are ready for the next question. Some eye contact with the jury is always helpful as they are the people you would need to convince on issues of fact. You should avoid a one-to-one 'conversation' with either the defence or the prosecution counsel as this is likely to be extremely irritating to the jury (they may feel distanced from the proceedings).

The defence may use a variety of approaches such as trailer questions, multiple questions, hypothetical questions, topic hopping, or out-of-sequence chronology. These should be dealt with one at a time. It is important to portray yourself to the jury as a competent professional.

The defence counsel will sometimes attempt to persuade juries that collusion has occurred between officers and that adjustments have been made to match their accounts. It is important that you limit yourself to recollections about matters that you have personal knowledge of, and can convey directly to the court, and do not adjust your evidence to correspond with another's. Imagine if you truthfully recalled in your evidence to the jury your recollection that the car you saw was green and your colleague following you into the witness box had said it was red? Both of you are telling the truth, one possibly mistaken, but this would be far better than you 'changing your recall' to having seen a red car—when the car was in fact later proved to be green! (See 10.2.3 on 'conferring with others' and your PNB.)

There will be occasions when your evidence as a police officer is favourable to the defendant, and naturally enough the defence will want to make use of this. You should expect to be questioned about how you conducted the investigation, about the evidence you have already given, and asked for any additional facts which you have not already given. It is often not what you say that is fertile territory for the cross-examination—but rather what you did not say.

26.5.3.4 Creating the right impression

The impression a police officer creates in court, as we have noted earlier, will influence his/her credibility, particularly as some members of the jury might be subjective and 'go by feel', rather than by objective fact. A variety of factors will contribute to the impression given. Imagine the situation:

> **Prosecutor:** Please tell the court what happened next.
>
> **Sergeant:** Well, John, when I got down to the edge of the, like, disco area, there was your man biggin' it up and asking all comers, like, if they wanted a piece of him, and he said 'you're 'aving a laugh', and I turned round to him and said 'you're nicked', and this other bloke says 'Nah', and he said to him 'you're a cocky sod, ain't you?' and swung a punch, like, so I stopped the music, sort of thing, and took them all in.
>
> **Prosecutor:** Then what?
>
> **Sergeant:** We got down the station and Pete Finch was on custody, no, hang on a minute, it was Debbie Johnson, I think. Just a sec. [He consults his PNB.] I got it down here somewhere.
>
> **Judge:** Sergeant, have you or have you not a record of this very confusing scene? Whom did you arrest? On what charge?
>
> **Sergeant:** Sorry, your Worship, I've got it on a bit of paper somewhere, I arrested the bloke in the dock, 'Smasher' Higgins. We know him all right, he's got a record as long as your arm. Put him away twice myself.

This exchange is deliberately exaggerated, of course, but the poor impression which the sergeant gives is not just of himself, but also of his force and the police in general. No one listening to this exchange would give the police officer any credibility and he is dangerously close to contempt of court. You might have noticed too that the sergeant reveals that the accused has a police record and has served a prison term. The defence counsel would almost certainly have intervened at this point and lodged a strong objection to the 'evidence' being given, as it is likely to prejudice the case against the accused (it does not meet any of the requirements for introducing BCE, see 26.4.5.2). A retrial might be required and the whole court process would begin afresh. This would certainly call for an inquiry and could have serious implications for the officer, and be costly for the force. In addition, the prosecution might well be abandoned.

A police officer giving evidence should always watch his/her general attitude, because an obvious bias against a defendant will actually aid the defence. More importantly, it will be deeply unhelpful to the prosecution case.

No one would advise you to talk like a legal textbook when giving your evidence but you should be careful about using jargon or slang expressions. Not only will some of these not be understood but they can give the impression of being too relaxed, or even complacent. The language of 'street cred' should be used only when expressing the flavour of an idiom, such as the language used by the accused. Another temptation is to say too much and to keep on talking. Instead, keep your answers to questions short and to the point:

Prosecutor: Constable Winn, did you see the injuries?

PC Winn: Yes, I did. This was at first during the initial interview, when Ms Bent showed me an extensive bruise to her left eye and cheekbone. She was then examined by the custody nurse for other injuries.

Prosecutor: What did you do next?

PC Winn: I arranged for the custody nurse to examine Ms Bent and prepare a body map of injuries, and arranged for them to be photographed.

Prosecutor: With what result?

PC Winn: We have the injuries photographed and listed. She was advised to attend A and E immediately after the interview, and I have obtained a doctor's report and statement.

Prosecutor: Your Honour, I refer to the statement taken from Dr Salim Khan, A and E House Officer at Albright Hospital, in bundle 6, document 44A.

Notice that PC Winn gives clear answers, but does not elaborate (she knows that the prosecution—or the defence—will follow up with another question if there is more to be said). Note too that she does not try to give a medical opinion, nor to paraphrase Dr Khan's evidence or statement. This would be inappropriate because PC Winn has no medical qualifications and knows that she cannot speak with any authority. However, the court may allow PC Winn to comment on whether the apparent injuries were consistent with assault, based on her knowledge and experience as a police officer. The temptation to use someone else's evidence in your answers can be strong, especially if you know the case well and have carefully read all the statements and written evidence, but you must resist.

The use of acronyms (eg BCU, TIC, ETA, SIO) and overly technical words (eg 'haematoma' (a bruise) or 'lacerations' (cuts)) should also be avoided as they may confuse and irritate the jury. You might appear to be trying too hard to impress if you say something like this (especially if your grasp of the meaning of words is a little shaky):

I proceeded in a southerly direction towards the connurbative encompassment of commercial premises which is characterized by the soubriquet of 'shopping mall'. The chronological observation which was then essayed by myself was recorded contemporaneously as 13.45 hours, British Summer Time. It was at that juncture that I espied the trio of adult males engaging in what I deemed to be behaviour which warranted a sufficiency of explanation as to make my legitimated suspicions subside...

Perhaps all you needed to say was:

> I was on patrol in the shopping centre at 13.45 when I saw three men behaving suspiciously, so I challenged them.

Even this is fairly formal, but it has the great merit of being brief. Remember the impression you are creating as a concise, well-prepared professional.

You certainly need to be organized and to appear to be organized: 'Um...I will just check...' or 'Um, I seem to have mislaid it...' are likely to irritate the jury and lose their attention. The statement 'May I please refer to document 24 in the bundle, M'Lord?' is far more professional and courteous. Using the correct terminology to address the court will certainly help create a good impression:

- 'Maam' or 'Sir' for the lawyers on either side;
- 'Your Honour', 'My Lady', or 'My Lord' for the Judge in the Crown Court (depending on the status of the Crown Court); and
- 'Your Worship' for the magistrates' court (or even 'Sir' or 'Maam').

It would be easy for us to ignore your appearance through some sense of 'politeness' and respect for individual personal style, but non-verbal communication (see 6.11.2) is a powerful influence—you need to look as smart as you sound. A smart uniform, polished shoes, and neat hair can seem petty restrictions, but they help you assert your authority (see 3.5) and will boost your confidence in the witness box. Actions also convey attitudes; hands in pockets, fiddling with buttons or your glasses, and constantly shifting through documents (maybe to track an entry you wish to use in a statement or report) create a poor impression.

You will experience, at some point in your career, an attack on your integrity, and this may happen in court. We looked at cross-examination in outline earlier. How would you respond to this?

> **Defence:** I put it to you, officer, that your whole account of what passed between you and the defendant is a tissue of invention from beginning to end. You have said that the defendant admitted en route to the police station in the police car, that he had assaulted Nina Bent with his fists on the evening of May 16, but that is not true, is it?
>
> **PC Winn:** It is true, sir. The defendant did say the things I recorded in my pocket notebook as significant statements, and these were then offered to him to sign as accurate. However, as I said in evidence-in-chief, he declined to sign my pocket notebook and I noted that fact. I raised the matter in the formal interview as I am required to do and he replied 'No comment'.
>
> **Defence:** I'll tell you what is true. You are mistaken in your evidence, you are confused about the events, and you have constructed an account after the event in order to improve your arrest figures and increase conviction rates, to move up the league table, is that not the case? I put it to you that you embellished your account, added a little here and there to make the evidence more compelling. Is that not the case?
>
> **PC Winn:** None of those things is true. I have told the truth.
>
> **Defence:** You continue to be mistaken, do you not, and now find you cannot change your story?
>
> **PC Winn:** No, sir, I am not mistaken.
>
> **Judge:** Mr Moyne, I think you have made your point. Do you wish to continue to challenge the integrity of the police officer or suggest wrongdoing? There are implications for your client if you persist.

You will recall (or if not, you will soon experience) abuse from people you have arrested, or when you have intervened in a fight or attended a domestic violence incident. You will have been called names, spat at, sworn at, jeered at, and belittled, and if you could keep your temper then, you will be able to keep it in court. If in court you appear intolerant or impatient, or reply in kind, then your credibility as a police officer on oath or affirmation in court would be at risk. Police officers are subject to personal scrutiny (as any other witness can be); your record, your training, your job performance, and even your personal life may be closely investigated by the defence. Anything which can undermine your credibility or make the jury dubious about the reliability of your testimony may be exploited by a defence lawyer, who will not hesitate to confront you with it during cross-examination.

TASK 6 What rule must you follow if your training, your integrity, and your standing as a police officer were to be so fundamentally challenged?

26.5.3.5 After giving evidence

You should wait in the witness box until the magistrate or judge gives you permission to leave. If you are in doubt about whether you are being 'stood down' or 'discharged' (see 26.5.2.3) you must speak to the CPS lawyer prosecuting the case at a convenient moment, and remain available within the court building.

If you wish to remain in court you are entitled to do so, and can sit in the public gallery. However, witnesses and family for the accused could also be there, so you might not feel particularly comfortable. You should also avoid making eye contact or nodding in agreement; this sort of action on your part might encourage the defence to question any influence you may be having on the jury or the magistrates, and could easily lead to criticism of your conduct in open court.

You would also need to take care in relation to other witnesses who have not yet given evidence. Imagine you travelled to court with a colleague and that you have given evidence and been discharged, but she is going to give evidence the following morning. You travelled together by car and intend to return home the same way; however, you would need to take care not to talk about the case. The following morning she may be asked about how she travelled, who with, and whether the case was discussed. The defence may look for forms of collusion, or inconsistency between her written statement and the evidence she gives orally, and suggest that any differences are an indication that she changed her account to suit others.

26.6 Answers to Tasks

TASK 1 A police officer attending an incident is a potential witness for both the prosecution and the defence. If he/she talks to witnesses or potential witnesses, their details and what they observed in relation to the incident should be recorded. If there are groups of people milling around, the officer might decide to stay in the area in case of any further trouble; such observations and any decision taken should be recorded. In the case of an arrest, any assistance provided to an arresting officer should be recorded. On the other hand, if it is clear that his/her colleagues require no further assistance, this should also be recorded as a PNB entry.

TASK 2

1. Unused material.
2. A disclosure officer is responsible for examining the records created during the investigation (and any criminal proceedings arising from the investigation).
3. It is revealed to the prosecutor on Schedules MG 6C and MG 6D (forms from the Manual of Guidance series of forms). It must be described in sufficient detail and with sufficient information to enable the prosecutor to make an informed decision as to whether or not the item contains anything which might undermine the prosecution case.

TASK 3 You might have referred to the 'continuity of evidence'. You will remember from many examples in this Handbook that this is a mundane but vital part of case preparation.

TASK 4 The exceptions usually agreed to be taken as evidence are declarations on the point of death; and statements made as confessions (if the witness heard the confession him/herself).

TASK 5 Form MG 16 is used.

TASK 6 Perhaps one rule to follow is 'do not allow yourself to be provoked'.

Different police officers have different strategies to achieve this. Some mentally count to three before responding to allow themselves time to compose a calm response. If you remain calm and collected, you will impress those watching and listening with your professionalism.

Bibliography and References

ACPO (2001), *ACPO Investigation of Volume Crime Manual* (London: The Stationery Office).

——(2005a), *Guidance on the Management, Recording and Investigation of Missing Persons* available at <http://www.gpdg.co.uk/pact_old/pdf/MissingPersonsInteractive.pdf> (accessed 11 March 2014).

——(2005b), *Hate Crime: Delivering a quality service, good practice and tactical guidance* available at <http://www.bedfordshire.police.uk/pdf/tacticalguidance.pdf> (accessed 11 March 2014).

——(2006a), *Murder Investigation Manual*, 3rd edn (Wyboston: National Centre for Policing Excellence).

——(2006b), *Practice Advice on Search Management and Procedures 2006* available at <http://www.kent.police.uk/about_us/policies/n/documents/n37search%2Bmanagement.pdf> (accessed 23 January 2014).

——(2006c), *Practice Advice on Stop and Search 2006* available at <http://content.met.police.uk/cs/Satellite?blobcol=urldata&blobheadername1=Content-Type&blobheadername2=Content-Disposition&blobheadervalue1=application%2Fpdf&blobheadervalue2=inline%3B+filename%3D%22436%2F865%2FPractice_Advice_on_Stop_and_Search.pdf%22&blobkey=id&blobtable=MungoBlobs&blobwhere=1283565271771&ssbinary=true> (accessed 19 March 2014).

——(2007a), *Good Practice Guide for Computer-based Electronic Evidence* available at <http://www.7safe.com/electronic_evidence/ACPO_guidelines_computer_evidence.pdf> (accessed 16 April 2012).

——(2007b), *Practice Advice on Critical Incident Management* available at <http://www.acpo.police.uk/documents/crime/2007/200708-cba-critical-incident-management.pdf> (accessed 11 March 2014).

——(2008), *Practice Advice on Analysis* available at <http://www.acpo.police.uk/documents/crime/2008/200804CRIPAA01.pdf> (accessed 17 April 2011).

——(2009), *ACPO Guidance on Investigating Child Abuse and Safeguarding Children*, 2nd edn, available at <http://ceop.police.uk/Documents/ACPOGuidance2009.pdf> (accessed 11 March 2014).

——(2010a), *Guidance on Investigating and Prosecuting Rape* (abridged edn) available at <http://www.acpo.police.uk/documents/crime/2011/20110303%20CBA.%20Guidance%20for%20Investigating%20and%20Prosecuting%20Rape_Public%20Facing_2010.pdf> (accessed 20 December 2013).

——(2010b), *Guidance on the Investigation, Cautioning and Charging of Knife Crime Offences 2009* available at <http://www.acpo.police.uk/documents/crime/2009/200907CRIKCO01.pdf> (accessed 8 April 2010).

——(2010c), *Guidance on the Management, Recording and Investigation of Missing Persons* available at <http://www.acpo.police.uk/documents/crime/2011/201103CRIIMP02.pdf> (accessed 14 April 2011).

——(2010d), *Manual of Guidance on Data Protection*, Version 3.0 (London: ACPO) available at <http://www.acpo.police.uk/documents/information/2010/201002-im-data-protection-mog.pdf> (accessed 11 March 2014).

——(2010e), *Manual of Guidance on Keeping the Peace* available at <http://www.acpo.police.uk/documents/uniformed/2010/201010UNKTP01.pdf> (accessed 5 February 2012).

—— (2011a), *ACPO Uniformed Operations Policing the Roads—5 Year Strategy 2011–2015* available at <http://library.college.police.uk/docs/ACPO/ACPO-policing-the-roads-2011.pdf> (accessed 3 March 2013).

——(2011b), *Annex A ACPO's Statement of Risk Principles* available at <http://knowsleychildcare.proceduresonline.com/pdfs/acpo_statement_risk.pdf> (accessed 27 February 2014).

——(2011c), *Guidance on the Management of Police Information* available at <http://www.acpo.police.uk/documents/information/2010/201004INFMOPI01.pdf> (accessed 11 March 2014).

——(2011d), *Prosecution Team Manual of Guidance* available at <http://library.college.police.uk/docs/appref/MoG-final-2011-july.pdf> (accessed 21 December 2013).

—— (2012a), *ACPO Good Practice Guide for Digital Evidence March 2012* available at <http://library.npia.police.uk/docs/acpo/digital-evidence-2012.pdf> (accessed 3 March 2013).

——(2012b), *The National Decision Model* available at <http://www.acpo.police.uk/documents/president/201201PBANDM.pdf> (accessed 27 February 2014).

——(2013), *Interim Guidance on the Management, Recording and Investigation of Missing Persons 2013* available at <http://www.acpo.police.uk/documents/crime/2013/201303-cba-int-guid-missing-persons.pdf> (accessed 11 March 2014).

ACPO Centrex (2005), *Practice Advice on Core Investigative Doctrine* (Camborne: National Centre for Policing Excellence).

Aitken, C, Connolly, T, Gammerman, A, Zhang, G, and Oldfield, R (1995), *Predicting an Offender's Characteristics: An evaluation of statistical modelling*, Police Research Group Special Interest Series 4 (London: Home Office).

Akers, S (2009), *ACPO Gangs Network* Letter to the LGA, 21 January 2009. Was available at <http://www.lga.gov.uk/lga/aio/874167> (accessed 14 April 2011) but is no longer available: please try other library resources.

Alderson, J (1998), *Principled Policing: Protecting the public with integrity* (Winchester: Waterside Press).

APCCS (2013), *Police and Crime Commissioners* available at <http://www.apccs.police.uk/page/pcc-candidates> (accessed 13 February 2013).

Audit Commission (1993), *Helping with Enquiries: Tackling crime effectively* (London: Audit Commission).

Banton, M (1964), *The Policeman in the Community* (London: Tavistock).

Belviso, M, De Donno, A, Vitale, L, and Introna, F (2003), 'Positional asphyxia: reflection on 2 cases', American Journal of Forensic Medicine and Pathology 24(3), 292–7.

Berne, E (1968), *Games People Play: The psychology of human relationships* (Harmondsworth: Penguin).

Bichard, Sir M (2004), *Return to an Address of the Honourable the House of Commons dated 22nd June 2004 for the Bichard Inquiry*, Report HC 653 (London: The Stationery Office).

Blackburn, R (1995), *The Psychology of Criminal Conduct: Theory, research and practice* (Chichester: Wiley & Sons).

Blair, Sir I (2005), *The Richard Dimbleby Lecture 2005: Sir Ian Blair* available at <http://www.bbc.co.uk/pressoffice/pressreleases/stories/2005/11_november/16/dimbleby.shtml> (accessed 13 April 2011).

Bloom, B, Engelhart, M, Furst, E, Hill, W, and Krathwohl, D (1956), *Taxonomy of Educational Objectives: The classification of educational goals; Handbook I: Cognitive Domain* (New York: Longmans).

Bottoms, A and Tankebe, J (2012), 'Beyond procedural justice: A dialogic approach to legitimacy in criminal justice', Journal of Criminal Law and Criminology 102(1), 119–70.

Bowers, KJ, Johnson, SD, and Pease, K (2004), 'Prospective hot-spotting: The future of crime mapping?', British Journal of Criminology 44(5), 641–58.

——, Hirschfield, A, and Johnson, S (1998), 'Victimisation revisited: A case study of non-residential repeat burglary in Merseyside', British Journal of Criminology 38(3), 429–52.

Bowling, B, Parmar, P, and Philips, C (2008), 'Policing ethnic minority communities' in T Newburn (ed), *Handbook of Policing*, 2nd edn (Cullompton: Willan), pp 611–41.

Bradford, B, Jackson, J, and Stanko, E (2009), 'Public encounters with the police: On the use of public opinion surveys to improve contact and confidence', Policing and Society 19(1), 20–46.

Bradley, The Rt Hon Lord (2009), *Lord Bradley's Review of People with Mental Health Problems and Learning Disabilities in the Criminal Justice System* (London: Department of Health).

Bryant, R (2008), *Investigating Digital Crime* (Chichester: John Wiley & Sons).

——and Bryant, S (2014), *Policing Digital Crime* (Farnham: Ashgate Publishing).

Bullock, K and Tilley, N (2003), *Crime Reduction and Problem-oriented Policing* (Cullompton: Willan).

Caless, B (2008a), 'Corruption in the police: The reality of the "dark side"', The Police Journal 80(1), 3–84.

——(2008b), 'Persistent dark matter: Police corruption in the last ten years', Ethics in Policing 1(2), 16–28.

Campbell, A and Muncer, S (1989), 'Them and Us: A comparison of the cultural context of American gangs and British subcultures', Deviant Behaviour 10, 271–88.

Canter, D and Alison, L (2000), *Precursors to Investigative Psychology: Criminal detection and the psychology of crime* (Aldershot: Ashgate).

——and Fritzon, K (1998), 'Differentiating arsonists: A model of firesetting actions and characteristics', Legal and Criminological Psychology 3, 73–96.

Center for Problem-Oriented Policing (2009), *Community Safety, Crime & Drugs Audit, 2004*. Was available at <http://www.popcenter.org/problems/residential_car_theft/PDFs/BrightonHove.pdf> (accessed 23 July 2009) but is no longer available: please try other library resources.

Centrex (2005), Level 1 Investigator Professional Development Portfolio.

Chan, JBL (2003), *Fair Cop: Learning the art of policing* (Toronto: University of Toronto Press).

Chartered Institute of Arbitrators (2009), *Mediation* available at <http://www.ciarb.org/information-and-resources/jargon-buster/> (accessed 13 April 2011).

Chenery, S, Henshaw C, and Pease, K (1999), *Illegal Parking in Disabled Bays: A means of offender targeting*, Police and Reducing Crime Briefing Note 1/99 (London: Home Office).

City of London Police (2005), *Cheque and Credit Card Fraud Investigation Policy* available at <http://www.cityoflondon.police.uk/NR/rdonlyres/3528E395-EDE9-4B8C-A8BA-829C00982E0D/0/chequecreditcardfraudinvestigationFOI.pdf> (accessed 3 April 2012).

Clarke, C and Milne, R (2001), *A National Evaluation of the PEACE Investigative Interviewing Course*, Home Office Report PRAS/149 (London: Home Office).

——, ——, and Bull, R (2011), 'Interviewing suspects of crime: The impact of PEACE training, supervision and the presence of a legal advisor', Journal of Investigative Psychology and Offender Profiling 8(2), 149–62.

Clarke, RV (1999), *Hot Products: Understanding, anticipating and reducing demand for stolen goods*, Police Research Series Paper 112 (London: Home Office).

College of Policing (2013a), *FAQs* available at <http://www.college.police.uk/en/18060.htm> (accessed 11 February 2013).

——(2013b), *Management of incidents* available at <http://www.app.college.police.uk/app-content/road-policing-2/management-of-incidents/> (accessed 5 January 2014).

—— (2013c), *OSPRE® Part 2* available at <http://www.college.police.uk/en/15228.htm> (accessed 11 February 2013).

——(2013d), *Police Promotion Framework* available at <http://www.college.police.uk/en/11621.htm> (accessed 11 February 2013).

—— (2013e), *Pre-Join to Policing Programmes* available at <http://www.college.police.uk/en/18826.htm> (accessed 11 February 2013).

—— (2013f), *Sergeants' 2012 Subject Areas* available at <http://www.college.police.uk/en/13498.htm> (accessed 11 February 2013).

—— (2013g), *Sergeants' OSPRE® Part II Police Promotion Assessment Centre 2012 Notes of Guidance for Part II Assessment Centre Candidates*. Was available at <http://www.college.police.uk/en/19425.htm> (accessed 11 February 2013) but is no longer available: please try other library resources.

——(2014a), *Certificate in Knowledge of Policing: approved pre-join providers* available at <http://www.college.police.uk/en/20027.htm> (accessed 11 March 2014).

——(2014b), *High Potential Development Scheme* available at <http://www.college.police.uk/en/8563.htm> (accessed 11 March 2014).

——(2014c), *High Potential Development Scheme (HPDS) Manual of Guidance* available at <http://www.college.police.uk/en/docs/HPDS_MoG_2013_final.pdf> (accessed 11 March 2014).

——(2014d), *HPDS Programme Details* available at <http://www.college.police.uk/en/10634.htm> (accessed 11 March 2014).

—— (2014e), *Investigating road deaths* available at <http://www.app.college.police.uk/app-content/road-policing-2/investigating-road-deaths/> (accessed 2 February 2014).

——(2014f), *Pre-Join Strategy Equality Impact Assessment* available at <http://www.college.police.uk/en/docs/Pre-join_Equality_Impact_Assessment.pdf> (accessed 11 March 2014).

——(2014g), *Professional Entry to Policing* available at <http://www.college.police.uk/en/docs/Professional_Entry_to_Policing_Strategy.pdf> (accessed 11 March 2014).

——(2014h), *Rules and Syllabus* available at <http://www.college.police.uk/en/docs/Rules_Syllabus_2014.pdf> (accessed 4 April 2014).

Cope, N, Fielding, N, and Innes, M (2005), 'The appliance of science? The theory and practice of crime intelligence analysis', British Journal of Criminology 45(1), 39–55.

Cottrell, S (2013), *The Study Skills Handbook (Palgrave Study Skills)*, 4th edn (Basingstoke: Palgrave Macmillan).

CPS (2004), *Prosecution Team Manual of Guidance*, 2004 edn, available at <http://tna.europarchive.org/20100419081706/http://www.police.homeoffice.gov.uk/publications/prosecution/prosecution-team-manual/indexbafb.html?view=Standard&pubID=656164> (accessed 14 July 2010).

——(2006), *Disclosure Manual* available at <http://www.cps.gov.uk/legal/d_to_g/disclosure_manual/> (accessed 23 July 2009).

——(2007), *Acquisition and Disclosure of Communications Data Code of Practice* available at <https://www.gov.uk/government/uploads/system/uploads/attachment_data/file/97961/code-of-practice-acquisition.pdf> (accessed 11 March 2014).

——(2009a), *Guidance on Prosecuting Cases of Domestic Violence* available at <http://www.cps.gov.uk/publications/prosecution/domestic/domv_guidance.html> (accessed 22 May 2010).

——(2009b), *Offences Against the Person, Incorporating Charging Standard* available at <http://www.cps.gov.uk/legal/l_to_o/offences_against_the_person/index.html> (accessed 10 July 2010).

——(2012a), *Perjury* available at <http://www.cps.gov.uk/legal/s_to_u/sentencing_manual/perjury/> (accessed 21 December 2013).

——(2012b), *S 67 Voyeurism* available at <http://www.cps.gov.uk/legal/s_to_u/sentencing_manual/s67__voyeurism/> (accessed 21 December 2013).

——(2014), *Hate Crime and Crime Against Older People* available at <http://www.cps.gov.uk/publications/equality/hate_crime/index.html> (accessed 11 March 2014).

Crawshaw, R, Devlin, B, and Williamson, T (1998), *Human Rights and Policing: Standards for good behaviour and a strategy for change* (The Hague: Kluwer Law International).

Croall, H (2011), *Crime and Society in Britain*, 2nd edn (Harlow: Pearson Education).

Cumbria Police (2014), *Making Cumbria an even safer place: A Police and Crime Plan for Cumbria 2013–2017* available at <http://www.cumbria-pcc.gov.uk/media/9811/Police%20and%20Crime%20Plan%202013-17.pdf> (accessed 12 February 2014).

Daly, M (2003), *My life as a secret policeman* available at <http://news.bbc.co.uk/1/hi/magazine/3210614.stm> (accessed 23 July 2009).

Davis, M (1996), 'Police, discretion, and the professions' in J Kleinig, *Handled with Discretion: Ethical issues in police decision making* (Lanham, MD: Rowman & Littlefield).

Defra (2009), *Dangerous Dogs Law Guidance for Enforcers* available at <https://www.gov.uk/government/publications/dangerous-dogs-law-guidance-for-enforcers> (accessed 11 March 2014).

Department for Transport (2013a), *Free-flow vehicle speeds on non-built-up roads by road type and vehicle type in Great Britain, 2012* available at <https://www.gov.uk/government/uploads/system/uploads/attachment_data/file/209007/spe0101.xls> (accessed 11 February 2014).

—— (2013b), *Reported Road Casualties in Great Britain: 2012 Annual Report* available at <https://www.gov.uk/government/uploads/system/uploads/attachment_data/file/245383/rrcgb2012-00.pdf> (accessed 11 February 2014).

Department of Health (2008), *Code of Practice: Mental Health Act 1983* available at <http://webarchive.nationalarchives.gov.uk/20130107105354/http://www.dh.gov.uk/en/Publicationsandstatistics/Publications/PublicationsPolicyAndGuidance/DH_084597> (accessed 26 February 2011).

Directgov (2011), *Uninsured Driving* available at <http://www.direct.gov.uk/en/Motoring/OwningAVehicle/Motorinsurance/DG_067639> (accessed 31 March 2011).

—— (2013), *Police officer recruitment update—February 2013* available at <http://www.dorset.police.uk/default.aspx?page=301> (accessed 3 March 2013).

Dunnighan, C and Norris, C (1996), 'A risky business: Exchange, bargaining and risk in the recruitment and running of informers by English police officers', Journal of Police Studies 19(2), 1–25.

——and ——(1999), 'The detective, the snout, and the Audit Commission: The real costs in using informants', The Howard Journal 38(1), 67–86.

Eddlestone, J (2012), *Blind Justice: Miscarriages of Justice in 20th Century Britain*, e-book, Bibliofile publishers.

Ede, R and Shepherd, E (2000), *Active Defence: Lawyer's guide to police and defence investigation and prosecution and defence disclosure in criminal cases* (London: Law Society Publishing).

Ekblom, P (2001), *The Conjunction of Criminal Opportunity: A framework for crime reduction toolkits* at <http://webarchive.nationalarchives.gov.uk/20100413151441/crimereduction.homeoffice.gov.uk/learningzone/cco.htm> (accessed 11 March 2014).

Elliott, J, Kusher, S, Alexandrou, A, Dwyfor Davies, J, Wilkinson, S, and Zamorski, B (2003), *Review of the Learning Requirement for Police Probationer Training in England & Wales* (University of East Anglia and University of the West of England).

Emsley, C (1996), *The English Police: A Political and Social History*, 2nd edn (Harlow: Pearson Education).

Environmental Audit Committee (2012), *Wildlife Crime* available at <http://www.publications.parliament.uk/pa/cm201213/cmselect/cmenvaud/140/140.pdf> (accessed 30 January 2013).

Everson, S and Pease, K (2001), 'Crime against the same person and place: Detection opportunity and offender targeting' in G Farrell and K Pease (eds), *Crime Prevention Studies*, vol 12 (Monsey, NY: CRC Press).

Farrall, S and Gadd, D (2004), 'Evaluating crime fears: A research note on a pilot study to improve the measurement of the "Fear of Crime" as a performance indicator', Evaluation 10(4), 493–502.

Fielding, NG (2005), *The Police & Social Conflict: Rhetoric and reality*, 2nd edn (London: Routledge-Cavendish).

Fineman, K (1995), 'A model for the qualitative analysis of child and adult fire deviant behaviour', American Journal of Forensic Psychology 13, 31–60.

Flanagan, Sir R (2004), *A Report on the Investigation by Cambridgeshire Constabulary into the Murders of Jessica Chapman and Holly Wells at Soham on 4 August 2002* (London: HMIC).

Flatley, J, Kershaw, C, Smith, K, Chaplin, R, and Moon, D (2010), *Crime in England and Wales 2009/10* Home Office Statistical Bulletin 12/10 (London: Home Office).

Francis, B, Barry, J, Bowater, R, Miller, N, Soothill, K, and Ackerley, E (2004), 'Using homicide data to assist murder investigation', Home Office Online Report 26/04 (London: Home Office).

Fuller, E (ed) (2008), *Drug Use, Smoking and Drinking among Young People in England in 2007* (National Centre for Social Research, National Foundation for Educational Research).

GMC (2008), *Licensing and Revalidation* available at <http://www.gmc-uk.org/7a_Licensing_and_Revalidation.pdf_25399016.pdf> (accessed 11 March 2014).

Goldstein, H (1990), *Problem-orientated Policing* (New York: McGraw Hill).

Gudjonsson, G, Sigurdsson, J, and Einarsson, E (2004), 'The role of personality in relation to confessions and denials', Psychology, Crime & Law 10(2), 125–35.

Haigh, J (2006), 'Forensic science and the legal process' available at <http://www.maths.sussex.ac.uk/Staff/JH/Fslp/FSLPnotes.pdf> (accessed 23 July 2009).

Harfield, C and Harfield, K (2005), *Covert Investigation* (Oxford: Oxford University Press).

——and ——(2008), *Intelligence: Investigation, Community, and Partnership* (Oxford: Oxford University Press).

Harris, D, Turner, R, Garrett, I, and Atkinson, S (2011), *Understanding the Psychology of Gang Violence: Implications for designing effective violence interventions*, Ministry of Justice Research Series 2/11, March.

Heaton, R (2000), 'The prospects for intelligence-led policing: Some historical and quantitative considerations', Policing & Society 9, 337–55.

——(2008), 'Measuring crime reduction: Geographical effects', The Police Journal 81(2), 95.

Herbert, N The Rt Hon (2011), 'Restorative justice, policing and the Big Society', Restorative Justice Council, Manchester, 22 February.

Herring, J (2007), *Family Law*, 3rd edn (Cambridge: Pearson).

Highway Code (2004) available at <http://www.direct.gov.uk/en/TravelAndTransport/Highwaycode/DG_070190> (accessed 11 March 2014).

HMIC (2002), *Training Matters* (London: HMSO).

——(2003), *Diversity Matters* (London: HMSO).

——(2005a), *Inspection of Kingston upon Hull BCU Humberside Police July 2005* available at <http://www.humberside.police.uk/about-us/inspection-reports/basic-command-unit-bcu-inspection-reports> (accessed 11 March 2014).

——(2005b), *Police National Computer Data Quality and Timeliness Second Report on the Inspection by HM Inspectorate of Constabulary* (London: HMSO).

——(2006), *PNC Compliance Report: City of London (Aug 2005)* (London: HMSO).

——(2009), *Adapting to Protest* available at <http://www.hmic.gov.uk/media/adapting-to-protest-20090705.pdf> (accessed 4 April 2012).

——(2010), *Anti-social Behaviour: Stop the rot* available at <http://www.hmic.gov.uk/media/stop-the-rot-20100923.pdf> (accessed 2 March 2011).

——(2011), *Policing Public Order* available at <http://www.hmic.gov.uk/media/policing-public-order-20110208.pdf> (accessed 19 March 2014).

——(2012), *A Review of National Police Units which Provide Intelligence on Criminality Associated with Protest* available at <http://www.hmic.gov.uk/publication/review-of-national-police-units-which-provide-intelligence-on-criminality-associated-with-protest-20120202/> (accessed 6 March 2012).

——(2013), *Crime Recording in Kent: A report commissioned by the Police and Crime Commissioner for Kent* available at <http://www.hmic.gov.uk/media/crime-recording-in-kent-130617.pdf> (accessed 11 March 2014).

Home Office (1989), *Criminal and Custodial Careers of those Born in 1953, 1958 and 1963*, Home Office Statistical Bulletin 32/89 (London: Home Office).

——(1997), *Police Health and Safety, Volume 2: A guide for police managers*, Police Policy Directorate (London: Home Office).

——(1998), *Speaking up for Justice* available at <http://www.nationalarchives.gov.uk/ERORecords/HO/421/2/P2/CPD/PVU/SUFJ.PDF> (accessed 19 March 2014).

——(2001), *Policing a New Century: A blueprint for reform*, Cm 5326 (London: Home Office).

——(2004), *Initial Police Learning and Development Programme* (IPLDP) Version 1 (London: Home Office).

——(2005a), *Code of Practice for Victims of Crime* available at <http://webarchive.nationalarchives.gov.uk/20100418065544/http://homeoffice.gov.uk/documents/victims-code-of-practice2835.pdf?view=Binary> (accessed 3 April 2012).

——(2005b), *Initial Police Learning and Development Programme (IPLDP), Letter to Chief Police Officers 7 November 2005* (London: Home Office).

——(2005c), *IPLDP Central Author Practitioner Guidance*, Community Engagement & Professional Development Units (London: Home Office).

——(2005d), *PIP Guidance for Completion of the Professional Development Portfolio Investigators and Assessors* (London: Home Office).

——(2005e), *Rationale for Changing the Overall Module Structure of the IPLDP*, IPLDP Central Authority Executive Services (London: Home Office).

——(2005f), *The Criminal Justice and Police Act (s.1–11), Penalty Notices for disorder, Police Operational Guidance March 2005* available at <http://www.unlock.org.uk/userfiles/file/IAG/penalty-notices-police-guidance2835.pdf> (accessed 21 January 2011).

——(2007), *Safer Communities: Towards Effective Arson Control* available at <http://webarchive.nationalarchives.gov.uk/20120919132719/http://www.communities.gov.uk/publications/fire/safercommunitiestowards> (accessed 13 April 2011).

——(2009a), *Explanatory Memorandum to the Criminal Justice and Immigration Act 2008 (Violent Offender Orders) (Notification Requirements) Regulations 2009 No. 2019* available at <http://www.legislation.gov.uk/uksi/2009/2019/pdfs/uksiem_20092019_en.pdf> (accessed 20 December 2013).

——(2009b), *Guidance On Designated Public Place Orders (DPPOs): for Local Authorities in England and Wales* available at <http://tna.europarchive.org/20100413151441/http://www.crimereduction.homeoffice.gov.uk/alcoholorders/alcoholorders016.htm> (accessed 7 July 2010).

——(2009c), *National Domestic Violence Delivery Plan Annual Progress Report 2008/2009* available at <http://webarchive.nationalarchives.gov.uk/20100418065544/http://www.homeoffice.gov.uk/documents/dom-violence-delivery-plan-08-09.html> (accessed 10 July 2010).

——(2009d), *Together We Can End Violence against Women and Girls: A strategy* available at <http://webarchive.nationalarchives.gov.uk/20100413151441/http://homeoffice.gov.uk/documents/vawg-strategy-2009/end-violence-against-women2835.pdf?view=Binary> (accessed 10 July 2010).

——(2010a), *Call to end violence against women and girls: strategic vision* available at <https://www.gov.uk/government/publications/call-to-end-violence-against-women-and-girls-strategic-vision> (accessed 9 February 2014).

——(2010b), *Drinking Banning Orders (DBOs) on Conviction*. Was available at <http://webarchive.nationalarchives.gov.uk/+/http://www.homeoffice.gov.uk/about-us/home-office-circulars/circulars-2010/003-2010/> (accessed 4 April 2011) but is no longer available: please try other library resources.

——(2010c), *Policing in the 21st Century: Reconnecting police and the people* (London: Home Office), available at <http://www.homeoffice.gov.uk/publications/consultations/policing-21st-century/> (accessed 19 May 2011).

——(2010d), *Statutory Guidance: Injunctions to prevent gang-related violence* available at <http://www.official-documents.gov.uk/document/other/9780108509599/9780108509599.pdf> (accessed 5 February 2011).

——(2011a), *Home Office Counting Rules for Recorded Crime*. Was available at <http://www.homeoffice.gov.uk/publications/science-research-statistics/research-statistics/crime-research/counting-rules> (accessed 13 April 2011) but is no longer available: please try other library sources.

——(2011b), *Missing Children and Adults* available at <https://www.gov.uk/government/uploads/system/uploads/attachment_data/file/117793/missing-persons-strategy.pdf> (accessed 11 March 2014).

——(2011c), *Three Steps to Escaping Violence Against Women and Girls* available at <http://www.homeoffice.gov.uk/publications/crime/3-steps-escaping-dv/english-3-steps?view=Binary> (accessed 1 March 2012).

—— (2012a), *Crime in England and Wales: Quarterly Update to September 2011–19* available at <http://www.homeoffice.gov.uk/publications/science-research-statistics/research-statistics/crime-research/hosb0112/hosb0112?view=Binary> (accessed 10 January 2013).

—— (2012b), *Domestic violence disclosure scheme pilot: guidance* available at <http://www.homeoffice.gov.uk/publications/crime/dvds-interim-guidance?view=Binary> (accessed 21 December 2012).

—— (2012c), *Ending Gang and Youth Violence: one year on* available at <http://www.official-documents.gov.uk/document/cm84/8493/8493.pdf> (accessed 10 January 2013).

—— (2012d), *The Police Act 1996 (Equipment) Regulations 2011 and the Police Act 1996 (Services) Regulations 2011 Impact Assessment* available at <http://www.homeoffice.gov.uk/publications/consultations/cons-2010-police-procurement/police-act-ia?view=Binary> (accessed 7 March 2012).

—— (2013a), *Crime Survey for England and Wales* available at <http://www.ons.gov.uk/ons/dcp171778_318761.pdf> (accessed 11 March 2014).

—— (2013b), *Direct Entry to the Police—WMS* available at <http://www.homeoffice.gov.uk/publications/about-us/parliamentary-business/written-ministerial-statement/direct-entry-to-police-wms/> (accessed 11 February 2013).

—— (2013c), *Domestic violence and abuse: new definition* available at <https://www.gov.uk/domestic-violence-and-abuse> (accessed 20 December 2013).

—— (2013d), *Home Office Counting Rules for Recorded Crime* available at <https://www.gov.uk/government/uploads/system/uploads/attachment_data/file/267387/count-general-dec-2013.pdf> (accessed 11 March 2014).

—— (2013e), *Penalty Notices for Disorder (PNDs)* available at <http://www.justice.gov.uk/downloads/oocd/pnd-guidance-oocd.pdf> (accessed 11 March 2014).

—— (2013f), *Surveillance Camera Code of Practice* available at <https://www.gov.uk/government/uploads/system/uploads/attachment_data/file/204775/Surveillance_Camera_Code_of_Practice_WEB.pdf> (accessed 11 March 2014).

—— (2014), *National DNA Strategy Board Annual Report 2012–2013* available at <https://www.gov.uk/government/uploads/system/uploads/attachment_data/file/252885/NDNAD_Annual_Report_2012-13.pdf> (accessed 6 March 2014).

House of Commons Library (2014), *Police Service Strength* available at <http://www.parliament.uk/briefing-papers/sn00634> (accessed 3 March 2014).

Ingleton, R (2002), *Policing Kent 1800–2000* (Chichester: Phillimore).

Innes, M (2004), 'Crime as a signal, crime as a memory', Journal for Crime, Conflict and the Media 1(2), 15–22.

—— (2005), 'What's your problem? Signal crimes and citizen-focused problem solving', Criminology & Public Policy 4(2), 187–200.

IPCC (2013), *Statutory Guidance to the police service on the handling of complaints* available at <https://www.ipcc.gov.uk/sites/default/files/Documents/statutoryguidance/2013_statutory_guidance_english.pdf> (accessed 11 March 2014).

—— (2014), *Police Officers Subject of a Complaint* available at <http://www.ipcc.gov.uk/page/police-officers-being-subject-complaint> (accessed 24 March 2014).

Jackson, J, Bradford, B, Stanko, B, and Hohl, K (2013), *Just Authority? Trust in the police in England and Wales* (London: Routledge).

Johnston, D and Hutton, G (2005), *Blackstone's Police Manual, Volume 2: Evidence and Procedure* (Oxford: Oxford University Press).

Jones, T and Newburn, T (1998), *Private Security and Public Policing* (Oxford: Clarendon Press).

Joyce, P (2011), *Policing: Development & Contemporary Practice* (London: Sage Publications).

Junger, M, West, R, and Timman, R (2001), 'Crime and risk behaviour in traffic', Journal of Research in Crime & Delinquency 38(4), 439–59.

Justice (2011), *Mediation and alternatives to court* available at <http://www.justice.gov.uk/courts/mediation> (accessed 21 December 2012).

Kent Police (2010), *Neighbourhood Watch* available at <http://www.kent.police.uk/advice/community_safety/initiatives/nwatch.html> (accessed 13 April 2011).

Kershaw, C, Nicholas, S, and Walker, A (eds) (2008), *Crime in England and Wales 2007/08: Findings from the British Crime Survey and police recorded crime*, Home Office Statistical Bulletin 07/08 (London: Home Office).

Kolb, D (1984), *Experiential Learning: Experience as the source of learning and development* (Upper Saddle River, NJ: Prentice Hall).

Lee, M and South, N (2003), 'Drugs policing' in T Newburn (ed), *Handbook of Policing* (Cullompton: Willan).

Leishman, F and Mason, P (2003), *Policing and the Media: Facts, fictions and factions* (Cullompton: Willan).

Lincolnshire Police (2011), *Drugs and Alcohol* available at <http://www.lincs.police.uk/Youth-Lincs/Teen-Lincs/Drugs-and-Alcohol.html> (accessed 7 April 2011).

London Evening Standard (2012), *Notting Hill Carnival: 'Body armour' gang held on way to festival* available at <http://www.standard.co.uk/news/crime/notting-hill-carnival-body-armour-gang-held-on-way-to-festival-one-man-remains-critical-8083875.html> (accessed 20 February 2013).

Luft, J (1970), *Group Processes: An introduction to group dynamics* (Palo Alto, CA: National Press Books).

Mackie, L (1978), 'Race causes an initial confusion', *The Guardian*, 14 June.

Macpherson, Sir W (1999), *The Stephen Lawrence Inquiry* available at <https://www.gov.uk/government/publications/the-stephen-lawrence-inquiry> (accessed 4 April 2014).

Marshall, B, Webb, B, and Tilley, N (2005), *Rationalisation of current research on guns, gangs and other weapons: Phase 1* (London: University College London/Jill Dando Institute of Crime Science).

Matassa, M and Newburn, T (2003), 'Policing and terrorism' in T Newburn (ed), *The Handbook of Policing* (Cullompton: Willan).

Mawby, RC (2008), 'Community policing' in T Newburn and P Neyroud (eds), *Dictionary of Policing* (Cullompton: Willan), pp 40–1.

Metropolitan Police Authority (2010), *Update on the Proposed New Model of Recruitment and Training for Police Officers* available at <http://policeauthority.org/Metropolitan/committees/mpa/2010/100930/07/index.html> (accessed 29 March 2011).

Miller, J (2003), *Police Corruption in England and Wales: An assessment of current evidence*, Home Office Online Report 11/03 available at <http://webarchive.nationalarchives.gov.uk/20110218135832/http://rds.homeoffice.gov.uk/rds/pdfs2/rdsolr1103.pdf> (accessed 23 July 2009).

Milne, R and Bull, R (1999), *Investigative Interviewing: Psychology and practice* (Chichester: John Wiley & Sons).

MIND (2010), *Achieving Justice for Victims and Witnesses with Mental Distress* available at <https://www.cps.gov.uk/publications/docs/mind_toolkit_for_prosecutors_and_advocates.pdf> (accessed 27 February 2014).

——(2013), *Police and Mental Health: How to get it right locally* available at <http://www.mind.org.uk/media/618027/2013-12-03-Mind_police_final_web.pdf> (accessed 27 February 2014).

Ministry of Justice (2010), *Offences Of Stirring Up Hatred On The Grounds Of Sexual Orientation* available at <http://www.banksr.co.uk/images/Other%20Documents/Judicial%20material/circular-2010-05-sexual-orientation-hatred.pdf> (accessed 11 March 2014).

——(2013), *Code of Practice for Victims of Crime* available at <https://www.gov.uk/government/uploads/system/uploads/attachment_data/file/254459/code-of-practice-victims-of-crime.pdf> (accessed 11 March 2014).

——(2014), *Multi-Agency Public Protection Arrangements Annual Report 2012/13* available at <https://www.gov.uk/government/uploads/system/uploads/attachment_data/file/253983/mappa-annual-report-2012-13.pdf> (accessed 11 March 2014).

Ministry of Justice, Home Office, and Office for National Statistics (2013), *An Overview of Sexual Offending in England and Wales* available at <https://www.gov.uk/government/uploads/system/uploads/attachment_data/file/214970/sexual-offending-overview-jan-2013.pdf> (accessed 20 December 2013).

Morris, W, Burden, A, and Weekes, A (2004), *The Case for Change: People in the Metropolitan Police Service* (Morris Inquiry) available at <http://www.policeauthority.org/Metropolitan/downloads/scrutinites/morris/morris-report.pdf> (accessed 19 July 2010).

Moses, D (1997), *The Watford Rail Incident—Inter-Agency De-briefing Report*. Was available at <http://www.herts.police.uk/FOI/Significant_Information/r_Watford_rail_crash-REDACTED.pdf> (23 July 2009) but is no longer available: please try other library resources.

Myhill, A and Bradford, B (2011), 'Can police enhance public confidence by improving quality of service? Results from two surveys in England and Wales', Policing and Society First 1–29.

National Audit Office (2012), *Home Office and National Policing Improvement Agency Mobile Technology in Policing Report by the Comptroller and Auditor General*, HC 1765, Session 2010–2012, 27 January (London: The Stationery Office).

Neighbourhood Watch (2014), *Our mission* available at <http://www.ourwatch.org.uk/about_us/our_mission/> (accessed 11 March 2014).

Newburn, T (1999), *Understanding and Preventing Police Corruption: Lessons from the literature*, Police Research Series Paper 110 (London: Home Office).

——(2007), *Criminology* (Cullompton: Willan).

——and Neyroud, P (2008), *Dictionary of Policing* (Cullompton: Willan).

——(2011), *Review of Police Leadership and Training: Volume One* (London: Home Office), available at <http://www.homeoffice.gov.uk/publications/consultations/rev-police-leadership-training/report?view=Binary> (accessed 11 April 2011).

Neyroud, P and Beckley, A (2001), *Policing, Ethics and Human Rights* (Cullompton: Willan).

Nozick, R (1974), *Anarchy, State and Utopia* (Oxford: Blackwell (2003 print)).

NPIA (2007), *Practice Advice on Critical Incident Management* available at <http://www.acpo.police.uk/documents/crime/2007/200708-cba-critical-incident-management.pdf> (accessed 16 March 2011).

——(2008a), *Guidance on Investigating Domestic Abuse* available at <http://www.acpo.police.uk/documents/crime/2008/2008-cba-inv-dom-abuse.pdf> (accessed 20 May 2010).

——(2008b), *National Policing Improvement Agency Circular NPIA(WSU)(RAP)(08)1*. Was available at <http://policerecruitment.homeoffice.gov.uk/documents/npia-08-012835.pdf?view=Binary> (accessed 17 March 2011) but is no longer available: please try other library resources.

——(2008c), *Subject Area Breakdown—OSPRE® Part I Inspectors' Examination 2008 OSPRE® Part I*. Was available at <http://www.npia.police.uk/en/11795.htm> (23 July 2009) but is no longer available: please try other library resources.

——(2009a), *Guidance on Command and Control* available at <http://www.acpo.police.uk/documents/crime/2009/200907CRICCG01.pdf> (accessed 29 March 2011).

——(2009b), *Guidance on Emergency Procedures* available from <http://www.acpo.police.uk/documents/uniformed/2009/200904UNGEP01.pdf> (accessed 16 March 2011).

——(2010a), *Guidance on Responding to People with Mental Ill Health or Learning Disabilities* available at <http://www.acpo.police.uk/documents/edhr/2010/201004EDHRMIH01.pdf> (accessed 23 January 2011).

——(2010b), *Initial Police Learning and Development Programme, Programme Handbook*, March, Final Draft Version, National Police Improvement Agency.

——(2010c), *Missing Persons: Data and Analysis 2009/10*. Was available at <http://www.npia.police.uk/en/docs/Missing_Persons_Data_and_Analysis_2009-10.pdf> (accessed 14 April 2011) but is no longer available: please try other library resources.

——(2010d), *National Investigators' Examination Rules and Syllabus—2010*. Was available at <http://www.npia.police.uk/en/15231.htm> (accessed 2 July 2010) but is no longer available: please try other library resources.

——(2011a), *Initial Police Learning and Development, Review and Guidance on Pre Join Programmes in England and Wales 2011*. Was available at <http://www.npia.police.uk/en/docs/Pre_Join_Guidance_0111_CA_HA_Ful_doc__6_.pdf> (accessed 13 April 2011) but is no longer available: please try other library resources.

——(2011b), *Neighbourhood Partnerships* Was available at <http://cfnp.npia.police.uk/1521.aspx> (accessed 13 April 2011) but is no longer available: please try other library resources.

——(2011c), *Penalty Notice Processing*. Was available at <http://www.npia.police.uk/en/11260.htm> (accessed 6 April 2011) but is no longer available: please try other library resources.

——(2011d), *Road Death Investigation Manual 2007* available at <http://webarchive.nationalarchives.gov.uk/20120405043115/http:/www.npia.police.uk/en/docs/Road_Death_Investigation_Manual_2007_PA.pdf> (accessed 6 April 2011).

——(2011e), *Rules and Syllabus Qualifying for Promotion to the Ranks of Sergeant and Inspector*. Was available at <http://www.npia.police.uk/en/docs/RulesSyllabus2011V2.pdf> (accessed 1 March 2011) but is no longer available: please try other library resources.

—— (2012), *Professional Entry to Policing Pre-Join Strategy & Guidance Document May 2012 Version 1.01*. Was available at <http://www.npia.police.uk/en/18826.htm> (accessed 11 February 2013) but is no longer available: please try other library resources.

——/ACPO (2009), *Practice Advice on the Management of Priority and Volume Crime (The Volume Crime Management Model)*, 2nd edn, available at <http://www.acpo.police.uk/documents/crime/2010/201002CRIPVC01.pdf> (accessed 13 July 2010).

NPT (1995), *Police Probationer Training Foundation Course Notes* (Police Central Planning & Training Unit, a division of National Police Training), p 4.

Office for National Statistics (2013), *Statistical bulletin: Crime in England and Wales, Year Ending June 2013* available at <http://www.ons.gov.uk/ons/dcp171778_331209.pdf> (accessed 19 December 2013).

——(2014), *Crime in England and Wales, Year Ending September 2013* available at <http://www.ons.gov.uk/ons/rel/crime-stats/crime-statistics/period-ending-september-2013/stb-crime-in-england-and-wales--year-ending-sept-2013.html#tab-Offences-involving-knives-and-sharp-instruments> (accessed 11 March 2014).

Ofqual (2013a), *View Qualification: OCR Level 3 Certificate in Knowledge of Policing (QCF)* available at <http://register.ofqual.gov.uk/Qualification/Details/600_7054_7> (accessed 30 January 2013).

——(2013b), *View Qualification : SFJ Awards Level 3 Diploma in Policing (QCF)* available at <http://register.ofqual.gov.uk/Qualification/Details/600_5980_1> (accessed 11 April 2013).

PCeU (2014), *What we do* available at <http://content.met.police.uk/Article/What-we-do/1400015320495/1400015320495> (accessed 11 March 2014).

Pease, K (1997), 'Crime prevention' in M Maguire, R Morgan, and R Reiner (eds), *The Oxford Handbook of Criminology*, 2nd edn (Oxford: Oxford University Press).

——(2002), 'Crime reduction' in M Maguire, R Morgan, and R Reiner (eds), *The Oxford Handbook of Criminology*, 3rd edn (Oxford: Oxford University Press), pp 947–79.

Peters, R (1973), *Authority, Responsibility and Education* (London: Allen & Unwin).

Police Federation (2011), *Policing the Riots* available at <http://www.polfed.org/documents/PR_Policing_the_riots_submission_to_HMIC_011211.pdf> (accessed 11 March 2014).

PredPol (2014), *Policing Meets big data* available at <http://www.predpol.com/about/> (accessed 11 March 2014).

Rawlings, PJ (2002), *Policing: A short history* (Cullompton: Willan).

——(2000), *The Politics of the Police*, 3rd edn (Oxford: Oxford University Press).

Re-Solv (2013), *Working to prevent VSA* available at <http://www.re-solv.org/> (accessed 11 March 2014).

Rogers, A (1996), *Teaching Adults*, 2nd edn (Buckingham: Open University Press).

Rogers, C (2006), *Crime Reduction Partnerships* (Oxford: Oxford University Press).

Rose, G (2000), 'The criminal histories of serious traffic offenders', HORS 206 (London: Home Office).

Rowe, M (2002), 'Policing diversity: Themes and concerns from the recent British experience', Police Quarterly 5(4), 424–46.

Scarman, Lord (1981), *Report into the Brixton Disorders*, Cmnd, 8427 (London: HMSO).

Sentencing Council (2012), *Assault Definitive Guidance* available at <http://sentencingcouncil.judiciary.gov.uk/docs/Assault_definitive_guideline_-_Crown_Court.pdf> (accessed 6 February 2012).

Sentencing Guidelines Council (2007), *Sexual Offences Act 2003, Definitive Guidance* available at <http://webarchive.nationalarchives.gov.uk/+/http://www.sentencingcouncil.org.uk/docs/web_0000_SexualOffencesAct1.pdf> (accessed 23 December 2012).

——(2012), *Offences taken into consideration and totality-definitive guideline* available at <http://sentencingcouncil.judiciary.gov.uk/docs/Definitive_guideline_TICs__totality_Final_web.pdf> (accessed 11 March 2014).

SFO (2010), *Perjury* available at <http://www.sfo.gov.uk/media/103061/perjury%20web%201.pdf> (accessed 21 December 2013).

Shepherd, E and Griffiths, A (2013), *Investigative Interviewing: The conversation management approach*, 2nd edn (Oxford: Oxford University Press).

Shorter Oxford English Dictionary (2002), 5th edn (Oxford: Oxford University Press).

Simmons, AJ (2001), *Justification and Legitimacy: Essays on rights and obligations* (Cambridge: Cambridge University Press).

Skills for Justice (2007a), *Police Assessment Support Project, End of Project Report*, May 2007. No longer available.

——(2011), *Policing Professional Framework* available at <http://www.skillsforjustice-ppf.com/?r_id=1> (accessed 3 April 2012).

Smith, MJ and Tilley, N (2005), *Crime Science: New approaches to preventing and detecting crime* (Cullompton: Willan).

Stelfox, P (1998), 'Policing lower levels of organised crime in England and Wales', The Howard Journal 37(4), 393–406.

Stone, V and Pettigrew, N (2000), *The Views of the Public on Stops and Searches* (London: Home Office).

Taylor, D (1999), 'Cannabis cautioning notice pilot programme training module—Bunbury and Mirrabooka', 5–6 (Alcohol and Drug Coordination Unit).

Taylor, M (1986), 'Learning for self-direction in the classroom: The pattern of a transition process', Studies in Higher Education 11(1), 55–72.

Taylor, P and Bond, S (eds) (2012), *Crime Detection in England & Wales* (London: ONS).

Thornton, S (2007), 'Introduction' in *ACPO Practice Advice: Introduction to Intelligence-led policing*, ACPO Centrex.

Tilley, N (2008a), 'Modern Approaches to Policing: Community, problem-orientated and intelligence-led' in T Newburn (ed), *Handbook of Policing* (Collumpton: Willan), pp 373–403.

——(2008b), 'Problem-orientated Policing' in T Newburn and P Neyroud (eds), *Dictionary of Policing*, pp 225–7.

Tong, S (2008), 'Interagency Approaches to Policing' in T Newburn and P Neyroud (eds), *Dictionary of Policing* (Cullompton: Willan), pp 148–9.

Tyler, TR (2003), 'Procedural justice, legitimacy, and the effective rule of law' in M Tonry (ed), *Crime and Justice: A Review of Research*, volume 30 (Chicago, IL: Chicago University Press), pp 431–505.

UK Parliament (2013), *Clare's law: The Domestic Violence Disclosure Scheme—Commons Library Standard Note* available at <http://www.parliament.uk/business/publications/research/briefing-papers/SN06250/clares-law-the-domestic-violence-disclosure-scheme> (accessed 20 December 2013).

Vrij, A (2008), *Detecting Lies and Deceit: Pitfalls and opportunities*, 2nd edn (Chichester: Wiley-Blackwell).

Waddington, PAJ (1999), *Policing Citizens* (London: UCL Press).

——, Stenson, K, and David, D (2004), 'In proportion: Race, and police stop and search', British Journal of Criminology 44, 889–914.

Wadham, J (2004), 'Conference on data protection and information sharing', 15 July (London).

Walby, S and Allen, J (2004), *Domestic violence, sexual assault and stalking: Findings from the British Crime Survey*, Home Office Research Study 276.

Walker, A, Flatley, J, Kershaw, C, and Moon, D (2009), *Crime in England and Wales 2008/09 Volume 1, Findings from the British Crime Survey and Police Recorded Crime*, Home Office Statistical Bulletin.

Walsh, D and Milne, R (2008), 'Keeping the PEACE? A study of investigative interviewing practices in the public sector', Legal and Criminological Psychology 13(1) February 2008, 395–7 (19).

West Yorkshire Police (2009), *IPLDP Programme* available at <http://www.bishopgarth.com/programme.html> (accessed 23 July 2009).

Wilson, J and Kelling, G (1982), 'Broken windows', Atlantic Monthly, March, pp 29–38.

Wilson, JQ (1996), 'On deterrence' in J Muncie, E McLaughlin, and M Langan (eds), *Criminological Perspectives: A reader* (London: Sage).

Wiltshire Police (no date), *What is a major incident?* available at <http://www.wiltshire.police.uk/index.php?option=com_content&view=article&id=173&Itemid=393> (accessed 30 January 2014).

Wolfenden Report (1957), *Report of the Committee on Homosexual Offences and Prostitution*, Cmnd 247 (London: HMSO).

Women's Aid (2006), *How common is domestic violence?* available at <http://www.womensaid.org.uk/domestic-violence-articles.asp?section=00010001002200410001&itemid=1280> (accessed 13 February 2013).

Woodhouse, J (2013), *Extreme Pornography Commons Library Standard Note SN/HA/5078* available at <http://www.parliament.uk/business/publications/research/briefing-papers/SN05078/extreme-pornography> (accessed 27 February 2014).

Wright, A (2002), *Policing: An introduction to concepts and practice* (Cullompton: Willan).

Index

Diploma in Policing 8.4
discrimination and equality 5.4, 6.2
health and safety 6.12
information, gathering and
    submitting 26.2
initial support for victims and
    witnesses 5.4, 5.4.2, 17.1
interpersonal communication 6.11
interviews 24.1
investigations 23.1, 25.1
National Intelligence Model 22.1–22.1.1
NOS units 1.4.3–1.4.4, 7.3
PACE 5.6
personal safety training 6.12.5
pre-join programmes 1.4.1, 1.4.4, 7.2.1
QCF 1.4.4, 7.3
searches 9.4, 9.6
theft 16.1
units 1.4.4, 7.3
CHALETS mnemonic 11.5.2
Charges
    bail 10.13.6
    cautions 10.13.6
    charging a suspect 10.10.3
    Crown Prosecution Service 26.1
    custody officers 10.10.3, 10.13.6
    refused charge 10.13.8
    road and traffic policing 19.12.1, 19.12.3
    written charges 10.13.1
**Chemical, biological, radiological or
    nuclear (CBRN) incidents** 11.6.3
**Child Sex Offender (CSO) Disclosure
    Scheme** 17.1
Children and young people
    see also **Children, safeguarding;
    Schools; Sexual offences and
    children**
    appropriate adult 24.4.2, 24.5.1, 25.6.1.1
    air weapons 18.6.1–18.6.2
    anti-social behaviour 14.2.4.2
    arrest 10.6.4, 10.6.4.3
    burglary, use for 16.4.1
    care, absences of children in 13.4.1.3
    containment 14.3.4
    entry and search, powers of 9.5.1.3
    firearms 18.3.6, 18.5, 18.6.1–18.6.2
    fireworks 14.9–14.9.1
    gangs 15.9.1
    human trafficking 13.5.3
    local child curfews 14.2.3
    missing persons 13.4.1.3
    Penalty Notice for Disorder (PND)
        Scheme 10.13.2–10.13.2.1
    reprimands and warnings 3.6.1, 10.13.4
    victims, supporting 13.6.2.1
    youth cautions 10.13.4
    Youth Court 5.5.2
    Youth Offending Teams 3.3.4
Children, safeguarding 13.3–13.3.3.4
    see also **Sexual offences and children**
    abuse, investigating child 13.3.1–13.3.2,
        13.3.3
    age definition 13.3
    alcohol 12.1, 12.2.2, 12.2.5, 12.3–12.3.2,
        12.4.4
    animals, transfer by sale or prize
        of 13.7.1.5
    Child Abuse Investigation Unit 13.3.1
    child commissioner, creation of role
        of 13.3
    child cruelty 13.3.2.1
    Child Exploitation and Online Protection
        (CEOP) Centre 3.4.8
    Children Act 1989 13.3, 13.3.1, 13.3.3,
        13.3.3.3

cigarettes and young people 13.3.2.2
corporal punishment 15.5
designated officer 13.3.3.1
domestic violence 15.7.2, 15.7.2.3
drunk in charge of children 12.2.2
harm, definition of 13.3.2
heating appliances, injuries from 13.3.2.3
initiating officer, role of 13.3.3.1, 13.3.3.2
licensed premises 12.4.3
Local Safeguarding Children Boards 13.3
multi-agency approach 3.3, 13.3
National Specialist Child Abuse
    Investigation Development
    Programme (SCAIDP) 13.3.1
NSPCC 3.4.6
parental responsibility 13.3.3.3
Police Central e-Crime Unit (PCeU) 3.4.8
police protection 13.3.3–13.3.3.4
seatbelts 19.5.3.5
Specialist Child Abuse Investigation
    Unit 13.3.3
suitable accommodation 13.3.3.4
tobacco to young people, selling 13.3.2.2
witnesses, special measures for 26.5.2.4
CHIS *see* **Covert Human Intelligence
    Sources (CHIS)**
Cigarettes 4.2.3, 14.2.6
Citizen's arrest 10.6.5
Civil courts 5.5.2, 14.1, 14.6, 14.8.5
Civil disputes 14.1, 14.8.5
Civil liberties 3.5.3 *see also* **Human Rights
    Act 1998**
Civil Nuclear Constabulary (CNC) 3.4.3
Civil trespass 14.8.5
CKP *see* **Certificate in Knowledge of
    Policing (CKP)**
Claire's Law 15.7
Clampers 3.4.7, 19.11.1
Classification of offences 5.5.1
Clothing
    crime scenes, attending 11.2.3.1, 11.2.4
    protective clothing 11.2.1.1, 11.2.3.1,
        11.2.4
    samples 25.6.1.5
    stop and search 9.4.3.2
Coaching 8.6.3
Code of Ethics for policing 3.5.1.1
Cognitive learning domain 8.6.5.1
Colleagues, communication with 6.11.4
College of Policing 3.1, 3.5.1.1, 3.7.2,
    3.7.4, 6.11.4.1, 7.2.1, 7.6.3–7.6.3.1
**Colleges and universities, pre-join
    schemes at** 1.4.1, 7.2
Collusion 2.2, 26.5.3.3, 26.5.3.5
Commitment, warrants of 9.5.1.1
Common Approach Path (CAP) 11.2.2,
    11.2.3.1, 11.6.2, 25.5.2.1
Communication *see* **Personal
    communication**
Communications data 22.3.3
**Community (neighbourhood)
    policing** 3.9.1–3.9.1.1, 3.9.1.3–3.9.1.4
    Community Impact Assessment 11.7.1
    Community Liaison Officers, role
        of 7.6.1.3
    Community Support Officers 3.4.4, 8.3,
        8.4.2
    crime prevention 4.6.3
    diversity 7.6.1.3, 8.6.6
    Family Liaison Officer, role of 7.6.1.3
    watch schemes 3.9.1.4, 4.6.3, 11.2,
        13.6.2.3
**Community Safety Partnerships
    (CSPs)** 3.3, 3.3.2, 22.6
Community Safety Units (CSUs) 3.3.3

Complaints *see* **Misconduct and
    complaints procedures**
Computers
    child welfare and protection 3.4.8, 17.1,
        17.4.2
    Cloud storage 25.5.5.2
    cybercrime 3.4.8
    deletion of data 25.5.5.2
    Digital Forensics Unit 9.8.1,
        25.7.3–25.7.3.2
    entry and search, powers of 9.6–9.6.2, 9.7
    evidence 3.4.8, 9.6–9.6.2, 9.7, 25.5,
        25.5.5.2, 26.4.3
    High-Tech Crime Unit 3.4.8
    intelligence, software for analysis
        of 22.5.2
    Internet 3.4.8, 6.9, 17.1, 22.4
    IT and communications systems,
        operation of 6.9–6.9.3
    National Cyber Crime Unit 3.4.8
    packaging 25.7.3.3
    Penalty Notices for Disorder, issue
        of 10.13.2
    Police Central e-Crime Unit (PCeU) 3.4.8
    pornography 17.4.2
    power supply, interruption
        of 25.7.3–25.7.3.2
    searches 9.8.1
    seizure 25.7.3–25.7.3.3
Conciliation 5.7–5.7.2.1
Condition of vehicles 19.5, 19.5.3.1,
    19.8.1, 19.12, 19.12.1
Conditions of Service *see* **Police Regulations
    and Conditions of Service**
Conduct Matters *see* **Misconduct and
    complaints procedures**
Conferring on PNB entries 10.2.3
Confessions 24.1, 24.5.1–24.5.1.1, 24.5.8
Confidentiality 6.1, 6.3.1, 6.8–6.8.1, 26.2.5
Confirmation as constable 8.4.2,
    8.4.3–8.4.4.3, 8.5.1, 8.5.4, 8.6
Conflict management 6.11.4.2, 6.12.5
Consent, policing by 3.5.3.1–3.5.3.2
Conservation areas, protection of 20.6
**Construction and use of
    vehicles** 19.5–19.5.4
    brakes, maintenance of 19.5.3.1
    condition of vehicles 19.5, 19.5.3.1,
        19.8.1, 19.12, 19.12.1
    emissions 19.5.3.1, 19.5.3.3
    engine running when stationary 19.5.3.3
    exhaust systems, maintenance of 19.5.3.1
    eye protection for motorcyclists 19.5.3.4
    helmets for motorcyclists 19.5.3.4
    horns (audible warning devices)
        19.5.3.1–19.5.3.2
    incorrect use of vehicle 19.5.3.2
    injury, danger of 19.5.3–19.5.3.5
    lights 19.5.2–19.5.2.5
    loads, carrying 19.5.3.2
    maintenance 19.5.3.1
    MOT test certificates 19.3.3, 19.4.2.2
    noise 19.5.3.2
    number plates, display of 19.5.4
    passengers, number of 19.5.3.2
    seatbelts 19.5.3.5
    stationary vehicle offences 19.5.3.3
    trailers, danger of injury
        from 19.5.3–19.5.3.5
    tyres 19.5.1–19.5.1.1
    Vehicle Defect Rectification Scheme
        (VDRS) 19.12, 19.12.1
    vehicle identification regulations 19.5.4
    wipers and washers, maintenance
        of 19.5.3.1